A-Z LO

CONTENTS

Key to Map Pages	2-3	Index to Streets	164-325
Map Pages @ approx. 3" to 1 mile	4-138	Index to selected Places of Interest	326-327
Large Scale Map Pages @ 5¾" to 1 mile	139-157	Index to Stations	328-330
Railway Connections Map	158-159	Index to Hospitals & Health Centres	331-336
West End Cinema & Theatre Maps	160-161	Underground Railway Map	Back Cover
Index to Places & Areas	162-163		

REFERENCE

Motorway — M1	**Railway** — Tunnel / Level Crossing / Station
A Road — A2	**Docklands Light Railway** — Station DLR
Under Construction	**Underground Station** ●
Proposed	**Croydon Tramlink** — Tunnel / Station
B Road — B408	The boarding of Tramlink trains at stations may be limited to a single direction, indicated by the arrow.
Dual Carriageway	
One Way Street — Traffic flow on A Roads is indicated by a heavy line on the drivers' left.	**Church or Chapel** †
Junction Name — MARBLE ARCH	**Disabled Toilet** ♿
Pedestrianized Road	**Fire Station** ■
Restricted Access	**Hospital** H
Track & Footpath	**House Numbers** A & B Roads only 51 22 19 48
Residential Walkway	
Map Continuation 56 / Large Scale Map Pages 140	**Information Centre** i
	National Grid Reference ^{5}30
Built Up Area — BANK / STREET	**Police Station** ▲
	Post Office ★

SCALE

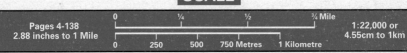

Pages 4-138
2.88 inches to 1 Mile

0   ¼   ½   ¾ Mile
0   250   500   750 Metres   1 Kilometre

1:22,000 or
4.55cm to 1km

Copyright of Geographers' A-Z Map Company Limited

Head Office : Fairfield Road, Borough Green, Sevenoaks, Kent TN15 8PP   Tel: 01732 781000
Showrooms : 44 Gray's Inn Road, London WC1X 8HX   Tel: 020 7440 9500

Every possible care has been taken to ensure that the information given in this publication is accurate and whilst the publishers would be grateful to learn of any errors, they regret they cannot accept any responsibility for loss thereby caused.

Based upon Ordnance Survey mapping with the permission of The Controller of Her Majesty's Stationery Office.

© 1998 Edition 4 1999 Edition 4A (part revision)
2000 Edition 4B (part revision)

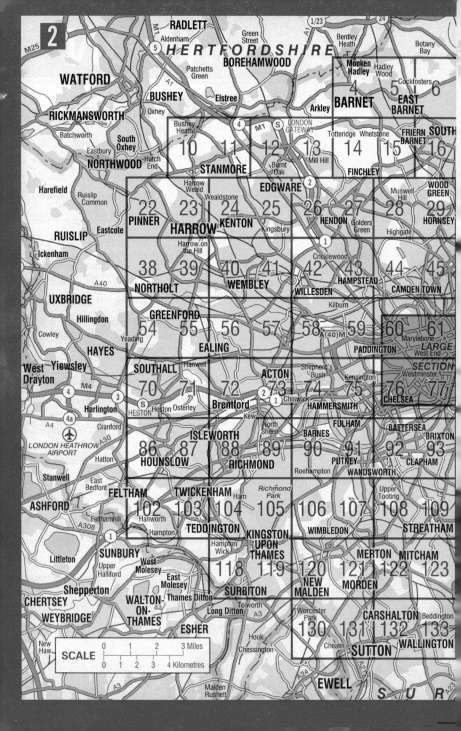

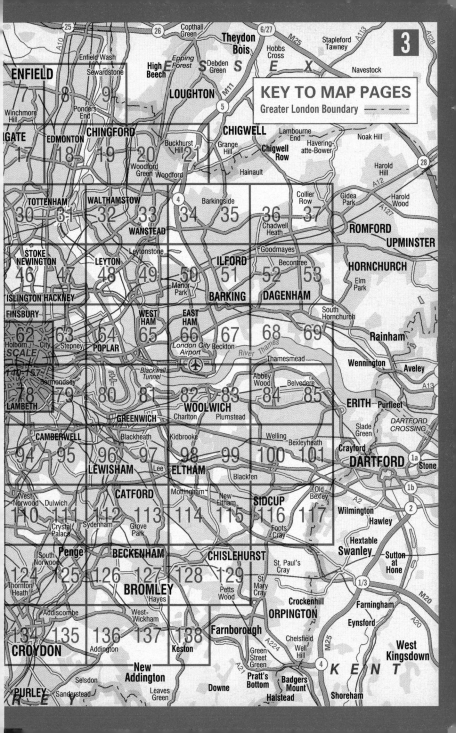

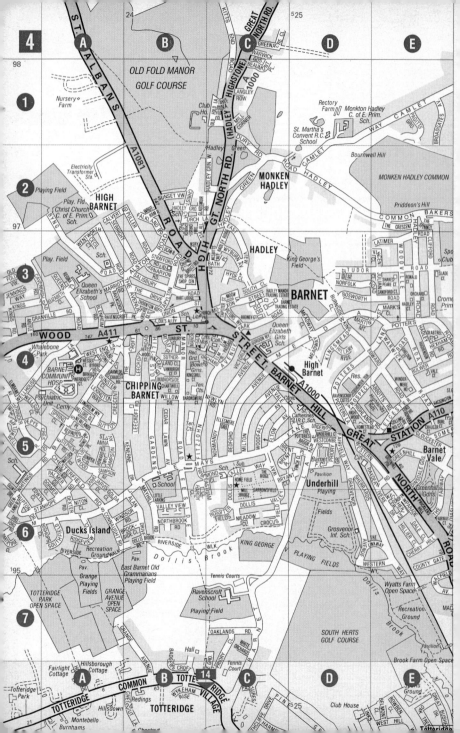

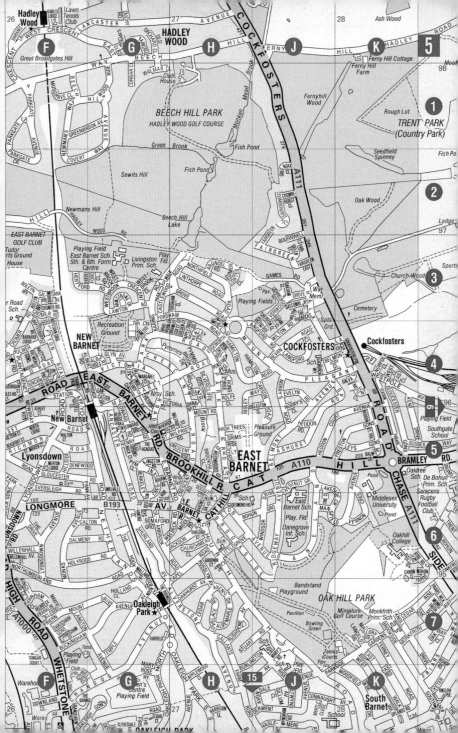

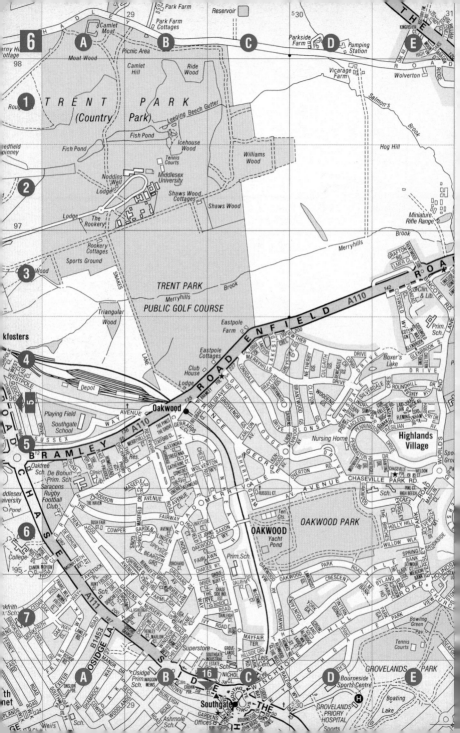

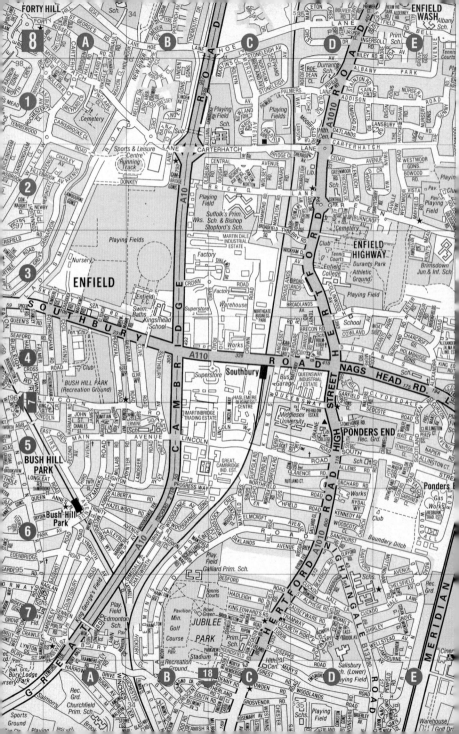

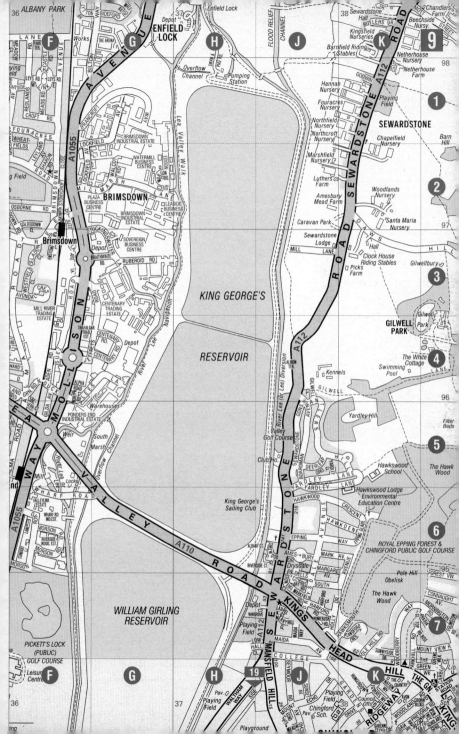

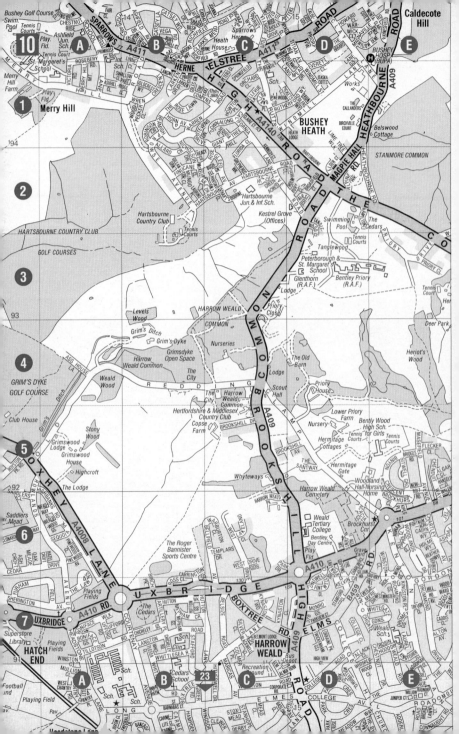

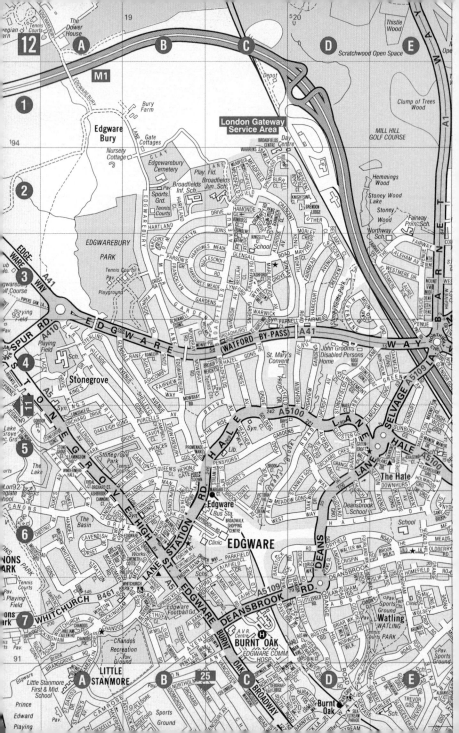

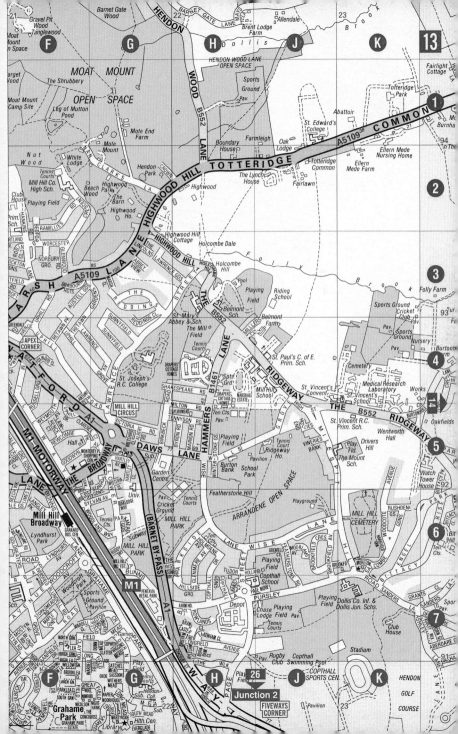

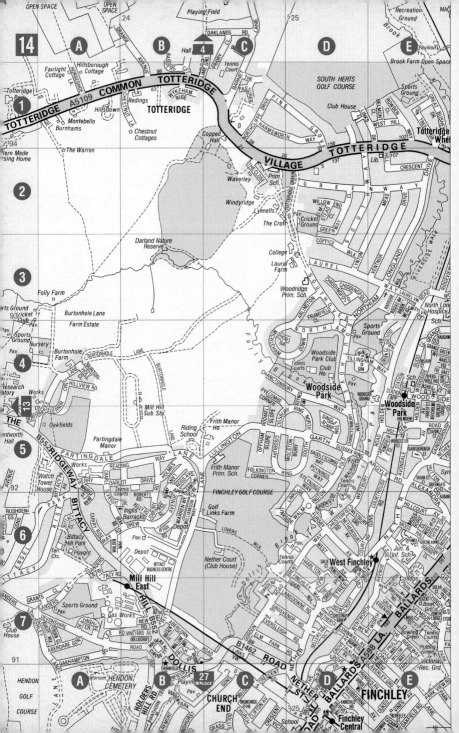

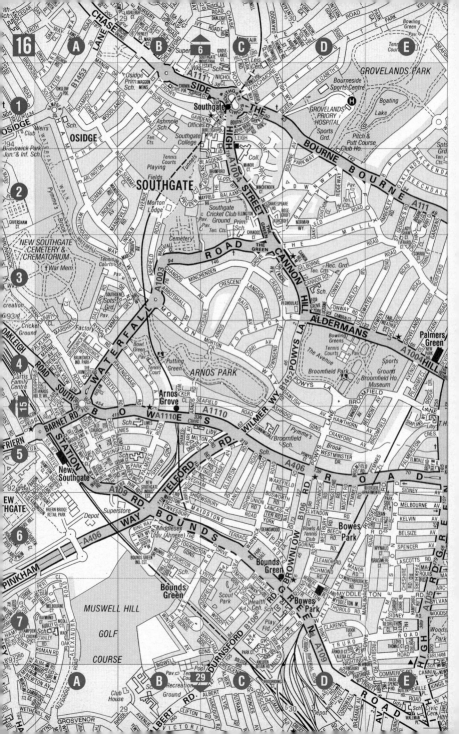

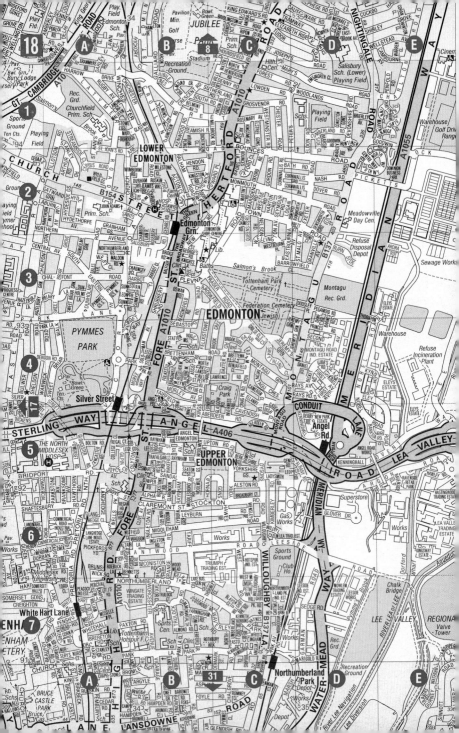

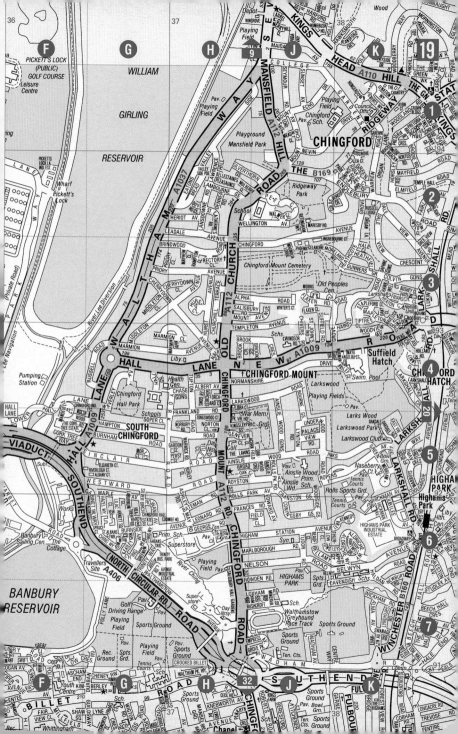

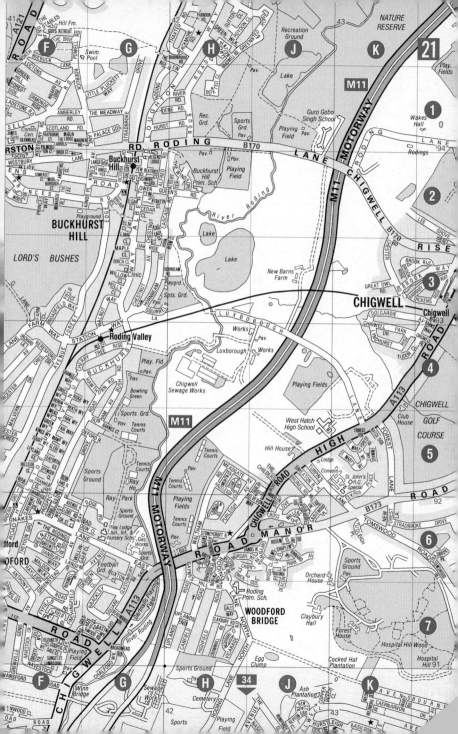

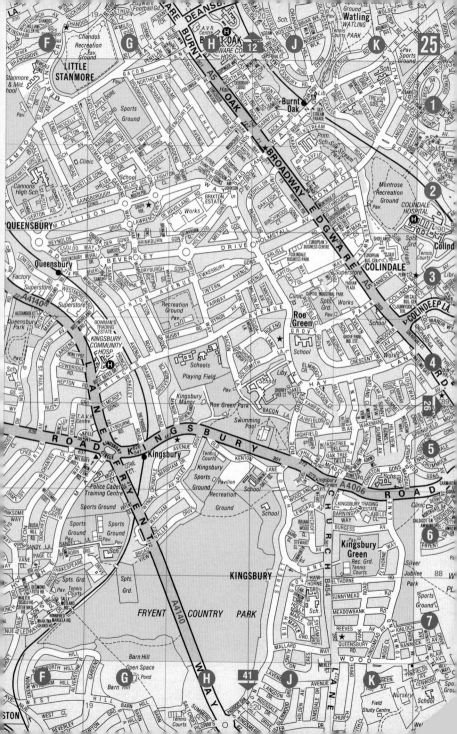

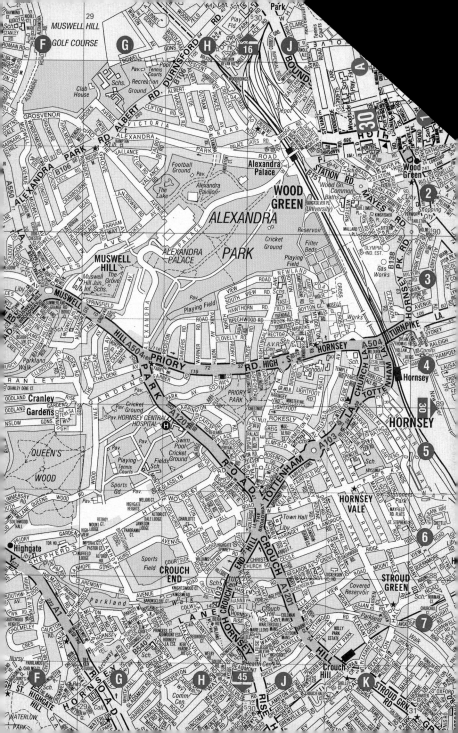

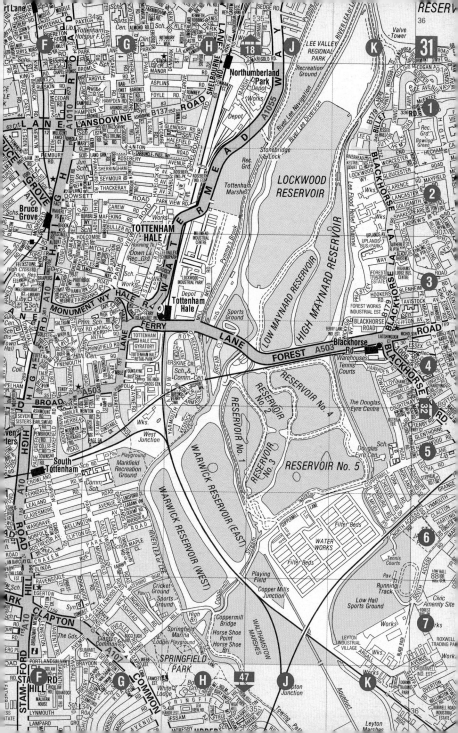

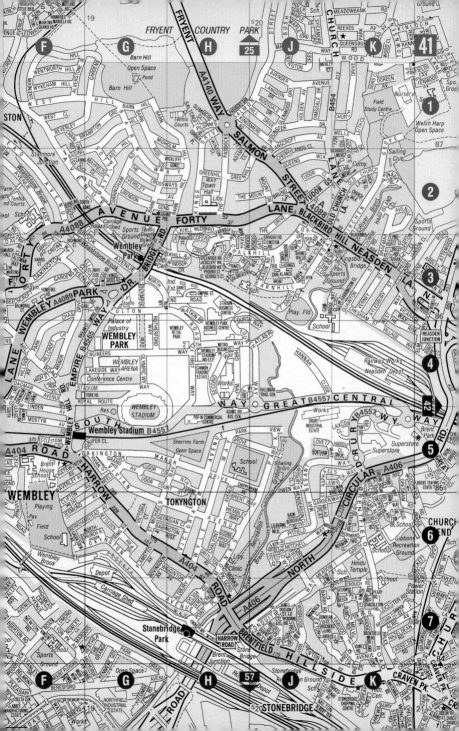

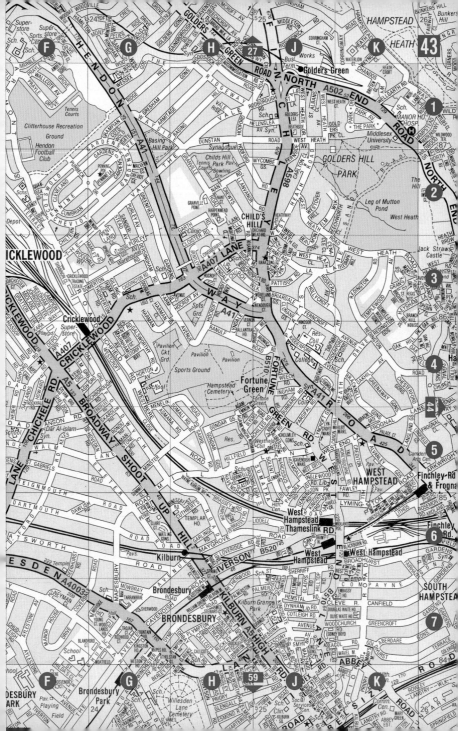

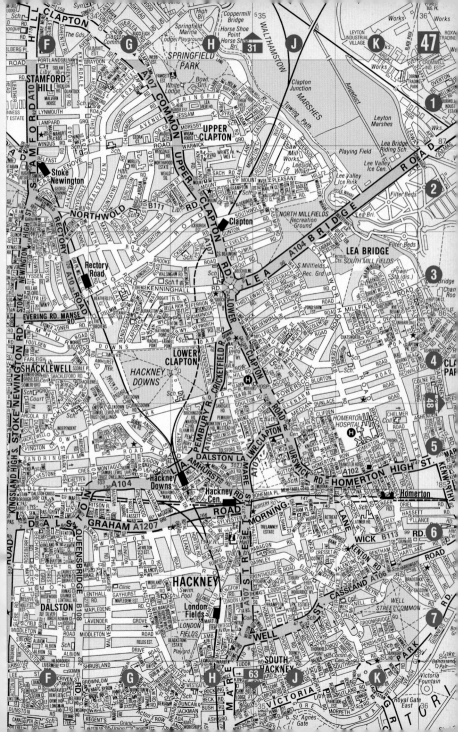

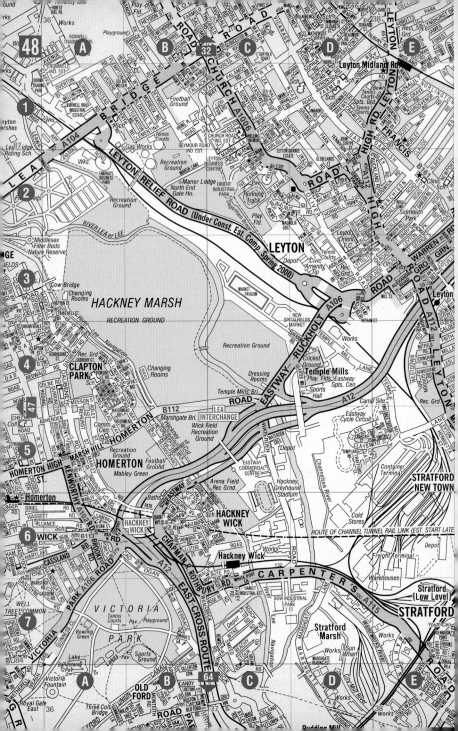

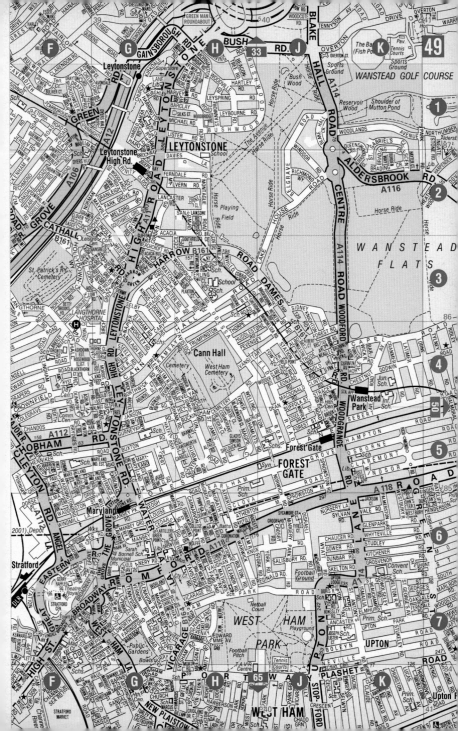

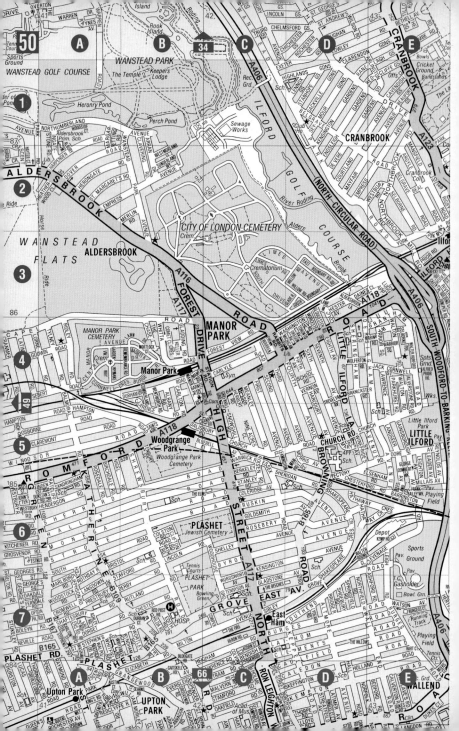

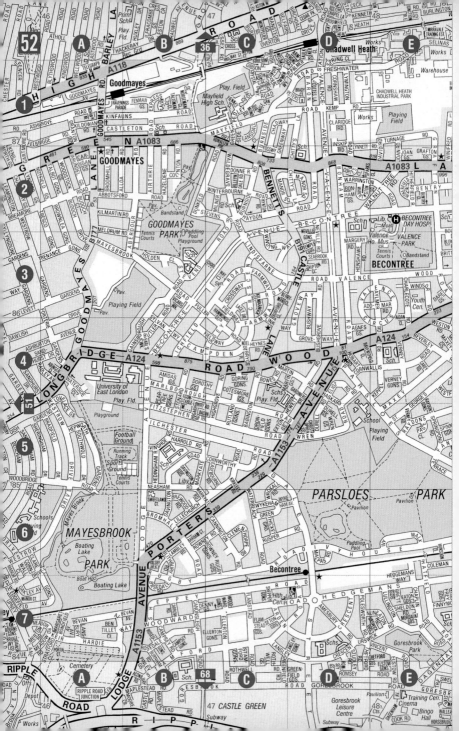

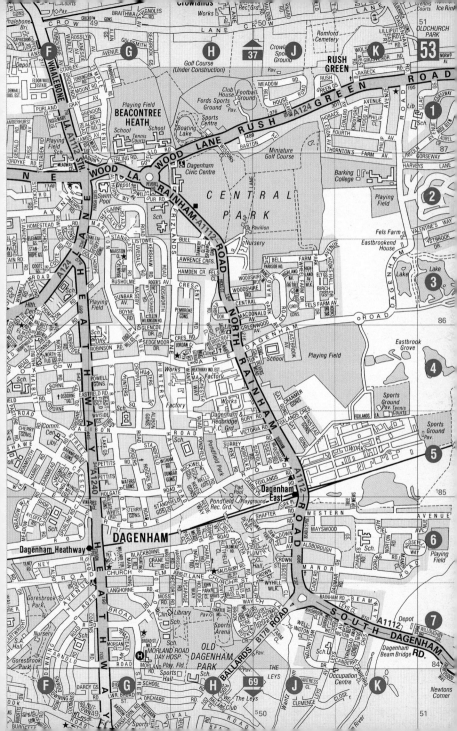

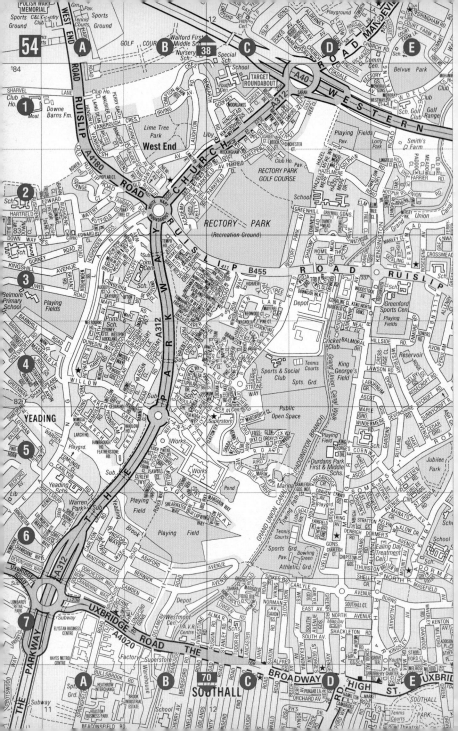

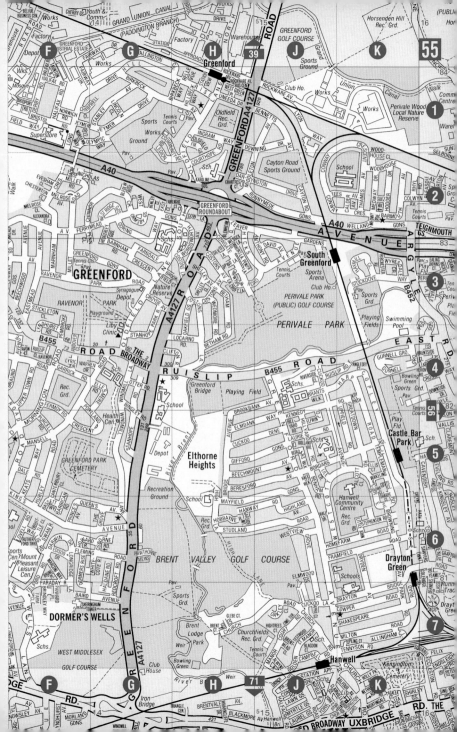

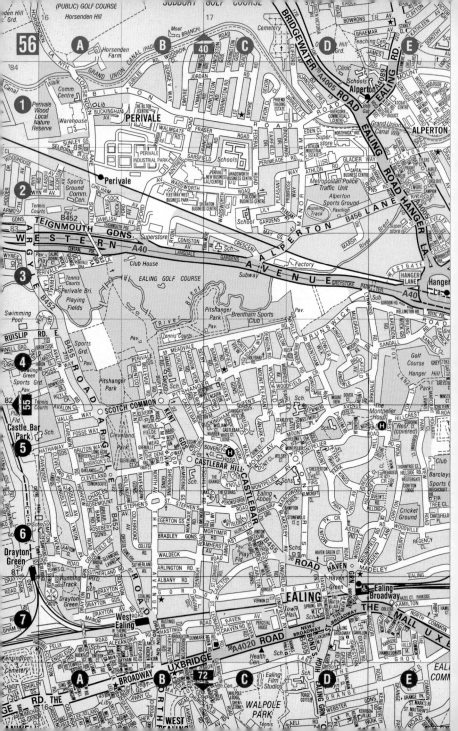

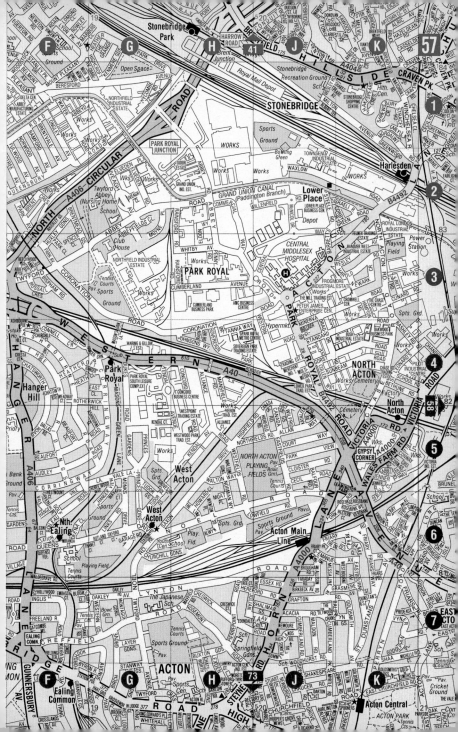

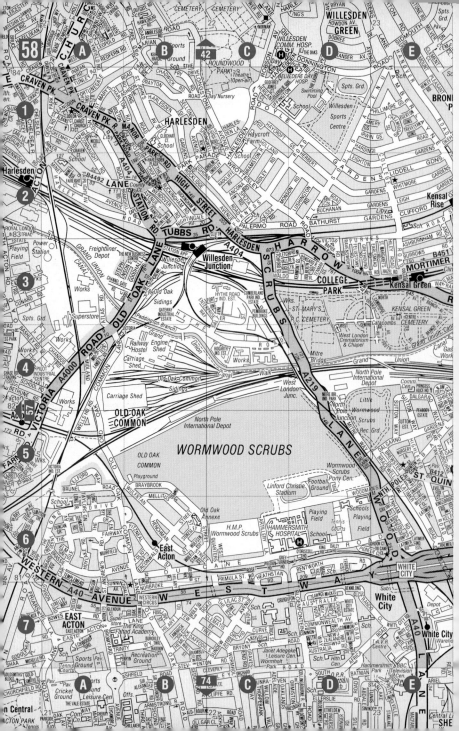

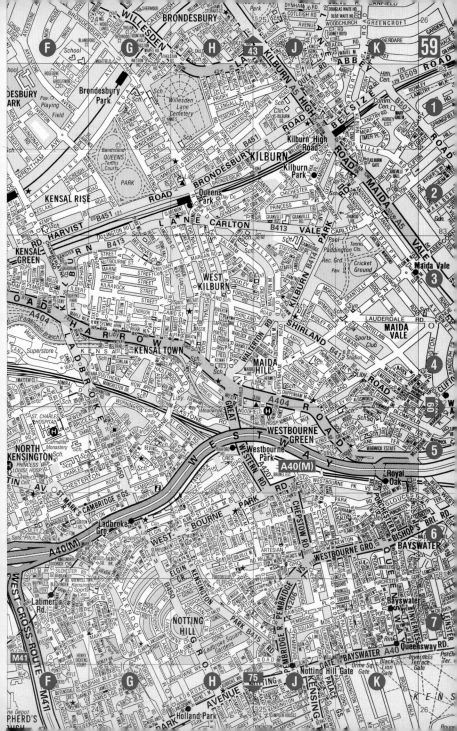

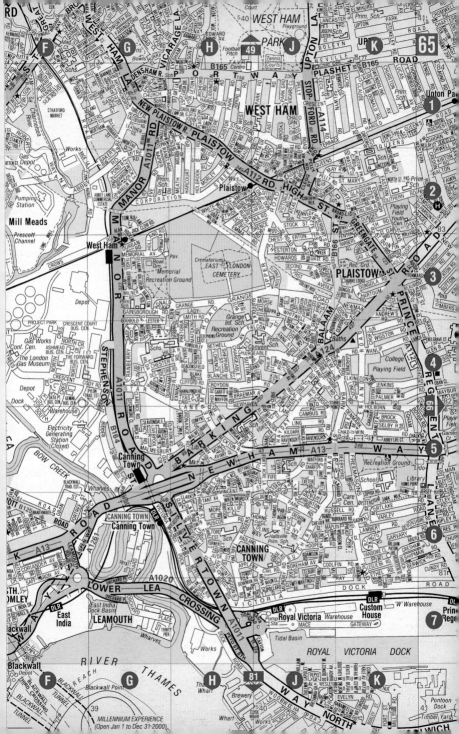

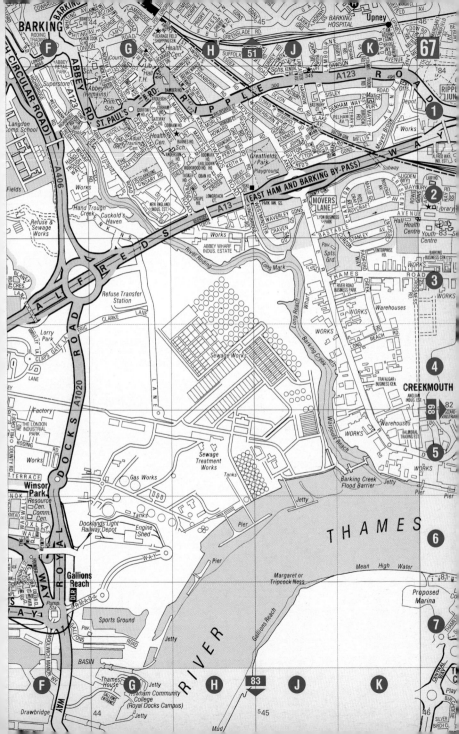

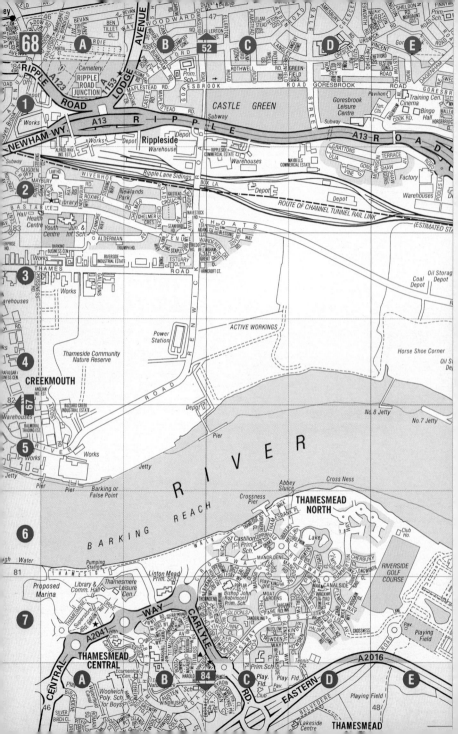

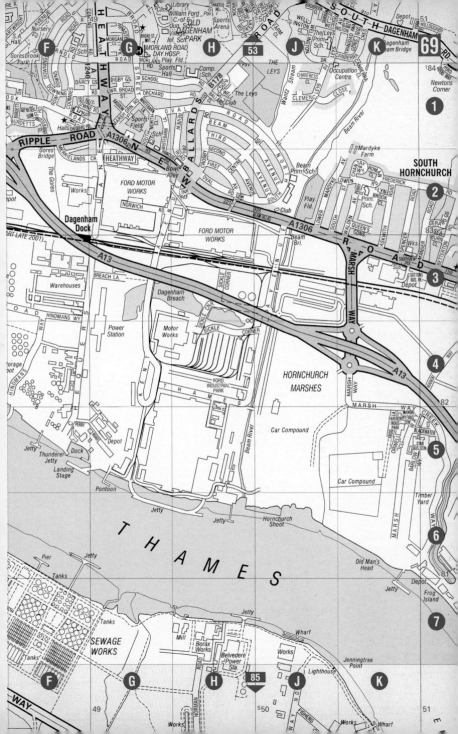

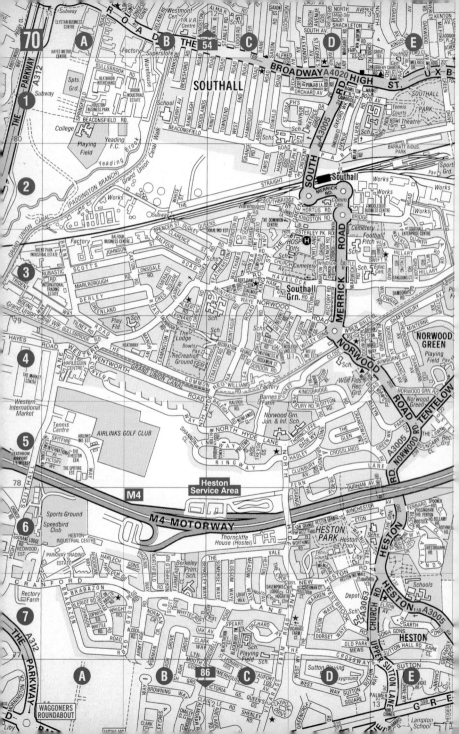

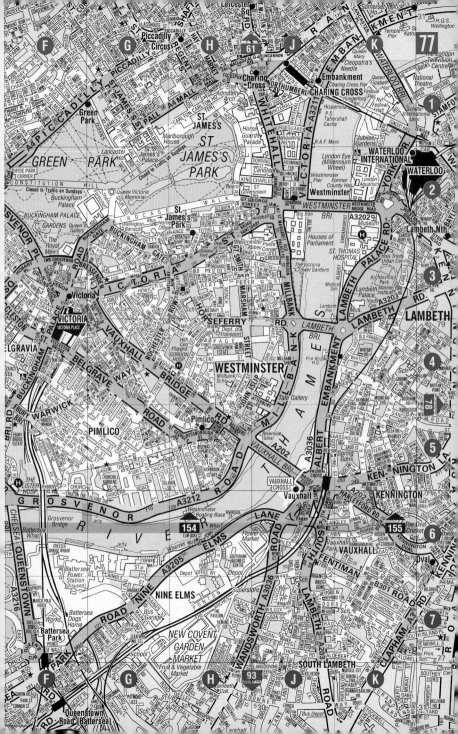

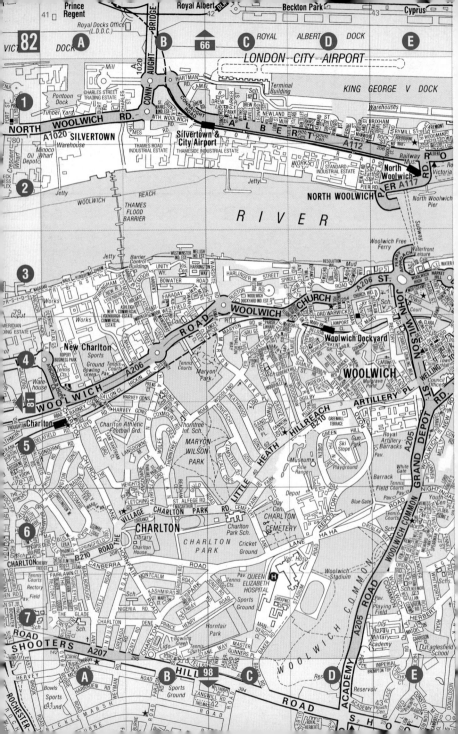

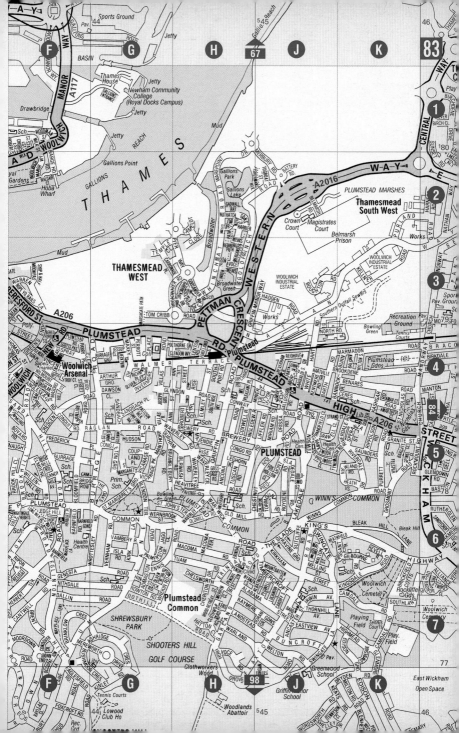

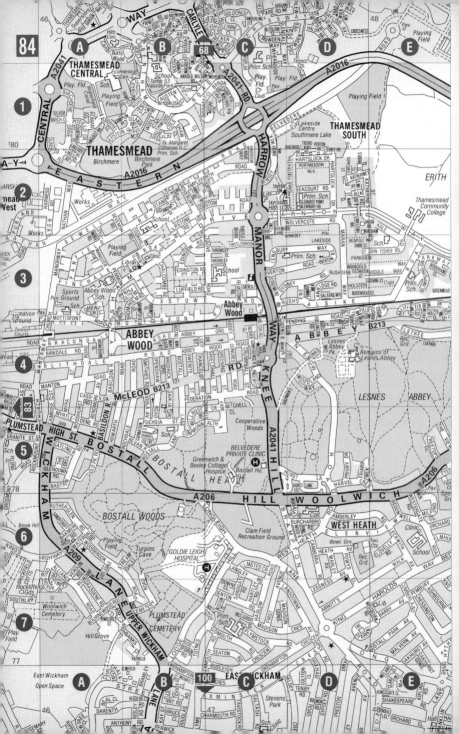

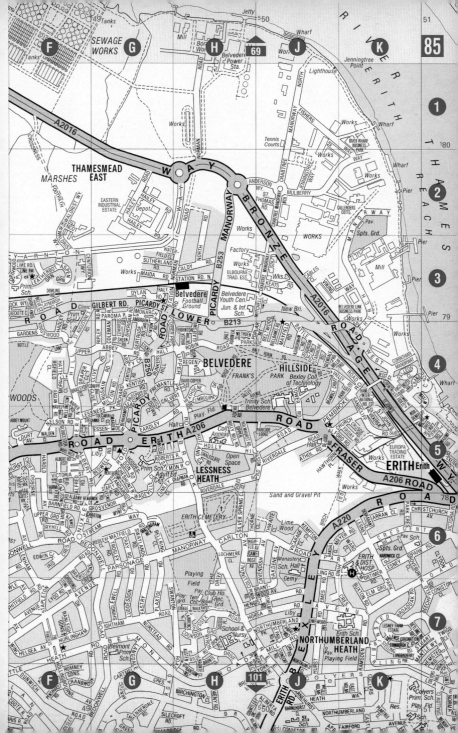

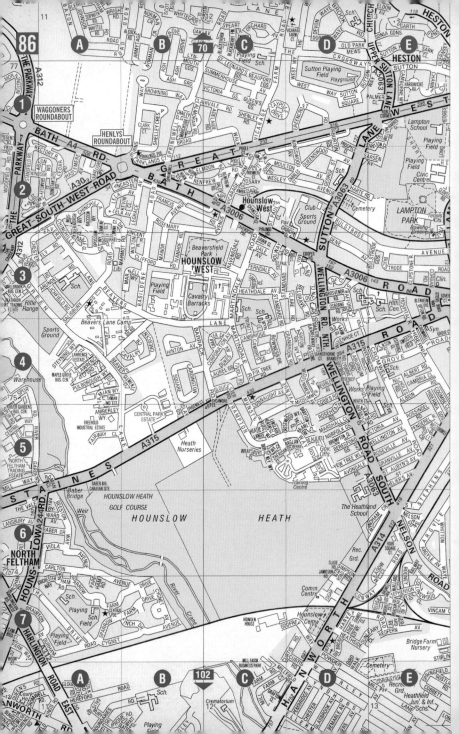

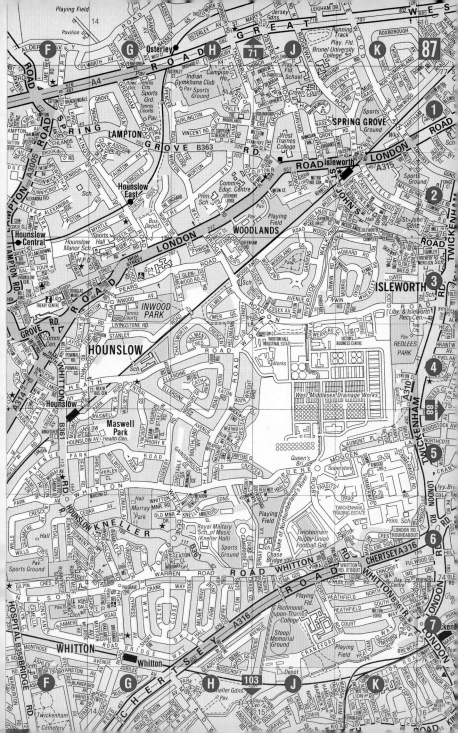

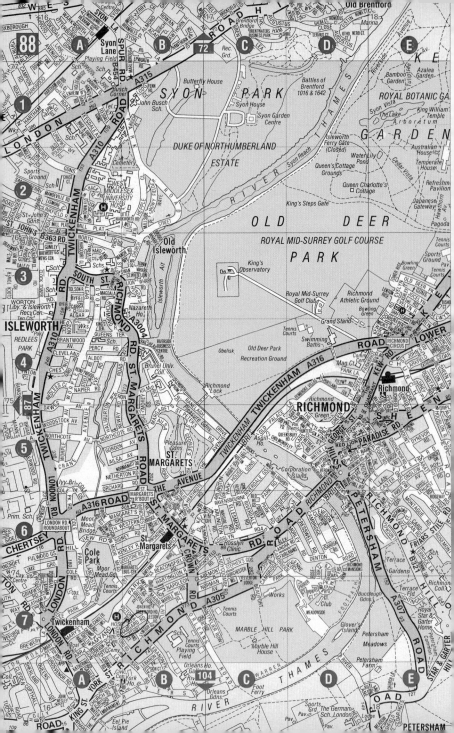

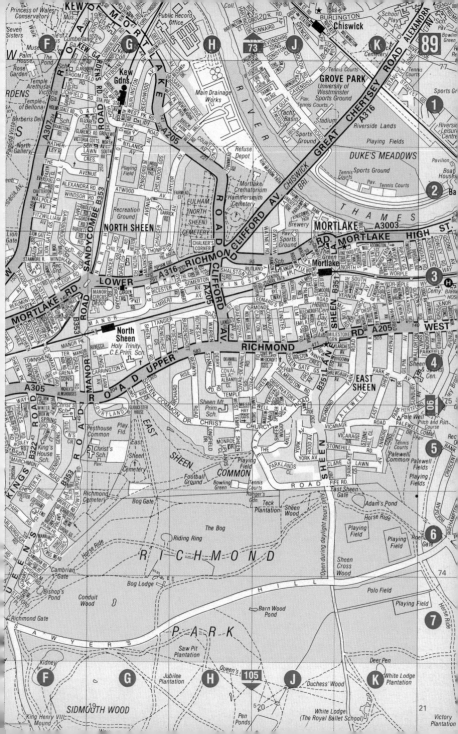

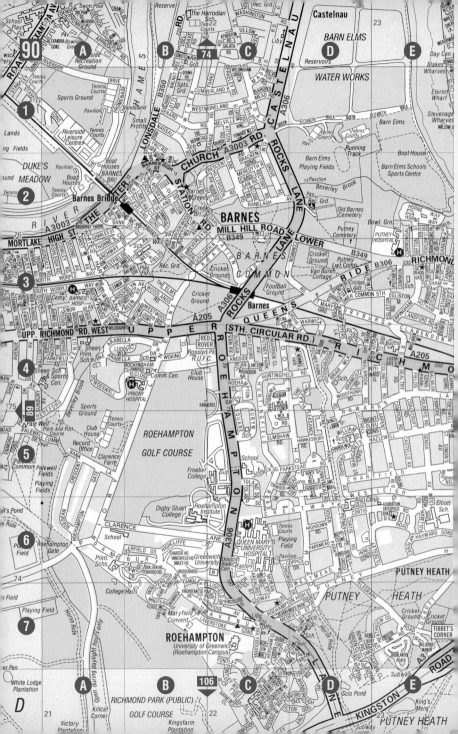

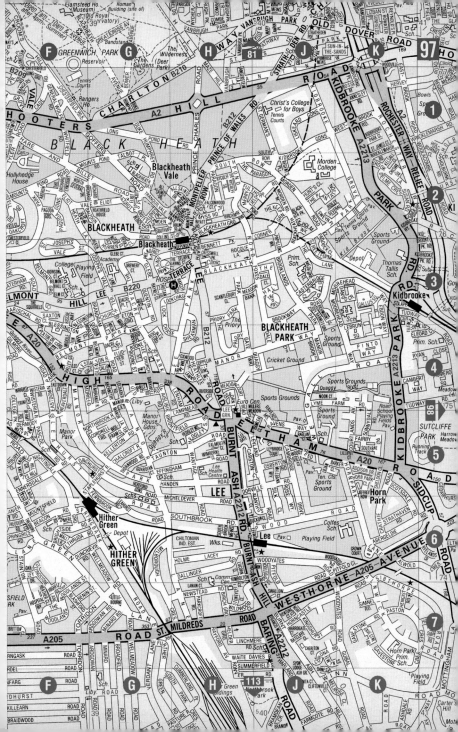

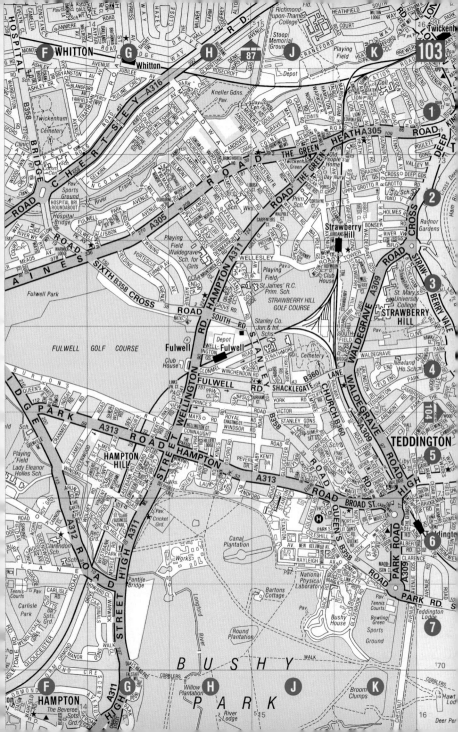

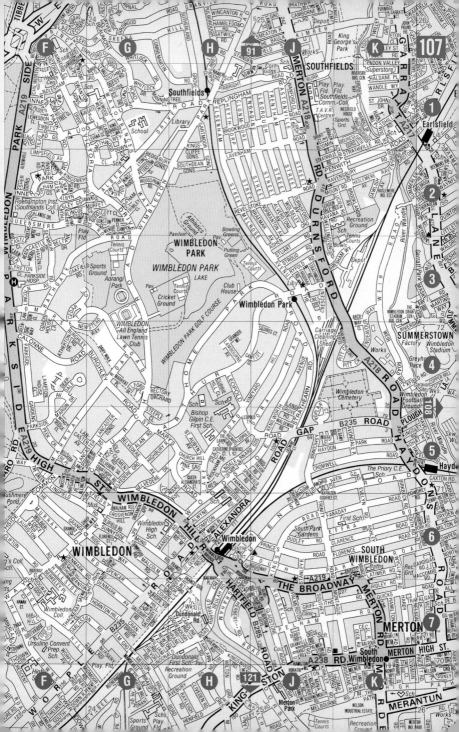

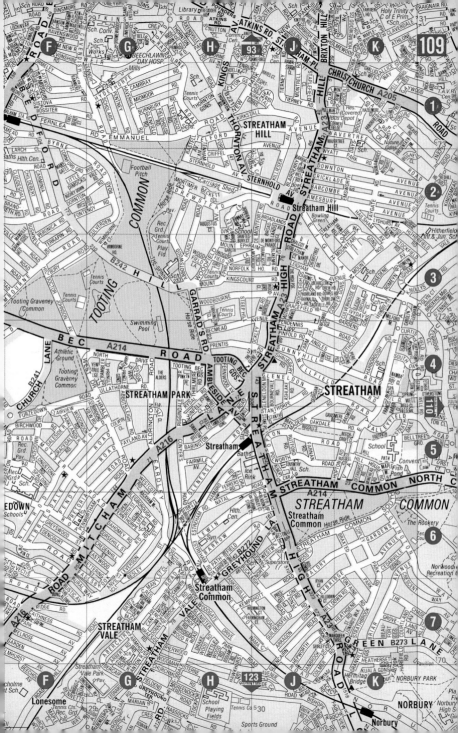

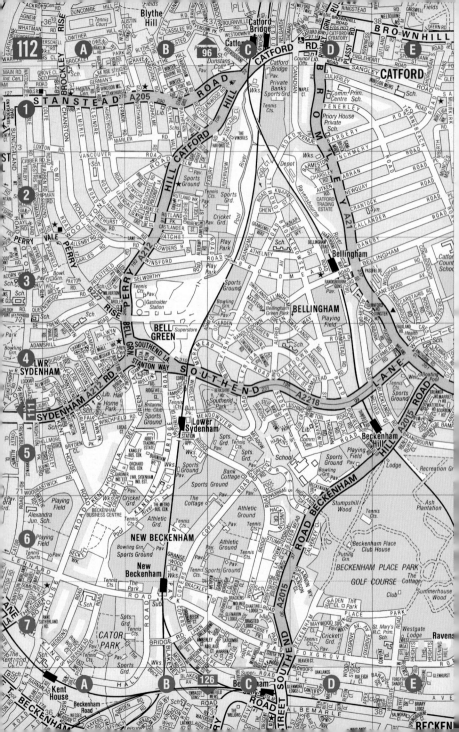

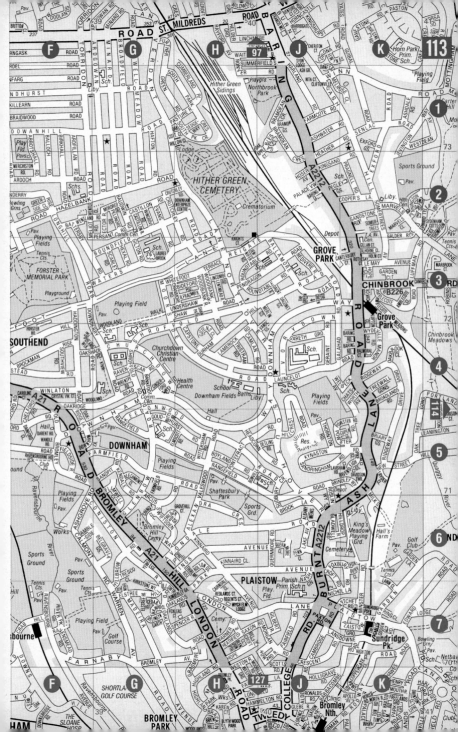

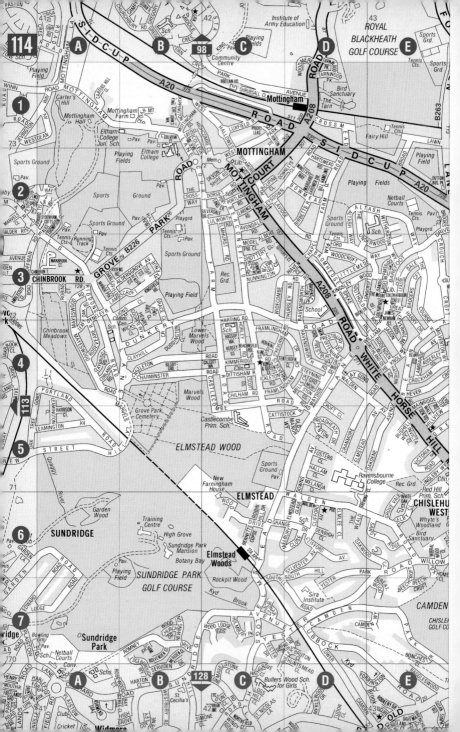

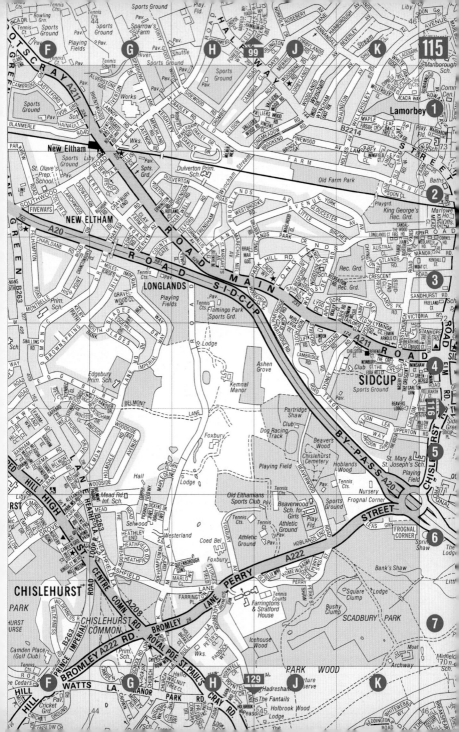

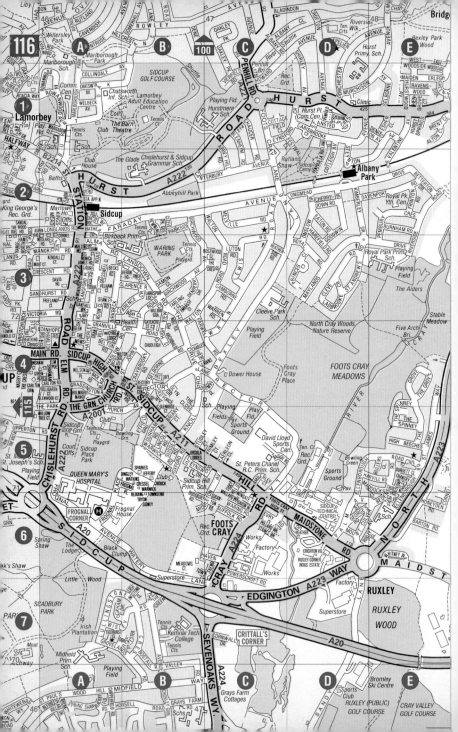

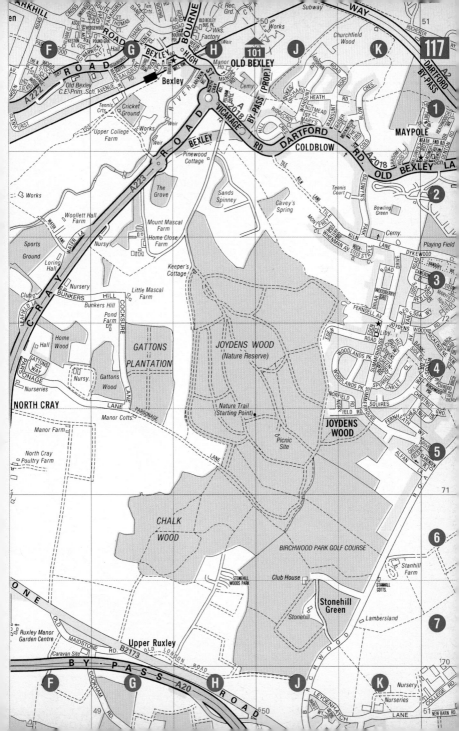

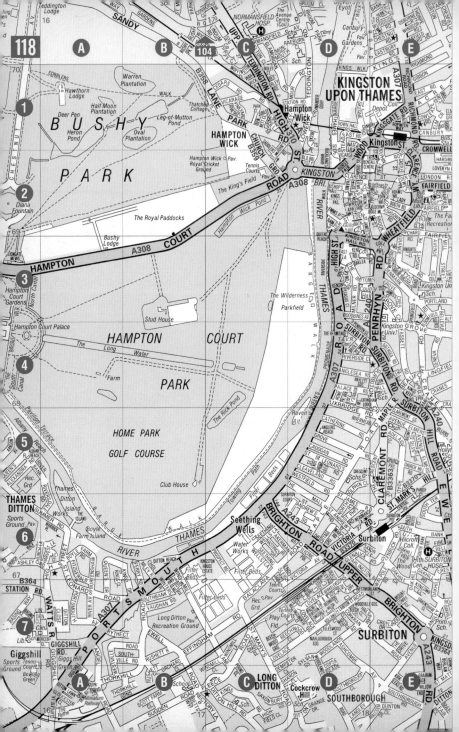

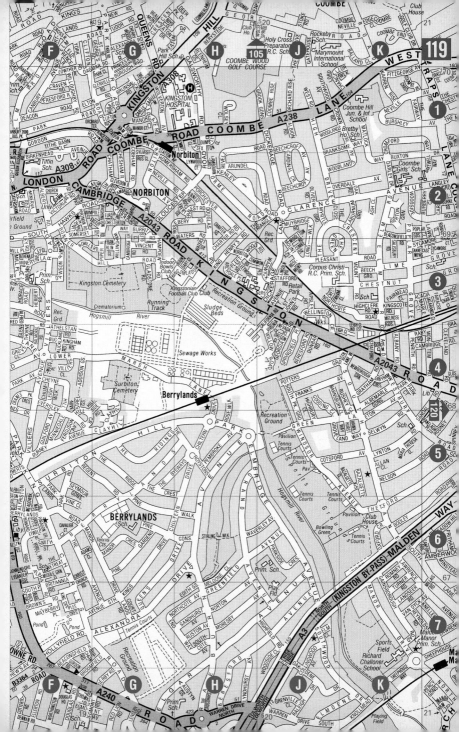

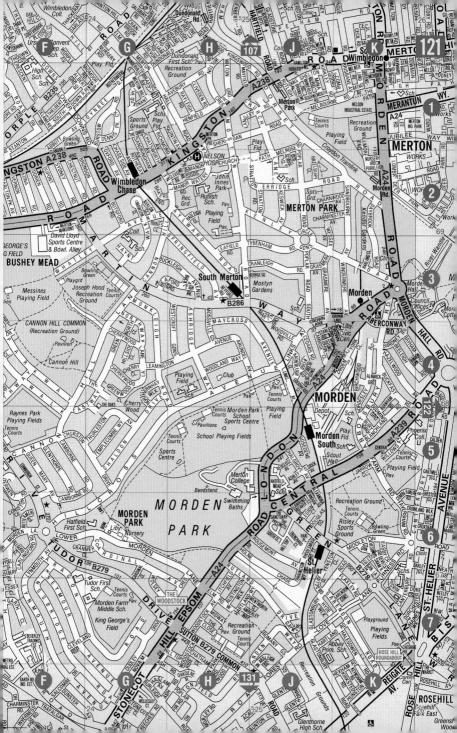

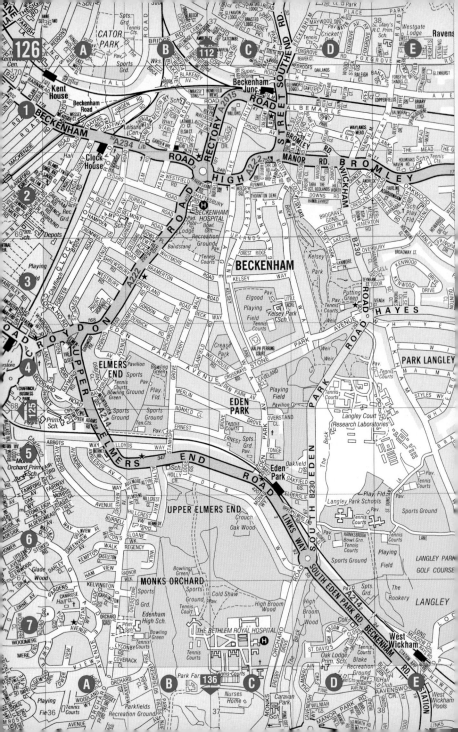

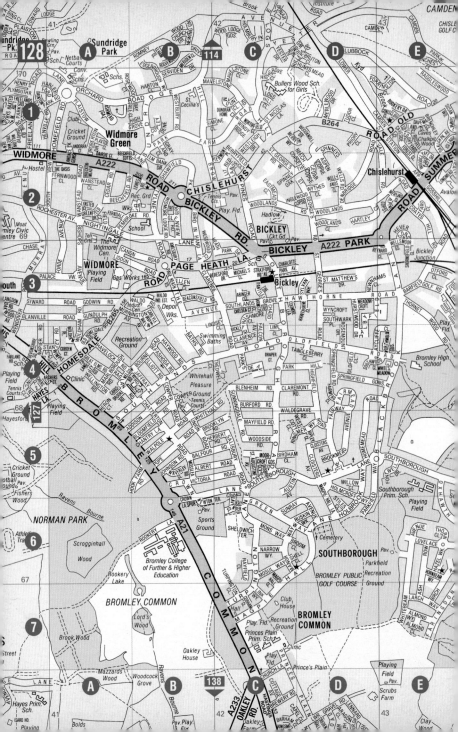

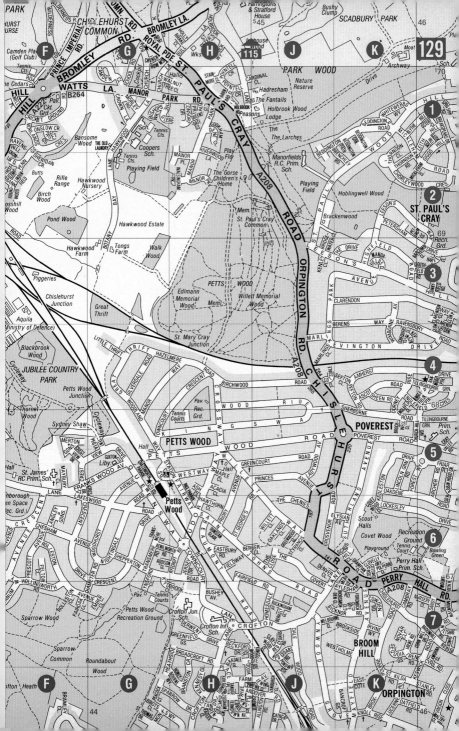

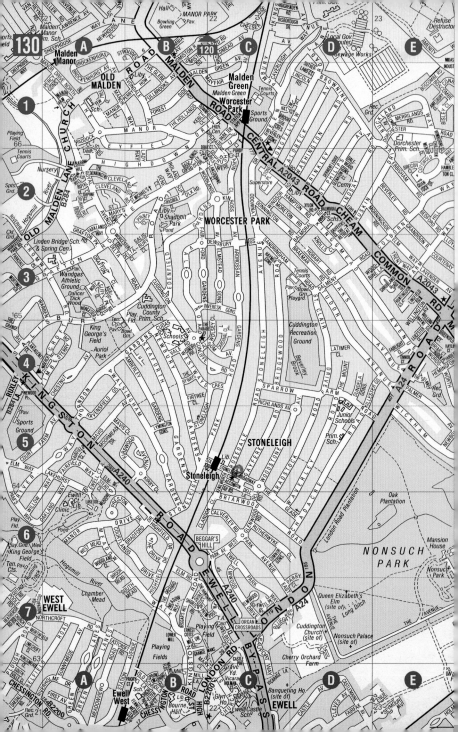

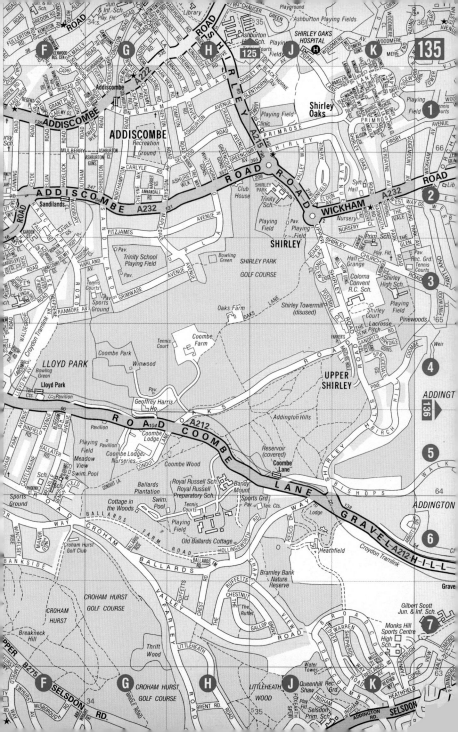

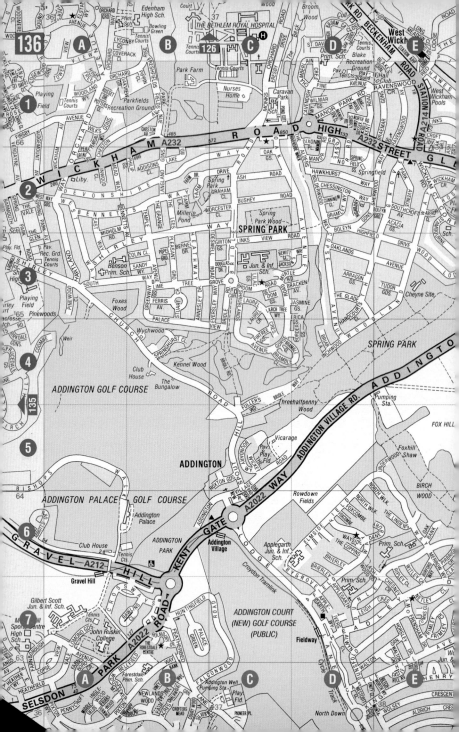

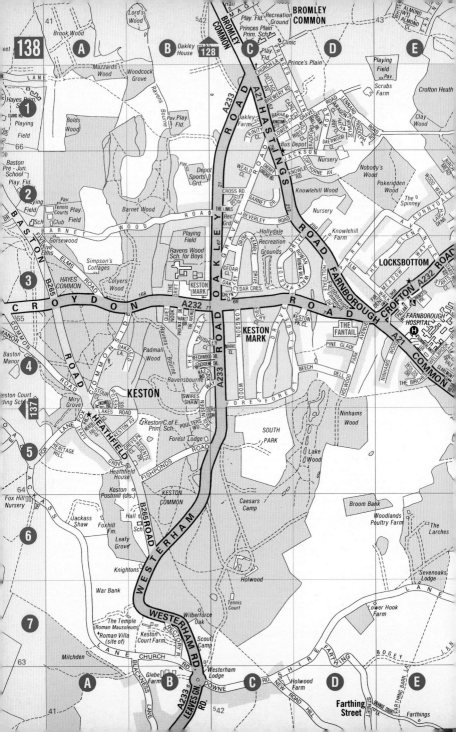

LARGE SCALE SECTION

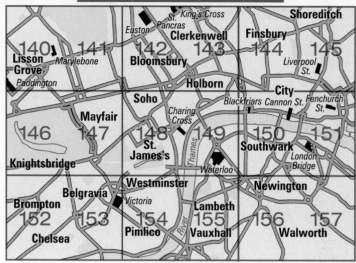

REFERENCE

Motorway	-A40(M)-
A Road	A41
B Road	B524
Dual Carriageway	
One Way Street Traffic flow on A Roads is indicated by a heavy line on the drivers' left.	→
House Numbers A & B Roads only	37 20 3 14
Footpath	- - - - - -
Page Continuation	Large Scale **146** **76**

Buildings Hospital Open to the Public Places of Interest	
Church or Chapel	†
Fire Station	■
Information Centre	🛈
National Grid Reference	^{5}27
Police Station	▲
Post Office	★
Railway Station	⇄
Docklands Light Railway Station	DLR
Underground Station	⊖

SCALE

5¾ inches to 1 mile   **1:11,000**   **9.1cm to 1km**

0 50 100 200 300 Yards ¼   ½ Mile

0 50 100 200 300 400 500   750 Metres   1 Kilometre

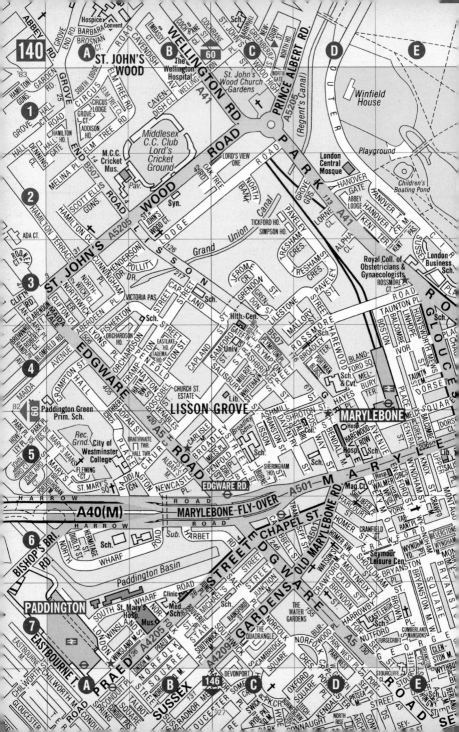

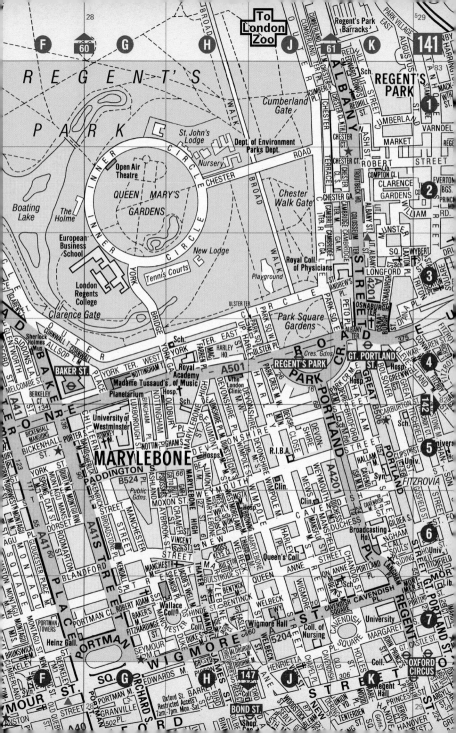

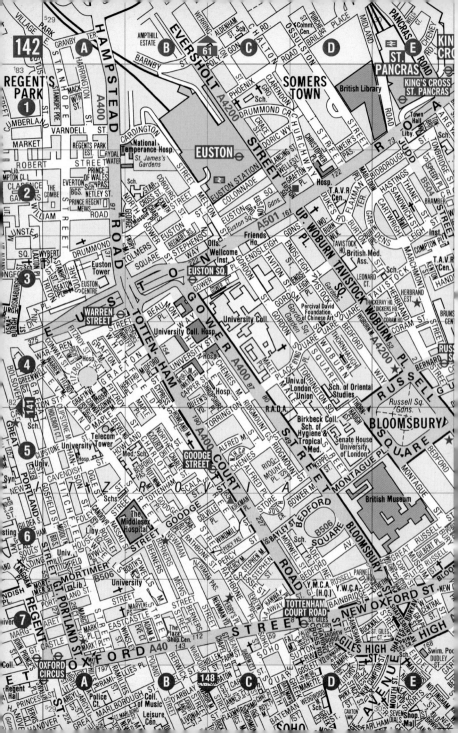

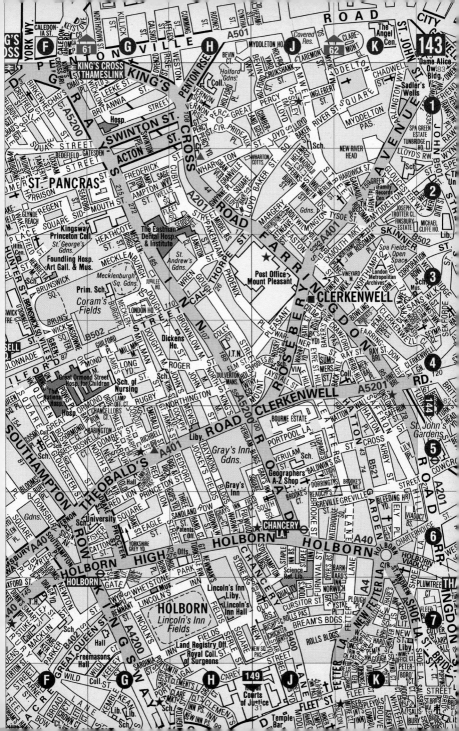

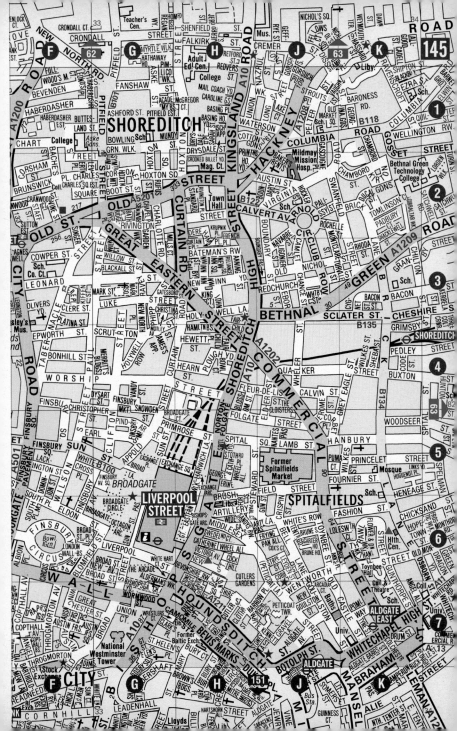

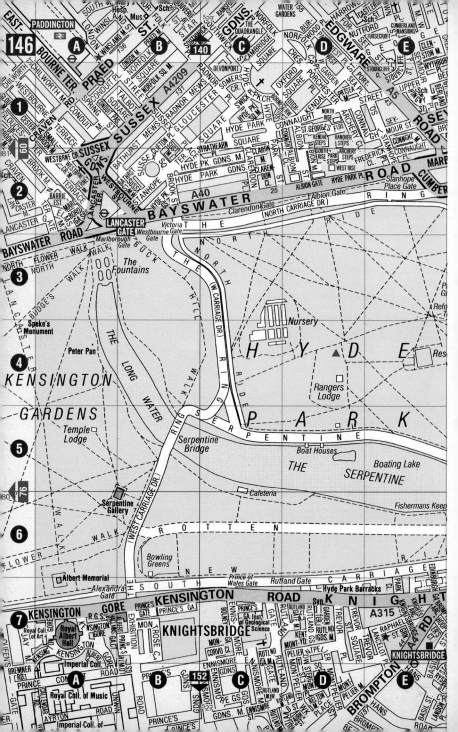

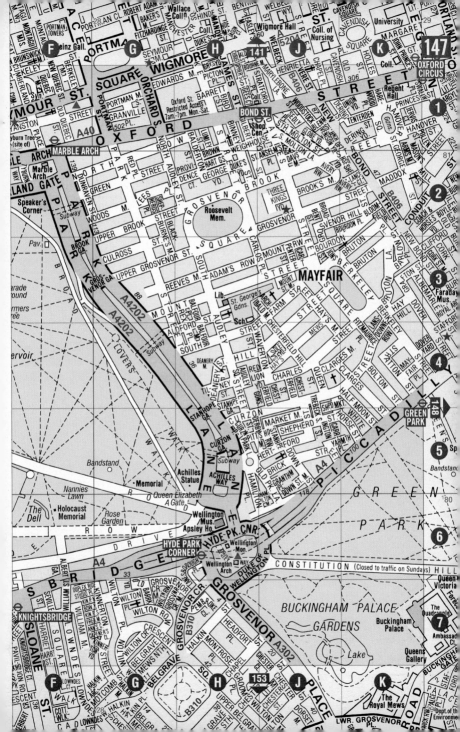

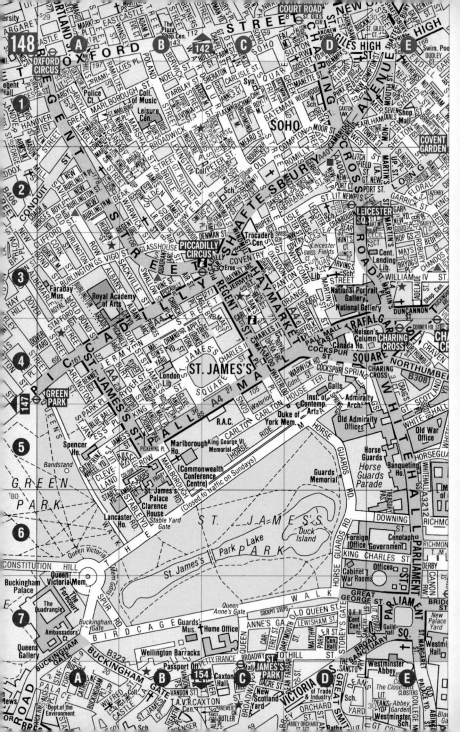

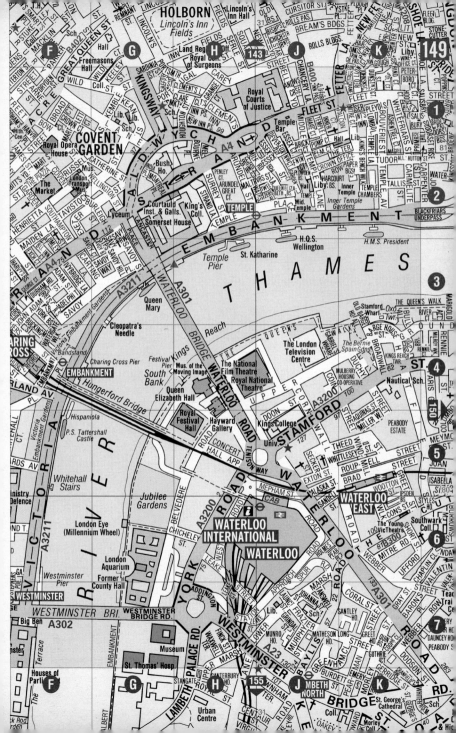

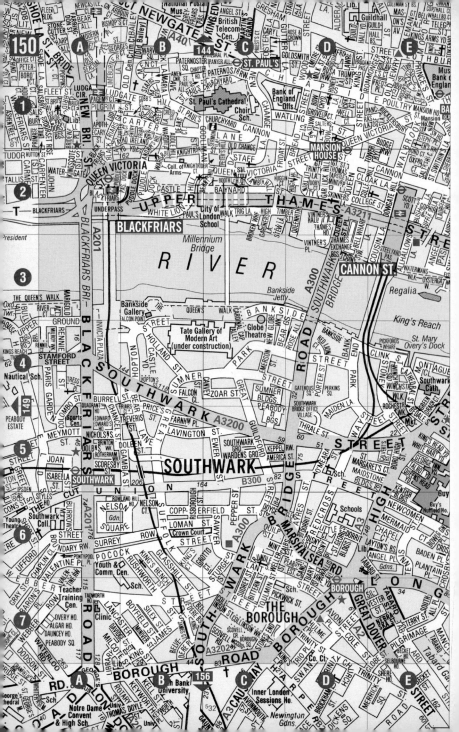

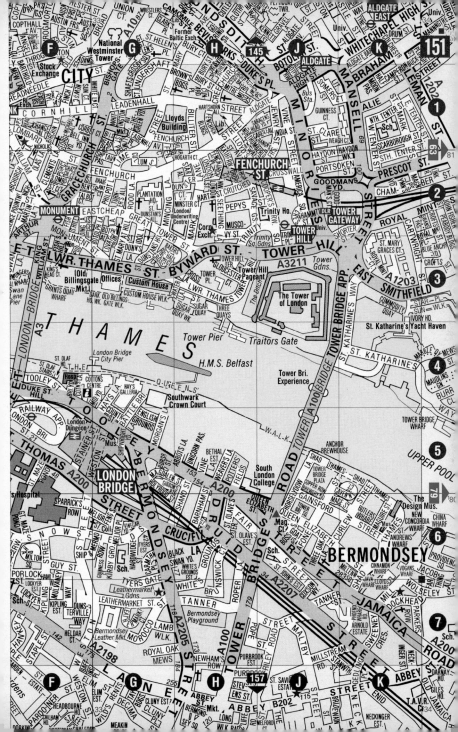

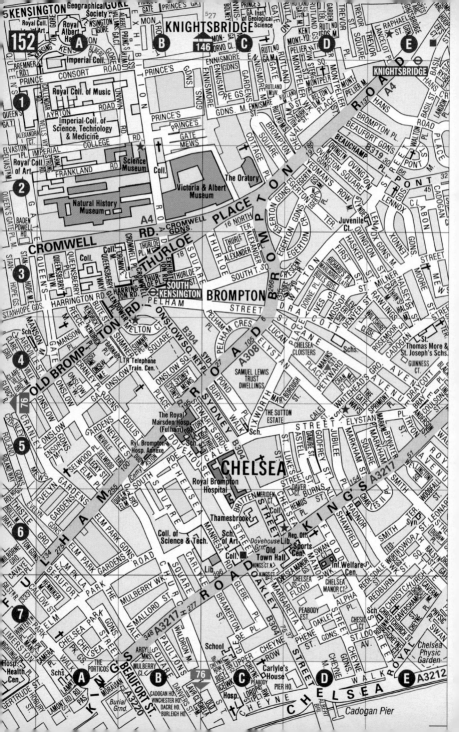

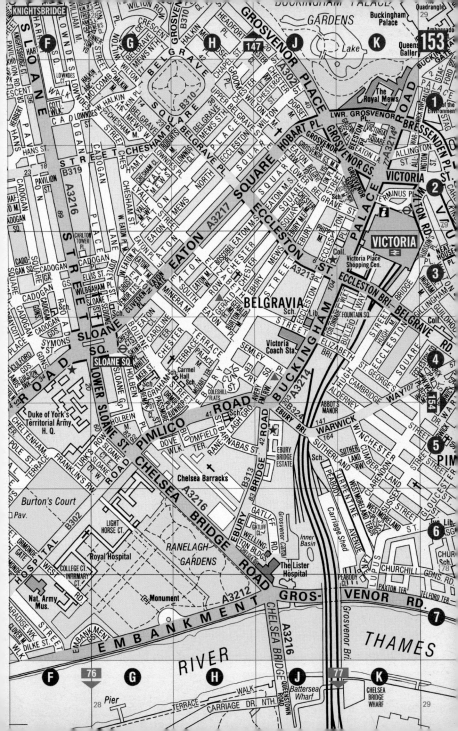

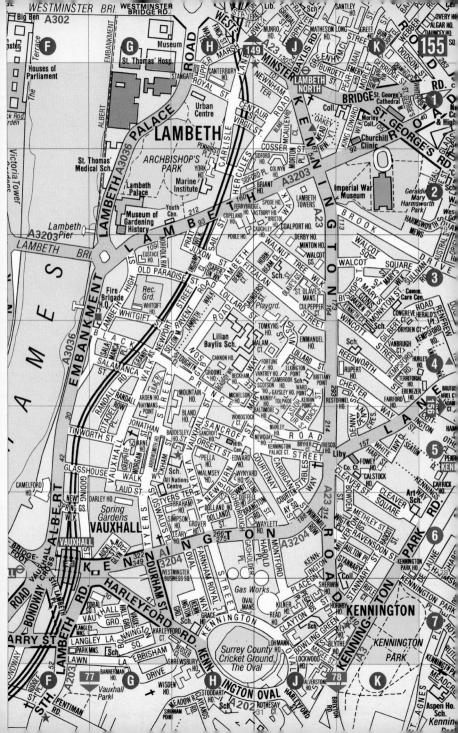

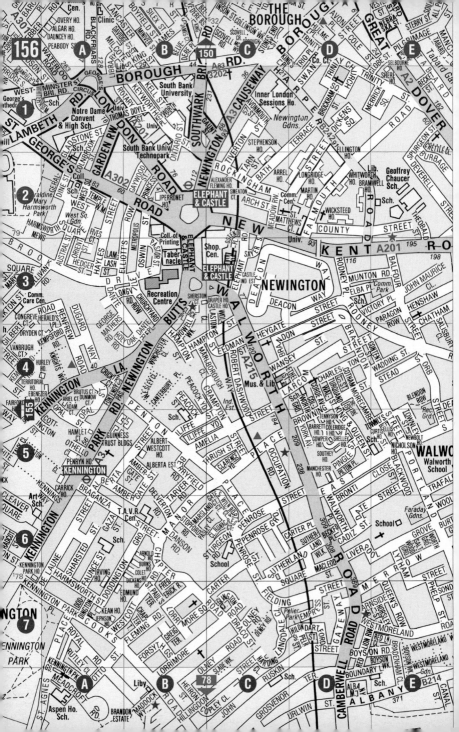

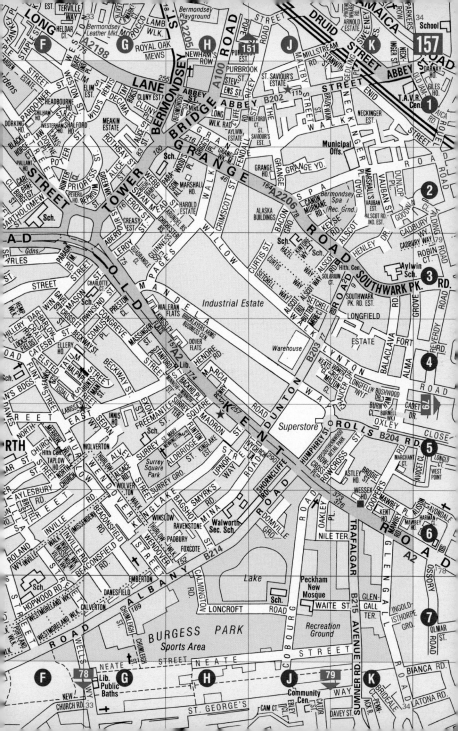

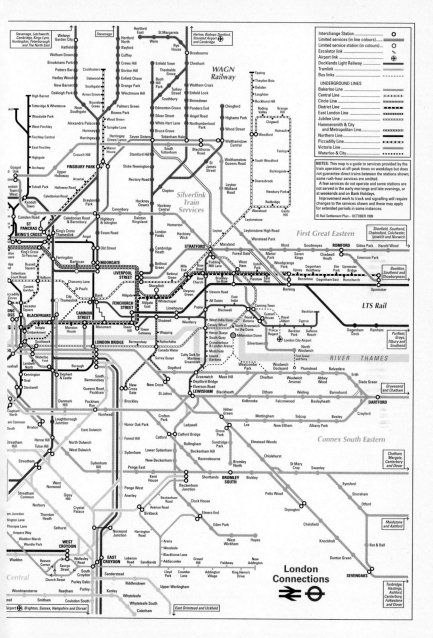

London Connections

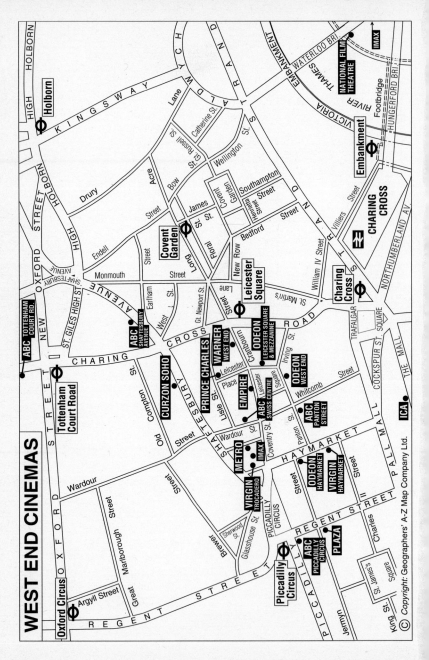

WEST END CINEMAS

160

© Copyright: Geographers' A-Z Map Company Ltd.

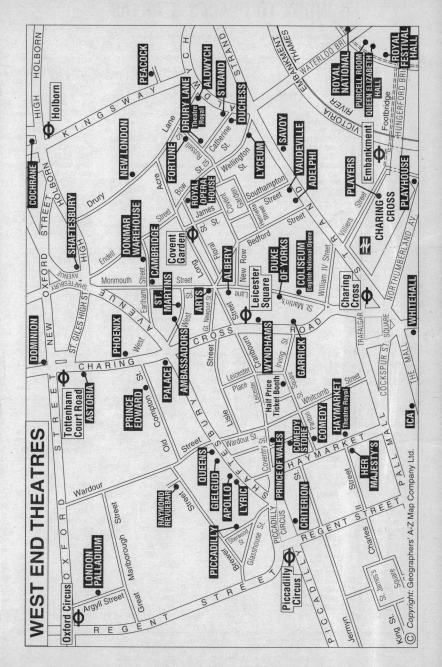

WEST END THEATRES

INDEX TO PLACES & AREAS

Names in this index shown in CAPITAL LETTERS, followed by their Postcode District(s), are Posttowns.

ABBEY WOOD. (SE2) —4C 84
ACTON. (W3) —1J 73
Acton Green. —4K 73
ADDINGTON. (CR0) —5C 136
ADDISCOMBE. (CR0) —1G 135
Aldborough Hatch. —4K 35
Aldersbrook. —2K 49
Alperton. —1E 56
ANERLEY. (SE20) —2H 125
Angell Town. —1A 94
Avery Hill. —6H 99

BALHAM. (SW12) —1F 109
Bandonhill. —5H 133
BARKING. (IG11) —7G 51
BARKINGSIDE. (IG6) —3G 35
BARNEHURST. (DA7) —3J 101
BARNES. (SW13) —2B 90
BARNET. (EN4 & EN5) —4B 4
Barnet Vale. —5E 4
Barnsbury. —7K 45
Barons Court. —5G 75
BATTERSEA. (SW11) —1B 92
Bayswater. —7A 60
Beacontree Heath. —2G 53
BECKENHAM. (BR3) —1C 126
Beckton. —5D 66
Beckton Park. —6D 66
Becontree. —2E 52
BEDDINGTON. (CR0 & SM6)
            —3J 133
Beddington Corner. —7E 122
Bedford Park. —3K 73
Belgravia. —3E 76 (2H 153)
Bell Green. —4B 112
Bellingham. —3D 112
Belmont. —1B 124
BELVEDERE. (DA17) —3G 85
Benhilton. —2K 131
BERMONDSEY. (SE1 & SE16)
            —2F 79 (7K 151)
BERRYLANDS. (KT5) —6G 119
BETHNAL GREEN. (E2) —3H 63
BEXLEY. (DA5) —7H 101
BEXLEYHEATH. (DA4 & DA7)
            —4G 101
BICKLEY. (BR1) —3C 128
Blackfen. —6A 100
BLACKHEATH. (SE3) —2H 97
Blackheath Park. —4H 97
Blackheath Vale. —2H 97
Blackwall. —7E 64
Blendon. —6D 100
Bloomsbury. —5J 61 (5E 142)
Blythe Hill. —7B 96
Borough, The. —2D 78 (6E 150)
Boston Manor. —5B 72
Bounds Green. —5C 16
BOW. (E3) —3C 64
Bow Common. —5C 64
Bowes Park. —7D 16
BRENTFORD. (TW8) —6D 72
Brent Cross. —7E 26
Brentford End. —7B 72
BRIMSDOWN. (EN3) —2F 9
BRIXTON. (SW2) —4K 93
Broadgate. —5E 62 (6G 145)
Broad Green. —7B 124
BROCKLEY. (SE4) —4B 96
Bromley. —3D 64
  (Bow)

BROMLEY. (BR1 & BR2) —2J 127
  (Kent)
Bromley Common. —1C 138
Bromley Park. —1G 127
Brompton. —2D 76 (2D 152)
Brondesbury. —7H 43
Brondesbury Park. —1G 59
Brook Green. —4F 75
Broom Hill. —4K 129
Brownswood Park. —2B 46
Brunswick Park. —3K 15
BUCKHURST HILL. (IG9) —2G 21
Burnt Oak. —1J 25
BUSHEY. (WD2) —1A 10
Bushey Heath. —1C 10
Bushey Mead. —3F 121
Bush Hill Park. —6A 8

CAMBERWELL. (SE5) —1D 94
CAMDEN TOWN. (NW1) —1F 61
Cann Hall. —4G 49
Canning Town. —6H 65
Canonbury. —6C 46
Canons Park. —7K 11
CARSHALTON. (SM5) —4E 132
Carshalton Beeches. —7C 132
Carshalton on the Hill. —7E 132
Castelnau. —6D 74
CATFORD. (SE6) —7D 96
CHADWELL HEATH. (RM6)
            —7D 36
Chalk Farm. —7E 44
Chapel End. —1C 32
CHARLTON. (SE7) —6B 82
Chase Side. —1J 7
CHEAM. (SM2 & SM3) —6G 131
CHELSEA. (SW3)
            —5C 76 (6D 152)
CHIGWELL. (IG7) —3K 21
Child's Hill. —3J 43
CHINGFORD. (E4) —1K 19
Chingford Green. —1A 20
Chingford Hatch. —4A 20
Chingford Mount. —4H 19
Chipping Barnet. —4B 4
CHISLEHURST. (BR7) —7G 115
Chislehurst West. —5E 114
CHISWICK. (W4) —6K 73
CHURCH END. (N3) —1H 27
  (Finchley)
Church End. —6A 42
  (Willesden)
CITY OF LONDON. (EC1 to EC4)
            —6D 62 (1F 150)
CLAPHAM. (SW4) —4G 93
Clapham Common. —5F 93
Clapham Junction. —4C 92
Clapham Park. —6H 93
Clapton Park. —4K 47
Clayhall. —2D 34
Clerkenwell. —4A 62 (4A 144)
COCKFOSTERS. (EN4) —4K 5
Coldblow. —1J 117
Cole Park. —6A 88
Colindale. —3A 26
College Park. —3D 58
COLLIER ROW. (RM5) —1H 37
Collier's Wood. —7B 108
Colney Hatch. —6J 15
Coney Hall. —3G 137
Coombe. —7K 105

Copse Hill. —7D 106
Cottenham Park. —1D 120
Covent Garden. —7J 61 (2F 149)
Cranbrook. —1D 50
Cranley Gardens. —4F 29
Creekmouth. —4A 68
CRICKLEWOOD. (NW2) —4F 43
Crofton Park. —5B 96
Crouch End. —5J 29
CROYDON. (CR0) —2C 134
Crystal Palace. —6F 111
Cubitt Town. —4E 80
Custom House. —6A 66
Cyprus. —7E 66

DAGENHAM. (RM8 to RM10)
            —6G 53
Dalston. —6F 47
Dartmouth Park. —3F 45
De Beauvoir Town. —7E 46
DEPTFORD. (SE8) —7C 80
Dollis Hill. —3C 42
Dormer's Wells. —7F 55
Downham. —5F 113
Ducks Island. —6A 4
Dudden Hill. —6D 42
DULWICH. (SE21) —2E 110
Dulwich Village. —7E 94

EALING. (W5) —7D 56
EARL'S COURT. (SW5) —5J 75
Earlsfield. —1A 108
East Acton. —7A 58
EAST BARNET. (EN4) —6H 5
Eastcote. —7A 22
EAST DULWICH. (SE22) —4F 95
EAST FINCHLEY. (N2) —4C 28
EAST HAM. (E6) —1D 66
East Sheen. —4J 89
East Village. —5A 22
East Wickham. —1C 100
EDEN PARK. (BR3) —5C 126
EDGWARE. (HA8) —6B 12
Edgware Bury. —1A 12
Edmonton. —4B 18
ELMERS END. (BR3) —4A 126
ELMSTEAD. (BR7) —6D 114
ELTHAM. (SE9) —6D 98
Eltham Park. —4E 98
Elthorne Heights. —5H 55
ENFIELD. (EN1 to EN3) —3J 7
Enfield Highway. —2E 8
Enfield Town. —3J 7
EWELL. (KT17) —7B 130

FAIR CROSS. —5J 51
Fairlop. —1K 35
Falconwood. —4J 99
Fallow Corner. —7F 15
Farthing Street. —7D 138
FINCHLEY. (N3) —1J 27
Finsbury. —3A 62 (2A 143)
FINSBURY PARK. (N4) —2A 46
Foots Cray. —6J 116
Forestdale. —7B 136
FOREST GATE. (E7) —5K 49
FOREST HILL. (SE23) —2J 111
Fortis Green. —3E 28
Fortune Green. —4J 43

Forty Hill. —1K 7
Friday Hill. —2B 20
Friern Barnet. —5J 15
FULHAM. (SW6) —2G 91
Fulwell. —4H 103
Fulwell Cross. —2G 35
Furzedown. —5F 109

GANTS HILL. —6E 34
Giggshill. —7A 118
Gilwell Park. —3K 9
Globe Town. —3K 63
GOLDERS GREEN. (NW11)
            —6G 27
Goodmayes. —1A 52
Gospel Oak. —4E 44
Grahame Park. —1B 26
Grange Park. —6G 7
GREENFORD. (UB6) —3G 55
Greenford Green. —6J 39
Greenhill. —5K 23
GREENWICH. (SE10) —7E 80
Grove Park. —1J 89
  (Chiswick)
Grove Park. —3K 113
  (Lee)
Gunnersbury. —4H 73

HACKBRIDGE. (SM6) —2E 132
HACKNEY. (E8) —6H 47
Hackney Wick. —6C 48
Hadley. —2C 4
Hadley Wood. —1F 5
Haggerston. —2F 63
Hale End. —6A 20
Hale, The. —5E 12
HAM. (TW10) —3C 104
HAMMERSMITH. (W6) —4E 74
HAMPSTEAD. (NW3) —4A 44
Hampstead Garden Suburb.
            —5A 28
HAMPTON. (TW12) —7F 103
Hampton Court. —3A 118
HAMPTON HILL. (TW12)
            —5G 103
HAMPTON WICK. (KT1) —1C 118
Hanger Hill. —4F 57
HANWELL. (W7) —1K 71
HANWORTH. (TW13) —4B 102
Harlesden. —2B 58
Harringay. —5B 30
HARROW. (HA1 to HA3) —6J 23
Harrow on the Hill. —1J 39
HARROW WEALD. (HA3) —7D 10
HATCH END. (HA5) —1D 22
HAYES. (BR2) —1K 137
Headstone. —4G 23
HENDON. (NW4) —5D 26
HERNE HILL. (SE24) —6C 94
Heston. —7E 70
Higham Hill. —2A 32
Highams Park. —6A 20
HIGH BARNET. (EN5) —3B 4
HIGHBURY. (N5) —4B 46
HIGHGATE. (N6) —1F 45
Highlands Village. —5E 6
Highwood Hill. —3J 13
Hither Green. —6G 97
Holborn. —5A 62 (6J 143)
Holders Hill. —2F 27

Holland Park. —1H 75
HOLLOWAY. (N7) —3J 45
HOMERTON. (E9) —5A 48
Honor Oak. —6K 95
Honor Oak Park. —7A 96
Horn Park. —5K 97
HORNSEY. (N8) —4J 29
Hornsey Vale. —5K 29
HOUNSLOW. (TW3 to TW6)
            —3F 87
Hounslow West. —2C 86
Hoxton. —2E 62
Hurlingham. —3K 91
Hyde Park. —1D 76 (4E 146)
HYDE, THE. (NW9) —5B 26

ILFORD. (IG1 to IG6) —3F 51
Iseldon Village. —3A 46
ISLEWORTH. (TW7) —3A 88
ISLINGTON. (N1) —7B 46

JOYDENS WOOD. —4K 117

KENNINGTON. (SE11) —6A 78
Kensal Green. —3E 58
Kensal Rise. —2F 59
Kensal Town. —4G 59
KENSINGTON. (W8) —2K 75
KENTISH TOWN. (NW5) —5F 45
KENTON. (HA3) —5C 24
KESTON. (BR2) —5A 138
Keston Mark. —3B 138
KEW. (TW9) —7G 73
Kidbrooke. —2K 97
KILBURN. (NW6) —1J 59
Kingsbury. —6J 25
Kingsbury Green. —5J 25
King's Cross. —2J 61
Kingsland. —6E 46
KINGSTON UPON THAMES.
      (KT1 & KT2) —2E 118
Kingston Vale. —4A 106
Knightsbridge. —2D 76 (7E 146)

LADYWELL. —5D 96
LAMBETH. (SE1 & SE11)
            —3K 77 (2G 155)
Lamorbey. —1K 115
Lampton. —1F 87
Lea Bridge. —3K 47
Leamouth. —7G 65
LEE. (SE12) —5H 97
Lessness Heath. —5G 85
LEWISHAM. (SE13) —3E 96
LEYTON. (E10) —3E 48
LEYTONSTONE. (E11) —1G 49
Limehouse. —6B 64
Lisson Grove. —5C 60 (5D 140)
Little Ealing. —4D 72
LITTLE HEATH. (RM6) —4B 36
Little Ilford. —7B 50
Little Stanmore. —7A 12
LOCKSBOTTOM. (BR6) —3E 138
London City Airport. —1C 82
Lonesome. —1G 123
LONG DITTON. (KT6) —7C 118
Longlands. —3H 115
LOWER CLAPTON. (E5) —4H 47

Index to Places & Areas

LOWER EDMONTON. (N9)
—3B 18
Lower Holloway. —5K 45
Lower Place. —2J 57
Lower Sydenham. —4A 112
Loxford. —5G 51
Lyonsdown. —5F 5

MAIDA HILL. (W9) —4H 59
Maida Vale. —3K 59
Malden Green. —1C 130
MANOR PARK. (E12) —4C 50
Marks Gate. —2E 36
Marling Park. —7D 102
Marylebone. —5E 60 (5H 141)
Maswell Park. —5G 87
Mawney. —3H 37
Mayfair. —7F 61 (3J 147)
Maypole. —1K 117
Merry Hill. —1A 10
Merton. —7K 107
Merton Park. —2J 121
Mid Beckton. —5D 66
Mile End. —3A 64
MILL HILL. (NW7) —5G 13
Mill Meads. —2F 65
Millwall. —4D 80
MITCHAM. (CR4) —3D 122
Monken Hadley. —1D 4
Monks Orchard. —7A 126
MORDEN. (SM4) —3K 121
Morden Park. —6G 121
MORTLAKE. (SW14) —3K 89
Motspur Park. —6C 120
Mottingham. —2C 114
MUSWELL HILL. (N10) —3F 29

Nash. —6J 137
Neasden. —3A 42
NEW BARNET. (EN4 & EN5)
—4F 5
New Beckenham. —6B 112
Newbury Park. —6H 35
New Charlton. —4A 82
NEW CROSS. (SE14) —7B 80
New Cross Gate. —1K 95
New Eltham. —2G 115
Newington. —3C 78 (2C 156)
Newlands. —5K 95
(Brockley)
Newlands. —3K 11
(Edgware)
NEW MALDEN. (KT3) —4A 120
NEW SOUTHGATE. (N11) —5A 16
Nine Elms. —7G 77
Noel Park. —2B 30
NORBITON. (KT1 & KT2)
—2G 119
Norbury. —2K 123
North Acton. —4K 57
North Beckton. —5C 66
NORTH CHEAM. (SM3) —4F 131
North Cray. —5E 116
North End. —2A 44
Northfields. —3B 72
NORTH FINCHLEY. (N12) —5F 15
NORTH HARROW. (HA2) —6F 23
NORTH KENSINGTON. (W10)
—5F 59
NORTHOLT. (UB5) —7E 38
North Sheen. —3G 89
NORTHUMBERLAND HEATH.
(DA8) —7J 85
North Wembley. —2B 40

North Woolwich. —2E 82
NORWOOD. (SE19) —6E 110
Norwood Green. —4E 70
Norwood New Town. —6C 110
NOTTING HILL. (W11) —7H 59
Nunhead. —3H 95

Oakleigh Park. —1G 15
Oakwood. —6C 6
Old Bexley. —7H 101
Old Brentford. —7D 72
Old Ford. —2B 64
Old Isleworth. —3B 88
Old Malden. —1B 130
Old Oak Common. —5A 58
ORPINGTON. (BR5 & BR6)
—7K 129
Osidge. —1A 16
Osterley. —7H 71

PADDINGTON. (W2)
—6B 60 (1A 146)
PALMERS GREEN. (N13) —4F 17
PARK LANGLEY. (BR3) —4E 126
Park Royal. —3H 57
Parson's Green. —1J 91
PECKHAM. (SE15) —1G 95
Penge. —7J 111
Pentonville. —2K 61
Perivale. —1C 56
Petersham. —1E 104
PETTS WOOD. (BR5) —5G 129
Pimlico. —5G 77 (6A 154)
PINNER. (HA5) —3C 22
Pinner Green. —2A 22
Pinnerwood Park. —1A 22
Plaistow. —7J 113
(Bromley)
PLAISTOW. (E13) —3K 65
(Newham)
Plashet. —6C 50
Plumstead. —4J 83
Plumstead Common. —6H 83
Ponders End. —5D 8
POPLAR. (E14) —7D 64
Poverest. —4K 129
Preston. —1E 40
Primrose Hill. —1E 60
PUTNEY. (SW15) —4G 91
Putney Heath. —6E 90
Putney Vale. —3C 106

Queensbury. —3F 25

Ratcliff. —6A 64
Rayners Lane. —1E 38
Raynes Park. —4E 120
Redbridge. —6C 34
Regent's Park. —2F 61 (1K 141)
RICHMOND. (TW9 & TW10)
—5D 88
Richmond Park. —1J 105
Rippleside. —1B 68
Rise Park. —1K 37
Roe Green. —4J 25
Roehampton. —7C 90
Rosehill. —1A 132
ROTHERHITHE. (SE16) —2J 79
Roundshaw. —7J 133
Roxeth. —2H 39
RUSH GREEN. (RM7) —1K 53
Ruxley. —7E 116

St Helier. —7C 122
St James's. —1H 77 (4C 148)
St John's. —2C 96
ST JOHN'S WOOD. (NW8)
—2B 60
St Luke's. —4C 62 (3D 144)
St Margarets. —6B 88
St Pancras. —3J 61 (1E 142)
Sands End. —1A 92
Seething Wells. —6C 118
Selhurst. —6D 124
Seven Kings. —1J 51
Sewardstone. —1K 9
Shacklewell. —4F 47
Shadwell. —7J 63
SHEPHERD'S BUSH. (W12)
—2E 74
SHIRLEY. (CR0) —2K 135
Shirley Oaks. —1H 135
Shooters Hill. —1E 98
Shoreditch. —3E 62 (2H 145)
SHORTLANDS. (BR2) —2G 127
SIDCUP. (DA14 & DA15)
—4A 116
Silvertown. —1B 82
Snaresbrook. —5J 33
Soho. —6H 61 (1C 148)
Somers Town. —3H 61 (1C 142)
South Acton. —3H 73
SOUTHALL. (UB1 & UB2) —1D 70
Southall Green. —3C 70
South Barnet. —1K 15
South Beddington. —6H 133
SOUTHBOROUGH. (BR1 & BR2)
(Bromley) —6C 128
Southborough. —7E 118
(Surbiton)
South Bromley. —6F 65
South Chingford. —6G 19
SOUTH CROYDON. (CR2)
—5D 134
Southend. —4E 112
Southfields. —1J 107
Southgate. —1C 16
South Hackney. —1J 63
South Hampstead. —7A 44
SOUTH HARROW. (HA2) —3G 39
SOUTH KENSINGTON. (SW7)
—4B 76 (3B 152)
SOUTH LAMBETH. (SW8) —7J 77
SOUTH NORWOOD. (SE25)
—4F 125
SOUTH RUISLIP. (HA4) —4A 38
SOUTH TOTTENHAM. (N15)
—5F 31
SOUTHWARK. (SE1)
—1D 78 (4E 150)
South Wimbledon. —6K 107
SOUTH WOODFORD. (E18)
—2J 33
Spencer Park. —5B 92
Spitalfields. —5F 63 (5J 145)
Spring Grove. —2J 87
Spring Park. —3C 136
Stamford Hill. —1F 47
STANMORE. (HA7) —5G 11
STEPNEY. (E1) —5K 63
STOCKWELL. (SW9) —2K 93
STOKE NEWINGTON. (N16)
—3F 47
Stonegrove. —4A 12
STONELEIGH. (KT19) —5C 130
Stoneybridge. —1K 57
Strand on the Green. —6H 73
STRATFORD. (E15) —7F 49
Stratford Marsh. —7D 48

Stratford New Town. —5F 49
Strawberry Hill. —3K 103
STREATHAM. (SW16) —4J 109
Streatham Common. —6J 109
Streatham Hill. —1J 109
Streatham Park. —4G 109
Streatham Vale. —7G 109
Stroud Green. —7K 29
Sudbury. —5B 40
Suffield Hatch. —4K 19
Summerstown. —3A 108
Sundridge. —6A 114
SUNDRIDGE PARK. (BR1)
—7A 114
SURBITON. (KT5 & KT6)
—6D 118
SUTTON. (SM1 to SM3) —5K 131
SYDENHAM. (SE26) —4J 111
Syon Park. —1C 88

TEDDINGTON. (TW11) —5A 104
Temple Fortune. —5H 27
Temple Mills. —5D 48
THAMES DITTON. (KT7) —6A 118
THAMESMEAD. (SE28) —2A 84
Thamesmead Central. —1A 84
Thamesmead East. —2G 85
Thamesmead North. —6C 68
Thamesmead South. —2D 84
Thamesmead South West.
—2K 83
Thamesmead West. —3H 83
THORNTON HEATH. (CR7)
—4B 124
Tokyngton. —6H 41
TOOTING. (SW17) —5C 108
Tooting Bec. —3E 108
Tooting Graveney. —6D 108
TOTTENHAM. (N17) —2F 31
Tottenham Hale. —3G 31
Totteridge. —1B 14
Tufnell Park. —4G 45
Tulse Hill. —1B 110
Turnham Green. —5K 73
TWICKENHAM. (TW1 & TW2)
—1A 104

Underhill. —5D 4
UPPER CLAPTON. (E5) —2H 47
UPPER EDMONTON. (N18)
—5C 18
UPPER ELMERS END. (BR3)
—5B 126
UPPER HOLLOWAY. (N19)
—2G 45
Upper Norwood. —1E 124
Upper Ruxley. —7G 117
Upper Shirley. —4K 135
Upper Sydenham. —3H 111
Upper Tooting. —3D 108
Upper Walthamstow. —4F 33
Upton. —5D 100
(Bexleyheath)
Upton. —7J 49
(Plaistow)
Upton Park. —2B 66

Vale of Health. —2A 44
Vauxhall. —5J 77

Waddon. —3A 134
Walham Green. —7K 75

Wallend. —1E 66
WALLINGTON. (SM6) —6G 133
WALTHAMSTOW. (E17) —4C 32
WALWORTH. (SE17)
—5C 78 (5E 156)
WANDSWORTH. (SW18) —5K 91
Wandsworth Common. —1D 108
Wanstead. —7K 33
Wapping. —1H 79
Watling. —7E 12
WEALDSTONE. (HA3) —3J 23
WELLING. (DA16) —3B 100
WEMBLEY. (HA9 & HA0)
—5E 40
Wembley Park. —5G 41
West Acton. —6G 57
West Barnes. —4D 120
West Beckton. —6B 66
West Green. —6H 59
Westbourne Green. —6B 60
WEST BROMPTON. (SW10)
—6A 76
West Dulwich. —2D 110
WEST EALING. (W13) —7B 56
West End. —2B 54
WEST EWELL. (KT19) —7A 130
West Green. —4B 30
West Ham. —1J 65
West Hampstead. —6K 43
West Harrow. —7G 23
West Heath. —7D 84
West Hendon. —7C 26
West Hill. —6H 91
WEST KENSINGTON. (W14)
—4H 75
West Kilburn. —3H 59
WESTMINSTER. (SW1)
—2J 77 (7E 148)
WEST NORWOOD. (SE27)
—4C 110
WEST WICKHAM. (BR4)
—1E 138
Whetstone. (N20) —2F 15
Whitechapel. —6G 63
White City. —7D 58
WHITTON. (TW2) —7G 87
Widmore. —3B 128
WILLESDEN. (NW10) —6C 42
Willesden Green. —6D 42
WIMBLEDON. (SW19) —6G 107
Wimbledon Park. —3J 107
WINCHMORE HILL (N21) —7F 7
Winsor Park. —5F 67
Woodcote Green. —7G 133
Wood End. —5H 39
Woodford. —6E 20
Woodford Bridge. —6H 21
WOODFORD GREEN. (IG8)
—6D 20
Woodford Side. —5C 20
Woodford Wells. —3E 20
WOOD GREEN. (N22) —2A 30
Woodlands. —2J 87
Woodside. —6G 125
Woodside Park. —4D 14
WOOLWICH. (SE18) —3E 82
WORCESTER PARK. (KT4)
—1C 130
World's End. —3E 6
Wrythe, The. —3D 132

Yeading. —4A 54

INDEX TO STREETS

ALSO INCLUDING INDUSTRIAL ESTATES, JUNCTION NAMES & SELECTED SUBSIDIARY ADDRESSES

HOW TO USE THIS INDEX

1. Each street name is followed by its Postal District (or, if outside the London Postal Districts, by its Posttown or Postal Locality), and then by its map reference;
e.g. Abbeville Rd. *SW4* —6G **93** is in the South West 4 Postal District and is found in square 6G on page **93**. The page number being shown in bold type.
A strict alphabetical order is followed in which Av., Rd., St. etc. (though abbreviated) are read in full and as part of the street name; e.g. Abbotstone Rd. appears after Abbots Ter. but before Abbot St.

2. Streets and a selection of Subsidiary names not shown on the Maps, appear in this index in *Italics* with the thoroughfare to which it is connected shown in brackets;
e.g. *Abbeydale Ct. S'hall* —6F **55** (off Dormers Rise)

3. The page references shown in brackets indicate those streets that appear on the large scale map pages 140-157; e.g. Abbey Lodge. *NW1* —3C **60** (2D **140**) appears in the large scale section in square 2D on page **140** and, where space allows, also appears in square 3C on page **60**.

4. With the now general usage of Postcodes for addressing mail, it is not recommended that this index be used for such a purpose.

GENERAL ABBREVIATIONS

All : Alley	Chyd : Churchyard	Ga : Gate	M : Mews	Sta : Station
App : Approach	Circ : Circle	Gt : Great	Mt : Mount	St : Street
Arc : Arcade	Cir : Circus	Grn : Green	N : North	Ter : Terrace
Av : Avenue	Clo : Close	Gro : Grove	Pal : Palace	Trad : Trading
Bk : Back	Comn : Common	Ho : House	Pde : Parade	Up : Upper
Boulevd : Boulevard	Cotts : Cottages	Ind : Industrial	Pk : Park	Vs : Villas
Bri : Bridge	Ct : Court	Junct : Junction	Pas : Passage	Wlk : Walk
B'way : Broadway	Cres : Crescent	La : Lane	Pl : Place	W : West
Bldgs : Buildings	Dri : Drive	Lit : Little	Quad : Quadrant	Yd : Yard
Bus : Business	E : East	Lwr : Lower	Rd : Road	
Cvn : Caravan	Embkmt : Embankment	Mnr : Manor	Shop : Shopping	
Cen : Centre	Est : Estate	Mans : Mansions	S : South	
Chu : Church	Gdns : Gardens	Mkt : Market	Sq : Square	

POSTTOWN AND POSTAL LOCALITY ABBREVIATIONS

Act V : Acton Vale Ind. Pk.	*Croy* : Croydon	*Hanw* : Hanworth	*N Mald* : New Malden	*Stan* : Stanmore
Bark : Barking	*Dag* : Dagenham	*Harr* : Harrow	*N Har* : North Harrow	*S'leigh* : Stoneleigh
B'side : Barkingside	*Dart* : Dartford	*Har W* : Harrow Weald	*N'holt* : Northolt	*Sun* : Sunbury-on-Thames
B'hurst : Barnehurst	*Dit H* : Ditton Hill	*Hay* : Hayes (Middlesex)	*N Hth* : Northumberland Heath	*Surb* : Surbiton
Barn : Barnet	*E Barn* : East Barnet	*Hayes* : Hayes (Surrey)	*Orp* : Orpington	*Sutt* : Sutton
Beck : Beckenham	*Eastc* : Eastcote	*H End* : Hatch End	*Pet W* : Petts Wood	*Swan* : Swanley
Bedd : Beddington	*E Mol* : East Molesey	*High Bar* : High Barnet	*Pinn* : Pinner	*Tedd* : Teddington
Belv : Belvedere	*Edgw* : Edgware	*Houn* : Hounslow	*Purf* : Purfleet	*Th Dit* : Thames Ditton
Bex : Bexley	*Els* : Elstree	*Ilf* : Ilford	*Purl* : Purley	*T Hth* : Thornton Heath
Bexh : Bexleyheath	*Enf* : Enfield	*Iswth* : Isleworth	*Rain* : Rainham	*Twic* : Twickenham
Bren : Brentford	*Eps* : Epsom	*Kent* : Kenton	*Rich* : Richmond	*Wall* : Wallington
Brom : Bromley	*Eri* : Erith	*Kes* : Keston	*R'way* : Ridgeway, The	*W'stone* : Wealdstone
Buck H : Buckhurst Hill	*Ewe* : Ewell	*Kew* : Kew	*Romf* : Romford	*Well* : Welling
Bush : Bushey	*Farn* : Farnborough (Kent)	*King T* : Kingston Upon Thames	*Ruis* : Ruislip	*Wemb* : Wembley
Cars : Carshalton	*F'boro* : Farnborough (Hants)	*L Hth* : Little Heath	*Rush G* : Rush Green	*W Ewe* : West Ewell
Chad H : Chadwell Heath	*Felt* : Feltham	*Lou* : Loughton	*St P* : St Pauls Cray	*W'way E* : Westway Estate
Cheam : Cheam	*Gnfd* : Greenford	*Mawn* : Mawneys	*S'hall* : Southall	*W Wick* : West Wickham
Chig : Chigwell	*Hack* : Hackbridge	*Mitc* : Mitcham	*S Croy* : South Croydon	*Whit* : Whitton
Chst : Chislehurst	*Ham* : Ham	*Mit J* : Mitcham Junction	*S Harr* : South Harrow	*Wilm* : Wilmington
Cockf : Cockfosters	*Hamp* : Hampton	*Mord* : Morden	*S Ruis* : South Ruislip	*Wfd G* : Woodford Green
Col R : Collier Row	*Hamp H* : Hampton Hill	*New Ad* : New Addington	*Short* : Shortlands	*Wor Pk* : Worcester Park
Cray : Crayford	*Hamp W* : Hampton Wick	*New Bar* : New Barnet	*Sidc* : Sidcup	

INDEX TO STREETS

Abberley M. *SW4* —3F **93**

Abbess Clo. *E6* —5C **66**

Abbess Clo. *SW2* —1B **110**

Abbeville M. *SW4* —4H **93**

Abbeville Rd. *N8* —4H **29**

Abbeville Rd. *SW4* —6G **93**

Abbey Av. *Wemb* —2E **56**

Abbey Bus. Cen. *SW8* —1G **93**

Abbey Clo. *N'holt* —3D **54**

Abbey Clo. *Pinn* —3A **22**

Abbey Ct. *Hamp* —7E **102**

Abbey Cres. *Belv* —4G **85**

Abbeydale Ct. *E17* —3F **33**

Abbeydale Ct. S'hall —6F **55** (off Dormers Rise)

Abbeydale Rd. *Wemb* —1F **57**

Abbey Dri. *SW17* —5E **108**

Abbey Est. *NW8* —1K **59**

Abbeyfield Est. *SE16* —4J **79**

Abbeyfield Est. *SE16* —4J **79** (in two parts)

Abbeyfields Clo. *NW10* —2G **57**

Abbey Gdns. *NW8* —2A **60**

Abbey Gdns. *SE16* —4G **79**

Abbey Gdns. *W6* —6G **75**

Abbey Gro. *SE2* —4B **84**

Abbey Hill Rd. *Sidc* —2C **116**

Abbey La. *E15* —2E **64**

Abbey La. *Beck* —7C **112**

Abbey La. Commercial Est. *E15* —2G **65**

Abbey Life Ct. *E16* —5K **65**

Abbey Lodge. *NW1* —3C **60** (2D **140**)

Abbey Manufacturing Est. *Wemb* —1F **57**

Abbey M. *E17* —5C **32**

Abbey Mt. *Belv* —5F **85**

Abbey Orchard St. *SW1* —3H **77** (1C **154**)

Abbey Orchard St. Est. *SW1* —3H **77** (1D **154**)

Abbey Pde. *NW10* —3F **57**

Abbey Pde. SW19 —7A **108** (off Merton High St.)

Abbey Pk. *Beck* —7C **112**

Abbey Retail Pk. *Bark* —1F **67**

Abbey Rd. *E15* —2F **65**

Abbey Rd. *NW6 & NW8* —7K **43**

Abbey Rd. *NW10* —2H **57**

Abbey Rd. *SE2 & Belv* —4D **84**

Abbey Rd. *SW19* —7A **108**

Abbey Rd. *Bexh* —4E **100**

Abbey Rd. *Croy* —3B **134**

Abbey Rd. *Enf* —5K **7**

Abbey Rd. *Ilf* —5H **35**

Abbey St. *E13* —4J **65**

Abbey St. *SE1* —3E **78** (1H **157**)

Abbey Ter. *SE2* —4C **84**

Abbey Trad. Est. SE26 —5B 112
Abbey View. NW7 —3G 13
Abbey Wharf Ind. Est. Bark
—3H 67
Abbey Wood Rd. SE2 —4B 84
Abbot Ct. SW8 —7J 77
(off Hartington Rd.)
Abbotsbury Clo. E15 —2E 64
Abbotsbury Clo. W14 —2H 75
Abbotsbury Gdns. Pinn —7A 22
Abbotsbury M. SE15 —3J 95
Abbotsbury Rd. W14 —2G 75
Abbotsbury Rd. Brom —2H 137
Abbotsbury Rd. Mord —5K 121
Abbots Clo. Orp —7G 129
Abbots Clo. Ruis —3B 38
Abbots Dri. Harr —2E 38
Abbotsford Av. N15 —4C 30
Abbotsford Gdns. Wfd G —7D 20
Abbotsford Rd. Ilf —2A 52
Abbots Gdns. N2 —4B 28
Abbots Gdns. W8 —3K 75
Abbotshade Rd. SE16 —1K 79
Abbotshall Av. N14 —3B 16
Abbotshall Rd. SE6 —1F 113
Abbots La. SE1
—1E 78 (5H 151)
Abbotsleigh Clo. Sutt —7K 131
Abbotsleigh Rd. SW16 —4G 109
Abbot's Mnr. SW1
—5F 77 (5J 153)
Abbots Pk. SW2 —1A 110
Abbot's Pl. NW6 —1K 59
Abbot's Rd. E6 —1B 66
Abbots Rd. Edgw —7D 12
Abbots Ter. N8 —6J 29
Abbotstone Rd. SW15 —3E 90
Abbot St. E8 —6F 47
Abbots Wlk. W8 —3K 75
(off Stone Hall Gdns.)
Abbots Way. Beck —5A 126
Abbotswell Rd. SE4 —5B 96
Abbotswood Clo. Belv —3E 84
Abbotswood Gdns. Ilf —3D 34
Abbotswood Rd. SE22 —4E 94
Abbotswood Rd. SW16 —3H 109
Abbotswood Way. Hayes —1A 70
Abbott Av. SW20 —1F 121
Abbott Clo. Hamp —6C 102
Abbott Clo. N'holt —6D 38
Abbott Rd. E14 —5E 64
(in two parts)
Abbotts Clo. N1 —6C 46
Abbotts Clo. SE28 —7C 68
Abbotts Clo. Romf —3H 37
Abbotts Cres. E4 —4A 20
Abbotts Cres. Enf —2G 7
Abbotts Dri. Wemb —2B 40
Abbott's Grn. Croy —6K 135
Abbottsmede Clo. Twic —2K 103
Abbotts Pk. Rd. E10 —7E 32
Abbotts Rd. Mitc —4G 123
Abbotts Rd. New Bar —4E 4
Abbotts Rd. S'hall —1C 70
Abbotts Rd. Sutt —4G 131
Abbott's Wlk. Bexh —7D 84
Abchurch La. EC4
—7D 62 (2F 151)
Abchurch Yd. EC4
—7D 62 (2E 150)
Abdale Rd. W12 —1D 74
Abel Ho. SE11 —6A 78 (7K 155)
Aberavon Rd. E3 —3A 64
Abercairn Rd. SW16 —7G 109
Aberconway Rd. Mord —4K 121

Abercorn Clo. NW7 —7B 14
Abercorn Clo. NW8 —3A 60
Abercorn Commercial Cen. Wemb
—1D 56
Abercorn Cres. Harr —1F 39
Abercorn Gdns. Harr —7D 24
Abercorn Gdns. Romf —6B 36
Abercorn Pl. NW8 —3A 60
Abercorn Rd. NW7 —7B 14
Abercorn Rd. Stan —7H 11
Abercorn Way. SE1 —5G 79
Abercrombie Dri. Enf —1B 8
Abercrombie St. SW11 —2C 92
Aberdare Clo. W Wick —2E 136
Aberdare Gdns. NW6 —7K 43
Aberdare Gdns. NW7 —7A 14
Aberdare Rd. Enf —4B 8
Aberdeen La. N5 —5C 46
Aberdeen Pde. N18 —5C 18
(off Aberdeen Rd.)
Aberdeen Pk. N5 —5C 46
Aberdeen Pl. NW8
—4B 60 (3A 140)
Aberdeen Rd. N5 —4C 46
Aberdeen Rd. N18 —5C 18
Aberdeen Rd. NW10 —5B 42
Aberdeen Rd. Croy —4D 134
Aberdeen Rd. Harr —2K 23
Aberdeen Ter. SE3 —2F 97
Aberdour Rd. Ilf —3B 52
Aberdour St. SE1
—4E 78 (3G 157)
Aberfeldy Ho. SE5 —7B 78
Aberfeldy St. E14 —6E 64
(in two parts)
Aberford Gdns. SE18 —1C 98
Aberfoyle Rd. SW16 —7H 109
Abergeldie Rd. SE12 —6K 97
Abernethy Rd. SE13 —4G 97
Abersham Rd. E8 —5F 47
Abery St. SE18 —4J 83
Abingdon Clo. NW1 —6H 45
Abingdon Clo. SW19 —6A 108
Abingdon Ct. W8 —3J 75
(off Abingdon Vs.)
Abingdon Gdns. W8 —3J 75
Abingdon Lodge. W8 —3J 75
Abingdon Rd. N3 —2A 28
Abingdon Rd. SW16 —2J 123
Abingdon Rd. W8 —3J 75
Abingdon St. SW1
—3J 77 (1E 154)
Abingdon Vs. W8 —3J 75
Abinger Av. Sutt —7E 130
Abinger Clo. Bark —4A 52
Abinger Clo. Brom —3C 128
Abinger Clo. Wall —5J 133
Abinger Ct. W5 —7C 56
Abinger Ct. Wall —5J 133
Abinger Gdns. Iswth —3J 87
Abinger Gro. SE8 —6B 80
Abinger M. W9 —4J 59
Abinger Rd. W4 —3A 74
Ablett St. SE16 —5J 79
Abney Gdns. N16 —2F 47
Aboyne Dri. SW20 —2C 120
Aboyne Rd. NW10 —3A 42
Aboyne Rd. SW17 —3B 108
Abridge Way. Bark —2B 68
Abyssinia Clo. SW11 —4C 92
Abyssinia Ct. N8 —5K 29
Acacia Av. N17 —7J 17
Acacia Av. Bren —7B 72
Acacia Av. Rich —2F 89
Acacia Av. Wemb —5E 40

Acacia Bus. Cen. E11 —3G 49
(off Howard Rd.)
Acacia Clo. SE20 —2G 125
Acacia Clo. Orp —5H 129
Acacia Clo. Stan —6D 10
Acacia Ct. Harr —5F 23
Acacia Dri. Sutt —1J 131
Acacia Gdns. NW8 —2B 60
Acacia Gdns. W Wick —2E 136
Acacia Gro. SE21 —2D 110
Acacia Gro. N Mald —3K 119
Acacia Ho. N22 —1A 30
(off Douglas Rd.)
Acacia Pl. NW8 —2B 60
Acacia Rd. E11 —2G 49
Acacia Rd. E17 —6A 32
Acacia Rd. N22 —1A 30
Acacia Rd. NW8 —2B 60
Acacia Rd. SW16 —1K 123
Acacia Rd. W3 —7J 57
Acacia Rd. Beck —3B 126
Acacia Rd. Enf —1J 7
Acacia Rd. Hamp —6E 102
Acacia Rd. Mitc —2E 122
Acacias, The. Barn —5G 5
Acacia Way. Sidc —1K 115
Academy Bldgs. N1
—3E 62 (1G 145)
Academy Gdns. Croy —1F 135
Academy Gdns. N'holt —2B 54
Academy Pl. SE18 —1D 98
Academy Rd. SE18 —1D 98
Acanthus Dri. SE1 —5G 79
Acanthus Rd. SW11 —3E 92
Accommodation Rd. NW11
—1H 43
Accommodation Rd. Wor Pk
—5C 130
A.C. Court. Th Dit —6A 118
Acer Av. Hayes —5C 54
Acfold Rd. SW6 —1K 91
Achilles Clo. SE1 —5G 79
Achilles Rd. NW6 —5J 43
Achilles St. SE14 —7B 80
Achilles Way. W1
—1E 76 (5H 147)
Acklam Rd. W10 —5G 59
Acklington Dri. NW9 —1A 26
Ackmar Rd. SW6 —1J 91
Ackroyd Dri. E3 —5B 64
Ackroyd Rd. SE23 —7K 95
Acland Clo. SE18 —7H 83
Acland Cres. SE5 —3D 94
Acland Ho. SW9 —2K 93
Acland Rd. NW2 —6D 42
Acol Ct. NW6 —7J 43
(off Acol Rd.)
Acol Cres. Ruis —5A 38
Acol Rd. NW6 —7J 43
Aconbury Rd. Dag —1B 68
Acorn Clo. E4 —5J 19
Acorn Clo. Chst —5G 115
Acorn Clo. Enf —1G 7
Acorn Clo. Hamp —6F 103
Acorn Clo. Stan —7G 11
Acorn Ct. E6 —7C 50
Acorn Ct. Ilf —6J 35
Acorn Gdns. SE19 —1F 125
Acorn Gdns. W3 —5K 57
Acorn Pde. SE15 —7H 79
Acorn Production Cen. N7
—7J 45
Acorn Wlk. SE16 —1A 80
Acorn Way. SE23 —3K 111
Acre Dri. SE22 —4G 95

Acrefield Ho. NW4 —4F 27
(off Belle Vue Est.)
Acre La. SW2 —4J 93
Acre La. Cars & Wall —4E 132
Acre Path. N'holt —6C 38
(off Arnold Rd.)
Acre Rd. SW19 —6B 108
Acre Rd. Dag —7H 53
Acre Rd. King T —1E 118
Acris St. SW18 —5A 92
Acton Central Ind. Est. W3
—1H 73
Acton Clo. N9 —2B 18
Acton Hill M. W3 —1H 73
Acton La. NW10 —3J 57
Acton La. W3 —2J 73
Acton La. W4 & W3 —4J 73
(in three parts)
Acton M. E8 —1F 63
Acton St. Est. W3 —2K 73
Acton St. WC1 —3K 61 (2G 143)
Acton Vale Ind. Pk. W3 —1B 74
Acuba Rd. SW18 —2A 107
Acworth Clo. N9 —7D 8
Ada Ct. W9 —3A 60 (2A 140)
Ada Gdns. E14 —6F 65
Ada Gdns. E15 —1H 65
Adair Clo. SE25 —3H 125
Adair Rd. W10 —4G 59
Adair Tower. W10 —4G 59
(off Appleford Rd.)
Adam Clo. SE6 —4C 112
Adam Ct. SE11 —4B 78 (4A 156)
Adam Ct. SW7 —4A 76
(off Gloucester Rd.)
Adam & Eve Ct. W1
—6G 61 (7B 142)
Adam & Eve M. W8 —3J 75
Adam Rd. E4 —6G 19
Adams Bri. Bus. Cen. Wemb
—5H 41
Adams Clo. N3 —7D 14
Adams Clo. NW9 —2H 41
Adams Clo. Surb —6F 119
Adams Ct. E14 —6A 32
Adams Ct. EC2 —6E 62 (7F 145)
Adams Ct. Wemb —6H 41
Adams Gdns. Est. SE16 —2J 79
Adamson Ct. N2 —3C 28
Adamson Rd. E16 —6J 65
Adamson Rd. NW3 —7B 44
Adams Pl. E14 —1D 80
(off N. Colonnade)
Adams Pl. N7 —5K 45
Adamsrill Clo. Enf —6J 7
Adamsrill Rd. SE26 —4K 111
Adams Rd. N17 —2D 30
Adams Rd. Beck —5A 126
Adam's Row. W1
—7E 60 (3H 147)
Adams Sq. Bexh —3E 100
Adam St. WC2 —7J 61 (3F 149)
Adams Wlk. King T —2E 118
Adams Way. Croy —6F 125
Adam Wlk. SW6 —7E 74
(off Crabtree La.)
Ada Pl. E2 —1H 63
Adare Wlk. SW16 —3K 109
Ada Rd. SE5 —7E 78
Ada Rd. Wemb —3D 40
Ada St. E8 —1H 63
Ada Workshops. E8 —1H 63
Adderley Gdns. SE9 —4E 114
Adderley Gro. SW11 —5E 92

Adderley Rd. Harr —1K 23
Adderley St. E14 —6E 64
Addey Ho. SE8 —7B 80
Addington Ct. SW14 —3K 89
Addington Dri. N12 —6G 15
Addington Gro. SE26 —4A 112
Addington Ho. SW9 —2K 93
(off Stockwell Rd.)
Addington Rd. E3 —3C 64
Addington Rd. E16 —4G 65
Addington Rd. N4 —6A 30
Addington Rd. Croy —1A 134
Addington Rd. S Croy —7K 135
Addington Rd. W Wick —4E 136
Addington Sq. SE5 —6D 78
Addington St. SE1
—2K 77 (7H 149)
Addington Village Rd. Croy
(in two parts) —6B 136
Addis Clo. Enf —1E 8
Addiscombe Av. Croy —1G 135
Addiscombe Clo. Harr —5C 24
Addiscombe Ct. Rd. Croy
—1E 134
Addiscombe Gro. Croy —2E 134
Addiscombe Rd. Croy —2E 134
Addison Av. N14 —6A 6
Addison Av. W11 —1G 75
Addison Av. Houn —1G 87
Addison Bri. Pl. W14 —4H 75
Addison Clo. Orp —6G 129
Addison Ct. E2 —2G 63
(off Pritchard's Rd.)
Addison Cres. W14 —3G 75
Addison Dri. SE12 —5K 97
Addison Gdns. Surb —4F 119
Addison Gro. W4 —3A 74
Addison Ho. NW8
—3B 60 (1A 140)
Addison Pl. SE25 —4G 125
Addison Pl. W11 —1G 75
Addison Pl. S'hall —7E 54
Addison Rd. E11 —6J 33
Addison Rd. E17 —5D 32
Addison Rd. SE25 —4G 125
Addison Rd. W14 —2G 75
Addison Rd. Brom —5B 128
Addison Rd. Enf —1D 8
Addison Rd. Ilf —1G 35
Addison Rd. Tedd —6B 104
Addisons Clo. Croy —2B 136
Addison Ter. W4 —4J 73
(off Chiswick Rd.)
Addle Hill. EC4 —6B 62 (1B 150)
Addle St. EC2 —6C 62 (7D 144)
Addmar Rd. Dag —3E 52
Addy Ho. SE16 —4J 79
Adela Av. N Mald —5D 120
Adelaide Av. SE4 —4B 96
Adelaide Clo. Enf —1K 7
Adelaide Clo. Stan —4F 11
Adelaide Ct. W7 —2K 71
Adelaide Ct. Beck —7B 112
Adelaide Gdns. Romf —5E 36
Adelaide Gro. W12 —1C 74
Adelaide Ho. E15 —2H 65
Adelaide Ho. E17 —2B 32
Adelaide Ho. SE5 —2E 94
Adelaide Rd. E10 —3E 48
Adelaide Rd. NW3 —7B 44
Adelaide Rd. Chst —5F 115
Adelaide Rd. Houn —1C 86

Adelaide Rd. *Ilf* —2F **51**
Adelaide Rd. *Rich* —4F **89**
Adelaide Rd. *S'hall* —4C **70**
Adelaide Rd. *Surb* —5E **118**
Adelaide Rd. *Tedd* —6K **103**
Adelaide St. *WC2*
　　　—7J **61** (3E **148**)
Adelaide Ter. *Bren* —5D **72**
Adelaide Wlk. *SW9* —4A **95**
Adela St. *W10* —4G **59**
Adelina Gro. *E1* —5J **63**
Adelina M. *SW12* —1H **109**
Adeline Pl. *WC1*
　　　—5H **61** (6D **142**)
Adelphi Ct. *W4* —6K **73**
Adelphi Ter. *WC2*
　　　—7J **61** (3F **149**)
Adeney Clo. *W6* —6F **75**
Aden Gro. *N16* —4D **46**
Adenmore Rd. *SE6* —7C **96**
Aden Rd. *Enf* —4F **9**
Aden Rd. *Ilf* —7F **35**
Aden Ter. *N16* —4D **46**
Adie Rd. *W6* —3E **74**
Adinc Rd. *E13* —4K **65**
Adler St. *E1* —6G **63**
Adley St. *E5* —5A **48**
Adlington Clo. *N18* —5K **17**
Admaston Rd. *SE18* —7G **83**
Admiral Ct. *SW10* —1A **92**
　　(off Admiral Sq.)
Admiral Ct. *Cars* —1C **132**
Admiral Ho. *Tedd* —4A **104**
Admiral Hyson Ind. Est. *SE16*
　　　—5H **79**
Admiral M. *W10* —4F **59**
Admiral Pl. *SE16* —1A **80**
Admirals Clo. *E18* —4K **33**
Admiral Seymour Rd. *SE9*
　　　—4D **98**
Admiral Sq. *SW10* —1A **92**
Admiral St. *SE8* —1C **96**
Admirals Wlk. *NW3* —3A **44**
Admirals Way. *E14* —2C **80**
Admiralty Clo. *SE8* —7C **80**
Admiralty Rd. *Tedd* —6K **103**
Admiral Wlk. *W9* —5J **59**
Adolf St. *SE6* —4D **112**
Adolphus Rd. *N4* —2B **46**
Adolphus St. *SE8* —7B **80**
Adpar St. *W2* —5B **60** (5A **140**)
Adrian Av. *NW2* —1D **42**
Adrian Ho. *N1* —1K **61**
　　(off Barnsbury Est.)
Adrian Ho. *SW8* —7J **77**
　　(off Wyvil Rd.)
Adrian M. *SW10* —6K **75**
Adrienne Av. *S'hall* —4D **54**
Aduent Way. *N18* —5D **18**
Advance Rd. *SE27* —4C **110**
Adys Lawn. *NW2* —6F **43**
Ady's Rd. *SE15* —3F **95**
Aerodrome Rd. *NW9 & NW4*
　　　—3B **26**
Aerodrome Way. *Houn* —6A **70**
Aeroville. *NW9* —2A **26**
Affleck St. *N1* —2K **61** (1G **143**)
Afghan Rd. *SW11* —2C **92**
Agamemnon Rd. *NW6* —5H **43**
Agar Gro. *NW1* —7G **45**
Agar Gro. Est. *NW1* —7H **45**
Agar Pl. *NW1* —7G **45**
Agar St. *WC2* —7J **61** (3E **148**)
Agate Clo. *E16* —6B **66**
Agate Rd. *W6* —3E **74**

Agatha Clo. *E1* —1H **79**
Agaton Rd. *SE9* —2G **115**
Agave Rd. *NW2* —4E **42**
Agdon St. *EC1* —4B **62** (3A **144**)
Agincourt Rd. *NW3* —4D **44**
Agnes Av. *Ilf* —4E **35**
Agnes Clo. *E6* —7E **66**
Agnesfield Clo. *N12* —6H **15**
Agnes Gdns. *Dag* —4D **52**
Agnes Rd. *W3* —1B **74**
Agnes St. *E14* —6B **64**
Agnew Rd. *SE23* —7K **95**
Agricola Pl. *Enf* —5A **8**
Aidan Clo. *Dag* —3E **52**
Aigburth Mans. *SW9* —7A **78**
　　(off Mowll St.)
Aileen Wlk. *E15* —7H **49**
Ailsa Av. *Twic* —5A **88**
Ailsa Rd. *Twic* —5B **88**
Ailsa St. *E14* —5E **64**
Ainger M. *NW3* —7D **44**
　　(off Ainger Rd.)
Ainger Rd. *NW3* —7D **44**
Ainsdale Clo. *Orp* —7H **129**
Ainsdale Cres. *Pinn* —3C **22**
Ainsdale Dri. *SE1* —5G **79**
Ainsdale Rd. *W5* —4D **56**
Ainsley Av. *Romf* —6H **37**
Ainsley Clo. *N9* —1K **17**
Ainsley St. *E2* —3H **63**
Ainslie Clo. *Wemb* —2E **56**
Ainslie Wlk. *SW12* —7F **93**
Ainslie Wood Cres. *E4* —5J **19**
Ainslie Wood Gdns. *E4* —4J **19**
Ainslie Wood Rd. *E4* —5H **19**
Ainsty Est. *SE16* —2K **79**
Ainsty St. *SE16* —2J **79**
Ainsworth Clo. *NW2* —3C **42**
Ainsworth Clo. *SE15* —2E **94**
Ainsworth Rd. *E9* —7J **47**
Ainsworth Rd. *Croy* —2B **134**
Ainsworth Way. *NW8* —1K **59**
Aintree Av. *E6* —1C **66**
Aintree Cres. *Ilf* —2G **35**
Aintree Est. *SW6* —7G **75**
　　(off Aintree St.)
Aintree Rd. *Gnfd* —2B **56**
Aintree St. *SW6* —7G **75**
Airbourne Ho. *Wall* —4G **133**
　　(off Maldon Rd.)
Air Call Bus. Cen. *NW9* —3K **25**
Airdrie Clo. *N1* —7K **45**
Airdrie Clo. *Hayes* —5C **54**
Airedale Av. *W4* —4B **74**
Airedale Av. S. *W4* —5B **74**
Airedale Rd. *SW12* —7D **92**
Airedale Rd. *W5* —3C **72**
Airlie Gdns. *W8* —1J **75**
Airlie Gdns. *Ilf* —1F **51**
Airlinks Ind. Est. *Houn* —5A **70**
Air St. *W1* —7G **61** (3B **148**)
Airthrie Rd. *Ilf* —2B **52**
Aisgill Av. *W14* —5H **75**
　　(in two parts)
Aisher Rd. *SE28* —7C **68**
Aislibie Rd. *SE12* —4G **97**
Aiten Pl. *W6* —4C **74**
Aitken Clo. *E8* —1G **63**
Aitken Clo. *Mitc* —7D **122**
Aitken Rd. *SE6* —2D **112**
Ajax Av. *NW9* —3A **26**
Ajax Rd. *NW6* —5H **43**
Akabusi Clo. *Croy* —6G **125**
Akehurst St. *SW15* —6C **90**
Akenside Rd. *NW3* —5B **44**

Akerman Rd. *SW9* —2B **94**
Akerman Rd. *Surb* —6C **118**
Alabama St. *SE18* —7H **83**
Alacross Rd. *W5* —2C **72**
Aland Ct. *SE16* —3A **80**
Alan Dri. *Barn* —6B **4**
Alan Gdns. *Romf* —7G **37**
Alan Hocken Way. *E15* —2G **65**
Alan Rd. *SW19* —5G **107**
Alanthus Clo. *SE12* —6J **97**
Alaska Bldgs. *SE1*
　　　—3F **79** (2J **157**)
Alaska St. *SE1* —1A **78** (5J **149**)
Alba Clo. *Hayes* —4B **54**
Albacore Cres. *SE13* —6D **96**
Alba Gdns. *NW11* —6G **27**
Albany. *N12* —6E **14**
Albany. *W1* —7G **61** (3A **148**)
Albany Clo. *N15* —4B **30**
Albany Clo. *SW14* —4H **89**
Albany Clo. *Bex* —7C **100**
Albany Ct. *E4* —5G **19**
Albany Ct. *E10* —7C **32**
Albany Ct. *NW9* —1K **25**
Albany Ct. Yd. *W1*
　　　—7G **61** (3B **148**)
Albany Cres. *Edgw* —7B **12**
Albany M. *N1* —7A **46**
Albany M. *SE5* —6C **78** (7D **156**)
Albany M. *Brom* —6J **113**
Albany M. *King T* —6D **104**
Albany M. *Sutt* —5K **131**
Albany Pde. *Bren* —6E **72**
Albany Pk. Av. *Enf* —1D **8**
Albany Pk. Rd. *King T* —6D **104**
Albany Pas. *Rich* —5E **88**
Albany Pl. *N7* —4A **46**
Albany Pl. *Bren* —6D **72**
Albany Reach. *Th Dit* —5A **118**
Albany Rd. *E10* —7C **32**
Albany Rd. *E12* —4B **50**
Albany Rd. *E17* —6A **32**
Albany Rd. *N4* —6A **30**
Albany Rd. *N18* —5C **18**
Albany Rd. *SE5* —6C **78** (7D **156**)
Albany Rd. *SW19* —5K **107**
Albany Rd. *W13* —7B **56**
Albany Rd. *Belv* —6F **85**
Albany Rd. *Bex* —7C **100**
Albany Rd. *Bren* —6D **72**
Albany Rd. *Chst* —5F **115**
Albany Rd. *N Mald* —4K **119**
Albany Rd. *Rich* —5F **89**
Albany Rd. *Romf* —6F **37**
Albany Rd. *SW1* —2F **61** (1J **141**)
Albany Ter. *Rich* —5F **89**
　　(off Albany Pas.)
Albany, The. *Wfd G* —4C **20**
Albany View. *Buck H* —1D **20**
Alba Pl. *W11* —6H **59**
Albatross. *NW9* —2A **26**
Albatross Ct. *SE8* —6B **80**
　　(off Childers St.)
Albatross St. *SE18* —7J **83**
Albatross Way. *SE16* —2K **79**
Albemarle. *SW19* —2F **107**
Albemarle App. *Ilf* —6F **35**
Albemarle Av. *Twic* —1D **102**
Albemarle Gdns. *Ilf* —6F **35**
Albemarle Gdns. *N Mald*
　　　—4K **119**
Albemarle Pk. *Beck* —1D **126**
Albemarle Pk. *Stan* —5H **11**
Albemarle Rd. *Beck* —1D **126**
Albemarle Rd. *E Barn* —7H **5**

Albemarle St. *W1*
　　　—7F **61** (3K **147**)
Albemarle Way. *EC1*
　　　—4B **62** (4A **144**)
Albermarle Ho. *SW9* —3A **94**
Alberon Gdns. *NW11* —4H **27**
Alberta Av. *Sutt* —4G **131**
Alberta Est. *SE17*
　　　—5B **78** (5B **156**)
Alberta Rd. *Enf* —6A **8**
Alberta Rd. *Eri* —1J **101**
Alberta St. *SE17*
　　　—5B **78** (5A **156**)
Albert Av. *E4* —4H **19**
Albert Av. *SW8* —7K **77**
Albert Bigg Point. *E15* —1E **64**
　　(off Godfrey St.)
Albert Bri. *SW3 & SW11*
　　　—6C **76** (7D **152**)
Albert Bri. Rd. *SW11* —7C **76**
Albert Carr Gdns. *SW16* —5J **109**
Albert Clo. *E9* —1H **63**
Albert Clo. *N22* —1H **29**
Albert Cotts. *E1* —5G **63**
　　(off Deal St.)
Albert Ct. *E7* —4J **49**
Albert Ct. *SW7* —2B **76** (7A **146**)
Albert Cres. *E4* —4H **19**
Albert Dane Cen. *S'hall* —3C **70**
Albert Dri. *SW19* —2G **107**
Albert Embkmt. *SE1*
　　　—5J **77** (6F **155**)
Albert Gdns. *E1* —6K **63**
Albert Ga. *SW1* —2D **76** (6F **147**)
Albert Gro. *SW20* —1F **121**
Albert Hall Mans. *SW7*
　　　—2B **76** (7A **146**)
Albert Ho. *E18* —3K **33**
　　(off Albert Rd.)
Albert M. *N4* —1K **45**
Albert M. *SE4* —4A **96**
Albert M. *W8* —3A **76**
Albert Pl. *N17* —3F **31**
Albert Pl. *W8* —2K **75**
Albert Rd. *E10* —2E **48**
Albert Rd. *E16* —1C **82**
Albert Rd. *E17* —5C **32**
Albert Rd. *E18* —3K **33**
Albert Rd. *N4* —1K **45**
Albert Rd. *N15* —6E **30**
Albert Rd. *N22* —1G **29**
Albert Rd. *NW4* —4F **27**
Albert Rd. *NW6* —2H **59**
Albert Rd. *NW7* —5G **13**
Albert Rd. *SE9* —3C **114**
Albert Rd. *SE20* —6K **111**
Albert Rd. *SE25* —4G **125**
Albert Rd. *W5* —4B **56**
Albert Rd. *Belv* —5F **85**
Albert Rd. *Bex* —6G **101**
Albert Rd. *Brom* —5B **128**
Albert Rd. *Buck H* —2G **21**
Albert Rd. *Dag* —1G **53**
Albert Rd. *Hamp* —5G **103**
Albert Rd. *Harr* —3G **23**
Albert Rd. *Houn* —4E **86**
Albert Rd. *Ilf* —3F **51**
Albert Rd. *King T* —2F **119**
Albert Rd. *Mitc* —3D **122**
Albert Rd. *N Mald* —4B **120**
Albert Rd. *Rich* —5E **88**
Albert Rd. *S'hall* —3B **70**
Albert Rd. *Sutt* —5B **132**

Albert Rd. *Tedd* —6K **103**
Albert Rd. *Twic* —1K **103**
Albert Rd. Est. *Belv* —5F **85**
Albert Sq. *E15* —5G **49**
Albert Sq. *SW8* —7K **77**
Albert St. *N12* —5F **15**
Albert St. *NW1* —1F **61**
　　(off Haddonfield)
Albert Starr Ho. *SE8* —4K **79**
　　(off Haddonfield)
Albert Studios. *SW11* —1D **92**
Albert Ter. *NW1* —1E **60**
Albert Ter. *NW10* —1J **57**
Albert Ter. *Buck H* —2H **21**
Albert Ter. M. *NW1* —1E **60**
Albert Victoria Ho. *N22* —1A **30**
　　(off Pellatt Gro.)
Albert Wlk. *E16* —2E **82**
Albert Westcott Ho. *SE17*
　　　—5B **78** (5B **156**)
Albert Whicker Ho. *E17* —4E **32**
Albert Yd. *SE19* —6F **111**
Albion Av. *N10* —1E **28**
Albion Av. *SW8* —2H **93**
Albion Clo. *W2* —7C **60** (2D **146**)
Albion Clo. *Romf* —6K **37**
Albion Dri. *E8* —7F **47**
　　(in two parts)
Albion Est. *SE16* —2K **79**
Albion Gdns. *W6* —4D **74**
Albion Ga. *W2* —7C **60** (2D **146**)
Albion Gro. *N16* —4E **46**
Albion Ho. *E16* —1F **83**
　　(off Church St.)
Albion M. *N1* —1A **62**
Albion M. *NW6* —7H **43**
Albion M. *W2* —7C **60** (2D **146**)
Albion M. *W6* —4D **74**
Albion Pl. *EC1* —5B **62** (5A **144**)
Albion Pl. *EC2* —5D **62** (6F **145**)
Albion Pl. *SE25* —3G **125**
Albion Pl. *W6* —4D **74**
Albion Rd. *E17* —3E **32**
Albion Rd. *N16* —4D **46**
Albion Rd. *N17* —2F **31**
Albion Rd. *Bexh* —4F **101**
Albion Rd. *Houn* —4E **86**
Albion Rd. *King T* —1J **119**
Albion Rd. *Sutt* —6B **132**
Albion Rd. *Twic* —1J **103**
Albion Sq. *E8* —7F **47**
Albion St. *SE16* —2J **79**
Albion St. *W2* —6C **60** (1D **146**)
Albion St. *Croy* —1B **134**
Albion Ter. *E4* —4J **9**
Albion Ter. *E8* —7F **47**
Albion Vs. Rd. *SE26* —3J **111**
Albion Way. *EC1*
　　　—5C **62** (6C **144**)
Albion Way. *SE13* —4E **96**
Albion Way. *Wemb* —3G **41**
Albion Yd. *N1* —2J **61**
Albrighton Rd. *SE22* —3E **94**
Albuhera Clo. *Enf* —1F **7**
Albury Av. *Bexh* —2E **100**
Albury Av. *Iswth* —7K **71**
Albury Clo. *Hamp* —6F **103**
Albury Ct. *N'holt* —3A **54**
　　(off Canberra Dri.)
Albury Ct. *Sutt* —4A **132**
Albury Dri. *Pinn* —1A **22**
Albury M. *E12* —1A **50**
Albury St. *SE8* —6C **80**
Albyfield. *Brom* —4D **128**
Albyn Rd. *SE8* —1C **96**
Alcester Cres. *E5* —2H **47**

Alcester Rd. *Wall* —4F **133**
Alcock Clo. *Wall* —7H **133**
Alcock Rd. *Houn* —7B **70**
Alconbury. *Bexh* —5H **101**
Alconbury Rd. *E5* —2G **47**
Alcorn Clo. *Sutt* —2J **131**
Alcott Clo. *W7* —5K **55**
Alcuin Ct. *Stan* —7H **11**
Aldam Pl. *N16* —2F **47**
Aldborough Ct. *Ilf* —5K **35**
 (off Aldborough Rd. N.)
Aldborough Rd. *Dag* —6J **53**
Aldborough Rd. N. *Ilf* —5K **35**
Aldborough Rd. S. *Ilf* —1J **51**
Aldbourne Rd. *W12* —1B **74**
Aldbridge St. *SE17*
 —5E **78** (5H **157**)
Aldburgh M. *W1* —6E **60** (7H **141**)
Aldbury Av. *Wemb* —7H **41**
Aldbury M. *N9* —7J **7**
Aldebert Ter. *SW8* —7J **77**
Aldeburgh Clo. *E5* —2H **47**
Aldeburgh Pl. *Wfd G* —4D **20**
Aldeburgh St. *SE10* —5J **81**
Alden Av. *E15* —4H **65**
Alden Ct. *Croy* —3E **134**
Aldenham St. *NW1*
 —2G **61** (1B **142**)
Aldensley Rd. *W6* —3D **74**
Alderbrook Rd. *SW12* —6F **93**
Alderbury Rd. *SW13* —6C **74**
Alder Clo. *SE15* —6F **79**
Alder Gro. *NW2* —2C **42**
Aldergrove Gdns. *Houn* —2C **86**
Alderholt Way. *SE15* —7E **78**
Alder Ho. *SE4* —3C **96**
Alder Ho. *SE15* —6F **79**
 (off Alder Clo.)
Alder Lodge. *SW6* —1F **91**
Alderman Av. *Bark* —3A **68**
Aldermanbury. *EC2*
 —6C **62** (7D **144**)
Aldermanbury Sq. *EC2*
 —5C **62** (6D **144**)
Alderman Judge Mall. *King T*
 —2E **118**
Aldermans Hill. *N13* —4D **16**
Aldermans Wlk. *EC2*
 —5E **62** (6G **145**)
Aldermary Rd. *Brom* —1J **127**
Alder M. *N19* —2G **45**
Alderminster Rd. *SE1* —5G **79**
Aldermoor Rd. *SE6* —3B **112**
Alderney Av. *Houn* —7F **71**
Alderney Gdns. *N'holt* —7D **38**
Alderney Ho. *Enf* —1E **8**
Alderney Rd. *E1* —4K **63**
Alderney St. *SW1*
 —4F **77** (4K **153**)
Alder Rd. *SW14* —3K **89**
Alder Rd. *Sidc* —3K **115**
Alders Av. *Wfd G* —6B **20**
Aldersbrook Av. *Enf* —2K **7**
Aldersbrook Dri. *King T* —6F **105**
Aldersbrook La. *E12* —3D **50**
Aldersbrook Rd. *E11 & E12*
 —2K **49**
Alders Clo. *E11* —2K **49**
Alders Clo. *W5* —3D **72**
Alders Clo. *Edgw* —5D **12**
Aldersey Gdns. *Bark* —6H **51**
Aldersford Clo. *SE4* —5K **95**
Aldersgate St. *EC1*
 —5C **62** (5C **144**)
Aldersgrove Av. *SE9* —3B **114**

Aldershot Rd. *NW6* —1H **59**
Aldersmead Av. *Croy* —6K **125**
Aldersmead Rd. *Beck* —7A **112**
Alderson Pl. *S'hall* —1G **71**
Alderson St. *W10* —4G **59**
Alders Rd. *Edgw* —5D **12**
Alders, The. *N21* —6G **7**
Alders, The. *SW16* —4G **109**
Alders, The. *Felt* —4C **102**
Alders, The. *Houn* —6D **70**
Alders, The. *W Wick* —2D **136**
Alderton Clo. *NW10* —3K **41**
Alderton Cres. *NW4* —5D **26**
Alderton Rd. *SE24* —3C **94**
Alderton Rd. *Croy* —7F **125**
Alderton Way. *NW4* —5D **26**
Alderville Rd. *SW6* —2H **91**
Alder Wlk. *Ilf* —5G **51**
Alderwick Dri. *Houn* —3H **87**
Alderwood Rd. *SE9* —6H **99**
Aldford St. *W1* —1E **76** (4H **147**)
Aldgate. *EC3* —6G **62** (1H **151**)
Aldgate. (Junct.) —6F **63**
Aldgate Av. *E1* —6F **63** (7J **145**)
Aldgate Barrs. *E1*
 —6F **63** (7K **145**)
Aldgate High St. *EC3*
 —6F **63** (1J **151**)
Aldham Ho. *SE4* —1B **96**
Aldine Ct. *W12* —2E **74**
 (off Aldine St.)
Aldine Pl. *W12* —2E **74**
Aldine St. *W12* —2E **74**
Aldington Clo. *Dag* —1C **52**
Aldington Ct. *E8* —7G **47**
Aldington Rd. *SE18* —3B **82**
Aldis M. *SW17* —5C **108**
Aldis St. *SW17* —5C **108**
Aldred Rd. *NW6* —5J **43**
Aldren Rd. *SW17* —3A **108**
Aldrich Cres. *New Ad* —7E **136**
Aldriche Way. *E4* —6K **19**
Aldrich Gdns. *Sutt* —3H **131**
Aldrich Ter. *SW18* —2A **108**
Aldridge Av. *Edgw* —3C **12**
Aldridge Av. *Ruis* —2A **38**
Aldridge Av. *Stan* —1E **24**
Aldridge Rise. *N Mald* —7A **120**
Aldridge Rd. Vs. *W11* —5H **59**
Aldridge Wlk. *N14* —7D **6**
Aldrington Rd. *SW16* —5G **109**
Aldsworth Dri. *W9* —4K **59**
Aldwick Clo. *SE9* —3H **115**
Aldwick Rd. *Croy* —3K **133**
Aldworth Gro. *SE13* —6E **96**
Aldworth Rd. *E15* —7G **49**
Aldwych. *WC2* —6K **61** (2G **149**)
Aldwych Av. *Ilf* —4G **35**
Aldwyn Ho. *SW8* —7J **77**
 (off Davidson Gdns.)
Alers Rd. *Bexh* —5D **100**
Alesia Clo. *N22* —7D **16**
Alestan Beck Rd. *E16* —6B **66**
Alexa Ct. *W8* —4K **75**
Alexa Ct. *Sutt* —6J **131**
Alexander Av. *NW10* —7D **42**
Alexander Clo. *Barn* —4G **5**
Alexander Clo. *Brom* —1J **137**
Alexander Clo. *Sidc* —6J **99**
Alexander Clo. *S'hall* —1G **71**
Alexander Clo. *Twic* —2K **103**
Alexander Ct. *SE16* —1B **80**
Alexander Ct. *Beck* —1F **127**
Alexander Ct. *Stan* —3F **25**

Alexander Evans M. *SE23*
 —2K **111**
Alexander Fleming Ho. *SE1*
 —3C **78** (2C **156**)
Alexander M. *W2* —6K **59**
Alexander Pl. *SW7*
 —4C **76** (3C **152**)
Alexander Rd. *N19* —3J **45**
Alexander Rd. *Bexh* —2D **100**
Alexander Rd. *Chst* —6F **115**
Alexander Sq. *SW3*
 —4C **76** (3C **152**)
Alexander St. *W2* —6J **59**
Alexander Studios. *SW11* —4B **92**
 (off Haydon Way)
Alexandra Av. *N22* —1H **29**
Alexandra Av. *SW11* —1E **92**
Alexandra Av. *W4* —7K **73**
Alexandra Av. *Harr* —1D **38**
Alexandra Av. *S'hall* —7D **54**
Alexandra Av. *Sutt* —3J **131**
Alexandra Clo. *Harr* —3E **38**
Alexandra Cotts. *SE14* —1B **96**
Alexandra Ct. *N14* —5B **6**
Alexandra Ct. *SW7*
 —3A **76** (1A **152**)
Alexandra Ct. *Gnfd* —2F **55**
Alexandra Ct. *Houn* —2F **87**
Alexandra Cres. *Brom* —6H **113**
Alexandra Dri. *SE19* —5E **110**
Alexandra Dri. *Surb* —7G **119**
Alexandra Gdns. *N10* —4F **29**
Alexandra Gdns. *W4* —7A **74**
Alexandra Gdns. *Houn* —2F **87**
Alexandra Gro. *N4* —1B **46**
Alexandra Gro. *N12* —5E **14**
Alexandra M. *N2* —3D **28**
Alexandra M. *SW19* —6H **107**
Alexandra Pal. Way. *N22* —4G **29**
Alexandra Pde. *Harr* —4F **39**
Alexandra Pk. Rd. *N10* —2F **29**
Alexandra Pk. Rd. *N22* —1G **29**
Alexandra Pl. *NW8* —1A **60**
Alexandra Pl. *SE25* —5D **124**
Alexandra Pl. *Croy* —1E **134**
Alexandra Rd. *E6* —3E **66**
Alexandra Rd. *E10* —3E **48**
Alexandra Rd. *E17* —6B **32**
Alexandra Rd. *E18* —3K **33**
Alexandra Rd. *N8* —3A **30**
Alexandra Rd. *N9* —7C **8**
Alexandra Rd. *N10* —1F **29**
Alexandra Rd. *N15* —5D **30**
Alexandra Rd. *NW4* —4F **27**
Alexandra Rd. *NW8* —1A **60**
Alexandra Rd. *SE26* —6K **111**
Alexandra Rd. *SW14* —3K **89**
Alexandra Rd. *SW19* —6H **107**
Alexandra Rd. *W4* —2K **73**
Alexandra Rd. *Bren* —6D **72**
Alexandra Rd. *Chad H* —6E **36**
Alexandra Rd. *Croy* —1E **134**
Alexandra Rd. *Enf* —4E **8**
Alexandra Rd. *Houn* —2F **87**
Alexandra Rd. *King T* —7G **105**
Alexandra Rd. *Mitc* —7C **108**
Alexandra Rd. *Rich* —2F **89**
Alexandra Rd. *Th Dit* —5A **118**
Alexandra Rd. *Twic* —6C **88**
Alexandra Rd. Ind. Est. *Enf* —4E **8**
Alexandra Sq. *Mord* —5J **121**
Alexandra St. *E16* —5J **65**
Alexandra St. *SE14* —7A **80**
Alexandra Wlk. *SE19* —5E **110**

Alexandra Yd. *E9* —1K **63**
Alexandria Rd. *W13* —7A **56**
Alexis St. *SE16* —4G **79**
Alfan La. *Dart* —5K **117**
Alfearn Rd. *E5* —4J **47**
Alford Grn. *New Ad* —6F **137**
Alford Ho. *N6* —6G **29**
Alford Pl. *N1* —2C **62** (1D **144**)
Alford Rd. *Eri* —5J **85**
Alfoxton Av. *N15* —4B **30**
Alfreda St. *SW11* —1F **93**
Alfred Clo. *W4* —4K **73**
Alfred Finlay Ho. *N22* —2B **30**
Alfred Gdns. *S'hall* —7C **54**
Alfred Ho. *E9* —5A **48**
 (off Homerton Rd.)
Alfred M. *W1* —5H **61** (5C **142**)
Alfred Prior Ho. *E12* —4E **50**
Alfred Rd. *E15* —5H **49**
Alfred Rd. *SE25* —5G **125**
Alfred Rd. *SW8* —1H **93**
Alfred Rd. *W2* —5J **59**
Alfred Rd. *W3* —1J **73**
Alfred Rd. *Belv* —5F **85**
Alfred Rd. *Buck H* —2G **21**
Alfred Rd. *Felt* —2A **102**
Alfred Rd. *King T* —3E **118**
Alfred Rd. *Sutt* —5A **132**
Alfred's Gdns. *Bark* —2J **67**
Alfred St. *E3* —3B **64**
Alfreds Way. *Bark* —3F **67**
Alfred's Way Ind. Est. *Bark*
 —2A **68**
Alfreton Clo. *SW19* —3F **107**
Alfriston. *Surb* —6F **119**
Alfriston Av. *Croy* —7J **123**
Alfriston Av. *Harr* —6E **22**
Alfriston Clo. *Surb* —5F **119**
Alfriston Rd. *SW11* —5D **92**
Algar Clo. *Iswth* —3A **88**
Algar Clo. *Stan* —5E **10**
Algar Ho. *SE1* —2B **78** (7A **150**)
Algar Rd. *Iswth* —3A **88**
Algarve Rd. *SW18* —1K **107**
Algernon Rd. *NW4* —6C **26**
Algernon Rd. *NW6* —1J **59**
Algernon Rd. *SE13* —4D **96**
Algiers Rd. *SE13* —4C **96**
Alibon Gdns. *Dag* —5G **53**
Alibon Rd. *Dag* —5F **53**
Alice Burrell Cen. *E10* —2E **48**
 (off Sidmouth Rd.)
Alice Ct. *SW15* —4H **91**
Alice Gilliatt Ct. *W14* —6H **75**
 (off Star Rd.)
Alice La. *E3* —1B **64**
Alice M. *Tedd* —5K **103**
Alice St. *SE1* —3E **78** (2G **157**)
Alice Thompson Clo. *SE12*
 —2A **114**
Alice Walker Clo. *SE24* —4B **94**
Alice Way. *Houn* —4F **87**
Alicia Av. *Harr* —4B **24**
Alicia Clo. *Harr* —5C **24**
Alicia Gdns. *Harr* —4B **24**
Alicia Ho. *Well* —1B **100**
Alie St. *E1* —6F **63** (1K **151**)
Alington Cres. *NW9* —7J **25**
Alington Gro. *Wall* —7G **133**
Alington Rd. Ind. Est. *Enf* —4E **8**
Alison Clo. *E6* —6E **66**
Alison Clo. *Croy* —1K **135**
Alison Ct. *SE1* —5G **79** (6K **157**)
Aliwal Rd. *SW11* —4C **92**
Alkerden Rd. *W4* —5A **74**

Alkham Rd. *N16* —2F **47**
Allan Barclay Clo. *N15* —6F **31**
Allan Clo. *N Mald* —5K **119**
Allandale Av. *N3* —3G **27**
Allanson Ct. *E10* —2C **48**
Allan Way. *W3* —5J **57**
Allard Cres. *Bush* —1B **10**
Allard Gdns. *SW4* —5H **93**
Allardyce St. *SW4* —4K **93**
Allbrook Clo. *Tedd* —5J **103**
Allcroft Rd. *NW5* —5E **44**
Allenby Clo. *Gnfd* —3E **54**
Allenby Rd. *SE23* —3A **112**
Allenby Rd. *S'hall* —6E **54**
Allen Clo. *Mitc* —1G **123**
Allen Ct. *E17* —6C **32**
Allen Ct. *Gnfd* —5K **39**
Allendale Av. *S'hall* —6E **54**
Allendale Clo. *SE5* —2D **94**
Allendale Clo. *SE26* —5K **111**
Allendale Rd. *Gnfd* —6B **40**
Allen Edwards Dri. *SW8* —1J **93**
Allenford Ho. *SW15* —6A **90**
 (off Tunworth Cres.)
Allen Rd. *E3* —1B **64**
Allen Rd. *N16* —4E **46**
Allen Rd. *Beck* —2K **125**
Allen Rd. *Croy* —1A **134**
Allensbury Pl. *NW1* —7H **45**
Allens Rd. *Enf* —5D **8**
Allen St. *W8* —3J **75**
Allenswood Rd. *SE9* —3C **98**
Allerford Ct. *Harr* —5G **23**
Allerford Rd. *SE6* —3D **112**
Allerton Rd. *N16* —2C **46**
Allerton Wlk. *N7* —2K **45**
Allestree Rd. *SW6* —7G **75**
Alleyn Cres. *SE21* —2D **110**
Alleyndale Rd. *Dag* —2C **52**
Alleyn Pk. *SE21* —2D **110**
Alleyn Pk. *S'hall* —5E **70**
Alleyn Rd. *SE21* —3D **110**
Allfarthing La. *SW18* —6K **91**
Allgood Clo. *Mord* —6F **121**
Allgood St. *E2* —2F **63** (1K **145**)
Allhallows La. *EC4*
 —7D **62** (3E **150**)
Allhallows Rd. *E6* —5C **66**
All Hallows Rd. *N17* —1E **30**
Alliance Clo. *Wemb* —4D **40**
Alliance Ct. *W3* —5H **57**
Alliance Rd. *E13* —5A **66**
Alliance Rd. *SE18* —6A **84**
Alliance Rd. *W3* —4H **57**
Allied Ind. Est. *W3* —2A **74**
Allied Way. *W3* —2A **74**
Allingham Clo. *W7* —7K **55**
Allingham St. *N1* —2C **62**
Allington Av. *N17* —6K **17**
Allington Clo. *SW19* —5F **107**
Allington Clo. *Gnfd* —7G **39**
Allington Ct. *SW8* —2G **93**
Allington Ct. *Enf* —5E **8**
Allington Rd. *NW4* —5D **26**
Allington Rd. *W10* —3G **59**
Allington Rd. *Harr* —5G **23**
Allington St. *SW1*
 —3F **77** (2K **153**)
Allison Clo. *SE10* —1E **96**
Allison Gro. *SE21* —1E **110**
Allison Rd. *N8* —5A **30**
Allison Rd. *W3* —6J **57**
Allitsen Rd. *NW8* —2C **60**
Allnutt Way. *SW4* —5H **93**

Alloa Rd. *SE8* —5K **79**
Alloa Rd. *Ilf* —2A **52**
Allom Ho. *W11* —1G **59**
  (off Clarendon Rd.)
Allonby Gdns. *Wemb* —1C **40**
Alloway Rd. *E3* —3A **64**
All Saints Clo. *N9* —2A **18**
All Saints Ct. *Houn* —1B **86**
  (off Springwell Rd.)
All Saints Dri. *SE3* —2G **97**
All Saints M. *Harr* —6D **10**
All Saints Pas. *SW18* —5J **91**
All Saints Rd. *SW19* —7A **108**
All Saints Rd. *W3* —3J **73**
All Saints Rd. *W11* —5H **59**
All Saints Rd. *Sutt* —3K **131**
All Saints St. *N1* —2K **61**
All Saints Tower. *E10* —7D **32**
All Seasons Ct. *E1* —1G **79**
  (off Aragon M.)
Allsop Pl. *NW1* —4D **60** (4F **141**)
All Souls Av. *NW10* —2D **58**
All Souls' Pl. *W1*
  —5F **61** (6K **141**)
Allum Way. *N20* —1F **15**
Allwood Clo. *SE26* —4K **111**
Alma Av. *E4* —7K **19**
Almack Rd. *E5* —4J **47**
Alma Clo. *N10* —1F **29**
Alma Ct. *Harr* —2G **39**
Alma Cres. *Sutt* —5G **131**
Alma Gro. *SE1* —4F **79** (4K **157**)
Alma Ho. *Bren* —6E **72**
Alma Pl. *NW10* —3D **58**
Alma Pl. *SE19* —7F **111**
Alma Pl. *T Hth* —5A **124**
Alma Rd. *N10* —7A **16**
Alma Rd. *SW18* —4A **92**
Alma Rd. *Cars* —5C **132**
Alma Rd. *Enf* —5F **9**
Alma Rd. *Sidc* —3A **116**
Alma Rd. *S'hall* —7C **54**
Alma Rd. Ind. Est. *Enf* —4E **8**
Alma Row. *Harr* —1H **23**
Alma St. *E15* —6F **49**
Alma Ter. *NW5* —6F **45**
Alma Ter. *SW18* —7B **92**
Alma Ter. *W8* —3J **75**
Almeida St. *N1* —1B **62**
Almeric Rd. *SW11* —4D **92**
Almer Rd. *SW20* —7C **106**
Almington St. *N4* —1K **45**
Almond Av. *W5* —3D **72**
Almond Av. *Cars* —2D **132**
Almond Clo. *SE15* —2G **95**
Almond Clo. *Brom* —7E **128**
Almond Gro. *Bren* —7B **72**
Almond Rd. *N17* —7B **18**
Almond Rd. *SE16* —4H **79**
Almonds Av. *Buck H* —2D **20**
Almondsbury Ct. *SE15* —7E **78**
  (off Lynbrook Clo.)
Almond Way. *Brom* —7E **128**
Almond Way. *Harr* —2F **23**
Almond Way. *Mitc* —5H **123**
Almorah Rd. *N1* —7D **46**
Almorah Rd. *Houn* —1B **86**
Alnmouth Ct. *S'hall* —6G **55**
  (off Fleming Rd.)
Alnwick. *N17* —7C **18**
Alnwick Gro. *Mord* —4K **121**
Alnwick Rd. *E16* —6A **66**
Alnwick Rd. *SE12* —7K **97**
Alperton La. *Gnfd & Wemb*
  —3C **56**

Alperton St. *W10* —4H **59**
Alphabet Gdns. *Cars* —6B **122**
Alphabet Sq. *E3* —5C **64**
Alpha Bus. Cen. *E17* —5B **32**
Alpha Clo. *NW1* —4C **60** (3D **140**)
Alpha Clo. *E14* —2C **80**
Alpha Pl. *NW6* —2J **59**
Alpha Pl. *SW3* —6C **76** (7D **152**)
Alpha Pl. *Mord* —1F **131**
Alpha Rd. *E4* —3H **19**
Alpha Rd. *N18* —6B **18**
Alpha Rd. *SE14* —1B **96**
Alpha Rd. *Croy* —1E **134**
Alpha Rd. *Enf* —4F **9**
Alpha Rd. *Surb* —6F **119**
Alpha Rd. *Tedd* —5H **103**
Alpha Rd. *Uxb* —7A **38**
Alpha St. *SE15* —2G **95**
Alphea Clo. *SW19* —7C **108**
Alpine Bus. Cen. *E6* —5E **66**
Alpine Clo. *Croy* —3E **134**
Alpine Copse. *Brom* —2E **128**
Alpine Rd. *SE16* —4K **79**
  (in two parts)
Alpine View. *Sutt* —5C **132**
Alpine Wlk. *Stan* —2D **10**
Alpine Way. *E6* —5E **66**
Alric Av. *NW10* —7K **41**
Alric Av. *N Mald* —3A **120**
Alroy Rd. *N4* —7A **30**
Alsace Rd. *SE17*
  —5E **78** (5G **157**)
Alscot Rd. *SE1* —4F **79** (3J **157**)
  (in two parts)
Alscot Rd. Ind. Est. *SE16*
  —1G **77** (5B **148**)
  —3F **79** (2K **157**)
Alscot Way. *SE1* —4F **79** (3J **157**)
Alsike Rd. *Eri* —3D **84**
Alsom Av. *Wor Pk* —4C **130**
Alston Clo. *Surb* —7B **118**
Alston Rd. *N18* —5C **18**
Alston Rd. *SW17* —4B **108**
Alston Rd. *Barn* —3B **4**
Altair Clo. *N17* —6A **18**
Altash Way. *SE9* —2D **114**
Altenburg Av. *W13* —3B **72**
Altenburg Gdns. *SW11* —4D **92**
Alt Gro. *SW19* —7H **107**
Altham Rd. *Pinn* —1C **22**
Althea St. *SW6* —2K **91**
Althorne Gdns. *E18* —4H **33**
Althorne Way. *Dag* —2G **53**
Althorp Rd. *SW17* —1B **92**
  (in two parts)
Althorpe M. *SW11* —1B **92**
Althorpe Rd. *Harr* —5G **23**
Althorp Rd. *SW17* —1D **108**
Altior Ct. *N6* —6G **29**
Altmore Av. *E6* —7D **50**
Alton Av. *Stan* —7E **10**
Alton Clo. *Bex* —1E **116**
Alton Clo. *Iswth* —2K **87**
Alton Gdns. *Beck* —7C **112**
Alton Gdns. *Twic* —7H **87**
Alton Rd. *N17* —3D **30**
Alton Rd. *SW15* —1C **106**
Alton Rd. *Croy* —3A **134**
Alton Rd. *Rich* —4E **88**
Alton St. *E14* —6D **64**
Altyre Clo. *Beck* —5B **126**
Altyre Rd. *Croy* —2D **134**
Altyre Way. *Beck* —5B **126**
Aluna Ct. *SE15* —3J **95**
Alvanley Gdns. *NW6* —5K **43**
Alverstone Av. *SW19* —2J **107**
Alverstone Av. *E Barn* —7H **5**
Alverstone Gdns. *SE9* —1G **115**

Alverstone Ho. *SE11*
  —6A **78** (7J **155**)
Alverstone Rd. *E12* —4E **50**
Alverstone Rd. *NW2* —7E **42**
Alverstone Rd. *N Mald* —4B **120**
Alverstone Rd. *Wemb* —1F **41**
Alverston Gdns. *SE25* —5E **124**
Alverton Rd. *N16* —2C **46**
Alverton St. *SE8* —5B **80**
Alveston Av. *Harr* —3B **24**
Alvey St. *SE17* —5E **78** (5G **157**)
Alvia Gdns. *Sutt* —4A **132**
Alvington Cres. *E8* —5F **47**
Alwold Cres. *SE12* —6K **97**
Alwyn Av. *W4* —5K **73**
Alwyn Clo. *New Ad* —7D **136**
Alwyne La. *N1* —7B **46**
Alwyne Pl. *N1* —6C **46**
Alwyne Rd. *SW19* —6H **107**
Alwyne Rd. *W7* —7J **55**
Alwyne Sq. *N1* —6C **46**
Alwyne Vs. *N1* —7B **46**
Alwyn Gdns. *NW4* —4C **26**
Alwyn Gdns. *W3* —6H **57**
Alyth Gdns. *NW11* —6J **27**
Amalgamated Dri. *Bren* —6A **72**
Amar Ct. *SE18* —4K **83**
Amar Deep Ct. *SE18* —5K **83**
Amazon St. *E1* —6G **63**
Ambassador Clo. *Houn* —2C **86**
Ambassador Gdns. *E6* —5D **66**
Ambassador's Ct. *SW1*
  —1G **77** (5B **148**)
Ambassador Sq. *E14* —4D **80**
Amber Av. *E17* —1A **32**
Amberden Av. *N3* —3J **27**
Ambergate St. *SE17*
  —5B **78** (5B **156**)
Amber Gro. *NW2* —1E **42**
Amberley Ct. *Beck* —7B **112**
Amberley Ct. *Sidc* —5C **116**
Amberley Gdns. *Enf* —7K **7**
Amberley Gdns. *Eps* —4B **130**
Amberley Gro. *SE26* —5H **111**
Amberley Gro. *Croy* —7F **125**
Amberley Rd. *E10* —7C **32**
Amberley Rd. *N13* —2E **16**
Amberley Rd. *SE2* —6D **84**
Amberley Rd. *W9* —5J **59**
Amberley Rd. *Buck H* —1F **21**
Amberley Rd. *Enf* —7A **8**
Amberley Way. *Houn* —5A **86**
Amberley Way. *Mord* —7H **121**
Amberley Way. *Romf* —4H **37**
Amberside Clo. *Iswth* —6H **87**
Amber St. *E15* —7F **49**
Amberwood Rise. *N Mald*
  —6A **120**
Amblecote Clo. *SE12* —3K **113**
Amblecote Meadows. *SE12*
  —3K **113**
Amblecote Rd. *SE12* —3K **113**
Ambler Rd. *N4* —3B **46**
Ambleside. *Brom* —6F **113**
Ambleside Av. *SW16* —4H **109**
Ambleside Av. *Beck* —5A **126**
Ambleside Clo. *E9* —5J **47**
Ambleside Clo. *E10* —7D **32**
Ambleside Cres. *Enf* —3E **8**
Ambleside Gdns. *SW16*
  —5H **109**
Ambleside Gdns. *Sutt* —6A **132**
Ambleside Gdns. *Wemb* —1D **40**

Ambleside Point. *SE15* —7J **79**
  (off Tustin Est.)
Ambleside Rd. *NW10* —7B **42**
Ambleside Rd. *Bexh* —2G **101**
Ambrooke Rd. *Belv* —3G **85**
Ambrosden Av. *SW1*
  —3G **77** (2B **154**)
Ambrose Av. *NW11* —7G **27**
Ambrose Clo. *E6* —5D **66**
Ambrose M. *SW11* —2D **92**
Ambrose St. *SE16* —4H **79**
Ambrose Wlk. *E3* —2C **64**
AMC Bus. Cen. *NW10* —3H **57**
Amelia St. *SE17*
  —5B **78** (5B **156**)
Amen Corner. *EC4*
  —6B **62** (1B **150**)
Amen Corner. *SW17* —6E **108**
Amen Ct. *EC4* —6B **62** (1B **150**)
Amenity Way. *Mord* —7E **120**
America Sq. *EC3*
  —7F **63** (2J **151**)
America St. *SE1*
  —1C **78** (5C **150**)
Amerland Rd. *SW18* —5H **91**
Amersham Gro. *SE14* —7B **80**
Amersham Rd. *SE14* —1B **96**
Amersham Rd. *Croy* —6C **124**
Amersham Vale. *SE14* —7B **80**
Amery Gdns. *NW10* —1D **58**
Amery Rd. *Harr* —2A **40**
Amesbury Av. *SW2* —2J **109**
Amesbury Clo. *Wor Pk* —1E **130**
Amesbury Ct. *Enf* —2F **7**
Amesbury Dri. *E4* —6J **9**
Amesbury Rd. *Brom* —3B **128**
Amesbury Rd. *Dag* —7D **52**
Amesbury Rd. *Felt* —2B **102**
Amesbury Tower. *SW8* —2G **93**
Amethyst Rd. *E15* —4F **49**
Amherst Av. *W13* —6C **56**
Amherst Dri. *Orp* —4K **129**
Amherst Rd. *W13* —6C **56**
Amhurst Gdns. *Iswth* —2K **87**
Amhurst Pk. *N16* —7D **30**
Amhurst Pas. *E8* —5G **47**
Amhurst Rd. *E8* —5H **47**
Amhurst Rd. *N16 & E8* —4F **47**
Amhurst Ter. *E8* —4G **47**
Amhurst Wlk. *SE28* —1A **84**
Amidas Gdns. *Dag* —4B **52**
Amiel St. *E1* —4J **63**
Amies St. *SW11* —3D **92**
Amina Way. *SE16* —3G **79**
Amity Gro. *SW20* —1D **120**
Amity Rd. *E15* —1H **65**
Ammanford Grn. *NW9* —6A **26**
Amner Rd. *SW11* —6E **92**
Amor Rd. *W6* —3E **74**
Amos Est. *SE16* —1K **79**
Amott Rd. *SE15* —3G **95**
Amoy Pl. *E14* —7C **64**
Ampere Way. *Bedd* —7J **123**
  (in two parts)
Ampleforth Rd. *SE2* —2B **84**
Ampthill Est. *NW1*
  —2G **61** (1B **142**)
Ampton Pl. *WC1*
  —3K **61** (2G **143**)
Ampton St. *WC1*
  —3K **61** (2G **143**)
Amroth Clo. *SE23* —1H **111**
Amroth Grn. *NW9* —6A **26**
Amsterdam Rd. *E14* —3E **80**

Amunsden Ho. *NW10* —7K **41**
  (off Stonebridge Pk.)
Amwell Clo. *Enf* —5J **7**
Amwell Ct. Est. *N4* —2C **46**
Amwell St. *EC1* —3A **62** (1J **143**)
Amyand Cotts. *Twic* —6B **88**
Amyand La. *Twic* —7B **88**
Amyand Pk. Gdns. *Twic* —7B **88**
Amyand Pk. Rd. *Twic* —7A **88**
Amy Clo. *SE3* —4A **98**
Amy Johnson. *Edgw* —2H **25**
Amyruth Rd. *SE4* —5C **96**
Anatola Rd. *N19* —2G **45**
Ancaster Cres. *N Mald* —6C **120**
Ancaster M. *Beck* —3K **125**
Ancaster Rd. *Beck* —3K **125**
Ancaster St. *SE18* —7J **83**
Anchorage Clo. *SW19* —5J **107**
Anchor Brewhouse. *SE1*
  —1F **79** (5J **151**)
Anchor Bus. Cen. *Croy* —3J **133**
Anchor Ct. *Enf* —5K **7**
Anchor M. *SW12* —6F **93**
Anchor St. *SE16* —4H **79**
Anchor Yd. *EC1* —4C **62** (3D **144**)
Ancill Clo. *W6* —6F **75**
Ancona Rd. *NW10* —2C **58**
Ancona Rd. *SE18* —5H **83**
Andace Pk. Gdns. *Brom* —2A **128**
Andalus Rd. *SW9* —3J **93**
Ander Clo. *Wemb* —4D **40**
Anderson Clo. *W3* —6K **57**
Anderson Clo. *NW2* —1E **42**
Anderson Ho. *Bark* —2H **67**
Anderson Pl. *Houn* —4F **87**
Anderson Rd. *E9* —6K **47**
Anderson Rd. *Wfd G* —3B **34**
Anderson St. *SW3*
  —5D **76** (5E **152**)
Anderson Way. *Belv* —2H **85**
Anderton Clo. *SE5* —3D **94**
Anderton Ct. *N22* —2H **29**
Andorra Ct. *Brom* —1A **128**
Andover Av. *E16* —6B **66**
Andover Clo. *Gnfd* —4F **55**
Andover Pl. *NW6* —2K **59**
Andover Rd. *N7* —2K **45**
Andover Rd. *Orp* —7J **129**
Andover Rd. *Twic* —1H **103**
Andoversford Ct. *SE15* —6E **78**
  (off Bibury Clo.)
Andreck Ct. *Beck* —2D **126**
Andre St. *E8* —5G **47**
Andrew Borde St. *WC2*
  —6H **61** (7D **142**)
Andrew Clo. *Dart* —5K **101**
Andrew Ct. *SE23* —2K **111**
Andrewes Gdns. *E6* —6C **66**
Andrewes Highwalk. *EC2*
  —5C **62** (6D **144**)
Andrewes Ho. *EC2*
  —5C **62** (6D **144**)
Andrewes Ho. *Sutt* —4J **131**
Andrew Pl. *SW8* —1H **93**
Andrews Clo. *Buck H* —2F **21**
Andrews Clo. *Harr* —7H **23**
Andrews Clo. *Wor Pk* —2F **131**
Andrews Crosse. *WC2*
  —6A **62** (1J **149**)
Andrews Path. *E9* —6F **99**
Andrew's Rd. *E8* —1H **63**
Andrew St. *E14* —6E **64**
Andrews Wlk. *SE17* —6B **78**

Ashdale Way. *Twic* —7F **87**
Ashdene. *SE15* —1H **95**
Ashdene. *Pinn* —3A **22**
Ashdon Clo. *Wfd G* —6E **20**
Ashdon Rd. *NW10* —1B **58**
Ashdown. *W13* —5B **56**
  (off Clivedon Ct.)
Ashdown Clo. *Beck* —2D **126**
Ashdown Clo. *Bex* —7J **101**
Ashdown Ct. *Sutt* —6A **132**
Ashdown Cres. *NW5* —5E **44**
Ashdowne Ct. *N17* —1G **31**
Ashdown Est. *E11* —4F **49**
Ashdown Rd. *Enf* —2D **8**
Ashdown Rd. *King T* —2E **118**
Ashdown Wlk. *E14* —4C **80**
  (off Copeland Dri.)
Ashdown Wlk. *Romf* —1H **37**
Ashdown Way. *SW17* —2E **108**
Ashenden Rd. *E5* —5A **48**
Ashen Gro. *SW19* —3J **107**
Ashentree Ct. *EC4*
  —6A **62** (1K **149**)
Asher Loftus Way. *N11* —6J **15**
Asher Way. *E1* —7G **63**
Ashfield Av. *Bush* —1B **10**
Ashfield Av. *Felt* —1A **102**
Ashfield Clo. *Beck* —7C **112**
Ashfield Clo. *Rich* —1E **104**
Ashfield La. *Chst* —6F **115**
  (in three parts)
Ashfield Pde. *N14* —1C **16**
Ashfield Rd. *N4* —6C **30**
Ashfield Rd. *N14* —3B **16**
Ashfield Rd. *W3* —1B **74**
Ashfield St. *E1* —5H **63**
Ashford Av. *N8* —4J **29**
Ashford Av. *Hayes* —6B **54**
Ashford Clo. *E17* —6B **32**
Ashford Ct. *Edgw* —3C **12**
Ashford Cres. *Enf* —2D **8**
Ashford Ho. *SE8* —6B **80**
Ashford Ho. *SW9* —4B **94**
Ashford Pas. *NW2* —4F **43**
Ashford Rd. *E6* —7E **50**
Ashford Rd. *E18* —2K **33**
Ashford Rd. *NW2* —4F **43**
Ashford St. *N1* —3E **62** (1G **145**)
Ash Gro. *E8* —1H **63**
Ash Gro. *N13* —3H **17**
Ash Gro. *NW2* —4F **43**
Ash Gro. *SE12* —1J **113**
Ash Gro. *SE20* —2J **125**
Ash Gro. *W5* —2E **72**
Ash Gro. *Enf* —7K **7**
Ash Gro. *Houn* —1B **86**
Ash Gro. *S'hall* —5E **54**
Ash Gro. *Wemb* —4A **40**
Ash Gro. *W Wick* —2E **136**
Ashgrove Rd. *Brom* —6F **113**
Ashgrove Rd. *Ilf* —1K **51**
Ash Hill Clo. *Bush* —1A **10**
Ash Hill Dri. *Pinn* —3A **22**
Ashingdon Clo. *E4* —3K **19**
Ashington Rd. *SW6* —2H **91**
Ashlake Rd. *SW16* —4J **109**
Ashland Pl. *W1* —5E **60** (5G **141**)
Ashlar Pl. *SE18* —4F **83**
Ashleigh Commercial Est. *SE7*
  —3A **82**
Ashleigh Ct. *N14* —7B **6**
Ashleigh Ct. *W7* —4D **72**
  (off Murray Rd.)
Ashleigh Gdns. *Sutt* —2K **131**
Ashleigh Point. *SE23* —3K **111**

Ashleigh Rd. *SE20* —3H **125**
Ashleigh Rd. *SW14* —3A **90**
Ashley Av. *Ilf* —2F **35**
Ashley Av. *Mord* —5J **121**
Ashley Clo. *NW4* —2E **26**
Ashley Ct. *NW4* —2E **26**
Ashley Ct. *Barn* —5F **5**
Ashley Cres. *N22* —2A **30**
Ashley Cres. *SW11* —3E **92**
Ashley Dri. *Iswth* —6J **71**
Ashley Dri. *Twic* —7F **87**
Ashley Gdns. *N13* —4H **17**
Ashley Gdns. *SW1*
  —3G **77** (2B **154**)
Ashley Gdns. *Rich* —2D **104**
Ashley Gdns. *Wemb* —2E **40**
Ashley La. *NW4* —2E **26**
Ashley La. *Croy* —4B **134**
Ashley Pl. *SW1* —3G **77** (2A **154**)
Ashley Rd. *E4* —6H **19**
Ashley Rd. *E7* —7A **50**
Ashley Rd. *N17* —3G **31**
Ashley Rd. *N19* —1J **45**
Ashley Rd. *SW19* —6K **107**
Ashley Rd. *Enf* —2D **8**
Ashley Rd. *Hamp* —7E **102**
Ashley Rd. *Rich* —3E **88**
Ashley Rd. *Th Dit* —6A **118**
Ashley Rd. *T Hth* —4K **123**
Ashley Wlk. *NW7* —7K **13**
Ashling Rd. *Croy* —1G **135**
Ashlin Rd. *E15* —4F **49**
Ashlone Rd. *SW15* —3F **91**
Ashmead. *N14* —5B **6**
Ashmead Bus. Cen. *E16* —4F **65**
Ashmead Ga. *Brom* —1A **128**
Ashmead Ho. *E9* —5A **48**
  (off Homerton Rd.)
Ashmead Rd. *SE8* —2C **96**
Ashmere Av. *Beck* —2F **127**
Ashmere Clo. *Sutt* —5F **131**
Ashmere Gro. *SW2* —4J **93**
Ashmill St. *NW1*
  —5C **60** (5C **140**)
Ashmole Pl. *SW8* —6K **77**
Ashmole St. *SW8* —6K **77**
Ashmore Ct. *N11* —6J **15**
Ashmore Ct. *Houn* —6E **70**
Ashmore Gro. *Well* —3H **99**
Ashmore Rd. *W9* —3H **59**
Ashmount Est. *N19* —7H **29**
Ashmount Rd. *N15* —5F **31**
Ashmount Rd. *N19* —7G **29**
Ashmount Ter. *W5* —4D **72**
Ashmour Gdns. *Romf* —2K **37**
Ashneal Gdns. *Harr* —3H **39**
Ashness Gdns. *Gnfd* —6B **40**
Ashness Rd. *SW11* —5D **92**
Ashridge Clo. *Harr* —6C **24**
Ashridge Ct. *N14* —5B **6**
Ashridge Ct. *S'hall* —6G **55**
  (off Redcroft Rd.)
Ashridge Cres. *SE18* —7G **83**
Ashridge Gdns. *N13* —5C **16**
Ashridge Gdns. *Pinn* —4C **22**
Ashridge Way. *Mord* —4H **121**
Ash Rd. *E15* —5G **49**
Ash Rd. *Croy* —2C **136**
Ash Row. *Brom* —7E **128**
Ashstead Rd. *N16* —7G **31**
Ashtead Rd. *E5* —7G **31**
Ashton Clo. *Sutt* —4J **131**
Ashton Ct. *Harr* —3K **39**
Ashton Gdns. *Houn* —4D **86**

Ashton Gdns. *Romf* —6E **36**
Ashton Heights. *SE23* —1J **111**
Ashton Ho. *SW9* —7A **78**
Ashton Rd. *E15* —5F **49**
Ashton St. *E14* —7E **64**
Ashtree Av. *Mitc* —2B **122**
Ashtree Dell. *NW9* —5K **25**
Ash Tree Way. *Croy* —5K **125**
Ashurst Clo. *SE20* —1H **125**
Ashurst Dri. *Ilf* —6F **35**
Ashurst Gdns. *SW2* —1A **110**
Ashurst Rd. *N12* —5H **15**
Ashurst Wlk. *Croy* —2H **135**
Ashvale Rd. *SW17* —5D **108**
Ashville Rd. *E11* —2F **49**
Ash Wlk. *Wemb* —3C **40**
Ashwater Clo. *NW9* —5K **25**
Ashwater Rd. *SE12* —1J **113**
Ashwell Clo. *E6* —6C **66**
Ashwin St. *E8* —6F **47**
Ashwood Gdns. *New Ad*
  —6D **136**
Ashwood Rd. *E4* —3A **20**
Ashworth Clo. *SE5* —2D **94**
Ashworth Est. *Croy* —1H **133**
Ashworth Mans. *W9* —3K **59**
  (off Elgin Av.)
Ashworth Rd. *W9* —3K **59**
Asilone Rd. *SW15* —3E **90**
Asker Ho. *N7* —4J **45**
Askern Clo. *Bexh* —4D **100**
Aske St. *N1* —3E **62** (1G **145**)
Askew Cres. *W12* —2B **74**
Askew Est. *W12* —1B **74**
  (off Uxbridge Rd.)
Askew Rd. *W12* —1B **74**
Askham Ct. *W12* —1C **74**
Askham Rd. *W12* —1C **74**
Askill Dri. *SW15* —5G **91**
Askwith Rd. *Rain* —3K **69**
Asland Rd. *E15* —1G **65**
Aslett St. *SW18* —7K **91**
Asmara Rd. *NW2* —5G **43**
Asmuns Hill. *NW11* —5J **27**
Asmuns Pl. *NW11* —5H **27**
Asolando Dri. *SE17*
  —4C **78** (5D **156**)
Aspen Clo. *N19* —2G **45**
Aspen Clo. *W5* —2F **73**
Aspen Copse. *Brom* —2D **128**
Aspen Ct. *E8* —6F **47**
Aspen Dri. *Wemb* —3A **40**
Aspen Gdns. *W6* —5D **74**
Aspen Gdns. *Mitc* —5E **122**
Aspen Grn. *Eri* —3F **85**
Aspen Ho. *Sidc* —3A **116**
Aspen La. *N'holt* —3C **54**
Aspenlea Rd. *W6* —6F **75**
Aspen Way. *E14* —7C **64**
Aspen Way. *Felt* —3A **102**
Aspern Gro. *NW3* —5C **44**
Aspinall Rd. *SE4* —3K **95**
Aspinden Rd. *SE16* —4H **79**
Aspley Rd. *E17* —5B **32**
Aspley Rd. *SW18* —5K **91**
Asplins Rd. *N17* —1G **31**
Asquith Clo. *Dag* —1C **52**
Assam St. *E1* —6G **63**
Assata M. *N1* —6B **46**
Assembly Pas. *E1* —5J **63**
Assembly Wlk. *Cars* —7C **122**
Ass Ho. La. *Harr* —4A **10**
Astall Clo. *Harr* —1J **23**

Astbury Ho. *SE11*
  —3A **78** (2J **155**)
Astbury Rd. *SE15* —1J **95**
Astell St. *SW3* —5C **76** (5D **152**)
Aste St. *E14* —2E **80**
Astey's Row. *N1* —7C **46**
Asthall Gdns. *Ilf* —4G **35**
Astins Ho. *E17* —4D **32**
Astle St. *SW11* —2E **92**
Astley Av. *NW2* —5E **42**
Astley Ho. *SE1* —5F **79** (5K **157**)
Aston Av. *Harr* —7C **24**
Aston Clo. *Sidc* —3A **116**
Aston Ct. *Wfd G* —6D **20**
Aston Grn. *Houn* —2A **86**
Aston Ho. *SW8* —1H **93**
Aston M. *Romf* —7C **36**
Aston Rd. *SW20* —2E **120**
Aston Rd. *W5* —6D **56**
Aston St. *E14* —5A **64**
Astonville St. *SW18* —1J **107**
Astor Av. *Romf* —6J **37**
Astor Clo. *King T* —6H **105**
Astoria Mans. *SW16* —3J **109**
Astoria Wlk. *SW9* —3A **94**
Astrop M. *W6* —3E **74**
Astrop Ter. *W6* —2E **74**
Astwood M. *SW7* —4A **76**
Asylum Rd. *SE15* —7H **79**
Atalanta St. *SW6* —7F **75**
Atbara Rd. *Tedd* —6B **104**
Atcham Rd. *Houn* —4G **87**
Atcost Rd. *Bark* —5A **68**
Atcraft Cen. *Wemb* —1E **56**
Atheldene Rd. *SW18* —1K **107**
Athelney St. *SE6* —3C **112**
Athelstane Gro. *E3* —2B **64**
Athelstane M. *N4* —1A **46**
Athelstan Gdns. *NW6* —7G **43**
Athelstan Rd. *King T* —4F **119**
Athelstone Rd. *Harr* —2H **23**
Athena Clo. *Harr* —2H **39**
Athena Clo. *King T* —3F **119**
Athenaeum Ct. *N5* —4C **46**
Athenaeum Pl. *N10* —3F **29**
Athenaeum Rd. *N20* —1F **15**
Athenlay Rd. *SE15* —5H **97**
Atherden Rd. *E5* —4J **47**
Atherfold Rd. *SW9* —3J **93**
Atherley Way. *Houn* —7D **86**
Atherstone M. *SW7* —4A **76**
Atherton Dri. *SW19* —4F **107**
Atherton Heights. *Wemb* —6C **40**
Atherton M. *E7* —6H **49**
Atherton Pl. *Harr* —3H **23**
Atherton Pl. *S'hall* —7E **54**
Atherton Rd. *E7* —6H **49**
Atherton Rd. *SW13* —7C **74**
Atherton Rd. *Ilf* —2C **34**
Atherton St. *SW11* —2C **92**
Athlone Clo. *E5* —5H **47**
Athlone Ct. *E17* —3F **33**
Athlone Rd. *SW2* —7K **93**
Athlone St. *NW5* —6E **44**
Athlon Ind. Est. *Wemb* —2D **56**
Athlon Rd. *Wemb* —2D **56**
Athol Clo. *Pinn* —1A **22**
Athole Gdns. *Enf* —5K **7**
Athol Gdns. *Pinn* —1A **22**
Atholl Rd. *Ilf* —7A **36**
Athol Rd. *Eri* —5J **85**
Athol Sq. *E14* —6E **64**
Atkins Dri. *W Wick* —2F **137**
Atkinson Ct. *E10* —7D **32**
  (off Kings Clo.)

Atkinson Rd. *E16* —5A **66**
Atkins Rd. *E10* —6D **32**
Atkins Rd. *SW12* —7G **93**
Atlantic Rd. *SW9* —4A **94**
Atlas Bus. Cen. *NW2* —2D **42**
Atlas Gdns. *SE7* —4A **82**
Atlas M. *E8* —6F **47**
Atlas M. *N7* —6K **45**
Atlas Rd. *E13* —2J **65**
Atlas Rd. *NW10* —3A **58**
Atlas Rd. *Wemb* —4J **41**
Atlas Wharf. *E9* —6C **48**
Atley Rd. *E3* —1C **64**
Atlip Rd. *Wemb* —1E **56**
Atney Rd. *SW15* —4G **91**
Atterbury Rd. *N4* —6B **30**
Atterbury St. *SW1*
  —4J **77** (4D **154**)
Attewood Av. *NW10* —3A **42**
Attewood Rd. *N'holt* —6C **38**
Attfield Clo. *N20* —2G **15**
Attleborough Ct. *SE23* —2H **111**
Attlee Clo. *Croy* —6C **124**
Attlee Rd. *SE28* —7B **68**
Attlee Ter. *E17* —4D **32**
Attneave St. *WC1*
  —3A **62** (2J **143**)
Atwater Clo. *SW2* —1A **110**
Atwell Clo. *E10* —6D **32**
Atwell Rd. *SE15* —2G **95**
Atwood Av. *Rich* —2G **89**
Atwood Rd. *W6* —4D **74**
Atwoods All. *Rich* —1G **89**
Aubert Ct. *N5* —4B **46**
Aubert Pk. *N5* —4B **46**
Aubert Rd. *N5* —4B **46**
Aubrey Gdns. *NW8* —2A **60**
  (off Abbey Rd.)
Aubrey Moore Point. *E15* —2E **64**
  (off Abbey La.)
Aubrey Pl. *NW8* —2A **60**
Aubrey Rd. *E17* —3C **32**
Aubrey Rd. *N8* —5J **29**
Aubrey Rd. *W8* —1H **75**
Aubrey Wlk. *W8* —1H **75**
Auburn Clo. *SE14* —7A **80**
Aubyn Hill. *SE27* —4C **110**
Aubyn Sq. *SW15* —5C **90**
Auckland Clo. *SE19* —1F **125**
Auckland Ct. *Hayes* —4A **54**
Auckland Gdns. *SE19* —1E **124**
Auckland Hill. *SE27* —4C **110**
Auckland Rd. *W12* —7D **58**
  (off White City Est.)
Auckland Rise. *SE19* —1E **124**
Auckland Rd. *E10* —3D **48**
Auckland Rd. *SE19* —1F **125**
Auckland Rd. *SW11* —4D **92**
Auckland Rd. *Ilf* —1F **51**
Auckland Rd. *King T* —4F **119**
Auckland St. *SE11*
  —5K **77** (6G **155**)
Auden Pl. *NW1* —1E **60**
  (in two parts)
Auden Pl. *Cheam* —4E **130**
Audleigh Pl. *Chig* —6K **21**
Audley Clo. *N10* —7A **16**
Audley Clo. *SW11* —3E **92**
Audley Ct. *E18* —4H **33**
Audley Ct. *N'holt* —3A **54**
Audley Ct. *Pinn* —2A **22**
Audley Dri. *E16* —1K **81**
Audley Gdns. *Ilf* —2K **51**
Audley Pl. *Sutt* —7K **131**

Audley Rd. NW4 —5C **26**
Audley Rd. W5 —5F **57**
Audley Rd. Enf —2G **7**
Audley Rd. Rich —5F **89**
Audley Sq. W1 —1E **76** (4H **147**)
Audrey Clo. Beck —6D **126**
Audrey Gdns. Wemb —2B **40**
Audrey Rd. Ilf —3F **51**
Audrey St. E2 —2G **63**
Audric Clo. King T —1G **119**
Augurs La. E13 —3K **65**
Augusta Rd. Twic —2G **103**
Augusta St. E14 —6D **64**
Augustine Rd. W14 —3F **75**
Augustine Rd. Harr —1F **23**
Augustus Clo. Bren —7C **72**
Augustus Ct. SW16 —2H **109**
Augustus Ct. Felt —4D **102**
Augustus Rd. SW19 —1F **107**
Augustus St. NW1
    —2F **61** (1K **141**)
Aultone Way. Cars —3D **132**
Aultone Way. Sutt —2K **131**
Aulton Pl. SE11
    —5A **78** (6K **155**)
Aurelia Gdns. Croy —5K **123**
Aurelia Rd. Croy —6J **123**
Auriel Av. Dag —6K **53**
Auriga M. N1 —5E **46**
Auriol Av. Wor Pk —3A **130**
Auriol Dri. Gnfd —7H **39**
Auriol Pk. Rd. Wor Pk —3A **130**
Auriol Rd. W14 —4G **75**
Austell Gdns. NW7 —3F **13**
Austen Clo. SE28 —1B **84**
Austen Rd. Eri —7H **85**
Austen Rd. Harr —2F **39**
Austin Av. Brom —5C **128**
Austin Clo. SE23 —7B **96**
Austin Clo. Twic —5C **88**
Austin Ct. E6 —1A **66**
Austin Ct. SE15 —3G **95**
    (off Philip Wlk.)
Austin Ct. Enf —5K **7**
Austin Friars. EC2
    —6D **62** (7F **145**)
Austin Friars Pas. EC2
    —6D **62** (7F **145**)
Austin Friars Sq. EC2
    —6D **62** (7F **145**)
Austin St. SW11 —1E **92**
Austin St. E2 —3F **63** (2J **145**)
Austral Clo. Sidc —3K **115**
Australia Rd. W12 —7D **58**
Austral St. SE11
    —4B **78** (3A **156**)
Austyn Gdns. Surb —7H **119**
Autumn Clo. SW19 —6A **108**
Autumn Clo. Enf —1B **8**
Autumn St. E3 —1C **64**
Avalon Clo. SW20 —2G **121**
Avalon Clo. W13 —5A **56**
Avalon Clo. Enf —2F **7**
Avalon Rd. SW6 —1K **91**
Avalon Rd. W13 —4A **56**
Avarn Rd. SW17 —6D **108**
Avebury Ct. N1 —1D **62**
    (off Colville Est.)
Avebury Pk. Surb —7D **118**
Avebury Rd. E11 —1F **49**
Avebury Rd. SW19 —1H **121**
Avebury St. N1 —1D **62**
Aveley Mans. Bark —7F **51**
    (off Whiting Av.)
Aveley Rd. Romf —4K **37**

Aveline St. SE11
    —5A **78** (5H **155**)
Aveling Pk. Rd. E17 —2C **32**
Ave Maria La. EC4
    —6B **62** (1B **150**)
Avenell Rd. N5 —3B **46**
Avening Rd. SW18 —7J **91**
Avening Ter. SW18 —7J **91**
Avenons Rd. E13 —4J **65**
Avenue Clo. N14 —6B **6**
Avenue Clo. NW8 —1C **60**
Avenue Ct. N14 —6B **6**
Avenue Ct. NW2 —3H **43**
Avenue Cres. W3 —2H **73**
Avenue Elmers. Surb —5E **118**
Avenue Gdns. SE25 —2G **125**
Avenue Gdns. SW14 —3A **90**
Avenue Gdns. W3 —2H **73**
Avenue Gdns. Tedd —7K **103**
Avenue Ind. Est. E4 —6G **19**
Avenue Mans. NW3 —5K **43**
    (off Finchley Rd.)
Avenue M. N10 —3F **29**
Avenue Pde. N21 —7J **7**
Avenue Pk. Rd. SE27 —2B **110**
Avenue Rd. E7 —4K **49**
Avenue Rd. N6 —7G **29**
Avenue Rd. N12 —4F **15**
Avenue Rd. N14 —7B **6**
Avenue Rd. N15 —5D **30**
Avenue Rd. NW3 & NW8 —7B **44**
Avenue Rd. NW10 —2B **58**
Avenue Rd. SE20 & Beck
    —1J **125**
Avenue Rd. SE25 —2F **125**
Avenue Rd. SW16 —2H **123**
Avenue Rd. SW20 —2D **120**
Avenue Rd. W3 —2H **73**
Avenue Rd. Belv —4H **85**
Avenue Rd. Bexh —3E **100**
Avenue Rd. Bren —5C **72**
Avenue Rd. Chad H —7C **36**
Avenue Rd. Eri —7J **85**
    (in three parts)
Avenue Rd. Iswth —1K **87**
Avenue Rd. King T —3E **118**
Avenue Rd. N Mald —4A **120**
Avenue Rd. Pinn —3C **22**
Avenue Rd. S'hall —1D **70**
Avenue Rd. Tedd —7A **104**
Avenue Rd. Wfd G —6F **21**
Avenue S. Surb —7G **119**
Avenue Ter. N Mald —3J **119**
Avenue, The. E4 —4B **20**
Avenue, The. E11 —5K **33**
Avenue, The. N3 —2J **27**
Avenue, The. N8 —3A **30**
Avenue, The. N10 —2G **29**
Avenue, The. N11 —5A **16**
Avenue, The. N17 —2E **30**
Avenue, The. NW6 —1G **59**
Avenue, The. SE7 —7A **82**
Avenue, The. SE9 —6D **98**
Avenue, The. SE10 —7F **81**
Avenue, The. SW4 —5F **93**
Avenue, The. SW18 —7C **92**
Avenue, The. W4 —3A **74**
Avenue, The. W13 —6B **56**
Avenue, The. Barn —3B **4**
Avenue, The. Beck —1D **126**
Avenue, The. Bex —7D **100**
Avenue, The. Brom —3B **128**
Avenue, The. Buck H —2F **21**
Avenue, The. Cars —7E **132**

Avenue, The. Croy —3E **134**
Avenue, The. Eps & Sut —7D **130**
Avenue, The. Hamp —6D **102**
Avenue, The. Harr —1K **23**
Avenue, The. Houn —5F **87**
Avenue, The. Kes —3B **138**
Avenue, The. Pinn —7D **22**
Avenue, The. Rich —2F **89**
Avenue, The. Romf —4K **37**
Avenue, The. St P —7B **116**
Avenue, The. Surb —7G **119**
Avenue, The. Sutt —7G **131**
Avenue, The. Twic —5B **88**
Avenue, The. Wemb —2F **41**
Avenue, The. W Wick —7G **127**
Avenue, The. Wor Pk —2A **130**
Averil Gro. SW16 —6B **110**
Averill St. W6 —6F **75**
Avery Farm Row. SW1
    —4F **77** (4J **153**)
Avery Gdns. Ilf —5D **34**
Avery Hill Rd. SE9 —6H **99**
Avery Row. W1 —7F **61** (2J **147**)
Aviary Clo. E16 —5H **65**
Aviemore Clo. Beck —5B **126**
Aviemore Way. Beck —5A **126**
Avignon Rd. SE4 —3K **95**
Avington Gro. SE20 —7J **111**
Avington Way. SE15 —7F **79**
Avion Cres. NW9 —1C **26**
Avis Sq. E1 —6K **63**
Avoca Rd. SW17 —4E **108**
Avocet Clo. SE1 —5G **79**
Avocet M. SE28 —3H **83**
Avon Clo. Hayes —4A **54**
Avon Clo. Sutt —4A **132**
Avon Clo. Wor Pk —2C **130**
Avon Ct. E4 —1K **19**
Avon Ct. N12 —5E **14**
Avon Ct. Buck H —1E **20**
Avon Ct. Gnfd —4F **55**
Avondale Av. N12 —5E **14**
Avondale Av. NW2 —3A **42**
Avondale Av. Barn —1J **15**
Avondale Av. Wor Pk —1B **130**
Avondale Ct. E11 —1G **49**
Avondale Ct. E16 —5G **65**
Avondale Ct. E18 —1K **33**
Avondale Cres. Enf —3F **9**
Avondale Cres. Ilf —5B **34**
Avondale Gdns. Houn —5D **86**
Avondale Ho. SE1
    —5G **79** (6K **157**)
Avondale Pk. Gdns. W11 —7G **59**
Avondale Pk. Rd. W11 —7G **59**
Avondale Rise. SE15 —3F **95**
Avondale Rd. E16 —5G **65**
Avondale Rd. E17 —7C **32**
Avondale Rd. N3 —1A **28**
Avondale Rd. N13 —2F **17**
Avondale Rd. N15 —5B **30**
Avondale Rd. SE9 —2C **114**
Avondale Rd. SW14 —3A **90**
Avondale Rd. SW19 —5K **107**
Avondale Rd. Brom —6H **113**
Avondale Rd. Harr —3K **23**
Avondale Rd. S Croy —6C **134**
Avondale Rd. Well —2C **100**
Avondale Sq. SE1
    —5G **79** (6K **157**)
Avonfield Ct. E17 —3F **33**
Avon Ho. W8 —3J **75**
    (off Allen St.)
Avonley Rd. SE14 —7J **79**
Avon M. Pinn —1D **22**

Avonmore Gdns. W14 —4H **75**
Avonmore Pl. W14 —4H **75**
    (off Avonmore Rd.)
Avonmore Rd. W14 —4G **75**
Avonmouth St. SE1
    —3C **78** (1C **156**)
Avon Path. S Croy —6C **134**
Avon Pl. SE1 —2C **78** (7D **150**)
Avon Rd. E17 —3F **33**
Avon Rd. SE4 —3C **96**
Avon Rd. Gnfd —4E **54**
Avon Way. E18 —3J **33**
Avonwick Rd. Houn —2F **87**
Avril Way. E4 —5K **19**
Avro Way. Wall —7J **133**
Awfield Av. N17 —1D **30**
Awliscombe Rd. Well —2K **99**
Axe Ct. E2 —3F **63** (1J **145**)
Axe St. Bark —1G **67**
    (in two parts)
Axholme Av. Edgw —1G **25**
Axminster Cres. Well —1C **100**
Axminster Rd. N7 —3J **45**
Aybrook St. W1 —5E **60** (6G **141**)
Aycliffe Clo. Brom —4D **128**
Aycliffe Rd. W12 —1C **74**
Ayerst Ct. E10 —7E **32**
Aylands Clo. Wemb —2E **40**
Aylesbury Clo. E7 —6H **49**
Aylesbury Ct. Sutt —3A **132**
Aylesbury Rd. SE17
    —5D **78** (6F **157**)
Aylesbury Rd. Brom —3J **127**
Aylesbury St. EC1
    —4B **62** (4A **144**)
Aylesbury St. NW10 —3K **41**
Aylesford Av. Beck —5A **126**
Aylesford St. SW1
    —5H **77** (5C **154**)
Aylesham Cen., The. SE15
    —1G **95**
Aylesham Clo. NW7 —7H **13**
Aylesham Rd. Orp —7K **129**
Aylestone Av. NW6 —7F **43**
Aylett Rd. SE25 —4H **125**
Aylett Rd. Iswth —2J **87**
Ayley Croft. Enf —5B **8**
Ayliffe Clo. King T —2G **119**
Aylmer Clo. Stan —4F **11**
Aylmer Ct. N2 —5D **28**
Aylmer Dri. Stan —4F **11**
Aylmer Pde. N2 —5D **28**
Aylmer Rd. E11 —1H **49**
Aylmer Rd. N2 —5C **28**
Aylmer Rd. W12 —2B **74**
Aylmer Rd. Dag —3E **52**
Ayloffe Rd. Dag —6F **53**
Aylton Est. SE16 —3J **79**
Aylward Rd. SE23 —2K **111**
Aylward Rd. SW20 —2H **121**
Aylwards Rise. Stan —4F **11**
Aylward St. E1 —6J **63**
Aylwin Est. SE1 —3E **78** (1H **157**)
Aynhoe Mans. W14 —4F **75**
    (off Aynhoe Rd.)
Aynhoe Rd. W14 —4F **75**
Aynscombe Path. SW14 —2J **89**
Ayr Ct. W3 —5G **57**
Ayres Clo. E13 —3J **65**
Ayres Cres. NW10 —7K **41**
Ayres St. SE1 —2C **78** (6D **150**)
Ayr Grn. Romf —1K **37**
Ayrsome Rd. N16 —3E **46**
Ayrton Rd. SW7 —3B **76** (1A **152**)
Ayr Way. Romf —1K **37**

Aysgarth Ct. Sutt —3K **131**
Aysgarth Rd. SE21 —7E **94**
Ayton Ho. SE5 —7D **78**
    (off Edmund St.)
Aytoun Pl. SW9 —2K **93**
Aytoun Rd. SW9 —2K **93**
Azalea Clo. W7 —1K **71**
Azalea Ct. W7 —1K **71**
Azalea Clo. Ilf —5F **51**
Azalia Clo. Ilf —5F **51**
Azenby Rd. SE15 —2F **95**
Azof St. SE10 —4G **81**

B

Baalbec Rd. N5 —5B **46**
Babbacombe Gdns. Ilf —4C **34**
Babbacombe Rd. Brom —1J **127**
Baber Bri. Cvn. Site. Felt —3A **86**
Baber Dri. Felt —6A **86**
Babington Ct. WC1
    —5K **61** (5G **143**)
Babington Rise. Wemb —6G **41**
Babington Rd. NW4 —4D **26**
Babington Rd. SW16 —5H **109**
Babington Rd. Dag —5C **52**
Babmaes St. SW1
    —7H **61** (3C **148**)
Bacchus Wlk. N1 —2E **62**
    (off Hoxton St.)
Back All. EC3 —6E **62** (1H **151**)
Back Church La. E1 —6G **63**
Back Hill. EC1 —4A **62** (4K **143**)
Backhouse Pl. SE17
    —4E **78** (4H **157**)
Back La. E15 —2F **65**
Back La. N8 —5J **29**
Back La. NW3 —4A **44**
Back La. Bark —1G **67**
Back La. Bex —7G **101**
Back La. Bren —6D **72**
Back La. Edgw —1J **25**
Back La. Rich —2C **104**
    (in two parts)
Back La. Romf —7D **38**
Backley Gdns. SE25 —6G **125**
Back Rd. Sidc —4A **116**
Back Rd. Tedd —7J **103**
Bacon Gro. SE1 —3F **79** (2J **157**)
Bacon La. NW9 —4H **25**
Bacon La. Edgw —1G **25**
Bacons La. N6 —1E **44**
Bacon St. E1 & E2
    —4F **63** (3K **145**)
Bacon Ter. Dag —5B **52**
Bacton St. E2 —3J **63**
Baddesley Ho. SE11
    —5K **77** (5H **155**)
Baddow Clo. Dag —1G **69**
Baddow Clo. Wfd G —6G **21**
Baddow Wlk. N1 —1C **62**
    (off Basire St.)
Baden. Belv —3G **85**
Baden Pl. SE1 —2D **78** (6E **150**)
Baden Powell Ho. SW7
    —4A **76** (2A **152**)
Baden Rd. N8 —4J **29**
Baden Rd. Ilf —5F **51**
Badger Clo. Houn —3A **86**
Badger Clo. Ilf —6G **35**
Badgers Clo. Enf —2G **7**
Badgers Clo. Harr —6H **23**
Badgers Copse. Wor Pk —2B **130**
Badgers Croft. N20 —7B **4**
Badgers Croft. SE9 —3E **114**
Badgers Hole. Croy —4K **135**

Badgers Wlk. N Mald —2A 120
Badlis Rd. E17 —3C 32
Badminton Clo. Harr —4J 23
Badminton Clo. N'holt —6E 38
Badminton M. E16 —1J 81
Badminton Rd. SW12 —6E 92
Badsworth Rd. SE5 —1C 94
Baffins Pl. SE1 —3D 78 (1F 157)
Baffin Way. E14 —1E 80
(off Blackwall Way)
Bagford St. N1 —1D 62
Bagley's La. SW6 —1K 91
Bagleys Spring. Romf —4E 36
Bagshot Ct. SE18 —1E 98
Bagshot Rd. Enf —7A 8
Bagshot St. SE17
—5E 78 (6H 157)
Baildon St. SE8 —7B 80
Bailey Clo. E4 —4K 19
Bailey Clo. N11 —1H 29
Bailey Pl. SE26 —6K 111
Baillies Wlk. W5 —2D 72
Bainbridge Rd. Dag —4F 53
Bainbridge St. WC1
—6H 61 (7D 142)
Baines Clo. S Croy —5D 134
Baird Av. S'hall —7F 55
Baird Clo. NW9 —6J 25
Baird Ho. W12 —7D 58
(off White City Est.)
Baird Rd. Enf —3C 8
Baird St. EC1 —4C 62 (3D 144)
Baizdon Rd. SE3 —2G 97
Baker Ho. W7 —1K 71
Baker La. Mitc —2E 122
Baker M. N16 —2F 47
Baker NW10 —1A 58
Baker Rd. SE18 —7C 82
Bakers Av. E17 —6D 32
Bakers Ct. SE25 —3E 124
Baker's Field. N7 —4J 45
Bakers Gdns. Cars —2C 132
Bakers Hall Ct. EC3
—7E 62 (3G 151)
Bakers Hill. E5 —1J 47
Bakers Hill. New Bar —2E 4
Bakers Ho. W5 —1D 72
(off Grove, The)
Bakers La. N6 —6D 28
Baker's M. W1 —6E 60 (7G 141)
Bakers Pas. NW3 —4A 44
(off Heath St.)
Baker's Rents. E2
—3F 63 (2J 145)
Baker's Row. E15 —2G 65
Baker's Row. EC1
—4A 62 (4J 143)
Baker St. NW1 & W1
—4D 60 (4F 141)
Baker Street. (Junct.) —5D 60
Baker St. Enf —3J 7
Baker's Yd. EC1
—4A 62 (4J 143)
Bakery Clo. SW9 —7K 77
Bakery Path. Edgw —5C 12
(off St Margaret's Rd.)
Bakery Pl. SW11 —4D 92
Bakewell Ct. E5 —3A 48
Bakewell Way. N Mald —2A 120
Balaam Ho. Sutt —4J 131
Balaams La. N14 —2C 16
Balaam St. E13 —4J 65

Balaclava Rd. SE1
—4F 79 (4K 157)
Balaclava Rd. Surb —7C 118
Balben Path. E9 —7J 47
Balcaskie Rd. SE9 —5D 98
Balchen Rd. SE3 —2B 98
Balchier Rd. SE22 —6H 95
Balcombe Clo. Bexh —4D 100
Balcombe St. NW1
—4D 60 (3E 140)
Balcon Ct. W5 —6F 57
Balcorne St. E9 —7J 47
Balder Rise. SE12 —2K 113
Balderton St. W1
—6E 60 (1H 147)
Baldock St. E3 —2D 64
Baldry Gdns. SW16 —6J 109
Baldwin Cres. SE5 —1C 94
Baldwin Ho. SW2 —1A 110
Baldwin's Gdns. EC1
—5A 62 (5J 143)
Baldwin St. EC1 —3D 62 (2E 144)
Baldwin Ter. N1 —2C 62
Baldwyn Gdns. W3 —7K 57
Baldwyn's Pk. Bex —2K 117
Baldwyn's Rd. Bex —2K 117
Bales Ter. N9 —3A 18
Balfern Gro. W4 —5A 74
Balfern St. SW11 —2C 92
Balfe St. N1 —2J 61
Balfour Tower. E14 —6E 64
Balfour Av. W7 —1K 71
Balfour Bus. Cen. S'hall —3A 70
Balfour Gro. N20 —3J 15
Balfour Ho. W10 —5F 59
(off St Charles Sq.)
Balfour M. N9 —3B 18
Balfour M. W1 —1E 76 (4H 147)
Balfour Pl. SW15 —4D 90
Balfour Pl. W1 —7E 60 (3H 147)
Balfour Rd. N5 —4C 46
Balfour Rd. SE25 —4G 125
Balfour Rd. SW19 —7K 107
Balfour Rd. W3 —5J 57
Balfour Rd. W13 —2A 72
Balfour Rd. Brom —5B 128
Balfour Rd. Cars —7D 132
Balfour Rd. Harr —5H 23
Balfour Rd. Houn —3F 87
Balfour Rd. Ilf —2F 51
Balfour Rd. S'hall —3B 70
Balfour St. SE17 —4D 78 (3E 156)
Balfour Ter. N3 —2K 27
Balgonie Rd. E4 —1A 20
Balgowan Clo. N Mald —5A 120
Balgowan Rd. Beck —2A 126
Balgowan St. SE18 —4K 83
Balham Continental Mkt. SW12
(off Shipka Rd.) —1F 109
Balham Gro. SW12 —7E 92
Balham High Rd. SW17 & SW12
—3E 108
Balham Hill. SW12 —7F 93
Balham New Rd. SW12 —7F 93
Balham Pk. Rd. SW12 —1D 108
Balkan Wlk. E1 —7H 63
Ballater Wlk. E14 —5D 64
Ballamore Rd. Brom —3J 113
Ballance Rd. E9 —6K 47
Ballantine St. SW18 —4A 92
Ballantine Ho. NW2 —4H 43
Ballantrae Ho. NW2 —4H 43
Ballard Clo. King T —7K 105

Ballards Clo. Dag —1H 69
Ballards Farm Rd. S Croy & Croy
—6G 135
Ballards La. N3 & N12 —1J 27
Ballards M. Edgw —6B 12
Ballards Rise. S Croy —6G 135
Ballards Rd. NW2 —2C 42
Ballards Rd. Dag —2H 69
Ballards Way. S Croy & Croy
—6G 135
Ballast Quay. SE10 —5F 81
Ballater Rd. SW2 —4J 93
Ballater Rd. S Croy —5F 135
Ballina St. SE23 —7K 95
Ballingdon Rd. SW11 —6E 92
Balliol Av. E4 —4B 20
Balliol Rd. N17 —1E 30
Balliol Rd. W10 —6E 58
Balliol Rd. Well —2B 100
Balloch Rd. SE6 —1F 113
Ballogie Av. NW10 —4A 42
Ballow Clo. SE5 —7E 78
Ball's Pond Pl. N1 —6D 46
Balls Pond Rd. N1 —6D 46
Balmain Clo. W5 —1D 72
Balmain Ct. Houn —1F 87
Balmer Rd. E3 —2B 64
Balmes Rd. N1 —1D 62
Balmoral Av. N11 —5A 16
Balmoral Av. Beck —4A 126
Balmoral Clo. SW15 —6F 91
Balmoral Ct. SE12 —4K 113
Balmoral Ct. SE27 —4C 110
Balmoral Ct. Beck —1E 126
Balmoral Ct. Sutt —7J 131
Balmoral Ct. Wemb —3F 41
Balmoral Ct. Wor Pk —2D 130
Balmoral Dri. S'hall —4D 54
Balmoral Gdns. W13 —3A 72
Balmoral Gdns. Bex —7F 101
Balmoral Gdns. Ilf —1K 51
Balmoral Gro. N7 —6K 45
Balmoral M. W12 —3B 74
Balmoral Rd. E7 —4A 50
Balmoral Rd. E10 —2D 48
Balmoral Rd. NW2 —6D 42
Balmoral Rd. Harr —4E 38
Balmoral Rd. King T —4F 119
Balmoral Rd. Wor Pk —3D 130
Balmoral Trad. Est. Bark —5K 67
Balmore Cres. Barn —5K 5
Balmore St. N19 —2F 45
Balmuir Gdns. SW15 —4E 90
Balnacraig Av. NW10 —4A 42
Balniel Ga. SW1 —5H 77 (5D 154)
Baltic Cen., The. Bren —5D 72
Baltic Clo. SW19 —7B 108
Baltic Ct. SE16 —2K 79
Baltic Ho. SE5 —2C 94
Baltic St. E. EC1 —4C 62 (4C 144)
Baltic St. W. EC1
—4C 62 (4C 144)
Baltimore Pl. Well —2K 99
Balvaird Pl. SW1
—5H 77 (6D 154)
Balvernie Gro. SW18 —7H 91
Bamber Ho. Bark —1G 67
Bamborough Gdns. W12 —2E 74
Bamburgh. N17 —7D 18
Bamford Av. Wemb —1F 57
Bamford Rd. Bark —6G 51
Bamford Rd. Brom —5E 112
Bampfylde Clo. Wall —3G 133
Bampton Clo. W5 —6D 56
Bampton Rd. SE23 —3K 111

Banavie Gdns. Beck —1E 126
Banbury Clo. Enf —1G 7
Banbury Ct. WC2
—7J 61 (2E 148)
Banbury Ct. Sutt —7J 131
Banbury Ho. E9 —7K 47
Banbury Rd. E9 —7K 47
Banbury Rd. E17 —7E 18
Banbury St. SW11 —2C 92
Banbury Wlk. N'holt —2E 54
(off Brabazon Rd.)
Banchory Rd. SE3 —7K 81
Bancroft Av. N2 —5C 28
Bancroft Av. Buck H —2D 20
Bancroft Ct. SW8 —7J 77
(off Allen Edwards Dri.)
Bancroft Gdns. Harr —1G 23
Bancroft Gdns. Orp —7K 129
Bancroft Rd. E1 —3K 63
Bancroft Rd. Harr —2G 23
Bandon Rise. Wall —5H 133
Bangalore St. SW15 —3E 90
Bangor Clo. N'holt —5F 39
Banim St. W6 —4D 74
Banister Ho. E9 —5K 47
Banister Rd. W10 —3F 59
Bank Av. Mitc —2B 122
Bank Bldgs. E4 —6A 20
Bank End. SE1 —1C 78 (4D 150)
Bankfoot Rd. Brom —4G 113
Bankhurst Rd. SE6 —7B 96
Bank La. SW15 —5A 90
Bank La. King T —7E 104
Bank M. Sutt —6A 132
Banksian Wlk. Iswth —1J 87
Banksia Rd. N18 —5D 18
Bankside. SE1 —6C 62 (3C 150)
Bankside. Enf —1G 7
Bankside. S'hall —1B 70
Bankside. S Croy —6F 135
Bankside. Bex —4K 117
Bankside Clo. Iswth —4K 87
Bankside Clo. Cars —6C 132
Bankside Rd. Ilf —5G 51
Bankside Way. SE19 —6E 110
Bankton Rd. SW2 —4A 94
Bankwell Rd. SE13 —4G 97
Banner St. EC1 —4C 62 (4D 144)
Banning St. SE10 —5G 81
Bannister Clo. SW2 —1A 110
Bannister Clo. Gnfd —5H 39
Bannockburn Rd. SE18 —4J 83
Bantock Ho. W10 —3G 59
Banton Clo. Enf —2C 8
Bantry St. SE5 —7D 78
Banwell Rd. Bex —6D 100
Banyard Rd. SE16 —3H 79
Baptist Gdns. NW5 —6E 44
Barandon Wlk. W11 —7F 59
Barbara Brosnan Ct. NW8
—2B 60 (1A 140)
Barbara Hucklesby Clo. N22
—2B 30

Barbauld Rd. N16 —3E 46
Barber Clo. N21 —7F 7
Barbers All. E13 —3K 65
Barbers Rd. E15 —2D 64
Barbican Rd. Gnfd —6F 55
Barb M. W6 —3E 74
Barbon Clo. WC1
—5K 61 (5F 143)
Barchard St. SW18 —5K 91
Barchester Clo. W7 —1K 71
Barchester Rd. Harr —2H 23
Barchester St. E14 —5D 64
Barclay Clo. SW6 —7J 75
Barclay Oval. Wfd G —4D 20
Barclay Path. E17 —5E 32
Barclay Rd. E11 —1H 49
Barclay Rd. E13 —4A 66
Barclay Rd. E17 —5E 32
Barclay Rd. N18 —6J 17
Barclay Rd. SW6 —7J 75
Barclay Rd. Croy —3D 134
Barclay Way. SE22 —1G 111
Barcombe Av. SW2 —2J 109
Barcombe Clo. Orp —3K 129
Barden St. SE18 —7J 83
Bardfield Av. Romf —3D 36
Bardney Rd. Mord —4K 121
Bardolph Av. Croy —7A 136
Bardolph Rd. N7 —4J 45
Bardolph Rd. Rich —3F 89
Bard Rd. W10 —7F 59
Bardsey Wlk. N1 —6C 46
Bardsley Clo. Croy —3F 135
Bardsley La. SE10 —6E 80
Barfett St. W10 —4H 59
Barfield Av. N20 —2J 15
Barfield Rd. E11 —1H 49
Barfield Rd. Brom —3E 128
Barfleur Ho. SE8 —5B 80
Barford Clo. NW4 —2C 26
Barford St. N1 —1A 62
Barforth Rd. SE15 —3H 95
Barfreston Way. SE20 —1H 125
Bargate Clo. SE18 —5K 83
Bargate Clo. N Mald —7C 120
Barge Ho. Rd. E16 —2F 83
Barge Ho. St. SE1
—1A 78 (3K 149)
Bargery Rd. SE6 —1D 112
Barge Wlk. King T —1D 118
Bargrove Clo. SE20 —7G 111
Bargrove Cres. SE6 —2B 112
Barham Clo. Brom —1C 138
Barham Clo. Chst —5F 115
Barham Clo. Romf —2H 37
Barham Clo. Wemb —6B 40
Barham Rd. SW20 —7C 106
Barham Rd. Chst —5F 115
Barham Rd. S Croy —5C 134
Baring Clo. SE12 —2J 113
Baring Rd. SE12 —7J 97
Baring Rd. Cockf —4G 5
Baring Rd. Croy —1G 135
Baring St. N1 —1D 62
Barington Ho. N1 —2K 61
(off Collier St.)
Barker Dri. NW1 —7G 45
Barker M. SW4 —4F 93
Barkers Arc. W8 —2K 75
Barker St. SW10 —6A 76
Barker Wlk. SW16 —3H 109
Barker Way. SE22 —7G 95
Barkham Rd. N17 —7J 17
Barking Bus. Cen. Bark —3A 68

Barking Northern Relief Rd. *Bark*
—7F **51**

Barking Rd. *E16, E13 & E6*
—5H **65**

Bark Pl. *W2*—7K **59**
Barkston Gdns. *SW5*—4K **75**
Barkway Ct. *N4*—2C **46**
Barkwood Clo. *Romf*—5J **37**
Barkworth Rd. *SE16*—5H **79**
Barlborough St. *SE14*—7K **79**
Barlby Gdns. *W10*—4F **59**
Barlby Rd. *W10*—5E **58**
Barleycorn Way. *E14*—7B **64**
Barleyfields Clo. *Romf*—6B **36**
Barley La. *Ilf & Romf*—7A **36**
Barley Mow Pas. *EC1*
—5B **62** (5B **144**)
Barley Mow Pas. *W4*—5K **73**
Barlings Ho. SE4—4K **95**
(off Frendsbury Rd.)
Barlow Clo. *Wall*—6J **133**
Barlow Ho. W11—7G **59**
(off Walmer Rd.)
Barlow Pl. *W1*—7F **61** (3K **147**)
Barlow Rd. *NW6*—6H **43**
Barlow Rd. *W3*—1H **73**
Barlow Rd. *Hamp*—7E **102**
Barlow St. *SE17*—4D **78** (4F **157**)
Barlow Way. *Rain*—5K **69**
Barmeston Rd. *SE6*—2D **112**
Barmor Clo. *Harr*—2F **23**
Barmouth Av. *Gnfd*—2K **55**
Barmouth Rd. *SW18*—6A **92**
Barmouth Rd. *Croy*—2K **135**
Barnabas Ct. *N21*—5G **7**
Barnabas Rd. *E9*—5K **47**
Barnaby Clo. *Harr*—2G **39**
Barnaby Clo. *NW9*—3A **26**
Barnaby Ct. SE16—2G **79**
(off Lidgett Cres.)
Barnaby Pl. *SW7*
—4B **76** (4A **152**)
Barnaby Way. *Chig*—3K **21**
Barnard Clo. *SE18*—3E **82**
Barnard Clo. *Chst*—1H **129**
Barnard Clo. *Wall*—7H **133**
Barnard Gdns. *Hayes*—4A **54**
Barnard Gdns. *N Mald*—4C **120**
Barnard Gro. *E15*—7H **49**
Barnard Hill. *N10*—1F **29**
Barnard Lodge. *New Bar*—4F **5**
Barnard M. *SW11*—4C **92**
Barnardo Dri. *Ilf*—4G **35**
Barnardo Gdns. *E1*—7K **63**
Barnardo St. *E1*—6K **63**
Barnardos Village. *B'side*—3G **35**
Barnard Rd. *SW11*—4C **92**
Barnard Rd. *Enf*—2C **8**
Barnard Rd. *Mitc*—3E **122**
Barnards Inn. *EC1*
—6A **62** (6K **143**)
Barnard's Wharf. *SE16*—2B **80**
Barnby Sq. *E15*—1G **65**
Barnby St. *E15*—1G **65**
Barnby St. *NW1*
—2G **61** (1B **142**)
Barn Clo. *N'holt*—2A **54**
Barn Cres. *Stan*—6H **11**
Barnehurst Av. *Eri & Bexh*
—1J **101**
Barnehurst Clo. *Eri*—1J **101**
Barnehurst Rd. *Bexh*—2J **101**
Barn Elms Pk. *SW15*—3E **90**
Barnes Av. *SW13*—7C **74**
Barnes Av. *S'hall*—4D **70**

Barnes Clo. *E12*—4B **50**
Barnes Ct. *E16*—5A **66**
Barnes Ct. *Wfd G*—5G **21**
Barnes End. *N Mald*—5C **120**
Barnes High St. *SW13*—2B **90**
Barnes Ho. *Bark*—1H **67**
Barnes Pikle. *W5*—7D **56**
Barnes Rd. *N18*—4D **18**
Barnes Rd. *Ilf*—5G **51**
Barnes St. *E14*—6A **64**
Barnes Wallis Ct. *Wemb*—3J **41**
Barnet Dri. *Brom*—2C **138**
Barnet Ga. La. *Barn*—1H **13**
Barnet Gro. *E2*—3G **63** (1K **145**)
Barnet Hill. *Barn*—4C **4**
Barnet Ho. *N20*—2F **15**
Barnet La. *N20 & Barn*—1C **14**
Barnet Trad. Est. *High Bar*—3C **4**
Barnetts Ct. *Harr*—3F **39**
Barnett St. *E1*—6H **63**
Barnet Way. *NW7*—3E **12**
Barnet Wood Rd. *Brom*—2A **138**
Barney Clo. *SE7*—5A **82**
Barn Field. *NW3*—5D **44**
Barnfield. *N Mald*—6A **120**
Barnfield Av. *Croy*—2J **135**
Barnfield Av. *King T*—4D **104**
Barnfield Av. *Mitc*—3F **123**
Barnfield Clo. *N4*—7J **29**
Barnfield Clo. *SW17*—3B **108**
Barnfield Gdns. *SE18*—6F **83**
Barnfield Gdns. *King T*—4E **104**
Barnfield Pl. *E14*—4C **80**
Barnfield Rd. *SE18*—6F **83**
(in two parts)
Barnfield Rd. *W5*—4C **56**
Barnfield Rd. *Belv*—6F **85**
Barnfield Rd. *Edgw*—1J **25**
Barnfield Rd. *S Croy*—7E **134**
Barnfield Wood Clo. *Beck*
—6F **127**
Barnfield Wood Rd. *Beck*
—6F **127**
Barnham Rd. *Gnfd*—3G **55**
Barnham St. *SE1*
—2E **78** (6H **151**)
Barnhill. *Pinn*—5A **22**
Barn Hill. *Wemb*—1G **41**
Barnhill Av. *Brom*—5H **127**
Barnhill La. *Hayes*—4A **54**
Barnhill Rd. *Hayes*—3A **54**
Barnhill Rd. *Wemb*—3J **41**
Barningham Way. *NW9*—6K **25**
Barnlea Clo. *Felt*—2C **102**
Barnmead Gdns. *Dag*—5F **53**
Barnmead Rd. *Beck*—1K **125**
Barnmead Rd. *Dag*—5F **53**
Barn M. *S Harr*—3E **38**
Barn Rise. *Wemb*—1G **41**
Barnsbury Clo. *N Mald*—4J **119**
Barnsbury Est. *N1*—1A **62**
Barnsbury Gro. *N7*—7K **45**
Barnsbury M. *N1*—7A **46**
Barnsbury Pk. *N1*—7A **46**
Barnsbury Rd. *N1*—2A **62**
Barnsbury Sq. *N1*—7A **46**
Barnsbury St. *N1*—7A **46**
Barnsbury Ter. *N1*—7K **45**
Barnscroft. *SW20*—3D **120**
Barnsdale Av. *E14*—4D **80**
Barnsdale Rd. *W9*—4H **59**
Barnsley St. *E1*—4H **63**
Barnstable Ho. SE12—5H **97**
(off Taunton Rd.)
Barnstable La. *SE13*—4E **96**

Barnstaple Rd. *Ruis*—3A **38**
Barn St. *N16*—2E **46**
Barn Way. *Wemb*—1G **41**
Barnwell Rd. *SW2*—5A **94**
Barnwood Clo. *W9*—4K **59**
Baron Clo. *N1*—2A **62**
Baron Clo. *N11*—5A **16**
Baroness Rd. *E2*
—3F **63** (1K **145**)
Baronet Gro. *N17*—1G **31**
Baronet Rd. *N17*—1G **31**
Baron Gdns. *Ilf*—3G **35**
Baron Gro. *Mitc*—4C **122**
Baron Rd. *Dag*—1D **52**
Baronsclere Ct. *N6*—7G **29**
Barons Ct. *Ilf*—2H **51**
Barons Ct. *Wall*—3H **133**
Baron's Ct. Rd. *W14*—5G **75**
Baronsfield Rd. *Twic*—6B **88**
Barons Ga. *W4*—3J **73**
Barons Ga. *Barn*—6H **5**
Barons Keep. *W14*—5G **75**
Barons Mead. *Harr*—4J **23**
Baronsmead Rd. *SW13*—1C **90**
Baronsmede. *W5*—2F **73**
Baronsmere Ct. *Barn*—4B **4**
Baronsmere Rd. *N2*—4C **28**
Barons Pl. *SE1*—2A **78** (7K **149**)
Barons, The. *Twic*—6B **88**
Baron St. *N1*—2A **62**
Baron's Wlk. *Croy*—6A **126**
Baron Wlk. *E16*—5H **65**
Baron Wlk. *Mitc*—4C **122**
Barque M. *SE8*—6C **80**
Barrack Rd. *Houn*—4B **86**
Barratt Av. *N22*—2K **29**
Barratt Ind. Est. *S'hall*—1E **70**
Barratt Ind. Pk. *E3*—4E **64**
Barratt Ind. Pk. *S'hall*—2E **70**
Barratt Way. *Harr*—2H **23**
Barrenger Rd. *N10*—1D **28**
Barrett Ho. *SE17*
—5C **78** (5D **156**)
Barrett Ho. SW9—3K **93**
(off Benedict Rd.)
Barrett Rd. *E17*—4E **32**
Barrett's Grn. Rd. *NW10*—3J **57**
Barrett's Gro. *N16*—5E **46**
Barrett St. *W1*—6E **60** (1H **147**)
Barrhill Rd. *SW2*—2J **109**
Barrie Ct. *New Bar*—5F **5**
(off Lyonsdown Rd.)
Barriedale. *SE14*—2A **96**
Barrie Est. *W2*—7B **60** (2A **146**)
Barrie Ho. W3—2J **73**
(off Castle Clo.)
Barrier App. *SE7*—3B **82**
Barringer Sq. *SW17*—4E **108**
Barrington Clo. *NW5*—5E **44**
Barrington Clo. *Ilf*—1D **34**
Barrington Clo. *NW5*—5E **44**
Barrington Ct. *W3*—2H **73**
(off Cheltenham Pl.)
Barrington Rd. *E12*—6E **50**
Barrington Rd. *N8*—5H **29**
Barrington Rd. *SW9*—3B **94**
Barrington Rd. *Bexh*—2D **100**
Barrington Rd. *Sutt*—2J **131**
Barrington Vs. *SE18*—1E **98**
Barrow Av. *Cars*—7D **132**
Barrow Clo. *N21*—3G **17**
Barrowdene Clo. *Pinn*—2C **22**
Barrowell Grn. *N21*—2G **17**
Barrowfield Clo. *N9*—3C **18**
Barrowgate Rd. *W4*—5J **73**

Barrow Hedges Clo. *Cars*
—7C **132**
Barrow Hedges Way. *Cars*
—7C **132**
Barrowhill. *Wor Pk*—2A **130**
Barrowhill Clo. *Wor Pk*—2A **130**
Barrow Hill Est. NW8—2C **60**
(off Barrow Hill Rd.)
Barrow Hill Rd. *NW8*
—2C **60** (1C **140**)
Barrow Point Av. *Pinn*—2C **22**
Barrow Point La. *Pinn*—2C **22**
Barrow Rd. *SW16*—6H **109**
Barrow Rd. *Croy*—5A **134**
Barrow Wlk. *Bren*—6C **72**
Barrs Rd. *NW10*—7K **41**
Barry Av. *N15*—6F **31**
Barry Av. *Bexh*—7E **84**
Barrydene. *N20*—1G **15**
Barry Rd. *E6*—6C **66**
Barry Rd. *NW10*—7J **41**
Barry Rd. *SE22*—6G **95**
Barset Rd. *SE15*—3J **95**
(in three parts)
Barson Clo. *SE20*—7J **111**
Barston Rd. *SE27*—3C **110**
Barstow Cres. *SW2*—1K **109**
Barter St. *WC1*—5J **61** (6F **143**)
Barters Wlk. *Pinn*—3C **22**
Bartholomew Clo. *EC1*
—5C **62** (6B **144**)
Bartholomew Clo. *SW18*—4A **92**
Bartholomew Ct. *Edgw*—7J **11**
Bartholomew La. *EC2*
—6D **62** (1F **151**)
Bartholomew Pl. *EC1*
—5C **62** (6C **144**)
Bartholomew Rd. *NW5*—6G **45**
Bartholomew Sq. *E1*—4H **63**
Bartholomew Sq. *EC1*
—4C **62** (3D **144**)
Bartholomew St. *SE1*
—3D **78** (2F **157**)
Bartholomew Vs. *NW5*—6G **45**
Barth Rd. *SE18*—4J **83**
Bartle Av. *E6*—2C **66**
Bartle Rd. *W11*—6G **59**
Bartlett Clo. *E14*—6C **64**
Bartlett Ct. *EC4*—6A **62** (7K **143**)
Bartlett Houses. Dag—7H **53**
(off Vicarage Rd.)
Bartlett St. *S Croy*—5D **134**
Bartlow Gdns. *Romf*—1K **37**
Barton Av. *Romf*—1H **53**
Barton Clo. *E6*—6D **66**
Barton Clo. *E9*—5J **47**
Barton Clo. *NW4*—4C **26**
Barton Clo. *SE15*—3H **95**
Barton Clo. *Bexh*—5E **100**
Barton Ct. *W14*—5G **75**
(off Barons Ct. Rd.)
Barton Ho. *N Mald*—2K **119**
Barton Ho. N1—7B **46**
(off Sable St.)
Barton Ho. SW6—3K **91**
(off Wandsworth Bri. Rd.)
Barton Meadows. *Ilf*—4F **35**
Barton Rd. *W14*—5G **75**
Barton Rd. *Sidc*—6E **116**
Barton St. *SW1*—3J **77** (1E **154**)
Bartram Rd. *SE4*—5A **96**
Bartrams La. *Barn*—1F **5**
Barts Clo. *Beck*—5C **126**
Barville Clo. *SE4*—4A **96**

Barwick Ho. *W3*—2J **73**
(off Strafford Rd.)
Barwick Rd. *E7*—4K **49**
Barwood Av. *W Wick*—1D **136**
Basden Gro. *Felt*—2E **102**
Basden Ho. *Felt*—2E **102**
Basedale Rd. *Dag*—7B **52**
Baseing Clo. *E6*—7E **66**
Bashley Rd. *NW10*—4K **57**
Basil Av. *E6*—3C **66**
Basildene Rd. *Houn*—3B **86**
Basildon Av. *Ilf*—1E **34**
Basildon Clo. *Sutt*—7K **131**
Basildon Rd. *SE2*—5A **84**
Basil Gdns. *SE27*—5C **110**
Basil Gdns. *Croy*—1K **135**
Basil Ho. SW8—7J **77**
(off Wyvil Rd.)
Basilon Rd. *Bexh*—2E **100**
Basil Spence Ho. *N22*—1K **29**
Basil St. *SW3*—3D **76** (1E **152**)
Basing Clo. *Th Dit*—7A **118**
Basing Ct. *SE15*—1F **95**
Basingdon Way. *SE5*—4D **94**
Basing Dri. *Bex*—6F **101**
Basinghall Av. *EC2*
—6D **62** (6E **144**)
Basinghall Gdns. *Sutt*—7K **131**
Basinghall St. *EC2*
—6D **62** (7E **144**)
Basing Hill. *NW11*—1H **43**
Basing Hill. *Wemb*—2F **41**
Basing Ho. Bark—1H **67**
(off St Margarets)
Basing Ho. Yd. *E2*
—3E **62** (1H **145**)
Basing Pl. *E2*—3E **62** (1H **145**)
Basing St. *W11*—6H **59**
Basing Way. *N3*—3J **27**
Basing Way. *Th Dit*—7A **118**
Basire St. *N1*—1C **62**
Baskerville Rd. *SW18*—7C **92**
Basket Gdns. *SE9*—5C **98**
Baslow Clo. *Harr*—1H **23**
Baslow Wlk. *E5*—4K **47**
Basnett Rd. *SW11*—3E **92**
Bassano St. *SE22*—5F **95**
Bassant Rd. *SE18*—6K **83**
Bassein Pk. Rd. *W12*—2B **74**
Bassett Gdns. *Iswth*—7G **71**
Bassett Rd. *E7*—4B **50**
Bassett Rd. *W10*—6F **59**
Bassett St. *NW5*—6E **44**
Bassett Way. *Gnfd*—6F **55**
Bassingham Rd. *SW18*—7A **92**
Bassingham Rd. *Wemb*—6D **40**
Bassishaw Highwalk. *EC2*
—5D **62** (6D **144**)
Basswood Clo. *SE15*—3H **95**
Bastable Av. *Bark*—2J **67**
Bastion Highwalk. *EC2*
—5C **62** (6C **144**)
Bastion Rd. *SE2*—5A **84**
Bastion Mnr. Rd. *Brom*—3K **137**
Baston Rd. *Brom*—2K **137**
Bastwick St. *EC1*
—4C **62** (3C **144**)
Basuto Rd. *SW6*—1J **91**
Batavia Ho. *SE14*—7A **80**
(off Batavia Rd.)
Batavia M. *SE14*—7A **80**
Batavia Rd. *SE14*—7A **80**
Batchelor St. *N1*—1A **62**
Bateman Clo. *Bark*—6G **51**
Bateman Rd. *E4*—6H **19**

Bateman's Bldgs. *W1*
　—6H **61** (1C **148**)
Bateman's Row. *EC2*
　—4E **62** (3H **145**)
Bateman St. *W1*
　—6H **61** (1C **148**)
Bates Cres. *SW16* —7G **109**
Bates Cres. *Croy* —5A **134**
Bateson St. *SE18* —4J **83**
Bates Point. *E13* —1J **65**
　(off Pelly Rd.)
Bate St. *E14* —7B **64**
Bath Clo. *SE15* —1J **95**
Bath Ct. *EC1* —4A **62** (4J **143**)
Bath Ct. *SE26* —3G **111**
　(off Droitwich Clo.)
Bathgate Rd. *SW19* —3F **107**
Bath Ho. *Rd. Bedd* —1J **133**
Bath Pas. *King T* —2D **118**
Bath Pl. *EC2* —3E **62** (2G **145**)
Bath Pl. *W6* —5E **74**
　(off Fulham Pal. Rd.)
Bath Pl. *Barn* —3C **4**
Bath Rd. *E7* —6B **50**
Bath Rd. *N9* —2C **18**
Bath Rd. *W4* —4A **74**
Bath Rd. *Mitc* —3B **122**
Bath Rd. *Houn* —1A **86**
Bath Rd. *Romf* —6E **36**
Baths App. *SW6* —7H **75**
Baths Rd. *Brom* —4B **128**
Bath St. *EC1* —3C **62** (2D **144**)
Bath Ter. *SE1* —3C **78** (2C **156**)
Bathurst Av. *SW19* —1K **121**
Bathurst Gdns. *NW10* —2D **58**
Bathurst M. *W2* —7B **60** (2B **146**)
Bathurst Rd. *Ilf* —1F **51**
Bathurst St. *W2* —7B **60** (2B **146**)
Bathway. *SE18* —4E **82**
Batley Clo. *Mitc* —7D **122**
Batley Pl. *N16* —3F **47**
Batley Rd. *N16* —3F **47**
Batley Rd. *Enf* —1H **7**
Batman Clo. *W12* —1D **74**
Batoum Gdns. *W6* —3E **74**
Batson Ho. *E1* —6G **63**
　(off Fairclough St.)
Batson St. *W12* —2C **74**
Batsworth Rd. *Mitc* —3B **122**
Battenberg Wlk. *SE19* —6E **110**
Batten Clo. *E6* —6D **66**
Batten Ho. *SW4* —5G **93**
Batten St. *SW11* —3C **92**
Battersby Rd. *SE6* —2F **113**
Battersea Bri. *SW3 & SW11*
　—7B **76**
Battersea Bri. Rd. *SW11* —7C **76**
Battersea Chu. Rd. *SW11* —1B **92**
Battersea High St. *SW11* —1B **92**
Battersea Pk. *Rd. SW11 & SW8*
　—2C **92**
Battersea Rise. *SW11* —5C **92**
Battersea Sq. *SW11* —1B **92**
Battery Rd. *SE28* —2J **83**
Batteson St. *SE18* —4J **83**
Battishill St. *N1* —7B **46**
Battis, The. *Romf* —6K **37**
Battishill St. *N1* —7B **46**
Battlebridge Ct. *N1* —2J **61**
　(off Wharfdale Rd.)
Battle Bri. La. *SE1*
　—1E **78** (5G **151**)
Battle Bri. Rd. *NW1* —2J **61**
Battle Clo. *SW19* —6A **108**
Battledean Rd. *N5* —5B **46**
Battle Rd. *Belv & Eri* —4J **85**

Batty St. *E1* —6G **63**
Baudwin Rd. *SE6* —2G **113**
Baugh Rd. *Sidc* —5C **116**
Baulk, The. *SW18* —7J **91**
Bavant Rd. *SW16* —2J **123**
Bavaria Rd. *N19* —2J **45**
Bavent Rd. *SE5* —2C **94**
Bawdale Rd. *SE22* —5F **95**
Bawdsey Av. *Ilf* —4K **35**
Bawtree Rd. *SE14* —7A **80**
Bawtry Rd. *N20* —3J **15**
Baxendale. *N20* —2F **15**
Baxendale St. *E2*
　—3G **63** (1K **145**)
Baxter Rd. *E16* —6A **66**
Baxter Rd. *N1* —6D **46**
Baxter Rd. *N18* —4C **18**
Baxter Rd. *Ilf* —5F **51**
Bayard Ct. *Bexh* —4H **101**
Bay Ct. *W5* —3E **72**
Baycroft Clo. *Pinn* —3A **22**
Baydon Ct. *Short* —3H **127**
Bayes Clo. *SE26* —5J **111**
Bayfield Ho. *SE4* —4K **95**
　(off Coston Wlk.)
Bayfield Rd. *SE9* —4B **98**
Bayford M. *E8* —7H **47**
　(off Bayford St.)
Bayford Rd. *NW10* —3F **59**
Bayford St. *E8* —7H **47**
Bayham Pl. *NW1* —1G **61**
Bayham Rd. *W4* —3K **73**
Bayham Rd. *W13* —7B **56**
Bayham Rd. *Mord* —4K **121**
Bayham St. *NW1* —1G **61**
Bayleaf Clo. *Hamp H* —5H **103**
Bayley St. *WC1* —5H **61** (6C **142**)
Bayley Wlk. *SE2* —5E **84**
Baylin Rd. *SW18* —6K **91**
Baylis Rd. *SE1* —2A **78** (7J **149**)
Bayliss Av. *SE28* —7D **68**
Bayliss Clo. *N21* —5D **6**
Bayne Clo. *E6* —6D **66**
Baynes Clo. *Enf* —1B **8**
Baynes M. *NW3* —6B **44**
Baynes St. *NW1* —7G **45**
Baynes St. *NW1* —7G **45**
Baynham Clo. *Bex* —6F **101**
Bayonne Rd. *W6* —6G **75**
Bays Ct. *Edgw* —5C **12**
Bayshill Rise. *N'holt* —6F **39**
Bayston Rd. *N16* —3F **47**
Bayswater Rd. *W2* —7K **59**
Baythorne St. *E3* —4B **112**
Bay Tree Clo. *Brom* —1B **128**
Baytree Clo. *Sidc* —1K **115**
Baytree Ct. *SW2* —4K **93**
Baytree Ho. *E4* —7J **9**
Baytree Rd. *SW2* —4K **93**
Bazalgette Clo. *N Mald* —5K **119**
Bazalgette Gdns. *N Mald*
　—5K **119**
Bazely St. *E14* —7E **64**
Bazile Rd. *N21* —6F **7**
Beacham Clo. *SE7* —5B **82**
Beachborough Rd. *Brom*
　—4E **112**
Beachcroft Rd. *E11* —3G **49**
Beachcroft Way. *N19* —1H **45**
Beach Gro. *Felt* —2E **102**
Beach Ho. *Felt* —2E **102**
Beachy Rd. *E3* —7C **48**
Beacon Ga. *SE14* —2K **95**
Beacon Gro. *Cars* —4E **132**
Beacon Hill. *N7* —5J **45**

Beacon Rd. *SE13* —6F **97**
Beacons Clo. *E6* —5C **66**
Beaconsfield Clo. *N11* —5K **15**
Beaconsfield Clo. *SE3* —6J **81**
Beaconsfield Clo. *W4* —5J **73**
Beaconsfield Pde. *SE9* —4C **114**
Beaconsfield Rd. *E10* —3E **48**
Beaconsfield Rd. *E16* —4H **65**
Beaconsfield Rd. *E17* —6B **32**
Beaconsfield Rd. *N9* —3B **18**
Beaconsfield Rd. *N11* —3K **15**
Beaconsfield Rd. *N15* —4E **30**
Beaconsfield Rd. *NW10* —6B **42**
Beaconsfield Rd. *SE3* —7H **81**
Beaconsfield Rd. *SE9* —2C **114**
Beaconsfield Rd. *SE17*
　—5D **78** (6G **157**)
Beaconsfield Rd. *W4* —3K **73**
Beaconsfield Rd. *W5* —2C **72**
Beaconsfield Rd. *Bex* —2K **117**
Beaconsfield Rd. *Brom* —3B **128**
Beaconsfield Rd. *Croy* —6D **124**
Beaconsfield Rd. *Hayes* —1A **70**
Beaconsfield Rd. *N Mald*
　—2K **119**
Beaconsfield Rd. *S'hall* —1B **70**
Beaconsfield Rd. *Surb* —7F **119**
Beaconsfield Rd. *Twic* —6B **88**
Beaconsfield Ter. *Romf* —6D **36**
Beaconsfield Ter. Rd. *W14*
　—3G **75**
Beaconsfield Wlk. *E6* —6E **66**
Beaconsfield Wlk. *SW6* —1H **91**
Beacontree Av. *E17* —1F **33**
Beacontree Rd. *E11* —7H **33**
Beadle's Pde. *Dag* —6J **53**
Beadlow Clo. *Cars* —6B **122**
Beadman Pl. *SE27* —4B **110**
Beadman St. *SE27* —4B **110**
Beadnell Rd. *SE23* —1K **111**
Beadon Rd. *W6* —4E **74**
Beadon Rd. *Brom* —4J **127**
Beaford Gro. *SW20* —3G **121**
Beak St. *W1* —7G **61** (2B **148**)
Beal Clo. *Well* —1A **100**
Beale Clo. *N13* —5G **17**
Beale Pl. *E3* —2B **64**
Beale Rd. *E3* —1B **64**
Beal Rd. *Ilf* —2E **50**
Beam Av. *Dag* —1H **69**
Beaminster Gdns. *Ilf* —2F **35**
Beaminster Ho. *SW8* —7K **77**
　(off Dorset Rd.)
Beamish Dri. *Bush* —1B **10**
Beamish Ga. *NW1* —7H **45**
Beamish Rd. *N9* —1B **18**
Beam Vs. *Dag* —2K **69**
Beamway. *Dag* —7K **53**
Beanacre Clo. *E9* —6B **48**
Bean Rd. *Bexh* —4D **100**
Beanshaw. *SE9* —4E **114**
Beansland Gro. *Romf* —3E **36**
Bear All. *EC4* —6B **62** (7A **144**)
Beardell St. *SE19* —6F **111**
Beardow Gro. *N14* —6B **6**
Beard Rd. *King T* —5F **105**
Beardsfield. *E13* —2J **65**
Beardsley Ter. *Dag* —5B **52**
　(off Fitzstephen Rd.)
Beardsley Way. *W3* —2K **73**
Beard's Rd. *King T* —7E **104**
Bear Gdns. *SE1* —1C **78** (4C **150**)
Bear La. *SE1* —1B **78** (4B **150**)
Bear Rd. *Felt* —4B **102**

Bearsted Rise. *SE4* —5B **96**
Bearsted Ter. *Beck* —1C **126**
Bear St. *WC2* —7H **61** (2D **148**)
Beatrice Av. *SW16* —3K **123**
Beatrice Av. *Wemb* —5E **40**
Beatrice Clo. *E13* —4J **65**
Beatrice Ct. *Buck H* —2G **21**
Beatrice Pl. *W8* —3K **75**
Beatrice Rd. *E17* —5C **32**
Beatrice Rd. *N4* —7A **30**
Beatrice Rd. *N9* —7D **8**
Beatrice Rd. *SE1* —4G **79**
Beatrice Rd. *Rich* —5F **89**
Beatrice Rd. *S'hall* —1D **70**
Beatson Wlk. *SE16* —1A **80**
Beattock Rise. *N10* —4F **29**
Beatty Ho. *E14* —2C **80**
　(off Admirals Way)
Beatty Rd. *N16* —4E **46**
Beatty Rd. *Stan* —6H **11**
Beatty St. *NW1* —2G **61**
Beattyville Gdns. *Ilf* —4E **34**
Beauchamp Clo. *W4* —3J **73**
Beauchamp Ct. *Stan* —5H **11**
Beauchamp Pl. *SW3*
　—3C **76** (1D **152**)
Beauchamp Rd. *E7* —7K **49**
Beauchamp Rd. *SE19* —1D **124**
Beauchamp Rd. *SW11* —4C **92**
Beauchamp Rd. *Sutt* —4J **131**
Beauchamp Rd. *Twic* —7A **88**
Beauchamp St. *EC1*
　—5A **62** (6J **143**)
Beauchamp Ter. *SW15* —3D **90**
Beauclerc Rd. *W6* —3D **74**
Beauclerk Clo. *Felt* —1A **102**
Beauclerk Ho. *SW16* —3J **109**
Beaufort. *E6* —5E **66**
Beaufort Av. *Harr* —4A **24**
Beaufort Clo. *E4* —6J **19**
Beaufort Clo. *SW15* —7D **90**
Beaufort Clo. *W5* —5F **57**
Beaufort Clo. *Romf* —4J **37**
Beaufort Ct. *N11* —5A **16**
　(off Limes Av., The)
Beaufort Ct. *New Bar* —5F **5**
Beaufort Ct. *Rich* —4C **104**
Beaufort Dri. *NW11* —4J **27**
Beaufort Gdns. *NW4* —6E **26**
Beaufort Gdns. *SW3*
　—3C **76** (1D **152**)
Beaufort Gdns. *SW16* —7K **109**
Beaufort Gdns. *Houn* —1C **86**
Beaufort Gdns. *Ilf* —1E **50**
Beaufort M. *SW6* —6H **75**
Beaufort Pk. *NW11* —4J **27**
Beaufort Rd. *W5* —5F **57**
Beaufort Rd. *King T* —4E **118**
Beaufort Rd. *Rich* —4C **104**
Beaufort Rd. *Twic* —7C **88**
Beaufort St. *SW3*
　—6B **76** (7A **152**)
Beaufort Way. *Eps* —7C **130**
Beaufoy Ho. *SE27* —3B **110**
Beaufoy Rd. *N17* —7K **17**
Beaufoy Wlk. *SE11*
　—4K **77** (4H **155**)
Beaulieu Av. *E16* —1K **81**
Beaulieu Av. *SE26* —4H **111**
Beaulieu Clo. *NW9* —4A **26**
Beaulieu Clo. *SE5* —3D **94**
Beaulieu Clo. *Houn* —5D **86**
Beaulieu Clo. *Mitc* —1E **122**
Beaulieu Clo. *Twic* —6D **88**
Beaulieu Ct. *W5* —5E **56**

Beaulieu Dri. *Pinn* —6B **22**
Beaulieu Gdns. *N21* —7H **7**
Beaulieu Pl. *W4* —3J **73**
Beaumanor Gdns. *SE9* —4E **114**
Beaumaris Dri. *Wfd G* —7G **21**
Beaumaris Grn. *NW9* —6A **26**
Beaumaris Tower *W3* —2H **73**
　(off Park Rd. N.)
Beaumont Av. *W14* —5H **75**
Beaumont Av. *Harr* —6F **23**
Beaumont Av. *Rich* —3F **89**
Beaumont Av. *Wemb* —5C **40**
Beaumont Clo. *King T* —7G **105**
Beaumont Ct. *E5* —3H **47**
Beaumont Ct. *W4* —5J **73**
Beaumont Cres. *W14* —5H **75**
Beaumont Gdns. *NW3* —3J **43**
Beaumont Gro. *E1* —4K **63**
Beaumont Ho. *E10* —7D **32**
Beaumont Ho. *E15* —1H **65**
　(off John St.)
Beaumont M. *W1*
　—5E **60** (5H **141**)
Beaumont Pl. *W1*
　—4G **61** (3B **142**)
Beaumont Pl. *Barn* —1C **4**
Beaumont Pl. *Iswth* —5K **87**
Beaumont Rise. *N19* —1H **45**
Beaumont Rd. *E10* —7D **32**
Beaumont Rd. *E13* —3K **65**
Beaumont Rd. *SE19* —6C **110**
Beaumont Rd. *SW19* —7G **91**
Beaumont Rd. *W4* —3J **73**
Beaumont Rd. *Orp* —6H **129**
Beaumont Sq. *E1* —5K **63**
Beaumont St. *W1*
　—5E **60** (5H **141**)
Beaumont Wlk. *NW3* —7D **44**
Beauvais Ter. *N'holt* —3B **54**
Beauval Rd. *SE22* —6F **95**
Beaux Arts Building. *N7* —3J **45**
Beav Callender Clo. *SW8* —3F **93**
Beaverbank Rd. *SE9* —1H **115**
Beaver Clo. *SE20* —7G **111**
Beaver Clo. *Hamp* —7F **103**
Beavercote Wlk. *Belv* —5F **85**
Beaver Ct. *Beck* —7D **112**
Beaver Gro. *N'holt* —3C **54**
Beavers Cres. *Houn* —4A **86**
Beavers La. *Houn* —2A **86**
Beavers Lodge. *Sidc* —4K **115**
Beavor Gro. *W6* —5C **74**
　(off Beavor La.)
Beavor La. *W6* —4C **74**
Bebbington Rd. *SE18* —4J **83**
Beccles Dri. *Bark* —6J **51**
Beccles St. *E14* —7B **64**
Bec Clo. *Ruis* —3B **38**
Bechervaise Ct. *E10* —1D **48**
Beck Clo. *SE13* —1D **96**
Beck Ct. *Beck* —3K **125**
Beckenham Bus. Cen. *Beck*
　—6A **112**
Beckenham Gdns. *N9* —3K **17**
Beckenham Gro. *Brom* —2F **127**
Beckenham Hill Est. *Beck*
　—5D **112**
Beckenham Hill Rd. *Beck & SE6*
　—6D **112**
Beckenham La. *Brom* —2G **127**
Beckenham Pl. Pk. *Beck* —7D **112**
Beckenham Rd. *Beck* —1K **125**
Beckenham Rd. *W Wick* —7E **126**

Beckers, The. N16 —3G 47
Becket Av. E6 —3E 66
Becket Clo. SE25 —6G 125
Becket Clo. SW19 —1K 121
(off High Path)
Becket Fold. Harr —5K 23
Becket Ho. SE1 —2D 78 (7E 150)
Becket Rd. N18 —4D 18
Becket St. SE1 —3D 78 (1E 156)
Beckett Clo. NW10 —6A 42
Beckett Clo. SW16 —2H 109
Beckett Clo. Belv —3F 85
Beckett Ho. SW9 —2J 93
Becketts Ho. Ilf —3E 50
Becketts Pl. Hamp W —1D 118
Beckett Wlk. Beck —6A 112
Beckford Dri. Orp —7H 129
Beckford Ho. N16 —5E 46
Beckford Pl. SE17
   —5C 78 (6D 156)
Beckford. Croy —6F 125
Beckham Ho. SE11
   —4K 77 (4H 155)
Beck La. Beck —3K 125
Becklow Gdns. W12 —1C 74
(off Becklow Rd.)
Becklow M. W12 —2C 74
(off Becklow Rd.)
Becklow Rd. W12 —2B 74
Beck River Pk. Beck —1C 126
Beck Rd. E8 —1H 63
Becks Rd. Sidc —3A 116
Beckton Retail Pk. E6 —5E 66
Beckton Rd. E16 —5H 65
Beck Way. Beck —3B 126
Beckway Rd. SW16 —2H 123
Beckway St. SE17
   —4E 78 (4F 157)
Beckwith Rd. SE24 —5D 94
Beclands Rd. SW17 —6E 108
Becmead Av. SW16 —4H 109
Becmead Av. Harr —5B 24
Becondale Rd. SE19 —5E 110
Becontree Av. Dag —4B 52
Bective Pl. SW15 —4H 91
Bective Rd. E7 —4J 49
Bective Rd. SW15 —4H 91
Becton Pl. Eri —7H 85
Bedale Rd. Enf —1H 7
Bedale St. SE1 —1D 78 (5E 150)
Beddalls Farm Ct. E6 —5C 66
Beddington Farm Rd. Croy
   —7J 123
Beddington Gdns. Cars & Wall
(in two parts)   —6E 132
Beddington Grn. Orp —1K 129
Beddington Gro. Wall —5H 133
Beddington La. Croy —5G 123
Beddington Pk. Cotts. Wall
   —3H 133
Beddington Path. St P —1K 129
Beddington Rd. Ilf —7K 35
Beddington Rd. Orp —1J 129
Beddington Ter. Croy —7K 123
Beddington Trad. Est. Croy
   —1J 133
Bede Clo. Pinn —1B 22
Bedefield. WC1 —3J 61 (2F 143)
Bede Ho. SE14 —1B 96
Bedenham Way. SE15 —7F 79
Bedens Rd. Sidc —6E 116
Bede Rd. Romf —6C 36
Bedfont Clo. Mitc —2E 122
Bedford Av. WC1
   —5H 61 (6D 142)

Bedford Av. Barn —5C 4
Bedford Av. Hayes —5A 54
Bedfordbury. WC2
   —7J 61 (2E 148)
Bedford Clo. N10 —7K 15
Bedford Corner. W4 —4A 74
(off South Pde.)
Bedford Ct. WC2
   —7J 61 (3E 148)
Bedford Gdns. W8 —1J 75
Bedford Hill. SW12 & SW16
   —1F 109
Bedford Ho. SW4 —4J 93
(off Solon New Rd. Est.)
Bedford Pk. Croy —1C 134
Bedford Pk. Corner. W4 —4A 74
Bedford Pk. Mans. W4 —4K 73
Bedford Pas. SW6 —7G 75
(off Dawes Rd.)
Bedford Pas. W1
   —5G 61 (5B 142)
Bedford Pl. WC1
   —5J 61 (5E 142)
Bedford Pl. Croy —1D 134
Bedford Rd. E6 —1E 66
Bedford Rd. E17 —2C 32
Bedford Rd. E18 —2J 33
Bedford Rd. N2 —3C 28
Bedford Rd. N8 —6H 29
Bedford Rd. N9 —7C 8
Bedford Rd. N15 —4E 30
Bedford Rd. N22 —1J 29
Bedford Rd. NW7 —2F 13
Bedford Rd. SW4 —4J 93
Bedford Rd. W4 —3K 73
Bedford Rd. W13 —7B 56
Bedford Rd. Harr —6G 23
Bedford Rd. Ilf —3F 51
Bedford Rd. Sidc —3J 115
Bedford Rd. Twic —3H 103
Bedford Rd. Wor Pk —2E 130
Bedford Row. WC1
   —5K 61 (5H 143)
Bedford Sq. WC1
   —5H 61 (6D 142)
Bedford St. WC2
   —7J 61 (2E 148)
Bedford Ter. SW2 —5J 93
Bedford Way. WC1
   —4H 61 (4D 142)
Bedgebury Gdns. SW19 —2G 107
Bedgebury Rd. SE9 —4B 98
Bedivere Rd. Brom —3J 113
Bedlow Way. Croy —4K 133
Bedonwell Rd. SE2 & Belv
   —6E 84
Bedonwell Rd. Bexh —6G 85
Bedser Clo. SE11
   —6K 77 (7H 155)
Bedser Clo. T Hth —3C 124
Bedser Dri. Gnfd —5H 39
Bedwardine Rd. SE19 —7E 110
Bedwell Ct. Romf —7D 36
(off Broomfield Rd.)
Bedwell Ho. SW9 —2A 94
Bedwell Rd. N17 —1E 30
Bedwell Rd. Belv —5G 85
Beeby Rd. E16 —5K 65
Beech Av. N20 —1H 15
Beech Av. W3 —1A 74
Beech Av. Bren —7B 72
Beech Av. Ruis —1A 38
Beech Av. Sidc —7A 100
Beech Clo. N9 —6B 8

Beech Clo. SE8 —6C 80
Beech Clo. SW15 —7C 90
Beech Clo. SW19 —6E 106
Beech Clo. Cars —2D 132
Beech Copse. Brom —2D 128
Beech Copse. S Croy —5E 134
Beech Ct. Beck —7B 112
Beech Ct. N'holt —1C 54
Beech Ct. Surb —7D 118
Beech Cres. Ct. N5 —4B 46
Beechcroft. Chst —7E 114
Beechcroft Av. NW11 —7H 27
Beechcroft Av. Bexh —1K 101
Beechcroft Av. Harr —7E 22
Beechcroft Av. N Mald —1J 119
Beechcroft Av. S'hall —1D 70
Beechcroft Clo. SW16 —5K 109
Beechcroft Clo. Houn —7C 70
Beechcroft Ct. NW11 —7H 27
(off Beechcroft Av.)
Beechcroft Gdns. Wemb —3F 41
Beechcroft Ho. W5 —6E 56
Beechcroft Lodge. Sutt —7K 131
Beechcroft Rd. E18 —2K 33
Beechcroft Rd. SW14 —3J 89
Beechcroft Rd. SW17 —2C 108
Beechdale. N21 —2E 16
Beechdale Rd. SW2 —6K 93
Beech Dell. Kes —4D 138
Beech Dri. N2 —2D 28
Beechen Cliff Way. Iswth —2K 87
Beechen Gro. Pinn —3D 22
Beechen Pl. SE23 —2K 111
Beeches Av. Cars —7C 132
Beeches Clo. SE20 —1J 125
Beeches Rd. SW17 —3C 108
Beeches Rd. Sutt —1G 131
Beeches, The. E12 —7D 50
Beeches, The. Houn —1F 87
Beeches, The. S Croy —5D 134
Beeches Wlk. Cars —7B 132
Beechfield Cotts. Brom —2A 128
Beechfield Gdns. Romf —7J 37
Beechfield Rd. N4 —6C 30
Beechfield Rd. SE6 —1B 112
Beechfield Rd. Brom —2A 128
Beechfield Rd. Eri —7K 85
Beech Gdns. W5 —2E 72
Beech Gdns. Dag —7J 53
Beech Gro. Mitc —5H 123
Beech Gro. N Mald —3K 119
Beech Hale Cres. E4 —7A 20
Beech Haven Ct. Dart —5K 101
(off London Rd.)
Beech Hill. Barn —1G 5
Beech Hill Av. Barn —1F 5
Beech Ho. E17 —3F 33
Beech Ho. Rd. Croy —3D 134
Beechhill Rd. SE9 —5E 98
Beech La. Buck H —2E 20
Beech Lawns. N12 —5G 15
Beechmont Clo. Brom —5G 113
Beechmore Gdns. Sutt —2F 131
Beechmore Rd. SW11 —1D 92
Beechmount Av. W7 —5H 55
Beecholme. N12 —2F 47
Beecholme Av. Mitc —1F 123
Beecholme Est. E5 —3H 47
Beech Rd. N11 —6D 16
Beech Rd. SW16 —2K 123
Beech Row. Ham —4E 104
Beech St. EC2 —5C 62 (5C 144)
Beech St. Romf —4J 37
Beech Tree Clo. N1 —7A 46

Beech Tree Clo. Stan —5H 11
Beech Tree Glade. E4 —1C 20
Beech Tree Pl. Sutt —5J 131
Beechvale Clo. N12 —5H 15
Beech Wlk. NW7 —6F 13
Beech Way. NW10 —7K 41
Beechway. Bex —6D 100
Beechwood Av. N3 —3H 27
Beechwood Av. Gnfd —3F 55
Beechwood Av. Harr —3F 39
Beechwood Av. Rich —1G 89
Beechwood Av. T Hth —4B 124
Beechwood Circ. Harr —3F 39
Beechwood Clo. N2 —4D 28
(off Western Rd.)
Beechwood Clo. NW7 —5F 13
Beechwood Clo. Surb —7C 118
Beechwood Ct. SE19 —5F 111
Beechwood Ct. W4 —6K 73
Beechwood Ct. Cars —4D 132
Beechwood Cres. Bexh —3D 100
Beechwood Dri. Kes —4B 138
Beechwood Dri. Wfd G —5C 20
Beechwood Gdns. NW10 —3F 57
Beechwood Gdns. Harr —3F 39
Beechwood Gdns. Ilf —5D 34
Beechwood Gro. W3 —7A 58
Beechwood Gro. Surb —7C 118
Beechwood Hall. N3 —3H 27
Beechwood M. N9 —2B 18
Beechwood Pk. E18 —3J 33
Beechwood Rise. Chst —4F 115
Beechwood Rd. E8 —6F 47
Beechwood Rd. N8 —4H 29
Beechwood Rd. S Croy —7E 134
Beechwood Rd. Wfd G —5C 20
Beechworth Clo. NW3 —2J 43
Beecroft Rd. SE4 —5A 96
Beehive Clo. E8 —7F 47
Beehive La. Ilf —5D 34
Beehive Pl. SW9 —3A 94
Beeleigh Rd. Mord —4K 121
Beemans Row. SW18 —2A 108
Beeston Clo. E8 —5G 47
Beeston Pl. SW1
   —3F 77 (1K 153)
Beeston Rd. Barn —6G 5
Beeston Way. Felt —6A 86
Beethoven St. W10 —3G 59
Beeton Clo. Pinn —1E 22
Beggar's Hill. Eps —7B 130
Beggar's Hill. (Junct.) —6B 130
Beggars Roost La. Sutt —6J 131
Begonia Clo. E6 —4D 66
Begonia Pl. Hamp —6E 102
Begonia Wlk. W12 —6B 58
Beira St. SW12 —7F 93
Bekesbourne St. E14 —6A 64
Belcombe Av. Wor Pk —1E 130
Belcroft Clo. Brom —7H 113
Beldanes Lodge. NW10 —7C 42
Belfairs Dri. Romf —7C 36
Belfast Gdns. SE3 —6H 81
Belfast Rd. N16 —2F 47
Belfast Rd. SE25 —4H 125
Belfield Rd. Eps —7A 138
Belfont Wlk. N7 —4J 45
Belford Gro. SE18 —4E 82
Belford Ho. E8 —1F 63
Belfort Rd. SE15 —2J 95
Belfry Clo. SE16 —5H 79
Belgrade Rd. N16 —4E 46

Belgrave Clo. N14 —5B 6
Belgrave Clo. W3 —2H 73
Belgrave Ct. E13 —4A 66
Belgrave Ct. W4 —5J 73
Belgrave Cres. Sun —7A 102
Belgrave Gdns. N14 —4C 6
Belgrave Gdns. NW8 —1K 59
Belgrave Gdns. Stan —5H 11
Belgrave Ho. SW9 —7A 78
Belgrave M. N. SW1
   —2E 76 (7G 147)
Belgrave M. S. SW1
   —3E 76 (1H 153)
Belgrave M. W. SW1
   —3E 76 (1G 153)
Belgrave Pl. SW1
   —3E 76 (1H 153)
Belgrave Rd. E10 —1E 48
Belgrave Rd. E11 —2J 49
Belgrave Rd. E13 —4A 66
Belgrave Rd. E17 —5C 32
Belgrave Rd. SE25 —4F 125
Belgrave Rd. SW1
   —4F 77 (4K 153)
Belgrave Rd. SW13 —7B 74
Belgrave Rd. Houn —3D 86
Belgrave Rd. Ilf —1D 50
Belgrave Rd. Mitc —3B 122
Belgrave Rd. Sun —7A 102
Belgrave Sq. SW1
   —3E 76 (1G 153)
Belgrave St. E1 —6K 63
Belgrave Ter. Wfd G —3D 20
Belgrave Wlk. Mitc —3B 122
Belgrave Yd. SW1
   —3F 77 (2J 153)
Belgravia Gdns. Brom —6G 113
Belgravia Ho. SW4 —6H 93
Belgravia M. King T —4D 118
Belgravia Workshops. N19
   (off Marlborough Rd.) —2J 45
Belgrove St. WC1
   —3J 61 (1F 143)
Belham Wlk. SE5 —1D 94
Belinda Rd. SW9 —3B 94
Belitha Vs. N1 —7K 45
Bellamy Clo. W14 —5H 75
Bellamy Ct. Edgw —2D 12
Bellamy Ct. Stan —1B 24
Bellamy Dri. Stan —1B 24
Bellamy Ho. Houn —6E 70
Bellamy Rd. E4 —6J 19
Bellamy Rd. Enf —2J 7
Bellamy St. SW12 —7F 93
Bellasis Av. SW2 —2J 109
Bell Clo. Pinn —2A 22
Bell Ct. NW4 —4E 26
Bell Dri. SW18 —7G 91
Bellefields Rd. SW9 —3K 93
Bellegrove Clo. Well —2K 99
Bellegrove Pde. Well —3K 99
Bellegrove Rd. Well —2J 99
Bellenden Rd. SE15 —3F 95
Bellestaines Pleasaunce. E4
   —2H 19
Belleville Rd. SW11 —5C 92
Belle Vue. Gnfd —1H 55
Belle Vue La. Bush —1C 10
Bellevue M. N11 —5K 15
Bellevue Pk. T Hth —3C 124
Bellevue Pl. E1 —4J 63
Bellevue Rd. E17 —2F 33
Bellevue Rd. N11 —4K 15
Belle Vue Rd. NW4 —4F 27

Bellevue Rd. *SW13* —2C **90**
Bellevue Rd. *SW17* —1C **108**
Bellevue Rd. *W13* —4B **56**
Bellevue Rd. *Bexh* —5F **101**
Bellevue Rd. *King T* —3E **118**
Beliew St. *SW17* —3A **108**
Bell Farm Av. *Dag* —3J **53**
Bellfield. *Croy* —7A **136**
Bellfield Av. *Harr* —6C **10**
Bellflower Clo. *E6* —5C **66**
Bellgate M. *NW5* —4F **45**
Bell Grn. *SE26* —3B **112**
Bell Grn. La. *SE26* —5B **112**
Bell Hill. *Croy* —2C **134**
Bell Ho. Rd. *Romf* —1J **53**
Bellina M. *NW5* —4F **45**
Bell Ind. Est. *W4* —4J **73**
Bellingham. *N17* —7C **18**
 (off Park La.)
Bellingham Ct. *Bark* —3B **68**
Bellingham Grn. *SE6* —3C **112**
Bellingham Rd. *SE6* —3C **112**
Bellingham Trad. Est. *SE6*
 —3D **112**
Bell Inn Yd. *EC3*
 —6D **62** (1F **151**)
Bell Junct. *Houn* —3F **87**
Bell La. *E1* —5F **63** (6J **145**)
Bell La. *E16* —1J **81**
Bell La. *NW4 & NW11* —4E **26**
Bell La. *Enf* —1E **8**
Bell La. *Twic* —1A **104**
Bell La. *Wemb* —3D **40**
Bell Meadow. *SE19* —5E **110**
Bell Moor. NW3 —3A **44**
 (off E. Heath Rd.)
Bello Clo. *SE24* —1B **110**
Bellot St. *SE10* —5G **81**
Bellring Clo. *Belv* —6G **85**
Bell Rd. *Enf* —1J **7**
Bell Rd. *Houn* —3F **87**
Bells All. *SW6* —2J **91**
Bells Hill. *Barn* —5A **4**
Bell St. *NW1* —5C **60** (5C **140**)
Bell, The. (Junct.) —3C **32**
Belltrees Gro. *SW16* —5K **109**
Bell Water Ga. *SE18* —3E **82**
Bell Wharf La. *EC4*
 —7C **62** (3D **150**)
Bellwood Rd. *SE15* —4K **95**
Bell Yd. *WC2* —6A **62** (1J **149**)
Belmarsh Rd. *SE28* —2J **83**
Belmont Av. *N9* —1B **18**
Belmont Av. *N13* —5E **16**
Belmont Av. *N17* —3C **30**
Belmont Av. *Barn* —5J **5**
Belmont Av. *N Mald* —5C **120**
Belmont Av. *S'hall* —3C **70**
Belmont Av. *Well* —3J **99**
Belmont Av. *Wemb* —1F **57**
Belmont Circ. *Harr* —1B **24**
Belmont Clo. *E4* —5A **20**
Belmont Clo. *N20* —1E **14**
Belmont Clo. *SW4* —3G **93**
Belmont Clo. *Cockf* —4J **5**
Belmont Clo. *Wfd G* —4E **20**
Belmont Ct. *N5* —4C **46**
Belmont Ct. *NW11* —5H **27**
Belmont Gro. *SE13* —3F **97**
Belmont Gro. *W4* —4K **73**
Belmont Hall Ct. *SE13* —3F **97**
Belmont Hill. *SE13* —3E **96**
Belmont La. *Chst* —5G **115**
 (in two parts)
Belmont La. *Stan* —7H **11**

Belmont Lodge. *Har W* —7C **10**
Belmont Pde. *Chst* —5G **115**
Belmont Pk. *SE13* —4F **97**
Belmont Pk. Clo. *SE13* —4G **97**
Belmont Pk. Rd. *E10* —6D **32**
Belmont Rise. *Sutt* —6H **131**
Belmont Rd. *N15 & N17* —4C **30**
Belmont Rd. *SE25* —5H **125**
Belmont Rd. *SW4* —3G **93**
Belmont Rd. *W4* —4K **73**
Belmont Rd. *Beck* —2B **126**
Belmont Rd. *Chst* —5F **115**
Belmont Rd. *Eri* —7G **85**
Belmont Rd. *Harr* —3K **23**
Belmont Rd. *Ilf* —3G **51**
Belmont Rd. *Twic* —2H **103**
Belmont Rd. *Wall* —5F **133**
Belmont St. *NW1* —7E **44**
Belmont Ter. *W4* —4K **73**
Belmore Av. *N7* —5H **45**
Belmore La. *N7* —5H **45**
Belmore St. *SW8* —1H **93**
Beloe Clo. *SW15* —4C **90**
Belsham St. *E9* —6J **47**
Belsize Av. *N13* —6E **16**
Belsize Av. *SW16* —7G **109**
Belsize Av. *W13* —3B **72**
Belsize Ct. *NW3* —5B **44**
Belsize Ct. Garages. NW3 —5B **44**
 (off Belsize La.)
Belsize Cres. *NW3* —5B **44**
Belsize Gdns. *Sutt* —4A **131**
Belsize Gro. *NW3* —6C **44**
Belsize La. *NW3* —6B **44**
Belsize M. *NW3* —6B **44**
Belsize Pk. *NW3* —6B **44**
Belsize Pk. Gdns. *NW3* —6B **44**
Belsize Pk. M. *NW3* —6B **44**
Belsize Pl. *NW3* —5B **44**
Belsize Rd. *NW6* —1J **59**
Belsize Rd. *Harr* —7C **10**
Belsize Sq. *NW3* —6B **44**
Belsize Ter. *NW3* —6B **44**
Belson Rd. *SE18* —4D **82**
Beltane Dri. *SW19* —3F **107**
Belthorn Cres. *SW12* —7G **93**
Belton Rd. *E7* —7K **49**
Belton Rd. *E11* —4G **49**
Belton Rd. *N17* —3E **30**
Belton Rd. *NW2* —6C **42**
Belton Rd. *Sidc* —4A **116**
Belton Way. *E3* —5C **64**
Beltran Rd. *SW6* —2K **91**
Beltwood Rd. *Belv* —4J **85**
Belvedere Av. *SW19* —5G **107**
Belvedere Av. *Ilf* —2F **35**
Belvedere Bldgs. *SE1*
 —2B **78** (7B **150**)
Belvedere Clo. *Tedd* —5J **103**
Belvedere Ct. *Belv* —3F **85**
Belvedere Dri. *SW19* —5G **107**
Belvedere Gro. *SW19* —5G **107**
Belvedere Link Bus. Pk. *Eri*
 —3K **85**
Belvedere M. *SE15* —3J **95**
Belvedere Pl. *SE1*
 —2B **78** (7B **150**)
Belvedere Rd. *E10* —1A **48**
Belvedere Rd. *SE1*
 —2K **77** (6H **149**)
Belvedere Rd. *SE2* —1C **84**
Belvedere Rd. *SE19* —7F **111**
Belvedere Rd. *W7* —3K **71**
Belvedere Rd. *Bexh* —3F **101**
Belvedere Sq. *SW19* —5G **107**
Belvedere Strand. *NW9* —2B **26**

Belvedere, The. *SW10* —1A **92**
 (off Chelsea Harbour)
Belvedere Way. *Harr* —6E **24**
Belvoir Clo. *SE9* —3C **114**
Belvoir Rd. *SE22* —7G **95**
Belvue Bus. Cen. *N'holt* —7F **39**
Belvue Clo. *N'holt* —7E **38**
Belvue Rd. *N'holt* —7E **38**
Bembridge Clo. *NW6* —7G **43**
Bembridge Ho. SE8 —4B **80**
 (off Longshore)
Bemersyde Point. E13 —3K **65**
 (off Dongola Rd. W.)
Bemerton Est. *N1* —7J **45**
Bemerton St. *N1* —1K **61**
Bemish Rd. *SW15* —3F **91**
Bemsted Rd. *E17* —3B **32**
Benares Rd. *SE18* —4K **83**
Benbow Rd. *W6* —3D **74**
Benbow St. *SE8* —6B **80**
Benbury Clo. *Brom* —5E **112**
Bence Ho. *SE8* —5A **80**
Bench Field. *S Croy* —5F **135**
Bench, The. *Rich* —3C **104**
Bencroft Rd. *SW16* —7G **109**
Bencurtis Pk. *W Wick* —3F **137**
Bendall M. *NW1*
 —5C **60** (5D **140**)
Bendemeer Rd. *SW15* —3F **91**
Benden Ho. SE13 —5E **96**
 (off Monument Gdns.)
Bendish Rd. *E6* —7C **50**
Bendmore Av. *SE2* —5A **84**
Bendon Valley. *SW18* —7K **91**
Benedict Clo. *Belv* —3E **84**
Benedict Rd. *SW9* —3K **93**
Benedict Rd. *Mitc* —3B **122**
Benedict Way. *N2* —3A **28**
Benedict Wharf. *Mitc* —3B **122**
Benenden Grn. *Brom* —5J **127**
Benett Gdns. *SW16* —2J **123**
Ben Ezra Ct. SE17
 —4C **78** (4D **156**)
 (off Asolando Dri.)
Benfleet Clo. *Sutt* —3A **132**
Benfleet Ct. *E8* —1F **63**
Bengal Rd. *Ilf* —3F **51**
Bengarth Dri. *Harr* —2H **23**
Bengarth Rd. *N'holt* —1C **54**
Bengeworth Rd. *SE5* —3C **94**
Bengeworth Rd. *Harr* —2A **40**
Ben Hale Clo. *Stan* —5G **11**
Benham Clo. *SW11* —3B **92**
Benham Gdns. *Houn* —5D **86**
Benham Rd. *W7* —5J **55**
Benham's Pl. *NW3* —4A **44**
Benhill Av. *Sutt* —4K **131**
Benhill Rd. *SE5* —7D **78**
Benhill Rd. *Sutt* —3A **132**
Benhill Wood Rd. *Sutt* —3A **132**
Benhilton Gdns. *Sutt* —3K **131**
Benhurst Ct. *SW16* —5A **110**
Benhurst La. *SW16* —5A **110**
Benin St. *SE13* —7F **97**
Benjafield Clo. *N18* —4C **18**
Benjamin Clo. *E8* —1G **63**
Benjamin Ct. *Belv* —6F **85**
Benjamin St. *EC1*
 —5B **62** (5A **144**)
Ben Jonson Ct. *N1* —2E **62**
Ben Jonson Ho. *EC2*
 —5C **62** (5D **144**)
Ben Jonson Pl. *EC2*
 —5C **62** (5D **144**)
Ben Jonson Rd. *E1* —5K **63**

Benledi St. *E14* —6F **65**
Bennerley Rd. *SW11* —5C **92**
Bennet's Hill. *EC4*
 —7C **62** (2C **150**)
Bennet St. *SW1* —1G **77** (4A **148**)
Bennett Clo. *Hamp W* —1C **118**
Bennett Clo. *Well* —2A **100**
Bennett Ct. *N7* —3K **45**
Bennett Gro. *SE13* —1D **96**
Bennett Pk. *SE3* —3H **97**
Bennett Rd. *E13* —4A **66**
Bennett Rd. *Romf* —6E **36**
Bennetts Av. *Croy* —2A **136**
Bennetts Av. *Gnfd* —1J **55**
Bennett's Castle La. *Dag* —2C **52**
Bennetts Clo. *N17* —7A **18**
Bennetts Clo. *Mitc* —1F **123**
Bennetts Copse. *Chst* —6C **114**
Bennett's Rd. *N16* —4E **46**
Bennett St. *W4* —6A **74**
Bennetts Way. *Croy* —2A **136**
Bennett's Yd. *SW1*
 —3J **77** (2D **154**)
Bennilong Clo. *W12* —7D **58**
Benningholme Rd. *Edgw* —6F **13**
Bennington Rd. *E4* —7B **20**
Bennington Rd. *N17* —1E **30**
Benn St. *E9* —6A **48**
Benns Wlk. *Rich* —4E **88**
Benrek Clo. *Ilf* —1G **35**
Bensbury Clo. *SW15* —7D **90**
Bensham Clo. *T Hth* —4C **124**
Bensham Gro. *T Hth* —2C **124**
Bensham La. *T Hth & Croy*
 —5B **124**
Bensham Mnr. Rd. *T Hth*
 —4C **124**
Bensley Clo. *N11* —5J **15**
Ben Smith Way. *SE16* —3G **79**
Benson Av. *E6* —2A **66**
Benson Clo. *Houn* —4E **86**
Benson Quay. *E1* —7J **63**
Benson Rd. *SE23* —1J **111**
Benson Rd. *Croy* —3A **134**
Bentall Cen., The. *King T*
 —1D **118**
Bentfield Gdns. *SE9* —3B **114**
Benthal Rd. *N16* —3G **47**
Bentham Ct. N1 —7C **46**
 (off Ecclesbourne Rd.)
Bentham Rd. *E9* —6K **47**
Bentham Rd. *SE28* —7B **68**
Bentham Wlk. *NW10* —5J **41**
Ben Tillet Clo. *E16* —1D **82**
Ben Tillet Clo. *Bark* —7A **52**
Ben Tillet Ho. *N15* —3B **30**
Bentinck Clo. *NW8* —2C **60**
Bentinck M. *W1* —6E **60** (7H **141**)
Bentinck St. *W1* —6E **60** (7H **141**)
Bentley Dri. *NW2* —3H **43**
Bentley Dri. *Ilf* —6G **35**
Bentley Ho. SE5 —1E **94**
 (off Peckham Rd.)
Bentley Rd. *N1* —6E **46**
Bentley Way. *Stan* —5F **11**
Bentley Way. *Wfd G* —3D **20**
Benton Rd. *Ilf* —1H **51**
Bentons La. *SE27* —4C **110**
Bentons Rise. *SE27* —5D **110**
Bentry Clo. *Dag* —2E **52**
Bentry Rd. *Dag* —2E **52**
Bentworth Rd. *W12* —6D **58**
Benville Ho. SW8 —7K **77**
 (off Oval Pl.)
Benwell Rd. *N7* —5A **46**

Benwick Clo. *SE16* —4H **79**
Benworth St. *E3* —3B **64**
Benworth St. *E3* —3B **64**
Berber Rd. *SW11* —5D **92**
Bercta Rd. *SE9* —2G **115**
Berenger Tower. SW10 —7B **76**
 (off Worlds End Est.)
Berenger Wlk. SW10 —7B **76**
 (off Worlds End Est.)
Berens Ct. *Sidc* —4K **115**
Berens Rd. *NW10* —3F **59**
Berens Way. *Chst* —3K **129**
Beresford Av. *N20* —2J **15**
Beresford Av. *Surb* —7H **119**
Beresford Av. *Twic* —6C **88**
Beresford Av. *Wemb* —1F **57**
Beresford Dri. *Brom* —3C **128**
Beresford Dri. *Wfd G* —4F **21**
Beresford Gdns. *Enf* —4K **7**
Beresford Gdns. *Houn* —5D **86**
Beresford Gdns. *Romf* —5E **36**
Beresford M. *SW18* —6A **92**
Beresford Rd. *E4* —1B **20**
Beresford Rd. *E17* —1D **32**
Beresford Rd. *N2* —3C **28**
Beresford Rd. *N5* —5D **46**
Beresford Rd. *N8* —5A **30**
Beresford Rd. *Harr* —5H **23**
Beresford Rd. *King T* —1F **119**
Beresford Rd. *N Mald* —4J **119**
Beresford Rd. *S'hall* —1B **70**
Beresford Rd. *Sutt* —7H **131**
Beresford Sq. *SE18* —4F **83**
Beresford St. *SE18* —3C **82**
Beresford Ter. *N5* —5C **46**
Berestede Rd. *W6* —5B **74**
Bere St. *E1* —7K **63**
Bergen Ho. *SE5* —2C **94**
Bergen Sq. *SE16* —3A **80**
Berger Clo. *Orp* —6H **129**
Berger Rd. *E9* —6K **47**
Berger Sq. *E8* —7F **47**
Berghem M. *W14* —3F **75**
Bergholt Av. *Ilf* —5C **34**
Bergholt Cres. *N16* —7E **30**
Bergholt M. *NW1* —7G **45**
Bering Wlk. *E16* —6B **66**
Berkeley Av. *Bexh* —1D **100**
Berkeley Av. *Gnfd* —6J **39**
Berkeley Av. *Ilf* —2E **34**
Berkeley Av. *Romf* —1J **37**
Berkeley Clo. *Bren* —6A **72**
Berkeley Clo. *King T* —7E **104**
Berkeley Clo. *Orp* —7J **129**
Berkeley Ct. *N3* —1K **27**
Berkeley Ct. NW1
 —4D **60** (4F **141**)
Berkeley Ct. *NW11* —7H **27**
 (off Ravenscroft Av.)
Berkeley Ct. *W5* —7C **56**
 (off Gordon Rd.)
Berkeley Ct. *Surb* —7D **118**
Berkeley Ct. *Wall* —3G **133**
Berkeley Cres. *Barn* —5G **5**
Berkeley Gdns. *N21* —7J **7**
Berkeley Gdns. *W8* —1J **75**
Berkeley Ho. Bren —6D **72**
 (off Albany Rd.)
Berkeley M. *W1* —6D **60** (1F **141**)
Berkeley Pl. *SW19* —6F **107**
Berkeley Rd. *E12* —5C **50**
Berkeley Rd. *N8* —5H **29**
Berkeley Rd. *N15* —6D **30**
Berkeley Rd. *NW9* —4G **25**

Berkeley Rd. *SW13* —1C **90**
Berkeley Sq. *W1*
—7F **61** (3K **147**)
Berkeley St. *W1* —7F **61** (3K **147**)
Berkeley Wlk. *N7* —2K **45**
 (off Durham Rd.)
Berkeley Waye. *Houn* —6B **70**
Berkhampstead Rd. *Belv* —5G **85**
Berkhemsted Av. *Wemb* —6F **41**
Berkley Clo. *Twic* —3J **103**
 (off Wellesley Rd.)
Berkley Gro. *NW1* —7D **44**
Berkley Rd. *NW1* —7D **44**
Berkley Works. *NW1* —7D **44**
 (off Berkley Rd.)
Berkshire Ct. *W7* —4K **55**
 (off Copley Clo.)
Berkshire Gdns. *N13* —6F **17**
Berkshire Gdns. *N18* —5C **18**
Berkshire Ho. *SE6* —4C **112**
Berkshire Rd. *E9* —6B **48**
Berkshire Sq. *Mitc* —4J **123**
Berkshire Way. *Mitc* —4J **123**
Bermans Way. *NW10* —4A **42**
Bermondsey Sq. *SE1*
—3E **78** (1H **157**)
Bermondsey St. *SE1*
—1E **78** (5G **151**)
Bermondsey Trad. Est. *SE16*
—5J **79**
Bermondsey Wall E. *SE16*
—2G **79**
Bermondsey Wall W. *SE16*
—2G **79**
Bernal Clo. *SE28* —7D **68**
Bernard Ashley Dri. *SE7* —5K **81**
Bernard Av. *W13* —3B **72**
Bernard Cassidy St. *E16* —5H **65**
Bernard Gdns. *SW19* —5H **107**
Bernard Rd. *N15* —5F **31**
Bernard Rd. *Romf* —7J **37**
Bernard Rd. *Wall* —4F **133**
Bernard St. *WC1*
—4J **61** (4E **142**)
Bernays Clo. *Stan* —6H **11**
Bernay's Gro. *SW9* —4K **93**
Bernel Dri. *Croy* —3B **136**
Berne Rd. *T Hth* —5C **124**
Berners Dri. *W13* —7A **56**
Berners M. *W1* —5G **61** (6B **142**)
Berners Pl. *W1* —6G **61** (7B **142**)
Berners Rd. *N1* —1B **62**
Berners Rd. *N22* —1A **30**
Berners St. *W1* —5G **61** (6B **142**)
Berney Ho. *Beck* —5A **126**
Berney Rd. *Croy* —7D **124**
Bernville Way. *Harr* —5F **25**
Bernwell Rd. *E4* —3B **20**
Berridge Grn. *Edgw* —7B **12**
Berridge M. *NW6* —5J **43**
Berridge Rd. *SE19* —5D **110**
Berriman Rd. *N7* —3K **45**
Berriton Rd. *Harr* —1D **38**
Berrybank Clo. *E4* —2K **19**
Berry Clo. *N21* —1G **17**
Berry Clo. *NW10* —7A **42**
Berry Ct. *Houn* —5D **86**
Berrydale Rd. *Hayes* —4C **54**
Berryfield Clo. *E17* —4D **32**
Berryfield Clo. *Brom* —1C **128**
Berryfield Rd. *SE17*
—5B **78** (5B **156**)
Berryhill. *SE9* —4F **99**
Berry Hill. *Stan* —4J **11**
Berryhill Gdns. *SE9* —4F **99**

Berrylands. *SW20* —4E **120**
Berrylands. *Surb* —6F **119**
Berrylands Rd. *Surb* —6F **119**
Berry La. *SE21* —4D **110**
Berryman Clo. *Dag* —3C **52**
Berryman's La. *SE26* —4K **111**
Berrymead Gdns. *W3* —2J **73**
Berrymede Rd. *W4* —3K **73**
Berry Pl. *EC1* —3B **62** (2B **144**)
Berry St. *EC1* —4B **62** (3B **144**)
Berry Way. *W5* —3E **72**
Bertal Rd. *SW17* —4B **108**
Bertha Hollamby Ct. *Sidc*
 (off Sidcup Hill) —5C **116**
Berthons Gdns. *E17* —5F **33**
Berthon St. *SE8* —7C **80**
Bertie Rd. *NW10* —6C **42**
Bertie Rd. *SE26* —6K **111**
Bertram Cotts. *SW19* —7J **107**
Bertram Rd. *NW4* —6C **26**
Bertram Rd. *Enf* —4B **8**
Bertram Rd. *King T* —7G **105**
Bertram St. *N19* —3F **45**
Bertrand Ho. *SW16* —3J **109**
 (off Leigham Av.)
Bertrand St. *SE13* —3D **96**
Bertrand Way. *SE28* —7B **68**
Bert Rd. *T Hth* —5C **124**
Bert Way. *Enf* —4A **8**
Berwick Av. *Hayes* —6B **54**
Berwick Clo. *Stan* —6E **10**
Berwick Cres. *Sidc* —6J **99**
Berwick Ho. *N2* —2B **28**
Berwick Rd. *E16* —6K **65**
Berwick Rd. *N22* —1B **30**
Berwick Rd. *Well* —1B **100**
Berwick St. *W1* —6G **61** (7B **142**)
Berwick Tower. *SE14* —6A **80**
Berwyn Av. *Houn* —1F **87**
Berwyn Rd. *SE24* —1B **110**
Berwyn Rd. *Rich* —4H **89**
Beryl Av. *E6* —5C **66**
Beryl Rd. *W6* —5F **75**
Berystede. *King T* —7H **105**
Besant Ct. *N1* —5D **46**
Besant Ho. *NW8* —1A **60**
 (off Boundary Rd.)
Besant Rd. *NW2* —4G **43**
Besant Wlk. *N7* —2K **45**
Besant Way. *NW10* —5J **41**
Besley St. *SW16* —6G **109**
Bessant Dri. *Rich* —1G **89**
Bessborough Gdns. *SW1*
—5H **77** (5D **154**)
Bessborough Pl. *SW1*
—5H **77** (5D **154**)
Bessborough Rd. *Harr* —1H **39**
Bessborough Rd. *SW15* —1C **106**
Bessborough St. *SW1*
—5H **77** (5C **154**)
Bessemer Rd. *SE5* —2C **94**
Bessie Lansbury Clo. *E6* —6E **66**
Bessingham Wlk. *SE4* —4K **95**
 (off Aldersford Clo.)
Besson St. *SE14* —1J **95**
Bessy St. *E2* —3J **63**
Bestwood St. *SE8* —4K **79**
Beswick M. *NW6* —6K **43**
Betchworth Clo. *Sutt* —5B **132**
Betchworth Rd. *Ilf* —2J **51**
Betchworth Way. *New Ad*
—7E **136**
Bethal Est. *SE1* —1E **78** (5H **151**)
Betham Rd. *Gnfd* —4H **55**
Bethecar Rd. *Harr* —5J **23**

Bethell Av. *E16* —4H **65**
Bethell Av. *Ilf* —7E **34**
Bethel Rd. *Well* —3C **100**
Bethersden Clo. *Beck* —7B **112**
Bethnal Grn. Rd. *E1 & E2*
—4F **63** (3J **145**)
Bethune Av. *N11* —4J **15**
Bethune Clo. *N16* —1E **46**
Bethune Rd. *N16* —7D **30**
Bethune Rd. *NW10* —4K **57**
Bethwin Rd. *SE5* —7B **78**
Betjeman Clo. *Pinn* —4E **22**
Betony Clo. *Croy* —1K **135**
Betoyne Av. *E4* —4B **20**
Betstyle Cir. *N11* —4A **16**
Betstyle Ho. *N10* —7K **15**
Betstyle Rd. *N11* —4A **16**
Betterton Dri. *Sidc* —2E **116**
Betterton Rd. *Rain* —3K **69**
Betterton St. *WC2*
—6J **61** (1F **149**)
Bettons Pk. *E15* —1G **65**
Bettridge Rd. *SW6* —2H **91**
Betts Clo. *Beck* —2A **126**
Betts Ho. *E1* —7H **63**
 (off Betts St.)
Betts M. *E17* —6B **32**
Betts Rd. *E16* —7K **65**
Betts St. *E1* —7H **63**
Betts Way. *SE20* —1H **125**
Betts Way. *Surb* —7B **118**
Betty Brooks Ho. *E11* —3F **49**
Beulah Av. *T Hth* —2C **124**
Beulah Clo. *Edgw* —3C **12**
Beulah Cres. *T Hth* —2C **124**
Beulah Gro. *Croy* —6C **124**
Beulah Hill. *SE19* —6B **110**
Beulah Path. *E17* —5E **32**
Beulah Rd. *E17* —5D **32**
Beulah Rd. *SW19* —7H **107**
Beulah Rd. *Sutt* —4J **131**
Beulah Rd. *T Hth* —3C **124**
Bevan Av. *Bark* —7A **52**
Bevan Ct. *Croy* —5A **134**
Bevan Rd. *SE2* —5B **84**
Bevan Rd. *Barn* —4J **5**
Bevan St. *N1* —1C **62**
Bev Callender Clo. *SW8* —3F **93**
Bevenden St. *N1*
—3D **62** (1F **145**)
Bevercote Wlk. *Belv* —6F **85**
Beveridge Rd. *NW10* —7A **42**
Beverley Av. *SW20* —1B **120**
Beverley Av. *Houn* —4D **86**
Beverley Av. *Sidc* —7K **99**
Beverley Clo. *N21* —1H **17**
Beverley Clo. *SW11* —4B **92**
Beverley Clo. *SW13* —2C **90**
Beverley Clo. *Enf* —4K **7**
Beverley Ct. *N14* —7B **6**
Beverley Ct. *SE4* —3B **96**
Beverley Ct. *W4* —5J **73**
Beverley Ct. *Harr* —3H **23**
Beverley Ct. *Houn* —4D **86**
Beverley Ct. *Kent* —4C **24**
Beverley Cres. *Wfd G* —1K **33**
Beverley Dri. *Edgw* —3G **25**
Beverley Gdns. *NW11* —7G **27**
Beverley Gdns. *SW13* —3B **90**
Beverley Gdns. *Stan* —1A **24**
Beverley Gdns. *Wemb* —1F **41**
Beverley Gdns. *Wor Pk*
—1C **130**

Beverley Ho. *Brom* —5F **113**
 (off Brangbourne Rd.)
Beverley La. *SW15* —3B **106**
Beverley La. *King T* —7A **106**
Beverley M. *E4* —6A **20**
Beverley Path. *SW13* —2B **90**
Beverley Rd. *E4* —6A **20**
Beverley Rd. *E6* —3B **66**
Beverley Rd. *SE20* —2H **125**
Beverley Rd. *SW13* —3B **90**
Beverley Rd. *W4* —5B **74**
Beverley Rd. *Bexh* —2J **101**
Beverley Rd. *Brom* —2C **138**
Beverley Rd. *Dag* —4E **52**
Beverley Rd. *King T* —1C **118**
Beverley Rd. *Mitc* —4H **123**
Beverley Rd. *N Mald* —4C **120**
Beverley Rd. *Ruis* —3A **38**
Beverley Rd. *S'hall* —4C **70**
Beverley Rd. *Wor Pk* —2C **130**
Beverley Trad. Est. *Mord*
—7F **121**
Beverley Way. *N Mald & SW20*
—1B **120**
Beversbrook Rd. *N19* —3H **45**
Beverstone M. *W1*
—5D **60** (6E **140**)
Beverstone Rd. *SW2* —5K **93**
Beverstone Rd. *T Hth* —4A **124**
Bevill Allen Clo. *SW17* —5D **108**
Bevill Clo. *SE25* —3G **125**
Bevin Clo. *SE16* —1A **80**
Bevin Ct. *WC1* —3K **61** (1H **143**)
Bevington Rd. *W10* —5G **59**
Bevington Rd. *Beck* —2D **126**
Bevington St. *SE16* —2G **79**
Bevin Way. *WC1*
—2A **62** (1J **143**)
Bevis Marks. *EC3*
—6E **62** (7H **145**)
Bewcastle Gdns. *Enf* —4D **6**
Bew Ct. *SE22* —7G **95**
Bewdley St. *N1* —7A **46**
Bewick St. *SW8* —2F **93**
Bewley St. *E1* —7J **63**
Bewlys Rd. *SE27* —5B **110**
Bexhill Clo. *Felt* —2C **102**
Bexhill Rd. *N11* —5C **16**
Bexhill Rd. *SE4* —6B **96**
Bexhill Rd. *SW14* —3J **89**
Bexhill Wlk. *E15* —1G **65**
Bexley Gdns. *N9* —3J **17**
Bexley Gdns. *Chad H* —5B **36**
Bexley High St. *Bex* —7G **101**
Bexley Ho. *SE4* —4A **96**
Bexley La. *Dart* —5K **101**
Bexley La. *Sidc* —4C **116**
Bexley Rd. *SE9* —4B **114**
Bexley Rd. *Eri* —7J **85**
 (in two parts)
Beynon Rd. *Cars* —5D **132**
Bianca Rd. *SE15*
—6G **79** (7K **157**)
Bibsworth Rd. *N3* —2H **27**
Bibury Clo. *SE15* —6E **78**
Bicester Rd. *Rich* —3G **89**
Bickenhall Mans. *W1*
—5D **60** (5F **141**)
Bickenhall St. *W1*
—5D **60** (5F **141**)
Bickersteth Rd. *SW17* —6D **108**
Bickerton Rd. *N19* —2G **45**
Bickley Cres. *Brom* —4C **128**
Bickley Pk. Rd. *Brom* —3C **128**
Bickley Rd. *E10* —7D **32**

Bickley Rd. *Brom* —2B **128**
Bickley St. *SW17* —5C **108**
Bicknell Ho. *E1* —6G **63**
 (off Ellen St.)
Bicknell Rd. *SE5* —3C **94**
Bicknoller Rd. *Enf* —1K **7**
Bicknor Rd. *Orp* —7J **129**
Bidborough Clo. *Brom* —5H **127**
Bidborough St. *WC1*
—3J **61** (2E **142**)
Biddenden Way. *SE9* —4E **114**
Bidder St. *E16* —5G **65**
 (in two parts)
Biddestone Rd. *N7* —4K **45**
Biddulph Ho. *SE18* —4D **82**
Biddulph Mans. *W9* —3K **59**
 (off Elgin Av.)
Biddulph Rd. *W9* —3K **59**
Bideford Av. *Gnfd* —2B **56**
Bideford Clo. *Edgw* —1G **25**
Bideford Clo. *Felt* —3D **102**
Bideford Gdns. *Enf* —7K **7**
Bideford Rd. *Brom* —3H **113**
Bideford Rd. *Enf* —1G **9**
Bideford Rd. *Ruis* —3A **38**
Bideford Rd. *Well* —7B **84**
Bidwell Gdns. *N11* —7B **16**
Bidwell St. *SE15* —1H **95**
Bigbury Clo. *N17* —7J **17**
Biggerstaff Rd. *E15* —1E **64**
Biggerstaff St. *N4* —2A **46**
Biggin Av. *Mitc* —1D **122**
Biggin Hill. *SE19* —7B **110**
Biggin Hill Clo. *King T* —5C **104**
Biggin Way. *SE19* —7B **110**
Bigginwood Rd. *SW16* —7B **110**
Biggs Row. *SW15* —3F **91**
Big Hill. *E5* —1H **47**
Bigland St. *E1* —6H **63**
Bignell Rd. *SE18* —5F **83**
Bignold Rd. *E7* —4J **49**
Bigwood Ct. *NW11* —5K **27**
Bigwood Rd. *NW11* —5K **27**
Billet Clo. *Romf* —3D **36**
Billet Rd. *E17* —1K **31**
Billet Rd. *Romf* —3B **36**
Billets Hart Clo. *W7* —2J **71**
Bill Hamling Clo. *SE9* —2D **114**
Billingford Clo. *SE4* —4K **95**
Billing Pl. *SW10* —7K **75**
Billing Rd. *SW10* —7K **75**
Billingsgate Rd. *E14* —7C **64**
Billing St. *SW10* —7K **75**
Billington Rd. *SE14* —7K **79**
Billiter Sq. *EC3* —6E **62** (1H **151**)
Billiter St. *EC3* —6E **62** (1H **151**)
Billson St. *E14* —4E **80**
Bilsby Gro. *SE9* —4B **114**
Bilsby Lodge. *Wemb* —3J **41**
 (off Chalklands)
Bilton Cen., The. *Gnfd* —1B **56**
Bilton Rd. *Gnfd* —1A **56**
Bilton Way. *Enf* —1F **9**
Bina Gdns. *SW5* —4A **76**
Bincote Rd. *Enf* —3E **6**
Binden Rd. *W12* —3B **74**
Bindon Grn. *Mord* —4K **121**
Binfield Rd. *SW4* —1J **93**
Binfield Rd. *S Croy* —5F **135**
Bingfield St. *N1* —1J **61**
 (in two parts)
Bingham Pl. *W1*
—5E **60** (5G **141**)
Bingham Rd. *Croy* —1G **135**
Bingham St. *N1* —6D **46**

Bingley Rd. E16 —6A 66
Bingley Rd. Gnfd —4G 55
Binley Ho. SW15 —6B 90
Binney St. W1 —6E 60 (1H 147)
Binns Rd. W4 —5A 74
Binns Ter. W4 —5A 74
Binsey Wlk. SE2 —2C 84
Binyon Cres. Stan —5E 10
Birbetts Rd. SE9 —2D 114
Bircham Path. SE4 —4K 95
(off Aldersford Clo.)
Birchanger Rd. SE25 —5G 125
Birch Av. N13 —3H 17
Birch Clo. E16 —5G 65
Birch Clo. N19 —2G 45
Birch Clo. SE15 —2G 95
Birch Clo. Bren —7B 72
Birch Clo. Buck H —3G 21
Birch Clo. Iswth —3H 87
Birch Clo. Romf —3H 37
Birch Clo. Tedd —5A 104
Birch Ct. Wall —4F 133
Birchdale Gdns. Romf —7D 36
Birchdale Rd. E7 —5A 50
Birchdene Dri. SE28 —1A 84
Birchen Clo. NW9 —2K 41
Birchend Clo. S Croy —6D 134
Birchen Gro. NW9 —2K 41
Birches Clo. Mitc —3D 122
Birches Clo. Pinn —5C 22
Birches, The. E12 —4C 50
Birches, The. N21 —6E 6
Birches, The. SE7 —6K 81
Birches, The. Houn —7D 86
Birches, The. Orp —4E 138
Birchfield St. E14 —7C 64
Birch Gdns. Dag —3J 53
Birch Grn. NW9 —5E 10
Birch Gro. E11 —4G 49
Birch Gro. SE12 —7H 97
Birch Gro. W3 —1G 73
Birch Gro. Well —4A 100
Birch Hill. Croy —5K 135
Birch Ho. SE14 —1B 96
Birch Ho. SW2 —6A 94
(off Tulse Hill)
Birchington Clo. Bexh —1H 101
Birchington Ho. E5 —5H 47
Birchington Rd. N8 —6H 29
Birchington Rd. NW6 —1J 59
Birchington Rd. Surb —7F 119
Birchin La. EC3 —6D 62 (1F 151)
Birchlands Av. SW12 —7D 92
Birchmead. Orp —2E 138
Birchmead Av. Pinn —4A 22
Birchmere Lodge. SE16 —5H 79
(off Sherwood Gdns.)
Birchmere Row. SE3 —2H 97
Birchmore Hall. N5 —3C 46
Birchmore Wlk. N5 —3C 46
Birch 'Pk. Harr —7B 10
Birch Rd. Felt —5B 102
Birch Rd. Romf —3H 37
Birch Row. Brom —7E 128
Birch Tree Av. W Wick —5H 137
Birch Tree Way. Croy —2H 135
Birch Wlk. Eri —6J 85
Birch Wlk. Mitc —1F 123
Birchwood Av. N10 —3E 28
Birchwood Av. Beck —4B 126
Birchwood Av. Sidc —3B 116
Birchwood Av. Wall —3E 132
Birchwood Clo. Mord —4K 121
Birchwood Ct. N13 —5G 17
Birchwood Ct. Edgw —2J 25

Birchwood Dri. NW3 —3K 43
Birchwood Dri. Dart —4K 117
Birchwood Gro. Hamp —6E 102
Birchwood Pde. Wilm —4K 117
Birchwood Rd. SW17 —5F 109
Birchwood Rd. Orp —4H 129
Birchwood Rd. Swan & Dart
—7J 117
Birdbrook Clo. Dag —7J 53
Birdbrook Rd. SE3 —3A 98
Birdcage Wlk. SW1
—2G 77 (7A 148)
Birdham Clo. Brom —5C 128
Birdhurst Av. S Croy —4D 134
Birdhurst Gdns. S Croy —4D 134
Birdhurst Rise. S Croy —5E 134
Birdhurst Rd. SW18 —5A 92
Birdhurst Rd. SW19 —6C 108
Birdhurst Rd. S Croy —5E 134
Bird in Bush Rd. SE15 —7G 79
Bird in Hand La. Brom —2B 128
Bird-in-Hand Pas. SE23 —2J 111
Bird in Hand Yd. NW3 —4A 44
Birdlington Rd. N9 —7C 8
Birdlip Clo. SE15 —6E 78
Birdport Rd. Gnfd —1F 55
Birds Farm Av. Romf —1H 37
Birdsfield La. E3 —1B 64
Bird St. W1 —6E 60 (1H 147)
Bird Wlk. Twic —1D 102
Birdwood Clo. Tedd —4J 103
Birkbeck Av. W3 —7J 57
Birkbeck Av. Gnfd —1G 55
Birkbeck Gdns. Wfd G —2D 20
Birkbeck Gro. W3 —2K 73
Birkbeck Hill. SE21 —1B 110
Birkbeck M. E8 —5F 47
Birkbeck Pl. SE21 —2C 110
Birkbeck Rd. E8 —5F 47
Birkbeck Rd. N8 —4J 29
Birkbeck Rd. N12 —5F 15
Birkbeck Rd. N17 —1F 31
Birkbeck Rd. NW7 —5G 13
Birkbeck Rd. SW19 —5H 107
Birkbeck Rd. W3 —1K 73
Birkbeck Rd. W5 —4C 72
Birkbeck Rd. Beck —2J 125
Birkbeck Rd. Enf —1J 7
Birkbeck Rd. Ilf —5H 35
Birkbeck Rd. Romf —1K 53
Birkbeck Rd. Sidc —3A 116
Birkbeck St. E2 —3H 63
Birkbeck Way. Gnfd —1H 55
Birkdale Av. Pinn —3E 22
Birkdale Ct. S'hall —6G 55
(off Redcroft Rd.)
Birkdale Gdns. Croy —4K 135
Birkdale Rd. SE2 —4A 84
Birkdale Rd. W5 —4E 56
Birkenhead Av. King T —2F 119
Birkenhead St. WC1
—3J 61 (1F 143)
Birkhall Rd. SE6 —1F 113
Birkwood Clo. SW12 —7H 93
Birley Rd. N20 —2F 15
Birley St. SW11 —2E 92
Birling Rd. Eri —7K 85
Birnam Rd. N4 —2K 45
Birnbeck Ct. NW11 —5H 27
Birnbeck Ct. Barn —4A 4
Birrell Ho. SW9 —2K 93
(off Stockwell Rd.)
Birse Cres. NW10 —3A 42
Birstall Rd. N15 —5E 30

Biscay Rd. W6 —5F 75
Biscoe Clo. Houn —6E 70
Biscoe Way. SE13 —3F 97
Bisenden Rd. Croy —2E 134
Bisham Clo. Cars —1D 132
Bisham Gdns. N6 —1E 44
Bishop Ct. N12 —4E 14
Bishop Ken Rd. Harr —2K 23
Bishop King's Rd. W14 —4G 75
Bishop Rd. N14 —7A 6
Bishop's Av. E13 —1K 65
Bishop's Av. SW6 —2F 91
Bishops Av. Brom —2A 128
Bishops Av. Romf —6C 36
Bishops Av., The. N2 —6B 28
Bishop's Bri. Rd. W2 —6K 59
Bishops Clo. E17 —4D 32
Bishops Clo. N19 —3G 45
Bishop's Clo. SE9 —2G 115
Bishops Clo. W4 —5J 73
Bishops Clo. Barn —6A 4
Bishops Clo. Enf —2C 8
Bishops Clo. Rich —3D 104
Bishop's Clo. Sutt —3J 131
Bishop's Clo. EC4
Bishop's Ct. EC4
—6B 62 (7A 144)
Bishop's Ct. WC2
—6A 62 (7J 143)
Bishops Ct. Rich —3E 88
Bishops Dri. N'holt —1C 54
Bishopsford Rd. Mord —7A 122
Bishopsgate. EC2
—6E 62 (1G 151)
Bishopsgate Arc. EC2
—5E 62 (6H 145)
Bishopsgate Chu. Yd. EC2
—5E 62 (7G 145)
Bishops Grn. Brom —1A 128
(off Up. Park Rd.)
Bishop's Gro. N2 —6C 28
Bishop's Gro. Hamp —4D 102
Bishops Gro. Cvn. Site. Hamp
—4E 102
Bishop's Hall. King T —1D 118
Bishop's Mans. SW6 —2F 91
(in two parts)
Bishops Pk. Rd. SW6 —2F 91
Bishop's Pk. Rd. SW16 —1J 123
Bishops Rd. N6 —6E 28
Bishops Rd. SW6 —1G 91
Bishop's Rd. SW11 —7C 76
Bishops Rd. W7 —2J 71
Bishop's Rd. Croy —7B 124
Bishop's Ter. SE11
—4A 78 (3K 155)
Bishopsthorpe Rd. SE26
—4K 111
Bishop St. N1 —1C 62
Bishops View Ct. N10 —4F 29
Bishops Wlk. Chst —1G 129
Bishops Wlk. Croy —5K 135
Bishops Wlk. Pinn —3C 22
Bishop's Way. E2 —2H 63
Bishopswood Rd. N6 —7D 28
Bishop Way. NW10 —7A 42
Bishop Wilfred Wood Clo. SE15
—2H 95
Bisley Clo. Wor Pk —1E 130
Bison Ct. Felt —7A 86
Bispham Rd. NW10 —3F 57
Bisson Rd. E15 —2E 64
Bisterne Av. E17 —3F 33
Bittacy Bus. Cen. NW7 —6B 14
Bittacy Clo. NW7 —6A 14
Bittacy Ct. NW7 —7B 14

Bittacy Hill. NW7 —6A 14
Bittacy Pk. Av. NW7 —5A 14
Bittacy Rise. NW7 —6K 13
Bittacy Rd. NW7 —6A 14
Bittern Clo. Hayes —5B 54
Bittern Ct. NW9 —2A 26
Bittern Ct. SE8 —6C 80
Bittern Pl. N22 —2K 29
Bittern St. SE1 —2C 78 (7C 150)
Bittoms, The. King T —3D 118
Bixley Clo. S'hall —4D 70
Blackall St. EC2 —4E 62 (3G 145)
Blackberry Farm Clo. Houn
—7C 70
Blackberry Field. Orp —7A 116
Blackbird Ct. NW9 —2K 41
Blackbird Hill. NW9 —2J 41
Blackborne Rd. Dag —6G 53
Black Boy La. N15 —5C 30
Blackbrook La. Brom —5E 128
Blackburn. NW9 —2B 26
Blackburne's M. W1
—7E 60 (2G 147)
Blackburn Rd. NW6 —6K 43
Blackbush Av. Romf —5D 36
Blackbush Clo. Sutt —7K 131
Blackdown Clo. N2 —2A 28
Blackett St. SW15 —3F 91
Black Fan Clo. Enf —1H 7
Blackfen Pde. Sidc —6A 100
Blackfen Rd. Sidc —5J 99
Blackford Clo. S Croy —7B 134
Blackford's Path. SW15 —7C 90
Blackfriars Bri. SE1 & EC4
—7B 62 (2A 150)
Black Friars La. EC4
—7B 62 (2A 150)
Blackfriars Pas. EC4
—7B 62 (2A 150)
Blackfriars Rd. SE1
—2B 78 (4A 150)
Blackfriars Underpass. EC4
—7B 62 (2A 150)
Black Gates. Pinn —3D 22
Blackheath Bus. Est. SE10
(off Blackheath Hill) —1E 96
Blackheath Gro. SE3 —2H 97
Blackheath Hill. SE10 —1E 96
Blackheath Pk. SE3 —3H 97
Blackheath Rise. SE13 —2E 96
Blackheath Rd. SE10 —1D 96
Blackheath Vale. SE3 —2G 97
Blackheath Village. SE3 —2H 97
Black Horse Ct. SE1
—3D 78 (1F 157)
Blackhorse La. E17 —4K 31
Black Horse La. Croy —7G 125
Blackhorse M. E17 —3K 31
Blackhorse Rd. E17 —4K 31
Blackhorse Rd. SE8 —6A 80
Blackhorse Rd. Sidc —4A 116
Blackhorse Road. (Junct.)
—4K 31
Blacklands Rd. SE6 —4E 112
Blacklands Ter. SW3
—4D 76 (4E 152)
Black Lion La. W6 —4C 74
Black Lion M. W6 —4C 74
Blackmore Av. S'hall —1H 71
Blackmore Ho. N1 —1K 61
(off Barnsbury Est.)
Blackmore Rd. Buck H —1H 21

Blackmore's Gro. Tedd —6A 104
Blackmore Tower. W3 —3J 73
(off Stanley Rd.)
Blackness La. Kes —7B 138
Black Path. E10 —7K 31
Blackpool Rd. SE15 —2H 95
Black Prince Interchange. (Junct.)
—6H 101
Black Prince Rd. SE1 & SE11
—4K 77 (4G 155)
Blackshaw Pl. N1 —7E 46
Blackshaw Rd. SW17 —4A 108
Blacksmiths Clo. Romf —6C 36
Blacksmiths Ho. E17 —4C 32
Blacks Rd. W6 —5E 74
Blackstock M. N4 —2B 46
Blackstock Rd. N4 & N5 —2B 46
Blackstone Est. E8 —7H 47
Blackstone Rd. NW2 —5E 42
Black Swan Yd. SE1
—2E 78 (6H 151)
Blackthorn Ct. E15 —4F 49
Blackthorn Ct. Houn —7C 70
Blackthorne Av. Croy —1J 135
Blackthorne Ct. S'hall —1F 71
(off Dormers Wells La.)
Blackthorne Dri. E4 —4A 20
Blackthorn Gro. Bexh —3E 100
Blackthorn St. E3 —4C 64
Blacktree M. SW9 —3A 94
Blackwall La. SE10 —5G 81
(in two parts)
Blackwall Trad. Est. E14 —5F 65
Blackwall Tunnel. E14 & SE10
—1F 81
Blackwall Tunnel App. E14
—7E 64
Blackwall Tunnel Northern App.
E3 & E14 —2D 64
Blackwall Tunnel Southern App.
SE10 —3G 81
Blackwall Way. E14 —1G 81
Blackwater Clo. E7 —5H 49
Blackwater Clo. Rain —5K 69
Blackwater St. SE22 —5F 95
Blackwell Clo. E5 —4K 47
Blackwell Clo. Harr —7C 10
Blackwell Gdns. Edgw —3B 12
Blackwell Ho. SW4 —6H 93
Blackwood St. SE17
—5D 78 (5E 156)
Blade M. SW15 —4H 91
Blades Ct. SW15 —4H 91
Bladindon Dri. Bex —7C 100
Bladon Clo. SW16 —6J 109
Bladon Gdns. Harr —6F 23
Blagdens Clo. N14 —2C 16
Blagdens La. N14 —2C 16
Blagdon Ct. W7 —7J 55
Blagdon Rd. SE13 —6D 96
Blagdon Rd. N Mald —4B 120
Blagdon Wlk. Tedd —6C 104
Blagrove Rd. W10 —5G 59
Blair Av. NW9 —7A 26
Blair Clo. N1 —6C 46
Blair Clo. Sidc —5J 99
Blair Ct. NW8 —1B 60
(off Boundary Rd.)
Blair Ct. Beck —1D 126
Blairderry Rd. SW2 —2J 109
Blair Ho. SW9 —2K 93
Blair St. E14 —6E 64
Blake Av. Bark —1J 67

Blake Clo. *W10* —5E **58**
Blake Clo. *Cars* —1C **132**
Blake Clo. *Well* —1J **99**
Blake Gdns. *SW6* —1K **91**
Blake Hall Cres. *E11* —1J **49**
Blake Hall Rd. *E11* —7J **33**
Blakehall Rd. *Cars* —6D **132**
Blake Ho. E14 —2D *80*
 (off Admirals Way)
Blake Ho. *SE1* —3A **78** (1J **155**)
Blakeley Cotts. *SE10* —2F **81**
Blakemore Rd. *SW16* —3J **109**
Blakemore Rd. *T Hth* —5K **123**
Blakemore Way. *Belv* —3E **84**
Blakeney Av. *Beck* —1B **126**
Blakeney Clo. *E8* —5G **47**
Blakeney Clo. *N20* —1F **15**
Blakeney Rd. *NW1* —7H **45**
Blakeney Rd. *Beck* —7B **112**
Blakenham Rd. *SW17* —4D **108**
Blaker Ct. *SE7* —7A **82**
Blake Rd. *E16* —4H **65**
Blake Rd. *N11* —7B **16**
Blake Rd. *Croy* —2E **134**
Blake Rd. *Mitc* —3C **122**
Blaker Rd. *E15* —1E **64**
Blakes Av. *N Mald* —5B **120**
Blake's Grn. *W Wick* —1E **136**
Blakes La. *N Mald* —5B **120**
Blakesley Av. *W5* —6C **56**
Blakesley Wlk. *SW20* —2H **121**
Blake's Rd. *SE15* —7E **78**
Blakes Ter. *N Mald* —5C **120**
Blakesware Gdns. *N9* —7J **7**
Blakewood Clo. *Felt* —4A **102**
Blanchard Clo. *SE9* —3C **114**
Blanchard Way. *E8* —6G **47**
Blanch Clo. *SE15* —7J **79**
Blanchedowne. *SE5* —4D **94**
Blanche St. *E16* —4H **65**
Blanchland Rd. *Mord* —5K **121**
Blandfield Rd. *SW12* —7E **92**
Blandford Av. *Beck* —2A **126** .
Blandford Av. *Twic* —1F **103**
Blandford Clo. *N2* —4A **28**
Blandford Clo. *Croy* —3J **133**
Blandford Clo. *Romf* —4G **37**
Blandford Ct. *NW6* —7G **43**
Blandford Cres. *E4* —7K **9**
Blandford Ho. SW8 —7K *77*
 (off Richborne Ter.)
Blandford Rd. *W4* —3A **74**
Blandford Rd. *W5* —2D **72**
Blandford Rd. *Beck* —2J **125**
Blandford Rd. *S'hall* —4E **70**
Blandford Rd. *Tedd* —5H **103**
Blandford Sq. *NW1*
 —4C **60** (4D **140**)
Blandford St. *W1*
 —6D **60** (7F **141**)
Blandford Waye. *Hayes* —6A **54**
Bland Ho. *SE11* —5K **77** (5H **155**)
Bland St. *SE9* —4B **98**
Blaney Cres. *E6* —3F **67**
Blanmerle Rd. *SE9* —1F **115**
Blann Clo. *SE9* —6B **98**
Blantyre Rd. *SW10* —7B **76**
Blantyre Wlk. SW10 —7B *76*
 (off Worlds End Est.)
Blashford St. *SE13* —7F **97**
Blasker Wlk. *E14* —5D **80**
Blawith Rd. *Harr* —4J **23**
Blaxland Ho. W12 —7D *58*
 (off White City Est.)
Blaydon Clo. *N17* —7C **18**

Blaydon Ct. *N'holt* —6E **38**
Bleak Hill La. *SE18* —6K **83**
Bleasdale Av. *Gnfd* —2A **56**
Blechynden St. *W10* —7F **59**
Bleddyn Clo. *Sidc* —6C **100**
Bledlow Clo. *SE28* —7C **68**
Bledlow Rise. *Gnfd* —2G **55**
Bleeding Heart Yd. *EC1*
 —5A **62** (6K **143**)
Blegborough Rd. *SW16* —6G **109**
Blendon Dri. *Bex* —6D **100**
Blendon Path. *Brom* —7H **113**
Blendon Rd. *Bex* —6D **100**
Blendon Row. *SE17*
 —4D **78** (4E **156**)
Blendon Ter. *SE18* —5G **83**
Blendworth Way. *SE15* —7E **78**
Blenheim Av. *Ilf* —6E **34**
Blenheim Clo. *N21* —1H **17**
Blenheim Clo. *SW20* —3E **120**
Blenheim Clo. *Gnfd* —2H **55**
Blenheim Clo. *Romf* —4J **37**
Blenheim Clo. *Wall* —7G **133**
Blenheim Ct. *N19* —2J **45**
Blenheim Ct. *Brom* —4H **127**
Blenheim Ct. *Kent* —6A **24**
Blenheim Ct. *Sidc* —3H **115**
Blenheim Ct. *Sutt* —6A **132**
Blenheim Cres. *W11* —7G **59**
Blenheim Cres. *S Croy* —7C **134**
Blenheim Dri. *Well* —1K **99**
Blenheim Gdns. *NW2* —6E **42**
Blenheim Gdns. *SW2* —6K **93**
Blenheim Gdns. *King T* —7H **105**
Blenheim Gdns. *Wall* —6G **133**
Blenheim Gdns. *Wemb* —3E **40**
Blenheim Gro. *SE15* —2G **95**
Blenheim Ho. Houn —3E *86*
Blenheim Pk. Rd. S Croy
 —7C **134**
Blenheim Pas. NW8 —2A *60*
 (off Carlton Hill)
Blenheim Pl. *NW8* —2A **60**
Blenheim Rise. *N15* —4F **31**
Blenheim Rd. *E6* —3B **66**
Blenheim Rd. *E15* —4G **49**
Blenheim Rd. *E17* —3K **31**
Blenheim Rd. *NW8* —2A **60**
Blenheim Rd. *SE20* —7J **111**
Blenheim Rd. *SW20* —3E **120**
Blenheim Rd. *W4* —3A **74**
Blenheim Rd. *Barn* —3A **4**
Blenheim Rd. *Brom* —4C **128**
Blenheim Rd. *Harr* —6F **23**
Blenheim Rd. *N'holt* —6F **39**
Blenheim Rd. *Sidc* —1C **116**
Blenheim Rd. *Sutt* —3J **131**
Blenheim Shop. Cen. *SE20*
 —7J **111**
Blenheim St. *W1*
 —6F **61** (1J **147**)
Blenheim Ter. *NW8* —2A **60**
Blenheim Way. *Iswth* —1A **88**
Blenkarne Rd. *SW11* —6D **92**
Bleriot. NW9 —2B *26*
 (off Belvedere Strand)
Bleriot Rd. *Houn* —7A **70**
Blessbury Rd. *Edgw* —1J **25**
Blessington Clo. *SE13* —3F **97**
Blessington Rd. *SE13* —4F **97**
Blessing Way. *Bark* —3C **68**
Bletchingley Clo. *T Hth* —4B **124**
Bletchley St. *N1* —2C **62** (1D **144**)
Bletsoe Wlk. *N1* —2C **62**

Blewbury Ho. *SE2* —2D **84**
Blincoe Clo. *SW19* —2F **107**
Bliss Cres. *SE13* —2D **96**
Blissett St. *SE10* —1E **96**
Blisworth Clo. *Hayes* —4C **54**
Blithbury Rd. *Dag* —6B **52**
Blithdale Rd. *SE2* —4A **84**
Blithfield St. *W8* —3K **75**
Blockley Rd. *Wemb* —2B **40**
Bloemfontein Av. *W12* —1D **74**
Bloemfontein Rd. *W12* —7D **58**
Bloemfontein Way. *W12* —1D **74**
Blomfield Rd. *W9* —5K **59**
Blomfield St. *EC2*
 —5D **62** (6F **145**)
Blomfield Vs. *W2* —5K **59**
Blomville Rd. *Dag* —3E **52**
Blondel St. *SW11* —2E **92**
Blondin Av. *W5* —4C **72**
Blondin St. *E3* —2C **64**
Bloomburg St. *SW1*
 —4H **77** (4B **154**)
Bloomfield Ct. *N6* —6E **28**
Bloomfield Cres. *Ilf* —6F **35**
Bloomfield Pl. *W1*
 —7F **61** (2K **147**)
Bloomfield Rd. *N6* —6E **28**
Bloomfield Rd. *SE18* —5F **83**
Bloomfield Rd. *Brom* —5B **128**
Bloomfield Rd. *King T* —3E **118**
Bloomfields, The. *Bark* —6G **51**
Bloomfield Ter. *SW1*
 —5E **76** (5H **153**)
Bloom Gro. *SE27* —3B **110**
Bloomhall Rd. *SE19* —5D **110**
Bloom Pk. Rd. *SW6* —7H **75**
Bloomsbury Clo. *W5* —7F **57**
Bloomsbury Ct. *WC1*
 —5J **61** (6F **143**)
Bloomsbury Ct. *Pinn* —3D **22**
Bloomsbury Ho. *SW4* —6H **93**
Bloomsbury Pl. *SW18* —5A **92**
Bloomsbury Pl. *WC1*
 —5J **61** (5F **143**)
Bloomsbury Sq. *WC1*
 —5J **61** (6F **143**)
Bloomsbury St. *WC1*
 —5H **61** (6D **142**)
Bloomsbury Way. *WC1*
 —5J **61** (6E **142**)
Blore Clo. *SW8* —1H **93**
Blore Ct. *SW8* —1H **93**
Blore Ct. *W1* —7H **61** (1C **148**)
Blossom Clo. *W5* —2E **72**
Blossom Clo. *Dag* —1F **69**
Blossom Clo. *S Croy* —5F **135**
Blossom La. *Enf* —1H **7**
Blossom St. *E1* —4E **62** (4H **145**)
Blossom Waye. *Houn* —6C **70**
Blount St. *E14* —6A **64**
Bloxam Gdns. *SE9* —5C **98**
Bloxhall Rd. *E10* —1B **48**
Bloxham Cres. *Hamp* —7D **102**
Bloxworth Clo. *Wall* —3G **133**
Bloxworth Gro. *N1* —1K **61**
Blucher Rd. *SE5* —7C **78**
Blue Anchor All. *Rich* —4E **88**
Blue Anchor La. *SE16* —4G **79**
Blue Anchor Yd. *E1* —7G **63**
Blue Ball Yd. *SW1*
 —1G **77** (5A **148**)
Bluebell Av. *E12* —5B **50**
Bluebell Clo. *SE26* —4F **111**
Bluebell Clo. *Wall* —1F **133**
Bluebell Way. *Ilf* —6F **51**

Blueberry Clo. *Wfd G* —6D **20**
Bluebird Wlk. *Wemb* —3H **41**
Bluefield Clo. *Hamp* —5E **102**
Bluegates. *Ewe* —7C **130**
Bluehouse Rd. *E4* —3B **20**
Blue Riband Ind. Est. *Croy*
 —2B **134**
Blundell Ho. *SE14* —7A **80**
 (off Goodwood Rd.)
Blundell Rd. *Edgw* —1K **25**
Blundell St. *N7* —7J **45**
Blunden Clo. *Dag* —1C **52**
Blunt Rd. *S Croy* —5D **134**
Blunts Rd. *SE9* —5E **98**
Blurton Rd. *E5* —4J **47**
Blydon Ct. N21 —5E *6*
 (off Chaseville Pk. Rd.)
Blyth Clo. *E14* —4F **81**
Blyth Clo. *Twic* —6K **87**
Blythe Clo. *SE6* —7B **96**
Blythe Hill. *SE6* —7B **96**
Blythe Hill. *Orp* —1K **129**
Blythe Hill La. *SE6* —7B **96**
Blythe Ho. *SE11* —6A **78** (7J **155**)
Blythe M. *W14* —3F **75**
Blythe Rd. *W14* —3F **75**
Blythe St. *E2* —3H **63**
Blythe Vale. *SE6* —1B **112**
Blyth Rd. *E17* —7B **32**
Blyth Rd. *SE28* —7C **68**
Blyth Rd. *Brom* —1H **127**
Blythswood Rd. *Ilf* —1A **52**
Blyth Wood Pk. *Brom* —1H **127**
Blythwood Rd. *N4* —7J **29**
Blythwood Rd. *Pinn* —1B **22**
Boades M. *NW3* —4B **44**
Boadicea St. *N1* —1K **61**
Boakes Clo. *NW9* —4J **25**
Boardman Av. *E4* —5J **9**
Boarhound. NW9 —2B *26*
 (off Further Acre)
Boars Head Yd. *Bren* —7D **72**
Boathouse Wlk. *SE15* —7G **79**
Boat Lifter Way. *SE16* —3A **80**
Bob Anker Clo. *E13* —3J **65**
Bobbin Clo. *SW4* —3G **93**
Bob Marley Way. *SE24* —4A **94**
Bockhampton Rd. *King T*
 —7F **105**
Bocking St. *E8* —1H **63**
Boddicott Clo. *SW19* —2G **107**
Boddington Ho. SE14 —1J *95*
 (off Pomeroy St.)
Boddys Bri. *SE1* —1A **78** (4K **149**)
Bodenay Ho. SE5 —1E *94*
 (off Peckham Rd.)
Bodiam Clo. *Enf* —2K **7**
Bodiam Rd. *SW16* —7H **109**
Bodley Clo. *N Mald* —5A **120**
Bodley Mnr. Way. *SW2* —7A **94**
Bodley Rd. *N Mald* —6K **119**
Bodmin. *NW9* —2B **26**
 (off Further Acre)
Bodmin Gro. *Mord* —5K **121**
Bodmin St. *SW18* —1J **107**
Bodnant Gdns. *SW20* —3C **120**
Bodney Rd. *E8* —5H **47**
Boeing Way. *S'hall* —3A **70**
Boevey Path. *Belv* —5F **85**
Bogey La. *Orp* —7E **138**
Bognor Rd. *Well* —1D **100**
Bohemia Pl. *E8* —6J **47**
Bohun Gro. *Barn* —6H **5**
Boileau Pde. W5 —6F *57*
 (off Boileau Rd.)

Boileau Rd. *SW13* —7C **74**
Boileau Rd. *W5* —6F **57**
Boisragon Ct. *Sidc* —5E **38**
Boldero Pl. *NW8*
 —4C **60** (4C **140**)
Bolderwood Way. *W Wick*
 —2D **136**
Boldmere Rd. *Pinn* —7A **22**
Boleyn Av. *Enf* —1C **8**
Boleyn Clo. *E17* —4C **32**
Boleyn Ct. *Buck H* —1D **20**
Boleyn Dri. *Ruis* —2B **38**
Boleyn Gdns. *Dag* —7J **53**
Boleyn Gdns. *W Wick* —2D **136**
Boleyn Gro. *W Wick* —2E **136**
Boleyn Rd. *E6* —2B **66**
Boleyn Rd. *E7* —7J **49**
Boleyn Rd. *N16* —5E **46**
Boleyn Way. *Barn* —3F **5**
Bolina Rd. *SE16* —5J **79**
Bolingbroke Gro. *SW11* —4C **92**
Bolingbroke Rd. *W14* —3F **75**
Bolingbroke Wlk. *SW11* —1B **92**
Bolliger Ct. *NW10* —4J **57**
Bollo Bri. Rd. *W3* —3H **73**
Bollo Ct. W3 —3J *73*
 (off Bollo Bri. Rd.)
Bollo La. *W3* & *W4* —2H **73**
Bolney Ga. *SW7*
 —2C **76** (7C **146**)
Bolney St. *SW8* —7K **77**
Bolney Way. *Felt* —3C **102**
Bolsover St. *W1* —4F **61** (4K **141**)
Bolstead Rd. *Mitc* —1F **123**
Bolster Gro. *N22* —1H **29**
Bolt Ct. *EC4* —6A **62** (1K **149**)
Boltmore Clo. *NW4* —3F **27**
Bolton Clo. *SE20* —2G **125**
Bolton Cres. *SE5* —7B **78**
Bolton Gdns. *NW10* —2F **59**
Bolton Gdns. *SW5* —5K **75**
Bolton Gdns. *Brom* —6H **113**
Bolton Gdns. *Tedd* —6A **104**
Bolton Gdns. M. *SW10* —5A **76**
Bolton Ho. SE10 —5G *81*
 (off Trafalgar Rd.)
Bolton Pl. *SW10* —5A **76**
Bolton Rd. *E15* —6H **49**
Bolton Rd. *N18* —5A **18**
Bolton Rd. *NW8* —1K **59**
Bolton Rd. *NW10* —1A **58**
Bolton Rd. *W4* —7J **73**
Bolton Rd. *Harr* —4G **23**
Boltons, The. *SW10* —5A **76**
Boltons, The. *Wemb* —4K **39**
Bolton St. *W1* —1F **77** (4K **147**)
Bolton Wlk. N7 —2K *45*
 (off Durham Rd.)
Bombay St. *SE16* —4H **79**
Bomore Rd. *W11* —7G **59**
Bonar Pl. *Chst* —7C **114**
Bonar Rd. *SE15* —7G **79**
Bonchester Clo. *Chst* —7E **114**
Bonchurch Clo. *Sutt* —7K **131**
Bonchurch Rd. *W10* —5G **59**
Bonchurch Rd. *W13* —1B **72**
Bond Ct. *EC4* —6D **62** (1E **150**)
Bondfield Rd. *E6* —5D **66**
Bond Gdns. *Wall* —4G **133**
Bond Ho. SE14 —7A *80*
 (off Goodwood Rd.)
Bonding Yd. Wlk. *SE16* —3A **80**
Bond Rd. *E15* —1D **64**
Bond Rd. *Mitc* —2C **122**
Bond St. *E15* —5G **49**

Bond St. *W4* —4K 73
Bond St. *W5* —7D 56
Bond Way. *SW8* —6J 77 (7F 155)
Boneta Rd. *SE18* —3D 82
Bonfield Rd. *SE13* —4E 96
Bonham Gdns. *Dag* —2D 52
Bonham Rd. *SW2* —5K 93
Bonham Rd. *Dag* —2D 52
Bonheur Rd. *W4* —2K 73
Bonhill St. *EC2* —4D 62 (4F 145)
Boniface Gdns. *Harr* —7A 10
Boniface Wlk. *Harr* —7A 10
Bon Marche Ter. *SE27* —4E 110
Bonner Hill Rd. *King T* —2F 119
Bonner Rd. *E2* —2J 63
Bonnersfield Clo. *Harr* —6K 23
Bonnersfield La. *Harr* —6K 23
Bonner St. *E2* —2K 63
Bonneville Gdns. *SW4* —6G 93
Bonnington Ct. *N'holt* —2B 54
  (off Gallery Gdns.)
Bonnington Sq. *SW8*
  —6K 77 (7G 155)
Bonny St. *NW1* —7G 45
Bonser Rd. *Twic* —2K 103
Bonsor St. *SE5* —7E 78
Bonville Gdns. *NW4* —4D 26
Bonville Rd. *Brom* —5H 113
Bookbinders Cottage Homes. *N20*
  —3J 15
Booker Clo. *E14* —5B 64
Booker Rd. *N18* —5B 18
Book M. *WC2* —6H 61 (1D 148)
Boone Ct. *N9* —3D 18
Boones Rd. *SE13* —4G 97
Boone St. *SE13* —4G 97
Boord St. *SE10* —3G 81
Boothby Ct. *E4* —3K 19
Boothby Rd. *N19* —2H 45
Booth Clo. *E9* —1H 63
Booth Clo. *SE28* —1B 84
Booth La. *EC4* —7C 62 (2C 150)
Boothman Ho. *Kent* —3D 24
Booth Rd. *NW9* —2K 25
Booth Rd. *Croy* —2B 134
Booth's Pl. *W1* —5G 61 (6B 142)
Boot Pde. *Edgw* —6B 12
  (off High St. Edgware.)
Boot St. *N1* —3E 62 (2G 145)
Bordars Rd. *W7* —5J 55
Bordars Wlk. *W7* —5J 55
Borden Av. *Enf* —6J 7
Border Cres. *SE26* —5H 111
Border Gdns. *Croy* —4D 136
Bordergate. *Mitc* —1D 122
Border Rd. *SE26* —5H 111
Bordesley Rd. *Mord* —4K 121
Bordon Wlk. *SW15* —7C 90
Boreham Av. *E16* —6J 65
Boreham Clo. *E11* —1E 48
Boreham Rd. *N22* —2C 30
Borgard Rd. *SE18* —4D 82
Borland Rd. *SE15* —4J 95
Borland Rd. *Tedd* —7B 104
Borneo St. *SW15* —3E 90
Borough High St. *SE1*
  —2C 78 (7D 150)
Borough Hill. *Croy* —3B 134
Borough Rd. *SE1*
  —3B 78 (1B 156)
Borough Rd. *Iswth* —1J 87
Borough Rd. *King T* —1G 119
Borough Rd. *Mitc* —2C 122
Borough Sq. *SE1*
  —2C 78 (7C 150)

Borrett Clo. *SE17*
  —5C 78 (6C 156)
Borrodaile Rd. *SW18* —6K 91
Borrowdale Av. *Harr* —2A 24
Borrowdale Clo. *IIf* —4C 34
Borrowdale Ct. *Enf* —1H 7
Borthwick M. *E15* —4G 49
Borthwick Rd. *E15* —4G 49
Borthwick Rd. *NW9* —6B 26
Borthwick St. *SE8* —5C 80
Borwick Av. *E17* —3B 32
Bosbury Rd. *SE6* —3E 112
Boscastle Rd. *NW5* —3F 45
Boscobel Pl. *SW1*
  —4E 76 (3H 153)
Boscobel St. *NW8*
  —4B 60 (4B 140)
Boscombe Av. *E10* —7F 33
Boscombe Clo. *E5* —5A 48
Boscombe Gdns. *SW16* —6J 109
Boscombe Rd. *SW17* —6E 108
Boscombe Rd. *SW19* —1J 121
Boscombe Rd. *W12* —1C 74
Boscombe Rd. *Wor Pk* —1E 130
Bosgrove. *E4* —2K 19
Boss Ho. *SE1* —2F 79 (6J 151)
  (off Boss St.)
Boss St. *SE1* —2F 79 (6J 151)
Bostall Hill. *SE2* —5A 84
Bostall La. *SE2* —5B 84
Bostall Mnr. Way. *SE2* —4B 84
Bostall Pk. Av. *Bexh* —7E 84
Bostall Rd. *Orp* —7B 118
Bostal Row. *Bexh* —3F 101
Bostock Ho. *Houn* —6E 70
Boston Bus. Pk. *W7* —3J 71
Boston Gdns. *W4* —6A 74
Boston Gdns. *W7* —4A 72
Boston Gdns. *Bren* —4A 72
Boston Mnr. Rd. *Bren* —4A 72
Boston Pde. *W7* —4A 72
Boston Pk. Rd. *Bren* —5C 72
Boston Pl. *NW1*
  —4D 60 (4E 140)
Boston Rd. *E6* —3C 66
Boston Rd. *E17* —6C 32
Boston Rd. *W7* —1J 71
Boston Rd. *Croy* —6K 123
Boston Rd. *Edgw* —7D 12
Bostonthorpe Rd. *W7* —2J 71
Boston Vale. *W7* —4A 72
Boswell Ct. *WC1* —5J 61 (5F 143)
Boswell Rd. *T Hth* —4C 124
Boswell St. *WC1* —5J 61 (5F 143)
Bosworth Clo. *E17* —1B 32
Bosworth Rd. *N11* —6C 16
Bosworth Rd. *W10* —4G 59
Bosworth Rd. *Barn* —3D 4
Bosworth Rd. *Dag* —3G 53
Botany Bay La. *Chst* —2G 129
Botany Clo. *New Bar* —4H 5
Boteley Clo. *E4* —2A 20
Botham Clo. *Edgw* —7D 12
Botha Rd. *E13* —5K 65
Bothwell Clo. *E16* —5H 65
Bothwell St. *W6* —6F 75
Bothwick St. *SE8* —5C 80
Botolph All. *EC3* —7E 62 (2G 151)
Botolph La. *EC3* —7E 62 (2G 151)
Botsford Rd. *SW20* —2G 121
Botts M. *W2* —6J 59
Boucher Clo. *Tedd* —5K 103
Boughton Av. *Brom* —7H 127
Boughton Rd. *SE28* —3J 83
Boulcott St. *E1* —6K 63

Boulevard, The. *SW17* —2E 108
Boulevard, The. *Pinn* —4E 22
  (in two parts)
Boulogne Rd. *Croy* —6C 124
Boulter Ho. *SE14* —1J 95
  (off Kender St.)
Boulton Ho. *Bren* —5E 72
Boulton Rd. *Dag* —2E 52
Boultwood Rd. *E6* —6D 66
Bounces La. *N9* —2C 18
Bounces Rd. *N9* —2C 18
Boundaries Rd. *SW12* —2D 108
Boundaries Rd. *Felt* —1A 102
Boundary Av. *E17* —7B 32
Boundary Clo. *SE20* —2G 125
Boundary Clo. *IIf* —4J 51
Boundary Clo. *King T* —3H 119
Boundary Clo. *S'hall* —5E 70
Boundary Ho. *SE18* —6A 18
  (off Snells Pk.)
Boundary La. *SE17*
  —6C 78 (7D 156)
Boundary La. *E13* —4B 66
Boundary La. *SE17*
  —6C 78 (7D 156)
Boundary M. *NW8* —1A 60
  (off Boundary Rd.)
Boundary Pas. *E2*
  —4F 63 (3J 145)
Boundary Rd. *E13* —2A 66
Boundary Rd. *N2* —1B 28
Boundary Rd. *N9* —6D 8
Boundary Rd. *N22* —3B 30
Boundary Rd. *NW8* —1K 59
Boundary Rd. *SW19* —6B 108
Boundary Rd. *Bark* —2G 67
  (in two parts)
Boundary Rd. *Cars & Wall*
  —6F 133
Boundary Rd. *Pinn* —7B 22
Boundary Rd. *Sidc* —5J 99
Boundary Rd. *Wemb* —3D 40
Boundary Row. *SE1*
  —2B 78 (6A 150)
Boundary St. *E2* —3F 63 (2J 145)
Boundary Way. *Croy* —5C 136
Boundfield Rd. *SE6* —3G 113
Bounds Grn. Ct. *N11* —6C 16
  (off Bounds Grn. Rd.)
Bounds Grn. Ind. Est. *N11*
  —6B 16
Bounds Grn. Rd. *N11 & N22*
  —6B 16
Bourbon Ho. *SE6* —5E 112
Bourchier St. *W1*
  —7H 61 (2C 148)
Bourdon Pl. *W1* —7F 61 (2K 147)
Bourdon Rd. *SE20* —2J 125
Bourdon St. *W1* —7F 61 (3J 147)
Bourke Clo. *NW10* —6A 42
Bourke Clo. *SW4* —6J 93
Bourlet Clo. *W1* —5G 61 (6A 142)
Bourn Av. *N15* —4D 30
Bournbrook Rd. *SE3* —3B 98
Bourne Av. *N14* —2D 16
Bourne Av. *Barn* —5G 5
Bourne Av. *Ruis* —5A 38
Bourne Ct. *W4* —6J 73
Bourne Ct. *S Ruis* —5A 38
Bourne Ct. *Wfd G* —2B 34
Bourne Dri. *Mitc* —2B 122
Bourne Est. *EC1*
  —5A 62 (5J 143)
Bourne Gdns. *E4* —4J 19
Bourne Hill. *N13* —2D 16

Bourne Hill Clo. *N13* —2E 16
Bourne Ind. Pk., The. *Dart*
  —5K 101
Bourne Mead. *Bex* —5K 101
Bourne M. *W1* —6E 60 (7H 141)
Bournemouth Rd. *SE15* —2G 95
Bournemouth Rd. *SW19* —1J 121
Bourne Pde. *Bex* —7H 101
Bourne Pl. *W4* —5K 73
Bourne Rd. *E7* —3H 49
Bourne Rd. *N8* —6J 29
Bourne Rd. *Bex & Dart* —7H 101
Bourne Rd. *Brom* —4B 128
Bournes Ho. *N15* —6E 30
  (off Chisley Rd.)
Bourneside Cres. *N14* —1C 16
Bourneside Gdns. *SE6* —5E 112
Bourne St. *SW1* —4E 76 (4G 153)
Bourne St. *Croy* —2B 134
Bourne Ter. *W2* —5K 59
Bourne, The. *N14* —1C 16
Bourne Vale. *Brom* —1H 137
Bournevale Rd. *SW16* —4J 109
Bourne View. *Gnfd* —6K 39
Bourne Way. *Brom* —2H 137
Bourne Way. *Sutt* —5H 131
Bournewood Rd. *SE18* —7A 84
Bournville Rd. *SE6* —7C 96
Bournwell Clo. *Barn* —3J 5
Bousfield Rd. *SE14* —2K 95
Boutflower Rd. *SW11* —4C 92
Bouverie Gdns. *Harr* —6D 24
Bouverie M. *N16* —2E 46
Bouverie Pl. *W2* —6B 60 (7B 140)
Bouverie Rd. *N16* —2E 46
Bouverie Rd. *Harr* —6G 23
Bouverie St. *EC4*
  —6A 62 (1K 149)
Bouvier Rd. *Enf* —1D 8
Boveney Rd. *SE23* —7K 95
Bovill Rd. *SE23* —7K 95
Bovingdon Av. *Wemb* —6G 41
Bovingdon Clo. *N19* —2G 45
Bovingdon La. *NW9* —1A 26
Bovingdon Rd. *SW6* —1K 91
Bovingdon Sq. *Mitc* —4J 123
Bowater Clo. *NW9* —5K 25
Bowater Clo. *SW2* —6J 93
Bowater Pl. *SE3* —7K 81
Bowater Rd. *SE18* —3B 82
Bow Bri. Est. *E3* —3D 64
Bow Chyd. *EC4* —6C 62 (1D 150)
Bow Comn. La. *E3* —4A 64
Bowden St. *SE11*
  —5A 78 (6K 155)
Bowditch. *SE8* —4B 80
Bowdon Rd. *E17* —7C 32
Bowen Dri. *SE21* —3E 110
Bowen Rd. *Harr* —7G 23
Bowen St. *E14* —6D 64
Bower Av. *SE10* —1G 97
Bower Clo. *N'holt* —2A 54
Bower Clo. *Romf* —1K 37
Bowerdean St. *SW6* —1K 91
Bowerman Av. *SE14* —6A 80
Bowerman Ct. *N19* —2H 45
  (off St John's Way)
Bower St. *E1* —6K 63
Bowers Wlk. *E6* —6D 66
Bowes Clo. *Sidc* —6B 100
Bowe's Ho. *Bark* —7F 51
Bowes Rd. *N11 & N13* —5B 16
Bowes Rd. *W3* —7A 58
Bowes Rd. *Dag* —4C 52
Bowfell Rd. *W6* —6E 74

Bowford Av. *Bexh* —1E 100
Bowhill Clo. *SW9* —7A 78
Bowie Clo. *SW4* —7H 93
Bow Ind. Pk. *E15* —7C 48
Bow Interchange. (Junct.)
  —2D 64
Bowland Rd. *SW4* —4H 93
Bowland Rd. *Wfd G* —5F 21
Bowland Yd. *SW1*
  —2D 76 (7F 147)
Bow La. *EC4* —6C 62 (1D 150)
Bow La. *N12* —7F 15
Bow La. *Mord* —6G 121
Bowl Ct. *EC2* —4E 62 (4H 145)
Bowles Rd. *SE1* —6G 79
Bowley Clo. *SE19* —6F 111
Bowley La. *SE19* —5F 111
Bowling Grn. Clo. *SW15* —7D 90
Bowling Grn. Ct. *Wemb* —2F 41
Bowling Grn. La. *EC1*
  —4A 62 (3K 143)
Bowling Grn. Pl. *SE1*
  —2D 78 (6E 150)
Bowling Grn. Row. *SE18* —3D 82
Bowling Grn. St. *SE11*
  —6A 78 (7J 155)
Bowling Grn. Wlk. *N1*
  —3E 62 (1G 145)
Bowls Clo. *Stan* —5G 11
Bowman Av. *E16* —7H 65
Bowman M. *SW18* —1H 107
Bowmans Clo. *W13* —1B 72
Bowmans Lea. *SE23* —7J 95
Bowmans Meadow. *Wall* —3F 133
Bowman's M. *E1* —7G 63
Bowman's M. *N7* —3J 45
Bowman's Pl. *N7* —3J 45
Bowmead. *SE9* —2D 114
Bowmore Wlk. *NW1* —7H 45
Bowness Clo. *E8* —6H 47
  (off Beechwood Rd.)
Bowness Cres. *SW15* —5A 106
Bowness Dri. *Houn* —4C 86
Bowness Ho. *SE15* —7J 79
  (off Hillbeck Clo.)
Bowness Rd. *SE6* —7D 96
Bowness Rd. *Bexh* —2H 101
Bowood Rd. *SW11* —5E 92
Bowood Rd. *Enf* —2E 8
Bow Rd. *E3* —3B 64
Bowrons Av. *Wemb* —7D 40
Bow St. *E15* —5G 49
Bow St. *WC2* —6J 61 (1F 149)
Bow Triangle Bus. Cen. *E3*
  —4C 64
Bowyer Clo. *E6* —5D 66
Bowyer St. *E4* —1K 19
  (off Ridgeway, The)
Bowyer Ho. *N1* —1E 62
  (off Whitmore Est.)
Bowyer Pl. *SE5* —7C 78
Bowyer St. *SE5* —7C 78
Boxall Rd. *SE21* —6E 94
Boxgrove Rd. *SE2* —3C 84
Box La. *Bark* —2B 68
Boxley Rd. *Mord* —4A 122
Boxley St. *E16* —1K 81
Boxmoor Ho. *W11* —1F 75
  (off Queensdale Cres.)
Boxmoor Rd. *Harr* —4B 24
Boxoll Rd. *Dag* —4F 53
Box Tree. Clo. *Buck H* —1H 21
Box Tree Ho. *SE8* —5A 80
Boxtree La. *Harr* —1G 23
Boxtree Rd. *Harr* —7C 10

Boxworth Clo. N12 —5G 15
Boxworth Gro. N1 —1K 61
Boyard Rd. SE18 —5F 83
Boyce Way. E13 —4J 65
Boycroft Av. NW9 —6J 25
Boyd Av. S'hall —1D 70
Boyd Clo. King T —7G 105
Boydell Ct. NW8 —7B 44
Boyden Ho. E17 —3E 32
Boyd Rd. SW19 —6B 108
Boyd St. E1 —6G 63
Boyfield St. SE1 —2B 78 (7B 156)
Boyland Av. Brom —5H 113
Boyle Av. Stan —6F 11
Boyle Farm Rd. Th Dit —6A 118
Boyle St. W1 —7G 61 (2A 148)
Boyne Av. NW4 —4F 27
Boyne Rd. SE13 —3E 96
Boyne Rd. Dag —3G 53
Boyne Ter. M. W11 —1H 75
Boyseland Ct. Edgw —2D 12
Boyson Rd. SE17
 —6D 78 (7D 156)
Boyson Wlk. SE17
 —6D 78 (7E 156)
Boyton Clo. E1 —4J 63
Boyton Clo. N8 —3J 29
Boyton Rd. N8 —3J 29
Brabant Ct. EC3 —7E 62 (2G 151)
Brabant Rd. N22 —2K 29
Brabazon Av. Wall —7J 133
Brabazon Rd. Houn —7A 70
Brabazon Rd. N'holt —2E 54
Brabazon St. E14 —6D 64
Brabourne Clo. SE19 —5E 110
Brabourne Cres. Bexh —6F 85
Brabourne Heights. NW7 —3F 13
Brabourne Rise. Beck —5E 126
Brabourn Gro. SE15 —2J 95
Brabrook Ct. Wall —4F 133
Bracer Ho. N1 —2E 62
 (off Whitmore Est.)
Bracewell Av. Gnfd —5K 39
Bracewell Rd. W10 —5E 58
Bracewood Gdns. Croy —3F 135
Bracey M. N4 —2J 45
Bracey St. N4 —2J 45
Bracken Av. SW12 —6E 92
Bracken Av. Croy —3D 136
Brackenbridge Dri. Ruis —3B 38
Brackenbury. N4 —1A 46
 (off Osborne Rd.)
Brackenbury Gdns. W6 —3D 74
Brackenbury Rd. N2 —3A 28
Brackenbury Rd. W6 —3D 74
Bracken Clo. E6 —5D 66
Bracken Clo. Twic —7E 86
Brackendale. N21 —2E 16
Brackendale Clo. Houn —1F 87
Brackendene. Dart —4K 117
Bracken End. Iswth —5H 87
Brackenfield Clo. E5 —3H 47
Bracken Gdns. SW13 —2C 90
Bracken Hill Clo. Brom —1H 127
Bracken Hill La. Brom —1H 127
Bracken Ind. Est. W12 —1K 35
Bracken M. E4 —1K 19
Bracken M. Romf —6H 37
Brackens. Beck —7C 112
Brackens, The. Enf —7K 7
Bracken, The. E4 —2K 19
Brackley Clo. Wall —7J 133
Brackley Rd. W4 —5A 74
Brackley Rd. Beck —7B 112
Brackley Sq. Wfd G —7G 21

Brackley St. EC1
 —4C 62 (4D 144)
Brackley Ter. W4 —5A 74
Bracklyn Ct. N1 —2D 62
Bracklyn St. N1 —2D 62
Bracknell Clo. N22 —1A 30
Bracknell Gdns. NW3 —4K 43
Bracknell Ga. NW3 —5K 43
Bracknell Way. NW3 —4K 43
Bracondale Rd. SE2 —4A 84
Bradbourne Rd. Belv —7G 101
Bradbourne St. SW6 —2J 91
Bradbury Clo. S'hall —4D 70
Bradbury St. N16 —5E 46
Braddock Clo. Iswth —2K 87
Braddon Rd. Rich —3F 89
Braddyll St. SE10 —5G 81
Bradenham Av. Well —4A 100
Bradenham Clo. SE17
 —6D 78 (7E 156)
Bradenham Rd. Harr —4B 24
Braden St. W9 —4K 59
Bradfield Dri. Bark —5A 52
Bradfield Rd. E16 —2J 81
Bradfield Rd. Ruis —5C 38
Bradford Clo. N17 —6A 18
Bradford Clo. SE26 —4H 111
Bradford Clo. Brom —1D 138
Bradford Dri. Eps —6B 130
Bradford Rd. W3 —2A 74
Bradford Rd. Ilf —1H 51
Bradgate Rd. SE6 —6D 96
Brading Cres. E11 —2K 49
Brading Rd. SW2 —7K 93
Brading Rd. Croy —6K 123
Brading Ter. W6 —3C 74
Bradiston Rd. W9 —3H 59
Bradley Clo. N7 —6J 45
Bradley Gdns. W13 —6B 56
Bradley Ho. SE16 —4J 79
 (off Raymouth Rd.)
Bradley M. SW17 —1D 108
Bradley Rd. N22 —2K 29
Bradley Rd. SE19 —6C 110
Bradley's Clo. N1 —2A 62
Bradley Stone Rd. E6 —6D 66
Bradman Row. Edgw —7D 12
Bradmead. SW8 —7F 77
Bradmore Pk. Rd. W6 —4D 74
Bradshaw Clo. SW19 —6J 107
Bradshaws Clo. SE25 —3G 125
Bradstock Ho. E9 —7A 48
Bradstock Rd. E9 —6K 47
Bradstock Rd. Eps —5C 130
Bradstone Rd. Rich —1F 89
Brad St. SE1 —1A 78 (5K 149)
Bradwell Av. Dag —2G 53
Bradwell Clo. E18 —4H 33
Bradwell M. N18 —4B 18
Bradwell Rd. Buck H —1H 21
Brady Ct. Dag —1D 52
Bradymead. E6 —6E 66
Brady St. E1 —4H 63
Braeburn Ct. Barn —4H 5
Braemar Av. N22 —1J 29
Braemar Av. NW10 —3K 41
Braemar Av. SW19 —2J 107
Braemar Av. Bexh —4J 101
Braemar Av. S Croy —7C 134
Braemar Av. T Hth —3B 124
Braemar Av. Wemb —7D 40
Braemar Gdns. NW9 —1K 25
Braemar Gdns. Sidc —3H 115
Braemar Gdns. W Wick —1E 136
Braemar Rd. E13 —4H 65

Braemar Rd. N15 —5E 30
Braemar Rd. Bren —6D 72
Braemar Rd. Wor Pk —3D 130
Braemer Clo. SE16 —5H 79
 (off Masters Dri.)
Braeside. Beck —5C 112
Braeside Av. SW19 —1G 121
Braeside Cres. Bexh —4J 101
Braeside Rd. SW16 —7G 109
Braes St. N1 —7B 46
Braesyde Clo. Belv —4F 85
Brafferton Rd. Croy —4C 134
Braganza St. SE17
 —5B 78 (5A 156)
Bragg Rd. Tedd —6J 103
Braham Ho. SE11
 —5K 77 (6H 155)
Braham St. E1 —6F 63 (1K 151)
Braid Av. W3 —6A 58
Braid Clo. Felt —2D 102
Braid Ho. SE10 —1E 96
 (off Blackheath Hill)
Braidwood Rd. SE6 —1F 113
Brailsford Clo. Mitc —7C 108
Brailsford Rd. SW2 —5A 94
Brainton Av. Felt —7A 86
Braintree Av. Ilf —4C 34
Braintree Rd. Dag —3G 53
Braintree Rd. Ruis —4A 38
Braintree St. E2 —3J 63
Braithwaite Av. Romf —7G 37
Braithwaite Gdns. Stan —1C 24
Braithwaite Ho. E14 —6E 64
Braithwaite Rd. Enf —3G 9
Braithwaite Tower. W2
 —5B 60 (5B 140)
Bramah Grn. SW9 —1A 94
Bramalea Clo. N6 —6E 28
Bramall Clo. E15 —5H 49
Bramall Ct. N7 —6K 45
 (off Georges Rd.)
Bramber. WC1 —3J 61 (2E 142)
Bramber Ho. W5 —4E 72
Bramber Ct. Bren —4E 72
Bramber Rd. N12 —5H 15
Bramber Rd. W14 —6H 75
Brambleacres Clo. Sutt —7J 131
Bramblebury Rd. SE18 —5G 83
Bramble Clo. N15 —4G 31
Bramble Clo. Croy —4C 136
Bramble Clo. Stan —7J 11
Bramble Croft. Eri —4J 85
Brambledown Clo. W Wick
 —5G 127
Brambledown Rd. Cars & Wall
 —7E 132
Brambledown Rd. S Croy
 —7E 134
Bramble Gdns. W12 —7B 58
Bramble La. Hamp —6D 102
Brambles Clo. Iswth —7B 72
Brambles, The. SW19 —5H 107
 (off Woodside)
Bramblewood Clo. Cars —1C 132
Bramblings, The. E4 —4A 20
Bramcote Av. Mitc —4D 122
Bramcote Gro. SE16 —5J 79
Bramcote Rd. SW15 —4D 90
Bramdean Cres. SE12 —1J 113
Bramdean Gdns. SE12 —1J 113
Bramerton Rd. Beck —3B 126
Bramerton St. SW3
 —6C 76 (7C 152)
Bramfield Ct. N4 —3C 46
 (off Queens Dri.)

Bramfield Rd. SW11 —6C 92
Bramford Ct. N14 —2C 16
Bramford Rd. SW18 —4A 92
Bramham Gdns. SW5 —5K 75
Bramham Ho. SE22 —4E 94
Bramhope La. SE7 —6A 82
Bramlands Clo. SW11 —3C 92
Bramley Clo. E17 —2A 32
Bramley Clo. N14 —5A 6
Bramley Clo. Orp —7F 129
Bramley Clo. S Croy —5C 134
Bramley Clo. Twic —6G 87
Bramley Ct. E4 —1K 19
Bramley Ct. Barn —4H 5
Bramley Ct. S'hall —7F 55
 (off Baird Av.)
Bramley Ct. Well —1B 100
Bramley Cres. SW8 —7H 77
Bramley Cres. Ilf —6E 34
Bramley Hill. S Croy —5B 134
Bramley Ho. SW15 —6B 90
 (off Tunworth Cres.)
Bramley Ho. W10 —6F 59
Bramley Ho. Houn —4D 86
Bramley Pde. N14 —4B 6
Bramley Rd. N14 —5A 6
Bramley Rd. W5 —3C 72
Bramley Rd. W10 —7F 59
Bramley Rd. Cheam —7F 131
Bramley Rd. Sutt —5B 132
Bramley St. W10 —6F 59
Bramley Way. Houn —5D 86
Bramley Way. W Wick —2D 136
Brampton Clo. E5 —2H 47
Brampton Ct. NW4 —4D 26
Brampton Gdns. N15 —5C 30
Brampton Gro. NW4 —4D 26
Brampton Gro. Harr —4A 24
Brampton Gro. Wemb —1F 41
Brampton La. NW4 —4E 26
Brampton Pk. Rd. N22 —3A 30
Brampton Rd. E6 —3B 66
Brampton Rd. N15 —5C 30
Brampton Rd. NW9 —4G 25
Brampton Rd. Bexh & SE2
 —3D 100
Brampton Rd. Croy —6F 125
Bramshaw Rise. N Mald —6A 120
Bramshaw Rd. E9 —6K 47
Bramshill Gdns. NW5 —3F 45
Bramshill Rd. NW10 —2A 58
Bramshot Av. SE7 —6J 81
Bramston Rd. NW10 —2C 58
Bramston Rd. SW17 —3A 108
Bramwell Ho. SE1
 —3C 78 (2D 156)
Bramwell M. N1 —1K 61
Brancaster Dri. NW7 —7H 13
Brancaster Rd. E12 —4D 50
Brancaster Rd. SW16 —3J 109
Brancaster Rd. Ilf —6J 35
Brancepeth Gdns. Buck H —2D 20
Branch Hill. NW3 —3A 44
Branch Hill Ho. NW3 —3A 43
Branch Pl. N1 —1D 62
Branch Rd. E14 —7A 64
Branch St. SE15 —7F 79
Brancker Clo. Wall —7J 133
Brancker Rd. Harr —3D 24
Brancroft Way. Enf —1F 9
Brandlehow Rd. SW15 —4H 91
Brandon. NW9 —2B 26
 (off Further Acre)
Brandon Est. SE17
 —6B 78 (7A 156)

Brandon Ho. Beck —5D 112
 (off Beckenham Hill Rd.)
Brandon Mans. W14 —6G 75
 (off Queen's Club Gdns.)
Brandon M. EC2
 —5D 62 (6E 144)
Brandon Rd. E17 —4E 32
Brandon Rd. N7 —7J 45
Brandon Rd. S'hall —5D 70
Brandon Rd. Sutt —4K 131
Brandon St. SE17
 —4C 78 (4C 156)
Brandram Rd. SE13 —3G 97
Brandreth Ct. Harr —6K 23
Brandreth Rd. E6 —6D 66
Brandreth Rd. SW17 —2F 109
Brandries, The. Wall —3H 133
Brand St. SE10 —7E 80
Brandville Gdns. Ilf —4F 35
Brandy Way. Sutt —7J 131
Brangbourne Rd. Brom —5E 112
Brangton Rd. SE11
 —5A 78 (6H 155)
Brangwyn Ct. W14 —3G 75
 (off Blythe Rd.)
Brangwyn Cres. SW19 —1A 122
Branksea St. SW6 —7G 75
Branksome Av. N18 —6A 18
Branksome Rd. SW8 —7K 77
 (off Meadow Rd.)
Branksome Rd. SW2 —5J 93
Branksome Rd. SW19 —1J 121
Branksome Way. Harr —6D 24
Branksome Way. N Mald —1J 119
Branksome Ct. N2 —3A 28
Branscombe Ct. Brom —5H 127
Branscombe Gdns. N21 —7F 7
Branscombe St. SE13 —3D 96
Bransdale Clo. NW6 —1J 59
Bransgrove Rd. Edgw —1F 25
Branston Cres. Orp —7H 129
Branstone Rd. Rich —1F 89
Brants Wlk. W7 —4J 55
Brantwood Av. Eri —7K 85
Brantwood Av. Iswth —4A 88
Brantwood Clo. E17 —3E 32
Brantwood Gdns. Enf —4D 6
Brantwood Gdns. Ilf —4C 34
Brantwood Ho. SE5 —7C 78
 (off Wyndam Est.)
Brantwood Rd. N17 —6B 18
Brantwood Rd. SE24 —5C 94
Brantwood Rd. Bexh —2H 101
Brantwood Rd. S Croy —7C 134
Brasher Clo. Gnfd —5H 39
Brassett Point. E15 —1G 65
 (off Abbey Rd.)
Brassey Rd. NW6 —6H 43
Brassey Sq. SW11 —3E 92
Brassie Av. W3 —6A 58
Brass Tally All. SE16 —2K 79
Brasted Clo. SE26 —4J 111
Brasted Clo. Bexh —5D 100
Brasted Lodge. SE20 —7C 112
Brasted Rd. Eri —7K 85
Brathway Rd. SW18 —7K 91
Bratley St. E1 —4G 63
Bratten Ct. Croy —6D 124
Braund Av. Gnfd —4F 55
Braundton Av. Sidc —1K 115
Braunston Dri. Hayes —4C 54
Bravington Pl. W9 —4H 59
Bravington Rd. W9 —3H 59
Braxfield Rd. SE4 —4A 96
Braxted Pk. SW16 —6K 109

Brayards Rd. *SE15* —2H **95**
Brayards Rd. Est. *SE15* —2J **95**
(off Brayards Rd.)
Braybourne Dri. *iswth* —7K **71**
Braybrooke Gdns. *SE19* —7F **111**
Braybrook St. *W12* —5B **58**
Brayburne Av. *SW4* —2G **93**
Bray Cl. *SW16* —5J **109**
Bray Cres. *SE16* —2K **79**
Braydon Rd. *N16* —1G **47**
Bray Dri. *E16* —7H **65**
Brayfield Ter. *N1* —7A **46**
Brayford Sq. *E1* —6J **63**
Bray Pas. *E16* —7J **65**
Bray Pl. *SW3* —4D **76** (4E **152**)
Bray Rd. *NW7* —6A **14**
Brayton Rd. *Enf* —4C **6**
Braywood Rd. *SE9* —4H **99**
Brazil Clo. *Bedd* —7J **123**
Breach La. *Dag* —3G **69**
Bread St. *EC4* —6C **62** (1D **150**)
Breakspears Dri. *Orp* —7A **116**
Breakspears M. *SE4* —2B **96**
Breakspears Rd. *SE4* —4B **96**
Bream Clo. *N17* —4H **31**
Bream Gdns. *E6* —3E **66**
Breamore Clo. *SW15* —1C **106**
Breamore Rd. *Ilf* —2K **51**
Bream's Bldgs. *EC4*
        —6A **62** (7J **143**)
Bream St. *E3* —7C **48**
Breamwater Gdns. *Rich* —3B **104**
Brearley Clo. *Edgw* —7D **12**
Breasley Clo. *SW15* —4E **90**
Brecknock M. *N7* —5H **45**
Brecknock Rd. *N19 & N7* —4G **45**
Brecknock Est. *N19* —4G **45**
Breckonmead. *Brom* —2A **128**
Brecon Clo. *Mitc* —3J **123**
Brecon Clo. *Wor Pk* —2E **130**
Brecon Grn. *NW9* —6A **26**
Brecon Rd. *W6* —6G **75**
Brecon Rd. *Enf* —4D **8**
Brede Clo. *E6* —3E **66**
Bredgar Rd. *N19* —2G **45**
Bredhurst Clo. *SE20* —6J **111**
Bredo Ho. *Bark* —3B **68**
Bredon Rd. *Croy* —7F **125**
Breer St. *SW6* —3K **91**
Breezer's Hill. *E1* —7G **63**
Brember Rd. *Harr* —2G **39**
Bremer M. *E17* —4D **32**
Bremner Rd. *SW7*
        —3A **76** (1A **152**)
Brenchley Clo. *Brom* —6H **127**
Brenchley Clo. *Chst* —1E **128**
Brenchley Gdns. *SE23* —6J **95**
Brenchley Rd. *Orp* —2K **129**
Brenda Rd. *SW17* —2D **108**
Brendon Av. *NW10* —5A **42**
Brendon Ct. *S'hall* —4F **71**
Brendon Gdns. *Harr* —4F **39**
Brendon Gdns. *Ilf* —5J **35**
Brendon Gro. *N2* —2A **28**
Brendon Rd. *SE9* —2H **115**
Brendon Rd. *Dag* —1F **53**
Brendon St. *W1* —6C **60** (7D **140**)
Brendon Vs. *N21* —1H **17**
Brendon Way. *Enf* —7K **7**
Brenley Clo. *Mitc* —3E **122**
Brenley Gdns. *SE9* —4B **98**
Brennand Ct. *N19* —3G **45**
Brent Clo. *Bex* —1E **116**
Brentcot Clo. *W13* —4B **56**
Brent Ct. *NW11* —7F **27**

Brent Ct. *W7* —7H **55**
Brent Cres. *NW10* —2F **57**
Brent Cross Fly-Over. *NW2*
        —7F **27**
Brent Cross Gdns. *NW4* —6F **27**
Brent Cross Interchange. (Junct.)
        —7F **27**
Brent Cross Shop. Cen. *NW4*
        —7E **26**
Brentfield. *NW10* —7H **41**
Brentfield Clo. *NW10* —6K **41**
Brentfield Gdns. *NW2* —7F **27**
Brentfield Ho. *NW10* —7K **41**
Brentfield Rd. *NW10* —6K **41**
Brentford Bus. Cen. *Bren* —7C **72**
Brentford Clo. *Hayes* —4B **54**
Brentford Ho. *Twic* —7B **88**
Brent Grn. *NW4* —5E **26**
Brent Grn. Wlk. *Wemb* —3J **41**
Brentham Way. *W5* —4D **56**
Brenthouse Rd. *E9* —6J **47**
Brenthurst Rd. *NW10* —6B **42**
Brent Lea. *Bren* —7C **72**
Brentmead Clo. *W7* —7J **55**
Brentmead Gdns. *NW10* —2F **57**
Brentmead Pl. *NW11* —6F **27**
Brenton St. *E14* —6A **64**
Brent Pk. Ind. Est. *W7* —3A **70**
Brent Pk. Rd. *NW9 & NW4*
        (in two parts) —7C **26**
Brent Pl. *Barn* —5C **4**
Brent Rd. *E16* —6J **65**
Brent Rd. *SE18* —7F **83**
Brent Rd. *Bren* —6C **72**
Brent Rd. *S'hall* —3A **70**
Brent Rd. *S Croy* —7H **135**
Brent Side. *Bren* —6C **72**
Brentside Clo. *W13* —4A **56**
Brentside Executive Cen. *Bren*
        —6C **72**
Brent St. *NW4* —4E **26**
Brent Ter. *NW2* —1E **42**
Brent Trad. Cen. *NW10* —5A **42**
Brentvale Av. *S'hall* —1H **71**
Brentvale Av. *Wemb* —1F **57**
Brent View Rd. *NW9* —6C **26**
Brentwaters Bus. Pk. *Bren*
        —7C **72**
Brent Way. *N3* —6D **14**
Brent Way. *Bren* —7D **72**
Brent Way. *Wemb* —6H **41**
Brentwick Gdns. *Bren* —4E **72**
Brentwood Clo. *SE9* —1G **115**
Brentwood Lodge. *NW4* —5F **27**
(off Holmdale Gdns.)
Brereton Rd. *N17* —7A **18**
Bressenden Pl. *SW1*
        —3F **77** (1K **153**)
Bressey Av. *Enf* —1B **8**
Bressey Gro. *E18* —2H **33**
Breton Ho. *EC1* —5C **62** (4D **144**)
Brett Clo. *N16* —2E **46**
Brett Clo. *N'holt* —3B **54**
Brett Ct. *N9* —2D **18**
Brett Cres. *NW10* —1K **57**
Brettell St. *SE17* —5D **78** (6F **157**)
Brettenham Av. *E17* —1C **32**
Brettenham Rd. *E17* —2C **32**
Brettenham Rd. *N18* —4B **18**
Brett Gdns. *Dag* —7E **52**
Brett Ho. Clo. *SW15* —7F **91**
Brett Pas. *E8* —5H **47**
Brett Rd. *E8* —5H **47**
Brewer's Grn. *SW1*
        —3G **77** (1C **154**)

Brewers La. *Rich* —5D **88**
Brewer St. *W1* —7G **61** (2B **148**)
Brewery Clo. *Wemb* —5A **40**
Brewery La. *Twic* —7K **87**
Brewery M. Cen. *Iswth* —3A **88**
Brewery Rd. *N7* —7J **45**
Brewery Rd. *SE18* —5H **83**
Brewery Rd. *Brom* —1C **138**
Brewery Sq. *SE1* —1F **79** (5J **151**)
Brewhouse La. *E1* —1H **79**
Brewhouse Rd. *SE18* —4D **82**
Brewhouse St. *SW15* —3G **91**
Brewhouse Wlk. *SE16* —1A **80**
Brewhouse Yd. *EC1*
        —4B **62** (3A **144**)
Brewood Rd. *Dag* —6B **52**
Brewster Gdns. *W10* —5E **58**
Brewster Rd. *E10* —1D **48**
Brian Rd. *Romf* —5C **36**
Briant Ho. *SE1* —3K **77** (2J **155**)
Briant St. *SE14* —1K **95**
Briar Av. *SW16* —7K **109**
Briarbank Rd. *W13* —6A **56**
Briar Clo. *N2* —3K **27**
Briar Clo. *N13* —3H **17**
Briar Clo. *Buck H* —2G **21**
Briar Clo. *Hamp* —5D **102**
Briar Clo. *Iswth* —5K **87**
Briar Ct. *E8* —7F **47**
Briar Ct. *Sutt* —4E **130**
Briar Cres. *N'holt* —6F **39**
Briardale Gdns. *NW3* —3J **43**
Briarfield Av. *N3* —2K **27**
Briar Gdns. *Brom* —1H **137**
Briaris Clo. *N17* —7C **18**
Briar La. *Croy* —4D **136**
Briar Rd. *NW2* —4E **42**
Briar Rd. *SW16* —3J **123**
Briar Rd. *Bex* —3K **117**
Briar Rd. *Harr* —5C **24**
Briar Rd. *Twic* —1J **103**
Briars, The. *Bush* —1D **10**
Briar Wlk. *SW15* —4D **90**
Briar Wlk. *W10* —4G **59**
Briar Wlk. *Edgw* —7D **12**
Briarwood Clo. *NW9* —6J **25**
Briarwood Ct. *Wor Pk* —1C **130**
(off Avenue, The)
Briarwood Rd. *SW4* —5H **93**
Briarwood Rd. *Eps* —6C **130**
Briary Clo. *NW3* —7C **44**
Briary Ct. *Sidc* —5B **116**
Briary Gdns. *Brom* —5K **113**
Briary Gro. *Edgw* —2H **25**
Briary La. *N9* —3A **18**
Brick Ct. *EC4* —6A **62** (1J **149**)
Brick Farm Clo. *Rich* —1H **89**
Brickfield Clo. *Bren* —7C **72**
Brickfield Cotts. *SE18* —6K **83**
Brickfield Rd. *SW19* —4K **107**
Brickfield Rd. *T Hth* —1B **124**
Brickfields. *Harr* —2H **39**
        (in two parts)
Brick La. *E2 & E1*
        —3F **63** (2K **145**)
Brick La. *Enf* —2C **8**
Brick La. *Stan* —7J **11**
Bricklayers Arms. (Junct.)
        —3D **78**
Bricklayers Arms Bus. Cen. *SE1*
        —4E **78** (3H **157**)
Brick St. *W1* —1F **77** (5J **147**)
Brickwood Clo. *SE26* —3H **111**

Brickwood Rd. *Croy* —2E **134**
Brideale Clo. *SE15* —6F **79**
Bride Ct. *EC4* —6B **62** (1A **150**)
Bride La. *EC4* —6B **62** (1A **150**)
Bride St. *N7* —6K **45**
Bridewain St. *SE1*
        —3F **79** (1J **157**)
Bridewell Pl. *E1* —1H **79**
Bridewell Pl. *EC4*
        —6B **62** (1A **150**)
Bridford M. *W1* —5F **61** (5K **141**)
Bridge App. *NW1* —7E **44**
Bridge Av. *W6* —4E **74**
Bridge Clo. *W10* —6F **59**
Bridge Clo. *Enf* —2C **8**
Bridge Clo. *Romf* —6K **37**
Bridge Clo. *Tedd* —4K **103**
Bridge Ct. *E10* —1D **48**
Bridge Dri. *N13* —4E **16**
Bridge End. *E17* —1E **32**
Bridgefield Rd. *Sutt* —6J **131**
Bridge Foot. *SE1*
        —5J **77** (6F **155**)
Bridge Ga. *N21* —7H **7**
Bridge Ho. E9 —6K 47
        (off Shepherds La.)
Bridge Ho. *SE4* —4B **96**
Bridge Ho. Sutt —6K 131
        (off Bridge Rd.)
Bridge Ho. Quay. *E14* —1E **80**
Bridgeland Rd. *E16* —7J **65**
Bridge La. *NW11* —4G **27**
Bridge La. *SW11* —1C **92**
Bridgeman Rd. *N1* —7K **45**
Bridgeman Rd. *Tedd* —6A **104**
Bridgeman St. *NW8* —2C **60**
Bridge Meadows. *SE14* —6K **79**
Bridgend Rd. *SW18* —4A **92**
Bridgenhall Rd. *Enf* —1A **8**
Bridgen Rd. *Bex* —7E **100**
Bridgepark. *SW18* —5J **91**
Bridge Pl. *SW1* —4F **77** (3K **153**)
Bridge Pl. *Croy* —1D **134**
Bridgeport Pl. *E1* —1G **79**
Bridge Rd. *E6* —7D **50**
Bridge Rd. *E15* —7F **49**
Bridge Rd. *E17* —7B **32**
Bridge Rd. *N9* —3B **18**
Bridge Rd. *N22* —1J **29**
Bridge Rd. *NW10* —6A **42**
Bridge Rd. *Beck* —7B **112**
Bridge Rd. *Bexh* —2E **100**
Bridge Rd. *Houn & Iswth* —3H **87**
Bridge Rd. *S'hall* —2D **70**
Bridge Rd. *Sutt* —6K **131**
Bridge Rd. *Twic* —6B **88**
Bridge Rd. *Wall* —5G **133**
Bridge Rd. *Wemb* —3G **41**
Bridge Row. *Croy* —1D **134**
Bridges Ct. *SW11* —2B **92**
        (in two parts)
Bridges Ho. SE5 —7D 78
        (off Elmington Est.)
Bridges La. *Croy* —4J **133**
Bridges Pl. *SW6* —1H **91**
Bridges Rd. *SW19* —6K **107**
Bridges Rd. *Stan* —5E **10**
Bridges Rd. M. *SW19* —6K **107**
Bridge St. *SW1* —2J **77** (7E **148**)
Bridge St. *W4* —4K **73**
Bridge St. *Pinn* —3C **22**
Bridge St. *Rich* —5D **88**
Bridge Ter. *E15* —7F **49**
        (in two parts)

Bridge, The. *Harr* —4K **23**
Bridgetown Clo. *SE19* —5E **110**
Bridge View. *W6* —5E **74**
Bridgewalk Heights. *SE1*
        —2D **78** (6F **151**)
        (off Weston St.)
Bridgewater Clo. *Chst* —3J **129**
Bridgewater Gdns. *Edgw* —2F **25**
Bridgewater Highwalk. *EC2*
        —5C **62** (5C **144**)
Bridgewater Rd. *E15* —1E **64**
Bridgewater Rd. *Wemb* —6C **40**
Bridgewater Sq. *EC2*
        —5C **62** (5C **144**)
Bridgewater St. *EC2*
        —5C **62** (5C **144**)
Bridge Way. *N11* —3B **16**
Bridge Way. *NW11* —5H **27**
Bridgeway. *Bark* —7K **51**
Bridge Way. *Twic* —7G **87**
Bridge Way. *Wemb* —7E **40**
Bridge Wharf. *E3* —2K **63**
Bridge Wharfe Rd. *Iswth* —3B **88**
Bridge Wharf Rd. *Iswth* —3B **88**
Bridgewood Clo. *SE20* —7H **111**
Bridgewood Rd. *SW16* —7H **109**
Bridgewood Rd. *Wor Pk* —4C **130**
Bridge Yd. *SE1* —1D **78** (4F **151**)
Bridgman Rd. *W4* —3J **73**
Bridle Clo. *King T* —4D **118**
Bridle La. *W1* —7G **61** (2B **148**)
Bridle La. *Twic* —6B **88**
Bridle Path. *Croy* —3J **133**
Bridle Path, The. *E4* —7B **20**
Bridle Rd. *Croy* —3C **136**
        (in two parts)
Bridle Rd. *Pinn* —6A **22**
Bridle Rd. *S Croy* —7J **135**
Bridle Way. *Croy* —4C **136**
Bridleway, The. *Wall* —5G **133**
Bridlington Rd. *N9* —7C **8**
Bridport Av. *Romf* —6H **37**
Bridport Ho. N1 —1D 62
        (off Colville Est.)
Bridport Pl. *N1* —1D **62**
        (in two parts)
Bridport Rd. *N18* —5K **17**
Bridport Rd. *Gnfd* —1F **55**
Bridport Rd. *T Hth* —3A **124**
Bridport Ter. *SW8* —1H **93**
Bridstow Pl. *W2* —6J **59**
Brief St. *SE5* —1B **94**
Brierley. *New Ad* —6D **136**
        (in two parts)
Brierley Av. *N9* —1D **18**
Brierley Clo. *SE25* —4G **125**
Brierley Rd. *E11* —4F **49**
Brierley Rd. *SW12* —2G **109**
Brierly Gdns. *E2* —2J **63**
Brigade Clo. *Harr* —2H **39**
Brigade St. *SE3* —2H **97**
Brigadier Av. *Enf* —1H **7**
Brigadier Hill. *Enf* —1H **7**
Briggeford Clo. *E5* —2G **47**
Briggs Clo. *Mitc* —1F **123**
Bright Clo. *Belv* —4D **84**
Brightfield Rd. *SE12* —5G **97**
Brightling Rd. *SE4* —6B **96**
Brightlingsea Pl. *E14* —7B **64**
Brightman Rd. *SW18* —1B **108**
Brighton Av. *E17* —5B **32**
Brighton Dri. *N'holt* —6E **38**
Brighton Gro. *SE14* —1A **96**
Brighton Rd. *E6* —3E **66**

Brighton Rd. N2 —2A 28
Brighton Rd. N16 —4E 46
Brighton Rd. S Croy —5C 134
Brighton Rd. Surb —6C 118
Brighton Rd. Surb —7K 131
Brighton Ter. SW9 —4K 93
Brightside Rd. SE13 —6F 97
Brightside, The. Enf —1F 9
Bright St. E14 —6D 64
Brightwell Clo. Croy —1A 134
Brightwell Cres. SW17 —5D 108
Brig M. SE8 —6C 80
Brigstock Ho. SE5 —2C 94
Brigstock Rd. Belv —4H 85
Brigstock Rd. T Hth —5A 124
Brill Pl. NW1 —2H 61 (1D 142)
Brim Hill. N2 —4A 28
Brimpsfield Clo. SE2 —3B 84
Brimsdown Av. Enf —2F 9
Brimsdown Ind. Est. Enf —1G 9
(in two parts)
Brimstone Ho. E15 —7G 49
(off Victoria St.)
Brindle Ga. Sidc —1J 115
Brindley Clo. Bexh —3H 101
Brindley Ga. Gnfd —1D 56
Brindley St. SE14 —1B 96
Brindley Way. Brom —5J 113
Brindley Way. S'hall —7F 55
Brindwood Rd. E4 —3G 19
Brinkburn Clo. SE2 —4A 84
Brinkburn Clo. Edgw —3H 25
Brinkburn Gdns. Edgw —2G 25
Brinkley Rd. Wor Pk —2D 130
Brinklow Cres. SE18 —7F 83
Brinklow Ho. W2 —5K 59
(off Torquay St.)
Brinkworth Rd. Ilf —3C 34
Brinkworth Way. E9 —6B 48
Brinsdale Rd. NW4 —3F 27
Brinsley Rd. Harr —2H 23
Brinsley St. E1 —6H 63
Brinsworth Clo. Twic —2H 103
Brinsworth Ho. Twic —2H 103
Brinton Wlk. SE1
—1B 78 (5A 150)
Brion Pl. E14 —5E 64
Brisbane Av. SW19 —1K 121
Brisbane Rd. E10 —2D 48
Brisbane Rd. W13 —2A 72
Brisbane Rd. Ilf —7F 35
Brisbane St. SE5 —7D 78
Briscoe Clo. E11 —3H 49
Briscoe Rd. SW19 —6B 108
Briset Rd. SE9 —3B 98
Briset St. EC1 —5B 62 (5A 144)
Briset Way. N7 —2K 45
Bristol Gdns. SW15 —7E 90
Bristol Gdns. W9 —4K 59
Bristol Ho. SE11 —3A 78 (2J 155)
Bristol Ho. Bark —7A 52
(off Margaret Bondfield Av.)
Bristol M. W9 —4K 59
Bristol Pk. Rd. E17 —4A 32
Bristol Rd. E7 —6A 50
Bristol Rd. Gnfd —1F 55
Bristol Rd. Mord —5A 122
Briston Gro. N8 —6J 29
Briston M. NW7 —7H 13
Bristow Rd. SE19 —5E 110
Bristow Rd. Bexh —1E 100
Bristow Rd. Croy —4J 133
Bristow Rd. Houn —3G 87
Britannia Clo. SW4 —4H 93
Britannia Clo. N'holt —3B 54

Britannia Ga. E16 —1J 81
Britannia Junction. (Junct.)
—1F 61
Britannia La. Twic —7G 87
Britannia Rd. E14 —4C 80
Britannia Rd. N12 —3F 15
Britannia Rd. SW6 —7K 75
Britannia Rd. Ilf —3F 51
Britannia Rd. Surb —7F 119
Britannia Row. N1 —1B 62
Britannia St. WC1
—3K 61 (1G 143)
Britannia Wlk. N1
(in two parts) —2D 62 (1E 144)
Britannia Way. NW10 —4H 57
Britannia Way. SW6 —7K 75
Britannic Tower. EC2
—5D 62 (5E 144)
British Gro. W4 —5B 74
British Gro. Pas. W4 —5B 74
British Gro. S. W4 —5C 74
British Legion Rd. E4 —2C 20
British St. E3 —3B 64
British Wharf Ind. Est. SE14
—6K 79
Brittain Ho. SE9 —1C 114
Brittain Rd. Dag —3E 52
Brittania Junct. NW1 —1F 61
Brittany Point. SE11
—4A 78 (4J 155)
Britten Clo. NW11 —1K 43
Britten Ct. E15 —2F 65
Britten Dri. S'hall —6E 54
Brittens Ct. E1 —7G 63
Britten St. SW3 —5C 76 (6C 152)
Britton Clo. SE6 —7F 97
Britton St. EC1 —4B 62 (4A 144)
Brixham Gdns. Ilf —5J 51
Brixham Rd. Well —1D 100
Brixton Est. Edgw —2H 25
Brixton Hill. SW2 —7J 93
Brixton Hill Ct. SW2 —5K 93
Brixton Hill Pl. SW2 —7J 93
Brixton Oval. SW2 —4A 94
Brixton Rd. SW9 & SE11
—4A 94 (7J 155)
Brixton Sta. Rd. SW9 —3A 94
Brixton Water La. SW2 —5K 93
Broadbent Clo. N6 —1F 45
Broadbent St. W1
—7F 61 (2J 147)
Broadbridge Clo. SE3 —7J 81
Broadbury Ct. N18 —6C 18
Broad Comn. Est. N16 —1G 47
(off Osbaldeston Rd.)
Broadcoombe. S Croy —7K 135
Broad Ct. WC2 —6J 61 (1F 149)
Broadcroft Av. Stan —2D 24
Broadcroft Rd. Orp —7H 129
Broadfield Clo. NW2 —3E 42
Broadfield Clo. Croy —2J 133
Broadfield Ct. Bush —2D 10
Broadfield Ct. N Har —1F 23
(off Broadfields)
Broadfield Heights. NW7 —4C 12
Broadfield La. NW1 —7H 45
Broadfield Rd. SE6 —7G 97
Broadfields. Harr —2F 23
Broadfields Av. N21 —7F 7
Broadfields Av. Edgw —4C 12
Broadfields Cen. Edgw —1C 12
Broadfield Sq. Enf —2C 8
Broadfields Way. NW10 —5B 42
Broadfield Way. Buck H —3F 21

Broadgate. EC2 —4E 62 (5G 145)
Broadgate Circ. EC2
—5E 62 (6G 145)
Broadgate Ct. EC2
—5E 62 (5G 145)
Broadgate Rd. E16 —6B 66
Broadgates Av. Barn —1E 4
Broadgates Rd. SW18 —1B 108
Broad Grn. Av. Croy —7B 124
Broadhead Strand. NW9 —1B 26
Broadheath Dri. Chst —5D 114
Broadhinton Rd. SW4 —3F 93
Broadhurst Av. Edgw —4C 12
Broadhurst Av. Ilf —3K 51
Broadhurst Clo. NW6 —6A 44
Broadhurst Clo. Rich —5F 89
Broadhurst Gdns. NW6 —6K 43
Broadhurst Gdns. Ruis —2A 38
Broadlands. E17 —3A 32
Broadlands Av. SW16 —2J 109
Broadlands Av. Enf —3C 8
Broadlands Clo. N6 —7E 28
Broadlands Clo. SW16 —2J 109
Broadlands Clo. Enf —3D 8
Broadlands Ct. Rich —7G 73
(off Kew Gdns. Rd.)
Broadlands Lodge. N6 —7D 28
Broadlands Rd. N6 —7D 28
Broadlands Rd. Brom —4K 113
Broadlands, The. Felt —3E 102
Broadlands Way. N Mald
—6B 120
Broad La. EC2 —5E 62 (5G 145)
Broad La. N8 —5K 29
Broad La. N15 —4F 31
Broad La. Hamp —7D 102
Broad Lawn. SE9 —2E 114
Broadlawns Ct. Harr —1K 23
Broadley St. NW8
—5B 60 (5B 140)
Broadley Ter. NW1
—4C 60 (4D 140)
Broadmead. SE6 —3C 112
Broadmead Av. Wor Pk —7C 120
Broadmead Clo. Hamp —6E 102
Broadmead Clo. Pinn —1C 22
Broadmead Ct. Wfd G —6D 20
Broadmead Rd. Hayes & N'holt
—4C 54
Broadmead Rd. Wfd G —6D 20
Broad Oak. Wfd G —5E 20
Broad Oak Clo. E4 —5H 19
Broadoak Ct. SW9 —3A 94
Broadoak Rd. Eri —7K 85
Broadoaks Way. Brom —5H 127
Broad Sanctuary. SW1
—2H 77 (7D 148)
Broadstone Ho. SW8 —7K 77
(off Dorset Rd.)
Broadstone Pl. W1
—5E 60 (6G 141)
Broad St. Dag —7G 53
Broad St. Tedd —6K 103
Broad St. Av. EC2
—5E 62 (6G 145)
Broad St. Mkt. Dag —7H 53
Broad St. Pl. EC2
—5D 62 (6F 145)
Broad View. NW9 —6G 25
Broadview Rd. SW16 —7H 109
Broadwalk. E18 —3H 33
Broad Wlk. N21 —2E 16
Broad Wlk. NW1
—1E 60 (1H 141)
Broad Wlk. SE3 —2A 98

Broad Wlk. W2 & W1
—7D 60 (3F 147)
Broadwalk. Harr —5E 22
Broad Wlk. Houn —1B 86
Broad Wlk. Rich —7F 73
Broadwalk Ct. W8 —1K 75
(off Palace Gdns. Ter.)
Broad Wlk. La. NW11 —7H 27
Broadwalk Shop. Cen. Edgw
—6C 12
Broad Wlk., The. W8 —1K 75
Broad Wlk., The. E Mol —4A 118
Broadwall. SE1 —1A 78 (4K 149)
Broadwater Farm Est. N17
—2D 30
Broadwater Rd. N17 —1E 30
Broadwater Rd. SE28 —3H 83
Broadwater Rd. SW17 —4C 108
Broadway. E13 —2K 65
Broadway. E15 —7F 49
(in two parts)
Broadway. SW1 —3H 77 (7C 148)
Broadway. W7 & W13 —1J 71
Broadway. Bark —1G 67
Broadway. Bexh —4E 100
Broadway Arc. W6 —4E 74
(off Hammersmith B'way.)
Broadway Av. Croy —5D 124
Broadway Av. Twic —6B 88
Broadway Cen., The. W6 —4E 74
Broadway Ct. SW19 —6J 107
Broadway Ct. Beck —3E 126
Broadway Gdns. Mitc —4C 122
Broadway Ho. Brom —5F 113
(off Bromley Rd.)
Broadway Mkt. E8 —1H 63
Broadway Mkt. M. E8 —1H 63
Broadway M. E5 —7F 31
Broadway M. N13 —5E 16
Broadway M. N21 —1G 17
Broadway Pde. E4 —6K 19
Broadway Pde. N8 —6J 29
Broadway Pde. Harr —5F 23
Broadway Pl. SW19 —6H 107
Broadway Rd. Hayes & N'holt
—4C 54
Broadway Shop. Cen. Bexh
—4G 101
Broadway Shop. Mall. SW1
—3H 77 (1C 154)
Broadway, The. E4 —6A 20
Broadway, The. N8 —6J 29
Broadway, The. N9 —3B 18
Broadway, The. N14 —1C 16
(off Southgate Cir.)
Broadway, The. N22 —2A 30
Broadway, The. NW7 —5F 13
Broadway, The. NW9 —6B 26
Broadway, The. SW13 —2A 90
Broadway, The. SW19 —6J 107
Broadway, The. W3 —2G 73
Broadway, The. W5 —7D 56
Broadway, The. Cheam —6G 131
Broadway, The. Croy —4J 133
Broadway, The. Dag —2F 53
Broadway, The. Gnfd —4G 55
Broadway, The. S'hall —1C 70
Broadway, The. Stan —5H 11
Broadway, The. Sutt —5A 132
Broadway, The. W'stone —2J 23
Broadway, The. Wemb —3E 40
Broadway, The. Wfd G —6E 20
Broadwell Ct. Houn —1B 86
(off Springwell Rd.)

Broadwick St. W1
—7G 61 (2B 148)
Broadwood Ter. W8 —4H 75
(off Warwick Rd.)
Broad Yd. EC1 —4B 62 (4A 144)
Brocas Clo. NW3 —7C 44
Brockbridge Ho. SW15 —6B 90
Brockdene Dri. Kes —4B 138
Brockdish Av. Bark —5K 51
Brockenhurst Av. Wor Pk
—1A 130
Brockenhurst Gdns. NW7 —5F 13
Brockenhurst Gdns. Ilf —5G 51
Brockenhurst Rd. Croy —7H 125
Brockenhurst Way. SW16
—2H 123
Brocket Ho. SW8 —2H 93
Brockham Clo. SW19 —5H 107
Brockham Cres. New Ad —7E 137
Brockham Dri. SW2 —7K 93
Brockham Dri. Ilf —6F 35
Brockham Ho. SW2 —7K 93
(off Brockham Dri.)
Brockham St. SE1
—3C 78 (1D 156)
Brockhurst Clo. Stan —6E 10
Brockill Cres. SE4 —4A 96
Brocklebank Ho. E16 —1E 82
(off Glenister St.)
Brocklebank Rd. SE7 —4K 81
Brocklebank Rd. SW18 —7A 92
Brocklebank Rd. Ind. Est. SE7
—4J 81
Brocklehurst St. SE14 —7K 79
Brocklesby Rd. SE25 —4H 125
Brockley Av. Stan —3K 11
Brockley Clo. Stan —4K 11
Brockley Cres. Romf —1J 37
Brockley Cross. SE4 —3A 96
Brockley Cross Bus. Cen. SE4
—3A 96
Brockley Footpath. SE4 —5A 96
(in two parts)
Brockley Footpath. SE15 —4J 95
Brockley Gdns. SE4 —2B 96
Brockley Gro. SE4 —5B 96
Brockley Hall Rd. SE4 —5A 96
Brockley Hill. Stan —1H 11
Brockley M. SE4 —5A 96
Brockley M. SE22 —5A 96
Brockley Pk. SE23 —7A 96
Brockley Rise. SE23 —1A 112
Brockley Rd. SE4 —3B 96
Brockley Side. Stan —4K 11
Brockley View. SE23 —7A 96
Brockley Way. SE4 —5K 95
Brockman Rise. Brom —4F 113
Brockmer Ho. E1 —7H 63
(off Crowder St.)
Brock Pl. E3 —4D 64
Brock Rd. E13 —5K 65
Brocks Dri. Sutt —3G 131
Brockshot Clo. Bren —5D 72
Brock St. SE15 —3J 95
Brockway Clo. E11 —2G 49
Brockwell Clo. Orp —5K 129
Brockwell Ct. SW2 —5A 94
Brockwell Ho. SE11
—6K 77 (7H 155)
(off Vauxhall St.)
Brockwell Pk. Gdns. SE24
—7B 94
Brockworth Clo. SE15 —6E 78
Brodia Rd. N16 —3E 46
Brodie Rd. E4 —1K 19

Brodie Rd. Enf —1H 7
Brodie St. SE1 —5F 79 (5K 157)
Brodlove La. E1 —7K 63
Brodrick Gro. SE2 —4B 84
Brodrick Rd. SW17 —2C 108
Brograve Gdns. Beck —2D 126
Broken Wharf. EC4
—7C 62 (2C 150)
Brokesley St. E3 —3B 64
Broke Wlk. E8 —1G 63
Bromar Rd. SE5 —3E 94
Bromefield. Stan —1C 24
Bromell's Rd. SW4 —4G 93
Brome Rd. SE9 —3D 98
Bromfelde Rd. SW4 —3H 93
Bromfelde Wlk. SW4 —2H 93
Bromfield St. N1 —2A 62
Bromhall Rd. Dag —6B 52
Bromhead St. E1 —6J 63
Bromhedge. SE9 —3D 114
Bromholm Rd. SE2 —3B 84
Bromleigh Ct. SE23 —2H 111
Bromley Av. Brom —7G 113
Bromley Comn. Brom —4A 128
Bromley Cres. Brom —3H 127
Bromley Gdns. Brom —3H 127
Bromley Gro. Brom —2F 127
Bromley Hall Rd. E14 —5E 64
Bromley High St. E3 —3D 64
Bromley Hill. Brom —6G 113
Bromley Ind. Cen. Brom —3B 128
Bromley La. Chst —7G 115
Bromley Pk. Brom —1H 127
Bromley Pl. W1 —5G 61 (5A 142)
Bromley Rd. E10 —6D 32
Bromley Rd. E17 —3C 32
Bromley Rd. N17 —1F 31
Bromley Rd. N18 —3J 17
Bromley Rd. SE6 & Brom
—1D 112
Bromley Rd. Beck & Short
—1D 126
Bromley Rd. Chst —1F 129
Bromley St. E1 —5K 63
Brompton Arc. SW3
—2D 76 (7E 146)
Brompton Clo. SE20 —2G 125
Brompton Clo. Houn —5D 86
Brompton Gro. N2 —4C 28
Brompton Pk. Cres. SW6 —6K 75
Brompton Pl. SW3
—3C 76 (1D 152)
Brompton Rd. SW3, SW7 &
SW11 —4C 76 (3C 152)
Brompton Sq. SW3
—3C 76 (1C 152)
Brompton Ter. SE18 —1D 98
Bromwich Av. N6 —2E 44
Bromyard Av. W3 —7A 58
Brondesbury M. NW6 —7J 43
Brondesbury Pk. NW2 & NW6
—6D 42
Brondesbury Rd. NW6 —2H 59
Brondesbury Vs. NW6 —2H 59
Bronsart Rd. SW6 —7G 75
Bronson Rd. SW20 —2F 121
Bronte Clo. E7 —4J 49
Bronte Clo. Eri —7H 85
Bronte Clo. Ilf —4E 34
Bronte Ho. N16 —5E 46
Bronte Ho. SW4 —7G 93
Bronti Clo. SE17
—5C 78 (5D 156)
Bronze Age Way. Belv —2H 85
Bronze St. SE8 —7C 80

Brook Av. Dag —7H 53
Brook Av. Edgw —6C 12
Brook Av. Wemb —3F 41
Brookbank Av. W7 —4H 55
Brookbank Rd. SE13 —3C 96
Brook Clo. NW7 —7B 14
Brook Clo. SW20 —3D 120
Brook Clo. W3 —1G 73
Brook Ct. E11 —4G 49
Brook Ct. E15 —5D 48
(off Clays La.)
Brook Ct. E17 —3A 32
Brook Ct. Edgw —5C 12
Brook Cres. E4 —4H 19
Brook Cres. N9 —4C 18
Brookdale. N11 —4B 16
Brookdale Rd. E17 —3C 32
Brookdale Rd. SE6 —7D 96
Brookdale Rd. Bex —6E 100
Brookdales. NW4 —4G 27
Brookdene Rd. SE18 —4K 83
Brook Dri. SE11 —3A 78 (2K 155)
Brook Dri. Harr —4G 23
Brooke Av. Harr —3G 39
Brooke Clo. Bush —1B 10
Brookehowse Rd. SE6 —2C 112
Brookend Rd. Sidc —1J 115
Brooke Rd. E5 —3G 47
Brooke Rd. E17 —4E 32
Brooke Rd. N16 —3F 47
Brooke's Ct. EC1
—5A 62 (6J 143)
Brooke's Mkt. EC1
—5A 62 (5K 143)
Brooke St. EC1 —5A 62 (6J 143)
Brooke Way. Bush —1B 10
Brookfield. N6 —3E 44
Brookfield Av. E17 —4E 32
Brookfield Av. NW7 —6J 13
Brookfield Av. W5 —4D 56
Brookfield Av. Sutt —4C 132
Brookfield Clo. NW7 —6J 13
Brookfield Ct. Gnfd —3G 55
Brookfield Cres. NW7 —6J 13
Brookfield Cres. Harr —5E 24
Brookfield Pk. NW5 —3F 45
Brookfield Path. E4 —6B 20
Brookfield Path. Wfd G —6B 20
Brookfield Rd. E9 —6A 48
Brookfield Rd. N9 —3B 18
Brookfield Rd. W4 —2K 73
Brookfields. Enf —4E 8
Brookfields Av. Mitc —5C 122
Brook Gdns. E4 —4J 19
Brook Gdns. SW13 —3B 90
Brook Gdns. King T —1J 119
Brook Ga. W1 —7D 60 (3F 147)
Brook Grn. W6 —3F 75
Brook Hill Clo. SE18 —5F 83
Brookhill Clo. E Barn —5H 5
Brookhill Rd. SE18 —5F 83
Brookhill Rd. Barn —5H 5
Brookhouse Gdns. E4 —4B 20
Brook Ind. Est. Hayes —1B 70
Brooking Rd. E7 —5J 49
Brookland Clo. NW11 —4J 27
Brookland Garth. NW11 —4J 27
Brookland Hill. NW11 —4K 27
Brookland Rise. NW11 —4J 27
Brooklands App. Romf —4K 37
Brooklands Av. SW19 —2K 107
Brooklands Av. Sidc —2H 115
Brooklands Clo. Romf —4K 37
Brooklands Ct. N21 —5J 7
Brooklands Ct. Mitc —2B 122

Brooklands Dri. Gnfd —1D 56
Brooklands La. Romf —4K 37
Brooklands Pk. SE3 —3J 97
Brooklands Pas. SW8 —1H 93
Brooklands Rd. Romf —4K 37
Brooklands St. SW8 —1H 93
Brooklands, The. Iswth —1H 87
Brook La. SE3 —2K 97
Brook La. Bex —6D 100
Brook La. Brom —6J 113
Brook La. Bus. Cen. Bren —5D 72
Brook La. N. Bren —5D 72
(in two parts)
Brooklea Clo. NW9 —1A 26
Brook Lodge. Romf —4K 37
(off Brooklands Rd.)
Brooklyn Av. SE25 —4H 125
Brooklyn Clo. Cars —2C 132
Brooklyn Gro. SE25 —4H 125
Brooklyn Rd. SE25 —4H 125
Brooklyn Rd. Brom —5B 128
Brookmarsh Ind. Est. SE10
—7D 80
Brook Mead. Eps —6A 130
Brookmead Av. Brom —5D 128
Brookmead Ind. Est. Croy
—6G 123
Brook Meadow. N12 —3E 14
Brook Meadow Clo. Wfd G
—6B 20
Brookmead Rd. Croy —6G 123
Brook M. N. W2 —7A 60 (2A 146)
Brookmill Rd. SE8 —1C 96
Brook Pde. Chig —3K 21
Brook Pk. Clo. N21 —6G 7
Brook Pas. SW6 —7J 75
Brook Path. Barn —5D 4
Brook Rise. Chig —3K 21
Brook Rd. N2 —7H 15
Brook Rd. N8 —4J 29
Brook Rd. N22 —3K 29
Brook Rd. NW2 —2B 42
Brook Rd. Buck H —2D 20
Brook Rd. Ilf —6J 35
Brook Rd. T Hth —4C 124
Brook Rd. Twic —6A 88
Brook Rd. Bren —6D 72
Brooks Av. E6 —4D 66
Brooksbank St. E9 —6K 47
Brooksby M. N1 —7A 46
Brooksby St. N1 —7A 46
Brooksby's Wlk. E9 —5K 47
Brooks Clo. SE9 —2E 114
Brooks Clo. SW8 —7G 77
(off Cringle St.)
Brookscroft. E17 —3D 32
Brookscroft Rd. E17 —1D 32
(in two parts)
Brookshill. Harr —5C 10
Brookshill Av. Harr —5C 10
Brookshill Dri. Harr —5C 10
Brookside. N21 —6E 6
Brookside. Cars —5E 132
Brookside. E Barn —6H 5
Brookside. Orp —7K 129
Brookside Clo. Barn —6B 4
Brookside Clo. Kent —5D 24
Brookside Clo. S Harr —4C 38
Brookside Cres. Wor Pk —1C 130
Brookside Rd. N9 —4C 18
Brookside Rd. N19 —2G 45
Brookside Rd. NW11 —6G 27
Brookside Rd. Hayes —7A 54
Brookside S. E Barn —7K 5

Brookside Wlk. N12 —6D 14
Brookside Way. Croy —6K 125
Brooks La. W4 —6G 73
Brook's M. W1 —7F 61 (2J 147)
Brooks Rd. E13 —1J 65
Brooks Rd. W4 —5G 73
Brookstone Ct. SE15 —4H 95
Brook St. N17 —2F 31
Brook St. W1 —7F 61 (2J 147)
Brook St. W2 —7B 60 (2B 146)
Brook St. Belv & Eri —5H 85
Brook St. King T —2E 118
Brooksville Av. NW6 —1G 59
Brookview Ct. Enf —5K 7
Brookview Rd. SW16 —5G 109
Brookville Rd. SW6 —7H 75
Brook Wlk. N2 —1B 28
Brook Wlk. Edgw —6E 12
Brookway. SE3 —3J 97
Brook Way. Chig —3K 21
Brookwood Av. SW13 —2B 90
Brookwood Clo. Brom —4H 127
Brookwood Rd. SW18 —1H 107
Brookwood Rd. Houn —2D 87
Broom Clo. Brom —6C 128
Broom Clo. Tedd —7E 104
Broomcroft Av. N'holt —3A 54
Broome Rd. Hamp —7D 102
Broome Way. SE5 —7D 78
Broomfield. E17 —7B 32
Broomfield Av. N13 —5E 16
Broomfield Clo. SE16 —3G 79
(off John Roll Way)
Broomfield La. N13 —4D 16
Broomfield Pl. W13 —1B 72
Broomfield Rd. N13 —5D 16
Broomfield Rd. W13 —1B 72
Broomfield Rd. Beck —3B 126
Broomfield Rd. Bexh —5G 101
Broomfield Rd. Rich —1F 89
Broomfield Rd. Romf —7D 36
Broomfield Rd. Surb —7F 119
Broomfield Rd. Tedd —6C 104
Broomfield St. E14 —5C 64
Broom Gdns. Croy —3C 136
Broomgrove Gdns. Edgw —1G 25
Broomgrove Rd. SW9 —2K 93
Broomhall Rd. S Croy —7D 134
Broomhill Ct. Wfd G —6D 20
Broom Hill Rise. Bexh —5G 101
Broomhill Rd. SW18 —5J 91
Broomhill Rd. Ilf —2A 52
Broomhill Rd. Orp —7K 129
Broomhill Rd. Wfd G —6D 20
(in two parts)
Broomhill Wlk. Wfd G —7C 20
Broomhouse La. SW6 —2J 91
Broomhouse Rd. SW6 —2J 91
Broomloan La. Sutt —2J 131
Broom Lock. Tedd —6C 104
Broom Mead. Bexh —5G 101
Broom Pk. Tedd —7D 104
Broom Rd. Croy —3C 136
Broom Rd. Tedd —5B 104
Broomsleigh Bus. Pk. SE26
(off Worsley Bri. Rd.) —5B 112
Broomsleigh St. NW6 —5H 43
Broom Water. Tedd —6C 104
Broom Water W. Tedd —5C 104
Broomwood Clo. Bex —1K 117
Broomwood Clo. Croy —5K 125

Broomwood Rd. SW11 —6D 92
Broseley Gro. SE26 —5A 112
Broster Gdns. SE25 —3F 125
Brougham Rd. E8 —1G 63
Brougham Rd. W3 —6J 57
Brougham St. SW11 —2D 92
Broughton Av. N3 —3G 27
Broughton Av. Rich —3B 104
Broughton Ct. W13 —7B 56
Broughton Dri. SW9 —4B 94
Broughton Gdns. N6 —6G 29
Broughton Rd. SW6 —2K 91
Broughton Rd. W13 —7B 56
Broughton Rd. T Hth —6A 124
Broughton Rd. SW8 —2E 92
Brouncker Rd. W3 —2J 73
Browells La. Felt —2A 102
Brown Bear Ct. Felt —4B 102
Brown Clo. Wall —7J 133
Brownfield St. E14 —6D 64
Brownhill Rd. SE6 —7D 96
Brownhill Ter. N17 —1G 31
Browning Av. W7 —6K 55
Browning Av. Sutt —4C 132
Browning Av. Wor Pk —1D 130
Browning Clo. W9 —4A 60
Browning Clo. Col R —1F 37
Browning Clo. Hamp —4D 102
Browning Clo. Well —1J 99
Browning M. W1
—5F 61 (6H 141)
Browning Rd. E11 —7H 33
Browning Rd. E12 —5D 50
Browning Rd. Enf —1J 7
Browning St. SE17
—5C 78 (5D 156)
Browning Way. Houn —1B 86
Brownlea Gdns. Ilf —2A 52
Brownlow Ct. N2 —5B 28
Brownlow Ct. N11 —6D 16
(off Brownlow Rd.)
Brownlow M. WC1
—4K 61 (4H 143)
Brownlow Rd. E7 —4J 49
Brownlow Rd. E8 —1G 63
Brownlow Rd. N3 —7E 14
Brownlow Rd. N11 —6D 16
Brownlow Rd. NW10 —7A 42
Brownlow Rd. W13 —1A 72
Brownlow Rd. Croy —4E 134
Brownlow St. WC1
—5K 61 (6H 143)
Brown's Bldgs. EC3
—6E 62 (1H 151)
Browns La. NW5 —5F 45
Brownspring Dri. SE9 —4F 115
Browns Rd. E17 —3C 32
Brown's Rd. Surb —7F 119
Brown St. W1 —6D 60 (7E 140)
Brownswell Rd. N2 —2B 28
Brownswood Rd. N4 —3B 46
Broxash Rd. SW11 —6E 92
Broxbourne Av. E18 —4K 33
Broxbourne Rd. E7 —3J 49
Broxbourne Rd. Orp —7K 129
Broxholme Rd. SW6 —1K 91
(off Harwood Rd.)
Broxholm Rd. SE27 —3A 110

Broxted Rd. SE6 —2B 112
Broxwood Way. NW8 —1C 60
Bruce Castle Ct. N17 —1F 31
(off Lordship La.)
Bruce Castle Rd. N17 —1F 31
Bruce Clo. W10 —5F 59
Bruce Clo. Well —1B 100
Bruce Ct. Sidc —4K 115
Bruce Gdns. N20 —3J 15
Bruce Gro. N17 —1E 30
Bruce Hall M. SW17 —4E 108
Bruce Rd. E3 —3D 64
Bruce Rd. NW10 —7K 41
Bruce Rd. SE25 —4D 124
Bruce Rd. Barn —3B 4
Bruce Rd. Harr —2J 23
Bruce Rd. Mitc —7E 108
Bruckner St. W10 —3H 59
Brudenell Rd. SW17 —3D 108
Bruffs Meadow. N'holt —6C 38
Bruges Pl. NW1 —7G 45
Brummel Clo. Bexh —3J 101
Brune Ho. E1 —5F 63 (6J 145)
Brunel Clo. SE19 —6F 111
Brunel Clo. N'holt —3D 54
Brunel Est. W2 —5J 59
Brunel Pl. S'hall —7F 55
Brunel Rd. E17 —6A 32
Brunel Rd. SE16 —2J 79
Brunel Rd. W'way E —5A 58
Brunel Rd. Wfd G —5J 21
Brunel St. E16 —6H 65
Brunel Wlk. N15 —4E 30
Brunel Wlk. Twic —7E 86
Bruner Rd. W5 —4D 56
Brune St. E1 —5F 63 (6J 145)
Brunner Clo. NW11 —5K 27
Brunner Ho. SE6 —4E 112
Brunner Rd. E17 —5A 32
Brunner Rd. W5 —4D 56
Bruno Pl. NW9 —2J 41
Brunswick Av. N11 —3K 15
(in two parts)
Brunswick Centre. WC1
—4J 61 (3E 142)
Brunswick Clo. Bexh —4D 100
Brunswick Clo. Pinn —6C 22
Brunswick Clo. Twic —3H 103
Brunswick Clo. Est. EC1
—3B 62 (2A 144)
Brunswick Ct. EC1
—3B 62 (2A 144)
(off Tompion St.)
Brunswick Ct. SE1
—2E 78 (7H 151)
Brunswick Ct. Barn —5G 5
Brunswick Ct. Sutt —4K 131
Brunswick Cres. N11 —3K 15
Brunswick Gdns. W5 —4E 56
Brunswick Gdns. W8 —1J 75
Brunswick Gdns. Ilf —1G 35
Brunswick Gro. N11 —3K 15
Brunswick Ho. N3 —1H 27
Brunswick Ind. Pk. N11 —4A 16
Brunswick M. SW16 —6H 109
Brunswick M. W1
—6D 60 (7F 141)
Brunswick Pk. SE5 —1E 94
Brunswick Pk. Gdns. N11 —2K 15
Brunswick Pk. Rd. N11 —2K 15
Brunswick Pl. N1
—3D 62 (2F 145)
Brunswick Pl. SE19 —7G 111
Brunswick Quay. SE16 —3K 79
Brunswick Rd. E10 —1E 48

Brunswick Rd. E14 —6E 64
Brunswick Rd. N15 —4E 30
(in two parts)
Brunswick Rd. W5 —4D 56
Brunswick Rd. Bexh —4D 100
Brunswick Rd. King T —1G 119
Brunswick Rd. Sutt —4K 131
Brunswick Sq. N17 —6A 18
Brunswick Sq. WC1
—4J 61 (3F 143)
Brunswick St. E17 —5E 32
Brunswick Vs. SE5 —1E 94
Brunswick Way. N11 —4A 16
Brunton Pl. E14 —6A 64
Brushfield St. E1
—5E 62 (5H 145)
Brussels Rd. SW11 —4B 92
Bruton Clo. Chst —7D 114
Bruton La. W1 —7F 61 (3K 147)
Bruton Pl. W1 —7F 61 (3K 147)
Bruton Rd. Mord —4A 122
Bruton St. W1 —7F 61 (3K 147)
Bruton Way. W13 —5A 56
Brutus Ct. SE11 —4B 78 (4A 156)
Bryan Av. NW10 —7D 42
Bryan Ho. SE16 —2B 80
Bryan Rd. SE16 —2B 80
Bryanston Av. Twic —1F 103
Bryanston Clo. S'hall —4D 70
Bryanston Ct. W1
—6D 60 (7E 140)
Bryanstone Ct. Sutt —4A 132
Bryanstone Rd. N8 —6H 29
Bryanston M. E. W1
—5D 60 (6E 140)
Bryanston M. W. W1
—5D 60 (6E 140)
Bryanston Pl. W1
—5D 60 (6E 140)
Bryanston Sq. W1
—5D 60 (6E 140)
Bryanston St. W1
—6D 60 (1E 146)
Bryant Clo. Barn —5C 4
Bryant Ct. E2 —2F 63
(off Whiston Rd.)
Bryant Rd. N'holt —5A 54
Bryant St. E15 —7F 49
Bryantwood Rd. N7 —5A 46
Brycedale Cres. N14 —4C 16
Bryce Rd. Dag —4C 52
Bryden Clo. SE26 —5A 112
Brydges Pl. WC2
—7J 61 (3E 148)
Brydges Rd. E15 —5F 49
Brydon Wlk. N1 —1J 61
Bryer Ct. EC2 —5C 62 (5C 144)
Bryet Rd. N7 —3J 45
Bryher Ct. SE11 —5A 78 (5J 155)
Brymay Clo. E3 —2C 64
Brynmaer Rd. SW11 —1D 92
Brynmawr Rd. Enf —4A 8
Bryony Rd. W12 —7C 58
Buccleugh Ho. E5 —7G 31
Buchanan Clo. N21 —5E 6
Buchanan Ct. SE16 —4K 79
(off Worgan St.)
Buchanan Gdns. NW10 —2D 58
Buchan Rd. SE15 —3J 95
Bucharest Rd. SW18 —7A 92
Buckden Clo. N2 —4D 28
Buckden Clo. SE12 —6H 97
Buckfast St. W13 —7A 56
Buckfast Rd. Mord —4K 121
Buckfast St. E2 —3G 63

Buck Hill Wlk. W2
—7B 60 (3B 146)
Buckhold Rd. SW18 —6J 91
Buckhurst Av. Cars —1C 132
Buckhurst Ct. Buck H —2G 21
(off Albert Rd.)
Buckhurst Hill Ho. Buck H
—2E 20
Buckhurst Ho. N7 —5H 45
Buckhurst St. E1 —4H 63
Buckhurst Way. Buck H —4G 21
Buckingham Arc. WC2
—7J 61 (3E 148)
Buckingham Av. Gnfd —1A 56
Buckingham Av. T Hth —1A 124
Buckingham Av. Well —4J 99
Buckingham Clo. W5 —5C 56
Buckingham Clo. Enf —2K 7
Buckingham Clo. Hamp —5D 102
Buckingham Clo. Orp —7J 129
Buckingham Ct. NW4 —3C 26
Buckingham Ct. N'holt —2C 54
Buckingham Dri. Chst —5G 115
Buckingham Gdns. Edgw —7A 12
Buckingham Gdns. T Hth
—2A 124
Buckingham Ga. SW1
—3G 77 (1A 154)
Buckingham La. SE23 —7A 96
Buckingham Mans. NW6 —5K 43
(off W. End La.)
Buckingham M. N1 —6E 46
(off Culford St.)
Buckingham M. NW10 —2B 58
Buckingham M. SW1
—3G 77 (1A 154)
Buckingham Pal. Rd. SW1
—4F 77 (4J 153)
Buckingham Pde. Stan —5H 11
Buckingham Pl. SW1
—3G 77 (1A 154)
Buckingham Rd. E10 —3D 48
Buckingham Rd. E11 —5A 34
Buckingham Rd. E15 —5H 49
Buckingham Rd. E18 —1H 33
Buckingham Rd. N1 —6E 46
Buckingham Rd. N22 —1J 29
Buckingham Rd. NW10 —2B 58
Buckingham Rd. Edgw —7A 12
Buckingham Rd. Hamp —4D 102
Buckingham Rd. Harr —5H 23
Buckingham Rd. Ilf —2H 51
Buckingham Rd. King T —4F 119
Buckingham Rd. Mitc —5J 123
Buckingham Rd. Rich —2D 104
Buckingham St. WC2
—1J 77 (4F 149)
Buckingham Way. Wall —7G 133
Buckland Ct. N1 —2E 62
(off St Johns Est.)
Buckland Cres. NW3 —7B 44
Buckland Rise. Pinn —1A 22
Buckland Rd. E10 —2E 48
Bucklands Rd. Tedd —6C 104
Buckland St. N1 —2D 62
Buckland's Wharf. King T
—2D 118
Buckland Wlk. W3 —2J 73
Buckland Wlk. Mord —4A 122
Buckland Way. Wor Pk —1E 130
Buck La. NW9 —5K 25
Buckleigh Av. SW20 —3G 121

Buckleigh Rd. SW16 —6H 109
Buckleigh Way. SE19 —7F 111
Buckler Gdns. SE9 —3D 114
Bucklers All. SW6 —6H 75
Bucklersbury. EC4
—6D 62 (1E 150)
Bucklers Way. Cars —3D 132
Buckles Ct. Belv —4D 84
Buckle St. E1 —6F 63 (7K 145)
Buckley Clo. NW6 —7H 43
Buckley Rd. NW6 —7H 43
Buckmaster Clo. SW9 —3A 94
Buckmaster Ho. N7 —4K 45
Buckmaster Rd. SW11 —4C 92
Bucknall St. WC2
—6J 61 (7D 142)
Bucknell Clo. SW2 —4K 93
Buckner Rd. SW2 —4K 93
Buckrell Rd. E4 —2A 20
Buckstone Clo. SE23 —6J 95
Buckstone Rd. N18 —5B 18
Buck St. NW1 —7F 45
Buckters Rents. SE16 —1A 80
Buckthorne Rd. SE4 —5A 96
Buckthorn Ho. Sidc —3K 115
(off Longlands Rd.)
Buckwheat Ct. Eri —3D 84
Budd Clo. N12 —4E 14
Buddings Circ. Wemb —3J 41
Budd's All. Twic —5C 88
Budge La. Mitc —7D 122
Budge Row. EC4
—7D 62 (1E 150)
Budge's Wlk. W2 —1A 76
(off North Wlk.)
Budleigh Cres. Well —1C 100
Budoch Ct. Ilf —2A 52
Budoch Dri. Ilf —2A 52
Buer Rd. SW6 —2G 91
Bugsby's Way. SE10 & SE7
—4H 81
Bulganak Rd. T Hth —4C 124
Bulinga St. SW1 —4J 77 (4E 154)
Bullace Row. SE5 —1D 94
Bull All. SE1 —7A 62 (3K 149)
Bull All. Well —3B 100
Bullard Rd. Tedd —6J 103
Bullard's Pl. E2 —3K 63
Bullbanks Rd. Belv —4J 85
Bulleid Way. SW1
—4F 77 (4K 153)
Bullen St. SW11 —2C 92
Buller Clo. SE15 —7G 79
Buller Rd. N17 —2G 31
Buller Rd. N22 —2A 30
Buller Rd. NW10 —3F 59
Buller Rd. Bark —7J 51
Buller Rd. T Hth —2D 124
Bullers Clo. Sidc —5E 116
Bullers Wood Dri. Chst —7D 114
Bullescroft Rd. Edgw —3B 12
Bullingham Mans. W8 —2J 75
Bull Inn Ct. WC2 —7J 61 (3F 149)
Bullivant St. E14 —7E 64
Bull La. N18 —5K 17
Bull La. Chst —7H 115
Bull La. Dag —3H 53
Bull Rd. E15 —2H 65
Bullrush Clo. SE25 —6E 124
Bull's All. SW14 —2K 89
Bullsbridge Rd. S'hall —4A 70
Bullsbrook Rd. Hayes —1A 70
Bulls Gdns. SW3
—4C 76 (3D 152)

Bull's Head Pas. EC3
—6E 62 (1G 151)
Bull Yd. SE15 —1G 95
Bulmer Gdns. Harr —7D 24
Bulmer M. W11 —7J 59
Bulmer Pl. W11 —1J 75
Bulow Est. SW6 —1K 91
(off Pearscroft Rd.)
Bulstrode Av. Houn —2D 86
Bulstrode Gdns. Houn —3E 86
Bulstrode Pl. W1
—5E 60 (6H 141)
Bulstrode Rd. Houn —3E 86
Bulstrode St. W1
—6E 60 (7H 141)
Bulwer Ct. E11 —1F 49
Bulwer Ct. Rd. E11 —1F 49
Bulwer Gdns. Barn —4F 5
Bulwer Rd. E11 —7F 33
Bulwer Rd. N18 —4K 17
Bulwer Rd. Barn —4E 4
Bulwer St. W12 —1E 74
Bunce's La. Wfd G —7C 20
Bungalow Rd. SE25 —4E 124
Bungalows, The. E10 —6E 32
Bungalows, The. SW16 —7F 109
Bungalows, The. Ilf —1J 35
Bunhill Row. EC1
—4D 62 (3E 144)
Bunhouse Pl. SW1
—5E 76 (5H 153)
Bunkers Hill. NW11 —7A 28
Bunkers Hill. Belv —4G 85
Bunkers Hill. Sidc —3F 117
Bunning Way. N7 —7J 45
Bunns La. NW7 —6F 13
(in two parts)
Bunsen St. E3 —2A 64
Buntingbridge Rd. Ilf —5H 35
Bunting Clo. N9 —1E 18
Bunting Clo. Mitc —5D 122
Bunting Ct. NW9 —2A 26
Bunton St. SE18 —3E 82
Bunyan Ct. EC2 —5C 62 (5C 144)
Bunyan Rd. E17 —3A 32
Buonaparte M. SW1
—5H 77 (5C 154)
Burbage Clo. SE1
—3D 78 (2E 156)
Burbage Ho. N1 —1D 62
(off Poole St.)
Burbage Rd. SE24 & SE21
—6C 94
Burberry Clo. N Mald —2A 120
Burbridge Way. N17 —2G 31
Burcham St. E14 —6D 64
Burcharbro Rd. SE2 —6D 84
Burchell Ct. Bush —1B 10
Burchell Ho. SE11
—5K 77 (4H 155)
Burchell Rd. E10 —1D 48
Burchell Rd. SE15 —1H 95
Burchett Way. Romf —6F 37
Burchwall Clo. Romf —1J 37
Burcote Rd. SW18 —7B 92
Burden Clo. Bren —5C 72
Burden Ho. SW8 —7J 77
(off Thorncroft St.)
Burdenshott Av. Rich —4H 89
Burden Way. E11 —2K 49
Burder Clo. N1 —6E 46
Burder Rd. N1 —6E 46
Burdett Av. SW20 —1C 120
Burdett Clo. W7 —1K 71
Burdett Clo. Sidc —5E 116

Burdett M. NW3—6B 44
Burdett M. W2—6K 59
Burdett Rd. E3 & E14—4A 64
Burdett Rd. Croy—6D 124
Burdett Rd. Rich—2F 89
Burdetts Rd. Dag—1F 69
Burdett St. SE1—3A 78 (1J 155)
Burdock Clo. Croy—1K 135
Burdock Rd. N17—3G 31
Burdon La. Sutt—7G 131
Burdon Pk. Sutt—7H 131
Bure Ct. New Bar—5E 4
Burfield Clo. SW17—4B 108
Burford Clo. Dag—3C 52
Burford Clo. Ilf—4G 35
Burford Gdns. N13—3E 16
Burford Ho. Bren—5E 72
Burford Rd. E6—3C 66
Burford Rd. E15—1F 65
Burford Rd. SE6—2B 112
Burford Rd. Bren—5E 72
Burford Rd. Brom—4C 128
Burford Rd. Sutt—2J 131
Burford Rd. Wor Pk—7B 120
Burford Wlk. SW6—7A 76
Burford Way. New Ad—6E 136
Burge Rd. E7—4B 50
Burges Gro. SW13—7D 74
Burges Rd. E6—7C 50
Burgess Av. NW9—6K 25
Burgess Clo. Felt—4C 102
Burgess Ct. E6—7E 50
Burgess Ct. S'hall—6F 55
(off Fleming Rd.)
Burgess Hill. NW2—4J 43
Burgess Ind. Pk. SE15—7D 78
Burgess Rd. E15—4G 49
Burgess Rd. Sutt—4K 131
Burgess St. E14—5D 64
Burge St. SE1—3D 78 (2F 157)
Burghill Rd. SE26—4A 112
Burghley Av. N Mald—1K 119
Burghley Hall Clo. SW19
—1G 107
Burghley Pl. Mitc—5D 122
Burghley Rd. E11—1G 49
Burghley Rd. N8—3A 30
Burghley Rd. NW5—4F 45
Burghley Rd. SW19—4F 107
Burghley Tower. W3—7B 58
Burgh St. N1—2B 62
Burgon Clo. EC4—6B 62 (1B 150)
Burgos Clo. Croy—6A 134
Burgos Gro. SE10—1D 96
Burgoyne Rd. N4—6B 30
Burgoyne Rd. SE25—4F 125
Burgoyne Rd. SW9—3K 93
Burham Clo. SE20—7J 111
Burhill Gro. Pinn—2C 22
Burke Clo. SW15—4A 90
Burke Lodge. E13—3A 65
Burke St. E16—5H 65
Burket Clo. S'hall—4C 70
Burland Rd. SW11—5D 92
Burleigh Av. Sidc—5K 99
Burleigh Av. Wall—3E 132
Burleigh Gdns. N14—1B 16
Burleigh Ho. SW3—6B 76
(off Beaufort St.)
Burleigh Ho. W10—3G 59
(off St Charles Sq.)
Burleigh Pl. SW15—5F 91
Burleigh Rd. Enf—4K 7
Burleigh Rd. Sutt—1G 131

Burleigh St. WC2
—7K 61 (2G 149)
Burleigh Wlk. SE6—1E 112
Burleigh Way. Enf—3J 7
Burley Clo. E4—5H 19
Burley Clo. SW16—2H 123
Burley Rd. E16—6A 66
Burlington Arc. W1
—7G 61 (3A 148)
Burlington Av. Rich—1G 89
Burlington Av. Romf—6H 37
Burlington Clo. E6—6C 66
Burlington Clo. W9—4J 59
Burlington Clo. Pinn—3A 22
Burlington Gdns. W1
—7G 61 (3A 148)
Burlington Gdns. W3—1J 73
Burlington Gdns. W4—5J 73
Burlington Gdns. Romf—7E 36
Burlington La. W4—7J 73
Burlington M. W3—1J 73
Burlington Pl. SW6—2G 91
Burlington Pl. Wfd G—3E 20
Burlington Rise. E Barn—7H 5
Burlington Rd. N10—3E 28
Burlington Rd. N17—1G 31
Burlington Rd. SW6—2G 91
Burlington Rd. W4—5J 73
Burlington Rd. Enf—1J 7
Burlington Rd. Iswth—1H 87
Burlington Rd. N Mald—4B 120
Burlington Rd. T Hth—2C 124
Burma M. N16—4D 46
Burma Rd. N16—4D 46
Burmarsh. NW5—6F 45
Burmarsh Ct. SE20—1J 125
Burma Ter. SE19—5E 110
Burmester Rd. SW17—3A 108
Burnaby Cres. W4—6J 73
Burnaby Gdns. W4—6H 73
Burnaby St. SW10—7A 76
Burnard Pl. N7—5K 45
Burnaston Ho. E5—3G 47
Burnbrae Clo. N12—6E 14
Burnbury Rd. SW12—1G 109
Burncroft Av. Enf—2D 8
Burne Jones Ho. W14—4G 75
(off N. End Rd.)
Burnell Av. Rich—5C 104
Burnell Av. Well—2A 100
Burnell Gdns. Stan—2D 24
Burnell Rd. Sutt—4K 131
Burnell Wlk. SE1
—5F 79 (5K 157)
Burnels Av. E6—3E 66
Burness Clo. N7—6K 45
Burne St. NW1—5B 60 (5C 140)
Burnett Clo. E9—5J 47
Burnett Ho. SE13—2E 96
(off Lewisham Hill)
Burney Av. Surb—5F 119
Burney St. SE10—7E 80
Burnfoot Av. SW6—1G 91
Burnham Clo. NW7—7H 13
Burnham Clo. SE1
—5F 79 (4K 157)
Burnham Clo. Enf—1K 7
Burnham Clo. W'stone—4A 24
Burnham Cres. E11—4A 34
Burnham Dri. Wor Pk—2F 131
Burnham Gdns. Croy—7F 125
Burnham Rd. E4—5G 19
Burnham Rd. Dag—7B 52
Burnham Rd. Mord—4K 121
Burnham Rd. Romf—3K 37
Burnham Rd. Sidc—2E 116

Burnham St. E2—3J 63
Burnham St. King T—1G 119
Burnham Way. SE26—5B 112
Burnham Way. W13—4B 72
Burnhill Clo. SE15—7H 79
Burnhill Rd. Beck—2C 126
Burnley Rd. NW10—5B 42
Burnley Rd. SW9—2K 93
Burnsall St. SW3
—5C 76 (6D 152)
Burns Av. Chad H—7C 36
Burns Av. Sidc—6B 100
Burns Av. S'hall—7E 54
Burnsbury Ho. SW4—6H 93
Burns Clo. SW19—6B 108
Burns Clo. Well—1K 99
Burns Ho. SE17—5B 78 (6B 156)
Burn Side. N9—3D 18
Burnside Av. E4—6G 19
Burnside Clo. SE16—1K 79
Burnside Clo. Barn—3D 4
Burnside Clo. Twic—6A 88
Burnside Cres. Wemb—1D 56
Burnside Rd. Dag—2C 52
Burns Rd. NW10—1B 58
Burns Rd. SW11—2D 92
Burns Rd. W13—2B 72
Burns Rd. Wemb—2E 56
Burns Way. Houn—2B 86
Burnt Ash Hill. SE12—6H 97
(in two parts)
Burnt Ash La. Brom—7J 113
Burnt Ash Rd. SE12—5H 97
Burnthwaite Rd. SW6—7H 75
Burnt Oak B'way. Edgw—7C 12
Burnt Oak Fields. Edgw—1J 25
Burnt Oak La. Sidc—6A 100
Burntwood Clo. SW18—1C 108
Burntwood Grange Rd. SW18
—1B 108
Burntwood View. SE19—5F 111
Buross St. E1—6H 63
Burrage Ct. SE16—4K 79
(off Worgan St.)
Burrage Gro. SE18—4G 83
Burrage Pl. SE18—5F 83
Burrage Rd. SE18—5G 83
Burrard Rd. E16—6K 65
Burrard Rd. NW6—5J 43
Burr Clo. E1—1G 79 (4K 151)
Burr Clo. Bexh—3F 101
Burrell Clo. Croy—6A 126
Burrell Clo. Edgw—2C 12
Burrell Row. Beck—2C 126
Burrell St. SE1—1B 78 (4A 150)
Burrell's Wharf Sq. E14—5D 80
Burrell Towers. E10—7C 32
Burritt Rd. King T—2G 119
Burrmill Ct. SE16—4K 79
(off Worgan St.)
Burroughs Gdns. NW4—4D 26
Burroughs Pde. NW4—4D 26
Burroughs, The. NW4—4D 26
Burrow Ho. SW9—2K 93
(off Stockwell Pk. Rd.)
Burrow Rd. SE22—4E 94
Burrows M. SE1
—2B 78 (6A 150)
Burrows Rd. NW10—3E 58
Burrow Wlk. SE21—7C 94
Bursar St. SE1—1E 78 (5G 151)
Bursdon Clo. Sidc—2K 115
Bursland Rd. Enf—4E 8

Burslem St. E1—6G 63
Burstock Rd. SW15—4G 91
Burston Rd. SW15—5F 91
Burstow Rd. SW20—1G 121
Burtenshaw Rd. Th Dit—7A 118
Burtley Clo. N4—1C 46
Burton Ct. Beck—2J 125
Burton Gdns. Houn—1D 86
Burton Gro. SE17
—5D 78 (6E 156)
Burtonhole Clo. NW4—4A 14
Burtonhole La. NW7—5K 13
Burton Ho. SE16—2H 79
(off Cherry Garden St.)
Burton La. SW9—2A 94
(in two parts)
Burton M. SW1—4E 76 (4H 153)
Burton Pl. WC1—4H 61 (2D 142)
Burton Rd. E18—3K 33
Burton Rd. NW6—7H 43
Burton Rd. SW9—2A 94
(in two parts)
Burton Rd. King T—7E 104
Burtons Ct. E15—7F 49
Burton's Rd. Hamp—4F 103
Burton St. WC1—3H 61 (2D 142)
Burtonwood Ho. N4—7D 30
Burt Ind. Est. E10—1A 48
Burt Rd. E16—1A 82
Burtwell La. SE27—4D 110
Burwash Rd. SE18—5H 83
Burwell Av. Gnfd—6J 39
Burwell Clo. E1—6H 63
Burwell Rd. E10—1A 48
Burwell Rd. Ind. Est. E10—1A 48
Burwood Av. Brom—2K 137
Burwood Av. Pinn—5A 22
Burwood Ho. SW9—4B 94
Burwood Pl. W2
—6C 60 (7D 140)
Bury Clo. SE16—1K 79
Bury Ct. EC3—6E 62 (7H 145)
Bury Gro. Mord—5K 121
Bury Hall Vs. N9—1A 18
Bury Pl. WC1—5J 61 (6E 142)
Bury Rd. E4—1B 20
Bury Rd. N22—2A 30
Bury Rd. Dag—5H 53
Bury St. EC3—6E 62 (1H 151)
Bury St. N9—7J 8
Bury St. SW1—1G 77 (4B 148)
Bury St. W. N9—7J 7
Bury Wlk. SW3—4C 76 (4C 152)
Busby M. NW5—6H 45
Busby Pl. NW5—6H 45
Busch Clo. Iswth—1B 88
Bushbaby Clo. SE1
—3E 78 (2G 157)
Bushberry Rd. E9—6A 48
Bush Clo. Ilf—5H 35
Bush Cotts. SW18—5J 91
Bush Ct. N14—1C 16
Bush Ct. W12—2F 75
Bushell Clo. SW2—2K 109
Bushell Grn. Bush—2C 10
Bushell St. E1—1G 79
Bushell Way. Chst—5E 114
Bushey Av. E18—3H 33
Bushey Av. Orp—7H 129
Bushey Clo. E4—3K 19
Bushey Ct. SW20—2D 120
Bushey Down. SW12—2F 109
Bushey Hill Rd. SE5—1E 94
Bushey La. Sutt—4J 131
Bushey Rd. E13—2A 66

Bushey Rd. N15—6E 30
Bushey Rd. SW20—3D 120
Bushey Rd. Croy—2C 136
Bushey Rd. Sutt—4J 131
Bushey Way. Beck—6F 127
Bush Fair Ct. N14—6A 6
Bushfield Clo. Edgw—2C 12
Bushfield Cres. Edgw—2C 12
Bush Gro. NW9—7J 25
Bush Gro. Stan—7J 11
Bushgrove Rd. Dag—4D 52
Bush Hill. N21—7H 7
Bush Hill Rd. N21—6J 7
Bush Hill Rd. Harr—6F 25
Bush Ind. Est. N19—3G 45
Bush Ind. Est. NW10—4K 57
Bushmead Clo. N15—4F 31
Bushmoor Cres. SE18—7F 83
Bushnell Rd. SW17—2F 109
Bush Rd. E8—1H 63
Bush Rd. E11—7H 33
Bush Rd. SE8—4K 79
Bush Rd. Buck H—4G 21
Bush Rd. Rich—6F 73
Bushway. Dag—4D 52
Bushwood. E11—7H 33
Bushwood Dri. SE1
—4F 79 (4K 157)
Bushwood Rd. Rich—6G 73
Bushy Ct. King T—1C 118
(off Up. Teddington Rd.)
Bushy Lees. Sidc—6K 99
Bushy Pk. Gdns. Tedd—5H 103
Bushy Pk. Rd. Tedd—7B 104
(in two parts)
Bushy Rd. Tedd—6K 103
Butcher Row. E14 & E1—7K 63
Butchers Rd. E16—6J 65
Bute Av. Rich—2E 104
Bute Ct. Wall—5G 133
Bute Gdns. W6—4F 75
Bute Gdns. Wall—5G 133
Bute Gdns. W. Wall—5G 133
Bute Rd. Croy—1A 134
Bute Rd. Ilf—5F 35
Bute Rd. Wall—4G 133
Bute St. SW7—4B 76 (3A 152)
Bute Wlk. N1—6D 46
Butler Ct. Wemb—4A 40
Butler Pl. SW1—3H 77 (1C 154)
Butler Rd. NW10—7A 42
Butler Rd. Dag—4B 52
Butler Rd. Harr—7G 23
Butlers Dri. E4—1K 9
Butler St. E2—3J 63
Butlers Wharf. SE1
—2F 79 (5K 151)
Butterfield Clo. SE16—2H 79
Butterfield Clo. Twic—6A 87
Butterfields. E17—5E 32
Butterfield Sq. E6—6D 66
Butterfly La. SE9—6F 99
Butterfly Wlk. SE5—2D 94
Butter Hill. Wall—4H 133
Butteridges Clo. Dag—1F 69
Buttermere Clo. SE1
—4F 79 (3J 157)
Buttermere Clo. Mord—6F 121
Buttermere Ct. NW8—1B 60
Buttermere Dri. SW15—5G 91
Buttermere Wlk. E8—6F 47
Butterwick. W6—4E 74
Butterworth Gdns. Wfd G—5D 20

Buttesland St. N1
—3D 62 (1F 145)
Buttfield Clo. Dag —6H 53
Buttmarsh Clo. SE18 —5F 83
Buttsbury Rd. Ilf —5G 51
(in two parts)
Butts Cotts. Felt —3C 102
Butts Cres. Felt —3E 102
Butts Rd. Brom —5G 113
Butts, The. Bren —6D 72
Buxted Rd. E8 —7F 47
Buxted Rd. N12 —5H 15
Buxted Rd. SE22 —4E 94
Buxton Clo. Wfd G —6G 21
Buxton Ct. N1 —3C 62 (1D 144)
Buxton Cres. Sutt —4G 131
Buxton Dri. E11 —4G 33
Buxton Dri. N Mald —2K 119
Buxton Gdns. W3 —7H 57
Buxton Ho. E11 —4G 33
Buxton Rd. E4 —1A 20
Buxton Rd. E6 —3C 66
Buxton Rd. E15 —5G 49
Buxton Rd. E17 —4A 32
Buxton Rd. N19 —1H 45
Buxton Rd. NW2 —6D 42
Buxton Rd. SW14 —3A 90
Buxton Rd. Eri —7K 85
Buxton Rd. Ilf —6J 35
Buxton Rd. T Hth —5B 124
Buxton St. E1 —4F 63 (4K 145)
Buzzard Creek Ind. Est. Bark
—5A 68
Byam St. SW6 —2A 92
Byards Ct. SE16 —4K 79
(off Worgan St.)
Byards Croft. SW16 —1H 123
Byatt Wlk. Hamp —6C 102
Bychurch End. Tedd —5K 103
Bycroft Rd. S'hall —4E 54
Bycroft St. SE20 —7K 111
Bycullah Av. Enf —3G 7
Bycullah Rd. Enf —2G 7
Byegrove Rd. SW19 —6B 108
Byelands Clo. SE16 —1K 79
Bye, The. W3 —6A 58
Byeways. Twic —3F 103
Byeways, The. Surb —5G 119
Byeway, The. SW14 —3J 89
Bye Way, The. Harr —1K 23
Byfeld Gdns. SW13 —1C 90
Byfield Clo. SE16 —3A 80
Byfield Pas. Iswth —3A 88
Byfield Rd. Iswth —3A 88
Byford Clo. E15 —7G 49
Byford Ho. Barn —4A 4
Bygrove. New Ad —6C 136
Bygrove St. E14 —6D 64
Byland Clo. N21 —7E 6
Bylands Clo. SE2 —3B 84
Byne Rd. SE26 —6J 111
Byne Rd. Cars —2C 132
Bynes Rd. S Croy —7D 134
Byng Pl. WC1 —4H 61 (4D 142)
Byng Rd. Barn —2A 4
Byng St. E14 —2C 80
Bynon Av. Bexh —3F 101
Byre Rd. N14 —6A 6
Byre Rd., The. N14 —6A 6
Byrne Rd. SW12 —1F 109
Byron Av. E12 —6C 50
Byron Av. E18 —3H 33
Byron Av. NW9 —4H 25
Byron Av. N Mald —5C 120
Byron Av. Sutt —4B 132

Byron Av. E. Sutt —4B 132
Byron Clo. E8 —1G 63
Byron Clo. SE20 —3H 125
Byron Clo. SE26 —5A 112
Byron Clo. SE28 —1C 84
Byron Clo. Hamp —4D 102
Byron Ct. E11 —4K 33
(off Makepiece Rd.)
Byron Ct. W7 —4A 72
(off Boston Rd.)
Byron Ct. Enf —2G 7
Byron Ct. Harr —6J 23
Byron Dri. N2 —6B 28
Byron Dri. Eri —7H 85
Byron Gdns. Sutt —4B 132
Byron Hill Rd. Harr —1H 39
Byron Ho. Dart —5K 101
Byron M. NW3 —5D 44
Byron Rd. E10 —1D 48
Byron Rd. E17 —3C 32
Byron Rd. NW2 —2D 42
Byron Rd. NW7 —5H 13
Byron Rd. W5 —1F 73
Byron Rd. Harr —6J 23
Byron Rd. W'stone —2K 23
Byron Rd. Wemb —2C 40
Byron St. E14 —6E 64
Byron Ter. N9 —6D 8
Byron Way. N'holt —3C 54
Bysouth Clo. Ilf —1F 35
Bythorn St. SW9 —3K 93
Byton Rd. SW17 —6D 108
Byward Av. Felt —6A 86
Byward St. EC3 —7E 62 (3H 151)
Bywater Pl. SE16 —1A 80
Bywater St. SW3
—5D 76 (5E 152)
Byway. E11 —5A 34
Byway, The. Eps —4B 130
Byway, The. Sutt —7B 132
Bywell Pl. W1 —5G 61 (6A 142)
Bywood Av. Croy —6J 125
Byworth Wlk. N19 —1J 45

Cabbell St. NW1
—5C 60 (6C 140)
Cabinet Way. E4 —5G 19
Cable Pl. SE10 —1E 96
Cables Clo. Belv —3J 85
Cable St. E1 —7G 63
Cabot Ct. SE16 —4K 79
(off Worgan St.)
Cabot Sq. E14 —1C 80
Cabot Way. E6 —1B 66
Cab Rd. SE1 —2A 78 (5H 149)
Cabul Rd. SW11 —2C 92
Cactus Clo. SE15 —2E 94
Cactus Wlk. W12 —6B 58
Cadbury Clo. Iswth —1A 88
Cadbury Way. SE16
(in two parts) —4F 79 (2K 157)
Caddington Clo. Barn —5H 5
Caddington Rd. NW2 —3G 43
Caddis Clo. Stan —7E 10
Cadell Clo. E2 —2F 63 (1K 145)
Cade Rd. SE10 —1F 97
Cader Rd. SW18 —6A 92
Cadet Pl. SE10 —5G 81
Cadiz Rd. Dag —7J 53
Cadiz St. SE17 —5C 78 (6D 156)
Cadley Ter. SE23 —2J 111
Cadman Clo. SW9 —7B 78
Cadman Ct. W4 —5H 73
(off Chaseley Dri.)

Cadmer Clo. N Mald —4A 120
Cadmus Clo. SW4 —3H 93
Cadogan Clo. Beck —1F 127
Cadogan Clo. Harr —4F 39
Cadogan Clo. Tedd —5J 103
Cadogan Ct. Sutt —6K 131
Cadogan Gdns. E18 —3K 33
Cadogan Gdns. N3 —1K 27
Cadogan Gdns. N21 —5F 7
Cadogan Gdns. SW3
—4D 76 (3F 153)
Cadogan Ga. E9 —7B 48
Cadogan Ga. SW1
—4D 76 (3F 153)
Cadogan Ho. SW3 —6B 76
Cadogan La. SW1
—3E 76 (2G 153)
Cadogan Pl. SW1
—3D 76 (1F 153)
Cadogan Rd. Surb —5D 118
Cadogan Sq. SW1
—3D 76 (2E 152)
Cadogan St. SW3
—4D 76 (4E 152)
Cadogan Ter. E9 —6B 48
Cadoxton Av. N15 —6F 31
Cadwallon Rd. SE9 —2F 115
Caedmon Rd. N7 —4K 45
Caerleon Clo. Sidc —5C 116
Caerleon Ter. SE2 —4B 84
Caernarvon Clo. Mitc —3J 123
Caernarvon Dri. Ilf —1E 34
Caesars Wlk. Mitc —5D 122
Cahill St. EC1 —4C 62 (4D 144)
Cahir St. E14 —4D 80
Cain Ct. W5 —5C 56
(off Castlebar M.)
Caine Ho. W3 —2H 73
(off Hanbury Rd.)
Caird St. W10 —3G 59
Cairn Av. W5 —1D 72
Cairndale Clo. Brom —7H 113
Cairnfield Av. NW2 —3A 42
Cairngorm Clo. Tedd —5A 104
Cairns Av. Wfd G —6H 21
Cairns Rd. SW11 —5C 92
Cairn Way. Stan —6E 10
Cairo New Rd. Croy —2B 134
Cairo Rd. E17 —4C 32
Caister Ho. N7 —6K 45
Caistor M. SW12 —7F 93
Caistor Pk. Rd. E15 —1H 65
Caistor Rd. SW12 —7F 93
Caithness Gdns. Sidc —6K 99
Caithness Ho. N1 —1K 61
(off Twyford St.)
Caithness Rd. W14 —3F 75
Caithness Rd. Mitc —7F 109
Calabria Rd. N5 —6B 46
Calais Ga. SE5 —1B 94
Calais St. SE5 —1B 94
Calbourne Rd. SW12 —7D 92
Calcott Ct. W14 —3G 75
(off Blythe Rd.)
Calcott Wlk. SE9 —4C 114
Caldbeck Av. Wor Pk —2D 130
Caldecote Gdns. Bush —1D 10
Caldecot Rd. SE5 —2C 94
Caldecott Way. E5 —3K 47
Calder Av. Gnfd —2K 55
Calder Clo. Enf —3K 7
Calder Ct. SE16 —1A 80
Calder Gdns. Edgw —3G 25
Calderon Pl. W10 —5E 58
Calderon Rd. E11 —4E 48

Calder Rd. Mord —5A 122
Caldervale Rd. SW4 —5H 93
Calderwood St. SE18 —4E 82
Caldew St. SE5 —7D 78
Caldwell St. SW9 —7K 77
Caldy Rd. Belv —3H 85
Caldy Wlk. N1 —6C 46
Caleb St. SE1 —2C 78 (6C 150)
Caledonian Clo. Ilf —1B 52
Caledonian Rd. N1
—2J 61 (1F 143)
Caledonian Wharf. E14 —4F 81
Caledonia St. N1 —2J 61 (1F 143)
Caledon Rd. E6 —1D 66
Caledon Rd. Wall —4E 132
Cale St. SW3 —5C 76 (5C 152)
Caletock Way. SE10 —5H 81
Caliban Tower. N1 —2E 62
(off Arden Est.)
Calico Row. SW11 —3A 92
Calidore Clo. SW2 —6K 93
California Ct. Bush —1C 10
(off High Rd.)
California La. Bush —1C 10
California Rd. N Mald —3J 119
Callaby Ter. N1 —6D 46
Callaghan Clo. SE13 —4G 97
Callander Rd. SE6 —2D 112
Callanders, The. Bush —1D 10
Callard Av. N13 —4G 17
Callcott Ct. NW6 —7H 43
Callcott Rd. NW6 —7H 43
Callcott St. W8 —1J 75
Callendar Rd. SW7
—3B 76 (1A 152)
Callenders Cotts. Belv —2K 85
Callingham Clo. E14 —5B 64
Callis Rd. E17 —6B 32
Callonfield. E17 —4A 32
Callow St. SW3 —6B 76 (7A 152)
Callum Welch Ho. EC1
—4C 62 (4C 144)
(off Goswell Rd.)
Calmington Rd. SE5
—6E 78 (7H 157)
Calmont Rd. Brom —6F 113
Calne Av. Ilf —1F 35
Calonne Rd. SW19 —4F 107
Calshot St. N1 —2K 61 (1G 143)
Calshot Way. Enf —3G 7
Calstock Ho. SE11
—5A 78 (5K 155)
Calthorpe Gdns. Edgw —5K 11
Calthorpe Gdns. Sutt —3A 132
Calthorpe St. WC1
—4K 61 (3H 143)
Calton Av. SE21 —6E 94
Calton Rd. New Bar —6F 5
Calverley Clo. Beck —6D 112
Calverley Cres. Dag —2G 53
Calverley Gdns. Harr —7D 24
Calverley Gro. N19 —1H 45
Calverley Rd. Eps —6C 130
Calvert Av. E2 —3F 63 (2H 145)
Calvert Clo. Belv —4G 85
Calvert Clo. Sidc —6E 116
Calverton. SE17 —6E 78 (7G 157)
Calverton Rd. E6 —1E 66
Calvert Rd. SE10 —5H 81
Calvert Rd. Barn —2A 4
Calvert's Bldgs. SE1
—1D 78 (5E 150)
Calvert St. NW1 —1E 60
Calvin St. E1 —4F 63 (4J 145)

Calydon Rd. SE7 —5K 81
Calypso Way. SE16 —3B 80
Camac Rd. Twic —1H 103
Cambalt Rd. SW15 —5F 91
Camber Ho. SE15 —6J 79
Camberley Av. SW20 —2E 120
Camberley Av. Enf —4K 7
Camberley Clo. Sutt —3F 131
Cambert Way. SE3 —4K 97
Camberley Av. Enf —4K 7
Camberwell Chu. St. SE5 —1D 94
Camberwell Glebe. SE5 —1E 94
Camberwell Grn. SE5 —1D 94
Camberwell Green. (Junct.)
—1D 94
Camberwell Gro. SE5 —1D 94
Camberwell New Rd. SE5 —6A 78
Camberwell Pl. SE5 —1C 94
Camberwell Rd. SE17 & SE5
—6C 78 (7D 156)
Camberwell Sta. Rd. SE5 —1C 94
Camberwell Trad. Est. SE5
—1C 94
Cambeys Rd. Dag —5H 53
Camborne Av. W13 —2B 72
Camborne M. W11 —6G 59
Camborne Rd. SW18 —7J 91
Camborne Rd. Croy —7G 125
Camborne Rd. Mord —5F 121
Camborne Rd. Sidc —3C 116
Camborne Rd. Sutt —7J 131
Camborne Rd. Well —2K 99
Camborne Way. Houn —1E 86
Cambourne Av. N9 —7E 8
Cambourne M. W11 —6G 59
(off St Mark's Rd.)
Cambourne Wlk. Rich —6D 88
Cambrai Ct. N13 —3D 16
Cambray Rd. SW12 —1G 109
Cambray Rd. Orp —7K 129
Cambria Clo. Houn —4E 86
Cambria Clo. Sidc —1H 115
Cambria Ct. Felt —7A 86
Cambria Ho. SE26 —4G 111
(off High Level Dri.)
Cambrian Av. Ilf —5J 35
Cambrian Grn. NW9 —5A 26
(off Snowden Dri.)
Cambrian Rd. E10 —7C 32
Cambrian Rd. Rich —6F 89
Cambria Rd. SE5 —3C 94
Cambria St. SW6 —7K 75
Cambridge Av. NW6 —2J 59
Cambridge Av. NW10 —3E 58
Cambridge Av. N Mald —3A 120
(in two parts)
Cambridge Av. Well —4K 99
Cambridge Av. Gnfd —5K 39
Cambridge Cir. WC2
—6H 61 (1D 148)
Cambridge Clo. N22 —1A 30
Cambridge Clo. NW10 —3K 41
Cambridge Clo. SW20 —1D 120
Cambridge Clo. Houn —4C 86
Cambridge Cotts. Rich —6G 73
Cambridge Ct. N16 —7E 30
(off Amhurst Pk.)
Cambridge Cres. E2 —2H 63
Cambridge Cres. Tedd —5A 104
Cambridge Dri. SE12 —5J 97
Cambridge Dri. Ruis —2A 38
Cambridge Gdns. N10 —1E 28
Cambridge Gdns. N17 —7J 17
Cambridge Gdns. N21 —7J 7

Cambridge Gdns. NW6 —2J 59
Cambridge Gdns. W10 —6F 59
Cambridge Gdns. Enf —2B 8
Cambridge Gdns. King T
　—2G 119
Cambridge Ga. NW1
　—4F 61 (3J 141)
Cambridge Ga. M. NW1
　—4F 61 (3K 141)
Cambridge Grn. SE9 —1F 115
Cambridge Gro. SE20 —1H 125
Cambridge Gro. W6 —4D 74
Cambridge Gro. Rd. King T
　—3G 119
Cambridge Heath Rd. E1 & E2
　—4H 63
Cambridge Ho. W13 —6A 56
Cambridge Lodge Vs. E8 —1H 63
Cambridge Pde. Enf —1B 8
Cambridge Pk. E11 —7J 33
Cambridge Pk. Twic —6C 88
Cambridge Pk. Ct. Twic —7D 88
Cambridge Pk. Rd. E11 —7H 33
Cambridge Pl. NW6 —3J 59
Cambridge Pl. W8 —2K 75
Cambridge Rd. E4 —1A 20
Cambridge Rd. E11 —6H 33
Cambridge Rd. NW6 —2J 59
　(in three parts)
Cambridge Rd. SE20 —3H 125
Cambridge Rd. SW11 —1D 92
Cambridge Rd. SW13 —2B 90
Cambridge Rd. SW20 —1C 120
Cambridge Rd. W7 —2K 71
Cambridge Rd. Bark —7G 51
Cambridge Rd. Brom —7J 113
Cambridge Rd. Cars —6C 132
Cambridge Rd. Hamp —7D 102
Cambridge Rd. Harr —5E 22
Cambridge Rd. Houn —4C 86
Cambridge Rd. Ilf —1J 51
Cambridge Rd. King T —2F 119
Cambridge Rd. Mitc —3G 123
Cambridge Rd. N Mald —4A 120
Cambridge Rd. Rich —7G 73
Cambridge Rd. Sidc —4J 115
Cambridge Rd. S'hall —1D 70
Cambridge Rd. Tedd —4K 103
Cambridge Rd. Twic —6D 88
Cambridge Rd. N. W4 —5H 73
Cambridge Rd. S. W4 —5H 73
Cambridge Row. SE18 —5F 83
Cambridge Sq. W2
　—6C 60 (7C 140)
Cambridge St. SW1
　—4F 77 (4K 153)
Cambridge Ter. N9 —7A 8
Cambridge Ter. NW1
　—3F 61 (2J 141)
Cambridge Ter. M. NW1
　—3F 61 (2K 141)
Cambus Clo. Hayes —5C 54
Cambus Rd. E16 —5J 65
Cam Ct. SE15 —6F 79 (7J 157)
Camdale Rd. SE18 —7K 83
Camden Av. Felt —1A 102
Camden Av. Hayes —7B 54
Camden Clo. Chst —1G 129
Camden Ct. Belv —5G 85
Camden Est. SE15 —1F 95
Camden Gdns. NW1 —7F 45
Camden Gdns. Sutt —5K 131
Camden Gdns. T Hth —3B 124
Camden Gro. Chst —6F 115
Camden High St. NW1 —7F 45

Camden Hill Rd. SE19 —6E 110
Camden Ho. SE8 —5B 80
Camdenhurst St. E14 —6A 64
Camden La. N7 —5H 45
Camden Lock Pl. NW1 —7F 45
Camden M. NW1 —7G 45
Camden Pk. Rd. NW1 —6H 45
Camden Pk. Rd. Chst —7D 114
Camden Pas. N1 —1B 62
Camden Rd. E11 —6K 33
Camden Rd. E17 —6B 32
Camden Rd. NW1 & N7 —7G 45
Camden Rd. Bex —1F 117
Camden Rd. Cars —4D 132
Camden Rd. Sutt —5K 131
Camden Row. SE3 —2G 97
Camden Row. Pinn —3A 22
Camden Sq. NW1 —6H 45
Camden Sq. SE15 —1F 95
Camden St. NW1 —7G 45
Camden Ter. NW1 —6H 45
Camden Wlk. N1 —1B 62
Camden Way. Chst —7D 114
Camden Way. T Hth —3B 124
Cameford Ct. SW12 —7J 93
Camelford Ct. W11 —6G 59
Camelford Ho. SE1
　—5J 77 (5F 155)
Camelford Wlk. W11 —6G 59
Camellia Ho. SE8 —7B 80
　(off Idonia St.)
Camellia Pl. Twic —7F 87
Camellia St. SW8 —7J 77
Camelot Clo. SE28 —2H 83
Camelot Clo. SW19 —4J 107
Camel Rd. E16 —1B 82
Camera Pl. SW10
　—6B 76 (7A 152)
Cameron Clo. N18 —4C 18
Cameron Clo. N20 —2G 15
Cameron Clo. Bex —3K 117
Cameron Ho. SE5 —7C 78
Cameron Pl. E1 —6H 63
Cameron Rd. SE6 —2B 112
Cameron Rd. Brom —5J 127
Cameron Rd. Croy —6B 124
Cameron Rd. Ilf —1J 51
Cameron Sq. Mitc —1C 122
Cameron Ter. SE12 —3K 113
Camerton Clo. E8 —6F 47
Camilla Rd. SE16 —4H 79
Camille Clo. SE25 —3G 125
Camlan Rd. Brom —4H 113
Camlet St. E2 —4F 63 (3J 145)
Camlet Way. Barn —2D 4
Camley St. NW1 —7H 45
Camm Gdns. King T —2F 119
Camomile Av. Mitc —1D 122
Camomile St. EC3
　—6E 62 (7G 145)
Campana Rd. SW6 —1J 91
Campbell Av. Ilf —4F 35
Campbell Clo. SE18 —1E 98
Campbell Clo. SW16 —4H 109
Campbell Clo. Twic —1H 103
Campbell Clo. N17 —1F 31
Campbell Clo. SE22 —1G 111
Campbell Ct. SE14 —3A 76
　(off Gloucester Rd.)
Campbell Croft. Edgw —5B 12
Campbell Gordon Way. NW2
　—4D 42
Campbell Ho. W12 —7D 58
　(off White City Est.)

Campbell Rd. E3 —3C 64
Campbell Rd. E6 —1C 66
Campbell Rd. E15 —4H 49
Campbell Rd. E17 —4B 32
Campbell Rd. N17 —1F 31
Campbell Rd. W7 —7J 55
Campbell Rd. Croy —7B 124
Campbell Rd. Twic —2H 103
Campbell Wlk. N1 —1J 61
　(off Outram Pl.)
Campdale Rd. N7 —3H 45
Campden Cres. Dag —4B 52
Campden Cres. Wemb —3B 40
Campden Gro. W8 —2J 75
Campden Hill. W8 —2J 75
Campden Hill Ct. W8 —2G 75
　(off Campden Hill Rd.)
Campden Hill Gdns. W8 —1J 75
Campden Hill Ga. W8 —2J 75
Campden Hill Pl. W11 —1H 75
Campden Hill Rd. W8 —1J 75
Campden Hill Sq. W8 —1H 75
Campden Ho. Clo. W8 —2J 75
Campden Houses. W8 —1J 75
Campden Rd. S Croy —5E 134
Campden St. W8 —1J 75
Campe Ho. N10 —7K 15
Campen Clo. SW19 —2G 107
Camperdown St. E1
　—6F 63 (1K 151)
Campfield Rd. SE9 —7B 98
Campion Clo. E6 —7D 66
Campion Clo. Croy —4E 134
Campion Clo. Harr —6F 25
Campion Ct. Wemb —2E 56
Campion Gdns. Wfd G —5D 20
Campion Pl. SE28 —1A 84
Campion Rd. SW15 —4E 90
Campion Rd. Iswth —1K 87
Campion Ter. NW2 —3F 43
Camplin Rd. Harr —5E 24
Camplin St. SE14 —7K 79
Camp Rd. SW19 —5D 106
Campsbourne Rd. N8 —3J 29
　(in two parts)
Campsbourne, The. N8 —4J 29
Campsey Gdns. Dag —7B 52
Campsey Rd. Dag —7B 52
Campsfield Rd. N8 —3J 29
Campshill Pl. SE13 —5E 96
Campshill Rd. SE13 —5E 96
Campus Rd. E17 —6B 32
Campus Way. NW4 —3D 26
Camp View. SW19 —5D 106
Cam Rd. E15 —1F 65
Camrose Av. Edgw —2F 25
Camrose Av. Eri —6H 85
Camrose Av. Felt —4A 102
Camrose Clo. Croy —7A 126
Camrose Clo. Mord —4J 121
Camrose St. SE2 —5A 84
Canada Av. N18 —6H 17
Canada Cres. W3 —4J 57
Canada Est. SE16 —3J 79
Canada Gdns. SE13 —5E 96
Canada Rd. W3 —5J 57
Canada Sq. E14 —1D 80
Canada St. SE16 —2K 79
Canada Way. W12 —7D 58
Canada Wharf. SE16 —1B 80
Canadian Av. SE6 —7D 96
Canal App. SE8 —6A 80
Canal Bridge. (Junct.) —6G 79
Canal Clo. E1 —4A 64
Canal Clo. W10 —4F 59

Canal Gro. SE15 —6G 79
Canal Head. SE15 —1G 95
Canal Path. E2 —1F 63
Canal Rd. E3 —4A 64
Canalside. SE28 —7D 68
Canal St. SE5 —6D 78 (7E 156)
Canal Wlk. N1 —1D 62
Canal Wlk. SE26 —5J 111
Canal Wlk. Croy —6F 125
Canal Way. W10 —4F 59
Canberra Clo. NW4 —3C 26
Canberra Clo. Dag —1K 69
Canberra Cres. Dag —7K 53
Canberra Dri. N'holt —3A 54
Canberra Rd. E6 —1D 66
Canberra Rd. SE7 —7A 82
Canberra Rd. W13 —1A 72
Canberra Rd. Bexh —6D 84
Canbury 2000 Bus. Pk. King T
　—1E 118
Canbury Av. King T —1F 119
Canbury M. SE26 —3G 111
Canbury Pk. Rd. King T
　—1E 118
Canbury Pas. King T —1D 118
Canbury Pl. King T —1E 118
Cancell Rd. SW9 —1A 94
Candahar Rd. SW11 —2C 92
Candler M. Twic —7A 88
Candler St. N15 —6D 30
Candover St. W1
　—5G 61 (6A 142)
Candy St. E3 —1B 64
Cane Clo. Wall —7J 133
Caney M. NW2 —2F 43
Canfield Dri. Ruis —5A 38
Canfield Gdns. NW6 —7K 43
Canfield Ho. N15 —6E 30
　(off Albert Rd.)
Canfield Pl. NW6 —6A 44
Canfield Rd. Wfd G —7H 21
Canford Av. N'holt —1D 54
Canford Clo. Enf —2F 7
Canford Gdns. N Mald —6A 120
Canford Pl. Tedd —6C 104
Canford Rd. SW11 —5E 92
Canham Rd. SE25 —3E 124
Canham Rd. W3 —2A 74
Canmore Gdns. SW16 —7G 109
Cann Hall Rd. E11 —4G 49
Canning Cres. N22 —1K 29
Canning Cross. SE5 —2E 94
Canning Ho. W12 —7D 58
　(off White City Est.)
Canning Pas. W8 —3A 76
Canning Pl. W8 —3A 76
Canning Pl. M. W8 —3A 76
　(off Canning Pl.)
Canning Rd. E15 —2F 65
Canning Rd. E17 —4A 32
Canning Rd. N5 —3B 46
Canning Rd. Croy —2F 135
Canning Rd. Harr —3J 23
Canning Town. (Junct.) —5G 65
Cannizaro Rd. SW19 —6E 106
Cannock Ho. N4 —7C 30
Cannon Clo. SW20 —4E 120
Cannon Clo. Hamp —6F 103
Cannon Dri. E14 —7C 64
Cannon Hill. N14 —3D 16
Cannon Hill. NW6 —5J 43
Cannon Hill La. SW20 —5F 121
Cannon Hill M. N14 —3D 16

Cannon Ho. SE11
　—4K 77 (4H 155)
Cannon La. NW3 —3B 44
Cannon La. Pinn —5C 22
Cannon Pl. NW3 —3B 44
Cannon Pl. SE7 —5C 82
Cannon Rd. N14 —3D 16
Cannon Rd. Bexh —1F 101
Cannon St. EC4 —6C 62 (1C 150)
Cannon St. Rd. E1 —6H 63
Cannon Trad. Est. Wemb —4H 41
Cannon Wharf Bus. Pk. SE8
　—4A 80
Canon Av. Romf —5C 36
Canon Beck Rd. SE16 —2J 79
Canonbie Rd. SE23 —7J 95
Canonbury Bus. Cen. N1 —1C 62
Canonbury Cres. N1 —7C 46
Canonbury Gro. N1 —7C 46
Canonbury La. N1 —7B 46
Canonbury Pk. N. N1 —6C 46
Canonbury Pk. S. N1 —6C 46
Canonbury Pl. N1 —6B 46
Canonbury Rd. N1 —6B 46
Canonbury Rd. Enf —1K 7
Canonbury Sq. N1 —7B 46
Canonbury St. N1 —7C 46
Canonbury Vs. N1 —7B 46
Canon Mohon Clo. N14 —6A 6
Canon Murnane Rd. SE1
　—3F 79 (2J 157)
Canon Rd. Brom —3A 128
Canon Row. SW1
　—2J 77 (7E 148)
Canon's Clo. N2 —7B 28
Canons Clo. Edgw —6A 12
Canons Corner. Edgw —4K 11
Canons Ct. Edgw —6A 12
Canons Dri. Edgw —6K 11
Canonsleigh Rd. Dag —7B 52
Canons Pk. Stan —6J 11
Canon St. N1 —1C 62
Canon's Wlk. Croy —3K 135
Canrobert St. E2 —2H 63
Cantelowes Rd. NW1 —6H 45
Canterbury Av. Ilf —7C 34
Canterbury Av. Sidc —2B 116
Canterbury Clo. E6 —6D 66
Canterbury Clo. SE5 —2C 94
Canterbury Clo. Beck —1D 126
Canterbury Clo. Gnfd —5F 55
Canterbury Ct. NW9 —2A 26
Canterbury Ct. SE12 —3K 113
Canterbury Cres. SW9 —3A 94
Canterbury Gro. SE27 —4A 110
Canterbury Ho. SE1
　—3K 77 (1H 155)
Canterbury Ho. SE15 —7A 78
Canterbury Ho. Bark —7A 52
　(off Margaret Bondfield Av.)
Canterbury Ind. Est. SE15 —6J 79
Canterbury Pl. SE17
　—4B 78 (4B 156)
Canterbury Rd. E10 —7E 32
Canterbury Rd. NW6 —2J 59
Canterbury Rd. Croy —7K 123
Canterbury Rd. Felt —2C 102
Canterbury Rd. Harr —5F 23
Canterbury Rd. Mord —7K 121
Canterbury Ter. NW6 —2J 59
Canthus Dri. SE1 —5G 79
Cantium Retail Pk. SE1 —6G 79
　(off Olmar St.)
Cantley Gdns. SE19 —1F 125
Cantley Gdns. Ilf —6G 35

Cantley Rd. *W7* —3A **72**
Canton St. *E14* —6C **64**
Cantrell Rd. *E3* —4B **64**
Cantwell Rd. *SE18* —7F **83**
Canute Gdns. *SE16* —4K **79**
Canvey St. *SE1* —1C **78** (4C **150**)
Cape Clo. *Bark* —7F **51**
Capel Av. *Wall* —5K **133**
Capel Clo. *N20* —3F **15**
Capel Clo. *Brom* —1C **138**
Capel Ct. *SE20* —1J **125**
Capel Gdns. *Ilf* —4K **51**
Capel Gdns. *Pinn* —4D **22**
Capel Rd. *E7 & E12* —4K **49**
Capel Rd. *Barn* —6H **5**
Capener's Clo. *SW1*
　　　　　—2E **76** (7F **147**)
Capern Rd. *SW18* —1A **108**
Cape Rd. *N17* —3G **31**
Cape Yd. *E1* —7G **63**
Capital Bus. Cen. *Wemb* —2D **56**
Capital Interchange Way. *Bren*
　　　　　—5G **73**
Capital Pl. *Croy* —5K **133**
*Capital Wharf. E1 —1G **79**
　(off High St. Wapping.)*
Capitol Ind. Pk. *NW9* —3J **25**
Capitol Way. *NW9* —3J **25**
Capland St. *NW8*
　　　　　—4B **60** (3B **140**)
Caple Rd. *NW10* —2B **58**
Capper St. *WC1* —4G **61** (4B **142**)
Caprea Clo. *Hayes* —5B **54**
Capricorn Cen. *Dag* —7F **37**
Capri Ho. *E17* —2B **32**
Capri Rd. *Croy* —1E **135**
Capstan Clo. *Romf* —6B **36**
Capstan Ride. *Enf* —2F **7**
Capstan Rd. *SE8* —4B **80**
Capstan Sq. *E14* —2E **80**
Capstan Way. *SE16* —1A **80**
Capstone Rd. *Brom* —4H **113**
Capthorne Av. *Harr* —1C **38**
Capuchin Clo. *Stan* —6G **11**
Capulet M. *E16* —1J **81**
Capworth St. *E10* —1C **48**
Caradoc Clo. *W2* —6J **59**
*Caradoc Evans Clo. N11 —5A **16**
　(off Springfield Rd.)*
Caradoc St. *SE10* —5G **81**
Caradon Clo. *E11* —1G **49**
Caradon Way. *N15* —4D **30**
Carage Clo. *Eri* —6J **85**
Caravel Clo. *E14* —3C **80**
Caravelle Gdns. *N'holt* —3B **54**
Caravel M. *SE8* —6C **80**
Caraway Clo. *E13* —5K **65**
Caraway Pl. *Wall* —3F **133**
Carberry Rd. *SE19* —6E **110**
Carbery Av. *W3* —2F **73**
Carbis Clo. *E4* —1A **20**
Carbis Rd. *E14* —6B **64**
Carbuncle Pas. Way. *N17* —2G **31**
Carburton St. *W1*
　　　　　—5F **61** (5K **141**)
Cardale St. *E14* —2E **80**
Carden Rd. *SE15* —3H **95**
Cardiff Rd. *W7* —3A **72**
Cardiff Rd. *Enf* —4C **8**
Cardiff St. *SE18* —7J **83**
*Cardigan Ct. W7 —4K **55**
　(off Copley Clo.)*
Cardigan Gdns. *Ilf* —2A **52**
Cardigan Rd. *E3* —2B **64**
Cardigan Rd. *SW13* —2C **90**

Cardigan Rd. *SW19* —6A **108**
Cardigan Rd. *Rich* —6E **88**
Cardigan St. *SE11*
　　　　　—5A **78** (5J **155**)
Cardigan Wlk. *N1* —7C **46**
　(off Ashby Gro.)
Cardinal Av. *King T* —5E **104**
Cardinal Av. *Mord* —6G **121**
Cardinal Bourne St. *SE1*
　　　　　—3D **78** (2F **157**)
Cardinal Cap All. *SE1*
　　　　　—1C **78** (3C **150**)
Cardinal Clo. *Chst* —1J **129**
Cardinal Clo. *Edgw* —7E **12**
Cardinal Clo. *Mord* —6G **121**
Cardinal Clo. *Wor Pk* —4C **130**
Cardinal Cres. *N Mald* —2J **119**
Cardinal Dri. *Ilf* —2C **34**
Cardinal Pl. *SW15* —4F **91**
Cardinal Rd. *Felt* —1A **102**
Cardinal Rd. *Ruis* —1B **38**
Cardinals Wlk. *Hamp* —7G **103**
Cardinals Way. *N19* —1H **45**
Cardinal Way. *Harr* —3J **23**
Cardine M. *SE15* —7H **79**
Cardington Sq. *Houn* —4B **86**
Cardington St. *NW1*
　　　　　—3G **61** (1B **142**)
Cardozo Rd. *N7* —5J **45**
Cardrew Av. *N12* —5G **15**
Cardrew Clo. *N12* —5H **15**
Cardrew Ct. *N12* —5G **15**
Cardross St. *W6* —3D **74**
Cardwell Rd. *N7* —4J **45**
Cardwell Rd. *SE18* —4E **82**
Carew Clo. *N7* —2K **45**
Carew Mnr. Cotts. *Wall* —3H **133**
Carew Rd. *N17* —2G **31**
Carew Rd. *W13* —2C **72**
Carew Rd. *Mitc* —2E **122**
Carew Rd. *T Hth* —4B **124**
Carew Rd. *Wall* —6G **133**
Carew St. *SE5* —2C **94**
Carey Ct. *Bexh* —5H **101**
Carey Gdns. *SW8* —1G **93**
Carey La. *EC2* —6C **62** (7C **144**)
Carey Pl. *SW1* —4H **77** (4C **154**)
Carey Rd. *Dag* —4E **52**
Carey St. *WC2* —6K **61** (1H **149**)
Carey Way. *Wemb* —4H **41**
Carfax Pl. *SW4* —4H **93**
Carfree Clo. *N1* —7A **46**
Cargill Rd. *SW18* —1K **107**
Cargreen Pl. *SE25* —4F **125**
Cargreen Rd. *SE25* —4F **125**
Cargrey Ho. *Stan* —5H **11**
Carholme Rd. *SE23* —1B **112**
Carillon Ct. *W5* —7D **56**
Carina M. *SE27* —4C **110**
Carisbrooke Av. *Bex* —1D **116**
Carisbrooke Clo. *Enf* —1A **8**
Carisbrooke Clo. *Stan* —2D **24**
*Carisbrooke Ct. W3 —2J **73**
　(off Brouncker Rd.)*
Carisbrooke Ct. *Cheam* —7H **131**
*Carisbrooke Ct. N'holt —1D **54**
　(off Eskdale Av.)*
Carisbrooke Gdns. *SE15* —7F **79**
Carisbrooke Rd. *E17* —4A **32**
Carisbrooke Rd. *Brom* —4A **128**
Carisbrooke Rd. *Mitc* —4H **123**
Carker's La. *NW5* —5F **45**
Carleton Av. *Wall* —7H **133**
Carleton Gdns. *N19* —5G **45**
Carleton Rd. *N7* —5H **45**

Carleton Vs. *NW5* —5G **45**
Carlile Clo. *E3* —2B **64**
Carlina Gdns. *Wfd G* —5E **20**
Carlingford Gdns. *Mitc* —7E **108**
Carlingford Rd. *N15* —3B **30**
Carlingford Rd. *NW3* —4B **44**
Carlingford Rd. *Mord* —6F **121**
Carlisle Av. *EC3* —6F **63** (1J **151**)
Carlisle Av. *W3* —6A **58**
Carlisle Clo. *King T* —1G **119**
Carlisle Gdns. *Ilf* —6C **34**
Carlisle La. *SE1* —3K **77** (2H **155**)
*Carlisle Mans. SW1
　　　　—4G **77** (3A **154**)
　(off Carlisle Pl.)*
Carlisle M. *NW8*
　　　　　—5B **60** (5B **140**)
Carlisle M. *King T* —1G **119**
Carlisle Pl. *N11* —4A **16**
Carlisle Pl. *SW1* —3G **77** (2A **154**)
Carlisle Rd. *E10* —1C **48**
Carlisle Rd. *N4* —7A **30**
Carlisle Rd. *NW6* —1G **59**
Carlisle Rd. *NW9* —3J **25**
Carlisle Rd. *Hamp* —7F **103**
Carlisle Rd. *Sutt* —6H **131**
Carlisle St. *W1* —6H **61** (1C **148**)
Carlisle Wlk. *E8* —6F **47**
Carlisle Way. *SW17* —5E **108**
Carlos Pl. *W1* —7E **60** (3H **147**)
Carlow St. *NW1* —2G **61**
Carlton Av. *Felt* —6A **86**
Carlton Av. *Harr* —5B **24**
Carlton Av. *S Croy* —7E **134**
Carlton Av. E. *Wemb* —2D **40**
Carlton Av. W. *Wemb* —2B **40**
Carlton Clo. *NW3* —2J **43**
Carlton Clo. *N'holt* —5G **39**
Carlton Ct. *SE20* —1H **125**
Carlton Ct. *SW9* —1B **94**
Carlton Ct. *Ilf* —3H **35**
Carlton Cres. *Sutt* —4G **131**
Carlton Dri. *SW15* —5F **91**
Carlton Dri. *Ilf* —3H **35**
Carlton Gdns. *SW1*
　　　　　—1H **77** (5C **148**)
Carlton Gdns. *W5* —6C **56**
Carlton Grn. *SE15* —1H **95**
Carlton Hill. *NW8* —2K **59**
*Carlton Ho. Ter. SW1
　　　　　—1H **77** (5C **148**)*
Carlton Lodge. *N4 —7A **30**
　(off Carlton Rd.)*
Carlton Mans. *W9* —3K **59**
Carlton Pk. Av. *SW20* —2F **121**
Carlton Rd. *E11* —1H **49**
Carlton Rd. *E12* —4B **50**
Carlton Rd. *E17* —1A **32**
Carlton Rd. *N4* —7A **30**
Carlton Rd. *N11* —5K **15**
Carlton Rd. *SW14* —3J **89**
Carlton Rd. *W4* —2K **73**
Carlton Rd. *W5* —7C **56**
Carlton Rd. *Eri* —6H **85**
Carlton Rd. *N Mald* —2A **120**
Carlton Rd. *Sidc* —5K **115**
Carlton Rd. *S Croy* —6D **134**
Carlton Rd. *Well* —3B **100**
Carlton Sq. *E1* —4K **63**
　(in two parts)
Carlton St. *SW1* —7H **61** (3C **148**)
Carlton Ter. *E7* —7A **50**

Carlton Ter. *E11* —5K **33**
Carlton Ter. *N18* —3J **17**
Carlton Ter. *SE26* —3J **111**
Carlton Tower Pl. *SW1*
　　　　　—4D **76** (3F **153**)
Carlton Vale. *NW6* —2H **59**
Carlwell St. *SW17* —5C **108**
Carlyle Av. *Brom* —3B **128**
Carlyle Av. *S'hall* —7D **54**
Carlyle Clo. *N2* —6A **28**
Carlyle Clo. *NW10* —1K **57**
*Carlyle Ct. SW6 —1K **91**
　(off Maltings Pl.)*
Carlyle Ct. *SW10 —1A **92**
　(off Chelsea Harbour)*
Carlyle Gdns. *S'hall* —7D **54**
Carlyle Pl. *SW15* —4F **91**
Carlyle Rd. *E12* —4C **50**
Carlyle Rd. *SE28* —7B **68**
Carlyle Rd. *W5* —5C **72**
Carlyle Rd. *Croy* —2G **135**
Carlyle Sq. *SW3* —5B **76** (6B **152**)
Carlyon Av. *Harr* —4D **38**
Carlyon Clo. *Wemb* —1E **56**
Carlyon Rd. *Hayes* —5A **54**
(in two parts)
Carlyon Rd. *Wemb* —2E **56**
Carlys Clo. *SE20* —2K **125**
Carmalt Gdns. *SW15* —4E **90**
Carmarthen Ct. *W7 —4K **55**
　(off Copley Clo.)*
Carmarthen Grn. *NW9* —5A **26**
Carmarthen Pl. *SE1*
　　　　　—2E **78** (6G **151**)
Carmel Ct. *W8 —2K **75**
　(off Holland St.)*
Carmelite Clo. *Harr* —1G **23**
Carmelite Rd. *Harr* —1G **23**
Carmelite St. *EC4*
　　　　　—7A **62** (2K **149**)
Carmelite Wlk. *Harr* —1G **23**
Carmelite Way. *Harr* —2G **23**
Carmen St. *E14* —6D **64**
Carmichael Clo. *SW11* —3B **92**
Carmichael M. *SW18* —7B **92**
Carmichael Rd. *SE25* —5G **125**
Carminia Rd. *SW17* —2F **109**
Carnaby St. *W1* —6G **61** (1A **148**)
Carnac St. *SE27* —4D **110**
Carnanton Rd. *E17* —1F **33**
Carnarvon Av. *Enf* —3A **8**
Carnarvon Rd. *E10* —5E **32**
Carnarvon Rd. *E15* —6H **49**
Carnarvon Rd. *E18* —1H **33**
Carnarvon Rd. *Barn* —3B **4**
Carnation St. *SE2* —5B **84**
Carnbrook Rd. *SE3* —3B **98**
Carnecke Gdns. *SE9* —5C **98**
Carnegie Pl. *SW19* —3F **107**
Carnegie Rd. *Harr* —7K **23**
Carnegie St. *N1* —1K **61**
Carnforth Rd. *SW16* —7H **109**
Carnie Hall. *SW17* —3F **109**
Carnoustie Dri. *N1* —7J **45**
Carnwath Rd. *SW6* —3J **91**
Caroe Ct. *N9* —1C **18**
Carolina Clo. *E15* —5G **49**
Carolina Rd. *T Hth* —2B **124**
Caroline Clo. *N10* —2F **29**
Caroline Clo. *SW16* —3K **109**
*Caroline Clo. W2 —7K **59**
　(off Bayswater Rd.)*
Caroline Clo. *Croy* —4E **134**
Caroline Clo. *Iswth* —7H **71**
Caroline Ct. *Brom* —4F **113**

Caroline Ct. *Stan* —6F **11**
Caroline Gdns. *E2*
　　　　　—3E **62** (1H **145**)
Caroline Gdns. *SE15* —7G **79**
Caroline Pl. *SW11* —2E **92**
Caroline Pl. *W2* —7K **59**
Caroline Pl. M. *W2* —7K **59**
Caroline Rd. *SW19* —7H **107**
Caroline St. *E1* —6K **63**
Caroline Ter. *SW1*
　　　　　—4E **76** (4G **153**)
Caroline Wlk. *W6* —6G **75**
Carol St. *NW1* —1G **61**
Carpenter Gdns. *N21* —2G **17**
Carpenter Ho. *NW11* —6A **28**
Carpenters Ct. *Twic* —2J **103**
Carpenters M. *N7* —5J **45**
Carpenters Pl. *SW4* —4H **93**
Carpenter's Rd. *E15* —6C **48**
*Carpenter St. W1
　　　　　—7F **61** (3J **147**)*
Carrara Wlk. *SW9* —4A **94**
Carr Gro. *SE18* —4C **82**
Carr Ho. *Dart* —5K **101**
Carriage Dri. E. *SW11* —7E **76**
Carriage Dri. N. *SW11* —7D **76**
(in two parts)
Carriage Dri. S. *SW11* —1D **92**
Carriage Dri. W. *SW11* —7D **76**
Carriage M. *Ilf* —2G **51**
Carrick Clo. *Iswth* —3A **88**
Carrick Dri. *Ilf* —1G **35**
Carrick Gdns. *N17* —7K **17**
*Carrick Ho. N7 —6K **45**
　(off Caledonian Rd.)*
Carrick Ho. *SE11*
　　　　　—5B **78** (5A **156**)
Carrick M. *SE8* —6C **80**
Carrill Way. *Belv* —3D **84**
Carrington Av. *Houn* —5F **87**
Carrington Clo. *Croy* —7A **126**
Carrington Clo. *King T* —5J **105**
Carrington Gdns. *E7* —4J **49**
Carrington Rd. *Rich* —4G **89**
Carrington Sq. *Harr* —6B **10**
Carrington St. *W1*
　　　　　—1F **77** (5J **147**)
Carrol Clo. *NW5* —4F **45**
Carroll Clo. *E15* —5H **49**
*Carroll Ct. W3 —3H **73**
　(off Osborne Rd.)*
Carronade Pl. *SE28* —3G **83**
Carron Clo. *E14* —6D **64**
Carroun Rd. *SW8* —7K **77**
Carroway La. *Gnfd* —3H **55**
Carrow Rd. *Dag* —7B **52**
Carr Rd. *E17* —2B **32**
Carr Rd. *N'holt* —6E **38**
Carrs La. *N21* —5H **7**
Carr St. *E14* —5A **64**
(in two parts)
Carshalton Gro. *Sutt* —4B **132**
Carshalton Pk. Rd. *Cars* —5D **132**
Carshalton Pl. *Cars* —5E **132**
Carshalton Rd. *Mitc* —4E **122**
Carshallon Rd. *Sutt & Cars*
　　　　　—5A **132**
Carslake Rd. *SW15* —6E **90**
Carson Rd. *E16* —4J **65**
Carson Rd. *SE21* —2D **110**
Carson Rd. *Cockf* —4J **5**
Carstairs Rd. *SE6* —3E **112**
Carston Clo. *SE12* —5H **97**
Carswell Clo. *Ilf* —4B **34**
Carswell Rd. *SE6* —7E **96**

Carter Clo. *Wall* —7H 133
Carter Ct. *EC4* —6B 62 (1A 150)
C^rter Dri. *Romf* —1H 37
Carteret St. *SW1*
　　　—2H 77 (7C 148)
Carteret Way. *SE8* —4A 80
Carterhatch La. *Enf* —1A 8
Carterhatch Rd. *Enf* —2D 8
Carter Ho. *E1* —5F 63 (6J 145)
Carter La. *EC4* —6B 62 (1B 150)
Carter Pl. *SE17* —5C 78 (6D 156)
Carter Rd. *E13* —1K 65
Carter Rd. *SW19* —6B 108
Carters Clo. *Wor Pk* —1F 131
Carters Hill Clo. *SE9* —1A 114
Carters La. *SE23* —2A 112
Carter St. *SE17* —6C 78 (7C 156)
Carter's Yd. *SW18* —5J 91
Carthew Rd. *W6* —3D 74
Carthew Vs. *W6* —3D 74
Carthusian St. *EC1*
　　　—5C 62 (5C 144)
Cartier Circ. *E14* —1D 80
Carting La. *WC2* —7J 61 (3F 149)
Cart La. *E4* —1B 20
Cartmel Clo. *N17* —7C 18
Cartmel Ct. *N'holt* —6C 38
Cartmell Gdns. *Mord* —5A 122
Cartmel Rd. *Bexh* —1G 101
Carton Ho. *SE16*
　　　—3G 79 (1K 157)
Cartwright Gdns. *WC1*
　　　—3J 61 (2E 142)
Cartwright Rd. *Dag* —7F 53
Cartwright St. *E1*
　　　—7F 63 (2K 151)
Cartwright Way. *SW13* —7D 74
Carvelle Gdns. *N'holt* —3B 54
Carver Rd. *SE24* —6C 94
Carville Cres. *Bren* —4E 72
Cary Rd. *E11* —4G 49
Carysfort Rd. *N8* —5H 29
Carysfort Rd. *N16* —3D 46
Cascade Av. *N10* —4G 29
Cascade Clo. *Buck H* —2G 21
Cascade Rd. *Buck H* —2G 21
Cascades Tower. *E14* —1B 80
Casella Rd. *SE14* —7K 79
Casewick Rd. *SE27* —5A 110
Casimir Rd. *E5* —2J 47
Casino Av. *SE24* —5C 94
Caspian St. *SE5* —7D 78
Caspian Wlk. *E16* —6B 66
Cassandra Clo. *N'holt* —4H 39
Casselden Rd. *NW10* —7K 41
Cassell Ho. *SW9* —2K 93
　(off Stockwell Gdns. Est.)
Cassidy Rd. *SW6* —7J 75
Cassilda Rd. *SE2* —4A 84
Cassilis Rd. *Twic* —5B 88
Cassiobury Rd. *E17* —5A 32
Cassland Rd. *E9* —7K 47
Cassland Rd. *T Hth* —4D 124
Casslee Rd. *SE6* —7B 96
Casson St. *E1* —5G 63
Castalia Sq. *E14* —2E 80
Castellain Mans. *W9* —4K 59
　(off Castellain Rd.)
Castellain Rd. *W9* —4K 59
Castellane Clo. *Stan* —7E 10
Castell Ho. *SE8* —7C 80
Castello Av. *SW15* —5E 90
Castelnau. *SW13* —1C 90
Castelnau Gdns. *SW13* —6D 74
Castelnau Pl. *SW13* —6D 74

Castelnau Row. *SW13* —6D 74
Casterbridge Rd. *SE3* —3J 97
Casterton St. *E8* —6H 47
Castile Rd. *SE18* —4E 82
Castillon Rd. *SE6* —2G 113
Castlands Rd. *SE6* —2B 112
Castle Av. *E4* —5A 20
Castle Av. *Eps* —7D 130
Castlebar Ct. *W5* —5C 56
Castlebar Hill. *W5* —5C 56
Castlebar M. *W5* —5C 56
Castlebar Pk. *W5* —4B 56
Castlebar Rd. *W5* —5C 56
Castle Baynard St. *EC4*
　　　—7B 62 (2B 150)
Castle Clo. *E9* —5A 48
Castle Clo. *SW19* —3F 107
Castle Clo. *W3* —2H 73
Castle Clo. *Brom* —3G 127
Castlecombe Dri. *SW19* —7F 91
Castlecombe Rd. *SE9* —4C 114
Castle Ct. *SE26* —4A 112
Castledine Rd. *SE20* —7H 111
Castle Dri. *Ilf* —6C 34
Castleford Av. *SE9* —1F 115
Castleford Clo. *N17* —6A 18
Castlegate. *Rich* —3F 89
Castlehaven Rd. *NW1* —7F 45
Castle Hill Av. *New Ad* —7D 136
Castle Ho. *SE1* —4C 78 (3C 156)
Castle La. *SW1* —3G 77 (1B 154)
Castleleigh Ct. *Enf* —5J 7
Castlemaine Av. *Eps* —7D 130
Castlemaine Av. *S Croy* —5F 135
Castle Mead. *SE5* —7C 78
　(off Camberwell Rd.)
Castle Mead. *SE17* —7C 78
Castle M. *N12* —5F 15
Castle M. *NW1* —6F 45
Castle Pde. *Eps* —7C 130
Castle Pl. *NW1* —6F 45
Castle Pl. *W4* —4A 74
Castle Point. *E13* —2A 66
　(off Boundary Rd.)
Castlereagh St. *W1*
　　　—6C 60 (7D 140)
Castle Rd. *N12* —5F 15
Castle Rd. *NW1* —6F 45
Castle Rd. *Dag* —1B 68
Castle Rd. *Enf* —1F 9
Castle Rd. *Iswth* —2K 87
Castle Rd. *N'holt* —6F 39
Castle Rd. *S'hall* —3D 70
Castle Row. *W4* —5K 73
Castle Way. *SW19* —3F 107
Castle Way. *Felt* —4A 102
Castlewood Dri. *SE9* —2D 98
Castlewood Rd. *N15 & N16*
　　　—6G 31
Castlewood Rd. *Cockf* —3G 5
Castle Yd. *N6* —7E 28

Castle Yd. *SE1* —1B 78 (4B 150)
Castle Yd. *Rich* —5D 88
Castor La. *E14* —7D 64
Caterham Av. *Ilf* —2D 34
Caterham Rd. *SE13* —3E 96
Catesby St. *SE17*
　　　—4D 78 (4F 157)
Catford B'way. *SE6* —7D 96
Catford Gyratory. (Junct.)
　　　—7D 96
Catford Hill. *SE6* —2B 112
Catford M. *SE6* —7D 96
Catford Rd. *SE6* —7C 96
Catford Trad. Est. *SE6* —2D 112
Cathall Rd. *E11* —2F 49
Cathay Ho. *SE16* —2H 79
Cathay St. *SE16* —2H 79
Cathay Wlk. *N'holt* —2E 54
　(off Brabazon Rd.)
Cathcart Dri. *Orp* —7J 129
Cathcart Hill. *N19* —3G 45
Cathcart Rd. *SW10* —6K 75
Cathcart St. *NW5* —6F 45
Cathedral Lodge *EC1*
　　　—5C 62 (5C 144)
　(off Aldersgate St.)
Cathedral Piazza. *SW1*
　　　—3G 77 (2A 154)
Cathedral Pl. *EC4*
　　　—6C 62 (7C 144)
Cathedral St. *SE1*
　　　—1D 78 (4E 150)
Catherall Rd. *N5* —3C 46
Catherine Ct. *N14* —5B 6
Catherine Ct. *SW19* —5H 107
Catherine Ct. *Ilf* —6J 35
Catherine Dri. *Rich* —4E 88
Catherine Gdns. *Houn* —4H 87
Catherine Griffiths Ct. *EC1*
　(off Pine St.) —4A 62 (3K 143)
Catherine Gro. *SE10* —1D 96
Catherine Ho. *N1* —1E 62
　(off Whitmore Est.)
Catherine Howard Ct. *SE9*
　　　—6H 99
Catherine of Aragon. *SE9* —6H 99
Catherine Parr Ct. *SE9* —6H 99
Catherine Pl. *SW1*
　　　—3G 77 (1A 154)
Catherine Rd. *Surb* —5D 118
Catherine St. *WC2*
　　　—7K 61 (2G 149)
Catherine Wheel All. *E1*
　　　—5E 62 (6H 145)
Catherine Wheel Rd. *Bren*
　　　—7D 72
Catherine Wheel Yd. *SW1*
　　　—1G 77 (5A 148)
Catherwood Ct. *N1*
　　　—3D 62 (1E 144)
Cat Hill. *Barn* —6H 5
Cathles Rd. *SW12* —6F 93
Cathnor Hall Ct. *W12* —2D 74
Cathnor Rd. *W12* —2D 74
Catling Clo. *SE23* —3J 111
Catlin's La. *Pinn* —3A 22
Catlin St. *SE16* —5G 79
Cator La. *Beck* —1B 126
Cato Rd. *SW4* —3H 93
Cator Rd. *SE26* —6K 111
Cator Rd. *Cars* —5D 132
Cato St. *W1* —6C 60 (6D 140)
Catsey La. *Bush* —1B 10
Catsey Wood. *Bush* —1B 10

Cattistock Rd. *SE9* —5D 114
Cattistock Rd. *SE12* —5C 114
Cattley Clo. *Barn* —4B 4
Catton St. *WC1* —5K 61 (6G 143)
Caughley Ho. *SE11*
　　　—3A 78 (2J 155)
Caulfield Rd. *E6* —1C 66
Caulfield Rd. *SE15* —2H 95
Causeway, The. *N2* —4C 28
Causeway, The. *SW18* —5K 91
Causeway, The. *SW19* —5E 106
Causeway, The. *Cars* —2E 132
Causeway, The. *Felt & Houn*
　　　—4A 86
Causeway, The. *Sutt* —7A 132
Causeway, The. *Tedd* —6K 103
Causeyware Rd. *N9* —7D 8
Causton Rd. *N6* —7F 29
Causton St. *SW1*
　　　—4H 77 (4D 154)
Cautley Av. *SW4* —5G 93
Cavalier Clo. *Romf* —4D 36
Cavalier Ct. *Surb* —6F 119
Cavalry Cres. *Houn* —4B 86
Cavalry Gdns. *SW15* —5H 91
Cavan Pl. *Pinn* —1D 22
Cavaye Pl. *SW10*
　　　—5A 76 (6A 152)
Cavell Dri. *Enf* —2F 7
Cavell Rd. *N17* —7J 17
Cavell St. *E1* —5H 63
Cavendish Av. *N3* —2J 27
Cavendish Av. *NW8*
　　　—2B 60 (1B 140)
Cavendish Av. *W13* —5A 56
Cavendish Av. *Eri* —6J 85
Cavendish Av. *Harr* —4H 39
Cavendish Av. *N Mald* —5D 120
Cavendish Av. *Ruis* —5A 38
Cavendish Av. *Sidc* —7A 100
Cavendish Av. *Well* —3K 99
Cavendish Av. *Wfd G* —1K 33
Cavendish Clo. *N18* —5C 18
Cavendish Clo. *NW6* —6H 43
Cavendish Clo. *NW8*
　　　—3B 60 (1B 140)
Cavendish Ct. *EC3*
　　　—6E 62 (7H 145)
Cavendish Dri. *E11* —1F 49
Cavendish Dri. *Edgw* —6A 12
Cavendish Gdns. *SW4* —6G 93
Cavendish Gdns. *Bark* —5J 51
Cavendish Gdns. *Ilf* —1E 50
Cavendish Gdns. *Romf* —5E 36
Cavendish Mans. *NW6* —5J 43
Cavendish M. N. *W1*
　　　—5F 61 (5K 141)
Cavendish M. S. *W1*
　　　—5F 61 (6K 141)
Cavendish Pde. *Houn* —2C 86
Cavendish Pl. *W1*
　　　—6F 61 (7K 141)
Cavendish Rd. *E4* —6K 19
Cavendish Rd. *N4* —6B 30
Cavendish Rd. *N18* —5C 18
Cavendish Rd. *NW6* —7G 43
Cavendish Rd. *SW12* —6F 93
Cavendish Rd. *SW19* —7B 108
Cavendish Rd. *W4* —1J 89
Cavendish Rd. *Barn* —3A 4
Cavendish Rd. *Croy* —1B 134
Cavendish Rd. *N Mald* —4B 120
Cavendish Rd. *Sutt* —7A 132
Cavendish Sq. *W1*
　　　—6F 61 (7K 141)

Cavendish St. *N1* —2D 62
Cavendish Way. *W Wick*
　　　—1D 136
Cavenham Gdns. *Ilf* —3H 51
Caverleigh Way. *Wor Pk* —1C 130
Cave Rd. *E13* —3K 65
Cave Rd. *Rich* —4C 104
Caversham Av. *N13* —3F 17
Caversham Av. *Sutt* —2G 131
Caversham Ct. *N11* —2K 15
Caversham Ho. *N15* —4C 30
　(off Caversham Rd.)
Caversham M. *SW3*
　　　—6D 76 (7E 152)
Caversham Rd. *N15* —4C 30
Caversham Rd. *NW5* —6G 45
Caversham Rd. *King T* —2F 119
Caversham St. *SW3*
　　　—6D 76 (7E 152)
Caverswall St. *W12* —6E 58
Cawdor Cres. *W7* —4A 72
Cawnpore St. *SE19* —5E 110
Caxton Ct. *SW11* —2C 92
Caxton Gro. *E3* —3C 64
Caxton M. *Bren* —6D 72
Caxton Rd. *N22* —2A 29
Caxton Rd. *SW19* —5A 108
Caxton Rd. *W12* —2F 75
Caxton Rd. *S'hall* —3B 70
Caxton St. *SW1* —3H 77 (1C 154)
Caxton St. N. *E16* —6H 65
Caxton St. S. *E16* —7J 65
Caxton Wlk. *WC2*
　　　—6H 61 (1D 148)
Cayenne Ct. *SE1*
　　　—2F 79 (6K 151)
Caygill Clo. *Brom* —4H 127
Cayley Clo. *Wall* —7J 133
Cayton Rd. *EC1* —3D 62 (2E 144)
Cayton Rd. *Gnfd* —2J 55
Cayton St. *EC1* —3D 62 (2E 144)
Cazenove Rd. *E17* —1C 32
Cazenove Rd. *N16* —2F 47
Cearns Ho. *E6* —1B 66
Cecil Av. *Bark* —7H 51
Cecil Av. *Enf* —4A 8
Cecil Av. *Wemb* —5F 41
Cecil Clo. *W5* —5D 56
Cecil Ct. *WC2* —7J 61 (3E 148)
Cecil Ct. *Barn* —3A 4
Cecile Pk. *N8* —6J 29
Cecil Ho. *E17* —1C 32
Cecilia Clo. *N2* —3A 28
Cecilia Rd. *E8* —5F 47
Cecil Pk. *Pinn* —4C 22
Cecil Pl. *Mitc* —5D 122
Cecil Rd. *E11* —3H 49
Cecil Rd. *E13* —1J 65
Cecil Rd. *E17* —1C 32
Cecil Rd. *N10* —2F 29
Cecil Rd. *N14* —1B 16
Cecil Rd. *NW9* —3A 26
Cecil Rd. *NW10* —1A 58
Cecil Rd. *SW19* —7K 107
Cecil Rd. *W3* —5J 57
Cecil Rd. *Croy* —6K 123
Cecil Rd. *Enf* —4H 7
Cecil Rd. *Harr* —3J 23
Cecil Rd. *Houn* —2G 87
Cecil Rd. *Ilf* —4F 51
Cecil Rd. *Romf* —7D 36
Cecil Rd. *Sutt* —6H 131
Cecil Rosen Ct. *Wemb* —3B 40

Cecil Way. Brom —1J 137
Cedar Av. Barn —7H 5
Cedar Av. Enf —2D 8
Cedar Av. Romf —5E 36
Cedar Av. Ruis —5A 38
Cedar Av. Sidc —7A 100
Cedar Av. Twic —6F 87
Cedar Clo. SE21 —1C 110
Cedar Clo. SW15 —4K 105
Cedar Clo. Brom —3C 138
Cedar Clo. Buck H —2G 21
Cedar Clo. Cars —6D 132
Cedar Clo. Romf —4J 37
Cedar Copse. Brom —2D 128
Cedar Ct. E8 —7F 47
Cedar Ct. E18 —1J 33
Cedar Ct. N1 —7C 46
Cedar Ct. N10 —2C 28
Cedar Ct. N11 —5R 16
Cedar Ct. N20 —1G 15
Cedar Ct. SE7 —6A 82
Cedar Ct. SW19 —3F 107
Cedar Ct. Bren —6D 72
(off Boston Mnr. Rd.)
Cedar Ct. Sutt —6A 132
Cedar Cres. Brom —3C 138
Cedar Dri. N2 —4C 28
Cedar Dri. Pinn —6A 10
Cedar Gdns. Sutt —6A 132
Cedar Grange. Enf —5K 7
Cedar Gro. W5 —3E 72
Cedar Gro. Bex —6D 100
Cedar Gro. S'hall —5E 54
Cedar Heights. Rich —1E 104
Cedar Ho. N22 —1A 30
(off Acacia Rd.)
Cedar Ho. SE14 —1K 95
Cedar Ho. W8 —3K 75
(off Marloes Rd.)
Cedar Ho. Hayes —4A 54
Cedarhurst. Brom —7G 113
Cedarhurst Cotts. Bex —1G 117
Cedarhurst Dri. SE9 —5A 98
Cedarland Ter. SW20 —7D 106
Cedar Lawn Av. Barn —5B 4
Cedar Mt. SE9 —1B 114
Cedarne Rd. SW6 —7K 75
Cedar Pk. Gdns. Romf —7D 36
Cedar Pk. Rd. Enf —1H 7
Cedar Pl. SE7 —5A 82
Cedar Rise. N14 —7K 5
Cedar Rd. N17 —1F 31
Cedar Rd. NW2 —4E 42
Cedar Rd. Brom —2A 128
Cedar Rd. Croy —2E 134
Cedar Rd. Enf —1G 7
Cedar Rd. Houn —2A 86
Cedar Rd. Romf —4J 37
Cedar Rd. Sutt —6A 132
Cedar Rd. Tedd —5A 104
Cedars Av. E17 —5C 32
Cedars Av. Mitc —4E 122
Cedars Clo. NW4 —3F 27
Cedars Ct. N9 —2K 17
Cedars Ilo. E17 —3D 32
Cedars M. SW4 —4F 93
(in two parts)
Cedars Rd. E15 —6G 49
Cedars Rd. N9 —2B 18
Cedars Rd. N21 —2G 17
Cedars Rd. SW4 —3F 93
Cedars Rd. SW13 —2C 90
Cedars Rd. W4 —6J 73
Cedars Rd. Beck —2A 126
Cedars Rd. Croy —3J 133

Cedars Rd. Hamp W —1C 118
Cedars Rd. Mord —4J 121
Cedars, The. W13 —6C 56
Cedars, The. Buck H —1D 20
Cedars, The. Tedd —6K 103
Cedars, The. Wall —4G 133
Cedar Ter. Rich —4E 88
Cedar Tree Gro. SE27 —5B 110
Cedarville Gdns. SW16 —6K 109
Cedar Vista. Rich —2E 88
Cedar Way. NW1 —7H 45
Cedar Way Ind. Est. NW1 —7H 45
Cedra Ct. N16 —1G 47
Cedric Rd. SE9 —3G 115
Celadon Clo. Enf —3F 9
Celandine Clo. E14 —5C 64
Celandine Ct. E4 —3J 19
Celandine Dri. SE28 —1B 84
Celandine Way. E15 —3G 65
Celbridge M. W2 —5K 59
Celestial Gdns. SE13 —4F 97
Celia Ho. N1 —2E 62
(off Arden Est.)
Celia Rd. N19 —4G 45
Celtic Av. Brom —3G 127
Celtic St. E14 —5D 64
Cemetery La. SE7 —6C 82
Cemetery Rd. E7 —4H 49
Cemetery Rd. N17 —7K 17
Cemetery Rd. SE2 —7B 84
Cenacle Clo. NW3 —3J 43
Centaurs Bus. Cen. Iswth —6A 72
Centaur St. SE1 —3K 77 (1H 155)
Centenary Rd. Enf —4G 9
Centenary Trad. Est. Enf —4G 9
Central Av. E11 —2F 49
Central Av. N2 —2B 28
(East Finchley)
Central Av. N2 —2K 27
(St Marylebone Cemetery)
Central Av. N9 —3K 17
Central Av. SW11 —7D 76
Central Av. Enf —2C 8
Central Av. Houn —4G 87
Central Av. Pinn —6D 22
Central Av. Wall —5J 133
Central Av. Well —2K 99
Central Bus. Cen. NW10 —5A 42
Central Cir. NW4 —5D 26
Central Gdns. Mord —5K 121
Central Hill. SE19 —6D 110
Central Ho. E15 —2E 64
Central Mans. NW4 —6D 26
(off Watford Way)
Central Pde. E17 —4C 32
Central Pde. SE20 —7K 111
(off High St. Penge,)
Central Pde. W3 —2H 73
Central Pde. Enf —2D 8
Central Pde. Felt —7A 86
Central Pde. Gnfd —3A 56
Central Pde. Harr —5K 23
Central Pde. Ilf —6K 35
Central Pde. Surb —6E 118
Central Pk. Av. Dag —3H 53
Central Pk. Est. Houn —5B 86
Central Pk. Rd. E6 —2B 66
Central Pl. SE25 —5G 125
Central Rd. Mord —6J 121
Central Rd. Wemb —5B 40
Central Rd. Wor Pk —1C 130
Central School Path. SW14
—3J 89
Central Sq. NW11 —6K 27
Central Sq. Wemb —5E 40

Central St. EC1 —3C 62 (1C 144)
Central Ter. Beck —3K 125
Central Way. NW10 —3J 57
Central Way. SE28 —1A 84
Central Way. Cars —7C 132
Central Way. Felt —5A 86
Centre Av. N2 —2C 28
Centre Av. NW10 —3E 58
Centre Av. W3 —1K 73
Centre Comn. Rd. Chst —6G 115
Centre Ct. SW19 —6H 107
Centre Ct. W2 —7A 60
(off Princes Sq.)
Centre Ct. Shop. Cen. SW19
—6H 107
Centre Dri. E7 —4A 50
Centre Point. SE1 —5G 79
Centrepoint. WC2
—6H 61 (7D 142)
(off St Giles High St.)
Centre Rd. E11 & E7 —2J 49
Centre Rd. Dag —2H 69
Centre St. E2 —2H 63
Centre, The. Houn —3F 87
Centre Way. E17 —7K 19
Centre Way. N9 —2D 18
Centre Way. Ilf —2G 51
Centric Clo. NW1 —1E 60
Centro Ct. E6 —4D 66
Centurion Clo. N7 —7K 45
Centurion Ct. Hack —2F 133
Centurion La. E3 —2B 64
Centurion Way. Eri —3F 85
Century Clo. NW4 —6E 26
Century Ho. SW15 —4F 91
Century Rd. E17 —3A 32
Cephas Av. E1 —4J 63
Cephas St. E1 —4J 63
Ceres Rd. SE18 —4K 83
Cerise Rd. SE15 —1G 95
Cerne Clo. Hayes —7A 54
Cerne Rd. Mord —6A 122
Cerney M. W2 —7B 60 (2A 146)
Cervantes Ct. N2 —2K 59
Cester St. E2 —1G 63
Ceylon Rd. W14 —3F 75
Chadacre Av. Ilf —3D 34
Chadacre Ct. E13 —1J 65
(off Vicars Clo.)
Chadacre Ho. SW9 —4B 94
(off Loughborough Pk.)
Chadacre Rd. Eps —6D 130
Chadbourn St. E14 —5D 64
Chadbury Ct. NW7 —7H 13
Chadd Dri. Brom —3C 128
Chadd Grn. E13 —1J 65
(in two parts)
Chadville Gdns. Romf —5D 36
Chadway. Dag —1C 52
Chadwell Av. Romf —7B 36
Chadwell Heath Ind. Pk. Dag
—1E 52
Chadwell Heath La. Chad H
—4B 36
Chadwell St. EC1
—3A 62 (1K 143)
Chadwick Av. E4 —4A 20
Chadwick Av. N21 —5E 6
Chadwick Av. SW19 —6J 107
Chadwick Clo. W7 —5K 55
Chadwick Clo. Tedd —6A 104
Chadwick Rd. E11 —7G 33
Chadwick Rd. NW10 —1B 58
Chadwick Rd. SE15 —2F 95
Chadwick Rd. Ilf —3F 51

Chadwick St. SW1
—3H 77 (2C 154)
Chadwick Way. SE28 —7D 68
Chadwin Rd. E13 —5K 65
Chadworth Ho. N4 —1C 46
Chaffinch Av. Croy —6K 125
Chaffinch Bus. Pk. Beck —4K 125
Chaffinch Clo. N9 —1E 18
Chaffinch Clo. Croy —5K 125
Chaffinch Rd. Beck —1A 126
Chafford Way. Romf —4C 36
Chagford St. NW1
—4D 60 (4E 140)
Chailey Av. Enf —2A 8
Chailey Clo. Houn —1B 86
Chailey St. E5 —3J 47
Chalbury Wlk. N1 —2A 62
Chalcombe Rd. SE2 —3B 84
Chalcot Clo. Sutt —7J 131
Chalcot Cres. NW1 —1D 60
Chalcot Gdns. NW3 —6D 44
Chalcot M. SW16 —3J 109
Chalcot Rd. NW1 —7E 44
Chalcot Sq. NW1 —7E 44
Chalcroft Rd. SE13 —5G 97
Chaldon Ct. SE19 —1D 124
Chaldon Rd. SW6 —7G 75
Chale Rd. SW2 —6J 93
Chalet Clo. Bex —4K 117
Chalfont Av. Wemb —6H 41
Chalfont Ct. NW9 —3B 26
Chalfont Ct. Harr —6K 23
(off Northwick Pk. Rd.)
Chalfont Grn. N9 —3K 17
Chalfont Ho. SE16 —3H 79
(off Keetons Rd.)
Chalfont Rd. N9 —3K 17
Chalfont Rd. SE25 —3F 125
Chalfont Wlk. Pinn —2A 22
Chalfont Way. W13 —3B 72
Chalford Rd. SE21 —4D 110
Chalford Wlk. Wfd G —1B 34
Chalgrove Av. Mord —5J 121
Chalgrove Cres. Ilf —2C 34
Chalgrove Gdns. N3 —3G 27
Chalgrove Rd. N17 —1H 31
Chalgrove Rd. Sutt —7B 132
Chalice Clo. Wall —6H 133
Chalice Ct. N2 —4C 28
Chalkenden Clo. SE20 —7H 111
Chalker's Corner. (Junct.)
—3H 89
Chalk Farm Rd. NW1 —7E 44
Chalkhill Dri. Enf —3C 8
Chalkhill Rd. W6 —4F 75
Chalkhill Rd. Wemb —3G 41
Chalklands. Wemb —3J 41
Chalk La. Barn —3J 5
Chalkley Clo. Mitc —2D 122
Chalk Pit Cvn. Site. Sidc —7F 117
Chalk Pit Way. Sutt —6A 132
Chalk Rd. E13 —5K 65
Chalkstone Clo. Well —1A 100
Chalkwell Pk. Av. Enf —4K 7
Challice Way. SW2 —1K 109
Challin St. SE20 —1J 125
Challis Rd. Bren —5D 72
Challoner Clo. N2 —2B 28
Challoner Cres. W14 —5H 75
Challoner St. W14 —5H 75
Chalmers Ho. E17 —5D 32
Chalmers Wlk. SE17
—6B 78 (7B 156)
Chalsey Rd. SE4 —4B 96
Chalton Dri. N2 —6B 28

Chalton St. NW1
—2G 61 (1C 142)
Chamberlain Clo. SE28 —3H 83
Chamberlain Cotts. SE5 —1D 94
Chamberlain Cres. W Wick
—1D 136
Chamberlain Pl. E17 —3A 32
Chamberlain Rd. N2 —2A 28
Chamberlain Rd. N9 —3B 18
Chamberlain Rd. W13 —2A 72
Chamberlain St. NW1 —7D 44
Chamberlain Wlk. Felt —4C 102
Chamberlain Way. Pinn —3A 22
Chamberlain Way. Surb —7E 118
Chamberlayne Rd. NW10 —7E 42
Chambers Gdns. N2 —1B 28
Chambers La. NW10 —7D 42
Chambers Rd. N7 —4J 45
Chambers St. SE16 —2G 79
Chambers, The. SW10 —1A 92
(off Chelsea Harbour)
Chamber St. E1 —7F 63 (2K 151)
Chambers Wharf. SE16 —2G 79
Chambon Pl. W6 —4C 74
Chambord St. E2
—3F 63 (2K 145)
Chamomile Ct. E17 —6C 32
(off Yunus Khan Clo.)
Champion Cres. SE26 —4A 112
Champion Gro. SE5 —3D 94
Champion Hill. SE5 —3D 94
Champion Hill Est. SE5 —3E 94
Champion Pk. SE5 —2D 94
Champion Rd. SE26 —4A 112
Champlain Ho. W12 —7D 58
(off White City Est.)
Champness Clo. SE27 —4D 110
Champneys Clo. Sutt —7H 131
Chancel Ind. Est. NW10 —6B 42
Chancellor Gdns. S Croy
—7B 134
Chancellor Gro. SE21 —2C 110
Chancellor Pas. E14 —1C 80
Chancellor Pl. NW9 —2B 26
Chancellors Ct. WC1
—5K 61 (5G 143)
Chancellor's Rd. W6 —5E 74
Chancellor's St. W6 —5E 74
Chancellors Wharf. W6 —5E 74
Chancelot Rd. SE2 —4B 84
Chancel St. SE1 —1B 78 (5A 150)
Chancery La. WC2
—6A 62 (6H 143)
Chancery La. Beck —2D 126
Chance St. E2 & E1
—4F 63 (3J 145)
Chanctonbury Clo. SE9 —3F 115
Chanctonbury Gdns. Sutt
—7K 131
Chanctonbury Way. N12 —4C 14
Chandler Av. E16 —5J 65
Chandler Clo. Hamp —7E 102
Chandlers Dri. Eri —4K 85
Chandlers M. E14 —2C 80
Chandler St. E1 —1H 79
Chandlers Way. SW2 —7A 94
Chandler Way. SE15 —7F 79
Chandon Lodge. Sutt —7A 132
Chandos Av. E17 —2C 32
Chandos Av. N14 —3B 16
Chandos Av. N20 —1F 15
Chandos Av. W5 —4C 72
Chandos Clo. Buck H —2E 20
Chandos Ct. N14 —2C 16
Chandos Ct. Edgw —7A 12

Chandos Cres. *Edgw* —7A **12**
Chandos Pde. *Edgw* —7A **12**
Chandos Pl. *WC2*
　　　—7J **61** (3E **148**)
Chandos Rd. *E15* —5F **49**
Chandos Rd. *N2* —2B **28**
Chandos Rd. *N17* —2E **30**
Chandos Rd. *NW2* —5E **42**
Chandos Rd. *NW10* —4A **58**
Chandos Rd. *Harr* —5G **23**
Chandos Rd. *Pinn* —7B **22**
Chandos Way. *NW11* —1K **43**
Change All. *EC3* —6D **62** (1F **151**)
Channel Clo. *Houn* —1E **86**
Channel Ga. Rd. *NW10* —3A **58**
Channelsea Rd. *E15* —1F **65**
Chantree Grn. *W4* —4J **73**
Chantress Clo. *Dag* —1J **69**
Chantrey Rd. *SW9* —3K **93**
Chantry Clo. *W9* —4H **59**
Chantry Clo. *Enf* —1H **7**
Chantry Clo. *Harr* —5F **25**
Chantry Clo. *Sidc* —5E **116**
Chantry La. *Brom* —5B **128**
Chantry Pl. *Harr* —1F **23**
Chantry Rd. *Harr* —1F **23**
Chantry Sq. *W8* —3K **75**
Chantry St. *N1* —1B **62**
Chantry, The. *E4* —1K **19**
Chantry Way. *Mitc* —3B **122**
Chantry Way. *Rain* —2K **69**
Chant Sq. *E15* —7F **49**
Chant St. *E15* —7F **49**
Chapel Clo. *Dart* —5K **101**
Chapel Ct. *N2* —3C **28**
Chapel Ct. *SE1* —2D **78** (6E **150**)
Chapel Farm Rd. *SE9* —3D **114**
Chapel Hill. *N2* —2C **28**
Chapel Hill. *Dart* —5K **101**
Chapel Ho. St. *E14* —5D **80**
Chapel La. *Pinn* —3B **22**
Chapel La. *Romf* —7D **36**
Chapel Mkt. *N1* —2A **62**
Chapel Path. E11 —6J 33
　(off Woodbine Pl.)
Chapel Pl. *EC2* —3E **62** (2G **145**)
Chapel Pl. *N1* —2A **62**
Chapel Pl. *N17* —7A **18**
Chapel Pl. *W1* —6F **61** (1J **147**)
Chapel Rd. *SE27* —4B **110**
Chapel Rd. *W13* —1B **72**
Chapel Rd. *Bexh* —4G **101**
Chapel Rd. *Houn* —3F **87**
Chapel Rd. *Ilf* —3E **50**
Chapel Rd. *Twic* —7B **88**
Chapel Side. *W2* —7K **59**
Chapel Stones. *N17* —1F **31**
Chapel St. *SE1* —5C **60** (6C **140**)
Chapel St. *SW1* —3E **76** (1H **153**)
Chapel St. *Enf* —3J **7**
Chapel View. *S Croy* —6J **135**
Chapel Wlk. *NW4* —4D **26**
　(in two parts)
Chapel Wlk. *Croy* —2C **134**
Chapel Way. *N7* —3K **45**
Chapel Yd. SW18 —5J 91
　(off Wandsworth High St.)
Chaplemount Rd. *Wfd G* —6J **21**
Chaplin Clo. *SE1*
　　　—2B **78** (6K **149**)
Chaplin Clo. *Wemb* —6D **40**
Chaplin Rd. *E15* —2H **65**
Chaplin Rd. *N17* —3F **31**
Chaplin Rd. *NW2* —6C **42**

Chaplin Rd. *Dag* —7E **52**
Chaplin Rd. *Wemb* —6C **40**
Chaplin Sq. *N12* —7G **15**
Chapman Cres. *Harr* —6E **24**
Chapman Rd. *E9* —6B **48**
Chapman Rd. *Belv* —5H **85**
Chapman Rd. *Croy* —1A **134**
Chapmans Grn. *N22* —1A **30**
Chapman's La. *SE2 & Belv*
　　　—4D **84**
Chapmans Pk. Ind. Est. *NW10*
　　　—6B **42**
Chapman St. *E1* —7H **63**
Chapone Pl. *W1*
　　　—6H **61** (1C **148**)
Chapter Clo. *W4* —3J **73**
Chapter Ho. Ct. *EC4*
　　　—6C **62** (1B **150**)
Chapter Rd. *NW2* —5C **42**
Chapter Rd. *SE17*
　　　—5B **78** (6B **156**)
Chapter St. *SW1*
　　　—4H **77** (4C **154**)
Chapter Ter. *SE17*
　　　—6B **78** (7B **156**)
Chapter Way. *Hamp* —4E **102**
Chara Pl. *W4* —6K **73**
Charcroft Ct. W14 —2F 75
　(off Minford Gdns.)
Charcroft Gdns. *Enf* —4E **8**
Chardin Rd. *W4* —4A **74**
Chardmore Rd. *N16* —1G **47**
Chardwell Clo. *E6* —6D **66**
Charecroft Way. *W12* —2F **75**
Charfield Ct. W9 —4K 59
　(off Shirland Rd.)
Charford Rd. *E16* —5J **65**
Chargeable La. *E13* —4H **65**
Chargeable St. *E16* —4H **65**
Chargrove Clo. *SE16* —2K **79**
Charing Ct. *Short* —2G **127**
Charing Cross. *SW1*
　　　—1J **77** (4E **148**)
Charing Cross Rd. *WC2*
　　　—6H **61** (7D **142**)
Charlbert Ct. NW8 —2C 60
　(off Charlbert St.)
Charlbert St. *NW8* —2C **60**
Charlbury Av. *Stan* —5J **11**
Charlbury Gdns. *Ilf* —2K **51**
Charlbury Gro. *W5* —6C **56**
Charldane Rd. *SE9* —3F **115**
Charlecote Gro. *SE26* —3H **111**
Charlecote Rd. *Dag* —3E **52**
Charlemont Rd. *E6* —3D **66**
Charles Barry Clo. *SW4* —3G **93**
Charles Bradlaugh Ho. N17
　(off Haynes Clo.) —7C **18**
Charles Clo. *Sidc* —4B **116**
Charles Cres. *Harr* —7H **23**
Charle Sevright Dri. *NW7* —5A **14**
Charlesfield. *SE9* —3A **114**
Charles Flemwell M. *E16* —1J **81**
Charles Grinling Wlk. *SE18*
　　　—4E **82**
Charles Hocking Ho. W3 —2H 73
　(off Bollo Bri. Rd.)
Charles Ho. N15 —7A 18
　(off Love La.)
Charles La. *NW8* —2C **60**
Charles Pl. *NW1*
　　　—3G **61** (2B **142**)
Charles Rd. *E7* —7A **50**
Charles Rd. *SW19* —1J **121**
Charles Rd. *W13* —6A **56**

Charles Rd. *Dag* —6K **53**
Charles Rd. *Romf* —6D **36**
Charles Rowan Ho. WC1
　　　—3A **62** (2J **143**)
　(off Margery St.)
Charles II Pl. *SW3*
　　　—5C **76** (6E **152**)
Charles II St. *SW1*
　　　—1H **77** (4C **148**)
Charles Sq. *N1* —3D **62** (2F **145**)
Charles Sq. Est. *N1*
　　　—3D **62** (2F **145**)
Charles St. *E16* —1A **82**
Charles St. *SW13* —2A **90**
Charles St. *W1* —1F **77** (4J **147**)
Charles St. *Croy* —3C **134**
Charles St. *Enf* —5A **8**
Charles St. *Houn* —2D **86**
Charles St. Trad. Est. *E16* —1A **82**
Charleston St. *SE17*
　　　—4C **78** (4D **156**)
Charles Uton Ct. *E8* —4G **47**
Charles Whincup Rd. *E16* —1K **81**
Charleville Cir. *SE26* —5G **111**
Charleville Mans. W14 —5G 75
　(off Charleville Rd.)
Charleville Rd. *W14* —5G **75**
Charlie Brown's Roundabout.
　　(Junct.) —2A **34**
Charlieville Rd. *Eri* —7J **85**
Charlmont Rd. *SW17* —6C **108**
Charlotte Clo. *Bexh* —5E **100**
Charlotte Ct. *N8* —6H **29**
Charlotte Ct. *SE17*
　　　—4E **78** (3G **157**)
Charlotte Ct. *Ilf* —6D **34**
Charlotte Despard Av. *SW11*
　　　—1E **92**
Charlotte M. *W1*
　　　—5G **61** (5B **142**)
Charlotte M. *W10* —6F **59**
Charlotte M. *W14* —4G **75**
Charlotte Pk. Av. *Brom* —3C **128**
Charlotte Pl. *NW9* —5J **25**
Charlotte Pl. *SW1*
　　　—4G **77** (4A **154**)
Charlotte Pl. *W1*
　　　—5G **61** (6B **142**)
Charlotte Rd. *EC2*
　　　—3E **62** (2G **145**)
Charlotte Rd. *SW13* —1B **90**
Charlotte Rd. *Dag* —6H **53**
Charlotte Rd. *Wall* —6G **133**
Charlotte Row. *SW4* —3G **93**
Charlotte Sq. *Rich* —6F **89**
Charlotte St. *W1*
　　　—5G **61** (5B **142**)
Charlotte Ter. *N1* —1K **61**
Charlow Clo. *SW6* —2A **92**
Charlton Chu. La. *SE7* —5A **82**
Charlton Ct. *E2* —1F **63**
Charlton Cres. *Bark* —2K **67**
Charlton Dene. *SE7* —7A **82**
Charlton Ho. *Bren* —6E **72**
Charlton King's Rd. *NW5* —5H **45**
Charlton La. *SE7* —4B **82**
Charlton Pk. La. *SE7* —7B **82**
Charlton Pk. Rd. *SE7* —6B **82**
Charlton Pl. *N1* —2B **62**
Charlton Rd. *N9* —1E **18**
Charlton Rd. *NW10* —1A **58**
Charlton Rd. *SE3 & SE7* —7J **81**
Charlton Rd. *Harr* —4D **24**
Charlton Rd. *Wemb* —1F **41**
Charlton Way. *SE3* —1G **97**

Charlwood. *Croy* —7B **136**
Charlwood Clo. *Harr* —6D **10**
Charlwood Pl. *SW1*
　　　—4G **77** (4B **154**)
Charlwood Rd. *SW15* —4F **91**
Charlwood Sq. *Mitc* —3B **122**
Charlwood St. *SW1*
　　　—5G **77** (6A **154**)
Charlwood Ter. *SW15* —4F **91**
Charmian Av. *Stan* —3D **24**
Charminster Av. *SW19* —2J **121**
Charminster Ct. *Surb* —7D **118**
Charminster Rd. *SE9* —4B **114**
Charminster Rd. *Wor Pk* —1F **131**
Charmouth Ct. *Rich* —5F **89**
Charmouth Ho. *SW8* —7K **77**
Charmouth Rd. *Well* —1C **100**
Charnock Rd. *E5* —3H **47**
Charnwood Av. *SW19* —2J **121**
Charnwood Clo. *N Mald* —4A **120**
Charnwood Dri. *E18* —3K **33**
Charnwood Gdns. *E14* —4C **80**
Charnwood Pl. *N20* —3F **15**
Charnwood Rd. *SE25* —5D **124**
Charnwood St. *E5* —2H **47**
Charrington Rd. *Croy* —2C **134**
Charrington St. *NW1* —2H **61**
Charsley Rd. *SE6* —2D **112**
Chart Clo. *Brom* —1G **127**
Chart Clo. *Croy* —6J **125**
Charter Av. *Ilf* —1H **51**
Charter Ct. *N4* —1A **46**
Charter Ct. *N22* —1H **29**
Charter Ct. *N Mald* —3A **120**
Charter Ct. *S'hall* —1E **70**
Charter Cres. *Houn* —4C **86**
Charter Dri. *Bex* —7E **100**
Charterhouse Av. *Wemb* —5C **40**
Charterhouse Bldgs. *EC1*
　　　—4B **62** (4B **144**)
Charterhouse M. *EC1*
　　　—5B **62** (5B **144**)
Charterhouse Sq. *EC1*
　　　—5B **62** (5B **144**)
Charterhouse St. *EC1*
　　　—5A **62** (6K **143**)
Charteris Rd. *N4* —1A **46**
Charteris Rd. *NW6* —1H **59**
Charteris Rd. *Wfd G* —7E **20**
Charter Rd. *King T* —3H **119**
Charter Rd., The. *Wfd G* —6B **20**
Charters Clo. *SE19* —5E **110**
Charter Sq. *King T* —2H **119**
Charter Way. *N3* —4H **27**
Charter Way. *N14* —6B **6**
Chartfield Av. *SW15* —5D **90**
Chartfield Sq. *SW15* —5F **91**
Chartham Ct. SW9 —3A 94
　(off Canterbury Cres.)
Chartham Gro. *SE27* —3B **110**
Chartham Rd. *SE25* —3H **125**
Chartley Av. *NW2* —3A **42**
Chartley Av. *Stan* —6E **10**
Chartres Ct. *Gnfd* —2H **55**
Chart St. *N1* —3D **62** (1F **145**)
Chartwell Clo. *SE9* —2H **115**
Chartwell Clo. *Croy* —1D **134**
Chartwell Clo. *Gnfd* —1F **55**
Chartwell Ct. *Barn* —4B **4**
Chartwell Dri. *Orp* —5H **129**
Chartwell Gdns. *Sutt* —4G **131**
Chartwell Lodge. *Beck* —7C **112**
Chartwell Pl. *Harr* —2H **39**
Chartwell Pl. *Sutt* —3H **131**

Chartwell Way. *SE20* —1H **125**
Charville Ct. *Harr* —6K **23**
Char Wood. *SW16* —4A **110**
Chase Bank Ct. N14 —6B 6
　(off Avenue Rd.)
Chase Cen., The. *NW10* —3K **57**
Chase Ct. *Iswth* —2A **88**
Chase Ct. Gdns. *Enf* —3H **7**
Chase Cross Rd. *Romf* —1J **37**
Chasefield Rd. *SW17* —4D **108**
Chase Gdns. *E4* —4H **19**
Chase Gdns. *Twic* —7H **87**
Chase Grn. *Enf* —3H **7**
Chase Grn. Av. *Enf* —2G **7**
Chase Hill. *Enf* —3H **7**
Chase La. *Ilf* —5H **35**
　(in two parts)
Chaseley Dri. *W4* —5H **73**
Chaseley St. *E14* —6A **64**
Chasemore Clo. *Mitc* —7D **122**
Chasemore Gdns. *Croy*
　　　—5A **134**
Chase Ridings. *Enf* —2F **7**
Chase Rd. *N14* —5B **6**
Chase Rd. *NW10* —4K **57**
Chase Rd. Trad. Est. *NW10*
　　　—4K **57**
Chase Side. *N14* —5K **5**
Chase Side. *Enf* —2H **7**
Chase Side Av. *Enf* —2H **7**
Chase Side Cres. *Enf* —1H **7**
Chase Side Pl. *Enf* —2H **7**
Chase Side Works Ind. Est. *N14*
　　　—7C **6**
Chase, The. *E12* —4B **50**
Chase, The. *SW4* —4F **93**
Chase, The. *SW16* —7K **109**
Chase, The. *SW20* —1G **121**
Chase, The. *Bexh* —3H **101**
Chase, The. *Brom* —3K **127**
Chase, The. *Chad H* —6E **36**
Chase, The. *Eastc* —6A **22**
Chase, The. *Edgw* —1H **25**
Chase, The. *Pinn* —4D **22**
Chase, The. *Romf* —3K **37**
Chase, The. *Stan* —6F **11**
Chase, The. *Sun* —7A **100**
Chase, The. *Wall* —5K **133**
Chaseville Pde. *N21* —5E **6**
Chaseville Pk. Rd. *N21* —5D **6**
Chase Way. *N14* —2A **16**
Chaseways Vs. *Romf* —1F **37**
Chasewood Av. *Enf* —2G **7**
Chasewood Ct. *NW7* —5E **12**
Chasewood Pk. *Harr* —3J **39**
Chaston St. NW5 —5E 44
　(off Grafton Ter.)
Chatfield Rd. *SW11* —3A **92**
Chatfield Rd. *Croy* —1B **134**
Chatham Av. *Brom* —7H **127**
Chatham Clo. *NW11* —5J **27**
Chatham Clo. *Sutt* —7H **121**
Chatham Pl. *E9* —6J **47**
Chatham Rd. *E17* —3A **32**
Chatham Rd. *E18* —2H **33**
Chatham Rd. *SW11* —6D **92**
Chatham Rd. *King T* —2G **119**
Chatham St. *SE17*
　　　—4D **78** (3E **156**)
Chatsfield Pl. *W5* —6E **56**
Chatsworth Av. *NW4* —2E **26**
Chatsworth Av. *SW20* —1G **121**
Chatsworth Av. *Brom* —4K **113**
Chatsworth Av. *Sidc* —1A **116**

Chatsworth Av. Wemb —5F 41
Chatsworth Clo. NW4 —2E 26
Chatsworth Clo. W4 —6J 73
Chatsworth Clo. W Wick
—1H 137
Chatsworth Ct. W8 —4J 75
(off Pembroke Rd.)
Chatsworth Ct. Stan —5H 11
Chatsworth Cres. Houn —4H 87
Chatsworth Dri. Enf —7B 8
Chatsworth Est. E5 —4K 47
Chatsworth Gdns. W3 —1H 73
Chatsworth Gdns. Harr —1F 39
Chatsworth Gdns. N Mald
—5B 120
Chatsworth Lodge. W4 —5K 73
(off Bourne Pl.)
Chatsworth Pde. Orp —5G 129
Chatsworth Pl. Mitc —3D 122
Chatsworth Pl. Tedd —4A 104
Chatsworth Rise. W5 —4F 57
Chatsworth Rd. E5 —3J 47
Chatsworth Rd. E15 —5H 49
Chatsworth Rd. Harr —6E 42
Chatsworth Rd. W4 —6J 73
Chatsworth Rd. W5 —4F 57
Chatsworth Rd. Croy —4D 134
Chatsworth Rd. Hayes —4A 54
Chatsworth Rd. Sutt —5F 131
Chatsworth Way. SE27 —3B 110
Chatterton Ct. Rich —2F 89
Chatterton Rd. N4 —3B 46
Chatterton Rd. Brom —4B 128
Chatto Rd. SW11 —5D 92
Chaucer Av. Rich —3G 89
Chaucer Clo. N11 —5B 16
Chaucer Ct. New Bar —5E 4
Chaucer Dri. SE1
—4F 79 (4K 157)
Chaucer Gdns. Sutt —3J 131
Chaucer Grn. Croy —7H 125
Chaucer Ho. Barn —4A 4
Chaucer Ho. Sutt —3J 131
(off Chaucer Gdns.)
Chaucer Mans. W14 —6G 75
(off Queen's Club Gdns.)
Chaucer Rd. E7 —6J 49
Chaucer Rd. E11 —6J 33
Chaucer Rd. E17 —2E 32
Chaucer Rd. W3 —1J 73
Chaucer Rd. Sidc —1C 116
Chaucer Rd. Sutt —4J 131
Chaucer Rd. Well —1J 99
Chaucer Way. SW19 —6B 108
Chauncey Clo. N9 —3B 18
Chaundrye Clo. SE9 —6D 98
Chauntler Clo. E16 —7K 65
Chaville Ho. N11 —4K 15
Cheam Comn. Rd. Wor Pk
—2D 130
Cheam Mans. Sutt —7G 131
Cheam Pk. Way. Sutt —6G 131
Cheam Rd. Sutt —6H 131
Cheam St. SE15 —3J 95
Cheam Village. (Junct.) —6G 131
Cheapside. EC2 —6C 62 (1D 150)
Cheapside. N13 —4J 17
Cheapside. N22 —3A 30
Cheddington Rd. N18 —3K 17
Chedworth Clo. E16 —6H 65
Cheeseman Clo. Hamp —6C 102
Cheesemans Ter. W14 —5H 75
(in two parts)
Chelford Rd. Brom —5F 113

Chelmer Cres. Bark —2B 68
Chelmer Rd. E9 —5A 47
Chelmsford Clo. E6 —6D 66
Chelmsford Clo. W6 —6F 75
Chelmsford Ct. N14 —7C 6
(off Chelmsford Rd.)
Chelmsford Gdns. Ilf —7C 34
Chelmsford Ho. N7 —4K 45
(off Holloway Rd.)
Chelmsford Rd. E11 —1F 49
Chelmsford Rd. E17 —6C 32
Chelmsford Rd. E18 —1H 33
Chelmsford Rd. N14 —7B 6
Chelmsford Sq. NW10 —1E 58
—4H 61 (4C 142)
Chelsea Bri. SW1 & SW8
—6F 77 (7J 153)
Chelsea Bri. Bus. Cen. SW8
—7F 77
Chelsea Bri. Rd. SW1
—5E 76 (5G 153)
Chelsea Bri. Wharf. SW8 —6F 77
Chelsea Cloisters. SW3
—4C 76 (4D 152)
Chelsea Clo. NW10 —1K 57
Chelsea Clo. Edgw —2G 25
Chelsea Clo. Hamp —5G 103
Chelsea Clo. Wor Pk —7C 120
Chelsea Ct. Brom —4C 128
Chelsea Cres. SW10 —1A 92
Chelsea Garden Mkt. SW10
—1A 92
Chelsea Gdns. SW1
—5E 76 (6H 153)
Chelsea Gdns. Sutt —4G 131
Chelsea Harbour. SW10 —1A 92
Chelsea Harbour Dri. SW10
—1A 92
Chelsea Mnr. Ct. SW3
—6C 76 (7D 152)
Chelsea Mnr. Gdns. SW3
—5C 76 (6D 152)
Chelsea Mnr. St. SW3
—5C 76 (6D 152)
Chelsea Pk. Gdns. SW3
—6B 76 (7A 152)
Chelsea Reach Tower. SW10
(off Worlds End Est.) —7B 76
Chelsea Sq. SW3
—5B 76 (5B 152)
Chelsea Towers. SW3
—6C 76 (7D 152)
Chelsea Wharf. SW10 —7B 76
(off Lots Rd.)
Chelsfield Av. N9 —7E 8
Chelsfield Gdns. SE26 —3J 111
Chelsfield Grn. N9 —7E 8
Chelsham Rd. SW4 —3H 93
Chelsham Rd. S Croy —7D 134
Chelsiter Ct. Sidc —4K 115
Chelsworth Dri. SE18 —6H 83
Cheltenham Av. Twic —7A 88
Cheltenham Clo. N Mald —3J 119
Cheltenham Clo. N'holt —6F 39
Cheltenham Ct. Stan —5H 11
(off Marsh La.)
Cheltenham Gdns. E6 —2C 66
Cheltenham Pl. W3 —1H 73
Cheltenham Pl. Harr —4E 24
Cheltenham Rd. E10 —6E 32
Cheltenham Rd. SE15 —4J 95
Cheltenham Ter. SW3
—5D 76 (5F 153)
Chelverton Rd. SW15 —4F 91
Chelwood. N20 —2G 15
Chelwood Clo. E4 —6J 9

Chelwood Gdns. Rich —2G 89
Chelwood Gdns. Pas. Rich
—2G 89
Chelwood Wlk. SE4 —4A 96
Chenappa Clo. E13 —3J 65
Chenduit Way. Stan —5E 10
Cheney Ct. SE23 —1K 111
Cheney Rd. N1 —2J 61 (1E 142)
Cheney Row. E17 —1B 32
Cheneys Rd. E11 —3G 49
Cheney St. Pinn —4A 22
Chenies Ho. W4 —6B 74
(off Corney Reach Way)
Chenies M. WC1
Chenies Pl. NW1 —2H 61
Chenies St. WC1
—5H 61 (5C 142)
Chenies, The. Orp —6J 129
Cheniston Gdns. W8 —3K 75
Chepstow Clo. SW15 —5G 91
Chepstow Cres. W11 —7J 59
Chepstow Cres. Ilf —6J 35
Chepstow Gdns. S'hall —6D 54
Chepstow Pl. W2 —6J 59
Chepstow Rise. Croy —3E 134
Chepstow Rd. W2 —6J 59
Chepstow Rd. W7 —3A 72
Chepstow Rd. Croy —3E 134
Chepstow Vs. W11 —7H 59
Chepstow Way. SE15 —1F 95
Chequers. Buck H —1E 20
Chequers Clo. NW9 —3A 26
Chequers Clo. Orp —4K 129
Chequers La. Dag —5F 69
Chequers Pde. N13 —5H 17
Chequers Pde. Dag —1F 69
Chequers, The. Pinn —3B 22
Chequer St. EC1
—4C 62 (4D 144)
Chequers Way. N13 —5G 17
Cherbury Clo. SE28 —6D 68
Cherbury St. N1 —2D 62
Cherchefelle M. Stan —5G 11
Cherington Rd. W7 —1K 71
Cheriton Av. Brom —5H 127
Cheriton Av. Ilf —2D 34
Cheriton Clo. W5 —5C 56
Cheriton Clo. Barn —4J 5
Cheriton Ct. SE12 —7J 97
Cheriton Dri. SE18 —7H 83
Cheriton Sq. SW17 —2E 108
Cherry Av. S'hall —1B 70
Cherry Clo. E17 —5D 32
Cherry Clo. SW2 —7A 94
Cherry Clo. W5 —3D 72
Cherry Clo. Cars —2D 132
Cherry Clo. Mord —4G 121
Cherry Ct. W3 —1A 74
Cherry Ct. Pinn —2B 22
Cherry Cres. Bren —7B 72
Cherry Dale. Stan —6G 11
Cherry Gdns. N'holt —7F 39
Cherry Gdns. Dag —5F 53
Cherry Garden St. SE16 —2H 79
Cherry Garth. Bren —5D 72
Cherry Hill. Harr —6E 10
Cherry Hill. New Bar —6E 4
Cherry Hill Gdns. Croy —4K 133
Cherrylands Clo. NW9 —2J 41
Cherry Laurel Wlk. SW2 —6K 93
Cherry Orchard. SE7 —6A 82

Cherry Orchard Gdns. Croy
—1E 134
Cherry Orchard Rd. Brom
—2C 138
Cherry Orchard Rd. Croy
—2D 134
Cherry Rd. Enf —1D 8
Cherry St. Romf —5K 37
Cherry Tree Clo. Wemb —4A 40
Cherry Tree Ct. NW9 —4J 25
Cherry Tree Ct. SE7 —6A 82
Cherrytree Dri. SW16 —3J 109
Cherry Tree Hill. N2 —5C 28
Cherry Tree Rise. Buck H
—4F 21
Cherry Tree Rd. E15 —5G 49
Cherry Tree Rd. N2 —4D 28
Cherry Tree Wlk. EC1
—4C 62 (4D 144)
Cherry Tree Wlk. Beck —4B 126
Cherry Tree Wlk. W Wick
—4H 137
Cherrytree Way. Stan —6G 11
Cherry Wlk. Brom —1J 137
Cherrywood Clo. E3 —3A 64
Cherry Wood Clo. King T
—7G 105
Cherrywood Ct. Tedd —5A 104
Cherrywood Dri. SW15 —5F 91
Cherrywood La. Mord —4G 121
Cherry Wood Way. W5 —5G 57
Chertsey Dri. Sutt —2G 131
Chertsey Rd. E11 —2F 49
Chertsey Rd. Ilf —4H 51
Chertsey Rd. Twic —2F 103
Chertsey St. SW17 —5E 108
Chervil M. SE28 —1B 84
Cheryls Clo. SW6 —1K 91
Cheseman St. SE26 —3H 111
Chesfield Rd. King T —7E 104
Chesham Av. Orp —6F 129
Chesham Clo. SW1
—3E 76 (2G 153)
Chesham Clo. Romf —4K 37
Chesham Cres. SE20 —1J 125
Chesham M. SW1
—3E 76 (1G 153)
Chesham Pl. SW1
—3E 76 (2G 153)
Chesham Rd. SE20 —2J 125
Chesham Rd. SW19 —5B 108
Chesham Rd. King T —2G 119
Chesham St. NW10 —3K 41
Chesham St. SW1
—3E 76 (2G 153)
Chesham Ter. W13 —2B 72
Cheshire Clo. SE4 —2B 96
Cheshire Clo. Mitc —3J 123
Cheshire Ho. Mord —7K 121
Cheshire Rd. N22 —7E 16
Cheshire St. E2 —4F 63 (3K 145)
Cheshir Ho. NW4 —4E 26
Chesholm Rd. N16 —3E 46
Cheshunt Rd. E7 —6K 49
Cheshunt Rd. Belv —5G 85
Chesil Ct. E2 —2J 63
Chesil Ct. SW3 —6C 76 (7D 152)
Chesilton Rd. SW6 —1H 91
Chesley Gdns. E6 —2B 66
Chesney Cres. New Ad —7E 136
Chesney Ho. SE13 —4F 97
(off Mercator Rd.)
Chesney St. SW11 —1E 92
Chesnut Gro. N17 —3F 31
Chesnut Rd. N17 —3F 31

Chessing Ct. N2 —3D 28
(off Fortis Grn.)
Chessington Av. N3 —3G 27
Chessington Av. Bexh —7E 84
Chessington Clo. N3 —3H 27
(off Charter Way)
Chessington Ct. Pinn —4D 22
Chessington Ho. SW8 —2H 93
Chessington Lodge. N3 —3H 27
Chessington Mans. E10 —7C 32
Chessington Mans. E11 —7G 33
Chessington Rd. Eps & Ewe
—7A 130
Chessington Way. W Wick
—2D 136
Chesson Rd. W14 —6H 75
Chesswood Way. Pinn —2B 22
Chestbrook Ct. Enf —5K 7
(off Forsyth Pl.)
Chester Av. Rich —6F 89
Chester Av. Twic —1D 102
Chester Clo. SW1
—2F 77 (7J 147)
Chester Clo. SW15 —3D 90
Chester Clo. Rich —6F 89
Chester Clo. Sutt —2J 131
Chester Clo. N. NW1
—3F 61 (1K 141)
Chester Clo. S. NW1
—3F 61 (2K 141)
Chester Cotts. SW1
—4E 76 (4G 153)
Chester Ct. NW1
—3F 61 (1K 141)
Chester Cres. E8 —5F 47
Chester Dri. Harr —6D 22
Chesterfield Clo. SE13 —2F 97
Chesterfield Flats. Barn —5A 4
(off Bells Hill)
Chesterfield Gdns. N4 —5B 30
Chesterfield Gdns. SE10 —7F 81
Chesterfield Gdns. W1
—1F 77 (4J 147)
Chesterfield Gro. SE22 —5F 95
Chesterfield Hill. W1
—1F 77 (4J 147)
Chesterfield Lodge. N21 —7E 6
(off Church Hill)
Chesterfield Rd. E10 —6E 32
Chesterfield Rd. N3 —6D 14
Chesterfield Rd. W4 —6J 73
Chesterfield Rd. Barn —5A 4
Chesterfield St. W1
—1F 77 (4J 147)
Chesterfield Wlk. SE10 —1F 97
Chesterfield Way. SE15 —7J 79
Chesterford Gdns. NW3 —4K 43
Chesterford Rd. E12 —5D 50
Chester Gdns. W13 —6B 56
Chester Gdns. Enf —6C 8
Chester Gdns. Mord —6A 122
Chester Ga. NW1
—3F 61 (2J 141)
Chester Ho. SE8 —6B 80
Chester Ho. SW9 —7A 78
(off Brixton Rd.)
Chesterman Ct. W4 —7A 74
(off Corney Reach Way)
Chester M. SW1 —3F 77 (1J 153)
Chester Pl. NW1 —3F 61 (1J 141)
Chester Rd. E7 —7B 50
Chester Rd. E11 —6K 33
Chester Rd. E16 —4G 65
Chester Rd. E17 —5K 31
Chester Rd. N9 —1C 18

Chester Rd. N17 —3D 30
Chester Rd. N19 —2F 45
Chester Rd. NW1
—3E 60 (2H 141)
Chester Rd. SW19 —6E 106
Chester Rd. Chig —3K 21
Chester Rd. Houn —3A 86
Chester Rd. Ilf —1K 51
Chester Rd. Sidc —5J 99
Chester Row. SW1
—4E 76 (4G 153)
Chester Sq. SW1
—4E 76 (3H 153)
Chester Sq. M. SW1
—3F 77 (2J 153)
Chesters, The. N Mald —1A 120
Chester St. E2 —4G 63
(Vallance Rd.)
Chester St. E2 —1G 63
(Whiston Rd.)
Chester St. SW1
—3E 76 (1H 153)
Chester Ter. NW1
—3F 61 (1J 141)
Chester Ter. Bark —6H 51
Chesterton Clo. SW18 —5J 91
Chesterton Gro. Gnfd —2F 55
Chesterton Ct. W3 —3H 73
(off Hanbury Rd.)
Chesterton Clo. W5 —5D 56
Chesterton Rd. E13 —3J 65
Chesterton Rd. W10 —5F 59
Chesterton Sq. W8 —4H 75
Chesterton Ter. E13 —3J 65
Chesterton Ter. King T —2G 119
Chester Way. SE11
—4A 78 (4K 155)
Chesthunte Rd. N17 —1C 30
Chestnut All. SW6 —6H 75
Chestnut Av. E7 —4K 49
Chestnut Av. N8 —5J 29
Chestnut Av. SW14 —3K 89
Chestnut Av. Bren —4D 72
Chestnut Av. Buck H —3G 21
Chestnut Av. E Mol & Tedd
—3A 118
Chestnut Av. Edgw —6K 11
Chestnut Av. Eps —4A 130
Chestnut Av. Hamp —7E 102
Chestnut Av. Wemb —5B 40
Chestnut Av. W Wick —5G 137
Chestnut Av. N. E17 —4F 33
Chestnut Av. S. E17 —5E 32
Chestnut Clo. N14 —5B 6
Chestnut Clo. N16 —2D 46
Chestnut Clo. SE6 —5E 112
Chestnut Clo. SW16 —4A 110
Chestnut Clo. Buck H —3G 21
Chestnut Clo. Cars —1D 132
Chestnut Clo. Sidc —1K 115
Chestnut Clo. N8 —5J 29
Chestnut Clo. SW6 —6H 75
Chestnut Clo. Felt —5B 102
Chestnut Dri. E11 —6J 33
Chestnut Dri. Bexh —4D 100
Chestnut Dri. Harr —7E 10
Chestnut Dri. Pinn —6B 22
Chestnut Gro. SE20 —7H 111
Chestnut Gro. SW12 —7E 92
Chestnut Gro. W5 —3D 72
Chestnut Gro. Barn —5J 5
Chestnut Gro. Dart —5K 117
Chestnut Gro. Iswth —4A 88
Chestnut Gro. Mitc —5H 123
Chestnut Gro. N Mald —3K 119

Chestnut Gro. S Croy —7H 135
Chestnut Gro. Wemb —5B 40
Chestnut Ho. W4 —4A 74
(off Orchard, The)
Chestnut La. N20 —1B 14
Chestnut Rise. SE18 —6H 83
Chestnut Rise. Bush —1A 10
Chestnut Rd. SE27 —3B 110
Chestnut Rd. SW20 —2F 121
Chestnut Rd. King T —7E 104
Chestnut Rd. Twic —2J 103
Chestnut Row. N3 —7D 14
Chestnut Row. N5 —4C 46
(off Highbury Grange)
Chestnuts, The. Pinn —1D 22
Chestnut Ter. Sutt —4K 131
Chestnut Wlk. Wfd G —5D 20
Chestnut Way. Felt —3A 102
Cheston Av. Croy —2A 136
Chettle Clo. SE1 —3D 78 (1E 156)
Chettle Ct. N8 —6A 30
Chetwode Rd. SW17 —3D 108
Chetwood Wlk. E6 —5C 66
(off Greenwich Cres.)
Chetwynd Av. E Barn —1J 15
Chetwynd Rd. NW5 —4F 45
Chevalier Clo. Stan —4K 11
Cheval Pl. SW7 —3C 76 (1D 152)
Cheval St. E14 —3C 80
Cheveney Wlk. Brom —3J 127
Chevening Rd. NW6 —2F 59
Chevening Rd. SE10 —5H 81
Chevening Rd. SE19 —6D 110
Chevenings, The. Sidc —3C 116
Cheverton Rd. N19 —1H 45
Chevet St. E9 —5A 48
Cheviot. N17 —1C 18
(off Northumberland Pk.)
Cheviot Clo. Bexh —2K 101
Cheviot Clo. Enf —2J 7
Cheviot Clo. Sutt —7B 132
Cheviot Ct. S'hall —4F 71
Cheviot Gdns. NW2 —2C 43
Cheviot Gdns. SE27 —4B 110
Cheviot Ga. NW2 —2G 43
Cheviot Rd. SE27 —5A 110
Cheviot Way. Ilf —5J 35
Chevron Clo. E16 —6J 65
Chevy Rd. S'hall —2G 71
Chewton Rd. E17 —4A 32
Cheyne Av. E18 —3H 33
Cheyne Av. Twic —1D 102
Cheyne Clo. NW4 —5E 26
Cheyne Clo. Brom —3C 138
Cheyne Ct. SW3
—6D 76 (7E 152)
Cheyne Gdns. SW3
—6C 76 (7D 152)
Cheyne Hill. Surb —4F 119
Cheyne Path. W7 —6K 55
Cheyne Pl. SW3
—6D 76 (7E 152)
Cheyne Row. SW3
—6C 76 (7C 152)
Cheyne Wlk. N21 —5G 7
Cheyne Wlk. NW4 —6E 26
Cheyne Wlk. SW10 & SW3
(in three parts) —7B 76
Cheyne Wlk. Croy —2G 135
Cheyneys Av. Edgw —6J 11
Chichele Gdns. Croy —4E 134
Chichele Rd. NW2 —5F 43
Chicheley Gdns. Harr —7B 10
(in two parts)
Chicheley Rd. Harr —7B 10

Chicheley St. SE1
—2K 77 (6H 149)
Chichester Bldgs. SE1
—3E 78 (2G 157)
Chichester Clo. E6 —6C 66
Chichester Clo. SE3 —1A 98
Chichester Clo. Hamp —6D 102
Chichester Ct. Edgw —6B 12
(off Whitchurch La.)
Chichester Ct. Eps —7B 130
Chichester Ct. N'holt —1C 54
Chichester Ct. Stan —3E 24
Chichester Gdns. Ilf —7C 34
Chichester Ho. SW9 —7A 78
(off Brixton Rd.)
Chichester M. SE27 —4A 110
Chichester Rents. WC2
—6A 62 (7J 143)
Chichester Rd. E11 —3G 49
Chichester Rd. N9 —1B 18
Chichester Rd. NW6 —2J 59
Chichester Rd. W2 —5K 59
Chichester Rd. Croy —3E 134
Chichester St. SW1
—5G 77 (6B 154)
Chichester Way. E14 —4F 81
Chichester Way. Felt —7A 86
Chicksand St. E1
—5F 63 (6K 145)
Chiddingfold. N12 —3D 14
Chiddingstone. SE13 —5E 96
Chiddingstone Av. Bexh —7F 85
Chiddingstone St. SW6 —2J 91
Chieveley Pde. Bexh —4H 101
Chieveley Rd. Bexh —4H 101
Chignell Pl. W13 —1A 72
Chigwell Hill. E1 —7H 63
Chigwell Hurst Ct. Pinn —3B 22
Chigwell Pk. Chig —4K 21
Chigwell Pk. Dri. Chig —4K 21
Chigwell Rise. Chig —2K 21
Chigwell Rd. E18 & Wfd G
—3K 33
Chilcot Clo. E14 —6D 64
Childebert Rd. SW17 —2F 109
Childeric Rd. SE14 —7A 80
Childerley St. SW6 —1G 91
Childers St. SE8 —6A 80
Childers, The. Wfd G —5J 21
Childs Hill Wlk. NW2 —3H 43
(off Cricklewood La.)
Child's La. SE19 —6E 110
Child's Pl. SW5 —4J 75
Child's St. SW5 —4J 75
Child's Wlk. SW5 —4J 75
Childs Way. NW11 —5H 27
Chilham Clo. Bex —7F 101
Chilham Clo. Gnfd —2A 56
Chilham Ho. SE1
—3D 78 (1F 157)
Chilham Rd. SE9 —4C 114
Chilham Way. Brom —7J 127
Chillerton Rd. SW17 —5E 108
Chillingworth Gdns. Twic
—1K 103
Chillingworth Rd. N7 —5A 46
Chilmark Gdns. N Mald —6C 120
Chilmark Rd. SW16 —2H 123
Chiltern Av. Twic —1E 102
Chiltern Clo. Bexh —1K 101
Chiltern Clo. Croy —3E 134
Chiltern Clo. Wor Pk —2E 130
Chiltern Ct. N10 —2E 28
Chiltern Ct. Harr —5H 23

Chiltern Ct. New Bar —5F 5
Chiltern Dene. Enf —4E 6
Chiltern Dri. Surb —6G 119
Chiltern Gdns. NW2 —3F 43
Chiltern Gdns. Brom —4H 127
Chiltern Ho. SE17
—6D 78 (7F 157)
(off Portland St.)
Chiltern Ho. W5 —5E 56
Chiltern Rd. E3 —4C 64
Chiltern Rd. Ilf —5J 35
Chiltern Rd. Pinn —5A 22
Chiltern St. W1 —5E 60 (5G 141)
Chiltern Way. Wfd G —3D 20
Chilthorne Clo. SE6 —7B 96
Chilton Av. W5 —4D 72
Chilton Gro. SE8 —4K 79
Chiltonian Ind. Est. SE12
—6H 97
Chilton Rd. Edgw —6B 12
Chilton Rd. Rich —3G 89
Chiltons, The. E18 —2J 33
Chilton St. E2 —4F 63 (3K 145)
Chilver St. SE10 —5H 81
Chilworth Ct. SW19 —1F 107
Chilworth Gdns. Sutt —3A 132
Chilworth M. W2
—6B 60 (1A 146)
Chilworth St. W2 —6A 60
Chimes Av. N13 —5F 17
Chimney Ct. E1 —1H 79
(off Brewhouse La.)
China Wharf. SE1
—2G 79 (6K 151)
Chinbrook Cres. SE12 —3K 113
Chinbrook Rd. SE12 —3K 113
Chinchilla Dri. Houn —2A 86
Chine, The. N10 —4G 29
Chine, The. N21 —6G 7
Chine, The. Wemb —5C 40
Ching Ct. WC2 —6J 61 (1E 148)
(off Monmouth St.)
Chingdale Rd. E4 —3B 20
Chingford Av. E4 —3H 19
Chingford Hall Est. E4 —6G 19
Chingford Ind. Est. E4 —5F 19
Chingford La. Wfd G —4B 20
Chingford Mt. Rd. E4 —4H 19
Chingford Rd. E4 —6H 19
Chingford Rd. E17 —1D 32
Chingley Clo. Brom —6G 113
Ching Way. E4 —6G 19
Chinnery Clo. Enf —1A 8
Chinnor Cres. Gnfd —2F 55
Chipka St. E14 —2E 80
Chipley St. SE14 —6A 80
Chipmunk Gro. N'holt —3C 54
Chippendale St. E5 —3K 47
Chippenham Av. Wemb —5H 41
Chippenham Gdns. NW6 —3J 59
Chippenham M. W9 —4J 59
Chippenham Rd. W9 —4J 59
Chipperfield Rd. Orp —7A 116
Chipping Clo. Barn —3B 4
Chipstead Av. T Hth —4B 124
Chipstead Clo. SE19 —7F 111
Chipstead Clo. Sutt —7K 131
Chipstead Gdns. NW2 —2D 42
Chipstead St. SW6 —1J 91
Chip St. SW4 —3H 93
Chirk Clo. Hayes —4C 54
Chisenhale Rd. E3 —2A 64
Chisholm Rd. Croy —2E 134
Chisholm Rd. Rich —6F 89

Chisledon Wlk. E9 —6B 48
(off Eastway)
Chislehurst Av. N12 —7F 15
Chislehurst Rd. Brom & Chst
—2B 128
Chislehurst Rd. Orp —4J 129
Chislehurst Rd. Rich —5E 88
Chislehurst Rd. Sidc —5A 116
Chislet Clo. Beck —7C 112
Chisley Rd. N15 —6E 30
Chiswell Sq. SE3 —2K 97
Chiswell St. EC1
—5D 62 (5E 144)
Chiswick Bri. SW14 & W4
—2J 89
Chiswick Clo. Croy —3K 133
Chiswick Comn. Rd. W4 —4K 73
Chiswick Ct. Pinn —3D 22
Chiswick High Rd. Bren & W4
(in two parts) —5G 73
Chiswick La. N. W4 —5A 74
Chiswick La. S. W4 —6B 74
Chiswick Mall. W4 & W6 —6B 74
Chiswick Plaza. W4 —6J 73
Chiswick Quay. W4 —1J 89
Chiswick Rd. N9 —2B 18
Chiswick Rd. W4 —4J 73
Chiswick Roundabout. (Junct.)
—5G 73
Chiswick Sq. W4 —6A 74
Chiswick Staithe. W4 —7H 73
Chiswick Ter. W4 —4J 73
Chiswick Village. W4 —6G 73
Chiswick Wharf. W4 —6B 74
Chitty's La. Dag —2D 52
Chitty St. W1 —5G 61 (5B 142)
Chivalry Rd. SW11 —5C 92
Chive Clo. Croy —1K 135
Chivenor Gro. King T —5D 104
Chivers Rd. E4 —3J 19
Chiver St. SE10 —5H 81
Choats Mnr. Way. Dag —2F 69
Choats Rd. Bark & Dag —2C 68
Chobham Gdns. SW19 —2F 107
Chobham Rd. E15 —5F 49
Cholmeley Cres. N6 —7F 29
Cholmeley Lodge. N6 —1F 45
Cholmeley Pk. N6 —1F 45
Cholmley Gdns. NW6 —5J 43
Cholmley Rd. Th Dit —6B 118
Cholmondeley Av. NW10 —2C 58
Cholmondeley Wlk. Rich —5C 88
Choppin's Ct. E1 —1H 79
Chopwell Clo. E15 —7G 49
Chorleywood Cres. Orp —2K 129
Choumert Gro. SE15 —2G 95
Choumert Rd. SE15 —3F 95
Choumert Sq. SE15 —2G 95
Chow Sq. E8 —5F 47
(off Arcola St.)
Chrisp St. E14 —5D 64
(in two parts)
Christabel Clo. Iswth —3J 87
Christchurch Av. N12 —6F 15
Christchurch Av. NW6 —1F 59
Christchurch Av. Eri —6K 85
Christchurch Av. Harr —4K 23
Christchurch Av. Tedd —5A 104
Christchurch Av. Wemb —6E 40
Christchurch Clo. N12 —7G 15
Christchurch Clo. SW19 —7B 108
Christchurch Ct. NW10 —1A 58
Christchurch Ct. Hayes —4A 54
(off Dunedin Way)
Christchurch Gdns. Harr —4A 24

Christchurch Grn. *Wemb* —6E **40**
Christchurch Hill. *NW3* —3B **44**
Christchurch Ho. SW2 —1K **109**
(off Christchurch Rd.)
Christchurch La. *Barn* —2B **4**
Christchurch Pk. *Sutt* —7A **132**
Christchurch Pas. *NW3* —3A **44**
Christchurch Pas. *High Bar*
—2B **4**
Christchurch Pl. *SW8* —2H **93**
Christchurch Rd. *N8* —6J **29**
Christchurch Rd. *SW2* —1K **109**
Christ Chu. Rd. *SW14* —5H **89**
Christchurch Rd. *SW19* —7B **108**
Christ Chu. Rd. *Beck* —2C **126**
Christchurch Rd. *Ilf* —1F **51**
Christchurch Rd. *Sidc* —4K **115**
Christchurch Rd. *Surb* —6F **119**
Christchurch Sq. *E9* —1J **63**
Christchurch St. *SW3*
—6D **76** (7E **152**)
Christchurch Ter. *SW3*
—6D **76** (7E **152**)
Christchurch Way. *SE10* —5G **81**
Christian Ct. *SE16* —1B **80**
Christian Fields. *SW16* —7A **110**
Christian Pl. E1 —6G **63**
(off Burslem St.)
Christian St. *E1* —6G **63**
Christie Ct. *N19* —2J **45**
Christie Dri. *Croy* —5G **125**
Christie Gdns. *Romf* —6B **36**
Christie Rd. *E9* —6A **48**
Christina Sq. *N4* —1B **46**
Christina St. *EC2*
—4E **62** (3G **145**)
Christopher Av. *W7* —3A **72**
Christopher Clo. *SE16* —2K **79**
Christopher Clo. *Sidc* —6K **99**
Christopher Gdns. *Dag* —5D **52**
Christopher Ho. Sidc —2A **116**
(off Station Rd.)
Christopher Pl. *NW1*
—3H **61** (1D **142**)
Christophers M. *W11* —1G **75**
Christopher St. *EC2*
—4D **62** (4F **145**)
Chryssell Rd. *SW9* —7A **78**
Chubworthy St. *SE14* —6A **80**
Chudleigh. *Sidc* —4B **116**
Chudleigh Cres. *Ilf* —4J **51**
Chudleigh Gdns. *Sutt* —3A **132**
Chudleigh Rd. *NW6* —7F **43**
Chudleigh Rd. *SE4* —5B **96**
Chudleigh Rd. *Twic* —6J **87**
Chudleigh St. *E1* —6K **63**
Chulsa Rd. *SE26* —5H **111**
Chumleigh St. *SE5*
—6E **78** (7G **157**)
Chumleigh Wlk. *Surb* —4F **119**
Church All. *Croy* —1A **134**
Church App. *SE21* —3D **110**
Church Av. *E4* —6A **20**
Church Av. *N2* —2B **28**
Church Av. *NW1* —6F **45**
Church Av. *SW14* —3K **89**
Church Av. *Beck* —1C **126**
Church Av. *N'holt* —5D **38**
Church Av. *Pinn* —6C **22**
Church Av. *Sidc* —5A **116**
Church Av. *S'hall* —3C **70**
Churchbank. E17 —4C **32**
(off Teresa M.)
Churchbury Clo. *Enf* —2K **7**
Churchbury La. *Enf* —3J **7**

Churchbury Rd. *SE9* —7B **98**
Churchbury Rd. *Enf* —2K **7**
Church Cloisters. *EC3*
—7E **62** (3G **151**)
Church Clo. *N20* —3H **15**
Church Clo. *W8* —2K **75**
Church Clo. *Edgw* —5D **12**
Church Clo. *Houn* —3D **86**
Church Ct. *Rich* —5D **88**
Church Ct. *Wfd G* —6F **21**
Church Cres. *E9* —7K **47**
Church Cres. *N3* —1H **27**
Church Cres. *N10* —4F **29**
Church Cres. *N20* —3H **15**
Churchcroft Clo. *SW12* —7E **92**
Churchdown. *Brom* —4G **113**
Church Dri. *NW9* —1K **41**
Church Dri. *Harr* —6E **22**
Church Dri. *W Wick* —3G **137**
Church Elm La. *Dag* —6G **53**
Church End. *E17* —4D **32**
Church End. *NW4* —3D **26**
Church Entry. *EC4*
—6B **62** (1B **150**)
Church Farm La. *Sutt* —6G **131**
Churchfield Av. *N12* —6G **15**
Churchfield Clo. *Harr* —4G **23**
Churchfield Mans. SW6 —2H **91**
(off New King's Rd.)
Churchfield Rd. *W3* —1J **73**
Churchfield Rd. *W7* —2J **71**
Churchfield Rd. *W13* —1B **72**
Churchfield Rd. *Well* —3A **100**
Churchfields. *E18* —1J **33**
Churchfields. *SE10* —6E **80**
Churchfields Av. *Felt* —3D **102**
Churchfields Rd. *Beck* —2K **125**
Churchfield Way. *N12* —6F **15**
Church Gdns. *W5* —2D **72**
Church Gdns. *Wemb* —4A **40**
Church Ga. *SW6* —3G **91**
Church Gro. *SE13* —5D **96**
Church Gro. *King T* —1C **118**
Church Hill. *E17* —4C **32**
Church Hill. *N21* —7E **6**
Church Hill. *SE18* —3D **82**
Church Hill. *SW19* —5H **107**
Church Hill. *Cars* —5D **132**
Church Hill. *Cray* —4K **101**
Church Hill. *Harr* —1J **39**
Church Hill Rd. *E17* —4D **32**
Church Hill Rd. *Barn* —6H **5**
Church Hill Rd. *Surb* —5E **118**
Church Hill Rd. *Sutt* —3F **131**
Church Hill Wood. *Orp* —5K **129**
Church Hyde. *SE18* —6J **83**
Churchill Av. *Harr* —6B **24**
Churchill Ct. *N4* —7A **30**
Churchill Ct. *W5* —4F **57**
Churchill Ct. *N'holt* —5E **38**
Churchill Ct. *Pinn* —1C **22**
Churchill Ct. *S Harr* —5F **23**
Churchill Gdns. *SW1*
—5G **77** (6A **154**)
Churchill Gdns. *W3* —6G **57**
Churchill Gdns. Rd. *SW1*
—5F **77** (6K **153**)
Churchill M. *Wfd G* —6C **20**
Churchill Pl. *E14* —1D **80**
Churchill Pl. *Harr* —4J **23**
Churchill Rd. *E16* —6A **66**
Churchill Rd. *NW2* —6D **42**
Churchill Rd. *NW5* —4F **45**
Churchill Rd. *Edgw* —6A **12**
Churchill Rd. *S Croy* —7C **134**

Churchills M. *Wfd G* —6C **20**
Churchill Ter. *E4* —4H **19**
Churchill Wlk. *E9* —5J **47**
Churchill Way. *Brom* —3J **127**
Church La. *E11* —1G **49**
Church La. *E17* —4D **32**
Church La. *N2* —3B **28**
Church La. *N8* —4K **29**
Church La. *N9* —2B **18**
Church La. *N17* —1E **30**
Church La. *NW9* —6J **25**
Church La. *SW17* —5D **108**
Church La. *SW19* —1J **121**
Church La. *W5* —2C **72**
Church La. *Brom* —1C **138**
Church La. *Chst* —1G **129**
Church La. *Dag* —7J **53**
Church La. *Enf* —3J **7**
Church La. *Harr* —1K **23**
Church La. *Pinn* —3C **22**
Church La. *Rich* —1E **104**
Church La. *Tedd* —5K **103**
Church La. *Th Dit* —6A **118**
Church La. *Twic* —1A **104**
Church La. *Wall* —3H **133**
Church La. *Wfd G* —4C **20**
Church Manorway. *SE2* —4A **84**
Church Manorway. *Eri* —4K **85**
Churchmead Clo. *E Barn* —6H **5**
Churchmead Rd. *NW10* —6C **42**
Churchmore Rd. *SW16* —1G **123**
Church Mt. *N2* —5B **28**
Church Pas. *Barn* —4C **4**
Church Pas. *Surb* —5E **118**
Church Pas. *Twic* —1B **104**
Church Path. *E11* —5J **33**
Church Path. *E17* —4D **32**
Church Path. *N5* —5B **46**
Church Path. *N17* —1E **30**
Church Path. *N20* —4F **15**
Church Path. *NW10* —7A **42**
Church Path. *SW14* —3K **89**
(in two parts)
Church Path. *SW19* —2H **121**
Church Path. *W4 & W3* —3J **73**
Church Path. *W7* —1J **71**
Church Path. *Bark* —1G **67**
Church Path. *Barn* —4B **4**
Church Path. *Croy* —2C **134**
Church Path. *Mitc* —3C **122**
Church Path. *Romf* —5K **37**
Church Path. *S'hall* —1E **70**
(Southall)
Church Path. *S'hall* —3D **70**
(Southall Green)
Church Pl. *SW1* —7G **61** (3B **148**)
Church Pl. *W5* —2D **72**
Church Pl. *Mitc* —3C **122**
Church Rise. *SE23* —2K **111**
Church Rd. *E10* —1C **48**
Church Rd. *E12* —5C **50**
Church Rd. *E17* —2A **32**
Church Rd. *N6* —6E **28**
Church Rd. *N17* —1E **30**
Church Rd. *NW4* —4D **26**
Church Rd. *NW10* —7A **42**
Church Rd. *SE19* —1E **124**
Church Rd. *SW13* —2B **90**
Church Rd. *SW19 & Mitc*
(Merton) —1B **122**
Church Rd. *SW19* —5G **107**
(Wimbledon)
Church Rd. *W3* —1J **73**
Church Rd. *W7* —7H **55**
Church Rd. *Bark* —6G **51**

Church Rd. *Bexh* —2F **101**
Church Rd. *Brom* —2J **127**
Church Rd. *Buck H* —1E **20**
Church Rd. *Cran* —6A **70**
Church Rd. *Croy* —3C **134**
(in two parts)
Church Rd. *Enf* —6D **8**
Church Rd. *Eri* —5K **85**
Church Rd. *Felt* —5B **102**
Church Rd. *Ham* —4D **104**
Church Rd. *Houn* —7E **70**
Church Rd. *Ilf* —6J **35**
Church Rd. *Iswth* —1H **87**
Church Rd. *Kes* —7B **138**
Church Rd. *King T* —2F **119**
Church Rd. *N'holt* —2B **54**
Church Rd. *Rich* —4E **88**
Church Rd. *Short* —3G **127**
Church Rd. *Sidc* —4A **116**
Church Rd. *S'hall* —3D **70**
Church Rd. *Stan* —5G **11**
Church Rd. *Sutt* —6G **131**
Church Rd. *Tedd* —4J **103**
Church Rd. *Wall* —3H **133**
Church Rd. *Well* —2B **100**
Church Rd. *W Ewe* —7A **130**
Church Rd. *Wor Pk* —1A **130**
Church Rd. Almshouses. *E10*
—2D **48**
Church Rd. Ind. Est. *E10* —1C **48**
Church Row. *N2* —2B **28**
Church Row. *Chst* —1G **129**
Church Row M. *Chst* —7G **115**
Church St. *E15* —1G **65**
Church St. *E16* —1F **83**
Church St. *N9* —7J **7**
Church St. *W2 & NW8*
—5B **60** (5B **140**)
Church St. *W4* —6B **74**
Church St. *Croy* —2B **134**
Church St. *Dag* —6H **53**
Church St. *Enf* —3H **7**
Church St. *Ewe* —7C **130**
Church St. *Hamp* —7G **103**
Church St. *Iswth* —3B **88**
Church St. *King T* —2D **118**
Church St. *Sutt* —5K **131**
Church St. *Twic* —1A **104**
Church St. Est. *NW8*
—4B **60** (4B **140**)
Church St. N. *E15* —1G **65**
Church St. Pas. *E15* —1G **65**
Church Stretton Rd. *Houn*
—5G **87**
Church Ter. *NW4* —3D **26**
Church Ter. *SE13* —3G **97**
Church Ter. *Rich* —5D **88**
Church Vale. *N2* —3D **28**
Church Vale. *SE23* —2K **111**
Church View. *Rich* —5E **88**
Churchview Rd. *Twic* —1H **103**
Church Wlk. *N6* —3E **44**
Church Wlk. *N16* —3D **46**
Church Wlk. *NW2* —3H **43**
Church Wlk. *NW4* —3E **26**
Church Wlk. *NW9* —2K **41**
Church Wlk. *SW13* —1C **90**
Church Wlk. *SW15* —5D **90**
Church Wlk. *SW16* —2G **123**
Church Wlk. *SW20* —3E **120**
Church Wlk. *Bren* —6C **72**
(in two parts)
Church Wlk. *Enf* —3J **7**

Church Wlk. *Rich* —5D **88**
Church Wlk. *Th Dit* —6A **118**
Churchward Ho. *W14* —5H **75**
(off Ivatt Pl.)
Church Way. *N20* —3H **15**
Churchway. *NW1*
—3H **61** (1D **142**)
Church Way. *Barn* —4J **5**
Church Way. *Edgw* —6B **12**
Churchwell Path. *E9* —5J **47**
Churchwood Gdns. *Wfd G*
—4D **20**
Churchyard Pas. *SE5* —1D **94**
Churchyard Row. *SE11*
—4B **78** (3B **156**)
Churnfield. *N4* —2A **46**
Churston Av. *E13* —1K **65**
Churston Clo. *SW2* —1A **110**
Churston Dri. *Mord* —5F **121**
Churston Gdns. *N11* —6B **16**
Churton Pl. *SW1*
—4G **77** (4B **154**)
Churton St. *SW1*
—4G **77** (4B **154**)
Chusan Pl. *E14* —6B **64**
Chute Ho. *SW9* —2A **94**
(off Stockwell Pk. Rd.)
Chyngton Clo. *Sidc* —3K **115**
Cibber Rd. *SE23* —2K **111**
Cicada Rd. *SW18* —6A **92**
Cicely Rd. *SE15* —1G **95**
Cinderford Way. *Brom* —4G **113**
Cinnamon Clo. *Croy* —7J **123**
Cinnamon Row. *SW11* —3A **92**
Cinnamon St. *E1* —1H **79**
Cinnamon Wharf. *SE1*
—2F **79** (6K **151**)
Cintra Pk. *SE19* —7F **111**
Circle Gdns. *SW19* —2J **121**
Circle, The. *NW2* —3A **42**
Circle, The. *NW7* —6E **12**
Circuits, The. *Pinn* —4A **22**
Circular Rd. *N2* —2B **28**
Circular Rd. *N17* —3F **31**
Circular Way. *SE18* —6D **82**
Circus Lodge. *NW8*
—3B **60** (1A **140**)
Circus M. *W1* —5D **60** (5E **140**)
Circus Pl. *EC2* —5D **62** (6F **145**)
Circus Rd. *NW8* —3B **60** (1A **140**)
Circus St. *SE10* —7E **80**
Cirencester St. *W2* —5K **59**
Cissbury Ho. *SE26* —3G **111**
Cissbury Ring N. *N12* —5C **14**
Cissbury Ring S. *N12* —5C **14**
Cissbury Rd. *N15* —5D **30**
Citadel Pl. *SE11* —5K **77** (5G **155**)
Citizen Rd. *N7* —4A **46**
City Garden Row. *N1*
—2B **62** (1B **144**)
City Heights. SE1
—1E **78** (5H **151**)
(off Tooley St.)
City Ho. Wall —1E **132**
(off Corbet Clo.)
City Rd. *EC1* —2B **62** (1A **144**)
City View Ct. *SE22* —7H **95**
Civic Way. *Ilf* —4G **35**
Clabon M. *SW1* —3D **76** (2E **152**)
Clack St. *SE16* —2J **79**
Clacton Rd. *E6* —3B **66**
Clacton Rd. *E17* —6A **32**
Clacton Rd. *N17* —2F **31**
Claigmar Gdns. *N3* —1K **27**
Claire Ct. *N12* —4F **15**

Claire Ct. *NW2* —6G **43**
Claire Ct. *Bush* —1C **10**
Claire Gdns. *Stan* —5H **11**
Claire Ho. *Edgw* —2J **25**
 (off Burnt Oak B'way.)
Claire Pl. *E14* —3C **80**
Clairvale Rd. *Houn* —1C **86**
Clairview Rd. *SW16* —5F **109**
Clairville Gdns. *W7* —1J **71**
Clairville Point. *SE23* —3K **111**
 (off Dacres Rd.)
Clamp Hill. *Stan* —4C **10**
Clancarty Rd. *SW6* —2J **91**
Clandeboyne Ho. *E15* —1H **65**
 (off John St.)
Clandon Clo. *W3* —2H **73**
Clandon Clo. *Eps* —6B **130**
Clandon Gdns. *N3* —3J **27**
Clandon Rd. *Ilf* —2J **51**
Clandon St. *SE8* —2C **96**
Clandon Ter. *SW20* —1F **121**
Clanfield Way. *SE15* —7F **79**
Clanricarde Gdns. *W2* —7J **59**
Clapham Common. (Junct.)
 —4G **93**
Clapham Comn. N. Side. *SW4*
 —4D **92**
Clapham Comn. S. Side. *SW4*
 —6F **93**
Clapham Comn. W. Side. *SW4*
 —4D **92**
Clapham Cres. *SW4* —4H **93**
Clapham High St. *SW4* —4H **93**
Clapham Junction App. *SW11*
 —4C **92**
Clapham Mnr. Ct. *SW4* —3G **93**
Clapham Mnr. St. *SW4* —3G **93**
Clapham Pk. Est. *SW4* —6H **93**
Clapham Pk. Rd. *SW4* —4H **93**
Clapham Rd. *SW9* —3J **93**
Clapham Rd. Est. *SW4* —3J **93**
Clap La. *Dag* —2H **53**
Claps Ga. La. *E6 & Bark* —4F **67**
 (in two parts)
Clapton Comn. *E5* —7F **31**
Clapton Pk. Est. *E5* —4K **47**
Clapton Pas. *E5* —5J **47**
Clapton Sq. *E5* —5J **47**
Clapton Ter. *N16* —1G **47**
Clapton Way. *E5* —4G **47**
Clara Nehab Ho. *NW11* —5H **27**
 (off Leeside Cres.)
Clara Pl. *SE18* —4E **82**
Clare Clo. *N2* —3A **28**
Clare Corner. *SE9* —7F **99**
Claredale St. *E2* —2G **63**
Clare Gdns. *E7* —4J **49**
Clare Gdns. *W11* —6G **59**
Clare Gdns. *Bark* —6K **51**
Clare La. *N1* —7C **46**
Clare Lawn Av. *SW14* —5K **89**
Clare Mkt. *WC2* —6K **61** (1H **149**)
Clare M. *SW6* —7K **75**
Claremont Av. *Harr* —5E **24**
Claremont Av. *N Mald* —5C **120**
Claremont Clo. *E16* —1E **82**
Claremont Clo. *N1*
 —2A **62** (1K **143**)
Claremont Clo. *SW2* —1J **109**
Claremont Gro. *W4* —7A **74**
Claremont Gdns. *Ilf* —2J **51**
Claremont Gdns. *Surb* —5E **118**
Claremont Gro. *Wfd G* —6F **21**
Claremont Pk. *N3* —1G **27**

Claremont Rd. *E7* —5K **49**
Claremont Rd. *E11* —3F **49**
Claremont Rd. *E17* —2A **32**
Claremont Rd. *N6* —7G **29**
Claremont Rd. *NW2* —7F **27**
Claremont Rd. *W9* —2G **59**
Claremont Rd. *W13* —5A **56**
Claremont Rd. *Brom* —4C **128**
Claremont Rd. *Croy* —1G **135**
Claremont Rd. *Harr* —2J **23**
Claremont Rd. *Surb* —5E **118**
Claremont Rd. *Tedd* —5K **103**
Claremont Rd. *Twic* —7B **88**
Claremont Sq. *N1*
 —2A **62** (1J **143**)
Claremont St. *E16* —2E **82**
Claremont St. *N18* —6B **18**
Claremont St. *SE10* —6D **80**
Claremont Way. *NW2* —1E **42**
 (in two parts)
Claremont Way Ind. Est. *NW2*
 —1E **42**
Clarence Av. *SW4* —7H **93**
Clarence Av. *Brom* —4C **128**
Clarence Av. *N Mald* —2J **119**
Clarence Clo. *Bush* —1E **10**
Clarence Ct. *NW7* —5G **13**
Clarence Cres. *SW4* —6H **93**
Clarence Cres. *Sidc* —3B **116**
Clarence Gdns. *NW1*
 —3F **61** (2K **141**)
Clarence La. *SW15* —6A **90**
Clarence M. *E5* —5H **47**
Clarence M. *SE16* —7K **63**
Clarence Pl. *E5* —5H **47**
Clarence Rd. *E5* —4H **47**
Clarence Rd. *E12* —5B **50**
Clarence Rd. *E16* —4G **65**
Clarence Rd. *E17* —2K **31**
Clarence Rd. *N15* —5C **30**
Clarence Rd. *N22* —7D **16**
Clarence Rd. *NW6* —7H **43**
Clarence Rd. *SE9* —2C **114**
Clarence Rd. *SW19* —6K **107**
Clarence Rd. *W4* —5G **73**
Clarence Rd. *Bexh* —4E **100**
Clarence Rd. *Brom* —3B **128**
Clarence Rd. *Croy* —7D **124**
Clarence Rd. *Enf* —5D **8**
Clarence Rd. *Rich* —1F **89**
Clarence Rd. *Sidc* —3B **116**
Clarence Rd. *Sutt* —5K **131**
Clarence Rd. *Tedd* —6K **103**
Clarence Rd. *Wall* —5F **133**
Clarence St. *King T* —2D **118**
Clarence St. *Rich* —4E **88**
Clarence St. *S'hall* —3B **70**
Clarence Ter. *NW1*
 —4D **60** (3F **141**)
Clarence Ter. *Houn* —4F **87**
Clarence Wlk. *SW4* —2J **93**
Clarence Way. *NW1* —7F **45**
Clarence Yd. *SE17*
 —5C **78** (5C **156**)
Clarenden Pl. *Wilm* —5K **117**
Clarendon Clo. *W2*
 —7C **60** (2C **146**)
Clarendon Clo. *St P* —3K **129**
Clarendon Clo. *NW11* —4H **27**
Clarendon Ct. *Beck* —1D **126**
 (off Albemarle Rd.)
Clarendon Ct. *Rich* —1F **89**
Clarendon Cres. *Twic* —3H **103**
Clarendon Cross. *W11* —7G **59**

Clarendon Dri. *SW15* —4E **90**
Clarendon Gdns. *NW4* —3C **26**
Clarendon Gdns. *W9* —4A **60**
Clarendon Gdns. *Ilf* —7D **34**
Clarendon Gdns. *Wemb* —3D **40**
Clarendon Grn. *Orp* —4K **129**
Clarendon Gro. *NW1*
 —3H **61** (1C **142**)
Clarendon Gro. *Mitc* —3D **122**
Clarendon Gro. *St P* —4K **129**
Clarendon M. *W2*
 —7C **60** (2C **146**)
Clarendon M. *Bex* —1H **117**
Clarendon Path. *St P* —4K **129**
 (in two parts)
Clarendon Pl. *W2*
 —7C **60** (2C **146**)
Clarendon Rise. *SE13* —4E **96**
Clarendon Rd. *E11* —1F **49**
Clarendon Rd. *E17* —6D **32**
Clarendon Rd. *E18* —3J **33**
Clarendon Rd. *N8* —3K **29**
Clarendon Rd. *N15* —4C **30**
Clarendon Rd. *N18* —6B **18**
Clarendon Rd. *N22* —2K **29**
Clarendon Rd. *SW19* —7C **108**
Clarendon Rd. *W5* —4E **56**
Clarendon Rd. *W11* —7G **59**
Clarendon Rd. *Croy* —2B **134**
Clarendon Rd. *Wall* —6G **133**
Clarendon St. *SW1*
 —5F **77** (5K **153**)
Clarendon Ter. *W9*
 —4A **60** (3A **140**)
Clarendon Wlk. *W11* —6G **59**
Clarendon Way. *N21* —6H **7**
Clarendon Way. *Chst & St M*
 —3K **129**
Clarens St. *SE6* —2B **112**
Clare Pl. *SW15* —7B **90**
Clare Rd. *E11* —6F **33**
Clare Rd. *NW10* —7C **42**
Clare Rd. *SE14* —2B **96**
Clare Rd. *Gnfd* —6H **39**
Clare Rd. *Houn* —3D **86**
Clare St. *E2* —2H **63**
Claret Gdns. *SE25* —3E **124**
Clareville Gro. *SW7*
 —4A **76** (4A **152**)
Clareville Gro. M. *SW7*
 —4A **76** (4A **152**)
Clareville St. *SW7* —4A **76**
Clare Way. *Bexh* —1E **100**
Clarewood Wlk. *SW9* —4A **94**
Clarges M. *W1* —1F **77** (4J **147**)
Clarges St. *W1* —1F **77** (4H **147**)
Claribel Rd. *SW9* —2B **94**
Clarice Way. *Wall* —7J **133**
Claridge Ct. *SW6* —2H **91**
Claridge Rd. *Dag* —1D **52**
Clarissa Rd. *Romf* —7D **36**
Clarissa St. *E8* —1F **63**
Clarke Ct. *NW10* —7J **41**
Clarke Mans. *Bark* —7K **51**
 (off Upney La.)
Clarke Path. *N16* —1G **47**
Clarkes Av. *Wor Pk* —1F **131**
Clarke's M. *W1* —5E **60** (5H **141**)
Clarks Mead. *Bush* —1B **10**
Clarkson Rd. *E16* —6H **65**
Clarkson Row. *NW1* —2G **61**
 (off Mornington Ter.)
Clarksons, The. *Bark* —2G **67**
Clarkson St. *E2* —3H **63**
Clarks Pl. *EC2* —6E **62** (7G **145**)

Clarks Rd. *Ilf* —2H **51**
Clark St. *E1* —5J **63**
Clark Way. *Houn* —7B **70**
Claude Rd. *E10* —2E **48**
Claude Rd. *E13* —1K **65**
Claude Rd. *SE15* —2H **95**
Claude St. *E14* —4C **80**
Claudia Jones Ho. *N17* —1C **30**
Claudia Jones Way. *SW2* —6J **93**
Claudia Pl. *SW19* —1G **107**
Claughton Rd. *E13* —2A **66**
Clauson Av. *N'holt* —5F **39**
Clavell St. *SE10* —6E **80**
Claverdale Rd. *SW2* —7K **93**
Clavering Av. *SW13* —6D **74**
Clavering Clo. *Twic* —4A **104**
Clavering Ho. *SE13* —4F **97**
 (off Blessington Rd.)
Clavering Ind. Est. *N9* —2D **18**
 (off Triangle Works)
Clavering Rd. *E12* —1B **50**
Claverley Gro. *N3* —1K **27**
Claverley Vs. *N3* —7E **14**
Claverton St. *SW1*
 —5G **77** (6B **154**)
Clave St. *E1* —1J **79**
Claxton Gro. *W6* —5F **75**
Claxton Path. *SE4* —4K **95**
 (off Coston Wlk.)
Clay Av. *Mitc* —2F **123**
Claybank Gro. *SE13* —3D **96**
Claybourne M. *SE19* —7E **110**
Claybridge Rd. *SE12* —4A **114**
Claybrook Clo. *N2* —3B **28**
Claybrook Rd. *W6* —6F **75**
Claybury B'way. *Ilf* —3C **34**
Claybury Rd. *Wfd G* —7H **21**
Clay Ct. *E17* —3F **33**
Claydon Dri. *Croy* —4J **133**
Claydon Ho. *NW4* —2F **27**
 (off Holders Hill Rd.)
Claydown M. *SE18* —5E **82**
Clay Farm Rd. *SE9* —2G **115**
Claygate Cres. *New Ad* —6E **136**
Claygate La. *Th Dit* —7A **118**
Claygate Rd. *W13* —3B **72**
Clayhall Av. *Ilf* —3C **34**
Clay Hill. *Enf* —1K **7**
Clayhill. *Surb* —5G **119**
Clayhill Cres. *SE9* —4B **114**
Claylands Pl. *SW8* —7A **78**
Claylands Rd. *SW8*
 —6K **77** (7H **155**)
Clay La. *Bush* —1D **10**
Clay La. *Edgw* —2B **12**
Claymore Clo. *Mord* —7J **121**
Claypole Ct. *E17* —6C **32**
 (off Yunus Khan Clo.)
Claypole Dri. *Houn* —1C **86**
Claypole Rd. *E15* —2E **64**
Clayponds Av. *W5 & Bren*
 —4E **72**
Clayponds Gdns. *W5* —4D **72**
Clayponds La. *Bren* —5E **72**
Clays La. *E15* —5D **48**
Clays La. Clo. *E15* —5D **48**
Clay St. *W1* —5D **60** (6F **141**)
Clayton Av. *Wemb* —7E **40**
Clayton Clo. *E6* —6D **66**
Clayton Ct. *E17* —2C **64**
Clayton Cres. *Bren* —5D **72**
Clayton Rd. *SE15* —1G **95**
Clayton Rd. *Iswth* —3J **87**
Clayton Rd. *Romf* —1J **53**

Clayton St. *SE11*
 —6A **78** (7J **155**)
Clayton Ter. *Hayes* —5C **54**
Claywood Clo. *Orp* —7J **129**
Clayworth Clo. *Sidc* —6B **100**
Cleadon Clo. *Enf* —3F **9**
Cleanthus Clo. *SE18* —1F **99**
Cleanthus Rd. *SE18* —1F **99**
Clearbrook Way. *E1* —6J **63**
Clearwell Dri. *W9* —4K **59**
Cleaveland Rd. *Surb* —5D **118**
Cleaverholme Clo. *SE25* —6H **125**
Cleaver Sq. *SE11*
 —5A **78** (6K **155**)
Cleaver St. *SE11*
 —5A **78** (5K **155**)
Cleeve Hill. *SE23* —1H **111**
Cleeve Pk, Gdns. *Sidc* —2B **116**
Clegg St. *E1* —1H **79**
Clegg St. *E13* —2J **65**
Clematis Gdns. *Wfd G* —5D **20**
Clematis St. *W12* —7C **58**
Clem Attlee Ct. *SW6* —6H **75**
Clem Attlee Est. *SW6* —6H **75**
Clem Attlee Pde. *SW6* —6H **75**
 (off N. End Rd.)
Clemence St. *Dag* —1J **69**
Clemence St. *E14* —5B **64**
Clement Av. *SW4* —4H **93**
Clement Clo. *NW6* —7E **42**
Clement Clo. *W4* —4K **73**
Clementhorpe Rd. *Dag* —6C **52**
Clement Ho. *SE8* —4A **80**
Clementina Rd. *E10* —1B **48**
Clementine Clo. *W13* —2B **72**
Clement Rd. *SW19* —5G **107**
Clement Rd. *Beck* —2K **125**
Clement's Av. *E16* —7J **65**
Clements Ct. *Houn* —4B **86**
Clements Ct. *Ilf* —3F **51**
Clement's Inn. *WC2*
 —6K **61** (1H **149**)
Clement's Inn Pas. *WC2*
 —6K **61** (1H **149**)
Clements La. *EC4*
 —7D **62** (2F **151**)
Clements La. *Ilf* —3F **51**
Clements Pl. *Bren* —5D **72**
Clements Rd. *E6* —7C **50**
Clement's Rd. *SE16* —3G **79**
Clements Rd. *Ilf* —3F **51**
Clemson Ho. *E8* —1F **63**
Clendon Way. *SE18* —4H **83**
Clennam St. *SE1*
 —2C **78** (6D **150**)
Clensham Ct. *Sutt* —2J **131**
Clensham La. *Sutt* —2J **131**
Clenston M. *W1* —6D **60** (7E **140**)
Clephane Rd. *N1* —6C **46**
Clephane Rd. N. *N1* —6C **46**
Clere Pl. *EC2* —4D **62** (3F **145**)
Clere St. *EC2* —4D **62** (3F **145**)
Clerkenwell Clo. *EC1*
 —4A **62** (3K **143**)
Clerkenwell Grn. *EC1*
 —4B **62** (4A **144**)
Clerkenwell Rd. *EC1*
 —4A **62** (4J **143**)
Clermont Rd. *E9* —1J **63**
Clevedon Clo. *N16* —3F **47**
Clevedon Mans. *NW5* —4E **44**
Clevedon Pas. *N16* —2F **47**
Clevedon Rd. *SE20* —1K **125**
Clevedon Rd. *King T* —2G **119**
Clevedon Rd. *Twic* —6D **88**

Cleveland Av. *SW20* —2H **121**
Cleveland Av. *W4* —4B **74**
Cleveland Av. *Hamp* —7D **102**
Cleveland Ct. *W13* —5B **56**
Cleveland Gdns. *N4* —5C **30**
Cleveland Gdns. *NW2* —2F **43**
Cleveland Gdns. *SW13* —2B **90**
Cleveland Gdns. *W2* —6A **60**
Cleveland Gdns. *Wor Pk* —2A **130**
Cleveland Gro. *E1* —4J **63**
Cleveland Ho. N2 —2B *28*
  (off Grange, The)
Cleveland La. *N9* —7C **8**
Cleveland Mans. SW9 —7A *78*
  (off Mowll St.)
Cleveland M. *W1*
  —5G **61** (5A **142**)
Cleveland Pk. Av. *E17* —4C **32**
Cleveland Pk. Cres. *E17* —4C **32**
Cleveland Pl. *SW1*
  —1G **77** (4B **148**)
Cleveland Rise. *Mord* —7F **121**
Cleveland Rd. *E18* —3J **33**
Cleveland Rd. *N1* —7D **46**
Cleveland Rd. *SW13* —2B **90**
Cleveland Rd. *W4* —3A **73**
Cleveland Rd. *W13* —5A **56**
Cleveland Rd. *Ilf* —3F **51**
Cleveland Rd. *Iswth* —4A **88**
Cleveland Rd. *N Mald* —4A **120**
Cleveland Rd. *Well* —2K **99**
Cleveland Rd. *Wor Pk* —2A **130**
Cleveland Row. *SW1*
  —1G **77** (5A **148**)
Cleveland Sq. *W2* —6A **60**
Clevelands, The. *Bark* —6G **51**
Cleveland St. *W1*
  —4F **61** (4K **141**)
Cleveland Ter. *W2* —6A **60**
Cleveland Way. *E1* —4J **63**
Cleveley Clo. *SE7* —4B **82**
Cleveley Cres. *W5* —2C **56**
Cleveleys Rd. *E5* —3H **47**
Cleverly Est. *W12* —1C **74**
Cleve Rd. *NW6* —7J **43**
Cleve Rd. *Sidc* —3D **116**
Cleves Av. *Eps* —7D **130**
Cleves Rd. *E6* —1B **66**
Cleves Rd. *Rich* —3C **104**
Cleves Wlk. *Ilf* —1G **35**
Cleves Way. *Hamp* —7D **102**
Cleves Way. *Ruis* —1B **38**
Clewer Ct. *E10* —1C **48**
Clewer Cres. *Harr* —1H **23**
Clewer Ho. SE2 —2D *84*
  (off Wolvercote Rd.)
Cley Ho. *SE4* —4K **95**
Clichy Est. *E1* —5J **63**
Clifden Rd. *E5* —5J **47**
Clifden Rd. *Bren* —6D **72**
Clifden Rd. *Twic* —1K **103**
Cliffe Rd. *S Croy* —5D **134**
Cliffe Wlk. Sutt —5A *132*
  (off Greyhound Rd.)
Clifford Av. *SW14* —3H **89**
Clifford Av. *Chst* —6D **114**
Clifford Av. *Ilf* —1F **35**
Clifford Av. *Wall* —4G **133**
Clifford Clo. *N'holt* —1C **54**
Clifford Dri. *SW9* —4B **94**
Clifford Gdns. *NW10* —2E **58**
Clifford Rd. *E16* —4H **65**
Clifford Rd. *E17* —2E **32**
Clifford Rd. *N9* —6D **8**
Clifford Rd. *SE25* —4G **125**

Clifford Rd. *Barn* —3E **4**
Clifford Rd. *Houn* —3B **86**
Clifford Rd. *Rich* —2D **104**
Clifford Rd. *Wemb* —7D **40**
Clifford's Inn Pas. *EC4*
  —6A **62** (1J **149**)
Clifford St. *W1* —7G **61** (3A **148**)
Clifford Way. *NW10* —4B **42**
Cliff Rd. *NW1* —6H **45**
Cliffsend Ho. SW9 —1A *94*
  (off Cowley Rd.)
Cliff Ter. *SE8* —2C **96**
Cliffview Rd. *SE13* —3C **96**
Cliff Vs. *NW1* —6H **45**
Cliff Wlk. *E16* —5H **65**
  (in two parts)
Clifton Av. *E17* —3K **31**
Clifton Av. *N3* —1H **27**
Clifton Av. *W12* —1B **74**
Clifton Av. *Felt* —3A **102**
Clifton Av. *Stan* —2B **24**
Clifton Av. *Wemb* —6F **41**
Clifton Copse. *SE8* —5B **80**
Clifton Ct. N4 —2A *46*
  (off Playford Rd.)
Clifton Ct. *SE15* —7H **79**
Clifton Ct. *W9* —4B **60** (3A **140**)
Clifton Ct. *Wfd G* —6D **20**
Clifton Cres. *SE15* —7H **79**
Clifton Est. *SE15* —1H **95**
Clifton Gdns. *N15* —6F **31**
Clifton Gdns. *NW11* —6H **27**
Clifton Gdns. *W4* —4K **73**
Clifton Gdns. *W9* —4A **60**
Clifton Gdns. *Enf* —4D **6**
Clifton Gro. *E8* —6G **47**
Clifton Hill. *NW8* —2K **59**
Clifton Ho. *E11* —2G **49**
Clifton Pde. *Felt* —4A **102**
Clifton Pk. Av. *SW20* —2E **120**
Clifton Pl. *SE16* —2J **79**
Clifton Pl. *W2* —6B **60** (1B **146**)
Clifton Rise. *SE14* —7A **80**
  (in two parts)
Clifton Rd. *E7* —6B **50**
Clifton Rd. *E16* —5G **65**
Clifton Rd. *N3* —1A **28**
Clifton Rd. *N8* —6H **29**
Clifton Rd. *N22* —1G **29**
Clifton Rd. *NW10* —2C **58**
Clifton Rd. *SE25* —4E **124**
Clifton Rd. *SW19* —6F **107**
Clifton Rd. *W9* —4A **60**
Clifton Rd. *Gnfd* —4G **55**
Clifton Rd. *Harr* —4F **25**
Clifton Rd. *Ilf* —6H **35**
Clifton Rd. *Iswth* —2J **87**
Clifton Rd. *King T* —7F **105**
Clifton Rd. *Sidc* —4J **115**
Clifton Rd. *S'hall* —4C **70**
Clifton Rd. *Tedd* —4J **103**
Clifton Rd. *Wall* —5F **133**
Clifton Rd. *Well* —3C **100**
Clifton St. *EC2* —5E **62** (5G **145**)
Clifton Ter. *N4* —2A **46**
Clifton Vs. *W9* —5A **60**
Cliftonville Ct. *SE12* —1J **113**
Clifton Wlk. W6 —4D *74*
  (off King St.)
Clifton Way. *SE15* —7J **79**
Clifton Way. *Wemb* —1E **56**
Clinch Ct. *E16* —5J **65**
  (off Plymouth Rd.)
Cline Rd. *N11* —6B **16**
Clinger Ct. *N1* —1E **62**

Clink St. *SE1* —1D **78** (4E **150**)
Clinton Av. *Well* —4A **100**
Clinton Ho. *SE8* —6C **80**
Clinton Rd. *E3* —3A **64**
Clinton Rd. *E7* —4J **49**
Clinton Rd. *N15* —4D **30**
Clipper Clo. *SE16* —2K **79**
Clipper Way. *SE13* —4E **96**
Clipstone M. *W1*
  —5G **61** (5A **142**)
Clipstone Rd. *Houn* —3E **86**
Clipstone St. *W1* —5F **61** (5K **141**)
Clissold Clo. *N2* —3D **28**
Clissold Ct. *N16* —2C **46**
Clissold Cres. *N16* —3D **46**
Clissold Rd. *N16* —3D **46**
Clitheroe Av. *Harr* —1E **38**
Clitheroe Rd. *SW9* —2J **93**
Clitherow Av. *W7* —3A **72**
Clitherow Rd. *Bren* —5C **72**
Clitherow Pas. *Bren* —5C **72**
Clitherow Rd. *Bren* —5B **72**
Clitterhouse Cres. *NW2* —1E **42**
Clitterhouse Rd. *NW2* —1E **42**
Clive Av. *N18* —6B **18**
Clive Clo. W9 —4A *60*
  (off Maida Vale)
Cliveden Clo. *N12* —4F **15**
Cliveden Pl. SW1
  —4E **76** (3G **153**)
Cliveden Rd. *SW19* —1H **121**
Clivedon Ct. *W13* —5B **56**
Clivedon Rd. *E4* —5B **20**
Clive Lloyd Ho. N15 —5C *30*
  (off Woodlands Pk. Rd.)
Clive Lodge. *NW4* —6F **27**
Clive Pas. *SE21* —3D **110**
Clive Rd. *SE21* —3D **110**
Clive Rd. *SW19* —6C **108**
Clive Rd. *Belv* —4G **85**
Clive Rd. *Enf* —4B **8**
Clive Rd. *Twic* —4A **104**
Clive Way. *Enf* —4B **8**
Cloak La. *EC4* —7C **62** (2D **150**)
Clochar Ct. *NW10* —1B **58**
Clock Ho. E17 —4F *33*
  (off Wood St.)
Clockhouse Av. *Bark* —1G **67**
Clockhouse Clo. *SW19* —2E **106**
Clockhouse Ct. *Beck* —2A **126**
Clockhouse La. *Romf* —1H **37**
Clockhouse Pde. *N13* —5F **17**
Clockhouse Pl. *SW15* —6G **91**
Clock Ho. Rd. *Beck* —3A **126**
Clock Pde. *Enf* —5J **7**
Clock Pl. *SE1* —4B **78** (3B **156**)
Clock Tower M. *N1* —1C **62**
Clock Tower Pl. *N7* —6J **45**
Clock Tower Rd. *Iswth* —3K **87**
Cloister Clo. *Tedd* —5B **104**
Cloister Gdns. *SE25* —6H **125**
Cloister Gdns. *Edgw* —5D **12**
Cloister Rd. *NW2* —3H **43**
Cloister Rd. *W3* —5J **57**
Cloisters Av. *Brom* —5D **128**
Cloisters Bus. Cen. SW8 —7F *77*
  (off Battersea Pk. Rd.)
Cloisters Ct. *Bexh* —3H **101**
Cloisters Mall. *King T* —2E **118**
Cloisters, The. *E1*
  —5F **63** (4J **145**)
Cloisters, The. *SW9* —1A **94**
Clonard Way. *Pinn* —6A **10**
Clonbrock Rd. *N16* —4E **46**
Cloncurry St. *SW6* —2F **91**

Clonmel Clo. *Harr* —2H **39**
Clonmell Rd. *N17* —3D **30**
Clonmel Rd. *SW6* —7H **75**
Clonmel Rd. *Tedd* —4H **103**
Clonmore St. *SW18* —1H **107**
Clorane Gdns. *NW3* —3J **43**
Close, The. *E4* —7K **19**
Close, The. *N10* —2F **29**
Close, The. *N14* —2C **16**
Close, The. *N20* —2C **14**
Close, The. *SE25* —6G **125**
Close, The. *Beck* —4A **126**
Close, The. *Bex* —6G **101**
Close, The. *Cars* —7C **132**
Close, The. *E Barn* —6J **5**
Close, The. *Eastc* —7A **22**
Close, The. *Harr* —2G **23**
Close, The. *Ilf* —6J **35**
Close, The. *Iswth* —2H **87**
Close, The. *Mitc* —4D **122**
Close, The. *N Mald* —2J **119**
Close, The. *Orp* —6J **129**
Close, The. *Pinn* —7D **22**
Close, The. *Rich* —3H **89**
Close, The. *Romf* —6E **36**
Close, The. *Sidc* —4B **116**
Close, The. *Sutt* —7H **121**
Close, The. *Wemb* —6E **40**
  (Wembley)
Close, The. *Wemb* —3J **41**
  (Wembley Park)
Cloth Ct. *EC1* —5B **62** (6B **144**)
Cloth Fair. *EC1* —5B **62** (6B **144**)
Clothier St. *E1* —6E **62** (7H **145**)
Cloth St. *EC1* —5C **62** (5C **144**)
Clothworkers Rd. *SE18* —7H **83**
Cloudesdale Rd. *SW17* —2F **109**
Cloudesley Pl. *N1* —1A **62**
Cloudesley Rd. *N1* —1A **62**
Cloudesley Rd. *Bexh* —1F **101**
Cloudesley Sq. *N1* —1A **62**
Cloudesley St. *N1* —1A **62**
Clouston Clo. *Wall* —5J **133**
Clova Rd. *E7* —6H **49**
Clove Cres. *E14* —7E **64**
Clove Hitch Quay. *SW11* —3A **92**
Clovelly Av. *NW9* —4B **26**
Clovelly Clo. *Pinn* —3A **22**
Clovelly Gdns. *SE19* —1F **125**
Clovelly Gdns. *Enf* —7K **7**
Clovelly Gdns. *Romf* —1H **37**
Clovelly Rd. *N8* —4H **29**
Clovelly Rd. *W4* —2K **73**
Clovelly Rd. *W5* —2C **72**
Clovelly Rd. *Bexh* —6E **84**
Clovelly Rd. *Houn* —2E **86**
Clovelly Way. *E1* —6J **63**
Clovelly Way. *Orp* —6K **129**
Clovelly Way. *S Harr* —2D **38**
Clover Clo. *E11* —2F **49**
Cloverdale Gdns. *Sidc* —6K **99**
Clover M. *SW3* —6D **76** (7F **153**)
Clover Way. *Wall* —1E **132**
Clove St. *E13* —4J **65**
Clowders Rd. *SE6* —3B **112**
Clowser Clo. *Sutt* —5A **132**
Cloysters Grn. *E1* —1G **79**
Cloyster Wood. *Edgw* —7J **11**
Club Gdns. Rd. *Hay* —7J **127**
Club Row. *E2* —4F **63** (3J **145**)
Clunbury Av. *S'hall* —5D **70**
Clunbury St. *N1* —2D **62**
Cluny Est. *SE1* —3E **78** (1G **157**)
Cluny M. *SW5* —4J **75**
Cluny Pl. *SE1* —3E **78** (1G **157**)

Clutton St. *E14* —5D **64**
Clydach Rd. *Enf* —4A **8**
Clyde Cir. *N15* —4E **30**
Clyde Ho. S15 —1G *79*
  (off Sumner Est.)
Clyde Pl. *E10* —7D **32**
Clyde Rd. *N15* —4E **30**
Clyde Rd. *N22* —1H **29**
Clyde Rd. *Croy* —2F **135**
Clyde Rd. *Sutt* —5J **131**
Clyde Rd. *Wall* —6G **133**
Clydesdale. *Enf* —4E **8**
Clydesdale Av. *Stan* —3D **24**
Clydesdale Clo. *Iswth* —3K **87**
Clydesdale Ct. *N20* —1G **15**
Clydesdale Gdns. *Rich* —4H **89**
Clydesdale Ho. Eri —2E *84*
  (off Kale Rd.)
Clydesdale Rd. *W11* —6H **59**
Clyde St. *SE8* —6B **80**
Clyde Ter. *SE23* —2J **111**
Clyde Vale. *SE23* —2J **111**
Clyde Way. *Romf* —1K **37**
Clyde Wharf. *E16* —1J **81**
Clydon Clo. *Eri* —6K **85**
Clynes Ho. Dag —3G *53*
  (off Uvedale Rd.)
Clyston St. *SW8* —2G **93**
Cmabrian Clo. *SE23* —3B **110**
Coach & Horses Yd. *W1*
  —7G **61** (2K **147**)
Coach Ho. La. *N5* —4B **46**
Coach Ho. La. *SW19* —4F **107**
Coach Ho. M. *SE20* —7H **111**
Coach Ho. M. *SE23* —6K **95**
Coach Ho. Yd. NW3 —4A *44*
  (off Hampstead High St.)
Coach Ho. Yd. *SW18* —4K **91**
Coaldale Wlk. *SE21* —7C **94**
Coalecroft Rd. *SW15* —4E **90**
Coalport Ho. *SE11*
  —4A **78** (2J **155**)
Coal Wharf Rd. *W12* —1F **75**
Coates Av. *SW18* —6C **92**
Coates Hill Rd. *Brom* —2E **128**
Coate St. *E2* —2G **63**
Coates Wlk. *Bren* —5E **72**
Cobalt Sq. *SW8* —6K **77** (7G **155**)
Cobbett Rd. *SE9* —3C **98**
Cobbett Rd. *Twic* —1E **102**
Cobbetts Av. *Ilf* —5B **34**
Cobbett St. *SW8* —7K **77**
Cobble La. *N1* —7B **46**
Cobblers Wlk. *Hamp & Tedd*
  —7G **103**
Cobblestone Pl. *Croy* —1C **134**
Cobbold M. *W12* —2B **74**
Cobbold Rd. *E11* —3H **49**
Cobbold Rd. *NW10* —6B **42**
Cobbold Rd. *W12* —2A **74**
Cobb's Ct. *EC4* —6B **62** (1B **150**)
Cobb's Rd. *Houn* —4D **86**
Cobb St. *E1* —5F **63** (6J **145**)
Cobden Ct. *Brom* —4A **128**
Cobden Ho. NW1 —2G *61*
  (off Arlington Rd.)
Cobden Rd. *E11* —3G **49**
Cobden Rd. *SE25* —5G **125**
Cobden St. *E14* —5D **64**
Cobham Av. *N Mald* —5C **120**
Cobham Clo. *SW11* —6C **92**
Cobham Clo. *Brom* —7C **128**
Cobham Clo. *Sidc* —6B **100**
Cobham Clo. *Wall* —6J **133**
Cobham Clo. *Mitc* —2B **122**

Cobham Ho. Bark —1G 67
(in two parts)
Cobham M. NW1 —7H 45
Cobham Pl. Bexh —4E 100
Cobham Rd. E17 —1E 32
Cobham Rd. N22 —3B 30
Cobham Rd. Houn —7A 70
Cobham Rd. Ilf —2J 51
Cobham Rd. King T —2G 119
Cobland Rd. SE12 —4A 114
Coborn Rd. E3 —3B 64
Coborn St. E3 —3B 64
Cobourg Rd. SE5
—6F 79 (7J 157)
Cobourg St. NW1
—3G 61 (2B 142)
Coburg Clo. SW1
—4G 77 (3B 154)
Coburg Cres. SW2 —1K 109
Coburg Rd. N22 —3K 29
Cochrane Clo. E14 —2C 80
(off Admirals Way)
Cochrane Clo. NW8
—2B 60 (1B 140)
Cochrane Ct. E10 —1C 48
Cochrane M. NW8 —2B 60
Cochrane Rd. SW19 —7H 107
Cochrane St. NW8
—2B 60 (1B 140)
Cockayne Way. SE8 —4A 80
Cockerell Rd. E17 —7A 32
Cockfosters Pde. Barn —4K 5
Cockfosters Rd. Pot B & Barn
—1H 5
Cockhill Rd. SE2 —3B 84
Cock La. EC1 —5B 62 (6A 144)
Cockpit Steps. SW1
—2H 77 (7C 148)
Cockpit Yd. WC1
—5K 61 (5H 143)
Cocks Cres. N Mald —4B 120
Cockspur Ct. SW1
—1H 77 (4D 148)
Cockspur St. SW1
—1H 77 (4D 148)
Cocksure La. Sidc —3G 117
Coda Cen., The. SW6 —1G 91
Code St. E1 —4F 63 (4K 145)
Codicote Ter. N4 —2C 46
Codling Clo. E1 —1G 79
Codling Way. Wemb —4D 40
Codrington Ct. E1 —4H 63
Codrington Ct. SE16 —1A 80
Codrington Hill. SE23 —7A 96
Codrington M. W11 —6G 59
Cody Clo. Harr —3D 24
Cody Clo. Wall —7H 133
Cody Rd. E16 —4F 65
Coe Av. SE25 —6G 125
Coe's All. Barn —4B 4
Cofers Circ. Wemb —3H 41
Cogan Av. E17 —1A 32
Coin St. SE1 —1A 78 (4J 149)
Coity Rd. NW5 —6E 44
Cokers La. SE21 —1D 110
Coke St. E1 —6G 63
Colas M. NW6 —1J 59
Colbeck M. SW7 —4K 75
Colbeck Rd. Harr —7G 23
Colberg Pl. N16 —7F 31
Colborne Way. Wor Pk —3E 130
Colburn Way. Sutt —3B 132
Colby M. SE19 —5E 110

Colby Rd. SE19 —5E 110
Colchester Av. E12 —3D 50
Colchester Dri. Pinn —5B 22
Colchester Rd. E10 —7E 32
Colchester Rd. E17 —6C 32
Colchester Rd. Edgw —7D 12
Colchester St. E1
—6F 63 (7K 145)
Coldbath Sq. EC1
—4A 62 (3J 143)
Coldbath St. SE13 —1D 96
Cold Blow Cres. Bex —1K 117
Cold Blow La. SE14 —7K 79
(in two parts)
Cold Blows. Mitc —3D 122
Coldershaw Rd. W13 —1A 72
Coldfall Av. N10 —2E 28
Coldham Ct. N22 —1B 30
Coldharbour. E14 —2E 80
Coldharbour Crest. SE9 —3E 114
Coldharbour La. SW9 & SE5
—4A 94
Coldharbour Pl. SE5 —2C 94
Coldharbour Rd. Croy —5A 134
Coldharbour Way. Croy —5A 134
Coldstream Gdns. SW18 —6H 91
Colebeck M. N1 —6B 46
Colebert Av. E1 —4J 63
Colebrook Clo. SW15 —7F 91
Colebrooke Av. W13 —6B 56
Colebrooke Ct. Sidc —4B 116
(off Granville Rd.)
Colebrooke Dri. E11 —7K 33
Colebrooke Pl. N1 —1B 62
Colebrooke Rise. Brom —2G 127
Colebrooke Row. N1 —2B 62
(in two parts)
Colebrook Rd. SW16 —1J 123
Colebrook Way. N11 —5A 16
Coleby Path. SE5 —7D 78
Cole Clo. SE28 —1B 84
Cole Ct. Twic —7A 88
Coledale Dri. Stan —1C 24
Coleford Rd. SW18 —5A 92
Colegrave Rd. E15 —5F 49
Colegrove Rd. SE15 —6F 79
Coleherne Ct. SW5 —5K 75
Coleherne M. SW10 —5K 75
Coleherne Rd. SW10 —5K 75
Colehill Gdns. SW6 —1G 91
Colehill La. SW6 —1G 91
Coleman Clo. SE25 —2F 125
Coleman Fields. N1 —1C 62
Coleman Mans. N8 —7J 29
Coleman Rd. SE5 —7E 78
Coleman Rd. Belv —4G 85
Coleman Rd. Dag —6E 52
Colemans Heath. SE9 —3E 114
Coleman St. EC2
—6D 62 (7E 144)
Coleman St. Bldgs. EC2
—6D 62 (7E 144)
Colenso Rd. E5 —4J 47
Colenso Rd. Ilf —1J 51
Cole Pk. Gdns. Twic —6A 88
Cole Pk. Rd. Twic —6A 88
Cole Pk. View. Twic —6A 88
Colepits Wood Rd. SE9 —5H 99
Coleraine Rd. N8 —3A 30
Coleraine Rd. SE3 —6H 81
Coleridge Av. E12 —6C 50
Coleridge Av. Sutt —4C 132
Coleridge Clo. SW8 —2F 93
Coleridge Ct. W14 —3F 75
(off Blythe Rd.)

Coleridge Ct. New Bar —5E 4
(off Station Rd.)
Coleridge Gdns. NW6 —7A 44
Coleridge Ho. SE17
—5C 78 (5D 156)
Coleridge La. N8 —6J 29
Coleridge Rd. E17 —4B 32
Coleridge Rd. N4 —2A 46
Coleridge Rd. N8 —6H 29
Coleridge Rd. N12 —5F 15
Coleridge Rd. Croy —7J 125
Coleridge Sq. W13 —6A 56
Coleridge Wlk. NW11 —4J 27
Cole Rd. Twic —6A 88
Colesbourne Ct. SE15 —7E 78
(off Birdlip Clo.)
Colesburg Rd. Beck —3B 126
Coles Cres. Harr —2F 39
Coles Grn. Bush —1B 10
Coles Grn. Ct. NW2 —2C 42
Coles Grn. Rd. NW2 —1C 42
Coleshill Flats. SW1
—5E 76 (4H 153)
Coleshill Rd. Tedd —6J 103
Colestown St. SW11 —2C 92
Cole St. SE1 —2C 78 (7D 150)
Colesworth Ho. Edgw —2J 25
(off Burnt Oak B'way.)
Colet Clo. N13 —6G 17
Colet Gdns. W14 —4F 75
Colet Ho. SE17 —5B 78 (6B 156)
(off Doddington Gro.)
Coley St. WC1 —4K 61 (4H 143)
Colfe & Hatcliffe Glebe. SE13
(off Lewisham High St.) —5E 96
Colfe Rd. SE23 —1A 112
Colina M. N15 —4B 30
Colina Rd. N15 —5B 30
Colin Clo. NW9 —4A 26
Colin Clo. Croy —3B 136
Colin Clo. W Wick —3H 137
Colin Cres. NW9 —4B 26
Colindale Av. NW9 —3K 25
Colindale Bus. Pk. NW9 —3J 25
Colindeep Gdns. NW4 —4C 26
Colindeep La. NW9 & NW4
—3A 26
Colin Dri. NW9 —5B 26
Colinette Rd. SW15 —4E 90
Colin Gdns. NW9 —4B 26
Colin Pde. NW9 —4A 26
Colin Pk. Rd. NW9 —4A 26
Colin Rd. NW10 —6C 42
Colinton Rd. Ilf —2B 52
Colin Winter Ho. E1 —4J 63
(off Nicholas Rd.)
Coliston Pas. SW18 —7J 91
Coliston Rd. SW18 —7J 91
Collamore Av. SW18 —1C 108
Collapit Clo. Harr —6F 23
Collard Pl. NW1 —7F 45
Collards Almshouses. E17
—5E 32

College Cross. N1 —7A 46
College Fields Bus. Cen. SW19
—1B 122
College Gdns. E4 —7J 9
College Gdns. N18 —5A 18
College Gdns. SE21 —1E 110
College Gdns. SW17 —2C 108
College Gdns. Enf —1J 7
College Gdns. Ilf —5C 34
College Gdns. N Mald —5B 120
College Grn. SE19 —7E 110
College Hill. EC4
—7C 62 (2D 150)
College La. NW5 —4F 45
College M. SW1 —3J 77 (1E 154)
College M. SW18 —5K 91
College Pk. Clo. SE13 —4F 97
College Pl. NW1 —1G 61
College Pl. SW10 —7A 76
College Point. E15 —6H 49
College Rd. E17 —5E 32
College Rd. N17 —6A 18
College Rd. N21 —2F 17
College Rd. NW10 —2E 58
College Rd. SW19 —6B 108
College Rd. W13 —6B 56
College Rd. Brom —1J 127
College Rd. Croy —2D 134
College Rd. Enf —2J 7
College Rd. Harr —6J 23
College Rd. Har W —1J 23
College Rd. Iswth —1K 87
College Rd. Swan —7K 117
College Rd. Wemb —1D 40
College Roundabout. King T
—3E 118
College Row. E9 —5K 47
College Slip. Brom —1J 127
College St. EC4 —7C 62 (2D 150)
College Ter. E3 —3B 64
College Ter. N3 —2H 27
College View. SE9 —1B 114
College Wlk. King T —3E 118
College Yd. NW5 —4F 45
Collent St. E9 —6J 47
Colleraine Rd. SE3 —6H 81
Colless Rd. N15 —5F 31
Collett Rd. SE16 —3H 79
Collett Way. S'hall —2F 71
Collier Clo. E6 —7F 67
Collier Dri. Edgw —2G 25
Collier Row La. Romf —1H 37
Collier Row Rd. Romf —1F 37
Colliers Ct. Croy —4D 134
Colliers Shaw. Kes —5B 138
Colliers Water La. T Hth —5A 124
Colliers Wood. (Junct.) —7B 108
Collindale Av. Eri —7H 85
Collindale Av. Sidc —1A 116
Collingbourne Rd. W12 —1D 74
Collingham Gdns. SW5 —4K 75
Collingham Pl. SW5 —4K 75
Collingham Rd. SW5 —4K 75
Collings Clo. N22 —6E 16
Collington St. SE10 —5F 81
Collingtree Rd. SE26 —4J 111
Collingwood Av. N10 —3E 28
Collingwood Av. Surb —7J 119
Collingwood Clo. SE20 —1H 125
Collingwood Clo. Twic —7E 86
Collingwood Ct. New Bar —5E 4

Collingwood Rd. E17 —6C 32
Collingwood Rd. N15 —4E 30
Collingwood Rd. Mitc —3C 122
Collingwood Rd. Sutt —3J 131
Collingwood St. E1 —4H 63
Collins Av. Stan —2E 24
Collins Ct. E8 —6F 47
Collins Dri. Ruis —2A 38
Collins Ho. E15 —1H 65
(off John St.)
Collinson St. SE1
—2C 78 (7C 150)
Collinson Wlk. SE1
—2C 78 (7C 150)
Collins Path. Hamp —6D 102
Collins Rd. N5 —4C 46
Collins Sq. SE3 —2H 97
Collins St. SE3 —3G 97
Collin's Yd. N1 —1B 62
Collis All. Twic —1J 103
Colls Rd. SE15 —1J 95
Collyer Av. Croy —4J 133
Collyer Pl. SE15 —1G 95
Collyer Rd. Bedd —4J 133
Colman Ct. N12 —6F 15
Colman Ct. Stan —6G 11
Colman Pde. Enf —3K 7
Colman Rd. E16 —5A 66
Colmar Clo. E1 —4K 63
Colmer Pl. Harr —7C 10
Colmer Rd. SW16 —1J 123
Colmore M. SE15 —1H 95
Colmore Rd. Enf —4D 8
Colnbrook St. SE1
—3B 78 (2A 156)
Colne Ct. W7 —6H 55
(off Hobbayne Rd.)
Colne Rd. E5 —4A 48
Colne Rd. N21 —7J 7
Colne Rd. Twic —1J 103
Colne St. E13 —3J 65
Colney Hatch La. N11 & N10
—6J 15
Cologne Rd. SW11 —4B 92
Colombo Rd. Ilf —7G 35
Colombo St. SE1
—1B 78 (5A 150)
Colomb St. SE10 —5G 81
Colonel's Wlk. Enf —3G 7
Colonial Av. Twic —5G 87
Colonial Dri. W4 —4J 73
Colonnade. WC1 —4J 61 (4F 143)
Colonnades, The. W2 —6K 59
Colonnade, The. SE8 —4B 80
Colonnade Wlk. SW1
—4F 77 (4J 153)
Colosseum Ter. NW1
—3F 61 (2K 141)
Colour Ct. SW1 —1G 77 (5B 148)
Colroy Ct. NW11 —5G 27
Colson Ct. Croy —2E 134
Colson Way. SW16 —4G 109
Colsterworth Rd. N15 —4F 31
(in two parts)
Colston Av. Cars —4C 132
Colston Ct. Cars —4D 132
(off West St.)
Colston Rd. E7 —6B 50
Colston Rd. SW14 —4J 91
Cotness Cres. SE2 —5B 84
Colton Gdns. N17 —3C 30
Colton Rd. Harr —5J 23
Columbia Av. Edgw —1H 25

Columbia Av. *Ruis* —1A **38**
Columbia Av. *Wor Pk* —7B **120**
Columbia Rd. *E2*
　　　　—3F **63** (1J **145**)
Columbia Rd. *E13* —4H **65**
Columbia Sq. *SW14* —4J **89**
Columbia Wharf. *SE16* —1B **80**
Columbine Av. *E6* —5C **66**
Columbine Av. *S Croy* —7B **134**
Columbine Way. *SE13* —2E **96**
Columbus Courtyard. *E14*
　　　　—1C **80**
Colva Wlk. *N19* —2F **45**
Colvestone Cres. *E8* —5F **47**
Colview Ct. *SE9* —1B **114**
Colville Est. *N1* —1E **62**
　(off Whitmore Rd.)
Colville Gdns. *W11* —6H **59**
　(in two parts)
Colville Houses. *W11* —6H **59**
Colville M. *W11* —6H **59**
Colville Pl. *W1* —5G **61** (6B **142**)
Colville Rd. *E11* —3E **48**
Colville Rd. *E17* —2A **32**
Colville Rd. *N9* —1C **18**
Colville Rd. *W3* —3H **73**
Colville Rd. *W11* —6H **59**
Colville Sq. *W11* —6H **59**
Colville Sq. M. *W11* —6H **59**
Colville Ter. *W11* —6H **59**
Colvin Clo. *SE26* —5J **111**
Colvin Gdns. *E4* —3K **19**
Colvin Gdns. *E11* —4K **33**
Colvin Rd. *E6* —7C **50**
Colvin Rd. *T Hth* —5A **124**
Colwall Gdns. *Wfd G* —5D **20**
Colwell Rd. *SE22* —5F **95**
Colwick Clo. *N6* —7H **29**
Colwith Rd. *W6* —6E **74**
Colwood Gdns. *SW19* —7B **108**
Colworth Gro. *SE17*
　　　　—4C **78** (4D **156**)
Colworth Rd. *E11* —6G **33**
Colworth Rd. *Croy* —1G **135**
Colwyn Av. *Gnfd* —2K **55**
Colwyn Clo. *SW16* —5G **109**
Colwyn Cres. *Houn* —1G **87**
Colwyn Grn. *NW9* —6A **26**
　(off Snowden Dri.)
Colwyn Ho. *SE1* —3A **78** (2J **155**)
Colwyn Rd. *NW2* —3D **42**
Colwyn Way. *N18* —5B **18**
Colyer Clo. *N1* —2K **61**
Colyer Clo. *SE9* —2F **115**
Colyers La. *Eri* —1J **101**
Colyers Wlk. *Eri* —1K **101**
Colyton Clo. *Well* —1D **100**
Colyton Clo. *Wemb* —6C **40**
Colyton Rd. *SE22* —5H **95**
Combe Av. *SE3* —7H **81**
Combedale Rd. *SE10* —5J **81**
Combe Lodge. *SE7* —6A **82**
Combemartin Rd. *SW18* —7G **91**
Combe M. *SE3* —7H **81**
Comber Clo. *NW2* —3D **42**
Comber Gro. *SE5* —7C **78**
Comber Ho. *SE5* —7C **78**
Combermere Rd. *SW9* —3K **93**
Combermere Rd. *Mord* —6K **121**
Comberton Rd. *E5* —2H **47**
Combeside. *SE18* —7K **83**
Combe, The. *NW1*
　　　　—3G **61** (2A **142**)

Combwell Cres. *SE2* —3A **84**
Comely Bank Rd. *E17* —5E **32**
Comeragh M. *W14* —5G **75**
Comeragh Rd. *W14* —5G **75**
Comer Cres. *S'hall* —2G **71**
　(off Windmill Av.)
Comerell Pl. *SE10* —5H **81**
Comerford Rd. *SE4* —4A **96**
Comet Clo. *E12* —4B **50**
Comet Pl. *SE8* —7C **80**
Comet St. *SE8* —7C **80**
Commerce Rd. *N22* —1K **29**
Commerce Rd. *Bren* —7C **72**
Commerce Way. *Croy* —2K **133**
Commercial Rd. *E1 & E14*
　　　　—6G **63** (7K **145**)
Commercial Rd. *N18* —6K **17**
Commercial Rd. Ind. Est. *N18*
　　　　—6A **18**
Commercial St. *E1*
　　　　—4F **63** (4J **145**)
Commercial Way. *NW10* —2H **57**
Commercial Way. *SE15* —7F **79**
Commerell St. *SE10* —5G **81**
Commodity Quay. *E1*
　　　　—7F **63** (3K **151**)
Commodore St. *E8* —1C **96**
　(off Albyn Rd.)
Commodore Sq. *SW10* —1A **92**
Commodore St. *E1* —4A **64**
Commondale. *SW15* —3E **90**
Commonfield La. *SW17* —5C **108**
Common Rd. *SW13* —3D **90**
Common Rd. *Stan* —4C **10**
Commonside. *Kes* —4A **138**
Commonside E. *Mitc* —3E **122**
Commonside W. *Mitc* —3D **122**
Common, The. *W5* —1E **72**
　(in two parts)
Common, The. *S'hall* —4B **70**
Common, The. *Stan* —3E **10**
Commonwealth Av. *W12* —7D **58**
　(in three parts)
Commonwealth Rd. *N17* —7B **18**
Commonwealth Way. *SE2*
　　　　—5B **84**
Community La. *N7* —5H **45**
Community Rd. *E15* —5F **49**
Community Rd. *Gnfd* —1G **55**
Como Rd. *SE23* —2A **112**
Como St. *Romf* —5K **37**
Compass Hill. *Rich* —6D **88**
Compass Point. *E14* —7B **64**
　(off Grenade St.)
Compayne Gdns. *NW6* —7K **43**
Compton Av. *E6* —2B **66**
Compton Av. *N1* —6B **46**
Compton Av. *N6* —7C **28**
Compton Clo. *E3* —5C **64**
Compton Clo. *NW1*
　　　　—3F **61** (2K **141**)
Compton Clo. *W13* —6A **56**
Compton Clo. *Edgw* —7D **12**
Compton Ct. *Sutt* —4A **132**
Compton Cres. *N17* —7H **17**
Compton Cres. *W4* —6J **73**
Compton Cres. *N'holt* —1B **54**
Compton Pas. *EC1*
　　　　—4B **62** (3B **144**)
Compton Pl. *WC1*
　　　　—4J **61** (3E **142**)
Compton Rise. *Pinn* —5C **22**
Compton Rd. *N1* —6B **46**
Compton Rd. *N21* —1F **17**

Compton Rd. *NW10* —3F **59**
Compton Rd. *SW19* —6H **107**
Compton Rd. *Croy* —1H **135**
Compton St. *EC1*
　　　　—4B **62** (3A **144**)
Compton Ter. *N1* —6B **46**
Compton Ter. *N21* —1F **17**
Comreddy Clo. *Enf* —1G **7**
Comus Pl. *SE17*
　　　　—4E **78** (4G **157**)
Comyn Rd. *SW11* —4C **92**
Comyns Clo. *E16* —5H **65**
Comyns Rd. *Dag* —7G **53**
Comyns, The. *Bush* —1B **10**
Concanon Rd. *SW2* —4K **93**
Concert Hall App. *SE1*
　　　　—1K **77** (5H **149**)
Concord Bus. Cen. *W3* —4H **57**
Concord Cen., The. *W12* —2F **75**
Concorde Clo. *N'holt* —3B **54**
Concorde Clo. *Houn* —2F **87**
Concorde Dri. *E6* —5D **66**
Concord Ho. *N17* —7A **18**
　(off Park La.)
Concord Rd. *W3* —4H **57**
Concord Rd. *Enf* —5C **8**
Concourse, The. *N9* —2C **18**
　(off Plevna Rd.)
Concourse, The. *NW9* —1A **26**
Condell Rd. *SW8* —1G **93**
Conder St. *E14* —6A **64**
Condor Path *N'holt* —2E **54**
　(off Union Rd.)
Condover Cres. *SE18* —7F **83**
Condray Pl. *SW11* —7C **76**
Conduit Ct. *WC2*
　　　　—7J **61** (2E **148**)
Conduit La. *N18* —5D **18**
Conduit La. *Croy* —5G **135**
Conduit La. *Enf* —7F **9**
Conduit La. *S Croy & Croy*
　　　　—5G **135**
Conduit M. *W2* —6B **60** (1A **146**)
Conduit Pas. *W2*
　　　　—6B **60** (1A **146**)
Conduit Pl. *W2* —6B **60** (1A **146**)
Conduit Rd. *SE18* —5F **83**
Conduit St. *W1* —7F **61** (2K **147**)
Conduit Way. *NW10* —7J **41**
Conewood St. *N5* —3B **46**
Coney Acre. *SE21* —1C **110**
Coney Burrows. *E4* —2B **20**
Coneygrove Path. *N'holt* —6C **38**
　(off Arnold Rd.)
Coney Hall Pde. *W Wick* —3G **137**
Coney Hill Rd. *W Wick* —2G **137**
Coney Way. *SW8* —6K **77**
Conference Clo. *E4* —2K **19**
Conference Rd. *SE2* —4C **84**
Congers Ho. *SE8* —7C **80**
Congleton Gro. *SE18* —5G **83**
Congo Rd. *SE18* —5H **83**
Congress Rd. *SE2* —4C **84**
Congreve Ct. *SE11*
　　　　—4A **78** (4K **155**)
Congreve Ho. *N16* —5E **46**
Congreve Rd. *SE9* —3D **98**
Congreve St. *SE17*
　　　　—4E **78** (4G **157**)
Congreve Wlk. *E16* —5B **66**
　(off Stansfield Rd.)
Conical Corner. *Enf* —2H **7**
Conifer Gdns. *SW16* —3K **109**
Conifer Gdns. *Enf* —6K **7**

Conifer Gdns. *Sutt* —2K **131**
Conifer Ho. *SE4* —4B **96**
　(off Brockley Rd.)
Conifers Clo. *Tedd* —7B **104**
Conifer Way. *Wemb* —3C **40**
Coniffe Ct. *SE9* —5F **99**
Coniger Rd. *SW6* —2J **91**
Coningham M. *W12* —1C **74**
Coningham Rd. *W12* —2D **74**
Coningsby Cotts. *W5* —2D **72**
Coningsby Gdns. *E4* —6J **19**
Coningsby Rd. *N4* —7B **30**
Coningsby Rd. *W5* —2D **72**
Coningsby Rd. *S Croy* —7C **134**
Conington Rd. *SE13* —2D **96**
Conisbee Ct. *N14* —5B **6**
Conisborough Cres. *SE6* —3E **112**
Coniscliffe Clo. *Chst* —1E **128**
Coniscliffe Rd. *N13* —3H **17**
Coniston Av. *Bark* —7J **51**
Coniston Av. *Gnfd* —3B **56**
Coniston Av. *Well* —3J **99**
Coniston Clo. *N20* —3G **15**
Coniston Clo. *SW13* —7B **74**
Coniston Clo. *SW20* —6F **121**
Coniston Clo. *W4* —7J **73**
Coniston Clo. *Bark* —7J **51**
Coniston Clo. *Bexh* —1J **101**
Coniston Clo. *Eri* —7K **85**
Coniston Ct. *NW7* —7J **45**
Coniston Gdns. *N9* —1D **18**
Coniston Gdns. *NW9* —5K **25**
Coniston Gdns. *Ilf* —4C **34**
Coniston Gdns. *Sutt* —6B **132**
Coniston Gdns. *Wemb* —1C **40**
Coniston Ho. *N10* —2F **29**
Coniston Ho. *N17* —6B **18**
Coniston Rd. *N10* —2F **29**
Coniston Rd. *N17* —6B **18**
Coniston Rd. *Bexh* —1J **101**
Coniston Rd. *Brom* —6G **113**
Coniston Rd. *Croy* —7G **125**
Coniston Rd. *Twic* —6F **87**
Coniston Wlk. *E9* —5J **47**
Conlan St. *W10* —4G **59**
Conley Rd. *NW10* —6A **42**
Conley St. *SE10* —5G **81**
Connaught Av. *E4* —7K **9**
Connaught Av. *SW14* —3J **89**
Connaught Av. *E Barn* —1J **15**
Connaught Av. *Enf* —2K **7**
Connaught Av. *Houn* —4C **86**
Connaught Brt. *E16* —1B **82**
Connaught Bus. Cen. *NW9*
　　　　—5B **26**
Connaught Clo. *E10* —2A **48**
Connaught Clo. *W2*
　　　　—6C **60** (1D **146**)
Connaught Clo. *Enf* —2K **7**
Connaught Clo. *Sutt* —2B **132**
Connaught Ct. *E17* —4D **32**
Connaught Dri. *NW11* —4J **27**
Connaught Gdns. *N10* —5F **29**
Connaught Gdns. *N13* —4G **17**
Connaught Gdns. *Mord* —4A **122**
Connaught La. *Ilf* —2G **51**
Connaught Lodge. *N4* —7A **30**
　(off Connaught Rd.)
Connaught M. *SE18* —5E **82**
Connaught M. *W2*
　　　　—6D **60** (1E **146**)
Connaught Pl. *W2*
　　　　—7D **60** (2E **146**)
Connaught Rd. *E4* —1B **20**
Connaught Rd. *E11* —1F **49**
Connaught Rd. *E16* —1B **82**
Connaught Rd. *E17* —5C **32**

Connaught Rd. *N4* —7A **30**
Connaught Rd. *NW10* —1A **58**
Connaught Rd. *SE18* —5E **82**
Connaught Rd. *W13* —7B **56**
Connaught Rd. *Barn* —6A **4**
Connaught Rd. *Harr* —1K **23**
Connaught Rd. *Ilf* —2H **51**
Connaught Rd. *N Mald* —4A **120**
Connaught Rd. *Rich* —5F **89**
Connaught Rd. *Sutt* —2B **132**
Connaught Rd. *Tedd* —5H **103**
Connaught Sq. *W2*
　　　　—6D **60** (1D **146**)
Connaught St. *W2*
　　　　—6C **60** (1D **146**)
Connaught Way. *N13* —4G **17**
Connell Cres. *W5* —4F **57**
Connington Cres. *E4* —3A **20**
Connor Ct. *SW11* —1F **93**
Connor Rd. *Dag* —4F **53**
Connor St. *E9* —1K **63**
Conolly Rd. *W7* —1J **71**
Conrad Dri. *Wor Pk* —1E **130**
Conrad Ho. *N16* —5E **46**
　(off Mayville Est.)
Conrad Ho. *SW8* —7J **77**
　(off Wyvil Rd.)
Conrad Towers. *W3* —3H **73**
　(off Bollo La.)
Consfield Av. *N Mald* —4C **120**
Consort M. *Iswth* —5H **87**
Consort Rd. *SE15* —1H **95**
Cons St. *SE1* —2A **78** (6K **149**)
Constable Av. *E16* —1K **81**
Constable Clo. *NW11* —6K **27**
Constable Ct. *W4* —5H **73**
　(off Chaseley Dri.)
Constable Cres. *N15* —5G **31**
Constable Gdns. *Edgw* —1G **25**
Constable Gdns. *Iswth* —5H **87**
Constable Ho. *E16* —6B **66**
Constable Ho. *N'holt* —2B **54**
　(off Gallery Gdns.)
Constable M. *Dag* —4B **52**
Constable Wlk. *SE21* —3E **110**
Constance Cres. *Brom* —7H **127**
Constance Rd. *Croy* —7B **124**
Constance Rd. *Enf* —6K **7**
Constance Rd. *Sutt* —4A **132**
Constance Rd. *Twic* —7F **87**
Constance St. *E16* —1C **82**
Constantine Rd. *NW3* —4C **44**
Constitution Hill. *SW1*
Constitution Rise. *SE18* —1E **98**
Content St. *SE17*
　　　　—4D **78** (4E **156**)
Convair Wlk. *N'holt* —3B **54**
Convent Clo. *Beck* —7E **112**
Convent Gdns. *W5* —4C **72**
Convent Gdns. *W11* —6G **59**
Convent Hill. *SE19* —6C **110**
Convent Way. *S'hall* —4A **70**
Conway Clo. *Stan* —6F **11**
Conway Cres. *Gnfd* —2J **55**
Conway Cres. *Romf* —6C **36**
Conway Dri. *Sutt* —6K **131**
Conway Gdns. *Enf* —1K **7**
Conway Gdns. *Mitc* —4J **123**
Conway Gdns. *Wemb* —7C **24**
Conway Gro. *W3* —5K **57**
Conway Ho. *E17* —5A **32**
　(off Mission Gro.)
Conway M. *W1* —4G **61** (4A **142**)
Conway Rd. *N14* —3D **16**

Conway Rd. N15 —5B 30
Conway Rd. NW2 —2E 42
Conway Rd. SE18 —4H 83
Conway Rd. Felt —5B 102
Conway Rd. Houn —7D 86
Conway St. W1 —4G 61 (4A 142)
(in two parts)
Conway Wlk. Hamp —6D 102
Conybeare. NW3 —7C 44
Conyers Clo. Wfd G —6B 20
Conyer's Rd. SW16 —5H 109
Conyer St. E3 —2A 64
Cooden Clo. Brom —7K 113
Cookes Clo. E11 —2H 49
Cookes La. Sutt —6G 131
Cookham Cres. SE16 —2K 79
Cookham Dene Clo. Chst
—1H 129
Cookham Rd. Swan —7G 117
Cookhill Rd. SE2 —2B 84
Cook Rd. Dag —1E 68
Cook's Clo. Romf —1J 37
Cooks Hole Rd. Enf —1G 7
Cookson Gro. Eri —7H 85
Cook's Rd. E15 —2D 64
Cook's Rd. SE17
—6B 78 (7A 156)
Coolfin Rd. E16 —6J 65
Coolgardie Av. E4 —5A 20
Coolgardie Av. Chig —3K 21
Coolhurst Rd. N8 —6H 29
Cool Oak La. NW9 —1A 42
Coomassie Rd. W9 —4H 59
Coombe Av. Croy —4E 134
Coombe Bank. King T —1A 120
Coombe Clo. Edgw —2F 25
Coombe Clo. Houn —4E 86
Coombe Corner. N21 —1G 17
Coombe Cres. Hamp —7D 102
Coombe Dri. Ruis —1A 38
Coombe End. King T —7K 105
Coombefield Clo. N Mald
—5A 120
Coombe Gdns. SW20 —2C 120
Coombe Gdns. N Mald —4B 120
Coombe Hill Glade. King T
—7A 106
Coombe Hill Rd. King T —7A 106
Coombe Ho. E4 —6G 19
Coombe Ho. N7 —5H 45
Coombe Ho. Chase. N Mald
—1K 119
Coombehurst Clo. Barn —2J 5
Coombe La. SW20 —1B 120
Coombe La. Croy —5H 135
Coombe La. King T —1H 119
Coombe La. Flyover. King T
—1B 120
Coombe Lane. (Junct.) —1B 120
Coombe La. W. King T —1H 119
Coombe Lea. Brom —3C 128
Coombe Neville. King T —7K 105
Coombe Pk. King T —5J 105
Coomber Ho. SW6 —3K 91
(off Wandsworth Bri. Rd.)
Coombe Ridings. King T —5J 105
Coombe Rise. King T —1J 119
Coombe Rd. N22 —2A 30
Coombe Rd. NW10 —3K 41
Coombe Rd. SE26 —4H 111
Coombe Rd. W4 —5A 74
Coombe Rd. W13 —3B 72
Coombe Rd. Croy —4D 134
Coombe Rd. Hamp —6D 102

Coombe Rd. King T —1G 119
Coombe Rd. N Mald —2A 120
Coomber Way. Croy —7H 123
Coombes Rd. Dag —1F 69
Coombe Wlk. Sutt —3K 131
Coombe Wood Dri. Romf —6F 37
Coombewood Rd. King T
—5J 105
Coombs St. N1 —2B 62 (1B 144)
Coomer M. SW6 —6H 75
Coomer Pl. SW6 —6H 75
Coomer Rd. SW6 —6H 75
Cooms Wlk. Edgw —1J 25
Cooperage Clo. N17 —6A 18
Cooper Av. E17 —1A 32
Cooper Clo. SE1
—2A 78 (7K 149)
Cooper Ct. E15 —5D 48
Cooper Cres. Cars —3D 132
Cooper Ho. Houn —3D 86
Cooper Rd. NW4 —6F 27
Cooper Rd. NW10 —5B 42
Cooper Rd. Croy —5A 134
Coopersale Clo. Wfd G —7F 21
Coopersale Rd. E9 —5K 47
Coopers Clo. E1 —4J 63
Coopers Clo. Dag —6H 53
Coopers Ct. Iswth —2K 87
(off Woodlands Rd.)
Coopers La. E10 —1D 48
Coopers La. NW1 —2H 61
Cooper's La. SE12 —2K 113
Cooper's Rd. SE1
—5F 79 (6K 157)
Cooper's Row. EC3
—7F 63 (2J 151)
Cooper St. E16 —5H 65
Coopers Wlk. E15 —5G 49
Cooper's Yd. SE19 —6E 110
Coote Gdns. Dag —3F 53
Coote Rd. Bexh —1F 101
Coote Rd. Dag —3F 53
Copeland Dri. E14 —4C 80
Copeland Ho. SE11
—3K 77 (2H 155)
Copeland Rd. E17 —6D 32
Copeland Rd. SE15 —2H 95
Copeman Clo. SE26 —5J 111
Copenhagen Gdns. W4 —2K 73
Copenhagen Ho. N1 —1A 62
(off Barnsbury Est.)
Copenhagen Pl. E14 —6B 64
Copenhagen St. N1 —1J 61
Cope Pl. W8 —3J 75
Copers Cope Rd. Beck —7B 112
Cope St. SE16 —4K 79
Copford Clo. Wfd G —6H 21
Copford Wlk. N1 —1C 62
(off Popham St.)
Copinger Wlk. Edgw —1H 25
Copland Av. Wemb —5D 40
Copland Clo. Wemb —5C 40
Copland M. Wemb —6E 40
Copland Rd. Wemb —6E 40
Copleston M. SE15 —2F 95
Copleston Pas. SE15 —2F 95
Copleston Rd. SE15 —3F 95
Copley Clo. SE17
—6C 78 (7C 156)
Copley Clo. W7 —4K 55
Copley Dene. Brom —1B 128
Copley Pk. SW16 —6K 109
Copley Rd. Stan —5H 11
Copley St. E1 —5K 63
Copnor Way. SE15 —7F 79

Coppelia Rd. SE3 —4H 97
Coppen Rd. Dag —7F 37
Copperas St. SE8 —6D 80
Copperbeech Clo. NW3 —5B 44
Copper Beech Clo. Ilf —1D 34
Copper Beeches Ct. Iswth
—1H 87
Copper Clo. SE19 —7F 111
Copperfield Dri. N15 —4F 31
Copperfield M. N18 —4K 17
Copperfield Rd. E3 —4A 64
Copperfield Rd. SE28 —6C 68
Copperfields. Beck —1E 126
Copperfields. Harr —7J 23
Copperfields Ct. W3 —2G 73
Copperfield St. SE1
—2B 78 (6B 150)
Copperfield Way. Chst —6G 115
Copperfield Way. Pinn —4D 22
Coppergate Clo. Brom —1K 127
Copper Mead Clo. NW2 —3E 42
Copper Mill Dri. Iswth —2K 87
Coppermill La. E17 —6J 31
Copper Mill La. SW17 —4A 108
Copper Row. SE1
—1F 79 (5J 151)
Coppetts Cen. N11 —7J 15
Coppetts Clo. N12 —7H 15
Coppetts Rd. N10 —7J 15
Coppice Clo. SW20 —3E 120
Coppice Clo. Stan —6E 10
Coppice Dri. SW15 —6D 90
Coppice, The. Enf —4G 7
Coppice, The. New Bar —6E 4
(off Gt. North Rd.)
Coppice Wlk. N20 —3D 14
Coppice Way. E18 —4H 33
Coppies Gro. N11 —4K 15
Copping Clo. Croy —4E 134
Coppins, The. Harr —6D 10
Coppins, The. New Ad —6D 136
Coppock Clo. SW11 —2C 92
Copse Av. W Wick —3D 136
Copse Clo. SE7 —6K 81
Copse Glade. Surb —7D 118
Copse Hill. SW20 —1C 120
Copse Hill. Sutt —7K 131
Copse, The. E4 —1C 20
Copse, The. N2 —3D 28
Copse View. S Croy —7K 135
Copsewood Clo. Sidc —6J 99
Coptefield Dri. Belv —3D 84
Copthall Av. EC2
—6D 62 (7F 145)
Copthall Bldgs. EC2
—6D 62 (7F 145)
Copthall Clo. EC2
—6D 62 (7F 144)
Copthall Dri. NW7 —7H 13
Copthall Gdns. NW7 —7H 13
Copthall Gdns. Twic —1K 103
Copthorne Av. SW12 —7H 93
Copthorne Av. Brom —2D 138
Coptic St. WC1 —5J 61 (6E 142)
Copwood Clo. N12 —4G 15
Coral Clo. Romf —4C 36
Coraline Clo. S'hall —3D 54
Coraline Wlk. SE2 —2C 84
Coral Row. SW11 —3A 92
Coral St. SE1 —2A 78 (7K 149)
Coram Ho. W4 —5A 74
(off Wood St.)
Coram Rd. WC1 —4J 61 (3E 142)
Coram St. WC1 —4J 61 (4E 142)
Coran Clo. N9 —7E 8

Corban Rd. Houn —3E 86
Corbar Clo. Barn —1G 5
Corbet Clo. Wall —1E 132
Corbet Ct. EC3 —6D 62 (1F 151)
Corbet Pl. E1 —5F 63 (5J 145)
Corbet Ct. SE26 —4B 112
Corbett Gro. N22 —7D 16
Corbett Rd. E11 —6A 34
Corbett Rd. E17 —3E 32
Corbetts La. SE16 —4J 79
(in two parts)
Corbetts Pas. SE16 —4J 79
(off Corbetts La.)
Corbett W. E11 —6A 34
Corbicum. E11 —7G 33
Corbiere Ct. SW19 —6F 107
Corbins La. Harr —3F 39
Corbridge. N17 —7C 18
Corbridge Cres. E2 —2H 63
Corby Cres. Enf —4D 6
Corbylands Rd. Sidc —1J 115
Corbyn St. N4 —1J 45
Corby Rd. NW10 —2K 57
Corby Way. E3 —4C 64
Cordelia Clo. SE24 —4B 94
Cordelia Ho. N1 —2E 62
(off Arden Est.)
Cordelia St. E14 —6D 64
Cordell Ho. N15 —5F 31
(off Newton Rd.)
Cording St. E14 —5D 64
Cordwainers Wlk. E13 —2J 65
Cord Way. E14 —3C 80
Cordwell Rd. SE13 —5G 97
Corelli Ct. SW5 —4J 75
(off W. Cromwell Rd.)
Corelli Rd. SE3 —2C 98
Corfe Av. Harr —4E 38
Corfe Clo. Hayes —6A 54
Corfe Ho. SW8 —7K 77
(off Dorset Rd.)
Corfe Tower. W3 —2J 73
Corfield St. E2 —3H 63
Corfton Lodge. W5 —5E 56
Corfton Rd. W5 —6E 56
Coriander Av. E14 —6F 65
Cories Clo. Dag —2D 52
Corinium Clo. Wemb —4F 41
Corinne Rd. N19 —4G 45
Corinthian Manorway. Eri —4K 85
Corinthian Rd. Eri —4K 85
Corkers Path. Ilf —2G 51
Corker Wlk. N7 —2K 45
Corkran Rd. Surb —7D 118
Corkscrew Hill. W Wick —2E 136
Cork Sq. E1 —1H 79
Cork St. W1 —7G 61 (3A 148)
Cork St. M. W1 —7G 61 (3A 148)
Cork Tree Est., The. E4 —5F 19
Cork Tree Way. E4 —5F 19
Corlett St. NW1 —5C 60 (5C 140)
Cormont Rd. SE5 —1B 94
Cormorant Clo. E17 —7E 18
Cormorant Ct. SE8 —6B 80
(off Pilot Clo.)
Cormorant Rd. E7 —5H 49
Cornbury Ho. SE8 —6B 80
(off Evelyn St.)
Cornbury Rd. Edgw —7J 11
Cornel Ho. Sidc —3A 116
Cornelia St. N7 —6K 45
Cornell Clo. Sidc —6E 116
Cornell Ho. S Harr —3D 38

Corner Fielde. SW2 —1K 109
Corner Grn. SE3 —2J 97
Corner Ho. St. WC2
—1J 77 (4E 148)
Corner Mead. NW9 —7G 13
Cornerstone Ho. Croy —7C 124
Corney Reach Way. W4 —6A 74
Corney Rd. W4 —6A 74
Cornfield Rd. N21 —5E 6
Cornflower La. Croy —1K 135
Cornflower Ter. SE22 —6H 95
Cornford Clo. Brom —5J 127
Cornford Gro. SW12 —2F 109
Cornhill. EC3 —6D 62 (1F 151)
Cornish Ct. N9 —7C 8
Cornish Gro. SE20 —1H 125
Cornish Ho. Bren —5F 73
Corn Mill Dri. Orp —7K 129
Cornmill La. SE13 —3E 96
Cornmow Dri. NW10 —5B 42
Cornshaw Rd. Dag —1D 52
Cornthwaite Rd. E5 —3J 47
Cornwall Av. E2 —3J 63
Cornwall Av. N3 —7D 14
Cornwall Av. N22 —1J 29
Cornwall Av. S'hall —5D 54
Cornwall Av. Well —3J 99
Cornwall Clo. Bark —6K 51
Cornwall Ct. W7 —4K 55
(off Copley Clo.)
Cornwall Ct. Pinn —1D 22
Cornwall Cres. W11 —6G 59
Cornwall Dri. Orp —7C 116
Cornwall Gdns. NW10 —6D 42
Cornwall Gdns. SE25 —5F 125
Cornwall Gdns. SW7 —3K 75
Cornwall Gdns. Wlk. SW7
—3K 75
Cornwall Ga. Purf —4J 85
Cornwall Gro. W4 —5A 74
Cornwallis Av. N9 —2C 18
Cornwallis Av. SE9 —2H 115
Cornwallis Ct. SW8 —1J 93
(off Lansdowne Grn.)
Cornwallis Gro. N9 —2C 18
Cornwallis Ho. W12 —7D 58
(off India Way)
Cornwallis Rd. E17 —4K 31
Cornwallis Rd. N9 —2C 18
Cornwallis Rd. N19 —2J 45
Cornwallis Rd. Dag —4D 52
Cornwallis Sq. N19 —2J 45
Cornwallis Wlk. SE9 —3D 98
Cornwall M. S. SW7 —3A 76
Cornwall M. W. SW7 —3K 75
Cornwall Rd. N4 —7A 30
Cornwall Rd. N15 —5D 30
Cornwall Rd. N18 —5B 18
Cornwall Rd. SE1
—1A 78 (4J 149)
Cornwall Rd. Croy —2B 134
Cornwall Rd. Harr —6G 23
Cornwall Rd. Pinn —1D 22
Cornwall Rd. Sutt —7H 131
Cornwall Rd. Twic —7A 88
Cornwall St. E1 —7H 63
Cornwall Ter. NW1
—4D 60 (4F 141)
Cornwall Ter. M. NW1
—4D 60 (4F 141)
Corn Way. E11 —3F 49
Cornwell Cres. E7 —4A 50
Cornwood Clo. N2 —5B 28
Cornwood Dri. E1 —6J 63
Cornworthy Rd. Dag —5C 52

201

Corona Rd. *SE12* —7J **97**
Coronation Av. *N16* —4F **47**
Coronation Clo. *Bex* —6D **100**
Coronation Clo. *Ilf* —4G **35**
Coronation Ct. *E15* —6H **49**
Coronation Ct. *Eri* —7K **85**
Coronation Rd. *E13* —3A **66**
Coronation Rd. *NW10* —3F **57**
Coronation Wlk. *Twic* —1E **102**
Coronet St. *N1* —3E **62** (2G **145**)
Corporate Ho. *Har W* —1J **23**
Corporation Av. *Houn* —4C **86**
Corporation Row. *EC1*
　　　　　—4A **62** (3K **143**)
Corporation St. *E15* —2G **65**
Corporation St. *N7* —5J **45**
Corrance Rd. *SW2* —4J **93**
Corri Av. *N14* —4C **16**
Corrib Ct. *N13* —3E **16**
Corrib Dri. *Sutt* —5C **132**
Corringham Ct. *NW11* —7J **27**
Corringham Rd. *NW11* —7J **27**
Corringham Rd. *Wemb* —2G **41**
Corringway. *NW11* —7K **27**
Corringway. *W5* —5F **57**
Corris Grn. *NW9* —6A **26**
Corscombe Clo. *King T* —5J **105**
Corsehill St. *SW16* —6G **109**
Corsham St. *N1* —3D **62** (2F **145**)
Corsica St. *N5* —6B **46**
Corsley Way. *E9* —6B **48**
　　(off Silkmills Sq.)
Cortayne Ct. *Twic* —2J **103**
Cortayne Rd. *SW6* —2H **91**
Cortis Rd. *SW15* —6D **90**
Cortis Ter. *SW15* —6D **90**
Corunna Rd. *SW8* —1G **93**
Corunna Ter. *SW8* —1G **93**
Corvette Sq. *SE10* —6F **81**
Coryton Path. *W9* —4H **59**
Cosbycote Av. *SE24* —5C **94**
Cosdach Av. *Wall* —7H **133**
Cosedge Cres. *Croy* —5A **134**
Cosgrove Clo. *N21* —2H **17**
Cosgrove Clo. *Hayes* —4C **54**
Cosmo Pl. *WC1* —5J **61** (5F **143**)
Cosmur Clo. *W12* —3B **74**
Cossall Wlk. *SE15* —2H **95**
Cosser St. *SE1* —3A **78** (1J **155**)
Costa St. *SE15* —2G **95**
Costons Av. *Gnfd* —3H **55**
Costons La. *Gnfd* —3H **55**
Coston Wlk. *SE4* —4K **95**
Cosway St. *NW1*
　　　　　—5C **60** (5D **140**)
Cotall St. *E14* —5C **64**
Coteford St. *SW17* —4D **108**
Cotelands. *Croy* —3E **134**
Cotesbach Rd. *E5* —3J **47**
Cotesmore Gdns. *Dag* —4C **52**
Cotford Rd. *T Hth* —4C **124**
Cotham St. *SE17*
　　　　　—4C **78** (4D **156**)
Cotherstone Rd. *SW2* —1K **109**
Cotleigh Av. *Bex* —2D **116**
Cotleigh Rd. *NW6* —7J **43**
Cotleigh Rd. *Romf* —6K **37**
Cotman Clo. *NW11* —6A **28**
Cotman Clo. *SW15* —6F **91**
Cotman Gdns. *Edgw* —2G **25**
Cotman Ho. *N'holt* —2B **54**
　　(off Academy Gdns.)
Cotman M. *Dag* —5C **52**
　　(off Highgrove Rd.)
Coton Rd. *Well* —3A **100**

Cotsford Av. *N Mald* —5J **119**
Cotswold Clo. *N11* —4K **15**
Cotswold Clo. *Bexh* —2K **101**
Cotswold Clo. *King T* —6J **105**
Cotswold Ct. *EC1*
　　　　　—4C **62** (3C **144**)
Cotswold Clo. *Gnfd* —2K **55**
　　(off Hodder Dri.)
Cotswold Gdns. *E6* —3B **66**
Cotswold Gdns. *NW2* —2F **43**
Cotswold Gdns. *Ilf* —7H **35**
Cotswold Ga. *NW2* —1G **43**
Cotswold Grn. *Enf* —4E **6**
Cotswold Rise. *Orp* —6K **129**
Cotswold Rd. *Hamp* —6E **102**
Cotswold St. *SE27* —4B **110**
Cotswold Way. *Enf* —4G **7**
Cotswold Way. *Wor Pk* —2E **130**
Cottage Av. *Brom* —1C **138**
Cottage Field Clo. *Sidc* —1C **116**
Cottage Grn. *SE5* —7D **78**
Cottage Gro. *SW9* —3J **93**
Cottage Gro. *Surb* —6D **118**
Cottage Pl. *SW3*
　　　　　—3C **76** (1C **152**)
Cottage Rd. *Eps* —7A **130**
Cottage St. *E14* —7D **64**
Cottage Wlk. *N16* —3F **47**
Cottage Wlk. *SE15* —1F **95**
Cottage Wlk. *SW1*
　　　　　—3D **76** (1F **153**)
Cottenham Dri. *SW20* —7D **106**
Cottenham Pde. *SW20* —2D **120**
Cottenham Pk. Rd. *SW20*
　　(in two parts) —1C **120**
Cottenham Pl. *SW20* —7D **106**
Cottenham Rd. *E17* —4B **32**
Cotterill Rd. *Surb* —7F **119**
Cottesbrook St. *SE14* —7A **80**
Cottesloe M. *SE1*
　　　　　—3A **78** (1K **155**)
　　(off Emery St.)
Cottesmore Av. *Ilf* —2E **34**
Cottesmore Ct. *W8* —3K **75**
　　(off Stanford Rd.)
Cottesmore Gdns. *W8* —3K **75**
Cottingham Rd. *SE20* —7K **111**
Cottingham Rd. *SW8* —7K **77**
Cottington Rd. *Felt* —4B **102**
Cottington St. *SE11*
　　　　　—5B **78** (5A **156**)
Cotton Av. *W3* —6K **57**
Cottongrass Clo. *Croy* —1K **135**
Cotton Hill. *Brom* —4E **112**
Cotton Ho. *SW2* —7J **93**
Cotton Row. *SW11* —3B **92**
Cottons App. *Romf* —5K **37**
Cottons Centre. *SE1*
　　　　　—1E **78** (4G **151**)
Cottons Ct. *Romf* —5K **37**
Cotton's Gdns. *E2*
　　　　　—3E **62** (1H **145**)
Cotton's La. *SE1*
　　　　　—1D **78** (4F **151**)
Cotton St. *E14* —7E **64**
Cotts Clo. *W7* —5K **55**
Couchmore Av. *Ilf* —2D **34**
Couldridge La. *Eri* —3D **84**
Coulgate St. *SE4* —3A **80**
Coulson Clo. *Dag* —1C **52**
Coulson St. *SW3*
　　　　　—5D **76** (5E **152**)
Coulter Clo. *Hayes* —4C **54**
Coulter Rd. *W6* —3D **74**

Coulthurst St. *SW16* —7J **109**
Councillor St. *SE5* —7C **78**
Counter St. *SE1* —1E **78** (5G **151**)
Countess Rd. *NW5* —5G **45**
Countisbury Av. *Enf* —7A **8**
Country Way. *Hanw* —6A **102**
County Gdns. *Bark* —2J **67**
County Ga. *SE9* —3G **115**
County Ga. *New Bar* —6E **4**
County Gro. *SE5* —1C **94**
County Pde. *Bren* —7D **72**
County Rd. *E6* —5F **67**
County Rd. *T Hth* —2B **124**
County St. *SE1* —3C **78** (2D **156**)
Coupland Pl. *SE18* —5G **83**
Courcy Rd. *N8* —3A **30**
Courland Gro. *SW8* —1H **93**
Courland St. *SW8* —1H **93**
　　(in two parts)
Course, The. *SE9* —3E **114**
Courtauld Clo. *SE28* —1A **84**
Courtauld Rd. *N19* —1J **45**
Court Av. *Belv* —5F **85**
Court Clo. *Harr* —3E **24**
Court Clo. *Twic* —3F **103**
Court Clo. *Wall* —7H **133**
Court Clo. Av. *Twic* —3F **103**
Court Downs Rd. *Beck* —2D **126**
Court Dri. *Croy* —4K **133**
Court Dri. *Stan* —4K **11**
Court Dri. *Sutt* —4C **132**
Courtenay Av. *N6* —7C **28**
Courtenay Av. *Harr* —7B **10**
Courtenay Av. *Sutt* —7J **131**
Courtenay Dri. *Beck* —2F **127**
Courtenay Gdns. *Harr* —2G **23**
Courtenay M. *E17* —5A **32**
Courtenay Pl. *E17* —5A **32**
Courtenay Rd. *E11* —3H **49**
Courtenay Rd. *E17* —4K **31**
Courtenay Rd. *SE20* —6K **111**
Courtenay Rd. *Wemb* —3D **40**
Courtenay Rd. *Wor Pk* —3E **130**
Courtenay Sq. *SE11*
　　　　　—5A **78** (6J **155**)
Courtenay St. *SE11*
　　　　　—5A **78** (5J **155**)
Courtens M. *Stan* —7H **11**
Court Farm Av. *Eps* —5A **130**
Court Farm La. *N'holt* —7E **38**
Court Farm Rd. *SE9* —2B **114**
Court Farm Rd. *N'holt* —7E **38**
Courtfield. *W5* —5C **56**
Courtfield Av. *Harr* —5K **23**
Courtfield Cres. *Harr* —5K **23**
Courtfield Gdns. *SW5* —4K **75**
Courtfield Gdns. *W13* —6A **56**
Courtfield M. *SW7* —4K **75**
Courtfield Rise. *W Wick* —3F **137**
Courtfield Rd. *SW7* —4A **76**
Court Gdns. *N1* —6B **46**
Courthill Rd. *SE13* —4E **96**
Courthope Ho. *SW8* —7J **77**
　　(off Hartington Rd.)
Courthope Rd. *NW3* —4D **44**
Courthope Rd. *SW19* —5G **107**
Courthope Rd. *Gnfd* —2H **55**
Courthope Vs. *SW19* —7G **107**
Court Ho. Gdns. *N3* —6D **14**
Courthouse Rd. *N12* —6E **14**
Courtland Av. *E4* —2C **20**
Courtland Av. *NW7* —2E **12**
Courtland Av. *SW16* —7K **109**
Courtland Av. *Ilf* —2D **50**
Courtland Gro. *SE28* —7D **68**

Courtland Rd. *E6* —1C **66**
Courtlands. *Rich* —5G **89**
Courtlands Av. *SE12* —5K **97**
Courtlands Av. *Brom* —1G **137**
Courtlands Av. *Hamp* —6D **102**
Courtlands Av. *Rich* —1H **89**
Courtlands Dri. *Eps* —6A **130**
Courtlands Rd. *Surb* —7G **119**
Courtleet Dri. *Eri* —1H **101**
Courtleigh. *NW11* —5H **27**
Courtleigh Gdns. *NW11* —4G **27**
Court Lodge. *Belv* —5G **85**
Courtman Rd. *N17* —7H **17**
Court Mead. *N'holt* —3D **54**
Courtmead Clo. *SE24* —6C **94**
Courtnell St. *W2* —6J **59**
Courtney Clo. *SE19* —6E **110**
Courtney Ct. *N7* —5A **46**
Courtney Cres. *Cars* —7D **132**
Courtney Ho. *NW4* —3E **26**
　　(off Mulberry Clo.)
Courtney Pl. *Croy* —3A **134**
Courtney Rd. *N7* —5A **46**
Courtney Rd. *SW19* —7C **108**
Courtney Rd. *Croy* —3A **134**
Court Pde. *Wemb* —3B **40**
　　(in two parts)
Courtrai Rd. *SE23* —6A **96**
Court Rd. *SE9* —6D **98**
Court Rd. *SE25* —2F **125**
Court Rd. *S'hall* —4D **70**
Courtside. *N8* —6H **29**
Courtside. *SE26* —3H **111**
Court St. *E1* —5H **63**
Court St. *Brom* —2J **127**
Court, The. *Ruis* —4C **38**
Court Way. *NW9* —4A **26**
Court Way. *W3* —5J **57**
Court Way. *Ilf* —3G **35**
Court Way. *Twic* —7K **87**
Court Way. *Wfd G* —5F **21**
Court Wood La. *Croy* —7B **136**
Court Yd. *SE9* —6D **98**
Courtyard, The. *N1* —7K **45**
Courtyard, The. *NW1* —7E **44**
Cousin La. *EC4* —7D **62** (3E **150**)
Couthurst Rd. *SE3* —7K **81**
Coutt's Cres. *NW5* —3E **44**
Coval Gdns. *SW14* —4H **89**
Coval La. *SW14* —4H **89**
Coval Pas. *SW14* —4J **89**
Coval Rd. *SW14* —4J **89**
Covelees Wall. *E6* —6E **66**
Covell Ct. *SE8* —7C **80**
Covell Ct. *Enf* —1E **6**
　　(off Ridgeway, The)
Coventry Rd. *SE25* —4G **125**
Covent Garden. *WC2*
　　　　　—7J **61** (2F **149**)
Coventry Clo. *E6* —6D **66**
Coventry Clo. *NW6* —2J **59**
Coventry Cross. *E3* —4E **64**
Coventry Hall. *SW16* —5J **109**
Coventry Rd. *E1 & E2* —4H **63**
Coventry Rd. *SE25* —4G **125**
Coventry Rd. *Ilf* —2F **51**
Coventry St. *W1*
　　　　　—7H **61** (3C **148**)
Coverack Clo. *N14* —6B **6**
Coverack Clo. *Croy* —7A **126**
Coverdale Clo. *Stan* —5G **11**
Coverdale Gdns. *Croy* —3F **135**
Coverdale Rd. *NW2* —7F **43**

Coverdale Rd. *W12* —2D **74**
Coverdales, The. *Bark* —2H **67**
Coverley Clo. *E1* —5G **63**
Coverton Rd. *SW17* —5C **108**
Covert, The. *SE19* —7F **111**
　　(off Fox Hill)
Covert, The. *Orp* —6J **129**
Covet Wood Clo. *Orp* —6K **129**
Covington Gdns. *SW16* —7B **110**
Covington Way. *SW16* —6K **109**
　　(in two parts)
Cowan Clo. *E6* —5C **66**
Cowbridge La. *Bark* —7F **51**
Cowbridge Rd. *Harr* —4F **25**
Cowcross St. *EC1*
　　　　　—5B **62** (5A **144**)
Cowdenbeath Path. *N1* —1K **61**
Cowden Rd. *Orp* —7K **129**
Cowden St. *SE6* —4C **112**
Cowdrey Clo. *Enf* —2K **7**
Cowdrey Rd. *SW19* —5K **107**
Cowdry Rd. *E9* —6A **48**
Cowen Av. *Harr* —2H **39**
Cowgate Rd. *Gnfd* —3H **55**
Cowick Rd. *SW17* —4D **108**
Cowings Mead. *N'holt* —6C **38**
Cowland Av. *Enf* —4D **8**
Cow La. *Gnfd* —2H **55**
Cow Leaze. *E6* —6E **66**
Cowleaze Rd. *King T* —1E **118**
Cowley La. *E11* —3G **49**
Cowley Pl. *NW4* —5E **26**
Cowley Rd. *E11* —5K **33**
Cowley Rd. *SW9* —1A **94**
Cowley Rd. *SW14* —3A **90**
Cowley Rd. *Act V* —1B **74**
Cowley Rd. *Ilf* —7D **34**
Cowley St. *SW1* —3J **77** (1E **154**)
Cowling Clo. *W11* —1G **59**
Cowper Av. *E6* —7C **50**
Cowper Av. *Sutt* —4B **132**
Cowper Clo. *Brom* —4B **128**
Cowper Clo. *Well* —5A **100**
Cowper Gdns. *N14* —6A **6**
Cowper Gdns. *Wall* —6G **133**
Cowper Ho. *SE17*
　　　　　—5C **78** (5D **156**)
Cowper Rd. *N14* —1A **16**
Cowper Rd. *N16* —5E **46**
Cowper Rd. *N18* —5B **18**
Cowper Rd. *SW19* —6A **108**
Cowper Rd. *W3* —1K **73**
Cowper Rd. *W7* —7K **55**
Cowper Rd. *Belv* —4G **85**
Cowper Rd. *Brom* —4B **128**
Cowper Rd. *King T* —5F **105**
Cowper St. *EC2* —4D **62** (3F **145**)
Cowper Ter. *W10* —5F **59**
Cowslip Rd. *E18* —2K **33**
Cowthorpe Rd. *SW8* —1H **93**
Coxe Pl. *W'stone* —4A **24**
Cox Ho. *W6* —6G **75**
　　(off Field Rd.)
Coxmount Rd. *SE7* —5B **82**
Cox's Ct. *E1* —5F **63** (6J **145**)
Coxson Way. *SE1*
　　　　　—2F **79** (7J **151**)
Cox's Wlk. *SE21 & SE26*
　　　　　—1G **111**
Coxwell Rd. *SE18* —5H **83**
Coxwell Rd. *SE19* —7E **110**
Crab Hill. *Beck* —7F **113**
Crabtree Av. *Romf* —4D **36**
Crabtree Av. *Wemb* —2E **56**

Crabtree Clo. E2 —2F **63**
Crabtree Ct. E15 —5D **48**
Crabtree Ct. New Bar —4E **4**
Crabtree La. SW6 —7E **74**
(in two parts)
Crabtree Manorway N. Belv
—2J **85**
Crabtree Manorway S. Belv
(in two parts) —3J **85**
Crabtree Wlk. SE15 —1F **95**
(off Exeter Rd.)
Crabtree Wlk. Croy —1G **135**
Crace St. NW1 —3H **61** (1C **142**)
Craddock Rd. Enf —3A **8**
Craddock St. NW5 —6E **44**
Cradley Rd. SE9 —1H **115**
Craigen Av. Croy —1H **135**
Craigerne Rd. SE3 —7K **81**
Craig Gdns. E18 —2H **33**
Craigholm. SE18 —2E **98**
Craigmuir Pk. Wemb —1F **57**
Craignair Rd. SW2 —7A **94**
Craignish Av. SW16 —2K **123**
Craig Pk. Rd. N18 —5C **18**
Craig Rd. Rich —4C **104**
Craig's Ct. SW1 —1J **77** (4E **148**)
Craigton Rd. SE9 —4D **98**
Craigweil Clo. Stan —5J **11**
Craigweil Dri. Stan —5J **11**
Crailey Av. Enf —2A **8**
Crail Row. SE17 —4D **78** (4F **157**)
Cramer St. W1 —5E **60** (6H **141**)
Crammond Clo. W6 —6G **75**
Cramonde Ct. Well —2A **100**
Crampton Rd. SE20 —6J **111**
Crampton St. SE17
—4C **78** (4C **156**)
Cranberry Clo. N'holt —2B **54**
Cranberry La. E16 —4G **65**
Cranborne Av. S'hall —4E **70**
Cranborne Rd. Bark —1H **67**
Cranborne Waye. Hayes —6A **54**
(in two parts)
Cranbourne Av. E11 —4K **33**
Cranbourne Clo. SW16 —3J **123**
Cranbourne Dri. Pinn —5B **22**
Cranbourne Gdns. NW11 —5G **27**
Cranbourne Gdns. Ilf —3G **35**
Cranbourne Rd. E12 —5C **50**
Cranbourne Rd. E15 —4E **48**
Cranbourne Rd. N10 —2F **29**
Cranbourn Ho. SE16 —2H **79**
(off Marigold St.)
Cranbourn Pas. SE16 —2H **79**
(off Wilson Gro.)
Cranbourn Pl. SE16 —2H **79**
Cranbourn St. WC2
—7H **61** (2D **148**)
Cranbrook Clo. Brom —6J **127**
Cranbrook Ct. Bren —6D **72**
(off Somerset Rd.)
Cranbrook Dri. Twic —1F **103**
Cranbrook Est. E2 —2K **63**
Cranbrook M. E17 —5B **32**
Cranbrook Pk. N22 —1A **30**
Cranbrook Point. E16 —1J **81**
Cranbrook Rise. Ilf —6D **34**
Cranbrook Rd. SE8 —1C **96**
Cranbrook Rd. SW19 —7G **107**
Cranbrook Rd. W4 —5A **74**
Cranbrook Rd. Barn —6G **5**
Cranbrook Rd. Bexh —1F **101**
Cranbrook Rd. Houn —4D **86**
Cranbrook Rd. Ilf —7E **34**
Cranbrook Rd. T Hth —2C **124**

Cranbrook St. E2 —2K **63**
Cranbury Rd. SW6 —2K **91**
Crandley Ct. SE8 —4A **80**
Crane Av. W3 —7J **57**
Crane Av. Iswth —5A **88**
Crane Clo. Dag —6G **53**
Crane Clo. Harr —3G **39**
Crane Ct. EC4 —6A **62** (1K **149**)
Craneford Clo. Twic —7K **87**
Craneford Way. Twic —7J **87**
Crane Gro. N7 —6A **46**
Crane Ho. Felt —3E **102**
Crane Lodge Rd. Houn —6A **70**
Cranemead. SE16 —4K **79**
Crane Mead Ct. Twic —7K **87**
Crane Pk. Rd. Twic —2F **103**
Crane Rd. Twic —1J **103**
Cranes Dri. Surb —4F **119**
Cranes Pk. Surb —4E **118**
Cranes Pk. Av. Surb —4E **118**
Cranes Pk. Cres. Surb —4F **119**
Crane St. SE10 —5F **81**
Craneswater Pk. S'hall —5D **70**
Crane Way. Twic —7G **87**
Cranfield Clo. SE27 —3C **110**
Cranfield Ct. W1
—5C **60** (6D **140**)
Cranfield Dri. NW9 —7F **13**
Cranfield Rd. SE4 —3B **96**
Cranfield Rd. E. Cars —7E **132**
Cranfield Rd. W. Cars —7E **132**
Cranfield Row. SE1
—3A **78** (1K **155**)
Cranford Av. N13 —5D **16**
Cranford Clo. SW20 —7D **106**
Cranford La. Houn —7A **70**
Cranford St. E1 —7K **63**
Cranford Way. N8 —4K **29**
Cranhurst Rd. NW2 —5E **42**
Cranleigh Clo. SE20 —1H **125**
Cranleigh Clo. Bex —6H **101**
Cranleigh Ct. Rich —3G **89**
Cranleigh Ct. S'hall —6D **54**
Cranleigh Gdns. N21 —5F **7**
Cranleigh Gdns. SE25 —3E **124**
Cranleigh Gdns. Bark —7H **51**
Cranleigh Gdns. Harr —5E **24**
Cranleigh Gdns. King T —6F **105**
Cranleigh Gdns. S'hall —6D **54**
Cranleigh Gdns. Sutt —3A **132**
Cranleigh Gdns. Ind. Est. S'hall
—6D **54**
Cranleigh M. SW11 —2C **92**
Cranleigh Rd. N15 —5C **30**
Cranleigh Rd. SW19 —3J **121**
Cranleigh St. NW1 —2G **61**
Cranley Dene Ct. N10 —4F **29**
Cranley Dri. Ilf —7G **35**
Cranley Gdns. N10 —4F **29**
Cranley Gdns. N13 —3E **16**
Cranley Gdns. SW7
—5A **76** (5A **152**)
Cranley Gdns. Wall —7G **133**
Cranley M. SW7
—5A **76** (5A **152**)
Cranley Pde. SE9 —4C **114**
(off Beaconsfield Rd.)
Cranley Pl. SW7 —4B **76** (4A **152**)
Cranley Rd. E13 —5K **65**
Cranley Rd. Ilf —6G **35**
Cranmer Av. W13 —3B **72**
Cranmer Clo. Mord —6F **121**
Cranmer Clo. Ruis —1B **38**
Cranmer Clo. Stan —7H **11**

Cranmer Ct. N3 —2G **27**
Cranmer Ct. SW3
—4C **76** (4D **152**)
Cranmer Ct. SW4 —3H **93**
Cranmere Ct. Enf —2F **7**
Cranmer Farm Clo. Mitc
—4D **122**
Cranmer Gdns. Dag —4J **53**
Cranmer Ho. SW9 —7A **78**
(off Brixton Rd.)
Cranmer Rd. E7 —4K **49**
Cranmer Rd. SW9 —7A **78**
Cranmer Rd. Croy —3B **134**
Cranmer Rd. Edgw —3C **12**
Cranmer Rd. Hamp —5F **103**
Cranmer Rd. King T —5E **104**
Cranmer Rd. Mitc —4D **122**
Cranmer Ter. SW17 —5B **108**
Cranmore Av. Iswth —7G **71**
Cranmore Rd. Brom —3H **113**
Cranmore Rd. Chst —5D **114**
Cranmore Way. N10 —4G **29**
Cranston Clo. Houn —2C **86**
Cranston Est. N1 —2D **62**
Cranston Gdns. E4 —6J **19**
Cranston Rd. SE23 —1A **112**
Cranswick Rd. SE16 —5H **79**
Crantock Rd. SE6 —2D **112**
Cranwell Clo. E3 —4D **64**
Cranwich Av. N21 —7J **7**
Cranwich Rd. N16 —7D **30**
Cranwood Ct. EC1
—3D **62** (2F **145**)
Cranwood St. EC1
—3D **62** (2F **145**)
Cranworth Cres. E4 —1A **20**
Cranworth Gdns. SW9 —1A **94**
Craster Rd. SW2 —7K **93**
Crathie Rd. SE12 —6K **97**
Craven Av. W5 —7C **56**
Craven Av. S'hall —5D **54**
Craven Clo. N16 —7G **31**
Craven Ct. NW10 —1A **58**
Craven Ct. Romf —6E **36**
Craven Gdns. SW19 —5J **107**
Craven Gdns. Bark —2J **67**
Craven Gdns. Ilf —2H **35**
Craven Hill. W2 —7A **60**
Craven Hill Gdns. W2 —7A **60**
(in four parts)
Craven Hill M. W2 —7A **60**
Craven M. SW11 —3E **92**
Craven Pk. NW10 —1K **57**
Craven Pk. M. NW10 —7A **42**
Craven Pk. Rd. N15 —6F **31**
Craven Pk. Rd. NW10 —1A **58**
Craven Pas. WC2
—1J **77** (4E **148**)
Craven Rd. NW10 —1K **57**
Craven Rd. W2 —7A **60** (2A **146**)
Craven Rd. W5 —7C **56**
Craven Rd. Croy —1H **135**
Craven Rd. King T —1F **119**
Craven St. WC2 —1J **77** (4E **148**)
Craven Ter. W2 —7A **60** (2A **146**)
Craven Wlk. N16 —7G **31**
Crawford Av. Wemb —5D **40**
Crawford Clo. Iswth —2J **87**
Crawford Est. SE5 —2C **94**
Crawford Gdns. N13 —3G **17**
Crawford Gdns. N'holt —3D **54**
Crawford M. W1
—5D **60** (6E **140**)
Crawford Pas. EC1
—4A **62** (4K **143**)
Crawford Pl. W1
—6C **60** (7D **140**)

Crawford Point. E16 —6H **65**
(off Wouldham Rd.)
Crawford Rd. SE5 —1C **94**
Crawford St. W1
—5C **60** (6E **140**)
Crawley Rd. E10 —1D **48**
Crawley Rd. N22 —2C **30**
Crawley Rd. Enf —7K **7**
Crawshay Ct. SW9 —1A **94**
Crawthew Gro. SE22 —4F **95**
Craybrooke Rd. Sidc —4B **116**
Craybury End. SE9 —2G **115**
Crayford Clo. E6 —6C **66**
Crayford Rd. N7 —4H **45**
Cray Rd. Belv —6G **85**
Cray Rd. Sidc —6C **116**
Cray Valley Rd. Orp —5K **129**
Crealock Gro. Wfd G —5C **20**
Crealock St. SW18 —6K **91**
Creasy Est. SE1 —3E **78** (2G **157**)
Crebor St. SE22 —6G **95**
Credenhall Dri. Brom —1D **138**
Credenhill Ho. SE15 —7H **79**
Credenhill St. SW16 —6G **109**
Crediton Hill. NW6 —5K **43**
Crediton Rd. E16 —6J **65**
Crediton Rd. NW10 —1F **59**
Credon Rd. E13 —2A **66**
Credon Rd. SE16 —5H **79**
Creechurch La. EC3
—6E **62** (1H **151**)
Creechurch Pl. EC3
—6E **62** (1H **151**)
Creed Ct. EC4 —6B **62** (1B **150**)
Creed La. EC4 —6B **62** (1B **150**)
Creek Rd. SE8 & SE10 —6C **80**
Creek Rd. Bark —3K **67**
Creekside. SE8 —7D **80**
Creek Way. Rain —5K **69**
Creeland Gro. SE6 —1B **112**
Crefeld Clo. W6 —6G **75**
Creffield Rd. W5 & W3 —7F **57**
Creighton Av. E6 —2B **66**
Creighton Av. N2 & N10 —3C **28**
Creighton Clo. W12 —7C **58**
Creighton Rd. N17 —7K **17**
Creighton Rd. NW6 —2F **59**
Creighton Rd. W5 —3D **72**
Cremer St. E2 —2F **63** (1J **145**)
Cremorne Gdns. Eps —7A **130**
Cremorne Rd. SW10 —7A **76**
Crescent. EC3 —7F **63** (2J **151**)
Crescent. Surb —5D **118**
Crescent Ct. Bus. Cen. E16
—4F **65**
Crescent Dri. Orp —6F **129**
Crescent E. Barn —1F **5**
Crescent Gdns. SW19 —3J **107**
Crescent Gdns. Ruis —1A **22**
Crescent Gro. SW4 —4G **93**
Crescent Gro. Mitc —5C **122**
Crescent La. SW4 —6G **93**
Crescent M. N22 —1J **29**
Crescent Pl. SW3
—4C **76** (3D **152**)
Crescent Rise. N22 —1H **29**
Crescent Rise. Barn —5H **5**
Crescent Rd. E4 —1B **20**
Crescent Rd. E6 —1A **66**
Crescent Rd. E10 —2D **48**
Crescent Rd. E13 —1J **65**
Crescent Rd. E18 —1A **34**
Crescent Rd. N3 —1H **27**
Crescent Rd. N8 —6H **29**
Crescent Rd. N9 —1B **18**

Crescent Rd. N11 —4J **15**
Crescent Rd. N15 —3B **30**
Crescent Rd. N22 —1H **29**
Crescent Rd. SE18 —5F **83**
Crescent Rd. SW20 —1F **121**
Crescent. Barn —4G **5**
Crescent. Beck —2D **126**
Crescent. Brom —7J **113**
Crescent. Dag —3H **53**
Crescent. King T —7G **105**
Crescent. Sidc —3K **115**
Crescent Row. EC1
—4C **62** (4C **144**)
Crescent Stables. SW15 —5G **91**
Crescent St. N1 —7K **45**
Crescent, The. E17 —5A **32**
Crescent, The. N9 —2C **18**
Crescent, The. N11 —4K **15**
Crescent, The. NW2 —3D **42**
Crescent, The. SW13 —2C **90**
Crescent, The. SW19 —3J **107**
Crescent, The. W3 —6A **58**
Crescent, The. Barn —2E **4**
Crescent, The. Beck —1C **126**
Crescent, The. Bex —7C **100**
Crescent, The. Croy —6D **124**
Crescent, The. Harr —1G **39**
Crescent, The. Ilf —6E **34**
Crescent, The. N Mald —2K **119**
Crescent, The. Sidc —4K **115**
Crescent, The. S'hall —2D **70**
Crescent, The. Surb —5E **118**
Crescent, The. Sutt —5B **132**
Crescent, The. Wemb —2B **40**
Crescent, The. W Wick —6G **127**
Crescent Way. N12 —6H **15**
Crescent Way. SE4 —3C **96**
Crescent Way. SW16 —6K **109**
Crescent W. Barn —1F **5**
Crescent Wharf. E16 —2K **81**
Crescent Wood Rd. SE26
—3G **111**
Cresford Rd. SW6 —1K **91**
Crespigny Rd. NW4 —6D **26**
Cressage Clo. S'hall —4E **54**
Cressage Ho. Bren —6E **72**
(off Ealing Rd.)
Cresset Rd. E9 —6J **47**
Cresset St. SW4 —3H **93**
Cressfel. Sidc —5B **116**
Cressfield Clo. NW5 —5E **44**
Cressida Rd. N19 —1G **45**
Cressingham Gdns. Est. SW2
—7A **94**
Cressingham Gro. Sutt —4A **132**
Cressingham Rd. SE13 —3E **96**
Cressingham Rd. Edgw —6E **12**
Cressington Clo. N16 —5E **46**
Cresswell. NW9 —2B **26**
Cresswell Gdns. SW5 —5A **76**
Cresswell Pk. SE3 —3H **97**
Cresswell Pl. SW10 —5A **76**
Cresswell Rd. SE25 —4G **125**
Cresswell Rd. Felt —3C **102**
Cresswell Rd. Twic —6D **88**
Cresswell Way. N21 —7F **7**
Cressy Ct. E1 —5J **63**
Cressy Ct. W6 —3D **74**
Cressy Houses. E1 —5J **63**
(off Hannibal Rd.)
Cressy Pl. E1 —5J **63**
Cressy Rd. NW3 —5D **44**
Cresta Ct. W5 —4F **57**
Crestbrook Av. N13 —3G **17**

Crestbrook Pl. N13 —3G 17
(off Green Lanes)
Crest Ct. NW4 —5E 26
Crest Dri. Enf —1D 8
Crestfield St. WC1
—3J 61 (1F 143)
Crest Gdns. Ruis —3A 38
Creston Way. Wor Pk —1F 131
Crest Rd. NW2 —2C 42
Crest Rd. Brom —7H 127
Crest Rd. S Croy —7H 135
Crest, The. N13 —4F 17
Crest, The. NW4 —5F 27
Crest, The. Surb —5G 119
Crest View. Pinn —4B 22
Crest View Dri. Pet W —5F 129
Crestway. SW15 —6C 90
Crestwood Way. Houn —5D 86
Creswick Ct. W3 —7H 57
Creswick Rd. W3 —7H 57
Creswick Wlk. E3 —3C 64
Creswick Wlk. NW11 —4H 27
Creton St. SE18 —3E 82
Crewdson Rd. SW9 —7A 78
Crewe Pl. NW10 —3B 58
Crews St. E14 —4C 80
Crewys Rd. NW2 —2H 43
Crewys Rd. SE15 —2H 95
Crichton Av. Wall —5H 133
Crichton Gdns. Romf —7G 37
Crichton Ho. Sidc —6D 116
Crichton Rd. Cars —7D 132
Crichton St. SW8 —2G 93
Cricketers Arms Rd. Enf —2H 7
Cricketers Clo. N14 —7B 6
Cricketers Clo. Eri —5K 85
Cricketer's Ct. SE11
—4B 78 (4A 156)
Cricketers Rd. Enf —2H 7
Cricketers Ter. Cars —3C 132
Cricketers Wlk. SE26 —5J 111
Cricketfield Rd. E5 —4H 47
Cricket Grn. Mitc —3D 122
Cricket Ground Rd. Chst —1F 129
Cricket La. Beck —6A 112
Cricklade Av. SW2 —2J 109
Cricklewood B'way. NW2 —3E 42
Cricklewood La. NW2 —4F 43
Cricklewood Trad. Est. NW2
—3F 43
Cridland St. E15 —1H 65
Crieff Ct. Tedd —7C 104
Crieff Rd. SW18 —6A 92
Criffel Av. SW2 —2H 109
Crimscott St. SE1
—3E 78 (2H 157)
Crimsworth Rd. SW8 —1H 93
Crinan St. N1 —2J 61
Cringle St. SW8 —7G 77
Crispe Ho. N1 —1K 61
(off Barnsbury Est.)
Crispe Ho. Bark —2H 67
Crispen Rd. Felt —4C 102
Crispian Clo. NW10 —4A 42
Crispin Clo. Croy —2J 133
Crispin Cres. Croy —3H 133
Crispin Lodge. N11 —5J 15
Crispin Rd. Edgw —6D 12
Crispin St. E1 —5F 63 (6J 145)
Crisp Rd. W6 —5E 74
Cristowe Rd. SW6 —2H 91
Criterion M. N19 —2H 45
Crittall's Corner. (Junct.)
—7C 116
Crockerton Rd. SW17 —2D 108

Crockham Way. SE9 —4E 114
Crocus Clo. Croy —1K 135
Crocus Field. Barn —6C 4
Croft Av. W Wick —1E 136
Croft Clo. NW7 —3F 13
Croft Clo. Belv —5F 85
Croft Clo. Chst —5D 114
Croft Ct. SE13 —6E 96
Croftdown Rd. NW5 —3E 44
Crofters Clo. Iswth —5H 87
Crofters Mead. Croy —7B 136
Crofters Way. NW1 —1H 61
Croft Gdns. W7 —2A 72
Croft Ho. E17 —4D 32
Croft Lodge Clo. Wfd G —6E 20
Croft M. N12 —3F 15
Crofton Av. W4 —7K 73
Crofton Av. Bex —7D 100
Croftongate Way. SE4 —5A 96
Crofton Gro. E4 —4A 20
Crofton La. Orp —7H 129
Crofton Pk. Rd. SE4 —6B 96
Crofton Rd. E13 —4K 65
Crofton Rd. SE5 —1E 94
Crofton Rd. Orp —3E 138
Crofton Ter. E5 —5A 48
Crofton Ter. Rich —4F 89
Crofton Way. Barn —6E 4
Crofton Way. Enf —2F 7
Croft Rd. SW16 —1A 124
Croft Rd. SW19 —7A 108
Croft Rd. Brom —6J 113
Croft Rd. Enf —1F 9
Croft Rd. Sutt —5C 132
Croftside. The. SE25 —3G 125
Crofts La. N22 —7F 17
Crofts St. E1 —7G 63 (3K 151)
Croft St. SE8 —4A 80
Crofts Wlk. Harr —6A 24
Croft, The. E4 —2B 20
Croft, The. NW10 —2B 58
Croft, The. W5 —5E 56
Croft, The. Barn —4B 4
Croft, The. Houn —7C 70
Croft, The. Pinn —7D 22
Croft, The. Ruis —4A 38
Croft, The. Wemb —5C 40
Croftway. NW3 —4J 43
Croftway. Rich —3B 104
Croft Way. Sidc —3J 115
Crogsland Rd. NW1 —7E 44
Croham Clo. S Croy —7E 134
Croham Mnr. Rd. S Croy
—7E 134
Croham Mt. S Croy —7E 134
Croham Pk. Av. S Croy —5F 135
Croham Rd. S Croy —5E 134
Croham Valley Rd. S Croy
—6G 135
Croindene Rd. SW16 —1J 123
Crokesley Ho. Edgw —2J 25
(off Burnt Oak B'way.)
Cromartie Rd. N19 —7H 29
Cromarty Ct. SW2 —5K 93
Cromarty Rd. Edgw —2C 12
Cromberdale Ct. N17 —1G 31
(off Spencer Rd.)
Crombie Clo. Ilf —5D 34
Crombie M. SW11 —2C 92
Crombie Rd. Sidc —1H 115
Crome Ho. N'holt —2B 54
(off Parkfield Dri.)
Cromer Pl. Orp —7H 129
Cromer Rd. E10 —7F 33

Cromer Rd. N17 —2G 31
Cromer Rd. SE25 —3H 125
Cromer Rd. SW17 —6E 108
Cromer Rd. Chad H —6E 36
Cromer Rd. New Bar —4F 5
Cromer Rd. Romf —6J 37
Cromer Rd. Wfd G —4G 20
Cromer St. WC1 —3J 61 (2E 142)
Cromer Ter. E8 —5G 47
Cromer Vs. Rd. SW18 —6H 91
Cromford Path. E5 —4K 47
Cromford Rd. SW18 —5J 91
Cromford Way. N Mald —2K 119
Cromlix Clo. Chst —2F 129
Crompton St. W2
—4B 60 (4A 140)
Cromwell Av. N6 —1F 45
Cromwell Av. Brom —4K 127
Cromwell Av. N Mald —5B 120
Cromwell Cen. NW10 —3K 57
Cromwell Cen., The. Dag —7F 37
(off Selinas La.)
Cromwell Clo. E1 —1G 79
Cromwell Clo. N2 —4B 28
Cromwell Clo. W3 —1J 73
(in two parts)
Cromwell Clo. Brom —4K 127
Cromwell Ct. Enf —5E 8
Cromwell Cres. SW5 —4J 75
Cromwell Gdns. SW7
—3B 76 (2B 152)
Cromwell Gro. W6 —3E 74
Cromwell Highwalk. EC2
—5C 62 (5D 144)
Cromwell Ind. Est. E10 —1A 48
Cromwell Lodge. Bexh —5E 100
Cromwell M. SW7
—4B 76 (3B 152)
Cromwell Pl. N6 —1F 45
Cromwell Pl. SW7
—4B 76 (3B 152)
Cromwell Pl. SW14 —3J 89
Cromwell Rd. E7 —7A 50
Cromwell Rd. E17 —5E 32
Cromwell Rd. N3 —1A 28
Cromwell Rd. N10 —7K 15
(in two parts)
Cromwell Rd. SW5 & SW7
—4J 75
Cromwell Rd. SW9 —1B 94
Cromwell Rd. SW19 —5J 107
Cromwell Rd. Beck —2A 126
Cromwell Rd. Croy —7D 124
Cromwell Rd. Felt —1A 102
Cromwell Rd. Houn —4E 86
Cromwell Rd. King T —1E 118
Cromwell Rd. Tedd —6A 104
Cromwell Rd. Wemb —2E 56
Cromwell Rd. Wor Pk —3A 130
Cromwell St. Houn —4E 86
Cromwell Tower. EC2
—5C 62 (5D 144)
Crondace Rd. SW6 —1J 91
Crondall Ct. N1 —2D 62 (1F 145)
Crondall St. N1 —2D 62 (1F 145)
Cronin St. SE15 —7F 79
(off Shanklin Way)
Crooked Billet. SW19 —6E 106
Crooked Billet. (Junct.) —1C 32
Crooked Billet Yd. E2
—3E 62 (2H 145)
Crooked Usage. N3 —3G 27
Crooke Rd. SE8 —5A 80
Crookham Rd. SW6 —1H 91

Crook Log. Bexh —3D 100
Crookston Rd. SE9 —3E 98
Croombs Rd. E16 —5A 66
Croom's Hill. SE10 —7E 80
Croom's Hill Gro. SE10 —7E 80
Cropley Ct. N1 —2D 62 (1E 144)
Croppath Rd. Dag —4G 53
Cropthorne Ct. W9 —3A 60
(off Maida Vale)
Crosbie. NW9 —3B 26
Crosbie Ho. E17 —3E 32
(off Prospect Hill)
Crosby Clo. Felt —3C 102
Crosby Ct. SE1 —2D 78 (6E 150)
Crosby Ho. E7 —6J 49
Crosby Rd. E7 —6J 49
Crosby Rd. Dag —2H 69
Crosby Row. SE1
—2D 78 (7E 150)
Crosby Sq. EC3 —6E 62 (1G 151)
Crosby Wlk. E8 —6F 47
Crosby Wlk. SW2 —7A 94
Crosby Way. SW2 —7A 94
Crosland Pl. SW11 —3E 92
Cross Av. SE10 —6F 81
Crossbow Ho. W13 —1B 72
(off Sherwood Clo.)
Crossbrook Rd. SE3 —3C 98
Cross Clo. SE15 —2H 95
Cross Deep. Twic —2K 103
Cross Deep Gdns. Twic —2K 103
Crossfield Ho. W11 —7G 59
(off Mary Pl.)
Crossfield Rd. NW3 —6B 44
Crossfield St. SE8 —7C 80
Crossford St. SW9 —2K 93
Cross Ga. Edgw —3B 12
Crossgate. Gnfd —6B 40
Cross Keys Clo. N9 —2B 18
(off Green, The)
Cross Keys Clo. W1
—5E 60 (6H 141)
Cross Lances Rd. Houn —4F 87
Crossland Rd. T Hth —6B 124
Crosslands Av. W5 —1F 73
Crosslands Av. S'hall —5D 70
Cross La. EC3 —7E 62 (3G 151)
Cross La. N8 —3K 29
(in two parts)
Cross La. Bex —7F 101
Crossleigh Ct. SE14 —7B 80
(off New Cross Rd.)
Crosslet St. SE17
—4D 78 (3F 157)
Crosslet Vale. SE10 —1D 96
Crossley St. N7 —6A 46
Crossmead. SE9 —1D 114
Crossmead Av. Gnfd —3E 54
Crossness Footpath. Eri —1F 85
Crossness La. SE28 —7D 68
Crossness Rd. Bark —3K 67
Cross Rd. E4 —1B 20
Cross Rd. N11 —5A 16
Cross Rd. N22 —7F 17
Cross Rd. SW19 —7J 107
Cross Rd. Brom —2C 138
Cross Rd. Chad H —7C 36
Cross Rd. Croy —1D 134
Cross Rd. Enf —4K 7
Cross Rd. Felt —4C 102
Cross Rd. Harr —4H 23
Cross Rd. King T —7F 105
Cross Rd. Mawn —4G 37
Cross Rd. Sidc —4B 116

Cross Rd. S Harr —3F 39
Cross Rd. Sutt —5B 132
Cross Rd. W'stone —2A 24
Cross Rd. Wfd G —6J 21
Cross St. N1 —1B 62
Cross St. N18 —5B 18
Cross St. SE5 —3D 94
Cross St. SW13 —2A 90
Cross St. Hamp —5G 103
Crossthwaite Av. SE5 —4D 94
Crosswall. EC3 —7F 63 (2J 151)
Crossway. N12 —6G 15
Crossway. N16 —5E 46
Crossway. NW9 —4B 26
Crossway. SE28 —7C 68
Crossway. SW20 —4E 120
Crossway. W13 —4A 56
Crossway. Dag —3C 52
Crossway. Enf —7K 7
Crossway. Orp —4H 129
Crossway. Pinn —2A 22
Crossway. Ruis —4A 38
Crossway. Wfd G —4F 21
Crossway Ct. SE4 —2A 96
Crossways. N21 —6H 7
Crossways. S Croy —7A 136
Crossways. Sutt —7B 132
Crossways Rd. Beck —4C 126
Crossways Rd. Mitc —3F 123
Crossways Ter. E5 —4J 47
Crossways, The. Houn —7D 70
Crossways, The. Surb —7H 119
Crossways, The. Wemb —2G 41
Crossway, The. N22 —7G 17
Crossway, The. SE9 —2B 114
Crossway, The. Harr —2J 23
Croston St. E8 —1G 63
Crothall Clo. N13 —3E 16
Crouch. Sidc —5B 116
Crouch Av. Bark —2B 68
Crouch Clo. Beck —6C 112
Crouch Croft. SE9 —3E 114
Crouch End Hill. N8 —7H 29
Crouch Hall Ct. N19 —1J 45
Crouch Hall Rd. N8 —6H 29
Crouch Hill. N8 & N4 —6J 29
Crouchman's Clo. SE26 —3F 111
Crouch Rd. NW10 —7K 41
Crowborough Rd. SW17
—6E 108
Crowborough Ct. Sutt —4K 131
(off St Nicholas Way)
Crowden Way. SE28 —7C 68
Crowder St. E1 —7H 63
Crowfield Ho. N5 —4C 46
Crowfoot Clo. E9 —5B 48
Crowhurst Clo. SW9 —2A 94
Crowhurst Ho. SW9 —2K 93
(off Aytoun Rd.)
Crowland Gdns. N14 —7D 6
Crowland Rd. N15 —5F 31
Crowland Rd. T Hth —4D 124
Crowlands Av. Romf —6H 37
Crowland Ter. N1 —7D 46
Crowland Wlk. Mord —6K 121
Crow La. Romf —7F 37
Crowley Cres. Croy —5A 134
Crowlin Wlk. N1 —6D 46
Crowmarsh Gdns. SE23 —7J 95
Crown Arc. King T —2D 118
Crownbourne Ct. Sutt —4K 131
Crown Bldgs. E4 —1A 20
Crown Clo. E3 —1C 64
Crown Clo. NW6 —6K 43
Crown Clo. NW7 —2G 13

Crown Clo. Bus. Cen. E3 —1C **64**
(off Crown Clo.)
Crown Cotts. Romf —1F **37**
Crown Ct. EC2 —6C **62** (1D **150**)
Crown Ct. N10 —7K **15**
Crown Ct. SE12 —6K **97**
Crown Ct. WC2 —6J **61** (1F **149**)
Crown Dale. SE19 —6B **110**
Crowndale Rd. NW1 —2G **61**
Crownfield Av. E4 —6J **35**
Crownfield Rd. E15 —4F **49**
Crown Hill. Croy —2C **134**
Crown Hill Rd. NW10 —1B **58**
Crownhill Rd. Wfd G —7H **21**
Crown La. N14 —1B **16**
Crown La. SW16 —5A **110**
Crown La. Brom —5B **128**
Crown La. Chst —1G **129**
Crown La. Mord —4J **121**
Crown La. Gdns. SW16 —5A **110**
Crown La. Spur. Brom —6B **128**
Crownmead Way. Romf —4H **37**
Crown M. E13 —1A **66**
Crown M. W6 —4C **74**
Crown Office Row. EC4
—7A **62** (2J **149**)
Crown Pde. N14 —1B **16**
Crown Pde. SE19 —6B **110**
Crown Pas. SW1
—1G **77** (5B **148**)
Crown Pas. King T —2D **118**
Crown Pl. NW5 —6F **45**
Crown Rd. N10 —7K **15**
Crown Rd. Enf —3B **8**
Crown Rd. Ilf —4H **35**
Crown Rd. Mord —4K **121**
Crown Rd. N Mald —1J **119**
Crown Rd. S Ruis —5B **38**
Crown Rd. Sutt —4K **131**
Crown Rd. Twic —6B **88**
Crownstone Ct. SW2 —5A **94**
Crownstone Rd. SW2 —5A **94**
Crown St. SE5 —7C **78**
Crown St. W3 —1H **73**
Crown St. Dag —6J **53**
(in two parts)
Crown St. Harr —1H **39**
Crown Ter. Rich —4F **89**
Crowntree Clo. Iswth —6K **71**
Crown Wlk. Wemb —3F **41**
Crown Woods. SE18 —2F **99**
Crown Woods Way. SE9 —5H **99**
Crown Yd. Houn —3G **87**
Crowshott Av. Stan —2C **24**
Crows Rd. E15 —3F **65**
Crowther Av. Bren —4E **72**
Crowther Rd. SE25 —4G **125**
Crowthorne Clo. SW18 —7H **91**
Crowthorne Rd. W10 —6F **59**
Croxden Clo. Edgw —3G **25**
Croxden Wlk. Mord —6A **122**
Croxford Gdns. N22 —7G **17**
Croxford Way. Romf —1K **53**
Croxley Grn. Orp —7B **116**
Croxley Rd. W9 —3H **59**
Croxted Clo. SE21 —7C **94**
Croxted Rd. SE24 —6C **94**
Croxted Rd. SE24 & SE21 —6C **94**
Croxteth Ho. SW8 —2H **93**
Croyde Av. Gnfd —3G **55**
Croyde Clo. Sidc —7H **99**
Croydon. N17 —2D **30**
(off Gloucester Rd.)
Croydon Flyover, The. Croy
—3C **134**

Croydon Gro. Croy —1B **134**
Croydon Rd. E13 —4H **65**
Croydon Rd. SE20 —2H **125**
Croydon Rd. Beck —4K **125**
Croydon Rd. Kes —3B **138**
Croydon Rd. Mitc & Bedd
—4E **122**
Croydon Rd. Wall & Croy
—4F **133**
Croydon Rd. W Wick & Brom
—3G **137**
Croydon Rd. Ind. Est. Beck
—4K **125**
Croyland Rd. N9 —1B **18**
Croylands Dri. Surb —7E **118**
Crozier Ho. SW8 —7K **77**
(off Wilkinson St.)
Crozier Ter. E9 —5K **47**
Crucible Clo. Romf —6B **36**
Crucifix La. SE1 —2E **78** (6H **151**)
Cruden St. N1 —1B **62**
Cruikshank Rd. E15 —4G **49**
Cruikshank St. WC1
—3A **62** (1J **143**)
Crummock Rd. NW9 —5A **26**
Crumpsall St. SE2 —4C **84**
Crundale Av. NW9 —5G **25**
Crunden Rd. S Croy —7D **134**
Crusader Gdns. Croy —3E **134**
Crusoe Rd. Eri —5K **85**
Crusoe Rd. Mitc —7D **108**
Crutched Friars. EC3
—7E **62** (2H **151**)
Crutchley Rd. SE6 —2G **113**
Crystal Pal. Pde. SE19 —6F **111**
Crystal Pal. Pk. Rd. SE26
—5G **111**
Crystal Pal. Rd. SE22 —6F **95**
Crystal Pal. Sta. Rd. SE19
—6G **111**
Crystal Ter. SE19 —6D **110**
Crystal View Ct. Brom —4F **113**
Crystal Way. Dag —1C **52**
Crystal Way. Harr —5K **23**
Cuba Dri. Enf —2D **8**
Cuba St. E14 —2C **80**
Cubitt Ho. SW4 —6G **93**
Cubitt Sq. S'hall —1G **71**
Cubitt Steps. E14 —1C **80**
Cubitt St. WC1 —3K **61** (2H **143**)
Cubitt St. Croy —5K **133**
Cubitt's Yd. WC2
—7J **61** (2F **149**)
Cubitt Ter. SW4 —3G **93**
Cuckoo Av. W7 —4J **55**
Cuckoo Dene. W7 —5H **55**
Cuckoo Hall La. N9 —7D **8**
Cuckoo Hall Rd. N9 —7D **8**
Cuckoo Hill. Pinn —3A **22**
Cuckoo Hill Dri. Pinn —3A **22**
Cuckoo Hill Rd. Pinn —4A **22**
Cuckoo La. W7 —7J **55**
Cudas Clo. Eps —4B **130**
Cuddington Av. Wor Pk —3B **130**
Cudham St. SE6 —7E **96**
Cudworth St. E1 —4H **63**
Cuff Cres. SE9 —6B **98**
Culford Gdns. SW3
—4D **76** (4F **153**)
Culford Gro. N1 —6E **46**
Culford M. N1 —6E **46**
Culford Rd. N1 —7E **46**
Culgaith Gdns. Enf —4D **6**
Cullen Way. NW10 —4J **57**
Culling Rd. SE16 —3J **79**

Cullington Clo. Harr —4A **24**
Cullingworth Rd. NW10 —5C **42**
Culloden Clo. SE16 —5G **79**
Culloden Rd. Enf —2G **7**
Culloden St. E14 —6E **64**
Cullum St. EC3 —7E **62** (2G **151**)
Culmington Rd. W13 —1C **72**
Culmington Rd. S Croy —7C **134**
Culmore Rd. SE15 —7H **79**
Culmstock Rd. SW11 —5E **92**
Culpepper Ct. SE11
—4A **78** (3J **155**)
Culross Clo. N15 —4C **30**
Culross Rd. Houn —7C **70**
Culross St. W1 —7E **60** (3G **147**)
Culverden Rd. SW12 —2G **109**
Culver Gro. Stan —2C **24**
Culverhouse Gdns. SW16
—3K **109**
Culverlands Clo. Stan —4G **11**
Culverley Rd. SE6 —1D **112**
Culvers Av. Cars —2D **132**
Culvers Retreat. Cars —2D **132**
Culverstone Clo. Hay —6H **127**
Culvers Way. Cars —2D **132**
Culvert Pl. SW11 —2E **92**
Culvert Rd. N15 —5E **30**
Culvert Rd. SW11 —2D **92**
Cumberland Av. NW10 —3H **57**
Cumberland Av. Well —3J **99**
Cumberland Bus. Pk. NW10
—3H **57**
Cumberland Clo. E8 —6F **47**
Cumberland Clo. SW20 —7F **107**
Cumberland Clo. Ilf —1G **35**
Cumberland Ct. Harr —3J **23**
(off Princes Dri.)
Cumberland Ct. Well —2J **99**
Cumberland Cres. W14 —4G **75**
(in two parts)
Cumberland Dri. Bexh —7E **84**
Cumberland Gdns. NW4 —1F **27**
Cumberland Gdns. WC1
—3A **62** (1J **143**)
Cumberland Ga. W1
—7D **60** (2E **146**)
Cumberland Ho. N9 —1D **18**
(off Cumberland Rd.)
Cumberland Ho. King T —7H **105**
Cumberland Mans. W1
—6D **60** (7E **140**)
Cumberland Mkt. NW1
—3F **61** (1K **141**)
Cumberland Mills Sq. E14 —5F **81**
Cumberland Pk. W3 —7J **57**
Cumberland Pk. Ind. Est. NW10
—3C **58**
Cumberland Pl. NW1
—3F **61** (1J **141**)
Cumberland Pl. SE6 —7H **97**
Cumberland Rd. E12 —4B **50**
Cumberland Rd. E13 —5K **65**
Cumberland Rd. E17 —2A **32**
Cumberland Rd. N9 —1D **18**
Cumberland Rd. N22 —2K **29**
Cumberland Rd. SE25 —6H **125**
Cumberland Rd. SW13 —1B **90**
Cumberland Rd. SW3 —7J **57**
Cumberland Rd. W7 —2K **71**
Cumberland Rd. Brom —4G **127**
Cumberland Rd. Harr —5F **23**
Cumberland Rd. Rich —7G **73**
Cumberland Rd. Stan —2F **25**
Cumberland St. SW1
—5F **77** (5K **153**)

Cumberland Ter. NW1
—2F **61** (1J **141**)
Cumberland Ter. M. NW1
—2F **61** (1J **141**)
Cumberland Vs. W3 —7J **57**
(off Cumberland Rd.)
Cumberlow Av. SE25 —3F **125**
Cumberton Rd. N17 —1D **30**
Cumbrian Gdns. NW2 —2F **43**
Cumming St. N1
—2K **61** (1H **143**)
Cumnor Gdns. Eps —6C **130**
Cumnor Rd. Sutt —6A **132**
Cunard Cres. N21 —6J **7**
Cunard Pl. EC3 —6E **62** (1H **151**)
Cunard Rd. NW10 —3K **57**
Cunard Wlk. SE16 —4K **79**
Cundy Rd. E16 —6A **66**
Cundy St. SW1 —4E **76** (4H **153**)
Cunliffe Pde. Eps —4B **130**
Cunliffe Rd. Eps —4B **130**
Cunliffe St. SW16 —6G **109**
Cunningham Clo. Romf —5C **36**
Cunningham Clo. W Wick
—2D **136**
Cunningham Ho. SE5 —7D **78**
(off Elmington Est.)
Cunningham Pk. Harr —5G **23**
Cunningham Pl. NW8
—4B **60** (3A **140**)
Cunningham Rd. N15 —4G **31**
Cunnington St. W4 —4J **73**
Cupar Rd. SW11 —1E **92**
Cupola Clo. Brom —5K **113**
Cureton St. SW1
—4H **77** (4D **154**)
Curfew Ho. Bark —1G **67**
Curie Gdns. NW9 —2A **26**
Curlew Clo. SE28 —7D **68**
Curlew Clo. Ilf —3E **34**
Curlew Ct. SE4 —4A **96**
(off St Norbert Rd.)
Curlew St. SE1 —2F **79** (6K **151**)
Curlew Way. Hayes —5B **54**
Curnick's La. SE27 —4C **110**
Curran Av. Sidc —5K **99**
Curran Av. Wall —3E **132**
Currey Rd. Gnfd —6H **39**
Curricle St. W3 —1A **74**
Currie Hill Clo. SW19 —4H **107**
Curry Rise. NW7 —6A **14**
Cursitor St. EC4 —6A **62** (7J **143**)
Curtain Pl. EC2 —4E **62** (3H **145**)
Curtain Rd. EC2 —4E **62** (2H **145**)
Curthwaite Gdns. Enf —4C **6**
Curtis Dri. W3 —6K **57**
Curtis Field Rd. SW16 —4K **109**
Curtis Ho. SE17 —5D **78** (5E **156**)
Curtis La. Wemb —5E **40**
Curtis Rd. Houn —7D **86**
Curtis St. SE1 —4F **79** (3J **157**)
Curtis Way. SE28 —7B **68**
Curtlington Ho. Edgw —2J **25**
(off Burnt Oak B'way.)
Curve, The. W12 —7C **58**
Curwen Av. E7 —4K **49**
Curwen Rd. W12 —2C **74**
Curzon Av. Enf —5E **8**
Curzon Av. Stan —1A **24**
Curzon Ct. SW6 —1K **91**
(off Maltings Pl.)
Curzon Cres. NW10 —7A **42**
Curzon Cres. Bark —2K **67**
Curzon Ga. W1 —1E **76** (5H **147**)

Curzon Pl. W1 —1E **76** (5H **147**)
Curzon Pl. Pinn —5A **22**
Curzon Rd. N10 —2F **29**
Curzon Rd. W5 —4B **56**
Curzon Rd. T Hth —6A **124**
Curzon St. W1 —1E **76** (5H **147**)
Cusack Clo. Twic —4K **103**
Custom Ho. Reach. SE16
—2B **80**
Custom Ho. Wlk. EC3
—7E **62** (3G **151**)
Cutbush Ho. N7 —5H **45**
Cutcombe Rd. SE5 —2C **94**
Cuthbert Gdns. SE25 —3E **124**
Cuthbert Rd. E17 —3E **32**
Cuthbert Rd. N18 —5B **18**
Cuthbert Rd. Croy —2B **134**
Cuthberts Rd. NW2 —6H **43**
Cuthbert St. W2 —5B **60** (4A **140**)
Cuthill Wlk. SE5 —1D **94**
Cutlers Gdns. E1
—6E **62** (6H **145**)
Cutlers Sq. E14 —4C **80**
Cutler St. E1 —6E **62** (7H **145**)
Cut, The. SE1 —2B **78** (6A **150**)
Cutthroat All. Rich —2C **104**
Cuxton. Pet W —5G **129**
Cuxton Clo. Bexh —5E **100**
Cyclamen Clo. Hamp —6E **102**
Cyclops M. E14 —4C **80**
Cygnet Av. Felt —7A **86**
Cygnet Clo. NW10 —5K **41**
Cygnets, The. Felt —4C **102**
Cygnet St. E1 —4F **63** (3K **145**)
Cygnet Way. Hayes —5B **54**
Cygnus Bus. Cen. NW10 —6B **42**
Cymbeline Ct. Harr —6K **23**
(off Gayton Rd.)
Cynthia St. N1 —2K **61** (1H **143**)
Cyntra Pl. E8 —7H **47**
Cypress Av. Twic —7G **87**
Cypress Gdns. SE4 —5A **96**
Cypress Ho. SE14 —1K **95**
Cypress Pl. W1 —4G **61** (4B **142**)
Cypress Rd. SE25 —2E **124**
Cypress Rd. Harr —2H **23**
Cypress Tree Clo. Sidc —1K **115**
Cyprus Av. N3 —2G **27**
Cyprus Clo. N4 —6B **30**
Cyprus Gdns. N3 —2G **27**
Cyprus Pl. E2 —2J **63**
Cyprus Pl. E6 —7E **66**
Cyprus Rd. N3 —2H **27**
Cyprus Rd. N9 —2A **18**
Cyprus St. E2 —2J **63**
(in two parts)
Cyrena Rd. SE22 —6F **95**
Cyril Lodge. Sidc —4A **116**
Cyril Mans. SW11 —1D **92**
Cyril Rd. Bexh —2E **100**
Cyril St. Orp —7K **129**
Cyrus St. EC1 —4B **62** (3B **144**)
Czar St. SE8 —6C **80**

Dabbs Hill La. N'holt —6D **38**
(in two parts)
Dabbs La. EC1 —4A **62** (4K **143**)
(off Farringdon Rd.)
Dabin Cres. SE10 —1E **96**
Dacca St. SE8 —6B **80**
Dace Rd. E3 —1C **64**
Dacre Av. Ilf —2E **34**
Dacre Clo. Gnfd —2F **55**
Dacre Gdns. SE13 —4G **97**

Dacre Ho. SW3 —6B **76**
(off Beaufort St.)
Dacre Pk. SE13 —3G **97**
Dacre Pl. SE13 —3G **97**
Dacre Rd. E11 —1H **49**
Dacre Rd. E13 —1K **65**
Dacre Rd. Croy —7J **123**
Dacre St. SW1 —3H **77** (1C **154**)
Dade Way. S'hall —5D **70**
Daerwood Clo. Brom —1D **138**
Daffodil Clo. Croy —1K **135**
Daffodil Gdns. Ilf —5F **51**
Daffodil Pl. Hamp —6E **102**
Daffodil St. W12 —7B **58**
Dafforne Rd. SW17 —3E **108**
Dagenham Av. Dag —1E **68**
(in two parts)
Dagenham Rd. E10 —1B **48**
Dagenham Rd. Dag & Romf
—4H **53**
Dagenham Rd. Rain —7K **53**
Dagenham Rd. Romf —7K **37**
Dagmar Av. Wemb —4F **41**
Dagmar Ct. E14 —3E **80**
Dagmar Gdns. NW10 —2F **59**
Dagmar M. S'hall —3C **70**
(off Dagmar Rd.)
Dagmar Pas. N1 —1B **62**
(off Cross St.)
Dagmar Rd. N4 —7A **30**
Dagmar Rd. N15 —4D **30**
Dagmar Rd. N22 —1H **29**
Dagmar Rd. SE5 —1E **94**
Dagmar Rd. SE25 —5E **124**
Dagmar Rd. Dag —7J **53**
Dagmar Rd. King T —1F **119**
Dagmar Rd. S'hall —3C **70**
Dagmar Ter. N1 —1B **62**
Dagnall Pk. SE25 —6D **124**
Dagnall Rd. SE25 —5E **124**
Dagnall St. SW11 —2D **92**
Dagnan Rd. SW12 —7F **93**
Dagonet Gdns. Brom —3J **113**
Dagonet Rd. Brom —3J **113**
Dahlia Gdns. Ilf —6F **51**
Dahlia Gdns. Mitc —4H **123**
Dahlia Rd. SE2 —4B **84**
Dahomey Rd. SW16 —6G **109**
Daimler Way. Wall —7J **133**
Dain Ct. W8 —4J **75**
(off Lexham Gdns.)
Daines Clo. E12 —3D **50**
Dainford Clo. Brom —5F **113**
Dainton Clo. Brom —1K **127**
Daintry Clo. Harr —4A **24**
Daintry Way. E9 —6B **48**
Dairsie Ct. Dare —2A **128**
Dairsie Rd. SE9 —3E **98**
Dairy Clo. T Hth —2C **124**
Dairy La. SE18 —4D **82**
Dairy M. SW9 —3J **93**
Dairy Wlk. SW19 —4G **107**
Daisy Clo. Croy —1K **135**
Daisy Dobbins Wlk. N19 —7J **29**
(off Jessie Blythe La.)
Daisy La. SW6 —3J **91**
Daisy Rd. E16 —4G **65**
Daisy Rd. E18 —2K **33**
Dakota Gdns. E6 —4C **66**
Dakota Gdns. N'holt —3C **54**
Dalberg Rd. SW2 —4A **94**
Dalberg Way. SE2 —3D **84**
Dalby Rd. SW18 —4A **92**
Dalbys Cres. N17 —6K **17**

Dalby St. NW5 —6F **45**
Dalcross Rd. Houn —2C **86**
Dale Av. Edgw —1F **25**
Dale Av. Houn —3C **86**
Dalebury Rd. SW17 —2D **108**
Dale Clo. SE3 —3J **97**
Dale Clo. New Bar —6E **4**
Dale Gdns. Wfd G —4E **20**
Dale Grn. Rd. N11 —3A **16**
Dale Gro. N12 —5F **15**
Daleham Gdns. NW3 —5B **44**
Daleham M. NW3 —6B **44**
Dale Ho. SE4 —4A **96**
Dale Lodge. N6 —6G **29**
Dalemain M. E16 —1J **81**
Dale Pk. Av. Cars —2D **132**
Dale Pk. Rd. SE19 —1D **124**
Dale Rd. NW5 —5E **44**
Dale Rd. SE17 —6B **78** (7B **156**)
Dale Rd. Sutt —4H **131**
Dale Row. W11 —6G **59**
Daleside Rd. SW16 —5F **109**
Dale St. W4 —5A **74**
Dale, The. Kes —4B **138**
Dale View Av. E4 —2K **19**
Dale View Cres. E4 —2K **19**
Dale View Gdns. E4 —3A **20**
Daleview Rd. N15 —6E **30**
Dalewood Gdns. Wor Pk
—2D **130**
Dale Wood Rd. Orp —7J **129**
Daley Ho. W12 —6D **58**
Daley St. E9 —6K **47**
Daley Thompson Way. SW8
—3F **93**
Dalgarno Gdns. W10 —5E **58**
Dalgarno Way. W10 —4E **58**
Dalgleish St. E14 —6A **64**
Daling Way. E3 —2B **64**
Dalkeith Gro. Stan —5J **11**
Dalkeith Rd. SE21 —1C **110**
Dalkeith Rd. Ilf —3G **51**
Dallas Rd. NW4 —7C **26**
Dallas Rd. SE26 —3H **111**
Dallas Rd. W5 —5F **57**
Dallas Rd. Sutt —6G **131**
Dallinger Rd. SE12 —6H **97**
Dalling Rd. W6 —4D **74**
Dallington St. EC1
—4B **62** (3B **144**)
Dallin Rd. SE18 —7F **83**
Dallin Rd. Bexh —4D **100**
Dalmain Rd. SE23 —1K **111**
Dalmally Rd. Croy —7F **125**
Dalmeny Av. N7 —4H **45**
Dalmeny Av. SW16 —2A **124**
Dalmeny Clo. Wemb —6C **40**
Dalmeny Cres. Houn —4H **87**
Dalmeny Rd. N7 —3H **45**
Dalmeny Rd. Cars —7E **132**
Dalmeny Rd. Eri —1H **101**
Dalmeny Rd. New Bar —6F **5**
Dalmeny Rd. Wor Pk —3D **130**
Dalmeyer Rd. NW10 —6B **42**
Dalmore Rd. SE21 —2C **110**
Dalrymple Clo. N14 —7C **6**
Dalrymple Rd. SE4 —4A **96**
Dalston Cross Shop. Cen. E8
—6F **47**
Dalston Gdns. Stan —1E **24**
Dalston La. E8 —6F **47**
Dalton Av. Mitc —2C **122**
Dalton Rd. W'stone —2H **23**
Dalton St. SE27 —2B **110**

Dalwood St. SE5 —1E **94**
Daly Ct. E15 —5D **48**
Dalyell Rd. SW9 —3K **93**
Damascene Wlk. SE21 —1C **106**
Damask Cres. E16 —4G **65**
Damer Ter. SW10 —7A **76**
Dames Rd. E7 —3J **49**
Dame St. N1 —2C **62**
Damien Ct. E1 —6H **63**
Damien St. E1 —6H **63**
Damon Clo. Sidc —3B **116**
Damsonwood Rd. S'hall —3E **70**
Danbrook Rd. SW16 —1J **123**
Danbury Clo. Romf —3D **36**
Danbury Mans. Bark —7F **51**
(off Whiting Av.)
Danbury M. Wall —4F **133**
Danbury St. N1 —2B **62**
Danbury Way. Wfd G —6F **21**
Danby Ct. Enf —3H **7**
(off Horseshoe La.)
Danby St. SE15 —3F **95**
Dancer Rd. SW6 —1H **91**
Dancer Rd. Rich —3G **89**
Dando Cres. SE3 —3K **97**
Dandridge Clo. SE10 —5H **81**
Danebury. New Ad —6D **136**
Danebury Av. SW15 —6A **90**
(in two parts)
Daneby Rd. SE6 —3D **112**
Dane Clo. Bex —7G **101**
Danecourt Gdns. Croy —3F **135**
Danecroft Rd. SE24 —5C **94**
Danehill Wlk. Sidc —3A **116**
Danehurst Gdns. Ilf —5C **34**
Danehurst St. SW6 —1G **91**
Daneland. Barn —6J **5**
Danemead Gro. N'holt —5F **39**
Danemere St. SW15 —3E **90**
Dane Pl. E3 —2B **64**
Dane Rd. N18 —4D **18**
Dane Rd. SW19 —1A **122**
Dane Rd. W13 —1C **72**
Dane Rd. Ilf —5G **51**
Dane Rd. S'hall —7C **54**
Danesbury Rd. Felt —1A **102**
Danescombe. SE12 —1J **113**
Danes Ct. Wemb —3H **41**
Danescourt Cres. Sutt —2A **132**
Danescroft. NW4 —5F **27**
Danescroft Av. NW4 —5F **27**
Danescroft Gdns. NW4 —5F **27**
Danesdale Rd. E9 —6A **48**
Danesfield. SE17
—6E **78** (7G **157**)
Danes Ga. Harr —3J **23**
Danes Rd. Romf —7J **37**
Dane St. WC1 —5K **61** (6G **143**)
Daneswood Av. SE6 —3E **112**
Danethorpe Rd. Wemb —6D **40**
Danette Gdns. Dag —2G **53**
Daneville Rd. SE5 —1D **94**
Dangan Rd. E11 —6J **33**
Daniel Bolt Clo. E14 —5D **64**
Daniel Clo. N18 —4D **18**
Daniel Clo. SW17 —6C **108**
Daniel Clo. Houn —7D **86**
Daniel Ct. NW9 —1A **26**
Daniel Gdns. SE15 —7F **79**
Daniel Ho. N1 —2D **62**
(off Cranston Est.)
Daniell Way. Croy —1J **133**
Daniel Pl. NW4 —7D **26**
Daniel Rd. W5 —7F **57**
Daniels Rd. SE15 —3J **95**

Danleigh Ct. N14 —7C **6**
Dan Leno Wlk. SW6 —7K **75**
Dansey Pl. W1 —7H **61** (2C **148**)
Dansington Rd. Well —4A **100**
Danson Cres. Well —3B **100**
Danson Interchange. (Junct.)
—6C **100**
Danson La. Well —4B **100**
Danson Mead. Well —3C **100**
Danson Rd. Bex & Bexh —5D **100**
(in two parts)
Danson Underpass. Sidc
—6C **100**
Dante Pl. SE11 —4B **78** (4B **156**)
Dante Rd. SE11 —4B **78** (3A **156**)
Danube St. SW3
—5C **76** (5D **152**)
Danvers Ho. E1 —6G **63**
(off Christian St.)
Danvers Rd. N8 —4H **29**
Danvers St. SW3
—6B **76** (7B **152**)
Da Palma Ct. SW6 —6J **75**
(off Anselm Rd.)
Daphne Ct. Wor Pk —2A **130**
Daphne Gdns. E4 —3K **19**
Daphne Ho. N22 —1A **30**
(off Acacia Rd.)
Daphne St. SW18 —6A **92**
Daplyn St. E1 —5G **63**
D'Arblay St. W1 —6G **61** (1B **148**)
Darcy Av. Wall —4G **133**
Darcy Clo. N20 —2G **15**
D'Arcy Dri. Harr —4D **24**
D'Arcy Gdns. Harr —4D **24**
D'Arcy Pl. Brom —4J **127**
Darcy Rd. SW16 —2J **123**
D'Arcy Rd. Iswth —1A **88**
D'Arcy Rd. Sutt —4F **131**
Dare Ct. E10 —7E **32**
Dare Gdns. Dag —3E **52**
Darell Rd. Rich —3G **89**
Darent Ho. Brom —5F **113**
Darenth Rd. N16 —7F **31**
Darenth Rd. Well —1A **100**
Darfield Rd. SE4 —5B **96**
Darfield Way. W10 —6F **59**
Darfur St. SW15 —3F **91**
Dargate Clo. SE19 —7F **111**
Darien Rd. SW11 —3B **92**
Dark Ho. Wlk. EC3
—7D **62** (3G **151**)
Darlan Rd. SW6 —7H **75**
Darlaston Rd. SW19 —7F **107**
Darley Clo. Croy —6A **126**
Darley Dri. N Mald —2K **119**
Darley Gdns. Mord —6A **122**
Darley Ho. SE11
—5K **77** (6G **155**)
Darley Rd. N9 —1A **18**
Darley Rd. SW11 —6D **92**
Darling Rd. SE4 —3C **96**
Darling Row. E1 —4H **63**
Darlington Rd. SE27 —5B **110**
Darmaine Clo. S Croy —7C **134**
Darnay Ho. SE16
—3G **79** (1K **157**)
Darndale Clo. N17 —2B **32**
Darnley Ho. E14 —6A **64**
Darnley Rd. E9 —6J **47**
Darnley Rd. Wfd G —1J **33**
Darnley Ter. W11 —1F **75**
Darrell Rd. SE22 —5G **95**

Darren Clo. N4 —7K **29**
Darris Clo. Hayes —4C **54**
Darsley Dri. SW8 —1H **93**
Dartford Av. N9 —6D **8**
Dartford By-Pass. Bex & Dart
—1K **117**
Dartford Gdns. Chad H —5B **36**
Dartford Rd. Bex —1J **117**
Dartford St. SE17
—6C **78** (7D **156**)
Dartington Ho. SW8 —2H **93**
(off Union Gro.)
Dartle Ct. SE16 —2G **79**
(off Dickens Est.)
Dartmoor Wlk. E14 —4C **80**
(off Charnwood Gdns.)
Dartmouth Clo. W11 —6J **59**
Dartmouth Ct. SE10 —1F **97**
Dartmouth Gro. SE10 —1E **96**
Dartmouth Hill. SE10 —1E **96**
Dartmouth Pk. Av. NW5 —3F **45**
Dartmouth Pk. Hill. N19 & NW5
—1F **45**
Dartmouth Pk. Rd. NW5 —4F **45**
Dartmouth Pl. SE23 —2J **111**
Dartmouth Pl. W4 —6A **74**
Dartmouth Rd. NW2 —6F **43**
Dartmouth Rd. NW4 —6C **26**
Dartmouth Rd. SE26 & SE23
—3H **111**
Dartmouth Rd. Brom —7J **127**
Dartmouth Row. SE10 —1E **96**
Dartmouth St. SW1
—2H **77** (7D **148**)
Dartmouth Ter. SE10 —1F **97**
Dartnell Rd. Croy —7F **125**
Darton Ct. W3 —1J **73**
Dartrey Tower. SW10 —7A **76**
(off Worlds End Est.)
Dartrey Wlk. SW10 —7B **76**
Dart St. W10 —3G **59**
Darville Rd. N16 —3F **47**
Darwell Clo. E6 —2E **66**
Darwin Clo. N11 —3A **16**
Darwin Dri. S'hall —6F **55**
Darwin Rd. N22 —1B **30**
Darwin Rd. W5 —5C **72**
Darwin Rd. Well —3K **99**
Darwin St. SE17
—4D **78** (3F **157**)
Daryngton Dri. Gnfd —2H **55**
Daryngton Ho. SW8 —7J **77**
(off Hartington Rd.)
Dashwood Clo. Bexh —5G **101**
Dashwood Rd. N8 —6K **29**
Dassett Rd. SE27 —5B **110**
Data Point Bus. Cen. E16 —4F **65**
Datchelor Pl. SE5 —1D **94**
Datchet Rd. SE6 —2B **112**
Datchworth Ct. Enf —5K **7**
Date St. SE17 —5D **78** (6D **156**)
Daubeney Gdns. N17 —7H **17**
Daubeney Rd. E5 —4A **48**
Daubeney Rd. N17 —7H **17**
Daubeney Tower. SE8 —5B **80**
(off Bowditch)
Dault Rd. SW18 —6A **92**
Dauncey Ho. SE1
—2B **78** (7A **150**)
Daventry Clo. Chst —1E **128**
Davenant Rd. N19 —2H **45**
Davenant Rd. Croy —4B **134**
Davenant St. E1 —5G **63**
Davenport Clo. Tedd —6A **104**
Davenport Lodge. Houn —7C **70**

Davenport Rd. *SE6* —6D **96**
Davenport Rd. *Sidc* —2E **116**
Daventer Dri. *Stan* —7E **10**
Daventry Av. *E17* —6C **32**
Daventry St. *NW1*
— 5C **60** (5C **140**)
Daver Ct. *SW3* —5C **76** (5D **152**)
Davern Clo. *SE10* —4H **81**
Davey Clo. *N7* —6K **45**
Davey Rd. *E9* —7C **48**
Davey's Ct. *WC2*
—7J **61** (2E **148**)
Davey St. *SE15* —6F **79** (7K **157**)
David Av. *Gnfd* —3J **55**
David Coffer Ct. *Belv* —4H **85**
David Ct. *N20* —3F **15**
Davidge St. *SE1* —2B **78** (7A **150**)
David Ho. SW8 —7J **77**
(off Wyvil Rd.)
David Ho. *Sidc* —3A **116**
David Lee Point. E15 —1G **65**
(off Leather Gdns.)
David M. *W1* —5D **60** (5F **141**)
David Rd. *Dag* —2E **52**
David's Ct. S'hall —6G **55**
(off Whitecote Rd.)
Davidson Gdns. *SW8* —7J **77**
Davidson La. *Harr* —7K **23**
Davidson Rd. *Croy* —7E **124**
Davidson Ter. E7 —5K **49**
(off Claremont Rd.)
Davidson Ter. E7 —5K **49**
(off Windsor Rd.)
Davidson Tower. *Brom* —5K **113**
David's Rd. *SE23* —1J **111**
David St. *E15* —6F **49**
Davies Clo. *Croy* —6G **125**
Davies La. *E11* —2G **49**
Davies M. *W1* —7F **61** (2J **147**)
Davies St. *W1* —6F **61** (1J **147**)
Davington Gdns. *Dag* —5B **52**
Davington Rd. *Dag* —6B **52**
Davinia Clo. *Wfd G* —6J **21**
Davis Rd. *W3* —1B **74**
Davis St. *E13* —2K **65**
Davisville Rd. *W12* —2C **74**
Davmor Ct. *Bren* —5C **72**
Dawes Av. *Iswth* —5A **88**
Dawes Rd. *SW6* —7G **75**
Dawes St. *SE17* —5D **78** (5F **157**)
Dawlish Av. *N13* —4D **16**
Dawlish Av. *SW18* —2K **107**
Dawlish Dri. *Ilf* —4J **51**
Dawlish Dri. *Pinn* —5C **22**
Dawlish Rd. *E10* —1E **48**
Dawlish Rd. *N17* —3G **31**
Dawlish Rd. *NW2* —6F **43**
Dawnay Gdns. *SW18* —2B **108**
Dawnay Rd. *SW18* —2A **108**
Dawn Clo. *Houn* —3C **86**
Dawn Cres. *E15* —1F **65**
Dawpool Rd. *NW2* —2B **42**
Daws Hill. *E4* —2K **9**
Daws La. *NW7* —5G **13**
Dawson Av. *Bark* —7J **51**
Dawson Clo. *SE18* —4G **83**
Dawson Gdns. *Bark* —7K **51**
Dawson Pl. *W2* —7J **59**
Dawson Rd. *NW2* —5E **42**
Dawson Rd. *King T* —3F **119**
Dawson Ter. *N9* —7D **8**
Daybrook Rd. *SW19* —2K **121**
Daylesford Av. *SW15* —4C **90**
Daymer Gdns. *Pinn* —4A **22**

Daysbrook Rd. *SW2* —1K **109**
Days La. *Sidc* —7J **99**
Dayton Gro. *SE15* —1J **95**
Deaconess Ct. N15 —4F **31**
(off Tottenham Grn. E.)
Deacon Est., The. *E4* —6G **19**
Deacon M. *N1* —7D **46**
Deacon Rd. *NW2* —5C **42**
Deacon Rd. *King T* —1F **119**
Deacons Clo. *Pinn* —2A **22**
Deacons Ct. *Twic* —2K **103**
Deacons Wlk. *Hamp* —4E **102**
Deacon Way. *SE17*
—4C **78** (3C **156**)
Deacon Way. *Wfd G* —6J **21**
Deal Cl. S'hall —6G **55**
(off Haldane Rd.)
Deal Porters Way. *SE16* —3J **79**
Deal Rd. *SW17* —6E **108**
Deal's Gateway. SE10 —1C **96**
Deal St. *E1* —5G **63**
Dealtry Rd. *SW15* —4E **90**
Deal Wlk. *SW9* —7A **78**
Dean Bradley St. *SW1*
—3J **77** (2E **154**)
Dean Clo. *E9* —5J **47**
Dean Clo. *SE16* —1K **79**
Dean Ct. SW8 —7J **77**
(off Thorncroft St.)
Dean Ct. *Edgw* —6C **12**
Dean Ct. *Romf* —5K **37**
Dean Ct. *Wemb* —3B **40**
Deancross St. *E1* —6J **63**
Dean Dri. *Stan* —2E **24**
Deane Av. *Ruis* —5A **38**
Deane Croft Rd. *Pinn* —6A **22**
Deanery Clo. *N2* —4C **28**
Deanery M. *W1* —1E **76** (4H **147**)
Deanery Rd. *E15* —7G **49**
Deanery St. *W1* —1E **76** (4H **147**)
Deane Way. *Ruis* —6A **22**
Dean Farrar St. *SW1*
—3H **77** (1D **154**)
Deanfield Gdns. *Croy* —4D **134**
Dean Gdns. *E17* —4F **33**
Deanhill Ct. *SW14* —4H **89**
Deanhill Rd. *SW14* —4H **89**
Dean Rd. *NW2* —6E **42**
Dean Rd. *Croy* —4D **134**
Dean Rd. *Hamp* —5E **102**
Dean Rd. *Houn* —5F **87**
Dean Ryle St. *SW1*
—4J **77** (3E **154**)
Deansbrook Clo. *Edgw* —7D **12**
Deansbrook Rd. *Edgw* —7C **12**
Dean's Bldgs. SE17
—4D **78** (4E **156**)
Deans Clo. *W4* —6H **73**
Deans Clo. *Croy* —3F **135**
Deans Clo. *Edgw* —6D **12**
Deans Ct. *EC4* —6B **62** (1B **150**)
Deanscroft Av. *NW9* —1J **41**
Deans Dri. *N13* —6G **17**
Deans Dri. *NW7* —5E **12**
Deans Dri. *Edgw* —5E **12**
Deans Ga. Clo. *SE23* —3K **111**
Deans La. W4 —6H **73**
(off Deans Clo.)
Deans La. *Edgw* —6D **12**
Dean's M. *W1* —6F **61** (7K **141**)
Dean's Pl. *SW1* —5H **77** (5C **154**)
Deans Rd. *W7* —1K **71**
Deans Rd. *Sutt* —3K **131**
Dean Stanley St. *SW1*
—3J **77** (2E **154**)

Deanston Wharf. *E16* —2K **81**
Dean St. *E7* —5J **49**
Dean St. *W1* —6H **61** (7C **142**)
Deansway. *N2* —4B **28**
Deansway. *N9* —3K **17**
—3H **77** (1D **154**)
Dean Trench St. *SW1*
—3J **77** (2E **154**)
Dean Wlk. *Edgw* —6D **12**
Dean Way. *S'hall* —2F **71**
Dearne Clo. *Stan* —5F **11**
De Barowe M. *N5* —4B **46**
Debden. N7 —2D **30**
(off Gloucester Rd.)
Debden Clo. *King T* —5D **104**
Debden Clo. *Wfd G* —7F **21**
De Beauvoir Cres. *N1* —1E **62**
De Beauvoir Est. *N1* —1E **62**
De Beauvoir Pl. *N1* —6E **46**
De Beauvoir Rd. *N1* —1E **62**
De Beauvoir Sq. *N1* —7E **46**
Debnams Rd. *SE16* —4J **79**
De Bohun Av. *N14* —6A **6**
Deborah Clo. *Iswth* —1J **87**
Deborah Ct. E18 —3K **33**
(off Victoria Rd.)
Deborah Lodge. *Edgw* —1H **25**
Debrabant Clo. *Eri* —6K **85**
De Brome Rd. *Felt* —1A **102**
De Bruin Ct. *E14* —5E **80**
De Burgh Rd. *SW19* —7A **108**
Debussy. *NW9* —2B **26**
Decima St. *SE1*
—3E **78** (1G **157**)
Decimus Clo. *T Hth* —4D **124**
Deck Clo. *SE16* —1K **79**
Decoy Av. *NW11* —5G **27**
De Crespigny Pk. *SE5* —2D **94**
Dee Ct. W7 —6H **55**
(off Hobbayne Rd.)
Deeley Rd. *SW8* —1H **93**
Deena Clo. *W3* —6F **57**
Deepdale. *SW19* —4F **107**
Deepdale Av. *Brom* —4H **127**
Deepdene. *W5* —4F **57**
Deepdene Av. *Croy* —3F **135**
Deepdene Clo. *E11* —4J **33**
Deepdene Ct. *N21* —6G **7**
Deepdene Gdns. *SW2* —7K **93**
Deepdene Point. *SE23* —3K **111**
Deepdene Rd. *SE5* —4D **94**
Deepdene Rd. *Well* —3A **100**
Deepwell Clo. *Iswth* —1A **88**
Deepwood La. *Gnfd* —3H **55**
Deerbrook Rd. *SE24* —1B **110**
Deerdale Rd. *SE24* —4C **94**
Deerfield Cotts. *NW9* —5B **26**
Deerhurst Cres. *Hamp H*
—5G **103**
Deerhurst Rd. *NW2* —6F **43**
Deerhurst Rd. *SW16* —5K **109**
Deerleap Gro. *E4* —5J **9**
Dee Rd. *Rich* —4F **89**
Deer Pk. Clo. *King T* —7H **105**
Deer Pk. Gdns. *Mitc* —4B **122**
Deer Pk. Rd. *SW19* —2K **121**
Deer Pk. Way. *W Wick* —2H **137**
Deeside Rd. *SW17* —3B **108**
Dee St. *E14* —6E **64**

Defiance Wlk. *SE18* —3D **82**
Defiant. *NW9* —2B **26**
(off Further Acre)
Defiant Way. *Wall* —7J **133**
Defoe Av. *Rich* —7G **73**
Defoe Clo. *SE16* —2B **80**
Defoe Clo. *SW17* —6C **108**
Defoe Ho. *EC2* —5C **62** (5D **144**)
Defoe Rd. *N16* —3E **46**
De Frene Rd. *SE26* —4K **111**
Degema Rd. *Chst* —5F **115**
Dehar Cres. *NW9* —7B **26**
De Havilland Clo. *N'holt* —3B **54**
De Havilland Rd. *Edgw* —2H **25**
De Havilland Rd. *Houn* —7A **70**
De Havilland Rd. *Wall* —7J **133**
Dekker Rd. *SE21* —6E **94**
Delacourt Rd. *SE3* —7K **81**
Delafield Ho. E1 —6G **63**
(off Christian St.)
Delafield Rd. *SE7* —5B **81**
Delaford Rd. *SE16* —5H **79**
Delaford St. *SW6* —7G **75**
Delamare Cres. *Croy* —6J **125**
Delamere Gdns. *NW7* —6E **12**
Delamere Rd. *SW20* —1F **121**
Delamere Rd. *W5* —2E **72**
Delamere Rd. *Hayes* —7B **54**
Delamere Rd. *W2* —5A **60**
Delamere Ter. *W2* —5K **59**
Delancey Pas. *NW1* —1F **61**
(off Delancey St.)
Delancey St. *NW1* —1F **61**
De Laune St. *SE17*
—5B **78** (6A **156**)
Delaware Mans. W9 —4K **59**
(off Delaware Rd.)
Delaware Rd. *W9* —4K **59**
Delawyk Cres. *SE24* —6C **94**
Delcombe Av. *Wor Pk* —1E **130**
Delderfield Ho. Romf —2K **37**
(off Portnoi Clo.)
Delft Way. *SE22* —5E **94**
Delhi Rd. *Enf* —7A **8**
Delhi St. *N1* —1J **61**
Delia St. *SW18* —7K **91**
Delius Clo. *E15* —2E **64**
Della Path. *E5* —3G **47**
Dell Clo. *E15* —1F **65**
Dell Clo. *Wall* —4H **133**
Dell Clo. *Wfd G* —3E **20**
Dellfield Clo. *Beck* —1E **126**
Dell La. *Eps* —5C **130**
Dellors Clo. *Barn* —5A **4**
Dellow Clo. *Ilf* —7H **35**
Dellow St. *E1* —7H **63**
Dell Rd. *Eps* —6C **130**
Dells Clo. *E4* —7J **9**
Dellwood Gdns. *Ilf* —3E **34**
Delmare Clo. *SW9* —4K **93**
Delme Cres. *SE3* —2K **97**
Delmey Clo. *Croy* —3F **135**
Deloraine Ho. *SE8* —1C **96**
Delorme St. *W6* —6F **75**
Delroy Ct. *N20* —7F **5**

Delta Bus. Pk. SW18 —4K **91**
(off Smugglers Way)
Delta Cen. *Wemb* —1F **57**
Delta Clo. *Wor Pk* —3B **130**
Delta Ct. *NW2* —2C **42**
Delta Est. *E2* —3G **63**
Delta Gro. *N'holt* —3B **54**
Delta Rd. *Wor Pk* —3A **130**
Delta St. *E2* —3G **63** (1K **145**)
De Luci Rd. *Eri* —5J **85**
De Lucy St. *SE2* —4B **84**
Delvan Clo. *SE18* —7E **82**
Delvers Mead. *Dag* —4J **53**
Delverton Rd. *SE17*
—5B **78** (6B **156**)
Delvino Rd. *SW6* —1J **91**
Demead Way. SE15 —7F **79**
(off Pentridge St.)
Demesne Rd. *Wall* —4H **133**
Demeta Clo. *Wemb* —3J **41**
De Montfort Pde. *SW16* —3J **109**
De Montfort Rd. *SW16* —2J **109**
De Morgan Rd. *SW6* —3K **91**
Dempster Clo. *Surb* —7C **118**
Dempster Rd. *SW18* —5A **92**
Denbar Pde. Romf —4J **37**
Denberry Dri. *Sidc* —3B **116**
Denbigh Clo. *NW10* —7A **42**
Denbigh Clo. *W11* —7H **59**
Denbigh Clo. *Chst* —6D **114**
Denbigh Clo. *S'hall* —6D **54**
Denbigh Clo. *Sutt* —5H **131**
Denbigh Ct. *E6* —3B **66**
Denbigh Ct. W7 —5K **55**
(off Copley Clo.)
Denbigh Gdns. *Rich* —5F **89**
Denbigh M. *SW1*
—4G **77** (4A **154**)
Denbigh Pl. *SW1*
—5G **77** (5A **154**)
Denbigh Rd. *E6* —3B **66**
Denbigh Rd. *W11* —7H **59**
Denbigh Rd. *W13* —7B **56**
Denbigh Rd. *Houn* —2F **87**
Denbigh Rd. *S'hall* —6D **54**
Denbigh St. *SW1*
—4G **77** (4A **154**)
Denbigh Ter. *W11* —7H **59**
Denbridge Rd. *Brom* —2D **128**
Denby Ct. *SE11*
—4K **77** (3H **155**)
Denchworth Ho. *SW9* —2A **94**
Den Clo. *Beck* —3F **127**
Dene Av. *Houn* —3D **86**
Dene Av. *Sidc* —7B **100**
Dene Clo. *SE4* —3A **96**
Dene Clo. *Brom* —1H **137**
Dene Clo. *Dart* —4K **117**
Dene Clo. *Wor Pk* —2B **130**
Dene Ct. *W5* —5C **56**
Dene Gdns. *Stan* —5H **11**
Denehurst Gdns. *NW4* —6E **26**
Denehurst Gdns. *W3* —1H **73**
Denehurst Gdns. *Rich* —4G **89**
Denehurst Gdns. *Twic* —7H **87**
Denehurst Gdns. *Wfd G* —4E **20**
Dene Rd. *N11* —1J **15**
Dene Rd. *Buck H* —1G **21**
Denesmead. *SE24* —5C **94**
Dene, The. *W13* —5B **56**
Dene, The. *Croy* —4K **135**
Dene, The. *Wemb* —4E **40**
Denewood. *New Bar* —5F **5**
Denewood Rd. *N6* —6D **28**
Denford St. *SE10* —5H **81**

Dengie Wlk. *N1* —1C **62**
(off Basire St.)
Denham Clo. *Well* —3C **100**
Denham Ct. SE26 —3H **111**
(off Kirkdale)
Denham Ct. S'hall —7G **55**
(off Baird Av.)
Denham Cres. *Mitc* —4D **122**
Denham Dri. *Ilf* —6G **35**
Denham Ho. W12 —7D **58**
(off White City Est.)
Denham Rd. *N20* —3J **15**
Denham Rd. *Felt* —7A **86**
Denham St. *SE10* —5J **81**
Denham Way. *Bark* —1J **67**
Denholme Rd. *W9* —3H **59**
Denison Clo. *N2* —3A **28**
Denison Rd. *SW19* —6B **108**
Denison Rd. *W5* —4C **56**
Deniston Av. *Bex* —1E **116**
Denis Way. *SW4* —3H **93**
Denleigh Gdns. *N21* —1F **17**
Denman Dri. *NW11* —5J **27**
Denman Dri. N. *NW11* —5J **27**
Denman Dri. S. *NW11* —5J **27**
Denman Pl. *W1* —1H **77** (2C **148**)
Denman Rd. *SE15* —1F **95**
Denman Av. *SW19* —7G **107**
Denman Ct. *Mord* —6J **121**
Denmark Gdns. *Cars* —3D **132**
Denmark Gro. *N1* —2A **62**
Denmark Hill. *SE5* —1D **94**
Denmark Hill Dri. *NW9* —4C **26**
Denmark Hill Est. *SE5* —4D **94**
Denmark Mans. *SE5* —2C **94**
Denmark Path. *SE25* —5H **125**
Denmark Pl. *WC2*
—6H **61** (7D **142**)
Denmark Rd. *N8* —4A **30**
Denmark Rd. *NW6* —2H **59**
(in two parts)
Denmark Rd. *SE5* —1C **94**
Denmark Rd. *SE25* —5G **125**
Denmark Rd. *SW19* —6F **107**
Denmark Rd. *W13* —7B **56**
Denmark Rd. *Brom* —1K **127**
Denmark Rd. *Cars* —3D **132**
Denmark Rd. *King T* —3E **118**
Denmark Rd. *Twic* —3H **103**
Denmark St. *E11* —3G **49**
Denmark St. *E13* —5K **65**
Denmark St. *N17* —1H **31**
Denmark St. *WC2*
—6H **61** (7D **142**)
Denmark Ter. *N2* —3D **28**
Denmark Wlk. *SE27* —4C **110**
Denmead Ho. SW15 —6B **90**
(off Highcliffe Dri.)
Denmead Rd. *Croy* —1B **134**
Denmore Ct. *Wall* —5F **133**
Dennan Rd. *Surb* —7F **119**
Denner Rd. *E4* —2H **19**
Denne Ter. *E8* —1F **63**
Dennett Rd. *Croy* —1A **134**
Dennetts Gro. *SE14* —1J **95**
Dennett's Rd. *SE14* —2K **95**
Denning Av. *Croy* —4A **134**
Denning Clo. *NW8*
—3A **60** (1A **140**)
Denning Clo. *Hamp* —5D **102**
Denning Rd. *NW3* —4B **44**
Dennington Clo. *E5* —2J **47**
Dennington Pk. Rd. *NW6*
—6J **43**

Dennings, The. *Wor Pk*
—2A **130**
Dennis Av. *Wemb* —5F **41**
Dennis Gdns. *Stan* —5H **11**
Dennis Ho. *Sutt* —4K **131**
Dennis La. *Stan* —3G **11**
Dennison Gro. *SW14* —3K **89**
Dennison Point. *E15* —7E **48**
Dennis Pde. *N14* —1C **16**
Dennis Pk. Cres. *SW20* —1G **121**
Dennis Reeve Clo. *Mitc* —1D **122**
Denny Clo. *E6* —5C **66**
Denny Cres. *SE11*
—5A **78** (5K **155**)
Denny Gdns. *Dag* —7C **52**
Denny Rd. *N9* —1C **18**
Denny St. *SE11* —5A **78** (5K **155**)
Den Rd. *Brom* —3F **127**
Densham Rd. *E15* —1G **65**
Densole Clo. *Beck* —1A **126**
Densworth Gro. *N9* —2D **18**
Denton. *NW1* —6E **44**
Denton Rd. *N8* —5K **29**
Denton Rd. *N18* —4K **17**
Denton Rd. *NW10* —7J **41**
Denton Rd. *Bex* —1K **117**
Denton Rd. *Twic* —6D **88**
Denton Rd. *Well* —7C **84**
Denton St. *SW18* —6K **91**
Denton Ter. *Bex* —2K **117**
Denton Way. *E5* —3K **47**
Dents Rd. *SW11* —6D **92**
Denver Clo. *Orp* —6J **129**
Denver Rd. *N16* —7E **30**
Denwood. *SE23* —3K **111**
Denyer St. *SW3* —4C **76** (4D **152**)
Denzil Rd. *NW10* —5B **42**
Deodara Clo. *N20* —3H **15**
Deodar Rd. *SW15* —4G **91**
Depot App. *NW2* —4F **43**
Depot Rd. *W12* —7E **58**
Depot Rd. *Houn* —3H **87**
Depot St. *SE5* —6D **78**
Deptford B'way. *SE8* —1C **96**
Deptford Chu. St. *SE8* —6C **80**
Deptford Ferry Rd. *E14* —4C **80**
Deptford Grn. *SE8* —6C **80**
Deptford High St. *SE8* —6C **80**
Deptford Pk. Bus. Cen. *SE8*
—5A **80**
Deptford Strand. *SE8* —4B **80**
Deptford Wharf. *SE8* —4B **80**
De Quincey M. *E16* —1J **83**
De Quincey Rd. *N17* —1D **30**
Derando Clo. *W12* —7D **58**
Derby Av. *N12* —5F **15**
Derby Av. *Romf* —6J **37**
Derby Est. *Houn* —4F **87**
Derby Ga. *SW1* —2J **77** (6E **148**)
Derby Hill. *SE23* —2J **111**
Derby Hill Cres. *SE23* —2J **111**
Derby Ho. *SE11* —4A **78** (3J **155**)
Derby Ho. *Pinn* —2B **22**
Derby Lodge. *N3* —2H **27**
Derby Rd. *E7* —7B **50**
Derby Rd. *E9* —1K **63**
Derby Rd. *E18* —1H **33**
Derby Rd. *N18* —5D **18**
Derby Rd. *SW14* —4H **89**
Derby Rd. *SW19* —7J **107**
Derby Rd. *Croy* —1B **134**
Derby Rd. *Enf* —5C **8**
Derby Rd. *Gnfd* —1F **55**

Derby Rd. *Houn* —4F **87**
Derby Rd. *Surb* —7G **119**
Derby Rd. *Sutt* —6H **131**
Derbyshire St. *E2* —3G **63**
Derby St. *W1* —1E **76** (5H **147**)
Dereham Ho. SE4 —4K **95**
(off Frendsbury Rd.)
Dereham Pl. *EC2*
—3E **62** (2H **145**)
Dereham Rd. *Bark* —5K **51**
Derek Av. *Wall* —4F **133**
Derek Av. *Wemb* —7H **41**
Derek Walcott Clo. *SE24* —5B **94**
Dericote St. *E8* —1H **63**
Derifall Clo. *E6* —5D **66**
Dering Pl. *Croy* —4C **134**
Dering Rd. *Croy* —4C **134**
Dering St. *W1* —6F **61** (1J **147**)
Dering Yd. *W1* —6F **61** (1H **147**)
Derinton Rd. *SW17* —4D **108**
Derley Rd. *S'hall* —3A **70**
Dermody Gdns. *SE13* —5F **97**
Dermody Rd. *SE13* —5F **97**
Deronda Est. *SW2* —1B **110**
Deronda Rd. *SE24* —1B **110**
Deroy Clo. *Cars* —6D **132**
Derrick Gdns. *SE7* —4A **82**
Derrick Rd. *Beck* —3B **126**
Derry Rd. *Croy* —3J **133**
Derry St. *W8* —2K **75**
Dersingham Av. *E12* —4D **50**
Dersingham Rd. *NW2* —3G **43**
Derwent Av. *N18* —5J **17**
Derwent Av. *NW7* —6E **12**
Derwent Av. *NW9* —5A **26**
Derwent Av. *SW15* —4A **106**
Derwent Av. *Barn* —1J **15**
Derwent Cres. *N20* —3F **15**
Derwent Cres. *Bexh* —2G **101**
Derwent Cres. *Stan* —2C **24**
Derwent Dri. *Orp* —7H **129**
Derwent Gdns. *Ilf* —4C **34**
Derwent Gdns. *Wemb* —7C **24**
Derwent Gro. *SE22* —4F **95**
Derwent Ho. SE20 —2H **125**
(off Derwent Rd.)
Derwent Lodge. *Iswth* —2H **87**
Derwent Lodge. *Wor Pk* —2D **130**
Derwent Rise. *NW9* —6A **26**
Derwent Rd. *N13* —4E **16**
Derwent Rd. *SE20* —2G **125**
Derwent Rd. *SW20* —5F **121**
Derwent Rd. *W5* —3C **72**
Derwent Rd. *S'hall* —6E **54**
Derwent Rd. *Twic* —6F **87**
Derwent St. *SE10* —5G **81**
Derwent Wlk. *Wall* —7F **133**
Derwentwater Rd. *W3* —1J **73**
Derwent Yd. W5 —3C **72**
(off Derwent Rd.)
Desborough Clo. *W2* —5K **59**
(off Bourne Ter.)
Desborough Ho. *W14* —6H **75**
(off N. End Rd.)
Desenfans Rd. *SE21* —6E **94**
Desford Rd. *E16* —4G **65**
Desmond Ho. *Barn* —6H **5**
Desmond St. *SE14* —7A **80**
Desmond Tutu Ho. *Wemb* —7F **25**
Despard Rd. *N19* —1G **45**
Detling Ho. *Brom* —5J **113**
Detling Rd. *Eri* —7K **85**
Detmold Rd. *E5* —2J **47**
Devalls Clo. *E6* —7F **67**
Devana End. *Cars* —3D **132**

Devas Rd. *SW20* —1E **120**
Devas St. *E3* —4D **64**
Devenay Rd. *E15* —7H **49**
Devenish Rd. *SE2* —2A **84**
Deventer Cres. *SE22* —5E **94**
De Vere Gdns. *W8* —2A **76**
De Vere Gdns. *Ilf* —2D **50**
Deverell St. *SE1*
—3D **78** (2E **156**)
De Vere M. W8 —3A **76**
(off De Vere Gdns.)
Devereux Ct. *WC2*
—6A **62** (1J **149**)
Devereux La. *SW13* —7D **74**
Devereux Rd. *SW11* —6D **92**
Deveron Way. *Romf* —1K **37**
Devey Clo. *King T* —7A **106**
Devon Av. *Twic* —1G **103**
Devon Clo. *N17* —3F **31**
Devon Clo. *Buck H* —2E **20**
Devon Clo. *Gnfd* —1C **56**
Devon Ct. W7 —5K **55**
(off Copley Clo.)
Devon Ct. *Hamp* —7E **102**
Devoncroft Gdns. *Twic* —7A **88**
Devon Gdns. *N4* —6B **30**
Devonhurst Pl. *W4* —5K **73**
Devonia Rd. *N1* —2B **62**
Devonia Gdns. *N18* —6H **17**
Devonport. *W2* —6C **60** (7C **140**)
Devonport Gdns. *Ilf* —6D **34**
Devonport M. *W12* —2D **74**
Devonport Rd. *W12* —1D **74**
Devonport St. *E1* —6K **63**
Devon Rise. *N2* —4B **28**
Devon Rd. *Bark* —1J **67**
Devon Rd. *Sutt* —7G **131**
Devons Est. *E3* —3D **64**
Devonshire Av. *Sutt* —7A **132**
Devonshire Clo. *E15* —4H **49**
Devonshire Clo. *N13* —3F **17**
Devonshire Clo. *W1*
—5F **61** (5J **141**)
Devonshire Ct. Pinn —1D **22**
(off Devonshire Rd.)
Devonshire Cres. *NW7* —7A **14**
Devonshire Dri. *SE10* —7D **80**
Devonshire Gdns. *N17* —6H **17**
Devonshire Gdns. *N21* —7H **7**
Devonshire Gdns. *W4* —7J **73**
Devonshire Gro. *SE15* —6H **79**
Devonshire Hill La. *N17* —6H **17**
Devonshire Ho. *Sutt* —7A **132**
Devonshire Ho. Bus. Cen. *Brom*
—4K **127**
Devonshire M. *N13* —4F **17**
Devonshire M. *W4* —5A **74**
Devonshire M. *W1*
—5F **61** (5J **141**)
Devonshire M. S. *W1*
—5F **61** (5J **141**)
Devonshire M. W. *W1*
—4E **60** (4H **141**)
Devonshire Pas. *W4* —5A **74**
Devonshire Pl. *NW2* —3J **43**
Devonshire Pl. *W1*
—4E **60** (4H **141**)
Devonshire Pl. *W4* —5A **74**
Devonshire Pl. *W8* —3K **75**
Devonshire Pl. M. *W1*
—5E **60** (4H **141**)
Devonshire Rd. *E15* —4G **49**
Devonshire Rd. *E16* —6K **65**
Devonshire Rd. *E17* —6C **32**
Devonshire Rd. *N9* —1D **18**

Devonshire Rd. *N13* —4E **16**
Devonshire Rd. *N17* —6H **17**
Devonshire Rd. *NW7* —7A **14**
Devonshire Rd. *SE9* —2C **114**
Devonshire Rd. *SE23* —1J **111**
Devonshire Rd. *SW19* —7C **108**
Devonshire Rd. *W4* —5A **74**
Devonshire Rd. *W5* —3C **72**
Devonshire Rd. *Bexh* —4E **100**
Devonshire Rd. *Cars* —4E **132**
Devonshire Rd. *Croy* —7D **124**
Devonshire Rd. *Eastc* —6A **22**
Devonshire Rd. *Felt* —3C **102**
Devonshire Rd. *Harr* —6H **23**
Devonshire Rd. *Ilf* —1J **35**
Devonshire Rd. *Orp* —7K **129**
Devonshire Rd. *Pinn* —1D **22**
Devonshire Rd. *S'hall* —6E **54**
Devonshire Rd. *Sutt* —7A **132**
Devonshire Row. *EC2*
—5E **62** (6H **145**)
Devonshire Row M. *W1*
—4F **61** (4K **141**)
Devonshire Sq. *EC2*
—6E **62** (6H **145**)
Devonshire Sq. *Brom* —4K **127**
Devonshire St. *W1*
—5E **60** (5H **141**)
Devonshire St. *W4*
—5E **60** (5H **141**)
Devonshire Ter. *W2* —6A **60**
Devonshire Way. *Croy* —2A **136**
Devonshire Way. *Hayes* —6A **54**
Devons Rd. *E3* —5C **64**
Devon St. *SE15* —6H **79**
Devon Waye. *Houn* —7D **70**
De Walden St. *W1*
—5E **60** (6H **141**)
Dewar St. *SE15* —3G **95**
Dewberry Gdns. *E6* —5C **66**
Dewberry St. *E14* —5E **64**
Dewey Rd. *N1* —2A **62**
Dewey Rd. *Dag* —6H **53**
Dewey St. *SW17* —5D **108**
Dewhurst Rd. *W14* —3F **75**
Dewsbury Clo. *Pinn* —6C **22**
Dewsbury Ct. *W4* —4J **73**
Dewsbury Gdns. *Wor Pk*
—3C **130**
Dewsbury Rd. *NW10* —5C **42**
Dewsbury Ter. *NW1* —1F **61**
Dexter Ho. *Eri* —3E **84**
(off Kale Rd.)
Dexter Rd. *Barn* —6A **4**
Deynecourt Gdns. *E11* —4A **34**
Deyncourt Rd. *N17* —1C **30**
D'Eynsford Rd. *SE5* —1D **94**
Diadem Ct. *W1* —6H **61** (7C **142**)
Dial Wlk., The. *W8* —2K **75**
(off Broad Wlk., The)
Diameter Rd. *Orp* —6G **129**
Diamond Clo. *Dag* —1C **52**
Diamond St. *SW17* —3C **108**
Diamond Rd. *Ruis* —4B **38**
Diamond St. *SE15* —7E **78**
Diamond Ter. *SE10* —1E **96**
Diana Clo. *E18* —1K **33**
Diana Ho. *SW13* —1B **90**
Diana Pl. *NW1* —4F **61** (3K **141**)
Diana Rd. *E17* —3B **32**
Dianne Way. *Barn* —4H **5**
Dianthus Clo. *SE2* —5B **84**
Dibden Ho. *SE5* —7E **78**
Dibden St. *N1* —1C **62**
Diblin Clo. *Sutt* —3J **131**
Dibdin Rd. *Sutt* —3J **131**

Dibdin Row. *SE1*
—3A 78 (1K 155)
Dicey Av. *NW2* —4E 42
Dickens Av. *N3* —1A 28
Dickens Clo. *Eri* —7H 85
Dickens Clo. *Rich* —2E 104
Dickens Ct. E11 —4J 33
(off Makepiece Rd.)
Dickens Dri. *Chst* —6G 115
Dickens Est. *SE16* —3G 79
Dickens Ho. *SE17*
—5B 78 (6B 156)
Dickens Ho. *WC1*
—4J 61 (3E 142)
Dickens La. *N18* —5K 17
Dickenson Clo. *N9* —1B 18
Dickenson Ho. *N8* —6K 29
Dickenson Rd. *N8* —7J 29
Dickenson Rd. *Felt* —5B 102
Dickensons La. *SE25* —6G 125
Dickensons Pl. *SE25* —6G 125
Dickenson St. *NW5* —6E 44
Dickens Rise. *Chig* —3K 21
Dickens Rd. *E6* —2B 66
Dickens Sq. *SE1*
—3C 78 (1D 156)
Dickens St. *SW8* —2F 93
Dickerage La. *N Mald* —3J 119
Dickerage Rd. *King T & N Mald*
—1J 119
Dickson Fold. *Pinn* —4B 22
Dickson Rd. *SE9* —3C 98
Didsbury Clo. *E6* —1D 66
Digby Cres. *N4* —2C 46
Digby Gdns. *Dag* —1G 69
Digby Mans. W6 —5D 74
(off Hammersmith Bri. Rd.)
Digby Pl. *Croy* —3F 135
Digby Rd. *E9* —6K 47
Digby Rd. *Bark* —7K 51
Digby St. *E2* —3J 63
Diggon St. *E1* —5K 63
Dighton Ct. *SE5*
—6C 78 (7C 156)
Dighton Rd. *SW18* —5A 92
Dignum St. *N1* —2A 62
Digswell St. *N7* —6A 46
Dilhorne Clo. *SE12* —3K 113
Dilke St. *SW3* —6D 76 (7F 153)
Dilloway La. *S'hall* —2C 70
Dillwyn Clo. *SE26* —4A 112
Dilston Clo. *N'holt* —3A 54
Dilston Gro. *SE16* —4J 79
Dilton Gdns. *SW15* —1C 106
Dilwyn Ct. *E17* —2A 32
Dimes Pl. *W6* —4D 74
Dimmock Dri. *Gnfd* —5H 39
Dimond Clo. *E7* —4J 49
Dimsdale Dri. *NW9* —1J 41
Dimsdale Dri. *Enf* —6B 8
Dimsdale Wlk. *E13* —2G 64
Dimson Cres. *E3* —3C 64
Dingle Gdns. *E14* —7C 64
Dingles Ct. *Pinn* —1B 22
Difigley. *Sidc* —3B 116
Dingley La. *SW16* —2H 109
Dingley Pl. *EC1* —3C 62 (2D 144)
Dingley Rd. *EC1*
—3C 62 (2C 144)
Dingwall Av. *Croy* —2C 134
Dingwall Gdns. *NW11* —6J 27
Dingwall Rd. *SW18* —7A 92
Dingwall Rd. *Cars* —7D 132
Dingwall Rd. *Croy* —1D 134
Dinmont Est. *E2* —2G 63

Dinmont St. *E2* —2H 63
Dinsdale Gdns. *SE25* —5E 124
Dinsdale Gdns. *New Bar* —5E 4
Dinsdale Rd. *SE3* —6H 81
Dinsmore Rd. *SW12* —7F 93
Dinton Rd. *SW19* —6B 108
Dinton Rd. *King T* —7F 105
Diploma Av. *N2* —4C 28
Diploma Ct. *N2* —4C 28
Dirleton Rd. *E15* —1H 65
Disbrowe Rd. *W6* —6G 75
Discovery Wlk. *E1* —7H 63
Dishforth La. *NW9* —7F 13
Disley Ct. S'hall —6F 55
(off Howard Rd.)
Disney Pl. *SE1* —2C 78 (6D 150)
Disney St. *SE1* —2C 78 (6D 150)
Dison Clo. *Enf* —1E 8
Disraeli Clo. *SE28* —1C 84
Disraeli Clo. *W4* —3K 73
Disraeli Gdns. *SW15* —4H 91
Disraeli Rd. *E7* —6J 49
Disraeli Rd. *NW10* —2K 57
Disraeli Rd. *SW15* —4G 91
Disraeli Rd. *W5* —1D 72
Diss St. *E2* —3F 63 (1J 145)
Distaff La. *EC4* —7C 62 (2C 150)
Distillery La. *W6* —5E 74
Distillery Rd. *W6* —5E 74
Distillery Wlk. *Bren* —6E 72
Distin St. *SE11* —4A 78 (4J 155)
District Rd. *Wemb* —5B 40
Ditch All. *SE10* —2D 96
Ditchburn St. *E14* —7E 64
Ditchfield Rd. *Hayes* —4C 54
Ditchley Ct. W7 —5K 55
(off Templeman Rd.)
Dittisham Rd. *SE9* —4C 114
Ditton Clo. *Th Dit* —7A 118
Ditton Lawn. *Th Dit* —7A 118
Ditton Pl. *SE20* —1H 125
Ditton Reach. *Th Dit* —6B 118
Ditton Rd. *Bexh* —5D 100
Ditton Rd. *S'hall* —5D 70
Ditton Rd. *Surb* —7E 118
Divis Way. SW15 —6D 90
(off Dover Pk. Dri.)
Dixon Clark Ct. *N1* —6B 46
Dixon Clo. *E6* —6D 66
Dixon Pl. *W Wick* —1D 136
Dixon Rd. *SE14* —1A 96
Dixon Rd. *SE25* —3E 124
Dixon's All. *SE16* —2H 79
Dobbin Clo. *Harr* —2A 24
Dobell Rd. *SE9* —5D 98
Dobree Av. *NW10* —7D 42
Dobson Clo. *NW6* —7B 44
Dobson Ho. SE5 —7D 78
(off Edmund St.)
Dockers Tanner Rd. *E14* —4C 80
Dockhead. *SE1* —2F 79 (7K 151)
Dock Hill Av. *SE16* —1K 79
Docklands Equestrian Cen., The.
—6E 66
Dockland St. *E16* —1E 82
Dockley Rd. SE16 —3G 79
Dockley Rd. Ind. Est. SE16
(off Dockley Rd.) —3G 79
Dock Rd. *E16* —7H 65
Dock Rd. *Bren* —7D 72
Dock St. *E1* —7G 63

Doctor Johnson Av. *SW17*
—3F 109
Doctors Clo. *SE26* —5J 111
Docwra's Bldgs. *N1* —6E 46
Dodbrooke Rd. *SE27* —3A 110
Doddington Gro. *SE17*
—6B 78 (7A 156)
Doddington Pl. *SE17*
—6B 78 (7A 156)
Dodsley Pl. *N9* —3D 18
Dodson St. *SE1* —2A 78 (7K 149)
Dod St. *E14* —6C 64
Doebury Wlk. SE18 —7A 84
(off Prestwood Clo.)
Doel Clo. *SW19* —7A 108
Dog and Duck Yd. *WC1*
—5K 61 (5G 143)
Doggett Rd. *SE6* —7C 96
Doggetts Courts. *Barn* —5H 5
Dog Kennel Hill. *SE22* —3E 94
Dog Kennel Hill Est. *SE22*
—3E 94
Dog La. *NW10* —4A 42
Doherty Rd. *E13* —4J 65
Dokal Ind. Est. *S'hall* —3C 70
Dolben Ct. *SE8* —4B 80
Dolben St. *SE1* —1B 78 (5A 150)
(in two parts)
Dolby Rd. *SW6* —2H 91
Dolland Ho. *SE11*
—5K 77 (6H 155)
Dolland St. *SE11*
—5K 77 (6H 155)
Dollis Av. *N3* —1H 27
Dollis Brook Wlk. *Barn* —6B 4
Dollis Cres. *Ruis* —1A 38
Dollis Hill Av. *NW2* —3D 42
Dollis Hill Est. *NW2* —3C 42
Dollis Hill La. *NW2* —4A 42
Dollis M. *N3* —1J 27
Dollis Pk. *N3* —1H 27
Dollis Rd. *NW7 & N3* —7B 14
Dollis Valley Way. *Barn* —6C 4
Dolman Clo. *N3* —1A 28
Dolman Rd. *W4* —4K 73
Dolman St. *SW4* —4K 93
Dolphin Clo. *SE16* —2K 79
Dolphin Clo. *SE28* —6D 68
Dolphin Clo. *Surb* —5D 118
Dolphin Ct. *NW11* —6G 27
Dolphin Est. SE8 —6B 80
(off Wotton Rd.)
Dolphin La. *E14* —7D 64
Dolphin Rd. *N'holt* —2D 54
Dolphin Sq. *SW1*
—5G 77 (6B 154)
Dolphin Sq. *W4* —7A 74
Dolphin St. *King T* —2E 118
Dolphin Tower. *SE8 —6B 80*
(off Abinger Gro.)
Dombey St. *WC1*
—5K 61 (5G 143)
Dome Hill Pk. *SE26* —4F 111
Domett Clo. *SE5* —4D 94
Domfe Pl. *E5* —4J 47
Domingo St. *EC1*
—4C 62 (3C 144)
Dominica Clo. *E6* —2B 66
Dominion Bus. Pk. *N9* —2E 18
Dominion Cen., The. *S'hall*
—2C 70
Dominion Pde. *Harr* —5K 23
Dominion Rd. *Croy* —7F 125
Dominion Rd. *S'hall* —2C 70

Dominion St. *EC2*
—5D 62 (5F 145)
Domitian Pl. *Enf* —5A 8
Domonic Dri. *SE9* —4F 115
Domville Clo. *N20* —2G 15
Domville Gro. *SE5*
—5F 79 (6J 157)
Donald Dri. *Romf* —5C 36
Donald Rd. *E13* —1K 65
Donald Rd. *Croy* —7K 123
Donaldson Rd. *NW6* —1H 59
Donaldson Rd. *SE18* —1E 98
Doncaster Dri. *N'holt* —5D 38
Doncaster Gdns. *N4* —6C 30
Doncaster Gdns. *N'holt* —5D 38
Doncaster Rd. *N9* —7C 8
Donegal St. *N1* —2K 61
Doneraile St. *SW6* —2F 91
Dongola Rd. *E13* —3K 65
Dongola Rd. *N17* —3E 30
Dongola Rd. *W. E13* —3K 65
Donington Av. *Ilf* —5G 35
Donkey All. *SE22* —7G 95
Donkey La. *Enf* —2B 8
Donne Ct. *SE24* —6C 94
Donnefield Av. *Edgw* —7K 11
Donnelly Ct. *SW6* —7G 75
(off Dawes Rd.)
Donne Pl. *SW3* —4C 76 (3D 152)
Donne Pl. *Mitc* —4F 123
Donne Rd. *Dag* —2C 52
Donnington Rd. *NW10* —7D 42
Donnington Rd. *Harr* —5D 24
Donnington Rd. *Wor Pk* —2C 130
Donnybrook Rd. *SW16* —7G 109
Donovan Av. *N10* —2F 29
Donovan Ct. *NW10* —7J 41
Don Phelan Clo. *SE5* —1D 94
Doone Clo. *Tedd* —6A 104
Doon St. *SE1* —1A 78 (5J 149)
Doral Way. *Cars* —5D 132
Doran Ct. *E6* —2D 66
Doran Gro. *SE18* —7J 83
Doran Mnr. N2 —5D 28
(off Gt. North Rd.)
Doran Wlk. *E15* —7E 48
Dora Rd. *SW19* —5J 107
Dora St. *E14* —6B 64
Dorchester Av. *N13* —4H 17
Dorchester Av. *Bex* —1D 116
Dorchester Av. *Harr* —6G 23
Dorchester Clo. *N'holt* —5F 39
Dorchester Clo. *Orp* —7B 116
Dorchester Ct. *E18* —1H 33
(off Buckingham Rd.)
Dorchester Ct. *N10* —3F 29
Dorchester Ct. *N14* —7A 6
Dorchester Ct. *NW2* —3F 43
Dorchester Ct. *SE24* —4C 94
Dorchester Ct. *SE24* —5C 94
Dorchester Gdns. *E4* —4H 19
Dorchester Gdns. *NW11* —4J 27
Dorchester Gro. *W4* —5A 74
Dorchester M. *N Mald* —4K 119
Dorchester M. *Twic* —6D 88
Dorchester Rd. *Mord* —7K 121
Dorchester Rd. *N'holt* —5F 39
Dorchester Rd. *Wor Pk* —1E 130
Dorchester Way. *Harr* —6F 25
Dorchester Waye. *Hayes* —6A 54
(in two parts)
Dorcis Av. *Bexh* —2E 100
Dordrecht Rd. *W3* —1A 74
Dore Av. *E12* —5E 50
Doreen Av. *NW9* —1K 41

Doreen Capstan Ho. *E11* —3G 49
Dore Gdns. *Mord* —7K 121
Dorell Clo. *S'hall* —5D 54
Doria Rd. *SW6* —2H 91
Doric Way. *NW1*
—3H 61 (1C 142)
Dorien Rd. *SW20* —2F 121
Dorinda St. *N7* —6A 46
Doris Av. *Eri* —1J 101
Doris Emmerton Ct. *SW11*
—4A 92
Doris Rd. *E7* —7J 49
Dorit M. *N18* —5K 17
Dorking Clo. *SE8* —6B 80
Dorking Clo. *Wor Pk* —2F 131
Dorking Ct. N17 —1G 31
(off Hampden La.)
Dorking Ho. *SE1*
—3D 78 (1F 157)
Dorlcote Rd. *SW18* —7C 92
Dorman Pl. *N9* —2B 18
Dorman Wlk. *NW10* —5K 41
Dorman Way. *NW8* —1B 60
Dorma Trad. Pk. *E10* —1K 47
Dormay St. *SW18* —5K 91
Dormer Clo. *E15* —6H 49
Dormer Clo. *Barn* —5A 4
Dormer's Av. *S'hall* —6E 54
Dormers Rise. *S'hall* —6F 55
Dormer's Wells La. *S'hall* —6E 54
Dornberg Clo. *SE3* —7J 81
Dornberg Rd. *SE3* —7R 81
Dorncliffe Rd. *SW6* —2G 91
Dorney Rise. *Orp* —4K 129
Dorney Way. *Houn* —5C 86
Dornfell St. *NW6* —5H 43
Dornton Rd. *SW12* —2F 109
Dornton Rd. *S Croy* —6D 134
Dorothy Av. *Wemb* —7E 40
Dorothy Evans Clo. *Bexh*
—4H 101
Dorothy Gdns. *Dag* —4B 52
Dorothy Pettingell Ho. Sutt
(off Angel Hill) —3K 131
Dorothy Rd. *SW11* —3D 92
Dorrell Pl. *SW9* —4A 94
Dorrien Wlk. *SW16* —2H 109
Dorrington Ct. *SE19* —2E 124
Dorrington St. *EC1*
—5A 62 (5J 143)
Dorris St. *SE1* —2C 78 (6D 150)
Dorrit Way. *Chst* —6G 115
Dorryn Ct. *SE26* —5K 111
Dors Clo. *NW9* —1K 41
Dorset Av. *Romf* —3K 37
Dorset Av. *S'hall* —4E 70
Dorset Av. *Well* —4K 99
Dorset Bldgs. *EC4*
—6B 62 (1A 150)
Dorset Clo. *NW1*
—5D 60 (5E 140)
Dorset Ct. W7 —5K 55
(off Copley Clo.)
Dorset Dri. *Edgw* —6A 12
Dorset Gdns. *Mitc* —4K 123
Dorset M. *N3* —1J 27
Dorset M. *SW1* —3F 77 (1J 153)
Dorset Pl. *E15* —6F 49
Dorset Rise. *EC4*
—6B 62 (1A 150)
Dorset Rd. *E7* —7A 50
Dorset Rd. *N15* —4D 30
Dorset Rd. *N22* —1J 29
Dorset Rd. *SE9* —2C 114
Dorset Rd. *SW8* —7J 77

Dorset Rd. SW19 —1J 121
Dorset Rd. W5 —3C 72
Dorset Rd. Beck —3K 125
Dorset Rd. Harr —6G 23
Dorset Rd. Mitc —2C 122
Dorset Sq. NW1
—4D 60 (4E 140)
Dorset St. W1 —5D 60 (6F 141)
Dorset Way. Twic —1H 103
Dorset Waye. Houn —7D 70
Dorville Cres. W6 —3D 74
Dorville Rd. SE12 —5H 97
Dothill Rd. SE18 —7G 83
Douai Gro. Hamp —7G 103
Doughty M. WC1
—4K 61 (4G 143)
Doughty St. WC1
—4K 61 (3G 143)
Douglas Av. E17 —1B 32
Douglas Av. N Mald —4D 120
Douglas Av. Wemb —7E 40
Douglas Clo. Stan —5F 11
Douglas Clo. Wall —6J 133
Douglas Cres. Hayes —4A 54
Douglas Dri. Croy —3C 136
Douglas Est. N1 —6C 46
Douglas Ho. Surb —7F 119
Douglas Johnston Ho. SW6
(off Clem Attlee Ct.) —6H 75
Douglas Mans. Houn —3F 87
Douglas M. NW2 —3G 43
Douglas Pl. E14 —4E 80
Douglas Rd. E4 —1B 20
Douglas Rd. E16 —5J 63
Douglas Rd. N1 —7C 46
Douglas Rd. N22 —1A 30
Douglas Rd. NW6 —1H 59
Douglas Rd. Houn —3F 87
Douglas Rd. Ilf —7A 36
Douglas Rd. King T —2H 119
Douglas Rd. Surb —7F 119
Douglas Rd. Well —1B 100
Douglas Rd. S. N1 —6C 46
Douglas Robinson Ct. SW16
—7J 109
Douglas Sq. Mord —6J 121
Douglas St. SW1
—4H 77 (4C 154)
Douglas Ter. E17 —1B 32
Douglas Waite Ho. NW6 —7K 43
Douglas Way. SE8 —7B 80
(in two parts)
Doulton M. NW6 —6K 43
Dounesforth Gdns. SW18
—1K 107
Douro Pl. W8 —3K 75
Douro St. E3 —2C 64
Douthwaite Sq. E1 —1G 79
Dove App. E6 —5C 66
Dove Clo. N'holt —4B 54
Dove Commercial Cen. NW5
—5G 45
Dovecot Clo. Pinn —5A 22
Dovecote Av. N22 —3A 30
Dovecote Gdns. SW14 —3K 89
Dove Ct. EC2 —6D 62 (1E 150)
Dovedale Av. Harr —6C 24
Dovedale Av. Ilf —2E 34
Dovedale Clo. Well —2A 100
Dovedale Rise. Mitc —7D 108
Dovedale Rd. SE22 —5H 95
Dovedon Clo. N14 —2D 16
Dovehouse Ct. N'holt —3B 54
(off Kittiwake Rd.)
Dove Ho. Gdns. E4 —2H 19

Dovehouse Mead. Bark —2H 67
Dovehouse St. SW3
—5B 76 (5B 152)
Dove M. SW5 —4A 76
Dove Pk. Pinn —1E 22
Dover Clo. NW2 —2F 43
Dover Clo. Romf —2J 37
Dover Ct. W5 —4D 56
Dovercourt Av. T Hth —5A 124
Dovercourt Est. N1 —6D 46
Dovercourt Gdns. Stan —5K 11
Dovercourt La. Sutt —3A 132
Dovercourt Rd. SE22 —6E 94
Doverfield Rd. SW2 —7J 93
Dover Flats. SE1
—4E 78 (4H 157)
Dover Gdns. Cars —3D 132
Dover Ho. SE15 —6J 79
Dover Ho. Rd. SW15 —4C 90
Doveridge Gdns. N13 —4G 17
Dove Rd. N1 —6D 46
Dove Row. E2 —1G 63
Dover Pk. Dri. SW15 —6D 90
Dover Patrol. SE3 —2K 97
Dover Rd. E12 —2A 50
Dover Rd. N9 —2D 18
Dover Rd. SE19 —6D 110
Dover Rd. Romf —6E 36
Dover St. W1 —7F 61 (3K 147)
Dover Yd. W1 —1G 77 (4A 148)
Doves Clo. Brom —2C 138
Doves Yd. N1 —1A 62
Dovet Ct. SW8 —1K 93
Doveton Rd. S Croy —5D 134
Doveton St. E1 —4J 63
Dove Wlk. SW1 —5E 76 (5G 153)
Dowanhill Rd. SE6 —1F 113
Dowdeswell Clo. SW15 —4A 90
Dowding Ho. N6 —7E 28
(off Hillcrest)
Dowding Pl. Stan —6F 11
Dowend Ct. SE15 —6E 78
(off Longhope Clo.)
Dower Av. Wall —7F 133
Dowes Ho. SW16 —3J 109
Dowgate Hill. EC4
—7D 62 (2E 150)
Dowland St. W10 —3G 59
Dowlas St. SE5 —7E 78
Dowler Ho. E1 —6G 63
(off Burslem St.)
Dowling Ho. Belv —3E 84
Dowman Clo. SW19 —1K 121
Downage. NW4 —3E 26
Downalong. Bush —1C 10
Downbank Av. Bexh —1H 101
Down Barns Rd. Ruis —3B 38
Downbury M. SW18 —5J 91
Down Clo. N'holt —2A 54
Downderry Rd. Brom —3F 113
Downe Rd. Well —7C 84
Down End. SE18 —7F 83
Downe Rd. Kes —7B 138
Downe Rd. Mitc —2D 122
Downer's Cottage. SW4 —4G 93
Downes Clo. Twic —6B 88
Downes Ct. N21 —1F 17
Downes Pl. SE15 —6G 79
Downe Ter. Rich —6E 88
Downfield. Wor Pk —1B 130
Downfield Clo. W9 —4K 59
Down Hall Rd. King T —1D 118
Downham Clo. Romf —1G 37
Downham Enterprise Cen. SE6
—2H 113

Downham La. Brom —5F 113
Downham Rd. N1 —7D 46
Downham Way. Brom —5F 113
Downhills Av. N17 —3D 30
Downhills Pk. Rd. N17 —3C 30
Downhills Way. N17 —3C 30
Downhurst Av. NW7 —5E 12
Downhurst Ct. NW4 —3E 26
Downing Clo. Harr —3G 23
Downing Dri. Gnfd —1H 55
Downing Rd. Dag —7F 53
Downings. E6 —6E 66
Downing St. SW1
—2J 77 (6E 148)
Downland Clo. N20 —1F 15
Downleys Clo. SE9 —2C 114
Downman Rd. SE9 —3C 98
Down Pl. W6 —4D 74
Down Rd. Tedd —6B 104
Downs Av. Chst —5D 114
Downs Av. Pinn —6C 22
Downsbridge Rd. Beck —1F 127
Downsell Rd. E15 —4E 48
Downsfield Rd. E17 —6A 32
Downshall Av. Ilf —6J 35
Downs Hill. Beck —7F 113
Downshire Hill. NW3 —4B 44
Downside. Twic —3K 103
Downside Clo. SW19 —6A 108
Downside Cres. NW3 —5C 44
Downside Cres. W13 —4A 56
Downside Rd. Sutt —6B 132
Downside Wlk. N'holt —3D 54
Downs La. E5 —4G 47
Downs Pk. Rd. E8 & E5 —5F 47
Downs Rd. E5 —4G 47
Downs Rd. Beck —2D 126
Downs Rd. Enf —4K 7
Downs Rd. T Hth —1C 124
Downs, The. SW20 —7F 107
Down St. W1 —1F 77 (5J 147)
Downs View. Iswth —1K 87
Downsview Gdns. SE19 —7B 110
Downsview Rd. SE19 —7C 110
Downsway, The. Sutt —7A 132
Downton Av. SW2 —2J 109
Downtown Rd. SE16 —2A 80
Downway. N12 —7H 15
Down Way. N'holt —3A 54
Dowrey St. N1 —1A 62
Dowsett Rd. N17 —2F 31
Dowson Clo. SE5 —4D 94
Dowson Ct. SE13 —3F 97
Doyce St. SE1 —2C 78 (6C 150)
Doyle Gdns. NW10 —1C 58
Doyle Rd. SE25 —4G 125
D'Oyley St. SW1
—4E 76 (3G 153)
Doynton St. N19 —2F 45
Draco Ga. SW15 —3E 90
Draco St. SE17 —6C 78 (7C 156)
Dragmire La. Mitc —4E 122
Dragonfly Clo. E13 —3K 65
Dragon Yd. WC1
—6J 61 (7F 143)
Dragoon Rd. SE8 —5B 80
Dragor Rd. NW10 —4J 57
Drake Clo. SE16 —2K 79
Drake Cres. SE28 —6C 68
Drakefell Rd. SE14 & SE4
—2K 95
Drakefield Rd. SW17 —3E 108
Drakeley Ct. N5 —4B 46
Drake Rd. SE4 —3C 96
Drake Rd. Croy —7K 123

Drake Rd. Harr —2D 38
Drake Rd. Mitc —6E 122
Drakes Ct. SE23 —1J 111
Drakes Courtyard. NW6 —7H 43
Drake St. WC1 —5K 61 (6G 143)
Drake St. Enf —1J 7
Drakes Wlk. E6 —1D 66
(in two parts)
Drakewood Rd. SW16 —7H 109
Draper Clo. Belv —4F 85
Draper Ct. Brom —4C 128
Draper Ho. SE1 —4C 78 (3C 156)
Draper Pl. N1 —1B 62
(off Dagmar Ter.)
Drapers' Cottage Homes. NW7
—4H 13
Draper's Gdns. EC2
—6D 62 (7F 145)
Drapers Rd. E15 —4F 49
Drapers Rd. N17 —3F 31
Drapers Rd. Enf —2G 7
Drappers Way. SE16 —4G 79
Drawdock Rd. SE10 —2F 81
Drawell Clo. SE18 —5J 83
Drax Av. SW20 —7C 106
Draxmont App. SW19 —6G 107
Draycot Rd. E11 —6K 33
Draycott Av. SW3
—4C 76 (3D 152)
Draycott Av. Harr —6B 24
Draycott Clo. Harr —6B 24
Draycott Pl. SW3
—4D 76 (4E 152)
Draycott Ter. SW3
—4D 76 (4F 153)
Dray Ct. Wor Pk —2C 130
Drayford Clo. W9 —4H 59
Dray Gdns. SW2 —5K 93
Draymans Way. Iswth —3K 87
Drayson M. W8 —2J 75
Drayton Av. W13 —7A 56
Drayton Bri. Rd. W7 & W13
—7K 55
Drayton Clo. Houn —5D 86
Drayton Clo. Ilf —1H 51
Drayton Gdns. N21 —7G 7
Drayton Gdns. SW10 —5A 76
Drayton Gdns. W13 —7A 56
Drayton Grn. W13 —7A 56
Drayton Grn. Rd. W13 —7B 56
Drayton Gro. W13 —7A 56
Drayton Ho. E11 —1F 49
Drayton Pk. N5 —4A 46
Drayton Pk. M. N5 —5A 46
Drayton Rd. E11 —1F 49
Drayton Rd. N17 —2E 30
Drayton Rd. NW10 —1B 58
Drayton Rd. W13 —6A 56
Drayton Rd. Croy —2B 134
Drayton Waye. Harr —6B 24
Dreadnought St. SE10 —3G 81
Dresden Clo. NW6 —6K 43
Dresden Rd. N19 —1G 45
Dressington Av. SE4 —6C 96
Drew Av. NW7 —6B 14
Drewery Ct. SE3 —3G 97
Drewett Ho. E1 —6G 63
(off Christian St.)
Drew Gdns. Gnfd —6K 39
Drew Ho. SW16 —3J 109
Drew Rd. E16 —1B 82
(in three parts)
Drewstead Rd. SW16 —2H 109
Driffield Ct. NW9 —1A 26
(off Pageant Av.)

Driffield Rd. E3 —2A 64
Drift, The. Brom —3B 138
Driftway, The. Mitc —1E 122
Drinkwater Ho. SE5 —7D 78
(off Picton St.)
Drinkwater Rd. Harr —2F 39
Drive Mans. SW6 —2G 91
(off Fulham Rd.)
Drive, The. E4 —1B 20
Drive, The. E17 —4D 32
Drive, The. E18 —3J 33
Drive, The. N3 —7D 14
Drive, The. N6 —5D 28
Drive, The. N7 —6K 45
Drive, The. NW10 —1B 58
Drive, The. NW11 —7G 27
Drive, The. SW16 —3K 123
Drive, The. SW20 —7E 106
Drive, The. W3 —6J 57
Drive, The. Bark —7K 51
Drive, The. Beck —1C 126
Drive, The. Bex —7D 100
Drive, The. Buck H —1F 21
Drive, The. Chst —3K 129
Drive, The. Col R —1K 37
Drive, The. Edgw —5C 12
Drive, The. Enf —1J 7
Drive, The. Eps —6B 130
Drive, The. Eri —7H 85
Drive, The. Felt —7A 86
Drive, The. Harr —7E 22
Drive, The. High Bar —3B 4
Drive, The. Houn & Iswth —2H 87
Drive, The. Ilf —7D 34
Drive, The. King T —7J 105
Drive, The. Mord —5B 122
Drive, The. New Bar —6F 5
Drive, The. Sidc —4B 116
Drive, The. Surb —7E 118
Drive, The. T Hth —4D 124
Drive, The. Wemb —2J 41
Drive, The. W Wick —7F 127
Driveway, The. E17 —6D 32
(off Hoe St.)
Droitwich Clo. SE26 —3G 111
Droitwich Ho. SE15 —7F 79
(off Commercial Way)
Dromey Gdns. Harr —7E 10
Dromore Rd. SW15 —6G 91
Dronfield Gdns. Dag —5C 52
Droop St. W10 —3F 59
Drover La. SE15 —7H 79
Drovers Pl. SE15 —7J 79
Drovers Rd. S Croy —5D 134
Druce Rd. SE21 —6E 94
Druid St. SE1 —2E 78 (6H 151)
Druids Way. Brom —4F 127
Druid Tower. SE14 —6A 80
Drumaline Ridge. Wor Pk
—2A 130
Drummond Av. Romf —4K 37
Drummond Cen. Croy —2C 134
Drummond Cres. NW1
—3H 61 (1C 142)
Drummond Dri. Stan —7E 10
Drummond Ga. SW1
—5H 77 (5D 154)
Drummond Pl. Croy —2C 134
Drummond Rd. E11 —6A 34
Drummond Rd. SE16 —3H 79
Drummond Rd. Croy —2C 134
Drummond Rd. Romf —4K 37
Drummonds, The. Buck H
(off Knighton La.) —2E 20

Drummond St. *NW1*
—4G 61 (3A 142)
Drum St. *E1* —6F 63 (7K 145)
Drury Cres. *Croy* —2A 134
Drury Ind. Est. *NW10* —5J 41
Drury La. *WC2* —6J 61 (7F 143)
Drury Rd. *Harr* —6J 23
Drury Way. *NW10* —5K 41
Dryad St. *SW15* —3F 91
Dryburgh Gdns. *NW9* —3G 25
Dryburgh Rd. *SW15* —3D 90
Dryden Av. *W7* —6K 55
Dryden Ct. *SE11*
—4B 78 (4A 156)
Dryden Mans. *W14* —6G 75
(off Queen's Club Gdns.)
Dryden Rd. *SW19* —6A 108
Dryden Rd. *Enf* —6K 7
Dryden Rd. *Harr* —1K 23
Dryden Rd. *Well* —1K 99
Dryden St. *WC2* —6J 61 (1F 149)
Dryfield Clo. *NW10* —6J 41
Dryfield Rd. *Edgw* —6D 12
Dryfield Wlk. *SE8* —6C 80
Dryhill Rd. *Belv* —6F 85
Drylands Rd. *N8* —6J 29
Drysdale Av. *E4* —7J 9
Drysdale Pl. *N1* —3E 62 (1H 145)
Drysdale St. *N1* —3E 62 (1H 145)
Dublin Av. *E8* —1G 63
Dublin Ct. *S Harr* —2H 39
Du Burstow Ter. *W7* —2J 71
Ducal St. *E2* —3F 63 (2K 145)
Du Cane Clo. *W12* —6D 58
Du Cane Rd. *W12* —6B 58
Ducavel Ho. *SW2* —1K 109
Duchess Clo. *N11* —5A 16
Duchess Gro. *Buck H* —2E 20
Duchess M. *W1* —5F 61 (6K 141)
Duchess of Bedford's Wlk. *W8*
—2J 75
Duchess St. *W1*
—5F 61 (6K 141)
Duchy Rd. *Barn* —1G 5
Duchy St. *SE1* —1A 78 (4K 149)
Ducie St. *SW4* —4K 93
Duckett Rd. *N4* —6A 30
Duckett St. *E1* —4K 63
Duck La. *W1* —6H 61 (1C 148)
Duck Lees La. *Enf* —4F 9
Ducks Wlk. *Twic* —5C 88
Du Cros Dri. *Stan* —6J 11
Du Cros Rd. *W3* —1A 74
Dudden Hill La. *NW10* —4B 42
Dudden Hill Pde. *NW10* —4B 42
Duddington Clo. *SE9* —4B 114
Dudley Av. *Harr* —3C 24
Dudley Ct. *NW11* —4H 27
Dudley Ct. *WC2* —6J 61 (7E 142)
Dudley Dri. *Mord* —1G 131
Dudley Dri. *Ruis* —5A 38
Dudley Gdns. *W13* —2B 72
Dudley Gdns. *Harr* —1H 39
Dudley Rd. *E17* —2C 32
Dudley Rd. *N3* —2K 27
Dudley Rd. *NW6* —2G 59
Dudley Rd. *SW19* —6J 107
Dudley Rd. *Harr* —2G 39
Dudley Rd. *Ilf* —4F 51
Dudley Rd. *King T* —3F 119
Dudley Rd. *Rich* —2F 89
Dudley St. *W2* —5B 60 (6A 140)
Dudlington Rd. *E5* —2J 47

Dudmaston M. *SW3*
—5B 76 (5B 152)
Dudsbury Rd. *Sidc* —6B 116
Duffell Ho. *SE11*
—5K 77 (6H 155)
Dufferin Av. *EC1*
—4D 62 (4E 144)
Dufferin St. *EC1*
—4C 62 (4D 144)
Duffield Clo. *Harr* —5K 23
Duffield Dri. *N15* —4F 31
Duff St. *E14* —6D 64
Dufour's Pl. *W1* —6G 61 (1B 148)
Dugard Way. *SE11*
—4B 78 (3A 156)
Duke Gdns. *Ilf* —4H 35
Duke Humphrey Rd. *SE3* —1G 97
(in two parts)
Duke of Cambridge Clo. *Twic*
—6H 87
Duke of Edinburgh Rd. *Sutt*
—2B 132
Duke of Wellington Pl. *SW1*
—2E 76 (6H 141)
Duke of York St. *SW1*
—1G 77 (4B 148)
Duke Rd. *W4* —5K 73
Duke Rd. *Ilf* —4H 35
Dukes Av. *N3* —1K 27
Duke's Av. *N10* —3F 29
Duke's Av. *W4* —5K 73
Duke's Av. *Edgw* —6A 12
Dukes Av. *Harr* —4J 23
Dukes Av. *Houn* —4C 86
Duke's Av. *N Mald* —3B 120
Dukes Av. *N Har* —6D 22
Dukes Av. *N'holt* —7C 38
Dukes Av. *Rich & King T*
—4C 104
Dukes Clo. *Hamp* —5D 102
Dukes Ct. *E6* —1E 66
Dukes Ct. *SE13* —2E 96
Dukes Head Pas. *Hamp* —7G 103
Duke's Head Yd. *N6* —1F 45
Duke Shore Pl. *E14* —7B 64
Duke's La. *W8* —2K 75
Dukes M. *N10* —3F 29
Duke's M. *W1* —6E 60 (7H 141)
Dukes Orchard. *Bex* —1J 117
Duke's Pas. *E17* —4E 32
Duke's Pl. *EC3* —6E 62 (1H 151)
Dukes Rd. *E6* —1E 66
Dukes Rd. *W3* —4G 57
Duke's Rd. *WC1*
—3H 61 (2D 142)
Dukesthorpe Rd. *SE26* —4K 111
Duke St. *SW1* —1G 77 (4B 148)
Duke St. *W1* —6E 60 (7H 141)
Duke St. *Rich* —4D 88
Duke St. *Sutt* —4B 132
Duke St. Hill. *SE1*
—1D 78 (4F 151)
Dukes Way. *W Wick* —3G 137
Duke's Yd. *W1* —7E 60 (2H 147)
Dulas St. *N4* —1A 46
Dulford St. *W11* —7G 59
Dulka Rd. *SW11* —5D 92
Dulverton Mans. *WC1*
—4K 61 (4H 143)
Dulverton Rd. *SE9* —2G 115
Dulwich Comn. *SE21 & SE22*
—1E 110
Dulwich Lawn Clo. *SE22* —5F 95
Dulwich Oaks Pl. *SE21* —3F 111
Dulwich Rise Gdns. *SE22* —5F 95

Dulwich Rd. *SE24* —5A 94
Dulwich Village. *SE21* —6E 94
Dulwich Wood Av. *SE19* —4E 110
Dulwich Wood Pk. *SE19* —4E 110
Dumbarton Ct. *SW2* —7J 93
Dumbarton Rd. *SW2* —6J 93
Dumbleton Clo. *King T* —1H 119
Dumbreck Rd. *SE9* —4D 98
Dumont Rd. *N16* —3E 46
Dumpton Pl. *NW1* —7E 44
Dunbar Av. *SW16* —2A 124
Dunbar Av. *Beck* —4A 126
Dunbar Av. *Dag* —3G 53
Dunbar Gdns. *Dag* —5G 53
Dunbar Rd. *E7* —6J 49
Dunbar Rd. *N22* —1A 30
Dunbar Rd. *N Mald* —4J 119
Dunbar St. *SE27* —3C 110
Dunbar Wharf. *E14* —7B 64
(off Narrow St.)
Dunblane Clo. *Edgw* —2C 12
Dunblane Rd. *SE9* —3C 98
Dunboyne Rd. *NW3* —5D 44
Dunbridge Ho. *SW15* —6B 90
(off Highcliffe Dri.)
Dunbridge St. *E2* —4G 63
Duncan Clo. *Barn* —4F 5
Duncan Ct. *N21* —1G 17
Duncan Gro. *W3* —6A 58
Duncannon St. *WC2*
—7J 61 (3E 148)
Duncan Rd. *E8* —1H 63
Duncan Rd. *Rich* —4E 88
Duncan St. *N1* —2B 62
Duncan Ter. *N1* —2B 62
Duncombe Hill. *SE23* —7A 96
Duncombe Rd. *N19* —1H 45
Duncrievie Rd. *SE13* —6F 97
Duncroft. *SE18* —7J 83
Dundalk Rd. *SE4* —3A 96
Dundas Rd. *SE15* —2J 95
Dundee Rd. *E13* —2K 65
Dundee Rd. *SE25* —5H 125
Dundee St. *E1* —1H 79
Dundee Wharf. *E14* —7B 64
Dundela Gdns. *Wor Pk* —4D 130
Dundonald Clo. *E6* —6C 66
Dundonald Rd. *NW10* —1F 59
Dundonald Rd. *SW19* —7G 107
Dundry Ho. *SE26* —3G 111
Dunedin Rd. *E10* —3D 48
Dunedin Rd. *Ilf* —1G 51
Dunedin Way. *Hayes* —4A 54
Dunelm Gro. *SE27* —3C 110
Dunelm St. *E1* —6K 63
Dunfield Gdns. *SE6* —5D 112
Dunfield Rd. *SE6* —5D 112
(in two parts)
Dunford Ct. *Pinn* —1D 22
Dunford Rd. *N7* —4K 45
Dungarvan Av. *SW15* —4C 90
Dunheved Clo. *T Hth* —6B 124
Dunheved Rd. N. *T Hth* —6A 124
Dunheved Rd. S. *T Hth* —6A 124
Dunheved Rd. W. *T Hth* —6A 124
Dunholme Grn. *N9* —3A 18
Dunholme La. *N9* —3A 18
Dunholme Rd. *N9* —3A 18
Dunkeld Rd. *SE25* —4D 124
Dunkeld Rd. *Dag* —2B 52
Dunkery Rd. *SE9* —4B 114
Dunkirk St. *SE27* —4C 110
Dunlace Rd. *E5* —4J 47
Dunleary Clo. *Houn* —7D 86
Dunley Dri. *New Ad* —7D 136

Dunloe Av. *N17* —3D 30
Dunloe Ct. *E2* —2F 63
Dunloe St. *E2* —2F 63
Dunlop Pl. *SE16* —3F 79 (2K 157)
Dunmore Rd. *NW6* —1G 59
Dunmore Rd. *SW20* —1E 120
Dunmow Clo. *Felt* —3C 102
Dunmow Clo. *Romf* —5C 36
Dunmow Ct. *SE11*
—4B 78 (4A 156)
Dunmow Rd. *E15* —4F 49
Dunmow Wlk. *N1* —1C 62
(off Popham St.)
Dunnage Cres. *SE16* —4A 80
Dunn Mead. *NW9* —7G 13
Dunnock Clo. *N9* —1E 18
Dunnock Rd. *E6* —6C 66
Dunn's Pas. *WC1*
—6J 61 (7F 143)
Dunn St. *E8* —5F 47
Dunollie Pl. *NW5* —5G 45
Dunollie Rd. *NW5* —5G 45
Dunoon Gdns. *SE23* —7K 95
Dunoon Ho. *N1* —1K 61
(off Bemerton Est.)
Dunoon Rd. *SE23* —7J 95
Dunraven Dri. *Enf* —2F 7
Dunraven Rd. *W12* —1C 74
Dunraven St. *W1*
—7D 60 (2F 147)
Dunsany Rd. *W14* —3F 75
Dunsdale Rd. *SE3* —6H 81
Dunsfold Way. *New Ad* —7D 136
Dunsford Way. *SW15* —6D 90
Dunsmore Clo. *Hayes* —4C 54
Dunsmore Rd. *N16* —1E 46
Dunspring La. *Ilf* —2F 35
Dunstable M. *W1*
—5E 60 (5H 141)
Dunstable Rd. *Rich* —4E 88
Dunstall Rd. *SW20* —6D 106
Dunstall Welling Est. *Well*
—2B 100
Dunstan Clo. *N2* —3A 28
Dunstan Glade. *Orp* —6H 129
Dunstan Houses. *E1* —5J 63
(off Stepney Grn.)
Dunstan Rd. *E8* —1F 63
Dunstan Rd. *NW11* —1H 43
Dunstan's Gro. *SE22* —6H 95
Dunstan's Rd. *SE22* —7G 95
Dunster Av. *Mord* —1F 131
Dunster Clo. *Barn* —4A 4
Dunster Clo. *Romf* —2J 37
Dunster Ct. *EC3* —7E 62 (2H 151)
Dunster Dri. *NW9* —1J 41
Dunster Gdns. *NW6* —7H 43
Dunster Ho. *SE6* —3E 112
Dunsterville Way. *SE1*
—2D 78 (7F 151)
Dunston Rd. *E8* —1F 63
Dunston Rd. *SW11* —2E 92
Dunston St. *E8* —1F 63
Dunton Clo. *Surb* —7E 118
Dunton Ct. *SE23* —2H 111
Dunton Rd. *E10* —7D 32
Dunton Rd. *SE1* —5F 79 (5J 157)
Dunton Rd. *Romf* —4K 37
Duntshill Rd. *SW18* —1K 107
Dunvegan Rd. *SE9* —4D 98
Dunwich Rd. *Bexh* —1F 101
Dunworth M. *W11* —6H 59
Duplex Ride. *SW1*
—2D 76 (7F 147)

Dupont Rd. *SW20* —2F 121
Dupont St. *E14* —6A 64
Duppas Av. *Croy* —4B 134
Duppas Hill La. *Croy* —4B 134
Duppas Hill Rd. *Croy* —4A 134
Duppas Hill Ter. *Croy* —3B 134
Duppas Rd. *Croy* —3A 134
Dupree Rd. *SE7* —5K 81
Duraden Clo. *Beck* —7D 112
Durand Clo. *Cars* —1D 132
Durand Gdns. *SW9* —1K 93
Durands Wlk. *SE16* —2B 80
Durand Way. *NW10* —7J 41
Durants Pk. Av. *Enf* —4E 8
Durants Rd. *Enf* —4D 8
Durant St. *E2* —2G 63
Durban Ct. *E7* —7B 50
Durban Gdns. *Dag* —7J 53
Durban Rd. *E15* —3G 65
Durban Rd. *E17* —1B 32
Durban Rd. *N17* —6K 17
Durban Rd. *SE27* —4C 110
Durban Rd. *Beck* —2B 126
Durban Rd. *Ilf* —7J 35
Durbin Rd. *S'hall* —6D 54
Durell Gdns. *Dag* —5D 52
Durell Rd. *Dag* —5D 52
Durford Cres. *SW15* —1D 106
Durham Av. *Brom* —4H 127
Durham Av. *Houn* —5D 70
Durham Av. *Wfd G* —5G 21
Durham Clo. *SW20* —2D 120
Durham Ct. *Tedd* —4H 103
Durham Hill. *Brom* —4H 113
Durham Ho. *Bark* —7A 52
(off Margaret Bondfield Av.)
Durham Ho. *Brom* —4G 127
Durham Ho. *Dag* —5J 53
Durham Ho. *WC2*
—7J 61 (3F 149)
Durham Pl. *SW3*
—5D 76 (6E 152)
Durham Pl. *Ilf* —4G 51
Durham Rise. *SE18* —5G 83
Durham Rd. *E12* —4B 50
Durham Rd. *E16* —4G 65
Durham Rd. *N2* —3C 28
Durham Rd. *N7* —2K 45
Durham Rd. *N9* —2B 18
Durham Rd. *SW20* —1D 120
Durham Rd. *W5* —3D 72
Durham Rd. *Brom* —3H 127
Durham Rd. *Dag* —5J 53
Durham Rd. *Felt* —7A 86
Durham Rd. *Harr* —5F 23
Durham Rd. *Sidc* —5B 116
Durham Row. *E1* —5K 63
Durham St. *SE11*
—5K 77 (6G 155)
Durham Ter. *W2* —6K 59
Durham Wharf. *Bren* —7C 72
Durham Yd. *E2* —3H 63
Durley Av. *Pinn* —7C 22
Durley Rd. *N16* —7E 30
Durlston Rd. *E5* —2G 47
Durlston Rd. *King T* —6E 104
Durnford Ho. *SE6* —3E 112
Durnford St. *N15* —5E 30
Durnford St. *SE10* —6E 80
Durning Rd. *SE19* —5D 110
Durnsford Av. *SW19* —2J 107
Durnsford Rd. *N11* —1H 29
Durnsford Rd. *SW19* —2J 107

Durrant Ct. *Har W* —2J **23**
Durrell Rd. *SW6* —2H **91**
Durrington Av. *SW20* —7E **106**
Durrington Pk. Rd. *SW20*
　—1E **120**
Durrington Rd. *E5* —4A **48**
Durrington Tower. *SW8* —2G **93**
Durrisdeer Ho. NW2 —4H **43**
　(off Lyndale)
Dursley Clo. *SE3* —2A **98**
Dursley Ct. SE15 —6E **78**
　(off Lydney Clo.)
Dursley Gdns. *SE3* —1B **98**
Dursley Rd. *SE3* —2A **98**
Durward St. *E1* —5H **63**
Durweston M. *W1*
　—5D **60** (5F **141**)
Durweston St. *W1*
　—5D **60** (6F **141**)
Dury Falls Ct. *Romf* —2J **37**
Dury Rd. *Barn* —1C **4**
Dutch Gdns. *King T* —6H **105**
Dutch Yd. *SW18* —5J **91**
Duthie St. *E14* —7E **64**
Dutton Bus. Pk. *SE9* —2E **114**
Dutton St. *SE10* —1E **96**
Duxberry Av. *Felt* —3A **102**
Duxberry Clo. *Brom* —5C **128**
Duxford Ho. S2 2D 84
　(off Wolvercote Rd.)
Dye Ho. La. *E3* —1C **64**
Dyer's Bldgs. *EC1*
　—5A **62** (6J **143**)
Dyers Hall Rd. *E11* —2G **49**
Dyers La. *SW15* —4D **90**
Dyke Ct. *E17* —5B **32**
Dykes Way. *Brom* —3H **127**
Dykewood Clo. *Bex* —3H **117**
Dylan Rd. *SE24* —4B **94**
Dylan Rd. *Belv* —3G **85**
Dylan Thomas Ho. *N8* —4K **29**
Dylways. *SE5* —4D **94**
Dymchurch Clo. *Ilf* —2E **34**
Dymes Path. *SW19* —2F **107**
Dymock Ct. SE15 —6E **78**
　(off Lydney Clo.)
Dymock St. *SW6* —3K **91**
Dyneley Rd. *SE12* —3A **114**
Dyne Rd. *NW6* —7G **43**
Dynevor Rd. *N16* —3E **46**
Dynevor Rd. *Rich* —5E **88**
Dynham Rd. *NW6* —7J **43**
Dyott St. *WC1* —6H **61** (7D **142**)
Dysart Av. *King T* —5C **104**
Dysart St. *EC2* —4D **62** (4G **145**)
Dyson Ct. *NW2* —7E **26**
Dyson Ct. *Wemb* —2A **40**
Dyson Ho. SE10 —5H **81**
　(off Blackwall La.)
Dyson Rd. *E11* —6G **33**
Dyson Rd. *E15* —6H **49**
Dysons Rd. *N18* —5C **18**

Eade Rd. *N4* —7C **30**
Eagans Clo. *N2* —3B **28**
Eagle Av. *Romf* —6E **36**
Eagle Clo. *Enf* —4D **8**
Eagle Clo. *Wall* —6J **133**
Eagle Ct. *E11* —4J **33**
Eagle Ct. *EC1* —5B **62** (5A **144**)
Eagle Dri. *NW9* —2A **26**
Eagle Hill. *SE19* —6D **110**
Eagle La. *E11* —4J **33**
Eagle Lodge. *NW11* —7H **27**

Eagle M. *N1* —6E **46**
Eagle Pl. *SW1* —7G **61** (3B **148**)
Eagle Pl. SW7 —5A **76**
　(off Rolandway)
Eagle Rd. *Wemb* —7D **40**
Eaglesfield Rd. *SE18* —1F **99**
Eagle St. *WC1* —5K **61** (6G **143**)
Eagle Ter. *Wtcl G* —7E **20**
Eagle Wharf E. E14 —7A **64**
　(off Narrow St.)
Eagle Wharf Rd. *N1* —2C **62**
Eagle Wharf W. E14 —7A **64**
　(off Narrow St.)
Ealdham Sq. *SE9* —4A **98**
Ealing B'way. Cen. *W5* —7D **56**
Ealing Common. (Junct.) —7F **57**
Ealing Downs Ct. *Gnfd* —3A **56**
Ealing Grn. *W5* —1D **72**
Ealing Pk. Gdns. *W5* —4C **72**
Ealing Rd. *Bren* —4D **72**
Ealing Rd. *N'holt* —1E **54**
Ealing Rd. *Wemb* —6E **40**
Ealing Rd. Trad. Est. *Bren*
　—5D **72**
Ealing Village. *W5* —6E **56**
Eamont Clo. NW8 —2C **60**
　(off Eamont St.)
Eamont St. *NW8* —2C **60**
Eardley Cres. *SW5* —5J **75**
Eardley Rd. *SW16* —5G **109**
Eardley Rd. *Belv* —5G **85**
Earl Clo. *N11* —5A **16**
Earldom Rd. *SW15* —4E **90**
Earle Gdns. *King T* —7E **104**
Earlham Gro. *E7* —5H **49**
Earlham Gro. *N22* —7E **16**
Earlham St. *WC2*
　—6J **61** (1D **148**)
Earl Rise. *SE18* —4H **83**
Earl Rd. *SW14* —4J **89**
Earls Ct. Gdns. *SW5* —4K **75**
Earl's Ct. Rd. *W8 & SW5* —3J **75**
Earl's Ct. Sq. *SW5* —5K **75**
Earls Cres. *Harr* —4J **23**
Earlsdown Ho. *Bark* —2H **67**
Earlsferry Way. *N1* —7K **45**
Earlsfield Rd. *SW18* —1A **108**
Earlshall Rd. *SE9* —4D **98**
Earlsmead. *Harr* —4D **38**
Earlsmead Rd. *N15* —5F **31**
Earlsmead Rd. *NW10* —3E **58**
Earls Ter. *W8* —3H **75**
Earlsthorpe M. *SW12* —6E **92**
Earlsthorpe Rd. *SE26* —4K **111**
Earlstoke St. *EC1*
　—3B **62** (1A **144**)
Earlston Gro. *E9* —1H **63**
Earl St. *EC2* —5D **62** (5F **145**)
Earls Wlk. *W8* —3J **75**
Earl's Wlk. *Dag* —4B **52**
Earlswood Av. *T Hth* —5A **124**
Earlswood Clo. *SE10* —6G **81**
Earlswood Gdns. *Ilf* —3E **34**
Earlswood St. *SE10* —5G **81**
Early M. *NW1* —1F **61**
Earne Rd. *W4* —6G **73**
Earnshaw St. *WC2*
　—6H **61** (7D **142**)
Earsby St. *W14* —4G **75**
　(in two parts)
Easby Cres. *Mord* —6K **121**
Easebourne Rd. *Dag* —5C **52**
Easley's M. *W1* —6E **60** (7H **141**)
E. Acton Ct. *W3* —7A **58**
E. Acton La. *W3* —1A **74**

East Arbour St. *E1* —6K **63**
East Av. *E12* —7C **50**
East Av. *E17* —4D **32**
East Av. *N2* —4K **27**
East Av. *S'hall* —7D **54**
East Av. *Wall* —5K **133**
E. Bank. *N16* —7E **30**
Eastbank Rd. *Hamp* —5G **103**
E. Barnet Rd. *Barn* —4G **5**
E. Beckton District Cen. *E6*
　—5D **66**
E. Boundary Rd. *E12* —3D **50**
Eastbourne Av. *W3* —6K **57**
Eastbourne Gdns. *SW14* —3J **89**
Eastbourne M. *W2* —6A **60**
Eastbourne Rd. *E6* —3E **66**
Eastbourne Rd. *E15* —1G **65**
Eastbourne Rd. *N15* —6E **30**
Eastbourne Rd. *SW17* —6E **108**
Eastbourne Rd. *W4* —6J **73**
Eastbourne Rd. *Bren* —5C **72**
Eastbourne Rd. *Felt* —2B **102**
Eastbourne Ter. *W2* —6A **60**
Eastbrook Av. *N9* —3C **18**
Eastbrook Av. *Dag* —4J **53**
Eastbrook Dri. *Romf* —2K **53**
Eastbrook Rd. *SE3* —1K **97**
E. Churchfield Rd. *W3* —1K **73**
Eastcheap. *EC3* —7D **62** (2G **151**)
East Clo. *W5* —4G **57**
East Clo. *Barn* —4K **5**
East Clo. *Gnfd* —2G **55**
Eastcombe Av. *SE7* —6K **81**
Eastcote. *Orp* —7K **129**
Eastcote Av. *Gnfd* —5A **40**
Eastcote Av. *Harr* —2F **39**
Eastcote La. *Harr* —4C **38**
Eastcote La. N. *N'holt* —6D **38**
Eastcote Rd. *Harr* —3G **39**
Eastcote Rd. *Pinn* —5B **22**
Eastcote Rd. *Well* —2H **99**
Eastcote St. *SW9* —2K **93**
Eastcote View. *Pinn* —4A **22**
East Ct. *Wemb* —2C **40**
East Cres. *N11* —4J **15**
East Cres. *Enf* —5A **8**
Eastcroft Rd. *Eps* —7A **130**
E. Cross Route. *E9 & E3* —7B **48**
Eastdown Ct. *SE13* —4F **97**
Eastdown Pk. *SE13* —4F **97**
East Dri. *Cars* —7C **132**
E. Dulwich Gro. *SE22* —6E **94**
E. Dulwich Rd. *SE22 & SE15*
　—4F **95**
E. End Farm. *Pinn* —3D **22**
E. End Rd. *N3 & N2* —2J **27**
E. End Way. *Pinn* —3C **22**

E. Entrance. *Dag* —2H **69**
Eastern Av. *E11* —6K **33**
Eastern Av. *Ilf & Romf* —6B **34**
Eastern Av. *Pinn* —7B **22**
Eastern Av. E. *Romf* —3K **37**
Eastern Av. W. *Romf* —4E **36**
　(in two parts)
Eastern Ind. Est. *Eri* —2G **85**
Eastern Rd. *E13* —2K **65**
Eastern Rd. *E17* —5E **32**
Eastern Rd. *N2* —3D **28**
Eastern Rd. *N22* —1J **29**
Eastern Rd. *SE4* —4C **96**
Easternville Gdns. *Ilf* —6G **35**
Eastern Way. *SE28* —2A **84**
E. Ferry Rd. *E14* —4D **80**
Eastfield Gdns. *Dag* —4G **53**
Eastfield Rd. *E17* —4C **32**
Eastfield Rd. *N8* —3J **29**
Eastfield Rd. *Dag* —4G **53**
Eastfield Rd. *Enf* —1E **8**
Eastfields. *Pinn* —5A **22**
Eastfields Rd. *W3* —5J **57**
Eastfields Rd. *Mitc* —2E **122**
East Gdns. *SW17* —6C **108**
Eastgate Clo. *SE28* —6D **68**
Eastglade. *Pinn* —3D **22**
E. Ham and Barking By-Pass. *Bark*
　—2J **67**
E. Ham Ind. Est. *E6* —4C **66**
E. Ham Mnr. Way. *E6* —6E **66**
E. Harding St. *EC4*
　—6A **62** (7K **143**)
E. Heath Rd. *NW3* —3A **44**
East Hill. *SW18* —5K **91**
East Hill. *Wemb* —2G **41**
Eastholm. *NW11* —4K **27**
East Holme. *Eri* —1K **101**
E. India Dock Ho. *E14* —6E **64**
E. India Dock Rd. *E14* —6C **64**
E. India Dock Wall Rd. *E14*
　—7F **65**
Eastlake Ho. *NW8*
　—4B **60** (4B **140**)
Eastlake Rd. *SE5* —2C **94**
Eastlands Cres. *SE21* —6F **95**
East La. *SE16* —2G **79**
East La. *King T* —3D **118**
East La. *Wemb* —3C **40**
Eastlea M. *E16* —4G **65**
Eastleigh Av. *Harr* —2F **39**
Eastleigh Clo. *NW2* —3A **42**
Eastleigh Clo. *Sutt* —7K **131**
Eastleigh Rd. *E17* —2B **32**
Eastleigh Rd. *Bexh* —3J **101**
Eastleigh Wlk. *SW15* —7C **90**
Eastman Ho. *SW4* —6G **93**
Eastman Rd. *W3* —2K **73**
East Mead. *Ruis* —3B **38**
Eastmead Av. *Gnfd* —3F **55**
Eastmead Clo. *Brom* —2C **128**
Eastmearn Rd. *SE21* —2C **110**
Eastmoor Pl. *SE7* —3B **82**
Eastmoor St. *SE7* —3B **82**
E. Mount St. *E1* —5H **63**
Eastney Rd. *Croy* —1B **134**
Eastney St. *SE10* —5F **81**
Eastnor Rd. *SE9* —1G **115**
Easton St. *WC1* —4A **62** (3J **143**)
East Pk. Clo. *Romf* —5D **36**
East Pas. *EC1* —5C **62** (5C **144**)
East Pier. *E1* —1H **79**
East Pl. *SE27* —4C **110**
East Point. *SE1* —5G **79**

E. Poultry Av. *EC1*
　—5B **62** (6A **144**)
East Rd. *E15* —1J **65**
East Rd. *N1* —3D **62** (2E **144**)
East Rd. *N2* —1C **28**
East Rd. *SW19* —6A **108**
East Rd. *Barn* —1K **15**
East Rd. *Chad H* —5E **36**
East Rd. *Edgw* —1H **25**
East Rd. *Enf* —1D **8**
East Rd. *King T* —1E **118**
East Rd. *Rush G* —7K **37**
East Rd. *Well* —2B **100**
E. Rochester Way. *Bex* —6H **101**
E. Rochester Way. *Sidc* —4J **99**
East Row. *E11* —6J **33**
East Row. *W10* —4G **59**
Eastry Av. *Brom* —6H **127**
Eastry Rd. *Eri* —7G **85**
E. Sheen Av. *SW14* —5K **89**
Eastside Rd. *NW11* —4H **27**
E. Smithfield. *E1*
　—7F **63** (3K **151**)
East St. *SE17* —5C **78** (5D **156**)
East St. *Bark* —1G **67**
East St. *Bexh* —4G **101**
East St. *Bren* —7C **72**
East St. *Brom* —2J **127**
E. Surrey Gro. *SE15* —7F **79**
E. Tenter St. *E1* —6F **63** (1K **151**)
East Ter. *Sidc* —1J **115**
East View. *E4* —5K **19**
East View. *Barn* —2C **4**
Eastview Av. *SE18* —7J **83**
Eastville Av. *NW11* —6H **27**
East Wlk. *E Barn* —7K **5**
Eastway. *E9* —6B **48**
East Way. *E11* —5K **33**
East Way. *Brom* —7J **127**
East Way. *Croy* —2A **136**
Eastway. *Mord* —5F **121**
Eastway. *Wall* —4G **133**
Eastway Commercial Cen. *E9*
　—5C **48**
Eastwell Clo. *Beck* —7A **112**
Eastwood Clo. *E18* —2J **33**
Eastwood Clo. *N17* —7C **18**
Eastwood Rd. *E18* —2J **33**
Eastwood Rd. *N10* —2E **28**
Eastwood Rd. *Ilf* —7A **36**
E. Woodside. *Bex* —1E **116**
Eastwood St. *SW16* —6G **109**
Eatington Rd. *E10* —5F **33**
Eaton Clo. *SW1* —4E **76** (4G **153**)
Eaton Clo. *Stan* —4G **11**
Eaton Dri. *SW9* —4B **94**
Eaton Dri. *King T* —7G **105**
Eaton Dri. *Romf* —1H **37**
Eaton Gdns. *Dag* —7E **52**
Eaton Ga. *SW1* —4E **76** (3G **153**)
Eaton Gro. *N19* —3H **45**
Eaton La. *SW1* —3F **77** (2K **153**)
Eaton M. N. *SW1*
　—4E **76** (3G **153**)
Eaton M. S. *SW1*
　—4E **76** (3H **153**)
Eaton M. W. *SW1*
　—4E **76** (3H **153**)
Eaton Pk. Rd. *N13* —2F **17**
Eaton Pl. *SW1* —4E **76** (2G **153**)
Eaton Rise. *E11* —5A **34**
Eaton Rise. *W5* —5D **56**
Eaton Rd. *NW4* —5E **26**

Eaton Rd. *Enf* —4K 7
Eaton Rd. *Houn* —4H 87
Eaton Rd. *Sidc* —2D 116
Eaton Rd. *Surt* —6A 132
Eaton Row. *SW1*
　　　　　—3F 77 (2J 153)
Eatons Mead. *E4* —2H 19
Eaton Sq. *SW1* —4E 76 (3H 153)
Eaton Ter. *E3* —3A 64
Eaton Ter. *SW1* —4E 76 (3G 153)
Eaton Ter. M. *SW1*
　　　　　—4E 76 (3G 153)
Eatonville Rd. *SW17* —2D 108
Eatonville Vs. *SW17* —2D 108
Eaton Wlk. SE15 —7F *79*
　(off Commercial Way)
Ebbisham Dri. *SW8*
　　　　　—6K 77 (7G 155)
Ebbisham Rd. *Wor Pk* —2E 130
Ebbsfleet Rd. *NW2* —5G 43
Ebdon Way. *SE3* —3K 97
Ebenezer Ho. *SE11*
　　　　　—4B 78 (4A 156)
Ebenezer St. *N1* —3D 62 (1E 144)
Ebenezer Wlk. *SW16* —1G 123
Ebley Clo. *SE15* —6F 79 (7J 157)
Ebner St. *SW18* —5K 91
Ebon Way. *SE3* —3K 97
Ebor Cotts. *SW15* —3A 106
Ebor St. *E1* —4F 63 (3J 145)
Ebrington Rd. *Harr* —6D 24
Ebsworth St. *SE23* —7K 95
Eburne Rd. *N7* —3J 45
Ebury Bri. *SW1* —5F 77 (5J 153)
Ebury Bri. Est. *SW1*
　　　　　—5F 77 (5J 153)
Ebury Bri. Rd. *SW1*
　　　　　—5E 76 (6H 153)
Ebury Clo. *Kes* —3C 138
Ebury M. *SE27* —3B 110
Ebury M. *SW1* —4F 77 (3J 153)
Ebury M. E. *SW1*
　　　　　—3F 77 (2J 153)
Ebury Sq. *SW1* —4E 76 (4H 153)
Ebury St. *SW1* —4E 76 (4H 153)
Ecclesbourne Clo. *N13* —5F 17
Ecclesbourne Gdns. *N13* —5F 17
Ecclesbourne Rd. *N1* —7C 46
Ecclesbourne Rd. *T Hth* —5C 124
Eccles Rd. *SW11* —4D 92
Eccleston Bri. *SW1*
　　　　　—4F 77 (3K 153)
Eccleston Clo. *Cockf* —4J 5
Eccleston Cres. *Romf* —7B 36
Ecclestone Ct. *Wemb* —5E 40
Ecclestone M. *Wemb* —5E 40
Ecclestone Pl. *Wemb* —5F 41
Eccleston Ho. *SW2* —6A 94
Eccleston M. *SW1*
　　　　　—3E 76 (2H 153)
Eccleston Pl. *SW1*
　　　　　—4F 77 (3J 153)
Eccleston Rd. *W13* —7A 56
Eccleston Sq. *SW1*
　　　　　—4F 77 (4K 153)
Eccleston Sq. M. *SW1*
　　　　　—4G 77 (4K 153)
Eccleston St. *SW1*
　　　　　—3F 77 (2J 153)
Echo Heights. *E4* —1J 19
Eckford St. *N1* —2A 62
Eckington Ho. N15 —6D *30*
　(off Fladbury Rd.)
Eckstein Rd. *SW11* —4C 92
Eclipse Rd. *E13* —5K 65

Ector Rd. *SE6* —2G 113
Edam Ct. *Sidc* —3A 116
Edans Ct. *W12* —2B 74
Edbrooke Rd. *W9* —4J 59
Eddington St. *N4* —1A 46
Eddisbury Ho. *SE26* —3G 111
Eddiscombe Rd. *SW6* —2H 91
Eddy Clo. *Romf* —6H 37
Eddystone Rd. *SE4* —5A 96
Eddystone Tower. *SE8* —5A 80
Ede Clo. *Houn* —3D 86
Edenbridge Clo. SE16 —5H *79*
　(off Masters Dri.)
Edenbridge Rd. *E9* —7K 47
Edenbridge Rd. *Enf* —6K 7
Eden Clo. *W8* —3J 75
Eden Clo. *Bex* —4K 117
Eden Clo. *Wemb* —1D 56
Edencourt Rd. *SW16* —6F 109
Edendale. *W3* —7H 57
Edendale Rd. *Bexh* —1K 101
Edenfield Gdns. *Wor Pk* —3B 130
Eden Gro. *E17* —5D 32
Eden Gro. *N7* —5K 45
Edenham Way. *W10* —4H 59
Edenhurst Av. *SW6* —3H 91
Eden M. *SW17* —3A 108
Eden Pk. Av. *Beck* —4A 126
Eden Rd. *E17* —5D 32
Eden Rd. *SE27* —4B 110
Eden Rd. *Beck* —4A 126
Eden Rd. *Bex* —4J 117
Eden Rd. *Croy* —4D 134
Edensor Gdns. *W4* —7A 74
Edensor Rd. *W4* —7A 74
Eden St. *King T* —2D 118
Edenvale Clo. *Mitc* —7E 108
Edenvale Rd. *Mitc* —7E 108
Edenvale St. *SW6* —2K 91
Eden Wlk. *King T* —2E 118
Eden Way. *Beck* —5B 126
Ederline Av. *SW16* —3K 123
Edgar Ct. *N Mald* —3A 120
Edgar Ho. E9 —5A *48*
　(off Homerton Rd.)
Edgar Ho. *E11* —7J 33
Edgar Ho. SW8 —7J *77*
　(off Wyvil Rd.)
Edgar Kail Way. *SE22* —4E 94
Edgarley Ter. *SW6* —1G 91
Edgar Rd. *E3* —3D 64
Edgar Rd. *Houn* —7D 86
Edgar Rd. *Romf* —7D 36
Edgeborough Way. *Brom*
　　　　　—7B 114
Edgebury. *Chst* —4F 115
Edgebury Wlk. *Chst* —4G 115
Edgecombe Clo. *King T*
　　　　　—7K 105
Edgecote Clo. *W3* —1J 73
Edgecot Gro. *N15* —5E 30
Edgefield Av. *Bark* —7K 51
Edgefield Ct. Bark —7K *51*
　(off Edgefield Av.)
Edgefoot Gro. *N15* —5E 30
Edge Hill. *SE18* —6F 83
Edge Hill. *SW19* —7F 107
Edgehill Av. *N3* —4J 27
Edge Hill Ct. *SW19* —7F 107
Edge Hill Ct. *Sidc* —4K 115
Edgehill Gdns. *Dag* —4G 53

Edgehill Ho. *SW9* —2B 94
Edgehill Rd. *W13* —5C 56
Edgehill Rd. *Chst* —3G 115
Edgehill Rd. *Mitc* —1F 123
Edgeley La. *SW4* —3H 93
Edgeley Rd. *SW4* —3H 93
Edgel St. *SW18* —4K 91
Edgepoint Clo. *SE27* —5B 110
Edge St. *W8* —1J 75
Edgewood Grn. *Croy* —1K 135
Edgeworth Av. *NW4* —5C 26
Edgeworth Clo. *NW4* —5C 26
Edgeworth Cres. *NW4* —5C 26
Edgeworth Rd. *SE9* —4A 98
Edgeworth Rd. *Cockf* —4H 5
Edgington Rd. *SW16* —6H 109
Edgington Way. *Sidc* —7C 116
Edgwarebury Gdns. *Edgw*
　　　　　—5B 12
Edgwarebury La. *Els & Edgw*
　(in three parts)　—1K 11
Edgware Ct. *Edgw* —6B 12
Edgware Rd. *NW2* —1D 42
Edgware Rd. *NW9* —2J 25
Edgware Rd. *W2*
　　　　　—4B 60 (4A 140)
Edgware Way. *Edgw* —1J 11
Edinburgh Clo. *E2* —2J 63
Edinburgh Ct. *SW20* —5F 121
Edinburgh Ct. *Eri* —7K 85
Edinburgh Ct. King T —3E *118*
　(off Watersplash Clo.)
Edinburgh Dri. *Romf* —4J 37
Edinburgh Ga. *SW1*
　　　　　—2D 76 (6E 146)
Edinburgh Ho. *NW4* —3E 26
Edinburgh Ho. W9 —1K *59*
　(off Maida Vale)
Edinburgh Ho. *E13* —2K 65
Edinburgh Ho. *E17* —5B 32
Edinburgh Ho. *N18* —5B 18
Edinburgh Ho. *W7* —2K 71
Edinburgh Rd. *Sutt* —2A 132
Edington Rd. *SE2* —3B 84
Edington Rd. *Enf* —2D 8
Edison Clo. *E17* —5C 32
Edison Dri. *S'hall* —6F 55
Edison Gro. *SE18* —7K 83
Edison Ho. Wemb —3J *41*
　(off Barnhill Rd.)
Edison Rd. *N8* —6H 29
Edison Rd. *Brom* —2J 127
Edison Rd. *Enf* —2G 9
Edison Rd. *Well* —1K 99
Edis St. *NW1* —1E 60
Edith Cavell Clo. *N19* —7J 29
Edith Gdns. *Surb* —7H 119
Edith Gro. *SW10* —6A 76
Edith Ho. W6 —5E *74*
　(off Queen Caroline St.)
Edithna St. *SW9* —3J 93
Edith Rd. *E6* —7B 50
Edith Rd. *E15* —5F 49
Edith Rd. *N11* —7C 16
Edith Rd. *SE25* —5D 124
Edith Rd. *SW19* —6K 107
Edith Rd. *W14* —4G 75
Edith Rd. *Romf* —7D 36
Edith Row. *SW6* —1K 91
Edith St. *E2* —2G 63
Edith Summerskill Ho. SW6
　(off Clem Attlee Est.)　—7H *75*
Edith Ter. *SW10* —7A 76
Edith Vs. *W14* —4H 75
Edith Yd. *SW10* —7A 76

Edmansons Clo. *N17* —1F 31
Edmeston Clo. *E9* —6A 48
Edmond Ct. *SE14* —1J 95
Edmonds Clo. *W13* —5A 56
Edmonton Grn. Shop. Cen. *N9*
　　　　　—2C 18
Edmund Ho. *SE17*
　　　　　—5B 78 (7B 156)
Edmund Rd. *Mitc* —3C 122
Edmund Rd. *Well* —3A 100
Edmundsbury Ct. Est. *SW9*
　　　　　—4K 93
Edmunds Clo. *Hayes* —5A 54
Edmund St. *SE5* —7D 78
Edmunds Wlk. *N2* —4C 28
Edna Rd. *SW20* —2F 121
Edna St. *SW11* —1C 92
Edred Ho. E9 —4A *48*
　(off Homerton Rd.)
Edrick Ho. *SW4* —1J 93
Edrick Rd. *Edgw* —6D 12
Edrick Wlk. *Edgw* —6D 12
Edric Rd. *SE14* —7K 79
Edridge Rd. *Croy* —3C 134
Edward Av. *E4* —6J 19
Edward Av. *Mord* —5B 122
Edward Clo. *N9* —7A 8
Edward Clo. *Hamp* —5G 103
Edward Clo. *N'holt* —2A 54
Edward Clo. *E16* —5J 65
Edward Edward's Ho. SE1
　　　　　—1B 78 (5A 150)
Edwardes Pl. *W8* —3H 75
Edwardes Sq. *W8* —3H 75
Edward Gro. *Barn* —5G 5
Edward Ho. *SE11*
　　　　　—5K 77 (5H 155)
Edward M. *NW1*
　　　　　—3F 61 (1K 141)
Edward Pl. *SE8* —6B 80
Edward Rd. *E17* —4K 31
Edward Rd. *SE20* —6K 111
Edward Rd. *Barn* —5G 5
Edward Rd. *Brom* —7K 113
Edward Rd. *Chst* —5F 115
Edward Rd. *Croy* —7E 124
Edward Rd. *Hamp* —5G 103
Edward Rd. *Harr* —3G 23
Edward Rd. *N'holt* —2A 54
Edward Rd. *Romf* —6E 36
Edward's Av. *Ruis* —6A 38
Edwards Clo. *Wor Pk* —2F 131
Edwards Cotts. *N1* —6B 46
Edwards Dri. *N11* —7C 16
Edwards La. *N16* —2E 46
Edwards Mans. Bark —7K *51*
　(off Upney La.)
Edwards M. *N1* —7A 46
Edwards M. *W1* —6E 60 (1G 147)
Edward Sq. *N1* —1K 61
Edward Sq. *SE16* —1A 80
Edwards Rd. *Belv* —4G 85
Edward St. *E16* —4J 65
Edward St. *SE8* —6B 80
Edward St. *SE14* —7A 80
Edwards Yd. *Wemb* —1E 56
Edward Temme Av. *E15* —7H 49
Edward Tyler Rd. *SE12* —2K 113
Edwina Gdns. *Ilf* —5C 34
Edwin Arnold Ct. *Sidc* —4K 115
Edwin Av. *E6* —2E 66
　(in two parts)
Edwin Clo. *Bexh* —6F 85
Edwin Pl. *Croy* —1E 134
Edwin Rd. *Edgw* —6E 12

Edwin Rd. *Twic* —1J 103
Edwin's Mead. *E9* —4A 48
Edwin St. *E1* —4J 63
Edwin St. *E16* —5J 65
Edwin Ware Ct. *Pinn* —2A 22
Edwis Ho. *SE15* —7G 79
Edwyn Clo. *Barn* —6A 4
Eel Pie Island. *Twic* —1A 104
Effie Pl. *SW6* —7J 75
Effie Rd. *SW6* —7J 75
Effingham Clo. *Sutt* —7K 131
Effingham Lodge. *King T*
　　　　　—4D 118
Effingham Rd. *N8* —5A 30
Effingham Rd. *SE12* —5G 97
Effingham Rd. *Croy* —7K 123
Effingham Rd. *Surb* —7B 118
Effort St. *SW17* —5C 108
Effra Ct. SW2 —5K *93*
　(off Brixton Hill)
Effra Pde. *SW2* —5A 94
Effra Rd. *SW2* —4A 94
Effra Rd. *SW19* —6K 107
Egbert St. *NW1* —1E 60
Egbury Ho. SW15 —6B *90*
　(off Tangley Gro.)
Egbwerts Way. *E4* —1K 19
Egerton Ct. *E11* —7F 33
Egerton Cres. *SW3*
　　　　　—4C 76 (3D 152)
Egerton Dri. *SE10* —1D 96
Egerton Gdns. *NW4* —4D 26
Egerton Gdns. *NW10* —1E 58
Egerton Gdns. *SW3*
　　　　　—3C 76 (2C 152)
Egerton Gdns. *W13* —6B 56
Egerton Gdns. *Ilf* —3K 51
Egerton Gdns. M. *SW3*
　　　　　—3C 76 (2D 152)
Egerton Pl. *SW3*
　　　　　—3C 76 (2D 152)
Egerton Rd. *N16* —7F 31
Egerton Rd. *SE25* —3E 124
Egerton Rd. *N Mald* —4B 120
Egerton Rd. *Twic* —7J 87
Egerton Rd. *Wemb* —7F 41
Egerton Ter. *SW3*
　　　　　—3C 76 (2D 152)
Eggardon Ct. *N'holt* —6G 39
Egham Clo. *SW19* —2G 107
Egham Clo. *Sutt* —2G 131
Egham Cres. *Sutt* —3F 131
Egham Rd. *E13* —5K 65
Eglantine Rd. *SW18* —5A 92
Egleston Rd. *Mord* —6K 121
Eglington Ct. *SE17*
　　　　　—6C 78 (7C 156)
Eglington Rd. *E4* —7A 10
Eglinton Hill. *SE18* —6F 83
Eglinton Rd. *SE18* —6E 82
Egliston M. *SW15* —3E 90
Egliston Rd. *SW15* —3E 90
Eglon M. *NW1* —7D 44
Egmont Av. *Surb* —7F 119
Egmont Rd. *N Mald* —4B 120
Egmont Rd. *Surb* —7F 119
Egmont Rd. *Sutt* —7A 132
Egmont St. *SE14* —7K 79
Egremont Rd. *SE27* —3A 110
Egret Way. *Hayes* —6B 54
Eider Clo. *E7* —5H 49
Eider Clo. *Hayes* —5B 54
Eighteenth Rd. *Mitc* —4J 123
Eighth Av. *E12* —4D 50

Eileen Rd. *SE25* —5D **124**
Eindhoven Clo. *Cars* —1E **132**
Einstein Ho. *Wemb* —3J **41**
Eisenhower Dri. *E6* —5C **66**
Elaine Gro. *NW5* —5E **44**
Elam Clo. *SE5* —2B **94**
Elam St. *SE5* —2B **94**
Elan Ct. *E1* —5H **63**
Eland Pl. *Croy* —3B **134**
Eland Rd. *SW11* —3D **92**
Eland Rd. *Croy* —3B **134**
Elba Pl. *SE17* —4C **78** (3D **156**)
Elberon Av. *Croy* —6G **123**
Elbe St. *SW6* —2A **92**
Elborough Rd. *SE25* —5G **125**
Elborough St. *SW18* —1J **107**
Elbourne Ct. *SE16* —4K **79**
  (off Worgan St.)
Elbury Dri. *E16* —6J **65**
Elcho St. *SW11* —7C **76**
Elcot Av. *SE15* —7H **79**
Eldenhall Ind. Est. *Dag* —1F **53**
Elder Av. *N8* —5J **29**
Elderberry Gro. *SE27* —4C **110**
Elderberry Rd. *W5* —2E **72**
Elder Clo. *Sidc* —1K **115**
Elder Ct. *Bush* —2D **10**
Elderfield Rd. *E5* —4J **47**
Elderfield Wlk. *E11* —5K **33**
Elderflower Way. *E15* —7G **49**
Elder Gdns. *SE27* —4C **110**
Elder Oak Clo. *SE20* —1H **125**
Elder Oak Ct. *SE20* —1G **125**
Elder Rd. *SE27* —4C **110**
Elderslie Clo. *Beck* —6D **126**
Elderslie Rd. *SE9* —5E **98**
Elder St. *E1* —4F **63** (4J **145**)
Elderton Rd. *SE26* —4A **112**
Eldertree Pl. *Mitc* —1G **123**
Eldertree Way. *Mitc* —1G **123**
Elder Wlk. *N1* —1B **62**
  (off Popham St.)
Elderwood Pl. *SE27* —5C **110**
Eldon Av. *Croy* —2J **135**
Eldon Av. *Houn* —7E **70**
Eldon Gro. *NW3* —5B **44**
Eldon Pk. *SE25* —4H **125**
Eldon Rd. *E17* —4B **32**
Eldon Rd. *N9* —1D **18**
Eldon Rd. *N22* —1B **30**
Eldon Rd. *W8* —3K **75**
Eldon St. *EC2* —5D **62** (6F **145**)
Eldon Wall Est. *Dag* —1F **53**
Eldon Way. *NW10* —1H **57**
Eldred Rd. *Bark* —1J **67**
Eldridge Ct. *SE16* —3G **79**
Eleanora Ter. *Sutt* —5A **132**
  (off Lind Rd.)
Eleanor Clo. *N15* —3F **31**
Eleanor Clo. *SE16* —2K **79**
Eleanor Cres. *NW7* —5A **14**
Eleanor Gdns. *Barn* —5A **4**
Eleanor Gdns. *Dag* —2F **53**
Eleanor Gro. *SW13* —3A **90**
Eleanor Rd. *E8* —6H **47**
Eleanor Rd. *E15* —6H **49**
Eleanor Rd. *N11* —6D **16**
Eleanor St. *E3* —3C **64**
Electric Av. *SW9* —4A **94**
Electric La. *SW9* & *SW2* —4A **94**
  (in two parts)
Electric Pde. *E18* —2J **33**
Electric Pde. *Ilf* —2K **51**
Electric Pde. *Surb* —6D **118**

Elephant & Castle. *SE1*
  —4B **78** (3B **156**)
Elephant & Castle. (Junct.)
  —3B **78**
Elephant La. *SE16* —2J **79**
Elephant Rd. *SE17*
  —4C **78** (3C **156**)
Elers Rd. *W13* —2C **72**
Eley Rd. *N18* —4D **18**
Eleys Est. *N18* —4E **18**
Elfindale Rd. *SE24* —5C **94**
Elfin Gro. *Tedd* —5K **103**
Elford Clo. *SE3* —4K **97**
Elford M. *SW4* —5G **93**
Elfort Rd. *N5* —4A **46**
Elfrida Cres. *SE6* —4C **112**
Elf Row. *E1* —7J **63**
Elfwine Rd. *W7* —5J **55**
Elgar. *N8* —3J **29**
  (off Boyton Clo.)
Elgar Av. *NW10* —6K **41**
  (in two parts)
Elgar Av. *SW16* —3J **123**
Elgar Av. *W5* —2E **72**
Elgar Av. *Surb* —7G **119**
Elgar Clo. *E13* —2A **66**
Elgar Clo. *SE8* —7C **80**
Elgar Clo. *Buck H* —2G **21**
Elgar Clo. *Els* —1H **11**
Elgar St. *SE16* —3A **80**
Elgin Av. *W9* —4H **59**
Elgin Av. *Harr* —2B **24**
Elgin Ct. *W9* —4K **59**
Elgin Cres. *W11* —7G **59**
Elgin Est. *W9* —4J **59**
  (off Elgin Av.)
Elgin M. *W11* —6G **59**
Elgin M. N. *W9* —3K **59**
Elgin M. S. *W9* —3K **59**
Elgin Rd. *N22* —2G **29**
Elgin Rd. *Croy* —2F **135**
Elgin Rd. *Ilf* —1J **51**
Elgin Rd. *Sutt* —3A **132**
Elgin Rd. *Wall* —6G **133**
Elgood Clo. *W11* —7G **59**
Elham Clo. *Brom* —7B **114**
Elham Ho. *E5* —5H **47**
Elia M. *N1* —2B **62** (1B **144**)
Elias Pl. *SW8* —6A **78**
Elia St. *N1* —2B **62** (1B **144**)
Elibank Rd. *SE9* —4D **98**
Elim Est. *SE1* —3E **78** (1G **157**)
Elim St. *SE1* —3D **78** (1F **157**)
Elim Way. *E13* —3H **65**
Eliot Bank. *SE23* —2H **111**
Eliot Cotts. *SE3* —2G **97**
Eliot Dri. *Harr* —2F **39**
Eliot Gdns. *SW15* —4C **90**
Eliot Hill. *SE13* —2E **96**
Eliot M. *NW8* —2A **60**
Eliot Pk. *SE13* —2E **96**
Eliot Pl. *SE3* —2G **97**
Eliot Rd. *Dag* —4D **52**
Eliot Vale. *SE3* —2F **97**
Elizabeth Av. *N1* —1C **62**
Elizabeth Av. *Enf* —3G **7**
Elizabeth Av. *Ilf* —2H **51**
Elizabeth Blackwell Ho. *N22*
  (off Progress Way) —1A **30**
Elizabeth Bri. *SW1*
  —4F **77** (4J **153**)
Elizabeth Clo. *E14* —6D **64**
Elizabeth Clo. *W9* —4A **60**

Elizabeth Clo. *Barn* —3A **4**
Elizabeth Clo. *Romf* —1H **37**
Elizabeth Clyde Clo. *N15* —4E **30**
Elizabeth Cotts. *Rich* —1F **89**
Elizabeth Ct. *E4* —5G **19**
Elizabeth Ct. *SW1*
  —3H **77** (2D **154**)
Elizabeth Ct. *Eri* —7K **85**
  (off Valence Rd.)
Elizabeth Ct. *Tedd* —5J **103**
Elizabeth Ct. *Wfd G* —7F **21**
Elizabeth Fry Rd. *E8* —7H **47**
Elizabeth Gdns. *W3* —1B **74**
Elizabeth Gdns. *Stan* —6H **11**
Elizabeth Garrett Anderson Ho.
  Belv —3G **85**
  (off Ambrooke Rd.)
Elizabeth Ind. Est. *SE14* —6K **79**
Elizabeth M. *NW3* —6C **44**
Elizabeth M. *Harr* —6J **23**
Elizabeth Pl. *N15* —4D **30**
Elizabeth Ride. *N9* —7C **8**
Elizabeth Rd. *E6* —1B **66**
Elizabeth Rd. *N15* —5E **30**
Elizabeth Sq. *SE16* —7A **64**
  (off Sovereign Cres.)
Elizabeth St. *SW1*
  —4E **76** (3H **153**)
Elizabeth Ter. *SE9* —6D **98**
Elizabeth Way. *SE19* —7D **110**
Elizabeth Way. *Felt* —4A **102**
Elkington Point. *SE11*
  —4A **78** (4J **155**)
Elkington Rd. *E13* —4K **65**
Elkstone Ct. *SE15* —6E **78**
  (off Birdlip Clo.)
Elkstone Rd. *W10* —5H **59**
Ellaline Rd. *W6* —6F **75**
Ellanby Cres. *N18* —4C **18**
Elland Rd. *SE15* —4J **95**
Ella Rd. *N8* —7J **29**
Ellement Clo. *Pinn* —5B **22**
Ellena Ct. *N14* —3D **16**
  (off Conway Rd.)
Ellenborough Ho. *W12* —7D **58**
  (off White City Est.)
Ellenborough Pl. *SW15* —4C **90**
Ellenborough Rd. *N22* —1C **30**
Ellenborough Rd. *Sidc* —5D **116**
Ellenbridge Way. *S Croy* —7E **134**
Ellen Clo. *Brom* —3B **128**
Ellen Ct. *E4* —1K **19**
  (off Ridgeway, The)
Ellen St. *E1* —6G **63**
Ellen Webb Dri. *W'stone* —3J **23**
Ellen Wilkinson Ho. *SW6* —6H **75**
  (off Lillie Rd.)
Ellen Wilkinson Ho. *Dag* —3G **53**
Elleray Rd. *Tedd* —6K **103**
Ellerby St. *SW6* —1F **91**
Ellerdale Clo. *NW3* —4A **44**
Ellerdale Rd. *NW3* —5A **44**
Ellerdale St. *SE13* —4D **96**
Ellerdine Rd. *Houn* —4G **87**
Ellerker Gdns. *Rich* —6E **88**
Ellerman Av. *Twic* —1D **102**
Ellerslie Gdns. *NW10* —1C **58**
Ellerslie Rd. *W12* —1D **74**
Ellerslie Sq. Ind. Est. *SW2* —5J **93**
Ellerton Gdns. *Dag* —7C **52**
Ellerton Lodge. *N3* —2J **27**
Ellerton Rd. *SW13* —1C **90**
Ellerton Rd. *SW18* —1B **108**
Ellerton Rd. *SW20* —7C **106**

Ellerton Rd. *Dag* —7C **52**
Ellerton Rd. *Surb* —7F **119**
Ellery Ho. *SE17* —4D **78** (4F **157**)
Ellery Rd. *SE19* —7D **110**
Ellery St. *SE15* —2H **95**
Ellesmere Av. *NW7* —3E **12**
Ellesmere Av. *Beck* —2E **126**
Ellesmere Clo. *E11* —5H **33**
Ellesmere Ct. *W4* —6K **73**
Ellesmere Gdns. *Ilf* —5C **34**
Ellesmere Gro. *Barn* —5C **4**
Ellesmere Rd. *E3* —2A **64**
Ellesmere Rd. *NW10* —5C **42**
Ellesmere Rd. *W4* —6J **73**
Ellesmere Rd. *Gnfd* —4G **55**
Ellesmere Rd. *Twic* —6C **88**
Ellesmere St. *E14* —6D **64**
Elleswood Ct. *Surb* —7D **118**
Ellingfort Rd. *E8* —7H **47**
Ellingham Rd. *E15* —4F **49**
Ellingham Rd. *W12* —2C **74**
Ellington Ct. *N14* —2C **16**
Ellington Ho. *SE1*
  —3C **78** (2E **156**)
Ellington Rd. *N10* —4F **29**
Ellington Rd. *Houn* —2F **87**
Ellington St. *N7* —6A **46**
Elliot Clo. *E15* —7G **49**
Elliot Rd. *NW4* —6D **26**
Elliott Clo. *Wemb* —3G **41**
Elliott Rd. *SW9* —7B **78**
Elliott Rd. *W4* —4A **74**
Elliott Rd. *Brom* —4B **128**
Elliott Rd. *Stan* —6F **11**
Elliott Rd. *T Hth* —4B **124**
Elliott's Pl. *N1* —1B **62**
Elliott Sq. *NW3* —7C **44**
Elliott's Row. *SE11*
  —4B **78** (3A **156**)
Ellis Clo. *NW10* —6D **42**
Ellis Clo. *SE9* —2G **115**
Elliscombe Rd. *SE7* —6A **82**
Ellis Ct. *W7* —5K **55**
Ellisfield Dri. *SW15* —7C **90**
Ellis Ho. *SE17* —5D **78** (5E **156**)
Ellis M. *SE7* —6A **82**
Ellison Gdns. *S'hall* —4D **70**
Ellison Rd. *SW13* —2B **90**
Ellison Rd. *SW16* —7H **109**
Ellison Rd. *Sidc* —1H **115**
Ellis Rd. *Mitc* —6D **122**
Ellis Rd. *S'hall* —1G **71**
Ellis St. *SW1* —4E **76** (3F **153**)
Ellora Rd. *SW16* —5H **109**
Ellsworth St. *E2* —3H **63**
Ellwood Ct. *W9* —4K **59**
  (off Clearwell Dri.)
Elmar Rd. *N15* —4D **30**
Elm Av. *W5* —1E **72**
Elm Av. *Ruis* —7A **22**
Elm Bank. *N14* —7D **6**
Elmbank Av. *Barn* —4A **4**
Elm Bank Dri. *Brom* —2A **128**
Elm Bank Gdns. *SW13* —2A **90**
Elmbank Way. *W7* —5H **55**
Elmbourne Dri. *Belv* —4H **85**
Elmbourne Rd. *SW17* —3F **109**
Elmbourne Trad. Est. *Belv*
  —3H **85**
Elmbridge Av. *Surb* —5H **119**
Elmbridge Wlk. *E8* —7G **47**
Elmbrook Gdns. *SE9* —4C **98**
Elmbrook Rd. *Sutt* —4H **131**
Elm Clo. *E11* —6K **33**
Elm Clo. *N19* —2G **45**

Elm Clo. *NW4* —5F **27**
Elm Clo. *SW20* —4E **120**
Elm Clo. *Buck H* —2G **21**
Elm Clo. *Cars* —1D **132**
Elm Clo. *Harr* —6F **23**
Elm Clo. *Romf* —1H **37**
Elm Clo. *S Croy* —6E **134**
Elm Clo. *Surb* —7J **119**
Elm Clo. *Twic* —2F **103**
Elmcote. *Pinn* —2B **22**
Elm Cotts. *Mitc* —2D **122**
Elm Ct. *EC4* —7A **62** (1J **149**)
Elm Ct. *SE13* —3F **97**
Elmcourt Rd. *SE27* —2B **110**
Elm Cres. *W5* —2E **72**
Elm Cres. *King T* —1E **118**
Elmcroft. *N6* —7G **29**
Elmcroft Av. *E11* —5K **33**
Elmcroft Av. *N9* —6C **8**
Elmcroft Av. *NW11* —7H **27**
Elmcroft Av. *Sidc* —7K **99**
Elmcroft Clo. *E11* —4K **33**
Elmcroft Clo. *N8* —5K **29**
Elmcroft Clo. *W5* —6D **56**
Elmcroft Cres. *NW11* —7G **27**
Elmcroft Cres. *Harr* —3E **22**
Elmcroft Gdns. *NW9* —4G **25**
Elmcroft St. *E5* —4J **47**
Elmdale Rd. *N13* —5E **16**
Elmdene. *Surb* —7J **119**
Elmdene Clo. *Beck* —6B **126**
Elmdene Rd. *SE18* —5F **83**
Elmdon Rd. *Houn* —2C **86**
Elm Dri. *Harr* —6F **23**
Elmer Clo. *Enf* —3E **6**
Elmer Gdns. *Edgw* —7C **12**
Elmer Gdns. *Iswth* —3H **87**
Elmer Rd. *SE6* —7E **96**
Elmers Dri. *Tedd* —6B **104**
Elmers End Rd. *SE20* & *Beck*
  —2J **125**
Elmerside Rd. *Beck* —4A **126**
Elmers Rd. *SE25* —7G **125**
Elmfield Av. *N8* —5J **29**
Elmfield Av. *Mitc* —1E **122**
Elmfield Av. *Tedd* —5K **103**
Elmfield Clo. *Harr* —2J **39**
Elmfield Ct. *Well* —1B **100**
Elmfield Ho. *N2* —2B **28**
  (off Grange, The)
Elmfield Pk. *Brom* —3J **127**
Elmfield Rd. *E4* —2K **19**
Elmfield Rd. *E17* —6K **31**
Elmfield Rd. *N2* —3B **28**
Elmfield Rd. *SW17* —2E **108**
Elmfield Rd. *Brom* —3J **127**
Elmfield Rd. *S'hall* —3C **70**
Elmfield Way. *S Croy* —7F **135**
Elm Friars Wlk. *NW1* —7H **45**
Elm Gdns. *N2* —3A **28**
Elm Gdns. *Mitc* —4H **123**
Elmgate Av. *Felt* —3A **102**
Elmgate Gdns. *Edgw* —5D **12**
Elm Grn. *W3* —6A **58**
Elmgreen Clo. *E15* —1G **65**
Elm Gro. *N8* —6J **29**
Elm Gro. *NW2* —4F **43**
Elm Gro. *SE15* —2F **95**
Elm Gro. *SW19* —7G **107**
Elm Gro. *Eri* —7K **85**
Elm Gro. *Harr* —7E **22**
Elm Gro. *King T* —1E **118**
Elm Gro. *Sutt* —4K **131**
Elm Gro. *Wfd G* —5C **20**
Elmgrove Cres. *Harr* —5K **23**

Elmgrove Gdns. Harr —5A 24
Elm Gro. Pde. Wall —3E 132
Elm Gro. Rd. SW13 —1C 90
Elm Gro. Rd. W5 —2E 72
Elmgrove Rd. Croy —7H 125
Elmgrove Rd. Harr —5K 23
Elmgrove Rd. Kent —5A 54
Elm Hall Gdns. E11 —6K 33
(in two parts)
Elm Hatch. Pinn —1D 22
(off Westfield Pk.)
Elmhurst. Belv —6B 84
Elmhurst Av. N2 —3B 28
Elmhurst Av. Mitc —7F 109
Elmhurst Dri. E18 —2J 33
Elmhurst Lodge. Sutt —7A 132
Elmhurst Mans. SW4 —3H 93
Elmhurst Rd. E7 —7K 49
Elmhurst Rd. N17 —2F 31
Elmhurst Rd. SE9 —2C 114
Elmhurst St. SW4 —3H 93
Elmington Clo. Bex —6H 101
Elmington Est. SE5 —7D 78
Elmington Rd. SE5 —7D 78
Elmira St. SE13 —3D 96
Elm La. SE6 —2B 112
Elm Lea Trad. Est. N17 —6C 18
Elmlee Clo. Chst —6D 114
Elmley Clo. E6 —5C 66
Elmley St. SE18 —5H 83
Elm Lodge. SW6 —1F 91
Elmore Clo. Wemb —2E 56
Elmore Rd. E11 —3E 48
Elmore Rd. Enf —1E 8
Elmore St. N1 —7C 46
Elm Pde. Sidc —4A 116
Elm Pk. SW2 —6K 93
Elm Pk. Stan —5G 11
Elm Pk. Av. N15 —5F 31
Elm Pk. Ct. Pinn —3A 22
Elm Pk. Gdns. NW4 —5F 27
Elm Pk. Gdns. SW10
—5B 76 (6A 152)
Elm Pk. La. SW3
—5B 76 (6A 152)
Elm Pk. Mans. SW10
—6A 76 (7A 152)
Elm Pk. Rd. E10 —1A 48
Elm Pk. Rd. N3 —7C 14
Elm Pk. Rd. N21 —7H 7
Elm Pk. Rd. SE25 —3F 125
Elm Pk. Rd. SW3
—6B 76 (7A 152)
Elm Pk. Rd. Pinn —2A 22
Elm Pas. Barn —4C 4
Elm Pl. SW7 —5B 76 (5A 152)
Elm Quay Ct. SW8
—6H 77 (7C 154)
Elm Rd. E7 —6H 49
Elm Rd. E11 —2F 49
Elm Rd. E17 —5E 32
Elm Rd. N22 —1B 30
Elm Rd. SW14 —3J 89
Elm Rd. Barn —4C 4
Elm Rd. Beck —2B 126
Elm Rd. Eps —6B 130
Elm Rd. King T —1F 119
Elm Rd. N Mald —2K 119
Elm Rd. Romf —7H 37
Elm Rd. Sidc —4A 116
Elm Rd. T Hth —4D 124
Elm Rd. Wall —1E 132
Elm Rd. Wemb —5E 40
Elm Rd. W. Sutt —7H 121

Elm Row. NW3 —3A 44
Elms Av. N10 —3F 29
Elms Av. NW4 —5F 27
Elmscott Gdns. N21 —6H 7
Elmscott Rd. Brom —5G 113
Elms Ct. Wemb —4A 40
Elms Cres. SW4 —6G 93
Elmsdale Rd. E17 —4B 32
Elms Gdns. Dag —4F 53
Elms Gdns. Wemb —4A 40
Elmshaw Rd. SW15 —5C 90
Elmshurst Cres. N2 —4B 28
Elmside. New Ad —6D 136
Elmside Rd. Wemb —3G 41
Elms La. Wemb —4A 40
Elmsleigh Av. Harr —4B 24
Elmsleigh Ct. Sutt —3K 131
Elmsleigh Ho. Twic —2H 103
(off Staines Rd.)
Elmsleigh Rd. Twic —2H 103
Elmslie Clo. Wfd G —6J 21
Elms M. W2 —7B 60 (2A 146)
Elms Pk. Av. Wemb —4A 40
Elms Rd. SW4 —5G 93
Elms Rd. Harr —7D 10
Elmstead Av. Chst —5D 114
Elmstead Av. Wemb —1E 40
Elmstead Clo. N20 —2D 14
Elmstead Clo. Eps —5A 130
Elmstead Gdns. Wor Pk —3C 130
Elmstead Glade. Chst —6D 114
Elmstead La. Chst —7C 114
Elmstead Rd. Eri —1K 101
Elmstead Rd. Ilf —2J 51
Elmsted Cres. Well —6C 84
Elms, The. E12 —5C 50
Elms, The. SW13 —3B 90
Elmstone Rd. SW6 —1J 91
Elm St. WC1 —4K 61 (4H 143)
Elmsworth Av. Houn —2F 87
Elm Ter. NW2 —3J 43
Elm Ter. NW3 —4C 44
Elm Ter. SE9 —6E 98
Elm Ter. Harr —1H 23
Elm Ter. Stan —5G 11
Elmton Way. E5 —3G 47
Elm Tree Clo. NW8
—3B 60 (1A 140)
Elm Tree Clo. N'holt —2D 54
Elm Tree Ct. SE7 —6A 82
Elm Tree Rd. NW8
—3B 60 (1A 140)
Elmtree Rd. Tedd —4J 103
Elm Wlk. NW3 —2J 43
Elm Wlk. SW20 —4E 120
Elm Wlk. Orp —3D 138
Elm Way. N11 —6K 15
Elm Way. NW10 —4A 42
Elm Way. Eps —5A 130
Elm Way. Wor Pk —3E 130
Elmwood Av. N13 —5D 16
Elmwood Av. Felt —3A 102
Elmwood Av. Harr —5A 24
Elmwood Clo. Eps —7C 130
Elmwood Clo. Wall —2F 133
Elmwood Ct. E10 —1C 48
(off Goldsmith Rd.)
Elmwood Ct. Wemb —3A 40
Elmwood Cres. NW9 —4J 25
Elmwood Dri. Bex —7E 100
Elmwood Dri. Eps —6C 130
Elmwood Gdns. W7 —6J 55
Elmwood Rd. SE24 —5D 94
Elmwood Rd. W4 —6J 73
Elmwood Rd. Croy —7B 124

Elmwood Rd. Mitc —3D 122
Elmworth Gro. SE21 —2D 110
Elnathan M. W9 —4K 59
Elphinstone Ct. SW16 —6J 109
Elphinstone Rd. E17 —2B 32
Elphinstone St. N5 —4B 46
Elrington Rd. E8 —6G 47
Elrington Rd. Wfd G —5D 20
Elsa Ct. Beck —1B 126
Elsa Rd. Well —2B 100
Elsa St. E1 —5A 64
Elsdale St. E9 —6J 47
Elsden M. E2 —2J 63
Elsden Rd. N17 —1F 31
Elsenham Rd. E12 —5E 50
Elsenham St. SW18 —1H 107
Elsham Rd. E11 —3G 49
Elsham Rd. W14 —2G 75
Elsham Ter. W14 —3G 75
(off Elsham Rd.)
Elsiedene Rd. N21 —7H 7
Elsiemaud Rd. SE4 —5B 96
Elsie Rd. SE22 —4F 95
Elsinore Gdns. NW2 —3G 43
Elsinore Ho. SE5 —2C 94
Elsinore Rd. SE23 —1A 112
Elsinore Way. Rich —3H 89
Elsley Rd. SW11 —3D 92
Elspeth Rd. SW11 —4D 92
Elspeth Rd. Wemb —5E 40
Elsrick Av. Mord —5J 121
Elstan Way. Croy —7A 126
Elstead Ct. Sutt —1G 131
Elstead Ho. SW2 —7K 93
(off Redlands Way)
Elsted St. SE17 —4D 78 (4F 157)
Elstow Clo. SE9 —5E 98
(in two parts)
Elstow Clo. Ruis —7B 22
Elstow Gdns. Dag —1E 68
Elstow Rd. Dag —1E 68
Elstree By-Pass. Els —1H 11
Elstree Gdns. N9 —1C 18
Elstree Gdns. Belv —4E 84
Elstree Gdns. Ilf —5G 51
Elstree Hill. Brom —7G 113
Elstree Hill S. Els —1J 11
Elstree Rd. Bush & Borwd
—1C 10
Elswick Rd. SE13 —2D 96
Elswick St. SW6 —2A 92
Elsworthy Rise. NW3 —7C 44
Elsworthy Rd. NW3 —1C 60
Elsworthy Ter. NW3 —7C 44
Elsynge Rd. SW18 —5B 92
Eltham Grn. SE9 —5B 98
Eltham Grn. Rd. SE9 —4A 98
Eltham High St. SE9 —6D 98
Eltham Hill. SE9 —5B 98
Eltham Pal. Rd. SE9 —6A 98
Eltham Pk. Gdns. SE9 —4E 98
Eltham Rd. SE12 & SE9 —5J 97
Elthiron Rd. SW6 —1J 91
Elthorne Av. W7 —2K 71
Elthorne Ct. Felt —1A 102
Elthorne Pk. Rd. W7 —2K 71
Elthorne Rd. N19 —2H 45
Elthorne Rd. NW9 —7K 25
Elthorne Way. NW9 —6K 25
Elthruda Rd. SE13 —6G 97
Eltisley Rd. Ilf —4F 51
Elton Av. Barn —5C 4
Elton Av. Gnfd —6J 39
Elton Av. Wemb —5B 40
Elton Clo. King T —7C 104

Elton Pl. N16 —5E 46
Elton Rd. King T —1F 119
Eltringham St. SW18 —4A 92
Elvaston M. SW7 —3A 76
Elvaston Pl. SW7 —3A 76
Elveden Ho. SE24 —5B 94
Elveden Pl. NW10 —2G 57
Elveden Rd. NW10 —2G 57
Elvendon Rd. N13 —6D 16
Elver Gdns. E2 —3G 63
Elverson Rd. SE8 —2D 96
Elverton St. SW1
—4H 77 (3C 154)
Elvington Grn. Brom —5H 127
Elvington La. NW9 —1A 26
Elvino Rd. SE26 —5A 112
Elvis Rd. NW2 —6E 42
Elwill Way. Beck —4E 126
Elwin St. E2 —3G 63 (1K 145)
Elwood St. N5 —3B 46
Elwyn Gdns. SE12 —7J 97
Ely Clo. SW20 —2B 120
Ely Clo. N Mald —2B 120
Ely Cotts. SW8 —7K 77
Ely Ct. EC1 —5A 62 (6K 143)
Ely Gdns. Dag —3J 53
Ely Gdns. Ilf —7C 34
Ely Pl. EC1 —5A 62 (6K 143)
Ely Pl. Wfd G —6K 21
Ely Rd. E10 —6E 32
Ely Rd. Croy —5D 124
Ely Rd. Houn —3A 86
Elysian Av. Orp —6K 129
Elysium Pl. SW6 —2H 91
(off Elysium St.)
Elysium St. SW6 —2H 91
Elystan Bus. Cen. Hayes —7A 54
Elystan Clo. Wall —7G 133
Elystan Pl. SW3 —5C 76 (5D 152)
Elystan St. SW3 —4C 76 (4C 152)
Elystan Wlk. N1 —1A 62
Emanuel Av. W3 —6J 57
Emanuel Dri. Hamp —5D 102
Embankment. SW15 —2F 91
Embankment Gdns. SW3
—6D 76 (7F 153)
Embankment Pl. WC2
—1J 77 (4F 149)
Embankment, The. Twic —1A 104
Embassy Ct. N11 —6C 16
(off Bounds Grn. Rd.)
Embassy Ct. NW8
—2B 60 (1B 140)
Embassy Ct. W5 —7F 57
Embassy Ct. Sidc —3B 116
Embassy Ct. Wall —6F 133
Embassy Ct. Well —3B 100
Embassy Gdns. Beck —1B 126
Embassy Ho. NW6 —7J 43
Emba St. SE16 —2G 79
Ember Clo. Orp —7G 129
Ember Ct. NW9 —2B 26
Emberton. SE17 —6E 78 (7G 157)
Emberton Ct. EC1
—3B 62 (2A 144)
(off Tompion St.)
Embleton Rd. SE13 —4D 96
Embleton Wlk. Hamp —5D 102
Embley Point. E5 —4H 47
(off Tiger Way)
Embroidery Bus. Cen. Wfd G
(off Southend Rd.) —2B 34
Embry Clo. Stan —4F 11
Embry Dri. Stan —6F 11

Embry Way. Stan —5F 11
Emden St. SW6 —1K 91
Emerald Clo. E16 —6B 66
Emerald Gdns. Dag —1G 53
Emerald Sq. S'hall —3B 70
Emerald St. WC1
—5K 61 (5G 143)
Emerson Gdns. Harr —6F 25
Emerson Rd. Ilf —7E 34
Emerson St. SE1
—1C 78 (4C 150)
Emerton Clo. Bexh —4E 100
Emery Hill St. SW1
—3G 77 (2B 154)
Emery St. SE1 —3A 78 (1K 155)
Emes Rd. Eri —7J 85
Emily Pl. N7 —4A 46
Emily St. E16 —6H 65
(off Jude St.)
Emlyn Gdns. W12 —2A 74
Emlyn Rd. W12 —2A 74
Emmanuel Ct. E10 —7D 32
Emmanuel Ho. SE11
—4A 78 (4J 155)
Emmanuel Rd. SW12 —1G 109
Emma Rd. E13 —2H 65
Emma St. E2 —2H 63
Emmaus Way. Chig —5K 21
Emmott Av. Ilf —5G 35
Emmott Clo. E1 —4A 64
Emmott Clo. NW11 —6A 28
Emms Pl. King T —2D 118
Emperor's Ga. SW7 —3A 76
Empire Av. N18 —5H 17
Empire Ct. Wemb —3H 41
Empire Pde. N18 —6J 17
Empire Pde. Wemb —3G 41
Empire Rd. Gnfd —1C 56
Empire Way. Wemb —4F 41
Empire Wharf Rd. E14 —4F 81
Empire Yd. N7 —3J 45
Empress Av. E4 —7J 19
Empress Av. E12 —2A 50
Empress Av. Ilf —2D 50
Empress Av. Wfd G —7C 20
Empress Dri. Chst —6F 115
Empress Pde. E4 —7J 19
(off Chingford Rd.)
Empress Pl. SW6 —5J 75
Empress St. SE17
—6C 78 (7D 156)
Empson St. E3 —4D 64
Emsworth Clo. N9 —1D 18
Emsworth Ct. SW16 —3J 109
Emsworth Ct. Ilf —2F 35
Emsworth St. SW2 —2K 109
Emu Rd. SW8 —2F 93
Ena Rd. SW16 —3J 123
Enbrook St. W10 —3G 59
Endale Clo. Cars —2D 132
Endeavour Way. SW19 —4K 107
Endeavour Way. Bark —4A 68
Endeavour Way. Croy —7J 123
Endell St. WC2 —6J 61 (7E 142)
Enderby St. SE10 —5G 81
Enderley Clo. Harr —2J 23
Enderley Rd. Harr —1J 23
Endersleigh Gdns. NW4 —4C 26
Endlebury Rd. E4 —2K 19
Endlesham Rd. SW12 —7E 92
Endsleigh Gdns. WC1
—4H 61 (3C 142)
Endsleigh Gdns. Ilf —2D 50
Endsleigh Gdns. Surb —6C 118
Endsleigh Ind. Est. S'hall —4C 70

Endsleigh Pl. *WC1*
—4H **61** (3D **142**)
Endsleigh Rd. *W13* —7A **56**
Endsleigh Rd. *S'hall* —4C **70**
Endsleigh St. *WC1*
—4H **61** (3D **142**)
End Way. *Surb* —7G **119**
Endwell Rd. *SE4* —2A **96**
Endymion Rd. *N4* —7A **30**
Endymion Rd. *SW2* —6K **93**
Enfield Ho. *SW9* —2J **93**
(off Stockwell Rd.)
Enfield Rd. *N1* —7E **46**
Enfield Rd. *W3* —2H **73**
Enfield Rd. *Bren* —5D **72**
Enfield Rd. *Enf* —4C **6**
Enfield Wlk. *Bren* —5D **72**
Enford St. *W1* —5D **60** (5E **140**)
Engadine Clo. *Croy* —3F **135**
Engadine St. *SW18* —1J **107**
Engate St. *SE13* —4E **96**
Engel Pk. *NW7* —6K **13**
Engineer Clo. *SE18* —6E **82**
Engineers Way. *Wemb* —4G **41**
England's La. *NW3* —6D **44**
Englefield Clo. *Croy* —6C **124**
Englefield Clo. *Enf* —2F **7**
Englefield Clo. *Orp* —4K **129**
Englefield Cres. *Orp* —4K **129**
Englefield Path. *Orp* —4K **129**
Englefield Rd. *N1* —7D **46**
Engleheart Rd. *SE6* —7D **96**
Englewood Rd. *SW12* —6F **93**
English Grounds. *SE1*
—1E **78** (5G **151**)
English St. *E3* —4B **64**
Enid St. *SE16* —3F **79** (1K **157**)
Enmore Av. *SE25* —5G **125**
Enmore Gdns. *SW14* —5K **89**
Enmore Rd. *SE25* —5G **125**
Enmore Rd. *SW15* —4E **90**
Enmore Rd. *S'hall* —4E **54**
Ennerdale Av. *Stan* —3C **24**
Ennerdale Clo. *Sutt* —4H **131**
Ennerdale Dri. *NW9* —5A **26**
Ennerdale Gdns. *Wemb* —1C **40**
Ennerdale Rd. *Bexh* —1G **101**
Ennerdale Rd. *Rich* —2F **89**
Ennersdale Rd. *SE13* —5F **97**
Ennismore Av. *W4* —4B **74**
Ennismore Av. *Gnfd* —6J **39**
Ennismore Gdns. *SW7*
—2C **76** (7C **146**)
Ennismore Gdns. M. *SW7*
—3C **76** (1C **152**)
Ennismore M. *SW7*
—3C **76** (7C **146**)
Ennismore St. *SW7*
—3C **76** (1C **152**)
Ennis Rd. *N4* —1A **46**
Ennis Rd. *SE18* —6G **83**
Ennor Ct. *Sutt* —4K **130**
Ensbury Ho. *SW8* —7K **77**
(off Carroun Rd.)
Ensign Dri. *N13* —3H **17**
Ensign Ind. Cen. *E1* —7G **63**
(off Ensign St.)
Ensign St. *E1* —7G **63**
Enslin Rd. *SE9* —7E **98**
Ensor M. *SW7* —5B **76** (5A **152**)
Enstone Rd. *Enf* —3F **9**
Enterprise Bus. Pk. *E14* —2C **80**
Enterprise Cen., The. *Beck*
—5A **112**
Enterprise Clo. *Croy* —1A **134**

Enterprise Ho. *Bark* —3K **67**
Enterprise Ind. Est. *SE16* —5J **79**
Enterprise Way. *NW10* —3B **58**
Enterprise Way. *SW18* —4J **91**
Enterprise Way. *Tedd* —6K **103**
Enterprize Way. *SE8* —4B **80**
Epcot M. *NW10* —3F **59**
Epirus M. *SW6* —7J **75**
Epirus Rd. *SW6* —7H **75**
Epping Clo. *E14* —4C **80**
Epping Clo. *Romf* —3H **37**
Epping Glade. *E4* —6K **9**
Epping New Rd. *Buck H & Lou*
—2E **20**
Epping Pl. *N1* —6A **46**
Epping Way. *E4* —6J **9**
Epple Rd. *SW6* —1H **91**
Epsom Clo. *Bexh* —3H **101**
Epsom Clo. *N'holt* —5D **38**
Epsom Rd. *E10* —6E **32**
Epsom Rd. *Croy* —4A **134**
Epsom Rd. *Ilf* —6K **35**
Epsom Rd. *Sutt & Mord* —7H **121**
Epstein Rd. *SE28* —1A **84**
Epworth Rd. *Iswth* —7B **72**
Epworth St. *EC2* —4D **62** (4F **145**)
Erasmus St. *SW1*
—4H **77** (4D **154**)
Erconwald St. *W12* —6B **58**
Eresby Dri. *Beck* —1C **136**
Eresby Pl. *NW6* —7J **43**
Erica Gdns. *Croy* —3D **136**
Erica Ho. *N22* —1A **30**
(off Acacia Rd.)
Erica Ho. *SE4* —3B **96**
Erica St. *W12* —7C **58**
Eric Clarke La. *Bark* —4F **67**
Eric Clo. *E7* —4J **49**
Ericcson Clo. *SW18* —5J **91**
Eric Fletcher Ct. *N1* —7C **46**
(off Essex Rd.)
Eric Rd. *E7* —4J **49**
Eric Rd. *NW10* —6B **42**
Eric Rd. *Romf* —7D **36**
Ericson Ho. *SE13* —4F **97**
(off Blessington Rd.)
Eric St. *E3* —4B **64**
Eridge Rd. *W4* —3K **73**
Erin Clo. *Brom* —7G **113**
Erindale. *SE18* —6H **83**
Erindale Ter. *SE18* —6H **83**
Erith Cres. *Romf* —1J **37**
Erith Rd. *Belv & Eri* —4H **101**
Erith Rd. *Bexh & N Hth* —4H **101**
Erlanger Rd. *SE14* —1K **95**
Erlesmere Gdns. *W13* —3A **72**
Ermine Clo. *Houn* —2A **86**
Ermine Rd. *N15* —6F **31**
Ermine Rd. *SE13* —4D **96**
Ermine Side. *Enf* —5B **8**
Ermington Rd. *SE9* —2G **115**
Ernald Av. *E6* —2C **66**
Erncroft Way. *Twic* —6K **87**
Ernest Av. *SE27* —4B **110**
Ernest Clo. *Beck* —5C **126**
Ernest Gdns. *W4* —6H **73**
Ernest Gro. *Beck* —5B **126**
Ernest Rd. *King T* —2H **119**
Ernest Sq. *King T* —2H **119**
Ernest St. *E1* —4K **63**
Ernle Rd. *SW20* —7D **106**
Ernshaw Pl. *SW15* —5G **91**
Erpingham Rd. *SW15* —3E **90**
Erridge Rd. *SW19* —2J **121**
Errington Rd. *W9* —4H **59**

Errol Gdns. *Hayes* —4A **54**
Errol Gdns. *N Mald* —4C **120**
Errol St. *EC1* —4C **62** (4D **144**)
Erskine Clo. *Sutt* —3C **132**
Erskine Cres. *N17* —4H **31**
Erskine Hill. *NW11* —4J **27**
Erskine Ho. *NW3* —7D **44**
(off Erskine Rd.)
Erskine Rd. *E17* —4B **32**
Erskine Rd. *NW3* —7D **44**
Erskine Rd. *Sutt* —4B **132**
Erwood Rd. *SE7* —5C **82**
Esam Way. *SW16* —5A **110**
Escott Gdns. *SE9* —4C **114**
Escreet Gro. *SE18* —4E **82**
Esher Av. *Romf* —6J **37**
Esher Av. *Sutt* —3F **131**
Esher Clo. *Bex* —1E **116**
Esher Gdns. *SW19* —2F **107**
Esher M. *Mitc* —3E **122**
Esher Rd. *Ilf* —3J **51**
Eskdale Av. *N'holt* —1D **54**
Eskdale Clo. *Wemb* —2D **40**
Eskdale Rd. *Bexh* —2G **101**
Eskmont Ridge. *SE19* —7E **110**
Esk Rd. *E13* —4J **65**
Esk Way. *Romf* —1K **37**
Esmar Cres. *NW9* —7C **26**
Esmeralda Rd. *SE1* —4G **79**
Esmond Gdns. *W4* —4K **73**
Esmond Rd. *NW6* —1H **59**
Esmond Rd. *W4* —4K **73**
Esmond St. *SW15* —4G **91**
Esparto St. *SW18* —7K **91**
Essan Ho. *W5* —5B **56**
Essenden Rd. *Belv* —5G **85**
Essenden Rd. *S Croy* —7E **134**
Essendine Rd. *W9* —4J **59**
Essex Av. *Iswth* —3J **87**
Essex Clo. *E17* —4A **32**
Essex Clo. *Mord* —7F **121**
Essex Clo. *Romf* —4H **37**
Essex Clo. *Ruis* —1B **38**
Essex Ct. *EC4* —6A **62** (1J **149**)
Essex Ct. *SW13* —2B **90**
Essex Gdns. *N4* —6B **30**
Essex Gro. *SE19* —6D **110**
Essex Hall. *E17* —1K **31**
Essex Mans. *E11* —7F **33**
Essex Pk. *N3* —6E **14**
Essex Pk. M. *W3* —1A **74**
Essex Pl. *W4* —4J **73**
Essex Pl. Sq. *W4* —4K **73**
Essex Rd. *E4* —1B **20**
Essex Rd. *E10* —6E **32**
Essex Rd. *E12* —5C **50**
Essex Rd. *E17* —6A **32**
Essex Rd. *E18* —2K **33**
Essex Rd. *N1* —1B **62**
Essex Rd. *NW10* —7A **42**
Essex Rd. *W3* —7J **57**
Essex Rd. *W4* —4K **73**
(in two parts)
Essex Rd. *Bark* —7H **51**
Essex Rd. *Chad H* —7C **36**
Essex Rd. *Dag* —5J **53**
Essex Rd. *Enf* —4J **7**
Essex Rd. *Romf* —4H **37**
Essex Rd. S. *E11* —7F **33**
Essex St. *E7* —5J **49**
Essex St. *WC2* —7A **62** (1J **149**)
Essex Vs. *W8* —2J **75**
Essex Wharf. *E5* —1K **47**
Essian St. *E1* —5A **64**
Essoldo Way. *Edgw* —3F **25**

Estate Way. *E10* —1B **48**
Estcourt Rd. *SE25* —6H **125**
Estcourt Rd. *SW6* —7H **75**
Estella Av. *N Mald* —4D **120**
Estelle Rd. *NW3* —4D **44**
Esterbrooke St. *SW1*
—4H **77** (4C **154**)
Este Rd. *SW11* —3C **92**
Esther Clo. *N21* —7F **7**
Esther Rd. *E11* —7G **33**
Estoria Clo. *SW2* —7A **94**
Estreham Rd. *SW16* —6H **109**
Estridge Clo. *Houn* —4E **86**
Estuary Clo. *Bark* —3B **68**
Eswyn Rd. *SW17* —4D **108**
Etchingham Ct. *N3* —7F **15**
Etchingham Pk. Rd. *N3* —7E **14**
Etchingham Rd. *E15* —4E **48**
Eternit Wlk. *SW6* —1F **91**
Etfield Gro. *Sidc* —5B **116**
Ethelbert Clo. *Brom* —2J **127**
Ethelbert Gdns. *Ilf* —5D **34**
Ethelbert Rd. *SW20* —1F **121**
Ethelbert Rd. *Brom* —3J **127**
Ethelbert Rd. *Eri* —7J **85**
Ethelbert St. *SW12* —1F **109**
Ethelburga St. *SW11* —1C **92**
Etheldene Av. *N10* —4G **29**
Ethelden Rd. *W12* —1D **74**
Ethel Rd. *E16* —6K **65**
Ethel St. *SE17* —4C **78** (4D **156**)
Etheridge Rd. *NW4* —7E **26**
Etherley Rd. *N15* —5C **30**
Etherow St. *SE22* —7G **95**
Etherstone Grn. *SW16* —4A **110**
Etherstone Rd. *SW16* —4A **110**
Ethnard Rd. *SE15* —6H **79**
Ethronvi Rd. *Bexh* —3E **100**
Etloe Rd. *E10* —2C **48**
Eton Av. *N12* —7F **15**
Eton Av. *NW3* —7B **44**
Eton Av. *Barn* —6H **5**
Eton Av. *Houn* —6D **70**
Eton Av. *N Mald* —5K **119**
Eton Av. *Wemb* —4B **40**
Eton Clo. *SW18* —7K **91**
Eton College Rd. *NW3* —6D **44**
Eton Ct. *Wemb* —4C **40**
Eton Garages. *NW3* —6C **44**
Eton Gro. *NW9* —3G **25**
Eton Gro. *SE13* —3G **97**
Eton Ho. *N5* —4B **46**
(off Leigh Rd.)
Eton Mnr. Ct. *E10* —2C **48**
Eton Pl. *NW3* —7E **44**
Eton Rise. *NW3* —6D **44**
Eton Rd. *NW3* —7D **44**
Eton Rd. *Ilf* —4G **51**
Eton St. *Rich* —5E **88**
Eton Vs. *NW3* —6D **44**
Etta St. *SE8* —6A **80**
Ettrick St. *E14* —6E **64**
(in two parts)
Etwell Pl. *Surb* —6F **119**
Eugenia Rd. *SE16* —4J **79**
Eureka Rd. *King T* —2G **119**
Eurolink Bus. Cen. *SW2* —5A **94**
Europa Pl. *EC1* —3C **62** (2C **144**)
Europa Trad. Est. *Eri* —5K **85**
European Bus. Cen. *NW9* —3J **25**
Europe Rd. *SE18* —3D **82**
Eustace Ho. *SE11*
—4K **77** (3G **155**)
Eustace Pl. *SE18* —4D **82**
Eustace Rd. *E6* —3C **66**

Eustace Rd. *SW6* —7J **75**
Eustace Rd. *Romf* —7D **36**
Euston Gro. *NW1*
—3H **61** (2C **142**)
Euston Rd. *NW1* —4F **61** (3A **142**)
Euston Rd. *Croy* —1A **134**
Euston Sq. *NW1*
—3H **61** (2C **142**)
Euston Sta. Colonnade. *NW1*
—3H **61** (2D **142**)
Euston St. *NW1* —3G **61** (2B **142**)
Euston Underpass. (Junct.)
—4G **61**
Evandale Rd. *SW9* —2A **94**
Evangelist Rd. *NW5* —4F **45**
Evans Clo. *E8* —6F **47**
Evans Gro. *Felt* —2E **102**
Evans Ho. *W12* —7D **58**
(off White City Est.)
Evans Ho. *Felt* —2E **102**
Evans Rd. *SE6* —2G **113**
Evanston Av. *E4* —7K **19**
Evanston Gdns. *Ilf* —6C **34**
Eva Rd. *Romf* —7C **36**
Evelina Mans. *SE5* —7D **78**
Evelina Rd. *SE15* —3H **95**
Evelina Rd. *SE20* —7J **111**
Eveline Rd. *Mitc* —1D **122**
Evelyn Av. *NW9* —4K **25**
Evelyn Clo. *Twic* —7F **87**
Evelyn Ct. *E8* —4G **47**
Evelyn Dennington Ct. *N1* —7B **46**
(off Upper St.)
Evelyn Dennington Rd. *E6*
—4C **66**
Evelyn Dri. *Pinn* —1B **22**
Evelyn Fox Ct. *W10* —5E **58**
Evelyn Gdns. *SW7*
—5A **76** (6A **152**)
Evelyn Gdns. *Rich* —4E **88**
Evelyn Gro. *W5* —1F **73**
Evelyn Gro. *S'hall* —6D **54**
Evelyn Ho. *W12* —2B **74**
(off Cobbold Rd.)
Evelyn Lowe Est. *SE16* —3G **79**
Evelyn Mans. *W14* —6G **75**
(off Queen's Club Gdns.)
Evelyn Rd. *E16* —1J **81**
Evelyn Rd. *E17* —4E **32**
Evelyn Rd. *SW19* —5K **107**
Evelyn Rd. *W4* —3K **73**
Evelyn Rd. *Cockf* —4J **5**
Evelyn Rd. *Ham* —3C **104**
Evelyn Rd. *Rich* —3E **88**
Evelyn St. *SE8* —4A **80**
Evelyn Ter. *Rich* —3E **88**
Evelyn Wlk. *N1* —2D **62** (1E **144**)
Evelyn Way. *Wall* —4H **133**
Evelyn Yd. *W1* —6H **61** (7C **142**)
Evening Hill. *Beck* —7E **112**
Evenlode Ho. *SE2* —2C **84**
Evenwood Clo. *SW15* —5G **91**
Everall Av. *SW6* —2K **91**
Everard Av. *Brom* —1J **137**
Everard Ct. *N13* —3E **16**
Everard Ho. *E1* —6G **63**
(off Boyd St.)
Everard Way. *Wemb* —3E **40**
Everatt Clo. *SW18* —6H **91**
Everdon Rd. *SW13* —6C **74**
Everest Pl. *E14* —5E **64**
Everest Rd. *SE9* —5D **98**
Everett Clo. *Bush* —1D **10**
Everett Wlk. *Belv* —5F **85**
Everglade Strand. *NW9* —1B **26**

Everilda St. N1 —1K 61
Evering Rd. N16 & E5 —3F 47
Everington Rd. N10 —2D 28
Everington St. W6 —6F 75
Everitt Rd. NW10 —3K 57
Everleigh St. N4 —1K 45
Eve Rd. E11 —4G 49
Eve Rd. E15 —2G 65
Eve Rd. N17 —3E 30
Eve Rd. Iswth —4A 88
Eversfield Gdns. NW7 —6F 13
Eversfield Rd. Rich —2F 89
Evershed Wlk. W4 —3J 73
Eversholt St. NW1
—2G 61 (1B 142)
Evershot Rd. N4 —1K 45
Eversleigh Rd. E6 —1B 66
Eversleigh Rd. N3 —7C 14
Eversleigh Rd. SW11 —3D 92
Eversleigh Rd. Barn —5F 5
Eversley Av. Bexh —2K 101
Eversley Av. Wemb —2G 41
Eversley Clo. N21 —6E 6
Eversley Cres. N21 —6F 7
Eversley Cres. Iswth —1H 87
Eversley Mt. N21 —6E 6
Eversley Pk. SW19 —6D 106
Eversley Pk. Rd. N21 —6E 6
Eversley Rd. SE7 —6A 80
Eversley Rd. SE19 —7D 110
Eversley Rd. Surb —4F 119
Eversley Way. Croy —3C 136
Everthorpe Rd. SE15 —3F 95
Everton Bldgs. NW1
—3G 61 (2A 142)
Everton Dri. Stan —3E 24
Everton Rd. Croy —1G 135
Evesham Av. E17 —2C 32
Evesham Clo. Gnfd —2F 55
Evesham Clo. Sutt —7J 131
Evesham Ct. W13 —1A 72
(off Tewkesbury Rd.)
Evesham Ct. Rich —6F 89
Evesham Grn. Mord —6K 121
Evesham Rd. E15 —7H 49
Evesham Rd. N11 —5B 16
Evesham Rd. Mord —6K 121
Evesham St. W11 —7F 59
Evesham Wlk. SE5 —2D 94
Evesham Wlk. SW9 —2A 94
Evesham Way. SW11 —3E 92
Evesham Way. Ilf —3E 34
Evry Rd. Sidc —6C 116
Ewald Rd. SW6 —2H 91
Ewanrigg Ter. Wfd G —5F 21
Ewart Gro. N22 —1A 30
Ewart Pl. E3 —2B 64
Ewart Rd. SE23 —7K 95
Ewe Clo. N7 —6J 45
Ewell By-Pass. Eps —7C 130
Ewell Ct. Av. Ewe —5A 130
Ewellhurst Rd. Ilf —2C 34
Ewell Pk. Gdns. Eps —7C 130
Ewell Pk. Way. Eps —6C 130
Ewell Rd. Dit H —7B 118
Ewell Rd. Surb —6E 118
Ewell Rd. Sutt —7F 131
Ewelme Rd. SE23 —1J 111
Ewen Cres. SW2 —1A 110
Ewen Ho. N1 —1K 61
(off Barnsbury Est.)
Ewer St. SE1 —1C 78 (5C 150)
Ewhurst Av. S Croy —7H 135
Ewhurst Clo. Sutt —7E 130
Ewhurst Rd. SE4 —6B 96

Exbury Ho. E9 —6J 47
Exbury Rd. SE6 —2C 112
Excel Ct. WC2 —7H 61 (3D 148)
Excelsior Clo. King T —2G 119
Excelsior Gdns. SE13 —2E 96
Exchange Arc. EC2
—5E 62 (5H 145)
Exchange Ct. WC2
—7J 61 (3F 149)
Exchange Mans. NW11 —7H 27
Exchange Pl. EC2
—5E 62 (5G 145)
Exchange Sq. EC2
—5E 62 (5G 145)
Exchange St. EC1
—3C 62 (2C 144)
Exchange St. Romf —5K 37
Exchange, The. Ilf —2F 51
Exeter Clo. E6 —6D 66
Exeter Gdns. Ilf —1C 50
Exeter Ho. Bark —7A 52
(off Margaret Bondfield Av.)
Exeter Ho. Felt —2C 102
(off Watermill Way)
Exeter M. NW6 —6K 43
Exeter Rd. E16 —5J 65
Exeter Rd. E17 —5C 32
Exeter Rd. N9 —2D 18
Exeter Rd. N14 —1A 16
Exeter Rd. NW2 —5G 43
Exeter Rd. SE15 —7F 79
Exeter Rd. Croy —7E 124
Exeter Rd. Dag —6H 53
Exeter Rd. Enf —3E 8
Exeter Rd. Felt —3D 102
Exeter Rd. Harr —2C 38
Exeter Rd. Well —2K 99
Exeter St. WC2 —7J 61 (2F 149)
Exeter Way. SE14 —7B 80
Exford Gdns. SE12 —1K 113
Exford Rd. SE12 —2K 113
Exhibition Clo. W12 —7E 58
Exhibition Rd. SW7
—2B 76 (7B 146)
Exmoor Clo. Ilf —1F 35
Exmoor St. W10 —5F 59
Exmouth Mkt. EC1
—4A 62 (3J 143)
Exmouth M. NW1
—3G 61 (3B 142)
Exmouth Pl. E8 —7H 47
Exmouth Rd. E17 —5B 32
Exmouth Rd. Ruis —3A 38
Exmouth Rd. Well —1C 100
Exmouth St. E1 —6J 63
Exning Rd. E16 —4H 65
Exon St. SE17 —5B 78 (5G 157)
Express Dri. Ilf —1B 52
Exton Cres. NW10 —7J 41
Exton Gdns. Dag —5C 52
Exton St. SE1 —1A 78 (5J 149)
Eyebright Clo. Croy —1K 135
Eyhurst Clo. NW2 —2C 42
Eylewood Rd. SE27 —5C 110
Eynella Rd. SE22 —7F 95
Eynham Rd. W12 —6E 58
Eynsford Clo. Orp —7G 129
Eynsford Cres. Bex —1C 116
Eynsford Ho. SE15 —6J 79
Eynsford Rd. Ilf —2J 51
Eynsham Dri. SE2 —4A 84
Eynswood Dri. Sidc —5B 116
Eyot Gdns. W6 —5B 74
Eyot Grn. W4 —5B 74
Eyre Ct. NW8 —2B 60

Eyre St. Hill. EC1
—4A 62 (4J 143)
Eysdown Rd. SE9 —2C 114
Eysham Ct. New Bar —5E 4
Eythorne Rd. SW9 —1A 94
Ezra St. E2 —3F 63 (1K 145)

Faber Gdns. NW4 —5C 26
Fabian Rd. SW6 —7H 75
Fabian St. E6 —4C 66
Factory La. N17 —2F 31
Factory La. Croy —1A 134
Factory Pl. E14 —5D 80
Factory Rd. E16 —1B 82
Factory Sq. SW16 —6J 109
Factory Yd. W7 —1J 71
Fairacre. N Mald —3A 120
Fairacres. SW15 —4C 90
Fair Acres. Brom —5J 127
Fair Acres. Croy —7B 136
Fairbairn Grn. SW9 —1B 94
Fairbank Est. N1
—3D 62 (1E 144)
Fairbanks Rd. N17 —3F 31
Fairbourne Rd. N17 —3E 30
Fairbridge Rd. N19 —2H 45
Fairbrook Clo. N13 —5F 17
Fairbrook Rd. N13 —6F 17
Fairburn Ct. SW15 —5G 91
Fairburn Ho. W14 —5H 75
(off Ivatt Pl.)
Fairby Rd. SE12 —5K 97
Faircharm Trad. Est. SE8 —7D 80
Fairchild Clo. SW11 —2B 92
Fairchild Ho. N3 —1J 27
Fairchild Pl. EC2
—4E 62 (4H 145)
Fairchild St. EC2
—4E 62 (3H 145)
Fair Clo. Bush —1A 10
Fairclough St. E1 —6G 63
Faircroft Ct. Tedd —6A 104
Faircross Av. Bark —6G 51
Faircross Av. Romf —1K 37
Faircross Pde. Bark —6J 51
Fairdale Gdns. SW15 —4D 90
Fairfax Av. Eps —7D 130
Fairfax Gdns. SE3 —1A 98
Fairfax M. E16 —1K 81
Fairfax Pl. NW6 —7A 44
Fairfax Pl. W14 —3G 75
Fairfax Rd. N8 —4A 30
Fairfax Rd. NW6 —7A 44
Fairfax Rd. W4 —3A 74
Fairfax Rd. Tedd —6A 104
Fairfax Way. N10 —7K 15
Fairfield. N20 —7G 5
Fairfield Av. NW4 —6D 26
Fairfield Av. Edgw —6C 12
Fairfield Av. Twic —1F 103
Fairfield Clo. N12 —4F 15
Fairfield Clo. Enf —4E 8
Fairfield Clo. Ewe —5A 130
Fairfield Clo. Mitc —7C 108
Fairfield Clo. Sidc —6K 99
Fairfield Ct. NW10 —1C 58
Fairfield Cres. Edgw —6C 12
Fairfield Dri. SW18 —5K 91
Fairfield Dri. Gnfd —1C 56
Fairfield Dri. Harr —3G 23
Fairfield E. King T —2E 118
Fairfield Gdns. N8 —5J 29
Fairfield Gro. SE7 —6B 82
Fairfield N. King T —2E 118
Fairfield Path. Croy —3D 134

Fairfield Pl. King T —3E 118
Fairfield Rd. E3 —2C 64
Fairfield Rd. E17 —2A 32
Fairfield Rd. N8 —5J 29
Fairfield Rd. N18 —4B 18
Fairfield Rd. Beck —2C 126
Fairfield Rd. Bexh —2F 101
Fairfield Rd. Brom —7J 113
Fairfield Rd. Croy —3D 134
Fairfield Rd. Ilf —6F 51
Fairfield Rd. King T —2E 118
Fairfield Rd. Orp —6H 129
Fairfield Rd. S'hall —6D 54
Fairfield Rd. Wfd G —6D 20
Fairfields. NW9 —5J 25
Fairfields Cres. NW9 —5J 25
Fairfield S. King T —3E 118
Fairfields Rd. Houn —3G 87
Fairfield St. SW18 —5K 91
Fairfield Way. Barn —5D 4
Fairfield Way. Eps —5A 130
Fairfield W. King T —2E 118
Fairfoot Rd. E3 —4C 64
Fairford. SE6 —1C 112
Fairford Av. Bexh —1K 101
Fairford Av. Croy —5K 125
Fairford Clo. Croy —5K 125
Fairford Ct. Sutt —7K 131
Fairford Gdns. Wor Pk —3B 130
Fairford Ho. SE11
—4A 78 (4K 155)
Fairgreen. Barn —3J 5
Fairgreen E. Barn —3J 5
Fairgreen Rd. T Hth —5B 124
Fairhaven Av. Croy —6K 125
Fairhazel Gdns. NW6 —6K 43
Fairholme. N3 —4G 27
Fairholme Gdns. N3 —3G 27
Fairholme Rd. W14 —5G 75
Fairholme Rd. Croy —7A 124
Fairholme Rd. Harr —5K 23
Fairholme Rd. Ilf —7D 34
Fairholme Rd. Sutt —6H 131
Fairholt Clo. N16 —1E 46
Fairholt Rd. N16 —1D 46
Fairholt St. SW7
—3C 76 (1D 152)
Fairland Ho. Brom —4K 127
Fairland Rd. E15 —6H 49
Fairlands Av. Buck H —2D 20
Fairlands Av. Sutt —2J 131
Fairlands Av. T Hth —4K 123
Fairlands Ct. SE9 —6D 98
Fairlawn. SE7 —6A 82
Fairlawn Av. N2 —4C 28
Fairlawn Av. W4 —4J 73
Fairlawn Av. Bexh —2D 100
Fairlawn Clo. N14 —6B 6
Fairlawn Clo. Felt —4D 102
Fairlawn Clo. King T —6J 105
Fairlawn Ct. SE7 —7A 82
Fairlawn Ct. W4 —4J 73
Fairlawn Dri. Wfd G —7D 20
Fairlawn Gro. W4 —4J 73
Fairlawn Mans. SE14 —1K 95
Fairlawn Pk. SE26 —5A 112
Fairlawn Rd. SW19 —7H 107
Fairlawns. Pinn —2B 22
Fairlawns. Twic —6D 88
Fairlawns. Wall —5F 133
Fairlea Pl. W5 —4D 56
Fairlie Gdns. SE23 —7J 95
Fairlight Av. E4 —2A 20

Fairlight Av. NW10 —2A 58
Fairlight Av. Wfd G —6D 20
Fairlight Clo. E4 —2A 20
Fairlight Clo. Wor Pk —4E 130
Fairlight Ct. NW10 —2A 58
Fairlight Ct. Gnfd —2G 55
Fairlight Rd. SW17 —4B 108
Fairline Ct. Beck —2E 126
Fairlop Ct. E11 —1F 49
Fairlop Gdns. Ilf —1G 35
Fairlop Rd. E11 —7F 33
Fairlop Rd. Ilf —2G 35
Fairman Ter. Kent —4D 24
Fairmead. Brom —4D 128
Fairmead Clo. Brom —4D 128
Fairmead Clo. Houn —7B 70
Fairmead Clo. N Mald —3K 119
Fairmead Ct. Rich —2H 89
Fairmead Cres. Edgw —3D 12
Fairmead Gdns. Ilf —5C 34
Fairmead Ho. E9 —4A 48
Fairmead Rd. N19 —3H 45
Fairmead Rd. Croy —7K 123
Fairmile Av. SW16 —5H 109
Fairmile Ho. Tedd —4A 104
Fairmont Clo. Belv —5F 85
Fairmount Rd. SW2 —6K 93
Fairoak Clo. Orp —7F 129
Fairoak Dri. SE9 —5H 99
Fairoak Gdns. Romf —2K 37
Fairseat Clo. Bush —2D 10
Fairstead Wlk. N1 —1C 62
(off Popham St.)
Fair St. SE1 —2E 78 (6H 151)
Fair St. Houn —3G 87
Fairthorn Rd. SE7 —5J 81
Fairview. Ruis —4A 38
Fairview Av. Wemb —6D 40
Fairview Clo. E17 —1A 32
Fairview Clo. SE26 —5A 112
Fairview Ct. NW4 —2F 27
Fairview Cres. Harr —1E 38
Fairview Gdns. Wfd G —1K 33
Fairview Ho. SW2 —7K 93
Fairview Ind. Pk. Rain —5K 69
Fairview Pl. SW2 —7K 93
Fairview Rd. N15 —5F 31
Fairview Rd. SW16 —1K 123
Fairview Rd. Enf —1F 7
Fairview Rd. Sutt —5C 132
Fairview Vs. E4 —7J 19
Fairview Way. Edgw —4B 12
Fairwall Ho. SE5 —1E 94
Fairwater Av. Well —4A 100
Fairwater Clo. N15 —4E 30
Fairway. SW20 —3E 120
Fairway. Bexh —5E 100
Fairway. Orp —5H 129
Fair Way. Wfd G —5F 21
Fairway. Av. NW9 —3H 25
Fairway Clo. NW11 —7A 28
Fairway Clo. Croy —5A 126
Fairway Clo. Houn —5A 86
Fairway Ct. NW7 —3E 12
Fairway Ct. New Bar —6E 4
Fairway Dri. Gnfd —7F 39
Fairway Gdns. Beck —6F 127
Fairway Gdns. Ilf —5G 51
Fairways. E17 —4E 32
Fairways. Iswth —1J 87
Fairways. Stan —2E 24
Fairways. Tedd —7D 104
Fairways Bus. Pk. E10 —2B 48
Fairway, The. N13 —3J 17
Fairway, The. N14 —6B 6

Fairway, The. NW7 —3E **12**
Fairway, The. W3 —6A **58**
Fairway, The. Brom —5D **128**
Fairway, The. New Bar —6E **4**
Fairway, The. N Mald —1K **119**
Fairway, The. N'holt —6G **39**
Fairway, The. Ruis —4A **38**
Fairway, The. Wemb —2B **40**
Fairweather Clo. N15 —4C **30**
Fairweather Ct. N13 —4E **16**
Fairweather Rd. N16 —6G **31**
Fairwyn Rd. SE26 —4A **112**
Fakenham Clo. NW7 —7H **13**
Fakenham Clo. N'holt —6D **38**
Fakruddin St. E1 —4G **63**
Falcon Av. Brom —4C **128**
Falconberg Ct. W1
　　　　—6H **61** (7D **142**)
Falconberg M. W1
　　　　—6H **61** (7D **142**)
Falcon Clo. SE1 —1B **78** (4B **156**)
Falcon Clo. W4 —6J **73**
Falcon Ct. E18 —3K **33**
　　(off Albert Rd.)
Falcon Ct. EC4 —6A **62** (1K **149**)
Falcon Ct. New Bar —4F **5**
Falcon Cres. Enf —5E **8**
Falconer Ct. N17 —7H **17**
Falconer Wlk. N7 —2K **45**
Falcon Gro. SW11 —3C **92**
Falcon La. SW11 —3D **92**
Falcon Point. SE1
　　　　—7B **62** (3B **150**)
Falcon Rd. SW11 —2C **92**
Falcon Rd. Enf —5E **8**
Falcon Rd. Hamp —7D **102**
Falcon St. E13 —4H **65**
Falcon Ter. SW11 —3C **92**
Falcon Way. E11 —4J **33**
Falcon Way. E14 —4D **80**
Falcon Way. NW9 —2A **26**
Falcon Way. Harr —5E **24**
Falconwood. (Junct.) —4G **99**
Falconwood Av. Well —2H **99**
Falconwood Ct. SE3 —2H **97**
Falconwood Pde. Well —4K **99**
Falconwood Rd. Croy —7B **136**
Falcourt Clo. Sutt —5K **131**
Falkirk Ho. W9 —3K **59**
　　(off Maida Vale)
Falkirk St. N1 —2E **62** (1H **145**)
Falkland Av. N3 —7D **14**
Falkland Av. N11 —4A **16**
Falkland Ho. SE6 —4E **112**
Falkland Ho. W8 —3K **75**
Falkland Pk. Av. SE25 —3E **124**
Falkland Pl. NW5 —5G **45**
Falkland Rd. N8 —4A **30**
Falkland Rd. NW5 —5G **45**
Falkland Rd. Barn —2B **4**
Fallaize Av. Ilf —4F **51**
Falloden Way. NW11 —4J **27**
Fallow Ct. Av. N12 —7F **15**
Fallowfield. Stan —4F **11**
Fallowfield Ct. Stan —3F **11**
Fallowfields Dri. N12 —6H **15**
Fallowhurst Path. N3 —7F **15**
Fallows Clo. N2 —2B **28**
Fallsbrook Rd. SW16 —6F **109**
Falman Clo. N9 —1B **18**
Falmer Rd. E17 —3D **32**
Falmer Rd. N15 —5C **30**
Falmer Rd. Enf —4K **7**
Falmouth Av. E4 —5A **20**
Falmouth Clo. N22 —7E **16**

Falmouth Clo. SE12 —5H **97**
Falmouth Ho. Pinn —1D **22**
Falmouth Rd. SE1
　　　　—3C **78** (2D **156**)
Falmouth St. E15 —5F **49**
Falstaff Ct. SE11
　　(off Opal St.) —4B **78** (4A **156**)
Falstaff Ho. N1 —2E **62**
　　(off Arden Est.)
Falstaff M. Hamp —7G **103**
Fambridge Clo. SE26 —4B **112**
Fambridge Ct. Romf —5K **37**
　　(off Marks Rd.)
Fambridge Rd. Dag —1G **53**
Fancett Ho. SE5 —4D **94**
Fane St. W14 —6H **75**
Fann St. EC1 —4C **62** (4C **144**)
Fanshawe Av. Bark —6G **51**
Fanshawe Cres. Dag —5E **52**
Fanshawe Rd. Rich —4C **104**
Fanshaw St. N1 —3E **62** (1G **145**)
Fantail, The. (Junct.) —3D **138**
Fanthorpe St. SW15 —3E **90**
Faraday Av. Sidc —2A **116**
Faraday Clo. N7 —6K **45**
Faraday Ho. Wemb —3J **41**
Faraday Rd. E15 —6H **49**
Faraday Rd. SW19 —6J **107**
Faraday Rd. W3 —7J **57**
Faraday Rd. W10 —5G **59**
Faraday Rd. S'hall —7F **55**
Faraday Rd. Well —3A **100**
Faraday Way. SE18 —3B **82**
Faraday Way. Croy —1K **133**
Fareham Rd. Felt —7A **86**
Fareham St. W1
　　　　—6H **61** (7C **142**)
Farewell Pl. Mitc —1C **122**
Faringdon Av. Brom —7E **128**
Faringford Rd. E15 —7G **49**
Farjeon Ho. NW6 —7B **44**
　　(off Hilgrove Rd.)
Farjeon Rd. SE3 —1B **98**
Farleigh Av. Brom —7H **127**
Farleigh Pl. N16 —4F **47**
Farleigh Rd. N16 —4F **47**
Farley Dri. Ilf —1J **51**
Farley Ho. SE26 —3H **111**
Farley Pl. SE25 —4G **125**
Farley Rd. SE6 —7D **96**
Farley Rd. S Croy —7G **135**
Farlington Pl. SW15 —7D **90**
Farlow Rd. SW15 —3F **91**
Farlton Rd. SW18 —7K **91**
Farm Av. NW2 —3G **43**
Farm Av. SW16 —4J **109**
Farm Av. Harr —7D **22**
Farm Av. Wemb —6C **40**
Farmborough Clo. Harr —7H **23**
Farm Clo. N14 —6A **6**
Farm Clo. NW4 —3C **26**
Farm Clo. Buck H —3F **21**
Farm Clo. Dag —7J **53**
Farm Clo. S'hall —7F **55**
Farm Clo. Sutt —7B **132**
Farm Clo. W Wick —3H **137**
Farmcote Rd. SE12 —1J **113**
Farm Ct. NW4 —3C **26**
Farmdale Rd. SE10 —5J **81**
Farmdale Rd. Cars —7C **132**
Farm Dri. Croy —2B **136**
Farmer Rd. E10 —1D **48**
Farmer's Rd. SE5 —7B **78**
Farmer St. W8 —1J **75**

Farmfield Rd. Brom —5G **113**
Farm Ho. Ct. NW7 —7H **13**
Farmhouse Rd. SW16 —7G **109**
Farmilo Rd. E17 —7B **32**
Farmington Av. Sutt —3B **132**
Farmlands. Enf —1F **7**
Farmlands, The. N'holt —6E **38**
Farmland Wlk. Chst —5F **115**
Farm La. N14 —6K **5**
Farm La. SW6 —6J **75**
Farm La. Croy —2B **136**
Farm La. Clo. SW6 —7J **75**
　　(off Farm La.)
Farmleigh. N14 —7B **6**
Farmleigh Ho. SE24 —5B **94**
Farm M. Mitc —2F **123**
Farm Pl. W8 —1J **75**
Farm Rd. N21 —1H **17**
Farm Rd. Edgw —6C **12**
Farm Rd. Houn —1C **102**
Farm Rd. Mord —5K **121**
Farm Rd. Sutt —7B **132**
Farmstead Rd. SE6 —4D **112**
Farmstead Rd. Harr —1H **23**
Farm St. W1 —7F **61** (3J **147**)
Farm Vale. Bex —6H **101**
Farm Wlk. NW11 —5H **27**
Farm Way. Buck H —4F **21**
Farmway. Dag —3C **52**
Farm Way. Wor Pk —3E **130**
Farnaby Rd. SE9 —4A **98**
Farnaby Rd. Brom —7F **113**
Farnan Av. E17 —2C **32**
Farnan Rd. SW16 —5J **109**
Farnborough Av. E17 —1H **31**
Farnborough Av. S Croy —7K **135**
Farnborough Clo. Wemb —2H **41**
Farnborough Comn. Orp
　　　　—3D **138**
Farnborough Cres. Brom
　　　　—1H **137**
Farnborough Cres. S Croy
　　　　—7A **136**
Farnborough Way. SE15 —7F **79**
Farncombe St. SE16 —2G **79**
Farndale Av. N13 —3G **17**
Farndale Cres. Gnfd —3G **55**
Farnell M. SW5 —5K **75**
Farnell Point. E5 —4J **47**
Farnell Rd. Iswth —3H **87**
Farnham Clo. N20 —7F **5**
Farnham Ct. S'hall —6G **55**
　　(off Redcroft Rd.)
Farnham Gdns. SW20 —2D **120**
Farnham Pl. SE1
　　　　—1B **78** (5B **150**)
Farnham Rd. Ilf —7K **35**
Farnham Rd. Well —2C **100**
Farnham Royal. SE11
　　　　—5K **77** (6H **155**)
Farningham Ct. SW16 —7H **109**
Farningham Ho. N4 —7D **30**
Farningham Rd. N17 —7B **18**
Farnley Ho. SW8 —2H **93**
Farnley Rd. E4 —1B **20**
Farnley Rd. SE25 —4D **124**
Faro Clo. Brom —2E **128**
Faroe Rd. W14 —3F **75**
Farorna Wlk. Enf —1F **7**
Farquhar Rd. SE19 —5F **111**
Farquhar Rd. SW19 —3J **107**
Farquharson Rd. Croy —1C **134**
Farrance Rd. Romf —7E **36**
Farrance St. E14 —6C **64**

Farrans Ct. Harr —7B **24**
Farrant Av. N22 —2A **30**
Farr Av. Bark —2A **68**
Farren Rd. SE23 —2A **112**
Farrer Ct. Twic —7D **88**
Farrer Ho. SE8 —7C **80**
Farrer M. N8 —4H **29**
Farrer Rd. N8 —4H **29**
Farrer Rd. Harr —5E **24**
Farrer's Pl. Croy —4K **135**
Farrier Rd. N'holt —2E **54**
Farrier St. NW1 —7F **45**
Farrier Wlk. SW10 —6A **76**
Farringdon La. EC1
　　　　—4A **62** (4K **143**)
Farringdon Rd. EC1
　　　　—4A **62** (3J **143**)
Farringdon St. EC4
　　　　—5B **62** (6A **144**)
Farrington Pl. Chst —7H **115**
Farrins Rents. SE16 —1A **80**
Farrow La. SE14 —7J **79**
Farrow Pl. SE16 —3A **80**
Farr Rd. Enf —1J **7**
Farthingale Wlk. E15 —7F **49**
Farthing All. SE1
　　　　—2G **79** (7K **151**)
Farthing Barn La. Orp —7E **138**
Farthing Fields. E1 —1H **79**
Farthings Clo. E4 —3B **20**
Farthings Clo. Pinn —6A **22**
Farthings, The. King T —1E **119**
Farthing St. Orp —7D **138**
Farwell Rd. Sidc —4B **116**
Farwig La. Brom —1H **127**
Fashion St. E1 —5F **63** (6J **145**)
Fashoda Rd. Brom —4B **128**
Fassett Rd. E8 —6G **47**
Fassett Rd. King T —4E **118**
Fassett Sq. E8 —6G **47**
Fauconberg Ct. W4 —6J **73**
　　(off Fauconberg Rd.)
Fauconberg Rd. W4 —6J **73**
Faulkner Clo. Dag —7D **36**
Faulkner's All. EC1
　　　　—5B **62** (5A **144**)
Faulkner St. SE14 —1J **95**
Fauna Clo. Romf —6C **36**
Faunce St. SE17
　　　　—5B **78** (6A **156**)
Favart Rd. SW6 —1J **91**
Faversham Av. E4 —1B **20**
Faversham Av. Enf —6J **7**
Faversham Rd. SE6 —7B **96**
Faversham Rd. Beck —2B **126**
Faversham Rd. Mord —6K **121**
Fawcett Clo. SW11 —2B **92**
Fawcett Est. E5 —1G **47**
Fawcett Rd. NW10 —1B **58**
Fawcett Rd. Croy —3C **134**
Fawcett St. SW10 —6A **76**
Fawe Pk. Rd. SW15 —4H **91**
Fawe St. E14 —5D **64**
Fawley Rd. NW6 —5K **43**
Fawnbrake Av. SE24 —5B **94**
Fawn Rd. E13 —2A **66**
Fawood Av. NW10 —7K **41**
Faygate Cres. Bexh —5G **101**
Faygate Rd. SW2 —2K **109**
Fayland Av. SW16 —5G **109**
Fearnley Cres. Hamp —5C **102**
Fearnley Ho. SE5 —2E **94**
Fearon St. SE10 —5J **81**
Featherbed La. Croy & Warl
　　　　—7B **136**

Feathers Pl. SE10 —6F **81**
Featherstone Av. SE23 —2J **111**
Featherstone Ho. Hayes —5A **54**
Featherstone Ind. Est. S'hall
　　(off Dominion Rd.) —3C **70**
Featherstone Rd. NW7 —6J **13**
Featherstone Rd. S'hall —3C **70**
Featherstone St. EC1
　　　　—4D **62** (3E **144**)
Featherstone Ter. S'hall —3C **70**
Featley Rd. SW9 —3B **94**
Federal Rd. Gnfd —1C **56**
Federation Rd. SE2 —4B **84**
Felbridge Av. Stan —1A **24**
Felbridge Clo. SW16 —4A **110**
Felbridge Clo. Sutt —7K **131**
Felbrigge Rd. Ilf —2K **51**
Felday Rd. SE13 —6D **96**
Felden Clo. Pinn —1C **22**
Felden St. SW6 —1H **91**
Feldman Clo. N16 —1G **47**
Felgate M. W6 —4D **74**
Felhampton Rd. SE9 —3F **115**
Felhurst Cres. Dag —4H **53**
Feline Ct. Barn —6H **5**
Felix Av. N8 —6J **29**
Felix Ct. E17 —5D **32**
Felix Mnr. Chst —6J **115**
Felix Rd. W13 —7A **56**
Felixstowe Rd. N9 —4B **18**
Felixstowe Rd. N17 —3F **31**
Felixstowe Rd. NW10 —3D **58**
Felixstowe Rd. SE2 —3B **84**
Felix St. E2 —2H **63**
Fellbrigg Rd. SE22 —5F **95**
Fellbrigg St. E1 —4H **63**
Fellbrook. Rich —3B **104**
Fellowes Clo. Hayes —4B **54**
Fellowes Rd. Cars —3C **132**
Fellows Ct. E2 —2E **63** (1J **145**)
Fellows Rd. NW3 —7B **44**
Felltram Way. SE7 —5J **81**
Fell Wlk. Edgw —1J **25**
Felmersham Clo. SW4 —4J **93**
Felmingham Rd. SE20 —2J **125**
Felnex Trad. Est. NW10 —2K **57**
Felsberg Rd. SW2 —7J **93**
Fels Clo. Dag —3H **53**
Fels Farm Av. Dag —3J **53**
Felsham Rd. SW15 —3E **90**
Felspar Clo. SE18 —5K **83**
Felstead Av. Ilf —1E **34**
Felstead Gdns. E14 —5E **80**
Felstead Rd. E11 —7J **33**
Felstead St. E9 —6B **48**
Felstead Wharf. E14 —5E **80**
Felsted Rd. E16 —6B **66**
Feltham Bus. Complex. Felt
　　　　—3A **102**
Felthambrook Ind. Est. Felt
　　　　—3A **102**
Felthambrook Way. Felt —3A **102**
Feltham Bus. Complex. Felt
　　　　—2A **102**
Felthamhill Rd. Felt —5A **102**
Feltham Rd. Mitc —2C **122**
Felton Clo. Orp —6F **129**
Felton Ct. N1 —1D **62**
Felton Gdns. Bark —1J **67**
Felton Ho. N1 —1D **62**
　　(off Colville Est.)
Felton Lea. Sidc —5K **115**
Felton Rd. W13 —2C **72**
Felton Rd. Bark —2J **67**
Fenchurch Av. EC3
　　　　—6E **62** (1G **151**)

Fenchurch Bldgs. *EC3*
—6E **62** (1H **151**)
Fenchurch Pl. *EC3*
—7E **62** (2H **151**)
Fenchurch St. *EC3*
—7E **62** (2G **151**)
Fen Ct. *EC3* —6E **62** (2G **151**)
Fendall St. *SE1* —3E **78** (2H **157**)
(in two parts)
Fendt Clo. *E16* —6H **65**
Fendyke Rd. *Belv* —4D **84**
Fenelon Pl. *W14* —4H **75**
Fen Gro. *Sidc* —5K **99**
Fenham Rd. *SE15* —7G **79**
Fenhurst Gdns. *Edgw* —6B **12**
Fenman Ct. *N17* —1H **31**
Fenman Gdns. *Ilf* —1B **52**
Fenn Clo. *Brom* —6J **113**
Fennel Clo. *E16* —4G **65**
Fennel Clo. *Croy* —1K **135**
Fennells Mead. *Eps* —7B **130**
Fennell St. *SE18* —6E **82**
Fenner Clo. *SE16* —4H **79**
Fenner Sq. *SW11* —3B **92**
Fen Ho. *Iswth* —1B **88**
Fenning St. *SE1* —2E **78** (6G **151**)
Fenn St. *E9* —5J **47**
Fenstanton Av. *N12* —5G **15**
Fen St. *E16* —7H **65**
Fenswood Clo. *Bex* —6G **101**
Fentiman Rd. *SW8*
—6J **77** (7F **155**)
Fenton Clo. *E8* —6F **47**
Fenton Clo. *SW9* —2K **93**
Fenton Clo. *Chst* —5D **114**
Fenton Ho. *SE14* —7A **80**
Fenton Ho. *Houn* —6E **70**
Fenton Rd. *N17* —7H **17**
Fentons Av. *E13* —3K **65**
Fenton St. *E1* —6H **63**
Fenwick Gro. *SE18* —6E **82**
Fenwick Pl. *SW9* —3J **93**
Fenwick Pl. *S Croy* —7B **134**
Fenwick Rd. *SE15* —3G **95**
Ferby Ct. *Sidc* —4K **115**
(off Main Rd.)
Ferdinand Pl. *NW1* —7E **44**
Ferdinand St. *NW1* —7E **44**
Ferguson Av. *Surb* —5F **119**
Ferguson Clo. *E14* —4C **80**
Ferguson Clo. *Brom* —3F **127**
Ferguson Dri. *W3* —6K **57**
Ferguson Ho. *E17* —6A **32**
Ferguson Ho. *SE10* —1E **96**
Fergus Rd. *N5* —5B **46**
Fermain Ct. E. *N1* —1E **62**
(off De Beauvoir Est.)
Fermain Ct. N. *N1* —1E **62**
(off De Beauvoir Est.)
Fermain Ct. W. *N1* —1E **62**
(off De Beauvoir Est.)
Ferme Pk. Rd. *N8 & N4* —5J **29**
Fermor Rd. *SE23* —1A **112**
Fermoy Rd. *W9* —4H **59**
Fermoy Rd. *Gnfd* —4F **55**
Fern Av. *Mitc* —4H **123**
Fernbank. *Buck H* —1E **20**
Fernbank Av. *Wemb* —4K **39**
Fernbank M. *SW12* —6F **93**
Fernbrook Av. *Sidc* —5J **99**
Fernbrook Cres. *SE13* —6G **97**
(off Fernbrook Rd.)
Fernbrook Dri. *Harr* —7F **23**
Fernbrook Rd. *SE13* —6G **97**

Ferncliff Rd. *E8* —5G **47**
Fern Clo. *N1* —2E **62**
Fern Clo. *SE14* —2K **95**
Fern Ct. *Bexh* —4G **101**
Ferncroft Av. *N12* —6J **15**
Ferncroft Av. *NW3* —3J **43**
Ferncroft Av. *Ruis* —2A **38**
Ferndale. *Brom* —2A **128**
Ferndale Av. *E17* —5F **33**
Ferndale Av. *Houn* —3C **86**
Ferndale Clo. *Bexh* —1E **100**
Ferndale Rd. *E7* —7K **49**
Ferndale Rd. *E11* —2G **49**
Ferndale Rd. *N15* —6F **31**
Ferndale Rd. *SE25* —5H **125**
Ferndale Rd. *SW4 & SW9* —4J **93**
Ferndale Rd. *Romf* —2J **37**
Ferndale St. *E6* —7F **67**
Ferndale Ter. *Harr* —4K **23**
Ferndell Av. *Bex* —3K **117**
Fern Dene *W13* —5B **56**
Ferndene Rd. *SE24* —4C **94**
Ferndown Av. *Orp* —7H **129**
Ferndown Clo. *Pinn* —1C **22**
Ferndown Clo. *Sutt* —6B **132**
Ferndown Ct. *S'hall* —6G **55**
(off Haldane Rd.)
Ferndown Rd. *SE9* —7B **98**
Ferney Meade Way. *Iswth*
—2A **88**
Ferney Rd. *E Barn* —7K **5**
Fernhall Dri. *Ilf* —5B **34**
Fernham Rd. *T Hth* —3C **124**
Fernhead Rd. *W9* —3H **59**
Fernheath Way. *Dart* —5K **117**
Fernhill Ct. *E17* —2F **33**
Fernhill Gdns. *King T* —5D **104**
Fernhill St. *E16* —1D **82**
Fernholme Rd. *SE15* —5K **95**
Fernhurst Gdns. *Edgw* —6B **12**
Fernhurst Rd. *SW6* —1G **91**
Fernhurst Rd. *Croy* —1H **135**
Fern La. *Houn* —5D **70**
Fernlea Rd. *SW12* —1F **109**
Fernlea Rd. *Mitc* —2E **122**
Fernleigh Clo. *Croy* —4A **134**
Fernleigh Ct. *Harr* —2F **23**
Fernleigh Ct. *Romf* —5J **37**
Fernleigh Ct. *Wemb* —2E **40**
Fernleigh Rd. *N21* —2F **17**
Fernsbury St. *WC1*
—3A **62** (2J **143**)
Fernshaw Rd. *SW10* —6A **76**
Fernside. *NW11* —2J **43**
Fernside. *Buck H* —1E **20**
Fernside Av. *NW7* —3E **12**
Fernside Av. *Felt* —4A **102**
Fernside Ct. *NW4* —2F **27**
Fernside Rd. *SW12* —1D **108**
Ferns Rd. *E15* —6H **49**
Fern St. *E3* —4C **64**
Fernthorpe Rd. *SW16* —6G **109**
Ferntower Rd. *N5* —5D **46**
Fern Wlk. *SE16* —5G **79**
(off Argyle Way)
Fernways. *Ilf* —4G **51**
Fernwood. *Croy* —7A **136**
Fernwood Av. *SW16* —4H **109**
Fernwood Av. *Wemb* —6C **40**
Fernwood Clo. *Brom* —2A **128**
Fernwood Cres. *N20* —3J **15**
Ferny Hill. *Barn* —1J **5**
Ferranti Clo. *SE18* —4B **82**
Ferraro Clo. *Houn* —6E **70**

Ferrers Av. *Wall* —4H **133**
Ferrers Rd. *SW16* —5H **109**
Ferrestone Rd. *N8* —4K **29**
Ferriby Clo. *N1* —7A **46**
Ferrier Ind. Est. *SW18* —4K **91**
(off Ferrier St.)
Ferrier Point. *E16* —5J **65**
(off Forty Acre La.)
Ferrier St. *SW18* —4K **91**
Ferring Clo. *Harr* —1G **39**
Ferrings. *SE21* —3E **110**
Ferris Av. *Croy* —3B **136**
Ferris Rd. *SE22* —4G **95**
Ferron Rd. *E5* —3H **47**
Ferry App. *SE18* —3E **82**
Ferrybridge Ho. *SE11*
—3K **77** (2H **155**)
Ferrydale Lodge. *NW4* —4E **26**
(off Church Rd.)
Ferry Ho. *E5* —1H **47**
(off Harrington Hill)
Ferry Island Retail Pk. *N17*
—3G **31**
Ferry La. *N17* —4G **31**
Ferry La. *SW13* —6B **74**
Ferry La. *Bren* —6E **72**
Ferry La. *Rich* —6F **73**
Ferry La. Ind. Est. *E17* —4K **31**
Ferrymead Av. *Gnfd* —3E **54**
Ferrymead Dri. *Gnfd* —2E **54**
Ferrymead Gdns. *Gnfd* —2F **55**
Ferrymoor. *Rich* —3B **104**
Ferry Pl. *SE18* —3E **82**
Ferry Rd. *SW13* —7C **74**
Ferry Rd. *Tedd* —5B **104**
Ferry Rd. *Th Dit* —6B **118**
Ferry Rd. *Twic* —1A **104**
Ferry Sq. *Bren* —7E **72**
Ferry St. *E14* —5E **80**
Festing Rd. *SW15* —3F **91**
Festival Clo. *Bex* —1D **116**
Festival Wlk. *Cars* —5D **132**
Fetter La. *EC4* —6A **62** (1K **149**)
Finch St. *SE8* —7C **80**
Field Clo. *E4* —6J **19**
Field Clo. *Brom* —2A **128**
Field Clo. *Buck H* —3F **21**
Field Clo. *Houn* —2A **86**
Field Clo. *SW19* —3J **107**
Field Ct. *WC1* —5K **61** (6H **143**)
Field End. *N'holt* —6G **38**
Field End. *Ruis* —6A **38**
Field End. *Twic* —4K **103**
Fieldend Rd. *SW16* —1G **123**
Field End Rd. *Eastc & Ruis*
—6A **22**
Fielders Clo. *Enf* —4K **7**
Fielders Clo. *Harr* —1G **39**
Fieldfare Rd. *SE28* —7C **68**
Fieldgate La. *Mitc* —2C **122**
Fieldgate Mans. *E1* —5G **63**
(off Fieldgate St.)
Fieldgate St. *E1* —5G **63**
Fieldhouse Clo. *E18* —1K **33**
Fieldhouse Rd. *SW12* —1G **109**
Fielding Av. *Twic* —3G **103**
Fielding Ho. *W4* —6A **74**
(off Devonshire Rd.)
Fielding M. *SW13* —6D **74**
(off Castelnau Rd.)
Fielding Rd. *W4* —3K **73**
Fielding Rd. *W14* —3F **75**
Fieldings, The. *SE23* —1J **111**
Fielding St. *SE17*
—6C **78** (7C **156**)

Fielding Ter. *W5* —7F **57**
Field La. *Bren* —7C **72**
Field La. *Tedd* —5A **104**
Field Mead. *NW9 & NW7*
—7F **13**
Field Pl. *N Mald* —6B **120**
Field Point. *E7* —4H **49**
Field Rd. *E7* —4H **49**
Field Rd. *N17* —3D **30**
Field Rd. *W6* —5G **75**
Field Rd. *Felt* —6A **86**
Fieldsend Rd. *Sutt* —5G **131**
Fields Est. *E8* —7G **47**
Fieldside Rd. *Brom* —5F **113**
Fields Pk. Cres. *Romf* —5D **36**
Field St. *WC1* —3K **61** (1G **143**)
Fieldsway Ho. *N5* —5A **46**
Fieldview. *SW18* —1B **108**
Field Way. *NW10* —7J **41**
Fieldway. *Dag* —3C **52**
Field Way. *Gnfd* —1F **55**
Field Way. *New Ad* —7D **136**
Fieldway. *Orp* —6H **129**
Fieldway Cres. *N5* —5A **46**
Fiennes Clo. *Dag* —1C **52**
Fife Rd. *E16* —5J **65**
Fife Rd. *N22* —7G **17**
Fife Rd. *SW14* —5J **89**
Fife Rd. *King T* —2E **118**
Fife Ter. *N1* —2K **61**
Fifield Path. *SE23* —3K **111**
Fifth Av. *E12* —4D **50**
Fifth Av. *W10* —3G **59**
Fifth Cross Rd. *Twic* —2H **103**
Fifth Way. *Wemb* —4H **41**
Figges Rd. *Mitc* —7E **108**
Fig Tree Clo. *NW10* —1A **58**
Filanco Ct. *W7* —1K **71**
(off Uxbridge Rd.)
Filey Av. *N16* —1G **47**
Filey Clo. *Sutt* —7A **132**
Filigree Ct. *SE16* —1A **80**
Fillebrook Av. *Enf* —2K **7**
Fillebrook Rd. *E11* —1G **49**
Filmer Rd. *SW6* —1G **91**
Filston Rd. *Eri* —5J **85**
Filton Ct. *SE15* —6E **78**
(off Brockworth Clo.)
Finborough Rd. *SW10* —5K **75**
Finborough Rd. *SW17* —6D **108**
Finchale Rd. *SE2* —3A **84**
Finch Av. *SE27* —4D **110**
Finch Clo. *NW10* —6K **41**
Finch Clo. *Barn* —5D **4**
Finch Ct. *Sidc* —3B **116**
Finchdean Ho. *SW15* —7B **90**
Finchdean Way. *SE15* —7F **79**
Finch Dri. *Felt* —7B **86**
Finchingfield Av. *Wfd G* —7F **21**
Finch La. *EC3* —6D **62** (1F **151**)
Finchley Ct. *N3* —6E **14**
Finchley Ind. Est. *N12* —4F **15**
Finchley La. *NW4* —4E **26**
Finchley Pk. *N12* —4F **15**
Finchley Pl. *NW8* —2B **60**
Finchley Rd. *NW3* —4J **43**
Finchley Rd. *NW8* —1B **60**
Finchley Rd. *NW11 & NW2*
—4H **27**
Finchley Way. *N3* —7D **14**
Finch's Ct. *E14* —7D **64**
Finck St. *SE1* —2K **77** (7H **149**)
Finden Rd. *E7* —5A **50**
Findhorn Av. *Hayes* —5A **54**
Findhorn St. *E14* —6E **64**

Findon Clo. *SW18* —6J **91**
Findon Clo. *Harr* —3F **39**
Findon Rd. *N9* —1C **18**
Findon Rd. *W12* —2C **74**
Fingal St. *SE10* —5H **81**
Finland Rd. *SE4* —3A **96**
Finland St. *SE16* —3A **80**
Finlay St. *SW6* —1F **91**
Finmere Ho. *N4* —7C **30**
Finnis St. *E2* —3H **63**
Finnymore Rd. *Dag* —7E **52**
Finsbury Av. *EC2*
—5D **62** (6F **145**)
Finsbury Av. Sq. *EC2*
—5E **62** (5G **145**)
Finsbury Cir. *EC2*
—5D **62** (6F **145**)
Finsbury Cotts. *N22* —7D **16**
Finsbury Est. *EC1*
—3A **62** (2K **143**)
Finsbury Ho. *N22* —1J **29**
Finsbury Mkt. *EC2*
(in two parts) —4E **62** (4G **145**)
Finsbury Pk. Av. *N4* —6C **30**
Finsbury Pk. Rd. *N4* —2B **46**
Finsbury Pavement. *EC2*
—5D **62** (5F **145**)
Finsbury Rd. *N22* —7E **16**
Finsbury Sq. *EC2*
—4D **62** (5F **145**)
Finsbury St. *EC2*
—5D **62** (5E **144**)
Finsbury Way. *Bex* —6F **101**
Finsen Rd. *SE5* —4C **94**
Finstock Rd. *W10* —6F **59**
Finucane Rise. *Bush* —2B **10**
Fiona Ct. *NW6* —2H **59**
Firbank Clo. *E16* —5B **66**
Firbank Clo. *Enf* —4H **7**
Firbank Rd. *SE15* —2H **95**
Fircroft Gdns. *Harr* —3J **39**
Fircroft Rd. *SW17* —2D **108**
Fir Dene. *Orp* —3E **138**
Fire Bell La. *Surb* —6E **118**
Firecrest Dri. *NW3* —3K **43**
Firefly Clo. *Wall* —7J **133**
Firefly Gdns. *E6* —4C **66**
Fire Sta. All. *High Bar* —3B **4**
Fire Sta. M. *Beck* —1D **126**
Fir Gro. *N Mald* —6B **120**
Firhill Rd. *SE6* —4C **112**
Fir Rd. *Felt* —5B **102**
Fir Rd. *Sutt* —1H **131**
Firs Av. *N10* —3E **28**
Firs Av. *N11* —6J **15**
Firs Av. *SW14* —4J **89**
Firsby Av. *Croy* —1K **135**
Firsby Rd. *N16* —1G **47**
Firs Clo. *N10* —4E **28**
Firs Clo. *SE23* —7A **96**
Firs Clo. *Mitc* —1F **123**
Firscroft. *N13* —3H **17**
Firs Ho. *N22* —1A **30**
(off Acacia Rd.)
Firside Gro. *Sidc* —1K **115**
Firs La. *N13 & N21* —3H **17**
Firs La. *N21* —7H **7**
Firs Pk. Av. *N21* —1J **17**
Firs Pk. Gdns. *N21* —1J **17**
First Av. *E12* —4C **50**
First Av. *E13* —3J **65**
(in two parts)
First Av. *E17* —5C **32**
First Av. *N18* —4D **18**
First Av. *N21* —6A **8**

First Av. *NW4* —4E **26**
First Av. *SW14* —3A **90**
First Av. *W3* —1B **74**
First Av. *W10* —4H **59**
First Av. *Bexh* —7C **84**
First Av. *Dag* —2H **69**
First Av. *Enf* —5A **8**
First Av. *Eps* —7A **130**
First Av. *Romf* —5C **36**
First Av. *Wemb* —2D **40**
First Cross Rd. *Twic* —2J **103**
Firs, The. *E6* —7C **50**
Firs, The. *N20* —1G **15**
Firs, The. *SE26* —5H **111**
  (Lawrie Pk. Gdns.)
Firs, The. *SE26* —5J **111**
  (Venner Rd.)
Firs, The. *W5* —5D **56**
Firs, The. *Bex* —1K **117**
Firs, The. *Sidc* —3K **115**
First St. *SW3* —4C **76** (3D **152**)
Firstway. *SW20* —2E **120**
First Way. *Wemb* —4H **41**
Firs Wlk. *Wfd G* —5D **20**
Firswood Av. *Eps* —5B **130**
Firth Gdns. *SW6* —1G **91**
Firtree Av. *Mitc* —2E **122**
Firtree Clo. *SW16* —5G **109**
Fir Tree Clo. *W5* —6C **56**
Firtree Clo. *Ewe* —4B **130**
Fir Tree Clo. *Romf* —3K **37**
Firtree Gdns. *Croy* —4C **136**
Fir Tree Gro. *Cars* —7D **132**
Fir Tree Rd. *Houn* —4C **86**
Fir Trees Clo. *SE16* —1A **80**
Fir Tree Wlk. *Dag* —3J **53**
Fir Tree Wlk. *Enf* —3J **7**
Fir Wlk. *Sutt* —6F **131**
Fisher Clo. *Croy* —1F **135**
Fisher Clo. *Gnfd* —3E **54**
Fisher Ho. *N1* —1A **62**
  (off Barnsbury Est.)
Fisherman Clo. *Rich* —4C **104**
Fishermans Dri. *SE16* —2K **79**
Fisherman's Pl. *W4* —6B **74**
Fisherman's Wlk. *E14* —1C **80**
Fishermans Wlk. *SE28* —2J **83**
Fisher Rd. *Harr* —2K **23**
Fishers Ct. *SE14* —1K **95**
Fisher's La. *W4* —4K **73**
Fisher St. *E16* —5J **65**
Fisher St. *WC1* —5K **61** (6G **143**)
Fishers Way. *Belv* —1J **85**
Fisherton St. *NW8*
  —4B **60** (4A **140**)
Fishmongers Hall Wharf. *EC4*
  —7D **62** (3F **151**)
Fishponds Rd. *SW17* —4C **108**
Fishponds Rd. *Kes* —5B **138**
Fish St. Hill. *EC3*
  —7D **62** (3F **151**)
Fiske Ct. *N17* —1G **31**
Fiske Ct. *Bark* —2H **67**
Fisons Rd. *E16* —1J **81**
Fitzalan Rd. *N3* —3J **26**
Fitzalan St. *SE11*
  —4A **78** (3H **155**)
Fitzgeorge Av. *W14* —4G **75**
Fitzgeorge Av. *N Mald* —1K **119**
Fitzgerald Av. *SW14* —3A **90**
Fitzgerald Ct. *E10* —1D **48**
Fitzgerald Ho. *SW9* —2A **94**
Fitzgerald Rd. *E11* —5J **33**
Fitzgerald Rd. *SW14* —3K **89**
Fitzgerald Rd. *Th Dit* —6A **118**

Fitzhardinge St. *W1*
  —6E **60** (7G **141**)
Fitzhugh Gro. *SW18* —6B **92**
Fitzjames Av. *W14* —4G **75**
Fitzjames Av. *Croy* —2G **135**
Fitzjohn Av. *Barn* —5B **4**
Fitzjohn's Av. *NW3* —4A **44**
Fitzmaurice Pl. *W1*
  —1F **77** (4K **147**)
Fitzneal St. *W12* —6B **58**
Fitzroy Clo. *N6* —1D **44**
Fitzroy Ct. *N6* —6G **29**
Fitzroy Ct. *W1* —4G **61** (4B **142**)
Fitzroy Cres. *W4* —7K **73**
Fitzroy Gdns. *SE19* —7E **110**
Fitzroy M. *W1* —4G **61** (4A **142**)
Fitzroy Pk. *N6* —1D **44**
Fitzroy Rd. *NW1* —1E **60**
Fitzroy Sq. *W1* —4G **61** (4A **142**)
Fitzroy St. *W1* —4G **61** (4A **142**)
Fitzroy Yd. *NW1* —1E **60**
  (off Fitzroy Rd.)
Fitzstephen Rd. *Dag* —5B **52**
Fitzwarren Gdns. *N19* —1G **45**
Fitzwilliam Av. *Rich* —2F **89**
Fitzwilliam Heights. *SE23*
  —2J **111**
Fitzwilliam Ho. *Rich* —4D **88**
Fitzwilliam M. *E16* —1J **81**
Fitzwilliam Rd. *SW4* —3G **93**
Fitzwygram Clo. *Hamp* —5G **103**
Five Acre. *NW9* —2B **26**
Fiveacre Clo. *T Hth* —6A **124**
Five Elms Rd. *Brom* —2K **137**
Five Elms Rd. *Dag* —3F **53**
Fives Ct. *SE11* —3B **78** (2A **156**)
Fiveways. (Junct.) —2F **115**
Fiveways Corner. (Junct.)
  (Hendon) —1C **26**
Fiveways Corner. (Junct.)
  (Waddon) —4A **134**
Fiveways Rd. *SW9* —2A **94**
Flack Ct. *E10* —7D **32**
Fladbury Rd. *N15* —6D **30**
Fladgate Rd. *E11* —6G **33**
Flag Clo. *Croy* —1K **135**
Flambard Rd. *Harr* —6A **24**
Flamborough Ho. *SE15* —1G **95**
  (off Oliver Goldsmith Est.)
Flamborough St. *E14* —6A **64**
Flamingo Ct. *SE8* —7C **80**
  (off Hamilton St.)
Flamingo Gdns. *N'holt* —3C **54**
Flamstead Gdns. *Dag* —7C **52**
Flamstead Rd. *Dag* —7C **52**
Flamstead Av. *Wemb* —6G **41**
Flamsted Rd. *SE7* —5C **82**
Flanchford Rd. *W12* —3B **74**
Flanders Ct. *E17* —6A **32**
Flanders Cres. *SW17* —7D **108**
Flanders Mans. *W4* —4B **74**
Flanders Rd. *E6* —2D **66**
Flanders Rd. *W4* —4A **74**
Flanders Way. *E9* —6K **47**
Flank St. *E1* —7G **63**
Flask Wlk. *NW3* —4A **44**
Flatford Ho. *SE6* —4E **112**
Flavell M. *SE10* —5G **81**
Flaxen Clo. *E4* —3J **19**
Flaxen Rd. *E4* —3J **19**
Flaxley Rd. *Mord* —7K **121**
Flaxman Ct. *W1*
  —6H **61** (1C **148**)
Flaxman Ct. *Belv* —5G **85**
  (off Hoddesdon Rd.)

Flaxman Ho. *W4* —5A **74**
  (off Devonshire St.)
Flaxman Rd. *SE5* —3B **94**
Flaxman Ter. *WC1*
  —3H **61** (2D **142**)
Flaxmore Pl. *Beck* —6F **127**
Flaxton Rd. *SE18* —7J **83**
Flecker Clo. *Stan* —5E **10**
Fleece Dri. *N9* —4B **18**
Fleece Rd. *Surb* —7C **118**
Fleece Wlk. *N7* —6J **45**
Fleeming Clo. *E17* —2B **32**
Fleeming Rd. *E17* —2B **32**
Fleet Bldgs. *EC4*
  —6B **62** (7A **144**)
Fleet Pl. *EC4* —6B **62** (7A **144**)
Fleet Rd. *NW3* —5C **44**
Fleet Sq. *WC1* —3K **61** (2H **143**)
Fleet St. *EC4* —6A **62** (1J **149**)
Fleet St. Hill. *E1* —4G **63**
Fleetway Bus. Cen. *NW2* —1B **42**
Fleetway W. Bus. Pk. *Gnfd*
  —2B **56**
Fleetwood Clo. *E16* —5B **66**
Fleetwood Clo. *Croy* —3F **135**
Fleetwood Ct. *E6* —5D **66**
  (off Evelyn Dennington Rd.)
Fleetwood Rd. *NW10* —5C **42**
Fleetwood Rd. *King T* —3H **119**
Fleetwood Sq. *King T* —3H **119**
Fleetwood St. *N16* —2E **46**
Fleming Ct. *W2* —5B **60** (5A **140**)
Fleming Ct. *Croy* —5A **134**
Fleming Dri. *N21* —5E **6**
Fleming Ho. *N4* —1C **46**
Fleming Ho. *SE16* —2G **79**
  (off George Row)
Fleming Ho. *Wemb* —3J **41**
  (off Barnhill Rd.)
Fleming Mead. *Mitc* —7D **108**
Fleming Rd. *SE17*
  —6B **78** (7B **156**)
Fleming Rd. *S'hall* —6F **55**
Fleming Wlk. *NW9* —3B **26**
Fleming Way. *SE28* —7D **68**
Fleming Way. *Iswth* —4K **87**
Flempton Rd. *E10* —1A **48**
Fletcher Clo. *E6* —7F **67**
Fletcher La. *E10* —7E **32**
Fletcher Path. *SE8* —7C **80**
Fletcher Rd. *W4* —3J **73**
Fletchers Clo. *Brom* —4K **127**
Fletching Rd. *E5* —3J **47**
Fletching Rd. *SE7* —6B **82**
Fletton Rd. *N11* —7D **16**
Fleur de Lis Ct. *EC4*
  —6A **62** (1K **149**)
Fleur-de-Lis St. *E1*
  —4F **63** (4H **145**)
Fleur Gates. *SW19* —7F **91**
Flexmere Rd. *N17* —1D **30**
Flight App. *NW9* —2B **26**
Flimwell Clo. *Brom* —5G **113**
Flintmill Cres. *SE3* —2C **98**
Flinton St. *SE17* —5E **78** (5H **157**)
Flint St. *SE17* —4D **78** (4F **157**)
Flitcroft St. *WC2*
  —6H **61** (1D **148**)
Flock Mill Pl. *SW18* —1K **107**
Flockton St. *SE16* —2G **79**
Flodden Rd. *SE5* —1C **94**
Flood La. *Twic* —1A **104**
Flood Pas. *SE18* —3D **82**
Flood St. *SW3* —5C **76** (6D **152**)

Flood Wlk. *SW3*
  —6C **76** (7D **152**)
Flora Clo. *E14* —6D **64**
Flora Gdns. *W6* —4D **74**
  (off Albion Gdns.)
Flora Gdns. *Romf* —6C **36**
Floral Pl. *N1* —5D **46**
Floral St. *WC2* —7J **61** (2E **148**)
Flora St. *Belv* —5F **85**
Florence Av. *Enf* —3H **7**
Florence Av. *Mord* —5A **122**
Florence Ct. *E5* —3G **47**
Florence Ct. *E11* —4K **33**
Florence Ct. *N1* —7B **46**
Florence Ct. *SW19* —6G **107**
Florence Ct. *W9* —3A **60**
  (off Maida Vale)
Florence Dri. *Enf* —3H **7**
Florence Gdns. *W4* —6J **73**
Florence Mans. *NW4* —5D **26**
  (off Vivian Av.)
Florence Rd. *E6* —1A **66**
Florence Rd. *E13* —2H **65**
Florence Rd. *N4* —7K **29**
  (in two parts)
Florence Rd. *SE2* —4D **84**
Florence Rd. *SE14* —1B **96**
Florence Rd. *SW19* —6K **107**
Florence Rd. *W4* —3K **73**
Florence Rd. *W5* —7E **56**
Florence Rd. *Beck* —2A **126**
Florence Rd. *Brom* —1J **127**
Florence Rd. *Felt* —1A **102**
Florence Rd. *King T* —7F **105**
Florence Rd. *S'hall* —4B **70**
Florence Rd. *S Croy* —7D **134**
Florence St. *E16* —4H **65**
Florence St. *N1* —7B **46**
Florence St. *NW4* —4E **26**
Florence Ter. *SE14* —1B **96**
Florence Ter. *SW15* —3A **106**
Florence Way. *SW12* —1D **108**
Florfield Pas. *E8* —6H **47**
  (off Florfield Rd.)
Florfield Rd. *E8* —6H **47**
Florian. *SE5* —1E **94**
Florian Av. *Sutt* —4B **132**
Florian Rd. *SW15* —4G **91**
Florida Clo. *Bush* —2C **10**
Florida Rd. *T Hth* —1B **124**
Florida St. *E2* —3G **63**
Florin Ct. *N18* —5K **17**
Floriston Clo. *Stan* —1B **24**
Floriston Ct. *N'holt* —5F **39**
Floriston Gdns. *Stan* —1B **24**
Floss St. *SW15* —2E **90**
Flower & Dean Wlk. *E1*
  —5F **63** (6K **145**)
Flower La. *NW7* —5G **13**
Flowersmead. *SW17* —2E **108**
Flowers M. *N19* —2G **45**
Flower Wlk., The. *SW7*
  —2A **76** (6A **146**)
Floyd Rd. *SE7* —5A **82**
Fludyer St. *SE13* —4G **97**
Foley St. *W1* —5G **61** (6A **142**)
Folgate St. *E1* —5E **62** (5H **145**)
Foliot St. *W12* —6B **58**
Folkestone Ct. *N'holt* —5F **39**
  (off Newmarket Av.)
Folkestone Rd. *E6* —2E **66**
Folkestone Rd. *E17* —4D **32**
Folkestone Rd. *N18* —4B **18**
Folkingham La. *NW9* —1K **25**
Folkington Corner. *N12* —5C **14**

Folland. *NW9* —2B **26**
  (off Hundred Acre)
Follett St. *E14* —6E **64**
Folly La. *E17* —7G **19**
Folly M. *W11* —6H **59**
Folly Wall. *E14* —2E **80**
Fontaine Rd. *SW16* —7K **109**
Fontarabia Rd. *SW11* —4E **92**
Fontayne Av. *Romf* —2K **37**
Fontenelle. *SE5* —1E **94**
Fontenoy Ho. *SE11*
  —4B **78** (4A **156**)
  (off Kennington La.)
Fontenoy Pas. *SE11*
  —4B **78** (4A **156**)
Fontenoy Rd. *SW12* —2F **109**
Fonteyne Gdns. *Wfd G* —2B **34**
Fonthill Clo. *SE20* —2G **125**
Fonthill M. *N4* —2A **46**
Fonthill Rd. *N4* —1K **45**
Font Hills. *N2* —2A **28**
Fontley Way. *SW15* —7C **90**
Fontwell Clo. *Harr* —7D **10**
Fontwell Clo. *N'holt* —6E **38**
Fontwell Dri. *Brom* —5E **128**
Football La. *Harr* —1K **39**
Footpath, The. *SW15* —5C **90**
Foots Cray High St. *Sidc*
  —6C **116**
Foots Cray La. *Sidc* —1C **116**
Footscray Rd. *SE9* —6E **98**
Forbes Clo. *NW2* —2C **42**
Forbes St. *E1* —6G **63**
Forburg Rd. *N16* —1G **47**
Ford Clo. *E3* —2A **64**
Ford Clo. *Harr* —7H **23**
Ford Clo. *T Hth* —5B **124**
Forde Av. *Brom* —3A **128**
Fordel Rd. *SE6* —1F **113**
Ford End. *Wfd G* —6E **20**
Fordham Clo. *Barn* —3A **5**
Fordham Rd. *Barn* —3B **5**
Fordham St. *E1* —6G **63**
Fordhook Av. *W5* —1F **73**
Ford Ho. *Barn* —5E **4**
Ford Ind. Pk. *Dag* —4H **69**
Fordingley Rd. *W9* —3H **59**
Fordington Ho. *SE26* —3G **111**
Fordington Rd. *N6* —5D **28**
Fordmill Rd. *SE6* —2C **112**
Ford Rd. *E3* —2B **64**
Ford Rd. *Dag* —7F **53**
Fords Gro. *N21* —1H **17**
Fords Pk. Rd. *E16* —6J **65**
Ford Sq. *E1* —5H **63**
Ford St. *E3* —1A **64**
Ford St. *E16* —6H **65**
Fordwich Clo. *Orp* —7K **129**
Fordwych Rd. *NW2* —4G **43**
Fordyce Rd. *SE13* —6E **96**
Foreland Ct. *NW4* —1F **27**
Foreland Ho. *W11* —7G **59**
  (off Walmer Rd.)
Foreland St. *SE18* —4H **83**
Foreman Ct. *W6* —4E **74**
Foreman Ct. *Twic* —1K **103**
Foreshore. *SE8* —4B **80**
Forest App. *E4* —1B **20**
Forest App. *Wfd G* —7C **20**
Forest Av. *E4* —1B **20**
Forest Bus. Pk. *E17* —7A **32**
Forest Clo. *E11* —5J **33**

Forest Clo. *Chst* —1E **128**
Forest Clo. *Wfd G* —3E **20**
Forest Ct. *E4* —1C **20**
Forest Ct. *E11* —4G **33**
Forest Ct. *N12* —4E **14**
Forest Croft. *SE23* —2H **111**
Forestdale. *N14* —4C **16**
Forestdale Cen., The. *Croy*
—7B **136**
Forest Dene Ct. *Sutt* —6A **132**
Forest Dri. *E12* —3B **50**
Forest Dri. *Kes* —4C **138**
Forest Dri. *Wfd G* —7A **20**
Forest Dri. E. *E11* —7F **33**
Forest Dri. W. *E11* —7E **32**
Forest Edge. *Buck H* —4F **21**
Forester Rd. *SE15* —3H **95**
Foresters Clo. *Wall* —7H **133**
Foresters Cres. *Bexh* —4H **101**
Foresters Dri. *E17* —4F **33**
Foresters Dri. *Wall* —7H **133**
Forest Gdns. *N17* —2F **31**
Forest Ga. *NW9* —4A **26**
Forest Glade. *E4* —4B **20**
Forest Glade. *E11* —6G **33**
Forest Gro. *E8* —6F **47**
Forest Hill Bus. Cen. *SE23*
—2J **111**
Forest Hill Ind. Est. *SE23*
—2J **111**
Forest Hill Rd. *SE22 & SE23*
—5H **95**
Forestholme Clo. *SE23* —2J **111**
Forest Ind. Pk. *Ilf* —1J **35**
Forest La. *E15 & E7* —6G **49**
Forest La. *Chig* —5K **21**
Forest Lodge. SE23 —3J 111
(off Dartmouth Rd.)
Forest Mt. Rd. *E4* —7A **20**
Forest Point. E7 —5K 49
(off Windsor Rd.)
Fore St. *EC2* —5C **62** (6D **144**)
Fore St. *N18 & N9* —6A **18**
Fore St. Av. *EC2* —5D **62** (6E **144**)
Forest Ridge. *Beck* —3C **126**
Forest Ridge. *Kes* —4C **138**
Forest Rise. *E17* —5F **33**
Forest Rd. *E7* —4J **49**
Forest Rd. *E8* —6F **47**
Forest Rd. *E11* —7F **33**
Forest Rd. *E17* —4J **31**
Forest Rd. *N9* —1C **18**
Forest Rd. *N17 & E17* —4J **31**
Forest Rd. *Felt* —2A **102**
Forest Rd. *Ilf* —2H **35**
Forest Rd. *Rich* —7G **73**
Forest Rd. *Romf* —3H **37**
Forest Rd. *Sutt* —1J **131**
Forest Rd. *Wfd G* —3D **20**
Forest Side. *E4* —1C **20**
Forest Side. *E7* —4K **49**
Forest Side. *Buck H* —1F **21**
Forest Side. *Wor Pk* —1B **130**
Forest St. *E7* —5J **49**
Forest Ter. *Chig* —5K **21**
Forest, The. *E11* —4G **33**
Forest Trad. Est. *E17* —3K **31**
Forest View. *E4* —7K **9**
Forest View. *E11* —7H **33**
Forest View Av. *E10* —5F **33**
Forest View Rd. *E12* —4C **50**
Forest View Rd. *E17* —1E **32**
Forest Way. *E11* —7H **33**
Forest Way. *N19* —2G **45**
Forest Way. *Orp* —5K **129**

Forest Way. *Sidc* —7H **99**
Forest Way. *Wfd G* —4E **20**
Forest Works Ind. Est. *E17*
—3K **31**
Forfar Rd. *N22* —1B **30**
Forfar Rd. *SW11* —1E **92**
Forge Clo. *Brom* —1J **137**
Forge Cotts. *W5* —1D **72**
Forge La. *Felt* —5C **102**
Forge La. *Sutt* —7G **131**
Forge Pl. *NW1* —6E **44**
Forlong Path. N'holt —6C 38
(off Arnold Rd.)
Forman Pl. *N16* —4F **47**
Formby Av. *Stan* —3C **24**
Formby Ct. N7 —5A 46
(off Morgan Rd.)
Formosa St. *W9* —4K **59**
Formunt Clo. *E16* —5H **65**
Fofres Gdns. *NW11* —6J **27**
Forrester Path. *SE26* —4J **111**
Forrest Gdns. *SW16* —3K **123**
Forset St. *W1* —6C **60** (7D **140**)
Forstal Clo. *Brom* —3J **127**
Forster Ho. *Brom* —3F **113**
Forster Rd. *E17* —6A **32**
Forster Rd. *N17* —3F **31**
Forster Rd. *SW2* —7J **93**
Forster Rd. *Beck* —3A **126**
Forsters Clo. *Romf* —6F **37**
Forston St. *N1* —2C **62**
Forsyte Cres. *SE19* —1E **124**
Forsythe Shades Ct. *Beck*
—1E **126**
Forsyth Gdns. *SE17*
—6B **78** (7B **156**)
Forsythia Clo. *Ilf* —5F **51**
Forsyth Pl. *Enf* —5K **7**
Forterie Gdns. *Ilf* —3A **52**
Fortescue Av. *E8* —7H **47**
Fortescue Av. *Twic* —3G **103**
Fortescue Rd. *SW19* —7B **108**
Fortescue Rd. *Edgw* —1K **25**
Fortess Gro. *NW5* —5G **45**
Fortess Rd. *NW5* —5F **45**
Fortess Wlk. *NW5* —5F **45**
Fortess Yd. *NW5* —5F **45**
Forthbridge Rd. *SW11* —4E **92**
Fortis Clo. *E16* —6A **66**
Fortis Ct. *N10* —3E **28**
Fortis Grn. *N2 & N10* —4C **28**
Fortis Grn. Av. *N2* —3D **28**
Fortis Grn. Rd. *N10* —3E **28**
Fortismere Av. *N10* —3E **28**
Fortnam Rd. *N19* —2H **45**
Fortnum's Acre. *Stan* —6E **10**
Fort Rd. *SE1* —4F **79** (4K **157**)
Fort Rd. *N'holt* —7E **38**
Fortrose Gdns. *SW2* —1J **109**
Fort St. *E1* —5E **62** (6H **145**)
Fort St. *E16* —1K **81**
Fortuna Clo. *N7* —6A **46**
Fortunegate Rd. *NW10* —1A **58**
Fortune Grn. Rd. *NW6* —4J **43**
Fortunes Mead. *N'holt* —6C **38**
Fortune St. *EC1*
—4C **62** (4D **144**)
Fortune Wlk. SE28 —3H 83
(off Broadwater Rd.)
Fortune Way. *NW10* —3C **58**
Forty Acre La. *E16* —5J **65**
Forty Av. *Wemb* —3F **41**
Forty Clo. *Wemb* —3F **41**
Forty Footpath. *SW14* —3J **89**
Forty Foot Rd. *SE9* —7G **99**

Forty Hill. *Enf* —1K **7**
Forty La. *Wemb* —2H **41**
Forumside. *Edgw* —6B **12**
Forum Way. *Edgw* —6B **12**
Forval Clo. *Mitc* —5D **122**
Forward Bus. Cen. *E16* —4F **65**
Forward Dri. *Harr* —4K **23**
Fosbrooke Ho. SW8 —7J 77
(off Davidson Gdns.)
Fosbury M. *W2* —7K **59**
Foscote M. *W9* —4J **59**
Foscote Rd. *NW4* —6D **26**
Foskett M. *SW6* —2H **91**
Foss Av. *Croy* —5A **134**
Fossdene Rd. *SE7* —5K **81**
Fossdyke Clo. *Hayes* —5C **54**
Fosset Lodge. *Bexh* —1J **101**
Fosse Way. *W13* —5A **56**
Fossil Rd. *SE13* —3C **96**
Fossington Rd. *Belv* —4D **84**
Foss Rd. *SW17* —4B **108**
Fossway. *Dag* —2C **52**
Foster Ct. *NW4* —4E **26**
Foster Ho. *SE14* —1B **96**
Foster La. *EC2* —6C **62** (7C **144**)
Foster Rd. *E13* —4J **65**
Foster Rd. *W3* —7A **58**
Foster Rd. *W4* —5K **73**
Fosters Clo. *E18* —1K **33**
Fosters Clo. *Chst* —5D **114**
Foster St. *NW4* —4E **26**
Foster's Way. *SW18* —7K **91**
Foster Wlk. *NW4* —4E **26**
Fothergill Clo. *E13* —2J **65**
Fothergill Dri. *N21* —5D **6**
Fotheringham Rd. *Enf* —4A **8**
Foubert's Pl. *W1*
—6G **61** (1A **148**)
Foulden Rd. *N16* —4F **47**
Foulden Ter. *N16* —4F **47**
Foulis Ter. *SW7* —5B **76** (5B **152**)
Foulser Rd. *SW17* —3D **108**
Foulsham Rd. *T Hth* —3D **124**
Founder Clo. *E6* —6F **67**
Founders Ct. *EC2*
—6D **62** (7E **144**)
Founders Gdns. *SE19* —7C **110**
Foundry Clo. *SE16* —1A **80**
Foundry M. *NW1*
—4G **61** (3B **142**)
Fountain Ct. *EC4*
—7A **62** (2J **149**)
Fountain Ct. *SE23* —2K **111**
Fountain Ct. SW1
—4F **77** (4J **153**)
(off Buckingham Pal. Rd.)
Fountain Ct. *Sidc* —6B **100**
Fountain Dri. *SE19* —4F **111**
Fountain Dri. *Cars* —7D **132**
Fountain Grn. Sq. *SE16* —2G **79**
Fountain Ho. *NW6* —7G **43**
Fountain M. N5 —4C 46
(off Highbury Grange)
Fountain M. *NW3* —6D **44**
Fountain Pl. *SW9* —1A **94**
Fountain Rd. *SW17* —5B **108**
Fountain Rd. *T Hth* —2C **124**
Fountain Roundabout. *N Mald*
—4A **120**
Fountains Av. *Felt* —3D **102**
Fountains Clo. *Felt* —2D **102**
(in two parts)
Fountains Cres. *N14* —7D **6**
Fountain Sq. *SW1*
—4F **77** (3K **153**)

Fountains, The. *N3* —7E **14**
(off Ballards La.)
Fountayne Bus. Cen. *N15* —4G **31**
Fountayne Rd. *N15* —4G **31**
Fountayne Rd. *N16* —2F **47**
Fount St. *SW8* —7H **77**
Fouracres. *Enf* —1E **9**
Fourland Wlk. *Edgw* —6D **12**
Fournier St. *E1* —5F **63** (5K **145**)
Four Seasons Cres. *Sutt*
—2H **131**
Four Sq. Ct. *Houn* —6E **86**
Fourth Av. *E12* —4D **50**
Fourth Av. *W10* —3G **59**
Fourth Av. *Romf* —1K **53**
Fourth Cross Rd. *Twic* —2H **103**
Fourth Way. *Wemb* —4J **41**
Four Wents, The. *E4* —1A **20**
Fovant Ct. *SW8* —2G **93**
Fowey Av. *Ilf* —5B **34**
Fowey Clo. *E1* —1H **79**
Fowey Ho. *SE11*
—5A **78** (5K **155**)
Fowler Clo. *SW11* —3B **92**
Fowler Rd. *E7* —4J **49**
Fowler Rd. *N1* —1B **62**
Fowler Rd. *Mitc* —2E **122**
Fowlers Clo. *Sidc* —5E **116**
Fowler's Wlk. *W5* —4D **56**
Fownes St. *SW11* —3C **92**
Foxberry Ct. *SE4* —4B **96**
Foxberry Rd. *SE4* —3A **96**
Foxborough Gdns. *SE4* —5C **96**
Foxbourne Rd. *SW17* —2E **108**
Foxbury Av. *Chst* —6H **115**
Foxbury Clo. *Brom* —6K **113**
Foxbury Rd. *Brom* —6J **113**
Fox Clo. *E1* —4J **63**
Fox Clo. *E16* —5J **65**
Foxcombe. *New Ad* —6D **136**
(in two parts)
Foxcombe Clo. *E6* —2B **66**
Foxcombe Rd. *SW15* —1C **106**
Foxcote. *SE17* —5E **78** (6H **157**)
Foxcroft Rd. *SE18* —1F **99**
Foxearth Spur. *S Croy* —7J **135**
Foxes Dale. *SE3* —3J **97**
Foxes Dale. *Brom* —3F **127**
Foxglove Clo. *S'hall* —7C **54**
Foxglove Ct. *Wemb* —2E **56**
Foxglove Gdns. *E11* —4A **34**
Foxglove St. *W12* —7B **58**
Foxglove Way. *Wall* —1F **133**
Foxgrove. *N14* —3D **16**
Foxgrove Av. *Beck* —7D **112**
Foxgrove Rd. *Beck* —7D **112**
Foxham Rd. *N19* —3H **45**
Fox Hill. *SE19* —7F **111**
Fox Hill. *Kes* —5A **138**
Fox Hill Gdns. *SE19* —7F **111**
Foxhole Rd. *SE9* —5C **98**
Fox Hollow Clo. *SE18* —5J **83**
Fox Hollow Dri. *Bexh* —3D **100**
Foxholt Gdns. *NW10* —7J **41**
Foxhome Clo. *Chst* —6E **114**
Fox Ho. Rd. *Belv* —4H **85**
(in two parts)
Fox & Knot St. *EC1*
—5B **62** (5B **144**)
Foxlands Cres. *Dag* —5J **53**
Foxlands La. *Dag* —5K **53**
Foxlands Rd. *Dag* —5J **53**
Fox La. *N13* —2E **16**
Fox La. *W5* —4E **56**
Fox La. *Kes* —5K **137**

Foxleas Ct. *Brom* —7G **113**
Foxlees. *Wemb* —4A **40**
Foxley Clo. *E8* —5G **47**
Foxley Ct. *Sutt* —7A **132**
Foxley Rd. *SW9* —7A **78**
Foxley Rd. *T Hth* —4B **124**
Foxley Sq. *SW9* —1B **94**
Foxmead Clo. *Enf* —3E **6**
Foxmore St. *SW11* —1D **92**
Fox Rd. *E16* —5H **65**
Fox's Path. *Mitc* —2C **122**
Foxton Gro. *Mitc* —2B **122**
Foxton Ho. E16 —2E 82
(off Albert Rd.)
Foxwell M. *SE4* —3A **96**
Foxwell St. *SE4* —3A **96**
Foxwood Clo. *NW7* —4F **13**
Foxwood Grn. Clo. *Enf* —6K **7**
Foxwood Rd. *SE3* —4H **97**
Foyle Rd. *N17* —1G **31**
Foyle Rd. *SE3* —6H **81**
Framborough Clo. *Harr* —7H **23**
Framfield Clo. *N12* —3D **14**
Framfield Ct. Enf —6K 7
(off Queen Annes Gdns.)
Framfield Rd. *N5* —5B **46**
Framfield Rd. *W7* —6J **55**
Framfield Rd. *Mitc* —7E **108**
Framlingham Clo. *E5* —2J **47**
Framlingham Cres. *SE9* —4C **114**
Frampton Clo. *Sutt* —7J **131**
Frampton Ct. W3 —2J 73
(off Cheltenham Pl.)
Frampton Pk. Est. *E9* —7J **47**
Frampton Pk. Rd. *E9* —6J **47**
Frampton Rd. *Houn* —5D **86**
Frampton St. *NW8*
—4B **60** (4B **140**)
Francemary Rd. *SE4* —5C **96**
Frances Ct. *E17* —6C **32**
Frances Rd. *E4* —6H **19**
Frances St. *SE18* —4D **82**
Francesca Ct. The. *SW17* —3A **108**
Francis Av. *Bexh* —2G **101**
Francis Av. *Ilf* —2H **51**
Francis Barber Clo. *SW16*
—5K **109**
Franciscan Rd. *SW17* —5D **108**
Francis Chichester Way. *SW11*
—1E **92**
Francis Clo. *EC1* —5B **62** (5A **144**)
Francis Ct. NW7 —5J 15
(off Watford Way)
Francis Gro. *SW19* —6H **107**
(in two parts)
Francis Ho. *E10* —1B **48**
Francis M. *SE12* —7J **97**
Francis Rd. *E10* —1E **48**
Francis Rd. *N2* —4D **28**
Francis Rd. *Croy* —7B **124**
Francis Rd. *Gnfd* —2B **56**
Francis Rd. *Harr* —5A **24**
Francis Rd. *Houn* —2B **86**
Francis Rd. *Ilf* —2H **51**
Francis Rd. *Pinn* —5A **22**
Francis Rd. *Wall* —6G **133**
Francis St. *E15* —5G **49**
Francis St. *SW1*
—4G **77** (3A **154**)
Francis St. *Ilf* —2H **51**
Francis Ter. *N19* —3G **45**
Francis Wlk. *N1* —1K **61**
Francklyn Gdns. *Edgw* —3B **12**
Franconia Rd. *SW4* —5H **93**

Frank Bailey Wlk. E12 —6E 50
Frank Beswick Ho. SW6 —6H 75
(off Clem Attlee Ct.)
Frank Burton Clo. SE7 —5K 81
Frank Dixon Clo. SE21 —7E 94
Frank Dixon Way. SE21 —1E 110
Frankel Mt. SE9 —5B 98
Frankfurt Rd. SE24 —5C 94
Frankham Ho. SE8 —7C 80
(off Frankham St.)
Frankham St. SE8 —7C 80
Frank Ho. SW8 —7J 77
(off Wyvil Rd.)
Frankland Clo. SE16 —4H 79
Frankland Clo. Wfd G —5F 21
Frankland Rd. E4 —5H 19
Frankland Rd. SW7
—3B 76 (2A 152)
Franklin Clo. N20 —7F 5
Franklin Clo. SE13 —1D 96
Franklin Clo. SE27 —3B 110
Franklin Clo. King T —3G 119
Franklin Cotts. Stan —4G 11
Franklin Cres. Mitc —4G 123
Franklin Pas. SE9 —3C 98
Franklin Rd. SE20 —7J 111
Franklin Rd. ?.xh —1E 100
Franklins M. Harr —2G 39
Franklin Sq. W14 —5H 75
Franklin's Row. SW3
—5D 76 (5F 153)
Franklin St. E3 —3D 64
Franklin St. N15 —6E 30
Franklin Way. Croy —7J 123
Franklyn Rd. NW10 —6B 42
Franks Av. N Mald —4J 119
Frank Soskice Ho. SW6 —6H 75
(off Clem Attlee Ct.)
Frank St. E13 —4J 65
Franks Wood Av. Orp —5F 129
Frank Welsh Ct. Pinn —4A 22
Franlaw Cres. N13 —4H 17
Fransfield Gro. SE26 —3H 111
Frans Hals Ct. E14 —3F 81
Frant Clo. SE20 —7J 111
Franthorne Way. SE6 —2D 112
Frant Rd. T Hth —5B 124
Fraser Clo. E6 —6C 66
Fraser Clo. Bex —1J 117
Fraser Ho. Bren —5F 73
Fraser Rd. E17 —5D 32
Fraser Rd. N9 —3C 18
Fraser Rd. Eri —5K 85
Fraser Rd. Gnfd —1B 56
Fraser St. W4 —5A 74
Frating Cres. Wfd G —6E 20
Frazer Av. Ruis —5A 38
Frazier St. SE1 —2A 78 (7J 149)
Frean St. SE16 —3G 79 (1K 157)
Freda Corbett Clo. SE15 —7G 79
Frederica Rd. E4 —1A 20
Frederica St. N7 —7K 45
Frederick Clo. W2
—7C 60 (2D 146)
Frederick Clo. Sutt —4H 131
Frederick Cres. SW9 —7B 78
Frederick Cres. Enf —2D 8
Frederick Gdns. Sutt —5H 131
Frederick Pl. SE18 —5F 83
Frederick Rd. SE17
—6B 78 (7B 156)
Frederick Rd. Rain —2K 69
Frederick Rd. Sutt —5H 131
Frederick's Pl. EC2
—6D 62 (1E 150)

Fredericks Pl. N12 —4F 15
Frederick Sq. SE16 —7A 64
(off Sovereign Cres.)
Frederick's Row. EC1
—3B 62 (1A 144)
Frederick St. WC1
—3K 61 (2G 143)
Frederick Ter. E8 —7F 47
Frederic M. SW1
—2D 76 (7F 147)
Frederic St. E17 —5A 32
Freedom Clo. E17 —4K 31
Freedom Rd. N17 —2D 30
Freedom St. SW11 —2D 92
Freegrove Rd. N7 —5J 45
(in two parts)
Freehold Ind. Cen. Houn —5A 86
Freeland Ct. Sidc —3A 116
Freeland Pk. NW4 —2G 27
Freeland Rd. W5 —7F 57
Freelands Av. S Croy —7K 135
Freelands Gro. Brom —1K 127
Freelands Rd. Brom —1K 127
Freeling St. N1 —7J 45
(in two parts)
Freeman Clo. N'holt —7C 38
Freeman Rd. Mord —5B 122
Freemantle Av. Enf —5E 8
Freemantle St. SE17
—5E 78 (5G 157)
Freemasons Rd. E16 —5K 65
Freemasons Rd. Croy —1E 134
Freethorpe Clo. SE19 —1E 124
Free Trade Wharf. E1 —7K 63
Freke Rd. SW11 —3E 92
Fremantle Rd. Belv —4G 85
Fremantle Rd. Ilf —2F 35
Fremont St. E9 —1J 63
French Ordinary Ct. EC3
—7E 62 (2H 151)
French Pl. E1 —4E 62 (2H 145)
Frendsbury Rd. SE4 —4A 96
Frensham Clo. S'hall —4D 54
Frensham Dri. SW15 —3B 106
Frensham Dri. New Ad —7E 136
Frensham Rd. SE9 —2H 115
Frensham St. SE15 —6G 79
Frere St. SW11 —2C 92
Freshfield Av. Wall —5K 133
Freshfield Clo. SE13 —4F 97
Freshfield Dri. N14 —7A 6
Freshfields. Croy —1B 136
Freshford St. SW18 —3A 108
Freshwater Clo. SW17 —6E 108
Freshwater Ct. S'hall —3E 54
Freshwater Rd. SW17 —6E 108
Freshwater Rd. Dag —1D 52
Freshwell Av. Romf —4C 36
Fresh Wharf Rd. Bark —1F 67
Freshwood Clo. Beck —1D 126
Freshwood Way. Wall —7F 133
Freston Gdns. Barn —5K 5
Freston Pk. N3 —2H 27
Freston Rd. W10 & W11 —7F 59
Freta Rd. Bexh —5H 101
Frewing Clo. Chst —6D 114
Frewin Rd. SW18 —1B 108
Friar M. SE27 —3B 110
Friar Rd. Hayes —4B 54
Friar Rd. Orp —5K 129
Friars Av. N20 —3H 15
Friars Av. SW15 —3B 106
Friars Clo. E4 —3K 19
Friars Clo. SE1 —1B 78 (4B 150)
Friars Clo. N'holt —3B 54

Friars Ct. E17 —1B 32
Friars Gdns. W3 —6K 57
Friars Ga. Clo. Wfd G —4D 20
Friars La. Rich —5D 88
Friars Mead. E14 —3E 80
Friars M. SE9 —5E 98
Friars Pl. La. W3 —7K 57
Friars Rd. E6 —1B 66
Friars Stile Pl. Rich —6E 88
Friars Stile Rd. Rich —6E 88
Friar St. EC4 —6B 62 (1B 150)
Friars Wlk. N14 —7A 6
Friars Wlk. SE2 —5D 84
Friars Way. W3 —6K 57
Friarswood. Croy —7A 136
Friary Ct. SW1 —1G 77 (5B 148)
Friary Est. SE15 —6G 79
Friary La. Wfd G —4D 20
Friary Pk. Ct. W3 & W3 —6J 57
Friary Rd. N12 —4G 15
Friary Rd. SE15 —6G 79
Friary Rd. W3 —6J 57
Friary Way. N12 —4F 15
Friday Hill. E4 —2B 20
Friday Hill E. E4 —3B 20
Friday Hill W. E4 —2B 20
Friday Rd. Eri —5K 85
Friday Rd. Mitc —7D 108
Friday St. EC4 —7C 62 (2C 150)
Frideswide Pl. NW5 —5G 45
Friendly Pl. SE10 —1D 96
Friendly St. SE8 —2C 96
Friendly St. M. SE8 —2C 96
Friendship Wlk. N'holt —3B 54
Friends Rd. Croy —3D 134
Friend St. EC1 —3B 62 (1A 144)
Friern Barnet La. N20 & N11
—2G 15
Friern Barnet Rd. N11 —5J 15
Friern Bri. Retail Pk. N11 —6A 16
Friern Ct. N20 —3G 15
Friern Mt. Dri. N20 —7F 5
Friern Pk. N12 —5F 15
Friern Rd. SE22 —7G 95
Friern Watch Av. N12 —4F 15
Frigate M. SE8 —6C 80
Frimley Av. Wall —5K 133
Frimley Clo. SW19 —2G 107
Frimley Clo. New Ad —7E 136
Frimley Ct. Sidc —5C 116
Frimley Cres. New Ad —7E 136
Frimley Gdns. Mitc —3D 122
Frimley Rd. Ilf —3J 51
Frimley Way. E1 —4K 63
Frinsted Rd. Eri —7K 85
Frinton Dri. Wfd G —7A 20
Frinton M. Ilf —6E 34
Frinton Rd. E6 —3B 66
Frinton Rd. N15 —6E 30
Frinton Rd. SW17 —6E 108
Frinton Rd. Sidc —2E 116
Friston St. SW6 —2K 91
Friswell Pl. Bexh —4G 101
Fritham Clo. N Mald —6A 120
Frith Ct. NW7 —7B 14
Frith La. NW7 —7B 14
Frith Rd. E11 —4E 48
Frith Rd. Croy —2C 134
Frith St. W1 —6H 61 (1C 148)
Frithville Gdns. W12 —1E 74
Frizlands La. Dag —2H 53
Frobisher Clo. Pinn —7B 22

Frobisher Ct. NW9 —2A 26
Frobisher Ct. SE23 —2H 111
Frobisher Ct. W12 —2E 74
(off Lime Gro.)
Frobisher Pas. E14 —1C 80
Frobisher Rd. E6 —6D 66
Frobisher Rd. N8 —4A 30
Frobisher St. SE10 —6G 81
Frogley Rd. SE22 —4F 95
Frogmore. SW18 —5J 91
Frogmore Clo. Sutt —3G 131
Frogmore Ct. S'hall —4D 70
Frogmore Gdns. Sutt —4G 131
Frogmore Ind. Est. N5 —4C 46
Frogmore Ind. Est. NW10 —3J 57
Frognal. NW3 —4A 44
Frognal Av. Sidc —6A 116
Frognal Clo. NW3 —5A 44
Frognal Corner. (Junct.) —6K 115
Frognal Ct. NW3 —6A 44
Frognal Gdns. NW3 —4A 44
Frognal La. NW3 —5K 43
Frognal Pde. NW3 —6A 44
Frognal Pl. Sidc —6A 116
Frognal Rise. NW3 —3A 44
Frognal Way. NW3 —4A 44
Froissart Rd. SE9 —5B 98
Frome Rd. N22 —3B 30
Frome St. N1 —2C 62
Fromondes Rd. Sutt —5G 131
Frostic Wlk. E1 —5G 63 (6K 145)
Froude St. SW8 —2F 93
Fryatt Rd. N17 —7J 17
(in two parts)
Fryatt St. E14 —6G 65
Fryent Clo. NW9 —6G 25
Fryent Cres. NW9 —6A 26
Fryent Fields. NW9 —6A 26
Fryent Gro. NW9 —6A 26
Fryent Way. NW9 —5G 25
Frye's Bldgs. N1 —2A 62
Fry Ho. E6 —7A 50
Frying Pan All. E1
—5F 63 (6J 145)
Fry Rd. E6 —7B 50
Fry Rd. NW10 —1B 58
Fryston Av. Croy —2G 135
Fuchsia St. SE2 —5B 84
Fulbeck Dri. NW9 —1A 26
Fulbeck Rd. N19 —4G 45
Fulbeck Way. Harr —2G 23
Fulbourne Rd. E17 —1E 32
Fulbourne St. E1 —5H 63
Fulbrook M. N19 —4G 45
Fulcher Ho. SE8 —5B 80
Fulford St. SE16 —2H 79
Fulham B'way. SW6 —7J 75
Fulham Broadway. (Junct.)
—7J 75
Fulham High St. SW6 —2H 91
Fulham Pal. Rd. W6 & SW6
—5E 74
Fulham Pk. Gdns. SW6 —2H 91
Fulham Pk. Rd. SW6 —2H 91
Fulham Rd. SW6 —2G 91
Fulham Rd. SW10 & SW3
—6A 76 (5A 152)
Fullbrooks Av. Wor Pk —1B 130
Fuller Clo. E2 —4G 63
Fuller Clo. Dag —3B 52
Fullers Av. Wfd G —7C 20
Fullers Clo. Romf —1J 37
Fullers La. Romf —1J 37

Fullers Rd. E18 —1H 33
Fuller St. NW4 —4E 26
Fuller's Wood. Croy —4C 136
Fullerton Rd. SW18 —5A 92
Fullerton Rd. Cars —7C 132
Fullerton Rd. Croy —7F 125
Fullwell Av. Ilf —1D 34
Fullwell Ct. S'hall —7F 55
(off Baird Av.)
Fullwell Cross. Ilf —2H 35
Fullwood's M. N1
—3D 62 (1F 145)
Fulmar Ct. Surb —6F 119
Fulmead St. SW6 —1K 91
Fulmer Clo. Hamp —5C 102
Fulmer Rd. E16 —5B 66
Fulmer Way. W13 —3B 72
Fulready Rd. E10 —5F 33
Fulstone Clo. Houn —4D 86
Fulthorp Rd. SE3 —2H 97
Fulton M. W2 —7A 60
(off Porchester Ter.)
Fulton Rd. Wemb —3G 41
Fulwell Pk. Av. Twic —2F 103
Fulwell Rd. Tedd —4H 103
Fulwood Av. Wemb —1F 57
Fulwood Ct. Kent —6A 24
Fulwood Gdns. Twic —6K 87
Fulwood Pl. WC1
—5K 61 (6H 143)
Fulwood Wlk. SW19 —1G 107
Furber St. W6 —3D 74
Furham Field. Pinn —7A 10
Furley Rd. SE15 —7G 79
Furlong Clo. Wall —1F 133
Furlong Rd. N7 —6A 46
Furmage St. SW18 —7K 91
Furneaux Av. SE27 —5B 110
Furness Rd. NW10 —2C 58
Furness Rd. SW6 —2K 91
Furness Rd. Harr —7F 23
Furness Rd. Mord —6K 121
Furnival St. EC4 —6A 62 (7J 143)
Furrow La. E9 —5J 47
Fursby Av. N3 —6D 14
Fursecroft. W1 —6D 60 (7E 140)
Further Acre. NW9 —2B 26
Furtherfield Clo. Croy —6A 124
Further Grn. Rd. SE6 —7G 97
Furzedown Dri. SW17 —5F 109
Furzedown Rd. SW17 —5F 109
Furze Farm Clo. Romf —2E 36
Furzefield Clo. Chst —6F 115
Furzefield Rd. SE3 —7K 81
Furze Rd. T Hth —3C 124
Furze St. E3 —5C 64
Fyfe Way. Brom —2J 127
Fyfield. N4 —2A 46
(off Six Acres Est.)
Fyfield Clo. Brom —4F 127
Fyfield Ct. E7 —6J 49
Fyfield Rd. E17 —3F 33
Fyfield Rd. SW9 —3A 94
Fyfield Rd. Enf —3K 7
Fyfield Rd. Wfd G —7F 21
Fynes St. SW1 —4H 77 (3C 154)

Gable Clo. Pinn —1E 22
Gable Ct. SE26 —4H 111
Gables Clo. SE5 —1E 94
Gables Clo. SE12 —1J 113
Gables Lodge. Barn —1F 5
Gables, The. N10 —3E 28
(off Fortis Grn.)

Gables, The. *Bark* —6G 51
Gables, The. *Brom* —7K 113
Gables, The. *Wemb* —3G 41
Gabriel Clo. *Felt* —4C 102
Gabrielle Clo. *Wemb* —3F 41
Gabrielle Ct. *NW3* —6B 44
Gabriel St. *SE23* —7K 95
Gabriel's Wharf. *SE1*
　　　　　　—1A 78 (4J 149)
Gad Clo. *E13* —3K 65
Gaddesden Av. *Wemb* —6F 41
Gadsbury Clo. *NW9* —6B 26
Gadwall Clo. *E16* —6K 65
Gadwall Way. *SE28* —2H 83
Gage Rd. *E16* —5G 65
Gage St. *WC1* —5J 61 (5F 143)
Gainford St. *N1* —1A 62
Gainsboro Gdns. *Gnfd* —5J 39
Gainsborough Av. *E12* —5E 50
Gainsborough Clo. *Beck* —7C 112
Gainsborough Ct. *N12* —5E 14
Gainsborough Ct. *SE21* —2E 110
Gainsborough Ct. *W4* —5H 73
　(off Chaseley Dri.)
Gainsborough Ct. *W12* —2E 74
Gainsborough Gdns. *NW3*
　　　　　　—3B 44
Gainsborough Gdns. *NW11*
　　　　　　—7H 27
Gainsborough Gdns. *Edgw*
　　　　　　—2F 25
Gainsborough Gdns. *Iswth*
　　　　　　—5H 87
Gainsborough Ho. *Dag* —4B 52
　(off Gainsborough Rd.)
Gainsborough Lodge. *Harr*
　(off Hindes Rd.)
Gainsborough M. *SE26* —3H 111
Gainsborough Rd. *E11* —7G 33
Gainsborough Rd. *E15* —3G 65
Gainsborough Rd. *N12* —5E 14
Gainsborough Rd. *W4* —4B 74
Gainsborough Rd. *Dag* —4B 52
Gainsborough Rd. *N Mald*
　　　　　　—7K 119
Gainsborough Rd. *Rich* —2F 89
Gainsborough Sq. *Bexh* —3D 100
Gainsborough Tower. *N'holt*
　(off Academy Gdns.) —2B 54
Gainsford Ct. *E11* —3F 49
Gainsford Rd. *E17* —4B 32
Gainsford St. *SE1*
　　　　　　—2F 79 (6J 151)
Gairloch Rd. *SE5* —2E 94
Gaisford St. *NW5* —6G 45
Gaitskell Ho. *E6* —1B 66
Gaitskell Ho. *E17* —3D 32
Gaitskell Rd. *SE9* —1G 115
Galahad Rd. *Brom* —4J 113
Galata Rd. *SW13* —7C 74
Galatea Sq. *SE15* —3H 95
Galba Ct. *Bren* —7D 72
Galbraith St. *E14* —3E 80
Galdana Av. *Barn* —3F 5
Galeborough Av. *Wfd G* —7A 20
Gale Clo. *Hamp* —6C 102
Gale Clo. *Mitc* —3B 122
Galena Rd. *W6* —4D 74
Galen Pl. *WC1* —5J 61 (6F 143)
Galesbury Rd. *SW18* —6A 92
Gales Gdns. *E2* —3H 63
Gale St. *E3* —5C 64
Gale St. *Dag* —5C 52
Gales Way. *Wfd G* —7H 21

Galgate Clo. *SW19* —1G 107
Gallants Farm Rd. *E Barn* —7H 5
Galleon Clo. *SE16* —2K 79
Galleon Clo. *Eri* —4K 85
Gallery Gdns. *N'holt* —2B 54
Gallery Rd. *SE21* —1D 110
Galleywall Rd. *SE16* —4H 79
Galliard Clo. *N9* —6D 8
Galliard Ct. *N9* —6D 8
　　　　　　—3A 60 (1A 140)
Galliard Rd. *N9* —7G 8
Gallia Rd. *N5* —5B 46
Gallions Clo. *Bark* —3A 68
Gallions Entrance. *E16* —1G 83
Gallions Rd. *E16* —7F 67
Gallions Rd. *SE7* —4K 81
Galliver Pl. *E5* —4H 47
Gallon Clo. *SE7* —4A 82
Gallop, The. *S Croy* —7H 135
Gallop, The. *Sutt* —7B 132
Gallosson Rd. *SE18* —4J 83
Galloway Path. *Croy* —4D 134
Galloway Rd. *W12* —1C 74
Gallus Clo. *N21* —6E 6
Gallus Sq. *SE3* —3K 97
Galpin's Rd. *T Hth* —5J 123
Galsworthy Av. *Romf* —7B 36
Galsworthy Clo. *SE28* —1B 84
Galsworthy Ct. *W3* —3H 73
　(off Bollo Bri. Rd.)
Galsworthy Cres. *SE3* —1A 98
Galsworthy Rd. *NW2* —4G 43
Galsworthy Rd. *King T* —1H 119
Galsworthy Ter. *N16* —3E 46
Galton St. *W10* —3G 59
Galva Clo. *Barn* —4K 5
Galvani Way. *Croy* —1K 133
Galveston Rd. *SW15* —5H 91
Galway Clo. *SE16* —5H 79
　(off Masters Dri.)
Galway Ho. *EC1* —3C 62 (2D 144)
Galway St. *EC1* —3C 62 (2D 144)
Galy. *NW9* —2B 26
Gambetta St. *SW8* —2F 93
Gambia St. *SE1* —1B 78 (5B 150)
Gamble Rd. *SW17* —4C 108
Games Rd. *Barn* —3J 5
Gamlen Rd. *SW15* —4F 91
Gamuel Clo. *E17* —6C 32
Gander Grn. La. *Sutt* —2G 131
Gandhi Clo. *E17* —6C 32
Ganton St. *W1* —7G 61 (2A 148)
Gants Hill. (Junct.) —6E 34
Gantshill Cres. *Ilf* —5E 34
Gants Hill Cross. *Ilf* —6E 34
Gap Rd. *SW19* —5J 107
Garage Rd. *W3* —6G 57
Garbutt Pl. *W1* —5E 60 (5H 141)
Garden Av. *Bexh* —3G 101
Garden Av. *Mitc* —7F 109
Garden City. *Edgw* —6B 12
Garden Clo. *E4* —5H 19
Garden Clo. *SE12* —3K 113
Garden Clo. *SW15* —7E 90
Garden Clo. *Hamp* —5D 102
Garden Clo. *N'holt* —1C 54
Garden Clo. *Wall* —5J 133
Garden Ct. *EC4* —7A 62 (2J 149)
Garden Ct. *W4* —3J 73
Garden Ct. *Croy* —3F 135
Garden Ct. *Hamp* —5D 102
Garden Ct. *Rich* —1F 89
Garden Ct. *Stan* —5H 11
Gardener Gro. *Felt* —2D 102
Gardeners Clo. *N11* —2K 15
Gardeners Rd. *Croy* —1B 134

Garden Ho. *N2* —2B 28
　(off Grange, The)
Gardenia Rd. *Enf* —6K 7
Gardenia Way. *Wfd G* —5D 20
Garden La. *SW2* —1K 109
Garden La. *Brom* —6K 113
Garden M. *W2* —7J 59
Garden Rd. *NW8*
　　　　　　—3A 60 (1A 140)
Garden Rd. *SE20* —1J 125
Garden Rd. *Brom* —7K 113
Garden Rd. *Rich* —3G 89
Garden Row. *SE1*
　　　　　　—3B 78 (2A 156)
Gardens, The. *N8* —4J 29
　(in two parts)
Gardens, The. *SE22* —4G 95
Gardens, The. *Beck* —2F 127
Gardens, The. *Harr* —6G 23
Gardens, The. *Pinn* —6D 22
Garden St. *E1* —5K 63
Garden Ter. *SW1*
　　　　　　—5H 77 (5C 154)
Garden Ter. *SW7*
　　　　　　—2C 76 (7D 146)
Garden View. *E7* —4A 50
Garden Wlk. *EC2*
　　　　　　—3E 62 (2G 145)
Garden Wlk. *Beck* —1B 126
Garden Way. *NW10* —6J 41
Gardiner Av. *NW2* —5E 42
Gardiner Clo. *Enf* —6E 8
Gardiner Ct. *S Croy* —6C 134
Gardiners Clo. *Dag* —4D 52
Gardner Clo. *E11* —6K 33
Gardner Ho. *Felt* —2D 102
Gardner Ho. *S'hall* —7B 54
　(off Broadway, The)
Gardner Ind. Est. *Beck* —5A 112
Gardners La. *EC4*
　　　　　　—7C 62 (2C 150)
Gardnor Rd. *NW3* —4B 44
Gard St. *EC1* —3B 62 (1B 144)
Garendon Gdns. *Mord* —7K 121
Garendon Rd. *Mord* —7K 121
Gareth Clo. *Wor Pk* —2F 131
Gareth Clo. *SE16* —3H 109
Gareth Gro. *Brom* —4J 113
Garfield. *Enf* —5J 7
　(off Private Rd.)
Garfield M. *SW11* —3F 93
Garfield Rd. *E4* —1A 20
Garfield Rd. *E13* —4H 65
Garfield Rd. *SW11* —3E 92
Garfield Rd. *SW19* —5A 108
Garfield Rd. *Enf* —4D 8
Garfield Rd. *Twic* —1A 104
Garford St. *E14* —7C 64
Garganey Ct. *NW10* —6K 41
　(off Elgar Av.)
Garganey Wlk. *SE28* —7C 68
Garibaldi St. *SE18* —4J 83
Garland Rd. *SE18* —7H 83
Garland Rd. *Stan* —1E 24
Garlick Hill. *EC4*
　　　　　　—7C 62 (2D 150)
Garlies Rd. *SE23* —3A 112
Garlinge Rd. *NW2* —6H 43
Garman Clo. *N18* —5J 17
Garman Rd. *N17* —7D 18
Garnault M. *EC1*
　　　　　　—3A 62 (2K 143)
Garnault Pl. *EC1*
　　　　　　—3A 62 (2K 143)

Garnault Rd. *Enf* —1A 8
Garner Rd. *E17* —1E 32
Garner St. *E2* —2G 63
Garnet Rd. *NW10* —6A 42
Garnet Rd. *T Hth* —4C 124
Garnet St. *E1* —7J 63
Garnett Clo. *SE9* —3D 98
Garnett Rd. *NW3* —5D 44
Garnett Way. *E17* —1A 32
Garnet Wlk. *E6* —5C 66
Garnham Clo. *N16* —2F 47
Garnham St. *N16* —2F 47
Garnies Clo. *SE15* —7F 79
Garrad's Rd. *SW16* —3H 109
Garrard Clo. *Bexh* —3G 101
Garrard Clo. *Chst* —5F 115
Garrard Wlk. *NW10* —6A 42
Garrat Rd. *Edgw* —7B 12
Garratt Clo. *Croy* —4J 133
Garratt Ct. *SW18* —7K 91
Garratt La. *SW18 & SW17*
　　　　　　—6K 91
Garratts Rd. *Bush* —1B 10
Garratt Ter. *SW17* —4C 108
Garrett Clo. *W3* —5K 57
Garrett St. *EC1* —4C 62 (3D 144)
Garrick Av. *NW11* —6G 27
Garrick Clo. *SW18* —4A 92
Garrick Clo. *W5* —4E 56
Garrick Clo. *Rich* —5D 88
Garrick Cres. *Croy* —2E 134
Garrick Dri. *NW4* —2C 26
Garrick Dri. *SE28* —3H 83
Garrick Ho. *W4* —6A 74
Garrick Ind. Est. *NW4* —4E 26
Garrick Pk. *NW4* —2F 27
Garrick Rd. *NW9* —6B 26
Garrick Rd. *Gnfd* —4F 55
Garrick Rd. *Rich* —2G 89
Garrick St. *WC2* —7J 61 (2E 148)
Garrick Way. *NW4* —4F 27
Garrick Yd. *WC2*
　　　　　　—7J 61 (2E 148)
Garrison Clo. *SE18* —7E 82
Garrowsfield. *Barn* —6C 4
Garry Way. *Romf* —1K 37
Garside Clo. *SE28* —3H 83
Garside Clo. *Hamp* —6F 103
Garside Dri. *Stan* —3F 25
Garside Grn. *SE9* —2D 98
Garsington M. *SE4* —3B 96
Garter Way. *SE16* —2K 79
Garth Clo. *W4* —5K 73
Garth Clo. *King T* —5F 105
Garth Clo. *Mord* —7F 121
Garth Clo. *Ruis* —1B 38
Garth Ct. *W4* —6K 73
Garth Ct. *Harr* —6K 23
　(off Northwick Pk. Rd.)
Garth M. *W5* —5K 11
Garthorne Rd. *SE23* —7K 95
Garth Rd. *NW2* —2H 43
Garth Rd. *W4* —5K 73
Garth Rd. *King T* —5F 105
Garth Rd. *Mord* —7E 120
Garth Rd. Ind. Est. *Mord* —1F 131
Garthside. *Ham* —5E 104
Garth, The. *Hamp* —6F 103
Garth, The. *Harr* —6C 25
Garthway. *N12* —6H 15
Gartmoor Gdns. *SW19* —1H 107
Gartmore Rd. *Ilf* —2K 51
Garton Pl. *SW18* —6A 92
Gartons Clo. *Enf* —4D 8
Gartons Way. *SW11* —3A 92

Garvary Rd. *E16* —6K 65
Garway Rd. *W2* —6J 59
Gascoigne Gdns. *Wfd G* —7B 20
Gascoigne Pl. *E2*
　　　　　　—3F 63 (1J 145)
Gascoigne Rd. *Bark* —1G 67
Gascoigne Rd. *New Ad* —7F 137
Gascony Av. *NW6* —7J 43
Gascoyne Ho. *E9* —7A 48
Gascoyne Rd. *E9* —7K 47
Gaselee St. *E14* —7E 64
Gasholder Pl. *SE11*
　　　　　　—5K 77 (6H 155)
Gaskarth Rd. *SW12* —6F 93
Gaskarth Rd. *Edgw* —1J 25
Gaskell Rd. *N6* —6D 28
Gaskell St. *SW4* —2J 93
Gaskin St. *N1* —1B 62
Gaspar Clo. *SW5* —4K 75
Gaspar Clo. *SW5* —4K 75
　(off Courtfield Gdns.)
Gaspar M. *SW5* —4K 75
Gassiot Rd. *SW17* —4D 108
Gassiot Way. *Sutt* —3B 132
Gastein Rd. *W6* —6F 75
Gaston Bell Clo. *Rich* —3F 89
Gaston Rd. *Mitc* —3E 122
Gataker St. *SE16* —3H 79
Gatcombe Ct. *Beck* —7C 112
Gatcombe M. *W5* —7F 57
Gatcombe Rd. *E16* —1J 81
Gatcombe Rd. *N19* —3H 45
Gatcombe Way. *Barn* —3J 5
Gateacre Ct. *Sidc* —4B 116
Gateforth St. *NW8*
　　　　　　—4C 60 (4C 140)
Gatehouse Clo. *King T* —7J 105
Gatehouse Sq. *SE1*
　　　　　　—1C 78 (4D 150)
Gateley Ho. *SE4* —4K 95
　(off Coston Wlk.)
Gateley Rd. *SW9* —3K 93
Gate M. *SW7* —2C 76 (7D 146)
Gater Dri. *Enf* —1J 7
Gates. *NW9* —2B 26
Gatesborough St. *EC2*
　　　　　　—4E 62 (3G 145)
Gates Ct. *SE17* —5C 78 (5C 156)
Gatesden. *WC1* —3J 61 (2F 143)
Gates Grn. Rd. *W Wick* —3H 137
Gateside Rd. *SW17* —3D 108
Gatestone Rd. *SE19* —6E 110
Gate St. *WC2* —6K 61 (7G 143)
Gateway. *SE17* —6D 78 (7D 156)
Gateway Ho. *Bark* —1G 67
Gateway Ind. Est. *NW10* —3B 58
Gateway M. *E8* —5F 47
Gateways Ct. *Wall* —5F 133
Gateways, The. *SW3*
　　　　　　—5C 76 (4D 152)
Gatfield Gro. *Felt* —2E 102
Gatfield Ho. *Felt* —2E 102
Gathorne Rd. *N22* —1A 30
Gathorne St. *E2* —2K 63
Gatliff Clo. *SW1* —5E 76 (6H 153)
Gatliff Rd. *SW1* —5F 77 (6J 153)
Gatling Rd. *SE2* —5A 84
Gatting Clo. *Edgw* —7D 12
Gattis Wharf. *N1* —2J 61
　(off New Wharf Rd.)
Gatton Rd. *SW17* —4C 108
Gattons Way. *Sidc* —4F 117
Gatward Clo. *N21* —6G 7
Gatward Grn. *N9* —2A 18
Gatwick Rd. *SW18* —7H 91

Gauden Clo. *SW4* —3H **93**	Geneva Rd. *T Hth* —5C **124**	Georgian Ct. *N3* —1H **27**	Gibson St. *SE10* —5G **81**	Gill St. *E14* —6B **64**
Gauden Rd. *SW4* —2H **93**	Genever Clo. *E4* —5H **19**	Georgian Ct. *NW4* —5D **26**	Gideon Clo. *Belv* —4H **85**	Gillum Clo. *E Barn* —1J **15**
Gauntlet. *NW9* —2B **26**	Genista Rd. *N18* —5C **18**	Georgian Ct. *SW16* —4J **109**	Gideon Rd. *SW11* —3E **92**	Gilmore Ct. *N11* —5J **15**
(off Five Acre)	Genoa Av. *SW15* —5E **90**	Georgian Ct. *New Bar* —4F **5**	Giesbach Rd. *N19* —2H **45**	Gilmore Rd. *SE13* —4F **97**
Gauntlet Clo. *N'holt* —7C **38**	Genoa Rd. *SE20* —1J **125**	Georgian Ct. *Wemb* —6G **41**	Giffard Rd. *N18* —6K **17**	Gilpin Av. *SW14* —4K **89**
Gauntlett Ct. *Wemb* —5B **40**	Genotin Rd. *Enf* —3J **7**	Georgian Way. *Harr* —2H **39**	Giffin St. *SE8* —7C **80**	Gilpin Clo. *Mitc* —2C **122**
Gauntlett Rd. *Sutt* —5B **132**	Genotin Ter. *Enf* —4J **7**	Georgia Rd. *T Hth* —1B **124**	Gifford Gdns. *W7* —5H **55**	Gilpin Cres. *N18* —5A **18**
Gaunt St. *SE1* —3C **78** (1C **156**)	Gentian Row. *SE13* —1E **96**	Georgina Gdns. *E2*	Gifford St. *N1* —7J **45**	Gilpin Cres. *Twic* —7F **87**
Gautrey Rd. *SE15* —2J **95**	Gentlemans Row. *Enf* —3H **7**	—3F **63** (1K **145**)	Gift La. *E15* —1H **65**	Gilpin Rd. *E5* —4A **48**
Gautrey Sq. *E6* —6D **66**	Gentry Gdns. *E13* —3J **65**	Geraint Rd. *Brom* —4J **113**	Giggs Hill. *Orp* —2K **129**	Gilpin St. *T Hth* —4D **124**
Gavel St. *SE17* —4D **78** (3F **157**)	Geoffrey Clo. *SE5* —2C **94**	Geraldine Rd. *SW18* —5A **92**	Giggshill Gdns. *Th Dit* —7A **118**	Gilstead Ho. *Bark* —2B **68**
Gavestone Cres. *SE12* —7K **97**	Geoffrey Ct. *SE4* —3B **96**	Geraldine Rd. *W4* —6G **73**	Giggshill Rd. *Th Dit* —7A **118**	Gilstead Rd. *SW6* —2K **91**
Gavestone Rd. *SE12* —7K **97**	Geoffrey Gdns. *E6* —2C **66**	Geraldine St. *SE11*	Gilbert Clo. *SE3* —1D **98**	Gilston Rd. *SW10* —5A **76**
Gaviller Pl. *E5* —4H **47**	Geoffrey Jones Ct. *NW10* —1C **58**	—3B **78** (2A **156**)	Gilbert Clo. *SW19* —1K **121**	Giltspur St. *EC1*
Gavina Clo. *Mord* —5C **122**	Geoffrey Rd. *SE4* —3B **96**	Gerald M. *SW1* —4E **76** (3H **153**)	(off High Path)	—6B **62** (7B **144**)
Gawber St. *E2* —3J **63**	George Beard Rd. *SE8* —4B **80**	Gerald Rd. *E16* —4H **65**	Gilbert Ct. *W5* —6F **57**	Gilwell Clo. *E4* —4J **9**
Gawsworth Clo. *E15* —5H **49**	George & Catherine Wheel All.	Gerald Rd. *SW1* —4E **76** (3H **153**)	(off Green Vale)	Gilwell La. *E4* —4J **9**
Gawthorne Av. *NW7* —5B **14**	*EC2* —5E **62** (5H **145**)	Gerald Rd. *Dag* —1F **53**	Gilbert Gro. *Edgw* —1K **25**	Ginsburg Yd. *NW3* —4A **44**
Gay Clo. *NW2* —5D **42**	George Comberton Wlk. *E12*	Gerard Av. *Houn* —7E **86**	Gilbert Ho. *E17* —3E **32**	Gippeswyck Clo. *Pinn* —1B **22**
Gaydon Ho. *W2* —5K **59**	—5E **50**	Gerard Gdns. *Rain* —2K **69**	Gilbert Ho. *EC2* —5C **62** (5D **144**)	Gipsy Corner. *W3* —5K **57**
(off Bourne Ter.)	George Ct. *WC2* —7J **61** (3F **149**)	Gerard Rd. *SW13* —1B **90**	Gilbert Ho. *SW8* —7J **77**	Gipsy Hill. *SE19* —4E **110**
Gaydon La. *NW9* —1A **26**	George Cres. *N10* —7K **15**	Gerard Rd. *Harr* —6A **24**	(off Wyvil Rd.)	Gipsy La. *SW15* —3D **90**
Gayfere Rd. *Eps* —5C **130**	George Cres. *Wfd G* —5E **20**	Gerards Clo. *SE16* —6J **79**	Gilbert Pl. *WC1* —5J **61** (6E **142**)	Gipsy Rd. *SE27* —4C **110**
Gayfere Rd. *Ilf* —3D **34**	George Downing Est. *N16*	Gerda Rd. *SE9* —2G **115**	Gilbert Rd. *SE11*	Gipsy Rd. *Well* —2D **100**
Gayfere St. *SW1* —3J **77** (2E **154**)	—2F **47**	Germander Way. *E15* —3G **65**	—4A **78** (4K **155**)	Gipsy Rd. Gdns. *SE27* —4C **110**
Gayford Rd. *W12* —2B **74**	George V Av. *Pinn* —2D **22**	Gernon Rd. *E3* —2A **64**	Gilbert Rd. *SW19* —7J **108**	Giralda Clo. *E16* —5B **66**
Gay Gdns. *Dag* —4J **53**	George V Clo. *Pinn* —3E **22**	Geron Way. *NW2* —2D **42**	Gilbert Rd. *Belv* —3G **85**	Giraud St. *E14* —6D **64**
Gay Ho. *N16* —5E **46**	George V Way. *Gnfd* —1B **56**	Gerrard Pl. *W1* —7H **61** (2D **148**)	Gilbert Rd. *Brom* —7J **113**	Girdler's Rd. *W14* —4G **75**
Gayhurst Ct. *N'holt* —3A **54**	George Gange Way. *Harr* —4J **23**	Gerrard Rd. *N1* —2B **62**	Gilbert Rd. *Pinn* —4B **22**	Girdlestone Wlk. *N19* —2G **45**
Gayhurst Rd. *E8* —7G **47**	George Gro. Rd. *SE20* —1G **125**	Gerrards Clo. *N14* —5B **6**	Gilbert St. *E15* —2K **49**	Girdwood Rd. *SW18* —7G **91**
Gaylor Rd. *N'holt* —5D **38**	George Inn Yd. *SE1*	Gerrards Ct. *W5* —3D **72**	Gilbert St. *E15* —4G **49**	Gironde Rd. *SW6* —7H **75**
Gaynesford Rd. *SE23* —2K **111**	—1D **78** (5E **150**)	Gerrard St. *W1* —7H **61** (2D **148**)	Gilbert St. *W1* —6E **60** (1H **147**)	Girtin Ho. *N'holt* —2B **54**
Gaynesford Rd. *Cars* —7D **132**	George La. *E18* —2J **33**	Gerridge St. *SE1*	Gilbert St. *Houn* —3F **87**	(off Academy Gdns.)
Gaynes Hill Rd. *Wfd G* —6H **21**	George La. *SE13* —6D **96**	—3A **78** (1K **155**)	Gilbert Way. *Croy* —3K **123**	Girton Av. *NW9* —3G **25**
Gay Rd. *E15* —2F **65**	George La. *Brom* —1K **137**	Gerry Raffles Sq. *E15* —7F **49**	Gilbey Rd. *SW17* —4C **108**	Girton Clo. *N'holt* —6G **39**
Gaysham Av. *Ilf* —5E **34**	George Lansbury Ho. *N22*	Gertrude Rd. *Belv* —4G **85**	Gilbeys Yd. *NW1* —7E **44**	Girton Gdns. *Croy* —3G **136**
Gaysham Hall. *Ilf* —3F **35**	—1A **30**	Gertrude St. *SW10* —6A **76**	Gilbourne Rd. *SE18* —6K **83**	Girton Rd. *SE26* —5K **111**
Gay St. *SW15* —3F **91**	(off Progress Way)	Gervase Clo. *Wemb* —3J **41**	Gilda Av. *Enf* —5F **9**	Girton Rd. *N'holt* —6G **39**
Gayton Ct. *Harr* —6K **23**	George Lindgren Ho. *SW6*	Gervase Rd. *Edgw* —1J **25**	Gilda Ct. *NW7* —1C **26**	Girton Vs. *W10* —6F **58**
Gayton Cres. *NW3* —4B **44**	—7H **75**	Gervase St. *SE15* —7H **79**	Gilda Cres. *N16* —1G **47**	Gisbourne Clo. *Wall* —3H **133**
Gayton Rd. *NW3* —4B **44**	(off Clem Attlee Ct.)	Gervis Ct. *Houn* —7G **71**	Gildea Clo. *Pinn* —1E **22**	Gisburn Rd. *N8* —4K **29**
Gayton Rd. *SE2* —3C **84**	George Lowe Ct. *W2* —5K **59**	Ghent St. *SE6* —2C **112**	Gildea St. *W1* —5F **61** (6K **141**)	Gissing Wlk. *N1* —7A **46**
Gayton Rd. *Harr* —6K **23**	(off Bourne Ter.)	Ghent Way. *E8* —6F **47**	Gilden Cres. *NW5* —5E **44**	Gittens Clo. *Brom* —4H **113**
Gayville Rd. *SW11* —6D **92**	George Mathers Rd. *SE11*	Giant Arches Rd. *SE24* —7C **94**	Gildersome St. *SE18* —6E **82**	Given Wilson Wlk. *E13* —2H **65**
Gaywood Clo. *SW2* —1K **109**	—4B **78** (4A **156**)	Giant Tree Hill. *Bush* —1C **10**	Giles Coppice. *SE19* —4F **111**	Glacier Way. *Wemb* —2D **56**
Gaywood Rd. *E17* —3C **32**	George M. *NW1*	Gibbfield Clo. *Romf* —3E **36**	Giles Ho. *SE16* —3G **79** (1K **157**)	Gladbeck Way. *Enf* —4G **7**
Gaywood St. *SE1*	—3G **61** (2B **142**)	Gibbins Rd. *E15* —7E **48**	Gilesmead. *SE5* —1D **94**	Gladding Rd. *E12* —4B **50**
—3B **78** (2B **156**)	George M. *Enf* —3J **7**	(in three parts)	Gilkes Cres. *SE21* —6E **94**	Glade Ct. *Ilf* —2D **34**
Gaza St. *SE17* —5B **78** (6A **156**)	(off Town, The)	Gibbon Rd. *SE15* —2J **95**	Gilkes Pl. *SE21* —6E **94**	Glade Gdns. *Croy* —7A **126**
Geariesville Gdns. *Ilf* —4F **35**	George Pl. *N17* —3E **30**	Gibbon Rd. *W3* —7A **58**	Gillan Ct. *SE12* —3K **113**	Glade La. *S'hall* —2F **71**
Geary Rd. *NW10* —5C **42**	George Rd. *E4* —6H **19**	Gibbon Rd. *King T* —1E **118**	Gillan Grn. *Bush* —2B **10**	Glade Rd. *E12* —3D **50**
Geary St. *N7* —5K **45**	George Rd. *King T* —7H **105**	Gibbon's Rents. *SE1*	Gillards M. *E17* —4C **32**	Gladeside. *N21* —6E **6**
Geddes Pl. *Bexh* —4G **101**	George Rd. *N Mald* —4B **120**	—1E **78** (5G **151**)	Gillards Way. *E17* —4C **32**	Gladeside. *Croy* —6K **125**
Gedeney Rd. *N17* —1C **30**	George Row. *SE16*	Gibbons Rd. *NW10* —6A **42**	Gill Av. *E16* —6J **65**	Gladesmore Rd. *N15* —6F **31**
Gedling Pl. *SE1* —3F **79** (1K **157**)	—2G **79** (7K **151**)	Gibbon Wlk. *SW15* —4C **90**	Gillender St. *E3 & E14* —4E **64**	Glades Pl. *Brom* —2J **127**
Geere Rd. *E15* —1H **65**	George Sq. *SW19* —3J **121**	Gibbs Av. *SE19* —5D **110**	Gillespie Rd. *N5* —3A **46**	Glades Shop. Cen., The. *Brom*
Gees Ct. *W1* —6E **60** (1H **147**)	George's Rd. *N7* —5K **45**	Gibbs Clo. *SE19* —5D **110**	Gillett Av. *E6* —2C **66**	—2J **127**
Gee St. *EC1* —4C **62** (3C **144**)	George's Sq. *SW6* —6H **75**	Gibbs Grn. *W14* —5H **75**	Gillette Corner. (Junct.) —7A **72**	Gladeswood Rd. *Belv* —4H **85**
Geffery's Ct. *SE9* —3C **114**	(off N. End Rd.)	Gibbs Grn. *Edgw* —5D **12**	Gillett Pl. *N16* —5E **46**	Glade, The. *N21* —7E **6**
Geffrye Ct. *N1* —2E **62**	George St. *E16* —6H **65**	Gibb's Rd. *N18* —4D **18**	Gillett Rd. *T Hth* —4D **124**	Glade, The. *SE7* —7A **82**
Geffrye Est. *N1* —2E **62**	George St. *W1* —6D **60** (7E **140**)	Gibbs Sq. *SE19* —5D **110**	Gillett St. *N16* —5E **46**	Glade, The. *Brom* —2B **128**
Geffrye St. *E2* —2F **63** (1J **145**)	George St. *W7* —1J **71**	Gibraltar Wlk. *E2*	Gillham Ter. *N17* —6B **18**	Glade, The. *Croy* —7A **126**
Geldart Rd. *SE15* —7H **79**	George St. *Bark* —7G **51**	—3F **63** (2K **145**)	Gillian Ho. *Har W* —6D **10**	Glade, The. *Eps* —6C **130**
Gellatly Rd. *SE14* —2J **95**	George St. *Croy* —2C **134**	Gibson Clo. *E1* —4J **63**	Gillian Pk. Rd. *Sutt* —1H **131**	Glade, The. *Ilf* —1D **34**
Gelsthorpe Rd. *Romf* —1H **37**	George St. *Houn* —2D **86**	Gibson Clo. *N21* —6F **7**	Gillian St. *SE13* —5D **96**	Glade, The. *Sutt* —7G **131**
Gemini Bus. Cen. *E16* —4F **65**	George St. *Rich* —5D **88**	Gibson Clo. *Iswth* —3J **87**	Gillies St. *NW5* —5E **44**	Glade, The. *W Wick* —3D **136**
Gemini Bus. Est. *SE14* —5K **79**	George St. *S'hall* —4C **70**	Gibson Gdns. *N16* —2F **47**	Gilling Ct. *NW3* —6C **44**	Glade, The. *Wfd G* —3E **20**
Gemini Gro. *N'holt* —3C **54**	Georgetown Clo. *SE19* —5E **110**	Gibson Ho. *Sutt* —4J **131**	Gillingham M. *SW1*	Gladiator St. *SE23* —7A **96**
General Gordon Pl. *SE18* —4F **83**	Georgette Pl. *SE10* —7E **80**	Gibson Rd. *SE11*	—4G **77** (3A **154**)	Glading Ter. *N16* —3F **47**
General Wolfe Rd. *SE10* —1F **97**	Georgeville Gdns. *Ilf* —4F **35**	—4K **77** (4H **155**)	Gillingham Rd. *NW2* —3G **43**	Gladioli Clo. *Hamp* —6E **102**
Genesta Rd. *SE18* —6F **83**	George Wyver Clo. *SW19*	Gibson Rd. *Dag* —1C **52**	Gillingham Row. *SW1*	Gladsmuir Rd. *N19* —1G **45**
Geneva Dri. *SW9* —4A **94**	—7G **91**	Gibson Sq. *N1* —1A **62**	—4G **77** (3A **154**)	Gladsmuir Rd. *Barn* —2B **4**
Geneva Gdns. *Romf* —5E **36**	George Yd. *EC3* —6D **62** (1F **151**)	Gibsons Hill. *SW16* —7A **110**	Gillingham St. *SW1*	Gladstone Av. *E12* —7C **50**
Geneva Rd. *King T* —4E **118**	George Yd. *W1* —7E **60** (2H **147**)	Gibson St. *SE10* —5G **81**	—4G **77** (3A **154**)	
	Georgiana St. *NW1* —1G **61**		Gillison Wlk. *SE16* —3H **79**	
	Georgian Clo. *Brom* —1K **137**		Gillman Dri. *E15* —1H **65**	
	Georgian Clo. *Stan* —7F **11**			

Gladstone Av. *N22* —2A **30**
Gladstone Av. *Twic* —7H **87**
Gladstone M. *N22* —2A **30**
Gladstone M. *NW6* —7H **43**
Gladstone M. *SE20* —7J **111**
Gladstone Pk. Gdns. *NW2*
—3D **42**
Gladstone Pl. *E3* —2B **64**
Gladstone Pl. *Barn* —4A **4**
Gladstone Rd. *SW19* —7J **107**
Gladstone Rd. *W4* —3K **73**
Gladstone Rd. *Buck H* —1F **21**
Gladstone Rd. *Croy* —7D **124**
Gladstone Rd. *King T* —3G **119**
Gladstone Rd. *S'hall* —2C **70**
Gladstone St. *SE1*
—3B **78** (1A **156**)
Gladstone Ter. *SW8* —1F **93**
Gladstone Way. *Harr* —3J **23**
Gladwell Rd. *N8* —6K **29**
Gladwell Rd. *Brom* —6J **113**
Gladwyn Rd. *SW15* —3F **91**
Gladys Dimson Ho. *E7* —5H **49**
Gladys Rd. *NW6* —7J **43**
Glaigmar Gdns. *N3* —1K **27**
Glaisher St. *SE10* —7E **80**
Glamis Av. *Enf* —2H **73**
Glamis Pl. *E1* —7K **63**
Glamis Rd. *E1* —7J **63**
Glamis Way. *N'holt* —6G **39**
Glamorgan Clo. *Mitc* —3J **123**
Glamorgan Rd. *W —7K **55**
(off Copley Clo.)
Glamorgan Rd. *King T* —7C **104**
Glanfield Rd. *Beck* —4B **126**
Glanleam Rd. *Stan* —4J **11**
Glanville Rd. *SW2* —5J **93**
Glanville Rd. *Brom* —3K **127**
Glasbrook Av. *Twic* —1D **102**
Glaserton Rd. *N16* —7E **30**
Glasford St. *SW17* —6D **108**
Glasfryn Ct. *Harr* —2H **39**
(off Roxeth Hill)
Glasfryn Ho. *Harr* —2H **39**
(off Roxeth Hill)
Glasgow Ho. *W9* —2K **59**
(off Maida Vale)
Glasgow Rd. *E13* —2K **65**
Glasgow Rd. *N18* —5C **18**
Glasgow Ter. *SW1*
—5G **77** (6A **154**)
Glasse Clo. *W13* —7A **56**
Glasshill St. *SE1*
—2B **78** (6B **150**)
Glasshouse Fields. *E1* —7K **63**
Glasshouse St. *W1*
—7G **61** (3B **148**)
Glasshouse Wlk. *SE11*
—5K **77** (5F **155**)
Glasshouse Yd. *EC1*
—4C **62** (4C **144**)
Glasslyn Rd. *N8* —5H **29**
Glassmill La. *Brom* —2H **127**
(in two parts)
Glass St. *E2* —4H **63**
Glass Yd. *SE18* —3E **82**
Glastonbury Av. *Wfd G* —7G **21**
Glastonbury St. *W13* —1A **72**
(off Talbot Rd.)
Glastonbury Ho. *SE13* —5H **97**
(off Wantage Rd.)
Glastonbury Rd. *N9* —1B **18**
Glastonbury Rd. *Mord* —7J **121**
Glastonbury St. *NW6* —5H **43**

Glaston Ct. *W5* —1D **72**
(off Grange Rd.)
Glaucus St. *E3* —5D **64**
Glazbury Rd. *W14* —4G **75**
Glazebrook Clo. *SE21* —2D **110**
Glazebrook Rd. *Tedd* —7K **103**
Glebe Av. *Enf* —3G **7**
Glebe Av. *Harr* —4E **24**
Glebe Av. *Mitc* —2C **122**
Glebe Av. *Ruis* —6A **38**
Glebe Av. *Wfd G* —6D **20**
Glebe Clo. *W4* —5A **74**
Glebe Cotts. *Felt* —3E **102**
Glebe Ct. *N13* —3F **17**
Glebe Ct. *SE3* —3G **97**
Glebe Ct. *W7* —7H **55**
Glebe Ct. *Mitc* —3D **122**
Glebe Ct. *Stan* —5H **11**
Glebe Cres. *NW4* —4E **26**
Glebe Cres. *Harr* —3E **24**
Glebe Gdns. *N Mald* —7A **120**
Glebe Ho. Dri. *Brom* —1K **137**
Glebe Hyrst. *SE19* —4E **110**
Glebelands. *E10* —2D **48**
Glebelands Av. *E18* —2J **33**
Glebelands Av. *Ilf* —7H **35**
Glebelands Clo. *SE5* —3E **94**
Glebe La. *Harr* —4E **24**
Glebe Path. *Mitc* —3D **122**
Glebe Pl. *SW3* —6C **76** (7C **152**)
Glebe Rd. *E8* —7F **47** (1J **151**)
Glebe Rd. *N3* —1A **28**
Glebe Rd. *N8* —4K **29**
Glebe Rd. *NW10* —6B **42**
Glebe Rd. *SW13* —2C **90**
Glebe Rd. *Brom* —1J **127**
Glebe Rd. *Cars* —6D **132**
Glebe Rd. *Dag* —6H **53**
Glebe Rd. *Stan* —5H **11**
Glebe Rd. *Sutt* —7G **131**
Glebe Side. *Twic* —6K **87**
Glebe Sq. *Mitc* —3D **122**
Glebe St. *W4* —5A **74**
Glebe Ter. *W4* —5A **74**
Glebe, The. *SE3* —3G **97**
Glebe, The. *SW16* —4J **109**
Glebe, The. *Chst* —1G **129**
Glebe, The. *Wor Pk* —1B **130**
Glebe Way. *Felt* —3E **102**
Glebe Way. *W Wick* —2E **136**
Glebe Way. *Wfd G* —5F **21**
Gledhow Gdns. *SW5* —4A **76**
Gledstanes Rd. *W14* —5G **75**
Gleed Av. *Bush* —2C **10**
Glegg Pl. *SW15* —4F **91**
Glenaffric Av. *E14* —4E **80**
Glen Albyn Rd. *SW19* —2F **107**
Glenalmond Rd. *Harr* —4E **24**
Glenalvon Way. *SE18* —4C **82**
Glena M. *Sutt* —4A **132**
Glenarm Rd. *E5* —4J **47**
Glenavon Ct. *Wor Pk* —2D **130**
Glenavon Lodge. *Beck* —7C **112**
Glenavon Rd. *E15* —7G **49**
Glenbarr Clo. *SE9* —3F **99**
Glenbow Rd. *Brom* —6G **113**
Glenbrook N. *Enf* —4E **6**
Glenbrook Rd. *NW6* —5J **43**
Glenbrook S. *Enf* —4E **6**
Glenbuck Rd. *Surb* —6D **118**
Glenburnie Rd. *SW17* —3D **108**
Glencairn Dri. *W5* —4C **56**
Glencairne Clo. *E16* —5B **66**
Glencairn Rd. *SW16* —1J **123**
Glencoe Av. *Ilf* —7H **35**

Glencoe Dri. *Dag* —4G **53**
Glenilla Rd. *NW3* —6C **44**
Glenister Pk. Rd. *SW16* —7H **109**
Glenister Rd. *SE10* —5H **81**
Glenister St. *E16* —1E **82**
Glenlea Rd. *SE9* —5D **98**
Glenloch Rd. *NW3* —6C **44**
Glenloch Rd. *Enf* —2D **8**
Glenluce Rd. *SE3* —6J **81**
Glenlyon Rd. *SE9* —5E **98**
Glenmead. *Buck H* —1E **21**
Glenmere Av. *NW7* —6H **13**
Glenmill. *Hamp* —5D **102**
Glenmore Lawns. *W13* —6A **56**
Glenmore Lodge. *Beck* —1D **126**
Glenmore Pde. *Wemb* —1E **56**
Glenmore Rd. *NW3* —6C **44**
Glenmore Rd. *Well* —7K **83**
Glenmore Way. *Bark* —2A **68**
Glenmount Path. *SE18* —5G **83**
Glennie Ho. *SE10* —1E **96**
(off Blackheath Hill)
Glennie Rd. *SE27* —3A **110**
Glenny Rd. *Bark* —6G **51**
Glenorchy Clo. *Hayes* —5C **54**
Glenparke Rd. *E7* —6K **49**
Glen Rise. *Wfd G* —6E **20**
Glen Rd. *E13* —4A **66**
Glen Rd. *E17* —5B **32**
Glen Rd. End. *Wall* —7F **133**
Glenrosa St. *SW6* —2A **92**
Glenrose Ct. *Sidc* —5B **116**
Glenroy St. *W12* —6E **58**
Glensdale Rd. *SE4* —3B **96**
Glenshaw Mans. *SW9* —7A **78**
(off Brixton Rd.)
Glenshiel Rd. *SE9* —5E **98**
Glentanner Way. *SW17* —3B **108**
Glentham Gdns. *SW13* —6D **74**
Glentham Rd. *SW13* —6C **74**
Glen, The. *Brom* —2G **127**
Glen, The. *Croy* —3K **135**
Glen, The. *Eastc* —5A **22**
Glen, The. *Enf* —4G **7**
Glen, The. *Orp* —3E **138**
Glen, The. *Pinn* —7C **22**
Glen, The. *S'hall* —5D **70**
Glen, The. *Wemb* —4D **40**
Glenthorne Av. *Croy* —1J **135**
Glenthorne Clo. *Sutt* —1J **131**
Glenthorne Gdns. *Ilf* —3F **35**
Glenthorne Gdns. *Sutt* —1J **131**
Glenthorne M. *W6* —4D **74**
Glenthorne Rd. *E17* —5A **32**
Glenthorne Rd. *N11* —5J **15**
Glenthorne Rd. *W6* —4D **74**
Glenthorne Rd. *King T* —4F **119**
Glenthorpe Rd. *Mord* —5F **121**
Glenton Rd. *SE13* —4G **97**
Glentworth St. *NW1*
—4D **60** (4F **141**)
Glenure Rd. *SE9* —5E **98**
Glenview. *SE2* —6D **84**
Glenview Rd. *Brom* —2B **128**
Glenville Av. *Enf* —1H **7**
Glenville Gro. *SE8* —7B **80**
Glenville M. *SW18* —7K **91**
Glenville Rd. *King T* —1G **119**
Glen Wlk. *Iswth* —5H **87**
Glenwood Av. *NW9* —1A **42**
Glenwood Clo. *Harr* —5K **23**
Glenwood Ct. *E18* —3J **33**
Glenwood Ct. *Sidc* —4A **116**
Glenwood Gdns. *Ilf* —5E **34**
Glenwood Gro. *NW9* —1J **41**

Glenwood Rd. *N15* —5B **30**
Glenwood Rd. *NW7* —3F **13**
Glenwood Rd. *SE6* —1C **112**
Glenwood Rd. *Eps* —6C **130**
Glenwood Rd. *Houn* —3H **87**
Glenwood Way. *Croy* —6K **125**
Glenworth Av. *E14* —4F **81**
Gliddon Rd. *W14* —4G **75**
Glimpsing Grn. *Eri* —3E **84**
Global App. *E3* —2E **64**
Globe Pond Rd. *SE16* —1A **80**
Globe Rd. *E2 & E1* —3J **63**
(in two parts)
Globe Rd. *E15* —5H **49**
Globe Rd. *Wfd G* —6F **21**
Globe Stairs. *SE16* —1K **79**
Globe St. *SE1* —3D **78** (1E **156**)
Globe Ter. *E2* —3J **63**
Globe Town Mkt. *E2* —3K **63**
Globe Yd. *W1* —6F **61** (1J **147**)
Glossop Rd. *S Croy* —7D **134**
Gloster Rd. *N Mald* —4A **120**
Gloucester Arc. *SW7* —4A **76**
Gloucester Av. *NW1* —7E **44**
Gloucester Av. *Sidc* —2J **115**
Gloucester Av. *Well* —4K **99**
Gloucester Cir. *SE10* —7E **80**
Gloucester Clo. *NW10* —7K **41**
Gloucester Clo. *Th Dit* —7A **118**
Gloucester Ct. *EC3*
—7E **62** (3H **151**)
Gloucester Ct. *NW11* —7H **27**
(off Golders Grn. Rd.)
Gloucester Ct. *W7* —5K **55**
(off Copley Clo.)
Gloucester Ct. *Harr* —3J **23**
Gloucester Ct. *Mitc* —5J **123**
Gloucester Ct. *Rich* —7G **73**
Gloucester Cres. *NW1* —1F **61**
Gloucester Dri. *N4* —2B **46**
Gloucester Dri. *NW11* —4J **27**
Gloucester Gdns. *NW11* —7H **27**
Gloucester Gdns. *W2* —6A **60**
Gloucester Gdns. *Cockf* —4K **5**
Gloucester Gdns. *Ilf* —7C **34**
Gloucester Gdns. *Sutt* —2K **131**
Gloucester Ga. *NW1* —2F **61**
Gloucester Ga. M. *NW1* —2F **61**
Gloucester Ho. *SW9 & SE5*
—7A **78**
Gloucester Ho. *Rich* —5G **89**
Gloucester M. *E10* —7C **32**
Gloucester M. *W2* —6A **60**
Gloucester M. W. *W2* —6A **60**
Gloucester Pde. *Sidc* —5A **100**
Gloucester Pl. *NW1 & W1*
—4D **60** (4E **140**)
Gloucester Pl. M. *W1*
—5D **60** (6F **141**)
Gloucester Rd. *E10* —7C **32**
Gloucester Rd. *E11* —5K **33**
Gloucester Rd. *E12* —3D **50**
Gloucester Rd. *E17* —2K **31**
Gloucester Rd. *N17* —2D **30**
Gloucester Rd. *N18* —5A **18**
Gloucester Rd. *SW7* —3A **76**
Gloucester Rd. *W3* —2J **73**
Gloucester Rd. *W5* —2C **72**
Gloucester Rd. *Barn* —5E **4**
Gloucester Rd. *Belv* —5F **85**
Gloucester Rd. *Croy* —7D **124**
Gloucester Rd. *Enf* —1H **7**
Gloucester Rd. *Felt* —1A **102**
Gloucester Rd. *Hamp* —7F **103**

Gloucester Rd. Harr —5F 23
Gloucester Rd. Houn —4C 86
Gloucester Rd. King T —2G 119
Gloucester Rd. Rich —7G 73
Gloucester Rd. Tedd —5J 103
Gloucester Rd. Twic —1G 103
Gloucester Sq. E2 —1G 63
Gloucester Sq. W2
—6B 60 (1B 146)
Gloucester St. SW1
—5G 77 (6A 154)
Gloucester Ter. W2 —6K 59
Gloucester Wlk. W8 —2J 75
Gloucester Way. EC1
—3A 62 (2A 143)
Glover Clo. SE2 —4C 84
Glover Dri. N18 —6D 18
Glover Ho. SE15 —4H 95
Glover Rd. Pinn —6B 22
Gloxinia Wlk. Hamp —6E 102
Glycena Rd. SW11 —3D 92
Glyn Av. Barn —4G 5
Glyn Clo. SE25 —2E 124
Glyn Ct. SE27 —3A 110
Glyndale Grange. Sutt —6K 131
Glyndebourne Ct. N'holt —3A 54
(off Canberra Ct.)
Glynde M. SW3 —3C 76 (2D 152)
Glynde Reach. WC1
—3J 61 (2F 143)
Glynde Rd. Bexh —3D 100
Glynde St. SE4 —6B 96
Glynde St. SE18 —4G 83
Glyn Dri. Sidc —4B 116
Glynfield Rd. NW10 —7A 42
Glyn Rd. N22 —2A 30
Glyn Rd. E5 —3K 47
Glyn Rd. Enf —4D 8
Glyn Rd. Wor Pk —2F 131
Glyn St. SE11 —5K 77 (6G 155)
Glynwood Ct. SE23 —2J 111
Goater's All. SW6 —7H 75
(off Dawes Rd.)
Goat Ho. Bri. SE25 —3G 125
Goat La. Enf —1A 8
Goat Rd. Mitc —7E 122
Goat St. SE1 —2F 79 (6J 151)
Goat Wharf. Bren —6E 72
Gobions Av. Romf —1K 37
Godalming Av. Wall —5J 133
Godalming Rd. E14 —5D 64
Godbold Rd. E15 —4G 65
Goddard Ct. W'stone —2A 24
Goddard Rd. Beck —4K 125
Goddards Way. Ilf —1H 51
Goddarts Ho. E17 —3C 32
Godfrey Av. N'holt —1C 54
Godfrey Av. Twic —7H 87
Godfrey Hill. SE18 —4C 82
Godfrey Rd. SE18 —4D 82
Godfrey St. E15 —2E 64
Godfrey St. SW3
—5C 76 (5D 152)
Godfrey Way. Houn —7D 86
Goding St. SE11
—5K 77 (5F 155)
Godley Rd. SW18 —1B 108
Godliman St. EC4
—6B 62 (1B 150)
Godman Rd. SE15 —2H 95
Godolphin Clo. N13 —6G 17
Godolphin Pl. W3 —7K 57
Godolphin Rd. W12 —1D 74
Godric Cres. New Ad —7F 137
Godson Rd. Croy —3A 134

Godson St. N1 —2A 62
Godstone Rd. Sutt —4A 132
Godstone Rd. Twic —6B 88
Godstow Rd. SE2 —2C 84
Godwin Clo. E4 —1K 9
Godwin Clo. N1 —2C 62
Godwin Rd. E7 —4K 49
Godwin Rd. Brom —3A 128
Goffers Rd. SE3 —1G 97
Goidel Clo. Wall —4H 133
Golborne Gdns. W10 —4G 59
Golborne Rd. W10 —5G 59
Golda Clo. Barn —6A 4
Goldbath St. SE13 —1D 96
Goldbeaters Gro. Edgw —6F 13
Goldbeaters Wlk. Wemb —3J 41
Goldcliff Clo. Mord —7J 121
Goldcrest Clo. E16 —5B 66
Goldcrest Clo. SE28 —7C 68
Goldcrest M. W5 —5D 56
Goldcrest Way. Bush —1B 10
Goldcrest Way. New Ad —7F 137
Golden Ct. Barn —4H 5
Golden Ct. Rich —5D 88
Golden La. EC1 —4C 62 (3C 144)
Golden La. EC1
—4C 62 (4C 144)
Golden Mnr. W7 —7J 55
Golden M. SE20 —1J 125
Golden Pde. E17 —3E 32
Golden Plover Clo. E16 —6J 65
Golden Sq. W1 —7G 61 (2B 148)
Golders Clo. Edgw —5C 12
Golders Ct. NW11 —7H 27
Golders Gdns. NW11 —7H 27
Golders Grn. Cres. NW11 —7H 27
Golders Grn. Rd. NW11 —6G 27
Golders Mnr. Dri. NW11 —6F 27
Golders Pk. Clo. NW11 —1J 43
Golders Rise. NW4 —5F 27
Golders Way. NW11 —7H 27
Golderton. NW4 —4E 26
(off Prince of Wales Clo.)
Goldeslea. NW11 —1J 43
Goldfinch Rd. SE28 —3H 83
Goldhawk Ind. Est. W6 —3D 74
Goldhawk M. W12 —2D 74
Goldhawk Rd. W6 & W12
—4B 74
Goldhaze Clo. Wfd G —7G 21
Gold Hill. Edgw —6E 12
Goldhurst Ter. NW6 —7K 43
Goldie Ho. N19 —7H 29
Golding Ct. Ilf —3E 50
Golding St. E1 —6G 63
Golding Ter. SW11 —2E 92
Goldington Ct. NW1 —1G 61
(off Royal College St.)
Goldington Cres. NW1 —2H 61
Goldington St. NW1 —2H 61
Gold La. Edgw —6E 12
Goldman Clo. E2
—4G 63 (3K 145)
Goldney Rd. W9 —4J 59
Goldsborough Cres. E4 —2J 19
Goldsborough Rd. SW8 —1H 93
Goldsdown Clo. Enf —2F 9
Goldsdown Rd. Enf —2E 8
Goldsmid St. SE18 —5J 83
Goldsmith Av. E12 —6C 50
Goldsmith Av. NW9 —5A 26
Goldsmith Av. W3 —7K 57
Goldsmith Av. Romf —7G 37
Goldsmith Clo. Harr —1F 39
Goldsmith La. NW9 —4H 25

Goldsmith Rd. E10 —1C 48
Goldsmith Rd. E17 —2K 31
Goldsmith Rd. N11 —5J 15
Goldsmith Rd. SE15 —1G 95
Goldsmith Rd. W3 —1K 73
Goldsmith's Bldgs. W3 —1K 73
Goldsmiths Clo. W3 —1K 73
Goldsmith's Pl. NW6 —1K 59
(off Springfield La.)
Goldsmith's Row. E2 —2G 63
Goldsmith's Sq. E2 —2G 63
Goldsmith St. EC2
—6C 62 (7D 144)
Goldsworthy Gdns. SE16 —5J 79
Goldwell Ho. SE22 —3E 94
Goldwell Rd. T Hth —4K 123
Goldwin Clo. SE14 —1J 95
Goldwing Clo. E16 —6J 65
Golf Clo. Stan —7H 11
Golf Clo. T Hlti —1A 124
Golf Club Dri. King T —7K 105
Golfe Rd. Ilf —3H 51
Golf Rd. W5 —6F 57
Golf Rd. Brom —3E 128
Golf Side. Twic —3H 103
Golfside Clo. N20 —3H 15
Golfside Clo. N Mald —2A 120
Goliath Clo. Wall —7J 133
Gollogly Ter. SE7 —5A 82
Gomer Gdns. Tedd —6A 104
Gomer Pl. Tedd —6A 104
Gomm Rd. SE16 —3J 79
Gomshall Av. Wall —5J 133
Gondar Gdns. NW6 —5H 43
Gonson St. SE8 —6D 80
Gonston Clo. SW19 —2G 107
Gonville Cres. N'holt —6F 39
Gonville Rd. T Hth —5K 123
Gonville St. SW6 —3G 91
Gooch Ho. E5 —3H 47
Goodall Ho. SE4 —4K 95
Goodall Rd. E11 —3E 48
Gooden Ct. Harr —3J 39
Goodenough Rd. SW19 —7H 107
Goodfellow Gdns. King T
—5J 105
Goodge Pl. W1 —5G 61 (6B 142)
Goodge St. W1 —5G 61 (6B 142)
Goodhall St. NW10 —3B 58
(in two parts)
Goodhart Pl. E14 —7A 64
Goodhart Way. W Wick —7G 127
Goodhew Rd. Croy —6G 125
Gooding Clo. N Mald —4J 119
Goodinge Clo. N7 —6J 45
Goodman Cres. SW2 —2J 109
Goodman Rd. E10 —7E 32
Goodman's Ct. E1
—7F 63 (2J 151)
Goodmans Ct. Wemb —4D 40
Goodmans Stile. E1
—6G 63 (7K 145)
Goodmans Yd. E1
—7F 63 (2J 151)
Goodmayes Av. Ilf —1A 52
Goodmayes La. Ilf —4A 52
Goodmayes Rd. Ilf —1A 52
Goodrich Ct. W10 —6F 59
Goodrich Rd. SE22 —6F 95
Goodson Rd. NW10 —7A 42
Goods Way. NW1 —2C 61
Goodway Gdns. E14 —6F 65
Goodwin Clo. SE16
—3G 79 (2K 157)
Goodwin Clo. Mitc —3B 122

Goodwin Ct. N8 —3J 29
(off Campsbourne Rd.)
Goodwin Ct. NW1 —2G 61
(off Chalton St.)
Goodwin Ct. SW19 —7C 108
Goodwin Ct. Barn —6H 5
Goodwin Dri. Sidc —3D 116
Goodwin Gdns. Croy —6B 134
Goodwin Ho. N9 —1B 18
Goodwin Rd. N9 —1E 18
Goodwin Rd. W12 —2C 74
Goodwin Rd. Croy —5B 134
Goodwins Ct. WC2
—7J 61 (2E 148)
Goodwin St. N4 —2A 46
Goodwood Clo. Mord —4J 121
Goodwood Clo. Stan —5H 11
Goodwood Dri. N'holt —6E 38
Goodwood Pde. Beck —4A 126
Goodwood Rd. SE14 —7A 80
Goodwyn Av. NW7 —5F 13
Goodwyns Vale. N10 —1E 28
Goodyear Pl. SE5 —6C 78
Goodyers Gdns. NW4 —5F 27
Goosander Clo. SE8 —6A 80
Goosander Way. SE28 —3H 83
Gooseacre La. Harr —5D 24
Gooseley La. E6 —3E 66
Goose Sq. E6 —6D 66
Goossens Clo. Sutt —5A 132
Gophir La. EC4 —7D 62 (2E 150)
Gopsall St. N1 —1D 62
Gordon Av. E4 —6B 20
Gordon Av. SW14 —4A 90
Gordon Av. N Mald —2B 120
Gordon Av. Stan —7E 10
Gordon Av. Twic —5A 88
Gordonbrock Rd. SE4 —5C 96
Gordon Clo. E17 —6C 32
Gordon Clo. N19 —2G 45
Gordon Ct. W12 —6E 58
Gordon Ct. Edgw —5A 12
Gordon Cres. Croy —1E 134
Gordondale Rd. SW19 —2J 107
Gordon Gdns. Edgw —2H 25
Gordon Gro. SE5 —2B 94
Gordon Hill. Enf —1H 7
Gordon Ho. E1 —7J 63
(off Glamis Rd.)
Gordon Ho. W5 —3E 56
Gordon Ho. Rd. NW5 —4E 44
Gordon Mans. WC1
—4H 61 (4C 142)
(off Torrington Pl.)
Gordon Pl. W8 —2J 75
Gordon Rd. E4 —1B 20
Gordon Rd. E11 —6J 33
Gordon Rd. E15 —4E 48
Gordon Rd. E18 —1K 33
Gordon Rd. N3 —7C 14
Gordon Rd. N9 —2C 18
Gordon Rd. N11 —7C 16
Gordon Rd. SE15 —2H 95
Gordon Rd. W4 —6H 73
Gordon Rd. W13 & W5 —7B 56
Gordon Rd. Bark —1J 67
Gordon Rd. Beck —3B 126
Gordon Rd. Belv —4J 85
Gordon Rd. Cars —6D 132
Gordon Rd. Enf —1H 7
Gordon Rd. Harr —3J 23
Gordon Rd. Houn —4G 87
Gordon Rd. Ilf —3H 51
Gordon Rd. King T —1F 119
Gordon Rd. Rich —2F 89

Gordon Rd. Romf —6F 37
Gordon Rd. Sidc —5J 99
Gordon Rd. S'hall —4C 70
Gordon Rd. Surb —7F 119
Gordon Sq. WC1
—4H 61 (3C 142)
Gordon St. E13 —3J 65
Gordon St. WC1
—4H 61 (3C 142)
Gordon Way. Barn —4C 4
Gordon Way. Brom —1J 127
Gore Ct. NW9 —5G 25
Gorefield Pl. NW6 —2J 59
Gore Rd. E9 —1J 63
Gore Rd. SW20 —2E 120
Goresbrook Rd. Dag —1B 68
Gorham Pl. W11 —7G 59
Goring Clo. Romf —1J 37
Goring Gdns. Dag —4C 52
Goring Rd. N11 —6D 16
Goring Rd. Dag —6K 53
Goring St. EC3 —6E 62 (7H 145)
Goring Way. Gnfd —2G 55
Gorleston Rd. N15 —5D 30
Gorleston St. W14 —4G 75
Gorman Rd. SE18 —4D 82
Gorringe Pk. Av. Mitc —7D 108
Gorse Clo. E16 —6J 65
Gorse Rise. SW17 —5E 108
Gorse Rd. Croy —4C 136
Gorseway. Romf —1K 53
Gorst Rd. NW10 —4J 57
Gorst Rd. SW11 —6D 92
Gorsuch Pl. E2 —3F 63 (1J 145)
Gorsuch St. E2 —3F 63 (1J 145)
Gosberton Rd. SW12 —1D 108
Gosfield Rd. Dag —2G 53
Gosfield St. W1 —5G 61 (6A 142)
Gosford Gdns. Ilf —5D 34
Goslett Yd. WC2
—6H 61 (1D 148)
Gosling Clo. Gnfd —3E 54
Gosling Ct. SE8 —6B 80
(off Wotton Rd.)
Gosling Way. SW9 —1A 94
Gospatrick Rd. N17 —7H 17
Gospel Oak Est. NW5 —5D 44
Gosport Rd. E17 —5B 32
Gosport Wlk. N17 —4H 31
Gosport Way. SE15 —7F 79
Gossage Rd. SE18 —5H 83
Gosset St. E2 —3F 63 (1K 145)
Gosshill Rd. Chst —2E 128
Gossington Clo. Chst —4F 115
Gosterwood St. SE8 —6A 80
Gostling Rd. Twic —1E 102
Goston Gdns. T Hth —3A 124
Goswell Pl. EC1 —3B 62 (2B 144)
Goswell Rd. EC1
—2B 62 (1A 144)
Gothic Rd. Twic —2H 103
Gottfried M. NW5 —4G 45
Goudhurst Rd. Brom —5G 113
Gough Rd. E15 —4H 49
Gough Rd. Enf —2C 8
Gough Sq. EC4 —6A 62 (7K 143)
Gough St. WC1 —4K 61 (3H 143)
Gough Wlk. E14 —6C 64
Goulding Gdns. T Hth —2C 124
Gould Rd. Twic —1J 103
Gould Ter. E8 —5H 47
Goulston St. E1 —6F 63 (7J 145)
Goulton Rd. E5 —4H 47
Gourley Pl. N15 —5E 30
Gourley St. N15 —5E 30

Gourock Rd. SE9 —5E 98
Govan St. E2 —1G 63
Gover Ct. SW4 —2J 93
Govier Clo. E15 —7G 49
Gowan Av. SW6 —1G 91
Gowan Rd. NW10 —6D 42
Gower Clo. SW4 —6G 93
Gower Ct. WC1 —4H 61 (3C 142)
Gower Ho. E17 —3C 32
Gower M. WC1 —5H 61 (6D 142)
Gower Pl. WC1 —4G 61 (3B 142)
Gower Rd. E7 —6J 49
Gower Rd. Iswth —6K 71
Gower St. WC1 —4G 61 (3B 142)
Gower's Wlk. E1 —6G 63
Gowland Pl. Beck —2B 126
Gowlett Rd. SE15 —3G 95
Gowrie Rd. SW11 —3E 92
Goy Mnr. Rd. SW19 —6F 107
Grace Av. Bexh —2F 101
Gracechurch Ct. EC3
　　　　　　—7D 62 (2F 151)
Gracechurch St. EC3
　　　　　　—7D 62 (2F 151)
Grace Clo. SE9 —3B 114
Grace Clo. Edgw —7D 12
Gracedale Rd. SW16 —5F 109
Gracefield Gdns. SW16 —3J 109
Grace Ho. SE11 —6K 77 (7H 155)
Grace Jones Clo. E8 —6G 47
Grace Path. SE26 —4J 111
Grace Pl. E3 —3D 64
Grace Rd. Croy —6C 124
Grace's All. E1 —7G 63
Graces M. NW8 —2A 60
Grace's M. SE5 —2E 94
Grace's Rd. SE5 —2E 94
Grace St. E3 —3D 64
Gradient, The. SE26 —4G 111
Graeme Rd. Enf —2J 7
Graemesdyke Av. SW14 —3H 89
Grafton Clo. W13 —6A 56
Grafton Clo. Houn —1C 102
Grafton Clo. Wor Pk —3A 130
Grafton Cres. NW1 —6F 45
Grafton Gdns. N4 —6C 30
Grafton Gdns. Dag —2E 52
Grafton Ho. SE8 —5B 80
Grafton M. N1 —2C 62
　　(off Frome St.)
Grafton M. W1 —4G 61 (4A 142)
Grafton Pk. Rd. Wor Pk
　　　　　　—2A 130
Grafton Pl. NW1
　　　　　—3H 61 (2D 142)
Grafton Rd. NW5 —5E 44
Grafton Rd. W3 —7J 57
Grafton Rd. Croy —1A 134
Grafton Rd. Dag —2E 52
Grafton Rd. Enf —3E 6
Grafton Rd. Harr —5G 23
Grafton Rd. N Mald —3A 120
Grafton Rd. Wor Pk —2E 130
Grafton Sq. SW4 —3G 93
Graftons, The. NW2 —3J 43
Grafton St. W1 —7F 61 (3K 147)
Grafton Ter. NW5 —5D 44
Grafton Way. W1 & WC1
　　　　　—4G 61 (4B 142)
Grafton Yd. NW5 —6F 45
Graham Av. W13 —2B 72
Graham Av. Mitc —1E 122
Graham Clo. Croy —2C 136
Graham Ct. N'holt —5D 38
Grahame Pk. Est. NW9 —1A 26

Grahame Pk. Way. NW7 & NW9
　　　　　　—7G 13
Grahame White Ho. Kent —3D 24
Graham Gdns. Surb —7E 118
Graham Ho. N9 —1D 18
　　(off Cumberland Rd.)
Graham Lodge. NW4 —6D 26
Graham Mans. Bark —7A 52
　　(off Lansbury Av.)
Graham Rd. E8 —6G 47
Graham Rd. E13 —4J 65
Graham Rd. N15 —3B 30
Graham Rd. NW4 —6D 26
Graham Rd. SW19 —7H 107
Graham Rd. W4 —3K 73
Graham Rd. Bexh —4F 101
Graham Rd. Hamp —4E 102
Graham Rd. Harr —3J 23
Graham Rd. Mitc —1E 122
Graham St. N1 —2B 62 (1C 144)
Graham Ter. SW1
　　　　　　—4E 76 (4G 153)
Graham Ter. Sidc —6B 100
　　(off Westerham Dri.)
Grainger Clo. N'holt —5G 39
Grainger Ct. SE5 —7C 78
Grainger Rd. N22 —1C 30
Grainger Rd. Iswth —2K 87
Gramer Clo. E11 —2F 49
Grampian Clo. Orp —6A 69
Grampian Gdns. NW2 —1G 43
Grampians, The. W6 —2F 75
　　(off Shepherd's Bush Rd.)
Granada St. SW17 —5C 108
Granard Av. SW15 —5D 90
Granard Bus. Cen. NW7 —6F 13
Granard Rd. E9 —6K 47
Granard Rd. SW12 —7D 92
Granary Clo. N9 —7D 8
Granary Rd. E1 —4H 63
Granary St. NW1 —1H 61
Granault Rd. Enf —1A 8
Granby Bldgs. SE11
　　　　　　—4K 77 (4G 155)
Granby Pl. SE1 —2A 78 (7J 149)
　　(off Lwr. Marsh)
Granby Rd. SE9 —2D 98
Granby St. E2 —4F 63 (3K 145)
Granby Ter. NW1
　　　　　　—2G 61 (1A 142)
Grand Arc. N12 —5F 15
Grand Av. EC1 —5B 62 (5B 144)
Grand Av. N10 —4E 28
Grand Av. Surb —5H 119
Grand Av. Wemb —5G 41
Grand Av. E. Wemb —5H 41
Grand Depot Rd. SE18 —5E 82
Grand Dri. SW20 —3E 120
Grand Dri. S'hall —2G 71
Granden Rd. SW16 —2J 123
Grandfield Ct. W4 —6K 73
Grandison Rd. SW11 —5D 92
Grandison Rd. Wor Pk —2E 130
Grand Junct. Wharf. N1 —2C 62
Grand Pde. N4 —5B 30
Grand Pde. Wemb —2G 41
Grand Pde. M. SW15 —5G 91
Grand Union Cen. W10 —4F 59
　　(off West Row)
Grand Union Cres. E8 —7G 47
Grand Union Ind. Est. NW10
　　　　　　—2H 57
Grand Union Wlk. NW1 —7F 45
　　(off Kentish Town Rd.)
Grand Wlk. E1 —4A 64

Granfield St. SW11 —1B 92
Grange Av. N12 —5F 15
Grange Av. N20 —7B 4
Grange Av. SE25 —2E 124
Grange Av. E Barn —1H 15
Grange Av. Stan —2B 24
Grange Av. Twic —2J 103
Grange Av. Wfd G —6D 20
Grangecliffe Gdns. SE25
　　　　　　—2E 124
Grange Clo. Edgw —5D 12
Grange Clo. Houn —6D 70
Grange Clo. Sidc —3A 116
Grange Clo. Wfd G —7D 20
Grange Ct. E8 —7F 47
Grange Ct. WC2
　　　　　　—6K 61 (1H 149)
Grange Ct. Harr —3K 39
Grange Ct. N'holt —2A 54
Grange Ct. Pinn —3C 22
Grange Ct. Sutt —7K 131
Grangecourt Rd. N16 —1E 46
Grange Cres. SE28 —6C 68
Grange Dri. Chst —6C 114
Grange Farm Clo. Harr —2G 39
Grange Gdns. N14 —1C 16
Grange Gdns. NW3 —3K 43
Grange Gdns. SE25 —2E 124
Grange Gdns. Pinn —3C 22
Grange Gro. N1 —6C 46
Grange Hill. SE25 —2E 124
Grange Hill. Edgw —5D 12
Grangehill Pl. SE9 —3D 98
Grangehill Rd. SE9 —4D 98
Grange Ho. SE1 —3F 79 (2J 157)
Grange La. SE21 —2F 111
Grange Lodge. SW19 —6F 107
Grange Mans. Eps —7B 130
Grangemill Rd. SE6 —3C 112
Grangemill Way. SE6 —2C 112
Grange Pk. E10 —2D 48
Grange Pk. W5 —1E 72
Grange Pk. Av. N21 —6H 7
Grange Pk. Pl. SW20 —7D 106
Grange Pk. Rd. E10 —1D 48
Grange Pk. Rd. T Hth —4D 124
Grange Pl. NW6 —7J 43
Grange Rd. E10 —1C 48
Grange Rd. E13 —3H 65
Grange Rd. E17 —5A 32
Grange Rd. N6 —6E 28
Grange Rd. N17 & N18 —6B 18
Grange Rd. NW10 —6D 42
Grange Rd. SE1 —3E 78 (2H 157)
Grange Rd. SE25 & SE19
　　　　　　—3D 124
Grange Rd. SW13 —1C 90
Grange Rd. W4 —5H 73
Grange Rd. W5 —1D 72
Grange Rd. Edgw —6E 12
Grange Rd. Harr —5A 24
Grange Rd. Ilf —4F 51
Grange Rd. King T —3E 118
Grange Rd. S'hall —2C 70
Grange Rd. S Croy —7C 134
Grange Rd. S Harr —2H 39
Grange Rd. Sutt —7J 131
Grange Rd. T Hth —4D 124
Grange St. N1 —1D 62
Grange, The. E17 —5B 32
　　(off Lynmouth Rd.)
Grange, The. N2 —2B 28
Grange, The. N20 —1F 15
Grange, The. SE1
　　　　　　—3F 79 (2J 157)

Grange, The. SW19 —6F 107
Grange, The. W3 —2H 73
Grange, The. W4 —5H 73
Grange, The. W5 —5C 56
Grange, The. Croy —2B 136
Grange, The. Wemb —7G 41
Grange, The. Wor Pk —4A 130
Grange Vale. Sutt —7K 131
Grangeview Rd. N20 —1F 15
Grange Wlk. SE1
　　　　　　—3E 78 (1H 157)
Grange Wlk. M. SE1
　　　　　　—3E 78 (2H 157)
Grange Way. N12 —4E 14
Grange Way. NW6 —7J 43
Grange Way. Wfd G —4F 21
Grangeway Gdns. Ilf —5C 34
Grangeway, The. N21 —6G 7
Grangewood. Bex —1F 117
Grangewood La. Beck —6B 112
Grangewood St. E6 —1B 66
Grangewood Ter. SE25 —2D 124
Grange Yd. SE1 —3F 79 (2J 157)
Granham Gdns. N9 —2A 18
Granite St. SE18 —5K 83
Granleigh Rd. E11 —2G 49
Gransden Av. E8 —7H 47
Gransden Ho. SE8 —5B 80
Gransden Rd. W12 —2B 74
Grantbridge St. N1 —2B 62
Grantchester. King T —2G 119
　　(off St Peters Rd.)
Grantchester Clo. Harr —3K 39
Grant Clo. N14 —7B 6
Grant Ct. E4 —1K 19
Grantham Clo. Edgw —3K 11
Grantham Ct. Romf —7F 37
Grantham Gdns. Romf —6F 37
Grantham Pl. W1
　　　　　　—1F 77 (5J 147)
Grantham Rd. E12 —4E 50
Grantham Rd. SW9 —2J 93
Grantham Rd. W4 —7A 74
Grantley Rd. Houn —2A 86
Grantley St. E1 —3K 63
Grantock Rd. E17 —1F 33
Granton Rd. SW16 —1G 123
Granton Rd. Ilf —1A 52
Granton Rd. Sidc —6C 116
Grant Pl. Croy —1F 135
Grant Rd. SW11 —4B 92
Grant Rd. Croy —1F 135
Grant Rd. Harr —3K 23
Grants Clo. NW7 —7K 13
Grants Quay Wharf. EC3
　　　　　　—7D 62 (3F 151)
Grant St. E13 —3J 65
Grant St. N1 —2A 62
Grantully Rd. W9 —3K 59
Grant Way. Iswth —6A 72
Granville Arc. SW9 —4A 94
Granville Av. N9 —3D 18
Granville Av. Houn —5E 86
Granville Clo. Croy —2E 134
Granville Ct. N1 —1E 62
Granville Ct. SE14 —7A 80
　　(off Nynehead St.)
Granville Gdns. SW16 —7K 109
Granville Gdns. W5 —1F 73
Granville Gro. SE13 —3E 96
Granville M. Sidc —4A 116
Granville Pk. SE13 —3E 96
Granville Pl. N12 —7F 15
Granville Pl. W1
　　　　　　—6E 60 (1G 147)

Granville Pl. Pinn —3B 22
Granville Point. NW2 —2H 43
Granville Rd. E17 —6D 32
Granville Rd. E18 —2K 33
Granville Rd. N4 —6K 29
Granville Rd. N12 —7E 14
Granville Rd. N13 —6E 16
Granville Rd. N22 —1B 30
Granville Rd. NW2 —2H 43
Granville Rd. NW6 —2J 59
　　(in two parts)
Granville Rd. SW18 —7H 91
Granville Rd. SW19 —7J 107
Granville Rd. Barn —4A 4
Granville Rd. Ilf —1F 51
Granville Rd. Sidc —4A 116
Granville Rd. Well —3C 100
Granville Sq. SE15 —7E 78
Granville Sq. WC1
　　　　　　—3K 61 (2H 143)
Granville St. WC1
　　　　　　—3K 61 (2H 143)
Granwood Ct. Iswth —1J 87
Grape St. WC2 —6J 61 (7E 142)
Graphite Sq. SE11
　　　　　　—5K 77 (5G 155)
Grasdene Rd. SE18 —7A 84
Grasmere Av. SW15 —4K 105
Grasmere Av. SW19 —3J 121
Grasmere Av. W3 —7K 57
Grasmere Av. Houn —6F 87
Grasmere Av. Wemb —7C 24
Grasmere Ct. N22 —6E 16
Grasmere Ct. SE26 —5G 111
Grasmere Ct. SW13 —6C 74
Grasmere Ct. Sutt —6A 132
Grasmere Gdns. Harr —2A 24
Grasmere Gdns. Ilf —5C 34
Grasmere Point. SE15 —7J 79
　　(off Old Kent Rd.)
Grasmere Rd. E13 —2J 65
Grasmere Rd. N10 —1F 29
Grasmere Rd. N17 —6B 18
Grasmere Rd. SE25 —5H 125
Grasmere Rd. SW16 —5K 109
Grasmere Rd. Bexh —2J 101
Grasmere Rd. Brom —1H 127
Grassington Rd. Sidc —4A 116
Grassmount. SE23 —2H 111
Grass Pk. N3 —1H 27
Grass Way. Wall —4G 133
Grasvenor Av. Barn —5D 4
Grately Way. SE15 —7F 79
Gratton Rd. W14 —3G 75
Gratton Ter. NW2 —3F 43
Gravel Hill. N3 —2H 27
Gravel Hill. Bexh —5H 101
Gravel Hill. Croy —6K 135
Gravel Hill Clo. Bexh —5H 101
Gravel La. E1 —6F 63 (7J 145)
Gravel Pit La. SE9 —5F 99
Gravel Rd. Brom —3C 138
Gravel Rd. Twic —1J 103
Gravelwood Clo. Chst —3G 115
Gravenel Gdns. SW17 —5C 108
　　(off Nutwell St.)
Graveney Gro. SE20 —7J 111
Graveney Rd. SW17 —4C 108
Gravesend Rd. W12 —7C 58
Gray Av. Dag —1F 53
Grayham Cres. N Mald —4K 119
Grayham Rd. N Mald —4K 119
Grayland Clo. Brom —1B 128
Grayling Clo. E16 —4G 65
Grayling Rd. N16 —2D 46

Grayling Sq. E2 —3G 63
(off Nelson Gdns.)
Grays Ct. Dag —7H 53
Grayscroft Rd. SW16 —7H 109
Grays Farm Rd. Orp —7B 116
Grayshott Rd. SW11 —2E 92
Gray's Inn Pl. WC1
—5K 61 (6H 143)
Gray's Inn Rd. WC1
—3J 61 (1F 143)
Gray's Inn Sq. WC1
—5K 61 (5J 143)
Grayson Ho. EC1
—3C 62 (2D 144)
Gray St. SE1 —2A 78 (7K 149)
Grayswood Gdns. SW20
—2D 120
Gray's Yd. W1 —6E 60 (1H 147)
Graywood Ct. N12 —7F 15
Grazebrook Rd. N16 —2D 46
Grazeley Clo. Bexh —5J 101
Grazeley Ct. SE19 —5E 108
Gt. Acre Ct. SW4 —4H 93
Gt. Bell All. EC2 —6D 62 (7E 144)
Gt. Brownings. SE21 —4F 111
Gt. Bushey Dri. N20 —1E 14
Gt. Cambridge Ind. Est. Enf
—5B 8
Great Cambridge Junction.
(Junct.) —4J 17
Gt. Cambridge Rd. N9 & Enf
—3J 17
Gt. Cambridge Rd. N17 & N18
—7J 17
Gt. Castle St. W1
—6F 61 (7K 141)
Gt. Central Av. Ruis —5A 38
Gt. Central St. NW1
—5D 60 (5E 140)
Gt. Central Way. Wemb & NW10
—4J 41
Gt. Chapel St. W1
—6H 61 (7C 142)
Gt. Chertsey Rd. W4 —2J 89
Gt. Chertsey Rd. Felt —3D 102
Gt. Church La. W6 —4F 75
Gt. College St. SW1
—3J 77 (1E 154)
Gt. Cross Av. SE10 —7G 81
Gt. Cumberland M. W1
—6D 60 (1E 146)
Gt. Cumberland Pl. W1
—6D 60 (7E 140)
Gt. Dover St. SE1
—2C 78 (7D 150)
Greatdown Rd. W7 —4K 55
Gt. Eastern Bldgs. E1 —5G 63
(off Fieldgate St.)
Gt. Eastern Enterprise Cen. E14
—2D 80
Gt. Eastern Rd. E15 —7F 49
Gt. Eastern St. EC2
—3E 62 (2G 145)
Gt. Eastern Wlk. EC2
—5E 62 (6H 145)
Gt. Elms Rd. Brom —4A 128
Gt. Field. NW9 —1A 26
Greatfield Av. E6 —4D 66
Greatfield Clo. N19 —4G 45
Greatfield Clo. SE13 —4C 96
Greatfields Rd. Bark —1H 67
Gt. Fleete Way. Bark —2C 68
Gt. Galley Clo. Bark —3C 68
Gt. George St. SW1
—2H 77 (7D 148)

Gt. Guildford St. SE1
—1C 78 (4C 150)
Greatham Wlk. SW15 —1C 106
Gt. Harry Dri. SE9 —3E 114
Gt. James St. WC1
—5K 61 (5G 143)
Gt. Marlborough St. W1
—6G 61 (1A 148)
Gt. Maze Pond. SE1
(in two parts) —2D 78 (5F 151)
Gt. Newport St. WC2
—7J 61 (2E 148)
Gt. New St. EC4 —6A 62 (7K 143)
Gt. North Rd. N2 & N6 —5C 28
Gt. North Rd. High Bar —2C 4
Gt. North Rd. New Bar —5D 4
Gt. North Way. NW4 —2D 26
Greatorex Ho. E1 —5G 63
(off Greatorex St.)
Greatorex St. E1 —5G 63
Gt. Ormond St. WC1
—5J 61 (5F 143)
Gt. Owl Rd. Chig —3K 21
Gt. Percy St. WC1
—3K 61 (1H 143)
Gt. Peter St. SW1
—3H 77 (2C 154)
Gt. Portland St. W1
—4F 61 (4K 141)
Gt. Pulteney St. W1
—7G 61 (2B 148)
Gt. Queen St. WC2
—6J 61 (1F 149)
Gt. Russell St. WC1
—6H 61 (7D 142)
Gt. St Helen's. EC3
—6E 62 (7G 145)
Gt. Saint Thomas Apostle. EC4
—7C 62 (2D 150)
Gt. Scotland Yd. SW1
—1J 77 (4E 148)
Gt. Smith St. SW1
—3H 77 (1D 154)
Gt. South W. Rd. Felt & Houn
—2A 86
Gt. Spilmans. SE22 —5E 94
Gt. Strand. NW9 —1B 26
Gt. Suffolk St. SE1
—1B 78 (5B 150)
Gt. Sutton St. EC1
—4B 62 (4B 144)
Gt. Swan All. EC2
—6D 62 (7E 144)
Gt. Thrift. Orp —4G 129
Gt. Titchfield St. W1
—5F 61 (4K 141)
Gt. Tower St. EC3
—7E 62 (2G 151)
Gt. Trinity La. EC4
—7C 62 (2D 150)
Gt. Turnstile. WC1
—5K 61 (6H 143)
Gt. Western Ind. Pk. S'hall
—2F 71
Gt. Western Rd. W9, W11 & W2
—5H 59
Gt. West Rd. W4 & W6 —5B 74
Gt. West Rd. Bren —7A 72
Gt. West Rd. Houn & Iswth
—2B 86
Gt. West Rd. Trad. Est. Bren
—6B 72
Gt. West Trad. Est. Bren —6B 72
Gt. Winchester St. EC2
—6D 62 (7F 145)

Gt. Windmill St. W1
—7H 61 (2C 148)
Greatwood. Chst —7E 114
Great Yd. SE1 —2E 78 (6H 151)
Greaves Clo. Bark —7H 51
Greaves Pl. SW17 —4C 108
Greaves Tower. SW10 —7A 76
(off Worlds End Est.)
Grebe Av. Hayes —6B 54
Grebe Clo. E7 —5H 49
Grebe Clo. E17 —7F 19
Grebe Ct. SE8 —6B 80
(off Dorking Clo.)
Grebe Ter. King T —3E 118
Grecian Cres. SE19 —6B 110
Greek Ct. W1 —6H 61 (1D 148)
Greek St. W1 —6H 61 (1D 148)
Greenacre Clo. Barn —1C 4
Greenacre Clo. N'holt —5D 38
Greenacre Gdns. E17 —4E 32
Greenacre Pl. Hack —2F 133
Greenacres. N3 —2H 27
Greenacres. SE9 —6E 98
Greenacres. Bush —2C 10
Green Acres. Croy —3F 135
Greenacres. Sidc —4A 116
Greenacres Dri. Stan —7G 11
Greenacre Sq. SE16 —2K 79
Greenacre Wlk. N14 —3C 16
Green Arbour Ct. EC1
—6B 62 (7A 144)
Green Av. NW7 —4E 12
Green Av. W13 —3B 72
Greenaway Gdns. NW3 —4K 43
Green Bank. E1 —1H 79
Greenbank. N12 —4E 14
Greenbank Av. Wemb —5A 40
Green Bank Clo. E4 —2K 19
Greenbank Cres. NW4 —4G 27
Greenbanks. Harr —4J 39
Greenbay Rd. SE7 —7B 82
Greenberry St. NW8
—2C 60 (1C 140)
Greenbrook Av. Barn —1F 5
Green Clo. NW9 —6J 25
Green Clo. NW11 —7A 28
Green Clo. Brom —3G 127
Green Clo. Cars —2D 132
Green Clo. Felt —5C 102
Greencoat Pl. SW1
—4G 77 (3B 154)
Greencourt Av. Croy —2H 135
Greencourt Av. Edgw —1H 25
Greencourt Gdns. Croy —2H 135
Greencourt Rd. Orp —5H 129
Greencrest Pl. NW2 —3C 42
Greencroft. Edgw —5D 12
Greencroft Av. Ruis —2A 38
Greencroft Clo. E6 —5B 66
Greencroft Gdns. NW6 —7K 43
Greencroft Gdns. Enf —3K 7
Greencroft Rd. Houn —1D 86
Green Dale. SE5 —4D 94
Green Dale. SE22 —5E 94
Greendale. Edgw —4F 13
Green Dale Clo. SE22 —5E 94
Green Dragon Ct. SE1
—1D 78 (4E 150)
Green Dragon La. N21 —6F 7
Green Dragon La. Bren —5E 72
Green Dragon Yd. E1
—5G 63 (6K 145)
Green Dri. S'hall —1E 70
Green End. N21 —2G 17
Greenend Rd. W4 —2A 74

Greener Ho. SW4 —3H 93
Grenfell Ho. SE5 —7C 78
(off Comber Gro.)
Grenfell St. SE10 —3G 81
Greenfield Av. Surb —7H 119
Greenfield Dri. N2 —4D 28
Greenfield Dri. Brom —2A 128
Greenfield Gdns. NW2 —2G 43
Greenfield Gdns. Dag —1D 68
Greenfield Gdns. Orp —7H 129
Greenfield Rd. E1 —5G 63
Greenfield Rd. N15 —5E 30
Greenfield Rd. Dag —1C 68
Greenfield Rd. Dart —5K 117
Greenfield Rd. Sutt —4K 131
Greenfields. S'hall —6E 54
Greenfield Way. Harr —3F 23
Greenford Av. W7 —4J 55
Greenford Av. S'hall —7D 54
Greenford Gdns. Gnfd —3F 55
Greenford Grn. Gnfd —6J 39
Greenford Ind. Est. N'holt —7F 39
Greenford Rd. Harr —4J 39
Greenford Rd. S'hall & Gnfd
—1G 71
Greenford Roundabout. (Junct.)
—2H 55
Greengate. Gnfd —6B 40
Greengate Lodge. E13 —2K 65
(off Hollybush St.)
Greengate St. E13 —2K 65
Greenhalgh Wlk. N2 —4A 28
Greenham Clo. SE1
—2A 78 (7J 149)
Greenham Cres. E4 —6G 19
Greenham Ho. Houn —3H 87
Greenham Rd. N10 —2E 28
Green Hedge. Twic —6C 88
Greenheys Dri. E18 —3H 33
Greenhill. NW3 —4B 44
Green Hill. SE18 —5D 82
Greenhill. Buck H —1F 21
Greenhill. Sutt —2A 132
Greenhill Gdns. N'holt —2D 54
Greenhill Gro. E12 —4C 50
Greenhill Pde. New Bar —5E 4
Greenhill Pk. NW10 —1A 58
Greenhill Pk. New Bar —5E 4
Greenhill Rd. NW10 —1A 58
Greenhill Rd. Harr —6J 23
Green Hill's Rents. EC1
—5B 62 (5A 144)
Greenhills Ter. N1 —6D 46
Greenhill Ter. SE18 —5D 82
Greenhill Ter. N'holt —2D 54
Greenhill Way. Harr —6J 23
Greenhill Way. Wemb —2H 41
Greenhithe Clo. Sidc —7J 99
Greenholm Rd. SE9 —5F 99
Green Hundred Rd. SE15 —6G 79
Greenhurst Rd. SE27 —5A 110
Greening St. SE2 —4C 84
Greenland Cres. S'hall —3A 70
Greenland M. SE8 —5K 79
Greenland Pl. NW1 —1F 61
Greenland Quay. SE16 —4A 80
Greenland Rd. NW1 —1F 61
Greenland Rd. Barn —6A 4
Greenland St. NW1 —1F 61
Green La. NW4 —4F 27
Green La. SE9 & Chst —1F 115
Green La. SE20 —7K 111
Green La. SW16 & T Hth
—7K 109

Green La. W7 —2J 71
Green La. Edgw —4A 12
Green La. Felt —5C 102
Green La. Harr —3J 39
Green La. Houn —3A 86
Green La. Ilf & Dag —2H 51
Green La. Mord —7E 120
(Battersea Cemetery)
Green La. Mord —6J 121
(Morden)
Green La. N Mald —5J 119
Green La. Stan —4G 11
Green La. Wor Pk —1C 130
Green La. Cotts. Stan —4G 11
Green La. Gdns. T Hth —2C 124
Green Lanes. N8, N4 & N16
—3B 30
Green Lanes. N13 & N21 —3F 17
Green Lanes. Eps —7A 130
(in two parts)
Greenlaw Ct. W5 —6D 56
(off Mount Pk. Rd.)
Greenlaw Gdns. N Mald —7B 120
Greenlawns. N3 —6E 14
Green Lawns. Ruis —1A 38
Greenlaw St. SE18 —3E 82
Green Leaf Av. Wall —4H 133
Greenleaf Clo. SW2 —7A 94
Greenleafe Dri. Ilf —3F 35
Greenleaf Rd. E6 —1A 66
Greenleaf Rd. E17 —3B 32
Greenlea Trad. Pk. SW19
—1B 122
Green Man Gdns. W13 —7A 56
Green Man La. W13 —7A 56
Green Man Pas. W13 —7A 56
(in two parts)
Green Man Roundabout. (Junct.)
—7H 33
Greenman St. N1 —7C 46
Greenmead. Eri —3E 84
Green Moor Link. N21 —7G 7
Greenmoor Rd. Enf —2D 8
Greenoak Clo. Cockf —2J 5
Greenoak Way. SW19 —4F 107
Greenock Rd. SW16 —1H 123
Greenock Rd. W3 —3H 73
Green Pde. Houn —5F 87
Greenpark Ct. Wemb —7C 40
Green Point. E15 —6G 49
Green Pond Clo. E17 —3A 32
Green Pond Rd. E17 —3A 32
Greenrigg Wlk. Wemb —3H 41
Green Rd. N14 —6A 6
Green Rd. N20 —3F 15
Green's Ct. W1 —7H 61 (2C 148)
Greensgate. Enf —2F 9
Greenshank Clo. E17 —4F 83
Greenshade Clo. E17 —7F 19
Greenshields Ind. Est. E16
—2J 81
Greenside. Bex —1E 116
Green Side. Dag —1C 52
Greenside Clo. N20 —2G 15
Greenside Clo. SE6 —2F 113
Greenside Rd. W12 —3C 74
Greenside Rd. Croy —7A 124
Greenslade Rd. Bark —7H 51
Greenstead Av. Wfd G —7F 21
Greenstead Clo. Wfd G —6F 21
Greenstead Gdns. SW15 —5D 90
Greenstead Gdns. Wfd G —6F 21
Greensted Rd. Lou —1H 21
Greenstone M. E11 —6J 33
Green St. E7 & E13 —6K 49

Green St. *W1* —7E **60** (2G **147**)
Green St. *Enf* —2D **8**
Green Ter. *EC1* —3A **62** (2K **143**)
Green, The, *E4* —1A **20**
—1D **96**
Green, The, *E11* —6K **33**
Green, The, *E15* —6H **49**
Green, The, *N9* —2B **18**
Green, The, *N14* —3C **16**
Green, The, *N17* —6H **17**
Green, The, *N21* —1F **17**
Green, The, *SW19* —5F **107**
Green, The, *W3* —6A **58**
Green, The, *W5* —1D **72**
Green, The, *Bexh* —1G **101**
Green, The, *Brom* —3J **113**
(in two parts)
Green, The, *Buck H* —1E **20**
Green, The, *Cars* —4E **132**
Green, The, *Croy* —7B **136**
Green, The, *Hay* —7J **127**
Green, The, *Houn* —6E **70**
Green, The, *Mord* —4G **121**
Green, The, *N Mald* —3J **119**
Green, The, *Rich* —5D **88**
Green, The, *Sidc* —4A **116**
Green, The, *S'hall* —2D **70**
Green, The, *St P* —7B **116**
Green, The, *Sutt* —3K **131**
Green, The, *Twic* —1J **103**
Green, The, *Well* —4J **89**
Green, The, *Wemb* —2A **40**
Green, The, *Wfd G* —5D **20**
Green Vale, *W5* —6F **57**
Green Vale, *Bexh* —5D **100**
Greenvale Rd. *SE9* —4D **98**
Green Verges. *Stan* —7J **11**
Greenview Av. *Beck* —6A **126**
Greenview Av. *Croy* —6A **126**
Green Wlk. *NW4* —5F **27**
Green Wlk. *SE1* —3E **78** (2G **157**)
Green Wlk. *Hamp* —6D **102**
Green Wlk. *Lou* —1H **21**
Green Wlk. *S'hall* —5E **70**
Green Wlk. *Wfd G* —6H **21**
Green Wlk., The. *E4* —1A **20**
Greenway. *N14* —2D **16**
Greenway. *N20* —2D **14**
Green Way. *SE9* —5B **98**
Greenway. *SW20* —4E **120**
Green Way. *Brom* —6C **128**
Greenway. *Chst* —5E **114**
Greenway. *Dag* —2C **52**
Greenway. *Hayes* —4A **54**
Greenway. *Kent* —5E **24**
Greenway. *Pinn* —2A **22**
Green Way. *Wall* —4G **133**
Green Way. *Wfd G* —5F **21**
Greenway Av. *E17* —4F **33**
Greenway Clo. *N4* —2C **46**
Greenway Clo. *N11* —6K **15**
Greenway Clo. *N15* —4F **31**
Greenway Clo. *N20* —2D **14**
Greenway Clo. *NW9* —2K **25**
Greenway Gdns. *NW9* —2K **25**
Greenway Gdns. *Croy* —3B **136**
Greenway Gdns. *Gnfd* —3E **54**
Greenway Gdns. *Harr* —2J **23**
Greenways. *Beck* —3C **126**
Greenways, The. *Twic* —6A **88**
Greenway, The. *NW9* —2K **25**
Greenway, The. *Houn* —4D **86**
Green Way, The. *Pinn* —6D **22**
Green Way, The. *W'stone* —1J **23**
Greenwell St. *W1*
—4F **61** (4K **141**)

Greenwich Chu. St. *SE10* —6E **80**
Greenwich Cres. *E6* —5C **66**
Greenwich High Rd. *SE10*
—1D **96**
Greenwich Mkt. *SE10* —6E **80**
Greenwich Pk. St. *SE10* —6F **81**
Greenwich S. St. *SE10* —1D **96**
Greenwich View Pl. *E14* —3D **80**
Greenwood Av. *Dag* —4H **53**
Greenwood Av. *Enf* —2F **9**
Greenwood Bus. Cen. *Croy*
—7F **125**
Greenwood Clo. *Bush* —1D **10**
Greenwood Clo. *Mord* —4G **121**
Greenwood Clo. *Orp* —6J **129**
Greenwood Clo. *Sidc* —2A **116**
Greenwood Ct. *SW1*
—5G **77** (5B **154**)
Greenwood Dri. *E4* —5A **20**
Greenwood Gdns. *N13* —3G **17**
Greenwood Gdns. *Ilf* —1G **35**
Greenwood Ho. *N22* —1A **30**
Greenwood Ho. *SE4* —4K **95**
Greenwood La. *Hamp* —5F **103**
Greenwood Mans. *Bark* —7A **52**
(off Lansbury Av.)
Greenwood Pk. *King T* —7A **106**
Greenwood Pl. *NW5* —5F **45**
Greenwood Rd. *E8* —6G **47**
Greenwood Rd. *E13* —2J **65**
Greenwood Rd. *Bex* —4K **117**
Greenwood Rd. *Croy* —7B **124**
Greenwood Rd. *Iswth* —3K **87**
Greenwood Rd. *Mitc* —3H **123**
Greenwoods, The. *S Harr* —2G **39**
Greenwood Ter. *NW10* —1K **57**
Green Wrythe Cres. *Cars*
—1C **132**
Green Wrythe La. *Cars* —6B **122**
Green Yd., The. *EC3*
—6E **62** (1G **151**)
Greer Rd. *Harr* —1G **23**
Greet Ho. *SE1* —2A **78** (7K **149**)
Greet St. *SE1* —1A **78** (5K **149**)
Greg Clo. *E10* —6E **32**
Gregor M. *SE3* —7J **81**
Gregory Clo. *Brom* —4H **127**
Gregory Cres. *SE9* —7B **98**
Gregory Pl. *W8* —2K **75**
Gregory Rd. *Romf* —4D **36**
Gregory Rd. *S'hall* —3E **70**
Greig Clo. *N8* —5J **29**
Greig Ter. *SE17* —6B **78** (7B **156**)
Grenaby Av. *Croy* —7D **124**
Grenaby Rd. *Croy* —7D **124**
Grenada Rd. *SE7* —7A **82**
Grenade St. *E14* —7B **64**
Grenadier St. *E16* —1E **82**
Grena Gdns. *Rich* —4F **89**
Grena Rd. *Rich* —4F **89**
Grendon Gdns. *Wemb* —2G **41**
Grendon Lodge. *Edgw* —2D **12**
Grendon St. *NW8*
—4C **60** (3D **140**)
Grenfell Ct. *NW7* —6J **13**
Grenfell Gdns. *Harr* —7E **24**
Grenfell Gdns. *Ilf* —5K **35**
Grenfell Ho. *SE5* —7C **78**
Grenfell Rd. *W11* —7F **59**
Grenfell Rd. *Mitc* —6D **108**
Grenfell Tower. *W11* —7F **59**
Grenfell Wlk. *W11* —7F **59**
Grennell Clo. *Sutt* —2B **132**
Grennell Rd. *Sutt* —2A **132**
Grenoble Gdns. *N13* —6F **17**

Grenville Clo. *N3* —1G **27**
Grenville Clo. *Surb* —7J **119**
Grenville Ct. *W13* —5B **56**
Grenville Gdns. *Wfd G* —1A **34**
Grenville M. *SW7* —4A **76**
(off Harrington Gdns.)
Grenville M. *Hamp* —5F **103**
Grenville Pl. *NW7* —5E **12**
Grenville Pl. *SW7* —3A **76**
Grenville Rd. *N19* —1J **45**
Grenville St. *WC1*
—4J **61** (4F **143**)
Gresham Av. *N20* —4J **15**
Gresham Clo. *Bex* —6F **101**
Gresham Clo. *Enf* —3H **7**
Gresham Dri. *Romf* —5B **36**
Gresham Gdns. *NW11* —1G **43**
Gresham Lodge. *E17* —5D **32**
Gresham M. *W4* —3J **73**
Gresham Rd. *E6* —2D **66**
Gresham Rd. *E16* —6K **65**
Gresham Rd. *NW10* —5K **41**
Gresham Rd. *SE25* —4G **125**
Gresham Rd. *SW9* —3A **94**
Gresham Rd. *Beck* —2A **126**
Gresham Rd. *Edgw* —6A **12**
Gresham Rd. *Hamp* —6E **102**
Gresham Rd. *Houn* —1G **87**
Gresham St. *EC2*
—6C **62** (7C **144**)
Gresham Way. *SW19* —3K **107**
Gresley Clo. *E17* —6A **32**
Gresley Clo. *N15* —4D **30**
Gresley Rd. *N19* —1G **45**
Gressenhall Rd. *SW18* —6H **91**
Gresse St. *W1* —6H **61** (6C **142**)
Gresswell Clo. *Sidc* —3A **116**
Greswell St. *SW6* —1F **91**
Gretton Rd. *N17* —7A **18**
Greville Clo. *Twic* —7B **88**
Greville Ct. *Harr* —4J **39**
Greville Lodge. *E13* —1K **65**
Greville Lodge. *N12* —4E **14**
Greville Lodge. *Edgw* —4C **12**
(off Broadhurst Av.)
Greville M. *NW6* —1K **59**
(off Greville Rd.)
Greville Pl. *NW6* —2K **59**
Greville Rd. *E17* —4E **32**
Greville Rd. *NW6* —2K **59**
Greville Rd. *Rich* —6F **89**
Greville St. *EC1* —5A **62** (6J **143**)
Grey Clo. *NW11* —6A **28**
Grey Coat Gdns. *SW1*
—3H **77** (2C **154**)
(off Greycoat St.)
Greycoat Pl. *SW1*
—3H **77** (2C **154**)
Greycoat St. *SW1*
—3H **77** (2C **154**)
Greycot Rd. *Beck* —5C **112**
Grey Eagle St. *E1*
—4F **63** (4K **145**)
Greyfell Clo. *Stan* —5H **11**
Greyfriars. *SE26* —3G **111**
(off Wells Pk. Rd.)
Greyfriars Pas. *EC1*
—6B **62** (7B **144**)
Greyhound Ct. *WC2*
—7K **61** (2H **149**)
Greyhound Hill. *NW4* —3D **26**
Greyhound La. *SW16* —6H **109**
Greyhound Mans. *W6* —6G **75**
(off Greyhound Rd.)
Greyhound Rd. *N17* —3E **30**

Greyhound Rd. *NW10* —3D **58**
Greyhound Rd. *W6 & W14*
—6F **75**
Greyhound Rd. *Sutt* —5A **132**
Greyhound Rd. *SW16* —1G **123**
Grey Ho. *W12* —7D **58**
(off White City Est.)
Greyladies Gdns. *SE10* —2E **96**
Greys Pk. Clo. *Kes* —5B **138**
Greystead Rd. *SE23* —7J **95**
Greystoke Av. *Pinn* —3E **22**
Greystoke Ct. *W5* —4F **57**
Greystoke Gdns. *W5* —4E **56**
Greystoke Gdns. *Enf* —4C **6**
Greystoke Lodge. *W5* —4F **57**
(off Hanger La.)
Greystoke Pk. Ter. *W5* —3D **56**
Greystoke Pk. Ter. *Gnfd* —2G **55**
Greystoke Pl. *EC4*
—6A **62** (7J **143**)
Greystone Gdns. *Harr* —6C **24**
Greystone Gdns. *Ilf* —2G **35**
Greystone Path. *E11* —7H **33**
(off Mornington Rd.)
Greyswood St. *SW16* —6F **109**
Grey Turner Ho. *W12* —6C **58**
Grierson Rd. *SE23* —7K **95**
Griffin Clo. *NW10* —5D **42**
Griffin Ct. *W4* —5B **74**
Griffin Ct. *Bren* —6E **72**
Griffin Mnr. Way. *SE28* —3H **83**
Griffin Rd. *N17* —2E **30**
Griffin Rd. *SE18* —5H **83**
Griffith Clo. *Dag* —1C **52**
Griffiths Clo. *Wor Pk* —2D **130**
Griffiths Rd. *SW19* —7J **107**
Griggs App. *Ilf* —2G **51**
Grigg's Pl. *SE1* —3E **78** (2H **157**)
Griggs Rd. *E10* —6E **32**
Grilse Clo. *N9* —4C **18**
Grimsby St. *E2* —4F **63** (4K **145**)
Grimsdyke Rd. *Pinn* —1C **22**
Grimsel Path. *SE5* —7B **78**
Grimshaw Clo. *N6* —7E **28**
Grimston Rd. *SW6* —2H **91**
Grimthorpe Ho. *EC1*
—4A **62** (3A **144**)
Grimwade Av. *Croy* —3G **135**
Grimwade Clo. *SE15* —3J **95**
Grimwood Rd. *Twic* —7K **87**
Grindall Clo. *Croy* —4B **134**
Grindal St. *SE1* —2A **78** (7J **149**)
Grindley Gdns. *Croy* —6F **125**
Grinling Pl. *SE8* —6C **80**
Grinstead Rd. *SE8* —5A **80**
Grittleton Av. *Wemb* —6H **41**
Grittleton Rd. *W9* —4J **59**
Grizedale Ter. *SE23* —2H **111**
—6F **77** (7J **153**)
Grocer's Hall Ct. *EC2*
—6D **62** (1E **150**)
Grocer's Hall Gdns. *EC2*
—6D **62** (1E **150**)
Grogan Clo. *Hamp* —6D **102**
Groombridge Clo. *Well* —5A **100**
Groombridge Rd. *E9* —7K **47**
Groom Cres. *SW18* —7B **92**
Groome Ho. *SE11*
—4K **77** (4H **155**)
Groomfield Clo. *SW17* —4E **108**
Groom Pl. *SW1* —3E **76** (1H **153**)
Grosmont Rd. *SE18* —6K **83**
Grosse Way. *SW15* —6D **90**
Grosvenor Av. *N5* —5C **46**
Grosvenor Av. *SW14* —3A **90**
Grosvenor Av. *Cars* —6D **132**

Grosvenor Av. *Harr* —6F **23**
Grosvenor Av. *Rich* —5E **88**
Grosvenor Cotts. *SW1*
—4E **76** (3G **153**)
Grosvenor Ct. *E10* —1D **48**
Grosvenor Ct. *N14* —7B **6**
Grosvenor Ct. *NW6* —1F **59**
Grosvenor Ct. *NW7* —5E **12**
(off Hale La.)
Grosvenor Ct. *W3* —1G **73**
Grosvenor Ct. *W5* —7E **56**
(off Grove, The.)
Grosvenor Ct. *Barn* —7B **6**
Grosvenor Cres. *NW9* —4G **25**
Grosvenor Cres. *SW1*
—2E **76** (7H **147**)
Grosvenor Cres. M. *SW1*
—2E **76** (7G **147**)
Grosvenor Est. *SW1*
—4H **77** (3D **154**)
Grosvenor Gdns. *E6* —3B **66**
Grosvenor Gdns. *N10* —3G **29**
Grosvenor Gdns. *N14* —5C **6**
Grosvenor Gdns. *NW2* —5E **42**
Grosvenor Gdns. *NW11* —6H **27**
Grosvenor Gdns. *SW1*
—3F **77** (1J **153**)
Grosvenor Gdns. *SW14* —3A **90**
Grosvenor Gdns. *King T*
—6D **104**
Grosvenor Gdns. *Wall* —7G **133**
Grosvenor Gdns. *Wfd G* —6D **20**
Grosvenor Gdns. M. E. *SW1*
—3F **77** (1K **153**)
Grosvenor Gdns. M. N. *SW1*
—3F **77** (2J **153**)
Grosvenor Gdns. M. S. *SW1*
—3F **77** (2K **153**)
Grosvenor Ga. *W1*
—7E **60** (3G **147**)
Grosvenor Hill. *SW19* —6G **107**
Grosvenor Hill. *W1*
—7F **61** (2J **147**)
Grosvenor Pk. *SE5* —7C **78**
Grosvenor Pk. Rd. *E17* —5C **32**
Grosvenor Pl. *SW1*
—2E **76** (7H **147**)
Grosvenor Rise E. *E17* —5D **32**
Grosvenor Rd. *E6* —1B **66**
Grosvenor Rd. *E7* —6K **49**
Grosvenor Rd. *E10* —1E **48**
Grosvenor Rd. *E11* —5K **33**
Grosvenor Rd. *N3* —7C **14**
Grosvenor Rd. *N9* —1C **18**
Grosvenor Rd. *N10* —1F **29**
Grosvenor Rd. *SE25* —4G **125**
Grosvenor Rd. *SW1*
—6F **77** (7J **153**)
Grosvenor Rd. *W4* —5H **73**
Grosvenor Rd. *W7* —1A **72**
Grosvenor Rd. *Belv* —6G **85**
Grosvenor Rd. *Bexh* —5D **100**
Grosvenor Rd. *Bren* —6D **72**
Grosvenor Rd. *Dag* —1F **53**
Grosvenor Rd. *Houn* —3D **86**
Grosvenor Rd. *Ilf* —3G **51**
Grosvenor Rd. *Orp* —6J **129**
Grosvenor Rd. *Rich* —5E **88**
Grosvenor Rd. *Romf* —7K **37**
Grosvenor Rd. *S'hall* —3D **70**
Grosvenor Rd. *Twic* —1A **104**
Grosvenor Rd. *Wall* —6F **133**
Grosvenor Rd. *W Wick* —1D **136**
Grosvenor Sq. *W1*
—7E **60** (2H **147**)

Grosvenor St. *W1*
—7F **61** (2J **147**)
Grosvenor Ter. *SE5* —7C **78**
Grosvenor Way. *E5* —2J **47**
Grosvenor Wharf Rd. *E14* —4F **81**
Grotes Bldgs. *SE3* —2G **97**
Grote's Pl. *SE3* —2G **97**
Groton Rd. *SW18* —2K **107**
Grotto Ct. *SE1* —2C **78** (6C **150**)
Grotto Pas. *W1* —5E **60** (5H **141**)
Grotto Rd. *Twic* —2K **103**
Grove Av. *N3* —7D **14**
Grove Av. *N10* —2G **29**
Grove Av. *W7* —6J **55**
Grove Av. *Pinn* —4C **22**
Grove Av. *Sutt* —6J **131**
Grove Av. *Twic* —1K **103**
Grovebury Clo. *Eri* —6K **85**
Grovebury Ct. *N14* —7C **6**
Grovebury Ct. *Bexh* —5H **101**
Grovebury Rd. *SE2* —2B **84**
Grove Clo. *N14* —7B **6**
Grove Clo. *SE23* —1A **112**
Grove Clo. *Brom* —2J **137**
Grove Clo. *Felt* —4C **102**
Grove Clo. *King T* —4F **119**
Grove Cotts. *W4* —6A **74**
Grove Ct. *NW8* —3B **60** (1A **140**)
Grove Ct. *Houn* —4E **86**
Grove Cres. *E18* —2H **33**
Grove Cres. *NW9* —4J **25**
Grove Cres. *SE5* —2E **94**
Grove Cres. *Felt* —4C **102**
Grove Cres. *King T* —3E **118**
Grove Cres. Rd. *E15* —6F **49**
Grovedale Rd. *N19* —2H **45**
Grove Dwellings. *E1* —5J **63**
Grove End. *E18* —2H **33**
Grove End. *NW3* —4F **45**
Grove End Rd. *NW8*
—2B **60** (1A **140**)
Grove Farm Ind. Est. *Mitc*
—5D **122**
Grovefield. *N11* —4A **16**
(off Coppies Gro.)
Grove Footpath. *Surb* —4E **118**
Grove Gdns. *E15* —6G **49**
Grove Gdns. *NW4* —5C **26**
Grove Gdns. *NW8*
—3C **60** (2D **140**)
Grove Gdns. *Dag* —3J **53**
Grove Gdns. *Enf* —1E **8**
Grove Gdns. *Rich* —6E **88**
Grove Gdns. *Tedd* —4A **104**
Grove Grn. Rd. *E11* —3E **48**
Grove Hall Ct. *NW8* —3A **60**
Grove Hill. *E18* —2H **33**
Grove Hill. *Harr* —1J **39**
Grovehill Ct. *Brom* —6H **113**
Grove Hill Rd. *SE5* —3E **94**
Grove Hill Rd. *Harr* —7K **23**
Grove Ho. Rd. *N8* —4J **29**
Groveland Av. *SW16* —7K **109**
Groveland Ct. *EC4*
—6C **62** (1D **150**)
Grovelands Clo. *SE5* —2E **94**
Grovelands Clo. *Harr* —3F **39**
Grovelands Ct. *N14* —7C **6**
Grovelands Rd. *N13* —4E **16**
Grovelands Rd. *N15* —6G **31**
Grovelands Rd. *Orp* —7A **116**
Groveland Way. *N Mald* —5J **119**
Grove La. *SE5* —1D **94**
Grove La. *King T* —4E **118**

Grove La. Ter. *SE5* —2D **94**
Grove Mkt. Pl. *SE9* —6D **98**
Grove M. *W6* —3E **74**
Grove M. *W11* —6H **59**
Grove Pk. *E11* —6K **33**
Grove Pk. *NW9* —4J **25**
Grove Pk. *SE5* —2E **94**
Grove Pk. Av. *E4* —7J **19**
Grove Pk. Bri. *W4* —7J **73**
Grove Pk. Gdns. *W4* —7H **73**
Grove Pk. Ind. Est. *NW9* —4K **25**
Grove Pk. M. *W4* —7J **73**
Grove Pk. Rd. *N15* —4E **30**
Grove Pk. Rd. *SE9* —3A **114**
Grove Pk. Rd. *W4* —7H **73**
Grove Pk. Ter. *W4* —7H **73**
Grove Pas. *E2* —2H **63**
Grove Pl. *NW3* —3B **44**
Grove Pl. *W3* —1J **73**
Grove Pl. *Bark* —1G **67**
Grover Ct. *SE13* —2D **96**
Grover Ho. *SE11*
—5K **77** (6H **155**)
Grove Rd. *E3* —1K **63**
Grove Rd. *E4* —4K **19**
Grove Rd. *E11* —7H **33**
Grove Rd. *E17* —6D **32**
Grove Rd. *E18* —2H **33**
Grove Rd. *N11* —5A **16**
Grove Rd. *N12* —5G **15**
Grove Rd. *N15* —5E **30**
Grove Rd. *NW2* —6E **42**
Grove Rd. *SW13* —2B **90**
Grove Rd. *SW19* —7A **108**
Grove Rd. *W3* —1J **73**
Grove Rd. *W5* —7D **56**
Grove Rd. *Belv* —6F **85**
Grove Rd. *Bexh* —4J **101**
Grove Rd. *Bren* —5C **72**
Grove Rd. *Cockf* —3H **5**
Grove Rd. *Edgw* —6B **12**
Grove Rd. *Houn* —4E **86**
Grove Rd. *Iswth* —1J **87**
Grove Rd. *L Hth* —7B **36**
Grove Rd. *Mitc* —3E **122**
Grove Rd. *Pinn* —5D **22**
Grove Rd. *Rich* —6F **89**
Grove Rd. *Surb* —5D **118**
Grove Rd. *Sutt* —6J **131**
Grove Rd. *T Hth* —4A **124**
Grove Rd. *Twic* —3H **103**
Groveside Clo. *W3* —5G **57**
Groveside Clo. *Cars* —2C **132**
Groveside Rd. *E4* —2B **20**
Grove St. *N18* —5A **18**
Grove St. *SE8* —4B **80**
Grove Ter. *NW5* —3E **44**
Grove Ter. *S'hall* —7E **54**
Grove Ter. *Tedd* —4A **104**
Grove Ter. M. *NW5* —3F **45**
Grove, The. *E15* —6G **49**
Grove, The. *N3* —7D **14**
Grove, The. *N4* —7K **29**
Grove, The. *N6* —1E **44**
Grove, The. *N8* —5H **29**
Grove, The. *N13* —4F **17**
(in two parts)
Grove, The. *N14* —5B **6**
Grove, The. *NW9* —5K **25**
Grove, The. *NW11* —7G **27**
Grove, The. *W5* —7E **56**
Grove, The. *Bexh* —4D **100**
Grove, The. *Edgw* —4C **12**
Grove, The. *Enf* —2F **7**
Grove, The. *Gnfd* —6G **55**

Grove, The. *Iswth* —1J **87**
Grove, The. *Sidc* —4B **116**
Grove, The. *Stan* —2F **11**
Grove, The. *Tedd* —4A **104**
Grove, The. *Twic* —6B **88**
Grove, The. *W Wick* —2E **136**
Grove, The. (Junct.) —1G **111**
Grove Vale. *SE22* —4F **95**
Grove Vale. *Chst* —6E **114**
Grove Vs. *E14* —7D **64**
Groveway. *SW9* —1K **93**
Groveway. *Dag* —3D **52**
Grove Way. *Wemb* —5H **41**
Grovewood. *Rich* —1G **89**
Grovewood Pl. *Wfd G* —6J **21**
Grummant Rd. *SE15* —1F **95**
Grundy St. *E14* —6D **64**
Gruneisen Rd. *N3* —7E **14**
Guardian Ct. *SE12* —5G **97**
Gubyon Av. *SE24* —5D **94**
Guerin Sq. *E3* —3B **64**
Guernsey Clo. *Houn* —7E **70**
Guernsey Gro. *SE24* —7C **94**
Guernsey Ho. *N1* —6C **46**
Guernsey Rd. *E11* —1F **49**
Guernsey Rd. *N1* —6C **46**
Guest St. *EC1* —4C **62** (4D **144**)
Guibal Rd. *SE12* —7K **97**
Guildersfield Rd. *SW16* —7J **109**
Guildersome St. *SE18* —6E **82**
Guildford Gro. *SE10* —1D **96**
Guildford Rd. *E6* —6D **66**
Guildford Rd. *E17* —1E **32**
Guildford Rd. *SW8* —1J **93**
Guildford Rd. *Croy* —6D **124**
Guildford Rd. *Ilf* —2J **51**
Guildford Way. *Wall* —5J **133**
Guildhall Bldgs. *EC2*
—6D **62** (7E **144**)
Guildhall Yd. *EC2*
—6C **62** (7D **144**)
Guildhouse St. *SW1*
—4G **77** (3A **154**)
Guildown Av. *N12* —4E **14**
Guild Rd. *SE7* —5B **82**
Guildsway. *E17* —1B **32**
Guilford Av. *Surb* —5F **119**
Guilford Pl. *WC1*
—4K **61** (4G **143**)
Guilford St. *WC1* —4J **61** (4E **142**)
Guilfoyle. *NW9* —2B **26**
Guillemot Ct. *SE8* —6B **80**
Guillemot Pl. *N22* —2K **29**
Guilsborough Clo. *NW10* —7A **42**
Guinness Clo. *E9* —7A **48**
Guinness Ct. *E1* —6F **63** (1K **151**)
Guinness Ct. *EC1*
—3C **62** (2D **144**)
Guinness Ct. *NW8* —1C **60**
Guinness Ct. *SE1*
—2E **78** (6G **151**)
Guinness Ct. *SW3*
—4D **76** (4E **152**)
Guinness Ct. *SW10* —7A **76**
Guinness Ct. *Croy* —2F **135**
Guinness Sq. *SE1*
—4E **78** (3G **157**)
Guinness Trust Bldgs. *SE17*
—5B **78** (5A **156**)
Guinness Trust Bldgs. *W6*
(off Fulham Pal. Rd.) —5F **75**
Guinness Trust Est. *N16* —1E **46**
Guion Rd. *SW6* —2H **91**
Gulland Wlk. *N1* —6C **46**
(off Oronsay Wlk.)

Gull Clo. *Wall* —7J **133**
Gulliver Clo. *N'holt* —1D **54**
Gulliver Rd. *Sidc* —2H **115**
Gulliver's Ho. *EC1*
—4C **62** (4C **144**)
Gulliver St. *SE16* —3A **80**
Gulston Wlk. *SW3*
—4D **76** (4F **153**)
Gumleigh Rd. *W5* —4C **72**
Gumley Gdns. *Iswth* —3A **88**
Gunderson Corner. *Mitc*
—3D **122**
Gundulph Rd. *Brom* —3A **128**
Gunmaker's La. *E3* —1A **64**
Gunnell Clo. *SE26* —4G **111**
Gunnell Clo. *Croy* —6F **125**
Gunner La. *SE18* —5E **82**
Gunnersbury Av. *W5, W3 & W4*
—1F **73**
Gunnersbury Clo. *W4* —5H **73**
Gunnersbury Ct. *W3* —2H **73**
Gunnersbury Cres. *W3* —2G **73**
Gunnersbury Dri. *W5* —2F **73**
Gunnersbury Gdns. *W3* —2G **73**
Gunnersbury La. *W3* —3G **73**
Gunnersbury Mnr. *W5* —1F **73**
Gunnersbury M. *W4* —5H **73**
Gunnersbury Park. (Junct.)
—3G **73**
Gunners Gro. *E4* —3K **19**
Gunners Rd. *SW18* —2B **108**
Gunning St. *SE18* —4J **83**
Gunstor Rd. *N16* —4E **46**
Gun St. *E1* —5F **63** (6J **145**)
Gunter Gro. *SW10* —6A **76**
Gunter Gro. *Edgw* —1K **25**
Gunterstone Rd. *W14* —4G **75**
Gunthorpe St. *E1*
—5F **63** (6K **145**)
Gunton Rd. *E5* —3H **47**
Gunton Rd. *SW17* —6E **108**
Gunwhale Clo. *SE16* —1K **79**
Gurdon Rd. *SE7* —5J **81**
Gurenne Ct. *E4* —1K **19**
Gurnell Gro. *W13* —4K **55**
Gurney Clo. *E15* —5G **49**
Gurney Clo. *E17* —1K **31**
Gurney Clo. *Bark* —6F **51**
Gurney Cres. *Croy* —1K **133**
Gurney Dri. *N2* —4A **28**
Gurney Rd. *E15* —5G **49**
Gurney Rd. *Cars* —4E **132**
Gurney Rd. *N'holt* —3A **54**
Guthrie Ct. *SE1* —2A **78** (7K **149**)
Guthrie St. *SW3*
—5B **76** (5C **152**)
Gutter La. *EC2* —6C **62** (7C **144**)
Guyatt Gdns. *Mitc* —2E **122**
Guy Barnett Gro. *SE3* —3J **97**
Guybon Av. *SE24* —5B **94**
Guy Rd. *Wall* —3H **133**
Guyscliff Rd. *SE13* —5E **96**
Guys Retreat. *Buck H* —1F **21**
Guy St. *SE1* —2D **78** (6F **151**)
Gwalior Rd. *SW15* —3F **91**
Gwendolen Av. *SW15* —4F **91**
Gwendolen Clo. *SW15* —5F **91**
Gwendoline Av. *E13* —1K **65**
Gwendwr Rd. *W14* —5G **75**
Gweneth Cotts. *Edgw* —6B **12**
Gwillim Clo. *Sidc* —5A **100**
Gwydor Rd. *Beck* —3K **125**
Gwydyr Rd. *Brom* —3H **127**
Gwyn Clo. *SW6* —7A **76**
Gwynne Av. *Croy* —7K **125**

Gwynne Clo. *W4* —6B **74**
Gwynne Pk. Av. *Wfd G* —6J **21**
Gwynne Pl. *WC1*
—3K **61** (2H **143**)
Gwynne Rd. *SW11* —2B **92**
Gylcote Clo. *SE5* —4D **94**
Gyles Pk. *Stan* —1C **24**
Gyllyngdune Gdns. *Ilf* —2K **51**
Gypsy Corner. (Junct.) —5K **57**

H

Haarlem Rd. *W14* —3F **75**
Haberdasher Est. *N1*
—3D **62** (1F **145**)
Haberdasher Pl. *N1*
—3D **62** (1F **145**)
Haberdashers Ct. *SE14* —2K **95**
Haberdasher St. *N1*
—3D **62** (1F **145**)
Habington Ho. *SE5* —7D **78**
(off Notley St.)
Haccombe Rd. *SW19* —6A **108**
Hackbridge Grn. *Wall* —2E **132**
Hackbridge Pk. *Cars* —2D **132**
Hackbridge Pk. Gdns. *Cars*
—2D **132**
Hackbridge Rd. *Wall* —2E **132**
Hackford Rd. *SW9* —1K **93**
Hackford Wlk. *SW9* —1K **93**
Hackington Cres. *Beck* —6C **112**
Hacklington Ct. *New Bar* —5E **4**
Hackney Gro. *E8* —6H **47**
Hackney Rd. *E2* —3F **63** (2J **145**)
Hackney Wick. (Junct.) —6A **48**
Hadden Rd. *SE28* —3J **83**
Hadden Way. *Gnfd* —6H **39**
Haddington Rd. *Brom* —3F **113**
Haddon Ct. *Enf* —6B **8**
Haddon Clo. *N Mald* —5B **120**
Haddon Ct. *W3* —7B **58**
Haddon Gro. *Sidc* —7K **99**
Haddon Rd. *Sutt* —4K **131**
Haddo St. *SE10* —6E **80**
Haden Ct. *N4* —2A **46**
Hadfield Clo. *S'hall* —3D **54**
Hadfield Ho. *E1* —6G **63**
(off Ellen St.)
Hadleigh Clo. *E1* —4J **63**
Hadleigh Clo. *SW20* —2H **121**
Hadleigh Ct. *E4* —1B **20**
Hadleigh Rd. *N9* —7C **8**
Hadleigh St. *E2* —3J **63**
Hadleigh Wlk. *E6* —6C **66**
Hadley Clo. *N21* —6F **7**
Hadley Comn. *Barn* —2D **4**
Hadley Ct. *N16* —1G **47**
Hadley Ct. *New Bar* —3E **4**
Hadley Gdns. *W4* —5K **73**
Hadley Gdns. *S'hall* —5D **70**
Hadley Grn. Rd. *Barn* —2C **4**
Hadley Grn. W. *Barn* —2C **4**
Hadley Gro. *Barn* —2B **4**
Hadley Highstone. *Barn* —1C **4**
Hadley Mnr. Trad. Est. *Barn*
—3C **4**
Hadley Ridge. *Barn* —3C **4**
Hadley Rd. *Barn* —2E **4**
(Barnet)
Hadley Rd. *Barn & Enf* —1K **5**
(Hadley Wood)
Hadley Rd. *Belv* —4F **85**
Hadley Rd. *Mitc* —4H **123**
Hadley St. *NW1* —6F **45**
Hadley Way. *N21* —6F **7**
Hadley Wood Rd. *Barn* —2F **5**

Hadlow Pl. SE19 —7G 111
Hadlow Rd. Sidc —4A 116
Hadlow Rd. Well —7C 84
Hadrian Clo. Wall —7J 133
Hadrian Ct. Sutt —7K 131
Hadrian Est. E2 —2G 63
Hadrians Ride. Enf —5A 8
Hadrian St. SE10 —5G 81
Hadyn Pk. Ct. W12 —2C 74
 (off Curwen Rd.)
Hadyn Pk. Rd. W12 —2C 74
Hafer Rd. SW11 —4D 92
Hafton Rd. SE6 —1G 113
Haggard Rd. Twic —7B 88
Hagger Ct. E17 —3F 33
Haggerston Rd. E8 & E2 —7F 47
Hague St. E2 —3G 63
Ha Ha Rd. SE18 —6D 82
Haig Pl. Mord —6J 121
Haig Rd. Stan —5H 11
 —5C 62 (6C 144)
Haig Rd. E. E13 —3A 66
Haig Rd. W. E13 —3A 66
Haigville Gdns. Ilf —4F 35
Hailes Clo. SW19 —6A 108
Haileybury Av. Enf —6A 8
Hailey Rd. Eri —2G 85
Hailsham Av. SW2 —2A 109
Hailsham Clo. Surb —7D 118
Hailsham Cres. Bark —5K 51
Hailsham Dri. Harr —3H 23
Hailsham Rd. SW17 —6E 108
Hailsham Ter. N18 —5J 17
Haimo Rd. SE9 —5B 98
Hainault Ct. E17 —4F 33
Hainault Gore. Romf —5E 36
Hainault Rd. E11 —1E 48
Hainault Rd. Chad H —6F 37
Hainault Rd. Col R —2J 37
Hainault Rd. L Hth —1B 36
Hainault St. SE9 —1F 115
Hainault St. Ilf —2G 51
Haines St. SW8 —7G 77
Haines Wlk. Mord —7K 121
Hainford Clo. SE4 —4A 95
Haining Clo. W4 —5G 73
Hainthorpe Rd. SE27 —3B 110
Hainton Clo. E1 —6H 63
Hainton Pl. E1 —6H 63
Halberd M. E5 —2H 47
Halbutt Gdns. Dag —3F 53
Halbutt St. Dag —4F 53
Halcomb St. N1 —1E 62
Halcot Av. Bexh —5H 101
Halcrow St. E1 —5H 63
Halcyon. Enf —5K 7
 (off Private Rd.)
Halcyon Ct. Wemb —3H 41
Haldane Clo. N10 —7A 16
Haldane Pl. SW18 —1K 107
Haldane Rd. E6 —3B 66
Haldane Rd. SE28 —7D 68
Haldane Rd. SW6 —7H 75
Haldane Rd. S'hall —7C 55
Haldan Rd. E4 —6K 19
Hale Clo. E4 —3K 19
Hale Clo. Edgw —5D 12
Hale Ct. Edgw —5D 12
Hale Dri. NW7 —6D 12
Hale End Rd. E17 —1F 33
Hale End Rd. Wfd G & E4
 —7A 20
Halefield Rd. N17 —1H 31
Hale Gdns. N17 —4G 31
Hale Gdns. W3 —1G 73

Hale Gro. Gdns. NW7 —5F 13
 (off Woodhouse Rd.)
Hale La. NW7 —5E 12 ·
Hale La. Edgw —5C 12
Hale Path. SE27 —4B 110
Hale Rd. E6 —4C 66
Hale Rd. N17 —3G 31
Halesowen Rd. Mord —7K 121
Hales St. SE8 —7C 80
Hale St. E14 —7D 64
Halesworth Clo. E5 —2J 47
Halesworth Rd. SE13 —3D 96
Hale, The. E4 —7A 20
Hale, The. N17 —3G 31
Hale Wlk. W7 —5J 55
Haley Rd. NW4 —6E 26
Half Acre. Bren —6D 72
Half Acre. Stan —6H 11
Half Acre Rd. W7 —1J 71
Half Moon Ct. EC1
 —5C 62 (6C 144)
Half Moon Cres. N1 —2K 61
Half Moon La. SE24 —6C 94
Half Moon Pas. E1
 —6F 63 (1K 151)
Half Moon St. W1
 —1F 77 (4K 147)
Halford Rd. E10 —5F 33
Halford Rd. SW6 —6J 75
Halford Rd. Rich —5E 88
Halfway St. Sidc —7H 99
Haliburton Rd. Twic —5A 88
Haliday Ho. N1 —6D 46
 (off Mildmay St.)
Haliday Wlk. N1 —6D 46
Halidon Clo. E9 —5J 47
Halifax. NW9 —2A 26
Halifax Rd. Enf —2H 7
Halifax Rd. Gnfd —1F 55
Halifax St. SE26 —3H 111
Halifield Dri. Belv —3E 84
Haling Down Pas. Purl —7C 134
Haling Gro. S Croy —7C 134
Haling Pk. Gdns. S Croy —6B 134
Haling Pk. Rd. S Croy —5B 134
Haling Rd. S Croy —6D 134
Halkin Arc. SW1
 —3D 76 (1F 153)
Halkin M. SW1 —3E 76 (1G 153)
Halkin Pl. SW1 —3E 76 (1G 153)
Halkin St. SW1 —2E 76 (7H 147)
Hallam Clo. Chst —5D 114
Hallam Gdns. Pinn —1C 22
Hallam M. W1 —5F 61 (5K 141)
Hallam Rd. N15 —4B 30
Hallam Rd. SW13 —3D 90
Hallam St. W1 —5F 61 (5K 141)
Hallane Ho. SE27 —5C 110
Hall Clo. W5 —5E 56
Hall Ct. Tedd —5K 103
Hall Dri. SE26 —5J 111
Hall Dri. W7 —6J 55
Halley Gdns. SE13 —4F 97
Halley Pl. E14 —5A 64
Halley Rd. E7 & E12 —6A 50
Halley St. E14 —5A 64
Hall Farm Clo. Stan —4G 11
Hall Farm Dri. Twic —7H 87
Hallfield Est. W2 —6A 60
Hall Gdns. E4 —4G 19
Hall Ga. NW8 —3B 60 (1A 140)
Halliday Sq. S'hall —1H 71
Halliford St. N1 —7C 46
Hallingbury Ct. E17 —3D 32
Halliwell Ct. SE22 —5G 95
Halliwell Rd. SW2 —6K 93

Halliwick Ct. Pde. N12 —6J 15
 (off Woodhouse Rd.)
Halliwick Rd. N10 —1E 28
Hall La. E4 —5F 19
Hall La. NW4 —1C 26
Hall Lane. (Junct.) —5E 18
Hallmark Trad. Cen. Wemb
 —4J 41
Hallmead Rd. Sutt —3K 131
Hall Oak Wlk. NW6 —6H 43
Hallowell Av. Croy —4J 133
Hallowell Clo. Mitc —3E 122
Hallowfield Way. Mitc —3B 122
Hall Pl. W2 —4B 60 (4A 140)
Hall Pl. Cres. Bex —5J 101
Hall Rd. E6 —1D 66
Hall Rd. E15 —4F 49
Hall Rd. NW8 —3A 60
Hall Rd. Chad H —6C 36
Hall Rd. Iswth —5H 87
Hall Rd. Wall —7F 133
Hallside Rd. Enf —1A 8
Hall St. EC1 —3B 62 (1B 144)
Hall St. N12 —5F 15
Hallsville Rd. E16 —6H 65
Hallswelle Pde. NW11 —5H 27
Hallswelle Rd. NW11 —5H 27
Hall, The. SE3 —3J 97
Hall Tower. W2 —3B 60 (5B 140)
Hall View. SE9 —2B 114
Hallywell Cres. E6 —5D 66
Halons Rd. SE9 —7E 98
Halpin Pl. SE17 —4D 78 (4F 157)
Halsbrook Rd. SE3 —3B 98
Halsbury Clo. Stan —4G 11
Halsbury Ct. Stan —4G 11
Halsbury Rd. W12 —1D 74
Halsbury Rd. E. N'holt —4G 39
Halsbury Rd. W. N'holt —5F 39
Halsey M. SW3 —4D 76 (3E 152)
Halsey St. SW3 —4D 76 (3E 152)
Halsmere Rd. SE5 —1B 94
Halstead Clo. Croy —3C 134
Halstead Gdns. N21 —1J 17
Halstead Rd. E11 —5J 33
Halstead Rd. N21 —1H 17
Halstead Rd. Enf —4K 7
Halstead Rd. Eri —1K 101
Halston Clo. SW11 —6D 92
Halstow Rd. NW10 —3F 59
Halstow Rd. SE10 —5J 81
Halton Cross St. N1 —1B 62
Halton Mans. N1 —7B 46
Halton Rd. N1 —7B 46
Halt Robin La. Belv —4H 85
Halt Robin Rd. Belv —4G 85
 (in two parts)
Hambalt Rd. SW4 —5G 93
Hambleden Ct. SE22 —4E 94
Hambleden Pl. SE21 —1E 110
Hambledon Ct. W5 —7E 56
Hambledon Gdns. SE25 —3F 125
Hambledon Rd. SW18 —7H 91
Hambledon Rd. Sidc —7H 99
Hamblehyrst. Beck —2D 126
Hamble St. SW6 —3K 91
Hambleton Clo. Wor Pk —2E 130
Hamble Wlk. N'holt —2E 54
 (off Brabazon Rd.)
Hamblin Ho. S'hall —7C 54
 (off Broadway, The)
Hambridge Way. SW2 —7A 94
Hambro Av. Brom —1J 137
Hambrook Rd. SE25 —3H 125
Hambro Rd. SW16 —6H 109

Hambrough Ho. Hayes —5A 54
Hambrough Rd. S'hall —1C 70
Hambury Ho. SW8 —7J 77
 (off Rite Rd.)
Ham Clo. Rich —3C 104
Ham Comn. Rich —3D 104
Hamden Cres. Dag —3H 53
Hamel Clo. Harr —4D 24
Hame Way. E6 —4E 66
Ham Farm Rd. Rich —4D 104
Hamfrith Rd. E15 —6H 49
Ham Ga. Av. Rich —3D 104
Hamilton Av. N9 —7B 8
Hamilton Av. Ilf —4F 35
Hamilton Av. Romf —2K 37
Hamilton Av. Sutt —2G 131
Hamilton Bldgs. EC2
 —4E 62 (4H 145)
Hamilton Clo. N17 —3F 31
Hamilton Clo. NW8
 —3B 60 (2A 140)
Hamilton Clo. SE16 —2A 80
Hamilton Clo. Cockf —4H 5
Hamilton Clo. Stan —2D 10
Hamilton Clo. SW15 —3G 91
Hamilton Clo. W5 —7F 57
Hamilton Ct. W9 —3A 60
 (off Maida Vale)
Hamilton Cres. N13 —4F 17
Hamilton Cres. Harr —3D 38
Hamilton Cres. Houn —5F 87
Hamilton Ho. NW8
 —3B 60 (1A 140)
Hamilton Ho. W4 —6A 74
Hamilton La. N5 —4B 46
Hamilton M. SW19 —1J 121
Hamilton M. W1 —2F 77 (6J 147)
Hamilton Pk. N5 —4B 46
Hamilton Pk. W. N5 —4B 46
Hamilton Pl. W1
 —1E 76 (5H 147)
Hamilton Rd. E15 —3G 65
Hamilton Rd. E17 —2A 32
Hamilton Rd. N2 —3A 28
Hamilton Rd. N9 —7B 8
Hamilton Rd. NW10 —5C 42
Hamilton Rd. NW11 —7F 27
Hamilton Rd. SE27 —4D 110
Hamilton Rd. SW19 —7K 107
Hamilton Rd. W4 —2A 74
Hamilton Rd. W5 —7E 56
Hamilton Rd. Bexh —2E 100
Hamilton Rd. Bren —6D 72
Hamilton Rd. Cockf —4H 5
Hamilton Rd. Harr —5J 23
Hamilton Rd. Ilf —4F 51
Hamilton Rd. Sidc —4A 116
Hamilton Rd. S'hall —1D 70
Hamilton Rd. T Hth —3D 124
Hamilton Rd. Twic —1J 103
Hamilton Rd. Ind. Est. SE27
 —4D 110
Hamilton Rd. M. SW19 —7K 107
Hamilton Sq. N12 —6G 15
Hamilton Sq. SE1
 —2D 78 (6F 151)
Hamilton St. SE8 —6C 80
Hamilton Ter. NW8 —2K 59
Hamilton Way. N3 —6D 14
Hamilton Way. N13 —4G 17
Hamilton Way. Wall —7H 133
Hamlea Clo. SE12 —5J 97
Hamlet Clo. SE13 —4G 97
Hamlet Clo. Romf —1G 37

Hamlet Ct. SE11
 —5B 78 (5A 156)
Hamlet Ct. W6 —4C 74
Hamlet Ct. Enf —5K 7
Hamlet Gdns. W6 —4C 74
Hamlet Ind. Est. E9 —7C 48
Hamlet International Ind. Est. Eri
 —4K 85
Hamlet Rd. SE19 —7F 111
Hamlet Rd. Romf —1G 37
Hamlet Sq. NW2 —3G 43
Hamlets Way. E3 —4B 64
Hamlet, The. SE5 —3D 94
Hamlet Way. SE1
 —2D 78 (6F 151)
Hamlin Cres. Pinn —5A 22
Hamlyn Clo. Edgw —3K 11
Hamlyn Gdns. SE19 —7E 110
Hammelton Grn. SW9 —1B 94
Hammelton Rd. Brom —1H 127
Hammers La. NW7 —5H 13
Hammersmith Bri. SW13 & W6
 —6D 74
Hammersmith Bri. Rd. W6
 (in two parts) —5D 74
Hammersmith B'way. W6 —4E 74
Hammersmith Broadway. (Junct.)
 —4E 74
 (off Hammersmith B'way.)
Hammersmith Flyover. W6
 —5E 74
Hammersmith Flyover. (Junct.)
 —5E 74
Hammersmith Gro. W6 —2E 74
Hammersmith Ind. Est. W6
 —6E 74
Hammersmith Rd. W6 & W14
 —4F 75
Hammersmith Ter. W6 —5C 74
Hammet Clo. Hayes —5B 54
Hammett St. EC3
 —7F 63 (2J 151)
Hammond Av. Mitc —2F 123
Hammond Clo. Barn —5B 4
Hammond Clo. Gnfd —5H 39
Hammond Ct. E10 —2D 48
Hammond Ct. E17 —5A 32
 (off Maude Rd.)
Hammond Ho. SE14 —7J 79
 (off Lubbock St.)
Hammond Rd. Enf —2C 8
Hammond Rd. S'hall —3C 70
Hammonds Clo. Dag —3C 52
Hammond St. NW5 —6G 45
Hammond Way. SE28 —7B 68
Hamond Clo. S Croy —7B 134
Hamonde Clo. Edgw —2C 12
Hamond Sq. N1 —2E 62
 (off Hoxton St.)
Ham Pk. Rd. E15 & E7 —7H 49
Hampden Av. Beck —2A 126
Hampden Clo. NW1 —2H 61
Hampden Clo. N10 —7K 15
Hampden Gurney St. W1
 —6D 60 (1E 146)
Hampden Ho. SW9 —2A 94
Hampden La. N17 —1F 31
Hampden Rd. N8 —4A 30
Hampden Rd. N10 —7K 15
Hampden Rd. N17 —1G 31
Hampden Rd. N19 —2H 45
Hampden Rd. Beck —2A 126
Hampden Rd. Harr —1G 23
Hampden Rd. King T —3G 119
Hampden Rd. Romf —1H 37

Hampden Sq. *N14* —1A **16**
Hampden Way. *N14* —1A **16**
Hampshire Clo. *N18* —5C **18**
Hampshire Hog La. *W6* —4D **74**
Hampshire Rd. *N22* —7E **16**
Hampshire St. *NW5* —6H **45**
Hampson Way. *SW8* —1K **93**
Hampstead Clo. *SE28* —1B **84**
Hampstead Gdns. *NW11* —6J **27**
Hampstead Gdns. *Chad H*
—5B **36**
Hampstead Grn. *NW3* —5C **44**
Hampstead Gro. *NW3* —3A **44**
Hampstead Heights. *N2* —3A **28**
Hampstead High St. *NW3*
—4B **44**
Hampstead Hill Gdns. *NW3*
—4B **44**
Hampstead La. *NW3 & N6*
—1B **44**
Hampstead Rd. *NW1*
—2G **61** (1A **142**)
Hampstead Sq. *NW3* —3A **44**
Hampstead Wlk. *E3* —1B **64**
Hampstead Way. *NW11* —5H **27**
Hampstead W. NW6 —6J **43**
(off Iverson Rd.)
Hampton Clo. *N11* —5A **16**
Hampton Clo. *NW6* —3J **59**
Hampton Clo. *SW20* —7E **106**
Hampton Ct. *N1* —6B **46**
Hampton Ct. *N22* —1G **29**
Hampton Ct. Rd. *E Mol & King T*
—3A **118**
Hampton Farm Ind. Est. *Felt*
—3C **102**
Hampton Ho. Bexh —2H **101**
(off Erith Rd.)
Hampton La. *Felt* —4C **102**
Hampton M. *NW10* —3K **57**
Hampton Rise. *Harr* —6E **24**
Hampton Rd. *E4* —5G **19**
Hampton Rd. *E7* —5K **49**
Hampton Rd. *E11* —1F **49**
Hampton Rd. *Croy* —6C **124**
Hampton Rd. *Hamp & Tedd*
—5H **103**
Hampton Rd. *Ilf* —4F **51**
Hampton Rd. *Twic* —3H **103**
Hampton Rd. *Wor Pk* —2D **130**
Hampton Rd. E. *Felt* —4D **102**
Hampton Rd. W. *Felt* —3C **102**
Hampton St. *SE17 & SE1*
—4B **78** (4B **156**)
Ham Ridings. *Rich* —5F **105**
Hamshades Clo. *Sidc* —3K **115**
Ham Sq. *Rich* —2C **104**
Ham St. *Rich* —1B **104**
Ham, The. *Bren* —7C **72**
Ham View. *Croy* —6A **126**
Ham Yd. *W1* —7H **61** (2C **148**)
Hanah Ct. *SW19* —7F **107**
Hanameel St. *E16* —1J **81**
Hanbury Ct. *Harr* —6K **23**
Hanbury Dri. *N21* —5E **6**
Hanbury Ho. E1 —5G **63**
(off Hanbury St.)
Hanbury M. *N1* —1C **62**
Hanbury Rd. *N17* —2H **31**
Hanbury Rd. *W3* —2H **73**
Hanbury St. *E1* —5F **63** (5K **145**)
Hanbury Wlk. *Bex* —3K **117**
Hancock Rd. *E3* —3E **64**
Hancock Rd. *SE19* —6D **110**
Handa Wlk. *N1* —6D **46**

Hand Ct. *WC1* —5K **61** (6H **143**)
Handcroft Rd. *Croy* —7B **124**
Handel Clo. *Edgw* —6A **12**
Handel Mans. *SW13* —7E **74**
Handel Pde. Edgw —7B **12**
(off Whitchurch La.)
Handel Pl. *NW10* —6K **41**
Handel St. *WC1* —4J **61** (3E **142**)
Handel Way. *Edgw* —7B **12**
Handen Rd. *SE12* —5G **97**
Handforth Rd. *SW9* —7A **78**
Handforth Rd. *Ilf* —3F **51**
Handley Rd. *E9* —1J **63**
Handowe Clo. *NW4* —4C **26**
Handside Clo. *Wor Pk* —1F **131**
Hands Wlk. *E16* —6J **65**
Handsworth Av. *E4* —6A **20**
Handsworth Rd. *N17* —3D **30**
Handtrough Way. *Bark* —2F **67**
Hanford Clo. *SW18* —1J **107**
Hanford Row. *SW19* —6E **106**
Hanger Ct. *W5* —4F **57**
Hanger Grn. *W5* —4G **57**
Hanger La. *W5* —5E **100**
Hanger La. (Junct.) —3E **56**
Hanger Vale La. *W5* —6F **57**
Hanger View Way. *W3* —6G **57**
Hanging Sword All. *EC4*
—6A **62** (1K **149**)
Hankey Pl. *SE1* —2D **78** (7F **151**)
Hankins La. *NW7* —2F **13**
Hanley Gdns. *N4* —1K **45**
Hanley Pl. *Beck* —7C **112**
Hanley Rd. *N4* —1J **45**
Hanmer Wlk. *N7* —2K **45**
Hannah Barlow Ho. *SW8* —1J **93**
Hannah Clo. *NW10* —4J **41**
Hannah Clo. *Beck* —3E **126**
Hannah Mary Way. *SE1* —4G **79**
Hannah M. *Wall* —7G **133**
Hannay La. *N8* —7H **29**
Hannay Wlk. *SW16* —2H **109**
Hannell Rd. *SW6* —7G **75**
Hannen Rd. *SE27* —3B **110**
Hannibal Rd. *E1* —5J **63**
Hannibal Way. *Croy* —5K **133**
Hannington Point. E9 —6B **48**
(off Eastway)
Hannington Rd. *SW4* —3F **93**
Hanover Av. *E16* —1J **81**
Hanover Clo. *Rich* —7G **73**
Hanover Clo. *Sutt* —4G **131**
Hanover Ct. *NW9* —3A **26**
Hanover Ct. *SW15* —4B **90**
Hanover Ct. W12 —1C **74**
(off Uxbridge Rd.)
Hanover Dri. *Chst* —4G **115**
Hanover Flats. W1
—7E **60** (2H **147**)
(off Binney St.)
Hanover Gdns. *SE11* —6A **78**
Hanover Gdns. *Ilf* —1G **35**
Hanover Ga. *NW1*
—3C **60** (2D **140**)
Hanover Ho. NW8
—2C **60** (1C **140**)
Hanover Ho. *SW9* —3A **94**
Hanover Mead. *NW11* —5G **27**
Hanover Pk. *SE15* —1G **95**
Hanover Pl. *WC2*
—6J **61** (1F **149**)
Hanover Rd. *N15* —4F **31**
Hanover Rd. *NW10* —7E **42**
Hanover Rd. *SW19* —7A **108**
Hanover Sq. *W1* —6F **61** (1K **147**)

Hanover Steps. *W2*
—6C **60** (1D **146**)
Hanover St. *W1* —6F **61** (1K **147**)
Hanover St. *Croy* —3B **134**
Hanover Ter. *NW1*
—3C **60** (2E **140**)
Hanover Ter. *Iswth* —1A **88**
Hanover Ter. M. *NW1*
—3C **60** (2D **140**)
Hanover Trad. Est. *N7* —5J **45**
Hanover Way. *Bexh* —3D **100**
Hanover W. Ind. Est. *NW10*
—3K **57**
Hanover Yd. N1 —2C **62**
(off Noel Rd.)
Hansard M. *W14* —2F **75**
Hansart Way. *Enf* —1F **7**
Hans Cres. *SW1*
—3D **76** (1E **152**)
Hanselin Clo. *Stan* —5E **10**
Hansen Dri. *N21* —5E **6**
Hanshaw Dri. *Edgw* —1K **25**
Hansler Rd. *SE22* —5F **95**
Hansol Rd. *Bexh* —5E **100**
Hanson Clo. *SW12* —7F **93**
Hanson Clo. *SW14* —3J **89**
Hanson Clo. *Beck* —4D **112**
Hanson Ct. *E17* —6D **32**
Hanson Gdns. *S'hall* —2C **70**
Hanson St. *W1* —5G **61** (5A **142**)
Hans Pl. *SW1* —3D **76** (1F **153**)
Hans Rd. *SW3* —3D **76** (1E **152**)
Hans St. *SW1* —3D **76** (2F **153**)
Hanway Pl. *W1* —6H **61** (7C **142**)
Hanway Rd. *W7* —6H **55**
Hanway St. *W1* —6H **61** (7C **142**)
Hanworth Ho. *SE5* —7B **78**
Hanworth Rd. *Felt* —1A **102**
Hanworth Rd. *Hamp* —4D **102**
Hanworth Rd. *Houn* —1C **102**
Hanworth Ter. *Houn* —4F **87**
Hanworth Trad. Est. *Felt* —3C **102**
Hapgood Clo. *Gnfd* —5H **39**
Harad's Pl. *E1* —7G **63**
Harben Rd. *NW6* —7A **44**
Harberson Rd. *E15* —1H **65**
Harberson Rd. *SW12* —1F **109**
Harberton Rd. *N19* —1G **45**
Harbet Rd. *N18 & E4* —5E **18**
Harbet Rd. *W2* —5B **60** (6B **146**)
Harbex Clo. *Bex* —7H **101**
Harbinger Rd. *E14* —4D **80**
Harbledown Rd. *SW6* —1J **91**
Harbord Clo. *SE5* —2D **94**
Harbord St. *SW6* —1F **91**
Harborough Av. *Sidc* —7K **99**
Harborough Rd. *SW16* —4K **109**
Harbour Av. *SW10* —1A **92**
Harbour Exchange Sq. *E14*
—2D **80**
Harbour Quay. *E14* —1E **80**
Harbour Rd. *SE5* —3C **94**
Harbour Yd. *SW10* —1A **92**
Harbridge Av. *SW15* —7B **90**
Harbury Rd. *Cars* —7C **132**
Harbut Rd. *SW11* —4B **92**
Harcombe Rd. *N16* —3E **46**
Harcourt Av. *E12* —4D **50**
Harcourt Av. *Edgw* —3D **12**
Harcourt Av. *Sidc* —6C **100**
Harcourt Av. *Wall* —4F **133**
Harcourt Bldgs. *EC4*
—7A **62** (2J **149**)
Harcourt Clo. *Iswth* —3A **88**
Harcourt Field. *Wall* —4F **133**

Harcourt Lodge. *Wall* —4F **133**
Harcourt Rd. *E15* —2H **65**
Harcourt Rd. *N22* —1H **29**
Harcourt Rd. *SE4* —3B **96**
Harcourt Rd. *SW19* —7J **107**
Harcourt Rd. *Bexh* —4E **100**
Harcourt Rd. *T Hth* —6K **123**
Harcourt Rd. *Wall* —4F **133**
Harcourt St. *W1*
—5C **60** (6D **140**)
Harcourt Ter. *SW10* —5K **75**
Hardcastle Clo. *Croy* —6G **125**
Hardcourts Clo. *W Wick* —3D **136**
Hardel Rise. *SW2* —1B **110**
Hardel Wlk. *SW2* —7A **94**
Harden Ho. *SE5* —2E **94**
Harden's Mnr. Way. *SE7* —3B **82**
Harders Rd. *SE15* —2H **95**
Hardess St. *SE24* —3C **94**
Hardie Clo. *NW10* —5K **41**
Hardie Rd. *Dag* —3J **53**
Harding Clo. *SE17*
—6C **78** (7C **156**)
Harding Clo. *Croy* —3F **135**
Hardinge La. *E1* —6J **63**
Hardinge Rd. *N18* —6K **17**
Hardinge Rd. *NW10* —1D **58**
Hardinge St. *E1* —6J **63**
Harding Rd. *Bexh* —2F **101**
Harding's Clo. *King T* —1E **118**
Hardings La. *SE20* —6K **111**
Hardman Rd. *SE7* —5K **81**
Hardman Rd. *King T* —2E **118**
Hardwick Clo. *Stan* —5H **11**
Hardwick Ct. *Eri* —6K **85**
Hardwicke Av. *Houn* —1E **86**
Hardwicke M. WC1
—3K **61** (2H **143**)
(off Lloyd Baker M.)
Hardwicke Rd. *N13* —6D **16**
Hardwicke Rd. *W4* —4K **73**
Hardwicke Rd. *Rich* —4C **104**
Hardwicke St. *Bark* —1G **67**
Hardwick Grn. *W13* —5B **56**
Hardwick St. *EC1*
—3A **62** (2K **143**)
Hardwicks Way. *SW18* —5J **91**
Hardwidge St. *SE1*
—2E **78** (6G **151**)
Hardy Av. *E16* —1J **81**
Hardy Av. *Ruis* —5A **38**
Hardy Clo. *SE16* —2K **79**
Hardy Clo. *Barn* —6B **4**
Hardy Clo. *Pinn* —7B **22**
Hardy Cotts. *SE10* —6F **81**
Hardy Ho. *SW4* —7G **93**
Hardying Ho. *E17* —4A **32**
Hardy Rd. *E4* —6G **19**
Hardy Rd. *SE3* —6H **81**
Hardy Rd. *SW19* —7K **107**
Hardy Way. *Enf* —1F **7**
Harebell Dri. *E6* —5E **66**
Hare & Billet Rd. *SE3* —1F **97**
Harecastle Clo. *Hayes* —4C **54**
Hare Ct. *EC4* —6A **62** (1J **149**)
Harecourt Rd. *N1* —6C **46**
Haredale Rd. *SE24* —4C **94**
Haredon Clo. *SE23* —7K **95**
Harefield Clo. *Enf* —1F **7**
Harefield Grn. *NW7* —6K **13**
Harefield M. *SE4* —3B **96**
Harefield Rd. *N8* —5H **29**
Harefield Rd. *SE4* —3B **96**
Harefield Rd. *SW16* —7K **109**
Harefield Rd. *Sidc* —3D **116**

Hare Marsh. *E2* —4G **63**
Hare Row. *E2* —2H **63**
Haresfield Rd. *Dag* —6G **53**
Hare St. *SE18* —3E **82**
Hare Wlk. *N1* —2E **62**
Harewood Av. *NW1*
—4C **60** (4D **140**)
Harewood Av. *N'holt* —7D **38**
Harewood Clo. *N'holt* —7D **38**
Harewood Dri. *Ilf* —2D **34**
Harewood Pl. *W1*
—6F **61** (1K **147**)
Harewood Rd. *SW19* —6C **108**
Harewood Rd. *Iswth* —7K **71**
Harewood Rd. *S Croy* —6E **134**
Harewood Row. *NW1*
—5C **60** (5D **140**)
Harewood Ter. *S'hall* —4D **70**
Harfield Gdns. *SE5* —3E **94**
Harfleur Ct. SE11
(off Opal St.) —4B **78** (4A **156**)
Harford Clo. *E4* —7J **9**
Harford Ho. *W11* —5H **59**
Harford Rd. *E4* —7J **9**
Harford St. *E1* —4A **64**
Harford Wlk. *N2* —4B **28**
Harfst Way. *Swan* —7J **117**
Hargood Clo. *Harr* —6E **24**
Hargood Rd. *SE3* —1A **98**
Hargrave Mans. *N19* —2H **45**
Hargrave Pk. *N19* —2G **45**
Hargrave Pl. *N7* —5H **45**
Hargrave Rd. *N19* —2G **45**
Hargraves Ho. W12 —7D **58**
(off White City Est.)
Hargwyne St. *SW9* —3K **93**
Haringey Pk. *N8* —6J **29**
Haringey Rd. *N8* —4J **29**
Harington Ter. *N9* —3J **17**
Harkett Clo. *Harr* —2K **23**
Harkett Ct. *W'stone* —2K **23**
Harkness Ho. *E1* —6G **63**
(off Christian St.)
Harland Av. *Croy* —3G **135**
Harland Av. *Sidc* —3H **115**
Harland Clo. *SW19* —3K **121**
Harland Rd. *SE12* —1J **113**
Harlech Gdns. *Houn* —6A **70**
Harlech Rd. *N14* —3D **16**
Harlech Tower. *W3* —2J **73**
Harlequin Av. *Bren* —6A **72**
Harlequin Cen. *S'hall* —4A **70**
Harlequin Clo. *Hayes* —5B **54**
Harlequin Clo. *Iswth* —5J **87**
Harlequin Ct. NW10 —6K **41**
(off Mitchellbrook Way)
Harlequin Ho. Eri —3E **84**
(off Kale Rd.)
Harlequin Rd. *Tedd* —7B **104**
Harlescott Rd. *SE15* —4K **95**
Harlesden Gdns. *NW10* —1B **58**
Harlesden La. *NW10* —1C **58**
Harlesden Plaza. *NW10* —2B **58**
Harlesden Rd. *NW10* —1C **58**
Harleston Clo. *E5* —2J **47**
Harley Clo. *Wemb* —6D **40**
Harley Ct. *E11* —7J **33**
Harley Ct. *N20* —3F **15**
Harley Ct. *Harr* —4H **23**
Harley Cres. *Harr* —4H **23**
Harleyford. *Brom* —1A **128**
Harleyford Ct. *SW8*
—6K **77** (7H **155**)
Harleyford Mnr. W3 —1J **73**
(off Edgecote Clo.)

Harleyford Rd. *SE11*
    —6K **77** (7G **155**)
Harleyford St. *SE11*
    —6A **78** (7J **155**)
Harley Gdns. *SW10* —5A **76**
Harley Gro. *E3* —3B **64**
Harley Ho. *E11* —7F **33**
Harley Ho. *NW1* —4E **60** (4H **141**)
Harley Pl. *W1* —5F **61** (6J **141**)
Harley Rd. *NW3* —7B **44**
Harley Rd. *NW10* —2A **58**
Harley Rd. *Harr* —4H **23**
Harley St. *W1* —4F **61** (4J **141**)
Harlinger St. *SE18* —3C **82**
Harlington Rd. *Bexh* —3E **100**
Harlington Rd. E. *Felt* —7A **86**
Harlington Rd. W. *Felt* —7A **86**
Harlow Clo. *E8* —1G **63**
Harlow Mans. Bark *—7F 51*
    (off Whiting Av.)
Harlow Rd. *N13* —3J **17**
Harman Av. *Wfd G* —6C **20**
Harman Clo. *E4* —4A **20**
Harman Clo. *NW2* —3G **43**
Harman Clo. *SE1*
    —5G **79** (6K **157**)
Harman Dri. *NW2* —3G **43**
Harman Dri. *Sidc* —6K **99**
Harman Rd. *Enf* —5A **8**
Harmon Ho. *SE8* —4B **80**
Harmony Clo. *NW11* —5G **27**
Harmony Clo. *Wall* —7J **133**
Harmony Way. *NW4* —4E **26**
Harmony Way. *Brom* —2J **127**
Harmood Gro. *NW1* —7F **45**
Harmood Pl. *NW1* —7F **45**
Harmood St. *NW1* —6F **45**
Harmsworth M. *SE11*
    —3B **78** (2A **156**)
Harmsworth St. *SE17*
    —6B **78** (6A **156**)
Harmsworth Way. *N20* —1C **14**
Harness Rd. *SE28* —2A **84**
Harold Av. *Belv* —5F **85**
Harold Est. *SE1* —3E **78** (2H **157**)
Harold Pl. *SE11* —5A **78** (6J **155**)
Harold Rd. *E4* —4K **19**
Harold Rd. *E11* —1G **49**
Harold Rd. *E13* —1K **65**
Harold Rd. *N8* —5K **29**
Harold Rd. *N15* —5F **31**
Harold Rd. *NW10* —3K **57**
Harold Rd. *SE19* —7D **110**
Harold Rd. *Sutt* —4B **132**
Harold Rd. *Wfd G* —1J **33**
Haroldstone Rd. *E17* —5K **31**
Harold Wilson Ho. *SE28* —1B **84**
Harold Wilson Ho. SW6 —6H **75**
    (off Clem Attlee Ct.)
Harp All. *EC4* —6B **62** (7A **144**)
Harp Bus. Cen. NW2 —2C **42**
    (off Apsley Way)
Harpenden Rd. *E12* —2A **50**
Harpenden Rd. *SE27* —3B **110**
Harpenmead Point. *NW2* —2H **43**
Harper Ho. *SW9* —3B **94**
Harper Rd. *E6* —6D **66**
Harper Rd. *SE1* —3C **78** (1D **156**)
Harper's Yd. *N17* —1F **31**
Harp Island Clo. *NW10* —2K **41**
Harp La. *EC3* —7E **62** (3G **151**)
Harpley Sq. *E1* —4K **63**
Harpour Rd. *Bark* —6G **51**
Harp Rd. *W7* —4K **55**
Harpsden St. *SW11* —1E **92**

Harpur M. *WC1* —5K **61** (5G **143**)
Harpur St. *WC1* —5K **61** (5G **143**)
Harraden Rd. *SE3* —1A **98**
Harrier Ho. King T —1E **118**
    (off Sigrist Sq.)
Harrier M. *SE28* —2H **83**
Harrier Rd. *NW9* —2A **26**
Harriers Clo. *W5* —7E **56**
Harrier Way. *E6* —5D **66**
Harries Rd. *Hayes* —4A **54**
Harriet Clo. *E8* —1G **63**
Harriet Gdns. *Croy* —2G **135**
Harriet St. *SW1* —2D **76** (7F **147**)
Harriet Tubman Clo. *SW2* —7K **93**
Harriet Wlk. *SW1*
    —2D **76** (7F **147**)
Harriet Way. *Bush* —1C **10**
Harringay Gdns. *N8* —4B **30**
Harringay Rd. *N15* —5B **30**
Harrington Clo. *NW10* —3K **41**
Harrington Clo. *Croy* —2J **133**
Harrington Gdns. *SW7* —4K **75**
Harrington Hill. *E5* —1H **47**
Harrington Rd. *E11* —1G **49**
Harrington Rd. *SE25* —4H **125**
Harrington Rd. *SW7*
    —4B **76** (3A **152**)
Harrington Sq. *NW1* —2G **61**
Harrington St. *NW1*
    —2G **61** (1A **142**)
Harrington Way. *SE18* —3B **82**
Harriott Clo. *SE10* —4H **81**
Harris Bldgs. E1 —6G **63**
    (off Burslem St.)
Harris Clo. *Enf* —1G **7**
Harris Clo. *Houn* —1E **86**
Harris Ct. *Wemb* —3F **41**
Harris Ho. SW9 —3C **94**
    (off St James's Cres.)
Harrison Clo. *N20* —1H **15**
Harrison Ho. *SW12* —7H **93**
Harrison Rd. *Dag* —6H **53**
Harrisons Rise. *Croy* —3B **134**
Harrison St. *WC1*
    —3J **61** (2F **143**)
Harris Rd. *Bexh* —1E **100**
Harris Rd. *Dag* —5F **53**
Harris St. *E17* —7B **32**
Harris St. *SE5* —7D **78**
Harrogate Ct. *SE12* —7J **97**
Harrogate Ct. *SE26* —3G **111**
    (off Droitwich Clo.)
Harrold Rd. *Dag* —5B **52**
Harrovian Bus. Village. *Harr*
    —7J **23**
Harrow Av. *Enf* —6A **8**
Harroway Rd. *SW11* —2B **92**
Harrowby St. *W1*
    —6C **60** (7D **140**)
Harrowdene Clo. *Wemb* —4D **40**
Harrowdene Gdns. Tedd
    —7A **104**
Harrowdene Rd. *Wemb* —3D **40**
Harrow Dri. *N9* —1A **18**
Harrowes Meade. *Edgw* —3B **12**
Harrow Fields Gdns. *Harr* —3J **39**
Harrow Grn. *E11* —3G **49**
Harrow La. *E14* —7E **64**
Harrow Mnr. Way. *SE2* —2C **84**
Harrow Pk. *Harr* —2J **39**
Harrow Pas. King T —2D **118**
Harrow Pl. *E1* —6E **62** (7H **145**)
Harrow Rd. *E6* —1C **66**

Harrow Rd. *E11* —3G **49**
Harrow Rd. *N9* —3C **58**
Harrow Rd. *W2* —5K **59**
Harrow Rd. *W10 & W9* —4F **59**
Harrow Rd. Bark —1J **67**
Harrow Rd. Cars —6C **132**
Harrow Rd. *Ilf* —4G **51**
Harrow Rd. Wemb —4K **39**
    (Sudbury)
Harrow Rd. Wemb —5G **41**
    (Wembley)
Harrow Road. (Junct.) —7H **41**
Harrow Rd. Bri. *W2* —5A **60**
Harrow View. *Harr* —2G **23**
Harrow View Rd. *W5* —4B **56**
Harrow Weald Pk. *Harr* —6C **10**
Harry Lambourn Ho. SE15
    (off Gervase St.) —7H **79**
Harte Rd. *Houn* —2D **86**
Hartfield Av. *N'holt* —2A **54**
Hartfield Cres. *SW19* —7H **107**
Hartfield Cres. *W Wick* —3J **137**
Hartfield Gro. *SE20* —1H **125**
Hartfield Rd. *SW19* —7H **107**
Hartfield Rd. *W Wick* —4J **137**
Hartfield Ter. *E3* —2C **64**
Hartford Av. *Harr* —3A **24**
Hartford Rd. *Bex* —6G **101**
Hart Gro. *W5* —1G **73**
Hart Gro. *S'hall* —5E **54**
Hart Gro. Ct. *W5* —1G **73**
Hartham Clo. *N7* —5J **45**
Hartham Clo. *Iswth* —1A **88**
Hartham Rd. *N7* —5J **45**
Hartham Rd. *N17* —2F **31**
Hartham Rd. *Iswth* —1K **87**
Harting Rd. *SE9* —3C **114**
Hartington Clo. *Harr* —4J **39**
Hartington Ct. *SW8* —1J **93**
Hartington Ct. *W4* —7H **73**
Hartington Rd. *E16* —6K **65**
Hartington Rd. *E17* —6A **32**
Hartington Rd. *SW8* —1J **93**
Hartington Rd. *W4* —7H **73**
Hartington Rd. *W13* —7B **56**
Hartington Rd. *S'hall* —3C **70**
Hartington Rd. *Twic* —7B **88**
Hartington Rd. *SW6* —7H **75**
Hartlake Rd. *E9* —6K **47**
Hartland Clo. *Edgw* —2B **12**
Hartland Dri. *Edgw* —2B **12**
Hartland Dri. *Ruis* —3A **38**
Hartland Rd. *E15* —7H **49**
Hartland Rd. *N11* —5J **15**
Hartland Rd. *NW1* —7F **45**
Hartland Rd. *NW6* —2H **59**
Hartland Rd. *Hamp* —4F **103**
Hartland Rd. *Iswth* —3A **88**
Hartland Rd. *Mord* —7J **121**
Hartlands Clo. *Bex* —6F **101**
Hartland Way. *Croy* —3A **136**
Hartland Way. *Mord* —7H **121**
Hartley Av. *E6* —1C **66**
Hartley Av. *NW7* —5G **13**
Hartley Clo. *NW7* —5G **13**
Hartley Clo. *Brom* —2D **128**
Hartley Rd. *E11* —1H **49**
Hartley Rd. *Croy* —7C **124**
Hartley Rd. *Well* —7C **84**
Hartley St. *E2* —3J **63**
    (in two parts)
Hart Lodge. High Bar —3B **4**
Hartman Rd. *E16* —1B **82**
Hartnoll St. *N7* —5K **45**

Harton Clo. *Brom* —1B **128**
Harton Rd. *N9* —2C **18**
Harton St. *SE8* —1C **96**
Hartop Point. SW6 —7G **75**
    (off Pellant Rd.)
Hartsbourne Av. *Bush* —2B **10**
Hartsbourne Clo. *Bush* —2C **10**
Hartsbourne Ct. S'hall —6G **55**
    (off Fleming Rd.)
Hartsbourne Pk. *Bush* —2D **10**
Hartsbourne Rd. *Bush* —2D **10**
Harts Gro. *Wfd G* —5D **20**
Hartshorn All. EC3
    —6E **62** (1H **151**)
Hartshorn Gdns. *E6* —4E **66**
Hart's La. *SE14* —1A **96**
Harts La. Bark —7F **51**
Hartslock Dri. *SE2* —2D **84**
Hartsmead Rd. *SE9* —2D **114**
Hart St. *EC3* —7E **62** (2H **151**)
Hartsway. *Enf* —4D **8**
Hartswood Gdns. *W12* —3B **74**
Hartswood Rd. *W12* —2B **74**
Hartsworth Clo. *E13* —2H **65**
Hartville Rd. *SE18* —4J **83**
Hartwell Dri. *E4* —6K **19**
Hartwell St. *E8* —6F **47**
Hartwood Grn. *Bush* —2C **10**
Harvard Ct. *NW6* —5K **43**
Harvard Hill. *W4* —6H **73**
Harvard La. *W4* —5J **73**
Harvard Rd. *SE13* —5E **96**
Harvard Rd. *W4* —5H **73**
Harvard Rd. *Iswth* —1J **87**
Harvel Clo. *Orp* —3K **129**
Harvel Cres. *SE2* —5D **84**
Harvest Bank Rd. W Wick
    —3H **137**
Harvesters Clo. *Iswth* —5H **87**
Harvest La. Th Dit —6A **118**
Harvey Ct. *E17* —5C **32**
Harvey Gdns. *E11* —1H **49**
Harvey Gdns. *SE7* —4B **82**
Harvey Ho. *N1* —1D **62**
    (off Colville Est.)
Harvey Ho. Bren —5E **72**
Harvey Ho. Romf —4D **36**
Harvey Point. E16 —5J **65**
    (off Fife Rd.)
Harvey Rd. *E11* —1G **49**
Harvey Rd. *N8* —5K **29**
Harvey Rd. *SE5* —1D **94**
    (in two parts)
Harvey Rd. *Houn* —7D **86**
Harvey Rd. *Ilf* —5F **51**
Harvey Rd. *N'holt* —7A **38**
Harvey's Bldgs. WC2
    —7J **61** (3F **149**)
Harveys La. *Romf* —2K **53**
Harvey St. *N1* —1D **62**
Harvill Rd. *Sidc* —5E **116**
Harvington Wlk. *E8* —7G **47**
Harvist Est. *N7* —4A **46**
Harvist Rd. *NW6* —2F **59**
Harwell Pas. *N2* —4D **28**
Harwich La. EC2
    —5E **62** (5H **145**)
Harwood Av. *Brom* —2K **127**
Harwood Av. *Mitc* —3C **122**
Harwood Clo. *N12* —6H **15**
Harwood Clo. *Wemb* —4D **40**
Harwood Ct. N1 —1D **62**
    (off Colville Est.)
Harwood Rd. *SW6* —7J **75**
Harwoods Yd. *N21* —7F **7**

Harwood Ter. *SW6* —1K **91**
Haselbury Rd. *N18 & N9* —4K **17**
Haseley End. *SE23* —7J **95**
Haselrigge Rd. *SW4* —4H **93**
Haseltine Rd. *SE26* —4B **112**
Haselwood Dri. *Enf* —4G **7**
Haskard Rd. *Dag* —4D **52**
Hasker St. *SW3* —4C **76** (3D **152**)
Haslam Av. *Sutt* —1G **131**
Haslam Clo. *N1* —7A **46**
Haslam Ct. *N11* —4A **16**
Haslam St. *SE15* —1F **95**
Haslemere Av. *NW4* —6F **27**
Haslemere Av. *SW18* —2K **107**
Haslemere Av. *W7 & W13*
    —3A **72**
Haslemere Av. Barn —1J **15**
Haslemere Av. *Houn* —2A **86**
Haslemere Av. *Mitc* —2B **122**
Haslemere Bus. Cen. *Enf* —5C **8**
Haslemere Clo. *Hamp* —5D **102**
Haslemere Clo. *Wall* —5J **133**
Haslemere Gdns. *N3* —3H **27**
Haslemere Rd. *N8* —7H **29**
Haslemere Rd. *N21* —2G **17**
Haslemere Rd. *Bexh* —2F **101**
Haslemere Rd. *Ilf* —2K **51**
Haslemere Rd. *T Hth* —5B **124**
Hasler Clo. *SE28* —7B **68**
Hasluck Gdns. New Bar —6F **5**
Hassard St. *E2* —2G **63** (1K **145**)
Hassendean Rd. *SE3* —6K **81**
Hassett Rd. *E9* —6K **47**
Hassocks Clo. *SE26* —3H **111**
Hassocks Rd. *SW16* —1H **123**
Hassock Wood. *Kes* —4B **138**
Hassop Rd. *NW2* —4F **43**
Hassop Wlk. *SE9* —4C **114**
Hasted Rd. *SE7* —5B **82**
Hastings Av. *Ilf* —4G **35**
Hastings Clo. *SE15* —7G **79**
Hastings Clo. Barn —4F **5**
Hastings Ct. Tedd —5H **103**
Hastings Dri. Surb —6C **118**
Hastings Ho. W12 —7D **58**
    (off White City Est.)
Hastings Ho. *W13* —7B **56**
Hastings Rd. *N11* —5C **16**
Hastings Rd. *N17* —3D **30**
Hastings Rd. *W13* —7B **56**
Hastings Rd. *Brom* —1C **138**
Hastings Rd. *Croy* —1F **135**
Hastings St. WC1
    —3J **61** (2E **142**)
Hastingwood Ct. *E17* —5D **32**
Hastingwood Trad. Est. *N18*
    —6E **18**
Hastlemere Ind. Est. *SW18*
    —2K **107**
Hastoe Clo. *Hayes* —4C **54**
Hatcham Pk. M. *SE14* —1K **95**
Hatcham Pk. Rd. *SE14* —1K **95**
Hatcham Rd. *SE15* —6J **79**
Hatchard Rd. *N19* —2H **45**
Hatchcliffe St. *SE10* —5H **81**
Hatchcroft. *NW4* —3D **26**
Hatchfield Ho. N15 —6E **30**
    (off Albert Rd.)
Hatch Gro. *Romf* —4E **36**
Hatch La. *E4* —4A **20**
    (in two parts)
Hatch Pl. King T —5F **105**
Hatch Rd. *SW16* —2J **123**
Hatch Side. *Chig* —5K **21**
Hatch, The. *Enf* —1E **8**

Hatchwood Clo. Wfd G —4C 20
Hatcliffe Clo. SE3 —3H 97
Hatfield Clo. SE14 —7K 79
Hatfield Clo. Ilf —3F 35
Hatfield Clo. Mitc —4B 122
Hatfield Ct. N'holt —3A 54
(off Canberra Dri.)
Hatfield Ho. EC1 —4C 62 (4C 144)
(off Golden La. Est.)
Hatfield Mead. Mord —5J 121
Hatfield Rd. E15 —5G 49
Hatfield Rd. W4 —2K 73
Hatfield Rd. W13 —1A 72
Hatfield Rd. Dag —6E 52
Hatfields. SE1 —1A 78 (4K 149)
Hathaway Clo. Brom —1D 138
Hathaway Clo. Stan —5F 11
Hathaway Cres. E12 —6D 50
Hathaway Gdns. W13 —5A 56
Hallaway Gdns. Romf —5D 36
Hathaway Ho. N1
—2E 62 (1G 145)
Hathaway Rd. Croy —7B 124
Hatherleigh Clo. Mord —4J 121
Hatherley Cres. Sidc —2A 116
Hatherley Gdns. E6 —3B 66
Hatherley Gdns. N8 —6J 29
Hatherley Gro. W2 —6K 59
Hatherley Ho. E17 —4C 32
Hatherley M. E17 —4C 32
Hatherley Rd. E17 —4B 32
Hatherley Rd. Rich —2F 89
Hatherley Rd. Sidc —4A 116
Hatherley St. SW1
—4G 77 (4B 154)
Hathern Gdns. SE9 —4E 114
Hatherop Rd. Hamp —7D 102
Hathersage Ct. N1 —5D 46
Hathorne Clo. SE15 —2H 95
Hathway St. SE15 —2K 95
Hathway Ter. SE14 —2K 95
(off Hathway St.)
Hatley Av. Ilf —4G 35
Hatley Clo. N11 —5J 15
Hatley Rd. N4 —2K 45
Hat & Mitre Ct. EC1
—4B 62 (4B 144)
Hatteraick St. SE16 —2J 79
Hattersfield Clo. Belv —4F 85
Hatton Clo. SE18 —7H 83
Hatton Garden. EC1
—5A 62 (5K 143)
Hatton Gdns. Mitc —5D 122
Hatton Pl. EC1 —5A 62 (5K 143)
Hatton Rd. Croy —1A 134
Hatton Row. NW8
—4B 60 (4B 140)
Hatton St. NW8 —4B 60 (4B 140)
Hatton Wall. EC1
—5A 62 (5K 143)
Haughmond. N12 —4E 14
Haunch of Venison Yd. W1
—6F 61 (1J 147)
Havana Rd. SW19 —2J 107
Havannah St. E14 —2C 80
Havant Rd. E17 —3E 32
Havant Way. SE15 —7F 79
Havelock Clo. W12 —7D 58
(off India Way)
Havelock Ct. S'hall —3D 70
(off Havelock Rd.)
Havelock Ho. SE23 —1J 111
Havelock Pl. Harr —6J 23
Havelock Rd. N17 —2G 31
Havelock Rd. SW19 —5A 108

Havelock Rd. Belv —4F 85
Havelock Rd. Brom —4A 128
Havelock Rd. Croy —2F 135
Havelock Rd. Harr —3J 23
Havelock Rd. S'hall —3C 70
Havelock St. N1 —1J 61
Havelock St. Ilf —2F 51
Havelock Ter. SW8 —7F 77
Havelock Wlk. SE23 —1J 111
Haven Clo. SE9 —3D 114
Haven Clo. SW19 —3F 107
Haven Clo. Sidc —6C 116
Haven Ct. Beck —2E 126
Haven Grn. W5 —6D 56
Haven Grn. Ct. W5 —6D 56
Havenhurst Rise. Enf —2F 7
Haven La. W5 —6E 56
Haven M. E3 —5B 64
Haven Pl. W5 —7D 56
Haven St. NW1 —7F 45
Haven, The. N14 —6A 6
Haven, The. Rich —3G 89
Haven Wood. Wemb —3H 41
Haverfield Gdns. Rich —7G 73
Haverfield Rd. E3 —3A 64
Haverford Way. Edgw —1F 25
Haverhill Rd. E4 —1K 19
Haverhill Rd. SW12 —1G 109
Havering Dri. Romf —4K 37
Havering Gdns. Romf —5C 36
Havering Rd. Romf —4K 37
Havering St. E1 —6K 63
Havering Way. Bark —3B 68
Haversham Clo. Twic —6D 88
Haversham Ct. Gnfd —6K 39
Haversham Pl. N6 —2D 44
Haverstock Hill. NW3 —5C 44
Haverstock Rd. NW5 —5E 44
Haverstock St. N1
—2B 62 (1B 144)
Havil St. SE5 —7E 78
Havisham Ho. SE16 —2G 79
Havisham Pl. SW16 & SE19
—6B 110
Hawarden Gro. SE24 —7C 94
Hawarden Hill. NW2 —3C 42
Hawarden Rd. E17 —4K 31
Hawbridge Rd. E11 —1F 49
Hawes Ho. E17 —4K 31
Hawes La. W Wick —1E 136
Hawes Rd. N18 —6C 18
Hawes Rd. Brom —1K 127
(in two parts)
Hawes St. N1 —7B 46
Hawgood St. E3 —5C 64
Hawkdene. E4 —6J 9
Hawke Ct. Hayes —4A 54
(off Perth Av.)
Hawke Pk. Rd. N22 —3B 30
Hawke Pl. SE16 —2K 79
Hawker. NW9 —1B 26
Hawker Clo. Wall —7J 133
Hawke Rd. SE19 —6D 110
Hawkesbury Rd. SW15 —5D 90
Hawkesfield Rd. SE23 —2A 112
Hawkesley Clo. Twic —4A 104
Hawkes Rd. Mitc —1C 122
Hawke Tower. SE14 —6A 80
Hawkfield Ct. Iswth —2J 87
Hawkhurst Way. SW16 —1H 123
Hawkhurst Way. N Mald —5K 119
Hawkhurst Way. W Wick
—2D 136

Hawkinge. N17 —2D 30
(off Gloucester Rd.)
Hawkins Clo. NW7 —5E 12
Hawkins Clo. Harr —7H 23
Hawkins Ct. SE18 —4C 82
Hawkins Ho. SE8 —6C 80
(off New King St.)
Hawkins Rd. Tedd —6B 104
Hawkins Way. SE6 —5C 112
Hawkley Gdns. SE27 —2B 110
Hawkridge Clo. Romf —6C 36
Hawksbrook La. Beck —6D 126
Hawkshaw Clo. SW2 —1J 109
Hawkshead. Brom —7G 113
Hawkshead Clo. NW10 —7B 42
Hawkshead Rd. W4 —2A 74
Hawkslade Rd. SE15 —5K 95
Hawksley Rd. N16 —3E 46
Hawks M. SE10 —7E 80
Hawksmoor Clo. E6 —6C 66
Hawksmoor Clo. SE18 —5J 83
Hawksmoor M. E1 —7H 63
Hawksmoor St. W6 —6F 75
Hawksmouth. E4 —7K 9
Hawks Rd. King T —2F 119
Hawkstone Rd. SE16 —4J 79
Hawkwell Ct. E4 —3K 19
Hawkwell Wlk. N1 —1C 62
(off Basire St.)
Hawkwood Cres. E4 —6J 9
Hawkwood La. Chst —1G 129
Hawkwood Mt. E5 —1H 47
Hawlands Dri. Pinn —7C 22
Hawley Clo. Hamp —6D 102
Hawley Cres. NW1 —7F 45
Hawley M. NW1 —7F 45
Hawley Rd. N18 —5E 18
Hawley Rd. NW1 —7F 45
(in three parts)
Hawley St. NW1 —7F 45
Hawstead Rd. SE6 —6D 96
Hawsted. Buck H —1E 20
Hawthordene Rd. Beck —2H 137
Hawthorn Av. N13 —5D 16
Hawthorn Av. Rich —2E 88
Hawthorn Cen. Harr —4K 23
Hawthorn Clo. Hamp —5E 102
Hawthorn Clo. Orp —6H 129
Hawthorn Cotts. Well —3A 100
(off Hook La.)
Hawthorn Ct. Pinn —2A 22
(off Rickmansworth Rd.)
Hawthorn Cres. SW17 —5E 108
Hawthornden Clo. N12 —6H 15
Hawthorndene Clo. Brom
—2H 137
Hawthorndene Rd. Brom
—2H 137
Hawthorn Dri. Harr —6E 22
Hawthorn Dri. W Wick —4G 137
Hawthorne Av. Cars —7E 132
Hawthorne Av. Harr —6A 24
Hawthorne Av. Mitc —2B 122
Hawthorne Av. Ruis —7A 22
Hawthorne Av. T Hth —1B 124
Hawthorne Clo. N1 —6E 46
Hawthorne Clo. Brom —3D 128
Hawthorne Clo. Sutt —2A 132
Hawthorne Farm Av. N'holt
—1C 54
Hawthorne Gro. NW9 —7J 25
Hawthorne M. Gnfd —6G 55
Hawthorne Rd. E17 —3C 32
Hawthorne Rd. Brom —3D 128
Hawthorn Gdns. W5 —3D 72

Hawthorn Gro. SE20 —1H 125
Hawthorn Gro. Enf —1J 7
Hawthorn Hatch. Bren —7B 72
Hawthorn M. NW7 —1G 27
Hawthorn Pl. Eri —5J 85
Hawthorn Rd. N8 —3H 29
Hawthorn Rd. N18 —6A 18
Hawthorn Rd. NW10 —7C 42
Hawthorn Rd. Bexh —4F 101
Hawthorn Rd. Bren —7B 72
Hawthorn Rd. Buck H —4G 21
Hawthorn Rd. Sutt —6C 132
Hawthorn Rd. Wall —7F 133
Hawthorn Way. N9 —2A 18
Hawthorns. Wfd G —3D 20
Hawthorns, The. Eps —7B 130
Hawthorn Wlk. W10 —4G 59
Hawthorn Way. N9 —2A 18
Hawtrey Av. N'holt —2B 54
Hawtrey Rd. NW3 —7C 44
Haxted Rd. Brom —1K 127
Hay Clo. E15 —7G 49
Haycroft Gdns. NW10 —1C 58
Haycroft Rd. SW2 —5J 93
Hay Currie St. E14 —6D 64
Hayday Rd. E16 —5J 65
Haydens M. W3 —6J 57
Hayden's Pl. W11 —6H 59
Hayden Way. Romf —2J 37
Haydock Av. N'holt —6E 38
Haydock Grn. N'holt —6E 38
Haydock Grn. Flats. N'holt
(off Haydock Grn.) —6E 38
Haydon Clo. NW9 —4J 25
Haydon Clo. Enf —6K 7
Haydon Pk. Rd. SW19 —5J 107
Haydon Rd. Dag —2C 52
Haydons Rd. SW19 —5K 107
Haydon St. EC3 —6F 63 (2J 151)
Haydon Wlk. E1 —6F 63 (1K 151)
Haydon Way. SW11 —4B 92
Hayes Chase. W Wick —6F 127
Hayes Clo. Brom —2J 137
Hayes Ct. SW2 —1J 109
Hayes Cres. NW11 —5H 27
Hayes Cres. Sutt —4F 131
Hayesford Pk. Dri. Brom
—5H 127
Hayes Garden. Brom —1J 137
Hayes Hill. Brom —1G 137
Hayes Hill Rd. Brom —1H 137
Hayes La. Beck —3E 126
Hayes La. Brom —5J 127
Hayes Mead Rd. Brom —1G 137
Hayes Metro Cen. Hayes —7A 54
Hayes Pl. NW1 —4C 60 (4D 140)
Hayes Rd. Brom —4J 127
Hayes Rd. S'hall —4A 70
Hayes St. Brom —1K 137
Hayes Way. Beck —4E 126
Hayes Wood Av. Brom —1K 137
Hayfield Pas. E1 —4J 63
Hayfield Yd. E1 —4K 63
Haygarth Pl. SW19 —5F 107
Haygreen Clo. King T —6H 105
Hay Hill. W1 —7F 61 (3K 147)
Hayland Clo. NW9 —4K 25
Hay La. NW9 —4J 25
Hayles St. SE11
—4B 78 (3A 156)
Haylett Gdns. King T —4D 118
Hayling Clo. N16 —5E 46
Hayling Ct. Sutt —4E 130
Haymans Point. SE11
—5K 77 (5G 155)
Hayman St. N1 —7B 46

Haymarket. SW1
—7H 61 (3C 148)
Haymarket Arc. SW1
—7H 61 (3C 148)
Haymer Gdns. Wor Pk —3C 130
Haymerle Rd. SE15 —6G 79
Haymill Clo. Gnfd —3K 55
Hayne Ho. W11 —1G 75
(off Penzance Pl.)
Hayne Rd. Beck —2B 126
Haynes Clo. N11 —3K 15
Haynes Clo. N17 —7C 18
Haynes Clo. SE3 —3J 97
Haynes La. SE19 —6E 110
Haynes Rd. Wemb —7E 40
Hayne St. EC1 —5B 62 (5B 144)
Haynt Wlk. SW20 —3G 121
Hays Galleria. SE1
—1E 78 (4G 151)
Hays La. SE1 —1E 78 (4G 151)
Haysleigh Gdns. SE20 —2G 125
Hay's M. W1 —1F 77 (4J 147)
Haysoms Clo. Romf —4K 37
Hay St. E2 —1G 63
Hayter Ct. E11 —2K 49
Hayter Rd. SW2 —5J 93
Hayton Clo. E8 —6F 47
Hayward Clo. SW19 —7K 107
Hayward Clo. Dart —5K 101
Hayward Ct. SW9 —2J 93
(off Clapham Rd.)
Hayward Gdns. SW15 —6E 90
Hayward Rd. N20 —2F 15
Haywards Clo. Chad H —5B 36
Hayward's Pl. EC1
—4B 62 (3A 144)
Haywards Yd. SE4 —5B 96
(off Lindal Rd.)
Haywood Clo. Pinn —2B 22
Haywood Lodge. N11 —6D 16
(off Oak La.)
Haywood Rd. Brom —4B 128
Hayworth Clo. Enf —2F 9
Hazel Bank. SE25 —2E 124
Hazelbank Rd. SE6 —2F 113
Hazelbourne Rd. SW12 —6F 93
Hazelbury Clo. SW19 —2J 121
Hazelbury Grn. N9 —3K 17
Hazelbury La. N9 —3K 17
Hazel Clo. N13 —3J 17
Hazel Clo. N19 —2G 45
Hazel Clo. SE15 —2G 95
Hazel Clo. Bren —7B 72
Hazel Clo. Croy —7K 125
Hazel Clo. Mitc —4H 123
Hazel Clo. Twic —7G 87
Hazel Ct. W5 —7B 56
Hazel Cres. Romf —1H 37
Hazel Croft. Pinn —6A 10
Hazeldean Rd. NW10 —7K 41
Hazeldene Dri. Pinn —3A 22
Hazeldene Rd. Ilf —2B 52
Hazeldene Rd. Well —2C 100
Hazeldon Rd. SE4 —5A 96
Hazeleigh Gdns. Wfd G —5H 21
Hazel Gdns. Edgw —4C 12
Hazelgreen Clo. N21 —1G 17
Hazel Gro. SE26 —4K 111
Hazel Gro. Romf —3E 36
Hazel Gro. Wemb —1E 56
Hazelhurst. Beck —1F 127
Hazelhurst Ct. SE6 —5E 112
(off Beckenham Hill Rd.)
Hazelhurst Rd. SW17 —4A 108
Hazel La. Rich —2E 104

Hazellville Rd. N19 —7H 29
Hazelmere Clo. N'holt —2D 54
Hazelmere Dri. N'holt —2D 54
Hazelmere Rd. NW6 —1H 59
Hazelmere Rd. N'holt —2D 54
Hazelmere Rd. Orp —4G 129
Hazelmere Wlk. N'holt —2D 54
Hazelmere Way. Brom —6J 127
Hazel Rd. E15 —5G 49
Hazel Rd. NW10 —3D 58
(in two parts)
Hazeltree La. N'holt —3C 54
Hazel Wlk. Brom —6E 128
Hazel Way. E4 —6G 19
Hazel Way. SE1 —4F 79 (3J 157)
Hazelwood Av. Mord —4K 121
Hazelwood Clo. W5 —2E 72
Hazelwood Clo. Harr —4F 23
Hazelwood Ct. N13 —4F 17
(off Hazelwood La.)
Hazelwood Ct. NW10 —3A 42
Hazelwood Ct. Surb —6E 118
Hazelwood Cres. N13 —4F 17
Hazelwood Ho. SE8 —4A 80
Hazelwood Houses. Short
—3G 127
Hazelwood La. N13 —4F 17
Hazelwood Rd. E17 —5A 32
Hazelwood Rd. Enf —6A 8
Hazlebury Rd. SW6 —2K 91
Hazledean Rd. Croy —2D 134
Hazledene Rd. W4 —6J 73
Hazlemere Ct. SW2 —1K 109
Hazlemere Gdns. Wor Pk
—1C 130
Hazlewell Rd. SW15 —5E 90
Hazlewood Clo. E5 —3A 48
Hazlewood Cres. W10 —4G 59
Hazlewood Tower. W10 —4H 59
(off Golborne Gdns.)
Hazlitt Clo. Felt —4C 102
Hazlitt M. W14 —3G 75
Hazlitt Rd. W14 —3G 75
Headbourne Ho. SE1
—3D 78 (1F 157)
Headcorn Pl. T Hth —4K 123
Headcorn Rd. N17 —7A 18
Headcorn Rd. Brom —5H 113
Headcorn Rd. T Hth —4K 123
Headfort Pl. SW1
—2E 76 (7H 147)
Headington Rd. SW18 —2A 108
Headlam Rd. SW4 —6H 93
Headlam St. E1 —4H 63
Headley App. Ilf —5F 35
Headley Av. Wall —5K 133
Headley Ct. SE26 —5J 111
Headley Dri. Ilf —6F 35
Headley Dri. New Ad —7D 136
Head's M. W11 —6J 59
Headstone Dri. Harr —3H 23
Headstone Gdns. Harr —4G 23
Headstone La. Harr —4E 22
Headstone Pde. Harr —4H 23
Headstone Rd. Harr —5J 23
Head St. E1 —6K 63
(in two parts)
Headway Clo. Rich —4C 104
Heald St. SE14 —1C 96
Healey Ho. SW9 —7A 78
Healey St. NW1 —6F 45
Hearne Rd. W4 —6G 73
Hearn Rise. N'holt —1B 54
Hearns Bldgs. SE17
—4D 78 (4F 157)

Hearn St. EC2 —4E 62 (4H 145)
Hearnville Rd. SW12 —1E 108
Heatham Pk. Twic —7K 87
Heath Av. Bexh —6D 84
Heathbourne Rd. Bush & Stan
—1D 10
Heath Brow. NW3 —3A 44
Heath Bus. Cen. Houn —4G 87
Heath Mill. N'holt —7K 27
Heath Clo. W5 —4F 57
Heathcote Av. Ilf —2D 34
Heathcote Gro. E4 —3K 19
Heathcote Rd. Twic —6B 88
Heathcote St. WC1
—4K 61 (3G 143)
Heath Ct. Houn —4D 86
Heathcroft. NW11 —1K 43
Heathcroft. W5 —4F 57
Heathdale Av. Houn —3C 86
Heathdene Dri. Belv —4H 85
Heathdene Rd. SW16 —7K 109
Heathdene Rd. Wall —7F 133
Heath Dri. NW3 —4K 43
Heath Dri. SW20 —4E 120
Heath Dri. Sutt —7A 132
Heathedge. SE26 —2H 111
Heath End Rd. Bex —1K 117
Heather Av. Romf —2K 37
Heatherbank. SE9 —2D 98
Heatherbank. Chst —2E 128
Heather Clo. E6 —6E 66
Heather Clo. SE13 —7F 97
Heather Clo. SW8 —3F 93
Heather Clo. Hamp —7D 102
Heather Clo. Iswth —5H 87
Heather Clo. Romf —1K 37
Heather Ct. Sidc —6D 116
Heatherdale Clo. King T —7G 105
Heatherdene Clo. N12 —1A 28
Heatherdene Clo. Mitc —4B 122
Heather Dri. E2 —7G 7
Heather Dri. Romf —2K 37
Heatherfield Pk. Dri. Romf
—5B 36
Heather Gdns. NW11 —6G 27
Heather Gdns. Romf —2K 37
Heather Gdns. Sutt —6J 131
Heather Glen. Romf —2K 37
Heatherley Ct. N16 —3G 47
Heatherley Dri. Ilf —3C 34
Heather Pk. Dri. Wemb —7G 41
Heather Rd. E4 —6G 19
Heather Rd. NW2 —2B 42
Heather Rd. SE12 —1J 113
Heatherset Gdns. SW16 —7K 109
Heatherside Rd. Eps —7A 130
Heatherside Rd. Sidc —3D 116
Heatherton Ter. N3 —2K 27
Heather Wlk. W10 —4G 59
Heather Wlk. Edgw —5C 12
Heather Wlk. Twic —7E 86
(off Stephenson Rd.)
Heather Way. Romf —2K 37
Heather Way. S Croy —7K 135
Heather Way. Stan —6E 10
Heatherwood Clo. E12 —2A 50
Heathfield. E4 —3K 19
Heathfield. Chst —6G 115
Heathfield Av. SW18 —7B 92
Heathfield Clo. E16 —5B 66
Heathfield Clo. Kes —5A 138
Heathfield Ct. SE20 —7J 111
Heathfield Ct. W4 —5K 73
Heathfield Dri. Mitc —1C 122

Heathfield Gdns. NW11 —6F 27
Heathfield Gdns. SW18 —6B 92
Heathfield Gdns. W4 —5J 73
Heathfield Gdns. Croy —4D 134
Heathfield Ho. SE3 —2G 97
Heathfield La. Chst —6F 115
Heathfield N. Twic —7J 87
Heathfield Pk. NW2 —6E 42
Heathfield Rd. SW18 —6A 92
Heathfield Rd. W3 —2H 73
Heathfield Rd. Bexh —4F 101
Heathfield Rd. Brom —7H 113
Heathfield Rd. Croy —4D 134
Heathfield Rd. Kes —5A 138
Heathfields Ct. Houn —5C 86
Heathfield S. Twic —7K 87
Heathfield Sq. SW18 —7B 92
Heathfield St. W11 —7G 59
(off Portland Rd.)
Heathfield Ter. SE18 —6J 83
Heathfield Ter. W4 —5J 73
Heathfield Vale. S Croy —7K 135
Heath Gdns. Twic —1K 103
Heathgate. NW11 —6K 27
Heathgate Pl. NW3 —5D 44
Heath Gro. SE20 —7J 111
Heath Ho. Sidc —4K 115
Heath Hurst Rd. NW3 —4C 44
Heathhurst Rd. S Croy —7E 134
Heathland Rd. N16 —1E 46
Heathlands Clo. Twic —2K 103
Heathlands Way. Houn —5C 86
Heath La. SE3 —2F 97
Heathlee Rd. SE3 —4H 97
Heathley End. Chst —6G 115
Heath Lodge. Bush —1D 10
Heathmans Rd. SW6 —1H 91
Heath Mead. SW19 —3F 107
Heath Pk. Dri. Brom —3C 128
Heath Pas. NW3 —1A 44
Heathpool Ct. E1 —4H 63
Heath Rise. SW15 —6F 91
Heath Rise. Brom —6H 127
Heath Rd. SW8 —2F 93
Heath Rd. Bex —1J 117
Heath Rd. Harr —7G 23
Heath Rd. Houn —4F 87
Heath Rd. Romf —7D 36
Heath Rd. T Hth —3C 124
Heath Rd. Twic —1K 103
Heaths Clo. Enf —2K 7
Heath Side. NW3 —4B 44
Heathside. NW11 —1J 43
Heathside. SE13 —2E 96
Heathside. Houn —7D 86
Heathside. Orp —7H 129
Heathside Av. Bexh —2E 100
Heathstan Rd. W12 —6C 58
Heath St. NW3 —3A 44
Heath, The. W7 —1J 71
Heath View. N2 —4A 28
Heathview Dri. SE2 —6D 84
Heathview Gdns. SW15 —7E 90
Heathview Rd. T Hth —4A 124
Heath Vs. NW3 —3B 44
Heath Vs. SE18 —5K 83
Heathville Rd. N19 —7J 29
Heathwall St. SW11 —3D 92
Heathway. SE3 —7J 81
Heathway. Croy —2B 136
Heathway. Dag —3F 53
Heath Way. Eri —1J 101
Heathway. S'hall —4B 70

Heath Way. Wfd G —5F 21
Heathway. (Junct.) —1G 69
Heathway Ct. NW3 —2J 43
Heathway Ind. Est. Dag —4H 53
Heathwood Gdns. SE7 —4C 82
Heathwood Point. SE23 —3K 111
Heathwood Wlk. Bex —1K 117
Heaton Clo. E4 —3K 19
Heaton Rd. SE15 —2H 95
Heaton Rd. Mitc —7E 108
Heaver Rd. SW11 —3B 92
Heavitree Clo. SE18 —5H 83
Heavitree Rd. SE18 —5H 83
Hebden Ct. E2 —1F 63
Hebden Ter. N17 —6K 17
—3C 62 (3D 144)
Heber Mans. W14 —6G 75
(off Queen's Club Gdns.)
Heber Rd. NW2 —5F 43
Heber Rd. SE22 —6F 95
Hebron Rd. W6 —3E 74
Hecham Clo. E17 —2A 32
Heckfield Pl. SW6 —7J 75
Heckford St. E1 —7K 63
Heckford St. Bus. Cen. E1
(off Heckford St.) —7K 63
Hector. NW9 —1B 26
(off Five Acre)
Hector Peterson Ho. Wemb
(off Wilson Dri.) —7F 25
Hector St. SE18 —4J 83
Heddington Gro. N7 —5K 45
Heddon Clo. Iswth —4A 88
Heddon Ct. Av. Barn —5J 5
Heddon Ct. Pde. Barn —5K 5
Heddon Rd. Cockf —5J 5
Heddon St. W1 —7G 61 (2A 148)
Hedge Hill. Enf —1G 7
Hedge La. N13 —3G 17
Hedgemans Rd. Dag —7D 52
Hedgemans Way. Dag —6E 52
Hedgerley Gdns. Gnfd —2G 55
Hedgers Gro. E9 —6A 48
Hedger St. SE11
—4B 78 (3A 156)
Hedge Wlk. SE6 —5D 112
Hedgewood Gdns. Ilf —5E 34
Hedgley. Ilf —4D 34
Hedgley M. SE12 —5H 97
Hedgley St. SE12 —5H 97
Hedingham Clo. N1 —7C 46
Hedingham Rd. Dag —5B 52
Hedley Rd. Twic —7E 86
Hedley Row. N5 —5D 46
Heenan Clo. Bark —6G 51
Heene Rd. Enf —1J 7
Heidegger Cres. SW13 —7D 74
Heigham Rd. E6 —7B 50
Heighton Gdns. Croy —5B 134
Heights Clo. SW20 —7D 106
Heights, The. SE7 —5B 82
Heights, The. Beck —7E 112
Heiron St. SE17 —6B 78 (7B 156)
Helby Rd. SW4 —6H 93
Heldar Ct. SE1 —2D 78 (7F 151)
Helder Gro. SE12 —7H 97
Helder St. S Croy —6D 134
Heldmann Clo. Houn —4H 87
Helena Clo. Wall —7K 133
Helena Ct. W5 —5D 56
Helena Pl. E9 —1H 63
Helena Rd. E13 —2H 65
Helena Rd. E17 —5C 32
Helena Rd. NW10 —5D 42

Helena Rd. W5 —5D 56
Helena Sq. SE16 —7A 64
(off Sovereign Cres.)
Helen Clo. N2 —3A 28
Helenslea Av. NW11 —1J 43
Helen's Pl. E2 —3J 63
Helen St. SE18 —4F 83
Helen Way. N13 —5A 56
Heliport Ind. Est. SW11 —2B 92
Helix Gdns. SW2 —6K 93
Helix Rd. SW2 —6K 93
Hellings St. E1 —1G 79
Helme Clo. SW19 —5H 107
Helmet Row. EC1
—3C 62 (3D 144)
Helmsdale Clo. Hayes —4C 54
Helmsdale Rd. SW16 —1H 123
Helmsley Pl. E8 —7H 47
Helmsley St. E8 —7H 47
Helsinki Sq. SE16 —3A 80
Helston Clo. Pinn —1D 22
Helston Ct. N15 —5E 30
(off Culvert Rd.)
Helvetia St. SE6 —2B 112
Hemans St. SW8 —7H 77
Hemans St. Est. SW8 —7H 77
Hemberton Rd. SW9 —3J 93
Hemery Rd. Gnfd —5H 39
Hemes Clo. W9 —4J 59
Hemingford Clo. N12 —5G 15
Hemingford Rd. N1 —1K 61
Hemingford Rd. Sutt —4E 130
Heming Rd. Edgw —7C 12
Hemington Av. N11 —5J 15
Hemlock Rd. W12 —7B 58
Hemming Clo. Hamp —7E 102
Hemmings Clo. Sidc —2B 116
Hemming St. E1 —4G 63
Hempstead Clo. Buck H —2D 20
Hempstead Rd. E17 —2F 33
Hemp Wlk. SE17
—4D 78 (3F 157)
Hemstal Rd. NW6 —7J 43
Hemsted Rd. Eri —7K 85
Hemswell Dri. NW9 —1A 26
Hemsworth Ct. N1 —2E 62
Hemsworth St. N1 —2E 62
Hemus Pl. SW3 —5C 76 (6D 152)
Henchman St. W12 —6B 58
Hendale Av. NW4 —3C 26
Henderson Clo. NW10 —6J 41
Henderson Dri. NW8
—4B 60 (3A 140)
Henderson Ho. Dag —3G 53
(off Kershaw Rd.)
Henderson Rd. E7 —6A 50
Henderson Rd. N9 —1C 18
Henderson Rd. SW18 —7C 92
Henderson Rd. Croy —6D 124
Hendham Rd. SW17 —2C 108
Hendon Av. N3 —1G 27
Hendon Hall Ct. NW4 —3F 27
Hendon Ho. NW4 —5F 27
Hendon La. N3 —3G 27
Hendon Lodge. NW4 —3D 26
Hendon Pk. Mans. NW4 —5E 26
Hendon Pk. Row. NW11 —6H 27
Hendon Rd. N9 —2B 18
Hendon Way. NW4 & NW2
—6D 26
Hendon Wood La. NW7 —1G 13
Hendre Clo. Gnfd —5H 39
Hendre Rd. SE1 —4E 78 (4H 157)
Hendrick Av. SW12 —7D 92
Hendy Ct. Enf —3J 7

Heneage La. EC3
—6E 62 (1H 151)
Heneage Pl. EC3
—6E 62 (1H 151)
Heneage St. E1 —5F 63 (5K 145)
Henfield Clo. N19 —1G 45
Henfield Clo. Bex —6G 101
Henfield Rd. SW19 —1H 121
Hengelo Gdns. Mitc —4B 122
Hengist Rd. SE12 —7K 97
Hengist Rd. Eri —7H 85
Hengist Way. Brom —4G 127
Hengrave Rd. SE23 —7J 95
Hengrove Ct. Bex —1E 116
Henham Ct. Romf —2J 37
Henley Av. Sutt —3G 131
Henley Clo. Gnfd —2G 55
Henley Clo. Iswth —1K 87
Henley Ct. N14 —7B 6
Henley Dri. SE1 —4F 79 (3K 157)
Henley Dri. King T —7B 106
Henley Gdns. Romf —5E 36
Henley Rd. E16 —2D 82
Henley Rd. N18 —4K 17
Henley Rd. NW10 —1E 58
Henley Rd. Ilf —4G 51
Henley St. SW11 —2E 92
Henley Way. Felt —5B 102
Henlow Pl. Rich —2D 104
Henlys Corner. (Junct.) —4H 27
Henlys Roundabout. (Junct.)
—2B 86
Hennel Clo. SE23 —3J 111
Henniker Gdns. E6 —3B 66
Henniker M. SW3
—6B 76 (7A 152)
Henniker Rd. E15 —5F 49
Henningham Rd. N17 —1D 30
Henning St. SW11 —1C 92
Henrietta Ho. N15 —6E 30
(off St Ann's Rd.)
Henrietta Ho. W6 —5E 74
(off Queen Caroline St.)
Henrietta M. WC1
—4J 61 (3F 143)
Henrietta Pl. W1 —6F 61 (1J 147)
Henrietta St. E15 —5E 48
Henrietta St. WC2
—7J 61 (2F 149)
Henriques St. E1 —6G 63
Henry Clo. Enf —1K 7
Henry Cooper Way. SE9 —3B 114
Henry Darlot Dri. NW7 —5A 14
Henry Dickens Ct. W11 —7F 59
Henry Hatch Wlk. Sutt —7A 132
Henry Ho. SW8 —7J 77
(off Wyvil Rd.)
Henry Jackson Rd. SW15 —3F 91
Henry Rd. E6 —2C 66
Henry Rd. N4 —1C 46
Henry Rd. Barn —5G 5
Henrys Av. Wfd G —5C 20
Henryson Rd. SE4 —5C 96
Henry St. Brom —1K 127
Henry's Wlk. Ilf —1H 35
Hensford Gdns. SE26 —4H 111
Henshall St. N1 —6D 46
Henshawe Rd. Dag —3D 52
Henshaw St. SE17
—4D 78 (3E 156)
Henslowe Rd. SE22 —5G 95
Henson Av. NW2 —5E 42
Henson Path. Harr —3D 24
Henson Pl. N'holt —1A 54
Henstridge Pl. NW8 —2C 60

Henty Clo. SW11 —7C 76
Henty Wlk. SW15 —5D 90
Henville Rd. Brom —1K 127
Henwick Rd. SE9 —3B 98
Henwood Rd. SE16 —3J 79
Henwood Side. Wfd G —6J 21
Hepburn Gdns. Brom —1G 137
Hepburn M. SW11 —5D 92
Hepple Clo. Iswth —2B 88
Hepplestone Clo. SW15 —6D 90
Hepscott Rd. E9 —6C 48
Hepworth Ct. NW3 —5C 44
Hepworth Gdns. Bark —4A 52
Hepworth Rd. SW16 —7J 109
Heracles. NW9 —1B 26
(off Five Acre)
Heracles Clo. Wall —7J 133
Herald Gdns. Wall —2F 133
Herald's Pl. SE11
—4B 78 (3A 156)
Herald St. E2 —4H 63
Herbal Hill. EC1 —4A 62 (4K 143)
Herbal Hill Gdns. EC1
—4A 62 (4K 143)
Herbal Pl. EC1 —4A 62 (4K 143)
Herbert Cres. SW1
—3D 76 (1F 153)
Herbert Gdns. NW10 —2D 58
Herbert Gdns. W4 —6H 73
Herbert Gdns. Romf —7D 36
Herbert Morrison Ho. SW6
(off Clem Attlee Ct.) —6H 75
Herbert Pl. SE18 —6F 83
Herbert Rd. E12 —4C 50
Herbert Rd. E17 —7B 32
Herbert Rd. N11 —7D 16
Herbert Rd. N15 —5F 31
Herbert Rd. NW9 —6C 26
Herbert Rd. SE18 —7E 82
Herbert Rd. SW19 —7H 107
(in two parts)
Herbert Rd. Bexh —2E 100
Herbert Rd. Brom —5B 128
Herbert Rd. Ilf —2J 51
Herbert Rd. King T —3F 119
Herbert Rd. S'hall —1D 70
Herbert St. E13 —2J 65
Herbert St. NW5 —6E 44
Herbert Ter. SE18 —7F 83
Herbrand Est. WC1
—4J 61 (3E 142)
Herbrand St. WC1
—4J 61 (3E 142)
Hercules Pl. N7 —3J 45
Hercules Rd. SE1
—3K 77 (2H 155)
Hercules St. N7 —3J 45
Hercules Tower. SE14 —6A 80
Hercules Yd. N7 —3J 45
Hereford Av. Barn —1J 15
Hereford Ct. W7 —5K 55
(off Copley Clo.)
Hereford Ct. Harr —3J 23
Hereford Ct. Sutt —7J 131
Hereford Gdns. SE13 —5G 97
Hereford Gdns. Ilf —7C 34
Hereford Gdns. Pinn —5C 22
Hereford Gdns. Twic —1G 103
Hereford M. W2 —6J 59
Hereford Pl. SE14 —7B 80
Hereford Retreat. SE15 —7G 79
Hereford Rd. E11 —5K 33
Hereford Rd. W2 —6J 59
Hereford Rd. W3 —7H 57

Hereford Rd. W5 —3C 72
Hereford Rd. Felt —1A 102
Hereford Sq. SW7 —4A 76
Hereford St. E2 —4G 63
Herent Dri. Ilf —4C 34
Hereward Gdns. N13 —5F 17
Hereward Rd. SW17 —4D 108
Herga Ct. Harr —3J 39
Herga Rd. Harr —4K 23
Heriot Av. E4 —2H 19
Heriot Rd. NW4 —5E 26
Heriots Clo. Stan —4F 11
Heritage Clo. SW9 —3B 94
Heritage Hill. Kes —5A 138
Heritage View. Harr —3K 39
Herlwyn Gdns. SW17 —4D 108
Herm Clo. Iswth —7G 71
Hermes Clo. W9 —4J 59
Hermes St. N1 —2A 62 (1J 143)
Hermes Wlk. N'holt —2E 54
Hermes Way. Wall —7H 133
Herm Ho. N1 —6C 46
Herm Ho. Enf —1E 8
Hermiston Av. N8 —5J 29
Hermitage Clo. E18 —4H 33
Hermitage Clo. Enf —2G 7
Hermitage Clo. SW14 —5K 89
Hermitage Ct. E18 —4J 33
Hermitage Ct. NW2 —3J 43
Hermitage Gdns. NW2 —3J 43
Hermitage Gdns. SE19 —7C 110
Hermitage Grn. SW16 —1J 123
Hermitage La. N18 —5J 17
Hermitage La. NW2 —3J 43
Hermitage La. SE25 —6G 125
(in two parts)
Hermitage La. SW16 —7K 109
Hermitage La. Croy & SE25
—7G 125
Hermitage Path. SW16 —1J 123
Hermitage Rd. N4 & N15 —7C 30
Hermitage Rd. SE19 —7C 110
Hermitage Row. E8 —5G 47
Hermitage St. W2
—5B 60 (6A 140)
Hermitage, The. SE13 —2E 96
Hermitage, The. SE23 —1J 111
Hermitage, The. SW13 —1B 90
Hermitage, The. King T —4D 118
Hermitage, The. Rich —5E 88
Hermitage Wlk. E18 —4H 33
Hermitage Wall. E1 —1G 79
Hermitage Way. Stan —1A 24
Hermit Pl. NW6 —1K 59
Hermit Rd. E16 —5H 65
Hermit St. EC1 —3B 62 (1A 144)
Hermon Hill. E11 & E18 —5J 33
Herndon Rd. SW18 —5A 92
Herne Clo. NW10 —5K 41
Herne Ct. Bush —1B 10
Herne Hill. SE24 —6C 94
Herne Hill Ho. SE24 —6B 94
(off Railton Rd.)
Herne Hill Rd. SE24 —3C 94
Herne M. N18 —4B 18
Herne Pl. SE24 —5B 94
Heron Clo. E17 —2B 32
Heron Clo. NW10 —6A 42
Heron Clo. Buck H —1D 20
Heron Ct. Brom —4A 128
Heron Cres. Sidc —3J 115
Herondale Av. SW18 —1B 108
Herongate Clo. Enf —2A 8
Herongate Rd. E12 —2A 50
Heron Hill. Belv —5F 85
Heron Ho. E6 —7C 50

Heron Ho. W13 —4A 56
Heron Ho. Sidc —3B 116
Heron Ind. Est. E15 —1D 64
Heron M. Ilf —2F 51
Heron Pk. Pde. SW19 —1H 121
Heron Quay. E14 —1C 80
Heron Quays Development. E14
—1D 80
Heron Rd. SE24 —4C 94
Heron Rd. Croy —2E 134
Heron Rd. Twic —4A 88
Heronsforde. W13 —6C 56
Herons Ga. Edgw —5B 12
Heron's Lea. N6 —6D 28
Heronslea Dri. Stan —5K 11
Heron's Pl. Iswth —3B 88
Heron Sq. Rich —5D 88
Herons Rise. New Bar —4H 5
Herons, The. E11 —6H 33
Heron Trad. Est. W3 —5H 57
Heron Way. Wfd G —4F 21
Herrick Rd. N5 —3C 46
Herrick St. SW1
—4H 77 (4D 154)
Herries St. W10 —3G 59
Herringham Rd. SE7 —3A 82
Herring St. SE5 —6E 78 (7H 157)
Herron Ct. Short —4H 127
Hersant Clo. NW10 —1C 58
Herschell M. SE5 —3C 94
Herschell Rd. SE23 —7A 96
Hersham Clo. SW15 —7C 90
Hertford Av. SW14 —5K 89
Hertford Clo. Barn —3D 4
Hertford Ct. E6 —3D 66
(off Vicarage La.)
Hertford Ct. N13 —3F 17
Hertford Pl. W1 —4G 61 (4B 142)
Hertford Rd. N1 —1E 62
Hertford Rd. N2 —3C 28
Hertford Rd. N9 —2C 18
Hertford Rd. Bark —7E 50
Hertford Rd. Barn —3F 5
Hertford Rd. Enf & Wal X —1C 18
Hertford Rd. Ilf —6J 35
Hertford Sq. Mitc —4J 123
Hertford St. W1 —1E 77 (5J 147)
Hertford Wlk. Belv —5G 85
Hertford Way. Mitc —4J 123
Hertslet Rd. N7 —3K 45
Hertsmere Rd. E14 —1C 80
Hervey Clo. N3 —1J 27
Hervey Pk. Rd. E17 —4A 32
Hervey Rd. SE3 —1K 97
Hervey Way. N3 —1J 27
Hesewall Clo. SW4 —2G 93
Hesketh Pl. W11 —7G 59
Hesketh Rd. E7 —3J 49
Heslop Rd. SW12 —1D 108
Hesper M. SW5 —4K 75
Hesperus Cres. E14 —4D 80
Hessel Rd. W13 —2A 72
Hessel St. E1 —6H 63
Hestercombe Av. SW6 —2G 91
Hesterman Way. Croy —1K 133
Hester Rd. N18 —5B 18
Hester Rd. SW11 —7C 76
Hester Ter. Rich —3G 89
Heston Av. Houn —6C 70
Heston Cen., The. Houn —5A 70
Heston Grange. Houn —6D 70
Heston Grange La. Houn —6D 70

Heston Ho. SE8 —1C 96
Heston Ind. Cen. Houn —6A 70
Heston Ind. Mall. Houn —7D 70
Heston Rd. Houn —7E 70
Heston St. SE14 —1C 96
Hetherington Rd. SW4 —4J 93
Hetley Gdns. SE19 —7F 111
Hetley Rd. W12 —1D 74
Hetley Ho. W12 —2D 74
(off Hetley Rd.)
Hetley Rd. W12 —1D 74
Heton Gdns. NW4 —4D 26
Hevelius Clo. SE10 —5H 81
Hever Croft. SE9 —4E 114
Hever Gdns. Brom —2E 128
Heverham Rd. SE18 —4J 83
Heversham Rd. Bexh —2G 101
Hewer St. W10 —5F 59
Hewett Clo. Stan —4G 11
Hewett Rd. Dag —4D 52
Hewett St. EC2 —4E 62 (4H 145)
Hewish Rd. N18 —4K 17
Hewison St. E3 —2B 64
Hewitt Av. N22 —2B 30
Hewitt Clo. Croy —3C 136
Hewitt Rd. N8 —5A 30
Hewlett Rd. E3 —2A 64
Hexagon, The. N6 —1D 44
Hexal Rd. SE6 —3G 113
Hexham Gdns. Iswth —7A 72
Hexham Rd. SE27 —2C 110
Hexham Rd. Barn —4E 4
Hexham Rd. Mord —1K 131
Heybourne Rd. N17 —7C 18
Heybridge Av. SW16 —7J 109
Heybridge Dri. Ilf —2H 35
Heybridge Way. E10 —7A 32
Heydon Ho. SE14 —1J 95
(off Kender St.)
Heyford Av. SW8 —7J 77
Heyford Av. SW20 —3H 121
Heyford Rd. Mitc —2C 122
Heyford Ter. SW8 —7J 77
Heygate St. SE17
—4C 78 (4C 156)
Heylyn Sq. E3 —3B 64
Heynes Rd. Dag —4C 52
Heysham La. NW3 —3K 43
Heysham Rd. N15 —6D 30
Heythorp St. SW18 —1H 107
Heywood Av. NW9 —1A 26
Heywood Ct. Stan —5H 11
Heyworth Rd. E5 —4H 47
Heyworth Rd. E15 —4H 49
Hibbert Rd. E17 —7B 32
Hibbert Rd. Harr —2K 23
Hibbert St. SW11 —3B 92
Hibernia Gdns. Houn —4E 86
Hibernia Point. SE2 —2D 84
(off Wolvercote Rd.)
Hibernia Rd. Houn —4E 86
Hichisson Rd. SE15 —5J 95
Hickey's Almshouses. Rich
—4F 89
Hickin Clo. SE7 —4B 82
Hickin St. E14 —3E 80
Hickling Rd. Ilf —5F 51
Hickman Av. E4 —6K 19
Hickman Clo. E16 —5B 66
Hickman Rd. Romf —7C 36
Hickmore Wlk. SW4 —3H 93
Hickory Clo. N9 —1B 18
Hicks Av. Gnfd —3H 55
Hicks Clo. SW11 —3C 92
Hicks Ct. Dag —3H 53
Hicks St. SE8 —5A 80

Hidcote Gdns. SW20 —3D 120
Hide. E6 —6E 66
Hide Pl. SW1 —4H 77 (4C 154)
Hide Rd. Harr —4G 23
Hides St. N7 —6K 45
Higgs Ind. Est. SE24 —3B 94
High Acres. Enf —3G 7
Higham Hill Rd. E17 —1A 32
Higham Pk. Ind. Est. E4 —6K 19
Higham Path. E17 —3A 32
Higham Pl. E17 —3A 32
Higham Rd. N17 —3D 30
Higham Rd. Wfd G —6D 20
Highams Ct. E4 —3A 20
Highams Lodge Bus. Cen. E17
　　　　　—3K 31
Higham Sta. Av. E4 —6H 19
Highams, The. E17 —1E 32
Higham St. E17 —3A 32
Highbanks Clo. Well —7B 84
Highbanks Rd. Pinn —6A 10
Highbank Way. N8 —4A 30
Higharrow Rd. Croy —1G 135
High Beech. N21 —6E 6
High Beech. S Croy —7E 134
High Beeches. Sidc —5E 116
High Birch Ct. New Bar —4H 5
(off Park Rd.)
High Bri. SE10 —5F 81
Highbridge Rd. Bark —1F 67
Highbrook Rd. SE3 —3B 98
High Broom Cres. W Wick
　　　　　—7D 126
Highbury Av. T Hth —2A 124
Highbury Barn. N5 —4B 46
Highbury Clo. N Mald —4J 119
Highbury Clo. W Wick —2D 136
Highbury Corner. (Junct.)
　　　　　—6B 46
Highbury Cres. N5 —5B 46
Highbury Est. N5 —5C 46
Highbury Gdns. Ilf —2J 51
Highbury Grange. N5 —4C 46
Highbury Gro. N5 —5B 46
Highbury Hill. N5 —3A 46
Highbury M. N7 —6A 46
Highbury New Pk. N5 —5C 46
Highbury Pk. N5 —3B 46
Highbury Pk. M. N5 —4C 46
Highbury Pl. N5 —6B 46
Highbury Quad. N5 —3C 46
Highbury Rd. SW19 —5G 107
Highbury Sta. Rd. N1 —6A 46
Highbury Ter. N5 —5B 46
Highbury Ter. M. N5 —5B 46
High Cedar Dri. SW20 —7E 106
Highclere Rd. N Mald —3A 119
Highclere St. SE26 —4A 112
Highcliffe. W13 —5B 56
(off Clivedon Ct.)
Highcliffe Dri. SW15 —6B 90
Highcliffe Gdns. Ilf —5C 34
Highcombe. SE7 —6K 81
Highcombe Clo. SE9 —1B 114
High Coombe Pl. King T —7K 105
High Croft. NW9 —5A 26
Highcroft Av. Wemb —7G 41
Highcroft Est. N19 —7J 29
Highcroft Gdns. NW11 —6H 27
Highcroft Rd. N19 —7J 29
High Cross Cen., The. N15
　　　　　—4G 31
High Cross Rd. N17 —3G 31
Highcross Way. SW15 —1C 106
Highdaun Dri. SW16 —4K 123

Highdown. Wor Pk —2A 130
Highdown Rd. SW15 —6D 90
High Dri. N Mald —1J 119
High Elms. Wfd G —5D 20
Highfield Av. NW9 —5J 25
Highfield Av. NW11 —7F 27
Highfield Av. Eri —6H 85
Highfield Av. Gnfd —5J 39
Highfield Av. Pinn —5D 22
Highfield Av. Wemb —3F 41
Highfield Clo. N22 —1A 30
Highfield Clo. NW9 —5J 25
Highfield Clo. Surb —7C 118
Highfield Ct. N14 —6B 6
Highfield Ct. NW11 —6G 27
Highfield Dri. Brom —4G 127
Highfield Dri. Eps —6B 130
Highfield Dri. W Wick —2D 136
Highfield Gdns. NW11 —6G 27
Highfield Hill. SE19 —7D 110
Highfield Rd. N21 —2G 17
Highfield Rd. NW11 —6G 27
Highfield Rd. W3 —5H 57
Highfield Rd. Bexh —5F 101
Highfield Rd. Brom —4D 128
Highfield Rd. Chst —3K 129
Highfield Rd. Iswth —1K 87
Highfield Rd. Surb —7J 119
Highfield Rd. Sutt —5C 132
Highfield Rd. Wfd G —7H 21
Highfields. Sutt —2J 131
Highfields Gro. N6 —1D 44
High Gables. Brom —2G 127
Highgate Av. N6 —7F 29
Highgate Clo. N6 —7E 28
Highgate Edge. N2 —5C 28
Highgate Heights. N6 —6G 29
Highgate High St. N6 —1E 44
Highgate Ho. N6 & N19 —1F 45
Highgate Ho. SE26 —3G 111
Highgate Rd. NW5 —3E 44
Highgate Spinney. N8 —6H 29
Highgate Wlk. SE23 —2J 111
Highgate W. Hill. N6 —2E 44
High Gro. SE18 —7H 83
High Gro. Brom —1B 128
Highgrove Clo. N11 —5K 15
Highgrove Clo. Chst —1C 128
Highgrove Ct. Beck —7C 112
Highgrove Ct. Sutt —6J 131
Highgrove M. Cars —3D 132
Highgrove Rd. Dag —5C 52
High Hill Est. E5 —1H 47
High Hill Ferry. E5 —1H 47
High Holborn. WC1
　　　　　—6J 61 (7E 142)
Highland Av. W7 —6J 55
Highland Av. Dag —3J 53
Highland Cotts. Wall —4G 133
Highland Ct. E18 —1K 33
Highland Croft. Beck —5D 112
Highland Dri. Bush —1A 10
Highland Rd. SE19 —6E 110
Highland Rd. Bexh —5G 101
Highland Rd. Brom —1H 127
Highlands. N20 —2H 15
Highlands Av. W3 —7J 57
Highlands Clo. N4 —7J 29
Highlands Clo. Houn —1F 87
Highlands Ct. SE19 —6E 110
Highlands Gdns. Ilf —1D 50
Highlands Heath. SW15 —7E 90
Highlands Rd. Barn —5D 4
Highlands, The. Edgw —2H 25
High La. W7 —5H 55

Highlea Clo. NW9 —7F 13
High Level Dri. SE26 —4G 111
Highlever Rd. W10 —5E 58
Highmead. N18 —5B 18
(off Alpha Rd.)
Highmead. SE18 —7J 83
High Mead. Harr —5J 23
High Mead. W Wick —2F 137
Highmead Cres. Wemb —7F 41
High Meadow Clo. Pinn —4A 22
High Meadow Cres. NW9 —5K 25
High Meads Rd. E16 —6B 66
Highmore Rd. SE3 —7G 81
High Mt. NW4 —6C 26
High Oaks. Enf —1E 6
High Pde., The. SW16 —3J 109
High Pk. Av. Rich —1G 89
High Pk. Rd. Rich —1G 89
High Path. SW19 —1K 121
Highpoint. N6 —7E 28
High Point. SE9 —3F 115
High Ridge Pl. Enf —1E 6
High Ridges. N10 —1F 29
High Rd. E18 —1J 33
High Rd. N11 —5A 16
High Rd. N15 & N17 —5F 31
High Rd. N22 —1K 29
High Rd. NW10 —6A 42
High Rd. Buck H & Lou —2E 20
High Rd. Bush —1C 10
High Rd. Chig —5K 21
High Rd. Eastc —4A 22
High Rd. Harr —7D 10
High Rd. Ilf & Romf —3F 51
(in five parts)
High Rd. Wemb —5D 40
High Rd. Wfd G —6C 20
High Rd. E. Finchley. N2 —1B 28
High Rd. Leyton. E10 & E15
　　　　　—6D 32
High Rd. Leytonstone. E11 & E15
　　　　　—4G 49
High Rd. N. Finchley. N12 —3F 15
High Rd. Whetstone. N20 —7F 5
High Sheldon. N6 —5D 28
Highshore Rd. SE15 —2G 95
Highstead Cres. Eri —1K 101
Highstone Av. E11 —6J 33
Highstone Ct. E11 —6H 33
(off New Wanstead)
High St. Acton. W3 —1H 73
High St. Barkingside. B'side
　　　　　—3G 35
High St. Barnet. Barn —3B 4
High St. Beckenham. Beck
　　　　　—2C 126
High St. Brentford. Bren —7C 72
High St. Bromley. Brom —2J 127
High St. Carshalton. Cars
　　　　　—4E 132
High St. Cheam. Cheam
　　　　　—6G 131
High St. Chislehurst. Chst
　　　　　—6F 115
High St. Colliers Wood. SW19
　　　　　—7B 108
High St. Cranford. Cran —6A 70
High St. Croydon. Croy —3C 134
High St. Ealing. W5 —1D 72
High St. Edgware. Edgw —6B 12
High St. Ewell. Ewe —7B 130
High St. Hampton. Hamp
　　　　　—7G 103
High St. Hampton Wick. Hamp W
　　　　　—1C 118

High St. Hampton Hill. Hamp H
　　　　　—6G 103
High St. Harlesden. NW10
　　　　　—2B 58
High St. Harrow. Harr —1J 39
High St. Hornsey. N8 —4J 29
High St. Hounslow. Houn —3F 87
High St. Kingston upon Thames,
　　　　　King T —3D 118
High St. M. SW19 —5G 107
High St. Mill Hill. NW7 —5J 13
High St. New Malden, N Mald
　　　　　—4A 120
High St. N. E12 & E6 —5C 50
High St. Orpington. Orp —7K 129
High St. Penge. SE20 —6J 111
High St. Pinner. Pinn —3C 22
High St. Plaistow, E13 —2J 65
High St. Ponders End. Enf —5D 8
High St. Romford. Romf —5K 37
High S. E6 —2D 66
High St. Southall. S'hall —1D 70
High St. Southgate, N14 —1C 16
High St. South Norwood, SE25
　　　　　—4F 125
High St. Stratford, E15 —2E 64
High St. Sutton, Sutt —4K 131
High St. Teddington, Tedd
　　　　　—5K 103
High St. Thames Ditton, Th Dit
　　　　　—6A 118
High St. Thornton Heath, T Hth
　　　　　—4C 124
High St. Walthamstow, E17
　　　　　—5A 32
High St. Wanstead, E11 —5J 33
High St. Wealdstone, W'stone
　　　　　—2J 23
High St. Wembley, Wemb —4F 41
High St. West Wickham, W Wick
　　　　　—1D 136
High St. Whitton, Whit —7G 87
High St. Wimbledon, SW19
　　　　　—5F 107
High Timber St. EC4
　　　　　—7C 62 (2C 150)
High Tor Clo. Brom —7K 113
High Trees. N20 —3F 15
High Trees. SW2 —1A 110
High Trees. Barn —5H 5
High Trees. Croy —1A 136
Hightrees Ct. W7 —7J 55
Highview. N6 —6G 29
Highview. NW7 —3E 12
Highview. N'holt —3C 54
High View. Pinn —4A 22
Highview Av. Edgw —4D 12
Highview Av. Wall —5K 133
High View Clo. SE19 —2F 125
High View Ct. Har W —7D 10
Highview Gdns. N3 —3G 27
Highview Gdns. N11 —5B 16
Highview Gdns. Edgw —4D 12
Highview Ho. Romf —4E 36
High View Rd. E18 —2H 33
High View Rd. N2 —1D 28
Highview Rd. SE19 —6D 110
Highview Rd. W13 —5A 56
High View Rd. Sidc —4B 116
Highway, The. E1 & E14 —7J 63
Highway, The. Stan —7F 11
Highway, The. Sutt —7A 132
Highway Trad. Cen., The. E1
(off Heckford St.)　—7K 63
Highwood. Short —3G 127

Highwood Av. N12 —4F 15
Highwood Ct. N12 —3F 15
Highwood Gdns. Ilf —5D 34
Highwood Gro. NW7 —5E 12
Highwood Hill. NW7 —2G 13
Highwood Rd. N19 —3J 45
High Worple. Harr —7D 22
Highworth Rd. N11 —6C 16
Hilary Av. Mitc —3E 122
Hilary Clo. E11 —5J 33
Hilary Clo. SW6 —7K 75
Hilary Clo. Eri —1H 101
Hilary Rd. W12 —7B 58
Hilbert Rd. Sutt —3F 131
Hilborough Ct. E8 —1F 63
Hilda Clo. Surb —7D 118
Hilda Rd. E6 —7B 50
Hilda Rd. E16 —4G 65
Hilda Ter. SW9 —2A 94
Hilda Vale Rd. Orp —4E 138
Hildenborough Gdns. Brom
　　　　　—6G 113
Hildenborough Ho. Beck —7B 112
(off Bethersden Clo.)
Hildenlea Pl. Brom —2G 127
Hildreth St. SW12 —1F 109
Hildyard Rd. SW6 —6J 75
Hiley Rd. NW10 —3E 58
Hilgrove Rd. NW6 —7A 44
Hiliary Gdns. Stan —2C 24
Hillary Rise. Barn —4D 4
Hillary Rd. S'hall —3E 70
Hillbeck Clo. SE15 —7J 79
Hillbeck Way. Gnfd —1H 55
Hillboro Ct. E11 —7F 33
Hillborough Clo. SW19 —7A 108
Hillbrook Rd. SW17 —3D 108
Hill Brow. Brom —1B 128
Hillbrow. N Mald —3B 120
Hill Brow Clo. Bex —4K 117
Hillbrow Rd. Brom —7G 113
Hillbury Av. Harr —5B 24
Hillbury Rd. SW17 —3F 109
Hill Clo. NW2 —3D 42
Hill Clo. NW11 —6J 27
Hill Clo. Chst —5F 115
Hill Clo. Harr —3J 39
Hill Clo. Stan —4G 11
Hillcote Av. SW16 —7A 110
Hill Ct. W5 —4F 57
Hill Ct. Barn —4H 5
Hill Ct. N'holt —5E 38
Hillcourt Av. N12 —6E 14
Hillcourt Est. N16 —1D 46
Hillcourt Rd. SE22 —6H 95
Hill Cres. N20 —2E 14
Hill Cres. Bex —1J 117
Hill Cres. Harr —5A 24
Hill Cres. Surb —5F 119
Hill Cres. Wor Pk —2E 130
Hillcrest. N6 —7E 28
Hillcrest. N21 —7F 7
Hillcrest. SE5 —4D 94
Hillcrest. Romf —1J 37
Hillcrest. Sidc —7A 100
Hillcrest Av. NW11 —5G 27
Hillcrest Av. Edgw —4C 12
Hillcrest Av. Pinn —4B 22
Hillcrest Clo. SE26 —4G 111
Hillcrest Clo. Beck —6B 126
Hillcrest Ct. Sutt —6B 132
Hillcrest Gdns. N3 —4G 27
Hillcrest Gdns. NW2 —3C 42
Hillcrest Rd. E17 —2F 33

Hillcrest Rd. E18 —2J 33
Hillcrest Rd. W3 —1G 73
Hillcrest Rd. W5 —5E 56
Hillcrest Rd. Brom —5J 113
Hillcrest View. Beck —6B 126
Hillcroft Av. Pinn —6D 22
Hillcroft Cres. W5 —6E 56
Hillcroft Cres. Ruis —3B 38
Hillcroft Cres. Wemb —4F 41
Hillcroft Rd. E6 —5F 67
Hillcroome Rd. Sutt —6B 132
Hillcross Av. Mord —6F 121
Hilldale Rd. Sutt —4H 131
Hilldown Ct. SW16 —7J 109
Hilldown Rd. SW16 —7J 109
Hilldown Rd. Brom —1G 137
Hill Dri. NW9 —1J 41
Hill Dri. SW16 —3K 123
Hilldrop Cres. N7 —5H 45
Hilldrop La. N7 —5H 45
Hilldrop Rd. N7 —5H 45
Hilldrop Rd. Brom —6K 113
Hillend. SE18 —1E 98
Hillersdon Av. SW13 —2C 90
Hillersdon Av. Edgw —5A 12
Hillery Clo. SE17
—4D 78 (4F 157)
Hill Farm Rd. W10 —5E 58
Hillfield Av. N8 —5J 29
Hillfield Av. NW9 —5A 26
Hillfield Av. Mord —6C 122
Hillfield Av. Wemb —7E 40
Hillfield Clo. Harr —4G 23
Hillfield Ct. NW3 —5C 44
Hillfield Pk. N5 —5C 46
Hillfield Pk. N10 —4F 29
Hillfield Pk. N21 —2F 17
Hillfield Pk. M. N10 —4F 29
Hillfield Rd. NW6 —5H 43
Hill Field Rd. Hamp —7D 102
Hillfoot Av. Romf —1J 37
Hillfoot Rd. Romf —1J 37
Hillgate Pl. SW12 —7F 93
Hillgate Pl. W8 —1J 75
Hillgate St. W8 —1J 75
Hill Gro. Felt —2D 102
Hill Gro. Romf —3K 37
Hill Ho. E5 —1H 47
(off Harrington Hill)
Hillhouse Av. Stan —7E 10
Hill Ho. Clo. N21 —7F 7
Hill Ho. Rd. SW16 —5K 109
Hilliards Ct. E1 —1J 79
Hillier Clo. New Bar —6E 4
Hillier Gdns. Croy —5A 134
Hillier Lodge. Tedd —5H 103
Hillier Rd. SW11 —6D 92
Hilliers La. Croy —3J 133
Hillingdon Ct. Harr —4D 24
Hillingdon Rd. Bexh —2J 101
Hillingdon St. SE5 & SE17
—7B 78
Hillington Gdns. Wfd G —2B 34
Hillman Dri. W10 —4E 58
Hillman St. E8 —6H 47
Hillmarton Rd. N7 —5J 45
Hillmead Dri. SW9 —4B 94
Hillmore Clo. SE13 —3F 97
(off Belmont Hill)
Hillmore Gro. SE26 —5A 112
Hill Path. SW16 —5K 109
Hillreach. SE18 —5D 82
Hill Rise. N9 —6C 8
Hillrise. N19 —7J 29
Hill Rise. NW11 —4K 27

Hill Rise. SE23 —1H 111
Hill Rise. Gnfd —1G 55
Hill Rise. Rich —5D 88
Hillrise Mans. N19 —7J 29
(off Warltersville Rd.)
Hill Rd. N10 —1D 28
Hill Rd. NW8 —3A 60
Hill Rd. Cars —6C 132
Hill Rd. Harr —5A 24
Hill Rd. Mitc —1F 123
Hill Rd. Pinn —5C 22
Hill Rd. Sutt —5K 131
Hill Rd. Wemb —3B 40
Hillsboro' Rd. SE22 —5E 94
Hillsgrove Clo. Well —7C 84
Hillside. N8 —6H 29
Hillside. NW5 —3E 44
Hillside. NW9 —4K 25
Hillside. NW10 —7J 41
Hillside. SW19 —6F 107
Hillside. Barn —5F 5
Hillside Av. N11 —6J 15
Hillside Av. Wemb —4F 41
Hillside Av. Wfd G —6F 21
Hillside Clo. NW6 —2K 59
Hillside Clo. NW8 —2K 59
Hillside Clo. Mord —4G 121
Hillside Clo. Wfd G —5F 21
Hillside Cres. Harr —1G 39
Hillside Dri. Edgw —6B 12
Hillside Est. N15 —6F 31
Hillside Gdns. E17 —3F 33
Hillside Gdns. N6 —6F 29
Hillside Gdns. N11 —6B 16
Hillside Gdns. SW2 —2A 110
Hillside Gdns. Barn —4B 4
Hillside Gdns. Edgw —4A 12
Hillside Gdns. Harr —7E 24
Hillside Gdns. Wall —7G 133
Hillside Gro. N14 —7C 6
Hillside Gro. NW7 —7H 13
Hillside La. Brom —2H 137
(in two parts)
Hillside Pas. SW16 —2K 109
Hillside Rd. N15 —7E 30
Hillside Rd. SW2 —2K 109
Hillside Rd. W5 —5E 56
Hillside Rd. Brom —3H 127
Hillside Rd. Croy —5B 134
Hillside Rd. Pinn —1A 22
Hillside Rd. S'hall —4E 54
Hillside Rd. Surb —4G 119
Hillside Rd. Sutt —7H 131
Hillsleigh Rd. W8 —1H 75
Hills M. W5 —7E 56
Hills Pl. W1 —6G 61 (1A 148)
Hills Rd. Buck H —1E 20
Hillstowe St. E5 —3J 47
Hill St. W1 —1E 76 (4H 147)
Hill St. Rich —5D 88
Hilltop. E17 —3D 32
Hilltop. NW11 —4K 27
Hill Top. Mord —6J 121
Hill Top. Sutt —7H 121
Hill Top Ct. Wfd G —6J 21
Hilltop Gdns. NW4 —2D 26
Hilltop Rd. NW6 —7J 43
Hill Top View. Wfd G —6J 21
Hilltop Way. Stan —3F 11
Hillview. SW20 —7D 106
Hillview Av. Harr —5E 24
Hill View Cres. IIf —6D 34
Hill View Dri. Well —2J 99
Hillview Gdns. NW4 —4F 27

Hill View Gdns. NW9 —5K 25
Hillview Gdns. Harr —3E 22
Hillview Rd. NW7 —4A 14
Hillview Rd. Chst —5E 114
Hillview Rd. Pinn —1D 22
Hillview Rd. Sutt —3A 132
Hill View Rd. Twic —6A 88
Hillway. N6 —2E 44
Hillway. NW9 —1A 42
Hillworth. Beck —2D 126
Hillworth Rd. SW2 —7A 94
Hillyard Ho. SW9 —1A 94
Hillyard Rd. W7 —5J 55
Hillyard St. SW9 —1A 94
Hillyfield. E17 —2A 32
Hilly Fields Cres. SE4 —3C 96
Hilsea St. E5 —4J 47
Hilton Av. N12 —5G 15
Hilton Ho. SE4 —4K 95
Hilversum Cres. SE22 —5E 94
Himley Rd. SW17 —5C 108
Hinchcliffe Clo. Wall —7K 133
Hinckley Rd. SE15 —4G 95
Hind Ct. EC4 —6A 62 (1K 149)
Hind Cres. N Hth —6K 85
Hinde M. W1 —6E 60 (7H 141)
Hindes Rd. Harr —5J 23
Hinde St. W1 —6E 60 (7H 141)
Hind Gro. E14 —6C 64
Hindhead Clo. N16 —1E 46
Hindhead Gdns. N'holt —1C 54
Hindhead Way. Wall —5J 133
Hindlip Ho. SW8 —1H 93
Hindmans Rd. SE22 —5G 95
Hindmans Way. Dag —4F 69
Hindmarsh Clo. E1 —7G 63
Hindrey Rd. E5 —5H 47
Hindsley's Pl. SE23 —2J 111
Hinkler Clo. Wall —7J 133
Hinkler Rd. Harr —3D 24
Hinksey Path. SE2 —3D 84
Hinstock Rd. SE18 —6G 83
Hinton Av. Houn —4B 86
Hinton Clo. SE9 —1C 114
Hinton Ct. E10 —2D 48
Hinton Ho. W13 —6C 56
Hinton Rd. N18 —4K 17
Hinton Rd. SE24 —3B 94
Hinton Rd. Wall —5G 133
Hippodrome M. W11 —7G 59
Hippodrome Pl. W11 —7G 59
Hiroshima Promenade. SE7
—3A 82
Hisocks Ho. NW10 —7J 41
Hitcham Rd. E17 —7B 32
Hitchin Sq. E3 —2A 64
Hitherfield Rd. SW16 —3K 109
Hitherfield Rd. Dag —2E 52
Hither Grn. La. SE13 —5E 96
Hitherwell Rd. Harr —1H 23
Hitherwood Dri. SE19 —4F 111
Hive Clo. Bush —2C 10
Hive Rd. Bush —2C 10
Hoadly Rd. SW16 —3H 109
Hobart Clo. N20 —2H 15
Hobart Clo. Hayes —4B 54
Hobart Dri. Hayes —4B 54
Hobart Gdns. T Hth —3D 124
Hobart La. Hayes —4B 54
Hobart Pl. SW1 —3F 77 (1J 153)
Hobart Pl. Rich —7F 89
Hobart Rd. Dag —4D 52
Hobart Rd. Hayes —4B 54
Hobart Rd. IIf —2G 35
Hobart Rd. Wor Pk —3D 130

Hobbayne Rd. W7 —6H 55
Hobbs Wlk. SW15 —5D 90
Hobbs Grn. N2 —3A 28
Hobbs M. IIf —2K 51
Hobbs Pl. N1 —1E 62
Hobbs Pl. Est. N1 —1E 62
(off Hobbs Pl.)
Hobbs Rd. SE27 —4C 110
Hobday St. E14 —6D 64
Hobill Wlk. Surb —6F 119
Hoblands End. Chst —6J 115
Hocker St. E2 —3F 63 (2J 145)
Hockett Clo. SE8 —4A 80
Hockley Av. E6 —2C 66
Hockley Ct. E18 —1J 33
Hocroft Av. NW2 —3H 43
Hocroft Ct. NW2 —3H 43
Hocroft Rd. NW2 —3H 43
Hocroft Wlk. NW2 —3H 43
Hodder Dri. Gnfd —2K 55
Hoddesdon Rd. Belv —5G 85
Hodford Rd. NW11 —1H 43
Hodgkin Clo. SE28 —7D 68
Hodister Clo. SE5 —7C 78
Hodnet Gro. SE16 —4K 79
Hodson Clo. Harr —3D 38
Hoecroft Ct. Enf —1D 8
(off Hoe La.)
Hoe La. Enf —1B 8
Hoe St. E17 —4C 32
Hoever Ho. SE6 —4E 112
Hofland Rd. W14 —3G 75
Hogan M. W2 —5A 60 (5A 140)
Hogan Way. E5 —2G 47
Hogarth Bus. Pk. W4 —6A 74
Hogarth Clo. E16 —5B 66
Hogarth Clo. W5 —5E 56
Hogarth Ct. EC3 —6E 62 (2H 151)
Hogarth Ct. SE19 —4F 111
Hogarth Ct. Houn —7C 70
Hogarth Cres. SW19 —1B 122
Hogarth Cres. Croy —7C 124
Hogarth Gdns. Houn —7E 70
Hogarth Hill. NW11 —4H 27
Hogarth Ho. N'holt —2B 54
(off Gallery Gdns.)
Hogarth La. W4 —6A 74
Hogarth Pl. SW5 —4K 75
Hogarth Rd. SW5 —4K 75
Hogarth Rd. Dag —6B 52
Hogarth Rd. Edgw —2G 25
Hogarth Roundabout. (Junct.)
—6A 74
Hogarth Ter. W4 —6A 74
Hog Hill Rd. Romf —1F 37
Hogshead Pas. E1 —7H 63
(off Pennington St.)
Holbeach Gdns. Sidc —6K 99
Holbeach M. SW12 —1F 109
Holbeach Rd. SE6 —7D 96
Holbeck Row. SE15 —7G 79
Holbein M. SW1
—5E 76 (5G 153)
Holbein Pl. SW1
—4E 76 (4G 153)
Holbein Ter. Dag —4C 52
(off Marlborough Rd.)
Holberton Gdns. NW10 —3D 58
Holborn. EC1 —5A 62 (6J 143)
Holborn Cir. EC1
—5A 62 (6K 143)
Holborn Pl. WC1
—5K 61 (6G 143)

Holborn Rd. E13 —5K 65
Holborn Viaduct. EC1
—5B 62 (6K 143)
Holbrook Clo. N19 —1F 45
Holbrook Clo. Enf —1A 8
Holbrooke Ct. N7 —3J 45
Holbrooke Pl. Rich —5D 88
Holbrook Ho. Chst —1H 129
Holbrook La. Chst —7H 115
Holbrook Rd. E15 —2H 65
Holbrook Way. Brom —6D 128
Holburne Clo. SE3 —1A 98
Holburne Gdns. SE3 —1B 98
Holburne Rd. SE3 —1A 98
Holcombe Hill. NW7 —3H 13
Holcombe Ho. SW9 —3J 93
(off Landor Rd.)
Holcombe Rd. N17 —3F 31
(in two parts)
Holcombe Rd. IIf —7E 34
Holcombe St. W6 —4D 74
Holcote Clo. Belv —3E 84
Holcroft Ct. W1
—5G 61 (5A 142)
Holcroft Rd. E9 —7J 47
Holden Av. N12 —5E 14
Holden Av. NW9 —1J 41
Holdenby Rd. SE4 —5A 96
Holden Clo. Dag —3B 52
Holden Ho. SE8 —7C 80
Holdenhurst Av. N12 —7F 15
Holden Rd. N12 —5E 14
Holden St. SW11 —2E 92
Holder Clo. N3 —7E 14
Holdernesse Clo. Iswth —1A 88
Holdernesse Rd. SW17 —3D 108
Holderness Way. SE27 —5B 110
Holder's Hill Av. NW4 —2F 27
Holder's Hill Cres. NW4 —2F 27
Holders Hill Dri. NW4 —3F 27
Holder's Hill Gdns. NW4 —2G 27
Holders Hill Rd. NW4 & NW7
—2F 27
Holford Pl. WC1
—3K 61 (1H 143)
Holford Rd. NW3 —3A 44
Holford St. WC1 —3K 61 (1J 143)
Holford Yd. WC1
—3A 62 (1J 143)
Holgate Av. SW11 —3B 92
Holgate Gdns. Dag —6G 53
Holgate Rd. Dag —5G 53
Holgate St. SE7 —3B 82
Hollam Ho. N8 —4K 29
Holland Av. SW20 —1B 120
Holland Av. Sutt —7J 131
Holland Clo. Brom —2H 137
Holland Clo. Romf —5J 37
Holland Clo. Stan —5G 11
Holland Ct. E17 —4E 32
(off Evelyn Rd.)
Holland Ct. NW7 —6H 13
Holland Dri. SE23 —3A 112
Holland Gdns. W14 —3G 75
Holland Gro. SW9 —7A 78
Holland Ho. E4 —4A 20
Holland La. W14 —3H 75
Holland Pk. W11 —1G 75
Holland Pk. Av. W11 —1F 75
Holland Pk. Av. IIf —6J 35
Holland Pk. Gdns. W14 —2G 75
Holland Pk. M. W11 —1G 75
Holland Pk. Rd. W14 —3H 75

Holland Park Roundabout.
(Junct.) —2F 75
Holland Pas. N1 —1C 62
(off Basire St.)
Holland Pl. W8 —2K 75
(off Kensington Chu. St.)
Holland Pl. Chambers. W8
(off Holland Pl.) —2K 75
Holland Rise Ho. SW9 —7K 77
(off Clapham Rd.)
Holland Rd. E6 —1D 66
Holland Rd. E15 —3G 65
Holland Rd. NW10 —1C 58
Holland Rd. SE25 —5G 125
Holland Rd. W14 —2F 75
Holland Rd. Wemb —6D 40
Hollands, The. Felt —4B 102
Hollands, The. Wor Pk —1B 130
Holland St. SE1 —1B 78 (4B 150)
Holland St. W8 —2J 75
Holland Vs. Rd. W14 —2G 75
Holland Wlk. N19 —1H 45
Holland Wlk. W8 —1H 75
Holland Wlk. Stan —5F 11
Holland Way. Brom —2H 137
Hollar Rd. N16 —3F 47
Hollen St. W1 —6H 61 (7C 142)
Holles Clo. Hamp —6E 102
Holles Ho. SW9 —2A 94
Holles St. W1 —6F 61 (7K 141)
Holley Rd. W3 —2A 74
Hollick Wood Av. N12 —6J 15
Holliday Sq. SW11 —3B 92
(off Fowler Clo.)
Hollidge Way. Dag —7H 53
Hollies Av. Sidc —2K 115
Hollies Clo. SW16 —6A 110
Hollies Clo. Twic —2K 103
Hollies End. NW7 —5J 13
Hollies Rd. W5 —4C 72
Hollies, The. E11 —5J 33
(off New Wanstead)
Hollies, The. N20 —1G 15
Hollies, The. Harr —4A 24
Hollies Way. SW12 —7E 92
Holligrave Rd. Brom —1J 127
Hollingbourne Av. Bexh —1F 101
Hollingbourne Gdns. W13
—5B 56
Hollingbourne Rd. SE24 —5C 94
Hollingsworth Ct. Surb —7D 118
Hollingsworth Rd. Croy —6H 135
Hollington Ct. Chst —6F 115
Hollington Cres. N Mald —6B 120
Hollington Rd. E6 —3D 66
Hollington Rd. N17 —2G 31
Hollingworth Rd. Orp —7F 129
Hollins Ho. N7 —4J 45
Hollman Gdns. SW16 —6B 110
Holloway Ho. NW2 —3E 42
Holloway Rd. E6 —3D 66
Holloway Rd. E11 —3F 49
Holloway Rd. N7 —4K 45
Holloway Rd. N19 & N7 —2H 45
Holloway St. Houn —3F 87
Hollowfield Wlk. N'holt —7C 38
Hollows, The. Bren —6F 73
Hollow, The. Wfd G —4C 20
Holly Av. Stan —2E 24
Hollybank Clo. Hamp —5E 102
Hollyberry La. NW3 —4A 44
Hollybrake Clo. Chst —7H 115
Hollybush Clo. E11 —5J 33
Hollybush Clo. Harr —1J 23
Hollybush Gdns. E2 —3H 63

Hollybush Hill. E11 —6H 33
Hollybush Hill. NW3 —4A 44
Hollybush Ho. E2 —3H 63
Hollybush La. Hamp —7D 102
Hollybush Pl. E2 —3H 63
Hollybush Rd. King T —5E 104
Hollybush Steps. NW3 —4A 44
(off Holly Mt.)
Hollybush St. E13 —2K 65
Holly Bush Vale. NW3 —4A 44
Holly Bush Wlk. SW9 —4B 94
Holly Clo. NW10 —7A 42
Holly Clo. Buck H —3G 21
Holly Clo. Felt —5C 102
Holly Clo. Wall —7F 133
Holly Ct. N15 —4E 30
Holly Ct. Sidc —4B 116
(off Sidcup Hill)
Holly Ct. Sutt —7J 131
Holly Cres. Beck —5B 126
Holly Cres. Wfd G —7A 20
Hollycroft Av. NW3 —3J 43
Hollycroft Av. Wemb —2F 41
Hollycroft Clo. S Croy —5E 134
Hollydale Clo. N'holt —4F 39
Hollydale Dri. Brom —3D 138
Hollydale Rd. SE15 —1J 95
Holly Dene. SE15 —1H 95
Holly Dri. E4 —7J 9
Holly Farm Rd. S'hall —5C 70
Hollyfield Av. N11 —5J 15
Hollyfield Rd. Surb —7F 119
Holly Gro. NW9 —7J 25
Holly Gro. SE15 —2F 95
Hollygrove. Bush —1C 10
Holly Gro. Pinn —1C 22
Hollygrove Clo. Houn —4D 86
Holly Hedge Ter. SE13 —5F 97
Holly Hill. N21 —6E 6
Holly Hill. NW3 —4A 44
Holly Hill Rd. Belv & Eri —5H 85
Holly Ho. Iswth —6C 72
Holly Lodge. Harr —5H 23
Holly Lodge Gdns. N6 —2E 44
Holly Lodge Mans. N6 —2E 44
Hollymead. Cars —3D 132
Holly M. SW10 —5A 76 (6A 152)
Holly Mt. NW3 —4A 44
Hollymount Clo. SE10 —1E 96
Holly Pk. N3 —3H 27
Holly Pk. N4 —7J 29
(in two parts)
Holly Pk. Est. N4 —7K 29
Holly Pk. Gdns. N3 —3J 27
Holly Pk. Rd. N11 —5K 15
Holly Pk. Rd. W7 —1K 71
Holly Pl. NW3 —4A 44
(off Holly Berry La.)
Holly Rd. E11 —1H 49
Holly Rd. W4 —4K 73
Holly Rd. Hamp —6G 103
Holly Rd. Houn —4F 87
Holly Rd. Twic —1K 103
Holly St. E8 —7F 47
Holly St. E8 —7F 47
Holly Ter. N6 —1E 44
Holly Ter. N20 —2F 15
Holly Tree Clo. SW19 —1F 107
Holly Tree Ho. SE4 —3B 96
(off Brockley Rd.)
Holly View Clo. NW4 —6C 26
Holly Village. N6 —2F 45
Holly Wlk. NW3 —4A 44
Holly Wlk. Enf —3H 7

Holly Way. Mitc —4H 123
Hollywood Ct. W5 —7F 57
Hollywood M. SW10 —6A 76
Hollywood Rd. E4 —5F 19
Hollywood Rd. SW10 —6A 76
Hollywood Way. Wfd G —7A 20
Holman Ct. Ewe —7C 130
Holman Hunt Ho. W6 —5G 75
(off Field Rd.)
Holman Rd. SW11 —2B 92
Holmbridge Gdns. Enf —4E 8
Holmbrook Dri. NW4 —5F 27
Holmbury Clo. Bush —2D 10
Holmbury Ct. SW17 —3D 108
Holmbury Ct. S Croy —5E 134
Holmbury Gro. Croy —7B 136
Holmbury Ho. SE24 —5B 94
Holmbury Mnr. Sidc —4A 116
Holmbury Pk. Brom —7C 114
Holmbury View. E5 —1H 47
Holmbush Rd. SW15 —6G 91
Holmcote Gdns. N5 —5C 46
Holm Ct. SE12 —3K 113
Holmcroft Ho. E17 —4D 32
Holmcroft Way. Brom —5D 128
Holmdale Gdns. NW4 —5F 27
Holmdale Rd. NW6 —5J 43
Holmdale Rd. Chst —5G 115
Holmdale Ter. N15 —7E 30
Holmdene. N12 —5E 14
Holmdene Av. NW7 —6H 13
Holmdene Av. SE24 —5C 94
Holmdene Av. Harr —3F 23
Holmdene Clo. Beck —2E 126
Holmead Rd. SW6 —7K 75
Holme Lacey Rd. SE12 —6H 97
Holme Rd. E6 —1C 66
Holmes Av. E17 —3B 32
Holmes Av. NW7 —5B 14
Holmesdale Av. SW14 —3H 89
Holmesdale Clo. SE25 —3F 125
Holmesdale Rd. N6 —7F 29
Holmesdale Rd. Bexh —2D 100
Holmesdale Rd. Croy & SE25
—5D 124
Holmesdale Rd. Rich —1F 89
Holmesdale Rd. Tedd —6C 104
Holmesley Rd. SE23 —6A 96
Holmes Pl. SW10 —6A 76
Holmes Rd. NW5 —5F 45
Holmes Rd. SW19 —7A 108
Holmes Rd. Twic —2K 103
Holmes Ter. SE1
—2A 78 (6J 149)
Holmeswood Ct. N22 —2A 30
Holme Way. Stan —6E 10
Holmewood Gdns. SW2 —7K 93
Holmewood Rd. SE25 —3E 124
Holmewood Rd. SW2 —7K 93
Holmfield Av. NW4 —5F 27
Holmfield Rd. NW3 —6C 44
Holmhurst Rd. Belv —5H 85
Holmleigh Ct. Enf —4D 8
Holmleigh Rd. N16 —1E 46
Holmleigh Rd. Est. N16 —1E 46
Holmoak Clo. SW15 —6H 91
Holm Oak M. SW4 —5J 93
Holmoaks Ho. Beck —2E 126
Holmsdale Ho. N11 —4A 16
(off Coppies Gro.)
Holmshaw Clo. SE26 —4A 112
Holmside Rd. SW12 —6E 92
Holmsley Clo. N Mald —6B 120
Holmsley Ho. SW15 —7B 90
(off Tangley Gro.)

Holmstall Av. Edgw —3J 25
Holmstall Pde. Edgw —2J 25
Holm Wlk. SE3 —2J 97
Holmwood Clo. Harr —3G 23
Holmwood Clo. N'holt —6F 39
Holmwood Clo. Sutt —7F 131
Holmwood Gdns. N3 —2J 27
Holmwood Gdns. Wall —6F 133
Holmwood Gro. NW7 —5E 12
Holmwood Rd. Ilf —2J 51
Holmwood Rd. Sutt —1E 130
Holmwood Vs. SE7 —5J 81
Holne Chase. N2 —6A 28
Holne Chase. Mord —6H 121
Holness Rd. E15 —6H 49
Holroyd Rd. SW15 —4E 90
Holstein Way. Eri —3D 84
Holst Mans. SW13 —7E 74
Holstock Rd. Ilf —2G 51
Holsworth Clo. Harr —5G 23
Holsworthy Sq. WC1
—4H 61 (4H 143)
Holt Clo. N10 —4E 28
Holt Clo. SE28 —7B 68
Holt Ct. E15 —5E 48
Holt Ho. SW2 —6A 94
Holton St. E1 —4K 63
Holt Rd. E16 —1C 82
Holt Rd. Wemb —3B 40
Holt, The. Mord —4J 121
Holt, The. Wall —4G 133
Holtwhites Av. Enf —2H 7
Holtwhite's Hill. Enf —1G 7
Holwell Pl. Pinn —4C 22
Holwood Pk. Av. Orp —4D 138
Holwood Pl. SW4 —4H 93
Holybourne Av. SW15 —7C 90
Holyhead Clo. E3 —3C 64
Holyhead Clo. E6 —5D 66
Holy Oake Ct. SE16 —2B 80
Holyoake Ho. W5 —4C 56
Holyoake Wlk. N2 —3A 28
Holyoake Wlk. W5 —4C 56
Holyoak Rd. SE11
—4B 78 (4A 156)
Holyport Rd. SW6 —7F 75
Holyrood Av. Harr —4C 38
Holyrood Gdns. Edgw —3H 25
Holyrood M. E16 —1J 81
(off Badminton M.)
Holyrood Rd. New Bar —6F 5
Holyrood St. SE1
—1E 78 (5G 151)
Holywell Clo. SE3 —6J 81
Holywell Clo. SE16 —5H 79
Holywell La. EC2
—4E 62 (3H 145)
Holywell Row. EC2
—4E 62 (4G 145)
Homan Ct. N12 —4G 15
Homebush Ho. E4 —7J 9
Home Clo. Cars —2D 132
Home Clo. N'holt —3D 54
Homecroft Rd. N22 —1C 30
Homecroft Rd. SE26 —5J 111
Homefarm Rd. W7 —6J 55
Home Field. Barn —5C 4
Homefield. Mord —4J 121
Homefield Av. Ilf —5J 35
Homefield Clo. NW10 —7J 41
Homefield Clo. Hayes —4B 54
Homefield Ct. SW16 —3J 109
Homefield Gdns. N2 —3B 28
Homefield Gdns. Mitc —2A 122
Homefield Rd. SE23 —3K 111

Homefield M. Beck —1C 126
Homefield Pk. Sutt —6K 131
Homefield Rd. SW19 —6G 107
Homefield Rd. W4 —4B 74
Homefield Rd. Brom —1A 128
Homefield Rd. Edgw —6E 12
Homefield Rd. Wemb —4A 40
Homefirs Ho. Wemb —3F 41
Home Gdns. Dag —3J 53
Homelands Dri. SE19 —7E 110
Homeleigh Rd. SE15 —5K 95
Home Mead. Stan —1C 24
Homemead Rd. Brom —5D 128
Homemead Rd. Croy —6H 123
Home Pk. Rd. SW19 —4H 107
Home Pk. Wlk. King T —4D 118
Homer Clo. Bexh —1J 101
Homer Dri. E14 —4C 80
Home Rd. SW11 —2C 92
Homer Rd. E9 —6A 48
Homer Rd. Croy —6K 125
Homer Row. W1
—5C 60 (6D 140)
Homersham Rd. King T —2G 119
Homer St. W1 —5C 60 (6D 140)
Homerton Gro. E9 —5K 47
Homerton High St. E9 —5K 47
Homerton Rd. E9 —5A 48
Homerton Row. E9 —5J 47
Homerton Ter. E9 —6J 47
Homesdale Clo. E11 —5J 33
Homesdale Rd. Brom —4A 128
Homesdale Rd. Orp —7J 129
Homesfield. NW11 —4J 27
Homestall Rd. SE22 —5J 95
Homestead Ct. Barn —5D 4
Homestead Paddock. N14 —5A 6
Homestead Pk. NW2 —3B 42
Homestead Rd. SW6 —7H 75
Homestead Rd. Dag —2F 53
Homesteads, The. N11 —4A 16
Homestead, The. Dart —5K 101
(off Crayford High St.)
Homewillow Clo. N21 —6G 7
Homewood Clo. Hamp —6D 102
Homewood Cres. Chst —6J 115
Homewoods. SW12 —7G 93
Homildon Ho. SE26 —3G 111
Honduras St. EC1
—4C 62 (3C 144)
Honeybourne Rd. NW6 —5K 43
Honeybourne Way. Orp —7H 129
Honeybrook Rd. SW12 —7G 93
Honey Clo. Dag —6H 53
Honeyden Rd. Sidc —6E 116
Honey La. EC2 —6C 62 (1D 150)
Honeyman Clo. NW6 —7F 43
Honeypot Bus. Cen. Stan —1E 24
Honeypot Clo. NW9 —4F 25
Honeypot La. Stan & NW9
—7J 11
Honeysett Rd. N17 —2F 31
Honeysuckle Clo. S'hall —7C 54
Honeysuckle Gdns. Croy
—7K 125
Honeysuckle La. N22 —2C 30
Honeywell Rd. SW11 —6D 92
Honeywood Rd. NW10 —2B 58
Honeywood Rd. Iswth —4A 88
Honeywood Wlk. Cars —4D 132
Honister Clo. Stan —1B 24
Honister Gdns. Stan —1B 24
Honister Pl. Stan —1B 24
Honiton Gdns. SE15 —2J 95
(off Gibbon Rd.)

Honiton Rd. NW6 —2H 59
Honiton Rd. Romf —6K 37
Honiton Rd. Well —2K 99
Honley Rd. SE6 —7D 96
Honor Oak Pk. SE23 —6J 95
Honor Oak Rise. SE23 —6J 95
Honor Oak Rd. SE23 —1J 111
Hood Av. N14 —6A 6
Hood Av. SW14 —5J 89
Hood Clo. Croy —1B 134
Hoodcote Gdns. N21 —7G 7
Hood Ct. EC4 —6A 62 (1K 149)
Hood Rd. SW20 —7B 106
Hood Wlk. Romf —1H 37
Hookers Rd. E17 —3K 31
Hook Farm Rd. Brom —5B 128
Hooking Grn. Harr —5F 23
Hook La. Well —5K 99
Hooks Clo. SE15 —1H 95
Hookshall Dri. Dag —3J 53
Hookstone Way. Wfd G —7G 21
Hooks Way. SE22 —1G 111
Hook, The. New Bar —6G 5
Hook Wlk. Edgw —6D 12
Hooper Rd. E16 —6J 65
Hooper's Ct. SW3
—2D 76 (7E 146)
Hooper's M. W3 —1J 73
Hooper St. E1 —6G 63
Hoop La. NW11 —7H 27
Hope Clo. N1 —6C 46
Hope Clo. SE12 —3K 113
Hope Clo. Chad H —4C 36
Hope Clo. Sutt —5A 132
Hope Clo. Wfd G —6F 21
Hopedale Rd. SE7 —6K 81
Hopefield Av. NW6 —2G 59
Hope Pk. Brom —7H 113
Hopes Clo. Houn —6E 70
Hope St. SW11 —3B 92
Hopetown St. E1
—5F 63 (6K 145)
Hopewell St. SE5 —7D 78
Hop Gdns. WC2 —7J 61 (3E 148)
Hopgood St. W12 —2E 74
Hopkins Clo. N10 —7K 15
Hopkins M. E15 —1H 65
Hopkinsons Pl. NW1 —1E 60
Hopkins St. W1 —6G 61 (1B 148)
Hoppers Rd. N13 & N21 —2F 17
Hoppett Rd. E4 —2B 20
Hopping La. N1 —6B 46
Hoppingwood Av. N Mald
—3A 120
Hopton Ct. Hay —1J 137
Hopton Gdns. N Mald —6C 120
Hopton Rd. SW16 —5K 109
Hopton's Gdns. SE1
—1B 78 (4B 150)
Hopton St. SE1 —1B 78 (4B 150)
Hopwood Clo. SW17 —3A 108
Hopwood Rd. SE17
—6D 78 (7F 157)
Hopwood Wlk. E8 —7G 47
Horace Av. Romf —1J 53
Horace Rd. E7 —4K 49
Horace Rd. Ilf —3G 35
Horace Rd. King T —3F 119
Horatio Pl. E14 —1E 80
(off Preston's Rd.)
Horatio Pl. SW19 —1J 121
Horatio St. E2 —2G 63
Horatius Way. Croy —5K 133
Horbury Cres. W11 —7J 59
Horbury M. W11 —7H 59

Horder Rd. SW6 —1G 91
Hordle Promenade E. SE15
—7F 79
Hordle Promenade N. SE15
—7E 78
Hordle Promenade S. SE15
—7F 79
Hordle Promenade W. SE15
—7E 78
Horizon Way. SE7 —4K 81
Horle Wlk. SE5 —2B 94
Horley Clo. Bexh —5G 101
Horley Rd. SE9 —4C 114
Hormead Rd. W9 —4H 59
Hornbeam Clo. SE11
—4A 78 (3J 155)
Hornbeam Clo. Buck H —3G 21
Hornbeam Clo. N'holt —5D 38
Hornbeam Cres. Bren —7B 72
Hornbeam Gro. E4 —3B 20
Hornbeam Ho. Buck H —3G 21
Hornbeam La. Bexh —2J 101
Hornbeam La. Buck H —3G 21
Hornbeam Rd. Hayes —5A 54
Hornbeams Rise. N11 —6K 15
Hornbeam Ter. Cars —1C 132
Hornbeam Wlk. Rich —4F 105
Hornbeam Way. Brom —6E 128
Hornblower Clo. SE16 —3A 80
Hornbuckle Clo. Harr —2H 39
Hornby Clo. NW3 —7B 44
Hornby Ho. SE11
—6A 78 (7J 155)
Horncastle Clo. SE12 —7J 97
Horncastle Rd. SE12 —7J 97
Hornchurch. N17 —2D 30
(off Gloucester Rd.)
Hornchurch Clo. King T —4D 104
Horndean Clo. SW15 —1C 106
Horndon Clo. Romf —1J 37
Horndon Grn. Romf —1J 37
Horndon Rd. Romf —1J 37
Horner La. N1 —2E 62
(off Whitmore Est.)
Horner La. Mitc —2B 122
Horne Way. SW15 —2E 90
Hornfair Rd. SE7 —6B 82
Horniman Dri. SE23 —1H 111
Horning Clo. SE9 —4C 114
Horn La. SE10 —4J 81
Horn La. W3 —1J 73
Horn La. Wfd G —6D 20
Hornpark Clo. SE12 —5K 97
Hornpark La. SE12 —5K 97
Horns End Pl. Pinn —4A 22
Hornsey La. N6 —1F 45
Hornsey La. Est. N19 —7H 29
Hornsey La. Gdns. N6 —7G 29
Hornsey Pk. Rd. N8 —3K 29
Hornsey Rise. N19 —7H 29
Hornsey Rise Gdns. N19 —7H 29
Hornsey Rd. N19 & N7 —1J 45
Hornsey St. N7 —5K 45
Hornshay St. SE15 —6J 79
Horns Rd. Ilf —5G 35
Hornton Pl. W8 —2K 75
Hornton St. W8 —2J 75
Horsa Clo. Wall —7J 133
Horsa Rd. SE12 —7A 98
Horsa Rd. Eri —7H 85
Horsebridge Clo. Dag —1E 68
Horsecroft Rd. Edgw —7E 12
Horse & Dolphin Yd. W1
—7H 61 (2D 148)
Horse Fair. King T —2D 118

Horseferry Pl. SE10 —6E 80
Horseferry Rd. E14 —7A 64
Horseferry Rd. SW1
—3H 77 (2C 154)
Horseferry Rd. Est. SW1
—3H 77 (2C 154)
Horseguards Av. SW1
—1J 77 (5E 148)
Horse Guards Rd. SW1
—1H 77 (5D 148)
Horse Leaze. E6 —6E 66
Horsell Rd. N5 —5A 46
Horsell Rd. Orp —7H 116
Horselydown La. SE1
—2F 79 (6J 151)
Horsenden Av. Gnfd —5J 39
Horsenden Cres. Gnfd —5K 39
Horsenden La. Gnfd —6J 39
Horsenden La. N. Gnfd —6K 39
Horsenden La. S. Gnfd —1A 56
Horse Ride. SW1
—2G 77 (5C 148)
Horseshoe Clo. E14 —5E 80
Horseshoe Clo. NW2 —2D 42
Horse Shoe Cres. N'holt —2E 54
Horse Shoe Grn. Sutt —2K 131
Horseshoe La. N20 —1A 14
Horseshoe La. Enf —3H 7
Horse Shoe Yd. W1
—7F 61 (2K 147)
Horsfeld Gdns. SE9 —5C 98
Horsfeld Rd. SE9 —5B 98
Horsford Rd. SW2 —5K 93
Horsham Av. N12 —5H 15
Horsham Ct. N17 —1G 31
(off Lansdowne Rd.)
Horsham Rd. Bexh —5G 101
Horsley Dri. King T —5D 104
Horsley Dri. New Ad —7E 136
Horsley Rd. E4 —2K 19
Horsley Rd. Brom —1K 127
Horsley St. SE17
—6D 78 (7E 156)
Horsman St. SE5 —6C 78
Horsmonden Clo. Orp —7K 129
Horsmonden Rd. SE4 —5B 96
Hortensia Rd. SW10 —7A 76
Horticultural Pl. W4 —5K 73
Horton Av. NW2 —4G 43
Horton Ho. SE15 —6J 79
Horton Ho. SW8 —7K 77
Horton Ho. W6 —5G 75
(off Field Rd.)
Horton Rd. E8 —6H 47
Horton St. SE13 —3D 96
Horton Way. Croy —5K 125
Hortus Rd. E4 —2K 19
Hortus Rd. S'hall —2D 70
Hosack Rd. SW17 —2E 108
Hoser Av. SE12 —2J 113
Hosier La. EC1 —5B 62 (6A 144)
Hoskins Clo. E16 —6A 66
Hoskins St. SE10 —5F 81
Hospital Bri. Rd. Twic —7F 87
Hospital Bridge Roundabout.
(Junct.) —2F 103
Hospital Rd. E9 —5K 47
Hospital Rd. Houn —3E 86
Hospital Way. SE13 —7F 96
Hotham Rd. SW15 —3E 90
Hotham Rd. SW19 —7A 108
Hotham Rd. M. SW19 —7A 108
Hotham St. E15 —1G 65

Hothfield Pl. SE16 —3J 79
Hotspur Ind. Est. N17 —6C 18
Hotspur Rd. N'holt —2E 54
Hotspur St. SE11
—5A 78 (5J 155)
Houblon Rd. Rich —5E 88
Houghton Clo. E8 —6F 47
Houghton Clo. Hamp —6C 102
Houghton Rd. N15 —4F 31
Houghton St. WC2
—6K 61 (1H 149)
Houlder Cres. Croy —6B 134
Houndsden Rd. N21 —6E 6
Houndsditch. EC3
—6E 62 (7H 145)
Houndsfield Rd. N9 —7C 8
Hounslow Av. Houn —5F 87
Hounslow Bus. Pk. Houn —4E 86
Hounslow Cen. Houn —3F 87
Hounslow Gdns. Houn —5F 87
Hounslow Rd. Felt —7A 86
Hounslow Rd. Hanw —4B 102
Hounslow Rd. Twic —6F 87
Hounslow Way. SE5 —7D 78
Houseman Way. SE5 —7D 78
Houston Bus. Pk. Hayes —1A 70
Houston Rd. SE23 —2A 112
Houston Ct. Houn —7D 70
Hove Av. E17 —6B 32
Hoveden Rd. NW2 —5G 43
Hove Gdns. Sutt —1K 131
Hoveton Rd. SE28 —7C 68
Howard Av. Bex —1C 116
Howard Bldgs. E1 —5G 63
(off Deal St.)
Howard Clo. N11 —2K 15
Howard Clo. NW2 —4G 43
Howard Clo. W3 —6H 57
Howard Clo. Bush —1D 10
Howard Clo. Hamp —7G 103
Howard Ct. Bark —1H 67
Howard Ho. SE8 —6B 80
(off Evelyn St.)
Howard Ho. SW9 —3B 94
(off Barrington Rd.)
Howard M. N5 —4B 46
Howard Rd. E6 —2D 66
Howard Rd. E11 —3G 49
Howard Rd. E17 —3C 32
Howard Rd. N15 —6E 30
Howard Rd. N16 —4D 46
Howard Rd. NW2 —4F 43
Howard Rd. SE20 —1J 125
Howard Rd. SE25 —5G 125
Howard Rd. Bark —1H 67
Howard Rd. Brom —7J 113
Howard Rd. Ilf —4F 51
Howard Rd. Iswth —3K 87
Howard Rd. N Mald —3A 120
Howard Rd. S'hall —6F 55
Howard Rd. Surb —6F 119
Howards Clo. Pinn —2A 22
Howards Crest Clo. Beck
—2E 126
Howard's La. SW15 —4D 90
Howards Rd. E13 —3J 65
Howard St. Th Dit —7B 118
Howard Wlk. N2 —4A 28
Howard Way. SE22 —1G 111
Howard Way. Barn —5A 4
Howarth Rd. SE2 —5A 84
Howberry Clo. Edgw —6J 11
Howberry Rd. Stan & Edgw
—6J 11
Howberry Rd. T Hth —1D 124
Howbury Rd. SE15 —3J 95

Howcroft Cres. N3 —7D 14
Howcroft La. Gnfd —3H 55
Howden Clo. SE28 —7D 68
Howden Ho. Houn —7C 86
Howden Rd. SE25 —2F 125
Howden St. SE15 —3G 95
Howe Clo. Romf —1G 37
Howell Clo. Romf —5D 36
Howell Ct. E10 —1D 48
Howell Wlk. SE17
—4B 78 (4B 156)
Howes Clo. N3 —3J 27
Howfield Pl. N17 —3F 31
Howgate Rd. SW14 —3K 89
Howick Pl. SW1
—3G 77 (2B 154)
Howie St. SW11 —7C 76
Howitt Clo. NW3 —6C 44
Howitt Rd. NW3 —6C 44
Howland Est. SE16 —3J 79
Howland Ho. SW16 —3J 109
Howland M. E. W1
—5G 61 (5B 142)
Howland St. W1
—5G 61 (5A 142)
Howland Way. SE16 —2A 80
Howlett's Rd. SE24 —6C 94
Howley Pl. W2 —5A 60
Howley Rd. Croy —3B 134
Howsman Rd. SW13 —6C 74
Howson Rd. SE4 —4A 96
Howson Ter. Rich —6E 88
How's St. E2 —2F 63
Howton Pl. Bush —1C 10
Hoxton Mkt. N1 —3E 62 (2G 145)
Hoxton Sq. N1 —3E 62 (2G 145)
Hoxton St. N1 —1E 62 (2H 145)
Hoylake Gdns. Mitc —3C 123
Hoylake Gdns. Ruis —1A 38
Hoylake Rd. W3 —6A 58
Hoyland Clo. SE15 —7H 79
Hoyle Rd. SW17 —5C 108
Hoy St. E16 —6H 65
Hubbard Rd. SE27 —4C 110
Hubbard St. E15 —1G 65
Hubert Clo. SW19 —1A 122
(off Nelson Gro. Rd.)
Hubert Gro. SW9 —3J 93
Hubert Rd. E6 —3B 66
Hubert Rd. Bexh —2F 101
Huddart St. E3 —5B 64
(in two parts)
Huddleston Clo. E2 —2J 63
Huddlestone Rd. E7 —4H 49
Huddlestone Rd. NW2 —6D 42
Huddleston Rd. N7 —3G 45
Hudson. NW9 —1B 26
(off Near Acre)
Hudson Clo. W12 —7D 58
Hudson Pl. SE18 —5G 83
Hudson Rd. Bexh —2F 101
Hudson's Pl. SW1
—4G 77 (3A 154)
Huggin Ct. EC4 —7C 62 (2C 150)
Huggin Hill. EC4
—7C 62 (2D 150)
Huggins Pl. SW2 —1K 109
Hughan Rd. E15 —5F 49
Hugh Astor Ct. SE1
—3B 78 (1B 156)
(off Keyworth St.)
Hugh Clark Ho. W13 —1A 72
(off Singapore Rd.)
Hugh Dalton Ho. SW6 —6H 75
(off Clem Attlee Ct.)
Hughenden Av. Harr —5B 24

Hughenden Gdns. N'holt —3A 54
Hughenden Rd. Wor Pk
—7C 120
Hughendon. New Bar —4E 4
Hughendon Ter. E15 —4E 48
Hughes Ct. N7 —5H 45
Hughes M. SW11 —5D 92
Hughes Rd. SE20 —7H 111
Hughes Ter. E16 —5H 65
(off Clarkson Rd.)
Hughes Wlk. Croy —7C 124
Hugh Gaitskell Ho. N16 —2F 47
Hugh Gaitskell Ho. SW6 —6H 75
(off Clem Attlee Ct.)
Hugh M. SW1 —4F 77 (4K 153)
Hugh St. SW1 —4F 77 (4K 153)
Hugon Rd. SW6 —3K 91
Hugo Rd. N19 —4G 45
Huguenot Pl. E1 —5F 63 (5K 145)
Huguenot Pl. SW18 —5A 92
Huguenot Sq. SE15 —3H 95
Hullbridge M. N1 —1D 62
Hull Clo. SE16 —2K 79
Hull St. EC1 —3C 62 (2C 144)
Hulme Pl. SE1 —2C 78 (7D 150)
Hulse Av. Bark —6H 51
Hulse Av. Romf —1H 37
Humber Ct. W7 —6H 55
(off Hobbayne Rd.)
Humber Dri. W10 —4F 59
Humber Rd. NW2 —2D 42
Humber Rd. SE3 —6H 81
Humberstone Rd. E13 —3A 66
Humberton Clo. E9 —5A 48
Humbolt Rd. W6 —6G 75
Hume Point. E16 —5A 66
Humes Av. W7 —3J 71
Hume Ter. E16 —6K 65
Humphrey Clo. Ilf —1D 34
Humphrey St. SE1
—5F 79 (5J 157)
Humphries Clo. Dag —4F 53
Hundred Acre. NW9 —2B 26
Hungerdown. E4 —1K 19
Hungerford La. WC2
—1J 77 (4F 149)
Hungerford Rd. N7 —6H 45
Hungerford St. E1 —6H 63
Hunsdon Clo. Dag —6E 52
Hunsdon Rd. SE14 —7K 79
Hunslett St. E2 —3J 63
Hunston Rd. Mord —1K 131
Hunt Ct. N14 —7A 6
Hunt Ct. N'holt —2B 54
(off Gallery Gdns.)
Hunter Clo. SE1 —3D 78 (2F 157)
Hunter Ho. King T —1E 118
(off Sigrist Sq.)
Hunter Rd. SW20 —1E 120
Hunter Rd. Ilf —5F 51
Hunter Rd. T Hth —3D 124
Hunters Clo. SW12 —1E 108
Hunters Clo. Bex —3K 117
Hunters Ct. Rich —5D 88
Hunters Gro. Harr —4C 24
Hunters Hall Rd. Dag —4G 53
Hunters Hill. Ruis —3A 38
Hunters Meadow. SE19 —4E 110
Hunters Sq. Dag —4G 53
Hunter St. WC1 —4J 61 (3F 143)
Hunter's Way. Croy —4E 134
Hunters Way. Enf —1F 7
Hunter Wlk. E13 —2J 65
Huntingdon Clo. Mitc —3J 123
Huntingdon Gdns. W4 —7J 73

Huntingdon Gdns. Wor Pk
—3E 130
Huntingdon Rd. N2 —3C 28
Huntingdon Rd. N9 —1D 18
Huntingdon St. E16 —6H 65
Huntingdon St. N1 —7K 45
Huntingfield. Croy —7B 136
Huntingfield Rd. SW15 —4C 90
Hunting Ga. Clo. Enf —3F 7
Hunting Ga. M. Sutt —3K 131
Hunting Ga. M. Twic —1J 103
Huntings Farm. Ilf —3H 51
Huntings Rd. Dag —6G 53
Huntley Dri. N3 —6D 14
Huntley St. WC1
—4G 61 (4B 142)
Huntley Way. SW20 —2C 120
Huntly Rd. SE25 —4E 124
Hunton St. E1 —5G 63 (5K 145)
Hunt Rd. S'hall —3E 70
Hunt's Clo. SE3 —2J 97
Hunt's Ct. WC2 —7H 61 (3D 148)
Hunts La. E15 —2E 64
Huntsman St. SE17
—4E 78 (4G 157)
Hunts Mead. Enf —3E 8
Huntsmead Clo. Chst —1D 128
Huntspill St. SW17 —3A 108
Hunts Slip Rd. SE21 —3E 110
Hunt St. W11 —1F 75
Huntsworth M. NW1
—4D 60 (3E 140)
Hunt Way. SE22 —1G 111
Hurdwick Pl. NW1 —2G 61
(off Harrington Sq.)
Hurleston Ho. SE8 —5B 80
Hurley Clo. W5 —6C 56
Hurley Cres. SE16 —2K 79
Hurley Ho. SE11 —4A 78 (4K 155)
Hurley Rd. Gnfd —6F 55
Hurlingham Bus. Pk. SW6 —3J 91
Hurlingham Ct. SW6 —3H 91
Hurlingham Gdns. SW6 —3H 91
Hurlingham Retail Pk. SW6
—3K 91
Hurlingham Rd. SW6 —2H 91
Hurlingham Rd. Bexh —7F 85
Hurlingham Sq. SW6 —3J 91
Hurlock St. N5 —3B 46
Hurlstone Rd. SE25 —5E 124
Hurn Ct. Houn —2B 86
Hurn Ct. Rd. Houn —2B 86
Huron Rd. SW17 —2E 108
Hurren Clo. SE3 —3G 97
Hurry Clo. E15 —7G 49
Hurst Av. E4 —4H 19
Hurst Av. N6 —6G 29
Hurstbourne Gdns. Bark —6J 51
Hurstbourne Ho. SW15 —6B 90
(off Tangley Gro.)
Hurstbourne Rd. SE23 —1A 112
Hurst Clo. E4 —3H 19
Hurst Clo. NW11 —6K 27
Hurst Clo. Brom —1H 137
Hurst Clo. N'holt —5D 38
Hurstcombe. Buck H —2D 20
Hurst Ct. Sidc —2A 116
Hurstcourt Rd. Sutt —2K 131
Hurstdene Av. Brom —1H 137
Hurstdene Gdns. N15 —7E 30
Hurstfield. Brom —5J 127
Hurst La. SE2 —5D 84
Hurst La. Est. SE2 —5D 84
Hurstleigh Gdns. Ilf —1D 34
Hurstmead Ct. Edgw —4C 12

Hurst Rise. Barn —3D 4
Hurst Rd. E17 —3D 32
Hurst Rd. N21 —1F 17
Hurst Rd. Buck H —1G 21
Hurst Rd. Croy —4D 134
Hurst Rd. Eri —1J 101
Hurst Rd. Sidc & Bex —2A 116
Hurst Springs. Bex —1E 116
Hurst St. SE24 —6B 94
Hurstview Grange. S Croy
—7B 134
Hurst View Rd. S Croy —7E 134
Hurst Way. S Croy —6E 134
Hurstway Wlk. W11 —7F 59
Hurstwood Av. E18 —4K 33
Hurstwood Av. Bex —1E 116
Hurstwood Ct. N12 —6H 15
Hurstwood Ct. NW11 —4H 27
Hurstwood Dri. Brom —3D 128
Hurstwood Rd. NW11 —4G 27
Huson Rd. NW3 —7C 44
Hussars Clo. Houn —3C 86
Husseywell Cres. Brom —1J 137
Hutchings St. E14 —2C 80
Hutchings Wlk. NW11 —4K 27
Hutchins Clo. E15 —7E 48
Hutchinson Ct. Romf —4D 36
Hutchinson Ho. SE14 —7J 79
Hutchinson Ter. Wemb —3D 40
Hutton Clo. Gnfd —5H 39
Hutton Clo. Wfd G —6E 20
Hutton Gdns. Harr —7B 10
Hutton Gro. N12 —5E 14
Hutton La. Harr —7B 10
Hutton Row. Edgw —7D 12
Hutton St. EC4 —6B 62 (2K 149)
Hutton Wlk. Harr —7B 10
Huxbear St. SE4 —5B 96
Huxley Clo. N'holt —1C 54
Huxley Dri. Romf —7B 36
Huxley Gdns. NW10 —3F 57
Huxley Pde. N18 —5J 17
Huxley Pl. N13 —3G 17
Huxley Rd. E10 —2E 48
Huxley Rd. N18 —4J 17
Huxley Rd. Well —3K 99
Huxley Sayze. N18 —5J 17
Huxley St. W10 —3G 59
Hyacinth Clo. Hamp —6E 102
Hyacinth Rd. SW15 —1C 106
Hyde Clo. E13 —2J 65
Hyde Clo. Barn —3C 4
Hyde Ct. N20 —3G 15
Hyde Cres. NW9 —5A 26
Hyde Est. Rd. NW9 —5B 26
Hydefield Clo. N21 —1J 17
Hydefield Ct. N9 —2A 18
Hyde Ind. Est. NW9 —5B 26
Hyde La. SW11 —1C 92
Hyde Pk. Av. N21 —2H 17
Hyde Pk. Corner. W1
—2E 76 (6H 147)
Hyde Park Corner. (Junct.)
—2E 76
Hyde Pk. Cres. W2
—6C 60 (1C 146)
Hyde Pk. Gdns. N21 —1H 17
Hyde Pk. Gdns. W2
—7B 60 (2B 146)

Hyde Pk. Gdns. M. W2
—7B 60 (2B 146)
Hyde Pk. Ga. SW7 —2A 76
(in two parts)
Hyde Pk. Ga. M. SW7 —2A 76
Hyde Pk. Mans. NW1
—5C 60 (6C 140)
(off Cabbell St.)
Hyde Pk. Pl. W2
—7C 60 (2D 146)
Hyde Pk. Sq. W2
—6C 60 (1C 146)
Hyde Pk. Sq. M. W2
—6C 60 (1C 146)
Hyde Pk. St. W2
—6C 60 (1C 146)
Hyde Pk. Towers. W2 —7A 60
Hyderabad Way. E15 —7G 49
Hyde Rd. N1 —1D 62
Hyde Rd. Bexh —2F 101
Hyde Rd. Rich —5F 89
Hydeside Gdns. N9 —2A 18
Hydes Pl. N1 —7B 46
Hyde St. SE8 —6C 80
Hyde, The. NW9 —5B 26
Hydethorpe Av. N9 —2A 18
Hydethorpe Rd. SW12 —1G 109
Hyde Vale. SE10 —7E 80
Hyde Wlk. Mord —7J 121
Hyde Way. N9 —2A 18
Hylands Rd. E17 —2F 33
Hylton St. SE18 —4K 83
Hyndewood. SE23 —3K 111
Hyndman Ho. Dag —3G 53
(off Kershaw Rd.)
Hyndman St. SE15 —6H 79
Hynton Rd. Dag —2C 52
Hyperion Ho. SW2 —6K 93
Hyrstdene. S Croy —5B 134
Hyson Rd. SE16 —5H 79
Hythe Av. Bexh —7E 84
Hythe Clo. N18 —4B 18
Hythe Clo. NW10 —3B 58
Hythe Rd. T Hth —2D 124
Hythe Rd. Ind. Est. NW10
—3C 58

I

Ian Ct. SE23 —2J 111
Ian Sq. Enf —1E 8
Ibberton Ho. SW8 —7K 77
(off Meadow Rd.)
Ibbotson Av. E16 —6H 65
Ibbott St. E1 —4J 63
Iberia Ho. N19 —7H 29
Iberian Av. Wall —4H 133
Ibis La. W4 —1J 89
Ibis Way. Hayes —6B 54
Ibrox Ct. Buck H —2F 21
Ibscott Clo. Dag —6J 53
Ibsley Gdns. SW15 —1C 106
Ibsley Way. Cockf —4H 5
Iceland Rd. E3 —1C 64
Ickburgh Est. E5 —2H 47
Ickburgh Rd. E5 —3H 47
Ickenham Rd. SE9 —4C 114
Icknield Dri. Ilf —5F 35
Ickworth Pk. Rd. E17 —4A 32
Ida Rd. N15 —4D 30
Ida St. E14 —6E 64
(in two parts)
Iden Clo. Brom —3G 127
Idlecombe Rd. SW17 —6E 108
Idmiston Rd. E15 —4H 49
Idmiston Rd. SE27 —3C 110

Idmiston Rd. Wor Pk —7B 120
Idmiston Sq. Wor Pk —7B 120
Idol La. EC3 —7E 62 (3G 151)
Idonia St. SE8 —7C 80
Iffley Rd. W6 —3D 74
Ifield Rd. SW10 —6K 75
Ifor Evans Pl. E1 —4K 63
Ightham Ho. Beck —7B 112
(off Bethersden Clo.)
Ightham Rd. Eri —7G 85
Ilbert St. W10 —3F 59
Ilchester Gdns. W2 —7K 59
Ilchester Pl. W14 —3H 75
Ilchester Rd. Dag —5B 52
Ildersly Gro. SE21 —2D 110
Ilderton Rd. SE16 & SE15
—5J 79
Ilex Rd. NW10 —6B 42
Ilex Way. SW16 —5A 110
Ilford Hill. Ilf —3E 50
Ilford Ho. N1 —6D 46
(off Dove Rd.)
Ilford La. Ilf —3F 51
Ilfracombe Gdns. Romf —7B 36
Ilfracombe Rd. Brom —3H 113
Iliffe St. SE17 —5B 78 (5B 156)
Iliffe Yd. SE17 —5B 78 (5B 156)
Ilkeston Ct. E5 —4K 47
(off Overbury St.)
Ilkley Clo. SE19 —6D 110
Ilkley Rd. E16 —5A 66
Illingworth Clo. Mitc —3B 122
Illingworth Way. Enf —5K 7
Ilmington Rd. Harr —6D 24
Ilminster Gdns. SW11 —4C 92
Imani Mans. SW11 —2B 92
Imber Clo. N14 —7B 6
Imber St. N1 —1D 62
Impact Ct. SE20 —2H 125
Imperial Av. N16 —4E 46
Imperial Clo. Harr —6E 22
Imperial College Rd. SW7
—3B 76 (2A 152)
Imperial Ct. N6 —6G 29
Imperial Ct. N20 —3F 15
Imperial Ct. NW8 —2C 60
(off Prince Albert Rd.)
Imperial Ct. S Harr —1E 22
Imperial Dri. Harr —1E 22
Imperial Gdns. Mitc —3F 123
Imperial M. E6 —2B 66
Imperial Pde. EC4
—6B 62 (1A 150)
(off New Bri. St.)
Imperial Rd. N22 —7D 16
Imperial Rd. SW6 —1K 91
Imperial Sq. SW6 —1K 91
Imperial St. E3 —3E 64
Imperial Way. Chst —4G 115
Imperial Way. Croy —6K 133
Imperial Way. Harr —6E 24
Inca Dri. SE9 —7F 99
Inchmery Rd. SE6 —2D 112
Inchwood. Croy —4D 136
Independent Pl. E8 —5F 47
Independents Rd. SE3 —3H 97
Inderwick Rd. N8 —5K 29
Indescon Ct. E14 —2C 80
India Pl. WC2 —7K 61 (2G 149)
India St. EC3 —6F 63 (1J 151)
India Way. W12 —7D 58
Indus Rd. SE7 —7A 82
Industry Ter. SW9 —3A 94
Infirmary Ct. SW3
—6D 76 (7F 153)

Ingal Rd. E13 —4J 65
Ingate Pl. SW8 —1F 93
Ingatestone Rd. E12 —1A 50
Ingatestone Rd. SE25 —4H 125
Ingatestone Rd. Wfd G —7E 20
Ingelow Rd. SW8 —2F 93
Ingersoll Rd. W12 —1D 74
Ingersoll Rd. Enf —1D 8
Ingestre Pl. W1 —6G 61 (1B 148)
Ingestre Rd. E7 —4J 49
Ingestre Rd. NW5 —4F 45
Ingham Rd. S Croy —7K 135
Ingham Rd. NW6 —4J 43
Ingham Rd. S Croy —7J 135
Inglebert St. EC1
　　　　　　　—3A 62 (1J 143)
Ingleborough St. N17 —3F 31
Ingleborough St. SW9 —2A 94
Ingleby Dri. Harr —3H 39
Ingleby Rd. N7 —3J 45
Ingleby Rd. Dag —6H 53
Ingleby Rd. Ilf —1F 51
Ingleby Way. Chst —5E 114
Ingleby Way. Wall —7H 133
Ingle Clo. Pinn —3C 22
Ingledew Rd. SE18 —5H 83
Inglehurst Gdns. Ilf —5D 34
Inglemere Rd. SE23 —3K 111
Inglemere Rd. Mitc —7D 108
Inglesham Wlk. E9 —6B 48
Ingleside Clo. Beck —7C 112
Ingleside Gro. SE3 —6H 81
Inglethorpe St. SW6 —1F 91
Ingleton Av. Well —5A 100
Ingleton Rd. N18 —6B 18
Ingleton St. Cars —7C 132
Ingleton St. SW9 —2A 94
Ingleway. N12 —6G 15
Inglewood. Croy —7A 136
Inglewood Clo. E14 —4C 80
Inglewood Copse. Brom —2C 128
Inglewood Rd. NW6 —5J 43
Inglewood Rd. Bexh —4K 101
Inglis St. W5 —7F 57
Inglis Rd. Croy —1F 135
Inglis St. SE5 —1B 94
Ingoldisthorpe Gro. SE15
　　　　　　　—6F 79 (7K 157)
Ingram Av. NW11 —7A 28
Ingram Clo. SE11
　　　　　　　—4K 77 (3H 155)
Ingram Clo. Stan —5H 11
Ingram Rd. N2 —4C 28
Ingram Rd. T Hth —1C 124
Ingram Way. Gnfd —1H 55
Ingrave Rd. Romf —4K 37
Ingrave St. SW11 —3B 92
Ingrebourne Ho. Brom —5F 113
　(off Brangbourne Rd.)
Ingresbourne Ct. E4 —3J 19
Ingress St. W4 —5A 74
Inigo Jones Rd. SE7 —7C 82
Inigo Pl. WC2 —7J 61 (2E 148)
Inkerman Rd. NW5 —6F 45
Inkerman Ter. W8 —3J 75
　(off Allen St.)
Inks Grn. E4 —5J 19
Inman Rd. NW10 —1A 58
Inman Rd. SW18 —7A 92
Inmans Row. Wfd G —4D 20
Inner Circ. NW1 —3E 60 (2G 141)
Inner Pk. Rd. SW19 —1F 107
Inner Staithe. W4 —1J 89
Inner Temple La. EC4
　　　　　　　—6A 62 (1J 149)

Innes Clo. SW20 —2G 121
Innes Gdns. SW15 —6D 90
Innis Ho. SE17 —5E 78 (5G 157)
Inniskilling Rd. E13 —2A 66
Innis Yd. Croy —3C 134
Inskip Clo. E10 —2D 48
Inskip Rd. Dag —1D 52
Institute Pl. E8 —5H 47
Instone Clo. Wall —7J 133
Integer Gdns. E11 —7F 33
Interface Ho. Houn —3E 86
　(off Staines Rd.)
International Av. Houn —5A 70
International Trad. Est. S'hall
　　　　　　　—3A 70
Inverary Pl. SE18 —6H 83
Inver Clo. E5 —2J 47
Inverclyde Gdns. Romf —4C 36
　(in two parts)
Inver Ct. W2 —6K 59
Inveresk Gdns. Wor Pk —3B 130
Inverforth Clo. NW3 —2A 44
Inverforth Rd. N11 —5A 16
Inverine Rd. SE7 —5K 81
Invermore Pl. SE18 —4G 83
Inverness Av. Enf —1K 7
Inverness Gdns. W8 —1K 75
Inverness M. W2 —7K 59
Inverness Pl. W2 —7K 59
Inverness Rd. N18 —5C 18
Inverness Rd. Houn —4D 86
Inverness Rd. S'hall —4C 70
Inverness Rd. Wor Pk —1F 131
Inverness St. NW1 —1F 61
Inverness Ter. W2 —6K 59
Inverton Rd. SE15 —4K 95
Invicta Clo. Chst —5E 114
Invicta Gro. N'holt —3D 54
Invicta Pde. Sidc —4B 116
Invicta Plaza. SE1
　　　　　　　—1B 78 (4A 150)
Invicta Rd. SE3 —7J 81
Inville Rd. SE17 —5D 78 (6F 157)
Inville Wlk. SE17
　　　　　　　—5D 78 (6F 157)
Inwen Ct. SE8 —5A 80
Inwood Av. Houn —3G 87
Inwood Bus. Cen. Houn —4F 87
Inwood Clo. Croy —2A 136
Inwood Rd. Houn —4F 87
Inworth St. SW11 —2C 92
Inworth Wlk. N1 —1C 62
　(off Popham St.)
Iona Clo. SE6 —7C 96
Ion Ct. E2 —2G 63
Ion Sq. E2 —2G 63
Ipsden Bldgs. SE1
　　　　　　　—2A 78 (6K 149)
Ipswich Ho. SE4 —5K 95
Ipswich Rd. SW17 —6E 108
Ireland Clo. E6 —5D 66
Ireland Pl. N22 —7D 16
Ireland Yd. EC4 —6B 62 (1B 150)
Irene M. W7 —1K 71
　(off Uxbridge Rd.)
Irene Rd. SW6 —1J 91
Irene Rd. Orp —7K 129
Ireton Clo. N10 —7K 15
Ireton Ho. SW9 —2A 94
Ireton St. E3 —4C 64
Iris Av. Bex —6E 100
Iris Clo. E6 —4C 66
Iris Clo. Croy —1K 135
Iris Clo. Surb —7F 119
Iris Cres. Bexh —6F 85

Iris Way. E4 —6G 19
Irkdale Av. Enf —1A 8
Iron Bri. Clo. NW10 —5A 42
Ironbridge Clo. S'hall —1G 71
Iron Mill Pl. SW18 —6K 91
Iron Mill Rd. SW18 —6K 91
Ironmonger La. EC2
　　　　　　　—6C 62 (1D 150)
Ironmonger Row. EC1
　　　　　　　—3C 62 (2D 144)
Ironmongers Pl. E14 —4C 80
Ironside Clo. SE16 —2K 79
Ironside Ho. E9 —4A 48
Irons Way. Romf —1J 37
Irvine Av. Harr —3A 24
Irvine Clo. N20 —2H 15
Irvine Ho. N7 —6K 45
　(off Caledonian Rd.)
Irving Av. N'holt —1B 54
Irving Gro. SW9 —2K 93
Irving Ho. SE17 —5B 78 (6A 156)
Irving Mans. W14 —6G 75
　(off Queen's Club Gdns.)
Irving M. N1 —6C 46
Irving Rd. W14 —3F 75
Irving St. WC2 —7H 61 (3D 148)
Irving Way. NW9 —6B 26
Irwell Ct. W7 —6H 55
　(off Hobbayne Rd.)
Irwell Est. SE16 —3J 79
Irwin Av. SE18 —7J 83
Irwin Gdns. NW10 —1D 58
Isabella Clo. N14 —7B 6
Isabella Ct. Rich —6F 89
Isabella Rd. E9 —5J 47
Isabella St. SE1 —1B 78 (5A 150)
Isabel St. SW9 —1K 93
Isambard M. E14 —3E 80
Isambard Pl. SE16 —1J 79
Isel Way. SE22 —5E 94
Isham Rd. SW16 —2J 123
Isis Clo. SW15 —4E 90
Isis Ct. W4 —7H 73
Isis Ho. N18 —6A 18
Isis St. SW18 —2A 108
Island Rd. Mitc —7D 108
Island Row. E14 —6B 64
Island, The. Th Dit —6A 118
Isla Rd. SE18 —6G 83
Islay Gdns. Houn —5B 86
Islay Wlk. N1 —6C 46
Isledon Rd. N7 —3A 46
Islehurst Clo. Chst —1E 128
Isleworth Bus. Complex. Iswth
　　　　　　　—2K 87
Isleworth Promenade. Twic
　　　　　　　—4B 88
Isley Ct. SW8 —2G 93
Islington Grn. N1 —1B 62
Islington High St. N1 —2A 62
Islington Pk. M. N1 —7B 46
Islington Pk. St. N1 —7A 46
Islip Gdns. Edgw —7E 12
Islip Gdns. N'holt —7C 38
Islip Mnr. Rd. N'holt —7C 38
Islip St. NW5 —5G 45
Ismailia Rd. E7 —7K 49
Isobel Ho. Harr —5K 23
Isom Clo. E13 —3K 65
Itaska Cotts. Bush —1D 10
Ivanhoe Dri. Harr —3A 24
Ivanhoe Rd. SE5 —3F 95
Ivanhoe Rd. Houn —3B 86

Ivatt Pl. W14 —5H 75
Ivatt Way. N17 —3C 30
Iveagh Av. NW10 —2G 57
Iveagh Clo. E9 —1K 63
Iveagh Clo. NW10 —2G 57
Iveagh Ct. E1 —6F 63 (1J 151)
Iveagh Ct. Beck —3E 126
Iveagh Ho. SW9 —2B 94
Iveagh Ter. NW10 —2G 57
　(off Iveagh Av.)
Ivedon Rd. Well —2C 100
Iveley Rd. SW4 —2G 93
Ivere Dri. New Bar —6E 4
Iverhurst Clo. Bexh —5D 100
Iverna Ct. W8 —3J 75
Iverna Gdns. W8 —3J 75
Iverson Rd. NW6 —6H 43
Ivers Way. New Ad —7D 136
Ives Rd. E16 —5G 65
Ives St. SW3 —4C 76 (3D 152)
Ivestor Ter. SE23 —7J 95
Ivimey St. E2 —3G 63
Ivinghoe Clo. Enf —1K 7
Ivinghoe Ho. N7 —5H 45
Ivinghoe Rd. Dag —5B 52
Ivor Ct. N8 —6J 29
Ivor Gro. SE9 —1F 115
Ivor Pl. NW1 —4D 60 (4E 140)
Ivor St. NW1 —7G 45
Ivorydown. Brom —4J 113
Ivory Ho. E1 —1F 79 (3K 151)
Ivory Sq. SW11 —3A 92
Ivybridge Clo. Twic —7A 88
Ivybridge Ct. Chst —1E 128
　(off Old Hill)
Ivybridge La. WC2
　　　　　　　—7J 61 (3F 149)
Ivychurch Clo. SE20 —7J 111
Ivychurch La. SE17
　　　　　　　—5F 79 (5J 157)
Ivy Clo. Harr —4D 38
Ivy Clo. Pinn —7A 22
Ivy Cotts. E14 —7D 64
Ivy Cres. W4 —4J 73
Ivydale Rd. SE15 —3K 95
Ivydale Rd. Cars —2D 132
Ivyday Gro. SW16 —3K 109
Ivydene Clo. Sutt —4A 132
Ivy Gdns. N8 —6J 29
Ivy Gdns. Mitc —3H 123
Ivyhouse Rd. Dag —6D 52
Ivy La. Houn —4D 86
Ivymount Rd. SE27 —3A 110
Ivy Rd. E16 —6J 65
Ivy Rd. E17 —6C 32
Ivy Rd. N14 —7B 6
Ivy Rd. NW2 —4E 42
Ivy Rd. SE4 —4B 96
Ivy Rd. SW17 —5C 108
Ivy Rd. Houn —4F 87
Ivy St. N1 —2E 62
Ivy Wlk. Dag —6E 52
Ixworth Pl. SW3
　　　　　　　—5C 76 (5C 152)
Izane Rd. Bexh —4F 101

Jacaranda Clo. N Mald —3A 120
Jackass La. Kes —5K 137
Jack Barnett Way. N22 —2K 29
Jack Clow Rd. E15 —2G 65
Jack Cook Ho. Bark —7F 51
Jack Cornwell St. E12 —4E 50

Jack Dash Way. E6 —4C 66
Jacklin Grn. Wfd G —4D 20
Jackman M. NW10 —3A 42
Jackman St. E8 —1H 63
Jackson Ct. E7 —6K 49
Jackson Rd. N7 —4K 45
Jackson Rd. Bark —1H 67
Jackson Rd. Barn —6H 5
Jackson Rd. Brom —2D 138
Jacksons La. N6 —7E 28
Jacksons Pl. Croy —1E 134
Jackson St. SE18 —6E 82
Jackson's Way. Croy —3C 136
Jackson Way. S'hall —2F 71
Jack Walker Ct. N5 —4B 46
Jacob Ho. Eri —2D 84
Jacobin Lodge. N7 —5J 45
Jacobs Clo. Dag —4H 53
Jacobs Ho. E13 —3A 66
　(off New City Rd.)
Jacob St. SE1 —2G 79 (6K 151)
Jacob's Well M. W1
　　　　　　　—6E 60 (6H 141)
Jacqueline Clo. N'holt —1C 54
Jacqueline Vs. E17 —5E 32
Jade Clo. E16 —6B 66
Jade Clo. NW2 —7E 26
Jade Clo. Dag —1C 52
Jaffe Rd. Ilf —1H 51
Jaffray Pl. SE27 —4B 110
Jaffray Rd. Brom —4B 128
Jaggard Way. SW12 —7D 92
Jago Clo. SE18 —6G 83
Jago Wlk. SE5 —7D 78
Jamaica Rd. SE1 & SE16
　　　　　　　—2F 79 (7K 151)
Jamaica Rd. T Hth —6B 124
Jamaica St. E1 —6J 63
James Anderson Ct. E2 —2E 62
　(off Kingsland Rd.)
James Av. NW2 —5E 42
James Av. Dag —1F 53
James Bedford Clo. Pinn —2A 22
James Boswell Clo. SW16
　　　　　　　—4K 109
James Clo. E13 —2J 65
James Clo. NW11 —6G 27
James Clo. Bush —1B 10
James Collins Clo. W9 —4H 59
James Ct. NW9 —2A 26
James Ct. N'holt —2C 54
　(off Church Rd.)
James Dudson Ct. NW10 —7J 41
James Est. Mitc —2D 122
James Gdns. N22 —7G 17
James Joyce Wlk. SE24 —4B 94
James La. E10 & E11 —7E 32
James Newham Ct. SE9 —3E 114
Jameson Ho. SE11
　　　　　　　—5K 77 (5G 155)
Jameson Lodge. N6 —6G 29
Jameson St. W8 —1J 75
James Pl. N17 —1F 31
James's Cotts. Rich —7G 73
James Stewart Ho. NW6 —7H 43
James St. W1 —6E 60 (7H 141)
James St. WC2 —7J 61 (1F 149)
James St. Bark —7G 51
James St. Beck —3B 126
James St. Enf —5A 8
James St. Houn —3H 87
Jamestown Rd. NW1 —1F 61
James Yd. E4 —6A 20
Jamieson Ho. Houn —6D 86
Jane Seymour Ct. SE9 —7H 99
Jane St. E1 —6H 63

Janet St. *E14* —3C **80**
Janeway Pl. *SE16* —2H **79**
Janeway St. *SE16* —2G **79**
Janice M. *Ilf* —2F **51**
Jansen Wlk. *SW11* —3B **92**
Janson Clo. *E15* —5G **49**
Janson Clo. *NW10* —3K **41**
Janson Rd. *E15* —5G **49**
Jansons Rd. *N15* —3E **30**
Japan Cres. *N4* —7K **29**
Japan Rd. *Romf* —6D **36**
Jardine Rd. *E1* —7K **63**
Jarrett Clo. *SW2* —1B **110**
Jarrow Clo. *Mord* —5K **121**
Jarrow Rd. *N17* —4H **31**
Jarrow Rd. *SE16* —4J **79**
Jarrow Rd. *Romf* —6C **36**
Jarrow Way. *E9* —4B **48**
Jarvis Clo. *Barn* —5A **4**
Jarvis Rd. *SE22* —4E **94**
Jarvis Rd. *S Croy* —6D **134**
Jashoda Ho. *SE18* —5E **82**
  (off Connaught M.)
Jasmin Ct. *SE12* —6J **97**
Jasmine Clo. *Ilf* —5F **51**
Jasmine Clo. *S'hall* —7C **54**
Jasmine Ct. *SW19* —5J **107**
Jasmine Gdns. *Croy* —3D **136**
Jasmine Gdns. *Harr* —2E **38**
Jasmine Gro. *SE20* —1H **125**
Jasmin Lodge. *SE16* —5H **79**
  (off Sherwood Gdns.)
Jason Ct. *W1* —6E **60** (7H **141**)
Jason Wlk. *SE9* —4E **114**
Jasper Clo. *Enf* —1D **8**
Jasper Pas. *SE19* —6F **111**
Jasper Rd. *E16* —6B **66**
Jasper Rd. *SE19* —5F **111**
Java Wharf. *SE1*
  —2F **79** (6K **151**)
Javelin Way. *N'holt* —3B **54**
Jaycroft. *Enf* —1F **7**
Jay Gdns. *Chst* —4D **114**
Jay M. *SW7* —2A **76** (7A **146**)
Jebb Av. *SW2* —6J **93**
Jebb St. *E3* —2C **64**
Jedburgh Rd. *E13* —3A **66**
Jedburgh St. *SW11* —4E **92**
Jeddo M. *W12* —2B **74**
Jeddo Rd. *W12* —2B **74**
Jefferson Clo. *W13* —3B **72**
Jefferson Clo. *Ilf* —5F **35**
Jefferson Wlk. *SE18* —6E **82**
Jeffery. *Sidc* —5B **116**
Jeffrey Row. *SE12* —5K **97**
Jeffrey's Pl. *NW1* —7G **45**
Jeffreys Rd. *SW4* —2J **93**
Jeffreys Rd. *Enf* —4F **9**
Jeffrey's St. *NW1* —7F **45**
Jeffreys Wlk. *SW4* —2J **93**
Jeffs Clo. *Hamp* —6F **103**
Jeffs Rd. *Sutt* —4H **131**
Jeger Av. *E2* —1F **63**
Jeken Rd. *SE9* —4A **98**
Jelf Rd. *SW2* —5A **94**
Jellicoe Gdns. *Stan* —6E **10**
  (in two parts)
Jellicoe Rd. *E13* —4J **65**
Jellicoe Rd. *N17* —7J **17**
Jemmett Clo. *King T* —1H **119**
Jem Paterson Ct. *Harr* —4J **39**
Jengar Clo. *Sutt* —4K **131**
Jenkins La. *Bark* —2G **67**
Jenkins Rd. *E13* —4K **65**
Jenner Av. *W3* —5K **57**

Jenner Clo. *W3* —5K **57**
Jenner Pl. *SW13* —6D **74**
Jenner Rd. *N16* —3F **47**
Jennett Rd. *Croy* —3A **134**
Jennifer Rd. *Brom* —3H **113**
Jennings Rd. *SE22* —6F **95**
Jennings Way. *Barn* —3A **4**
Jenningtree Way. *Belv* —2J **85**
Jenny Hammond Clo. *E11*
  —3H **49**
Jenson Way. *SE19* —7F **111**
Jenton Av. *Bexh* —2E **100**
Jephson Ct. *SW4* —2J **93**
Jephson Ho. *SE17*
  —6B **78** (7A **156**)
Jephson Rd. *E7* —7A **50**
Jephson St. *SE5* —1D **94**
Jephtha Rd. *SW18* —6J **91**
Jeppos La. *Mitc* —4D **122**
Jepson Ho. *SW6* —1K **91**
  (off Pearscroft Rd.)
Jerdan Pl. *SW6* —7J **75**
Jeremiah St. *E14* —6D **64**
Jeremy's Grn. *N18* —4C **18**
Jermyn St. *SW1*
  —1G **77** (4A **148**)
Jerningham Av. *Ilf* —2F **35**
Jerningham Ct. *SE14* —1A **96**
Jerningham Rd. *SE14* —2A **96**
Jerome Cres. *NW8*
  —4C **60** (3C **140**)
Jerome St. *E1* —5F **63** (5J **145**)
Jerome Tower. *W3* —2H **73**
Jerrard St. *SE13* —3D **96**
Jerrold St. *N1* —2E **62** (1H **145**)
Jersey Av. *Stan* —2B **24**
Jersey Dri. *Orp* —6H **129**
Jersey Ho. *N1* —6C **46**
Jersey Rd. *E11* —1F **49**
Jersey Rd. *E16* —6A **66**
Jersey Rd. *N1* —6C **46**
Jersey Rd. *SW17* —6F **109**
Jersey Rd. *W7* —2A **72**
Jersey Rd. *Houn & Iswth* —1F **87**
Jersey Rd. *Ilf* —4F **51**
Jersey St. *E2* —3H **63**
Jerusalem Pas. *EC1*
  —4B **62** (4A **144**)
Jervis Clo. *W1* —6F **61** (1K **147**)
Jervis Ct. *Dag* —6H **53**
Jerviston Gdns. *SW16* —6A **110**
Jesmond Av. *Wemb* —6F **41**
Jesmond Clo. *Mitc* —3F **123**
Jesmond Rd. *Croy* —7F **125**
Jesmond Way. *Stan* —5K **11**
Jessam Av. *E5* —1H **47**
Jessamine Rd. *W7* —1K **71**
Jesse Rd. *E10* —1E **48**
Jessett Clo. *Eri* —4K **85**
Jessica Rd. *SW18* —6A **92**
Jessie Blythe La. *N19* —7J **29**
Jessop Av. *S'hall* —4D **70**
Jessop Ct. *N1* —2B **62**
Jessop Rd. *SE24* —4B **94**
Jessops Way. *Croy* —6G **123**
Jessup Clo. *SE18* —4G **83**
Jetstar Way. *N'holt* —3C **54**
Jevington Way. *SE12* —1K **113**
Jewel Rd. *E17* —3C **32**
Jewry St. *EC3* —6F **63** (1J **151**)
Jew's Row. *SW18* —4K **91**
Jews Wlk. *SE26* —4H **111**
Jeymer Av. *NW2* —5D **42**
Jeymer Dri. *Gnfd* —1F **55**
Jeypore Pas. *SW18* —6A **92**

Jeypore Rd. *SW18* —7A **92**
Jillian Clo. *Hamp* —7E **102**
Jim Bradley Clo. *SE18* —4E **82**
Jim Griffiths Ho. *SW6* —6H **75**
  (off Clem Attlee Ct.)
Joan Cres. *SE9* —7B **98**
Joan Gdns. *Dag* —2E **52**
Joanna Wlk. *SW9* —1K **93**
Joan Rd. *Dag* —2E **52**
Joan St. *SE1* —1B **78** (5A **150**)
Jocelin Ho. *N1* —1K **61**
  (off Barnsbury Est.)
Jocelyn Rd. *Rich* —3E **88**
Jocelyn St. *SE15* —1G **95**
Jockey's Fields. *WC1*
  —5K **61** (5H **143**)
Jodane St. *SE8* —4B **80**
Jodrell Clo. *Iswth* —1A **88**
Jodrell Rd. *E3* —1B **64**
Joe Hunte Ct. *SE27* —5B **110**
Johanna St. *SE1*
  —2A **78** (7J **149**)
John Adams Ct. *N9* —2A **18**
John Adam St. *WC2*
  —7J **61** (3F **149**)
John Aird Ct. *W2*
  —5A **60** (5A **140**)
John Ashby Clo. *SW2* —6J **93**
John Baird Ct. *SE26* —4J **111**
John Barnes Wlk. *E15* —6H **49**
John Bradshaw Rd. *N14* —1C **16**
John Brent Ho. *SE8* —4K **79**
  (off Haddonfield)
John Burns Dri. *Bark* —7J **51**
John Campbell Rd. *N16* —5E **46**
John Carpenter St. *EC4*
  —7B **62** (2A **150**)
John Felton Rd. *SE16* —2G **79**
John Fisher St. *E1*
  —7G **63** (2K **151**)
John Gooch Dri. *Enf* —1G **7**
John Islip St. *SW1*
  —4H **77** (5D **154**)
John Kennedy Ct. *N1* —6D **46**
  (off Newington Grn. Rd.)
John Knight Lodge. *SW6* —7J **75**
  (off Vanston Pl.)
John Lamb Ct. *Harr* —1J **23**
John Masefield Ho. *N15* —6D **30**
  (off Fladbury Rd.)
John Maurice Clo. *SE17*
  —4D **78** (3E **156**)
John McKenna Wlk. *SE16*
  —3G **79**
John Newton Ct. *Well* —3B **100**
John Parker Clo. *Dag* —7H **53**
John Parker Sq. *SW11* —3B **92**
John Parry Ct. *N1* —2E **62**
  (off Hare Wlk.)
John Penn St. *SE13* —1D **96**
John Perrin Pl. *Harr* —7E **24**
John Pound Ho. *SW18* —7K **91**
John Prince's St. *W1*
  —6F **61** (7K **141**)
John Pritchard Ho. *E1* —4G **63**
  (off Buxton St.)
John Rennie Wlk. *E1* —7H **63**
John Roll Way. *SE16* —3G **79**
John Ruskin St. *SE5* —7B **78**
John's Av. *NW4* —4E **26**
John's Ct. *Sutt* —6K **131**
John Silkin La. *SE8* —5K **79**
John's La. *Mord* —5A **122**
John's M. *WC1* —4K **61** (4H **143**)
John Smith Av. *SW6* —7H **75**

Johnson Clo. *E8* —1G **63**
Johnson Mans. *W14* —6G **75**
  (off Queen's Club Gdns.)
Johnson Rd. *Brom* —5B **128**
Johnson Rd. *Croy* —7D **124**
Johnson Rd. *Houn* —7A **70**
Johnsons Clo. *Cars* —2D **132**
Johnsons Ct. *EC4*
  —6A **62** (1K **149**)
Johnson's Pl. *SW1*
  —5G **77** (6A **154**)
Johnson St. *E1* —7J **63**
Johnson St. *S'hall* —3A **70**
Johnsons Way. *NW10* —4H **57**
John Spencer Sq. *N1* —6B **46**
John's Pl. *E1* —6J **63**
John's Ter. *Croy* —1E **134**
Johnston Clo. *SW9* —1K **93**
Johnstone Ho. *SE13* —3F **97**
  (off Belmont Hill)
Johnstone Rd. *E6* —3D **66**
Johnston Rd. *Wfd G* —5D **20**
Johnston Ter. *NW2* —3F **43**
John Strachey Ho. *SW6* —6H **75**
  (off Clem Attlee Ct.)
John St. *E15* —1H **65**
John St. *SE25* —4G **125**
John St. *WC1* —4K **61** (4H **143**)
John St. *Enf* —5A **8**
John St. *Houn* —2C **86**
John Strype Ct. *E10* —2D **48**
John Trundle Ct. *EC2*
  —5C **62** (5C **144**)
John Wesley Ct. *Twic* —1A **104**
John Wheatley Ho. *SW6* —6H **75**
  (off Clem Attlee Ct.)
John Williams Clo. *SE14* —6K **79**
John Wilson St. *SE18* —3E **82**
John Woolley Clo. *SE13* —4G **97**
Joiners Arms Yd. *SE5* —1D **94**
Joiners Pl. *N5* —4D **46**
Joint Rd. *N2* —1C **28**
Jollys La. *Harr* —1H **39**
Jollys La. *Hayes* —5B **54**
Jonathan St. *SE11*
  —5K **77** (5G **155**)
Jones Rd. *E13* —4K **65**
Jones Rd. *E13* —4K **65**
Jones St. *W1* —7F **61** (3J **147**)
Jones Wlk. *Rich* —6F **89**
Jonquil Gdns. *Hamp* —6E **102**
Jonson Clo. *Mitc* —4F **123**
Jordan Clo. *Dag* —4H **53**
Jordan Clo. *S Harr* —3D **38**
Jordan Ho. *N1* —1D **62**
  (off Colville Est.)
Jordan Ho. *SE4* —4K **95**
  (off St Norbert Rd.)
Jordan Rd. *Gnfd* —1B **56**
Jordans Clo. *Iswth* —1J **87**
Jordans M. *Twic* —2J **103**
Joseph Av. *W3* —5K **57**
Joseph Ct. *N16* —7E **30**
  (off Amhurst Pk.)
Josephine Av. *SW2* —5K **93**
Joseph Lister Ct. *E7* —7J **49**
  (off Upton La.)
Joseph Powell Clo. *SW12* —6F **93**
Joseph Ray Rd. *E11* —2G **49**
Joseph St. *E3* —4B **64**
Joseph Trotter Clo. *EC1*
  —3A **62** (2K **143**)
Joshua St. *E14* —6E **64**
Joubert St. *SW11* —2D **92**
Jowett St. *SE15* —7F **79**

Joyce Av. *N18* —5A **18**
Joyce Butler Ho. *N22* —1K **29**
Joyce Dawson Way. *SE28*
  —7A **68**
Joyce Page Clo. *SE7* —6B **82**
Joyce Wlk. *SW2* —6A **94**
Joydens Wood Rd. *Bex* —4K **117**
Joydon Dri. *Romf* —6B **36**
Joyners Clo. *Dag* —4F **53**
Joystone Ct. *New Bar* —4H **5**
  (off Park Rd.)
Jubb Powell Ho. *N15* —6E **30**
Jubilee Av. *E4* —6K **19**
Jubilee Av. *Romf* —5H **37**
Jubilee Av. *Twic* —1G **103**
Jubilee Bldgs. *NW8* —1B **60**
  (off Queen's Ter.)
Jubilee Clo. *NW9* —6K **25**
Jubilee Clo. *King T* —1C **118**
Jubilee Clo. *Pinn* —2A **22**
Jubilee Clo. *Romf* —5H **37**
Jubilee Ct. *N10* —3E **28**
Jubilee Ct. *Harr* —7E **24**
Jubilee Ct. *Houn* —3G **87**
  (off Bristow Rd.)
Jubilee Cres. *E14* —3E **80**
Jubilee Cres. *N9* —1B **18**
Jubilee Dri. *Ruis* —4B **38**
Jubilee Gdns. *S'hall* —5E **54**
Jubilee Ho. *WC1*
  —4K **61** (3G **143**)
Jubilee Pl. *SW3* —5C **76** (5D **152**)
Jubilee Rd. *Gnfd* —1B **56**
Jubilee Rd. *Sutt* —7F **131**
Jubilee St. *E1* —6J **63**
Jubilee Ter. *N1* —7D **46**
Jubilee, The. *SE10* —7D **80**
Jubilee Way. *SW19* —1K **121**
Jubilee Way. *Sidc* —2A **116**
Judd St. *WC1* —3J **61** (2E **142**)
Jude St. *E16* —6H **65**
Judges Wlk. *NW3* —3A **44**
Juer St. *SW11* —7C **76**
Julia Ct. *E17* —5D **32**
Julia Gdns. *Bark* —2D **68**
Julia Garfield M. *E16* —1K **81**
Juliana Clo. *N2* —2A **28**
Julian Av. *W3* —7H **57**
Julian Clo. *New Bar* —3E **4**
Julian Hill. *Harr* —2J **39**
Julian Pl. *E14* —5D **80**
Julian Taylor Path. *SE23*
  —2H **111**
Julia St. *NW5* —4E **44**
Julien Rd. *W5* —4C **72**
Juliet Ho. *N1* —2E **62**
  (off Arden Est.)
Juliette Rd. *E13* —2J **65**
Junction App. *SE13* —3E **96**
Junction App. *SW11* —3C **92**
Junction M. *W2* —6C **60** (7C **140**)
Junction Pl. *W2* —6C **60** (7B **140**)
Junction Rd. *E13* —2K **65**
Junction Rd. *N9* —1B **18**
Junction Rd. *N17* —3G **31**
Junction Rd. *N19* —4G **45**
Junction Rd. *W5 & Bren* —4C **72**
Junction Rd. *Harr* —6J **23**
Junction Rd. *S Croy* —5D **134**
Junction Rd. *E. Romf* —7E **36**
Junction Rd. *W. Romf* —7E **36**
Juniper Clo. *Barn* —5A **4**
Juniper Clo. *Wemb* —5G **41**
Juniper Ct. *W8* —3K **75**
  (off St. Marys Pl.)

Juniper Ct. *Harr* —1K **23**
Juniper Cres. *NW1* —7E **44**
Juniper Gdns. *SW16* —1G **123**
Juniper La. *E6* —5C **66**
Juniper Rd. *Ilf* —3E **50**
Juniper St. *E1* —7J **63**
Juno Way. *SE14* —6K **79**
Juno Way Ind. Est. *SE14* —6K **79**
Jupiter Way. *N7* —6K **45**
Jupp Rd. *E15* —7F **49**
Jupp Rd. W. *E15* —1F **65**
Justice Wlk. *SW3*
　　　　—6C **76** (7C **152**)
Justin Clo. *Bren* —7D **72**
Justin Rd. *E4* —6G **19**
Jute La. *Enf* —3F **9**
Jutland Clo. *N19* —1J **45**
Jutland Ho. *SE5* —2C **94**
Jutland Rd. *E13* —4J **65**
Jutland Rd. *SE6* —7E **96**
Jutsums Av. *Romf* —6H **37**
Jutsums Ct. *Romf* —6H **37**
Jutsums La. *Romf* —6H **37**
Juxon Clo. *Harr* —1F **23**
Juxon St. *SE11* —4K **77** (3H **155**)
JVC Bus. Pk. *NW2* —1C **42**

Kale Rd. *Eri* —2E **84**
Kambala Rd. *SW11* —3B **92**
Kangley Bri. Rd. *SE26* —5B **112**
Kangley Bus. Cen. *SE26* —5B **112**
Kara Way. *NW2* —4F **43**
Karen Ct. *Brom* —1H **127**
Karen Ter. *E11* —2H **49**
Karoline Gdns. *Gnfd* —2H **55**
Kashgar Rd. *SE18* —4K **83**
Kashmir Rd. *SE7* —7B **82**
Kassala Rd. *SW11* —1D **92**
Katharine St. *Croy* —3C **134**
Katharine Clo. *SE16* —1K **79**
Katherine Ct. *SE23* —1J **111**
Katherine Gdns. *SE9* —4B **98**
Katherine Rd. *E7 & E6* —5A **50**
Katherine Rd. *Twic* —7A **88**
Katherine Sq. *W11* —1G **75**
Kathleen Av. *W3* —2J **93**
Kathleen Av. *Wemb* —7E **40**
Kathleen Godfree Ct. *SW19*
　　　　—5J **107**
Kathleen Rd. *SW11* —3D **92**
Kayemoor Rd. *Sutt* —6B **132**
Kay Rd. *SW9* —2A **93**
Kay St. *E2* —2G **63**
Kay St. *E15* —7F **49**
Kay St. *Well* —1B **100**
Kean Ho. *SE17* —6B **78** (7A **156**)
Kean St. *WC2* —6K **61** (1G **149**)
Keatley Grn. *E4* —6G **19**
Keats Av. *E16* —1K **81**
Keats Clo. *E11* —5K **33**
Keat's Clo. *NW3* —4C **44**
Keats Clo. *SE1* —4F **79** (4J **157**)
Keats Clo. *SW19* —6B **108**
Keats Clo. *Enf* —5E **8**
Keat's Gro. *NW3* —4C **44**
Keats Ho. *SE5* —7C **78**
　　(off Elmington Est.)
Keats Ho. *Cray* —5K **101**
　　(off Bexley La.)
Keats Rd. *Belv* —3J **85**
Keats Rd. *Well* —1J **99**
Keats Way. *Croy* —6J **125**

Keats Way. *Gnfd* —5F **55**
Kebbell Ter. *E7* —5K **49**
　　(off Claremont Rd.)
Keble Clo. *N'holt* —5G **39**
Keble Clo. *Wor Pk* —1B **130**
Keble St. *SW17* —4A **108**
Kechill Gdns. *Brom* —7J **127**
Kedeston Ct. *Sutt* —1K **131**
Kedleston Dri. *Orp* —5K **129**
Kedleston Wlk. *E2* —3H **63**
Kedyngton Ho. Edgw —2J **25**
　　(off Burnt Oak B'way.)
Keedonwood Rd. *Brom* —5G **113**
Keel Clo. *SE16* —1K **79**
Keeley Rd. *Croy* —2C **134**
Keeley St. *WC2* —6K **61** (1G **149**)
Keeling Rd. *SE9* —5B **98**
Keely Clo. *Barn* —5H **5**
Keemor Clo. *SE18* —7E **82**
Keens Clo. *SW16* —5H **109**
Keens Rd. *Croy* —4C **134**
Keepers M. *Tedd* —6C **104**
Keep, The. *SE3* —2J **97**
Keep, The. *King T* —6F **105**
Keeton's Rd. *SE16* —3H **79**
　　(in two parts)
Keevil Dri. *SW19* —7F **91**
Keighley Clo. *N7* —5J **45**
Keightley Dri. *SE9* —1G **115**
Keildon Rd. *SW11* —4D **92**
Keir Hardie Est. *E5* —1H **47**
Keir Hardie Ho. *N19* —7H **29**
Keir Hardie Way. *Bark* —7A **52**
Keir, The. *SW19* —5E **106**
Keith Connor Clo. *SW8* —3F **93**
Keith Gro. *W12* —2C **74**
Keith Rd. *E17* —1B **32**
Keith Rd. *Bark* —2H **67**
Kelbrook Rd. *SE3* —2C **98**
Kelby Path. *SE9* —3F **115**
Kelceda Clo. *NW2* —2C **42**
Kelfield Ct. *W10* —6F **59**
Kelfield Gdns. *W10* —6E **58**
Kelfield M. *W10* —6F **59**
　　(in two parts)
Kelland Clo. *N8* —5H **29**
Kelland Rd. *E13* —4J **65**
Kellaway Rd. *SE3* —2B **98**
Keller Cres. *W12* —4B **50**
Kellerton Rd. *SE13* —5G **97**
Kellett Ho. N1 —1E **62**
　　(off Colville Est.)
Kellett Rd. *SW2* —4A **94**
Kelling Gdns. *Croy* —7B **124**
Kellino St. *SW17* —4D **108**
Kellner Rd. *SE28* —3K **83**
Kell St. *SE1* —3B **78** (1B **156**)
Kelly Clo. *NW10* —3K **41**
Kelly Rd. *NW7* —6B **14**
Kelly St. *NW1* —6F **45**
Kelly Way. *Romf* —5E **36**
Kelman Clo. *SW4* —2H **93**
Kelmore Gro. *SE22* —4G **95**
Kelmscott Clo. *E17* —1B **32**
Kelmscott Gdns. *W12* —3C **74**
Kelmscott Rd. *SW11* —5C **92**
Kelross Pas. *N5* —4C **46**
Kelross Rd. *N5* —4C **46**
Kelsall Clo. *SE3* —2K **97**
Kelsey La. *Beck* —2D **126**
Kelsey La. *Beck* —2C **126**
Kelsey Pk. Av. *Beck* —2D **126**
Kelsey Pk. Rd. *Beck* —2C **126**

Kelsey Sq. *Beck* —2C **126**
Kelsey St. *E2* —4G **63**
Kelsey Way. *Beck* —3C **126**
Kelso Pl. *W8* —3K **75**
Kelso Rd. *Cars* —7A **122**
Kelston Rd. *Ilf* —2F **35**
Kelvedon Clo. *King T* —6G **105**
Kelvedon Ho. *SW8* —1J **93**
Kelvedon Rd. *SW6* —7H **75**
Kelvin Av. *N13* —6E **16**
Kelvin Av. *S Croy* —7D **134**
Kelvin Ct. *Sidc* —2J **87**
Kelvin Gdns. *Sutt* —2A **132**
Kelvin Gro. *SE26* —3H **111**
Kelvin Gro. *Chess* —3D **129**
Kelvin Cres. *Harr* —7D **10**
Kelvin Dri. *Twic* —6B **88**
Kelvin Gdns. *Croy* —7J **123**
Kelvin Gdns. *S'hall* —6E **54**
Kelvin Gro. *SE26* —3H **111**
Kelvin Gro. *Chess* —3D **129**
Kelvin Ind. Est. *Gnfd* —5G **39**
Kelvington Clo. *Croy* —7A **126**
Kelvington Rd. *SE15* —5K **95**
Kelvin Rd. *N5* —4C **46**
Kelvin Rd. *Well* —3A **100**
Kember St. *N1* —7K **45**
Kemble Dri. *Brom* —3C **138**
Kemble Ho. *SW9* —3B **94**
　　(off Barrington Rd.)
Kemble Rd. *N17* —1G **31**
Kemble Rd. *SE23* —1K **111**
Kemble Rd. *Croy* —3B **134**
Kemble St. *WC2*
　　　　—6K **61** (1G **149**)
Kemerton Rd. *SE5* —3C **94**
Kemerton Rd. *Beck* —2D **126**
Kemerton Rd. *Croy* —7F **125**
Kemeys St. *E9* —5A **48**
Kemnal Rd. *Chst* —7G **115**
Kemp. NW9 —1B **26**
　　(off Concourse, The)
Kemp Ct. SW8 —7J **77**
　　(off Hartington Rd.)
Kemp Rd. *NW6* —2F **59**
Kemp Gdns. *Croy* —6C **124**
Kemp Ho. *E6* —6E **50**
Kempis Way. *SE22* —5E **94**
Kemplay Rd. *NW3* —4B **44**
Kemp Rd. *Dag* —1D **52**
Kemps Dri. *E14* —7C **64**
Kempsford Gdns. *SW5* —5J **75**
Kempsford Rd. *SE11*
　　(in two parts) —4A **78** (4K **155**)
Kemps Gdns. *SE13* —5E **96**
Kempshott Rd. *SW16* —7H **109**
Kempson Rd. *SW6* —1J **91**
Kempthorne Rd. *SE8* —4B **80**
Kempton Av. *N'holt* —6E **38**
Kempton Av. *Sun* —7A **102**
Kempton Clo. *Eri* —6J **85**
Kempton Ct. *E1* —5H **63**
Kempton Ct. *Sun* —7A **102**
Kempton Rd. *E6* —1D **66**
Kempton Wlk. *Croy* —6A **126**
Kempt St. *SE18* —6E **82**
Kemsing Clo. *Bex* —7E **100**
Kemsing Clo. *Brom* —1H **137**
Kemsing Clo. *T Hth* —4C **124**
Kemsing Rd. *SE10* —5J **81**
Kemsley. *SE13* —1C **72**
Kenbury Gdns. *SE5* —2C **94**
Kenbury Mans. *SE5* —2C **94**
Kenbury St. *SE5* —2C **94**
Kenchester Clo. *SW8* —7J **77**
Kencot Way. *Eri* —2F **85**

Kendal Av. *N18* —4J **17**
Kendal Av. *W3* —4G **57**
　　(in two parts)
Kendal Av. *Bark* —1J **67**
Kendal Clo. *SW9* —7B **78**
Kendal Clo. *Wfd G* —2C **20**
Kendal Ct. *W3* —5G **57**
Kendale Rd. *Brom* —5G **113**
Kendal Gdns. *N18* —4J **17**
Kendal Gdns. *Sutt* —2A **132**
Kendal Ho. *SE20* —2H **125**
　　(off Derwent Rd.)
Kendall Av. *Beck* —2A **126**
Kendall Av. *S Croy* —7D **134**
Kendall Ct. *Sidc* —3A **116**
Kendall Gdns. *Sutt* —2A **132**
Kendall Pl. *W1* —5E **60** (6G **141**)
Kendall Rd. *Beck* —2A **126**
Kendall Rd. *Iswth* —2A **88**
Kendall Rd. *SW15* —5H **91**
Kendal Rd. *NW10* —4C **42**
Kendal Steps. *W2*
　　　　—6C **60** (1D **146**)
Kendal St. *W2* —6C **60** (1D **146**)
Kender St. *SE14* —7J **79**
Kendoa Rd. *SW4* —4H **93**
Kendon Clo. *E11* —5K **33**
Kendra Hall Rd. *S Croy* —7B **134**
Kendrey Gdns. *Twic* —7J **87**
Kendrick M. *SW7*
　　　　—4B **76** (3A **152**)
Kendrick Pl. *SW7*
　　　　—4B **76** (4A **152**)
Kenelm Clo. *Harr* —3A **40**
Kenerne Dri. *Barn* —5B **4**
Keniford Rd. *SW12* —7F **93**
Kenilworth Av. *E17* —2C **32**
Kenilworth Av. *SW19* —5J **107**
Kenilworth Av. *Harr* —4D **38**
Kenilworth Cres. *Enf* —1K **7**
Kenilworth Gdns. *Ilf* —2K **51**
Kenilworth Gdns. *S'hall* —3D **54**
Kenilworth Rd. *E3* —2A **64**
Kenilworth Rd. *NW6* —1H **59**
Kenilworth Rd. *SE20* —1K **125**
Kenilworth Rd. *W5* —1E **72**
Kenilworth Rd. *Edgw* —3D **12**
Kenilworth Rd. *Eps* —5C **130**
Kenilworth Rd. *Orp* —6G **129**
Kenley Av. *NW9* —1A **26**
Kenley Clo. *Barn* —4H **5**
Kenley Clo. *Bex* —7G **101**
Kenley Clo. *Chst* —3J **129**
Kenley Gdns. *T Hth* —4B **124**
Kenley Rd. *SW19* —2J **121**
Kenley Rd. *King T* —2H **119**
Kenley Rd. *Twic* —6B **88**
Kenley Wlk. *W11* —7G **59**
Kenley Wlk. *Sutt* —4F **131**
Kenlor Rd. *SW17* —5B **108**
Kenmare Dri. *Mitc* —7D **108**
Kenmare Gdns. *N13* —4H **17**
Kenmare Rd. *T Hth* —6A **124**
Kenmere Gdns. *Wemb* —1G **57**
Kenmere Rd. *Well* —2C **100**
Kenmont Gdns. *NW10* —3D **58**
Kenmore Av. *Harr* —4A **24**
Kenmore Clo. *Rich* —7G **73**
Kenmore Gdns. *Edgw* —2H **25**
Kenmore Rd. *Harr* —3D **24**
Kenmure Rd. *E8* —5H **47**
Kenmure Yd. *E8* —5H **47**
Kennacraig Clo. *E16* —1K **81**

Kennard Rd. *E15* —7F **49**
Kennard Rd. *N11* —5J **15**
Kennard St. *E16* —1D **82**
Kennard St. *SW11* —1E **92**
Kennedy Av. *Enf* —6D **8**
Kennedy Clo. *E13* —2J **65**
Kennedy Clo. *Mitc* —2E **122**
Kennedy Clo. *Orp* —7H **129**
Kennedy Ct. *Beck* —6B **126**
Kennedy Ct. *Bush* —2C **10**
Kennedy Ct. *Croy* —6B **126**
Kennedy Ho. *SE11*
　　　　—5K **77** (5G **155**)
Kennedy Path. *W7* —4K **55**
Kennedy Rd. *W7* —5J **55**
Kennedy Rd. *Bark* —1J **67**
Kennet Clo. *SW11* —4B **92**
Kenneth Av. *Ilf* —4F **51**
Kenneth Ct. *SE11*
　　　　—4A **78** (3K **155**)
Kenneth Cres. *NW2* —5D **42**
Kenneth Gdns. *Stan* —6F **11**
Kenneth More Rd. *Ilf* —3F **51**
Kenneth Rd. *Romf* —7D **36**
Kenneth Robbins Ho. *N17*
　　　　—7C **18**
Kenneth Younger Ho. SW6
　　(off Clem Attlee Ct.) —6H **75**
Kennet Clo. *Iswth* —3K **87**
Kennet Sq. *Mitc* —1C **122**
Kennet St. *E1* —1G **79**
Kennet Ct. *W4* —7H **73**
Kennett Dri. *Hayes* —5C **54**
Kenninghall. (Junct.) —5D **18**
Kenninghall Rd. *E5* —3G **47**
Kenninghall Rd. *N18* —5D **18**
Kenning St. *SE16* —2J **79**
Kennings Way. *SE11*
　　　　—5A **78** (5A **156**)
Kenning Ter. *N1* —1E **62**
Kennington Grn. *SE11*
　　　　—5A **78** (6J **155**)
Kennington Gro. *SE11*
　　　　—6K **77** (7H **155**)
Kennington La. *SE11*
　　　　—5K **77** (6G **155**)
Kennington Oval. *SE11*
　　　　—6K **77** (7H **155**)
Kennington Oval. (Junct.)
　　　　—6A **78**
Kennington Palace Ct. *SE11*
　　　　—5A **78** (5J **155**)
Kennington Pk. Gdns. *SE11*
　　　　—6B **78** (7A **156**)
Kennington Pk. Ho. *SE11*
　　　　—5A **78** (6K **155**)
Kennington Pk. Pl. *SE11*
　　　　—6A **78** (7K **155**)
Kennington Pk. Rd. *SE11*
　　　　—6A **78**
Kennington Rd. *SE1 & SE11*
　　　　—3A **78** (1J **155**)
Kennistoun Ho. *NW5* —5G **45**
Kennyland Ct. *NW4* —6D **26**
　　(off Hendon Way)
Kenny Rd. *NW7* —6B **14**
Kenrick Pl. *W1* —5E **60** (6G **141**)
Kensal Rd. *W10* —4G **59**
Kensington Av. *E12* —6C **50**
Kensington Av. *T Hth* —1A **124**
Kensington Cen. *W14* —4G **75**
　　(in two parts)
Kensington Chu. Ct. *W8* —2K **75**
Kensington Chu. St. *W8* —1J **75**

Kensington Chu. Wlk. *W8*
—2K 75
Kensington Clo. *N11* —6K 15
Kensington Ct. *W8* —2K 75
Kensington Ct. Gdns. *W8* —3K 75
(off Kensington Ct. Pl.)
Kensington Ct. M. *W8* —3K 75
(off Kensington Ct. Pl.)
Kensington Ct. Pl. *W8* —3K 75
Kensington Dri. *Wfd G* —2B 34
Kensington Gdns. *Ilf* —1D 50
Kensington Gdns. *King T*
—3D 118
Kensington Gdns. Sq. *W2*
—6K 59
Kensington Ga. *W8* —3A 76
Kensington Gore. *SW7*
—2A 76 (7A 146)
Kensington Hall Gdns. *W14*
—5H 75
Kensington Heights. *W8* —1J 75
Kensington High St. *W14 & W8*
—3H 75
Kensington Mall. *W8* —1J 75
Kensington Mans. *SW5* —5J 75
(off Trebovir Rd.)
Kensington Pal. Gdns. *W8*
—1K 75
Kensington Pk. Gdns. *W11*
—7H 59
Kensington Pk. M. *W11* —6H 59
Kensington Pk. Rd. *W11* —6H 59
Kensington Pl. *W8* —1J 75
Kensington Rd. *W8 & SW7*
—2A 76
Kensington Rd. *N'holt* —3E 54
Kensington Sq. *W8* —3K 75
Kensington Sq. *W8* —3K 75
Kensington Ter. *S Croy* —7D 134
Kensington W. *W14* —6G 75
Kenswick Ct. *SE13* —5D 96
Kent Av. *W13* —5B 56
Kent Av. *Dag* —4G 69
Kent Av. *Well* —5K 99
Kent Clo. *Mitc* —4J 123
Kent Ct. *E2* —2F 63
Kent Ct. *NW9* —2A 26
Kent Dri. *Cockf* —4K 5
Kent Dri. *Tedd* —5J 103
Kentford Way. *N'holt* —1C 54
Kent Gdns. *W13* —5B 56
Kent Ga. Way. *Croy* —6B 136
Kent Ho. *SE1* —5F 79 (6K 157)
Kent Ho. *W4* —5A 74
(off Devonshire St.)
Kent Ho. La. *Beck* —5A 112
Kent Ho. Rd. *SE26 & Beck*
—5A 112
Kentish Bldgs. *SE1*
—1D 78 (5E 150)
Kentish Rd. *Belv* —4G 85
Kentish Town Ind. Est. *NW5*
—5F 45
Kentish Town Rd. *NW1 & NW5*
—7F 45
Kentish Way. *Brom* —2J 127
Kentmere Mans. *W5* —4C 56
Kentmere Rd. *SE18* —4J 83
Kenton Av. *Harr* —7K 23
Kenton Av. *S'hall* —7E 54
Kenton Ct. *SE26* —4A 112
(off Adamsrill Rd.)
Kenton Ct. *W14* —3H 75
Kenton Ct. *Kent* —6B 24
Kenton Ct. *Twic* —6D 88

Kentone Ct. *SE25* —4H 125
Kenton Gdns. *Harr* —5C 24
Kenton La. *Harr* —6E 10
Kenton Pk. Av. *Harr* —4D 24
Kenton Pk. Clo. *Harr* —4C 24
Kenton Pk. Cres. *Harr* —4D 24
Kenton Pk. Mans. *Kent* —5C 24
(off Kenton Rd.)
Kenton Pk. Pde. *Harr* —5C 24
Kenton Pk. Rd. *Harr* —4C 24
Kenton Rd. *E9* —6K 47
Kenton Rd. *Harr* —7K 23
Kenton St. *WC1* —4J 61 (3E 142)
Kent Pas. *NW1* —4D 60 (3E 140)
Kent Rd. *N21* —1J 17
Kent Rd. *W4* —3J 73
Kent Rd. *Dag* —5H 53
Kent Rd. *King T* —3D 118
Kent Rd. *Rich* —7G 73
Kent Rd. *W Wick* —1D 136
Kent St. *E2* —2F 63
Kent St. *E13* —3A 66
Kent Ter. *NW1* —3C 60 (2D 140)
Kent View Gdns. *Ilf* —2J 51
Kent Wlk. *SW9* —4B 94
Kent Way. *SE15* —1F 95
Kentwell Clo. *SE4* —4A 96
Kentwode Grn. *SW13* —7C 74
Kent Yd. *SW7* —2C 76 (7D 146)
Kenver Av. *N12* —6G 15
Kenward Rd. *SE9* —5A 98
Kenway. *Romf* —2J 37
Kenway Rd. *SW5* —4K 75
Kenwood Av. *N14* —5C 6
Kenwood Av. *SE14* —1K 95
Kenwood Clo. *NW3* —1B 44
Kenwood Dri. *Beck* —3E 126
Kenwood Gdns. *E18* —3K 33
Kenwood Gdns. *Ilf* —4E 34
Kenwood Ho. *SW9* —4B 94
Kenwood Rd. *N6* —6D 28
Kenwood Rd. *N9* —1B 18
Kenworthy Rd. *E9* —5A 48
Kenwrick Ho. *N1* —1K 61
(off Barnsbury Est.)
Kenwyn Dri. *NW2* —2A 42
Kenwyn Lodge. *N2* —4D 28
Kenwyn Rd. *SW4* —4H 93
Kenwyn Rd. *SW20* —1E 120
Kenya Rd. *SE7* —7B 82
Kenyngton Pl. *Harr* —5C 24
Kenyon Mans. *W14* —6G 75
(off Queen's Club Gdns.)
Kenyon St. *SW6* —1F 91
Keogh Rd. *E15* —6G 49
Kepler Rd. *SW4* —4J 93
Keppel Ho. *SE8* —5B 80
Keppel Rd. *E6* —7D 50
Keppel Rd. *Dag* —4E 52
Keppel Row. *SE1*
—1C 78 (5C 150)
Keppel St. *WC1*
—5H 61 (5D 142)
Kerbela St. *E2* —4G 63 (3K 145)
Kerbey St. *E14* —6D 64
Kerfield Cres. *SE5* —1D 94
Kerfield Pl. *SE5* —1D 94
Kerridge Ct. *N1* —6E 46
(off Balls Pond Rd.)
Kerrin Point. *SE11*
—5A 78 (4J 155)
Kerrison Pl. *W5* —1D 72
Kerrison Rd. *E15* —1F 65
Kerrison Rd. *SW11* —3C 92
Kerrison Rd. *W5* —1D 72

Kerrison Vs. *W5* —1E 72
Kerry. *N7* —6J 45
Kerry Av. *Stan* —4H 11
Kerry Clo. *E16* —6K 65
Kerry Clo. *N13* —2E 16
Kerry Ct. *Stan* —4J 11
Kerry Path. *SE14* —6B 80
Kersey Gdns. *SE9* —4C 114
Kersfield Rd. *SW15* —6F 91
Kershaw Clo. *SW18* —6B 92
Kershaw Rd. *Dag* —3G 53
Kersley M. *SW11* —1D 92
Kersley Rd. *N16* —2E 46
Kersley St. *SW11* —2D 92
Kerswell Clo. *N15* —5E 30
Kerwick Clo. *N7* —7J 45
Keslake Mans. *NW10* —2F 59
(off Station Ter.)
Keslake Rd. *NW6* —2F 59
Kessock Clo. *N17* —5H 31
Kestlake Rd. *Bex* —6C 100
Keston Av. *Kes* —5A 138
Keston Clo. *N18* —3J 17
Keston Clo. *Well* —7C 84
Keston Gdns. *Kes* —4A 138
Keston Mark. (Junct.) —3C 138
Keston Pk. Clo. *Kes* —3D 138
Keston Rd. *N17* —3D 30
Keston Rd. *SE15* —3G 95
Keston Rd. *T Hth* —6A 124
Kestrel Av. *E6* —5C 66
Kestrel Av. *SE24* —5B 94
Kestrel Clo. *NW9* —2A 26
Kestrel Clo. *NW10* —5K 41
Kestrel Clo. *King T* —4D 104
Kestrel Ct. *E17* —2K 31
Kestrel Ct. *SE8* —6B 80
(off Abinger Gro.)
Kestrel Ct. *S Croy* —6C 134
Kestrel Ho. *King T* —1E 118
(off Sigrist Sq.)
Kestrel Way. *New Ad* —7F 137
Keswick Av. *SW15* —5A 106
Keswick Av. *SW19* —2J 121
Keswick Clo. *Sutt* —4A 132
Keswick Ct. *Short* —4H 127
Keswick Gdns. *Ilf* —4C 34
Keswick Gdns. *Wemb* —4E 40
Keswick Ho. *SE5* —2C 94
Keswick M. *W5* —1E 72
Keswick Rd. *SW15* —5G 91
Keswick Rd. *Bexh* —1G 101
Keswick Rd. *Orp* —7K 129
Keswick Rd. *Twic* —6G 87
Keswick Rd. *W Wick* —2G 137
Ketley Ho. *SE15* —7G 79
(off Sumner Est.)
Kettering St. *SW16* —6G 109
Kett Gdns. *SW2* —5K 93
Kettlebaston Rd. *E10* —1B 48
Kettleby Ho. *SW9* —3B 94
(off Barrington Rd.)
Kevan Ct. *E17* —4D 32
Kevan Ho. *SE5* —7C 78
Kevelioc Rd. *N17* —1D 30
Kevin Clo. *Houn* —2B 86
Kevington Clo. *Croy* —7A 126
Kevington Clo. *Orp* —4K 129
Kevington Dri. *Chst & Orp*
—4K 129
Kew Bri. *Bren & Kew* —6F 73
Kew Bridge. (Junct.) —5F 73
Kew Bri. Arches. *Rich & W4*
—6G 73
Kew Bri. Ct. *W4* —5G 73

Kew Bri. Distribution Cen. *Bren*
—5F 73
Kew Bri. Rd. *Bren* —6F 73
Kew Cres. *Sutt* —3G 131
Kew Foot Rd. *Rich* —4E 88
Kew Grn. Rich. *Rich* —7F 73
Kew Grn. *Rich* —6F 73
Kew Green. (Junct.) —7G 73
Kew Meadow Path. *Rich* —1H 89
Kew Rd. *Rich* —6G 73
Key Clo. *E1* —4J 63
Keyes Rd. *NW2* —5F 43
Key Ho. *SE11* —6A 78 (7K 155)
Keymer Rd. *SW2* —2K 109
Keynes Clo. *N2* —4D 28
Keynsham Av. *Wfd G* —4B 20
Keynsham Gdns. *SE9* —5C 98
Keynsham Rd. *SE9* —5B 98
Keynsham Rd. *Mord* —1K 131
Keynsham Wlk. *Mord* —1K 131
Keyse Rd. *SE1* —3F 79 (2J 157)
Keystone Cres. *N1*
—2J 61 (1F 143)
Keyworth Clo. *E5* —4A 48
Keyworth Pl. *SE1*
—3B 78 (1B 156)
Keyworth St. *SE1*
—3B 78 (1B 156)
Kezia St. *SE8* —5A 80
Khama Rd. *SW17* —4C 108
Khartoum Rd. *E13* —3K 65
Khartoum Rd. *SW17* —4B 108
Khartoum Rd. *Ilf* —5F 51
Khyber Rd. *SW11* —2C 92
Kibworth St. *SW8* —7K 77
Kidbrooke Est. *SE3* —3A 98
Kidbrooke Gdns. *SE3* —2J 97
Kidbrooke Gro. *SE3* —1J 97
Kidbrooke La. *SE9* —4C 98
Kidbrooke Pk. Clo. *SE3* —1K 97
Kidbrooke Pk. Rd. *SE3* —3A 98
Kidbrooke Way. *SE3* —2K 97
Kidderminster Rd. *Croy* —1B 134
Kidderpore Av. *NW3* —4J 43
Kidderpore Gdns. *NW3* —4J 43
Kidd Pl. *SE7* —5C 82
Kidlington Way. *NW9* —2K 25
Kidron Way. *E9* —1J 63
Kierbeck Bus. Complex. *E16*
—2K 81
Kier Hardie Ct. *NW10* —7B 42
Kiffen St. *EC2* —4D 62 (3F 145)
Kilberry Clo. *Iswth* —1H 87
Kilburn Bri. *NW6* —1J 59
Kilburn High Rd. *NW6* —7H 43
Kilburn La. *W10 & W9* —3F 59
Kilburn Pk. Rd. *NW6* —3J 59
Kilburn Pl. *NW6* —1J 59
Kilburn Priory. *NW6* —1K 59
Kilburn Sq. *NW6* —1J 59
Kilburn Vale. *NW6* —1K 59
Kilburn Vale Est. *NW6* —1K 59
(off Kilburn Vale)
Kildare Clo. *Ruis* —1A 38
Kildare Gdns. *W2* —6J 59
Kildare Rd. *E16* —5J 65
Kildare Ter. *W2* —6J 59
Kildare Wlk. *E14* —6C 64
Kildoran Rd. *SW2* —5J 93
Kildowan Rd. *Ilf* —1A 52
Kilgour Rd. *SE23* —6A 96
Kilkie St. *SW6* —2A 92
Killarney Rd. *SW18* —6A 92
Killearn Rd. *SE6* —1F 113

Killester Gdns. *Wor Pk* —4D 130
Killick Ho. *Sutt* —4K 131
Killick St. *N1* —2K 61 (1G 143)
Killieser Av. *SW2* —2J 109
Killigarth Ct. *Sidc* —4A 116
Killip Clo. *E16* —6H 65
Killowen Av. *N'holt* —5G 39
Killowen Rd. *E9* —6K 47
Killyon Rd. *SW8* —2G 93
Killyon Ter. *SW8* —2G 93
Kilmaine Rd. *SW6* —7G 75
Kilmarnock Gdns. *Dag* —3C 52
Kilmarsh Rd. *W6* —4E 74
Kilmartin Av. *SW16* —3A 124
Kilmartin Rd. *Ilf* —2A 52
Kilmeston Way. *SE15* —7F 79
Kilmington Rd. *SW13* —6C 74
Kilmorey Gdns. *Twic* —5B 88
Kilmorey Rd. *Twic* —4B 88
Kilmorie Rd. *SE23* —1A 112
Kilner Ho. *SE11* —6A 78 (7J 155)
Kilner St. *E14* —5C 64
Kiln M. *SW17* —5B 108
Kiln Pl. *NW5* —4E 44
Kilpatrick Way. *Hayes* —5C 54
Kilravock St. *W10* —3G 59
Kilronan. *W3* —6K 57
Kilsby Wlk. *Dag* —6B 52
Kimbell Gdns. *SW6* —1G 91
Kimberley Rd. *Beck* —2K 125
Kimberley Av. *E6* —2C 66
Kimberley Av. *SE15* —2H 95
Kimberley Av. *Ilf* —7H 35
Kimberley Av. *Romf* —6J 37
Kimberley Dri. *Sidc* —2D 116
Kimberley Gdns. *N4* —5B 30
Kimberley Gdns. *Enf* —3A 8
Kimberley Ga. *Brom* —7G 113
Kimberley Ind. Est. *E17* —1B 32
Kimberley Rd. *E4* —1B 20
Kimberley Rd. *E11* —2F 49
Kimberley Rd. *E16* —4H 65
Kimberley Rd. *E17* —1B 32
Kimberley Rd. *N17* —2G 31
Kimberley Rd. *N18* —6C 18
Kimberley Rd. *NW6* —1G 59
Kimberley Rd. *SW9* —2J 93
Kimberley Rd. *Beck* —2K 125
Kimberley Rd. *Croy* —6B 124
Kimberley Way. *E4* —1B 20
Kimber Rd. *SW18* —7J 91
Kimble Cres. *Bush* —1B 10
Kimble Rd. *SW19* —6B 108
Kimbolton Clo. *SE12* —6H 97
Kimbolton Row. *SW3* —4C 76
Kimmeridge Gdns. *SE9* —4C 114
Kimmeridge Rd. *SE9* —4C 114
Kimpton Ind. Est. *Sutt* —2H 131
Kimpton Rd. *SE5* —1D 94
Kimpton Rd. *Sutt* —2H 131
Kinburn St. *SE16* —2K 79
Kincaid Rd. *SE15* —7H 79
Kincardine Gdns. *W9* —4J 59
Kinch Gro. *Wemb* —7F 25
Kinder Clo. *SE28* —7C 68
Kinder Ho. *N1* —2D 62
(off Cranston Est.)
Kindersley Ho. *E1* —6G 63
(off Pinchin St.)
Kinder St. *E1* —6H 63
Kinefold Ho. *N7* —6J 45
Kinfauns Av. *N9* —2A 110
Kinfauns Rd. *Ilf* —1A 52
King Alfred Av. *SE6* —4C 112
(in two parts)
King Arthur Clo. *SE15* —7J 79

King Charles Cres. *Surb* —7F **119**
King Charles Ho. SW6 —7K **75**
  (off Wandon Rd.)
King Charles Rd. *Surb* —5F **119**
King Charles St. *SW1*
  —2H **77** (6D **148**)
King Charles Wlk. *SW19*
  —1G **107**
King Ct. E10 —7D **32**
Kingcup Clo. *Croy* —7K **125**
King David La. E1 —7J **63**
Kingdon Rd. NW6 —6J **43**
King Edward Mans. SW6 —7J **75**
  (off Fulham Rd.)
King Edward M. SW13 —1C **90**
King Edward Rd. E10 —1E **48**
King Edward Rd. E17 —3A **32**
King Edward Rd. *Barn* —4D **4**
King Edward's Gdns. W3 —1G **73**
King Edwards Gro. *Tedd* —6B **104**
King Edward's Pl. W3 —1G **73**
King Edward's Rd. E9 —1H **63**
King Edward's Rd. N9 —7C **8**
King Edwards Rd. *Bark* —1H **67**
King Edward's Rd. *Enf* —4E **8**
King Edward St. EC1
  —6C **62** (7C **144**)
King Edward III M. SE16 —1H **79**
King Edward Wlk. SE1
  —2B **78** (1K **155**)
Kingfield Rd. W5 —4D **56**
Kingfield St. E14 —4E **80**
Kingfisher Clo. SE28 —7C **68**
Kingfisher Clo. *Har W* —7E **10**
Kingfisher Ct. SW19 —2F **107**
Kingfisher Ct. *Enf* —1E **6**
Kingfisher Ct. *Houn* —5F **87**
Kingfisher Dri. *Rich* —4B **104**
Kingfisher M. SE13 —4D **96**
Kingfisher Pl. N22 —2K **29**
Kingfisher St. E6 —5C **66**
Kingfisher Wlk. NW9 —2A **26**
Kingfisher Way. NW10 —6K **41**
Kingfisher Way. *Beck* —5K **125**
King Frederick Ninth Tower. SE16
  —3B **80**
King Gdns. *Croy* —5B **134**
King George Av. E16 —6B **66**
King George Av. *Ilf* —5H **35**
King George Clo. *Romf* —3J **37**
King George's Dri. *S'hall* —5D **54**
King George VI Av. *Mitc*
  —4D **122**
King George Sq. *Rich* —6F **89**
King George St. SE10 —7E **80**
Kingham Clo. SW18 —7A **92**
King Harolds Way. *Bexh* —7D **84**
King Henry's Dri. *New Ad*
  —7D **136**
King Henry's Rd. NW3 —7D **44**
King Henry's Rd. *King T* —3H **119**
King Henry St. N16 —5E **46**
King Henry's Wlk. N1 —6E **46**
Kinghorn St. EC1
  —5C **62** (6C **144**)
King Ho. W12 —6D **58**
King James Ct. SE1
  —2B **78** (7B **150**)
King James St. SE1
  —2B **78** (7B **150**)
King John Ct. EC2
  —4E **62** (3H **145**)
King John's Wlk. SE9 —1B **114**
Kinglake Est. SE17
  —5E **78** (5H **157**)

Kinglake St. SE17
  —5E **78** (6G **157**)
Kingly Ct. W1 —7G **61** (2B **148**)
Kingly St. W1 —6G **61** (1A **148**)
King & Queen Clo. SE9 —4C **114**
King & Queen St. SE17
  —5C **78** (5D **156**)
Kingsand Rd. SE12 —2J **113**
Kings Arbour. *S'hall* —5C **70**
King's Arms All. *Bren* —6D **72**
Kings Arms Ct. E1 —5G **63**
  (off Whitechapel Rd.)
Kings Arms Yd. EC2
  —6D **62** (7E **144**)
Kingsash Dri. *Hayes* —4C **54**
King's Av. N10 —3E **28**
Kings Av. N21 —1G **17**
Kings Av. SW12 & SW4
  —1H **109**
Kings Av. W5 —6D **56**
Kings Av. *Brom* —6H **113**
King's Av. *Buck H* —2G **21**
King's Av. *Cars* —7C **132**
Kings Av. *Gnfd* —5F **55**
Kings Av. *Houn* —1F **87**
King's Av. *N Mald* —4A **120**
Kings Av. *Romf* —6F **37**
King's Av. *Wfd G* —6E **20**
King's Bench St. SE1
  —2B **78** (6B **150**)
King's Bench Wlk. EC4
  —7A **62** (1K **149**)
Kingsbridge Av. W3 —2F **73**
Kingsbridge Ct. E14 —3C **80**
  (off Dockers Tanner Rd.)
Kingsbridge Cres. *S'hall* —5D **54**
Kingsbridge Rd. W10 —6E **58**
Kingsbridge Rd. *Bark* —2H **67**
Kingsbridge Rd. *Mord* —7F **121**
Kingsbridge Rd. *S'hall* —4D **70**
Kingsbury Circ. NW9 —5G **25**
Kingsbury Rd. N1 —6E **46**
Kingsbury Rd. NW9 —5G **25**
Kingsbury Ter. N1 —6E **46**
Kingsbury Trad. Est. NW9 —6K **25**
Kings Chase View. *R'way* —2F **7**
Kingsclere Clo. SW15 —7C **90**
Kingsclere Ct. N12 —5H **15**
Kingscliffe Gdns. SW19 —1H **107**
Kings Clo. E10 —7D **32**
Kings Clo. NW4 —4F **27**
Kings Clo. *Dart* —4A **101**
King's Clo. *Th Dit* —6A **118**
King's College Rd. NW3 —7C **44**
Kingscote Rd. W4 —3K **73**
Kingscote Rd. *Croy* —7H **125**
Kingscote Rd. *N Mald* —3K **119**
Kingscote St. EC4
  —7B **62** (2A **150**)
King's Ct. E13 —1K **65**
King's Ct. SE1 —2B **78** (6B **150**)
Kings Ct. W6 —4C **74**
Kings Ct. *Buck H* —2G **21**
Kings Ct. N. SW3
  —5C **76** (6C **152**)
Kingscourt Rd. SW16 —3H **109**
Kings Ct. S. SW3
  —5C **76** (6C **152**)
King's Cres. N4 —3C **46**
Kings Cres. Est. N4 —2C **46**
Kingscroft. SW4 —6J **93**
Kingscroft Rd. NW2 —6H **43**
Kings Cross. (Junct.) —3J **61**
King's Cross Bri. N1
  —3J **61** (1F **143**)

King's Cross Rd. WC1
  —3K **61** (1G **143**)
Kingsdale Gdns. W11 —1F **75**
Kingsdale Rd. SE18 —7K **83**
Kingsdale Rd. SE20 —7K **111**
Kingsdown Av. W3 —7A **58**
Kingsdown Av. W13 —2B **72**
Kingsdown Av. *S Croy* —7C **134**
Kingsdown Clo. SE16 —5H **79**
  (off Masters Dri.)
Kingsdown Clo. W10 —6F **59**
Kingsdowne Rd. *Surb* —7E **118**
Kingsdown Ho. E8 —5G **47**
Kingsdown Rd. E11 —3G **49**
Kingsdown Rd. N19 —2J **45**
Kingsdown Rd. *Sutt* —5G **131**
Kingsdown Way. *Brom*
  —6J **127**
King's Dri. *Edgw* —4A **12**
King's Dri. *Surb* —7G **119**
Kings Dri. *Tedd* —5H **103**
Kings Dri. *Th Dit* —6B **118**
Kings Dri. *Wemb* —2H **41**
Kings Farm. E17 —1D **32**
Kings Farm Av. *Rich* —4G **89**
Kingsfield Av. *Harr* —4F **23**
Kingsfield Ho. SE9 —3B **114**
Kingsfield Rd. *Harr* —7H **23**
Kingsfield Ter. *Harr* —1H **39**
Kingsford Av. *Wall* —7J **133**
Kingsford St. NW5 —5D **44**
Kingsford Way. E6 —5D **66**
King's Gdns. NW6 —7J **43**
Kings Gdns. *Ilf* —1H **51**
Kings Garth M. SE23 —2J **111**
Kingsgate Av. N3 —3J **27**
Kingsgate Clo. *Bexh* —1E **100**
Kingsgate Est. N1 —6E **46**
Kingsgate Ho. SW9 —1A **94**
Kingsgate Pde. SW1
  —3G **77** (2B **154**)
Kingsgate Pl. NW6 —7J **43**
Kingsgate Rd. NW6 —7J **43**
Kingsgate Rd. *King T* —1E **118**
Kingsground. SE9 —7B **98**
King's Gro. SE15 —1H **95**
  (in two parts)
Kingshall M. SE13 —3E **96**
Kings Hall Rd. *Beck* —7A **112**
King's Head Ct. EC3
  —7D **62** (3F **151**)
Kings Head Hill. E4 —7J **9**
Kings Head Pas. SW4 —4H **93**
  (off Clapham Pk. Rd.)
King's Head Yd. SE1
  —1D **78** (5E **150**)
King's Highway. SE18 —6J **83**
Kingshill Av. *Harr* —4B **24**
Kingshill Av. *Hayes & N'holt*
  —3A **54**
Kingshill Av. *Wor Pk* —7C **120**
Kingshill Ct. *Barn* —4B **4**
Kingshill Dri. *Harr* —3B **24**
Kingshold Rd. E9 —7J **47**
Kingsholm Gdns. SE9 —4B **98**
Kingshurst Rd. SE12 —7J **97**
Kings Keep. *Brom* —3G **127**
Kings Keep. *King T* —4E **118**
Kingsland Grn. E8 —6E **46**
Kingsland Gro. N16 —6E **46**
Kingsland High St. E8 —6F **47**
Kingsland Pas. E8 —6E **46**

Kingsland Rd. E2
  —3E **62** (2H **145**)
Kingsland Rd. E13 —3A **66**
Kings La. *Sutt* —5B **132**
Kingslawn Clo. SW15 —5D **90**
Kingsleigh Pl. *Mitc* —3D **122**
Kingsleigh Wlk. *Brom* —4H **127**
Kingsley Av. W13 —5A **56**
Kingsley Av. *Houn* —2G **87**
Kingsley Av. *S'hall* —7E **54**
Kingsley Av. *Sutt* —4B **132**
Kingsley Clo. N2 —5A **28**
Kingsley Clo. *Dag* —4H **53**
Kingsley Ct. *Bexh* —5G **101**
Kingsley Ct. *Edgw* —2C **12**
Kingsley Ct. *Wor Pk* —2B **130**
  (off Avenue, The)
Kingsley Dri. *Wor Pk* —2B **130**
Kingsley Flats. SE1
  —4E **78** (4G **157**)
Kingsley Gdns. E4 —5H **19**
Kingsley Ho. SW3 —6B **76**
  (off Beaufort St.)
Kingsley M. E1 —7H **63**
Kingsley M. W8 —3K **75**
Kingsley M. *Chst* —6F **115**
Kingsley Pl. N6 —7E **28**
Kingsley Rd. E7 —7J **49**
Kingsley Rd. E17 —2E **32**
Kingsley Rd. N13 —4F **17**
Kingsley Rd. NW6 —1H **59**
Kingsley Rd. SW19 —5K **107**
Kingsley Rd. *Croy* —1A **134**
Kingsley Rd. *Harr* —4G **39**
Kingsley Rd. *Houn* —1F **87**
Kingsley Rd. *Ilf* —1G **35**
Kingsley Rd. *Pinn* —4D **22**
Kingsley St. SW11 —3D **92**
Kingsley Way. N2 —6A **28**
Kingsley Wood Dri. SE9 —3D **114**
Kingslyn Cres. SE19 —2E **124**
Kings Mall. W6 —4E **74**
Kingsman Pde. SE18 —3D **82**
Kingsman St. SE18 —3D **82**
Kingsmead. *Barn* —4D **4**
Kings Mead. *Rich* —6F **89**
Kingsmead Av. N9 —1C **18**
Kingsmead Av. NW9 —7K **25**
Kingsmead Av. *Mitc* —3G **123**
Kingsmead Av. *Wor Pk* —2D **130**
Kingsmead Clo. *Eps* —7A **130**
Kingsmead Clo. *Sidc* —2A **116**
Kingsmead Clo. *Tedd* —6B **104**
Kingsmead Cotts. *Brom* —1C **138**
Kingsmead Ct. N6 —7H **29**
Kingsmead Dri. *N'holt* —7D **38**
Kingsmead Ho. E9 —4A **48**
Kingsmeadow. *King T* —3H **119**
Kingsmead Rd. SW2 —2A **110**
King's Mead Way. E9 —4A **48**
Kingsmere Clo. SW15 —3F **91**
Kingsmere Pk. NW9 —1H **41**
Kingsmere Rd. SW19 —2F **107**
King's M. SW4 —5J **93**
King's M. WC1 —4K **61** (4H **143**)
Kingsmill Gdns. *Dag* —5F **53**
Kingsmill Rd. *Dag* —5F **53**
Kingsmill Ter. NW8 —2B **60**
Kingsnorth Ho. W10 —6F **59**
Kingsnympton Pk. *King T*
  —6H **105**
King's Orchard. SE9 —6C **98**
Kings Pde. N17 —3F **31**
Kingspark Ct. E18 —3J **33**

Kings Pas. E11 —7G **33**
Kings Pas. *King T* —2D **118**
King's Pl. SE1 —2C **78** (7C **150**)
King's Pl. W4 —5J **73**
Kings Pl. *Buck H* —2F **21**
King Sq. EC1 —3C **62** (2C **144**)
King's Quay. SW10 —1A **92**
  (off Chelsea Harbour)
Kings Reach Tower. SE1
  —1B **78** (4K **149**)
Kings Ride Ga. *Rich* —4G **89**
Kingsridge. SW19 —2G **107**
Kings Rd. E4 —1A **20**
Kings Rd. E6 —1A **66**
Kings Rd. E11 —7G **33**
King's Rd. N17 —1F **31**
Kings Rd. N18 —5B **18**
Kings Rd. N22 —1K **29**
King's Rd. NW10 —7D **42**
Kings Rd. SE25 —3G **125**
King's Rd. SW6 & SW10 —7K **75**
Kings Rd. SW14 —3K **89**
Kings Rd. SW19 —6J **107**
Kings Rd. W5 —5D **56**
Kings Rd. *Bark* —7G **51**
Kings Rd. *Barn* —3A **4**
Kings Rd. *Felt* —1A **102**
Kings Rd. *Harr* —2D **38**
King's Rd. *King T* —1E **118**
Kings Rd. *Mitc* —3E **122**
Kings Rd. *Rich* —6F **89**
King's Rd. *Surb* —7C **118**
King's Rd. *Tedd* —5H **103**
Kings Rd. *Twic* —6B **88**
Kings Rd. Bungalows. *S Harr*
  —3D **38**
King's Scholars Pas. SW1
  —3G **77** (2A **154**)
King Stairs Clo. SE16 —2H **79**
King's Ter. NW1 —1G **61**
King's Ter. *Iswth* —4A **88**
Kingsthorpe Rd. SE26 —4K **111**
Kingston Av. *Sutt* —3G **131**
Kingston Bri. *King T* —2D **118**
Kingston By-Pass. SW15 & SW20
  —5A **106**
Kingston Clo. *N'holt* —7D **38**
Kingston Clo. *Romf* —3E **36**
Kingston Clo. *Tedd* —6B **104**
Kingston Cres. *Beck* —1B **126**
Kingston Gdns. *Croy* —3J **133**
Kingston Hall Rd. *King T* —3D **118**
Kingston Hill. *King T* —1G **119**
Kingston Hill Av. *Romf* —2E **36**
Kingston Hill Pl. *King T* —4K **105**
Kingston Ho. NW6 —7G **43**
Kingston Ho. Est. *Surb* —6C **118**
Kingston La. *Tedd* —5A **104**
Kingston Pl. *Harr* —7E **10**
Kingston Rd. N9 —2B **18**
Kingston Rd. SW15 & SW19
  —2C **106**
Kingston Rd. SW20 & SW19
  —2E **120**
Kingston Rd. *Barn* —5G **5**
Kingston Rd. *Eps* —7B **130**
Kingston Rd. *Ilf* —4F **51**
Kingston Rd. *King T & N Mald*
  —3H **119**
Kingston Rd. *S'hall* —2D **70**
Kingston Rd. *Tedd* —5B **104**
Kingston Rd. *Eps* —5D **110**
Kingston Vale. SW15 —4K **105**
Kingstown St. NW1 —1E **60**
  (in two parts)

King St. E13 —4J 65
King St. EC2 —6C 62 (1D 150)
King St. N2 —3B 28
King St. N17 —1F 31
King St. SW1 —1G 77 (5B 148)
King St. W3 —1H 73
King St. W6 —4C 74
King St. WC2 —7J 61 (2E 148)
King St. Rich —5D 88
King St. S'hall —3C 70
King St. Twic —1A 104
King St. Pde. Twic —1A 104
(off King St.)
King's Wlk. King T —1D 118
Kingswater Pl. SW11 —7C 76
Kingsway. N12 —6F 15
Kingsway. SW14 —3H 89
Kingsway. WC2 —6K 61 (7G 143)
King's Way. Croy —5K 133
Kingsway. Enf —5C 8
Kings Way. Harr —4J 23
Kingsway. N Mald —5E 120
Kingsway. Orp —5H 129
Kingsway. Wemb —4E 40
Kings Way. W Wick —3G 137
Kings Way. Wfd G —5F 21
Kingsway Bus. Pk. Hamp
—4F 79 (3J 157)
Kingsway Cres. Harr —4G 23
Kingsway Est. N18 —6E 18
Kingsway Rd. Sutt —7G 131
Kingswear Rd. NW5 —3F 45
Kingswood Av. NW6 —1G 59
Kingswood Av. Belv —4F 85
Kingswood Av. Brom —4G 127
Kingswood Av. Hamp —6F 103
Kingswood Av. T Hth —5A 124
Kingswood Clo. N20 —7F 5
Kingswood Clo. SW8 —7J 77
Kingswood Clo. Enf —5K 7
Kingswood Clo. N Mald —6B 120
Kingswood Clo. Orp —7H 129
Kingswood Clo. Surb —7E 118
Kingswood Ct. E4 —5H 19
Kingswood Ct. NW6 —7J 43
(off W. End La.)
Kingswood Dri. SE19 —4E 110
Kingswood Dri. Cars —1D 132
Kingswood Dri. Sutt —7K 131
Kingswood Est. SE21 —4E 110
Kingswood Pk. N3 —1H 27
Kingswood Pl. SE13 —4G 97
Kingswood Rd. E11 —7G 33
Kingswood Rd. SE20 —6J 111
Kingswood Rd. SW2 —6J 93
Kingswood Rd. SW19 —7H 107
Kingswood Rd. W4 —3J 73
Kingswood Rd. Brom —4F 127
Kingswood Rd. Ilf —1A 52
Kingswood Rd. Wemb —3G 41
Kingswood Ter. W4 —3J 73
Kingswood Way. Wall —5J 133
Kingsworth Clo. Beck —5A 126
Kingsworthy Clo. King T —3F 119
Kingthorpe Rd. NW10 —7K 41
Kingthorpe Ter. NW10 —7K 41
(off Brentfield Rd.)
King William IV Gdns. SE20
—6J 111
King William La. SE10 —5G 81
King William St. EC4
—6D 62 (1F 151)
King William Wlk. SE10 —6E 80
(in two parts)

Kingwood Rd. SW6 —1G 91
Kinlet Rd. SE18 —1G 99
Kinloch Dri. NW9 —7K 25
Kinloch St. N7 —3K 45
Kinloss Ct. N3 —4H 27
Kinloss Gdns. N3 —3H 27
Kinloss Rd. Cars —7A 122
Kinnaird Av. W4 —7J 73
Kinnaird Av. Brom —6H 113
Kinnaird Clo. Brom —6H 113
Kinnaird Way. Wfd G —6J 21
Kinnear Rd. W12 —2B 74
Kinnerton Pl. N. SW1
—2D 76 (7F 147)
Kinnerton Pl. S. SW1
—2D 76 (7F 147)
Kinnerton St. SW1
—2E 76 (7G 147)
Kinnerton Yd. SW1
—2E 76 (7G 147)
Kinnoul Rd. W6 —6G 75
Kinross Av. Wor Pk —2C 130
Kinross Clo. Edgw —2C 12
Kinross Clo. Harr —5E 24
Kinsale Rd. SE15 —3G 95
Kintore Way. SE1
—4F 79 (3J 157)
Kintyre Clo. SW16 —2K 123
Kintyre Ct. SW2 —7J 93
Kinveachy Gdns. SE7 —5C 82
Kinver Rd. SE26 —4J 111
Kipling Clo. W7 —7K 55
Kipling Dri. SW19 —6B 108
Kipling Est. SE1 —2D 78 (7F 151)
Kipling Ho. SE5 —7C 78
(off Elmington Est.)
Kipling Pl. Stan —6E 10
Kipling Rd. Bexh —1E 100
Kipling St. SE1 —2D 78 (7F 151)
Kipling Ter. N9 —3J 17
Kipling Tower W3 —3J 73
(off Palmerston Rd.)
Kippington Dri. SE9 —1B 114
Kirby Clo. Eps —5B 130
Kirby Clo. Lou —1H 21
Kirby Est. SE16 —3H 79
Kirby Gro. SE1 —2E 78 (6G 151)
Kirby St. EC1 —5A 62 (5K 143)
Kirchen Rd. W13 —7B 56
Kirkdale. SE26 —2H 111
Kirkdale Rd. E11 —1G 49
Kirkfield Clo. W13 —1B 72
Kirkham Rd. E6 —6C 66
Kirkham St. SE18 —6J 83
Kirkland Av. Ilf —2E 34
Kirkland Clo. Sidc —6J 99
Kirkland Wlk. E8 —6F 47
Kirk La. SE18 —6G 83
Kirkleas Rd. Surb —7E 118
Kirklees Rd. Dag —5C 52
Kirklees Rd. T Hth —5A 124
Kirkley Rd. SW19 —1J 121
Kirkman Pl. W1 —5H 61 (6C 142)
Kirkmichael Rd. E14 —6E 64
Kirk Rise. Sutt —3K 131
Kirk Rd. E17 —6B 32
Kirkside Rd. SE3 —6J 81
Kirk's Pl. E14 —5B 64
Kirkstall Av. N17 —4D 30
Kirkstall Gdns. SW2 —1J 109
Kirkstall Rd. SW2 —1H 109
Kirksted Rd. Mord —1K 131
Kirkstone Way. Brom —7G 113
Kirk St. WC1 —4K 61 (4G 143)
Kirkton Rd. N15 —4E 30

Kirkwall Pl. E2 —3J 63
Kirkwood La. NW1 —7E 44
Kirkwood Rd. SE15 —2H 95
Kirrane Clo. N Mald —5B 120
Kirtley Rd. SE26 —4A 112
Kirtling St. SW8 —7G 77
Kirton Clo. W4 —4K 73
Kirton Gdns. E2 —3F 63 (2K 145)
Kirton Rd. E13 —2A 66
Kirton Wlk. Edgw —7D 12
Kirwyn Way. SE5 —7B 78
Kitcat Ter. E3 —3C 64
Kitchener Rd. E7 —6K 49
Kitchener Rd. E17 —1D 32
Kitchener Rd. N2 —3C 28
Kitchener Rd. N17 —3E 30
Kitchener Rd. Dag —6J 53
Kitchener Rd. T Hth —3D 124
Kite Pl. E2 —3G 63
(off Lampern St.)
Kite Yd. SW11 —1D 92
Kitley Gdns. SE19 —1F 125
Kitson Rd. SE5 —7D 78
Kitson Rd. SW13 —1C 90
Kittiwake Rd. N'holt —3B 54
Kittiwake Way. Hayes —5B 54
Kitto Rd. SE14 —2K 95
Kitts End Rd. Barn —1C 4
Kiver Rd. N19 —2H 45
Klea Av. SW4 —6G 93
Knapdale Clo. SE23 —2H 111
Knapmill Rd. SE6 —2C 112
Knapmill Way. SE6 —2D 112
Knapp Clo. NW10 —6A 42
Knapp Rd. E3 —4C 64
Knapton M. SW17 —6E 108
Knaresborough Dri. SW18
—1K 107
Knaresborough Pl. SW5 —4K 75
Knatchbull Rd. NW10 —1K 57
Knatchbull Rd. SE5 —1B 94
Knebworth Av. E17 —1C 32
Knebworth Ho. SW8 —1H 93
Knebworth Rd. N16 —4E 46
Knee Hill. SE2 —4C 84
Kneehill Cres. SE2 —4C 84
Kneller Gdns. Iswth —6H 87
Kneller Ho. N'holt —2B 54
(off Academy Gdns.)
Kneller Rd. SE4 —4A 96
Kneller Rd. N Mald —7A 120
Kneller Rd. Twic —6G 87
Knight Ct. N15 —5E 30
Knighten St. E1 —1H 79
Knighthead Point. E14 —2C 80
Knighthorpe Rd. NW10 —7K 41
Knightland Rd. E5 —2H 47
Knighton Clo. Romf —6K 37
Knighton Clo. S Croy —7B 134
Knighton Clo. Wfd G —4E 20
Knighton Dri. Wfd G —4E 20
Knighton Grn. Buck H —2E 20
Knighton La. Buck H —2E 20
Knighton Pk. Rd. SE26 —5K 111
Knighton Rd. E7 —3J 49
Knighton Rd. Romf —6J 37
Knightrider Ct. EC4
—7C 62 (2B 150)
Knightrider St. EC4
—6B 62 (2B 150)
Knights Arc. SW1
—2D 76 (7E 146)
Knights Av. W5 —2E 72
Knightsbridge. SW7 & SW1
—2C 76 (7C 146)

Knightsbridge Ct. SW1
—2D 76 (7F 147)
Knightsbridge Gdns. Romf
—5K 37
Knightsbridge Grn. SW1
—2D 76 (7E 146)
Knights Clo. E9 —5J 47
Knights Ct. E4 —1K 19
Knights Ct. Brom —3H 113
Knights Ct. King T —3E 118
Knights Hill. SE27 —5B 110
Knight's Hill Sq. SE27 —4B 110
Knights La. N9 —3B 18
Knight's Pk. King T —3E 118
Knight's Rd. E16 —2J 81
Knights Rd. Stan —4H 11
Knights Wlk. SE11
—4B 78 (4A 156)
Knightswood Clo. Edgw —2D 12
Knightswood Ct. N6 —7H 29
Knightswood Ho. N12 —6F 15
Knightwood Cres. N Mald
—6A 120
Knivet Rd. SW6 —6J 75
Knobs Hill Rd. E15 —1D 64
Knockholt Rd. SE9 —5B 98
Knole Clo. Croy —6J 125
Knole Ct. N'holt —3A 54
(off Broomcroft Av.)
Knole Ga. Sidc —3J 115
Knole, The. SE9 —4E 114
Knoll Dri. N14 —7K 5
Knoll Ho. Pinn —2B 22
Knollmead. Surb —7K 119
Knoll Rise. Orp —7K 129
Knoll Rd. SW18 —5A 92
Knoll Rd. Bex —7G 101
Knoll Rd. Sidc —5B 116
Knolls Clo. Wor Pk —3D 130
Knoll, The. W13 —5C 56
Knoll, The. Beck —1D 126
Knoll, The. Brom —1J 137
Knollys Clo. SW16 —3A 110
Knollys Rd. SW16 —3A 110
Knottisford St. E2 —3J 63
Knotts Grn. M. E10 —6D 32
Knotts Grn. Rd. E10 —6D 32
Knowle Av. Bexh —7E 84
Knowle Clo. SW9 —3A 94
Knowle Rd. Brom —2D 138
Knowle Rd. Twic —1J 103
Knowles Ct. Harr —6K 23
(off Gayton Rd.)
Knowles Hill Cres. SE13 —5F 97
Knowles Wlk. SW4 —3G 93
Knowlton Grn. Brom —5H 127
Knowlton Ho. SW9 —1B 94
(off Cowley Rd.)
Knowsley Av. S'hall —1F 71
Knowsley Rd. SW11 —2D 92
Knox Ct. SW4 —2J 93
Knox Rd. E7 —6H 49
Knox St. W1 —5D 60 (5E 140)
Knoyle St. SE14 —6A 80
Koblenz Ho. N8 —3J 29
(off Newland Rd.)
Kohat Rd. SW19 —5K 107
Komehather Ho. Ilf —5D 34
Kossuth St. SE10 —5G 81
Kotree Way. SE1 —4G 79
Kramer M. SW5 —5J 75
Kreedman Wlk. E8 —5G 47
Kreisel Wlk. Rich —6F 73
Kristina Ct. Sutt —7J 131
(off Overton Rd.)

Krupnik Pl. EC2 —4E 62 (2H 145)
Kuala Gdns. SW16 —1K 123
Kuhn Way. E7 —5J 49
Kydbrook Clo. Orp —7G 129
Kylemore Clo. E6 —2B 66
Kylemore Rd. NW6 —7J 43
Kymberley Rd. Harr —6J 23
Kymes Ct. S Harr —2H 39
Kynance Gdns. Stan —1C 24
Kynance M. SW7 —3K 75
Kynance Pl. SW7 —3A 76
Kynaston Av. N16 —3F 47
Kynaston Av. T Hth —5C 124
Kynaston Clo. Harr —7C 10
Kynaston Cres. T Hth —5C 124
Kynaston Rd. N16 —3E 46
Kynaston Rd. Brom —5J 113
Kynaston Rd. Enf —1J 7
Kynaston Rd. T Hth —5C 124
Kynaston Wood. Harr —7C 10
Kynnersley Clo. Cars —3D 132
Kynoch Rd. N18 —4D 18
Kyrle Rd. SW11 —6E 92
Kyverdale Rd. N16 —1F 47

Laburnam Av. N9 —2A 18
Laburnam Av. N17 —7J 17
Laburnam Av. Sutt —3C 132
Laburnam Clo. E4 —6G 19
Laburnam Clo. N11 —6K 15
Laburnam Clo. SE15 —7J 79
Laburnam Ct. E2 —1F 63
Laburnam Ct. SE16 —2J 79
(off Albion St.)
Laburnam Ct. SE19 —1F 125
Laburnam Ct. Harr —6F 23
Laburnam Ct. Stan —4H 11
Laburnam Gdns. N21 —2H 17
Laburnam Gdns. Croy —1K 135
Laburnam Gro. N21 —2H 17
Laburnam Gro. NW9 —7J 25
Laburnam Gro. Houn —4D 86
Laburnam Gro. N Mald —2K 119
Laburnam Gro. S'hall —4D 55
Laburnam Ho. Brom —1G 127
Laburnam Lodge. N3 —2H 27
Laburnam Rd. SW19 —7A 108
Laburnam Rd. Mitc —2E 122
Laburnams, The. E6 —4C 66
Laburnam Way. Brom —7C 128
Lacebark Clo. Sidc —7K 99
Lacey Clo. N9 —2B 18
Lacey Dri. Edgw —4A 12
Lacey Wlk. E3 —2C 64
Lackington St. EC2
—5D 62 (5F 145)
Lacland Pl. SW10 —7B 76
Lacock Clo. SW19 —6A 108
Lacock Ct. W13 —1A 72
(off Singapore Rd.)
Lacon Rd. SE22 —4G 95
Lacy Rd. Dag —3C 52
Lacy Rd. SW15 —4F 91
Ladas Rd. SE27 —4C 110
Ladbroke Cres. W11 —6G 59
Ladbroke Gdns. W11 —7H 59
Ladbroke Gro. W10 & W11
—4F 59
Ladbroke M. W11 —1G 75
Ladbroke Rd. W11 —1H 75
Ladbroke Rd. Enf —6A 8
Ladbroke Sq. W11 —7H 59
Ladbroke Ter. W11 —7H 59

247

Ladbroke Wlk. W11 —1H 75
Ladbrook Clo. Pinn —5D 22
Ladbrooke Cres. Sidc —3D 116
Ladbrook Rd. SE25 —4D 124
Ladderstile Ride. King T —5H 105
Laddenswood Way. N11 —5B 16
Ladlands. SE22 —7G 95
Lady Booth Rd. King T —2E 118
Ladycroft Rd. SE13 —3D 96
Ladycroft Wlk. Stan —1D 24
Lady Dock Wlk. SE16 —2A 80
Lady Hay. Wor Pk —2B 130
Lady Margaret Rd. NW5 & N19
—5G 45
Lady Margaret Rd. S'hall —7D 54
Lady Shaw Ct. N13 —2E 16
Ladyship Ter. SE22 —7G 95
Ladysmith Av. E6 —2C 66
Ladysmith Av. Ilf —7H 35
Ladysmith Rd. E16 —3H 65
Ladysmith Rd. N17 —2G 31
Ladysmith Rd. N18 —5C 18
Ladysmith Rd. SE9 —6E 98
Ladysmith Rd. Enf —3K 7
Ladysmith Rd. Harr —2J 23
Lady Somerset Rd. NW5 —4F 45
Ladywell Clo. SE4 —5C 96
Ladywell Heights. SE4 —6B 96
Ladywell Rd. SE13 —5C 96
Ladywell St. E15 —1H 65
Ladywood Av. Orp —5J 129
Lafone Av. Felt —2A 102
Lafone St. SE1 —2F 79 (6J 151)
Lagado M. SE16 —1K 79
Lagan Ho. SE15 —7G 79
(off Sumner Est.)
Laidlaw Dri. N21 —5E 6
Laing Dean. N'holt —1A 54
Laing Ho. SE5 —7C 78
Laings Av. Mitc —2D 122
Lainlock Pl. Houn —1F 87
Lainson St. SW18 —7J 91
Lairdale Clo. SE21 —1C 110
Lairs Clo. N7 —5J 45
Laitwood Rd. SW12 —1F 109
Lake Av. Brom —6J 113
Lake Bus. Cen. N17 —7B 18
Lake Clo. SW19 —5H 107
Lakedale Rd. SE18 —6J 83
Lake Dri. Bush —2B 10
Lakefield Rd. N22 —2B 30
Lake Footpath. SE2 —2D 84
Lake Gdns. Dag —5G 53
Lake Gdns. Rich —2B 104
Lake Gdns. Wall —3F 133
Lakehall Gdns. T Hth —5B 124
Lakehall Rd. T Hth —5B 124
Lake Ho. Rd. E11 —3J 49
Lakehurst Rd. Eps —5A 130
Lakeland Clo. Harr —6C 10
Lakenheath. N14 —5B 6
Laker Ct. SW4 —1J 93
Lake Rd. SW19 —5H 107
Lake Rd. Croy —2B 136
Lake Rd. Romf —4D 36
Laker Pl. SW15 —6H 91
Lakeside. N3 —2K 27
Lakeside. SE2 —3D 84
Lakeside. W13 —6C 56
Lakeside. Beck —3D 126
Lakeside. Enf —4C 6
Lakeside. Eps —6A 130
Lakeside. Wall —4F 133
Lakeside Av. SE28 —2A 84
Lakeside Av. Ilf —4B 34

Lakeside Clo. SE25 —2G 125
Lakeside Clo. Sidc —5C 100
Lakeside Ct. N4 —2C 46
Lakeside Cres. Barn —5J 5
Lakeside Dri. Brom —3C 138
Lakeside Rd. N13 —4E 16
Lakeside Rd. W14 —3F 75
Lakeside Ter. EC2
—5C 62 (5D 144)
Lakeside Way. Wemb —4G 41
Lakes Rd. Kes —5A 138
Lakeswood Rd. Orp —6G 129
Lake, The. Bush —1C 10
Lake View. Edgw —5A 12
Lake View Est. E3 —2A 64
Lakeview Rd. SE27 —5A 110
Lakeview Rd. Well —4B 100
Lakis Clo. NW3 —4A 44
Laleham Av. NW7 —3E 12
Laleham Rd. SE6 —7E 96
Lalor St. SW6 —2G 91
Lambarde Av. SE9 —4E 114
Lamberhurst Ho. SE15 —6J 79
Lamberhurst Rd. SE27 —4A 110
Lamberhurst Rd. Dag —1F 53
Lambert Av. Rich —3G 89
Lambert Ct. Eri —6J 85
(off Park Cres.)
Lambert Jones M. EC2
—5C 62 (5C 144)
Lambert Lodge. Bren —5D 72
(off Layton Rd.)
Lambert Rd. E16 —6K 65
Lambert Rd. N12 —5G 15
Lambert Rd. SW2 —5J 93
Lambert's Pl. Croy —1D 134
Lamberts Rd. Surb —5E 118
Lambert St. N1 —7A 46
Lambert Wlk. Wemb —3D 40
Lambert Way. N12 —5F 15
Lambeth Bri. SW1 & SE1
—4J 77 (3F 155)
Lambeth High St. SE1
—4K 77 (4G 155)
Lambeth Hill. EC4
—7C 62 (2C 150)
Lambeth Pal. Rd. SE1
—3K 77 (3G 155)
Lambeth Rd. SE1
—3K 77 (3G 155)
Lambeth Rd. Croy —1A 134
Lambeth Towers. SE11
—3A 78 (2J 155)
Lambeth Wlk. SE11
—4K 77 (3H 155)
Lambfold Ho. N7 —6J 45
Lamb La. E8 —7H 47
Lamble St. NW5 —5E 44
Lambley Rd. Dag —6B 52
Lambolle Pl. NW3 —6C 44
Lambolle Rd. NW3 —6C 44
Lambourn Clo. NW5 —4G 45
(off Lady Margaret Rd.)
Lambourn Clo. W7 —2K 71
Lambourne Av. SW19 —4H 107
Lambourne Ct. Wfd G —7F 21
Lambourne Gdns. E4 —2H 19
Lambourne Gdns. Bark —7K 51
Lambourne Gdns. Enf —2A 8
Lambourne Ho. SE16 —4K 79
Lambourne Pl. SE3 —1K 97
Lambourne Rd. E11 —7E 32
Lambourne Rd. Bark —7J 51
Lambourne Rd. Ilf —2J 51
Lambourn Gro. King T —2H 119

Lambourn Rd. SW4 —3F 93
Lamb Pas. Bren —6F 73
Lambrook Ho. SE15 —1G 95
Lambrook Ter. SW6 —1G 91
Lamb's Bldgs. EC1
—4D 62 (4E 144)
Lamb's Clo. N9 —2B 18
Lamb's Conduit Pas. WC1
—5K 61 (5G 143)
Lamb's Conduit St. WC1
—4K 61 (4G 143)
Lambscroft Av. SE9 —3A 114
Lambs Meadow. Wfd G —2B 34
Lamb's M. N1 —1B 62
Lamb's Pas. EC1
—4D 62 (4E 144)
Lamb St. E1 —5F 63 (5J 145)
Lamb's Wlk. Enf —2H 7
Lambton Pl. W11 —7H 59
Lambton Rd. N19 —1J 45
Lambton Rd. SW20 —1E 120
Lamb Wlk. SE1 —2E 78 (7G 151)
Lamerock Rd. Brom —4H 113
Lamerton Rd. Ilf —2F 35
Lamerton St. SE8 —6C 80
Lamford Clo. N17 —7J 17
Lamington St. W6 —4D 74
Lamlash St. SE11
—4B 78 (3A 156)
Lammas Av. Mitc —2E 122
Lammas Grn. SE26 —3H 111
Lammas Pk. Gdns. W5 —1C 72
Lammas Pk. Rd. W5 —2D 72
Lammas Rd. E9 —7K 47
Lammas Rd. E10 —2A 48
Lammas Rd. Rich —4C 104
Lammermoor Rd. SW12 —7F 93
Lamont Rd. SW10 —6A 76
Lamont Rd. Pas. SW10
—6B 76 (7A 152)
Lamorbey Clo. Sidc —1K 115
Lamorna Clo. E17 —2E 32
Lamorna Clo. Orp —7K 129
Lamorna Gro. Stan —1D 24
Lampard Gro. N16 —1F 47
Lampern Sq. E2 —3G 63
Lampeter Sq. W6 —6G 75
Lamplighter Clo. E1 —4J 63
Lampmead Rd. SE12 —4H 97
Lamp Office Ct. WC1
—4K 61 (4G 143)
Lamport Clo. SE18 —4D 82
Lamps Ct. SE5 —7C 78
Lampton Av. Houn —1F 87
Lampton Ct. Houn —1F 87
Lampton Ho. Clo. SW19 —4F 107
Lampton Pk. Rd. Houn —2F 87
Lampton Rd. Houn —2F 87
Lanacre Av. NW9 —1K 25
Lanain Ct. SE12 —7H 97
Lanark Clo. W5 —5C 56
Lanark Ct. N'holt —5E 38
(off Newmarket Av.)
Lanark Ho. SE1 —5G 79 (6K 157)
Lanark Pl. W9 —4A 60
Lanark Rd. W9 —2K 59
Lanark Sq. E14 —3D 80
Lanata Wlk. Hayes —4B 54
(off Alba Clo.)
Lanbury Rd. SE15 —4K 95
Lancashire Ct. W1
—7F 61 (2K 147)
Lancaster Av. E18 —4K 33
Lancaster Av. SE27 —2B 110

Lancaster Av. SW19 —5F 107
Lancaster Av. Bark —7J 51
Lancaster Av. Barn —1F 5
Lancaster Av. Mitc —5J 123
Lancaster Clo. N1 —7E 46
Lancaster Clo. N17 —7B 18
Lancaster Clo. SE27 —2B 110
Lancaster Clo. Brom —4H 127
Lancaster Clo. Croy —2J 133
Lancaster Clo. King T —5D 104
Lancaster Cotts. Rich —6E 88
Lancaster Ct. SE27 —2B 110
Lancaster Ct. SW6 —7H 75
Lancaster Ct. Sutt —7J 131
(off Mulgrave Rd.)
Lancaster Dri. E14 —1E 80
Lancaster Dri. NW3 —6C 44
Lancaster Gdns. SW19 —5G 107
Lancaster Gdns. W13 —2B 72
Lancaster Gdns. King T —5D 104
Lancaster Ga. W2 —7A 60
Lancaster Gro. NW3 —6B 44
Lancaster Ho. Enf —1J 7
Lancaster M. Rich —6E 88
Lancaster M. W2
—7A 60 (2A 146)
Lancaster M. SW18 —5K 91
Lancaster M. W2
Lancaster Pk. Rich —5E 88
Lancaster Pl. SW19 —5F 107
Lancaster Pl. WC2
—7K 61 (2G 149)
Lancaster Pl. Houn —2B 86
Lancaster Pl. Ilf —4G 51
Lancaster Pl. Twic —6A 88
Lancaster Rd. E7 —7J 49
Lancaster Rd. E11 —2G 49
Lancaster Rd. E17 —2K 31
Lancaster Rd. N4 —7K 29
Lancaster Rd. N11 —6C 16
Lancaster Rd. N18 —5A 18
Lancaster Rd. NW10 —5C 42
Lancaster Rd. SE25 —2F 125
Lancaster Rd. SW19 —5F 107
Lancaster Rd. W11 —6G 59
Lancaster Rd. Barn —4G 5
Lancaster Rd. Enf —1J 7
Lancaster Rd. Harr —5E 22
Lancaster Rd. N'holt —6G 39
Lancaster Rd. S'hall —7C 54
Lancaster Stables. NW3 —6C 44
Lancaster St. SE1
—2B 78 (7A 150)
Lancaster St. SE18 —7J 83
Lancaster Ter. W2
—7B 60 (2A 146)
Lancaster Wlk. W2 —1A 76
Lancefield Ct. W10 —2G 59
Lancefield Ho. SE15 —3H 95
Lancefield St. W10 —3H 59
Lancell St. N16 —2E 46
Lancelot Av. Wemb —4D 40
Lancelot Cres. Wemb —4D 40
Lancelot Gdns. E Barn —7K 5
Lancelot Pl. SW7
—2D 76 (7E 146)
Lancelot Rd. Well —4A 100
Lancelot Rd. Wemb —4D 40
Lance Rd. Harr —7G 23
Lancer Sq. W8 —2K 75
Lancey Clo. SE7 —4C 82
Lanchester Rd. N6 —5D 28
Lancing Gdns. N9 —1A 18

Lancing Rd. W13 —7B 56
Lancing Rd. Croy —7K 123
Lancing Rd. Ilf —6H 35
Lancing St. NW1
—3H 61 (2C 142)
Lancresse Ct. N1 —1E 62
(off De Beauvoir Est.)
Landcroft Rd. SE22 —5F 95
Landells Rd. SE22 —6F 95
Landford Rd. SW15 —3E 90
Landgrove Rd. SW19 —5J 107
Landmann Way. SE14 —5K 79
Landmark Commercial Cen. N18
—6K 17
Landon Pl. SW1 —3D 76 (1E 152)
Landon's Clo. E14 —1E 80
Landon Wlk. E14 —7D 64
Landor Rd. SW9 —3J 93
Landor Wlk. W12 —2C 74
Landport Way. SE15 —7F 79
Landra Gdns. N21 —6G 7
Landridge Rd. SW6 —2H 91
Landrock Rd. N8 —6J 29
Landscape Rd. Wfd G —7E 20
Landseer Av. E12 —5E 50
Landseer Clo. SW19 —1A 122
Landseer Clo. Edgw —2G 25
Landseer Ho. N'holt —2B 54
(off Parkfield Dri.)
Landseer Rd. N19 —3J 45
Landseer Rd. Enf —5B 8
Landseer Rd. N Mald —7K 119
Landseer Rd. Sutt —6J 131
Landstead Rd. SE18 —7H 83
Lane App. NW7 —5B 14
Lane Clo. NW2 —3D 42
Lane End. SW15 —6F 91
Lane End. Bexh —3H 101
Lane Gdns. Bush —1D 10
Lane M. E12 —3D 50
Lanercost Clo. SW2 —2A 110
Lanercost Gdns. N14 —7D 6
Lanercost Rd. SW2 —2A 110
Lanesborough Pl. SW1
—2E 76 (6H 147)
Laneside. Chst —5G 115
Laneside. Edgw —5D 12
Laneside Av. Dag —7F 37
Lane, The. NW8 —2A 60
Lane, The. SE3 —3J 97
Laneway. SW15 —5D 90
Lanfranc Ct. Harr —3K 39
Lanfranc Rd. E3 —2A 64
Lanfrey Pl. W14 —5H 75
Langbourne Av. N6 —2E 44
Langbourne Mans. N6 —2E 44
Langbrook Rd. SE3 —3B 98
Langcroft Clo. Cars —3D 132
Langdale Av. Mitc —3D 122
Langdale Clo. SE17
—6C 78 (7C 156)
Langdale Clo. SW14 —4H 89
Langdale Clo. Dag —1C 52
Langdale Cres. Bexh —5G 85
Langdale Gdns. Gnfd —3B 56
Langdale Mans. E1 —6H 63
(off Langdale St.)
Langdale Pde. Mitc —3D 122
Langdale Rd. SE10 —7E 80
Langdale Rd. T Hth —4A 124
Langdale St. E1 —6H 63
Langdon Ct. NW10 —1A 58
Langdon Cres. E6 —2E 66
Langdon Dri. NW9 —1J 41
Langdon Pk. Rd. N6 —7G 29

Langdon Pl. SW14 —3J 89
Langdon Rd. E6 —1E 66
Langdon Rd. Brom —3K 127
Langdon Rd. Mord —5A 122
Langdons Ct. S'hall —3E 70
Langdon Shaw. Sidc —5K 115
Langdon Way. SE1 —4G 79
Langford Clo. E8 —5G 47
Langford Clo. N15 —6E 30
Langford Clo. NW8 —2A 60
Langford Ct. NW8 —2A 60
(off Abbey Rd.)
Langford Cres. Cockf —4J 5
Langford Grn. SE5 —3E 94
Langford Ho. SE8 —6C 80
Langford Pl. NW8 —2A 60
Langford Pl. Sidc —3A 116
Langford Rd. SW6 —2K 91
Langford Rd. Cockf —4J 5
Langford Rd. Wfd G —6F 21
Langfords. Buck H —2G 21
Langham Clo. N15 —3B 30
(off Langham Rd.)
Langham Ct. NW4 —5F 27
Langham Dri. Romf —6B 36
Langham Gdns. N21 —5F 7
Langham Gdns. W13 —7B 56
Langham Gdns. Edgw —7D 12
Langham Gdns. Rich —4C 104
Langham Gdns. Wemb —2C 40
Langham Ho. Clo. Rich —4D 104
Langham Mans. SW5 —5K 75
(off Earl's Ct. Sq.)
Langham Pl. N15 —3B 30
Langham Pl. W1
—5F 61 (6K 141)
Langham Pl. W4 —6A 74
Langham Rd. N15 —3B 30
Langham Rd. SW20 —1E 120
Langham Rd. Edgw —6D 12
Langham Rd. Tedd —5B 104
Langham St. W1
—5F 61 (6K 141)
Langhedge Clo. N18 —6A 18
Langhedge La. N18 —6A 18
Langhedge La. Ind. Est. N18
—6A 18
Langholm Clo. SW12 —7H 93
Langholme. Bush —1B 10
Langhorne Ct. NW8 —7B 44
(off Dorman Way)
Langhorne Rd. Dag —7G 53
Lang Ho. SW8 —7J 77
(off Hartington Rd.)
Langland Cres. Stan —2D 24
Langland Dri. Pinn —1C 22
Langland Gdns. NW3 —5K 43
Langland Gdns. Croy —2B 136
Langland Ho. SE5 —7D 78
(off Edmund St.)
Langler Rd. NW10 —2E 58
Langley Av. Ruis —2A 38
Langley Av. Surb —7D 118
Langley Av. Wor Pk —2F 131
Langley Ct. WC2 —7J 61 (2E 148)
Langley Cres. E11 —7A 34
Langley Cres. Dag —7C 52
Langley Cres. Edgw —3D 12
Langley Dri. E11 —7K 33
Langley Dri. W3 —2H 73
Langley Gdns. Brom —4A 128
Langley Gdns. Dag —7D 52
Langley Gdns. Orp —6F 129
Langley Gro. N Mald —2A 120

Langley La. SW8
—6J 77 (7F 155)
Langley Mans. SW8
—6K 77 (7G 155)
Langley Pk. NW7 —6F 13
Langley Pk. Rd. Sutt —5A 132
Langley Rd. SW19 —1H 121
Langley Rd. Beck —4A 126
Langley Rd. Iswth —2K 87
Langley Rd. Surb —7E 118
Langley Rd. Well —6D 84
Langley Row. Barn —1C 4
Langley St. WC2
—6J 61 (1E 148)
Langley Way. W Wick —1F 137
Langmead Dri. Bush —1D 10
Langmead St. SE27 —4C 110
Langmore Ho. E1 —6G 63
(off Stutfield St.)
Langport Ho. SW9 —2B 94
Langridge M. Hamp —6D 102
Langroyd Rd. SW17 —2D 108
Langside Av. SW15 —4C 90
Langside Cres. N14 —3C 16
Langston Hughes Clo. SE24
—4B 94
Lang St. E1 —4J 63
Langthorn Ct. EC2
—6D 62 (7F 145)
Langthorne Ct. Brom —4E 112
Langthorne Rd. E11 —3E 48
Langthorne St. SW6 —7F 75
Langton Av. E6 —3E 66
Langton Av. N20 —7F 5
Langton Clo. WC1
—4K 61 (3H 143)
Langton Pl. SW18 —1J 107
Langton Rise. SE23 —7H 95
Langton Rd. NW2 —3E 42
Langton Rd. SW9 —7B 78
Langton Rd. Harr —7B 10
Langton Rd. SW10 —6A 76
Langton Way. SE3 —1H 97
Langton Way. Croy —4E 134
Langtry Rd. NW8 —1K 59
Langtry Rd. N'holt —2B 54
Langtry Wlk. NW8 —1K 59
Langwood Chase. Tedd —6C 104
Lanhill Rd. W9 —4J 59
Lanier Rd. SE13 —6F 97
Lanigan Dri. Houn —5F 87
Lankaster Gdns. N2 —1B 28
Lankers Dri. Harr —6D 22
Lankton Clo. Beck —1E 126
Lannoy Point. SW6 —7G 75
(off Pellant Rd.)
Lannoy Rd. SE9 —1G 115
Lanrick Rd. E14 —6F 65
Lanridge Rd. SE2 —3D 84
Lansbury Av. N18 —5J 17
Lansbury Av. Bark —7A 52
Lansbury Av. Felt —6A 86
Lansbury Av. Romf —5E 36
Lansbury Clo. NW10 —5J 41
Lansbury Est. E14 —6D 64
Lansbury Gdns. E14 —6F 65
Lansbury Rd. Enf —1E 8
Lansbury Wlk. N18 —5K 17
Lanscombe Wlk. SW8 —1J 93
Lansdell Ho. SW2 —5A 94
(off Tulse Hill)
Lansdell Rd. Mitc —2E 122
Lansdowne Av. Bexh —7D 84
Lansdowne Clo. SW20 —7F 107

Lansdowne Clo. Twic —1K 103
Lansdowne Ct. Wor Pk —2C 130
Lansdowne Cres. W11 —7G 59
Lansdowne Dri. E8 —6G 47
Lansdowne Gdns. SW8 —1J 93
Lansdowne Grn. SW8 —1J 93
Lansdowne Gro. NW10 —4A 42
Lansdowne Hill. SE27 —3B 110
Lansdowne La. SE7 —5B 82
Lansdowne M. SE7 —5B 82
Lansdowne M. W11 —1H 75
Lansdowne Pl. SE1
—3D 78 (1F 157)
Lansdowne Pl. SE19 —7F 111
Lansdowne Rise. W11 —7G 59
Lansdowne Rd. E4 —2H 19
Lansdowne Rd. E11 —2H 49
Lansdowne Rd. E17 —6C 32
Lansdowne Rd. E18 —3J 33
Lansdowne Rd. N3 —7D 14
Lansdowne Rd. N10 —2G 29
Lansdowne Rd. N17 —1G 31
Lansdowne Rd. SW20 —7E 106
Lansdowne Rd. W11 —7G 59
Lansdowne Rd. Brom —7J 113
Lansdowne Rd. Croy —2D 134
Lansdowne Rd. Harr —7J 23
Lansdowne Rd. Houn —3F 87
Lansdowne Rd. Ilf —1K 51
Lansdowne Rd. Stan —6H 11
Lansdowne Row. W1
—1F 77 (4K 147)
Lansdowne Ter. WC1
—4J 61 (4F 143)
Lansdowne Wlk. W11 —1H 75
Lansdowne Way. SW8 —1H 93
Lansdowne Wood Clo. SE27
—3B 110
Lansdown Rd. E7 —7A 50
Lansdown Rd. Sidc —3B 116
Lansfield Av. N18 —4B 18
Lantern Clo. SW15 —4C 90
Lantern Clo. Wemb —5D 40
Lanterns Ct. E14 —3C 80
Lant St. SE1 —2C 78 (6C 156)
Lanvanor Rd. SE15 —2J 95
Lanyard Ho. SE8 —4B 80
Lapford Clo. W9 —4H 59
Lappmann Wlk. Hayes —4B 54
Lapse Wood Wlk. SE23 —1H 111
Lapstone Gdns. Harr —6C 24
Lapwing Tower. SE8 —6B 80
(off Abinger Gro.)
Lapwing Way. Hayes —6B 54
Lapworth. N11 —4A 16
(off Coppies Gro.)
Lara Clo. SE13 —6E 96
Larbert Rd. SW16 —7G 109
Larch Av. W3 —1A 74
Larch Clo. E13 —4K 65
Larch Clo. N11 —7K 15
Larch Clo. N19 —2G 45
Larch Clo. SE8 —6B 80
Larch Clo. SW12 —2F 109
Larch Cres. Hayes —5A 54
Larch Dene. Orp —2E 138
Larch Dri. W4 —5G 73
Larches Av. SW14 —4K 89
Larches, The. N13 —3H 17
Larch Grn. NW9 —1A 26
Larch Gro. Sidc —1K 115
Larch Ho. Brom —1G 127
Larch Ho. Hayes —5A 54
Larch Rd. E10 —2C 48
Larch Rd. NW2 —4E 42

Larch Tree Way. Croy —3C 136
Larchvale Ct. Sutt —7K 131
Larch Way. Brom —7E 128
Larchwood Rd. SE9 —2F 115
Larcombe Clo. Croy —4F 135
Larcombe Ct. Sutt —7K 131
(off Worcester Rd.)
Larcom St. SE17
—4C 78 (4D 156)
Larden Rd. W3 —1A 74
Larissa St. SE17
—5D 78 (5F 157)
Larkbere Rd. SE26 —4A 112
Larken Clo. Bush —1B 10
Larken Dri. Bush —1B 10
Larkfield Av. Harr —3B 24
Larkfield Clo. Brom —2H 137
Larkfield Rd. Rich —4E 88
Larkfield Rd. Sidc —3K 115
Larkhall La. SW4 —2H 93
Larkhall Rise. SW4 —3G 93
Lark Row. E2 —1J 63
Larksfield Gro. Enf —1C 8
Larks Gro. Bark —7J 51
Larkshall Ct. Romf —2J 37
Larkshall Cres. E4 —4K 19
Larkshall Rd. E4 —5K 19
Larkspur Clo. E6 —5C 66
Larkspur Clo. N17 —7J 17
Larkspur Lodge. Sidc —3B 116
Larkswood Ct. E4 —5A 20
Larkswood Rise. Pinn —4A 22
Larkswood Rd. E4 —4H 19
Lark Way. Cars —7C 122
Larkway Clo. NW9 —4K 25
Larnach Rd. W6 —6F 75
Larpent Av. SW15 —5E 90
Larshall Rd. E4 —3A 20
Larwood Clo. Gnfd —5H 39
Lascelles Av. Harr —7H 23
Lascelles Clo. E11 —2F 49
Lascotts Rd. N22 —6E 16
Laseron Ho. N15 —4F 31
(off Tottenham Grn. E.)
Lassa Rd. SE9 —5C 98
Lassell St. SE10 —5F 81
Lasseter Pl. SE3 —6G 81
Latchett Rd. E18 —1K 33
Latchingdon Ct. E17 —4K 31
Latchingdon Gdns. Wfd G
—6H 21
Latchmere Clo. Rich —5E 104
Latchmere La. King T —6F 105
Latchmere Pas. SW11 —2C 92
Latchmere Rd. SW11 —2D 92
Latchmere Rd. King T —7E 104
Latchmere St. SW11 —2D 92
Lateward Rd. Bren —6D 72
Latham Clo. E6 —5C 66
Latham Clo. Twic —7A 88
Latham Ct. SW5 —4J 75
(off W. Cromwell Rd.)
Latham Ct. N'holt —3B 54
(off Seasprite Clo.)
Latham Rd. Bexh —5G 101
Latham Rd. Twic —7K 87
Latham's Way. Croy —1K 133
Lathkill Clo. Enf —7B 8
Lathkill Ct. Beck —1B 126
Lathom Rd. E6 —7C 50
Latimer Av. E6 —1D 66
Latimer Clo. Pinn —1A 22
Latimer Clo. Wor Pk —4D 130
Latimer Gdns. Pinn —1A 22
Latimer Ho. E9 —6K 47

Latimer Ind. Est. W10 —6E 58
Latimer Pl. W10 —6E 58
Latimer Rd. E7 —4K 49
Latimer Rd. N15 —6E 30
Latimer Rd. SW19 —6K 107
Latimer Rd. W10 —5E 58
Latimer Rd. Barn —3E 4
Latimer Rd. Croy —3B 134
Latimer Rd. Tedd —5K 103
Latona Rd. SE15 —6G 79
Lattimer Pl. W4 —6A 74
Latymer Ct. W6 —4F 75
Latymer Gdns. N3 —2G 27
Latymer Rd. N9 —1A 18
Latymer Way. N9 —2K 17
Lauder Clo. N'holt —2B 54
Lauder Ct. N14 —7D 6
Lauderdale Dri. Rich —3D 104
Lauderdale Mans. W9 —3K 59
(off Lauderdale Rd.)
Lauderdale Rd. W9 —3K 59
Lauderdale Tower. EC2
—5C 62 (5C 144)
Laud St. SE11 —5K 77 (5G 155)
Laud St. Croy —3C 134
Laughton Rd. N'holt —1B 54
Launcelot Rd. Brom —4J 113
Launcelot St. SE1
—2A 78 (7J 149)
Launceston Gdns. Gnfd —1C 56
Launceston Pl. W8 —3A 76
Launceston Rd. Gnfd —1C 56
Launch St. E14 —3D 80
Laundress La. N16 —3G 47
Laundry La. N1 —7C 46
Laundry Rd. W6 —6G 75
Laura Clo. E11 —5A 34
Laura Clo. Enf —5K 7
Lauradale Rd. N2 —4D 28
Laura Pl. E5 —4J 47
Laurel Av. Twic —1K 103
Laurel Bank Gdns. SW6 —2H 91
Laurel Bank Rd. Enf —1H 7
Laurel Bank Vs. W7 —1J 71
(off Lwr. Boston Rd.)
Laurelbrook. SE6 —3G 113
Laurel Clo. N19 —2G 45
Laurel Clo. SW17 —5C 108
Laurel Clo. Sidc —3A 116
Laurel Ct. E8 —6F 47
Laurel Ct. Wemb —2E 56
Laurel Cres. Croy —3C 136
Laurel Cres. Romf —1K 53
Laurel Dri. N21 —7F 7
Laurel Gdns. E4 —7J 9
Laurel Gdns. NW7 —3E 12
Laurel Gdns. W7 —1J 71
Laurel Gdns. Houn —4C 86
Laurel Gro. SE20 —7J 111
Laurel Gro. SE26 —4K 111
Laurel Ho. SE8 —6B 80
Laurel Ho. Brom —1G 127
Laurel Mnr. Sutt —7A 132
Laurel Pk. Harr —7E 10
Laurel Rd. SW13 —2C 90
Laurel Rd. SW20 —1D 120
Laurel Rd. Hamp —5H 103
Laurels, The. NW10 —1D 58
Laurels, The. Brom —2H 127
Laurels, The. Buck H —1F 21
Laurel St. E8 —6F 47
Laurel View. N12 —3E 14
Laurel Way. E18 —4H 33
Laurel Way. N20 —3D 14
Laurence Ct. E10 —7D 32

Laurence M. *W12* —2C **74**
Laurence Pountney Hill. *EC4*
   —7D **62** (2E **150**)
Laurence Pountney La. *EC4*
   —7D **62** (2E **150**)
Laurie Gro. *SE14* —1A **96**
Laurie Rd. *W7* —5J **55**
Laurier Rd. *NW5* —3F **45**
Laurier Rd. *Croy* —7F **125**
Laurimel Clo. *Stan* —6G **11**
Laurino Pl. *Bush* —2B **10**
Lauriston Rd. *E9* —7J **47**
Lauriston Rd. *SW19* —6F **107**
Lausanne Rd. *N8* —4A **30**
Lausanne Rd. *SE15* —1J **95**
Lavell St. *N16* —4D **46**
Lavender Av. *NW9* —1J **41**
Lavender Av. *Mitc* —1C **122**
Lavender Av. *Wor Pk* —3E **130**
Lavender Clo. *SW3*
   —6C **76** (7B **152**)
Lavender Clo. *Brom* —6C **128**
Lavender Clo. *Cars* —4F **133**
Lavender Gdns. *SW11* —4D **92**
Lavender Gdns. *Enf* —1G **7**
Lavender Gdns. *Harr* —6D **10**
Lavender Gro. *E8* —7G **47**
Lavender Gro. *Mitc* —1C **122**
Lavender Hill. *SW11* —4C **92**
Lavender Hill. *Enf* —1F **7**
Lavender Pl. *Ilf* —5F **51**
Lavender Rd. *SE16* —1A **80**
Lavender Rd. *SW11* —3B **92**
Lavender Rd. *Cars* —4E **132**
Lavender Rd. *Croy* —6K **123**
Lavender Rd. *Enf* —1J **7**
Lavender Rd. *Sutt* —4B **132**
Lavender Sq. *E11* —3F **49**
Lavender St. *E15* —6G **49**
Lavender Sweep. *SW11* —4D **92**
Lavender Ter. *SW11* —3C **92**
Lavender Vale. *Wall* —6H **133**
Lavender Wlk. *SW11* —4D **92**
Lavender Wlk. *Mitc* —3E **122**
Lavender Way. *Croy* —6K **125**
Lavengro Rd. *SE27* —2C **110**
Lavenham Rd. *SW18* —2H **107**
Lavernock Rd. *Bexh* —2G **101**
Lavers Rd. *N16* —3E **46**
Laverstoke Gdns. *SW15* —7B **90**
Laverton M. *SW5* —4K **75**
Laverton Pl. *SW5* —4K **75**
Lavidge Rd. *SE9* —2C **114**
Lavina Gro. *N1* —2K **61**
Lavington Rd. *W13* —1B **72**
Lavington Rd. *Croy* —3K **133**
Lavington St. *SE1*
   —1B **78** (5B **150**)
Lavisham Ho. *Brom* —5K **113**
Lawdons Gdns. *Croy* —4B **134**
Lawford Clo. *Wall* —7J **133**
Lawford Rd. *N1* —7E **46**
Lawford Rd. *NW5* —6G **45**
Lawford Rd. *W4* —7J **73**
Law Ho. *Bark* —2A **68**
Lawless St. *E14* —7D **64**
Lawley Rd. *N14* —7A **6**
Lawley St. *E5* —4J **47**
Lawn Clo. *N9* —7A **8**
Lawn Clo. *Brom* —6K **113**
Lawn Clo. *N Mald* —2A **120**
Lawn Cres. *Rich* —2G **89**
Lawn Dri. *E7* —4B **50**
Lawn Farm Gro. *Romf* —4E **36**
Lawn Gdns. *W7* —1J **71**

Lawn Ho. Clo. *E14* —2E **80**
Lawn La. *SW8* —6J **77** (7F **155**)
Lawn Pl. *SE15* —1F **95**
Lawn Rd. *NW3* —5D **44**
Lawn Rd. *Beck* —7B **112**
Lawns Ct. *Wemb* —2F **41**
Lawnside. *SE3* —4H **97**
Lawns, The. *E4* —5H **19**
Lawns, The. *SE3* —3H **97**
Lawns, The. *SE19* —1D **124**
Lawns, The. *SW19* —5H **107**
Lawns, The. *Pinn* —7A **10**
Lawns, The. *Sidc* —4C **116**
Lawns, The. *Sutt* —7G **131**
Lawnsway. *Romf* —1J **37**
Lawn Ter. *SE3* —3G **97**
Lawn, The. *S'hall* —5E **70**
Lawn Vale. *Pinn* —2C **22**
Lawrence Av. *E12* —4E **50**
Lawrence Av. *E17* —1K **31**
Lawrence Av. *N13* —4G **17**
Lawrence Av. *NW7* —4F **13**
Lawrence Av. *N Mald* —6K **119**
Lawrence Bldgs. *N16* —3F **47**
Lawrence Campe Clo. *N20*
   —3G **15**
Lawrence Clo. *E3* —3C **64**
Lawrence Clo. *N15* —3E **30**
Lawrence Clo. *W12* —7D **58**
Lawrence Ct. *NW7* —5G **13**
Lawrence Ct. *W3* —3J **73**
   (off Stanley Rd.)
Lawrence Cres. *Dag* —3H **53**
Lawrence Cres. *Edgw* —2G **25**
Lawrence Est. *Houn* —4A **86**
Lawrence Gdns. *NW7* —3G **13**
Lawrence Hill. *E4* —2H **19**
Lawrence La. *EC2*
   —6C **62** (1D **150**)
Lawrence Pl. *N1* —1J **61**
   (off Brydon Wlk.)
Lawrence Rd. *E6* —1C **66**
Lawrence Rd. *E13* —1K **65**
Lawrence Rd. *N18* —4C **18**
Lawrence Rd. *SE25* —4F **125**
Lawrence Rd. *W5* —4C **72**
Lawrence Rd. *Eri* —7H **85**
Lawrence Rd. *Hamp* —7D **102**
Lawrence Rd. *Houn* —4A **86**
Lawrence Rd. *Pinn* —6B **22**
Lawrence Rd. *Rich* —4C **104**
Lawrence Rd. *W Wick* —4J **137**
Lawrence St. *E16* —5H **65**
Lawrence St. *NW7* —4G **13**
Lawrence St. *SW3*
   —6C **76** (7C **152**)
Lawrence Way. *NW10* —3K **41**
Lawrence Weaver Clo. *Mord*
   —6J **121**
Lawrence Yd. *N15* —4E **30**
Lawrie Pk. Av. *SE26* —5H **111**
Lawrie Pk. Cres. *SE26* —5H **111**
Lawrie Pk. Gdns. *SE26* —4H **111**
Lawrie Pk. Rd. *SE26* —6H **111**
Lawson Clo. *E16* —5A **66**
Lawson Clo. *SW19* —3F **107**
Lawson Ct. *N4* —1K **45**
   (off Lorne Rd.)
Lawson Clo. *Surb* —7D **118**
Lawson Gdns. *Pinn* —3A **22**
Lawson Ho. *W12* —7D **58**
   (off White City Est.)
Lawson Rd. *Enf* —1D **8**
Lawson Rd. *S'hall* —4E **54**

Law St. *SE1* —3D **78** (1F **157**)
Lawton Rd. *E3* —3A **64**
   (in two parts)
Lawton Rd. *E10* —1E **48**
Lawton Rd. *Cockf* —3G **5**
Laxcon Clo. *NW10* —5K **41**
Laxley Clo. *SE5* —7B **78**
Laxton Pl. *NW1* —4F **61** (3K **141**)
Layard Rd. *SE16* —4H **79**
Layard Rd. *Enf* —1A **8**
Layard Rd. *T Hth* —2D **124**
Layard Sq. *SE16* —4H **79**
Laybourne Ho. *E14* —2D **80**
   (off Admirals Way)
Laybrook Lodge. *E18* —4H **33**
Laycock St. *N1* —6A **46**
Layer Gdns. *W3* —7G **57**
Layfield Clo. *NW4* —7D **26**
Layfield Cres. *NW4* —7D **26**
Layfield Rd. *NW4* —7D **26**
Layhams Rd. *W Wick & Kes*
   —4G **137**
Laymarsh Clo. *Belv* —3F **85**
Laymead Clo. *N'holt* —6C **38**
Laystall St. *EC1* —4A **62** (4J **143**)
Layton Ct. *Bren* —5D **72**
Layton Cres. *Croy* —5A **134**
Layton Rd. *N1* —2A **62**
Layton Rd. *Bren* —5D **72**
Layton Rd. *Houn* —4F **87**
Layton's Bldgs. *SE1*
   —2D **78** (6E **150**)
Layzell Wlk. *SE9* —1B **114**
Lazar Wlk. *N7* —2K **45**
Lazenby Ct. *WC2* —7J **61** (2E **148**)
Leabank Clo. *Harr* —3J **39**
Leabank Sq. *E9* —6C **48**
Leabank View. *N15* —6G **31**
Lea Bon Ct. *E15* —1H **65**
   (off Plaistow Gro.)
Leabourne Rd. *N16* —7G **31**
Lea Bri. Ind. Cen. *E10* —1B **48**
Lea Bri. Rd. *E5, E10 & E17*
   —3J **47**
Lea Ct. *E4* —2K **19**
Lea Ct. *E13* —3J **65**
Leacroft Av. *SW12* —7D **92**
Leadale Av. *E4* —2H **19**
Leadale Rd. *N15 & N16* —6G **31**
Leadbeaters Clo. *N11* —5J **15**
Leadbetter Ct. *NW10* —7K **41**
   (off Melville Rd.)
Leadenhall Pl. *EC3*
   —6E **62** (1G **151**)
Leadenhall St. *EC3*
   —6E **62** (1G **151**)
Leadenham Ct. *E3* —4C **64**
Leader Av. *E12* —5E **50**
Leadings, The. *Wemb* —3J **41**
Leaf Gro. *SE27* —5A **110**
Leafield Clo. *SW16* —6B **110**
Leafield Rd. *SW20* —3H **121**
Leafield Rd. *Sutt* —2J **131**
Leafy Gro. *Kes* —5A **138**
Leafy Oak Rd. *SE12* —4A **114**
Leafy Way. *Croy* —2F **135**
Lea Gdns. *Wemb* —5F **41**
Leagrave St. *E5* —3J **47**
Lea Hall Gdns. *E10* —1C **48**
Lea Hall Rd. *E10* —1C **48**
Leahurst Rd. *SE13* —5F **97**
Lea Interchange. (Junct.) —5C **48**
Leake St. *SE1* —2K **77** (7H **149**)
Leake St. *SE1* —2K **77** (6H **149**)

Lealand Rd. *N15* —6F **31**
Leamington Av. *E17* —5C **32**
Leamington Av. *Brom* —5A **114**
Leamington Av. *Mord* —4G **121**
Leamington Clo. *Brom* —4A **114**
Leamington Clo. *Houn* —5G **87**
Leamington Cres. *Harr* —3C **38**
Leamington Gdns. *Ilf* —2K **51**
Leamington Ho. *Edgw* —5A **12**
Leamington Pk. *W3* —5K **57**
Leamington Rd. *S'hall* —4B **70**
Leamington Rd. Vs. *W11* —5H **59**
Leamore St. *W6* —4E **74**
Leamouth Rd. *E6* —5C **66**
Leamouth Rd. *E14* —6F **65**
Leander Ct. *SE8* —1C **96**
Leander Rd. *SE16* —1B **80**
Leander Rd. *Surb* —7D **118**
Leander Rd. *SW2* —6K **93**
Leander Rd. *N'holt* —2E **54**
Leander Rd. *T Hth* —4A **124**
Lea Pk. Trad. Est. *E10* —1B **48**
Leapold M. *E9* —1J **63**
Learner Dri. *Harr* —2E **38**
Lea Rd. *Beck* —2C **126**
Lea Rd. *Enf* —1J **7**
Lea Rd. *S'hall* —4C **70**
Learoyd Gdns. *E6* —7E **66**
Leary Ho. *SE11* —5K **77** (6H **155**)
Leas Dale. *SE9* —3E **114**
Leas Grn. *Chst* —6K **115**
Leaside Av. *N10* —3E **28**
Leaside Bus. Cen. *Enf* —2G **9**
Leaside Mans. *N10* —3E **28**
   (off Fortis Grn.)
Leaside Rd. *E5* —1J **47**
Leasowes Rd. *E10* —1C **48**
Leatherbottle Grn. *Eri* —3F **85**
Leather Bottle La. *Belv* —4E **84**
Leather Clo. *Mitc* —2E **122**
Leatherdale St. *E1* —4J **63**
   (in two parts)
Leather Gdns. *E15* —1G **65**
Leatherhead Clo. *N16* —1F **47**
Leather La. *EC1* —5A **62** (5J **143**)
Leathermarket Ct. *SE1*
   —2E **78** (7G **151**)
Leathermarket St. *SE1*
   —2E **78** (7G **151**)
Leathersellers Clo. *Barn* —3B **4**
Leathsail Rd. *Harr* —3F **39**
Leathwaite Rd. *SW11* —4D **92**
Leathwell Rd. *SE8* —2D **96**
Lea Vale. *Dart* —4K **101**
Lea Valley Rd. *Enf & E4* —5F **9**
Lea Valley Trad. Est. *N18* —5F **19**
Lea Valley Viaduct. *N18 & E4*
   —5E **18**
Leaveland Clo. *Beck* —4C **126**
Leaver Gdns. *Gnfd* —2H **55**
Leavesden Rd. *Stan* —6F **11**
Leaves Grn. Rd. *Kes* —7B **138**
Lea View Ho. *E5* —1H **47**
Leaway. *E10* —1K **47**
Lebanon Av. *Felt* —5B **102**
Lebanon Gdns. *SW18* —6J **91**
Lebanon Pk. *Twic* —7B **88**
Lebanon Rd. *SW18* —5J **91**
Lebanon Rd. *Croy* —1E **134**
Lebrun Sq. *SE3* —4K **97**
Lechmere App. *Wfd G* —2A **34**
Lechmere Av. *Wfd G* —2B **34**
Lechmere Rd. *NW2* —6D **42**
Leckford Rd. *SW18* —2A **108**

Leckhampton Pl. *SW2* —7A **94**
Leckwith Av. *Bexh* —6E **84**
Lecky St. *SW7* —5B **76** (5A **152**)
Leconfield Av. *SW13* —3B **90**
Leconfield Rd. *N5* —4D **46**
Leda Av. *Enf* —1E **8**
Leda Rd. *SE18* —3D **82**
Ledbury M. N. *W11* —6J **59**
Ledbury M. W. *W11* —7J **59**
Ledbury Pl. *Croy* —4D **134**
Ledbury Rd. *W11* —6H **59**
Ledbury Rd. *Croy* —4D **134**
Ledbury St. *SE15* —7G **79**
Ledrington Rd. *SE19* —6G **111**
Ledway Dri. *Wemb* —7F **25**
Lee Av. *Romf* —6E **36**
Lee Bri. *SE13* —3E **96**
Leechcroft Av. *Sidc* —5K **99**
Leechcroft Rd. *Wall* —3E **132**
Lee Chu. St. *SE13* —4G **97**
Lee Clo. *E17* —1K **31**
Lee Clo. *Barn* —4F **5**
Lee Conservancy Rd. *E9* —5B **48**
Lee Ct. *SE13* —4F **97**
Leecroft Rd. *Barn* —5B **4**
Leeds Pl. *N4* —1K **45**
Leeds Rd. *Ilf* —1H **51**
Leeds St. *N18* —5B **18**
Leefern Rd. *W12* —2C **74**
Leegate. *SE12* —5H **97**
Lee Green. (Junct.) —5H **97**
Lee Gro. *Chig* —2K **21**
Lee High Rd. *SE13 & SE12*
   —3E **96**
Leeke St. *WC1* —3K **61** (1G **143**)
Leeland Rd. *W13* —1A **72**
Leeland Ter. *W13* —1A **72**
Leeland Way. *NW10* —4B **42**
Leemount Clo. *NW4* —4F **27**
Leemount Ho. *NW4* —4F **27**
Lee Pk. *SE3* —4H **97**
Lee Pk. Way. *N18, N9 & E4*
   —4E **18**
Leerdam Dri. *E14* —3E **80**
Lee Rd. *NW7* —7A **14**
Lee Rd. *SE3* —3H **97**
Lee Rd. *SW19* —1K **121**
Lee Rd. *Enf* —6B **8**
Lee Rd. *Gnfd* —1C **56**
Leeside. *Barn* —5B **4**
Leeside Cres. *NW11* —6G **27**
Leeside Ind. Est. *N17* —7D **18**
Leeside Rd. *N17* —6C **18**
Leeside Works. *N17* —7D **18**
Leeson Ho. *Twic* —7B **88**
Leeson Rd. *SE24* —4A **94**
Leesons Hill. *Chst & St M*
   —3J **129**
Leeson's Way. *Orp* —2K **129**
Lees Pl. *W1* —7E **60** (2G **147**)
Lees, The. *Croy* —2B **136**
Lee St. *E8* —1F **63**
Lee Ter. *SE13 & SE3* —3G **97**
Lee Valley Technopark. *N17*
   —3G **31**
Lee View. *Enf* —1G **7**
Leeward Ct. *E1* —7G **63**
Leeward Gdns. *SW19* —5G **107**
Leeway. *SE8* —5B **80**
Leeway Clo. *H End* —1D **22**
Leeway Clo. *SE12* —6H **97**
Lefevre Wlk. *E3* —1B **64**
Lefroy Rd. *W12* —2B **74**
Left Ho. *NW6* —7G **43**
Legard Rd. *N5* —3B **46**

Legatt Rd. *SE9* —5B **98**
Leggatt Rd. *E15* —2E **64**
Legge St. *SE13* —5E **96**
Leghorn Rd. *NW10* —2B **58**
Leghorn Rd. *SE18* —5H **83**
Legion Clo. *N1* —7A **46**
Legion Ct. *Mord* —6J **121**
Legion Rd. *Gnfd* —1G **55**
Legion Way. *N12* —7H **15**
Legrace Av. *Houn* —2B **86**
Leicester Av. *Mitc* —4J **123**
Leicester Clo. *Wor Pk* —4E **130**
Leicester Ct. *WC2*
—7H **61** (2D **148**)
Leicester Gdns. *Ilf* —7J **35**
Leicester Ho. SW9 —3B **94**
(off Loughborough Rd.)
Leicester Pl. *WC2*
—7H **61** (2D **148**)
Leicester Rd. *E11* —5K **33**
Leicester Rd. *N2* —3C **28**
Leicester Rd. *NW10* —7K **41**
Leicester Rd. *Barn* —5E **4**
Leicester Rd. *Croy* —7E **124**
Leicester Sq. *WC2*
—7H **61** (3D **148**)
Leicester St. *WC2*
—7H **61** (2D **148**)
Leigham Av. *SW16* —3J **109**
Leigham Clo. *SW16* —3K **109**
Leigham Ct. Rd. *SW16* —2J **109**
Leigham Dri. *Iswth* —7J **71**
Leigham Vale. *SW16 & SW2*
—3K **109**
Leigh Av. *Ilf* —4B **34**
Leigh Clo. *N Mald* —4K **119**
Leigh Clo. Ind. Est. *N Mald*
—4K **119**
Leigh Ct. *Harr* —1J **39**
Leigh Cres. *New Ad* —7D **136**
Leigh Gdns. *NW10* —2E **58**
Leigh Hunt Dri. *N14* —1C **16**
Leigh Orchard Clo. *SW16*
—3K **109**
Leigh Pl. *EC1* —5A **62** (5J **143**)
Leigh Pl. *Well* —2A **100**
Leigh Rd. *E6* —6E **50**
Leigh Rd. *E10* —7E **32**
Leigh Rd. *N5* —4B **46**
Leigh Rd. *Houn* —4H **87**
Leigh St. *WC1* —3J **61** (2E **142**)
Leighton Av. *E12* —5E **50**
Leighton Av. *Pinn* —3C **22**
Leighton Clo. *Edgw* —2G **25**
Leighton Cres. *NW5* —5G **45**
Leighton Gdns. *NW10* —2D **58**
Leighton Gdns. *Croy* —1B **134**
Leighton Gro. *NW5* —5G **45**
Leighton Pl. *NW5* —5G **45**
Leighton Rd. *NW5* —5G **45**
Leighton Rd. *W13* —2A **72**
Leighton Rd. *Enf* —5A **8**
Leighton Rd. *Har W* —2H **23**
Leighton St. *Croy* —1B **134**
Leila Parnell Pl. *SE7* —6A **82**
Leinster Av. *SW14* —3J **89**
Leinster Gdns. *W2* —6A **60**
Leinster M. *W2* —7A **60**
Leinster Pl. *W2* —6A **60**
Leinster Rd. *N10* —4F **29**
Leinster Rd. *NW6* —3J **59**
Leinster Sq. *W2* —6J **59**
Leinster Ter. *W2* —7A **60**
Leisure Way. *N12* —7G **15**

Leith Clo. *NW9* —1K **41**
Leithcote Gdns. *SW16* —4K **109**
Leithcote Path. *SW16* —3K **109**
Leith Hill. *Orp* —1K **129**
Leith Hill Grn. *Orp* —1K **129**
Leith Mans. W9 —3K **59**
(off Grantully Rd.)
Leith Rd. *N22* —1B **30**
Leith Towers. *Sutt* —7K **131**
Lela Av. *Houn* —2A **86**
Lelitia Clo. *E8* —1G **63**
Lely Ho. N'holt —2B **54**
(off Academy Gdns.)
Leman St. *E1* —6F **63** (1K **151**)
Lemark Clo. *Stan* —6H **11**
Le May Av. *SE12* —3K **113**
Lemmon Rd. *SE10* —6G **81**
Lemna Rd. *E11* —7G **33**
Lemonwell Dri. *SE9* —6G **99**
Lemsford Clo. *N15* —6G **31**
Lemsford Ct. *N4* —2C **46**
Lena Gdns. *W6* —3E **74**
Lena Kennedy Clo. *E4* —6K **19**
Lendal Ter. *SW4* —3H **93**
Lenelby Rd. *Surb* —7G **119**
Len Freeman Pl. *SW6* —7H **75**
Lenham Rd. *SE12* —4H **97**
Lenham Rd. *Bexh* —6F **85**
Lenham Rd. *Sutt* —4K **131**
Lenham Rd. *T Hth* —2D **124**
Lennard Av. *W Wick* —2G **137**
Lennard Clo. *W Wick* —2G **137**
Lennard Rd. SE20 & Beck
—6K **111**
Lennard Rd. *Brom* —1D **138**
Lennard Rd. *Croy* —1C **134**
Lennon Rd. *NW2* —5E **42**
Lennox Gdns. *NW10* —4B **42**
Lennox Gdns. *SW1*
—3D **76** (2E **152**)
Lennox Gdns. *Croy* —4B **134**
Lennox Gdns. *Ilf* —1D **50**
Lennox Gdns. M. *SW1*
—3D **76** (2E **152**)
Lennox Ho. Belv —3G **85**
(off Picardy St.)
Lennox Rd. *E17* —6B **32**
Lennox Rd. *N4* —2A **45**
Lenor Clo. *Bexh* —4E **100**
Lensbury Way. *SE2* —3C **84**
Lens Rd. *E7* —7A **50**
Lenthall Ho. *E8* —7F **47**
Lenthall Rd. *E8* —7G **47**
Lenthorp Rd. *SE10* —4H **81**
Lentmead Rd. *Brom* —3H **113**
Lenton Rise. *Rich* —3E **88**
Lenton St. *SE18* —4H **83**
Leo Ct. *Bren* —7D **72**
Leof Cres. *SE6* —5D **112**
Leominster Rd. *Mord* —6A **122**
Leominster Wlk. *Mord* —6A **122**
Leonard Av. *Mord* —5A **122**
Leonard Av. *Romf* —1K **53**
Leonard Ct. *WC1*
—4J **61** (3E **142**)
Leonard Ct. *Har W* —1J **23**
Leonard Rd. *E4* —6H **19**
Leonard Rd. *E7* —4J **49**
Leonard Rd. *N9* —3A **18**
Leonard Rd. *SW16* —1G **123**
Leonard Rd. *S'hall* —3B **70**
Leonard Robbins Path. SE28
(off Tawney Rd.) —7B **68**
Leonard St. *E16* —1C **82**

Leonard St. *EC2* —4D **62** (3F **145**)
Leontine Clo. *SE15* —7G **79**
Leopard's Ct. *EC1*
—5A **62** (5J **143**)
Leopold Av. *SW19* —5H **107**
Leopold M. *E9* —1J **63**
Leopold Rd. *E17* —5C **32**
Leopold Rd. *N2* —3B **28**
Leopold Rd. *N18* —5C **18**
Leopold Rd. *NW10* —7A **42**
Leopold Rd. *SW19* —4H **107**
Leopold St. *E3* —5B **64**
Leopold Ter. *SW19* —5J **107**
Leo St. *SE15* —7H **79**
Leo Yd. *EC1* —4B **62** (4B **144**)
Leppoc Rd. *SW4* —5H **93**
Leroy St. *SE1* —4E **78** (2G **157**)
Lerwick Ct. *Enf* —5K **7**
Lescombe Clo. *SE23* —3A **112**
Lescombe Rd. *SE23* —3A **112**
Lesley Clo. *Bex* —7H **101**
Leslie Gdns. *Sutt* —7J **131**
Leslie Gro. *Croy* —1E **134**
Leslie Gro. Pl. *Croy* —1E **134**
Leslie Prince Ct. *SE5* —7D **78**
Leslie Rd. *E11* —4E **48**
Leslie Rd. *E16* —6K **65**
Leslie Rd. *N2* —3B **28**
Leslie Smith Sq. *SE18* —6E **82**
Lesney Farm Est. *Eri* —7K **85**
Lesney Pk. *Eri* —6K **85**
Lesney Pk. Rd. *Eri* —6K **85**
Lessar Av. *SW4* —6G **93**
Lessingham Av. *SW17* —4D **108**
Lessingham Av. *Ilf* —3E **34**
Lessing St. *SE23* —7A **96**
Lessington Av. *Romf* —6J **37**
Lessness Av. *Bexh* —7D **84**
Lessness Pk. *Belv* —5F **85**
Lessness Rd. *Belv* —5G **85**
Lessness Rd. *Mord* —6A **122**
Lester Av. *E15* —4G **65**
Leswin Pl. *N16* —3F **47**
Leswin Rd. *N16* —3F **47**
Letchford Gdns. *NW10* —3C **58**
Letchford M. *NW10* —3C **58**
Letchford Ter. *Harr* —1F **23**
Letchworth Clo. *Brom* —5J **127**
Letchworth Dri. *Brom* —5J **127**
Letchworth St. *SW17* —4D **108**
Lethbridge Clo. *SE13* —1E **96**
Letterstone Rd. *SW6* —7H **75**
Lettice St. *SW6* —1H **91**
Lett Rd. *E15* —7F **49**
Lettsom St. *SE5* —2E **94**
Lettsom Wlk. *E13* —2J **65**
Leucha Rd. *E17* —5A **32**
Levana Clo. *SW19* —1G **107**
Levehurst Ho. *SE27* —5C **110**
Levendale Rd. *SE23* —2A **112**
Levenhurst Way. *SW4* —2J **93**
Leven Rd. *E14* —5E **64**
Leverett St. *SW3*
—4C **76** (3D **152**)
Leverholme Gdns. *SE9* —4E **114**
Leverington Pl. *N1*
—3E **62** (2F **145**)
Leverson St. *SW16* —6G **109**
Lever St. *EC1* —3B **62** (2B **144**)
Leverton Pl. *NW5* —5G **45**
Leverton St. *NW5* —5G **45**
Levett Gdns. *Ilf* —4K **51**
Levett Rd. *Bark* —6J **51**
Levine Gdns. *Bark* —2D **68**

Levison Way. *N19* —1H **45**
Lewen's Ct. *EC1*
—4C **62** (2C **144**)
Lewes Clo. *N'holt* —6E **38**
Lewesdon Clo. *SW19* —1F **107**
Lewes Rd. *N12* —5H **15**
Lewes Rd. *Brom* —2B **128**
Leweston Pl. *N16* —7F **31**
Lewgars Av. *NW9* —6J **25**
Lewing Clo. *Orp* —7J **129**
Lewin Rd. *SW14* —3K **89**
Lewin Rd. *SW16* —6H **109**
Lewin Rd. *Bexh* —4E **100**
Lewis Av. *E17* —1C **32**
Lewis Clo. *N14* —7B **6**
Lewis Cres. *NW10* —5K **41**
Lewis Gdns. *N2* —2B **28**
Lewis Gro. *SE13* —3E **96**
Lewisham Bus. Cen. *SE14*
—6K **79**
Lewisham Cen. *SE13* —3E **96**
Lewisham Heights. *SE23*
—1J **111**
Lewisham High St. *SE13* —6D **96**
Lewisham Hill. *SE13* —2D **96**
Lewisham Model Mkt. SE13
—4E **96**
(off Lewisham High St.)
Lewisham Pk. *SE13* —6E **96**
Lewisham Rd. *SE13* —1D **96**
Lewisham St. *SW1*
—2H **77** (7D **148**)
Lewisham Way. *SE14 & SE4*
—1B **96**
Lewis Hunt Dri. *N14* —7B **6**
Lewis Rd. *Mitc* —2B **122**
Lewis Rd. *Rich* —5D **88**
Lewis Rd. *Sidc* —3C **116**
Lewis Rd. *S'hall* —2C **70**
Lewis Rd. *Sutt* —4K **131**
Lewis Rd. *Well* —3C **100**
Lewis Silkin Ho. SE15 —6J **79**
(off Lovelinch Clo.)
Lewis St. *NW1* —7F **45**
(in two parts)
Lewis Way. *Dag* —6H **53**
Lexden Dri. *Romf* —6B **36**
Lexden Rd. *W3* —7H **57**
Lexden Rd. *Mitc* —4H **123**
Lexham Gdns. *W8* —4J **75**
Lexham Gdns. M. *W8* —3K **75**
Lexham Ho. Bark —1H **67**
(off St Margarets)
Lexham M. *W8* —4J **75**
Lexham Wlk. *W8* —3K **75**
Lexington Apartments. *EC1*
—4D **62** (3F **145**)
Lexington St. *W1*
—7G **61** (2B **148**)
Lexington Way. *Barn* —4A **4**
Lexton Gdns. *SW12* —1H **109**
Leyborne Pk. *Rich* —1G **89**
Leybourne Av. *W13* —2B **72**
Leybourne Clo. *Brom* —6J **127**
Leybourne Ho. *SE15* —6J **79**
Leybourne Pk. *Rich* —1G **89**
Leybourne Rd. *E11* —1H **49**
Leybourne Rd. *NW1* —7F **45**
Leybourne Rd. *NW9* —5G **25**
Leybourne St. *NW1* —7F **45**
Leybridge Ct. *SE12* —5J **97**
Leyburn Clo. *E17* —4D **32**
Leyburn Gdns. *Croy* —2E **134**
Leyburn Gro. *N18* —6B **18**
Leyburn Rd. *N18* —6B **18**

Leydenhatch La. *Swan* —7J **117**
Leyden Mans. *N19* —7J **29**
Leyden St. *E1* —5F **63** (6J **145**)
Leydon Clo. *SE16* —1K **79**
Leyes Rd. *E16* —6A **66**
Leyfield. *Wor Pk* —1A **130**
Leyland Av. *Enf* —2F **9**
Leyland Gdns. *Wfd G* —5F **21**
Leyland Rd. *SE12* —5J **97**
Leylang Rd. *SE14* —7K **79**
Leys Av. *Dag* —1J **69**
Leys Clo. *Dag* —7K **53**
(in two parts)
Leys Clo. *Harr* —5H **23**
Leys Ct. *SW9* —2A **94**
Leysdown Av. *Bexh* —4J **101**
Leysdown Rd. *SE9* —2C **114**
Leysfield Rd. *W12* —3C **74**
Leys Gdns. *Barn* —5K **5**
Leyspring Rd. *E11* —1H **49**
Leys Rd. E. *Enf* —1F **9**
Leys Rd. W. *Enf* —1F **9**
Leys Sq. *N3* —1K **27**
Leys, The. *N2* —4A **28**
Leys, The. *Harr* —6F **25**
Ley St. *Ilf* —2F **51**
Leyswood Dri. *Ilf* —5J **35**
Leythe Rd. *W3* —2J **73**
Leyton Bus. Cen. *E10* —2C **48**
Leyton Ct. *SE23* —1J **111**
Leyton Grange Est. *E10* —2C **48**
Leyton Grn. Rd. *E10* —6E **32**
Leyton Ind. Village. *E10* —1K **31**
Leyton Pk. Rd. *E10* —3E **48**
Leyton Rd. *E15* —5E **48**
Leyton Rd. *SW19* —7A **108**
Leytonstone Rd. *E15* —4G **49**
Leyton Way. *E11* —7G **33**
Leywick St. *E15* —2G **65**
Liardet St. *SE14* —6A **80**
Liberia Rd. *N5* —6B **46**
Liberty Av. *SW19* —1A **122**
Liberty M. *SW12* —6F **93**
Liberty St. *SW9* —1A **93**
Libra Ct. *E4* —4H **19**
Libra Rd. *E3* —1B **64**
Libra Rd. *E13* —2J **65**
Library Ct. *N17* —3F **31**
Library Pl. *E1* —7H **63**
Library St. *SE1* —2B **78** (1A **156**)
Library Way. *Twic* —7G **87**
Lichfield Clo. *Barn* —3J **5**
Lichfield Ct. *Rich* —4E **88**
Lichfield Gdns. *Rich* —4E **88**
Lichfield Gro. *N3* —1J **27**
Lichfield M. *E3* —3A **64**
Lichfield Rd. *E3* —3A **64**
Lichfield Rd. *E6* —3B **66**
Lichfield Rd. *N9* —2B **18**
Lichfield Rd. *NW2* —4G **43**
Lichfield Rd. *Dag* —4B **52**
Lichfield Rd. *Houn* —3A **86**
Lichfield Rd. *Rich* —1F **89**
Lichfield Rd. *Wfd G* —4B **20**
Lichfield Ter. *Rich* —5E **88**
Lickey Ho. W14 —6H **75**
(off N. End Rd.)
Lidbury Rd. *NW7* —6B **14**
Lidcote Gdns. *SW9* —2A **94**
Liddall Way. *W Dray* —1B **76**
Liddell Gdns. *NW10* —2E **58**
Liddell Rd. *NW6* —6J **43**
Lidding Rd. *Harr* —5D **24**
Liddington Rd. *E15* —1H **65**
Liddon Rd. *E13* —3K **65**

Liddon Rd. Brom —3A 128
Liden Clo. E17 —7B 32
Lidfield Rd. N16 —4D 46
Lidgate Rd. SE15 —7E 78
Lidiard Rd. SW18 —2A 108
Lidlington Pl. NW1 —2G 61
Lido Sq. N17 —2D 30
Lidyard Rd. N19 —1G 45
Liffler Rd. SE18 —5J 83
Liffords Pl. SW13 —2B 90
Lifford St. SW15 —4F 91
Light App. NW9 —2B 26
Lightcliffe Rd. N13 —4F 17
Lighter Clo. SE16 —4A 80
Lightermans Rd. E14 —2C 80
Lightermans Wlk. SW18 —4J 91
Lightfoot Rd. N8 —5J 29
Light Horse Ct. SW3
    —5E 76 (6G 153)
Lightley Clo. Wemb —1E 56
Ligonier St. E2 —4F 63 (3J 145)
Lilac Clo. E4 —6G 19
Lilac Ct. E13 —1A 66
Lilac Ct. Tedd —4K 103
Lilac Gdns. W5 —3D 72
Lilac Gdns. Croy —3C 136
Lilac Gdns. Romf —1K 53
Lilac Ho. SE4 —3C 96
Lilac Pl. SE11 —4K 77 (4G 155)
Lilac St. W12 —7C 58
Lilburne Gdns. SE9 —5C 98
Lilburne Rd. SE9 —5C 98
Lilburne Wlk. NW10 —6J 41
Lile Cres. W7 —5J 55
Lilestone St. NW8
    —4C 60 (3C 140)
Lilford Ho. SE5 —2C 94
Lilford Rd. SE5 —2C 94
Lilian Barker Clo. SE12 —5J 97
Lilian Board Way. Gnfd —5H 39
Lilian Clo. N16 —3E 46
Lilian Gdns. Wfd G —1K 33
Lilian Rd. SW16 —1G 123
Lillechurch Rd. Dag —6B 52
Lilleshall Rd. Mord —6B 122
Lilley Clo. E1 —1G 79
Lillian Av. W3 —2G 73
Lillian Rd. SW13 —6C 74
Lillie Mans. SW6 —6G 75
    (off Lillie Rd.)
Lillie Rd. SW6 —6F 75
Lillieshall Rd. SW4 —3F 93
Lillie Yd. SW6 —6J 75
Lillington Gdns. Est. SW1
    —4G 77 (4B 154)
Liliput Av. N'holt —1C 54
Liliput Ct. SE12 —5K 97
Liliput Rd. Romf —7K 37
Lily Clo. W14 —4F 75
    (in two parts)
Lily Gdns. Wemb —2C 56
Lily Pl. EC1 —5A 62 (5K 143)
Lily Rd. E17 —6C 32
Lilyville Rd. SW6 —1H 91
Limberg Ho. SE8 —4B 80
Limbourne Av. Dag —7F 37
Limburg Rd. SW11 —4C 92
Lime Clo. E1 —1G 79
Lime Clo. Brom —4C 128
Lime Clo. Cars —2D 132
Lime Clo. Harr —2A 24
Lime Clo. Romf —4J 37
Lime Ct. E11 —2G 49
    (off Trinity Clo.)

Lime Ct. E17 —5E 32
Lime Ct. SE9 —2F 115
Lime Ct. Harr —6K 23
Lime Ct. Mitc —2B 122
Limecroft Clo. Eps —7A 130
Limedene Clo. Pinn —1B 22
Lime Gro. N20 —1C 14
Lime Gro. W12 —2E 74
Lime Gro. N Mald —3K 119
Lime Gro. Sidc —6K 99
Lime Gro. Twic —6K 87
Limeharbour. E14 —3D 80
Limeharbour Ct. E14 —3D 80
Limehouse Causeway. E14
    —7B 64
Limehouse Fields Est. E14
    —5A 64
Limehouse Link. E14 —7B 64
Lime Kiln Dri. SE7 —6K 81
Limerick Clo. SW12 —7G 93
Lime Rd. Eri —3F 85
Lime Rd. Rich —4F 89
Lime Row. Eri —3F 85
Limerston St. SW10
    —6A 76 (7A 152)
Limes Av. E11 —4K 33
Limes Av. E12 —3C 50
Limes Av. N12 —4F 15
Limes Av. NW7 —6F 13
Limes Av. NW11 —7G 27
Limes Av. SE20 —7H 111
Limes Av. SW13 —2B 90
Limes Av. Cars —1D 132
Limes Av. Croy —3A 134
Limes Av., The. N11 —5A 16
Limes Clo. N11 —5B 16
Limesdale Gdns. Edgw —2J 25
Limes Field Rd. SW14 —3A 90
Limesford Rd. SE15 —4K 95
Limes Gdns. SW18 —6J 91
Limes Gro. SE13 —4E 96
Limes Pl. Croy —7D 124
Limes Rd. Beck —2D 126
Limes Rd. Croy —7D 124
Limes, The. SW18 —6J 91
Limes, The. W2 —7J 59
    (off Linden Gdns.)
Limes, The. Kes —2C 138
Limestone Wlk. Eri —2D 84
Lime St. E17 —4A 32
Lime St. EC3 —7E 62 (2G 151)
Lime St. Pas. EC3
    —6E 62 (1G 151)
Limes Wlk. SE15 —4J 95
Limes Wlk. W5 —2D 72
Lime Ter. W7 —7J 55
Limetree Clo. SW2 —1K 109
Limetree Ct. Pinn —1E 22
    (off Avenue, The)
Lime Tree Ct. S Croy —6C 134
Lime Tree Gro. Croy —3B 136
Lime Tree Pl. Mitc —1F 123
Lime Tree Rd. Houn —1F 87
Lime Tree Ter. SE6 —1B 112
Limetree Ter. Well —3A 100
Lime Tree Wlk. SW17 —5E 108
Lime Tree Wlk. Bush —1D 10
Lime Tree Wlk. Enf —1H 7
Lime Tree Wlk. W Wick —4H 137
Lime Wlk. E15 —1G 65
Limewood Clo. W13 —6B 56
Limewood Ct. Ilf —5D 34
Limewood Rd. Eri —7J 85
Limpsfield Av. SW19 —2F 107
Limpsfield Av. T Hth —5K 123

Linacre Rd. NW2 —6D 42
Linberry Wlk. SE8 —4B 80
Linchmere Rd. SE12 —7H 97
Lincoln Av. N14 —3B 16
Lincoln Av. SW19 —3F 107
Lincoln Av. Romf —2K 53
Lincoln Av. Twic —2G 103
Lincoln Clo. SE25 —6G 125
Lincoln Clo. Gnfd —1G 55
Lincoln Clo. Harr —5D 22
Lincoln Ct. N16 —7D 30
Lincoln Cres. Enf —5K 7
Lincoln Gdns. Ilf —7C 34
Lincoln Grn. Rd. Orp —5K 129
Lincoln Ho. SW3
    (off Basil St.) —2D 76 (7E 146)
Lincoln Ho. SW9 & SE5 —7A 78
Lincoln M. NW6 —1H 59
Lincoln M. SE21 —2D 110
Lincoln Rd. E7 —6B 50
Lincoln Rd. E13 —4K 65
Lincoln Rd. E18 —1H 33
Lincoln Rd. N2 —3C 28
Lincoln Rd. SE25 —3H 125
Lincoln Rd. Enf —4K 7
Lincoln Rd. Felt —3D 102
Lincoln Rd. Harr —5D 22
Lincoln Rd. Mitc —5J 123
Lincoln Rd. N Mald —3J 119
Lincoln Rd. Sidc —5B 116
Lincoln Rd. Wemb —6D 40
Lincoln Rd. Wor Pk —1D 130
Lincoln's Inn Fields. WC2
    —6K 61 (7G 143)
Lincolns, The. NW7 —3G 13
Lincoln St. E11 —2G 49
Lincoln St. SW3
    —4D 76 (4E 152)
Lincoln Way. Enf —5C 8
Lincombe Rd. Brom —3H 113
Lindal Cres. Enf —4D 6
Lindal Rd. SE4 —5B 96
Lindbergh Rd. Wall —7J 133
Linden Av. NW10 —2F 59
Linden Av. Enf —1B 8
Linden Av. Houn —5F 87
Linden Av. Ruis —1A 38
Linden Av. T Hth —4B 124
Linden Av. Wemb —5F 41
Linden Clo. N14 —6B 6
Linden Clo. Stan —5G 11
Linden Clo. Th Dit —7A 118
Linden Clo. W12 —1E 74
Linden Ct. Sidc —4J 115
Linden Cres. Gnfd —6K 39
Linden Cres. King T —2F 119
Linden Cres. Wfd G —6E 20
Lindenfield. Chst —2F 129
Linden Gdns. W2 —7J 59
Linden Gdns. W4 —5A 74
Linden Gdns. Enf —1B 8
Linden Gro. SE15 —3H 95
Linden Gro. SE26 —6J 111
Linden Gro. N Mald —3A 120
Linden Gro. Tedd —5K 103
Linden Gro. SE15 —3H 95
Linden Ho. Hamp —6F 103
Linden Lawns. Wemb —4F 41
Linden Lea. N2 —5A 28
Linden Leas. W Wick —2F 137
Linden M. N1 —5D 46
Linden M. W2 —7J 59
Linden Pl. Mitc —4C 122
Linden Rd. N10 —4F 29
Linden Rd. N11 —2J 15

Linden Rd. N15 —4C 30
Linden Rd. Hamp —7E 102
Lindens, The. E17 —4D 32
Lindens, The. N12 —5G 15
Lindens, The. W4 —1J 89
Lindens, The. New Ad —6E 136
Linden St. Romf —4K 37
Linden Wlk. N19 —2G 45
Linden Way. N14 —6B 6
Lindeth Clo. Stan —6G 11
Lindfield Gdns. NW3 —5K 43
Lindfield Rd. W5 —4C 56
Lindfield Rd. Croy —6F 125
Lindfield St. E14 —6C 64
Lindholme Ct. NW9 —1A 26
    (off Pageant Av.)
Lindisfarne Rd. SW20 —7C 106
Lindisfarne Rd. Dag —3C 52
Lindisfarne Way. E9 —4A 48
Lindley Ct. King T —1C 118
Lindley Est. SE15 —7G 79
Lindley Rd. E10 —2E 48
Lindley St. E1 —5J 63
Lindore Rd. SW11 —4D 92
Lindores Rd. Cars —1A 132
Lindo St. SE15 —2J 95
Lind Rd. Sutt —5A 132
Lindrop St. SW6 —2A 92
Lindsay Dri. Harr —6E 24
Lindsay Rd. Hamp —4F 103
Lindsay Rd. Wor Pk —2D 130
Lindsay Sq. SW1
    —5H 77 (5D 154)
Lindsell St. SE10 —1E 96
Lindsey Clo. Brom —3B 128
Lindsey Clo. Mitc —4J 123
Lindsey Ct. N13 —3F 17
    (off Green Lanes)
Lindsey M. N1 —7C 46
Lindsey Rd. Dag —4C 52
Lindsey St. EC1 —5B 62 (5B 144)
Lind St. SE8 —2C 96
Lindum Rd. Tedd —7C 104
Lindway. SE27 —5B 110
Lindwood Clo. E6 —6D 66
Linfield Clo. NW4 —4E 26
Linford Rd. E17 —3E 32
Linford St. SW8 —1G 93
Lingards Rd. SE13 —4E 96
Lingey Clo. Sidc —2K 115
Lingfield Av. King T —4E 118
Lingfield Clo. Enf —6K 7
Lingfield Clo. N'holt —2E 54
Lingfield Cres. SE9 —4H 99
Lingfield Gdns. N9 —7C 8
Lingfield Rd. SW19 —5F 107
Lingfield Rd. Wor Pk —3E 130
Lingham St. SW9 —2J 93
Lingholm Way. Barn —5A 4
Ling Rd. E16 —5J 65
Ling Rd. Eri —6J 85
Lingrove Gdns. Buck H —2E 20
Lings Coppice. SE21 —2D 110
Lingwell Rd. SW17 —3C 108
Lingwood. Bexh —2H 101
Lingwood Gdns. Iswth —7J 71
Lingwood Rd. E5 —7G 31
Linhope St. NW1
    —4D 60 (3E 140)
Linkenholt Mans. W6 —4B 74
    (off Stamford Brook Av.)
Linkfield. Hay —6J 127
Linkfield Rd. Iswth —2K 87
Link La. Wall —6H 133

Linklea Clo. NW9 —7F 13
Link Rd. E1 —7G 63
Link Rd. N8 —3A 30
Link Rd. N11 —4K 15
Link Rd. Dag —2H 69
Link Rd. Wall —1E 132
Links Av. Mord —4J 121
    (in two parts)
Links Dri. N20 —1D 14
Links Gdns. SW16 —7A 110
Linkside. N12 —6D 14
Linkside. N Mald —2A 120
Linkside Clo. Enf —3E 6
Linkside Gdns. Enf —3E 6
Links Rd. NW2 —2B 42
Links Rd. W3 —6G 57
Links Rd. SW17 —6E 108
Links Rd. W Wick —1E 136
Links Rd. Wfd G —5D 20
Links Side. Enf —3F 7
Links, The. E17 —4A 32
Link St. E9 —6J 47
Linksview. N2 —5D 28
    (off Gt. North Rd.)
Links View. N3 —7C 14
Links View Clo. Stan —7F 11
Links View Ct. Hamp —4H 103
Links View Rd. Croy —3C 136
Links View Rd. Hamp —5G 103
Linksway. NW4 —2F 27
Links Way. Beck —6C 126
Links Yd. E1 —5G 63
Link, The. SE9 —3E 114
    (off William Barefoot Dri.)
Link, The. W3 —6H 57
Link, The. Enf —1F 9
Link, The. Pinn —7A 22
Link, The. Tedd —6K 103
Link, The. Wemb —1C 40
Linkway. N4 —7C 30
Linkway. SW20 —3D 120
Link Way. Brom —7C 128
Linkway. Dag —4C 52
Link Way. Pinn —1B 22
Linkway. Rich —2B 104
Linkway, The. Barn —6E 4
Linkwood Wlk. NW1 —7H 45
Linky Ct. Sutt —4A 132
Linley Cres. Romf —3H 37
Linley Rd. N17 —2E 30
Linnell Clo. NW11 —6K 27
Linnell Dri. NW11 —6K 27
Linnell Rd. N18 —5B 18
Linnell Rd. SE5 —2E 94
Linnet Clo. N9 —1E 18
Linnet Clo. SE28 —7C 68
Linnet Clo. Bush —1B 10
Linnet M. SW12 —7E 92
Linnett Clo. E4 —4K 19
Linom Rd. SW4 —4J 93
Linscott Rd. E5 —4J 47
Linsdell Rd. Bark —1G 67
Linsey Ct. E10 —1C 48
    (off Grange Rd.)
Linsey St. SE16 —4G 79
    (in two parts)
Linslade Clo. Houn —5C 86
Linslade Ho. E2 —1G 63
Linstead St. NW6 —7J 43
Linstead Way. SW18 —7G 91
Lintaine Clo. W6 —6G 75
Linthorpe Av. Wemb —6C 40
Linthorpe Rd. N16 —7E 30
Linthorpe Rd. Cockf —3H 5

Linton Clo. *Mitc* —7D **122**
Linton Clo. *Well* —1B **100**
Linton Ct. *Romf* —2K **37**
Linton Gdns. *E6* —6C **66**
Linton Gro. *SE27* —5B **110**
Linton Rd. *Bark* —7G **51**
Lintons, The. *Bark* —7G **51**
Linton St. *N1* —1C **62**
Linver Rd. *SW6* —2J **91**
Linwood Clo. *SE5* —2F **95**
Linwood Cres. *Enf* —1B **8**
Linwood Way. *SE15* —7F **79**
Linzee Rd. *N8* —4J **29**
Lion Av. *Twic* —1K **103**
Lion Clo. *SE4* —6C **96**
Lion Ct. *SE1* —1E **78** *(5H 151)*
(off Magdalen St.)
Lionel Gdns. *SE9* —5B **98**
Lionel M. *W10* —5G **59**
Lionel Rd. *SE9* —5B **98**
Lionel Rd. *Bren* —3E **72**
(in two parts)
Lion Ga. Gdns. *Rich* —3F **89**
Liongate M. *E Mol* —3A **118**
Lion Mills. *E2* —2G **63**
Lion Rd. *E6* —5D **66**
Lion Rd. *N9* —2B **18**
Lion Rd. *Bexh* —4E **100**
Lion Rd. *Croy* —5C **124**
Lion Rd. *Twic* —1K **103**
Lions Clo. *SE9* —3B **114**
Lion Way. *Bren* —7D **72**
Lion Wharf Rd. *Iswth* —3B **88**
Lion Yd. *SW4* —4G **93**
Liphook Cres. *SE23* —7J **95**
Lipton Clo. *SE28* —7C **68**
Lipton Rd. *E1* —6K **63**
Lisbon Av. *Twic* —2G **103**
Lisburne Rd. *NW3* —4D **44**
Lisford St. *SE15* —1F **95**
Lisgar Ter. *W14* —4H **75**
Liskeard Clo. *Chst* —6G **115**
Liskeard Gdns. *SE3* —1J **97**
Lisle Ct. *NW2* —3G **43**
Lisle St. *WC2* —7H **61** *(2D 148)*
Lismore. SW19 —5H **107**
(off Woodside)
Lismore Cir. *NW5* —5E **44**
Lismore Clo. *Iswth* —2A **88**
Lismore Ho. *SE15* —3H **95**
Lismore Rd. *N17* —3D **30**
Lismore Rd. *S Croy* —6E **134**
Lismore Wlk. N1 —7C **46**
(off Clephane Rd.)
Lisselton Ho. NW4 —4F **27**
(off Belle Vue Est.)
Lissenden Gdns. *NW5* —4E **44**
Lissenden Mans. *NW5* —4E **44**
—4B **60** *(3B 140)*
Lisson Gro. *NW8 & NW1*
Lisson St. *NW1* —5C **60** *(5C 140)*
Liss Way. *SE15* —7F **79**
Lister Clo. *W3* —5K **57**
Lister Clo. *Mitc* —1C **122**
Lister Gdns. *N18* —5H **17**
Listergate Ct. *SW15* —4E **90**
Lister Ho. Wemb —3J **41**
(off Barnhill Rd.)
Lister M. *N7* —4K **45**
Lister Rd. *E11* —1G **49**
Lister St. *E13* —3J **65**
Lister Wlk. *SE28* —7D **68**
Liston Rd. *N17* —1G **31**
Liston Rd. *SW4* —3G **93**
Liston Way. *Wfd G* —7F **21**

Listowel Clo. *SW9* —7A **78**
Listowel Rd. *Dag* —3G **53**
Listria Pk. *N16* —2E **46**
Litchfield Av. *E15* —6G **49**
Litchfield Av. *Mord* —7H **121**
Litchfield Ct. *E17* —6C **32**
Litchfield Gdns. *NW10* —6C **42**
Litchfield Rd. *Sutt* —4A **132**
Litchfield St. *WC2*
—7H **61** *(2D 148)*
Litchfield Way. *NW11* —5K **27**
Lithos Rd. *NW3* —6K **43**
Lit. Acre. *Beck* —3C **126**
Lit. Albany St. *NW1*
(in two parts) —3F **61** *(2K 141)*
Lit. Argyll St. *W1*
—6G **61** *(1A 148)*
Lit. Birches. *Sidc* —2J **115**
Lit. Boltons, The. *SW5 & SW10*
—5K **75**
Lit. Bornes. *SE21* —4E **110**
Littlebourne. *SE13* —7G **97**
Lit. Britain. *EC1* —5B **62** *(6B 144)*
Littlebrook Clo. *Croy* —6K **125**
Lit. Brownings. *SE23* —2H **111**
Littlebury Rd. *SW4* —3H **93**
Lit. Bury St. *N9* —7J **7**
Lit. Bushey La. *Bush* —1C **10**
Lit. Cedars. *N12* —4F **15**
Lit. Chester St. *SW1*
—3F **77** *(1J 153)*
Little Cloisters *SW1*
—3J **77** *(1E 154)*
Lit. College St. *SW1*
—3J **77** *(1E 154)*
Littlecombe. *SE7* —6K **81**
Littlecombe Clo. *SW15* —6F **91**
Lit. Common. *Stan* —3F **11**
Littlecote Clo. *SW19* —7G **91**
Littlecote Pl. *Pinn* —1C **22**
Little Ct. *W Wick* —2G **137**
Lit. Croft. *SE9* —3E **98**
Littledale. *SE2* —6A **84**
Lit. Dean's Yd. *SW1*
—3J **77** *(1E 154)*
Lit. Dimocks. *SW12* —2F **109**
Lit. Dorrit Ct. *SE1*
—2C **78** *(6D 150)*
Lit. Ealing La. *W5* —4C **72**
Lit. Edward St. *NW1*
—3F **61** *(1K 141)*
Lit. Essex St. *WC2*
—7A **62** *(2J 149)*
Lit. Ferry Rd. *Twic* —1B **104**
Littlefield Clo. *N19* —4G **45**
Littlefield Rd. *King T* —2E **118**
Littlefield Rd. *Edgw* —7D **12**
Lit. Friday Rd. *E4* —2B **20**
Lit. Gearies. *Ilf* —4F **35**
Lit. George St. *SW1*
—2J **77** *(7E 148)*
Lit. Grange. *Gnfd* —3A **56**
Little Grn. *Rich* —4D **88**
Lit. Green St. *NW5* —4F **45**
Littlegrove. *E Barn* —6H **5**
Lit. Heath. *SE7* —6C **82**
Lit. Heath. *L Hth* —4B **36**
Lit. Heath Rd. *Bexh* —1F **101**
Littleheath Rd. *S Croy* —7H **135**
Lit. Holt. *E11* —5J **33**
Lit. Ilford La. *E12* —4D **50**
Lit. John Rd. *W7* —6K **55**
Lit. Larkins. *Barn* —6B **4**
Lit. Marlborough St. *W1*
—6G **61** *(1A 148)*

Littlemede. *SE9* —3D **114**
Littlemoor Rd. *Ilf* —3H **51**
Littlemore Rd. *SE2* —3A **84**
Lit. Moss La. *Pinn* —2C **22**
Lit. Newport St. *WC2*
—7H **61** *(2D 148)*
Lit. New St. *EC4* —6A **62** *(7K 143)*
Lit. Orchard Clo. *Pinn* —2C **22**
Lit. Park Dri. *Felt* —2C **102**
Lit. Park Gdns. *Enf* —3H **7**
Lit. Pluckett's Way. *Buck H*
—1G **21**
Lit. Portland St. *W1*
—6G **61** *(7K 141)*
Lit. Potters. *Bush* —1C **10**
Lit. Queen's Rd. *Tedd* —6K **103**
Lit. Redlands. *Brom* —2C **128**
Littlers Clo. *SW19* —2B **122**
Lit. Russell St. *WC1*
—5J **61** *(6E 142)*
Lit. St James's St. *SW1*
—1G **77** *(5A 148)*
Lit. St Leonard's. *SW14* —3J **89**
Lit. Sanctuary. *SW1*
—2H **77** *(7D 148)*
Lit. Smith St. *SW1*
—3H **77** *(1D 154)*
Lit. Somerset St. *E1*
—6F **63** *(1J 151)*
Littlestone Clo. *Beck* —6C **112**
Lit. Strand. *NW9* —2B **26**
Lit. Thrift. *Orp* —4G **129**
Lit. Titchfield St. *W1*
—5G **61** *(6A 142)*
Littleton Av. *E4* —1C **20**
Littleton Cres. *Harr* —2K **39**
Littleton Rd. *Harr* —2K **39**
Littleton St. *SW18* —2A **108**
Lit. Trinity La. *EC4*
—7C **62** *(2D 150)*
Lit. Turnstile. *WC1*
—5K **61** *(6G 143)*
Lit. Venice. *W2* —5A **60**
Lit. Warkworth Ho. *Iswth* —2B **88**
Littlewood. *SE13* —6E **96**
Littlewood Clo. *W13* —3B **72**
Lit. Wood St. *King T* —2D **118**
Livermere Rd. *E8* —1F **63**
Liverpool Gro. *SE17*
—5C **78** *(6D 156)*
Liverpool Rd. *E10* —6E **32**
Liverpool Rd. *E16* —5G **65**
Liverpool Rd. *N7 & N1* —5A **46**
Liverpool Rd. *W5* —2D **72**
Liverpool Rd. *King T* —7G **105**
Liverpool Rd. *T Hth* —3C **124**
Liverpool St. *EC2*
—5E **62** *(6G 145)*
Livesey Clo. *King T* —3F **119**
Livesey Pl. *SE15* —6G **79**
Livingstone College Towers. *E10*
—6E **32**
Livingstone Ct. *E10* —6E **32**
Livingstone Ct. *W'stone* —3K **23**
Livingstone Rd. *SW8* —1F **93**
Livingstone Ho. SE5 —7C **78**
(off Wyndam Rd.)
Livingstone Mans. W14 —6G **75**
(off Queen's Club Gdns.)
Livingstone Pl. *E14* —5E **80**
Livingstone Rd. *E15* —1E **64**
Livingstone Rd. *E17* —6D **32**
Livingstone Rd. *N13* —6D **16**
Livingstone Rd. *SW11* —3B **92**
Livingstone Rd. *Houn* —4G **87**
Livingstone Rd. *S'hall* —7B **54**

Livingstone Rd. *T Hth* —2D **124**
Livonia St. *W1* —6G **61** *(1B 148)*
Lizard St. *EC1* —3C **62** *(2D 144)*
Lizban St. *SE3* —7K **81**
Llanelly Rd. *NW2* —2H **43**
Llanover Rd. *SE18* —6E **82**
Llanover Rd. *Wemb* —3D **40**
Llanthony Rd. *Mord* —5B **122**
Llanvanor Rd. *NW2* —2H **43**
Llewellyn Ct. *SE20* —1J **125**
Llewellyn St. *SE16* —2G **79**
Lloyd Av. *SW16* —1J **123**
Lloyd Baker M. *WC1*
—3K **61** *(2H 143)*
Lloyd Baker St. *WC1*
—3A **62** *(2H 143)*
Lloyd Ct. *Pinn* —5B **22**
Lloyd Pk. Av. *Croy* —4F **135**
Lloyd Pk. Ho. *E17* —3C **32**
Lloyd Rd. *E6* —1D **66**
Lloyd Rd. *E17* —4K **31**
Lloyd Rd. *Dag* —7F **53**
Lloyd Rd. *Wor Pk* —3F **131**
Lloyd's Av. *EC3* —6E **62** *(1H 151)*
Lloyd's Pl. *SE3* —2G **97**
Lloyd Sq. *WC1* —3A **62** *(1J 143)*
Lloyd's Row. *EC1*
—3A **62** *(2K 143)*
Lloyd St. *WC1* —3A **62** *(1J 143)*
Lloyds Way. *Beck* —5A **126**
Lloyds Wharf. *SE1*
—2F **79** *(7K 151)*
Lloyd Thomas Ct. *N22* —7E **16**
Loampit Hill. *SE13* —2C **96**
Loampit Vale. *SE13* —3D **96**
Loampit Vale. (Junct.) —3E **96**
Loanda Clo. *E8* —1F **63**
Loats Rd. *SW2* —6J **93**
Lobelia Clo. *E6* —5C **66**
Locarno Rd. *W3* —1J **73**
Locarno Rd. *Gnfd* —4H **55**
Lochaber Rd. *SE13* —4G **97**
Lochaline St. *W6* —6E **74**
Lochan Clo. *Hayes* —4C **54**
Lochinvar St. *SW12* —7F **93**
Lochleven Ho. N2 —2B **28**
(off Grange, The)
Lochmere Clo. *Eri* —6H **85**
Lochnagar St. *E14* —5E **64**
Lock Chase. *SE3* —3E **97**
Lock Clo. *S'hall* —2G **71**
Lockesfield Pl. *E14* —5D **80**
Lockesley Dri. *Orp* —6K **129**
Lockesley Sq. *Surb* —6D **118**
Locket Rd. *Harr* —3J **23**
Lockfield Av. *Enf* —2F **9**
Lockgate Clo. *E9* —5B **48**
Lockhart Clo. *N7* —6K **45**
Lockhart Clo. *Enf* —5C **8**
Lockhart St. *E3* —4B **64**
Lockhurst St. *E5* —4K **47**
Lockie Pl. *SE25* —3G **125**
Lockier Wlk. *Wemb* —3D **40**
Lockington Rd. *SW8* —1F **93**
Lockmead Rd. *N15* —6G **31**
Lockmead Rd. *SE13* —3E **96**
Lock Rd. *Rich* —4C **104**
Locksfields. *SE17*
—4D **78** *(4F 157)*
Lockside. E14 —7A **64**
(off Narrow St.)
Locks La. *Mitc* —2E **122**
Locksley Est. *E14* —6B **64**
Locksley St. *E14* —5B **64**
Locksmeade Rd. *Rich* —4C **104**

Lockwood Clo. *SE26* —4K **111**
Lockwood Clo. *Cockf* —4J **5**
Lockwood Ho. *SE11*
—6A **78** *(7J 155)*
Lockwood Ind. Pk. *N17* —3H **31**
Lockwood Sq. *SE16* —3H **79**
Lockwood Way. *E17* —2K **31**
Lockyer Est. *SE1*
—2D **78** *(7F 151)*
Lockyer Ho. *SE1* —2D **78** *(7F 151)*
Locton Grn. *E3* —1B **64**
Loddiges Rd. *E9* —7J **47**
Loder St. *SE15* —7J **79**
Lodge Av. *SW14* —3A **90**
Lodge Av. *Croy* —3A **134**
Lodge Av. *Dag* —1A **68**
Lodge Av. *Harr* —4E **24**
Lodge Clo. *N18* —5H **17**
Lodge Clo. *Edgw* —6A **12**
Lodge Clo. *Iswth* —1B **88**
Lodge Clo. *Wall* —1E **132**
Lodge Ct. *Wemb* —6E **40**
Lodge Dri. *N13* —4F **17**
Lodge Gdns. *Beck* —5B **126**
Lodge Hill. *Ilf* —4C **34**
Lodge Hill. *Well* —7B **84**
Lodgehill Pk. Clo. *Harr* —2F **39**
Lodge La. *N12* —5F **15**
Lodge La. *Bex* —6D **100**
Lodge La. *New Ad* —6C **136**
Lodge La. *Romf* —1G **37**
Lodge Pl. *Sutt* —5K **131**
Lodge Rd. *NW4* —4E **26**
Lodge Rd. *NW8* —3B **60** *(2B 140)*
Lodge Rd. *Brom* —7A **114**
Lodge Rd. *Croy* —6B **124**
Lodge Rd. *Wall* —5F **133**
Lodge Vs. *Wfd G* —6C **20**
Lodore Gdns. *NW9* —5A **26**
Lodore St. *E14* —6E **64**
Loftie St. *SE16* —2G **79**
Lofting Rd. *N1* —7K **45**
Loftus Rd. *W12* —1D **74**
Logan Clo. *Enf* —1E **8**
Logan Clo. *Houn* —3D **86**
Logan M. *W8* —4J **75**
Logan Pl. *W8* —4J **75**
Logan Rd. *N9* —2C **18**
Logan Rd. *Wemb* —2D **40**
Loggetts. *SE21* —3E **110**
Logs Hill. *Chst & Brom* —7C **114**
Logs Hill Clo. *Chst* —1C **128**
Lohmann Ho. *SE11*
—6A **78** *(7J 155)*
Lolesworth Clo. *E1*
—5F **63** *(6J 145)*
Lollard St. *SE11*
(in two parts) —4K **77** *(3H 155)*
Loman St. *SE1* —2B **78** *(6B 150)*
Lomas Clo. *Croy* —7E **136**
Lomas Ct. *E8* —7F **47**
Lomas St. *E1* —5G **63**
Lombard Av. *Enf* —1D **8**
Lombard Av. *Ilf* —1J **51**
Lombard Bus. Cen., The. *SW11*
Lombard Bus. Pk. *Croy* —7K **123**
Lombard Ct. *EC3*
—7D **62** *(2F 151)*
Lombard Ct. Romf —4J **37**
(off Poplar St.)
Lombard La. *EC4*
—6A **62** *(1K 149)*
Lombard Rd. *N11* —5A **16**
Lombard Rd. *SW11* —2B **92**

Lombard Rd. SW19 —2K 121
Lombard Roundabout. (Junct.)
—7K 123
Lombard St. EC3
—6D 62 (1F 151)
Lombard Wall. SE7 —3K 81
(in two parts)
Lombardy Pl. W2 —7K 59
Lombardy Retail Pk. Hayes
—7A 54
Lomond Clo. N15 —5E 30
Lomond Clo. Wemb —7F 41
Lomond Gdns. S Croy —7A 136
Lomond Gro. SE5 —7D 78
Lomond Ho. SE5 —7D 78
Loncroft Rd. SE5
—6E 78 (7H 157)
Londesborough Rd. N16 —4E 46
London Bri. SE1 & EC4
—1D 78 (4F 151)
London Bri. St. SE1
—1D 78 (5F 151)
London City Airport. E16 —7C 66
Londonderry Pde. Eri —7K 85
London Fields E. Side. E8 —7H 47
London Fields W. Side. E8
—7G 47
London Ho. NW8 —2C 60
(off Avenue Rd.)
London Ho. WC1
—4K 61 (3G 143)
London Ind. Pk., The. E6 —5F 67
London La. E8 —7H 47
London La. Brom —7H 113
London Master Bakers
Almshouses. E10 —6D 32
London M. W2 —6B 60 (7B 140)
London Rd. E13 —2J 65
London Rd. SE1
—3B 78 (1A 156)
London Rd. SE23 —1H 111
London Rd. SW16 & T Hth
—1K 123
London Rd. Bark —7F 51
London Rd. Brom —7H 113
London Rd. Chad H & Romf
—6G 37
London Rd. Cray —5K 101
London Rd. Croy —6B 124
London Rd. Enf —5J 7
London Rd. Harr —2J 39
London Rd. Houn & Iswth
—3G 87
London Rd. Iswth & Bren —2K 87
London Rd. King T —2E 118
London Rd. Mitc & SW17
—4C 122
London Rd. Mord —5J 121
London Rd. Stan —5H 11
London Rd. Twic —5A 88
London Rd. Wall & Mitc —4F 133
London Rd. Wemb —5E 40
London Stile. W4 —5G 73
London St. EC3 —7E 62 (2H 151)
London St. W2 —6B 60 (7A 140)
London Ter. E2 —2G 63
London Underwriting Cen. EC3
—7E 62 (2H 151)
London Wall. EC2
—5C 62 (6D 144)
London Wall Bldgs. EC2
—5D 62 (6F 145)
London Wharf. E2 —1H 63
(off Wharf Pl.)

Lonesome Way. SW16 —1G 123
Long Acre. WC2 —7J 61 (2E 148)
Longacre Clo. Enf —3H 7
Long Acre Ct. W13 —5A 56
Longacre Pl. Cars —6E 132
Longacre Rd. E17 —1F 33
Longbeach Rd. SW11 —3D 92
Longberrys. NW3 —3H 43
Longboat Row. S'hall —6D 54
Longbourne Ct. E17 —6A 32
Longbridge Ho. Dag —4B 52
(off Gainsborough Rd.)
Longbridge Rd. Bark & Dag
—7G 51
Longbridge Way. SE13 —5E 96
Longcroft. SE9 —3E 114
Longcrofte Rd. Edgw —7J 11
Long Deacon Rd. E4 —1B 20
Longdon Wood. Kes —3C 138
Longdown Rd. SE6 —4C 112
Long Dri. W3 —6A 58
Long Dri. Gnfd —1F 55
Long Dri. Ruis —5A 38
Long Elmes. Harr —1F 23
Longfellow Rd. E3 —3A 64
Longfellow Rd. E17 —6B 32
Longfellow Rd. Wor Pk —1C 130
Longfellow Way. SE1
—4F 79 (4K 157)
Long Field. NW9 —7F 13
Longfield. Brom —1H 127
Longfield Av. E17 —4A 32
Longfield Av. NW7 —7H 13
Longfield Av. W5 —7C 56
Longfield Av. Wall —1E 132
Longfield Av. Wemb —1E 40
Longfield Cres. SE26 —3J 111
Longfield Dri. SW14 —5H 89
Longfield Dri. Mitc —1C 122
Longfield Est. SE1
—4F 79 (3K 157)
Longfield Ho. SE1
—3C 78 (2D 156)
Longfield Rd. W5 —6C 56
Longfield St. SW18 —7J 91
Longfield Wlk. W5 —6C 56
Longford Av. S'hall —7F 55
Longford Av. Hayes —7B 54
Longford Clo. Hamp —4E 102
Longford Clo. Hayes —7B 54
Longford Ct. NW4 —4F 27
Longford Ct. S'hall —1E 70
(off Uxbridge Rd.)
Longford Gdns. Hayes —7B 54
Longford Gdns. Sutt —3A 132
Longford Ho. Brom —5F 113
(off Brangbourne Rd.)
Longford Ho. Hamp —4E 102
Longford Rd. Twic —1E 102
Longford St. NW1
—4F 61 (3K 141)
Longford Wlk. SW2 —7A 94
Longhayes Av. Romf —4D 36
Longhayes Ct. Romf —4D 36
Longheath Gdns. Croy —5J 125
Longhedge Ho. SE26 —4G 111
(off High Level Dri.)
Long Hedges. Houn —2E 86
Longhedge St. SW11 —2E 92
Longhill Rd. SE6 —2F 113
Longhope Clo. SE15 —6E 78
Longhurst Rd. SE13 —5G 97
Longhurst Rd. Croy —6H 125
Longland Ct. SE1
—5G 79 (5K 157)
Longland Dri. N20 —3E 14
Longlands Ct. W11 —7H 59
(off Westbourne Gro.)

Longlands Ct. Sidc —2K 115
Longlands Pk. Cres. Sidc
—3J 115
Longlands Rd. Sidc —3J 115
Long La. EC1 —5B 62 (6B 144)
Long La. N2 & N3 —2A 28
Long La. N3 & N2 —1K 27
Long La. SE1 —2D 78 (7E 150)
Long La. Bexh —7D 84
Long La. Croy —6J 125
Longleat Rd. Enf —5K 7
Longleigh Ho. SE5 —1E 94
(off Peckham Rd.)
Longleigh La. Bexh —6C 84
Longley Av. Wemb —1F 57
Longley Ct. SW8 —1J 93
Longley Rd. SW17 —6C 108
Longley Rd. Croy —7B 124
Longley Rd. Harr —5G 23
Long Leys. E4 —6J 19
Longley St. SE1 —4G 79
Longley Way. NW2 —3E 42
Longman Ho. E8 —1F 63
Long Mark Rd. E16 —5B 66
Long Mead. NW9 —1B 26
Longmead. Chst —2E 128
Longmead Dri. Sidc —2D 116
Longmead Ho. SE27 —5C 110
Long Meadow. NW5 —5G 45
Long Meadow Clo. W Wick
—7E 126
Longmeadow Rd. Sidc —1J 115
Longmead Rd. SW17 —5D 108
Longmoore St. SW1
—4G 77 (4A 154)
Longmore Av. Barn —6F 5
Longnor Est. E1 —3K 63
Longnor Rd. E1 —3K 63
Long Pond Rd. SE3 —1G 97
Longreach Ct. Bark —2H 67
Long Reach Rd. Bark —4K 67
Longridge Ho. SE1
—3C 78 (2D 156)
Longridge La. S'hall —6F 55
Longridge Rd. SW5 —4J 75
Long Ridges. N2 —3E 28
(off Fortis Grn.)
Long Rd. SW4 —4F 93
Long's Ct. WC2 —7H 61 (3D 148)
Longs Ct. Rich —4F 89
Longshaw Rd. E4 —3A 20
Longshore. SE8 —4B 80
Longshott Ct. SW5 —4J 75
(off W. Cromwell Rd.)
Longstaff Cres. SW18 —7J 91
Longstaff Rd. SW18 —6J 91
Longstone Av. NW10 —7B 42
Longstone Rd. SW17 —5F 109
Long St. E2 —3F 63 (1J 145)
Longthornton Rd. SW16
—2G 123
Longton Av. SE26 —4G 111
Longton Gro. SE26 —4H 111
Longview Vs. Romf —1F 37
Longview Way. Romf —1K 37
Longville Rd. SE11
—4B 78 (3B 156)
Long Wlk. SE1 —3E 78 (1H 157)
Long Wlk. SE18 —6F 83
Long Wlk. SW13 —2B 90
Long Wlk. N Mald —3J 119
Long Wall. E15 —3F 65
Longwood Dri. SW15 —6C 90
Longwood Gdns. Ilf —4D 34
Longworth Clo. SE28 —6D 68
Long Yd. WC1 —4K 61 (4G 143)

Loning, The. NW9 —4B 26
Lonsdale Av. E6 —3B 66
Lonsdale Av. Romf —6J 37
Lonsdale Av. Wemb —5E 40
Lonsdale Clo. E6 —4C 66
Lonsdale Clo. SE9 —3B 114
Lonsdale Clo. Edgw —5A 12
Lonsdale Clo. Pinn —1C 22
Lonsdale Clo. Surb —7D 118
Lonsdale Cres. Ilf —6F 35
Lonsdale Dri. Enf —4C 6
Lonsdale Gdns. T Hth —4K 123
Lonsdale M. W11 —6H 59
(off Lonsdale Rd.)
Lonsdale M. Rich —1G 89
Lonsdale Pl. N1 —7A 46
Lonsdale Rd. E11 —7H 33
Lonsdale Rd. NW6 —2H 59
Lonsdale Rd. SE25 —4H 125
Lonsdale Rd. SW13 —1B 90
Lonsdale Rd. W4 —4B 74
Lonsdale Rd. W11 —6H 59
Lonsdale Rd. Bexh —2F 101
Lonsdale Rd. S'hall —3B 70
Lonsdale Sq. N1 —7A 46
Lonsdale Sq. W11 —7J 59
Loobert Rd. N15 —3E 30
Looe Gdns. Ilf —3F 35
Loop Rd. Chst —6G 115
Lopen Rd. N18 —4K 17
Lopez Ho. SW9 —3J 93
Lorac Ct. Sutt —7J 131
Loraine Clo. N12 —4E 14
Loraine Clo. Enf —5D 8
Loraine Ct. Chst —5F 115
Loraine Ho. Wall —4F 133
Loraine Rd. N7 —4K 45
Loraine Rd. W4 —6H 73
Lord Av. Ilf —4D 34
Lord Chancellor Wlk. King T
—1K 119
Lordell Pl. SW19 —6E 106
Lorden Wlk. E2 —3G 63 (2K 145)
Lord Gdns. Ilf —4D 34
Lord Hills Bri. W2 —5K 59
Lord Hills Rd. W2 —5K 59
Lord Holland La. SW9 —2A 94
Lord Napier Pl. W6 —5C 74
Lord North St. SW1
—3J 77 (2E 154)
Lord Roberts M. SW6 —7K 75
Lord Robert's Ter. SE18 —5E 82
Lords Clo. SE21 —2C 110
Lords Clo. Felt —2C 102
Lordship Gro. N16 —2D 46
Lordship La. N22 & N17 —2A 30
Lordship La. SE22 —4F 95
Lordship La. Est. SE22 —7G 95
Lordship Pk. N16 —2C 46
Lordship Pk. M. N16 —2C 46
Lordship Pl. SW3
—6C 76 (7C 152)
Lordship Rd. N16 —1D 46
Lordship Rd. N'holt —7C 38
Lordship Ter. N16 —2D 46
Lordsmead Rd. N17 —1E 30
Lord St. E16 —1C 82
Lords View One. NW8
—3C 60 (2C 140)
Lord Warwick St. SE18 —3D 82
Loreburn Ho. N7 —4K 45
Lorenzo St. WC1
—3K 61 (1G 143)
Loretto Gdns. Harr —4E 24
Loring Rd. N20 —2H 15

Loring Rd. Iswth —2K 87
Loris Rd. W6 —3E 74
Lorn Ct. SW9 —1A 94
Lorne Av. Croy —7K 125
Lorne Clo. NW8
—3C 60 (2D 140)
Lorne Gdns. E11 —4A 34
Lorne Gdns. W11 —2F 75
Lorne Gdns. Croy —7K 125
Lorne Rd. E7 —4K 49
Lorne Rd. E17 —5C 32
Lorne Rd. N4 —1K 45
Lorne Rd. Harr —2K 23
Lorne Rd. Rich —5F 89
Lorne Ter. N3 —2H 27
Lorn Rd. SW9 —2K 93
Lorraine Pk. Harr —7D 10
Lorrimore Rd. SE17
—6B 78 (7B 156)
Lorrimore Sq. SE17
—6B 78 (7B 156)
Lothair Rd. W5 —2D 72
Lothair Rd. N. N4 —6B 30
Lothair Rd. S. N4 —7A 30
Lothbury. EC2 —6D 62 (7E 144)
Lothian Av. Hayes —5A 54
Lothian Clo. Wemb —3A 40
Lothian Rd. SW9 —1B 94
Lothrop St. W10 —3G 59
Lots Rd. SW10 —7A 76
Lotus Clo. SE21 —3D 110
Loubet St. SW17 —6D 108
Loudoun Av. Ilf —5F 35
Loudoun Rd. NW8 —1A 60
Loughborough Est. SW9 —3B 94
Loughborough Pk. SW9 —4B 94
Loughborough Rd. SW9 —2A 94
Loughborough St. SE11
—5K 77 (5H 155)
Lough La. NW9 —5J 25
Lough Rd. N7 —5K 45
Loughton Way. Buck H —1G 21
Louisa Ct. Twic —2J 103
Louisa Gdns. E1 —4K 63
Louisa St. E1 —4K 63
Louise Bennett Clo. SE24 —4B 94
Louise Ct. N22 —1A 30
Louise Rd. E15 —6G 49
Louise White Ho. N19 —1H 45
Louis M. N10 —1F 29
Louisville Rd. SW17 —3E 108
Lousada Lodge. N14 —6B 6
(off Avenue Rd.)
Louvaine Rd. SW11 —4B 92
Lovage App. E6 —5C 66
Lovat Clo. NW2 —3B 42
Lovat La. EC3 —7E 62 (3G 151)
Lovatt Clo. Edgw —6C 12
Lovat Wlk. Houn —7C 70
Loveday Rd. W13 —2B 72
Lovegrove St. SE1 —5G 79
Lovegrove Wlk. E14 —1E 80
Lovekyn Clo. King T —2E 118
Lovelace Av. Brom —6E 128
Lovelace Gdns. Bark —4A 52
Lovelace Gdns. Surb —7D 118
Lovelace Grn. SE9 —3D 98
Lovelace Rd. SE21 —2C 110
Lovelace Rd. Barn —7H 5
Lovelace Rd. Surb —7C 118
Loveland Mans. Bark —7K 51
(off Upney La.)
Love La. EC2 —6C 62 (7D 144)
Love La. N17 —7A 18
Love La. SE18 —4E 82

Love La. SE25 —3H 125
(in two parts)
Love La. Bex —6F 101
Love La. Brom —3K 127
(off Elmfield Rd.)
Love La. Mitc —3C 122
(in two parts)
Love La. Mord —7J 121
Love La. Pinn —2B 22
Love La. Sutt —6G 131
Love La. Wfd G —6J 21
Lovel Av. Well —2A 100
Lovelinch Clo. SE15 —6J 79
Lovell Pl. SE16 —3A 80
Lovell Rd. Rich —3C 104
Lovell Rd. S'hall —6F 55
Loveridge M. NW6 —6H 43
Loveridge Rd. NW6 —6H 43
Lovers Wlk. NW7 & N3 —5E 14
Lovers Wlk. SE10 —6F 81
Lovers' Wlk. W1
—1E 76 (4G 147)
Lovett Dri. Cars —7A 122
Lovett Way. NW10 —5J 41
Love Wlk. SE5 —2D 94
Lowbrook Rd. Ilf —4F 51
Low Cross Wood La. SE21
—3F 111
Lowden Rd. N9 —1C 18
Lowden Rd. SE24 —4B 94
Lowden Rd. S'hall —7C 54
Lowe Av. E16 —5J 65
Lowell Ho. SE5 —7C 78
(off Wyndham Est.)
Lowell St. E14 —6A 64
Lowen Rd. Rain —2K 69
Lwr. Addiscombe Rd. Croy
—1E 134
Lwr. Addison Gdns. W14 —2G 75
Lwr. Belgrave St. SW1
—3F 77 (2J 153)
Lwr. Boston Rd. W7 —1J 71
Lwr. Broad St. Dag —1G 69
Lwr. Camden. Chst —7D 114
Lwr. Church St. Croy —2B 134
Lwr. Clapton Rd. E5 —3H 47
Lwr. Clarendon Wlk. W11
(off Clarendon Rd.) —6G 59
Lwr. Common S. SW15 —3D 90
Lwr. Coombe St. Croy —4C 134
Lwr. Downs Rd. SW20 —1F 121
Lwr. Drayton Pl. Croy —2B 134
Lwr. Fosters. NW4 —5E 26
(off New Brent St.)
Lwr. George St. Rich —5D 88
Lwr. Gravel Rd. Brom —1C 138
Lwr. Green W. Mitc —3C 122
Lwr. Grosvenor Pl. SW1
—3F 77 (1K 153)
Lwr. Grove Rd. Rich —6F 89
Lwr. Hall La. E4 —5F 19
Lwr. Ham Rd. King T —5D 104
Lwr. James St. W1
—7G 61 (2B 148)
Lwr. John St. W1
—7G 61 (2B 148)
Lwr. Kenwood Av. Enf —5C 6
Lwr. Lea Crossing. E14 —7G 65
Lwr. Maidstone Rd. N11 —6B 16
Lwr. Mall. W6 —5D 74
Lwr. Mardyke Av. Rain —2J 69
Lwr. Marsh. SE1
—2A 78 (7J 149)
Lwr. Marsh La. King T —4F 119
Lwr. Merton Rise. NW3 —7C 44

Lwr. Mill. Eps —7B 130
Lwr. Morden La. Mord —6E 120
Lwr. Mortlake Rd. Rich —4E 88
Lwr. Park Rd. N11 —5B 16
Lwr. Park Rd. Belv —4G 85
Lwr. Pk. Trad. Est. W5 —4J 57
Lwr. Place Bus. Cen. NW10
—2J 57
Lwr. Queen's Rd. Buck H —2G 21
Lwr. Richmond Rd. SW13 &
SW15 —3D 90
Lwr. Richmond Rd. Rich & SW14
—3G 89
Lower Rd. N11 —5A 16
Lower Rd. SE16 & SE8 —2J 79
(in two parts)
Lower Rd. Belv & Eri —3H 85
Lower Rd. Harr —1H 39
Lower Rd. Sutt —4A 132
Lwr. Robert St. WC2
—7J 61 (3F 149)
Lwr. Sloane St. SW1
—4E 76 (4G 153)
Lower Sq. Iswth —3B 88
Lower Sq., The. Sutt —5K 131
Lwr. Staithe. W4 —1J 89
Lwr. Strand. NW9 —2B 26
Lwr. Sydenham Ind. Est. SE26
—5B 112
Lwr. Teddington Rd. King T
—1D 118
Lower Ter. NW3 —3A 44
Lwr. Thames St. EC3
—7D 62 (3F 151)
Lowerwood Ct. W11 —6G 59
(off Westbourne Pk. Rd.)
Lowestoft Clo. E5 —2J 47
(off Southwold Rd.)
Loweswater Clo. Wemb —2D 40
Lowfield Rd. NW6 —7J 43
Lowfield Rd. W3 —6H 57
Low Hall Clo. E4 —7J 9
Lowhall La. E17 —6A 32
Low Hall Mnr. Bus. Cen. E17
—6A 32
Lowick Rd. Harr —4J 23
Lowlands Gdns. Romf —5H 37
Lowlands Rd. Harr —6J 23
Lowlands Rd. Pinn —7A 22
Lowman Rd. N7 —4K 45
Lowndes Clo. SW1
—3E 76 (2H 153)
Lowndes Ct. W1
—3D 76 (1F 153)
Lowndes Ct. W1
—6G 61 (1A 148)
Lowndes Pl. SW1
—3E 76 (2G 153)
Lowndes Sq. SW1
—2D 76 (7F 147)
Lowndes St. SW1
—3E 76 (1F 153)
Lowndes Ct. Brom —2J 127
Lowood St. E1 —7H 63
Lowry Cres. Mitc —2C 122
Lowry Ho. N17 —1F 31
(off Pembury Rd.)
Lowry Rd. Dag —5B 52
Lowshoe La. Romf —1G 37
Lowther Dri. Enf —4D 6
Lowther Gdns. SW7
—3B 76 (1B 152)
Lowther Hill. SE23 —7A 96
Lowther Rd. E17 —2A 32
Lowther Rd. N7 —5A 46

Lowther Rd. SW13 —1B 90
Lowther Rd. King T —1F 119
Lowther Rd. Stan —3F 25
Lowth Rd. SE5 —1C 94
Low Wlk. E17 —5B 32
Loxford Av. E6 —2B 66
Loxford La. Ilf —5G 51
Loxford Rd. Bark —6F 51
Loxford Ter. Bark —6G 51
Loxham Rd. E4 —7J 19
Loxham St. WC1
—3J 61 (2F 143)
Loxley Clo. SE26 —5K 111
Loxley Rd. SW18 —1B 108
Loxley Rd. Hamp —4D 102
Loxton Rd. SE23 —1K 111
Loxwood Rd. N17 —3E 30
Lubbock Rd. Chst —7D 114
Lubbock St. SE14 —7J 79
Lucan Ho. N1 —1D 62
(off Colville Est.)
Lucan Pl. SW3 —4C 76 (4C 152)
Lucan Rd. Barn —3B 4
Lucas Av. E13 —1K 65
Lucas Av. Harr —2E 38
Lucas Ct. SE26 —5A 112
Lucas Rd. SE20 —6J 111
Lucas Sq. NW11 —6J 27
Lucas St. SE8 —1C 96
Lucerne Clo. N13 —3D 16
Lucerne Ct. Eri —3E 84
Lucerne Gro. E17 —4F 33
Lucerne M. W8 —1J 75
Lucerne Rd. N5 —4B 46
Lucerne Rd. Orp —7K 129
Lucerne Rd. T Hth —4C 124
Lucey Rd. SE16 —3G 79
Lucey Way. SE16 —3G 79
(in two parts)
Lucien Rd. SW17 —4E 108
Lucien Rd. SW19 —2K 107
Lucinda Ct. Enf —4K 7
Lucknow St. SE18 —7J 83
Lucorn Clo. SE12 —6H 97
Luctons Av. Buck H —1F 21
Lucy Cres. W3 —5J 57
Lucy Gdns. Dag —3E 52
Luddesdon Rd. Eri —7G 85
Ludford Clo. NW9 —2A 26
Ludford Clo. Croy —3A 134
Ludgate B'way. EC4
—6B 62 (1A 150)
Ludgate Cir. EC4
—6B 62 (1A 150)
Ludgate Hill. EC4
—6B 62 (1A 150)
Ludgate Sq. EC4
—6B 62 (1B 150)
Ludham Clo. SE28 —6C 68
Ludlow Clo. Brom —3J 127
Ludlow Clo. Harr —4D 38
Ludlow Ct. W3 —2J 73
Ludlow Rd. W5 —4C 56
Ludlow St. EC1 —4C 62 (3C 144)
Ludlow Way. N2 —4A 28
Ludovick Wlk. SW15 —4B 90
Ludwick M. SE14 —7A 80
Luffield Rd. SE2 —3B 84
Luffman Rd. SE12 —3A 114
Lugard Rd. SE15 —2H 95
Lugg App. E12 —3E 50
Luke St. EC2 —4E 62 (3G 145)
Lukin Cres. E4 —3A 20
Lukin St. E1 —6J 63
Luley La. NW7 —5E 12

Lullingstone Clo. Orp —7B 116
Lullingstone Cres. Orp —7A 116
Lullingstone Rd. Belv —6F 85
Lullington Garth. N12 —5C 14
Lullington Garth. Brom —7G 113
Lullington Rd. SE20 —7H 111
Lullington Rd. Dag —7E 52
Lulot Gdns. N19 —2F 45
Lulworth Av. Houn —1F 87
Lulworth Av. Wemb —7C 24
Lulworth Clo. Harr —3D 38
Lulworth Cres. Mitc —2C 122
Lulworth Dri. Pinn —6B 22
Lulworth Gdns. Harr —2C 38
Lulworth Ho. SW8 —7K 77
Lulworth Rd. SE9 —2C 114
Lulworth Rd. SE15 —2H 95
Lulworth Rd. Well —2K 99
Lulworth Waye. Hayes —6A 54
Lumen Rd. Wemb —2D 40
Lumley Clo. Belv —5G 85
Lumley Ct. WC2 —7J 61 (3F 149)
Lumley Flats SW1
—5E 76 (5G 153)
(off Holbein Pl.)
Lumley Gdns. Sutt —5G 131
Lumley Rd. Sutt —5G 131
Lumley St. W1 —6E 60 (1H 147)
Luna Rd. T Hth —3C 124
Lund Point. E15 —1E 64
Lundy Wlk. N1 —6C 46
Lunham Rd. SE19 —6E 110
Lupin Clo. SW2 —2B 110
Lupin Clo. Croy —1K 135
Lupton Clo. SE12 —3K 113
Lupton St. NW5 —4G 45
Lupus St. SW1 —5F 77 (6K 153)
Luralda Gdns. E14 —5F 81
Lurgan Av. W6 —6F 75
Lurline Gdns. SW11 —1E 92
Luscombe Ct. Short —2G 127
Luscombe Way. SW8 —7J 77
Lushington Rd. NW10 —2D 58
Lushington Rd. SE6 —4D 112
Lushington Ter. E8 —5G 47
(off Wayland Av.)
Lusitania Building. E1 —7K 63
(off Jardine Rd.)
Lutea Ho. Sutt —7A 132
(off Walnut M.)
Luther Clo. Edgw —2D 12
Luther King Clo. E17 —6A 32
Luther Rd. Tedd —5K 103
Luton Pl. SE10 —7E 80
Luton Rd. E13 —4J 65
Luton Rd. E17 —3B 32
Luton Rd. Sidc —3C 116
Luton St. NW8 —4B 60 (4B 140)
Lutton Ter. NW3 —4A 44
(off Heath St.)
Luttrell Av. SW15 —5D 90
Lutwyche Rd. SE6 —2B 112
Luxborough La. Chig —3H 21
Luxborough St. W1
—5E 60 (5G 141)
Luxemburg Gdns. W6 —4F 75
Luxfield Rd. SE9 —1C 114
Luxford St. SE16 —4K 79
Luxmore St. SE4 —1B 96
Luxor St. SE5 —3C 94
Lyall Av. SE21 —4E 110
Lyall M. SW1 —3E 76 (2G 153)
Lyall M. W. SW1
—3E 76 (2G 153)
Lyall St. SW1 —3E 76 (2G 153)

Lyal Rd. E3 —2A 64
Lycett Pl. W12 —2C 74
Lychgate Mnr. Harr —7K 23
Lyconby Gdns. Croy —7A 126
Lydd Clo. Sidc —3J 115
Lydden Gro. SW18 —7K 91
Lydden Rd. SW18 —7K 91
Lydd Rd. Bexh —7F 85
Lydeard Rd. E6 —7D 50
Lydford Clo. N16 —5E 46
(off Pellerin Rd.)
Lydford Rd. N15 —5D 30
Lydford Rd. NW2 —6E 42
Lydford Rd. W9 —4H 59
Lydhurst Av. SW2 —2K 109
Lydia Ct. N12 —6F 15
Lydney Clo. SE15 —7E 78
Lydney Clo. SW19 —2G 107
Lydon Rd. SW4 —3G 93
Lydstep Rd. Chst —4E 114
Lyford Rd. SW18 —7B 92
Lyford St. SE7 —4C 82
Lygon Ho. SW6 —1G 91
(off Fulham Pal. Rd.)
Lygon Pl. SW1 —3F 77 (2J 153)
Lyham Clo. SW2 —6J 93
Lyham Rd. SW2 —5J 93
Lyle Clo. Mitc —7E 122
Lyme Farm Rd. SE12 —4J 97
Lyme Gro. E9 —7J 47
Lymer Av. SE19 —5F 111
Lyme Rd. Well —1B 100
Lymescote Gdns. Sutt —2J 131
Lyme St. NW1 —7G 45
Lyme Ter. NW1 —7G 45
Lyminge Clo. Sidc —4K 115
Lyminge Gdns. SW18 —1C 108
Lymington Av. N22 —2A 30
Lymington Clo. E6 —5D 66
Lymington Clo. SW16 —2H 123
Lymington Ct. Sutt —3K 131
Lymington Gdns. Eps —5B 130
Lymington Rd. NW6 —6K 43
Lymington Rd. Dag —1D 52
Lympne. N17 —2D 30
(off Gloucester Rd.)
Lympstone Gdns. SE15 —7G 79
Lynbridge Gdns. N13 —4G 17
Lynbrook Clo. SE15 —7E 78
Lynbrook Clo. Rain —2K 69
Lynch Wlk. SE8 —6B 80
Lyncott Cres. SW4 —4F 93
Lyncourt. SE3 —2F 97
Lyncroft Av. Pinn —5C 22
Lyncroft Gdns. NW6 —5J 43
Lyncroft Gdns. W13 —2C 72
Lyncroft Gdns. Houn —5G 87
Lyncroft Mans. NW6 —5J 43
Lyndale. NW2 —4H 43
Lyndale Av. NW2 —3H 43
Lyndale Clo. SE3 —6H 81
Lynde Ho. SW4 —3H 93
Lyndhurst Av. N12 —6G 15
Lyndhurst Av. NW7 —6F 13
Lyndhurst Av. SW16 —2H 123
Lyndhurst Av. Pinn —1A 22
Lyndhurst Av. S'hall —1F 71
Lyndhurst Av. Surb —7H 119
Lyndhurst Av. Twic —1D 102
Lyndhurst Clo. NW10 —3K 41
Lyndhurst Clo. Bexh —3H 101
Lyndhurst Clo. Croy —3F 135
Lyndhurst Ct. E18 —1J 33
Lyndhurst Dri. E10 —7E 32
Lyndhurst Dri. N Mald —7A 120

Lyndhurst Gdns. *N3* —1G 27
Lyndhurst Gdns. *NW3* —5B 44
Lyndhurst Gdns. *Bark* —6J 51
Lyndhurst Gdns. *Enf* —4K 7
Lyndhurst Gdns. *Ilf* —6H 35
Lyndhurst Gdns. *Pinn* —1A 22
Lyndhurst Gro. *SE15* —2E 94
Lyndhurst Rise. *Chig* —4K 21
Lyndhurst Rd. *E4* —7K 19
Lyndhurst Rd. *N18* —4B 18
Lyndhurst Rd. *N22* —6F 17
Lyndhurst Rd. *NW3* —5B 44
Lyndhurst Rd. *Bexh* —3H 101
Lyndhurst Rd. *Gnfd* —4F 55
Lyndhurst Rd. *T Hth* —4A 124
Lyndhurst Sq. *SE15* —1F 95
Lyndhurst Ter. *NW3* —5B 44
Lyndhurst Way. *SE15* —1F 95
Lyndhurst Way. *Sutt* —7J 131
Lyndon Av. *Sidc* —5K 99
Lyndon Av. *Wall* —3E 132
Lyndon Rd. *Belv* —4G 85
Lyne Cres. *E17* —1B 32
Lyneham Wlk. *E5* —5A 48
Lynette Av. *SW4* —6G 93
Lynford Clo. *Edgw* —1J 25
Lynford Gdns. *Edgw* —3C 12
Lynford Gdns. *Ilf* —2K 51
Lynford Ter. *N9* —1A 18
Lynmere Rd. *Well* —2B 100
Lyn M. *E3* —3B 64
Lynmouth Av. *Enf* —6A 8
Lynmouth Av. *Mord* —6F 121
Lynmouth Gdns. *Gnfd* —1B 56
Lynmouth Gdns. *Houn* —1B 86
Lynmouth Rd. *E17* —6A 32
Lynmouth Rd. *N2* —3D 28
Lynmouth Rd. *N16* —1F 47
Lynmouth Rd. *Gnfd* —1B 56
Lynn Clo. *Harr* —2H 23
Lynne Clo. *SE23* —7B 96
Lynett Rd. *Dag* —2D 52
Lynne Way. *NW10* —6A 42
Lynne Way. *N'holt* —2B 54
Lynn M. *E11* —2G 49
Lynn Rd. *E11* —2G 49
Lynn Rd. *SW12* —7F 93
Lynn Rd. *Ilf* —7H 35
Lynn St. *Enf* —1J 7
Lynscott Way. *S Croy* —7B 134
Lynstead Ct. *Beck* —2A 126
Lynsted Clo. *Bexh* —5H 101
Lynsted Clo. *Brom* —2A 128
Lynsted Ct. *Beck* —2A 126
Lynsted Gdns. *SE9* —4B 98
Lynton Av. *N12* —4G 15
Lynton Av. *NW9* —4B 26
Lynton Av. *W13* —6A 56
Lynton Av. *Romf* —1G 37
Lynton Clo. *NW10* —5A 42
Lynton Clo. *Iswth* —4K 87
Lynton Cres. *Ilf* —6F 35
Lynton Est. *SE1* —5G 79 (5K 157)
Lynton Gdns. *N11* —6C 16
Lynton Gdns. *Enf* —7K 7
Lynton Grange. *N2* —3D 28
Lynton Mead. *N20* —3D 14
Lynton Rd. *E4* —5J 19
Lynton Rd. *N8* —5H 29
(in two parts)
Lynton Rd. *NW6* —2H 59
Lynton Rd. *SE1* —4F 79 (4K 157)
Lynton Rd. *W3* —7G 57
Lynton Rd. *Croy* —6A 124
Lynton Rd. *Harr* —2C 38

Lynton Rd. *N Mald* —5K 119
Lynwood Clo. *E18* —1A 34
Lynwood Clo. *Harr* —3C 38
Lynwood Ct. *King T* —2H 119
Lynwood Dri. *Wor Pk* —2C 130
Lynwood Gdns. *Croy* —4K 133
Lynwood Gdns. *S'hall* —6D 54
Lynwood Gro. *N21* —1F 17
Lynwood Gro. *Orp* —7J 129
Lynwood Rd. *SW17* —3D 108
Lynwood Rd. *W5* —3E 56
Lyon Bus. Pk. *Bark* —2J 67
Lyon Ind. Est. *NW2* —2D 42
Lyon Meade. *Stan* —1C 24
Lyon Pk. Av. *Wemb* —6E 40
(in two parts)
Lyon Rd. *SW19* —1A 122
Lyon Rd. *Harr* —6K 23
Lyonsdown Av. *New Bar* —6F 5
(off Central St.)
Lyonsdown Rd. *Barn* —6F 5
Lyon's Pl. *NW8* —4B 60 (4A 140)
Lyon St. *N1* —7K 45
Lyons Wlk. *W14* —4G 75
Lyon Way. *Gnfd* —1J 55
Lyric Dri. *Gnfd* —4F 55
Lyric Rd. *SW13* —1B 90
Lysander Gdns. *Surb* —6F 119
Lysander Gro. *N19* —1H 45
Lysander Rd. *Croy* —6K 133
Lysias Rd. *SW12* —6F 93
Lysia St. *SW6* —7F 75
Lysons Wlk. *SW15* —4C 90
Lytchet Rd. *Brom* —7K 113
Lytchet Way. *Enf* —1D 8
Lytchgate Clo. *S Croy* —7E 134
Lytcott Gro. *SE22* —5E 94
Lytham Ct. *S'hall* —6F 55
(off Whitecote Rd.)
Lytham Gro. *W5* —3F 57
Lytham St. *SE17*
—6D 78 (6E 156)
Lyttelton Clo. *NW3* —7C 44
Lyttelton Ct. *N2* —5A 28
Lyttelton Rd. *E10* —3D 48
Lyttelton Rd. *N2* —5A 28
Lyttelton Ct. *Hayes* —4A 54
(off Dunedin Way)
Lyttleton Rd. *N8* —3A 30
Lytton Av. *N13* —2F 17
Lytton Av. *Enf* —1F 9
Lytton Clo. *N2* —6B 28
Lytton Clo. *N'holt* —7D 38
Lytton Gdns. *Wall* —4H 133
Lytton Gro. *SW15* —5F 91
Lytton Rd. *E11* —7G 33
Lytton Rd. *Barn* —4F 5
Lytton Rd. *Pinn* —1C 22
Lytton Strachey Path. *SE28*
—7B 68
Lyveden Rd. *SE3* —7K 81
Lyveden Rd. *SW17* —6D 108

Maberley Cres. *SE19* —7G 111
Maberley Rd. *SE19* —1G 125
Maberley Rd. *Beck* —3K 125
Mabledon Pl. *WC1*
—3H 61 (2D 142)
Mablethorpe Rd. *SW6* —7G 75
Mabley St. *E9* —5A 48
Mablin Lodge. *Buck H* —1F 21
McAdam Dri. *Enf* —2G 7
Macaret Clo. *N20* —7E 4
Macarthur Clo. *E7* —6J 49
Macarthur Ter. *SE7* —6B 82

Macaulay Ct. *SW4* —3F 93
Macaulay Rd. *E6* —2B 66
Macaulay Rd. *SW4* —3F 93
Macaulay Sq. *SW4* —4F 93
Macaulay Way. *SE28* —1B 84
McAuley Clo. *SE1*
—3A 78 (1J 155)
McAuley Clo. *SE9* —5E 98
Macaulay M. *SE13* —1E 96
Macbean St. *SE18* —3F 83
Macbeth Ho. *N1* —2E 62
Macbeth St. *W6* —5D 74
McCall Clo. *SW4* —2J 93
McCall Cres. *SE7* —5C 82
McCall Ho. *N7* —4J 45
McCarthy Rd. *Felt* —5B 102
Macclesfield Ho. *EC1*
—4C 62 (2C 144)
(off Central St.)
Macclesfield Rd. *EC1*
—3C 62 (1C 144)
Macclesfield Rd. *SE25* —5J 125
Macclesfield St. *W1*
—7H 61 (2D 148)
McCoid Way. *SE1*
—2C 78 (7C 150)
McCrone M. *NW3* —6B 44
McCullum Rd. *E3* —1B 64
McDermott Clo. *SW11* —3C 92
McDermott Rd. *SE15* —3G 95
Macdonald Av. *Dag* —3H 53
Macdonald Rd. *E7* —4J 49
Macdonald Rd. *E17* —2E 32
Macdonald Rd. *N11* —5J 15
Macdonald Rd. *N19* —2G 45
Macdonald Rd. *Dag* —3H 53
McDowall Clo. *E16* —5H 65
McDowall Rd. *SE5* —1C 94
Macduff Rd. *SW11* —1E 92
Mace Clo. *E1* —1H 79
Mace Gateway. *E16* —7J 65
McEntee Av. *E17* —1A 32
Mace St. *E2* —2K 63
Mace St. *SE1* —2F 79 (6J 151)
McEwen Way. *E15* —1F 65
Macfarlane La. *Iswth* —6K 71
Macfarlane Rd. *W12* —1E 74
Macfarren Pl. *NW1*
—4E 60 (4H 141)
McGrath Rd. *E15* —5H 49
McGregor Ct. *N1*
—3E 62 (1H 145)
MacGregor Rd. *E16* —5A 66
McGregor Rd. *W11* —5H 59
Machell Rd. *SE15* —3J 95
McIntosh Clo. *Romf* —3K 37
McIntosh Clo. *Wall* —7J 133
McIntosh Rd. *Romf* —3K 37
McIntyre Ct. *SE18* —4C 82
(off Prospect Vale)
Mackay Ho. *W12* —7D 58
(off White City Est.)
Mackay Rd. *SW4* —3F 93
McKay Rd. *SW20* —7D 106
McKay Trad. Est. *W10* —4G 59
McKellar Clo. *Bush* —2B 10
Mackennal St. *NW8* —2C 60
Mackenzie Clo. *W12* —7D 58
Mackenzie Ho. *NW2* —3C 42
Mackenzie Rd. *N7* —6K 45
Mackenzie Rd. *Beck* —2J 125
Mackenzie Wlk. *E14* —1C 80
McKerrell Rd. *SE15* —1G 95
Mackeson Rd. *NW3* —4D 44
Mackie Rd. *SW2* —7A 94

Mackintosh La. *E9* —5K 47
Macklin St. *WC2* —6J 61 (7F 143)
Mackrow Wlk. *E14* —7E 64
Mack's Rd. *SE16* —4G 79
Mackworth St. *NW1*
—3G 61 (1A 142)
Maclaren M. *SW15* —4E 90
Maclean Rd. *SE23* —6A 96
Macleod Rd. *N21* —5D 6
Macleod Rd. *SE2* —4B 84
McLeod's M. *SW7* —4K 75
Macleod St. *SE17*
—5C 78 (6D 156)
Maclise Rd. *W14* —3G 75
Macmillan Ct. *S Harr* —1E 38
McMillan Rd. *SE4* —3A 96
(off Arica Rd.)
McMillan St. *SE8* —6C 80
McNeil Rd. *SE5* —2E 94
McNicol Dri. *NW10* —2J 57
Macoma Rd. *SE18* —6H 83
Macoma Ter. *SE18* —6H 83
Maconochies Rd. *E14* —5D 80
Macquarie Way. *E14* —4D 80
McRae La. *Mitc* —7D 122
Macready Pl. *N7* —4J 45
Macroom Rd. *W9* —3H 59
Maddams St. *E3* —4D 64
Maddison Clo. *Tedd* —6K 103
Maddocks Clo. *Sidc* —5E 116
Maddox Way. *SE17*
—6B 78 (7B 156)
Madeira Av. *Brom* —7G 113
Madeira Gro. *Wfd G* —6F 21
Madeira Rd. *E11* —2F 49
Madeira Rd. *N13* —4G 17
Madeira Rd. *SW16* —5J 109
Madeira Rd. *Mitc* —4D 122
Madeley Rd. *W5* —6E 56
Madeline Gro. *Ilf* —5H 51
Madeline Rd. *SE20* —7G 111
Madge Gill Way. *E6* —1C 66
(off High St. N.)
Madinah Rd. *E8* —6G 47
Madison Cres. *Bexh* —7C 84
Madison Gdns. *Bexh* —7C 84
Madison Gdns. *Brom* —3H 127
Madras Pl. *N7* —6A 46
Madras Rd. *Ilf* —4F 51
Madrid Rd. *SW13* —1C 90
Madrigal La. *SE5* —7B 78
Madron St. *SE17*
—5E 78 (5H 157)
Maes Ho. *E17* —3D 32
Mafeking Av. *E6* —2C 66
Mafeking Av. *Bren* —6E 72
Mafeking Av. *Ilf* —7H 35
Mafeking Rd. *E16* —4H 65
Mafeking Rd. *N17* —2G 31
Mafeking Rd. *Enf* —3A 8
Magdala Av. *N19* —2G 45
Magdala Rd. *Iswth* —3A 88
Magdala Rd. *S Croy* —7D 134
Magdalene Clo. *SE15* —2H 95
Magdalene Gdns. *E6* —4E 66
Magdalen Pas. *E1*
—7F 63 (2K 151)
Magdalen Rd. *SW18* —1A 108
Magdalen St. *SE1*
—1E 78 (5G 151)
Magee St. *SE11* —6A 78 (7J 155)
Magellan Ct. *NW10* —7K 41
(off Stonebridge Pk.)
Magnaville Rd. *Bush* —1D 10

Magnet Rd. *Wemb* —2D 40
Magnin Clo. *E8* —1G 63
Magnolia Clo. *E10* —2C 48
Magnolia Clo. *King T* —6H 105
Magnolia Clo. *N'holt* —4J 54
Magnolia Ct. *Sutt* —7K 131
(off Grange Rd.)
Magnolia Ct. *Wall* —5F 133
Magnolia Gdns. *E10* —2D 48
(off Walnut Rd.)
Magnolia Ho. *SE8* —6B 80
Magnolia Lodge. *E4* —3J 19
Magnolia Pl. *SW4* —5J 93
Magnolia Pl. *W5* —5D 56
Magnolia Pl. *Harr* —7F 25
Magnolia Rd. *W4* —6H 73
Magpie All. *EC4* —6A 62 (1K 149)
Magpie Clo. *E7* —5H 49
Magpie Clo. *NW9* —2A 26
Magpie Clo. *Enf* —1B 8
Magpie Hall Clo. *Brom* —6C 128
Magpie Hall La. *Brom* —7C 128
Magpie Hall Rd. *Bush* —2D 10
Magri Wlk. *E1* —5J 63
Maguire Dri. *Rich* —4C 104
Maguire St. *SE1* —2F 79 (6K 151)
Mahatma Gandhi Ind. Est. *SE24*
—4B 94
Mahatma Ghandi Ho. *Wemb*
—7F 25
Mahlon Av. *Ruis* —5A 38
Mahogany Clo. *SE16* —1A 80
Mahon Clo. *Enf* —1A 8
Maida Av. *E4* —7J 9
Maida Av. *W2* —5A 60
Maida Rd. *Belv* —3G 85
Maida Vale. *W9* —2K 59
Maida Way. *E4* —7J 9
Maiden Erlegh Av. *Bex* —1E 116
Maiden La. *NW1* —7H 45
Maiden La. *SE1* —1C 78 (5D 150)
Maiden La. *WC2* —7J 61 (3F 149)
Maiden Pl. *NW5* —3F 45
Maiden Rd. *E15* —7G 49
Maidenstone Hill. *SE10* —1E 96
Maids of Honour Row. *Rich*
—5D 88
Maidstone Av. *Romf* —2J 37
Maidstone Bldgs. *SE1*
—1C 78 (5D 150)
Maidstone Rd. *N11* —6C 16
Maidstone Rd. *Sidc* —6D 116
Mail Coach Yd. *E2*
—3E 62 (1H 145)
Maidstone Rd. *N11* —6C 16
Main Av. *Enf* —5A 8
Main Dri. *Wemb* —3D 40
Mainridge Rd. *Chst* —4E 114
Main Rd. *Sidc* —3H 115
Main St. *Felt* —5B 102
Mais Ho. *SE26* —2H 111
Maismore St. *SE15* —6G 79
Maisonettes, The. *Sutt* —5H 131
Maitland Clo. *SE10* —7E 80
Maitland Clo. *Houn* —3D 86
Maitland Ct. *W2* —7B 60 (2A 146)
(off Lancaster Ter.)
Maitland Pk. Est. *NW3* —6D 44
Maitland Pk. Rd. *NW3* —6D 44
Maitland Pk. Vs. *NW3* —6D 44
Maitland Pl. *E5* —4H 47
Maitland Rd. *E15* —6H 49
Maitland Rd. *SE26* —6K 111
Maitland Yd. *W13* —1A 72
Majendie Rd. *SE18* —5H 83
Majestic Way. *Mitc* —2D 122

Major Rd. E15 —5F 49
Major Rd. SE16 —3G 79
Makepeace Av. N6 —2E 44
Makepeace Mans. N6 —2E 44
Makepeace Rd. N'holt —2C 54
Makepiece Rd. E11 —4J 33
Makins St. SW3
 —4C 76 (4D 152)
Malabar Ct. W12 —7D 58
 (off India Way)
Malabar St. E14 —2C 80
Malam Ct. SE11 —4A 78 (4J 155)
Malam Gdns. E14 —7D 64
Malbrook Rd. SW15 —4D 90
Malcolm Ct. E7 —6H 49
Malcolm Ct. NW4 —6C 26
Malcolm Cres. NW4 —6C 26
Malcolm Dri. Surb —7D 118
Malcolm Ho. N1 —2E 62
 (off Arden Est.)
Malcolm Pl. E2 —4J 63
Malcolm Rd. E1 —4J 63
Malcolm Rd. SE20 —7J 111
Malcolm Rd. SE25 —6G 125
Malcolm Rd. SW19 —6G 107
Malcolm Way. E11 —5J 33
Malden Av. SE25 —3H 125
Malden Av. Gnfd —5J 39
Malden Ct. N4 —6C 30
Malden Cres. NW1 —6E 44
Malden Grn. Av. Wor Pk —1B 130
Malden Hill. N Mald —3B 120
Malden Hill Gdns. N Mald
 —3B 120
Malden Junction. (Junct.)
 —6B 120
Malden La. NW1 —7H 45
Malden Pk. N Mald —6A 120
Malden Pl. NW5 —5E 44
Malden Rd. NW5 —5D 44
Malden Rd. N Mald & Wor Pk
 —5A 120
Malden Rd. Sutt —4F 131
Malden Way. N Mald —6A 120
Maldon Clo. E15 —5G 49
Maldon Clo. N1 —1C 62
Maldon Clo. SE5 —3E 94
Maldon Ct. E6 —1E 66
 (off Langdon Rd.)
Maldon Ct. Wall —5G 133
Maldon Rd. N9 —3A 18
Maldon Rd. W3 —7J 57
Maldon Rd. Romf —7J 37
Maldon Rd. Wall —5F 133
Maldon Wlk. Wfd G —6F 21
Malet Pl. WC1 —4H 61 (4C 142)
Malet St. WC1 —4H 61 (4C 142)
Maley Av. SE27 —2B 110
Malford Ct. E18 —2J 33
Malford Gro. E18 —4H 33
Malfort Rd. SE5 —3E 94
Malham Rd. SE23 —1K 111
Malham Ter. N18 —6C 18
 (off Dysons Rd.)
Malibu Ct. SE26 —3H 111
Mallams M. SW9 —3B 94
Mallard Clo. E9 —6B 48
Mallard Clo. NW6 —1J 59
Mallard Clo. W7 —2J 71
Mallard Clo. New Bar —6G 5
Mallard Clo. Twic —7E 86
Mallard Ct. E17 —3F 33

Mallard Path. SE28 —3H 83
 (off Goosander Way)
Mallard Pl. N22 —2K 29
Mallard Pl. Twic —3A 104
Mallards. E11 —7J 33
 (off Blake Hall Rd.)
Mallards Rd. Wfd G —7E 20
Mallard Wlk. Beck —5K 125
Mallard Wlk. Sidc —6C 116
Mallard Way. NW9 —7J 25
Mallard Way. Wall —7G 133
Mall Chambers. W8 —1J 75
 (off Kensington Mall)
Mallet Dri. N'holt —5D 38
Mallet Rd. SE13 —6F 97
Malling Clo. Croy —6J 125
Malling Gdns. Mord —6A 122
Malling Way. Brom —7H 127
Mallinson Rd. SW11 —5C 92
Mallinson Rd. Croy —3H 133
Mallord St. SW3
 —6B 76 (7B 152)
Mallory Clo. SE4 —4A 96
Mallory Gdns. E Barn —7K 5
Mallory St. NW8
 —4C 60 (3D 140)
Mallow Clo. Croy —1K 135
Mallow Mead. NW7 —7B 14
Mallow St. EC1 —4D 62 (3E 144)
Mall Rd. W6 —5D 74
Mall, The. E15 —7F 49
Mall, The. N14 —2D 16
Mall, The. SW1 —1H 77 (5D 148)
Mall, The. SW14 —5J 89
Mall, The. W5 —7E 56
Mall, The. Bexh —4G 101
Mall, The. Bren —6D 72
Mall, The. Brom —3J 127
Mall, The. Croy —2C 134
Mall, The. Dag —6G 53
Mall, The. Harr —6F 25
Mall, The. Surb —6D 118
Malmains Clo. Beck —4F 127
Malmains Way. Beck —4E 126
Malmesbury Rd. E3 —3B 64
Malmesbury Rd. E16 —5G 65
Malmesbury Rd. E18 —1H 33
Malmesbury Rd. Mord —7A 122
Malmesbury Ter. E16 —5H 65
Malmsey Ho. SE11
 —5K 77 (5H 155)
Malmsmead Ho. E9 —5A 48
 (off Homerton Rd.)
Malpas Dri. Pinn —5B 22
Malpas Rd. E8 —5H 47
Malpas Rd. SE4 —2B 96
Malpas Rd. Dag —6D 52
Malta Rd. E10 —1C 48
Malta St. EC1 —4B 62 (3B 144)
Maltby Clo. Orp —7K 129
Maltby Dri. Enf —1C 8
Maltby Rd. Chess —6G 131
Maltby St. SE1 —2F 79 (7J 151)
Malthouse Dri. W4 —6A 74
Malthouse Dri. Felt —5B 102
Malthouse Pas. SW13 —2B 90
 (off Maltings Clo.)
Malthus Path. SE28 —1C 84
Maltings. W4 —5G 73
Maltings Clo. SW13 —2B 90
Maltings Ct. E14 —7C 64
Maltings Lodge. W4 —6A 74
 (off Corney Reach Way)
Maltings M. Sidc —3A 116
Maltings Pl. SW6 —1K 91
Malting Way. Iswth —3K 87
Malton M. SE18 —6J 83

Malton M. W10 —6G 59
Malton Rd. W10 —6G 59
Malton St. SE18 —6J 83
Maltravers St. WC2
 —7K 61 (2H 149)
Malt St. SE1 —6G 79
Malva Clo. SW18 —5K 91
Malvern Av. E4 —7A 20
Malvern Av. Bexh —7E 84
Malvern Av. Harr —3C 38
Malvern Clo. SE20 —2G 125
Malvern Clo. W10 —5H 59
Malvern Clo. Mitc —3G 123
Malvern Ct. W12 —2C 74
 (off Hadyn Pk. Rd.)
Malvern Ct. Sutt —7J 131
Malvern Dri. Felt —5B 102
Malvern Dri. Ilf —4K 51
Malvern Dri. Wfd G —5F 21
Malvern Gdns. NW2 —2G 43
Malvern Gdns. Harr —4E 24
Malvern Ho. N16 —1F 47
Malvern M. NW6 —3J 59
Malvern Pl. NW6 —3H 59
Malvern Rd. E6 —1C 66
Malvern Rd. E8 —7G 47
Malvern Rd. E11 —2G 49
Malvern Rd. N8 —3A 30
Malvern Rd. N17 —3G 31
Malvern Rd. NW6 —3J 59
 (in two parts)
Malvern Rd. Hamp —7E 102
Malvern Rd. T Hth —4A 124
Malvern Ter. N1 —1A 62
Malvern Ter. N9 —1A 18
Malvern Way. W13 —5B 56
Malwood Rd. SW12 —6F 93
Malyons Rd. SE13 —6D 96
Malyons Ter. SE13 —5D 96
Managers St. E14 —1E 80
Manaton Clo. SE15 —3H 95
Manaton Cres. S'hall —6E 54
Manbey Gro. E15 —6G 49
Manbey Pk. Rd. E15 —6G 49
Manbey Rd. E15 —6G 49
Manbey St. E15 —6G 49
Manbre Rd. W6 —6E 74
Manbrough Av. E6 —3E 66
Manchester Dri. W10 —4G 59
Manchester Gro. E14 —5E 80
Manchester Ho. SE17
 —5C 78 (5D 156)
Manchester M. W1
 —5E 60 (6G 141)
Manchester Rd. E14 —5E 80
Manchester Rd. N15 —6D 30
Manchester Rd. T Hth —3C 124
Manchester Sq. W1
 —6E 60 (7G 141)
Manchester St. W1
 —5E 60 (6G 141)
Manchester Way. Dag —4H 53
Manchuria Rd. SW11 —6E 92
Manciple St. SE1
 —2D 78 (7E 150)
Mandalay Rd. SW4 —5G 93
Mandarin Ct. NW10 —6K 41
 (off Mitchellbrook Way)
Mandarin St. E14 —7C 64
Mandarin Way. Hayes —6B 54
Mandela Clo. NW10 —7J 41
Mandela Clo. W12 —7D 58
Mandela Ho. SE5 —2B 94
Mandela Rd. E16 —6J 65
Mandela St. NW1 —1G 61

Mandela St. SW9 —7A 78
Mandela Way. SE1
 —4E 78 (3G 157)
Mandeville Clo. SE3 —7H 81
Mandeville Clo. SW20 —1G 121
Mandeville Ct. E4 —4F 19
Mandeville Ho. SW4 —5G 93
Mandeville Pl. W1
 —6E 60 (7H 141)
Mandeville Rd. N14 —2A 16
Mandeville Rd. Iswth —2A 88
Mandeville Rd. N'holt —7E 38
Mandeville St. E5 —3A 48
Mandrake Rd. SW17 —2D 108
Mandrake Way. E15 —7G 49
Mandrell Rd. SW2 —5J 93
Manesty Ct. N14 —7C 6
 (off Ivy Rd.)
Manette St. W1 —6H 61 (1D 148)
Manfred Rd. SW15 —5H 91
Manger Rd. N7 —6J 45
Mangold Way. Eri —3D 84
Manilla St. E14 —2C 80
Manister Rd. SE2 —3A 84
Manley Ct. N16 —3F 47
Manley Ho. SE11
 —5A 78 (5J 155)
Manley St. NW1 —1E 60
Mann Clo. Croy —4C 124
Manningford Clo. EC1
 —3B 62 (1A 144)
Manning Gdns. Harr —7D 24
Manning Pl. Rich —6F 89
Manning Rd. E17 —5A 32
Manning Rd. Dag —6G 53
Manningtree Clo. SW19 —1G 107
Manningtree Rd. Ruis —4A 38
Manningtree St. E1
 —6G 63 (7K 145)
Mannin Rd. Romf —7B 36
Mannock Rd. N22 —3B 30
Mann's Clo. Iswth —5K 87
Manns Rd. Edgw —6B 12
Manny Shinwell Ho. SW6 —6H 75
 (off Clem Attlee Ct.)
Manoel Rd. Twic —3G 103
Manor Av. E7 —4A 50
Manor Av. SE4 —2B 96
Manor Av. Houn —3B 86
Manor Av. N'holt —7D 38
Manor Brook. SE3 —4J 97
Manor Circus. (Junct.) —3G 89
Manor Clo. E17 —2A 32
Manor Clo. NW7 —5E 12
Manor Clo. NW9 —5H 25
Manor Clo. SE28 —7C 68
Manor Clo. Barn —4B 4
Manor Clo. Cray —4K 101
Manor Clo. Dag —6K 53
Manor Clo. Wor Pk —1A 130
Manor Cotts. N2 —2A 28
Manor Cotts. App. N2 —2A 28
Manor Ct. E4 —1B 20
Manor Ct. E10 —1D 48
Manor Ct. N2 —5D 28
 (off Aylmer Rd.)
Manor Ct. N14 —2C 16
Manor Ct. N20 —3J 15
 (off York Way)
Manor Ct. SW2 —5K 93
Manor Ct. SW3 —3J 109
Manor Ct. W3 —4G 73
Manor Ct. Bark —7K 51
Manor Ct. Bexh —5H 101
Manor Ct. Harr —6K 23

Manor Ct. King T —1G 119
Manor Ct. Twic —2G 103
Manor Ct. Wemb —5E 40
Manor Ct. W Wick —1D 136
Manor Ct. Rd. W7 —7J 55
Manor Cres. Surb —6G 119
Manor Deerfield Cotts. NW9
 —5B 26
Manor Dene. SE28 —6C 68
Manordene Rd. SE28 —6D 68
Manor Dri. N14 —1A 16
Manor Dri. N20 —4H 15
Manor Dri. NW7 —5E 12
Manor Dri. Eps —6A 130
Manor Dri. Felt —5B 102
Manor Dri. Surb —6F 119
Manor Dri. Wemb —4F 41
Manor Dri. N. N Mald & Wor Pk
 —7K 119
Manor Dri., The. Wor Pk
 —1A 130
Manor Est. SE16 —4H 79
Manor Farm Clo. Wor Pk
 —1A 130
Manor Farm Ct. E6 —3D 66
 (off Holloway Rd.)
Manor Farm Dri. E4 —3B 20
Manor Farm Rd. SW16 —2A 124
Manor Farm Rd. Wemb —2D 56
Manorfield Clo. N19 —4G 45
 (off Fulbeck M.)
Manor Fields. SW15 —6F 91
Manorfields Clo. Chst —3K 129
Manor Gdns. N7 —3J 45
Manor Gdns. SW20 —2H 121
Manor Gdns. W3 —4G 73
Manor Gdns. W4 —5A 74
Manor Gdns. Hamp —7F 103
Manor Gdns. Rich —4F 89
Manor Gdns. Ruis —5A 38
Manor Gdns. S Croy —6F 135
Manor Ga. N'holt —7C 38
Manorgate Rd. King T —1G 119
Manor Gro. SE15 —6J 79
Manor Gro. Beck —2D 126
Manor Hall Av. NW4 —2F 27
Manor Hall Dri. NW4 —2F 27
Manorhall Gdns. E10 —1C 48
Manor House. (Junct.) —1C 46
Manor Ho. Dri. NW6 —7F 43
Manor Ho. Est. Stan —6G 11
Manor Ho. Way. Iswth —3B 88
Manor La. SE13 & SE12 —5G 97
Manor La. Sutt —5A 132
Manor La. Ter. SE13 —4G 97
Manor M. NW6 —2J 59
 (off Cambridge Av.)
Manor M. SE4 —2B 96
Manor Mt. SE23 —1J 111
Manor Pde. N16 —1F 47
Manor Pk. SE13 —4F 97
Manor Pk. Chst —2H 129
Manor Pk. Rich —4F 89
Manor Pk. Clo. W Wick —1D 136
Manor Pk. Cres. Edgw —6B 12
Manor Pk. Dri. Harr —3F 23
Manor Pk. Gdns. Edgw —5B 12
Manor Pk. Pde. SE13 —4F 97
 (off Lee High Rd.)
Manor Pk. Rd. E12 —4B 50
Manor Pk. Rd. N2 —3A 28
Manor Pk. Rd. NW10 —1B 58
Manor Pk. Rd. Chst —1G 129

Manor Pk. Rd. Sutt —5A 132
Manor Pk. Rd. W Wick —1D 136
Manor Pl. SE17 —5B 78 (6B 156)
Manor Pl. Chst —2H 129
Manor Pl. Mitc —3G 123
Manor Pl. Sutt —4K 131
Manor Rd. E10 —7C 32
Manor Rd. E15 & E16 —2G 65
Manor Rd. E17 —2A 32
Manor Rd. N16 —2D 46
Manor Rd. N17 —1G 31
Manor Rd. N22 —6D 16
Manor Rd. SE25 —4G 125
Manor Rd. SW20 —2H 121
Manor Rd. W13 —7A 56
Manor Rd. Bark —7K 51
Manor Rd. Barn —4B 4
Manor Rd. Beck —2D 126
Manor Rd. Bex —1H 117
Manor Rd. Chad H —6D 36
Manor Rd. Dag —6J 53
Manor Rd. Dart —4K 101
Manor Rd. Enf —2H 7
Manor Rd. Harr —6A 24
Manor Rd. Mitc —4G 123
Manor Rd. Rich —6K 89
Manor Rd. Sidc —3A 116
Manor Rd. Sutt —7H 131
Manor Rd. Tedd —5A 104
Manor Rd. Twic —2G 103
Manor Rd. Wall —4F 133
Manor Rd. W Wick —2D 136
Manor Rd. Wfd G & Chig —6J 21
Manor Rd. N. Harr —6A 24
Manor Rd. N. Wall —4F 133
Manorside. Barn —4B 4
Manorside Clo. SE2 —4C 84
Manor Sq. Dag —2C 52
Manor Vale. Bren —5C 72
Manor View. N3 —2K 27
Manor Way. E4 —4A 20
Manor Way. NW9 —4A 26
Manor Way. SE3 —4H 97
Manor Way. Beck —2C 126
Manor Way. Bex —1G 117
Manor Way. Bexh —3K 101
Manor Way. Brom —6C 128
Manorway. Enf —7K 7
Manor Way. Harr —4F 23
Manor Way. Mitc —3G 123
Manor Way. Orp —4G 129
Manor Way. Rain —4K 69
Manor Way. S'hall —4B 70
Manor Way. S Croy —6E 134
Manor Way. Wfd G —5F 21
Manor Way. Wor Pk —1A 130
Manor Way Bus. Cen. Rain
—5K 69
Manor Way, The. Wall —4F 133
Manpreet Ct. E12 —5D 50
Manresa Rd. SW3
—5C 76 (6C 152)
Mansard Beeches. SW17
—5E 108
Mansard Clo. Pinn —3B 22
Mansel Gro. E17 —1C 32
Mansell Rd. W3 —2K 73
Mansell Rd. Gnfd —5F 55
Mansell St. E1 —6F 63 (1K 151)
Mansel Rd. SW19 —6G 107
Mansergh Clo. SE18 —7C 82
Manse Rd. N16 —3F 47
Manse Rd. Rain —3K 69
Mansfield Av. N15 —4D 30
Mansfield Av. Barn —6J 5

Mansfield Clo. N9 —6B 8
Mansfield Heights. N2 —5D 28
Mansfield Hill. E4 —7J 9
Mansfield M. W1
—5F 61 (6J 141)
Mansfield Pl. NW3 —4A 44
Mansfield Rd. E11 —6K 33
Mansfield Rd. E17 —4B 32
Mansfield Rd. NW3 —5D 44
Mansfield Rd. W3 —4H 57
Mansfield Rd. Ilf —2E 50
Mansfield Rd. S Croy —6D 134
Mansfield St. W1
—5F 61 (6J 141)
Mansford St. E2 —2G 63
Manship Rd. Mitc —7E 108
Mansion Clo. SW9 —4A 84
Mansion Gdns. NW3 —3K 43
Mansion Ho. Pl. EC4
—6D 62 (1E 150)
Mansion Ho. St. EC2
—6D 62 (1E 150)
Mansions, The. SW5 —5K 75
Manson M. SW7
—4A 76 (4A 152)
Manson Pl. SW7
—4B 76 (4A 152)
Mansted Gdns. Romf —7C 36
Manston. N17 —2D 30
(off Adams Rd.)
Manston Av. S'hall —4E 70
Manston Clo. SE20 —1J 125
Manstone Rd. NW2 —5G 43
Manston Gro. King T —5D 104
Manthorp Rd. SE18 —5G 83
Mantilla Rd. SW17 —4E 108
Mantle Rd. SE4 —3A 96
Mantlet Clo. SW16 —7G 109
Manton Av. W7 —2K 71
Manton Rd. SE2 —4A 84
Mantua St. SW11 —3B 92
Mantus Clo. E1 —4J 63
Mantus Rd. E1 —4J 63
Manus Way. N20 —2F 15
Manville Gdns. SW17 —3F 109
Manville Rd. SW17 —2E 108
Manwood Rd. SE4 —5B 96
Manwood St. E16 —1D 82
Manygates. SW12 —2F 109
Mapesbury Rd. NW2 —7G 43
Mapeshill Pl. NW2 —6E 42
Mapes Ho. NW6 —7G 43
Mape St. E2 —4H 63
(in two parts)
Maple Av. E4 —5G 19
Maple Av. W3 —1A 74
Maple Av. Harr —2F 39
Maple Clo. N16 —6G 31
Maple Clo. SW4 —6H 93
Maple Clo. Buck H —3G 21
Maple Clo. Hamp —6D 102
Maple Clo. Hayes —3B 54
Maple Clo. Mitc —1F 123
Maple Clo. Orp —5H 129
Maple Ct. E6 —5E 66
Maple Ct. SE6 —1D 112
Maple Ct. N Mald —3K 119
Maple Cres. Sidc —6A 100
Maplecroft Clo. E6 —6B 66
Mapledale Av. Croy —2G 135
Mapledene. Chst —5G 115
Mapledene Est. E8 —7G 47
Mapledene Rd. E8 —7G 47
Maple Gdns. Edgw —7F 13

Maple Gro. NW9 —7J 25
Maple Gro. W5 —3D 72
Maple Gro. Bren —7B 72
Maple Gro. S'hall —5D 54
Maple Gro. Bus. Cen. Houn
—4A 86
Maple Ho. E17 —3D 32
Maple Ho. SE8 —7B 80
(off Idonia St.)
Maplehurst. Brom —2G 127
Maplehurst Clo. King T —4E 118
Maple Leaf Dri. Sidc —1K 115
Mapleleafe Gdns. Ilf —3F 35
Maple Leaf Sq. SE16 —2K 79
Maple M. NW6 —2K 59
Maple M. SW16 —5K 109
Maple Pl. W1 —4G 61 (5B 142)
Maple Rd. E11 —6G 33
Maple Rd. SE20 —1H 125
Maple Rd. Hayes —3A 54
Maple Rd. Surb —6D 118
Maples Pl. E1 —5H 63
Maplestead Rd. SW2 —7K 93
Maplestead Rd. Dag —1B 68
Maple St. W1 —5G 61 (5A 142)
Maple St. Romf —4J 37
Maplethorpe Rd. T Hth —4B 124
Mapleton Clo. Brom —6J 127
Mapleton Cres. SW18 —6K 91
Mapleton Cres. Enf —1D 8
Mapleton Rd. E4 —3K 19
Mapleton Rd. SW18 —6J 91
Mapleton Rd. Enf —2C 8
Maple Wlk. W10 —3F 59
Maplin Clo. N21 —6E 6
Maplin Ho. E16 —6J 65
(off Wolvercote Rd.)
Maplin Rd. E16 —6J 65
Maplin St. E3 —4B 64
Mapperley Clo. E11 —6H 33
Mapperley Dri. Wfd G —7B 20
Maran Way. Eri —3D 84
Marban Rd. W9 —3H 59
Marble Arch. W1
—7D 60 (2E 146)
Marble Arch. (Junct.) —7D 60
Marble Clo. W3 —1H 73
Marble Dri. NW2 —7E 26
Marble Hill Clo. Twic —7B 88
Marble Hill Gdns. Twic —7B 88
Marble Ho. W9 —4H 59
Marble Quay. E1
—1G 79 (4K 151)
Marbrook Ct. SE12 —3A 114
March. NW9 —1B 26
(off Concourse, The)
Marchant Rd. E11 —2F 49
Marchant St. SE14 —6A 80
Marchbank Rd. W14 —6H 75
Marchmont Rd. Rich —5F 89
Marchmont Rd. Wall —7G 133
Marchmont St. WC1
—4J 61 (3E 142)
March Rd. Twic —7A 88
Marchside Clo. Houn —1B 86
Marchwood Clo. SE5 —7E 78
Marchwood Cres. W5 —6C 56
Marcia Rd. SE1 —4E 78 (4H 157)
Marcilly Rd. SW18 —5B 92
Marcon Ct. E8 —5H 47
(off Amhurst Rd.)
Marconi Rd. E10 —1C 48
Marconi Way. S'hall —6F 55
Marcon Pl. E8 —5H 47
Marco Polo Ho. SW8 —7F 77

Marco Rd. W6 —3E 74
Marcourt Lawns. W5 —4E 56
Marcus Ct. E15 —1G 65
Marcus Garvey M. SE22 —5H 95
Marcus Garvey Way. SE24
—4A 94
Marcus St. E15 —1G 65
Marcus St. SW18 —6K 91
Marcus Ter. SW18 —6K 91
Mardale Dri. NW9 —5K 25
Mardell Rd. Croy —5K 125
Marden Av. Brom —6J 127
Marden Ct. SE8 —6C 80
Marden Cres. Bex —5J 101
Marden Cres. Croy —6K 123
Marden Ho. E8 —5H 47
Marden Rd. N17 —2E 30
Marden Rd. Croy —6K 123
Marden Sq. SE16 —3H 79
Marder Rd. W13 —2A 72
Marechal Niel Av. Sidc —3H 115
Marechal Niel Pde. Sidc —3H 115
(off Main Rd.)
Maresby Ho. E4 —2J 19
Mares Fields. Croy —2E 134
Maresfield Gdns. NW3 —5A 44
Mare St. E8 —1H 63
Marfleet Clo. Cars —2C 132
Margaret Av. E4 —6J 9
Margaret Bondfield Av. Bark
—7A 52
Margaret Bldgs. N16 —1F 47
Margaret Ct. W1
—6G 61 (7A 142)
Margaret Ct. Barn —4G 5
Margaret Gardner Dri. SE9
—2D 114
Margaret Herbison Ho. SW6
(off Clem Attlee Ct.) —6H 75
Margaret Ingram Clo. SW6
—7H 75
Margaret Rd. N16 —1F 47
Margaret Rd. Barn —4G 5
Margaret Rd. Bex —6D 100
Margaret St. W1 —6F 61 (7K 141)
Margaretta Ter. SW3
—6C 76 (7C 152)
Margaretting Rd. E12 —1A 50
Margaret Way. Ilf —6C 34
Margate Rd. SW2 —5J 93
Margery Fry Ct. N7 —3J 45
Margery Pk. Rd. E7 —6J 49
Margery Rd. Dag —3D 52
Margery St. WC1
—3A 62 (2J 143)
Margin Dri. SW19 —5F 107
Margravine Gdns. W6 —5F 75
Margravine Rd. W6 —5F 75
Marham Gdns. SW18 —1C 108
Marham Gdns. Mord —6A 122
Maria Clo. SE1 —4H 79
Marian Clo. Hayes —4B 54
Marian Ct. E9 —6J 47
Marian Ct. Sutt —5K 131
Marian Pl. E2 —2H 63
Marian Rd. SW16 —1G 123
Marian Sq. E2 —2H 63
Marian Way. NW10 —7B 42
Maria Ter. E1 —4A 64
Maria Theresa Clo. N Mald
—5K 119
Maricas Av. Harr —1H 23
Marie Lloyd Gdns. N19 —7J 29
Marie Lloyd Wlk. E8 —6F 47
Mariette Way. Wall —7J 133

Marigold All. SE1
—7B 62 (3A 150)
Marigold Clo. S'hall —7C 54
Marigold Rd. N17 —7D 18
Marigold St. SE16 —2H 79
Marigold Way. E4 —6G 19
Marigold Way. Croy —1K 135
Marina App. Hayes —5C 54
Marina Dri. Well —2J 99
Marina Gdns. Romf —6H 37
Marina Clo. Brom —3J 127
Marina Way. Tedd —7D 104
Marine Dri. SE18 —4D 82
Marine St. SE16 —3G 79
Marinefield Rd. SW6 —2K 91
Marinel Ho. SE5 —7C 78
Mariner Gdns. Rich —3C 104
Mariner Rd. E12 —4E 50
Mariners M. E14 —4F 81
Marine St. SE16 —3G 79
Marion Gro. Wfd G —5B 20
Marion Ho. NW7 —5H 13
Marion Rd. T Hth —5C 124
Marion Sq. E2 —2H 63
Marischal Rd. SE13 —3F 97
Maritime Ind. Est. SE7 —4K 81
Maritime St. E3 —4B 64
Marius Pas. SW17 —2E 108
Marius Rd. SW17 —2E 108
Marjorie Gro. SW11 —4D 92
Marjorie M. E1 —6K 63
Mark Av. E4 —6J 9
Mark Clo. Bexh —1E 100
Mark Clo. S'hall —7F 55
Marke Clo. Kes —4C 138
Market Cen., The. S'hall —4A 70
Market Ct. W1 —6G 61 (7A 142)
Market Entrance. SW8 —7G 77
Market Est. N7 —6J 45
Market Hill. SE18 —3E 82
Market La. Edgw —1J 25
Market Link. Romf —4K 37
Market Pde. E10 —6E 32
Market Pde. E17 —3B 32
Market Pde. Felt —3C 102
Market Pde. Sidc —4B 116
Market Pavilion. E10 —3C 48
Market Pl. N2 —3C 28
Market Pl. NW11 —4K 27
Market Pl. SE16 —4G 79
(in two parts)
Market Pl. W1 —6G 61 (7A 142)
Market Pl. W3 —1J 73
Market Pl. Bexh —4G 101
Market Pl. Bren —7C 72
Market Pl. Enf —3J 7
Market Pl. King T —2D 118
Market Pl. S'hall —1D 70
Market Rd. N7 —6J 45
Market Rd. Rich —3G 89
Market Row. SW9 —4A 94
Market Sq. E14 —6D 64
Market Sq. Brom —2J 127
Market Sq., The. N9 —2C 18
(off New Rd.)
Market St. E6 —2D 66
Market St. SE18 —4E 82
Market Ter. Bren —6E 72
(off Albany Rd.)
Market, The. Sutt —1A 132
Market Way. Wemb —5E 40
Markfield Gdns. E4 —7J 9
Markfield Rd. N15 —4G 31

Markham Ho. *Dag* —3G **53**
(off Uvedale Rd.)
Markham Pl. *SW3*
—5D **76** (5E **152**)
Markham Sq. *SW3*
—5D **76** (5E **152**)
Markham St. *SW3*
—5C **76** (5D **152**)
Markhole Clo. *Hamp* —7D **102**
Markhouse Av. *E17* —6A **32**
Markhouse Pas. *E17* —6B **32**
(off Markhouse Rd.)
Markhouse Rd. *E17* —6B **32**
Mark La. *EC3* —7E **62** (2H **151**)
Markmanor Av. *E17* —7A **32**
Mark Rd. *N22* —1B **30**
Marksbury Av. *Rich* —3G **89**
Marks Lodge. *Romf* —5K **37**
Mark Sq. *EC2* —4E **62** (3G **145**)
Marks Rd. *Romf* —5J **37**
Mark St. *E15* —7G **49**
Mark St. *EC2* —4E **62** (3G **145**)
Markwell Clo. *SE26* —4H **111**
Markyate Rd. *Dag* —5B **52**
Marlands Rd. *Ilf* —3C **34**
Marlborough Av. *E8* —1G **63**
(in two parts)
Marlborough Av. *N14* —3B **16**
Marlborough Av. *Edgw* —3C **12**
Marlborough Clo. *N20* —3J **15**
Marlborough Clo. *SE17*
—4C **78** (4B **156**)
Marlborough Clo. *SW19* —6C **108**
Marlborough Clo. *Orp* —6K **129**
Marlborough Ct. *W1*
—7G **61** (2A **148**)
Marlborough Ct. *W8* —4J **75**
(off Pembroke Rd.)
Marlborough Ct. *Buck H* —2F **21**
Marlborough Ct. *Enf* —5K **7**
Marlborough Ct. *Harr* —4H **23**
Marlborough Cres. *W4* —3K **73**
Marlborough Dri. *Ilf* —3C **34**
Marlborough Flats. *SW3*
—4C **76** (3D **152**)
Marlborough Gdns. *N20* —3J **15**
Marlborough Gdns. *Surb*
—7D **118**
Marlborough Ga. Stables. *W2*
—7B **60** (2A **146**)
Marlborough Gro. *SE1* —5G **79**
Marlborough Hill. *NW8* —1B **60**
Marlborough Hill. *Harr* —4H **23**
Marlborough La. *SE7* —7A **82**
Marlborough Mans. *NW6* —5J **43**
Marlborough Pk. Av. *Sidc*
—7A **100**
Marlborough Pl. *NW8* —2A **60**
Marlborough Rd. *E4* —6J **19**
Marlborough Rd. *E7* —7A **50**
Marlborough Rd. *E15* —4G **49**
Marlborough Rd. *E18* —2J **33**
Marlborough Rd. *N9* —1A **18**
Marlborough Rd. *N19* —2H **45**
Marlborough Rd. *N22* —7D **16**
Marlborough Rd. *SW1*
—1G **77** (5B **148**)
Marlborough Rd. *SW19* —6C **108**
Marlborough Rd. *W4* —5J **73**
Marlborough Rd. *W5* —2D **72**
Marlborough Rd. *Bexh* —3D **100**
Marlborough Rd. *Brom* —4A **128**
Marlborough Rd. *Dag* —4B **52**
Marlborough Rd. *Felt* —2B **102**
Marlborough Rd. *Hamp* —6E **102**

Marlborough Rd. *Iswth* —1B **88**
Marlborough Rd. *Rich* —6F **89**
Marlborough Rd. *Romf* —4G **37**
Marlborough Rd. *S'hall* —3A **70**
Marlborough Rd. *S Croy*
—7C **134**
Marlborough Rd. *Sutt* —3J **131**
Marlborough St. *SW3*
—4C **76** (4C **152**)
Marlborough Yd. *N19* —2H **45**
Marler Rd. *SE23* —1A **112**
Marley Av. *Bexh* —6D **84**
Marley Clo. *N15* —4B **30**
Marley Clo. *Gnfd* —3E **54**
Marley Wlk. *NW2* —5E **42**
Marlingdene Clo. *Hamp* —6E **102**
Marlings Clo. *Chst* —4J **129**
Marlings Pk. Av. *Chst* —4J **129**
Marlins Clo. *Sutt* —5A **132**
Marloes Clo. *Wemb* —4D **40**
Marloes Rd. *W8* —3K **75**
Marlow Clo. *SE20* —3H **125**
Marlow Ct. *N14* —7B **6**
Marlow Ct. *NW9* —3B **26**
Marlow Cres. *Twic* —6K **87**
Marlow Dri. *Sutt* —2F **131**
Marlowe Clo. *Chst* —6H **115**
Marlowe Clo. *Ilf* —1G **35**
Marlowe Gdns. *SE9* —6E **98**
Marlow Rd. *E17* —4E **32**
Marlowe Sq. *Mitc* —4G **123**
Marlowes, The. *NW8* —1B **60**
Marlowes, The. *Dart* —4K **101**
Marlowe Way. *Croy* —2J **133**
Marlow Rd. *E6* —3D **66**
Marlow Rd. *SE20* —3H **125**
Marlow Rd. *S'hall* —3D **70**
Marlow Way. *SE16* —2K **79**
Marl Rd. *SW18* —4A **92**
Marlton St. *SE10* —5H **81**
Marmadon Rd. *SE18* —4K **83**
Marmion App. *E4* —4H **19**
Marmion Av. *E4* —4G **19**
Marmion Clo. *E4* —4G **19**
Marmion M. *SW11* —3E **92**
Marmion Rd. *SW11* —4E **92**
Marmont Rd. *SE15* —1G **95**
Marmora Rd. *SE22* —6J **95**
Marmot Rd. *Houn* —3B **86**
Marne Av. *N11* —4A **16**
Marne Av. *Well* —3A **100**
Marne Ho. *SE15* —7G **79**
(off Sumner Est.)
Marnell Way. *Houn* —3B **86**
Marne St. *W10* —3G **59**
Marney Rd. *SW11* —4E **92**
Marnfield Cres. *SW2* —1K **109**
Marnham Av. *NW2* —4G **43**
Marnham Ct. *Wemb* —5C **40**
Marnham Cres. *Gnfd* —3F **55**
Marnock Rd. *SE4* —5B **96**
Maroon St. *E14* —5A **64**
Maroons Way. *SE6* —5C **112**
Marqueen Towers. *SW16*
—7J **109**
Marquess Rd. *N1* —6D **46**
Marquess Rd. N. *N1* —6D **46**
Marquess Rd. S. *N1* —6C **46**
Marquis Clo. *Wemb* —7F **41**
Marquis Ct. *N4* —7A **30**
(off Marquis Rd.)
Marquis Ct. *Bark* —5J **51**
Marquis Rd. *N4* —1K **45**
Marquis Rd. *N22* —6E **16**

Marquis Rd. *NW1* —6H **45**
Marrabon Clo. *Sidc* —1A **116**
Marrick Clo. *SW15* —4C **90**
Marriett Ho. *SE6* —4E **112**
Marrilyne Av. *Enf* —1G **9**
Marriott Rd. *E15* —1G **65**
Marriott Rd. *N4* —1K **45**
Marriott Rd. *N10* —1D **28**
Marriott Rd. *Barn* —3A **4**
Marriotts Clo. *NW9* —6B **26**
Marryat Pl. *SW19* —4G **107**
Marryat Rd. *SW19* —5F **107**
Marryat Sq. *SW6* —1G **91**
Marsala Rd. *SE13* —4D **96**
Marsden Rd. *N9* —2C **18**
Marsden Rd. *SE15* —3F **95**
Marsden St. *NW5* —6E **44**
Marshall Clo. *SW18* —6A **92**
Marshall Clo. *Harr* —7J **23**
Marshall Clo. *Houn* —5D **86**
Marshall Est. *NW7* —4H **13**
Marshall Ho. *N1* —2D **62**
(off Cranston Est.)
Marshall Ho. *SE1*
—3E **78** (2H **157**)
Marshall Ho. *Eri* —2D **84**
Marshall Path. *SE28* —7B **68**
Marshall Rd. *N17* —1D **30**
Marshalls Clo. *N11* —4A **16**
Marshalls Dri. *Romf* —3K **37**
Marshalls Gro. *SE18* —4C **82**
Marshall's Pl. *SE16*
—3F **79** (2K **157**)
Marshalls Rd. *Romf* —4K **37**
Marshall's Rd. *Sutt* —4K **131**
Marshall St. *W1* —6G **61** (1B **148**)
Marshalsea Rd. *SE1*
—2C **78** (6D **150**)
Marsham Clo. *Chst* —5F **115**
Marsham Ct. *SW1*
—4H **77** (3D **154**)
Marsham St. *SW1*
—3H **77** (2D **154**)
Marsh Av. *Mitc* —2D **122**
Marshbrook Clo. *SE3* —3B **98**
Marsh Clo. *NW7* —3G **13**
Marsh Ct. *E8* —7G **47**
Marsh Dri. *NW9* —6B **26**
Marsh Farm Rd. *Twic* —1K **103**
Marshfield St. *E14* —3E **80**
Marsh Ga. Bus. Cen. *E15* —2E **64**
Marshgate La. *E15* —7D **48**
Marshgate Path. *SE18* —3G **83**
Marshgate Trad. Est. *E15* —7D **48**
Marsh Grn. Rd. *Dag* —1G **69**
Marsh Hall. *Wemb* —3F **41**
Marsh Hill. *E9* —5A **48**
Marsh La. *E10* —2B **48**
Marsh La. *N17* —1H **31**
Marsh La. *NW7* —3F **13**
Marsh La. *Stan* —5H **11**
Marsh Rd. *Pinn* —4C **22**
Marsh Rd. *Wemb* —3D **56**
Marshside Clo. *N9* —1D **18**
Marsh St. *E14* —4D **80**
Marsh Wall. *E14* —1C **80**
Marsh Way. *Rain* —3K **69**
(in two parts)
Marsland Clo. *SE17*
—5B **78** (6B **156**)
Marston Av. *Dag* —2G **53**
Marston Clo. *NW6* —7A **44**
Marston Clo. *Dag* —3G **53**
Marston Ho. *SW9* —2A **94**
Marston Rd. *Ilf* —1C **34**

Marston Rd. *Tedd* —5B **104**
Marston Way. *SE19* —7B **110**
Marsworth Av. *Pinn* —1B **22**
Marsworth Clo. *Hayes* —5C **54**
Martaban Rd. *N16* —2F **47**
Martello St. *E8* —7H **47**
Martello Ter. *E8* —7H **47**
Martell Rd. *SE21* —3D **110**
Martel Pl. *E8* —6F **47**
Marten Rd. *E17* —2C **32**
Martens Av. *Bexh* —4H **101**
Martens Clo. *Bexh* —4H **101**
Martha Ct. *E2* —2H **63**
Martham Clo. *SE28* —7D **68**
Martha Rd. *E4* —6G **19**
Martha Rd. *E15* —6G **49**
Martha St. *E1* —6J **63**
Marthorne Cres. *Harr* —2H **23**
Martin Bowes Rd. *SE9* —3D **98**
Martinbridge Trad. Est. *Enf* —5B **8**
Martin Clo. *N9* —1E **18**
Martindale. *SW14* —5J **89**
Martindale Av. *E16* —7J **65**
Martindale Rd. *SW12* —7F **93**
Martindale Rd. *Houn* —3C **86**
Martin Dene. *Bexh* —5F **101**
Martin Dri. *N'holt* —5D **38**
Martineau Est. *E1* —6J **63**
Martineau M. *N5* —4B **46**
Martineau Rd. *N5* —4B **46**
Martingales Clo. *Rich* —3D **104**
Martin Gdns. *Dag* —4C **52**
Martin Gro. *Mord* —4J **121**
Martin Ho. *SE1* —3C **78** (2D **156**)
Martin Ho. *SW8* —7J **77**
(off Wyvil Rd.)
Martin La. *EC4* —7D **62** (2F **151**)
Martin Rise. *Bexh* —5F **101**
Martin Rd. *Dag* —4C **52**
Martins Clo. *W Wick* —2F **137**
Martins Mt. *New Bar* —4D **4**
Martin's Rd. *Brom* —2H **127**
Martins, The. *Wemb* —3F **41**
Martins Wlk. *N10* —1E **28**
Martin Way. *SW20 & Mord*
—3G **121**
Martlesham. *N17* —2E **30**
(off Adams Rd.)
Martlet Gro. *N'holt* —3B **54**
Martlett Ct. *WC2* —6J **61** (1F **149**)
Martley Dri. *Ilf* —5F **35**
Martock Clo. *Harr* —4A **24**
Marton Clo. *SE6* —3C **112**
Marton Rd. *N16* —2E **46**
Mart St. *WC2* —7J **61** (2F **149**)
Martynside. *NW9* —1B **26**
(off Concourse, The)
Martys Yd. *NW3* —4B **44**
Marvell Ho. *SE5* —7D **78**
(off Camberwell Rd.)
Marvels Clo. *SE12* —2K **113**
Marvels La. *SE12* —2K **113**
Marville Rd. *SW6* —7H **75**
Marvin St. *E8* —6H **47**
Marwell Clo. *W Wick* —2H **137**
Marwood Clo. *Well* —3B **100**
Mary Adelaide Clo. *SW15*
—4A **106**
Mary Ann Gdns. *SE8* —6C **80**
Maryatt Av. *Harr* —2F **39**
Mary Bank. *SE18* —4D **82**
Mary Clo. *Stan* —4F **25**
Mary Datchelor Clo. *SE5* —1D **94**

Maryfield Clo. *Bex* —3K **117**
Mary Grn. *NW8* —1K **59**
Maryland Ho. *E15* —6G **49**
(off Manbey Pk. Rd.)
Maryland Ind. Est. *E15* —5G **49**
(off Maryland Rd.)
Maryland Pk. *E15* —5G **49**
Maryland Rd. *E15* —5F **49**
Maryland Rd. *N22* —6E **16**
Maryland Rd. *T Hth* —1B **124**
Maryland Sq. *E15* —5G **49**
Marylands Rd. *W9* —4J **59**
Maryland St. *E15* —5F **49**
Maryland Wlk. *N1* —1C **62**
(off Popham St.)
Mary Lawrenson Pl. *SE3* —7J **81**
—5C **60** (6B **140**)
Marylebone Fly-Over. *W2 & NW8*
—5C **60**
Marylebone Fly-Over. (Junct.)
—5C **60**
Marylebone High St. *W1*
—5E **60** (5H **141**)
Marylebone La. *W1*
—5E **60** (6H **141**)
Marylebone M. *W1*
—5F **61** (6J **141**)
Marylebone Pas. *W1*
—6G **61** (7B **142**)
Marylebone Rd. *NW1*
—5C **60** (5D **140**)
Marylebone St. *W1*
—5E **60** (6H **141**)
Marylee Way. *SE11*
—4K **77** (4H **155**)
Mary Macarthur Ho. *W6* —6G **75**
Mary Macarthur Ho. *Dag* —3G **53**
(off Wythenshawe Rd.)
Maryon Gro. *SE7* —4C **82**
Maryon M. *NW3* —4C **44**
Maryon Rd. *SE7* —4C **82**
Maryon Rd. *SE18* —4C **82**
Mary Peters Dri. *Gnfd* —5H **39**
Mary Pl. *W11* —7G **59**
Mary Rose Clo. *Hamp* —7E **102**
Mary Rose Mall. *E6* —5D **66**
Mary Rose Way. *N20* —1G **15**
Mary Seacole Clo. *E8* —1F **63**
Mary's Ter. *Twic* —7A **88**
Mary St. *E16* —5H **65**
Mary St. *N1* —1C **62**
Mary Ter. *NW1* —1F **61**
Maryville. *Well* —2K **99**
Marzena Ct. *Houn* —6G **87**
Masbro Rd. *W14* —3F **75**
Mascalls Rd. *SE7* —6A **82**
Mascotte Rd. *SW15* —4F **91**
Mascotts Clo. *NW2* —3D **42**
Masefield Av. *S'hall* —7E **54**
Masefield Av. *Stan* —5E **10**
Masefield Ct. *New Bar* —4F **5**
Masefield Ct. *Surb* —7D **118**
Masefield Cres. *N14* —6B **6**
Masefield Gdns. *E6* —4E **66**
Masefield La. *Hayes* —4A **54**
Masefield Rd. *Hamp* —4D **102**
Mashie Rd. *W3* —6A **58**
Mashiters Hill. *Romf* —1K **37**
Maskall Clo. *SW2* —1A **110**
Maskani Wlk. *SW16* —7G **109**
Maskell Rd. *SW17* —3A **108**
Maskelyne Clo. *SW11* —1C **92**
Mason Clo. *E16* —7J **65**
Mason Clo. *SE16* —5G **79**
Mason Clo. *Bexh* —3H **101**
Mason Rd. *Wfd G* —4B **20**

Mason's Arms M. *W1*
　　—6F **61** (1K **147**)
Mason's Av. *EC2*
　　—6D **62** (7E **144**)
Masons Av. *Croy* —3D **134**
Masons Av. *Harr* —4K **23**
Masons Grn. La. *W5* —4G **57**
　(in two parts)
Masons Hill. *SE18* —4F **83**
Masons Hill. *Brom* —3J **127**
Mason's Pl. *EC1*
　　—3C **62** (1C **144**)
Masons Pl. *Mitc* —1D **122**
Mason St. *SE17* —4D **78** (3F **157**)
Masons Yd. *SW1*
　　—1G **77** (4B **148**)
Mason's Yd. *SW19* —5F **107**
Massey Clo. *N11* —5A **16**
Massey Ct. E6 —1A **66**
　(off Florence Rd.)
Massie Rd. *E8* —6G **47**
Massinger St. *SE17*
　　—4E **78** (4G **157**)
Massingham St. *E1* —4K **63**
Masson Av. *Ruis* —6A **38**
Master Gunners Pl. *SE18* —7C **82**
Masterman Rd. *E6* —3C **66**
Masters Dri. *SE16* —5H **79**
Master's St. *E1* —5K **63**
Masthouse Ter. *E14* —4C **80**
Mastmaker Ct. *E14* —2C **80**
Mastmaker Rd. *E14* —2C **80**
Maswell Pk. Cres. *Houn* —5G **87**
Maswell Pk. Rd. *Houn* —5F **87**
Matcham Rd. *E11* —3G **49**
Matchless Dri. *SE18* —7E **82**
Matfield Clo. *Brom* —5J **127**
Matfield Rd. *Belv* —6G **85**
Matham Gro. *SE22* —4F **95**
Matheson Long Ho. *SE1*
　　—2A **78** (7J **149**)
Matheson Rd. *W14* —4H **75**
Mathews Pk. Av. *E15* —6H **49**
Mathews Yd. *WC2*
　　—6J **61** (1E **148**)
Matilda Clo. *SE19* —7D **110**
Matilda St. *N1* —1K **61**
Matlock Clo. *Barn* —5A **4**
Matlock Ct. *SE5* —4C **94**
Matlock Cres. *Sutt* —4G **131**
Matlock Gdns. *Sutt* —4G **131**
Matlock Pl. *Sutt* —4G **131**
Matlock Rd. *E10* —6E **32**
Matlock St. *E14* —6A **64**
Matlock Way. *N Mald* —1H **119**
Matrimony Pl. *SW4* —2G **93**
Matson Ct. *E4* —7B **20**
Matthew Clo. *W10* —4F **59**
Matthew Ct. *E17* —3E **32**
Matthew Ct. *Mitc* —5H **123**
Matthew Parker St. *SW1*
　　—2H **77** (7D **148**)
Matthews Av. *E6* —2E **66**
Matthews Rd. *Gnfd* —5H **39**
Matthews St. *SW11* —2D **92**
Matthews Wlk. E17 —1C **32**
　(off Chingford Rd.)
Matthias Rd. *N16* —5E **46**
Mattingley Way. SE15 —7F **79**
　(off Longhope Clo.)
Mattison Rd. *N4* —6A **30**
Mattock La. *W13 & W5* —1B **72**
Maud Cashmore Way. *SE18*
　　—3D **82**
Maude Rd. *E17* —5A **32**

Maude Rd. *SE5* —1E **94**
Maude Ter. *E17* —5A **32**
Maud Gdns. *E13* —1H **65**
Maud Gdns. *Bark* —2K **67**
Maudlins Grn. *E1*
　　—1G **79** (4K **151**)
Maud Rd. *E10* —3E **48**
Maud Rd. *E13* —2H **65**
Maudslay Rd. *SE9* —3D **98**
Maudsley Ho. *Bren* —5E **72**
Maud St. *E16* —5H **65**
Maudsville Cotts. *W7* —1J **71**
Maugham Ct. W3 —3J **73**
　(off Palmerston Rd.)
Mauleverer Rd. *SW2* —5J **93**
Maundeby Wlk. *NW10* —6A **42**
Maunder Rd. *W7* —1K **71**
Maunsel St. *SW1*
　　—4H **77** (3C **154**)
Maureen Ct. *Beck* —2J **125**
Mauretania Building. E1 —7K **63**
　(off Jardine Rd.)
Maurice Av. *N22* —2B **30**
Maurice Brown Clo. *NW7* —5A **14**
Maurice Ct. *Bren* —7D **72**
Maurice St. *W12* —6D **58**
Maurice Wlk. *NW11* —4A **28**
Mauritius Rd. *SE10* —4G **81**
Maury Rd. *N16* —2G **47**
Mavelstone Clo. *Brom* —1C **128**
Mavelstone Rd. *Brom* —1B **128**
Maverton Rd. *E3* —1C **64**
Mavis Av. *Eps* —5A **130**
Mavis Clo. *Eps* —5A **130**
Mavis Wlk. E6 —5C **66**
　(off Greenwich Cres.)
Mawbey Ho. *SE1*
　　—5F **79** (6K **157**)
Mawbey Pl. *SE1* —5F **79** (6K **157**)
Mawbey Rd. *SE1*
　　—5F **79** (6K **157**)
Mawbey St. *SW8* —7J **77**
Mawney Clo. *Romf* —2H **37**
Mawney Rd. *Romf* —2H **37**
Mawson Clo. *SW20* —2G **121**
Mawson La. *W4* —6B **74**
Maxden Ct. *SE15* —3G **95**
Maxey Gdns. *Dag* —4E **52**
Maxey Rd. *SE18* —4G **83**
Maxey Rd. *Dag* —4E **52**
Maxfield Clo. *N20* —7F **5**
Maxilla Wlk. *W10* —6F **59**
Maximfeldt Rd. *Eri* —5K **85**
Maxim Rd. *N21* —6F **7**
Maxim Rd. *Eri* —4K **85**
Maxted Pk. *Harr* —7J **23**
Maxted Rd. *SE15* —3F **95**
Maxwell Clo. *Croy* —1J **133**
Maxwell Ct. *SW4* —5H **93**
Maxwell Rd. *SW6* —7K **75**
Maxwell Rd. *Well* —3K **99**
Maxwelton Av. *NW7* —5E **12**
Maxwelton Clo. *NW7* —5E **12**
Maya Angelou Ct. *E4* —4K **19**
Mayall Rd. *SE24* —4B **94**
Maya Rd. *N2* —4A **28**
Maybank Av. *E18* —2K **33**
Maybank Av. *Wemb* —5K **39**
Maybank Rd. *E18* —1K **33**
Maybells Commercial Est. *Bark*
　　—2D **68**
Mayberry Ct. *Beck* —7B **112**
Mayberry Pl. *Surb* —7F **119**
Maybourne Clo. *SE26* —6H **111**

Maybury Clo. *Orp* —5F **129**
Maybury Ct. *Harr* —6A **23**
Maybury Gdns. *NW10* —6D **42**
Maybury M. *N6* —7G **29**
Maybury Rd. *E13* —4A **66**
Maybury Rd. *Bark* —2K **67**
Maybury St. *SW17* —5C **108**
Maychurch Clo. *Stan* —7J **11**
Maycross Av. *Mord* —4H **121**
Mayday Gdns. *SE3* —2C **98**
Mayday Rd. *T Hth* —6B **124**
Mayerne Rd. *SE9* —5B **98**
Mayesbrook Rd. *Bark* —1K **67**
Mayesbrook Rd. *Ilf & Dag*
　　—3A **52**
Mayesford Rd. *Romf* —7C **36**
Mayes Rd. *N22* —2K **29**
Mayeswood Rd. *SE12* —4A **114**
Mayfair Av. *Bexh* —1D **100**
Mayfair Av. *Ilf* —2D **50**
Mayfair Av. *Romf* —6D **36**
Mayfair Av. *Twic* —7G **87**
Mayfair Av. *Wor Pk* —1C **130**
Mayfair Clo. *Beck* —1D **126**
Mayfair Clo. *Surb* —7E **118**
Mayfair Gdns. *N17* —6H **17**
Mayfair Gdns. *Wfd G* —7D **20**
Mayfair M. NW1 —7D **44**
　(off Regents Pk. Rd.)
Mayfair Pl. *W1* —1H **77** (4K **147**)
Mayfair Ter. *N14* —7C **6**
Mayfield. *Bexh* —3F **101**
Mayfield Av. *N12* —4F **15**
Mayfield Av. *N14* —2C **16**
Mayfield Av. *W4* —4A **74**
Mayfield Av. *W13* —3B **72**
Mayfield Av. *Harr* —5B **24**
Mayfield Av. *Orp* —7K **129**
Mayfield Av. *Wfd G* —6D **20**
Mayfield Clo. *E8* —6F **47**
Mayfield Clo. *SE20* —1H **125**
Mayfield Clo. *SW4* —5H **93**
Mayfield Cres. *N9* —6C **8**
Mayfield Cres. *T Hth* —4K **123**
Mayfield Dri. *Pinn* —4D **22**
Mayfield Gdns. *NW4* —6F **27**
Mayfield Gdns. *W7* —6H **55**
Mayfield Rd. *E4* —2K **19**
Mayfield Rd. *E8* —7F **47**
Mayfield Rd. *E13* —4H **65**
Mayfield Rd. *E17* —2A **32**
Mayfield Rd. *N8* —5K **29**
Mayfield Rd. *SW19* —1H **121**
Mayfield Rd. *W3* —7H **57**
Mayfield Rd. *W12* —2A **74**
Mayfield Rd. *Belv* —4J **85**
Mayfield Rd. *Brom* —5C **128**
Mayfield Rd. *Dag* —1C **52**
Mayfield Rd. *Enf* —2E **8**
Mayfield Rd. *S Croy* —7D **134**
Mayfield Rd. *Sutt* —6B **132**
Mayfield Rd. *T Hth* —4K **123**
Mayfield Rd. Flats. *N8* —6K **29**
Mayfields. *Wemb* —2G **41**
Mayfields Clo. *Wemb* —2G **41**
Mayflower Clo. *SE16* —4K **79**
Mayflower Ct. *SE16* —2H **79**
Mayflower Ho. Bark —1H **67**
　(off Westbury Rd.)
Mayflower Rd. *SW9* —3J **93**
Mayflower St. *SE16* —2J **79**
Mayfly Clo. *Eastc* —7A **22**
Mayfly Gdns. *N'holt* —3B **54**
Mayford Clo. *SW12* —7D **92**
Mayford Clo. *Beck* —3K **125**

Mayford Rd. *SW12* —7D **92**
May Gdns. *Wemb* —3G **56**
Maygood St. *N1* —2A **62**
Maygrove Rd. *NW6* —6H **43**
Mayhew Clo. *E4* —3H **19**
Mayhew Ct. *SE5* —4D **94**
Mayhill Rd. *SE7* —6K **81**
Mayhill Rd. *Barn* —6B **4**
Maylands Dri. *Sidc* —3D **116**
Maylands Dri. *Sidc* —3D **116**
Maynard Clo. *N15* —5E **30**
Maynard Clo. *SW6* —7K **75**
Maynard Path. *E17* —5E **32**
Maynard Rd. *E17* —5E **32**
Maynards Quay. *E1* —7J **63**
Maynooth Gdns. *Cars* —7D **122**
Mayo Ct. *W13* —3B **72**
Mayo Rd. *NW10* —6A **42**
Mayo Rd. *Croy* —5D **124**
Mayow Rd. *SE26 & SE23*
　　—4K **111**
Mayplace Clo. *Bexh* —3H **101**
Mayplace La. *SE18* —7F **83**
Mayplace Rd. E. *Bexh & Dart*
　　—3H **101**
Mayplace Rd. W. *Bexh* —4G **101**
May Rd. *E4* —6H **19**
May Rd. *E13* —2J **65**
May Rd. *Twic* —1J **103**
May's Bldgs. M. *SE10* —7F **81**
May's Ct. *SE10* —7F **81**
Mays Ct. *WC2* —7J **61** (3E **148**)
Mays Hill Rd. *Brom* —2G **127**
Mays La. *Barn* —1J **13**
　(in two parts)
Maysoule Rd. *SW11* —4B **92**
Mays Rd. *Tedd* —5H **103**
May St. *W14* —5H **75**
Mayswood Gdns. *Dag* —6J **53**
Mayton St. *N7* —3K **45**
Maytree Clo. *Edgw* —3D **12**
Maytree Ct. *N'holt* —3C **54**
Maytree Gdns. *W5* —2D **72**
May Tree Ho. SE4 —3B **96**
　(off Wickham Rd.)
Maytree La. *Stan* —7F **11**
Maytree Wlk. *SW2* —2A **110**
Mayville Est. *N16* —5E **46**
Mayville Rd. *E11* —2G **49**
Mayville Rd. *Ilf* —5F **51**
May Wlk. *E13* —2K **65**
Mayward Ho. SE5 —1E **94**
　(off Peckham Rd.)
Maywood Clo. *Beck* —7D **112**
Maze Hill. *SE10 & SE3* —6G **81**
Mazenod Av. *NW6* —7J **43**
Maze Rd. *Rich* —7G **73**
Mead Clo. *Harr* —1H **23**
Mead Ct. *NW9* —5J **25**
Mead Cres. *E4* —4K **19**
Mead Cres. *Sutt* —3C **132**
Meadcroft Rd. *SE11*
　　—6B **78** (7A **156**)
Meade Clo. *W4* —6G **73**
Meader Ct. *SE14* —7K **79**
Meadfield. *Edgw* —2C **12**
Mead Field. *Harr* —3F **38**
Meadfield Grn. *Edgw* —2C **12**
Meadfoot Rd. *SW16* —7G **109**
Meadgate Av. *Wfd G* —5H **21**
Mead Gro. *Romf* —3D **36**

Meadlands Dri. *Rich* —2D **104**
Mead Lodge. *W4* —2K **73**
Meadow Av. *Croy* —6K **125**
Meadow Bank. *N21* —6E **6**
Meadowbank. *NW3* —7D **44**
Meadow Bank. *SE3* —3H **97**
Meadowbank. *Surb* —6F **119**
Meadowbank Clo. *SW6* —7E **74**
Meadowbank Rd. *NW9* —7K **25**
Meadow Clo. *E4* —1J **19**
Meadow Clo. *E9* —5B **48**
Meadow Clo. *SE6* —5C **112**
Meadow Clo. *SW20* —4E **120**
Meadow Clo. *Barn* —6C **4**
Meadow Clo. *Bexh* —5F **101**
Meadow Clo. *Chst* —5F **115**
Meadow Clo. *Enf* —1F **9**
Meadow Clo. *Houn* —7E **86**
Meadow Clo. *N'holt* —2E **54**
Meadow Clo. *Rich* —1E **104**
Meadow Clo. *Sutt* —2A **132**
Meadow Ct. N1 —2E **62**
　(off Ivy St.)
Meadow Cft. *Houn* —6H **87**
Meadowcourt Rd. *SE3* —4H **97**
Meadowcroft. W4 —5G **73**
　(off Brooks Rd.)
Meadowcroft. *Brom* —3D **128**
Meadowcroft Clo. *N13* —2F **17**
Meadowcroft Rd. *N13* —2F **17**
Meadow Dri. *N10* —3F **29**
Meadow Dri. *NW4* —2C **26**
Meadow Garth. *NW10* —6J **41**
Meadow Hill. *N Mald* —6A **120**
Meadow M. *SW8* —6K **77**
Meadow Pl. *SW8* —7J **77**
Meadow Pl. *W4* —7A **74**
Meadow Rd. *SW8* —7K **77**
Meadow Rd. *SW19* —1A **122**
Meadow Rd. *Bark* —7K **51**
Meadow Rd. *Brom* —1G **127**
Meadow Rd. *Dag* —6F **53**
Meadow Rd. *Felt* —2C **102**
Meadow Rd. *Pinn* —4B **22**
Meadow Rd. *Romf* —1J **53**
Meadow Rd. *S'hall* —7D **54**
Meadow Rd. *Sutt* —4C **132**
Meadow Row. *SE1*
　　—3C **78** (2C **156**)
Meadows Clo. *E10* —2C **48**
Meadows Ct. *Sidc* —6B **116**
Meadowside. *SE9* —4A **98**
Meadowside. *Twic* —7D **88**
Meadow Stile. *Croy* —3C **134**
Meadowsweet Clo. *E16* —5B **66**
Meadow, The. *N10* —3F **29**
Meadow, The. *Chst* —6G **115**
Meadow View. *Harr* —1J **39**
Meadow View. *Sidc* —7B **100**
Meadowview Rd. *SE6* —5B **112**
Meadowview Rd. *Bex* —6E **100**
Meadowview Rd. *Eps* —7A **130**
Meadow View Rd. *T Hth* —5B **124**
Meadow Wlk. *E18* —4J **33**
Meadow Wlk. *Dag* —6F **53**
Meadow Wlk. *Eps* —6A **130**
　(Ewell)
Meadow Wlk. *Eps* —6A **130**
　(West Ewell)
Meadow Wlk. *Wall* —3F **133**
Meadow Way. *NW9* —5K **25**
Meadow Way. *Orp* —3E **138**
Meadow Way. *Ruis* —6A **22**
Meadow Way. *Wemb* —4D **40**

Meadow Waye. *Houn* —6C **70**
Meadow Way, The. *Harr* —1J **23**
Mead Path. *SW17* —4A **108**
Mead Pl. *E9* —6J **47**
Mead Pl. *Croy* —1C **134**
Mead Plat. *NW10* —6J **41**
Mead Rd. *Chst* —6G **115**
Mead Rd. *Edgw* —6B **12**
Mead Rd. *Rich* —3C **104**
Mead Row. *SE1* —3A **78** (1J **155**)
Meads Ct. *E15* —6H **49**
Meadside Clo. *Beck* —1A **126**
Meads La. *Ilf* —7J **35**
Meads Rd. *N22* —2B **30**
Meads Rd. *Enf* —1F **9**
Meads, The. *Edgw* —6E **12**
Meads, The. *Mord* —5C **122**
Mead Ter. *Wemb* —4D **40**
Mead, The. *N2* —2A **28**
Mead, The. *W13* —5B **56**
Mead, The. *Beck* —1E **126**
Mead, The. *Wall* —6H **133**
Meadvale Rd. *W5* —4B **56**
Meadvale Rd. *Croy* —7F **125**
Meadway. *N14* —2C **16**
Meadway. *NW11* —6J **27**
Meadway. *Barn* —4D **4**
Meadway. *Beck* —1E **126**
Mead Way. *Brom* —6H **127**
Mead Way. *Croy* —2A **136**
Meadway. *Ilf* —4J **51**
Meadway. *Twic* —1H **103**
Mead Way. *Wfd G* —5F **21**
Meadway Clo. *NW11* —6K **27**
Meadway Clo. *Barn* —4D **4**
Meadway Clo. *Pinn* —6A **10**
Meadway Ct. *NW11* —6K **27**
Meadway Ct. *W5* —4F **57**
Meadway Ct. *Dag* —2F **53**
Meadway Ct. *Tedd* —5C **104**
Meadway Ga. *NW11* —6J **27**
Meadway, The. *SE3* —2F **97**
Meadway, The. *Buck H* —1G **21**
Meaford Way. *SE20* —7H **111**
Meakin Est. *SE1*
  —3E **78** (1G **157**)
Meanley Rd. *E12* —4C **50**
Meard St. *W1* —6H **61** (1C **148**)
Meath Rd. *E15* —2H **65**
Meath Rd. *Ilf* —3G **51**
Meath St. *SW11* —1F **93**
Mechanics Path. *SE8* —7C **80**
Mecklenburgh Pl. *WC1*
  —4K **61** (3G **143**)
Mecklenburgh Sq. *WC1*
  —4K **61** (3G **143**)
Mecklenburgh St. *WC1*
  —4K **61** (3G **143**)
Medburn St. *NW1* —2H **61**
Medcroft Gdns. *SW14* —4J **89**
Medebourne Clo. *SE3* —3J **97**
Mede Ho. *Brom* —5K **113**
Medesenge Way. *N13* —6G **17**
Medfield St. *SW15* —7C **90**
Medhurst Clo. *E3* —2A **64**
Median Rd. *E5* —5J **47**
Medina Gro. *N7* —3A **46**
Medina Rd. *N7* —3A **46**
Medland Clo. *Wall* —1E **132**
Medlar Clo. *N'holt* —2B **54**
Medlar Ho. *Sidc* —3A **116**
Medlar St. *SE5* —1C **94**

Medley Rd. *NW6* —6J **43**
Medora Rd. *SW2* —7K **93**
Medora Rd. *Romf* —4K **37**
Medusa Rd. *SE6* —6D **96**
Medway Clo. *Croy* —6J **125**
Medway Clo. *Ilf* —5G **51**
Medway Dri. *Gnfd* —2K **55**
Medway Gdns. *Wemb* —4A **40**
Medway M. *E3* —2A **64**
Medway Pde. *Gnfd* —2K **55**
Medway Rd. *E3* —2A **64**
Medway St. *SW1*
  —3H **77** (2D **154**)
Medwin St. *SW4* —4K **93**
Meek Clo. *E8* —1H **63**
Meek Rd. *SW10* —7A **76**
  (off Tadema Rd.)
Meerbrook Rd. *SE3* —3A **98**
Meeson Rd. *E15* —1H **65**
Meeson St. *E5* —4A **48**
Meeting Field Path. *E9* —6J **47**
Meetinghouse All. *E1* —1H **79**
Meeting Ho. La. *SE15* —1H **95**
Mehetabel Rd. *E9* —6J **47**
Meister Clo. *Ilf* —1H **51**
Melancholy Wlk. *Rich* —2C **104**
Melanda Clo. *Chst* —5D **114**
Melanie Clo. *Bexh* —1E **100**
Melba Way. *SE13* —1D **96**
Melbourne Av. *N13* —6E **16**
Melbourne Av. *W13* —1A **72**
Melbourne Av. *Pinn* —3F **23**
Melbourne Clo. *SE20* —7G **111**
Melbourne Clo. *Orp* —7J **129**
Melbourne Clo. *Wall* —5G **133**
Melbourne Ct. *N10* —7A **16**
Melbourne Gdns. *Romf* —5E **36**
Melbourne Gro. *SE22* —4E **94**
Melbourne Ho. *Hayes* —4A **54**
Melbourne M. *SE6* —7E **96**
Melbourne M. *SW9* —1A **94**
Melbourne Pl. *WC2*
  —6K **61** (1H **149**)
Melbourne Rd. *E6* —2D **66**
Melbourne Rd. *E10* —7D **32**
Melbourne Rd. *E17* —4A **32**
Melbourne Rd. *SW19* —1J **121**
Melbourne Rd. *Ilf* —1F **51**
Melbourne Rd. *Tedd* —6C **104**
Melbourne Rd. *Wall* —5F **133**
Melbourne Way. *Enf* —6A **8**
Melbury Av. *S'hall* —3F **71**
Melbury Clo. *Chst* —6D **114**
Melbury Ct. *W8* —3H **75**
Melbury Dri. *SE5* —7E **78**
Melbury Gdns. *SW20* —1C **120**
Melbury Ho. *SW8* —7K **77**
  (off Richborne Ter.)
Melbury Rd. *W14* —3H **75**
Melbury Rd. *Harr* —5F **25**
Melbury Ter. *NW1*
  —4C **60** (4D **140**)
Melchester Ho. *N19* —3H **45**
  (off Wedmore St.)
Melcombe Gdns. *Harr* —6F **25**
Melcombe Ho. *SW8* —7K **77**
  (off Dorset Rd.)
Melcombe Pl. *NW1*
  —5D **60** (5E **140**)
Melcombe St. *NW1*
  —4D **60** (4F **141**)
Meldon Clo. *SW6* —1K **91**
Meldone Clo. *Surb* —6H **119**
Meldrum Rd. *Ilf* —2A **52**

Melfield Gdns. *SE6* —4E **112**
Melford Av. *Bark* —6J **51**
Melford Ct. *SE1* —3F **79** (1J **157**)
Melford Ct. *SE22* —1G **111**
Melford Pas. *SE22* —7G **95**
Melford Rd. *E6* —3D **66**
Melford Rd. *E11* —2G **49**
Melford Rd. *E17* —4A **32**
Melford Rd. *SE22* —7G **95**
Melford Rd. *Ilf* —2H **51**
Melfort Av. *T Hth* —3B **124**
Melfort Rd. *T Hth* —3B **124**
Melgund Rd. *N5* —5A **46**
Melina Clo. *SW15* —3C **90**
Melina Pl. *NW8* —3B **60** (2A **140**)
Melina Rd. *W12* —2D **74**
Melior Ct. *N6* —6G **29**
Melior Pl. *SE1* —2E **78** (6G **151**)
Melior St. *SE1* —2E **78** (6G **151**)
Meliot Rd. *SE6* —2F **113**
Meller Clo. *Croy* —3J **133**
Melling Dri. *Enf* —1B **8**
Melling St. *SE18* —6J **83**
Mellish Clo. *Bark* —1K **67**
Mellish Flats. *E10* —7C **32**
Mellish Gdns. *Wfd G* —5D **20**
Mellish Ind. Est. *SE18* —3B **82**
Mellish St. *E14* —3C **80**
Mellison Rd. *SW17* —5C **108**
Mellitus St. *W12* —5B **58**
Mellows Rd. *Ilf* —3D **34**
Mellows Rd. *Wall* —5H **133**
Mells Cres. *SE9* —4D **114**
Mell St. *SE10* —5G **81**
Melody La. *N5* —5B **46**
Melody Rd. *SW18* —5A **92**
Melon Pl. *W8* —2J **75**
Melon Rd. *E11* —3G **49**
Melon Rd. *SE15* —1G **95**
Melrose Av. *N22* —1B **30**
Melrose Av. *NW2* —5D **42**
Melrose Av. *SW16* —3A **124**
Melrose Av. *SW19* —2H **107**
Melrose Av. *Gnfd* —2F **55**
Melrose Av. *Mitc* —7F **109**
Melrose Av. *Twic* —7F **87**
Melrose Clo. *SE12* —1J **113**
Melrose Clo. *Gnfd* —2F **55**
Melrose Clo. *Hayes* —5A **54**
Melrose Dri. *S'hall* —1E **70**
Melrose Gdns. *W6* —3E **74**
Melrose Gdns. *Edgw* —3H **25**
Melrose Gdns. *N Mald* —3K **119**
Melrose Rd. *SW13* —2B **90**
Melrose Rd. *SW18* —6H **91**
Melrose Rd. *SW19* —1J **121**
Melrose Rd. *W3* —3J **73**
Melrose Rd. *Pinn* —4D **22**
Melrose Ter. *W6* —3E **74**
Melrose Tudor. *Wall* —5J **133**
  (off Plough La.)
Melsa Rd. *Mord* —6A **122**
Melthorne Dri. *Ruis* —3A **38**
Melthorpe Gdns. *SE3* —1C **98**
Melton Clo. *Ruis* —1A **38**
Melton Ct. *SW7* —4B **76** (4B **152**)
Melton Ct. *Sutt* —7A **132**
Melton Pl. *Eps* —7A **130**
Melton St. *NW1* —3G **61** (2B **142**)
Melville Av. *SW20* —7C **106**
Melville Av. *Gnfd* —5K **39**
Melville Av. *S Croy* —5F **135**
Melville Ct. *SE8* —4A **80**
Melville Ct. *W12* —2D **74**
  (off Goldhawk Rd.)
Melville Gdns. *N13* —5G **17**

Melville Ho. *SE10* —1E **96**
Melville Ho. *New Bar* —5G **5**
Melville Pl. *N1* —7C **46**
Melville Rd. *E17* —3B **32**
Melville Rd. *NW10* —7K **41**
Melville Rd. *SW13* —1C **90**
Melville Rd. *Romf* —1H **37**
Melville Rd. *Sidc* —2C **116**
Melvin Rd. *SE20* —1J **125**
Melyn Clo. *N7* —4G **45**
Memel Ct. *EC1* —4C **62** (4C **144**)
Memel St. *EC1* —4C **62** (4C **144**)
Memess Path. *SE18* —6E **82**
Memorial Av. *E15* —3G **65**
Memorial Clo. *Houn* —6D **70**
Mendip Clo. *SE26* —4J **111**
Mendip Clo. *SW19* —2G **107**
Mendip Clo. *Wor Pk* —2E **130**
Mendip Ct. *SW11* —3A **92**
Mendip Dri. *NW2* —2G **43**
Mendip Houses. *E2* —3J **63**
  (off Welwyn St.)
Mendip Rd. *SW11* —3A **92**
Mendip Rd. *Bexh* —1K **101**
Mendip Rd. *Ilf* —5J **35**
Mendora Rd. *SW6* —7G **75**
Menelik Rd. *NW2* —4G **43**
Menlo Gdns. *SE19* —7D **110**
Menlo Lodge. *N13* —3E **16**
  (off Crothall Clo.)
Menotti St. *E2* —4G **63**
Mentmore Clo. *Harr* —6C **24**
Mentmore Ter. *E8* —7H **47**
Meon Ct. *Iswth* —2J **87**
Meon Rd. *W3* —2J **73**
Meopham Rd. *Mitc* —1G **123**
Mepham Cres. *Harr* —7B **10**
Mepham Gdns. *Harr* —7B **10**
Mepham St. *SE1*
  —1A **78** (5H **149**)
Mera Dri. *Bexh* —4G **101**
Merantun Way. *SW19* —1K **121**
Merbury Clo. *SE13* —5F **97**
Merbury Rd. *SE28* —2J **83**
Mercator Rd. *SE13* —4F **97**
Mercer Clo. *Th Dit* —7A **118**
Merceron Houses. *E2* —3J **63**
  (off Globe Rd.)
Merceron St. *E1* —4H **63**
Mercer Pl. *Pinn* —2A **22**
Mercers Clo. *SE10* —4H **81**
Mercers Pl. *W6* —4E **74**
Mercers Rd. *N19* —3H **45**
Mercer St. *WC2* —6J **61** (1E **148**)
Merchant Ind. Est. *NW10* —4J **57**
Merchant Rd. *E1* —3B **64**
Merchants Lodge. *E17* —4C **32**
  (off Westbury Rd.)
Merchant St. *E3* —3B **64**
Merchiston Rd. *SE6* —2F **113**
Merchland Rd. *SE9* —1G **115**
Mercia Gro. *SE13* —4E **96**
Mercia Ho. *SE5* —2C **94**
Mercier Rd. *SW15* —5G **91**
Mercury. *NW9* —1B **26**
  (off Concourse, The)
Mercury Ho. *Bren* —6C **72**
Mercury Ho. *Bren* —6C **72**
  (off Glenhurst Rd.)
Mercury Way. *SE14* —6K **79**
Mercy Ter. *SE13* —5D **96**
Merebank La. *Croy* —5K **133**
Mere Clo. *SW15* —7F **91**
Meredith Av. *NW2* —5E **42**
Meredith Clo. *Pinn* —1B **22**
Meredith Ho. *N16* —5E **46**

Meredith M. *SE4* —4B **96**
Meredith St. *E13* —3J **65**
Meredith St. *EC1*
  —3B **62** (2A **144**)
Meredyth Rd. *SW13* —2C **90**
Mere End. *Croy* —7K **125**
Meretone Clo. *SE4* —4A **96**
Merevale Cres. *Mord* —6A **122**
Mereway Rd. *Twic* —1H **103**
Merewood Clo. *Brom* —2E **128**
Merewood Rd. *Bexh* —2J **101**
Mereworth Clo. *Brom* —5H **127**
Mereworth Dri. *SE18* —7F **83**
Mereworth Ho. *SE15* —6J **79**
Merganser Ct. *SE8* —6B **80**
  (off Edward St.)
Merganser Gdns. *SE28* —3H **83**
Meriden Clo. *Brom* —7B **114**
Meriden Clo. *Ilf* —1G **35**
Meriden Ct. *SW3*
  —5C **76** (6C **152**)
Meridian Ga. *E14* —2E **80**
Meridian Rd. *SE7* —7B **82**
Meridian Trad. Est. *SE7* —4K **81**
Meridian Wlk. *N17* —6K **17**
Meridian Way. *N18, N9 & Enf*
  —5D **18**
Merifield Rd. *SE9* —4A **98**
Merino Clo. *E11* —4A **34**
Merino Pl. *Sidc* —6A **100**
Merioneth Ct. *W7* —5K **55**
  (off Copley Clo.)
Merivale Rd. *SW15* —4G **91**
Merivale Rd. *Harr* —7G **23**
Merlewood Dri. *Chst* —1D **128**
Merlewood Pl. *SE9* —6D **98**
Merley Ct. *NW9* —1J **41**
Merlin. *NW9* —1B **26**
  (off Concourse, The)
Merlin Clo. *Croy* —4E **134**
Merlin Clo. *Mitc* —3C **122**
Merlin Clo. *N'holt* —3A **54**
Merlin Ct. *SE8* —6B **80**
Merlin Ct. *Short* —3H **127**
Merlin Cres. *Edgw* —1F **25**
Merlin Gdns. *Brom* —3J **113**
Merlin Gro. *Beck* —4B **126**
Merlin Rd. *E12* —2B **50**
Merlin Rd. *Well* —4A **100**
Merlin Rd. N. *Well* —4A **100**
Merlins Av. *Harr* —3D **38**
Merlin St. *WC1* —3A **62** (2J **143**)
Mermaid Ct. *SE1*
  —2D **78** (6E **150**)
Mermaid Ct. *SE16* —1B **80**
Mermaid Tower. *SE8* —6B **80**
  (off Abinger Gro.)
Meroe Ct. *N16* —2E **46**
Merredene St. *SW2* —6K **93**
Merriam Clo. *E4* —5K **19**
Merrick Ho. *S'hall* —3D **70**
Merrick Sq. *SE1*
  —3D **78** (1E **156**)
Merridene. *N21* —6G **7**
Merrielands Cres. *Dag* —2F **69**
Merrilands Rd. *Wor Pk* —1E **130**
Merrilees Rd. *Sidc* —7J **99**
Merriman Rd. *SE3* —1A **98**
Merrington Rd. *SW6* —6J **75**
Merrion Av. *Stan* —5J **11**
Merritt Rd. *SE4* —5B **96**
Merritt's Bldgs. *EC2*
  —4E **62** (4G **145**)
Merrivale. *N14* —6C **6**

Merrivale Av. Ilf —4B **34**
Merrow Rd. Sutt —7F **131**
Merrow St. SE17
　　　　　—6B **112**
Merrow Wlk. SE17
　　　—5D **78** (6E **156**)
Merrow Way. New Ad —6E **136**
Merrydown Way. Chst —1C **128**
Merryfield. SE3 —2H **97**
Merryfield Gdns. Stan —5H **11**
Merryfield Ho. SE9 —3A **114**
　(off Grove Pk. Rd.)
Merryfields Way. SE6 —7D **96**
Merryhill Clo. E4 —7J **9**
Merry Hill Mt. Bush —1A **10**
Merry Hill Rd. Bush —1A **10**
Merryhills Ct. N14 —5B **6**
Merryhills Dri. Enf —4C **6**
Merryweather Ct. N19 —3G **45**
Mersey Rd. E17 —3B **32**
Mersey Wlk. N'holt —2E **54**
Mersham Dri. NW9 —5G **25**
Mersham Pl. SE20 —1H **125**
Mersham Rd. T Hth —3D **124**
Merten Rd. Romf —7E **36**
Merthyr Ter. SW13 —6D **74**
Merton Av. W4 —4B **74**
Merton Av. N'holt —5G **53**
Merton Ct. Ilf —6C **34**
Merton Ct. Well —2B **100**
Merton Gdns. Orp —5F **129**
Merton Hall Gdns. SW20
　　　　　—1G **121**
Merton Hall Rd. SW19 —7G **107**
Merton High St. SW19 —7K **107**
Merton Ind. Pk. SW19 —1K **121**
Merton La. N6 —2D **44**
Merton Lodge. New Bar —5F **5**
Merton Mans. SW20 —2F **121**
Merton Pk. Ind. Est. SW19
　　　　　—1K **121**
Merton Pl. SW19 —1A **122**
　(off Nelson Gro. Rd.)
Merton Rise. NW3 —7C **44**
Merton Rd. E17 —5E **32**
Merton Rd. SE25 —5G **125**
Merton Rd. SW18 —6J **91**
Merton Rd. SW19 —7K **107**
Merton Rd. Bark —7K **51**
Merton Rd. Enf —1J **7**
Merton Rd. Harr —1G **39**
Merton Rd. Ilf —7K **35**
Merttins Rd. SE15 & SE4 —5K **95**
Meru Clo. NW5 —4E **44**
Mervan Rd. SW2 —4A **94**
Mervyn Av. SE9 —3G **115**
Mervyn Rd. W13 —3A **72**
Messaline Av. W3 —6J **57**
Messent Rd. SE9 —5A **98**
Messeter Pl. SE9 —6E **98**
Messina Av. NW6 —7J **43**
Messiter Ho. N1 —1K **61**
　(off Barnsbury Est.)
Metcalf Wlk. Felt —4C **102**
Meteor St. SW11 —4E **92**
Meteor Way. Wall —7J **133**
Metheringham Way. NW9
　　　　　—1A **26**
Methley St. SE11
　　　—5A **78** (6K **155**)
Methuen Clo. Edgw —7B **12**
Methuen Pk. N10 —3F **29**
Methuen Rd. Belv —4H **85**
Methuen Rd. Bexh —4F **101**
Methuen Rd. Edgw —7B **12**

Methwold Rd. W10 —5F **59**
Metro Bus. Cen., The. Beck
　　　　　—6B **112**
Metro Bus. Pk. Wemb —4H **41**
Metro Ind. Cen. Iswth —2J **87**
Metropolis. SE11
　　　　　—4B **78** (3B **156**)
Mews Pl. Wfd G —4D **20**
Mews St. E1 —1G **79** (4K **151**)
Mews, The. N1 —1C **62**
Mews, The. Ilf —5B **34**
Mews, The. Romf —4K **37**
Mews, The. Sidc —4A **116**
Mews, The. Twic —6B **88**
Mexfield Rd. SW15 —5H **91**
Meyer Grn. Enf —1B **8**
Meyer Rd. Eri —6K **85**
Meymott St. SE1
　　　　　—1B **78** (5A **150**)
Meynell Cres. E9 —7K **47**
Meynell Gdns. E9 —7K **47**
Meynell Rd. E9 —7K **47**
Meyrick Rd. NW10 —6C **42**
Meyrick Rd. SW11 —3B **92**
Miah Ter. E1 —1G **79**
Miall Wlk. SE26 —4A **112**
Micawber Ho. SE16 —2G **79**
　(off Llewellyn St.)
Micawber St. N1
　　　—3C **62** (1D **144**)
Michael Cliffe Ho. EC1
　　　—3A **62** (2K **143**)
Michael Gaynor Clo. W7 —1K **71**
Michael Manley Ind. Est. SW8
　　　　　—2H **93**
Michaelmas Clo. SW20 —3E **120**
Michael Rd. E11 —1G **49**
Michael Rd. SE25 —3E **124**
Michael Rd. SW6 —1K **91**
Michael's Clo. SE13 —4G **97**
Michael's Row. Rich —4E **88**
Michael Stewart Ho. SW6
　(off Clem Attlee Ct.) —6H **75**
Micheldever Rd. SE12 —6H **97**
Michelham Gdns. Twic —3K **103**
Michelle Ct. N12 —5F **15**
Michelle Ct. W3 —7K **57**
Michelson Ho. SE11
　　　—4K **77** (4H **155**)
Michel's Row. Rich —4E **88**
Michigan Av. E12 —4D **50**
Michigan Ho. E14 —4C **80**
Michleham Down. N12 —4C **14**
Mickleham Clo. Orp —2K **129**
Mickleham Gdns. Sutt —6G **131**
Mickleham Rd. Orp —1K **129**
Mickleham Way. New Ad
　　　　　—7F **137**
Micklethwaite Rd. SW6 —6J **75**
Midas Metropolitan Ind. Est. Mord
　　　　　—7E **120**
Middle Dene. NW7 —3E **12**
Middlefield. NW8 —1B **60**
Middlefielde. W13 —5B **56**
Middlefield Gdns. Ilf —6F **35**
Middlefields. Croy —7A **136**
Middle Grn. Clo. Surb —6F **119**
Middleham Gdns. N18 —6B **18**
Middleham Rd. N18 —6B **18**
Middle La. N8 —5J **29**
Middle La. Tedd —6K **103**
Middle La. M. N8 —5J **29**
Middle Pk. Av. SE9 —6B **98**
Middle Path. Harr —1H **39**
Middle Rd. E13 —2J **65**

Middle Rd. SW16 —2H **123**
Middle Rd. E Barn —6H **5**
Middle Rd. Harr —2H **39**
Middle Row. W10 —4G **59**
Middlesborough Rd. N18
　　　　　—6B **18**
Middlesex Bus. Cen. S'hall
　　　　　—2D **70**
Middlesex Ct. W4 —5B **74**
Middlesex Ct. Harr —5K **23**
Middlesex Pas. EC1
　　　　　—5B **62** (6B **144**)
Middlesex Rd. Mitc —5J **123**
Middlesex St. E1
　　　　　—5E **62** (6H **145**)
Middlesex Wharf. E5 —2J **47**
Middle St. EC1 —5C **62** (5C **144**)
Middle St. Croy —3C **134**
　(in two parts)
Middle Temple La. EC4
　　　　　—6A **62** (1J **149**)
Middleton Av. E4 —4G **19**
Middleton Av. Gnfd —2H **55**
Middleton Av. Sidc —6B **116**
Middleton Bldgs. W1
　　　　　—5G **61** (6A **142**)
Middleton Clo. E4 —3G **19**
Middleton Dri. SE16 —2K **79**
Middleton Gdns. Ilf —6F **35**
Middleton Gro. N7 —5J **45**
Middleton M. N7 —5J **45**
Middleton Rd. E8 —7F **47**
Middleton Rd. NW11 —7J **27**
Middleton Rd. Mord & Cars
　　　　　—6K **121**
Middleton Rd. N Mald —2J **119**
Middleton St. E2 —3H **63**
Middleton Way. SE13 —4F **97**
Middleway. NW11 —5K **27**
Middle Way. SW16 —2H **123**
Middle Way. Eri —3D **84**
Middle Way. Hayes —4A **54**
Middle Way, The. Harr —2K **23**
Middle Yd. SE1 —1E **78** (4G **151**)
Midfield Av. Bexh —3J **101**
Midfield Pl. Bexh —3J **101**
Midfield Way. Orp —7B **116**
Midford Ho. NW4 —4F **27**
　(off Belle Vue Est.)
Midford Pl. W1 —4G **61** (4B **142**)
Midholm. Wemb —1G **41**
Midholm. NW11 —4H **27**
Midholm Clo. NW11 —4K **27**
Midholm Rd. Croy —2A **136**
Midhope St. WC1
　　　　　—3J **61** (2F **143**)
Midhurst. SE26 —6J **111**
Midhurst Av. N10 —3E **28**
Midhurst Av. Croy —7A **124**
Midhurst Hill. Bexh —6G **101**
Midhurst Pde. N10 —3E **28**
　(off Fortis Grn.)
Midhurst Rd. W13 —2A **72**
Midland Cres. NW3 —6A **44**
Midland Pde. NW6 —6K **43**
Midland Pl. E14 —5E **80**
Midland Rd. E10 —7E **32**
Midland Rd. NW1
　　　　　—2H **61** (1D **142**)
Midland Ter. NW2 —3F **43**
Midland Ter. NW10 —4A **58**
Midlothian Rd. E3 —5B **64**
Midmoor Rd. SW12 —1G **109**
Midmoor Rd. SW19 —1G **121**
Midship Clo. SE16 —1K **79**

Midship Point. E14 —2C **80**
　(off Quarterdeck, The)
Midstrath Rd. NW10 —4A **42**
Midsummer Av. Houn —4D **86**
Midway. Sutt —7H **121**
Midway Ho. EC1 —3B **62** (1B **144**)
Midwinter Clo. Well —3A **100**
Midwood Clo. NW2 —3D **42**
Miers Clo. E6 —1E **66**
Mighell Av. Ilf —5B **34**
Milan Rd. S'hall —2D **70**
Milborne Gro. SW10 —5A **76**
Milborne St. E9 —6J **47**
Milborough Cres. SE12 —6G **97**
Milcote St. SE1 —2B **78** (7A **150**)
Mildenhall Rd. E5 —4J **47**
Mildmay Av. N1 —6D **46**
Mildmay Gro. N. N1 —5D **46**
Mildmay Gro. S. N1 —5D **46**
Mildmay Pk. N1 —5D **46**
Mildmay Pl. N16 —5E **46**
Mildmay Rd. N1 —5D **46**
Mildmay Rd. Ilf —3F **51**
Mildmay Rd. Romf —5J **37**
Mildmay St. N1 —6D **46**
Mildred Av. N'holt —5F **39**
Mildred Av. Eri —5K **85**
Mildura Ct. N8 —4K **29**
Mile End Pl. E1 —4K **63**
Mile End Rd. E1 & E3 —5J **63**
Mile End, The. E17 —1K **31**
Mile Rd. Wall —1F **133**
Miles Lodge. Harr —5H **23**
Milespit Hill. NW7 —5J **13**
Miles Pl. NW8 —5C **60** (5B **140**)
Miles Pl. Surb —4F **119**
Miles Rd. N8 —3J **29**
Miles Rd. Mitc —3C **122**
Miles St. SW8 —6J **77** (7E **154**)
Milestone Clo. N9 —2B **18**
Milestone Clo. Sutt —7B **132**
Milestone Green. (Junct.) —4J **89**
Milestone Rd. SE19 —6F **111**
Miles Way. N20 —2H **15**
Milfoil St. W12 —7C **58**
Milford Clo. SE2 —6E **84**
Milford Gdns. Croy —5K **125**
Milford Gdns. Edgw —7B **12**
Milford Gdns. Wemb —4D **40**
Milford Gro. Sutt —4A **132**
Milford La. WC2 —7A **62** (2J **149**)
Milford M. SW16 —3K **109**
Milford Rd. W13 —1B **72**
Milford Rd. S'hall —7E **54**
Milford Towers. SE6 —7D **96**
Milk St. E16 —1F **83**
Milk St. EC2 —6C **62** (1D **150**)
Milk St. Brom —6K **113**
Milkwell Gdns. Wfd G —7E **20**
Milkwell Yd. SE5 —1C **94**
Milkwood Rd. SE24 —5B **94**
Milk Yd. E1 —7J **63**
Millais Av. E12 —5E **50**
Millais Ct. N'holt —2B **54**
　(off Academy Gdns.)
Millais Gdns. Edgw —2G **25**
Millais Rd. E11 —4E **48**
Millais Rd. Enf —5A **8**
Millais Rd. N Mald —7A **120**
Millard Clo. N16 —5E **46**
Millard Ter. Dag —6G **53**
Millbank. SW1 —3J **77** (2E **154**)
Millbank Tower. SW1
　　　　　—4J **77** (4E **154**)

Millbank Way. SE12 —5J **97**
Millbourne Rd. Felt —4C **102**
Mill Bri. Barn —6C **4**
Millbrook Av. Well —4H **99**
Millbrook Gdns. Chad H —6F **37**
Millbrook Pas. SW9 —3B **94**
Millbrook Pl. NW1 —2G **61**
　(off Hampstead Rd.)
Millbrook Rd. N9 —1C **18**
Millbrook Rd. SW9 —3B **94**
Mill Clo. Cars —2E **132**
Mill Corner. Barn —1C **4**
Mill Ct. E10 —3E **48**
Millcroft Ho. SE6 —4D **112**
　(off Melfield Gdns.)
Millender Wlk. SE16 —4J **79**
Millenium Sq. SE1
　　　　　—2F **79** (6K **151**)
Millennium Pl. E2 —2H **63**
Miller Clo. Mitc —7D **122**
Miller Clo. Pinn —2A **22**
Miller Ct. Bexh —3H **101**
Miller Rd. SW19 —6B **108**
Miller Rd. Croy —1K **133**
Miller's Av. E8 —5F **47**
Millers Clo. NW7 —4H **13**
Miller's Ct. W4 —5B **74**
Millcroft Ho. SW8 —2E **56**
　(off Vicars Bri. Clo.)
Millers Grn. Clo. Enf —3G **7**
Millers Meadow Clo. SE12
　　　　　—5H **97**
Miller's Ter. E8 —5F **47**
Miller St. NW1 —2G **61**
Millers Way. W6 —2E **74**
Miller Wlk. SE1 —1A **78** (5K **149**)
Millet Rd. Gnfd —3F **55**
Mill Farm Bus. Pk. Houn —1C **102**
Mill Farm Clo. Pinn —2A **22**
Mill Farm Cres. Houn —1C **102**
Millfield. N4 —2A **46**
Millfield Av. E17 —1A **32**
Millfield La. N6 —1C **44**
Millfield Pl. N6 —2E **44**
Millfield Rd. Edgw —2J **25**
Millfield Rd. Houn —1C **102**
Millfields Rd. E5 —4J **47**
Mill Gdns. SE26 —3H **111**
Mill Grn. Mitc —7E **122**
Mill Grn. Rd. Mitc —7E **122**
Mill Grn. Bus. Pk. Mitc —7E **122**
Mill Grn. Rd. Mitc —7E **122**
Millgrove St. SW11 —1E **92**
Millharbour. E14 —2D **80**
Millhaven Clo. Romf —6B **36**
Mill Hill. SW13 —2C **90**
Mill Hill Circus. (Junct.) —5G **13**
Mill Hill Gro. W3 —1H **73**
Mill Hill Ind. Est. NW7 —6G **13**
Mill Hill Rd. SW13 —2C **90**
Mill Hill Rd. W3 —2H **73**
Mill Hill Ter. W3 —1H **73**
Mill Ho. Wfd G. W3 —2G **73**
Mill Ho. Wfd G —5C **8**
Millhouse Pl. SE27 —4B **110**
Millicent Fawcett Ct. N17 —1F **31**
Millicent Rd. E10 —1B **48**
Milligan St. E14 —7B **64**
Milling Rd. Edgw —7E **12**
Millington Ho. N16 —3D **46**
Mill La. E4 —3J **9**
Mill La. NW6 —5H **43**
Mill La. SE18 —5E **82**
Mill La. Cars —4D **132**
Mill La. Croy —3K **133**
Mill La. Eps —7B **130**

Mill La. *Romf* —6E 36
Mill La. *Wfd G* —5C 20
Millman M. *WC1*
   —4K 61 (4G 143)
Millman St. *WC1*
   —4K 61 (4G 143)
Millmark Gro. *SE14* —2A 96
Millmarsh La. *Enf* —2F 9
Millmead Ind. Cen. *N17* —3H 31
Mill Mead Rd. *N17* —3H 31
Mill Pl. *E14* —6A 64
Mill Pl. *Chst* —1F 129
Mill Pl. *King T* —3F 119
Mill Plat. *Iswth* —2A 88
(in two parts)
Mill Plat Av. *Iswth* —2A 88
Millpond Est. *SE16* —2H 79
Mill Ridge. *Edgw* —5A 12
Mill River Trad. Est. *Enf* —4F 9
Mill Rd. *E16* —1K 81
Mill Rd. *SE13* —3E 96
Mill Rd. *SW19* —7A 108
Mill Rd. *Eri* —7J 85
Mill Rd. *Ilf* —3E 50
Mill Rd. *Twic* —2G 103
Mill Row. *N1* —1E 62
Mill Row. *Bex* —7H 101
Mills Ct. *EC2* —4E 62 (3G 145)
Mills Gro. *E14* —6E 64
Mills Gro. *NW4* —3F 27
Mill Shot Clo. *SW6* —1E 90
Mills Ho. *E17* —3F 33
Millside. *Cars* —2D 132
Millside Pl. *Iswth* —2B 88
Millson Clo. *N20* —2G 15
Mills Row. *W4* —4K 73
Millstream Clo. *N13* —5F 17
Millstream Rd. *SE1*
   —2F 79 (7J 151)
Mill St. *SE1* —2F 79 (7K 151)
Mill St. *W1* —7F 61 (2A 148)
Mill St. *King T* —3E 118
Mill Trad. Est., The. *NW10*
   —3J 57
Mill Vale. *Brom* —2H 127
Mill View Clo. *Ewe* —7B 130
Mill View Gdns. *Croy* —3K 135
Millwall Dock Rd. *E14* —3C 80
Millway. *NW7* —4F 13
Mill Way. *Felt* —5A 86
Millway Gdns. *N'holt* —6D 38
Millwood Rd. *Houn* —5G 87
Millwood St. *W10* —5G 59
Mill Yd. *E1* —7G 63
Milman Clo. *Pinn* —3B 22
Milman Rd. *NW6* —2F 59
Milman's St. *SW10* —6B 76
Milne Gdns. *SE9* —5C 98
Milne Ho. *SE18* —4D 82
(off Ogilby St.)
Milner Dri. *Twic* —7H 87
Milner Pl. *N1* —1A 62
Milner Pl. *Cars* —4E 132
Milner Rd. *E15* —3G 65
Milner Rd. *SW19* —1K 121
Milner Rd. *Dag* —2C 52
Milner Rd. *King T* —3D 118
Milner Rd. *Mord* —6B 122
Milner Rd. *T Hth* —3D 124
Milner Sq. *N1* —7B 46
Milner St. *SW3* —4D 76 (3E 152)
Milner Wlk. *Sidc* —2H 115
Milnthorpe Rd. *W4* —6K 73
Milo Gdns. *SE22* —6F 95
Milo Rd. *SE22* —6F 95

Milroy Wlk. *SE1* —1B 78 (4A 150)
Milson Rd. *W14* —3F 75
Milstead Ho. *E5* —5H 47
Milton Av. *E6* —7B 50
Milton Av. *N6* —7G 29
Milton Av. *NW9* —3J 25
Milton Av. *NW10* —1J 57
Milton Av. *Barn* —6A 4
Milton Av. *Croy* —7D 124
Milton Av. *Sutt* —3B 132
Milton Clo. *N2* —5A 28
Milton Clo. *SE1* —4F 79 (4J 157)
Milton Clo. *Sutt* —3B 132
Milton Ct. *EC2* —5D 62 (5E 144)
Milton Ct. *SE14* —6B 80
Milton Ct. *SW18* —5J 91
Milton Ct. *Chad H* —7C 36
Milton Ct. *Twic* —3J 103
Milton Ct. Rd. *SE14* —6A 80
Milton Cres. *Ilf* —7F 35
Milton Garden Est. *N16* —4E 46
Milton Gro. *N11* —5B 16
Milton Gro. *N16* —4D 46
Milton Ho. *E17* —4C 32
Milton Ho. *SE5* —7D 78
(off Elmington Est.)
Milton Ho. *Sutt* —3J 131
Milton Lodge. *Sidc* —4A 116
Milton Lodge. *Twic* —7K 87
Milton Mans. *W14* —6G 75
(off Queen's Club Mans.)
Milton Pk. *N6* —7G 29
Milton Pl. *N7* —5A 46
Milton Rd. *E17* —4C 32
Milton Rd. *N6* —7G 29
Milton Rd. *N15* —4B 30
Milton Rd. *NW7* —5H 13
Milton Rd. *NW9* —7C 26
Milton Rd. *SE24* —5B 94
Milton Rd. *SW14* —3K 89
Milton Rd. *SW19* —6A 108
Milton Rd. *W3* —1K 73
Milton Rd. *W7* —7K 55
Milton Rd. *Belv* —4G 85
Milton Rd. *Croy* —7D 124
Milton Rd. *Hamp* —7E 102
Milton Rd. *Harr* —4J 23
Milton Rd. *Mitc* —7E 108
Milton Rd. *Sutt* —3J 131
Milton Rd. *Wall* —6G 133
Milton Rd. *Well* —1K 99
Milton St. *EC2* —5D 62 (5E 144)
Milverton Gdns. *Ilf* —2K 51
Milverton Ho. *SE6* —3A 112
Milverton Rd. *NW6* —7E 42
Milverton St. *SE11*
   —5A 78 (6K 155)
Milverton Way. *SE9* —4E 114
Milward Wlk. *E1* —5H 63
Milward Wlk. *SE18* —6E 82
Mimosa Ho. *Hayes* —5A 54
Mimosa Lodge. *NW10* —5B 42
Mimosa Rd. *Hayes* —5A 54
Mimosa St. *SW6* —1H 91
Minard Rd. *SE6* —7G 97
(in two parts)
Mina Rd. *SE17* —5E 78 (6H 157)
Mina Rd. *SW19* —1J 121
Minchenden Ct. *N14* —2C 16
Minchenden Cres. *N14* —3B 16
Mincing La. *EC3*
   —7E 62 (2G 151)
Minden Rd. *SE20* —1H 125
Minden Rd. *Sutt* —2H 131
Minehead Rd. *SW16* —5K 109

Minehead Rd. *Harr* —3E 38
Mineral St. *SE18* —4J 83
Minera M. *SW1* —4E 76 (3G 153)
Minerva Clo. *SW9* —7A 78
Minerva Clo. *Sidc* —3J 115
Minerva Rd. *E4* —7J 19
Minerva Rd. *NW10* —4J 57
Minerva Rd. *King T* —2F 119
Minerva St. *E2* —2H 63
Minet Av. *NW10* —2A 58
Minet Gdns. *NW10* —2A 58
Minet Rd. *SW9* —2B 94
Minford Gdns. *W14* —2F 75
Mingard Wlk. *N7* —2K 45
Ming St. *E14* —7C 64
Ministry Way. *SE9* —2D 114
Miniver Pl. *EC4* —7C 62 (2D 150)
Miniver St. *SE1* —2B 78 (7B 150)
Mink Ct. *Houn* —2A 86
Minniedale. *Surb* —5F 119
Minnow St. *SE17*
   —4E 78 (4H 157)
Minnow Wlk. *SE17*
   —4E 78 (4H 157)
Minoco Wharf. *E16* —2A 82
Minories. *EC3* —6F 63 (1J 151)
Minshaw Ct. *Sidc* —4A 116
Minshill St. *SW8* —1H 93
Minshull Pl. *Beck* —7C 112
Minson Rd. *E9* —1K 63
Minstead Gdns. *SW15* —7B 90
Minstead Way. *N Mald* —6A 120
Minster Av. *Sutt* —2J 131
Minster Ct. *EC3* —7E 62 (2H 151)
Minster Dri. *Croy* —4E 134
Minster Rd. *NW2* —5G 43
Minster Rd. *Brom* —7K 113
Minster Wlk. *N8* —4J 29
Minstrel Gdns. *Surb* —4F 119
Mintern Clo. *N13* —3G 17
Minterne Av. *S'hall* —4E 70
Minterne Rd. *Harr* —5F 25
Minterne Waye. *Hayes* —6A 54
Mintern St. *N1* —2D 62
Minton Ho. *SE11*
   —4A 78 (3J 155)
Minton M. *NW6* —6K 43
Mint Rd. *Wall* —4F 133
Mint St. *SE1* —2C 78 (6C 150)
Mint Wlk. *Croy* —3C 134
Mirabel Rd. *SW6* —7H 75
Miranda Clo. *E1* —5J 63
Miranda Ct. *W3* —6F 57
Miranda Rd. *N19* —1G 45
Mirfield St. *SE7* —4B 82
Miriam Rd. *SE18* —5J 83
Mirravale Trad. Est. *Dag* —7E 36
Mirren Clo. *Harr* —4D 38
Mirror Path. *SE9* —3A 114
Missenden. *SE17*
   —5D 78 (6F 157)
Missenden Gdns. *Mord* —6A 122
Mission Gro. *E17* —5J 33
Mission Pl. *SE15* —1G 95
Mission Sq. *Bren* —6E 72
Mistletoe Clo. *Croy* —1K 135
Mitali Pas. *E1* —6G 63
Mitcham Garden Village. *Mitc*
   —5E 122
Mitcham Ho. *SE5* —1C 94
Mitcham La. *SW16* —6G 109
Mitcham Pk. *Mitc* —4C 122
Mitcham Rd. *E6* —3C 66
Mitcham Rd. *SW17* —5D 108
Moira Clo. *N17* —2E 30

Mitcham Rd. *Croy* —6J 123
Mitcham Rd. *Ilf* —7K 35
Mitcheldean Ct. *SE15* —7E 78
(off Newent Clo.)
Mitchell. *NW9* —1B 26
(off Concourse, The)
Mitchellbrook Way. *NW10*
   —6K 41
Mitchell Clo. *SE2* —4C 84
Mitchell Clo. *Belv* —3J 85
Mitchell Ho. *W12* —7D 58
(off White City Est.)
Mitchell Rd. *N13* —5H 17
Mitchell St. *EC1* —4C 62 (3C 144)
Mitchell Wlk. *E6* —5B 66
(off Neats Ct. Rd.)
Mitchell Way. *NW10* —6J 41
Mitchell Way. *Brom* —1J 127
Mitchison Rd. *N1* —6D 46
Mitchley Rd. *N17* —3G 31
Mitford Rd. *N19* —2J 45
Mitre Bri. Ind. Pk. *W10* —4D 58
Mitre Clo. *Brom* —2H 127
Mitre Clo. *Sutt* —7A 132
Mitre Ct. *EC2* —6C 62 (7D 144)
Mitre Ct. *EC4* —6A 62 (1K 149)
Mitre Rd. *E15* —2G 65
Mitre Rd. *SE1* —2A 78 (6K 149)
Mitre Sq. *EC3* —6E 62 (1H 151)
Mitre St. *EC3* —6E 62 (1H 151)
Mitre, The. *E14* —7B 64
Mitre Way. *W10* —5D 58
Mitre Yd. *SW3* —4C 76 (3D 152)
Moat Ct. *SE9* —6D 98
Moat Cres. *N3* —3K 27
Moat Croft. *Well* —3C 100
Moat Dri. *E13* —2A 66
Moat Dri. *Harr* —4G 23
Moat Farm Rd. *N'holt* —6D 38
Moatfield. *NW6* —7G 43
Moat Gdns. *SE28* —7C 68
Moat Pl. *SW9* —2K 93
Moat Pl. *W3* —6H 57
Moat Side. *Enf* —4E 8
Moat Side *Felt* —4A 102
Moat, The. *N Mald* —1A 120
Moberley Rd. *SW4* —7H 93
Mobil Ct. *WC2* —6K 61 (1H 149)
(off Clement's Inn)
Moby Dick. (Junct.) —4E 36
Modbury Gdns. *NW5* —6E 44
Modder Pl. *SW15* —4F 91
Model Bldgs. *WC1*
   —3K 61 (2H 143)
Model Cotts. *SW14* —4J 89
Model Cotts. *W13* —2B 72
Model Farm Clo. *SE9* —3C 114
Modern Ct. *EC4* —6B 62 (7A 144)
Modern Wharf Rd. *SE10* —3G 81
Moelwyn. *N7* —5H 45
Moelyn M. *Harr* —5A 24
Moffat Ct. *SW19* —5J 107
Moffat Gdns. *Mitc* —3C 122
Moffat Ho. *SE5* —7C 78
Moffat Rd. *N13* —6D 16
Moffat Rd. *SW17* —4D 108
Moffat Rd. *T Hth* —2C 124
Mogden La. *Iswth* —5K 87
Mohammedi Pk. *N'holt* —1E 54
Mohmmad Khan Rd. *E11* —1H 49
Moiety Rd. *E14* —2C 80
Moineau. *NW9* —1B 26
(off Concourse, The)
Moira Rd. *SE9* —4D 98

Moira Rd. *SE9* —4D 98
Mokswell Ct. *N10* —1E 28
Moland Mead. *SE16* —5K 79
Molasses Ho. *SW11* —3A 92
(off Clove Hitch Quay)
Molasses Row. *SW11* —3A 92
Molescroft. *SE9* —3G 115
Molesey Dri. *Sutt* —2G 131
Molesford Rd. *SW6* —1J 91
Molesworth St. *SE13* —3E 96
Moliner Ct. *Beck* —7C 112
Mollison Dri. *Wall* —7H 133
Mollison Way. *Edgw* —2F 25
Molly Huggins Clo. *SW12* —7G 93
Molton Ho. *N1* —1K 61
(off Barnsbury Est.)
Molyneux St. *W1*
   —5C 60 (6D 140)
Monarch Clo. *W Wick* —4H 137
Monarch Ct. *N2* —5B 28
Monarch Dri. *E16* —5B 66
Monarch M. *E17* —6D 32
Monarch M. *SW16* —5A 110
Monarch Pde. *Mitc* —2D 122
Monarch Pl. *Buck H* —2F 21
Monarch Rd. *Belv* —3G 85
Mona Rd. *SE15* —2J 95
Monastery Gdns. *Enf* —2J 7
Mona St. *E16* —5H 65
Moncks Row. *SW18* —6H 91
(off West Hill Rd.)
Monck St. *SW1* —3H 77 (2D 154)
Monclar Rd. *SE5* —4D 94
Moncorvo Clo. *SW7*
   —2C 76 (7C 146)
Moncrieff Pl. *SE15* —2G 95
Moncrieff Clo. *E6* —6C 66
Moncrieff St. *SE15* —2G 95
Monega Rd. *E7 & E12* —6A 50
Monica Ct. *Enf* —5K 7
Monica James Ho. *Sidc* —3A 116
Monier Rd. *E3* —7C 48
Monivea Rd. *Beck* —7B 112
Monk Dri. *E16* —7J 65
Monkfrith Av. *N14* —6A 6
Monkfrith Clo. *N14* —7A 6
Monkfrith Way. *N14* —7K 5
Monkham's Av. *Wfd G* —5E 20
Monkham's Dri. *Wfd G* —5E 20
Monkham's La. *Wfd G* —5D 20
(in two parts)
Monkleigh Rd. *Mord* —3G 121
Monk Pas. *E16* —7J 65
(off Monk Dri.)
Monks Av. *Barn* —6F 5
Monks Clo. *SE2* —4D 84
Monks Clo. *Enf* —2H 7
Monks Clo. *Harr* —2E 38
Monks Clo. *Ruis* —4B 38
Monksdene Gdns. *Sutt* —3K 131
Monks Dri. *W3* —5G 57
Monks Orchard Rd. *Beck*
   —1C 136
Monks Pk. *Wemb* —6H 41
Monks Pk. Gdns. *Wemb* —7H 41
Monks Rd. *Enf* —2H 7
Monks St. *SE18* —4E 82
Monks Way. *NW11* —4H 27
Monks Way. *Beck* —6C 126
Monks Way. *Orp* —7G 129
Monkswood Gdns. *Ilf* —3E 34
Monkton Ho. *E5* —5H 47
Monkton Rd. *Well* —2K 99
Monkton St. *SE11*
   —4A 78 (3K 155)

Monkville Av. *NW11* —4H **27**
Monkville Pde. *NW11* —4H **27**
Monkwell Sq. *EC2*
    —5C **62** (6D **144**)
Monmouth Av. *E18* —3K **33**
Monmouth Av. *King T* —7C **104**
Monmouth Clo. *W4* —3J **73**
Monmouth Clo. *Mitc* —4J **123**
Monmouth Clo. *Well* —4A **100**
Monmouth Ct. W7 —5K **55**
  (off Copley Clo.)
Monmouth Gro. *Bren* —4E **72**
Monmouth Pl. W2 —6K **59**
  (off Monmouth Rd.)
Monmouth Rd. *E6* —3D **66**
Monmouth Rd. *N9* —2C **18**
Monmouth Rd. *W2* —6J **59**
Monmouth Rd. *Dag* —5F **53**
Monmouth St. *WC2*
    —6J **61** (1E **148**)
Monnery Rd. *N19* —3G **45**
Monnow Rd. *SE1* —4G **79**
Monoux Almshouses. *E17*
    —4D **32**
Monoux Gro. *E17* —1C **32**
Monroe Cres. *Enf* —1C **8**
Monroe Dri. *SW14* —5H **89**
Monro Gdns. *Harr* —7D **10**
Monsell Rd. *N4* —3B **46**
Monson Rd. *NW10* —2C **58**
Monson Rd. *SE14* —7K **79**
Mons Way. *Brom* —6C **128**
Montacute Rd. *SE6* —7B **96**
Montacute Rd. *Bush* —1D **10**
Montacute Rd. *Mord* —6B **122**
Montacute Rd. *New Ad* —7E **136**
Montagu Cres. *N18* —4C **18**
Montague Av. *SE4* —4B **96**
Montague Av. *W7* —1K **71**
Montague Clo. *SE1*
    —1D **78** (4E **150**)
Montague Ct. *Sidc* —3A **116**
Montague Gdns. *W3* —7G **57**
Montague Pl. *WC1*
    —5H **61** (5D **142**)
Montague Rd. *E8* —5G **47**
Montague Rd. *E11* —2H **49**
Montague Rd. *N8* —5K **29**
Montague Rd. *N15* —4G **31**
Montague Rd. *SW19* —7K **107**
Montague Rd. *W7* —1K **71**
Montague Rd. *W13* —6B **56**
Montague Rd. *Croy* —1B **134**
Montague Rd. *Houn* —3F **87**
Montague Rd. *Rich* —6E **88**
Montague Rd. *S'hall* —4C **70**
Montague Sq. *SE15* —7J **79**
Montague St. *EC1*
    —5C **62** (6C **144**)
Montague St. *WC1*
    —5J **61** (5E **142**)
Montague Ter. *Brom* —3H **127**
Montague Waye. *S'hall* —3C **70**
Montagu Gdns. *N18* —4C **18**
Montagu Gdns. *Wall* —4G **133**
Montagu Mans. *W1*
    —5D **60** (5F **141**)
Montagu M. N. *W1*
    —5D **60** (6F **141**)
Montagu M. S. *W1*
    —6D **60** (7F **141**)
Montagu M. W. *W1*
    —6D **60** (7F **141**)
Montagu Pl. *W1*
    —5D **60** (6E **140**)

Montagu Rd. *N18 & N9* —5C **18**
Montagu Rd. *NW4* —6C **26**
Montagu Rd. Ind. Est. *N18*
    —4D **18**
Montagu Row. *W1*
    —5D **60** (6F **141**)
Montagu Sq. *W1*
    —5D **60** (6F **141**)
Montagu St. *W1*
    —6D **60** (7F **141**)
Montalt Rd. *Wfd G* —5C **20**
Montana Gdns. *Sutt* —5A **132**
Montana Rd. *SW17* —3E **108**
Montana Rd. *SW20* —1E **120**
Montbelle Rd. *SE9* —3F **115**
Montcalm Clo. *Brom* —6J **127**
Montcalm Ho. *E14* —4B **80**
Montcalm Rd. *SE7* —7B **82**
Montclare St. *E2* —4F **63** (3J **145**)
Monteagle Av. *Bark* —6G **51**
Monteagle Ct. *N1* —2E **62**
Monteagle Way. *E5* —3G **47**
Monteagle Way. *SE15* —3H **95**
Montefiore St. *SW8* —2F **93**
Montego Clo. *SE24* —4A **94**
Monteith Rd. *E3* —1B **64**
Montem Rd. *SE23* —7B **96**
Montem Rd. *N Mald* —4A **120**
Montem St. *N4* —1K **45**
Montenotte Rd. *N8* —5G **29**
Monterey Clo. *Bex* —2J **117**
Monterey Pl. Shop. Cen. *NW7*
    —5F **13**
Montesole Ct. *Pinn* —2A **22**
Montesquieu Ter. E16 —6H **65**
  (off Clarkson Rd.)
Montford Pl. *SE11*
    —5A **78** (6J **155**)
Montfort Pl. *SW19* —1F **107**
Montgolfier Wlk. *N'holt* —3C **54**
Montgomery Clo. *Mitc* —4J **123**
Montgomery Clo. *Sidc* —6K **99**
Montgomery Rd. *W4* —4J **73**
Montgomery Rd. *Edgw* —6A **12**
Montholme Rd. *SW11* —6D **92**
Monthope Rd. *E1*
    —5G **63** (6K **145**)
Montolieu Gdns. *SW15* —5D **90**
Montpelier Av. *W5* —5C **56**
Montpelier Av. *Bex* —7D **100**
Montpelier Ct. *W5* —5D **56**
Montpelier Gdns. *E6* —3B **66**
Montpelier Gro. *NW5* —5G **45**
Montpelier M. *SW7*
    —3C **76** (1D **152**)
Montpelier Pl. *SW7*
    —3C **76** (1D **152**)
Montpelier Rise. *NW11* —7G **27**
Montpelier Rise. *Wemb* —1D **40**
Montpelier Rd. *N3* —1A **28**
Montpelier Rd. *SE15* —1H **95**
Montpelier Rd. *W5* —5D **56**
Montpelier Rd. *Sutt* —4A **132**
Montpelier Row. *SE3* —2H **97**
Montpelier Row. *Twic* —7C **88**
Montpelier Sq. *SW7*
    —2C **76** (7D **146**)
Montpelier St. *SW7*
    —3C **76** (1D **152**)
Montpelier Ter. *SW7*
    —2C **76** (7D **146**)
Montpelier Vale. *SE3* —2H **97**
Montpelier Wlk. *SW7*
    —3C **76** (1D **152**)

Montpelier Way. *NW11* —7G **27**
Montrave Rd. *SE20* —6J **111**
Montreal Pl. *WC2*
    —7K **61** (2G **149**)
Montreal Rd. *Ilf* —7G **35**
Montrell Rd. *SW2* —1J **109**
Montrose Av. *NW6* —2G **59**
Montrose Av. *Edgw* —2J **25**
Montrose Av. *Sidc* —7A **100**
Montrose Av. *Twic* —7F **87**
Montrose Av. *Well* —3H **99**
Montrose Clo. *Well* —3K **99**
Montrose Clo. *Wfd G* —4D **20**
Montrose Ct. *NW9* —2J **25**
Montrose Ct. *SW7*
    —2B **76** (7B **146**)
Montrose Ct. *Harr* —5F **23**
Montrose Cres. *N12* —6F **15**
Montrose Cres. *Wemb* —6E **40**
Montrose Gdns. *Mitc* —2D **122**
Montrose Gdns. *Sutt* —2K **131**
Montrose Ho. *E14* —3C **80**
Montrose Pl. *SW1*
    —2E **76** (7H **147**)
Montrose Rd. *Harr* —2J **23**
Montrose Wlk. *Stan* —6G **11**
Montrose Way. *SE23* —1K **111**
Montserrat Av. *Wfd G* —7A **20**
Montserrat Clo. *SE19* —5D **110**
Montserrat Rd. *SW15* —4G **91**
Monument Gdns. *SE13* —5E **96**
Monument St. *EC3*
    —7D **62** (2F **151**)
Monument Way. *N17* —3F **31**
Monza St. *E1* —7J **63**
Moodkee St. *SE16* —3J **79**
Moody St. *E1* —3K **63**
Moon Ct. *SE12* —4J **97**
Moon La. *Barn* —3C **4**
Moon St. *N1* —1B **62**
Moorcroft. *Edgw* —1H **25**
Moorcroft Gdns. *Brom* —5C **128**
Moorcroft Rd. *SW16* —3J **109**
Moorcroft Way. *Pinn* —5C **22**
Moordown. *SE18* —1E **98**
Moore Clo. *SW14* —3J **89**
Moore Clo. *Mitc* —2F **123**
Moore Clo. *Wall* —7J **133**
Moore Cres. *Dag* —1B **68**
Moore Ho. N8 —4J **29**
  (off Pembroke Rd.)
Mooreland Rd. *Brom* —7H **113**
Moore Pk. Rd. *SW6* —7J **75**
Moore Rd. *SE19* —6C **110**
Moore St. *SW3* —4D **76** (3E **152**)
Moore Wlk. *E7* —4J **49**
Moore Way. *Sutt* —7J **131**
Moorey Clo. *E15* —1H **65**
Moorfield Av. *W5* —4D **56**
Moorfield Rd. *N17* —2F **31**
Moorfield Rd. *Enf* —1D **8**
Moorfields. *EC2*
    —5D **62** (6E **144**)
Moorgate. *EC2* —6D **62** (7E **144**)
Moorgate Pl. *EC2*
    —6D **62** (7E **144**)
Moorgreen Ho. *EC1*
    —3B **62** (1A **144**)
Moorhead Way. *SE3* —3K **97**
Moorhouse. *NW9* —1B **26**
Moorhouse Rd. *W2* —6J **59**
Moorhouse Rd. *Harr* —3D **24**
Moorings, The. E16 —5A **66**
  (off Prince Regent La.)

Moorland Clo. *Romf* —1H **37**
Moorland Clo. *Twic* —7E **86**
Moorland Rd. *SW9* —4B **94**
Moorland Rd. *SW9* —4B **94**
    —5G **77** (5B **154**)
Moorlands. *N'holt* —1C **54**
Moorlands Av. *NW7* —6J **13**
Moor La. *EC2* —5D **62** (6E **144**)
Moormead Dri. *Eps* —5A **130**
Moor Mead Rd. *Twic* —6A **88**
Moor Pk. Gdns. *King T* —7A **106**
Moor Pl. *EC2* —5D **62** (6E **144**)
Moorside Rd. *Brom* —3G **113**
Moor St. *W1* —6H **61** (1D **148**)
Moot Ct. *NW9* —5G **25**
Morant Pl. *N22* —1K **29**
Morant St. *E14* —7C **64**
Mora Rd. *NW2* —4E **42**
Mora St. *EC1* —3C **62** (1D **144**)
Morat St. *SW9* —1K **93**
Moravian Clo. *SW10*
    —6B **76** (7A **152**)
Moravian Pl. *SW10* —6B **76**
Moravian St. *E2* —2J **63**
Moray Clo. *Edgw* —2C **12**
Moray Clo. *Romf* —1K **37**
Moray M. *N7* —2K **45**
Moray Rd. *N4* —2K **45**
Moray Way. *Romf* —1K **37**
Mordaunt Gdns. *Dag* —7E **52**
Mordaunt Rd. *NW10* —1K **57**
Mordaunt St. *SW9* —3K **93**
Morden Ct. *Mord* —4K **121**
Morden Ct. Pde. *Mord* —4K **121**
Morden Gdns. *Gnfd* —5K **39**
Morden Gdns. *Mitc* —4B **122**
Morden Hall Rd. *Mord* —3K **121**
Morden Hill. *SE13* —2E **96**
Morden La. *SE13* —1E **96**
Morden Rd. *SE3* —2J **97**
Morden Rd. *SW19* —1K **121**
Morden Rd. *Mord & Mitc*
    —4A **122**
Morden Rd. *Romf* —7E **36**
Morden Rd. M. *SE3* —2J **97**
Morden St. *SE13* —1D **96**
Morden Way. *Sutt* —7J **121**
Morden Wharf Rd. *SE10* —3G **81**
Mordon Rd. *Ilf* —7K **35**
Mordred Rd. *SE6* —2G **113**
Morecambe Clo. *E1* —5K **63**
Morecambe Gdns. *Stan* —4J **11**
Morecambe St. *SE17*
    —5C **78** (4D **156**)
Morecambe Ter. N18 —4J **17**
  (off Gt. Cambridge Rd.)
More Clo. *E16* —6H **65**
More Clo. *W14* —4F **75**
Morecoombe Clo. *King T*
    —7H **105**
Moree Way. *N18* —4B **18**
Moreland St. *EC1*
    —3B **62** (1B **144**)
Moreland Way. *E4* —3J **19**
Morella Rd. *SW12* —7D **92**
Moremead Rd. *SE6* —4B **112**
Morena St. *SE6* —7D **96**
Moresby Av. *Surb* —7H **119**
Moresby Rd. *E5* —1H **47**
Moresby Wlk. *SW8* —2G **93**
More's Gdns. SW3 —6B **76**
  (off Cheyne Wlk.)
Moreton Av. *Iswth* —1J **87**
Moreton Clo. *E5* —2H **47**
Moreton Clo. *N15* —6D **30**
Moreton Clo. *NW7* —6K **13**

Moreton Ct. *N'holt* —5G **39**
Moreton Gdns. *Wfd G* —5H **21**
Moreton Pl. *SW1*
    —5G **77** (5B **154**)
Moreton Rd. *N15* —6D **30**
Moreton Rd. *S Croy* —5D **134**
Moreton Rd. *Wor Pk* —2C **130**
Moreton St. *SW1*
    —5G **77** (5B **154**)
Moreton Ter. *SW1*
    —5G **77** (5B **154**)
Moreton Ter. M. N. *SW1*
    —5G **77** (5B **154**)
Moreton Ter. M. S. *SW1*
    —5G **77** (5B **154**)
Moreton Tower. *W3* —1H **73**
Morfe Way. *N18* —4B **18**
Morford Clo. *Ruis* —7A **22**
Morford Way. *Ruis* —7A **22**
Morgan Av. *E17* —4F **33**
Morgan Clo. *Dag* —7G **53**
Morgan Mans. N7 —5A **46**
  (off Morgan Rd.)
Morgan Rd. *N7* —5A **46**
Morgan Rd. *W10* —5H **59**
Morgan Rd. *Brom* —7J **113**
Morgan Rd. *Tedd* —6J **103**
Morgan's La. SE1
    —1E **78** (5G **151**)
Morgan St. *E3* —3A **64**
Morgan St. *E16* —5H **65**
Morgan St. *SE18* —3F **83**
Morgan Way. *Wfd G* —6H **21**
Moriatry Clo. *N7* —4J **45**
Morie St. *SW18* —5K **91**
Morieux Rd. *E10* —1B **48**
Moring Rd. *SW17* —4E **108**
Morkyns Wlk. *SE21* —3E **110**
Morland Av. *Croy* —1E **134**
Morland Clo. *NW11* —1K **43**
Morland Clo. *Hamp* —5D **102**
Morland Clo. *Mitc* —3C **122**
Morland Est. *E8* —7G **47**
Morland Gdns. *NW10* —7K **41**
Morland Gdns. *S'hall* —1F **71**
Morland M. *N1* —7A **46**
Morland Rd. *E17* —5K **31**
Morland Rd. *SE20* —6K **111**
Morland Rd. *Croy* —1E **134**
Morland Rd. *Dag* —7G **53**
Morland Rd. *Harr* —5E **24**
Morland Rd. *Ilf* —2F **51**
Morland Rd. *Sutt* —5A **132**
Morley Av. *E4* —7A **20**
Morley Av. *N18* —4B **18**
Morley Av. *N22* —2A **30**
Morley Ct. *E4* —5G **19**
Morley Ct. *Short* —4H **127**
Morley Cres. *Edgw* —2D **12**
Morley Cres. *Ruis* —2A **38**
Morley Cres. E. *Stan* —2C **24**
Morley Cres. W. *Stan* —3C **24**
Morley Hill. *Enf* —1J **7**
Morley Ho. *N16* —2G **47**
Morley Rd. *E10* —1E **48**
Morley Rd. *E15* —2H **65**
Morley Rd. *SE13* —4E **96**
Morley Rd. *Bark* —1H **67**
Morley Rd. *Chst* —1G **129**
Morley Rd. *Romf* —5E **36**
Morley Rd. *Sutt* —1H **131**
Morley Rd. *Twic* —6D **88**
Morley St. *SE1* —3A **78** (1K **155**)
Morna Rd. *SE5* —2C **94**
Morning La. *E9* —6J **47**

Morningside Rd. *Wor Pk*
—2E **130**
Mornington Av. *W14* —4H **75**
Mornington Av. *Brom* —3A **128**
Mornington Av. *W14* —7E **34**
Mornington Clo. *Wfd G* —4D **20**
Mornington Ct. *Bex* —1K **117**
Mornington Cres. *NW1* —2G **61**
Mornington Cres. *Houn* —1A **86**
Mornington Gro. *E3* —3C **64**
Mornington M. *SE1* —1C **94**
Mornington Pl. *NW1* —2F **61**
Mornington Rd. *E4* —7K **9**
Mornington Rd. *E11* —7H **33**
Mornington Rd. *SE8* —7B **80**
Mornington Rd. *Gnfd* —5F **55**
Mornington Rd. *Wfd G* —4C **20**
Mornington St. *NW1* —2F **61**
Mornington Ter. *NW1* —1F **61**
Mornington Wlk. *Rich* —4C **104**
Morocco St. *SE1*
—2E **78** (7G **151**)
Morpeth Gro. *E9* —1K **63**
Morpeth Mans. Ilf
—4G **77** (3A **154**)
(off Morpeth Ter.)
Morpeth Rd. *E9* —1J **63**
Morpeth St. *E2* —3K **63**
Morpeth Ter. *SW1*
—3G **77** (2A **154**)
Morpeth Wlk. *N17* —7C **18**
Morrab Gdns. *Ilf* —3K **51**
Morrell Clo. *New Bar* —3F **5**
Morris Av. *E12* —5D **50**
Morris Blitz Ct. *N16* —4F **47**
Morris Clo. *Croy* —5A **126**
Morris Ct. *E4* —3J **19**
Morris Gdns. *SW18* —7J **91**
Morrish Rd. *SW2* —7J **93**
Morrison Av. *N17* —3E **30**
Morrison Bldgs. N. E1 —6G 63
(off Commercial Rd.)
Morrison Bldgs. S. E1 —6G 63
(off Commercial Rd.)
Morrison Rd. *Bark* —2E **68**
Morrison St. *SW11* —3E **92**
Morris Pl. *N4* —2A **46**
Morris Rd. *E14* —5D **64**
Morris Rd. *E15* —4G **49**
Morris Rd. *Dag* —2F **53**
Morris Rd. *Iswth* —3K **87**
Morriss Ho. SE16 —2H 79
(off Cherry Garden St.)
Morris St. *E1* —6H **63**
Morse Clo. *E13* —3J **65**
Morshead Mans. W9 —3K 59
(off Morshead Rd.)
Morshead Rd. *W9* —3J **59**
Morson Rd. *Enf* —6F **9**
Morston Gdns. *SE9* —4D **114**
Mortain Ho. SE16 —4H 79
(off Roseberry St.)
Morten Clo. *SW4* —6H **93**
Morteyne Rd. *N17* —1D **30**
Mortgramit Sq. *SE18* —3E **82**
Mortham St. *E15* —1G **65**
Mortimer Clo. *NW2* —2H **43**
Mortimer Clo. *SW16* —2H **109**
Mortimer Cres. *NW6* —1K **59**
Mortimer Cres. *Wor Pk* —3A **130**
Mortimer Dri. *Enf* —5J **7**
Mortimer Est. NW6 —1K 59
(off Mortimer Pl.)
Mortimer Ho. W11 —1F 75
(off Queensdale Cres.)

Mortimer Mkt. *WC1*
—4G **61** (4B **142**)
Mortimer Pl. *NW6* —1K **59**
Mortimer Rd. *E6* —3D **66**
Mortimer Rd. *N1* —7E **46**
(in two parts)
Mortimer Rd. *NW10* —3E **58**
Mortimer Rd. *W13* —6C **56**
Mortimer Rd. *Eri* —6K **85**
Mortimer Rd. *Mitc* —1D **122**
Mortimer Sq. *W11* —7F **59**
Mortimer St. *W1*
—6G **61** (7K **141**)
Mortimer Ter. *NW5* —4F **45**
Mortlake Clo. *Croy* —3J **133**
Mortlake Dri. *Mitc* —1C **122**
Mortlake High St. *SW14* —3K **89**
Mortlake Rd. *E16* —6K **65**
Mortlake Rd. *Ilf* —4G **51**
Mortlake Rd. *Rich* —7G **73**
Mortlake Ter. Rich —7G 73
(off Mortlake Rd.)
Mortlock Clo. *SE15* —1H **95**
Mortlock Ct. *E12* —4B **50**
Morton Cres. *N14* —4C **16**
Morton Gdns. *Wall* —5G **133**
Morton M. *SW5* —4K **75**
Morton Pl. *SE1* —3A **78** (2J **155**)
Morton Rd. *E15* —7H **49**
Morton Rd. *N1* —7C **46**
Morton Rd. *Mord* —5B **122**
Morton Way. *N14* —3B **16**
Morvale Clo. *Belv* —4F **85**
Morval Rd. *SW2* —5A **94**
Morven Rd. *SW17* —3D **108**
Morville St. *E3* —2C **64**
Morwell St. *WC1*
—5H **61** (6C **142**)
Moscow Pl. *W2* —7K **59**
Moscow Rd. *W2* —7J **59**
Moselle Av. *N22* —2A **30**
Moselle Clo. *N8* —3K **29**
Moselle Ho. N17 —7A 18
(off William St.)
Moselle Pl. *N17* —7A **18**
Moselle St. *N17* —7A **18**
Mossborough Ct. *N12* —6E **14**
Mossbury Rd. *SW11* —3C **92**
Moss Clo. *E1* —5G **63**
Moss Clo. *Pinn* —2D **22**
Mossdown Clo. *Belv* —4G **85**
Mossford Ct. *Ilf* —2F **35**
Mossford Grn. *Ilf* —3F **35**
Mossford La. *Ilf* —2F **35**
Mossford St. *E3* —4B **64**
Moss Gdns. *S Croy* —7K **135**
Moss Hall Ct. *N12* —6E **14**
Moss Hall Cres. *N12* —6E **14**
Moss Hall Gro. *N12* —6E **14**
Mossington Gdns. *SE16* —4J **79**
Moss La. *Pinn* —1C **22**
Mosslea Rd. *SE20* —6J **111**
(in two parts)
Mosslea Rd. *Brom* —5B **128**
Mossop St. *SW3*
—4C **76** (3D **152**)
Moss Rd. *Dag* —7G **53**
Mossville Gdns. *Mord* —3H **121**
Moss Way. *Houn* —1B **86**
Mosswell Ho. *N10* —1E **28**
Mostyn Av. *Wemb* —5F **41**
Mostyn Gdns. *NW10* —2F **59**
Mostyn Gro. *E3* —2C **64**
Mostyn Rd. *SW9* —1A **94**
Mostyn Rd. *SW19* —1H **121**

Mostyn Rd. *Edgw* —7F **13**
Mosul Way. *Brom* —6C **128**
Mota M. *N3* —1J **27**
Motcomb St. *SW1*
—3E **76** (1G **153**)
Mothers Sq. *E5* —4J **47**
Motley Av. *EC2* —4E **62** (4G **145**)
Motley St. *SW8* —2G **93**
Motspur Pk. *N Mald* —6B **120**
Mottingham Gdns. *SE9* —1B **114**
Mottingham La. *SE12 & SE9*
—1A **114**
Mottingham Rd. *N9* —6E **8**
Mottingham Rd. *SE9* —2C **114**
Mottisfont Rd. *SE2* —3A **84**
Mott St. *E4 & Lou* —1K **9**
Moules Ct. *SE5* —7C **78**
Moulins Rd. *E9* —7J **47**
Moulsford Ho. *N7* —5H **45**
Moulton Av. *Houn* —2C **86**
Moundfield Rd. *N16* —6G **31**
Mound, The. *SE9* —3E **114**
Mountacre Clo. *SE26* —4F **111**
Mt. Adon Pk. *SE22* —7G **95**
Mountague Pl. *E14* —7E **64**
Mountain Ho. *SE11*
—5K **77** (4H **155**)
Mt. Angelus Rd. *SW15* —7B **90**
Mt. Ararat Rd. *Rich* —5E **88**
Mt. Arlington. Short —2G 127
(off Park Hill Rd.)
Mt. Ash Rd. *SE26* —3H **111**
Mount Av. *E4* —3H **19**
Mount Av. *W5* —5C **56**
Mount Av. *S'hall* —6E **54**
Mt. Baton Ct. W5 —5C 56
(off Mount Av.)
Mountbatten Clo. *SE18* —6J **83**
Mountbatten Clo. *SE19* —5E **110**
Mountbatten Ct. *Buck H* —2G **21**
Mountbatten Gdns. *Beck*
—4A **126**
Mountbatten Ho. N6 —7E 28
(off Hillcrest)
Mountbatten M. *SW18* —7A **92**
Mountbel Rd. *Stan* —1A **24**
Mount Clo. *W5* —5C **56**
Mount Clo. *Brom* —1C **128**
Mount Clo. *Cars* —7E **132**
Mount Clo. *Cockf* —4K **5**
Mountcombe Clo. *Surb* —7E **118**
Mount Ct. *SW15* —3G **91**
Mount Ct. *W Wick* —2G **137**
Mount Dri. *Bexh* —5E **100**
Mount Dri. *Harr* —5D **22**
Mount Dri. *Wemb* —2J **41**
Mountearl Gdns. *SW16* —3K **109**
Mt. Echo Av. *E4* —1J **19**
Mt. Echo Dri. *E4* —1J **19**
Mt. Ephraim La. *SW16* —3H **109**
Mt. Ephraim Rd. *SW16* —3H **109**
Mountfield Rd. *E6* —2E **66**
Mountfield Rd. *N3* —3K **27**
Mountfield Rd. *W5* —6D **56**
Mountford Rd. *E8* —5G **47**
Mountford St. *E1* —6G **63**
Mountfort Cres. *N1* —7A **46**
Mountfort Ter. *N1* —7A **46**
Mount Gdns. *SE26* —3H **111**
Mount Gro. *Edgw* —3D **12**
Mountgrove Rd. *N5* —3B **46**
Mounthurst Rd. *Brom* —7H **127**
Mountington Pk. Clo. Harr
—6D **24**

Mountjoy Clo. *SE2* —2B **84**
Mountjoy Ho. *EC2*
—5C **62** (6C **144**)
Mt. Lodge. *N6* —6G **29**
Mt. Mills. *EC1* —3B **62** (2B **144**)
Mt. Nod Rd. *SW16* —3K **109**
Mt. Olive Ct. *W7* —2J **71**
Mount Pde. *Barn* —4H **5**
Mount Pk. *Cars* —7E **132**
Mount Pk. Av. *Harr* —2H **39**
Mount Pk. Av. *S Croy* —7B **134**
Mount Pk. Cres. *W5* —6D **56**
Mount Pk. Rd. *W5* —5D **56**
Mount Pk. Rd. *Harr* —3H **39**
Mount Pl. *W3* —1H **73**
Mt. Pleasant. *SE27* —4C **110**
Mt. Pleasant. *WC1*
—4A **62** (4J **143**)
Mt. Pleasant. *Barn* —4H **5**
Mt. Pleasant. *Ilf* —5G **51**
Mt. Pleasant. *Ruis* —2A **38**
Mt. Pleasant. *Wemb* —1E **56**
Mt. Pleasant Cotts. N14 —1C 16
(off Wells, The)
Mt. Pleasant Cres. *N4* —1K **45**
Mt. Pleasant Hill. *E5* —2H **47**
Mt. Pleasant La. *E5* —2H **47**
Mt. Pleasant Pl. *SE18* —4H **83**
Mt. Pleasant Rd. *E17* —2A **32**
Mt. Pleasant Rd. *NW10* —7E **42**
Mt. Pleasant Rd. *SE13* —6D **96**
Mt. Pleasant Rd. *W5* —4C **56**
Mt. Pleasant Rd. *N Mald* —3J **119**
Mt. Pleasant Vs. *N4* —7K **29**
Mt. Pleasant Wlk. *Bex* —5J **101**
Mount Rd. *NW2* —3D **42**
Mount Rd. *NW4* —6C **26**
Mount Rd. *SW19* —2J **107**
Mount Rd. *Barn* —5H **5**
Mount Rd. *Bexh* —5D **100**
Mount Rd. *Dag* —1F **53**
Mount Rd. *Felt* —3C **102**
Mount Rd. *Ilf* —5F **51**
Mount Rd. *Mitc* —2B **122**
Mount Rd. *N Mald* —3K **119**
Mount Row. *W1*
—7F **61** (3J **147**)
Mountsfield Ct. *SE13* —6F **97**
Mountside. *Stan* —1K **23**
Mount Sq., The. *NW3* —3A **44**
Mt. Stewart Av. *Harr* —7D **24**
Mount St. *SE18* —4F **83**
Mount St. *W1* —7E **60** (3G **147**)
Mount St. M. *W1*
—7F **61** (3J **147**)
Mount Ter. *E1* —5H **63**
Mount, The. *E5* —2H **47**
Mount, The. *N20* —2F **15**
Mount, The. *NW3* —4A **44**
Mount, The. *W3* —1H **73**
Mount, The. *Bexh* —5H **101**
Mount, The. *N Mald* —3B **120**
Mount, The. *Wemb* —2J **41**
Mount, The. *Wor Pk* —4D **130**
Mt. Vernon. *NW3* —4A **44**
Mount View. *NW7* —3E **12**
Mount View. *W5* —4D **56**
Mount View. *Enf* —1E **6**
Mountview Ct. *N15* —4B **30**
Mt. View Rd. *E4* —7K **9**
Mt. View Rd. *N4* —7J **29**
Mt. View Rd. *NW9* —5K **25**

Mountview Rd. *Orp* —7K **129**
(in two parts)
Mount Vs. *SE27* —3B **110**
Mount Way. *Cars* —7E **132**
Movers La. *Bark* —1H **67**
Movers Lane. (Junct.) —2J **67**
Mowatt Clo. *N19* —1H **45**
Mowat Corner. *Wor Pk* —2B **130**
Mowat Ct. Wor Pk —2B 130
(off Avenue, The)
Mowatt Clo. *N19* —2H **45**
Mowbray Ct. *N22* —1A **30**
Mowbray Ct. *SE19* —7F **111**
Mowbray Gdns. *N'holt* —1E **54**
Mowbray Ho. N2 —2B 28
(off Grange, The)
Mowbray Pde. *Edgw* —4B **12**
Mowbray Pde. *N'holt* —1E **54**
Mowbray Rd. *NW6* —7G **43**
Mowbray Rd. *SE19* —1F **125**
Mowbray Rd. *Edgw* —4B **12**
Mowbray Rd. *New Bar* —4F **5**
Mowbray Rd. *Rich* —3C **104**
Mowbrays Clo. *Romf* —1J **37**
Mowbrays Rd. *Romf* —2J **37**
Mowlem St. *E2* —2H **63**
Mowlem Trad. Est. *N17* —7D **18**
Mowll St. *SW9* —7A **78**
Moxon Clo. *E13* —2H **65**
Moxon St. *W1* —5E **60** (6G **141**)
Moxon St. *Barn* —3C **4**
Moye Clo. *E2* —2G **63**
Moyers Rd. *E10* —7E **32**
Moylan Rd. *W6* —6G **75**
Moyne Ho. *SW4* —5B **94**
Moyne Pl. *NW10* —2G **57**
Moynihan Dri. *N21* —5D **6**
Moys Clo. *Croy* —6J **123**
Moyser Rd. *SW16* —5F **109**
Mozart St. *W10* —3H **59**
Mozart Ter. *SW1*
—4E **76** (4H **153**)
Muchelney Rd. *Mord* —6A **122**
Mudlarks Way. *SE10 & SE7*
—3H **81**
Muggeridge Clo. *S Croy*
—5D **134**
Muggeridge Rd. *Dag* —4H **53**
Muirdown Av. *SW14* —4K **89**
Muir Dri. *SW18* —6C **92**
Muirfield. *W3* —6A **58**
Muirfield Clo. *SE16* —5H **79**
Muirfield Cres. *E14* —3D **80**
Muirkirk Rd. *SE6* —1E **112**
Muir Rd. *E5* —4G **47**
Muir St. *E16* —1C **82**
Mulberry Bus. Pk. *SE16* —2K **79**
Mulberry Clo. *E4* —2H **19**
Mulberry Clo. *N8* —5J **29**
Mulberry Clo. *NW3* —4B **44**
Mulberry Clo. *NW4* —3E **26**
Mulberry Clo. *SE22* —5G **95**
Mulberry Clo. *SW3*
—6B **76** (7B **152**)
Mulberry Clo. *SW16* —4G **109**
Mulberry Clo. *Barn* —4G **5**
Mulberry Clo. *N'holt* —2C **54**
Mulberry Ct. *Bark* —7K **51**
Mulberry Ct. *Surb* —7D **118**
Mulberry Ct. *Twic* —3K **103**
Mulberry Cres. *Bren* —7B **72**
Mulberry Ho. *SE8* —6B **80**
Mulberry Ho. *Short* —2G **127**
Mulberry La. *Croy* —1F **135**
Mulberry M. *SE14* —1B **96**
Mulberry M. *Wall* —6G **133**

Mulberry Pl. *E14* —7E **64**
(off Clove Cres.)
Mulberry Pl. *W6* —5C **74**
Mulberry Rd. *E8* —7F **47**
Mulberry St. *E1* —6G **63**
Mulberry Wlk. *SW3*
—6B **76** (7B **152**)
Mulberry Way. *E18* —2K **33**
Mulberry Way. *Belv* —2J **85**
Mulberry Way. *Ilf* —4G **35**
Mulgrave Ct. *Sutt* —6K **131**
(off Mulgrave Rd.)
Mulgrave Rd. *NW10* —4B **42**
Mulgrave Rd. *SW6* —6H **75**
Mulgrave Rd. *Croy* —3D **134**
Mulgrave Rd. *Harr* —2A **40**
Mulgrave Rd. *Sutt* —7H **131**
Mulholland Clo. *Mitc* —2F **123**
Mulkern Rd. *N19* —1H **45**
Mullards Clo. *Mitc* —1D **132**
Muller Rd. *SW4* —6H **93**
Mullet Gdns. *E2* —3G **63**
Mullins Path. *SW14* —3K **89**
Mullion Clo. *Harr* —1F **23**
Mull Wlk. *N1* —6C **46**
(off Clephane Rd.)
Mulready St. *NW8*
—4C **60** (4C **140**)
Multimedia Ho. *NW10* —4J **57**
Multi Way. *W3* —2A **74**
Multon Rd. *SW18* —7B **92**
Mulvaney Way. *SE1*
—2D **78** (7F **151**)
Mumford Ct. *EC2*
—6C **62** (7D **144**)
Mumford Rd. *SE24* —5B **94**
Muncaster Rd. *SW11* —5D **92**
Muncies M. *SE6* —2E **112**
Mundania Rd. *SE22* —6H **95**
Munday Rd. *E16* —7J **65**
Munden St. *W14* —4G **75**
Mundford Rd. *E5* —2J **47**
Mundon Gdns. *Ilf* —1H **51**
Mund St. *W14* —5H **75**
Mundy St. *N1* —3E **62** (1G **145**)
Mungo Pk. Clo. *Bush* —2B **10**
Munnings Gdns. *Iswth* —5H **87**
Munro Dri. *N11* —6B **16**
Munro Ho. *SE1* —2A **78** (7J **149**)
Munro M. *W10* —5G **59**
Munro Ter. *SW10* —6B **76**
Munslow Gdns. *Sutt* —4B **132**
Munster Av. *Houn* —5C **86**
Munster Ct. *SW6* —2H **91**
Munster Ct. *Tedd* —6C **104**
Munster Gdns. *N13* —4G **17**
Munster Rd. *SW6* —7G **75**
Munster Rd. *Tedd* —6C **104**
Munster Sq. *NW1*
—3F **61** (2K **141**)
Munton Rd. *SE17*
—4C **78** (3D **156**)
Murchison Av. *Bex* —1D **116**
Murchison Rd. *E10* —2E **48**
Murdock Clo. *E16* —6H **65**
Murdock St. *SE15* —6H **79**
Murfett Clo. *SW19* —2G **107**
Muriel Ct. *E10* —7D **32**
Muriel St. *N1* —2K **61**
(in two parts)
Murillo Rd. *SE13* —4F **97**
Murphy St. *SE1* —2A **78** (7J **149**)
Murray Av. *Brom* —3K **127**
Murray Av. *Houn* —5F **87**

Murray Ct. *Harr* —6K **23**
Murray Ct. *Twic* —2H **103**
Murray Cres. *Pinn* —1B **22**
Murray Gro. *N1* —2C **62** (1D **144**)
Murray Ho. *SE18* —4D **82**
(off Rideout St.)
Murray M. *NW1* —7H **45**
Murray Rd. *SW19* —6F **107**
Murray Rd. *W5* —4C **72**
Murray Rd. *Rich* —2C **104**
Murray Sq. *E16* —6J **65**
Murray St. *NW1* —7G **45**
Murray Ter. *NW3* —4A **44**
Murray Ter. *W5* —4D **72**
Mursell Est. *SW8* —1K **93**
Musard Rd. *W6* —6G **75**
Musbury St. *E1* —6J **63**
Muscatel Pl. *SE5* —7E **78**
Muschamp Rd. *SE15* —3F **95**
Muschamp Rd. *Cars* —2C **132**
Muscovy Ho. *Eri* —2E **84**
(off Kale Rd.)
Muscovy St. *EC3*
—7E **62** (2H **151**)
Museum Path. *E2* —3J **63**
Museum St. *WC1*
—5J **61** (6E **142**)
Musgrave Clo. *Barn* —1F **5**
Musgrave Cres. *SW6* —7J **75**
Musgrave Rd. *Iswth* —1K **87**
Musgrove Rd. *SE14* —1K **95**
Musjid Rd. *SW11* —2B **92**
Musquash Way. *Houn* —2A **86**
Muston Rd. *E5* —2H **47**
Mustow Pl. *SW6* —2H **91**
Muswell Av. *N10* —1F **29**
Muswell Hill. *N10* —3F **29**
Muswell Hill B'way. *N10* —3F **29**
Muswell Hill Pl. *N10* —4F **29**
Muswell Hill Rd. *N6 & N10*
—6E **28**
Muswell M. *N10* —3F **29**
Muswell Rd. *N10* —3F **29**
Mutrix Rd. *NW6* —1J **59**
Mutton Pl. *NW1* —6E **44**
Muybridge Rd. *N Mald* —2J **119**
Myatt Rd. *SW9* —1B **94**
Mycenae Rd. *SE3* —7J **81**
Myddelton Av. *Enf* —1K **7**
Myddelton Clo. *Enf* —1A **8**
Myddelton Gdns. *N21* —7H **7**
Myddelton Pas. *EC1*
—3A **62** (1K **143**)
Myddelton Rd. *N8* —3J **29**
Myddelton Sq. *EC1*
—3A **62** (1K **143**)
Myddelton St. *EC1*
—3A **62** (2K **143**)
Myddleton Ho. *WC1*
—2A **62** (1J **143**)
Myddleton M. *N22* —7D **16**
Myddleton Rd. *N22* —7D **16**
Myers La. *SE14* —6K **79**
Mylis Clo. *SE26* —4H **111**
Mylius Clo. *SE14* —7J **79**
Mylne Clo. *W6* —5C **74**
Mylne St. *EC1* —3A **62** (1J **143**)
Myra St. *SE2* —4A **84**
Myrdle St. *E1* —5G **63**
Myrna Clo. *SW19* —7C **108**
Myron Pl. *SE13* —3E **96**
Myrtleberry Clo. *E8* —6F **47**
(off Beechwood Rd.)
Myrtle Clo. *E Barn* —1J **15**

Myrtledene Rd. *SE2* —5A **84**
Myrtle Gdns. *W7* —1J **71**
Myrtle Gro. *Enf* —1J **7**
Myrtle Gro. *N Mald* —2J **119**
Myrtle Rd. *E6* —1C **66**
Myrtle Rd. *E17* —6A **32**
Myrtle Rd. *N13* —3H **17**
Myrtle Rd. *W3* —1J **73**
Myrtle Rd. *Croy* —3C **136**
Myrtle Rd. *Hamp* —6G **103**
Myrtle Rd. *Houn* —2G **87**
Myrtle Rd. *Ilf* —2F **51**
Myrtle Rd. *Sutt* —5A **132**
Myrtle Wlk. *N1* —2E **62** (1G **145**)
Mysore Rd. *SW11* —4D **92**
Myton Rd. *SE21* —3D **110**
Mytton Ho. *SW8* —7K **77**
(off St Stephens Ter.)

N

Nadine Ct. *Wall* —7G **133**
Nadine St. *SE7* —5A **82**
Nagasaki Wlk. *SE7* —3K **81**
Nagle Clo. *E17* —2F **33**
Nag's Head. (Junct.) —3J **45**
Nags Head Ct. *EC1*
—4C **62** (4D **144**)
Nags Head La. *Well* —3B **100**
Nags Head Rd. *Enf* —4D **8**
Nags Head Shop. Cen. *N7*
—4K **45**
Nailsworth Ct. *SE15* —6E **78**
(off Birdlip Clo.)
Nairne Gro. *SE24* —5D **94**
Nairn Rd. *Ruis* —6A **38**
Nairn St. *E14* —5E **64**
Naish Ct. *N1* —7J **45**
Naldera Gdns. *SE3* —6J **81**
Nallhead Rd. *Felt* —5A **102**
Namba Roy Clo. *SW16* —4K **109**
Namton Dri. *T Hth* —4K **123**
Nan Clark's La. *NW7* —2F **13**
Nankin St. *E14* —6C **64**
Nansen Ho. *NW10* —7K **41**
(off Stonebridge Pk.)
Nansen Rd. *SW11* —3E **92**
Nansen Village. *N12* —4E **14**
Nant Ct. *NW2* —2H **43**
Nantes Clo. *SW18* —4A **92**
Nantes Pas. *E1* —5F **63** (5J **145**)
Nant Rd. *NW2* —2H **43**
Nant St. *E2* —3H **63**
Naoroji St. *WC1* —3A **62** (2J **143**)
Napier. *NW9* —1B **28**
Napier Av. *E14* —5C **80**
Napier Av. *SW6* —3H **91**
Napier Clo. *SE8* —7B **80**
Napier Clo. *W14* —3G **75**
Napier Ct. *SW6* —3H **91**
(off Ranelagh Gdns.)
Napier Ct. Hayes —4A **54**
(off Dunedin Way)
Napier Gro. *N1* —2C **62**
Napier Pl. *W14* —3H **75**
Napier Rd. *E6* —1E **66**
Napier Rd. *E11* —4G **49**
Napier Rd. *E15* —2G **65**
(in two parts)
Napier Rd. *N17* —3E **30**
Napier Rd. *NW10* —3D **58**
Napier Rd. *SE25* —4H **125**
Napier Rd. *W14* —3G **75**
Napier Rd. *Belv* —4F **85**
Napier Rd. *Brom* —4K **127**
Napier Rd. *Enf* —5E **8**

Napier Rd. *Iswth* —4A **88**
Napier Rd. *S Croy* —7D **134**
Napier Rd. *Wemb* —5D **40**
Napier Ter. *N1* —7B **46**
Napoleon Rd. *E5* —3H **47**
Napoleon Rd. *Twic* —7B **88**
Narbonne Av. *SW4* —5G **93**
Narborough St. *SW6* —2K **91**
Narcissus Rd. *NW6* —5J **43**
Nardini. *NW9* —1B **26**
(off Concourse, The)
Naresby Fold. *Stan* —6H **11**
Narford Rd. *E5* —3G **47**
Narrow St. *E14* —7A **64**
Narrow St. *W3* —1H **73**
Narrow Way. *Brom* —6C **128**
Narvic Ho. *SE5* —2C **94**
Nascot St. *W12* —6E **58**
Naseby Clo. *NW6* —7A **44**
Naseby Clo. *Iswth* —1J **87**
Naseby Ct. *Sidc* —4K **115**
Naseby Rd. *SE19* —6D **110**
Naseby Rd. *Dag* —3G **53**
Naseby Rd. *Ilf* —1D **34**
Naseby Tower. *SE14* —7A **80**
(off Desmond St.)
Nash Ct. *Kent* —6B **24**
Nash Grn. *Brom* —6J **113**
Nash Ho. *E17* —4D **32**
Nash La. *Kes* —7J **137**
Nash Pl. *E14* —1D **80**
Nash Rd. *N9* —2D **18**
Nash Rd. *SE4* —4A **96**
Nash Rd. *Romf* —4D **36**
Nash St. *NW1* —3F **61** (1K **141**)
Nash Way. *Kent* —6B **24**
Nasmyth St. *W6* —3D **74**
Nassau Path. *SE28* —1C **84**
Nassau Rd. *SW13* —1B **90**
Nassau St. *W1* —5G **61** (6A **142**)
Nassington Rd. *NW3* —4C **44**
Natalie M. *Twic* —3H **103**
Natal Rd. *N11* —6D **16**
Natal Rd. *SW16* —6H **109**
Natal Rd. *Ilf* —4F **51**
Natal Rd. *T Hth* —3D **124**
Nathan Ct. *N9* —7D **8**
(off Causeyware Rd.)
Nathaniel Clo. *E1*
—5F **63** (6K **145**)
Nathaniel Ct. *E17* —6A **32**
Nathans Rd. *Wemb* —1C **40**
Nathan Way. *SE28* —4J **83**
Nation Way. *E4* —1K **19**
Naval Row. *E14* —7E **64**
Naval Wlk. *Brom* —2J **127**
Navarino Gro. *E8* —6G **47**
Navarino Mans. *E8* —6G **47**
Navarino Rd. *E8* —6G **47**
Navarre Rd. *E6* —2C **66**
Navarre St. *E2* —4F **63** (3J **145**)
Navenby Wlk. *E3* —4C **64**
Navestock Clo. *E4* —3K **19**
Navestock Cres. *Wfd G* —7F **21**
Navestock Ho. *Bark* —2B **68**
Navigator Dri. *S'hall* —2G **71**
Navy St. *SW4* —3H **93**
Nayland Ho. *SE6* —4E **112**
Naylor Gro. *Enf* —5E **8**
Naylor Rd. *N20* —2F **15**
Naylor Rd. *SE15* —7H **79**
Nazareth Gdns. *SE15* —2G **95**
Nazrul St. *E2* —3F **63** (1J **145**)
Neagle Clo. *E7* —4J **49**

Neagle Ho. *NW2* —3E **42**
(off Stoll Clo.)
Neal Av. *S'hall* —4D **54**
Nealden St. *SW9* —3K **93**
Neale Clo. *N2* —3A **28**
Neal St. *WC2* —6J **61** (1E **148**)
Neal's Yd. *WC2* —6J **61** (1E **148**)
Near Acre. *NW9* —1B **28**
Neasden Clo. *NW10* —5A **42**
Neasden Junction. (Junct.)
—4A **42**
Neasden La. *NW10* —3A **42**
Neasden La. N. *NW10* —3K **41**
Neasham Rd. *Dag* —5B **52**
Neate St. *SE5* —6E **78** (7G **157**)
Neath Gdns. *Mord* —6A **122**
Neath Ho. *SE24* —6B **94**
(off Dulwich Rd.)
Neathouse Pl. *SW1*
—4G **77** (3A **154**)
Neatscourt Rd. *E6* —5B **66**
Nebraska St. *SE1*
—2D **78** (7E **150**)
Neckinger. *SE1* —3F **79** (1K **157**)
Neckinger Est. *SE16*
—3F **79** (1K **157**)
Neckinger St. *SE1*
—2F **79** (7K **151**)
Nectarine Way. *SE13* —2D **96**
Needham Rd. *W11* —6J **59**
Needham Ter. *NW2* —3F **43**
Needleman St. *SE16* —2K **79**
Needwood Ho. *N4* —1C **46**
Neeld Cres. *NW4* —5D **26**
Neeld Cres. *Wemb* —5G **41**
Neil Wates Cres. *SW2* —1A **110**
Nelgarde Rd. *SE6* —7C **96**
Nella Rd. *W6* —6F **75**
Nelldale Rd. *SE16* —4J **79**
Nello James Gdns. *SE27*
—4D **110**
Nelson Clo. *Croy* —1B **134**
Nelson Clo. *Romf* —1H **37**
Nelson Ct. *SE1* —2B **78** (6B **150**)
Nelson Gdns. *E2* —3G **63**
Nelson Gdns. *Houn* —6E **86**
Nelson Gro. Rd. *SW19* —1A **122**
Nelson Ind. Est. *SW19* —1K **121**
Nelson Mandela Clo. *N10* —2E **28**
Nelson Mandela Rd. *SE3* —3A **98**
Nelson Pas. *EC1*
—3C **62** (1D **144**)
Nelson Pl. *N1* —2B **62** (1B **144**)
Nelson Pl. *Sidc* —4A **116**
Nelson Rd. *E4* —6J **19**
Nelson Rd. *E11* —4J **33**
Nelson Rd. *N8* —5K **29**
Nelson Rd. *N9* —2C **18**
Nelson Rd. *N15* —4E **30**
Nelson Rd. *SE10* —6E **80**
Nelson Rd. *SW19* —7A **108**
Nelson Rd. *Belv* —5F **85**
Nelson Rd. *Brom* —4A **128**
Nelson Rd. *Enf* —6E **8**
Nelson Rd. *Harr* —1H **39**
Nelson Rd. *Houn* —6E **86**
Nelson Rd. *N Mald* —5K **119**
Nelson Rd. *Sidc* —4A **116**
Nelson Rd. *Stan* —6H **11**
Nelson Rd. *Twic* —6E **86**
Nelson Rd. M. *SW19* —7K **107**
Nelson Sq. *SE1*
—2B **78** (6A **150**)
Nelson's Row. *SW4* —4H **93**
Nelson St. *E1* —6H **63**

Nelson St. E6 —2D 66
(in two parts)
Nelson St. E16 —7H 65
(in two parts)
Nelsons Yd. NW1 —2G 61
(off Mornington Cres.)
Nelson Ter. N1 —2B 62 (1B 144)
Nelson Wlk. SE14 —1A 80
Nemoure Rd. W3 —7J 57
Nene Gdns. Felt —2D 102
Nepaul Rd. SW11 —3C 92
Nepean St. SW15 —6C 90
Neptune Rd. Harr —6H 23
Neptune St. SE16 —3J 79
Nero Ct. Bren —7D 72
Nesbit Rd. SE9 —4B 98
Nesbitt Clo. SE3 —3G 97
Nesbitts All. Barn —3C 4
Nesbitt Sq. SE19 —7E 124
Nesham St. E1 —1G 79
Ness St. SE16 —3G 79
Nesta Rd. Wfd G —6B 20
Nestor Av. N21 —6G 7
Netheravon Rd. W7 —1K 71
Netheravon Rd. N. W4 —4B 74
Netheravon Rd. S. W4 —5B 74
Netherbury Rd. W5 —3D 72
Netherby Gdns. Enf —4D 6
Netherby Rd. SE23 —7J 95
Nether Clo. N3 —7D 14
Nethercourt Av. N3 —6D 14
Netherfield Gdns. Bark —7H 51
Netherfield Rd. N12 —5E 14
Netherfield Rd. SW17 —3E 108
Netherford Rd. SW4 —2G 93
Netherhall Gdns. NW3 —6A 44
Netherhall Way. NW3 —5A 44
Netherlands Rd. New Bar —6G 5
Netherleigh Clo. N6 —1F 45
Nether St. N3 & N12 —1J 27
Netherton Gro. SW10 —6A 76
Netherton Rd. N15 —6D 30
Netherton Rd. Twic —5A 88
Netherwood. N2 —2B 28
Netherwood Rd. W14 —3F 75
Netherwood St. NW6 —7H 43
Nethewode Ct. Belv —3H 85
(off Lwr. Park Rd.)
Netley Clo. New Ad —7E 136
Netley Clo. Sutt —5F 131
Netley Gdns. Mord —7A 122
Netley Rd. E17 —5B 32
Netley Rd. Bren —6E 72
Netley Rd. Ilf —5H 35
Netley Rd. Mord —7A 122
Netley St. NW1 —3G 61 (2A 142)
Nettleden Av. Wemb —6G 41
Nettlefold Pl. SE27 —3B 110
Nettlestead Clo. Beck —7B 112
Nettleton Rd. SE14 —1K 95
Nettlewood Rd. SW16 —7H 109
Neuchatel Rd. SE6 —2B 112
Nevada Clo. N Mald —4J 119
Nevada St. SE10 —6E 80
Nevern Mans. SW5 —4J 75
(off Warwick Rd.)
Nevern Pl. SW5 —4J 75
Nevern Rd. SW5 —4J 75
Nevern Sq. SW5 —4J 75
Nevil Ho. SW9 —2B 94
(off Loughborough Est.)
Nevill Ct. EC4 —6A 62 (7K 143)
(off E. Harding St.)
Neville Av. N Mald —1K 119
Neville Clo. E11 —3H 49

Neville Clo. NW1
—2H 61 (1D 142)
Neville Clo. NW6 —2H 59
Neville Clo. SE15 —1G 95
Neville Clo. W3 —2J 73
Neville Clo. Houn —2F 87
Neville Clo. Sidc —4K 115
Neville Dri. N2 —6A 28
Neville Gdns. Dag —3D 52
Neville Gill Clo. SW18 —6J 91
Neville Ho. N11 —4K 15
Neville Ho. N22 —6E 16
(off Neville Pl.)
Neville Pl. N22 —1K 29
Neville Rd. E7 —7J 49
Neville Rd. NW6 —2H 59
Neville Rd. W5 —4D 56
Neville Rd. Croy —7D 124
Neville Rd. Dag —2D 52
Neville Rd. Ilf —1G 35
Neville Rd. King T —2G 119
Neville Rd. Rich —3C 104
Nevilles Ct. NW2 —3C 42
Neville St. SW7
—5B 76 (5A 152)
Neville Ter. SW7
—5B 76 (5A 152)
Neville Wlk. Cars —7C 122
Nevill Rd. N16 —4E 46
Nevin Dri. E4 —1J 19
Nevinson Clo. SW18 —6B 92
Nevis Rd. SW17 —2E 108
Nevitt Ho. N1 —2D 62
(off Cranston Est.)
Newark Cres. NW10 —3K 57
Newark Ho. SW9 —2B 94
Newark Knok. E6 —6E 66
Newark Pde. NW4 —3C 26
Newark Rd. S Croy —6D 134
Newark St. E1 —5H 63
(in two parts)
Newark Way. NW4 —4C 26
New Ash Clo. N2 —3B 28
New Barn Rd. Swan —7K 117
New Barns Av. Mitc —4H 123
New Barn St. E13 —4J 65
New Barns Way. Chig —3K 21
New Bentham Ct. N1 —7C 46
(off Ecclesbourne Rd.)
Newbolt Av. Sutt —5E 130
Newbolt Ho. SE17
—5D 78 (5E 156)
Newbolt Rd. Stan —5E 10
New Bond St. W1
—6F 61 (1J 147)
Newborough Grn. N Mald
—4K 119
New Brent St. NW4 —5E 26
Newbridge Point. SE23 —3K 111
(off Windrush La.)
New Bri. St. EC4
—6B 62 (1A 150)
New Broad St. EC2
—5E 62 (6G 145)
New B'way. W5 —7D 56
New B'way. Hamp —5H 103
Newburgh Rd. W3 —1J 73
Newburgh St. W1
—6G 61 (1B 148)
New Burlington M. W1
—7G 61 (2A 148)
New Burlington Pl. W1
—7G 61 (2A 148)
New Burlington St. W1
—7G 61 (2A 148)
Newdales Clo. N9 —2B 18

Newburn St. SE11
—5K 77 (5H 155)
Newbury Clo. N'holt —6D 38
Newbury Ct. Sidc —4K 115
Newbury Gdns. Eps —4B 130
Newbury Ho. N22 —1J 29
Newbury Ho. SW9 —2B 94
Newbury M. NW5 —6E 44
Newbury Rd. E4 —6K 19
Newbury Rd. Brom —3J 127
Newbury Rd. Ilf —6J 35
Newbury St. EC1
—5C 62 (6C 144)
Newbury Way. N'holt —6C 38
New Bus. Cen., The. NW10
—3B 58
New Butt La. SE8 —7C 80
(in two parts)
New Butt La. N. SE8 —7C 80
(off Reginald Rd.)
Newby Clo. Enf —2K 7
Newby Pl. E14 —7E 64
Newby St. SW8 —3F 93
New Caledonian Wharf. SE16
—3B 80
Newcastle Clo. EC4
—6B 62 (7A 144)
Newcastle Pl. W2
—5B 60 (5B 140)
Newcastle Row. EC1
—4A 62 (4K 143)
New Cavendish St. W1
—5E 60 (6H 141)
New Change. EC4
—6C 62 (1C 150)
New Charles St. EC1
—3B 62 (1B 144)
New Chu. Rd. SE5 —7C 78
(in two parts)
New City Rd. E13 —3A 66
New Clo. SW19 —3A 122
New Clo. Felt —5C 102
New Colebrooke Ct. Cars
(off Stanley Rd.) —7E 132
New College Ct. NW3 —6A 44
(off College Cres.)
New College M. N1 —7A 46
New College Pde. NW3 —6B 44
(off College Cres.)
Newcombe Gdns. SW16 —4J 109
Newcombe Pk. NW7 —5F 13
Newcombe Pk. Wemb —1F 57
Newcombe St. W8 —1J 75
Newcomen Rd. E11 —3H 49
Newcomen Rd. SW11 —3B 92
Newcomen St. SE1
—2D 78 (6E 150)
New Compton St. WC2
—6H 61 (1D 148)
New Concordia Wharf. SE1
—2G 79 (6K 151)
New Ct. EC4 —7A 62 (2J 149)
New Ct. N'holt —5F 39
Newcourt St. NW8
—2C 60 (1C 140)
New Covent Garden Mkt. SW8
—7H 77
New Coventry St. W1
—7H 61 (3D 148)
New Crane Pl. E1 —1J 79
New Cross. (Junct.) —1B 96
New Cross Gate. (Junct.) —1K 95
New Cross Rd. SE15 & SE14
—7J 79

Newdene Av. N'holt —2B 54
Newell St. E14 —6B 64
New And. NW3 —3A 44
New End Sq. NW3 —4B 44
New England Ind. Est. Bark
—2G 67
Newent Clo. SE15 —7E 78
New Era Est. N1 —1E 62
(off Phillipp St.)
New Farm Av. Brom —4J 127
New Fetter La. EC4
—6A 62 (7K 143)
Newfield Clo. Hamp —7E 102
Newfield Rise. NW2 —3D 42
New Forest La. Chig —6K 21
Newgale Gdns. Edgw —1F 25
Newgate. Croy —1C 134
Newgate Clo. Felt —3C 102
Newgate St. E4 —3B 20
Newgate St. EC1
—6B 62 (7B 144)
New Globe Wlk. SE1
—1C 78 (4C 150)
New Goulston St. E1
—6E 63 (7J 145)
Newham Grn. N22 —1A 30
Newham's Row. SE1
—2E 78 (7H 151)
Newham Way. E16 & E6 —5H 65
Newhaven Gdns. SE9 —4B 98
Newhaven La. E16 —4H 65
Newhaven Rd. SE25 —5D 124
New Heston Rd. Houn —7D 70
New Horizons Ct. Bren —6C 72
Newhouse Av. Romf —3D 36
Newhouse Clo. N Mald —7A 120
Newhouse Wlk. Mord —7A 122
Newick Clo. Bex —6H 101
Newick Rd. E5 —4H 47
Newing Grn. Brom —7B 114
Newington Barrow Way. N7
—3K 45
Newington Butts. SE11
—4B 78 (4B 156)
Newington Causeway. SE1
—3C 78 (2B 156)
Newington Grn. N16 & N1
—5D 46
Newington Grn. Mans. N16
—5D 46
Newington Grn. Rd. N1 —6D 46
New Inn B'way. EC2
—4E 62 (3H 145)
New Inn Pas. WC2
—6K 61 (1H 149)
New Inn Sq. EC2
—4E 62 (3H 145)
New Inn St. EC2
—4E 62 (3H 145)
New Inn Yd. EC2
—4E 62 (3H 145)
New Jubilee Ct. Wfd G —7D 20
New Kelvin Av. Tedd —6J 103
New Kent Rd. SE1
—3C 78 (2C 156)
New Kings Rd. SW6 —2H 91
New King St. SE8 —6C 80
Newland Ct. EC1
—4D 62 (3E 144)
Newland Dri. Enf —1C 8
Newland Gdns. W13 —2A 72
Newland Ho. N8 —3J 29
(off Newland Rd.)
Newland Rd. N8 —3J 29
Newlands Clo. Edgw —3K 11

Newlands Clo. S'hall —5C 70
Newlands Clo. Wemb —6C 40
Newlands Ct. SE9 —6E 98
Newlands Pk. SE26 —6J 111
Newlands Pl. Barn —5A 4
Newlands Quay. E1 —7J 63
Newlands Rd. SW16 —2J 123
Newlands Rd. Wfd G —2C 20
Newlands, The. Wall —7H 133
Newland St. E16 —1C 82
Newlands Wood. New Ad
—7B 136
Newling St. E6 —6D 66
New London St. EC3
—7E 62 (2H 151)
New Lydenburg Commercial Est.
SE7 —3A 82
New Lydenburg St. SE7 —3A 82
Newlyn Gdns. Harr —7D 22
Newlyn Ho. Pinn —1D 22
Newlyn Rd. N17 —1F 31
Newlyn Rd. Barn —4C 4
Newlyn Rd. Well —2K 99
Newman Pas. W1
—5G 61 (6B 142)
Newman Rd. E13 —3K 65
Newman Rd. E17 —5K 31
Newman Rd. Brom —1J 127
Newman Rd. Croy —1K 133
Newman Rd. Hayes —7A 54
Newman Rd. Ind. Est. Croy
—7K 123
Newman's Ct. EC3
—6D 62 (1F 151)
Newmans La. Surb —6D 118
Newman's Row. WC2
—5K 61 (6H 143)
Newman St. W1
—5G 61 (6B 142)
Newman's Way. Barn —1F 5
Newman Yd. W1
—6H 61 (7C 142)
Newmarket Av. N'holt —5E 38
Newmarket Grn. SE9 —7B 98
Newminster Rd. Mord —6A 122
New Mt. St. E15 —7F 49
Newnes Path. SW15 —4D 90
Newnet Clo. Cars —1D 132
Newnham Av. Ruis —1A 38
Newnham Clo. N'holt —6G 39
Newnham Clo. T Hth —2C 124
Newnham Gdns. N'holt —6G 39
Newnham Lodge. Belv —5G 85
Newnham M. N22 —7F 17
Newnham Rd. N22 —1K 29
Newnhams Clo. Brom —3D 128
Newnham Ter. SE1
—3A 78 (1J 155)
Newnham Way. Harr —5E 24
New North Pl. EC2
—4E 62 (3G 145)
New North Rd. N1
—7C 46 (1F 145)
New N. Rd. Ilf —1H 35
New North St. WC1
—5K 61 (5G 143)
Newnton Clo. N4 —7D 30
New Oak Rd. N2 —2A 28
New Orleans Wlk. N19 —7H 29
New Oxford St. WC1
—6H 61 (7D 142)
New Pk. Av. N13 —3H 17
New Pk. Clo. N'holt —6C 38
New Pk. Est. N18 —5D 18
New Pk. Ho. N13 —4E 16

New Pk. Rd. *SW2* —1H **109**
New Pl. *New Ad* —6C **136**
New Pl. Sq. *SE16* —3H **79**
New Plaistow Rd. *E15* —1G **65**
Newport Av. *E13* —4K **65**
Newport Ct. *WC2*
　　　　　—7H **61** (2D **148**)
Newport Lodge. Enf —5K 7
　(off Village Rd.)
Newport Pl. *WC2*
　　　　　—7H **61** (2D **148**)
Newport Rd. *E10* —2E **48**
Newport Rd. *E17* —4A **32**
Newport Rd. *SW13* —1C **90**
Newport St. *SE11*
　　　　　—4K **77** (4G **155**)
Newquay Cres. *Harr* —2C **38**
Newquay Ho. *SE11*
　　　　　—5A **78** (5H **155**)
Newquay Rd. *SE6* —2D **112**
New Quebec St. *W1*
　　　　　—6D **60** (1F **147**)
New Ride. *SW7 & SW1*
　　　　　—2B **76** (6B **146**)
New River Ct. *N5* —4C **46**
New River Cres. *N13* —4G **17**
New River Head. *EC1*
　　　　　—3A **62** (2K **143**)
New River Wlk. *N1* —6C **46**
New River Way. *N4* —7D **30**
New Rd. *E1* —5H **63**
New Rd. *E4* —4J **19**
New Rd. *N8* —5J **29**
New Rd. *N9* —3B **18**
New Rd. *N17* —1F **31**
New Rd. *N22* —1C **30**
New Rd. *NW7* —7B **14**
New Rd. *SE2* —4D **84**
New Rd. *Bren* —6D **72**
New Rd. *Dag & Rain* —2G **69**
New Rd. *Hanw* —5C **102**
New Rd. *Harr* —4K **39**
New Rd. *Houn* —4F **87**
New Rd. *Ilf* —2J **51**
New Rd. *King T* —7G **105**
New Rd. *Mitc* —1D **132**
New Rd. *Rich* —4C **104**
New Rd. *Well* —2B **100**
New Rd. Hill. *Kes & Orp* —7C **138**
New Rochford St. *NW5* —5D **44**
New Row. *WC2* —7J **61** (2E **148**)
Newry Rd. *Twic* —5A **88**
Newsam Av. *N15* —5D **30**
New Southgate Ind. Est. *N11*
　　　　　—5B **16**
New Spitalfields Mkt. *E10* —3D **48**
New Spring Gdns. Wlk. *SE11*
　　　　　—5J **77** (6F **155**)
New Sq. *WC2* —6K **61** (7J **143**)
New Sq. Pas. *WC2*
　　　　　—6A **62** (7J **143**)
Newstead Clo. *N12* —6H **15**
Newstead Ct. *N'holt* —3C **54**
Newstead Rd. *SE12* —7H **97**
Newstead Wlk. *Cars* —7J **121**
Newstead Way. *SW19* —4F **107**
New St. *EC2* —5E **62** (6H **145**)
New St. Hill. *Brom* —5K **113**
New St. Sq. *EC4*
　　　　　—6A **62** (7K **143**)
Newton Av. *N10* —1E **28**
Newton Av. *W3* —2J **73**
Newton Clo. *E17* —6A **32**
Newton Clo. *Harr* —2E **38**
Newton Gro. *W4* —4A **74**

Newton Ho. *E17* —3D **32**
　(off Prospect Hill)
Newton Ho. *SE20* —1K **125**
Newton Ind. Est. *Romf* —4D **36**
Newton Mans. *W14* —6G **75**
　(off Queen's Club Gdns.)
Newton Point. *E16* —6H **65**
　(off Clarkson Rd.)
Newton Rd. *E15* —5F **49**
Newton Rd. *N15* —5G **31**
Newton Rd. *NW2* —4E **42**
Newton Rd. *SW19* —7G **107**
Newton Rd. *W2* —6K **59**
Newton Rd. *Harr* —2J **23**
Newton Rd. *Iswth* —2K **87**
Newton Rd. *Well* —3A **100**
Newton Rd. *Wemb* —7F **41**
Newton St. *WC2* —6J **61** (7F **143**)
Newton's Yd. *SW18* —5J **91**
Newton Ter. *Brom* —6B **128**
Newton Wlk. *Edgw* —1H **25**
Newton Way. *N18* —5H **17**
Newtown St. *SW11* —1F **93**
New Trinity Rd. *N2* —3B **28**
New Turnstile. *WC1*
　　　　　—5K **61** (6G **143**)
New Union Clo. *E14* —3E **80**
New Union St. *EC2*
　　　　　—5D **62** (6E **144**)
New Wanstead. *E11* —6H **33**
New Way Rd. *NW9* —4A **26**
New Wharf Rd. *N1* —2J **61**
New Zealand Way. *W12* —7D **58**
Niagra Av. *W5* —4C **72**
Niagra Clo. *N1* —2C **62**
Nibthwaite Rd. *Harr* —5J **23**
Nicholas Clo. *Gnfd* —2F **55**
Nicholas Ct. W4 —6A 74
　(off Corney Reach Way)
Nicholas Gdns. *W5* —2D **72**
Nicholas La. *EC4*
　　　　　—7D **62** (2F **151**)
Nicholas Pas. *EC4*
　　　　　—7D **62** (1F **151**)
Nicholas Rd. *E1* —4J **63**
Nicholas Rd. *Croy* —4J **133**
Nicholas Rd. *Dag* —2F **53**
Nicholas St. *SE8* —1B **96**
Nicholay Rd. *N19* —1H **45**
Nichol Clo. *N14* —1C **16**
Nicholes Rd. *Houn* —4E **86**
Nichol La. *Brom* —7J **113**
Nicholl Ho. *N4* —1C **46**
Nichollsfield Wlk. *N7* —5K **45**
Nicholls Point. E15 —1J 65
　(off Park Gro.)
Nicholl St. *E2* —1G **63**
Nichols Clo. N4 —1A 46
　(off Osborne Rd.)
Nichols Grn. *W5* —5D **56**
Nicholson Ct. *E17* —4A **32**
Nicholson Dri. *Bush* —1B **10**
Nicholson Ho. *SE17*
　　　　　—5D **78** (5E **156**)
Nicholson Rd. *Croy* —1F **135**
Nicholson St. *SE1*
　　　　　—1B **78** (5A **150**)
Nichol's Sq. *E2* —2F **63** (1J **145**)
Nimrod Clo. *N'holt* —3B **54**
Nimrod Pas. *N1* —6E **46**
Nimrod Rd. *SW16* —6F **109**
Nine Acres Clo. *E12* —5C **50**
Nine Elms La. *SW8* —7G **77**
Nineteenth Rd. *Mitc* —4J **123**
Ninhams Wood. *Orp* —4E **138**
Nita Ct. *SE12* —1J **113**
Nithdale Rd. *SE18* —7F **83**

Nicol Clo. *Twic* —6B **88**
Nicoll Ct. *N10* —7A **16**
Nicoll Ct. *NW10* —1A **58**
Nicoll Pl. *NW4* —6D **26**
Nicoll Rd. *NW10* —1A **58**
Nicolson. *NW9* —1A **26**
Nicosia Rd. *SW18* —7C **92**
Niederwald Rd. *SE26* —4A **112**
Nigel Clo. *N'holt* —1C **54**
Nigel Ct. *N3* —7E **14**
Nigel M. *Ilf* —4F **51**
Nigel Playfair Av. *W6* —5D **74**
Nigel Rd. *E7* —5A **50**
Nigel Rd. *SE15* —3G **95**
Nigeria Rd. *SE7* —7A **82**
Nighthawk. *NW9* —1B **26**
Nightingale Av. *E4* —5B **20**
Nightingale Clo. *E4* —4A **20**
Nightingale Clo. *W4* —6J **73**
Nightingale Clo. *Cars* —2E **132**
Nightingale Clo. *Pinn* —5A **22**
Nightingale Ct. N4 —2K 45
　(off Tollington Pk.)
Nightingale Ct. SW6 —1K 91
　(off Maltings Pl.)
Nightingale Ct. *Short* —2G **127**
Nightingale Gro. *SE13* —5F **97**
Nightingale Heights. *SE18*
　　　　　—6F **83**
Nightingale Ho. *E1* —1G **79**
　(off Thomas More St.)
Nightingale Ho. N1 —1E 62
　(off Wilmer Gdns.)
Nightingale Ho. SE18 —5E 82
　(off Connaught M.)
Nightingale La. *E11* —5J **33**
Nightingale La. *N8* —4J **29**
Nightingale La. *SW12 & SW4*
　　　　　—7D **92**
Nightingale La. *Brom* —2A **128**
Nightingale La. *Rich* —7E **88**
Nightingale M. *E3* —2A **64**
Nightingale Pl. *SE18* —6E **82**
Nightingale Pl. *SW10*
　　　　　—6A **76** (7A **152**)
Nightingale Rd. *E5* —3H **47**
Nightingale Rd. *N9* —6D **8**
Nightingale Rd. *N22* —7D **16**
Nightingale Rd. *NW10* —2B **58**
Nightingale Rd. *W7* —1K **71**
Nightingale Rd. *Cars* —3D **132**
Nightingale Rd. *Hamp* —5E **102**
Nightingale Rd. *Orp* —6G **129**
Nightingale Sq. *SW12* —7E **92**
Nightingale Vale. *SE18* —6E **82**
Nightingale Wlk. *SW4* —6F **93**
Nightingale Way. *E6* —5C **66**
Nikols Wlk. *SW18* —4K **91**
Nile Clo. *N16* —3F **47**
Nile Path. *SE18* —6E **82**
Nile Rd. *E13* —2A **66**
Nile St. *N1* —3C **62** (1D **144**)
Nile Ter. *SE15* —5F **79** (6J **157**)
Nimegen Way. *SE22* —5E **94**
Nimmo Dri. *Bush* —1C **10**
Nimmo. *NW9* —1A **26**
Nimrod Clo. *N'holt* —3B **54**
Nimrod Pas. *N1* —6E **46**
Nimrod Rd. *SW16* —6F **109**
Nine Acres Clo. *E12* —5C **50**
Nine Elms La. *SW8* —7G **77**
Nineteenth Rd. *Mitc* —4J **123**
Ninhams Wood. *Orp* —4E **138**
Nita Ct. *SE12* —1J **113**
Nithdale Rd. *SE18* —7F **83**

Niton Clo. *Barn* —6A **4**
Niton Rd. *Rich* —3G **89**
Niton St. *SW6* —7F **75**
Nobel Ho. *SE5* —2C **94**
Nobel Rd. *N18* —4D **18**
Noble Corner. *Houn* —1E **86**
Noble Ct. E1 —7G 63
　(off Cable St.)
Noble Ct. *Mitc* —2B **122**
Noblefield Heights. *N2* —5C **28**
Noble St. *EC2* —6C **62** (7C **144**)
Noel. *NW9* —1A **26**
Noel Ct. *Houn* —3D **86**
Noel Pk. Rd. *N22* —2A **30**
Noel Rd. *E6* —4C **66**
Noel Rd. *N1* —2B **62**
Noel Rd. *W3* —7G **57**
Noel Sq. *Dag* —4C **52**
Noel St. *W1* —6G **61** (1B **148**)
Noel Ter. *SE23* —2J **111**
Noel Ter. *Sidc* —4B **116**
Nolan Way. *E5* —4G **47**
Nolton Pl. *Edgw* —1F **25**
Nonsuch Wlk. *Sutt* —7F **131**
Noorwood Gdns. *Hayes* —4A **54**
Nora Gdns. *NW4* —4F **27**
Norbiton Av. *King T* —1G **119**
Norbiton Comn. Rd. *King T*
　　　　　—3H **119**
Norbreck Gdns. *NW10* —3F **57**
Norbreck Pde. *NW10* —3E **56**
Norbroke St. *W12* —7B **58**
Norburn St. *W10* —5G **59**
Norbury Av. *SW16 & T Hth*
　　　　　—1K **123**
Norbury Av. *Houn* —4H **87**
Norbury Clo. *SW16* —1A **124**
Norbury Ct. Rd. *SW16* —3J **123**
Norbury Cres. *SW16* —1K **123**
Norbury Cross. *SW16* —3J **123**
Norbury Gdns. *Romf* —5D **36**
Norbury Gro. *NW7* —3F **13**
Norbury Hill. *SW16* —7A **110**
Norbury Rise. *SW16* —3J **123**
Norbury Rd. *E4* —5H **19**
Norbury Rd. *T Hth* —2C **124**
Norbury Trad. Est. *SW16*
　　　　　—2K **123**
Norcombe Gdns. *Harr* —6E **24**
Norcombe Ho. N19 —3H 45
　(off Wedmore St.)
Norcott Clo. *Hayes* —4A **54**
Norcott Rd. *N16* —2G **47**
Norcroft Gdns. *SE22* —7G **95**
Norcutt Rd. *Twic* —1J **103**
Nordenfeldt Rd. *Eri* —5K **85**
Norfield Rd. *Dart* —4J **117**
Norfolk Av. *N13* —6G **17**
Norfolk Av. *N15* —6F **31**
Norfolk Clo. *N2* —3C **28**
Norfolk Clo. *N13* —6G **17**
Norfolk Clo. *Barn* —4K **5**
Norfolk Clo. *Twic* —6B **88**
Norfolk Cres. *W2*
　　　　　—6C **60** (7C **140**)
Norfolk Cres. *Sidc* —7J **99**
Norfolk Gdns. *Bexh* —1F **101**
Norfolk Gdns. *Houn* —5D **86**
Norfolk Ho. *SE8* —1C **96**
Norfolk Ho. *Beck* —1J **125**
Norfolk Ho. Rd. *SW16* —3H **109**
Norfolk Mans. SW11 —1D 92
　(off Prince of Wales Dri.)
Norfolk Pl. *W2* —6B **60** (7B **140**)

Norfolk Pl. *Well* —2A **100**
Norfolk Rd. *E6* —1D **66**
Norfolk Rd. *E17* —2K **31**
Norfolk Rd. *NW8* —1B **60**
Norfolk Rd. *NW10* —7A **42**
Norfolk Rd. *SW19* —7C **108**
Norfolk Rd. *Bark* —7J **51**
Norfolk Rd. *Barn* —3D **4**
Norfolk Rd. *Dag* —5H **53**
Norfolk Rd. *Enf* —6C **8**
Norfolk Rd. *Felt* —1A **102**
Norfolk Rd. *Harr* —5F **23**
Norfolk Rd. *Ilf* —1J **51**
Norfolk Rd. *Romf* —6J **37**
Norfolk Rd. *T Hth* —3C **124**
Norfolk Row. *SE1*
　　　　　—4K **77** (3G **155**)
Norfolk Sq. *W2* —6B **60** (1B **146**)
Norfolk Sq. M. *W2*
　　　　　—6B **60** (1B **146**)
Norfolk St. *E7* —5J **49**
Norfolk Ter. *W6* —5G **75**
Norgrove St. *SW12* —7E **92**
Norhyrst Av. *SE25* —3F **125**
Norland Pl. *W11* —1G **75**
Norland Rd. *W11* —1F **75**
Norlands Cres. *Chst* —1F **129**
Norland Sq. *W11* —1G **75**
Norley Vale. *SW15* —1C **106**
Norlington Rd. *E10 & E11*
　　　　　—1E **48**
Norman Av. *N22* —1B **30**
Norman Av. *Felt* —2C **102**
Norman Av. *S'hall* —7C **54**
Norman Av. *Twic* —7C **88**
Normanby Clo. *SW15* —5H **91**
Normanby Rd. *NW10* —4B **42**
Norman Clo. *N22* —1C **30**
Norman Clo. *Romf* —1H **37**
Norman Ct. *N4* —7A **30**
Norman Ct. *NW10* —7C **42**
Norman Ct. W13 —1B 72
　(off Kirkfield Clo.)
Norman Ct. *Ilf* —7H **35**
Norman Cres. *Houn* —7B **70**
Norman Cres. *Pinn* —1A **22**
Normand Gdns. W14 —6G 75
　(off Greyhound Rd.)
Normand M. *W14* —6G **75**
Normand Rd. *W14* —6H **75**
Normandy Av. *Barn* —5C **4**
Normandy Rd. *SW9* —1A **94**
Normandy Ter. *E16* —6K **65**
Normandy Way. *Eri* —1K **101**
Norman Gro. *E3* —2A **64**
Norman Ho. SW8 —7J 77
　(off Wyvil Rd.)
Norman Ho. *Felt* —2D **102**
Normanhurst Av. *Bexh* —1D **100**
Normanhurst Dri. *Twic* —5A **88**
Normanhurst Rd. *SW2* —2K **109**
Norman Rd. *E6* —4D **66**
Norman Rd. *E11* —2F **49**
Norman Rd. *N15* —5F **31**
Norman Rd. *SE10* —7D **80**
Norman Rd. *SW19* —7A **108**
Norman Rd. *Belv* —3H **85**
Norman Rd. *Ilf* —5F **51**
Norman Rd. *Sutt* —5J **131**
Norman Rd. *T Hth* —5B **124**
Norman's Bldgs. EC1
　　　　　—3C **62** (2C **144**)
Norman's Clo. *NW10* —6K **41**
Normansfield Av. *Tedd* —7C **104**
Normanshire Av. *E4* —4K **19**

Normanshire Dri. *E4* —4H **19**
Norman's Mead. *NW10* —6K **41**
Norman St. *EC1* —3C **62** (2C **144**)
Normanton Av. *SW19* —2J **107**
Normanton Pk. *E4* —2B **20**
Normanton Rd. *S Croy* —6E **134**
Normanton St. *SE23* —2K **111**
Norman Way. *N14* —2D **16**
Norman Way. *W3* —5H **57**
Normington Clo. *SW16* —5A **110**
Norrice Lea. *N2* —5B **28**
Norris. *NW9* —1B **26**
 (off Concourse, The)
Norris St. *SW1* —7H **61** (3C **148**)
Norroy Rd. *SW15* —4F **91**
Norry's Clo. *Cockf* —4J **5**
Norry's Rd. *Cockf* —4J **5**
Norseman Clo. *Ilf* —1B **52**
Norseman Way. *Gnfd* —1F **55**
Norstead Pl. *SW15* —2C **106**
N. Access Rd. *E17* —6K **31**
North Acre. *NW9* —1A **26**
N. Acton Rd. *NW10* —2K **57**
Northall Rd. *Bexh* —2J **101**
Northampton Gro. *N1* —5D **46**
Northampton Pk. *N1* —6C **46**
Northampton Rd. *EC1*
 —4A **62** (3K **143**)
Northampton Rd. *Croy* —2G **135**
Northampton Rd. *Enf* —4F **9**
Northampton Row. *EC1*
 —4A **62** (3K **143**)
Northampton Sq. *EC1*
 —3B **62** (2A **144**)
Northampton St. *N1* —7C **46**
Northanger Rd. *SW16* —6J **109**
N. Audley St. *W1*
 —6E **60** (1G **141**)
North Av. *N18* —4B **18**
North Av. *NW10* —3E **58**
North Av. *W13* —5B **56**
North Av. *Cars* —7E **132**
North Av. *Harr* —6F **23**
North Av. *Rich* —1G **89**
North Av. *S'hall* —7D **54**
North Bank. *NW8*
 —3C **60** (2C **140**)
Northbank Rd. *E17* —2E **32**
N. Birkbeck Rd. *E11* —3F **49**
Northborough Rd. *SW16*
 —3H **123**
Northbourne. *Brom* —7J **127**
Northbourne Rd. *SW4* —5H **93**
N. Branch Av. *NW10* —3E **58**
Northbrook Rd. *N22* —7D **16**
Northbrook Rd. *SE13* —5G **97**
Northbrook Rd. *Barn* —6B **4**
Northbrook Rd. *Croy* —5D **124**
Northbrook Rd. *Ilf* —2E **50**
Northburgh St. *EC1*
 —4B **62** (4B **144**)
N. Carriage Dri. *W2*
 —7C **60** (2C **146**)
Northchurch. *SE17*
 —5D **78** (5F **157**)
Northchurch Rd. *N1* —7D **46**
Northchurch Rd. *Wemb* —6G **41**
Northchurch Ter. *N1* —7E **46**
N. Circular Rd. *E18* —2A **34**
N. Circular Rd. *N3* —4H **27**
N. Circular Rd. *N12* —1B **28**
N. Circular Rd. *N13* —5F **17**
N. Circular Rd. *NW2* —3A **42**
N. Circular Rd. *NW4* —1D **42**
N. Circular Rd. *NW10* —3F **57**

N. Circular Rd. *NW11* —6F **27**
Northcliffe Clo. *Wor Pk* —3A **130**
Northcliffe Dri. *N20* —1C **14**
North Clo. *Bexh* —4D **100**
North Clo. *Dag* —1G **69**
North Clo. *Mord* —4G **121**
N. Colonnade. *E14* —1C **80**
N. Common Rd. *W5* —7E **56**
Northcote. *Pinn* —2A **22**
Northcote Av. *W5* —7E **56**
Northcote Av. *Iswth* —5A **88**
Northcote Av. *S'hall* —7C **54**
Northcote Av. *Surb* —7H **119**
Northcote M. *SW11* —4C **92**
Northcote Rd. *E17* —4A **32**
Northcote Rd. *NW10* —7A **42**
Northcote Rd. *SW11* —5C **92**
Northcote Rd. *Croy* —6D **124**
Northcote Rd. *N Mald* —3J **119**
Northcote Rd. *Sidc* —4J **115**
Northcote Rd. *Twic* —5A **88**
Northcott Av. *N22* —1J **29**
N. Countess Rd. *E17* —2B **32**
North Ct. *SE24* —3B **94**
Northcourt. *W1* —5G **61** (5B **142**)
N. Cray Rd. *Sidc & Bex* —6E **116**
North Cres. *E16* —4F **65**
North Cres. *N3* —2H **27**
North Cres. *WC1*
 —5H **61** (5C **142**)
Northcroft Rd. *W13* —2B **72**
Northcroft Rd. *Eps* —7A **130**
N. Crofts. *SE23* —1H **111**
Northcroft Ter. *W4* —2B **72**
N. Cross Rd. *SE22* —5F **95**
N. Cross Rd. *Ilf* —4G **35**
Northdale Ct. *SE25* —3F **125**
North Dene. *NW7* —3E **12**
North Dene. *Houn* —1F **87**
Northdene Gdns. *N15* —6F **31**
Northdown Gdns. *Ilf* —5J **35**
Northdown Rd. *Well* —2B **100**
Northdown St. *N1*
 —2J **61** (1G **143**)
North Dri. *SW16* —4G **109**
North Dri. *Houn* —2G **87**
N. East Pier. *E1* —1H **79**
Northeast Pl. N1 —2A **62**
 (off Chapel Mkt.)
North End. *NW3* —2A **44**
North End. *Buck H* —1F **21**
North End. *Croy* —2C **134**
N. End Av. *NW3* —2A **44**
N. End Cres. *W14* —4H **75**
N. End Ho. *W14* —4G **75**
 (off Fitzjames Av.)
N. End Pde. W14 —4G **75**
 (off N. End Rd.)
N. End Rd. *NW11* —1J **43**
N. End Rd. *W14 & SW6* —4G **75**
N. End Rd. *Wemb* —3G **41**
N. End Way. *NW3* —2A **44**
Northern Av. *N9* —2K **17**
Northernhay Wlk. *Mord* —4G **121**
Northern Rd. *E13* —2K **65**
Northesk Ho. E1 —1H **47**
 (off Tent St.)
N. Eyot Gdns. *W6* —5B **74**
Northey St. *E14* —7A **64**
N. Feltham Trad. Est. *Felt* —5A **86**
Northfield Av. *W13 & W5* —1B **72**
Northfield Av. *Pinn* —4B **22**
Northfield Clo. *Brom* —1C **128**
Northfield Cres. *Sutt* —4G **131**
Northfield Gdns. *Dag* —4F **53**

Northfield Ho. *SE15* —6G **79**
Northfield Ind. Est. *NW10 & HA0*
 (in two parts) —3G **57**
Northfield Ind. Est. *Wemb*
 —1G **57**
Northfield Path. *Dag* —2F **53**
Northfield Rd. *E6* —7D **50**
Northfield Rd. *N16* —7E **30**
Northfield Rd. *W13* —2B **72**
Northfield Rd. *Barn* —3H **5**
Northfield Rd. *Dag* —4F **53**
Northfield Rd. *Enf* —5C **8**
Northfield Rd. *Houn* —6B **70**
Northfields. *SW18* —4J **91**
Northfields Prospect Bus. Cen.
 SW18 —4J **91**
Northfields Rd. *W3* —5H **57**
N. Flockton St. *SE16* —2G **79**
N. Flower Wlk. *W2* —7A **60**
North Gdns. *SW19* —7B **108**
North Ga. *NW8* —3C **60** (1C **140**)
Northgate Bus. Pk. *Enf* —3C **8**
Northgate Dri. *NW9* —6A **26**
N. Glade, The. *Bex* —1F **117**
N. Gower St. *NW1*
 —3G **61** (2B **142**)
North Grn. *NW9* —7F **13**
North Gro. *N6* —7E **28**
North Gro. *N15* —5D **30**
North Hill. *N6* —6D **28**
N. Hill Av. *N6* —6E **28**
North Ho. *NW8* —2C **60** (1C **140**)
North Ho. *SE8* —5B **80**
N. Hyde La. *S'hall & Houn*
 —5B **70**
Northiam. *N12* —4D **14**
 (in two parts)
Northiam St. *E8 & E9* —1H **63**
Northington St. *WC1*
 —4K **61** (4H **143**)
N. Kent Gro. *SE18* —4D **82**
Northlands St. *SE5* —2C **94**
North La. *Tedd* —6K **103**
Northleach Ct. SE15 —6E **78**
 (off Birdlip Clo.)
N. Lodge. *New Bar* —5F **5**
N. Lodge Clo. *SW15* —5F **91**
North Mall. *N9* —2C **18**
 (off Plevna Rd.)
North M. *WC1* —4K **61** (4H **143**)
North Mt. N20 —2F **15**
 (off High Rd.)
Northolm. *Edgw* —4E **12**
Northolme Gdns. *Edgw* —1G **25**
Northolme Rd. *N5* —4C **46**
Northolt. N17 —2E **30**
 (off Griffin Rd.)
Northolt Av. *Ruis* —5A **38**
Northolt Gdns. *Gnfd* —5K **39**
Northolt Rd. *Harr* —4F **39**
Northover. *Brom* —3H **113**
North Pde. *Edgw* —2G **25**
North Pde. *S'hall* —6E **54**
 (off North Rd.)
North Pk. *SE9* —6D **98**
North Pl. *SW18* —5J **91**
North Pl. *Mitc* —7D **108**
North Pl. *Tedd* —6K **103**
N. Pole La. *Kes* —6H **137**
N. Pole Rd. *W10* —5E **58**
Northport St. *N1* —1D **62**
North Ride. *W2* —7B **60** (3C **146**)
North Rise. *W2* —6C **60** (1D **146**)
North Rd. *N2* —2C **28**
North Rd. *N6* —7E **28**

North Rd. *N7* —6J **45**
North Rd. *N9* —1C **18**
North Rd. *SE18* —4J **83**
North Rd. *SW19* —6A **108**
North Rd. *W5* —3D **72**
North Rd. *Belv* —3H **85**
North Rd. *Bren* —6E **72**
North Rd. *Brom* —1K **127**
North Rd. *Chad H* —5E **36**
North Rd. *Edgw* —1H **25**
North Rd. *Ilf* —2J **51**
North Rd. *Rich* —3G **89**
North Rd. *S'hall* —7E **54**
North Rd. *Surb* —6D **118**
North Rd. *W Wick* —1D **136**
North Row. *W1* —7D **60** (2F **147**)
North Several. *SE3* —2F **97**
Northside Rd. *Brom* —1J **127**
North-South Route. *N17* —2H **31**
Northspur Rd. *Sutt* —3J **131**
North Sq. N9 —2C **18**
 (off Hertford Rd.)
North Sq. *NW11* —5J **27**
Northstead Rd. *SW2* —2A **110**
North St. *E13* —2K **65**
North St. *NW4* —5E **26**
North St. *SW4* —3G **93**
North St. *Bark* —6F **51**
North St. *Bexh* —4G **101**
North St. *Brom* —1J **127**
North St. *Cars* —3D **132**
North St. *Iswth* —3A **88**
North St. *Romf* —3K **37**
North St. Pas. *E13* —2K **65**
N. Tenter St. *E1* —6F **63** (1K **151**)
North Ter. *SW3* —3C **76** (2C **152**)
Northumberland All. *EC3*
 —6E **62** (1H **151**)
Northumberland Av. *E12* —1A **50**
Northumberland Av. *WC2*
 —1J **77** (4E **148**)
Northumberland Av. *Enf* —1C **8**
Northumberland Av. *Iswth*
 —1K **87**
Northumberland Av. *Well* —3J **99**
Northumberland Clo. *Eri* —7J **85**
Northumberland Gdns. *N9*
 —3A **18**
Northumberland Gdns. *Brom*
 —4E **128**
Northumberland Gdns. *Iswth*
 —7A **72**
Northumberland Gro. *N17*
 —7C **18**
Northumberland Pk. *N17* —7A **18**
Northumberland Pk. *Eri* —7J **85**
Northumberland Pk. Ind. Est. *N17*
 —7C **18**
Northumberland Pl. *W2* —6J **59**
Northumberland Pl. *Rich* —6D **88**
Northumberland Rd. *E6* —6C **66**
Northumberland Rd. *E17* —7C **32**
Northumberland Rd. *Harr*
 —5D **22**
Northumberland Rd. *New Bar*
 —6F **5**
Northumberland Row. *Twic*
 —1J **103**
Northumberland St. *WC2*
 —1J **77** (4E **148**)
Northumberland Way. *Eri*
 —1J **101**
Northumbria St. *E14* —6C **64**

N. Verbena Gdns. *W6* —5C **74**
Northview. *N7* —3J **45**
North View. *SW19* —5E **106**
North View. *W5* —4C **56**
North View. *Pinn* —7A **22**
N. View Cres. *NW10* —4B **42**
Northview Dri. *Wfd G* —2B **34**
N. View Rd. *N8* —4H **29**
North Vs. *NW1* —6H **45**
North Wlk. W2 —7K **59**
 (off Bayswater Rd.)
North Wlk. *New Ad* —6D **136**
 (in two parts)
North Way. *N9* —2E **18**
North Way. *N11* —6B **16**
North Way. *NW9* —3H **25**
Northway. *NW11* —5K **27**
Northway. *Mord* —4G **121**
North Way. *Pinn* —4B **22**
Northway. *Wall* —4G **133**
Northway Cir. *NW7* —4E **12**
Northway Cres. *NW7* —4E **12**
Northway Gdns. *NW11* —5K **27**
Northway Rd. *SE5* —3C **94**
Northway Rd. *Croy* —6F **125**
Northways Pde. NW3 —7B **44**
 (off College Cres.)
Northweald La. *King T* —5D **104**
N. West Pier. *E1* —1H **79**
Northwest Pl. *N1* —2A **62**
N. Wharf Rd. *W2*
 —5B **60** (6A **140**)
Northwick Av. *Harr* —6A **24**
Northwick Circ. *Harr* —6C **24**
Northwick Clo. *NW8*
 —4B **60** (3A **140**)
Northwick Pk. Rd. *Harr* —6K **23**
Northwick Rd. *Wemb* —1D **56**
Northwick Ter. *NW8*
 —4B **60** (3A **140**)
Northwick Wlk. *Harr* —7K **23**
Northwold Dri. *Pinn* —3A **22**
Northwold Est. *E5* —2G **47**
Northwold Rd. *N16 & E5* —2F **47**
N. Wood Ct. *SE25* —3G **125**
Northwood Gdns. *N12* —5G **15**
Northwood Gdns. *Gnfd* —5H **39**
Northwood Gdns. *Ilf* —4E **34**
Northwood Ho. *SE27* —4D **110**
Northwood Pl. *Eri* —3F **85**
Northwood Rd. *N6* —7F **29**
Northwood Rd. *SE23* —1B **112**
Northwood Rd. *Cars* —6E **132**
Northwood Rd. *T Hth* —2B **124**
Northwood Rd. *Wat* —6G **10**
N. Woolwich Rd. *E16* —1J **81**
N. Worple Way. *SW14* —3K **89**
Norton Av. *Surb* —7H **119**
Norton Clo. *E4* —5H **19**
Norton Clo. *Enf* —2C **8**
Norton Folgate. *E1*
 —5E **62** (5H **145**)
Norton Gdns. *SW16* —2J **123**
Norton Ho. SW9 —2K **93**
 (off Aytoun Rd.)
Norton Rd. *E10* —1B **48**
Norton Rd. *Dag* —6K **53**
Norton Rd. *Wemb* —6D **40**
Norval Rd. *Wemb* —2B **40**
Norway Ga. *SE16* —3A **80**
Norway Pl. *E14* —6B **64**
Norway St. *SE10* —6D **80**
Norwich M. *Ilf* —1A **52**
Norwich Pl. *Bexh* —4G **101**
Norwich Rd. *E7* —5J **49**

Norwich Rd. *Dag* —2G **69**
Norwich Rd. *Gnfd* —1F **55**
Norwich Rd. *T Hth* —3C **124**
Norwich St. *EC4* —6A **62** (7J **143**)
Norwich Wlk. *Edgw* —7D **12**
Norwood Av. *Romf* —7K **37**
Norwood Av. *Wemb* —1F **57**
Norwood Clo. *S'hall* —4E **70**
Norwood Clo. *Twic* —2H **103**
Norwood Dri. *Harr* —6D **22**
Norwood Gdns. *Hayes* —4A **54**
Norwood Gdns. *S'hall* —4D **70**
Norwood Grn. Rd. *S'hall* —4E **70**
Norwood High St. *SE27* —3B **110**
Norwood Pk. Rd. *SE27* —5C **110**
Norwood Rd. *SE24* —1B **110**
Norwood Rd. *SE27* —2B **110**
Norwood Rd. *S'hall* —3C **70**
Norwood Ter. *S'hall* —4F **71**
Noss Clo. *Sutt* —5C **132**
Notley St. *SE5* —7D **78**
Notson Rd. *SE25* —4H **125**
Notting Barn Rd. *W10* —4F **59**
Nottingdale Sq. *W11* —1G **75**
Nottingham Av. *E16* —5A **66**
Nottingham Ct. *WC2*
 —6J **61** (1E **148**)
Nottingham Pl. *W1*
 —5E **60** (4G **141**)
Nottingham Rd. *E10* —6E **32**
Nottingham Rd. *SW17* —1D **108**
Nottingham Rd. *Iswth* —2K **87**
Nottingham Rd. *S Croy* —4C **134**
Nottingham St. *W1*
 —5E **60** (5G **141**)
Nottingham Ter. *NW1*
 —4E **60** (4G **141**)
Notting Hill Ga. *W11* —1J **75**
Nottingwood Ho. W11 —7G 59
 (off Clarendon Rd.)
Nova M. *Sutt* —1G **131**
Novar Clo. *Orp* —7K **129**
Nova Rd. *Croy* —7B **124**
Novar Rd. *SE9* —1G **115**
Novello St. *SW6* —1J **91**
Nowell Rd. *SW13* —6C **74**
Nower Ct. *Pinn* —4D **22**
Nower Hill. *Pinn* —4D **22**
Noyna Rd. *SW17* —3D **108**
Nuding Clo. *SE13* —3C **96**
Nuffield Lodge. *N6* —6G **29**
Nugent Rd. *N19* —1J **45**
Nugent Rd. *SE25* —3F **125**
Nugents Ct. *Pinn* —1C **22**
Nugents Pk. *Pinn* —1C **22**
Nugent Ter. *NW8* —2A **60**
Numa Ct. *Bren* —7D **72**
Nun Ct. *EC2* —6D **62** (6E **144**)
Nuneaton Rd. *Dag* —7E **52**
Nunhead Cres. *SE15* —3H **95**
Nunhead Est. *SE15* —4H **95**
Nunhead Grn. *SE15* —3H **95**
Nunhead Gro. *SE15* —3H **95**
Nunhead La. *SE15* —3H **95**
Nunhead Pas. *SE15* —4H **95**
Nunnington Clo. *SE9* —3C **114**
Nunns Rd. *Enf* —2H **7**
Nupton Dri. *Barn* —6A **4**
Nursery App. *N12* —6H **15**
Nursery Av. *N3* —2A **28**
Nursery Av. *Bexh* —3F **101**
Nursery Av. *Croy* —2K **135**
Nursery Clo. *SE4* —2B **96**
Nursery Clo. *SW15* —4F **91**
Nursery Clo. *Croy* —2K **135**

Nursery Clo. *Enf* —1E **8**
Nursery Clo. *Orp* —7K **129**
Nursery Clo. *Romf* —6D **36**
Nursery Clo. *Wfd G* —5E **20**
Nursery Ct. *N17* —7A **18**
Nursery Ct. *W13* —5A **56**
Nursery Gdns. *Chst* —6F **115**
Nursery Gdns. *Enf* —1E **8**
Nursery La. *E2* —1F **63**
Nursery La. *E7* —6J **49**
Nursery La. *W10* —5E **58**
Nurserymans Rd. *N11* —2K **15**
Nursery Rd. *E9* —6J **47**
Nursery Rd. *N2* —1B **28**
Nursery Rd. *N14* —7B **6**
Nursery Rd. *SW9* —4K **93**
Nursery Rd. *SW19* —2K **121**
 (Merton)
Nursery Rd. *SW19* —7G **107**
 (Wimbledon)
Nursery Rd. *Pinn* —3A **22**
Nursery Rd. *Sutt* —4A **132**
Nursery Rd. *T Hth* —4D **124**
Nursery Row. *Barn* —3B **4**
Nursery St. *N17* —7A **18**
Nursery Wlk. *NW4* —3D **26**
Nursery Wlk. *Romf* —7K **37**
Nurstead Rd. *Eri* —7G **85**
Nutbourne St. *W10* —3G **59**
Nutbrook St. *SE15* —3G **95**
Nutbrowne Rd. *Dag* —1F **69**
Nutcroft Rd. *SE15* —7H **79**
Nutfield Clo. *N18* —6A **18**
Nutfield Clo. *Cars* —3C **132**
Nutfield Gdns. *IIf* —2K **51**
Nutfield Gdns. *N'holt* —2A **54**
Nutfield Rd. *E15* —4E **48**
Nutfield Rd. *NW2* —3C **42**
Nutfield Rd. *SE22* —4F **95**
Nutfield Rd. *T Hth* —4B **124**
Nutford Pl. *W1* —6D **60** (7D **140**)
Nuthatch Gdns. *SE28* —2H **83**
Nuthurst Av. *SW2* —2K **109**
Nutley Ter. *NW3* —6A **44**
Nutmead Clo. *Bex* —1J **117**
Nutmeg Clo. *E16* —4G **65**
Nutmeg La. *E14* —6F **65**
Nuttall St. *N1* —2E **62**
Nutter La. *E11* —6A **34**
Nutt Gro. *Edgw* —2J **11**
Nutt St. *SE15* —7F **79**
Nutwell St. *SW17* —5C **108**
Nuxley Rd. *Belv* —6F **85**
Nyanza St. *SE18* —6H **83**
Nye Bevan Est. *E5* —3K **47**
Nye Bevan Ho. SW6 —7H 75
 (off Clem Attlee Est.)
Nylands Av. *Rich* —1G **89**
Nymans Gdns. *SW20* —3D **120**
Nynehead St. *SE14* —7A **80**
Nyon Gro. *SE6* —2B **112**
Nyssa Clo. *Wfd G* —6J **21**
Nyssa Ct. *E15* —3G **65**
 (off Teasel Way)
Nyton Clo. *N19* —1J **45**

Oak Apple Ct. *SE12* —1J **113**
Oak Av. *N8* —4J **29**
Oak Av. *N10* —7A **16**
Oak Av. *N17* —7J **17**
Oak Av. *Croy* —2C **136**
Oak Av. *Enf* —1E **6**
Oak Av. *Hamp* —5C **102**
Oak Av. *Houn* —7B **70**

Oak Bank. *New Ad* —6E **136**
Oakbank Gro. *SE24* —4C **94**
Oakbrook Clo. *Brom* —4K **113**
Oakbury Rd. *SW6* —2K **91**
Oak Clo. *N14* —7A **6**
Oak Clo. *Sutt* —2A **132**
Oakcombe Clo. *N Mald* —1A **120**
Oak Cottage Clo. *SE6* —1H **113**
Oak Cotts. *W7* —2J **71**
Oak Ct. SE15 —7F 79
 (off Sumner Rd.)
Oak Cres. *E16* —5G **65**
Oakcroft Clo. *Pinn* —2A **22**
Oakcroft Rd. *SE13* —2F **97**
Oakdale. *N14* —1A **16**
Oakdale Av. *Harr* —5E **24**
Oakdale Ct. *E4* —5K **19**
Oakdale Gdns. *E4* —5K **19**
Oakdale Rd. *E7* —7K **49**
Oakdale Rd. *E11* —2F **49**
Oakdale Rd. *E18* —2K **33**
Oakdale Rd. *N4* —6C **30**
Oakdale Rd. *SE15 & SE4* —3J **95**
Oakdale Rd. *SW16* —5J **109**
Oakdale Rd. *Eps* —7A **130**
Oakdale Way. *Mitc* —7E **122**
Oak Dene. *SE15* —1H **95**
Oakdene. *W13* —5B **56**
Oakdene Av. *Chst* —5E **114**
Oakdene Av. *Eri* —6J **85**
Oakdene Av. *Th Dit* —7A **118**
Oakdene Clo. *Pinn* —1D **22**
Oakdene Dri. *Surb* —7J **119**
Oakdene Rd. *Sutt* —1H **131**
Oakdene Pk. *N3* —7C **14**
Oakdene Rd. *Orp* —5K **129**
Oakden St. *SE11*
 —4A **78** (3K **155**)
Oake Ct. *SW15* —5G **91**
Oakeford Av. *N14* —2D **16**
Oakend Ho. *N4* —7D **30**
Oakenholt Ho. *SE2* —1D **84**
Oakenshaw Clo. *Surb* —7E **118**
Oakes Clo. *E6* —6D **66**
Oakeshott Av. *N6* —2E **44**
Oakey La. *SE1* —3A **78** (1J **155**)
Oakfield. *E4* —5J **19**
Oakfield Av. *Harr* —3B **24**
Oakfield Cen. *SE20* —7H **111**
Oakfield Clo. *N Mald* —5B **120**
Oakfield Ct. *N8* —7J **29**
Oakfield Ct. *NW2* —7F **27**
Oakfield Gdns. *N18* —4K **17**
Oakfield Gdns. *SE19* —5E **110**
 (in two parts)
Oakfield Gdns. *Beck* —5D **126**
Oakfield Gdns. *Cars* —1C **132**
Oakfield Gdns. *Gnfd* —4H **55**
Oakfield La. *Kes* —4A **138**
Oakfield Lodge. IIf —3F 51
 (off Albert Rd.)
Oakfield Rd. *E6* —1C **66**
Oakfield Rd. *E17* —2A **32**
Oakfield Rd. *N3* —1K **27**
Oakfield Rd. *N4* —6A **30**
Oakfield Rd. *N14* —2D **16**
Oakfield Rd. *SE20* —7H **111**
Oakfield Rd. *SW19* —3F **107**
Oakfield Rd. *Croy* —1C **134**
Oakfield Rd. *IIf* —3F **51**
Oakfield Rd. Ind. Est. *SE20*
 —7H **111**
Oakfields Rd. *NW11* —6G **27**
Oakfield St. *SW10* —6A **76**
Oakford Rd. *NW5* —4G **45**

Oak Gdns. *Croy* —2C **136**
Oak Gdns. *Edgw* —2J **25**
Oak Gro. *NW2* —4F **43**
Oak Gro. *W Wick* —1E **136**
Oak Gro. Rd. *SE20* —1J **125**
Oakhall Ct. *E11* —6K **33**
Oak Hall Rd. *E11* —6K **33**
Oakham Clo. *SE6* —2B **112**
Oakham Clo. *Barn* —3J **5**
Oakham Dri. *Brom* —4H **127**
Oakhampton Rd. *NW7* —7A **14**
Oakhill. *Surb* —7E **118**
Oak Hill. *Wfd G* —7A **20**
Oakhill Av. *NW3* —4K **43**
Oakhill Av. *Pinn* —2C **22**
Oak Hill Clo. *Wfd G* —7A **20**
Oakhill Ct. *SE23* —6J **95**
Oakhill Ct. *SW19* —7F **107**
Oak Hill Cres. *Wfd G* —7A **20**
Oakhill Dri. *Surb* —7E **118**
Oak Hill Gdns. *Wfd G* —1G **33**
Oakhill Gro. *Surb* —6E **118**
Oak Hill Pk. *NW3* —4K **43**
Oak Hill Pk. M. *NW3* —4A **44**
Oakhill Path. *Surb* —6E **118**
Oakhill Pl. *SW15* —5J **91**
Oakhill Rd. *SW15* —5H **91**
Oakhill Rd. *SW16* —1K **123**
Oakhill Rd. *Beck* —2E **126**
Oakhill Rd. *Surb* —6E **118**
Oakhill Rd. *Sutt* —3K **131**
Oak Hill Way. *NW3* —4A **44**
Oak Ho. *N2* —2B **28**
Oakhouse Rd. *Bexh* —5G **101**
Oakhurst Av. *Barn* —7H **5**
Oakhurst Av. *Bexh* —7E **84**
Oakhurst Clo. *IIf* —1G **35**
Oakhurst Clo. *Tedd* —5J **103**
Oakhurst Gdns. *E4* —1C **20**
Oakhurst Gdns. *Bexh* —7E **84**
Oakhurst Gro. *SE22* —4G **95**
Oakington Av. *Harr* —7E **22**
Oakington Av. *Wemb* —3F **41**
Oakington Mnr. Dri. *Wemb*
 —5G **41**
Oakington Rd. *W9* —4J **59**
Oakington Way. *N8* —7J **29**
Oakland Rd. *E15* —4F **49**
Oaklands. *N21* —2E **16**
Oaklands. *W13* —5A **56**
Oaklands. *Beck* —1D **126**
Oaklands. *N9* —6C **8**
Oaklands. *Edgw* —2J **25**
Oaklands Av. *Iswth* —6K **71**
Oaklands Av. *Sidc* —7K **99**
Oaklands Av. *T Hth* —4A **124**
Oaklands Av. *W Wick* —3D **136**
Oaklands Clo. *Bexh* —5F **101**
Oaklands Clo. *Orp* —6J **129**
Oaklands Clo. *Wemb* —5D **40**
Oaklands Ct. NW10 —7K 41
 (off Nicoll Rd.)
Oaklands Ct. *Wemb* —5D **40**
Oaklands Dri. *Twic* —7G **87**
Oaklands Est. *SW4* —6G **93**
Oaklands Gro. *W12* —1C **74**
Oaklands Pk. Av. *IIf* —2G **51**
Oaklands Pl. *SW4* —4H **93**
Oaklands Rd. *N20* —7C **4**
Oaklands Rd. *NW2* —4F **43**
Oaklands Rd. *SW14* —3K **89**
Oaklands Rd. *W7* —2K **71**
Oaklands Rd. *Bexh* —4F **101**

Oaklands Rd. *Brom* —7G **113**
Oaklands Way. *Wall* —7H **133**
Oakland Way. *Eps* —6A **130**
Oak La. *E14* —7B **64**
Oak La. *N2* —2B **28**
Oak La. *N11* —6C **16**
Oak La. *Iswth* —4J **87**
Oak La. *Twic* —7A **88**
Oak La. *Wfd G* —4C **20**
Oaklea Pas. *King T* —3D **118**
Oakleafe Gdns. *IIf* —3F **35**
Oakleigh Av. *N20* —2G **15**
Oakleigh Av. *Edgw* —2H **25**
Oakleigh Av. *N20* —3J **15**
Oakleigh Ct. *Barn* —6H **5**
Oakleigh Ct. *Edgw* —2J **25**
Oakleigh Ct. *S'hall* —1D **70**
Oakleigh Cres. *N20* —2H **15**
Oakleigh Gdns. *N20* —1F **15**
Oakleigh Gdns. *Edgw* —5A **12**
Oakleigh M. *N20* —1F **15**
Oakleigh Pk. Av. *Chst* —1E **128**
Oakleigh Rd. N. *N20* —1G **15**
Oakleigh Pk. S. *N20* —2H **15**
Oakleigh Rd. N. *N20* —2G **15**
Oakleigh Rd. S. *N11* —3K **15**
Oakleigh Way. *Mitc* —1F **123**
Oakley Av. *W5* —7G **57**
Oakley Av. *Bark* —7K **51**
Oakley Av. *Croy* —4K **133**
Oakley Clo. *E4* —3K **19**
Oakley Clo. *E6* —6C **66**
Oakley Clo. *W7* —7J **55**
Oakley Clo. *Iswth* —1H **87**
Oakley Cres. *EC1*
 —2B **62** (1B **144**)
Oakley Dri. *SE9* —1H **115**
Oakley Dri. *Brom* —3C **138**
Oakley Gdns. *N8* —5K **29**
Oakley Gdns. *SW3*
 —6C **76** (7D **152**)
Oakley Grange. *Harr* —3G **39**
Oakley Ho. *W5* —7G **57**
Oakley Pk. *Bex* —7C **100**
Oakley Pl. *SE1* —5F **79** (6J **157**)
Oakley Rd. *N1* —7D **46**
Oakley Rd. *SE25* —5H **125**
Oakley Rd. *Brom* —3C **138**
Oakley Rd. *Harr* —6J **23**
Oakley Sq. *NW1* —2G **61**
Oakley St. *SW3* —6C **76** (7C **152**)
Oakley Wlk. *W6* —6F **75**
Oak Lodge. *E11* —6J **33**
Oak Lodge. W8 —3K 75
 (off Chantry Sq.)
Oak Lodge Clo. *Stan* —5H **11**
Oak Lodge Dri. *W Wick* —7D **126**
Oaklodge Way. *NW7* —6G **13**
Oakmead Av. *Brom* —6J **127**
Oakmead Ct. *Stan* —4H **11**
Oak Meade. *Pinn* —6A **10**
Oakmead Gdns. *Edgw* —4E **12**
Oakmead Pl. *Mitc* —1C **122**
Oakmead Rd. *SW12* —1E **108**
Oakmead Rd. *Croy* —6H **123**
Oakmede. *Barn* —4A **4**
Oakmere Rd. *SE2* —6A **84**
Oakmont Pl. *Orp* —7H **129**
Oak Pk. Gdns. *SW19* —1F **107**
Oak Pk. M. *N16* —3F **47**
Oak Pl. *SW18* —5K **91**
Oakridge Dri. *N2* —3B **28**
Oakridge La. *Brom* —5F **113**
Oakridge Rd. *Brom* —4F **113**
Oak Rise. *Buck H* —3G **21**

Oak Rd. *W5* —7D **56**
Oak Rd. *N Mald* —2K **119**
Oak Rd. *N Hth* —7J **85**
Oak Row. *SW16* —2G **123**
Oaks Av. *SE19* —5E **110**
Oaks Av. *Felt* —2C **102**
Oaks Av. *Romf* —2J **37**
Oaks Av. *Wor Pk* —3D **130**
Oaksford Av. *SE26* —3H **111**
Oaks Gro. *E4* —2B **20**
Oakshade Rd. *Brom* —4F **113**
Oakshaw Rd. *SW18* —7K **91**
Oaks La. *Croy* —3J **135**
Oaks La. *Ilf* —5J **35**
Oaks Rd. *Croy* —5H **135**
Oaks, The. *E4* —7B **20**
Oaks, The. *N12* —4E **14**
Oaks, The. *NW10* —7D **42**
Oaks, The. *SE18* —5G **83**
Oaks, The. Enf —3G **7**
(off Bycullah Rd.)
Oaks, The. *Mord* —4G **121**
Oak St. *Romf* —5J **37**
Oaks Way. *Cars* —7D **132**
Oakthorpe Ct. *N18* —5H **17**
Oakthorpe Pk. Est. *N13* —5H **17**
Oakthorpe Rd. *N13* —5F **17**
Oaktree Av. *N13* —3G **17**
Oak Tree Clo. *W5* —6C **56**
Oak Tree Clo. *Stan* —7H **11**
Oak Tree Ct. *W3* —7H **57**
Oak Tree Ct. *N'holt* —2A **54**
Oak Tree Dell. *NW9* —5K **25**
Oak Tree Dri. *N20* —1E **14**
Oak Tree Gdns. *Brom* —5K **113**
Oaktree Gro. Ilf —5H **51**
Oak Tree Rd. *NW8*
    —3C **60** (2B **140**)
Oakview Gdns. *N2* —4B **28**
Oakview Gro. *Croy* —1A **136**
Oakview Lodge. NW11 —7H **27**
(off Beechcroft Av.)
Oakview Rd. *SE6* —5D **112**
Oak Village. *NW5* —4E **44**
Oak Way. *N14* —7A **6**
Oak Way. *SW20* —4E **120**
Oak Way. *W3* —1A **74**
Oakway. *Brom* —2F **127**
Oak Way. *Croy* —6K **125**
Oakway Clo. *Bex* —6E **100**
Oakways. *SE9* —6F **99**
Oakwood. *Wall* —7F **133**
Oakwood Av. *N14* —7C **6**
Oakwood Av. *Beck* —2E **126**
Oakwood Av. *Brom* —3K **127**
Oakwood Av. *Mitc* —2B **122**
Oakwood Av. *S'hall* —7E **54**
Oakwood Bus. Pk. *NW10* —4K **57**
Oakwood Clo. *N14* —6B **6**
Oakwood Clo. *Chst* —6D **114**
Oakwood Clo. *Wfd G* —6H **21**
Oakwood Ct. *E6* —1C **66**
Oakwood Ct. *W14* —3H **75**
Oakwood Ct. *Harr* —6H **23**
Oakwood Cres. *N21* —6D **6**
Oakwood Cres. *Gnfd* —6A **40**
Oakwood Dri. *SE19* —6D **110**
Oakwood Dri. *Bexh* —4K **101**
Oakwood Dri. *Edgw* —6D **12**
Oakwood Dri. *S'hall* —7E **54**
Oakwood Gdns. *Ilf* —2K **51**
Oakwood Gdns. *Sutt* —2J **131**
Oakwood La. *W14* —3H **75**
Oakwood Lodge. N14 —6B **6**
(off Avenue Rd.)

Oakwood Pk. Rd. *N14* —7C **6**
Oakwood Pl. *Croy* —6A **124**
Oakwood Rd. *NW11* —4J **27**
Oakwood Rd. *SW20* —1C **120**
Oakwood Rd. *Croy* —6A **124**
Oakwood View. *N14* —6C **6**
Oakworth Rd. *W10* —5E **58**
Oasis, The. *Brom* —2A **128**
Oast Lodge. W4 —7A **74**
(off Corney Reach Way)
Oates Clo. *Brom* —3F **127**
Oatfield Ho. *N15* —6E **30**
(off Perry Ct.)
Oatfield Rd. *Orp* —7K **129**
Oatland Rise. *E17* —2A **32**
Oatlands Rd. *Enf* —1D **8**
Oat La. *EC2* —6C **62** (7D **144**)
Oban Clo. *E13* —4A **66**
Oban Ho. *Bark* —2H **67**
Oban Rd. *E13* —3A **66**
Oban Rd. *SE25* —4D **124**
Oban St. *E14* —6F **65**
Oberon Ho. N1 —2E **62**
(off Arden Est.)
Oberstein Rd. *SW11* —4B **92**
Oborne Clo. *SE24* —5B **94**
Observatory Gdns. *W8* —2J **75**
Observatory Rd. *SW14* —4J **89**
Occupation La. *SE18* —1F **99**
Occupation La. *W5* —4D **72**
Occupation Rd. *SE17*
    —5C **78** (5C **156**)
Occupation Rd. *W13* —2B **72**
Occupation Rd. *Eps* —7A **130**
Ocean Est. *E1* —4K **63**
(in two parts)
Ocean St. *E1* —5K **63**
Ockendon Rd. *N1* —6D **46**
Ockham Dri. *Orp* —7A **116**
Ockley Ct. *Sidc* —3J **115**
Ockley Ct. *Sutt* —4A **132**
Ockley Rd. *SW16* —4J **109**
Ockley Rd. *Croy* —7K **123**
Octagon Arc. *EC2*
    —5E **62** (6G **145**)
Octavia Clo. *Mitc* —5C **122**
Octavia Ho. W10 —4G **59**
(off Southern Row)
Octavia Rd. *Iswth* —3J **87**
Octavia St. *SW11* —1C **92**
Octavia Way. *SE28* —7B **68**
Octavius St. *SE8* —7C **80**
Oddmark Rd. *Bark* —2H **67**
Odeon Ct. *E16* —5J **65**
Odeon Ct. *NW10* —1A **58**
Odeon Pde. Gnfd —6B **40**
(off Allendale Rd.)
Odessa Rd. *E7* —3H **49**
Odessa Rd. *NW10* —2C **58**
Odessa St. *SE16* —3B **80**
Odger St. *SW11* —2D **92**
Odham's Wlk. *WC2*
    —6J **61** (1F **149**)
Odin Ho. *SE5* —2C **94**
O'Donnell Ct. *WC1*
    —4J **61** (3F **143**)
O'Driscoll Ho. *W12* —6D **58**
Odyssey Bus. Pk. *Ruis* —5A **38**
Offa's Mead. *E9* —4B **48**
Offenham Rd. *SE9* —4D **114**
Offenham Rd. *SE12* —4D **114**
Offerton Rd. *SW4* —3G **93**
Offham Slope. *N12* —5C **14**
Offley Rd. *SW9* —7A **78**
Offord Clo. *N17* —6B **18**

Offord Rd. *N1* —7K **45**
Offord St. *N1* —7K **45**
Ogden Ho. *Felt* —3C **102**
Ogilby St. *SE18* —4D **82**
Oglander Rd. *SE15* —4F **95**
Ogle St. *W1* —5G **61** (5A **142**)
Oglethorpe Rd. *Dag* —3G **53**
O'Grandy Ho. *E17* —3D **32**
Ohio Cotts. *Pinn* —2A **22**
Ohio Rd. *E13* —4H **65**
Oil Mill La. *W6* —5C **74**
Okeburn Rd. *SW17* —5E **108**
Okehampton Clo. *N12* —5G **15**
Okehampton Cres. Well
    —1B **100**
Okehampton Rd. *NW10* —1E **58**
Olaf St. *W11* —7F **59**
Oldacre M. *SW12* —7F **93**
Old Bailey. *EC4* —6B **62** (1B **150**)
Old Barge Ho. All. *SE1*
    —7A **62** (3K **149**)
Old Barn Clo. *Sutt* —7G **131**
Old Barn Way. *Bexh* —4K **101**
Old Barrack Yd. *SW1*
    —2E **76** (7G **147**)
Old Barrowfield. *E15* —1G **65**
Old Belgate Wharf. *E14* —3C **80**
Old Bell Ga. *E14* —3C **80**
Oldberry Rd. *Edgw* —6E **12**
Old Bethnal Grn. Rd. *E2* —3G **63**
Old Bexley Bus. Pk. *Bex* —7H **101**
Old Bexley La. Bex & Dart
(in two parts)   —2K **117**
Old Billingsgate Wlk. *EC3*
    —7E **62** (3G **151**)
Old Bond St. *W1*
    —7G **61** (3A **148**)
Oldborough Rd. *Wemb* —3C **40**
Old Brewer's Yd. *WC2*
    —6J **61** (1E **148**)
Old Brewery M. *NW3* —4B **44**
Old Bri. Clo. *N'holt* —2E **54**
Old Bri. St. *Hamp W* —2D **118**
Old Broad St. *EC2*
    —6D **62** (7F **145**)
Old Bromley Rd. *Brom* —5F **113**
Old Brompton Rd. *SW5 & SW7*
    —5J **75**
Old Bldgs. *WC2* —6A **62** (7J **143**)
Old Burlington St. *W1*
    —7G **61** (2A **148**)
Oldbury Pl. *W1* —5E **60** (5H **141**)
Oldbury Rd. *Enf* —2B **8**
Old Castle St. *E1* —6F **63** (7J **145**)
Old Cavendish St. *W1*
    —6F **61** (1K **147**)
Old Change Ct. *EC4*
    —6C **62** (1C **150**)
Old Chapel Pl. *SW9* —2A **94**
Old Chelsea M. *SW3*
    —6C **76** (7C **152**)
Old Church Gdns. *Romf* —7K **37**
Old Chu. La. *NW9* —2J **41**
Old Chu. La. *Gnfd* —3A **56**
Old Chu. La. *Stan* —5G **11**
Oldchurch Rise. *Romf* —7K **37**
Old Chu. Rd. *E1* —6K **63**
Old Chu. Rd. *E4* —4H **19**
Oldchurch Rd. *Romf* —7K **37**
Old Chu. St. *SW3*
    —5B **76** (6B **152**)
Old Compton St. *W1*
    —7H **61** (2C **148**)
Old Cote Dri. *Houn* —6E **70**

Old Ct. Pl. *W8* —2K **75**
Old Courtyard, The. Brom
    —1K **127**
Old Deer Pk. Gdns. *Rich* —3E **88**
Old Devonshire Rd. *SW12*
    —7F **93**
Old Dock Clo. *Rich* —6G **73**
Old Dover Rd. *SE3* —7J **81**
Oldegate Ho. *E6* —1B **66**
Old Farm Av. *N14* —7B **6**
Old Farm Av. *Sidc* —1H **115**
Old Farm Clo. *Houn* —4D **86**
Old Farm Rd. *N2* —1B **28**
Old Farm Rd. *Hamp* —6D **102**
Old Farm Rd. E. *Sidc* —2A **116**
Old Farm Rd. W. *Sidc* —2K **115**
Oldfield Clo. *Brom* —4D **128**
Oldfield Clo. *Gnfd* —5J **39**
Oldfield Clo. *Stan* —5F **11**
Old Farm Gdns. *Gnfd* —1H **55**
Oldfield Gro. *SE16* —4K **79**
Oldfield Ho. W4 —5A **74**
(off Devonshire Rd.)
Oldfield La. *Gnfd* —7H **39**
Oldfield La. N. *Gnfd* —2H **55**
Oldfield La. S. *Gnfd* —4G **55**
Oldfield M. *N6* —7G **29**
Oldfield Rd. *N16* —3E **46**
Oldfield Rd. *NW10* —7A **42**
Oldfield Rd. *SW19* —6G **107**
Oldfield Rd. *W3* —2B **74**
Oldfield Rd. *Bexh* —2E **100**
Oldfield Rd. *Brom* —4D **128**
Oldfield Rd. *Hamp* —7D **102**
Oldfields Cir. *N'holt* —6G **39**
Oldfields Rd. *Sutt* —3H **131**
Oldfields Trad. Est. *Sutt* —3J **131**
Old Fleet La. *EC4*
    —6B **62** (7A **144**)
Old Ford. (Junct.) —2C **64**
Old Fold Clo. *Barn* —1C **4**
Old Fold La. *Barn* —1C **4**
Old Fold View. *Barn* —3A **4**
Old Ford Rd. *E2 & E3* —3J **63**
Old Forge Clo. *Stan* —4F **11**
Old Forge M. *W12* —2D **74**
Old Forge Rd. *Enf* —1A **8**
Old Forge Way. *Sidc* —4B **116**
Old Gloucester St. *WC1*
    —5J **61** (5F **143**)
Old Hall Clo. *Pinn* —1C **22**
Old Hall Dri. *Pinn* —1C **22**
Oldham Ter. *W3* —1J **73**
Old Hill. *Chst* —1E **128**
Oldhill St. *N16* —1G **47**
Old Homesdale Rd. *Brom*
    —4A **128**
Old Hospital Clo. *SW17* —1D **108**
Old Ho. Clo. *SW19* —5G **107**
Old Ho. Gdns. *Twic* —6C **88**
Old Jamaica Rd. *SE16*
    —3G **79** (1K **157**)
Old James St. *SE15* —3H **95**
Old Jewry. *EC2* —6D **62** (1E **150**)
Old Kenton La. *NW9* —5H **25**
Old Kent Rd. *SE1*
    —4E **78** (3G **157**)
Old Laundry, The. *Chst* —1G **129**
Old Lodge Pl. *Twic* —6B **88**
Old Lodge Way. *Stan* —5F **11**
Old London Rd. *Sidc* —7H **117**
Old Maidstone Rd. *Sidc* —7H **117**
Old Malden La. *Wor Pk* —2A **130**
Old Mnr. Dri. *Iswth* —6G **87**
Old Mnr. Way. *Bexh* —2K **101**

Old Mnr. Way. *Chst* —5D **114**
Old Mnr. Yd. *SW5* —5K **75**
Old Market Sq. *E2*
    —3F **63** (1J **145**)
Old Marylebone Rd. *NW1*
    —5C **60** (6D **140**)
Oldmead Ho. *Dag* —6H **53**
Old M. *Harr* —5J **23**
Old Mill Clo. *E18* —3A **34**
Old Mill Pl. *Romf* —6K **37**
Old Mill Rd. *SE18* —6H **83**
Old Montague St. *E1*
    —5G **63** (6K **145**)
Old Nichol St. *E2*
    —4F **63** (3J **145**)
Old North St. *WC1*
    —5K **61** (5G **143**)
Old Oak Comn. La. *NW10 & W3*
    —5A **58**
Old Oak La. *NW10* —3A **58**
Old Oak Rd. *W3* —7B **58**
Old Orchard Clo. *Barn* —1G **5**
Old Orchard, The. *NW3* —4C **44**
Old Pal. La. *Rich* —5C **88**
Old Pal. Rd. *Croy* —3D **134**
Old Pal. Ter. *Rich* —5D **88**
Old Palace Yd. *SW1*
    —3J **77** (1E **154**)
Old Pal. Yd. *Rich* —5C **88**
Old Paradise St. *SE11*
    —4K **77** (3G **155**)
Old Pk. Av. *SW12* —6E **92**
Old Pk. Av. *Enf* —5H **7**
Old Pk. Gro. *Enf* —4H **7**
Old Pk. Ho. N13 —4E **16**
(off Old Park Rd.)
Old Pk. La. *W1* —1F **77** (5J **147**)
Old-Pk. M. *Houn* —7D **70**
Old Pk. Ridings. *N21* —6G **7**
Old Pk. Rd. *N13* —4E **16**
Old Pk. Rd. *SE2* —5A **84**
Old Pk. Rd. *Enf* —3G **7**
Old Pk. Rd. S. *Enf* —4G **7**
Old Pk. View. *Enf* —3F **7**
Old Perry St. *Chst* —6J **115**
Old Pound Clo. *Iswth* —2A **88**
Old Pye St. *SW1*
    —3H **77** (1C **154**)
Old Pye St. Est. *SW1*
    —3H **77** (1C **154**)
(off Old Pye St.)
Old Quebec St. *W1*
    —6D **60** (1F **147**)
Old Queen St. *SW1*
    —2H **77** (7D **148**)
Old Rectory Gdns. *Edgw* —6B **12**
Old Redding. *Harr* —5A **10**
Oldridge Rd. *SW12* —7E **92**
Old River Works. *N17* —6H **17**
Old Rd. *SE13* —4G **97**
Old Rd. *Enf* —1D **8**
Old Royal Free Pl. N1 —1A **62**
(off Liverpool Rd.)
Old Royal Free Sq. N1 —1A **62**
(off Old Royal Free Pl.)
Old Ruislip Rd. *N'holt* —2A **54**
Old School Clo. *SW19* —2J **121**
Old School Clo. *Beck* —2A **126**
Old Schools La. *Eps* —7B **130**
Old School Ter. *Sutt* —7F **131**
Old Seacoal La. *EC4*
    —6B **62** (1A **150**)
Old S. Clo. *H End* —1B **22**
Old S. Lambeth Rd. *SW8* —7J **77**

271

Old Sq. WC2 —6K 61 (7J 143)
Old Stable M. N5 —3C 46
Old Sta. Gdns. Tedd —6A 104
(off Victoria Rd.)
Oldstead Rd. Brom —4E 112
Old St. E13 —2K 65
Old St. EC1 —4C 62 (3C 144)
Old Street. (Junct.) —3D 62
(off Old St.)
Old Sungate Cotts. Romf —1F 37
Old Sun Wharf. E14 —7A 64
(off Narrow St.)
Old Swan Wharf. SW11 —1A 92
Old Swan Rd. Cars —4D 132
Old Town. SW4 —3G 93
Old Town. Croy —3B 134
Old Woolwich Rd. SE10 —6F 81
Old York Rd. SW18 —5K 91
O'Leary Sq. E1 —5J 63
Olinda Rd. N16 —6F 31
Oliphant St. W10 —3F 59
Oliver Av. SE25 —3F 125
Oliver Clo. E10 —3D 48
Oliver Clo. W4 —6H 73
Oliver Ct. SE18 —4G 83
Oliver Gdns. E6 —5C 66
Oliver Goldsmith Est. SE15
—1G 95
Oliver Gro. SE25 —4F 125
Oliver Ho. SE16 —2G 79
(off George Row)
Oliver Ho. SW8 —7J 77
(off Wyvil Rd.)
Olive Rd. E13 —3A 66
Olive Rd. NW2 —4E 42
Olive Rd. SW19 —1A 108
Olive Rd. W5 —3D 72
Oliver Rd. E10 —2D 48
Oliver Rd. E17 —5E 32
Oliver Rd. N Mald —2J 119
Oliver Rd. Sutt —4B 132
Olivers Yd. EC1 —4D 62 (3F 145)
Olivette St. SW15 —3F 91
Olive Waite Ho. NW6 —7K 43
Olivia Ct. Enf —1H 7
(off Chase Side)
Ollerton Grn. E3 —1B 64
Ollerton Rd. N11 —5C 16
Olley Clo. Wall —7J 133
Oligar Clo. W12 —1B 74
Olliffe St. E14 —3E 80
Olmar St. SE1 —6G 79 (7K 157)
Olney Rd. SE17 —6B 78 (7B 156)
Olron Cres. Bexh —5D 100
Olven Rd. SE18 —6G 83
Olveston Wlk. Cars —6B 122
Olwen M. Pinn —2B 22
Olyffe Av. Well —1A 100
Olyffe Dri. Beck —1E 126
(in two parts)
Olympia Ind. Est. N22 —3K 29
Olympia M. W2 —7K 59
Olympia Way. W14 —3G 75
Olympic Way. Gnfd —1G 55
Olympic Way. Wemb —3G 41
Olympus Sq. E5 —3G 47
O'Mahoney Ct. SW17 —3A 108
Oman Av. NW2 —4D 42
O'Meara St. SE1 —1C 78 (5D 150)
Omega Clo. E14 —3D 80
Omega Pl. N1 —2J 61 (1F 143)
Omega St. SE14 —1C 96
Ommaney Rd. SE14 —1K 95
Omnibus Way. E17 —2C 32

Ondine Rd. SE15 —4F 95
Onega Ga. SE16 —3A 80
101 Bus. Units. SW11 —3D 92
O'Neill Path. SE18 —6E 82
One Tree Clo. SE23 —6J 95
Ongar Clo. Romf —5C 36
Ongar Rd. SW6 —6J 75
Onra Rd. E17 —7C 32
Onslow Av. Rich —5E 88
Onslow Clo. E4 —2K 19
Onslow Dri. Sidc —2D 116
Onslow Gdns. E18 —3K 33
Onslow Gdns. N10 —5F 29
Onslow Gdns. N21 —5F 7
Onslow Gdns. SW7
—4B 76 (4A 152)
Onslow Gdns. Wall —6G 133
Onslow M. E. SW7
—4B 76 (4A 152)
Onslow M. W. SW7
—4B 76 (4A 152)
Onslow Pde. N14 —1A 16
Onslow Rd. Croy —7A 124
Onslow Rd. N Mald —4C 120
Onslow Rd. Rich —5E 88
Onslow Sq. SW7
—4B 76 (4B 152)
Onslow St. EC1 —4A 62 (4K 143)
Ontario St. SE1 —3B 78 (2B 156)
Ontario Way. E14 —1C 80
Opal Clo. E16 —6B 66
Opal M. NW6 —1H 59
Opal M. Ilf —2F 51
Opal St. SE11 —5B 78 (5A 156)
Openshaw Rd. SE2 —4B 84
Openview. SW18 —1A 108
Ophelia Gdns. NW2 —3G 43
Ophir Ter. SE15 —1G 95
Opossum Way. Houn —3A 86
Oppenheim Rd. SE13 —2E 96
Oppidans M. NW3 —7D 44
Oppidans Rd. NW3 —7D 44
Orange Ct. La. Orp —7E 138
Orange Gro. E11 —3G 49
(in two parts)
Orange Hill Rd. Edgw —7D 12
Orange Pl. SE16 —3J 79
Orangery La. SE9 —5D 98
Orange St. WC2
—7H 61 (3D 148)
Orange Yd. W1 —6H 61 (1D 148)
Oratory La. SW3
—5B 76 (5B 152)
Orbain Rd. SW6 —7G 75
Orbel St. SW11 —1C 92
Orbital Cen., The. Wfd G —2B 34
Orb St. SE17 —4D 78 (4E 156)
Orchard Av. N3 —3J 27
Orchard Av. N14 —6B 6
Orchard Av. N20 —2G 15
Orchard Av. Belv —6E 84
Orchard Av. Croy —1A 136
Orchard Av. Houn —7C 70
Orchard Av. Mitc —1E 132
Orchard Av. N Mald —3A 120
Orchard Av. S'hall —1D 70
Orchard Clo. E11 —4K 33
Orchard Clo. N1 —7C 46
Orchard Clo. NW2 —3C 42
Orchard Clo. SE23 —6J 95
Orchard Clo. SW20 —4E 120
Orchard Clo. W10 —5H 59

Orchard Clo. Bexh —1E 100
Orchard Clo. Bush —1C 10
Orchard Clo. Edgw —6K 11
Orchard Clo. N'holt —6G 39
Orchard Clo. Surb —7B 118
Orchard Clo. Wemb —1E 56
Orchard Ct. E10 —1D 48
Orchard Ct. N14 —6B 6
Orchard Ct. Edgw —5A 12
Orchard Ct. Iswth —7H 71
Orchard Ct. New Bar —3E 4
Orchard Ct. Twic —2H 103
Orchard Ct. Wor Pk —1C 130
Orchard Cres. Edgw —5D 12
Orchard Cres. Enf —1A 8
Orchard Dri. SE3 —2F 97
Orchard Dri. Edgw —5A 12
Orchard Gdns. Sutt —5J 131
Orchard Ga. NW9 —4A 26
Orchard Ga. Gnfd —6B 40
Orchard Gro. SE20 —7G 111
Orchard Gro. Croy —7A 126
Orchard Gro. Edgw —1G 25
Orchard Gro. Harr —5F 25
Orchard Hill. SE13 —2D 96
Orchard Hill. Cars —5D 132
Orchard Hill. Dart —5K 101
Orchard Ho. SE16 —3J 79
Orchard Ho. W12 —1C 74
Orchard La. SW20 —1D 120
Orchard La. Wfd G —4F 21
Orchardleigh Av. Enf —2D 8
Orchard Mead Ho. NW11 —2J 43
Orchardmede. N21 —6J 7
Orchard M. N1 —7D 46
Orchard Pl. E14 —7E 65
Orchard Pl. N17 —7A 18
Orchard Rise. Croy —1A 136
Orchard Rise. King T —1J 119
Orchard Rise. Rich —5H 89
Orchard Rise E. Sidc —5K 99
Orchard Rise W. Sidc —5J 99
Orchard Rd. N6 —7F 29
Orchard Rd. SE3 —2G 97
Orchard Rd. SE18 —4H 83
Orchard Rd. Barn —4C 4
Orchard Rd. Belv —4G 85
Orchard Rd. Bren —6C 72
Orchard Rd. Brom —1A 128
Orchard Rd. Dag —1G 69
Orchard Rd. Enf —5D 8
Orchard Rd. Hamp —7D 102
Orchard Rd. King T —2E 118
Orchard Rd. Mitc —1E 132
Orchard Rd. Rich —3G 89
Orchard Rd. Romf —1H 37
Orchard Rd. Sidc —4J 115
Orchard Rd. Sutt —5J 131
Orchard Rd. Twic —6A 88
Orchard Rd. Well —3B 100
Orchardson Ho. NW8
—4B 60 (3B 140)
Orchardson St. NW8
—4B 60 (4A 140)
Orchard Sq. W14 —5H 75
(off Sun Rd.)
Orchard St. E17 —4A 32
Orchard St. W1 —6E 60 (1G 147)
Orchard Ter. Enf —6B 8
Orchard, The. N14 —5A 6
Orchard, The. N21 —6J 7
Orchard, The. NW11 —5J 27
Orchard, The. SE3 —2F 97
Orchard, The. W4 —4K 73

Orchard, The. W5 —6D 56
(off Montpelier Rd.)
Orchard, The. Eps —7B 130
Orchard, The. Houn —2G 87
Orchard Way. Croy & Beck
—7A 126
Orchard Way. Enf —3K 7
Orchard Way. Sutt —4B 132
Orchid Clo. E6 —5C 66
Orchid Clo. S'hall —7C 54
Orchid Grange. N14 —7B 6
Orchid Rd. N14 —7B 6
Orchid St. W12 —7C 58
Orde. NW9 —1B 26
Orde Hall St. WC1
—5K 61 (4G 143)
Ordell Rd. E3 —2B 64
Ordnance Cres. SE10 —2G 81
Ordnance Hill. NW8 —1B 60
Ordnance M. NW8 —2B 60
Ordnance Rd. E16 —5H 65
Ordnance Rd. SE18 —6E 82
Oregano Dri. E14 —6F 65
Oregon Av. E12 —4D 50
Oregon Clo. N Mald —4J 119
Orestes M. NW6 —5J 43
Orford Ct. SE27 —2B 110
Orford Ct. Stan —6H 11
Orford Gdns. Twic —2K 103
Orford Rd. E17 —5C 32
Orford Rd. E18 —3K 33
Orford Rd. SE6 —3D 112
Organ Crossroads. (Junct.)
—7C 130
Organ La. E4 —2K 19
Oriel Clo. Mitc —4H 123
Oriel Ct. NW3 —4A 44
Oriel Ct. Croy —1D 134
Oriel Gdns. Ilf —3D 34
Oriel Pl. NW3 —4A 44
(off Heath St.)
Oriel Rd. E9 —6K 47
Oriel Way. N'holt —7F 39
Oriental Rd. E16 —1B 82
Orient Ind. Pk. E10 —2C 48
Orient St. SE11 —4B 78 (3A 156)
Orient Way. E5 —3K 47
Oriole Way. SE28 —7B 68
Orion Bus. Cen. SE14 —5K 79
Orion Cen., The. Croy —3J 133
Orissa Rd. SE18 —5J 83
Orkney Ho. N1 —1K 61
(off Bemerton Est.)
Orkney St. SW11 —2E 92
Orlando Rd. SW4 —3G 93
Orleans Clo. Twic —7B 88
Orleans Rd. SE19 —6D 110
Orleans Rd. Twic —7B 88
Orleston M. N7 —6A 46
Orleston Rd. N7 —6A 46
Orley Ct. Harr —4K 39
Orley Farm Rd. Harr —3J 39
Orlop St. SE10 —5G 81
Ormanton Rd. SE26 —4G 111
Orme Ct. W2 —7K 59
Orme Ct. M. W2 —7K 59
(off Orme La.)
Orme Ho. E8 —1F 63
Orme La. W2 —7K 59
Ormeley Rd. SW12 —1F 109
Orme Rd. King T —2H 119
Ormerod Gdns. Mitc —2E 122
Ormesby Clo. SE28 —7D 68
Ormesby Way. Harr —6F 25
Orme Sq. W2 —7K 59

Ormiston Gro. W12 —1D 74
Ormiston Rd. SE10 —5J 81
Ormond Av. Hamp —7F 103
Ormond Av. Rich —5D 88
Ormond Clo. WC1
—5J 61 (5F 143)
Ormond Cres. Hamp —7F 103
Ormond Dri. Hamp —7F 103
Ormonde Ga. SW3
—5D 76 (6E 152)
Ormonde Pl. SW1
—4E 76 (4G 153)
Ormonde Rise. Buck H —1F 21
Ormonde Rd. SW14 —3J 89
Ormonde Ter. NW8 —1D 60
Ormond M. WC1
—4J 61 (4F 143)
Ormond Rd. N19 —1J 45
Ormond Rd. Rich —5D 88
Ormond Yd. SW1
—1G 77 (4B 148)
Ormsby. Sutt —7K 131
Ormsby Gdns. Gnfd —2G 55
Ormsby Lodge. W4 —3A 74
Ormsby Pl. N16 —3F 47
Ormsby St. E2 —2F 63
Ormside St. SE15 —6J 79
Ornan Rd. NW3 —5C 44
Oronsay Wlk. N1 —7C 46
Orpen Wlk. N16 —3E 46
Orpheus St. SE5 —1D 94
Orpheus Tower. SE14 —7A 80
(off Desmond St.)
Orpington Gdns. N18 —3K 17
Orpington Mans. N21 —1F 17
Orpington Rd. N21 —1G 17
Orpington Rd. Chst —3J 129
Orpwood Clo. Hamp —6D 102
Orsett M. W2 —5K 59
(in two parts)
Orsett St. SE11 —5K 77 (5H 155)
Orsett Ter. W2 —6K 59
Orsett Ter. Wfd G —7F 21
Orsman Rd. N1 —1E 62
Orton St. E1 —1G 79
Orville Rd. SW11 —2B 92
Orwell Clo. Rain —5K 69
Orwell Ct. N5 —4C 46
Orwell Rd. E13 —1A 66
Osbaldeston Rd. N16 —2G 47
Osberton Rd. SE12 —5J 97
Osbert St. SW1 —4H 77 (4C 154)
Osborn Clo. E8 —1G 63
Osborne Clo. Beck —4A 126
Osborne Clo. Felt —5B 102
Osborne Ct. E10 —7D 32
Osborne Ct. W5 —5E 56
Osborne Gdns. T Hth —2C 124
Osborne Gro. E17 —4B 32
Osborne Gro. N4 —1A 46
Osborne M. E17 —4B 32
Osborne Pl. Sutt —5B 132
Osborne Rd. E7 —5K 49
Osborne Rd. E9 —6B 48
Osborne Rd. E10 —3D 48
Osborne Rd. N4 —1A 46
Osborne Rd. N13 —3F 17
Osborne Rd. NW2 —6D 42
Osborne Rd. W3 —3H 73
Osborne Rd. Belv —5F 85
Osborne Rd. Buck H —1E 20
Osborne Rd. Dag —5F 53
Osborne Rd. Enf —2F 9
Osborne Rd. Houn —3D 86
Osborne Rd. King T —7E 104

Osborne Rd. S'hall —6G 55
Osborne Rd. T Hth —2C 124
Osborne Sq. Dag —4F 53
Osborne Ter. SW17 —5E 108
  (off Church La.)
Osborn Gdns. NW7 —7A 14
Osborn La. SE23 —7A 96
Osborn St. E1 —5F 63 (6K 145)
Osborn Ter. SE3 —4H 97
Osbourne Clo. Cockf —3J 5
Osbourne Ct. Harr —4F 23
Osbourne Ho. Twic —2G 103
Oscar St. SE8 —2C 96
  (in two parts)
Oseney Cres. NW5 —5G 45
O'Shea Gro. E3 —1B 64
Osidge La. N14 —1K 15
Osier Ct. Romf —6K 37
Osier M. W4 —6A 74
Osiers Rd. SW18 —4J 91
Osier St. E1 —4J 63
Osier Way. E10 —3D 48
Osier Way. Mitc —5D 122
Oslac Rd. SE6 —5D 112
Oslo Ct. NW8 —2C 60
  (off Prince Albert Rd.)
Oslo Ho. SE5 —2C 94
Oslo Sq. SE16 —3A 80
Osman Clo. N15 —6D 30
Osman Rd. N9 —3B 18
Osman Rd. W6 —3E 74
Osmond Clo. Harr —2G 39
Osmond Gdns. Wall —5G 133
Osmund St. W12 —5B 58
Osnaburgh St. NW1
  —4F 61 (4K 141)
Osnaburgh Ter. NW1
  —4F 61 (3K 141)
Osney Ho. SE2 —2D 84
Osney Wlk. Cars —6B 122
Osprey Clo. E6 —5C 66
Osprey Clo. E11 —4J 33
Osprey Ct. Beck —7C 112
Osprey Est. SE16 —4K 79
Osprey M. Enf —5D 8
Ospringe Clo. SE20 —7J 111
Ospringe Rd. NW5 —4G 45
Osram Rd. Wemb —3D 40
Osric Path. N1 —2E 62
Ossian M. N4 —7K 29
Ossian Rd. N4 —7K 29
Ossington Bldgs. W1
  —5E 60 (5G 141)
Ossington Clo. W2 —7J 59
Ossington St. W2 —7K 59
Ossory Rd. SE1 —6G 79 (6K 157)
Ossulston St. NW1
  —2H 61 (1D 142)
Ossulton Pl. N2 —3A 28
Ossulton Way. N2 —4A 28
Ostade Rd. SW2 —7K 93
Ostend Pl. SE17
  —4C 78 (3C 156)
Osten M. SW7 —3K 75
Osterley Av. Iswth —7H 71
Osterley Clo. Orp —7A 116
Osterley Ct. Iswth —1H 87
Osterley Ct. N'holt —3A 54
  (off Canberra Dri.)
Osterley Cres. Iswth —1J 87
Osterley Gdns. S'hall —1G 71
Osterley Gdns. T Hth —2C 124
Osterley La. S'hall & Iswth
  —5E 70

Osterley Lodge. Iswth —7J 71
  (off Church Rd.)
Osterley Pk. Rd. S'hall —3D 70
Osterley Pk. View Rd. W7 —2J 71
Osterley Rd. N16 —4E 46
Osterley Rd. Iswth —7J 71
Osterley Views. S'hall —1G 71
Oster Ter. E17 —5K 31
Ostliffe Rd. N13 —5G 17
Oswald Rd. S'hall —1C 70
Oswald's Mead. E9 —4A 48
Oswald St. E5 —3K 47
Oswald Ter. NW2 —3E 42
Osward Pl. N9 —2C 18
Osward Rd. SW17 —2D 108
Oswin St. SE11 —4B 78 (3B 156)
Oswyth Rd. SE5 —2E 94
Otford Clo. SE20 —1J 125
Otford Clo. Bex —6H 101
Otford Clo. Brom —3B 128
Otford Cres. SE4 —6B 96
Otford Ho. SE15 —6J 79
  (off Lovelinch Clo.)
Othello Clo. SE11
  —5B 78 (5A 156)
Otho Ct. Bren —7D 72
Otis St. E3 —3E 64
Otley App. Ilf —6F 35
Otley Dri. Ilf —5F 35
Otley Ho. N5 —3B 46
Otley Rd. E16 —6A 66
Otley Ter. E5 —3K 47
Ottawa Gdns. Dag —7K 53
Ottaway Ct. E5 —3G 47
Ottaway St. E5 —3G 47
Otterbourne Rd. E4 —3A 20
Otterbourne Rd. Croy —2C 134
Otterburn Gdns. Iswth —7A 72
Otterburn St. SW17 —6D 108
Otterden St. SE6 —4C 112
Otter Rd. Gnfd —4G 55
Otto Clo. SE26 —3H 111
Otto St. SE17 —6B 78 (7A 156)
Oulton Clo. E5 —2J 47
Oulton Clo. SE28 —6C 68
Oulton Cres. Bark —5K 51
Oulton Rd. N15 —5D 30
Ouseley Rd. SW12 —1D 108
Outer Circ. NW1
  —3C 60 (1D 140)
Outgate Rd. NW10 —7B 42
Outram Pl. N1 —1J 61
Outram Rd. E6 —1C 66
Outram Rd. N22 —1H 29
Outram Rd. Croy —2F 135
Outwich St. EC3
  —6E 62 (7H 145)
Outwood Ho. SW2 —7K 93
  (off Deepdene Gdns.)
Oval Ct. Edgw —7D 12
Oval Mans. SE11
  —6K 77 (7H 155)
Oval Pl. SW8 —7K 77
Oval Rd. NW1 —1F 61
Oval Rd. Croy —2D 134
Oval Rd. N. Dag —1H 69
Oval Rd. S. Dag —2H 69
Oval, The. E2 —2H 63
Oval, The. Sidc —7A 100
Oval Way. SE11 —5K 77 (6H 155)
Overbrae. Beck —5C 112
Overbrook Wlk. Edgw —7B 12
  (in two parts)
Overbury Av. Beck —3D 126
Overbury Rd. N15 —6D 30

Overbury St. E5 —4K 47
Overcliff Rd. SE13 —3C 96
Overcourt Clo. Sidc —6B 100
Overdale Av. N Mald —2K 119
Overdale Rd. W5 —3C 72
Overdown Rd. SE6 —4C 112
Overhill Rd. SE22 —7G 95
Overhill Way. Beck —5F 127
Overlea Rd. E5 —7G 31
Overmead. Sidc —7H 99
Oversley Ho. W2 —5J 59
  (off Alfred Rd.)
Overstand Clo. Beck —5C 126
Overstone Gdns. Croy —7B 126
Overstone Rd. W6 —3E 74
Overstrand Mans. SW11 —1D 92
Overton Clo. NW10 —6J 41
Overton Clo. Iswth —1K 87
Overton Ct. E11 —7J 33
Overton Ct. Sutt —7J 131
Overton Dri. E11 —7J 33
Overton Dri. Chad H —7C 36
Overton Ho. SW15 —7B 90
  (off Tangley Gro.)
Overton Rd. E10 —1A 48
Overton Rd. N14 —5D 6
Overton Rd. SE2 —3C 84
Overton Rd. SW9 —2A 94
Overton Rd. Sutt —6J 131
Overton Rd. E. SE2 —3D 84
Overtons Yd. Croy —3C 134
Overy Ho. SE1 —2B 78 (7A 150)
Ovesdon Av. Harr —1D 38
Ovett Clo. SE19 —6E 110
Ovex Clo. E14 —2E 80
Ovington Gdns. SW3
  —3C 76 (2D 152)
Ovington M. SW3
  —3C 76 (2D 152)
Ovington Sq. SW3
  —3C 76 (2D 152)
Ovington St. SW3
  —4C 76 (3D 152)
Owen Clo. SE28 —1C 84
Owen Clo. Croy —6D 124
Owen Gdns. Wfd G —6H 21
Owen Ho. Twic —7B 88
Owenite St. SE2 —4B 84
Owen Mans. W14 —6G 75
  (off Queen's Club Gdns.)
Owen Rd. N13 —5H 17
Owen Rd. Hayes —3A 54
Owen's Ct. EC1 —3B 62 (1A 144)
Owen's Row. EC1
  —3B 62 (1A 144)
Owen St. EC1 —2B 62 (1A 144)
Owens Way. SE23 —7A 96
Owen Wlk. SE20 —7G 111
Owen Way. NW10 —5J 41
Owgan Clo. SE5 —7D 78
Oxberry Av. SW6 —2G 91
Oxendon St. SW1
  —7H 61 (3C 148)
Oxenford St. SE15 —3F 95
Oxenpark Av. Wemb —1E 40
Oxestall's Rd. SE8 —5A 80
Oxford Av. NW10 —3D 58
Oxford Av. SW20 —2G 121
Oxford Av. Houn —5E 70
Oxford & Cambridge Mans. NW1
  —5C 60 (6D 140)
  (off Old Marylebone Rd.)
Oxford Cir. W1 —6G 61 (1A 148)
Oxford Cir. Av. W1
  —6G 61 (1A 148)

Oxford Clo. N9 —2C 18
Oxford Clo. Mitc —3G 123
Oxford Ct. EC4 —7D 62 (2E 150)
Oxford Ct. W3 —6G 57
Oxford Ct. W4 —5H 73
Oxford Ct. W7 —5K 55
  (off Copley Clo.)
Oxford Ct. Felt —4B 102
Oxford Cres. N Mald —6K 119
Oxford Dri. Ruis —2A 38
Oxford Gdns. N20 —1G 15
Oxford Gdns. N21 —7H 7
Oxford Gdns. W4 —5G 73
Oxford Gdns. W10 —6E 58
Oxford Ga. W6 —4F 75
Oxford M. Bex —7G 101
Oxford Pl. NW10 —3K 41
  (off Neasden La. N.)
Oxford Rd. E15 —6F 49
  (in two parts)
Oxford Rd. N4 —1A 46
Oxford Rd. N9 —2C 18
Oxford Rd. NW6 —2J 59
Oxford Rd. SE19 —6D 110
Oxford Rd. SW15 —4G 91
Oxford Rd. W5 —7D 56
Oxford Rd. Cars —6C 132
Oxford Rd. Enf —5E 8
Oxford Rd. Harr —6G 23
Oxford Rd. Ilf —6G 51
Oxford Rd. Sidc —5B 116
Oxford Rd. Tedd —5H 103
Oxford Rd. Wall —5G 133
Oxford Rd. W'stone —3K 23
Oxford Rd. Wfd G —5G 21
Oxford Rd. N. W4 —5H 73
Oxford Rd. S. W4 —5G 73
Oxford Sq. W2 —6D 60 (1G 146)
Oxford St. W1 —6D 60 (1G 147)
Oxford Wlk. S'hall —1D 70
Oxford Way. Felt —4B 102
Oxgate Cen. NW2 —2C 42
Oxgate Ct. NW2 —2C 42
Oxgate Gdns. NW2 —3D 42
Oxgate La. NW2 —2D 42
Oxgate Pde. NW2 —2C 42
Oxhawth Cres. Brom —5C 128
Oxhey La. Wat & Harr —5A 10
Oxhey La. Wat & Harr —5A 10
Oxleas. E6 —6F 67
Oxleas Clo. Well —2H 99
Oxleay Rd. Harr —1E 38
Oxleigh Clo. N Mald —5A 120
Oxley Clo. SE1 —5F 79 (5K 157)
Oxleys Rd. NW2 —3D 42
Oxlip Clo. Croy —1K 135
Oxlow La. Dag —4F 53
Oxonian St. SE22 —4F 95
Oxted Clo. Mitc —3B 122
Oxtoby Way. SW16 —1H 123
Oystercatcher Clo. E16 —6K 65
Oystergate Wlk. EC4
  —7D 62 (3E 150)
Oyster Row. E1 —6J 63
Ozolins Way. E16 —6J 65

Pablo Neruda Clo. SE24 —3B 94
Pace Pl. E1 —6H 63
Pacific Rd. E16 —6J 65
Packington Rd. W3 —3J 73
Packington Sq. N1 —1C 62
Packington St. N1 —1B 62
Packmores Rd. SE9 —5H 99
Padbury. SE17 —5E 78 (6H 157)

Padbury Ct. E2 —3F 63 (2K 145)
Paddenswick Rd. W6 —3C 74
Paddington Clo. Hayes —4B 54
Paddington Ct. W7 —5K 55
  (off Copley Clo.)
Paddington Grn. W2
  —5B 60 (5A 140)
Paddington St. W1
  —5E 60 (5G 141)
Paddock Clo. SE3 —3J 97
Paddock Clo. SE26 —4K 111
Paddock Clo. N'holt —2E 54
Paddock Clo. Wor Pk —1A 130
Paddock Gdns. SE19 —6E 110
Paddock Pas. SE19 —6E 110
  (off Paddock Gdns.)
Paddock Rd. NW2 —2C 42
Paddock Rd. Bexh —4E 100
Paddock Rd. Ruis —3B 38
Paddocks Clo. Harr —4F 39
Paddocks Grn. NW9 —1H 41
Paddocks, The. W5 —3D 72
  (off Popes La.)
Paddocks, The. Cockf —3J 5
Paddocks, The. New Ad —5C 136
Paddocks, The. Wemb —2H 41
Paddock, The. NW9 —5G 25
Paddock Way. Chst —7H 115
Padfield Rd. SE5 —3C 94
Padnall Ct. Romf —3D 36
Padnall Rd. Chad H —3D 36
Padstow Rd. Enf —1G 7
Padua Rd. SE20 —1J 125
Pagden St. SW8 —1F 93
Pageant Av. NW9 —1A 26
Pageant Cres. SE16 —1B 80
Pageantmaster Ct. EC4
  —6B 62 (1A 150)
Pageant Wlk. Croy —3E 134
Page Clo. Dag —5E 52
Page Clo. Hamp —6C 102
Page Clo. Harr —6F 25
Page Cres. Croy —5B 134
Page Grn. Rd. N15 —5G 31
Page Grn. Ter. N15 —5F 31
Page Heath La. Brom —3B 128
Page Heath Vs. Brom —3B 128
Pagehurst Rd. Croy —7H 125
Page Meadow. NW7 —7J 13
Pages Hill. N10 —2E 28
Pages La. N10 —2E 28
Page St. NW7 —1C 26
Page St. SW1 —4H 77 (3D 154)
Pages Wlk. SE1 —4E 78 (3G 157)
Pages Yd. W4 —6A 74
Paget Av. Sutt —3B 132
Paget Clo. Hamp —4H 103
Paget Gdns. Chst —1F 129
Paget La. Iswth —3H 87
Paget Pl. King T —6J 105
Paget Rise. SE18 —6E 82
Paget Rd. N16 —1D 46
Paget Rd. Ilf —4F 51
Paget St. EC1 —3B 62 (1A 144)
Paget Ter. SE18 —6F 83
Pagin Ho. N15 —5E 30
  (off Braemar Rd.)
Pagitts Gro. Barn —1E 4
Pagnell St. SE14 —7B 80
Pagoda Av. Rich —3F 89
Pagoda Gdns. SE3 —2F 97
Pagoda Vista. Rich —2E 89
Paignton Rd. N15 —6E 30
Paines Clo. Pinn —3C 22
Paines La. Pinn —1C 22

Pain's Clo. *Mitc* —2F 123
Painsthorpe Rd. *N16* —3E 46
Painswick Ct. *SE15* —7F 79
 (off Daniel Gdns.)
Painters Rd. *Ilf* —3K 35
Paisley Rd. *N22* —1B 30
Paisley Rd. *Cars* —1B 132
Pakeman St. *N7* —3K 45
Pakenham Clo. *SW12* —1E 108
Pakenham St. *WC1*
 —3K 61 (2H 143)
Pakington Ho. *SW9* —2J 93
 (off Stockwell Gdns. Est.)
Palace Av. *W8* —2K 75
Palace Ct. *SE15* —7F 79
Palace Ct. *NW3* —5K 43
Palace Ct. *W2* —7K 59
Palace Ct. *Harr* —6E 24
Palace Ct. Gdns. *N10* —3G 29
Palace Gdns. *Buck H* —1G 21
Palace Gdns. *Enf* —4J 7
Palace Gdns. M. *W8* —1K 75
Palace Gdns. Shop. Cen. *Enf*
 —4J 7
Palace Gdns. Ter. *W8* —1J 75
Palace Ga. *W8* —2A 76
Palace Gates Rd. *N22* —1H 29
Palace Grn. *W8* —1K 75
Palace Grn. *Croy* —7B 136
Palace Gro. *SE19* —7F 111
Palace Gro. *Brom* —1K 127
Palace M. *E17* —4B 32
Palace M. *SW1* —4E 76 (4H 153)
Palace M. *SW6* —7H 75
Palace M. *Enf* —3J 7
Palace Pde. *E17* —4B 32
Palace Pl. *SW1* —3G 77 (1A 154)
Palace Pl. Mans. *W8* —2K 75
 (off Kensington Ct.)
Palace Rd. *N8* —5H 29
 (in two parts)
Palace Rd. *N11* —7D 16
Palace Rd. *SE19* —7F 111
Palace Rd. *SW2* —1K 109
Palace Rd. *Brom* —1K 127
Palace Rd. *King T* —4D 118
Palace Rd. *Ruis* —4C 38
Palace Sq. *SE19* —7F 111
Palace St. *SW1* —3G 77 (1A 154)
Palace View. *SE12* —2J 113
Palace View. *Brom* —3K 127
 (in two parts)
Palace View. *Croy* —4B 136
Palace View Rd. *E4* —5J 19
Palamos Rd. *E10* —1C 48
Palatine Av. *N16* —4E 46
Palatine Rd. *N16* —4E 46
Palermo Rd. *NW10* —2C 58
Palestine Gro. *SW19* —1B 122
Palewell Comn. Dri. *SW14*
 —5K 89
Palewell Pk. *SW14* —5K 89
Palfrey Pl. *SW8* —7K 77
Palgrave Av. *S'hall* —7E 54
Palgrave Ho. *SE5* —7C 78
 (off Wyndham Est.)
Palgrave Ho. *Twic* —7G 87
Palgrave Rd. *W12* —3B 74
Palissy St. *E2* —3F 63 (2J 145)
Pallant Ho. *SE1* —3D 78 (2F 157)
Pallant Way. *Orp* —3E 138
Pallet Way. *SE18* —1C 98
Palliser Rd. *W14* —5G 75
Pall Mall. *SW1* —1G 77 (5B 148)
Pall Mall E. *SW1*
 —1H 77 (4D 148)

Pall Mall Pl. *SW1*
 —1G 77 (5B 148)
Palmar Ct. *Bexh* —3G 101
Palmar Rd. *Bexh* —2G 101
Palm Av. *Sidc* —6D 116
Palm Clo. *E10* —3D 48
Palm Ct. *SE15* —7F 79
 (off Garnies Clo.)
Palmeira Rd. *Bexh* —3D 100
Palmer Av. *Sutt* —4E 130
Palmer Clo. *Houn* —1E 86
Palmer Clo. *W Wick* —2F 137
Palmer Cres. *King T* —3E 118
Palmer Pl. *N7* —5A 46
Palmer Rd. *E13* —4K 65
Palmer Rd. *Dag* —1D 52
Palmer's Ct. *N11* —5B 16
 (off Palmer's Rd.)
Palmers La. *Enf* —1C 8
Palmers Pas. *SW14* —3J 89
Palmers Rd. *E2* —2K 63
Palmers Rd. *N11* —5B 16
Palmers Rd. *SW14* —3J 89
Palmers Rd. *SW16* —2K 123
Palmerston Cen. *W'stone* —3K 23
Palmerston Ct. *Buck H* —2F 21
Palmerston Ct. *Surb* —7D 118
Palmerston Cres. *N13* —5E 16
Palmerston Cres. *SE18* —6G 83
Palmerston Gro. *SW19* —7J 107
Palmerston Mans. *W14* —6G 75
 (off Queen's Club Gdns.)
Palmerston Rd. *E7* —6K 49
Palmerston Rd. *E17* —3B 32
Palmerston Rd. *N22* —7E 16
Palmerston Rd. *NW6* —7H 43
 (in two parts)
Palmerston Rd. *SW14* —4J 89
Palmerston Rd. *SW19* —7J 107
Palmerston Rd. *W3* —3J 73
Palmerston Rd. *Bexh* —2F 100
Palmerston Rd. *Buck H* —2E 20
Palmerston Rd. *Cars* —4D 132
Palmerston Rd. *Croy* —5D 124
Palmerston Rd. *Harr* —3J 23
Palmerston Rd. *Sutt* —5A 132
Palmerston Rd. *Twic* —6K 87
Palmerston Way. *SW8* —7G 77
Palmer St. *SW1* —3H 77 (1C 154)
Palm Gro. *W5* —3E 72
Palm Rd. *Romf* —5J 37
Pamela Ct. *N12* —6E 14
Pamela Gdns. *Pinn* —5A 22
Pamela Wlk. *E8* —1G 63
Pampisford Rd. *Purl & S Croy*
 —7B 134
Pam's Way. *Eps* —6A 130
Pancras La. *EC4*
 —6C 62 (1E 150)
Pancras Rd. *NW1*
 —2H 61 (1E 142)
Pandora Rd. *NW6* —6J 43
Panfield M. *Ilf* —6E 34
Panfield Rd. *SE2* —3A 84
Pangbourne Av. *W10* —5E 58
Pangbourne Dri. *Stan* —5J 11
Panhard Pl. *S'hall* —7F 55
Pank Av. *Barn* —5F 5
Pankhurst Clo. *Iswth* —3K 87
Panmuir Rd. *SW20* —1D 120
Panmure Clo. *N5* —4B 46
Panmure Ct. *S'hall* —6F 55
 (off Osborne Rd.)
Panmure Rd. *SE26* —3H 111
Panorama Ct. *N6* —6G 29

Pansy Gdns. *W12* —7C 58
Panther Dri. *NW10* —5K 41
Pantiles Clo. *N13* —5G 17
Pantiles, The. *NW11* —5G 27
Pantiles, The. *Bexh* —7F 85
Pantiles, The. *Brom* —3C 128
Pantiles, The. *Bush* —1C 10
Panton St. *SW1* —7H 61 (3C 148)
Panyer All. *EC4* —6C 62 (7C 144)
Paper Bldgs. *EC4*
 —7A 62 (2K 149)
Papermill Clo. *Cars* —4E 132
Paper Mill Wharf. *E14* —7A 64
Papillons Wlk. *SE3* —3J 97
Papworth Gdns. *N7* —5K 45
Papworth Way. *SW2* —7A 94
Parade Mans. *NW4* —5D 26
Parade M. *SE27* —2B 110
Parade, The. *N4* —2A 46
Parade, The. *SE4* —2B 96
 (off Up. Brockley Rd.)
Parade, The. *SE26* —4H 111
 (off Wells Pk. Rd.)
Parade, The. *SW11* —7D 76
Parade, The. *Cars* —5D 132
 (off Beynon Rd.)
Parade, The. *Croy* —6J 123
Parade, The. *Gnfd* —5B 40
Parade, The. *Hamp* —5H 103
Parade, The. *Wor Pk* —4B 130
Paradise Ct. *Wemb* —3H 41
Paradise Pas. *N7* —5A 46
Paradise Pl. *SE18* —4C 82
Paradise Rd. *SW4* —2J 93
Paradise Rd. *Rich* —5D 88
Paradise Row. *E2* —3H 63
Paradise St. *SE16* —2H 79
Paradise Wlk. *SW3*
 —6D 76 (7F 153)
Paragon All. *SE1*
 —3E 78 (2H 157)
Paragon Clo. *E16* —6J 65
Paragon Gro. *Surb* —6F 119
Paragon M. *SE1* —4D 78 (3F 157)
Paragon Pl. *SE3* —2H 97
Paragon Pl. *Surb* —6F 119
Paragon Rd. *E9* —6J 47
Paragon Row. *SE17*
 —4D 78 (3E 156)
Paragon, The. *SE3* —2J 97
Paraside Pl. *SE18* —4C 82
Parbury Rd. *SE23* —6A 96
Parchmore Rd. *T Hth* —2B 124
Parchmore Way. *T Hth* —2B 124
Pardoner St. *SE1*
 —3D 78 (1F 157)
Pardon St. *EC1* —4B 62 (3B 144)
Parfett St. *E1* —5G 63
Parfitt Clo. *NW3* —1A 44
Parfrey St. *W6* —6E 74
Pargreaves Ct. *Wemb* —2G 41
Parham Dri. *Ilf* —6F 35
Parham Way. *N10* —2G 29
Paris Garden. *SE1*
 —1B 78 (4A 150)
Parish Cotts. *Dag* —2G 53
Parish Ct. *Surb* —6E 118
Parish Ga. Dri. *Sidc* —6J 99
Parish La. *SE20* —6K 111
Parish M. *SE20* —7H 111
Parish Wharf Pl. *SE18* —4C 82
Park App. *SE16* —3H 79
Park App. *Well* —4B 100
Park Av. *E6* —1E 66
Park Av. *E15* —6G 49

Park Av. *N3* —1K 27
Park Av. *N13* —3F 17
Park Av. *N18* —4B 18
Park Av. *N22* —2J 29
Park Av. *NW2* —5D 42
Park Av. *NW10* —2F 57
 (in two parts)
Park Av. *NW11* —1K 43
Park Av. *SW14* —4K 89
Park Av. *Bark* —6G 51
Park Av. *Brom* —6H 113
Park Av. *Cars* —6E 132
Park Av. *Enf* —5J 7
Park Av. *F'boro* —3D 138
Park Av. *Houn* —6F 87
Park Av. *Ilf* —1E 50
Park Av. *Mitc* —7F 109
Park Av. *S'hall* —2D 70
Park Av. *W Wick* —2E 136
Park Av. *Wfd G* —5E 20
Park Av. E. *Eps* —6C 130
Park Av. M. *Mitc* —7F 109
Park Av. N. *N8* —4H 29
Park Av. N. *NW10* —5D 42
Park Av. Rd. *N17* —7C 18
Park Av. S. *N8* —4H 29
Park Av. W. *Eps* —6C 130
Park Bus. Cen. *NW6* —3J 59
Park Chase. *Wemb* —4F 41
Park Clo. *E9* —1J 63
Park Clo. *N12* —4G 15
Park Clo. *NW2* —3D 42
Park Clo. *NW10* —3F 57
Park Clo. *SE7* —5C 82
Park Clo. *SW1* —2D 76 (7E 146)
Park Clo. *W4* —5K 73
Park Clo. *W14* —3H 75
Park Clo. *Cars* —6D 132
Park Clo. *Hamp* —7G 103
Park Clo. *Harr* —1J 23
Park Clo. *Houn* —5G 87
Park Clo. *King T* —1G 119
Park Clo. *E17* —5D 32
Park Clo. *N11* —7C 16
Park Clo. *N17* —7B 18
Park Clo. *SE26* —6H 111
Park Clo. *SW11* —1F 93
Park Clo. *Harr* —7E 24
Park Clo. *King T* —1C 108
Park Clo. *N Mald* —4K 119
Park Clo. *Wemb* —5E 40
Park Cres. *N3* —7E 14
Park Cres. *W1* —4F 61 (4J 141)
Park Cres. *Enf* —4J 7
Park Cres. *Eri* —6J 85
Park Cres. *Harr* —1J 23
Park Cres. *Twic* —1H 103
Park Cres. M. E. *W1*
 —4F 61 (4K 141)
Park Cres. M. W. *W1*
 —4F 61 (4J 141)
Park Cres. Rd. *Eri* —6K 85
Park Croft. *Edgw* —1J 25
Parkcroft Rd. *SE12* —7H 97
Parkdale. *N11* —6C 16
Parkdale Cres. *Wor Pk* —3A 130
Parkdale Rd. *SE18* —5J 83
Park Dri. *N21* —6H 7
Park Dri. *NW11* —1K 43
Park Dri. *SE7* —6C 82
Park Dri. *SW14* —5K 89
Park Dri. *W3* —3G 73
Park Dri. *Dag* —3J 53
Park Dri. *Har W* —6C 10

Park Dri. *N Har* —7E 22
Park Dri. *Romf* —4K 37
Park Dwellings. *NW3* —5D 44
Park End. *NW3* —4C 44
Park End. *Brom* —1H 127
Parker Clo. *E16* —1C 82
Parker Ho. *E14* —2C 80
 (off Admirals Way)
Parker M. *WC2* —6J 61 (7F 143)
Parke Rd. *SW13* —1C 90
Parker Rd. *Croy* —4C 134
Parker's Row. *SE1*
 —2G 79 (7K 151)
Parker St. *E16* —1C 82
Parker St. *WC2* —6J 61 (7F 143)
Park Farm Clo. *N2* —3A 28
Park Farm Clo. *Pinn* —5A 22
Park Farm Rd. *Brom* —1B 128
Park Farm Rd. *King T* —7E 104
Parkfield. *Iswth* —1J 87
Parkfield Av. *SW14* —4A 90
Parkfield Av. *Harr* —2G 23
Parkfield Av. *N'holt* —2B 54
Parkfield Clo. *Edgw* —6C 12
Parkfield Clo. *N'holt* —2C 54
Parkfield Cres. *Harr* —2G 23
Parkfield Cres. *Ruis* —2C 38
Parkfield Dri. *N'holt* —2B 54
Parkfield Gdns. *Harr* —3F 23
Parkfield Ho. *N Har* —1F 22
Parkfield Rd. *NW10* —7D 42
Parkfield Rd. *SE14* —1B 96
Parkfield Rd. *Harr* —3G 39
Parkfield Rd. *N'holt* —2C 54
Parkfields. *SW15* —4E 90
Parkfields. *Croy* —1B 136
Parkfields Av. *NW9* —1K 41
Parkfields Av. *SW20* —1D 120
Parkfields Clo. *Cars* —4E 132
Parkfields Rd. *King T* —5F 105
Parkfield St. *N1* —2A 62
Parkfield Way. *Brom* —6D 128
Park Gdns. *E10* —1C 48
Park Gdns. *NW9* —3K 25
Park Gdns. *Eri* —4K 85
Park Gdns. *King T* —5F 105
Park Ga. *N2* —3B 28
Park Ga. *N21* —7E 6
Park Ga. *SE3* —3H 97
Park Ga. *W5* —5D 56
Parkgate Av. *Barn* —1F 5
Park Ga. Clo. *King T* —6H 105
Parkgate Cres. *Barn* —1F 5
Parkgate Gdns. *SW14* —5K 89
Parkgate M. *N6* —7G 29
Parkgate Rd. *SW11* —7C 76
Parkgate Rd. *Wall* —5E 132
Park Gates. *Harr* —4E 38
Park Gro. *E15* —1J 65
Park Gro. *N11* —7C 16
Park Gro. *Bexh* —4J 101
Park Gro. *Brom* —1K 127
Park Gro. *Edgw* —5A 12
Park Gro. Rd. *E11* —2G 49
Parkhall Rd. *N2* —4C 28
Park Hall Rd. *SE21* —3D 110
Park Hall Trad. Est. *SE21*
 —3C 110
Parkham Ct. *Short* —2G 127
Parkham St. *SW11* —1C 92
Park Hill. *SE23* —2H 111
Park Hill. *SW4* —5H 93
Park Hill. *W5* —5D 56
Park Hill. *Brom* —4C 128
Park Hill. *Cars* —6C 132

Park Hill. Rich —6F 89
Park Hill Clo. Cars —5C 132
Park Hill Ct. SW17 —3D 108
Park Hill Rise. Croy —2E 134
Parkhill Rd. E4 —1K 19
Parkhill Rd. NW3 —5D 44
Park Hill Rd. Bex —7F 101
Park Hill Rd. Brom —2G 127
Park Hill Rd. Croy —4E 134
Park Hill Rd. Sidc —3J 115
Park Hill Rd. Wall —7F 133
Parkhill Wlk. NW3 —5D 44
Parkholme Rd. E8 —6G 47
Park Ho. N21 —7E 6
Park Ho. Gdns. Twic —5C 88
Park Ho. Pas. N6 —7E 28
Parkhouse St. SE5 —7D 78
Parkhurst Ct. N7 —4J 45
Parkhurst Gdns. Bex —7G 101
Parkhurst Rd. E12 —4E 50
Parkhurst Rd. E17 —4A 32
Parkhurst Rd. N7 —4J 45
Parkhurst Rd. N11 —4K 15
Parkhurst Rd. N17 —2G 31
Parkhurst Rd. N22 —6E 16
Parkhurst Rd. Bex —7G 101
Parkhurst Rd. Sutt —4B 132
Parkland Ct. E15 —5G 49
  (off Maryland Pk.)
Parkland Gdns. SW19 —1F 107
Parkland Rd. N22 —2K 29
Parkland Rd. Wfd G —7D 20
Parklands. N6 —7F 29
Parklands. Surb —5F 119
Parklands Clo. SW14 —5J 89
Parklands Clo. Barn —1G 5
Parklands Ct. Houn —2B 86
Parklands Dri. N3 —3G 27
Parklands Pde. Houn —2B 86
Parklands Way. Wor Pk —2A 130
Park La. E15 —1F 65
Park La. N9 —3K 17
Park La. N17 —7A 18
Park La. W1 —7D 60 (2F 147)
Park La. Cars & Wall —4E 132
Park La. Chad H —6D 36
Park La. Croy —3D 134
Park La. Harr —7F 39
Park La. Rich —4D 88
Park La. Stan —3F 11
Park La. Sutt —6G 131
Park La. Tedd —6K 103
Park La. Wemb —6E 40
Park La. Clo. N17 —7B 18
Park Lawns. Wemb —4F 41
Parklea Clo. NW9 —1A 26
Park Lee Ct. N16 —7E 30
Parkleigh Rd. SW19 —2K 121
Parkleys. Rich —4D 104
Park Mnr. Sutt —7A 132
  (off Christchurch Pk.)
Park Mans. NW4 —5D 26
Park Mans. SE26 —3J 111
  (off Sydenham Pk.)
Park Mans. SW1
  —2D 76 (7E 146)
  (off Brompton Rd.)
Park Mans. SW8
  —6J 77 (7F 155)
Park Mans. SW11 —1D 92
  (off Prince of Wales Dri.)
Parkmead. SW15 —6D 90
Park Mead. Harr —3F 39
Park Mead. Sidc —5B 100

Parkmead Gdns. NW7 —6G 13
Park M. SE24 —7C 94
Park M. W10 —2G 59
Park M. Chst —6F 115
Parkmore Clo. Wfd G —4D 20
Park Pde. NW10 —2B 58
Park Pde. W5 —3G 73
Park Pl. E14 —1C 80
Park Pl. SW1 —1G 77 (5A 148)
Park Pl. W3 —4G 73
Park Pl. W5 —1D 72
Park Pl. Hamp H —6G 103
Park Pl. Wemb —4F 41
Park Pl. Gdns. W2
  —5A 60 (5A 140)
Park Pl. Vs. W2 —5A 60 (5A 140)
Park Ridings. N8 —3A 30
Park Rise. SE23 —1A 112
Park Rise. Harr —1J 23
Park Rise Rd. SE23 —1A 112
Park Rd. E6 —1A 66
Park Rd. E10 —1C 48
Park Rd. E12 —1K 49
Park Rd. E15 —1J 65
Park Rd. E17 —5B 32
Park Rd. N2 —3B 28
Park Rd. N8 —4G 29
Park Rd. N11 —7C 16
Park Rd. N14 —1C 16
Park Rd. N15 —4B 30
Park Rd. N18 —4B 18
Park Rd. NW4 —7C 26
Park Rd. NW8 & NW1
  —3C 60 (2D 140)
Park Rd. NW9 —7K 25
Park Rd. NW10 —1A 58
Park Rd. SE25 —4E 124
Park Rd. SW19 —6B 108
Park Rd. W4 —7J 73
Park Rd. W7 —7K 55
Park Rd. Beck —7B 112
Park Rd. Brom —1K 127
Park Rd. Chst —6F 115
Park Rd. Felt —4B 102
Park Rd. Hack —2F 133
Park Rd. Hamp H —4F 103
Park Rd. Hamp W —1C 118
Park Rd. High Bar —4C 4
Park Rd. Houn —5F 87
Park Rd. Ilf —3H 51
Park Rd. Iswth —1B 88
Park Rd. King T —5F 105
Park Rd. New Bar —4G 5
Park Rd. N Mald —4K 119
Park Rd. Rich —6F 89
Park Rd. Surb —5F 119
Park Rd. Sutt —6G 131
Park Rd. Tedd —6K 103
Park Rd. Twic —6C 88
Park Rd. Wall —5F 133
Park Rd. Wemb —6E 40
Park Rd. E. W3 —2J 73
Park Rd. Ho. King T —7G 105
Park Rd. Ind. Est. Swan —3A 118
Park Rd. N. W3 —2H 73
Park Rd. N. W4 —5K 73
Park Row. SE10 —5F 81
Park Royal Junction. (Junct.)
  —1G 57
Pk. Royal Metro Cen. NW10
  —4H 57
Pk. Royal Rd. NW10 & W3
  —3J 57
Pk. Royal S. Leisure Complex. W3
  —4G 57

Parkshot. Rich —4D 88
Parkside. N3 —1K 27
Parkside. NW2 —3C 42
Parkside. NW7 —6H 13
Parkside. SE3 —7H 81
Parkside. SW19 —3F 107
Parkside. W3 —1A 74
Parkside. Buck H —2E 20
Parkside. Hamp —5H 103
Parkside. Sidc —2B 116
Parkside. Sutt —6G 131
Parkside Av. Bexh —2K 101
Parkside Av. Brom —4C 128
Parkside Av. Romf —3K 37
Parkside Clo. SE20 —7J 111
Parkside Ct. N22 —6E 16
Parkside Cres. N7 —3A 46
Parkside Cres. Surb —6J 119
Parkside Cross. Bexh —2K 101
Parkside Dri. Edgw —3B 12
Parkside Est. E9 —1K 63
Parkside Gdns. SW19 —5F 107
Parkside Gdns. E Barn —1J 15
Parkside Ho. Dag —3J 53
Parkside Lodge. Belv —5J 85
Parkside Rd. SW11 —1E 92
Parkside Rd. Belv —4H 85
Parkside Rd. Houn —5F 87
Parkside Ter. N18 —4J 17
Parkside Way. Harr —4F 23
Park Sq. E. NW1 —4F 61 (3J 141)
Park Sq. M. NW1
  —4F 61 (4J 141)
Park Sq. W. NW1
  —4F 61 (3J 141)
Parkstead Rd. SW15 —5C 90
Park Steps. W2 —7C 60 (2D 146)
Parkstone Av. N18 —6A 18
Parkstone Rd. E17 —3E 32
Parkstone Rd. SE15 —2G 95
Park St. SE1 —1C 78 (4C 150)
Park St. W1 —7E 60 (2G 147)
Park St. Croy —2C 134
Park St. Tedd —6J 103
Park Ter. Enf —1F 9
Park Ter. Wor Pk —1C 130
Park, The. N6 —6E 28
Park, The. NW11 —1K 43
Park, The. SE19 —7E 110
Park, The. SE23 —1J 111
Park, The. W5 —1D 72
Park, The. Cars —6D 132
Park, The. Sidc —5A 116
Parkthorne Clo. Harr —6F 23
Parkthorne Dri. Harr —6E 22
Parkthorne Rd. SW12 —7H 93
Park View. N5 —4C 46
Park View. N21 —7E 6
Park View. W3 —5J 57
Park View. Chad H —6D 36
Parkview. Eri —1D 84
Parkview. Gnfd —3A 56
  (off Perivale La.)
Park View. N Mald —3B 120
Park View. Pinn —1D 22
Park View. Wemb —5H 41
Park View Clo. SE20 —1H 125
Parkview Ct. SW18 —5J 91
Parkview Ct. Har W —7D 10
Park View Cres. N11 —4A 16
Parkview Dri. Mitc —2B 122
Park View Est. E2 —2K 63
Park View Gdns. N22 —1A 30

Park View Gdns. NW4 —5E 26
Park View Gdns. Ilf —4D 34
Park View Gdns. Bark —2J 67
Park View Ho. E4 —5H 19
Parkview Ho. N9 —7C 8
Park View Ho. SE24 —6B 94
  (off Hurst St.)
Park View Mans. N4 —7B 30
Park View Rd. N3 —1K 27
Park View Rd. N17 —3G 31
Park View Rd. NW10 —4B 34
Parkview Rd. SE9 —1F 115
Park View Rd. W5 —5E 56
Park View Rd. Croy —1G 135
Park View Rd. S'hall —1E 70
Park View Rd. Well —3C 100
Park Village E. NW1
  —2F 61 (1K 141)
Park Village W. NW1 —2F 61
Park Vs. Romf —6D 36
Parkville Rd. SW6 —7H 75
Park Vista. SE10 —6F 81
Park Wlk. N6 —7E 28
Park Wlk. SW10
  —6A 76 (7A 152)
Park Wlk. Barn —3G 5
Parkway. N14 —2D 16
Park Way. N20 —4J 15
Parkway. NW1 —1F 61
Park Way. NW11 —5G 27
Parkway. SW20 —4F 121
Park Way. Edgw —1H 25
Parkway. Eri —3E 84
Park Way. Felt —7A 86
Parkway. Ilf —3K 51
Park Way. Wfd G —5F 21
Parkway, The. Hayes & N'holt
  (in two parts) —1A 70
Parkway Trad. Est. Houn —6A 70
Park West. W2 —6C 60 (7D 140)
Park West Pl. W2
  —6C 60 (7D 140)
Parkwood. N20 —3J 15
Parkwood. Beck —7C 112
Parkwood Flats. N20 —3J 15
Parkwood M. N6 —6F 29
Parkwood Rd. SW19 —5H 107
Parkwood Rd. Bexh —7F 101
Parkwood Rd. Iswth —1K 87
Parliament Ct. E1
  —5E 62 (6H 145)
Parliament Hill. NW3 —4C 44
Parliament Hill Mans. NW5
  —4E 44
Parliament M. SW14 —2J 89
Parliament Sq. SW1
  —2J 77 (7E 148)
Parliament St. SW1
  —2J 77 (6E 148)
Parluke Clo. SE7 —5B 82
Parma Cres. SW11 —4D 92
Parmiter Ind. Cen. E2 —2H 63
  (off Parmiter St.)
Parmiter St. E2 —2H 63
Parmoor Ct. EC1
  —4C 62 (3C 144)
Parndon Ho. Lou —1H 21
Parnell Clo. Edgw —4C 12
Parnell Rd. E3 —1B 64
  (in two parts)
Parnham St. E14 —6A 64
Parolles Rd. N19 —1G 45
Paroma Rd. Belv —3G 85
Parr Clo. N9 & N18 —4C 18

Parr Ct. Felt —4A 102
Parrington Ho. SW4 —6H 93
Parrish Ct. NW6 —1F 59
Parr Rd. E6 —1B 66
Parr Rd. Stan —1E 24
Parrs Clo. S Croy —7D 134
Parrs Pl. Hamp —7E 102
Parr St. N1 —2D 62
Parry Av. E6 —6D 66
Parry Clo. Eps —7D 130
Parry Pl. SE18 —4F 83
Parry Rd. SE25 —3E 124
Parry Rd. W10 —3G 59
  (in two parts)
Parry St. SW8 —6J 77 (7F 155)
Parsifal Rd. NW6 —5J 43
Parsley Gdns. Croy —1K 135
Parsloes Av. Dag —4D 52
Parsonage Gdns. Enf —2H 7
Parsonage La. Enf —2H 7
Parsonage La. Sidc —4F 117
Parsonage Manorway. Belv
  —6G 85
Parsonage St. E14 —4E 80
Parson's Cres. Edgw —3B 12
Parson's Grn. SW6 —1J 91
Parson's Grn. La. SW6 —1J 91
Parson's Gro. Edgw —3B 12
Parsons Mead. Croy —1B 134
Parson's Rd. E13 —2A 66
Parson St. NW4 —4E 26
Parthenia Rd. SW6 —1J 91
Partingdale La. NW7 —5A 14
Partington Clo. N19 —1H 45
Partridge Clo. E16 —5B 66
Partridge Clo. Barn —6A 4
Partridge Clo. Bush —1B 10
Partridge Clo. Stan —4K 11
Partridge Ct. EC1
  —4B 62 (3A 144)
Partridge Grn. SE9 —3E 114
Partridge Rd. Hamp —6D 102
Partridge Rd. Sidc —4J 115
Partridge Sq. E6 —5C 66
Partridge Way. N22 —1J 29
Parvin St. SW8 —1H 93
Pascal St. SW8 —7H 77
Pascoe Rd. SE13 —5F 97
Pasley Clo. SE17
  —5C 78 (6C 156)
Pasquier Rd. E17 —3A 32
Passage, The. W6 —3E 74
Passage, The. Rich —5E 88
Passey Pl. SE9 —6D 98
Passfield Dri. E14 —5D 64
Passfield Path. SE28 —7B 68
Passfields. SE6 —3E 112
Passfields. W14 —5H 75
  (off May St.)
Passing All. EC1
  —5B 62 (4B 144)
Passingham Ho. Houn —6E 70
Passmore Gdns. N11 —6C 16
Passmore St. SW1
  —5E 76 (5G 153)
Pasteur Clo. NW9 —2A 26
Pasteur Gdns. N18 —5G 17
Paston Clo. E5 —3K 47
Paston Cres. SE12 —7K 97
Pastor Ct. N6 —6G 29
Pastor St. SE11 —4B 78 (3B 156)
  (in two parts)
Pasture Clo. Wemb —3B 40
Pasture Rd. SE6 —1H 113
Pasture Rd. Dag —4F 53

Pasture Rd. Wemb —2B 40
Pastures, The. N20 —1C 14
Patcham Ter. SW8 —1F 93
Patchway Ct. SE15 —6E 78
(off Newent Clo.)
Paternoster Row. EC4
—6C 62 (1C 150)
Paternoster Sq. EC4
—6B 62 (7B 144)
Paterson Ct. EC1
—3D 62 (2E 144)
Pater St. W8 —3J 75
Pathfield Rd. SW16 —6H 109
Path, The. SW19 —1K 121
Patience Rd. SW11 —2C 92
Patina Wlk. SE16 —1A 80
(off Capstan Way)
Patio Clo. SW4 —6H 93
Patmore Est. SW8 —1G 93
Patmore Ho. N16 —5E 46
Patmore Lodge. N6 —4D 28
Patmore St. SW8 —1G 93
Patmos Rd. SW9 —7B 78
Paton Clo. E3 —3C 64
Paton Ho. SW9 —2K 93
(off Stockwell Rd.)
Paton St. EC1 —3C 62 (2C 144)
Patricia Ct. Chst —1H 129
Patricia Ct. Well —7B 84
Patrick Connolly Gdns. E3
—3D 64
Patrick Pas. SW11 —2C 92
Patrick Rd. E13 —3A 66
Patriot Sq. E2 —2H 63
Patrol Pl. SE6 —6D 96
Patshull Pl. NW5 —6G 45
Patshull Rd. NW5 —6G 45
Patten All. Rich —5D 88
Pattenden Rd. SE6 —1B 112
Patten Ho. N4 —1C 46
Patten Rd. SW18 —7C 92
Patterdale Clo. Brom —6H 113
Patterdale SE15 —7J 79
Pattern Ho. EC1 —4B 62 (3A 144)
Patterson Ct. SE19 —7F 111
Patterson Rd. SE19 —6F 111
Pattinson Point. E16 —5J 65
(off Fife Rd.)
Pattison Rd. NW2 —3J 43
Pattison Wlk. SE18 —5G 83
Paul Byrne Ho. N2 —3A 28
Paul Clo. E15 —1G 65
Paul Ct. Romf —6J 37
Paulet Rd. SE5 —2B 94
Paul Gdns. Croy —3F 135
Paulhan Rd. Harr —4D 24
Pauline Cres. Twic —1G 103
Paul Julius Clo. E14 —7F 65
Paul Robeson Clo. E6 —3E 66
Paul St. E15 —1G 65
Paul St. EC2 —4D 62 (4F 145)
Paul's Wlk. EC4
—7C 62 (2B 150)
Paultons Sq. SW3
—6B 76 (7B 152)
Paultons St. SW3
—6B 76 (7B 152)
Pauntley St. N19 —1G 45
Paved Ct. Rich —5D 88
Paveley Dri. SW11 —7C 76
Paveley St. NW8
—3C 60 (2D 140)
Pavement M. Romf —7D 36
Pavement Sq. Croy —1G 135

Pavement, The. E11 —1E 48
Pavement, The. SW4 —4G 93
Pavement, The. W5 —3E 72
Pavement, The. Iswth —3A 88
(off South St.)
Pavet Clo. Dag —6H 53
Pavilion Lodge. Harr —1H 39
Pavilion M. N3 —2J 27
Pavilion Rd. SW1
—3D 76 (7F 147)
Pavilion Rd. Ilf —7D 34
Pavilion St. SW1
—3D 76 (2F 153)
Pavilion Ter. Ilf —5J 35
Pavilion Way. Edgw —7C 12
Pavilion Way. Ruis —2A 38
Pavillion Ter. W12 —6E 58
(off Wood La.)
Pavillion, The. SW8 —7H 77
Pawleyne Clo. SE20 —7J 111
Pawsey Clo. E13 —1K 65
Pawsons Rd. Croy —6C 124
Paxfold. Stan —6J 11
Paxford Rd. Wemb —2B 40
Paxton Clo. Rich —2F 89
Paxton Ct. SE26 —4A 112
(off Adamsrill Rd.)
Paxton Pl. SE27 —4E 110
Paxton Rd. N17 —7B 18
Paxton Rd. SE23 —3A 112
Paxton Rd. W4 —6A 74
Paxton Rd. Brom —7J 113
Paxton Ter. SW1
—6F 77 (7K 153)
Payne Ho. N1 —1K 61
(off Barnsbury Est.)
Payne Rd. E3 —2D 64
Paynesfield Av. SW14 —3K 89
Paynesfield Rd. Bush —1E 10
Payne St. SE8 —7B 80
Paynes Wlk. W6 —6G 75
Payzes Gdns. Wfd G —5C 20
Peabody Av. SW1
—5F 77 (5J 153)
Peabody Bldgs. E1 —7G 63
Peabody Bldgs. E2 —2H 63
(off Cambridge Cres.)
Peabody Bldgs. SE1
—1C 78 (4C 150)
Peabody Bldgs. SW3
—6C 76 (7C 152)
Peabody Clo. SE10 —1D 96
Peabody Clo. SW1
—6F 77 (7K 153)
Peabody Clo. Croy —1J 135
Peabody Cotts. N17 —1E 30
Peabody Ct. EC1
—4C 62 (4D 144)
(off Roscoe St.)
Peabody Ct. SE5 —1D 94
(off Kimpton Rd.)
Peabody Est. EC1
—4A 62 (4K 143)
(off Farringdon La.)
Peabody Est. N1 —1C 62
Peabody Est. SE1
(Hatfield St.) —1A 78 (5K 149)
Peabody Est. SE1
(off Mint St.) —2C 78 (6D 150)
Peabody Est. SE24 —7C 94
Peabody Est. SW1
—4G 77 (3B 154)
Peabody Est. SW3
—6C 76 (7D 152)

Peabody Est. SW6 —6J 75
(off Lillie Rd.)
Peabody Est. SW11 —4C 92
Peabody Est. W6 —5E 74
Peabody Est. W10 —4E 58
Peabody Hill. SE21 —1B 110
Peabody Sq. SE1
—2B 78 (7A 150)
Peabody Tower. EC1
—4C 62 (4D 144)
(off Golden La.)
Peabody Yd. N1 —1C 62
Peace Clo. N14 —5A 6
Peace Clo. SE25 —4E 124
Peace Gro. Wemb —3H 41
Peace St. SE18 —6E 82
Peaches Clo. Sutt —7G 131
Peach Rd. W10 —3F 59
Peachum Rd. SE3 —6H 81
Peacock Ind. Est. N17 —7A 18
Peacock St. SE17
—4B 78 (4B 156)
Peacock Wlk. E16 —6K 65
(off Mortlake Rd.)
Peacock Wlk. N6 —7F 29
Peacock Yd. SE17
—4B 78 (4B 156)
Peaketon Av. Ilf —4B 34
Peak Hill. SE26 —4J 111
Peak Hill Av. SE26 —4J 111
Peak Hill Gdns. SE26 —4J 111
Peak Ho. N4 —1C 46
(off Woodberry Down Est.)
Peak, The. SE26 —3J 111
Peal Gdns. W13 —3A 56
Peall Rd. Croy —6K 123
Peall Rd. Ind. Est. Croy —6K 123
Pearce Clo. Mitc —2E 122
Pearcefield Av. SE23 —1J 111
Pear Clo. NW9 —4K 25
Pear Clo. SE14 —7A 80
Pearcroft Rd. E11 —2F 49
Peardon St. SW8 —2F 93
Pearescroft Gdns. Stan —1D 24
Pearfield Rd. SE23 —3A 112
Pearl Clo. E6 —6E 66
Pearl Clo. NW2 —7E 26
Pearl Rd. E17 —3C 32
Pearl St. E1 —1H 79
Pearman St. SE1
—3A 78 (1K 155)
Pear Pl. SE1 —2A 78 (6J 149)
Pear Rd. E11 —3F 49
Pearscroft Ct. SW6 —1K 91
Pearscroft Rd. SW6 —1K 91
Pearson's Av. SE14 —1C 96
Pearson St. E2 —2F 63
Pears Rd. Houn —3G 87
Peartree Av. SW17 —3A 108
Pear Tree Clo. E2 —1F 63
Peartree Clo. Eri —1K 101
Peartree Clo. Mitc —2C 122
Pear Tree Ct. E18 —1K 33
Pear Tree Ct. EC1
—4A 62 (4K 143)
Peartree Gdns. Dag —4B 52
Peartree Gdns. Romf —2H 37
Pear Tree Ho. SE4 —4B 96
Peartree La. E1 —7J 63
Peartree Rd. Enf —3K 7
Pear Tree St. EC1
—4C 62 (3B 144)
Peary Ho. NW10 —7K 41
Peary Pl. E2 —3J 63
Peas Mead Ter. E4 —4K 19

Peatfield Clo. Sidc —3J 115
Pebworth Rd. Harr —2A 40
Peckarmans Wood. SE26
—3G 111
Peckett Sq. N5 —4C 46
Peckford Clo. SW9 —2A 94
Peckford Pl. SW9 —2A 94
Peckham Gro. SE15 —7E 78
Peckham High St. SE15 —1G 95
Peckham Hill St. SE15 —7G 79
Peckham Pk. Rd. SE15 —7G 79
Peckham Rd. SE5 & SE15
—1E 94
Peckham Rye. SE15 & SE22
—3G 95
Peckham Rye Ind. Est. SE15
—2F 95
Peckwater St. NW5 —5G 45
Pedhoulas. N14 —3D 16
Pedlar's Wlk. N7 —5K 45
Pedley Rd. Dag —1C 52
Pedley St. E1 —4F 63 (4K 145)
Pedro St. E5 —3K 47
Pedworth Gdns. SE16 —4J 79
Peebles Ct. S'hall —6G 55
(off Haldane Rd.)
Peel Clo. E4 —2J 19
Peel Clo. N9 —3B 18
Peel Dri. NW9 —3C 26
Peel Dri. Ilf —3C 34
Peel Gro. E2 —2J 63
(in two parts)
Peel La. NW9 —3C 26
Peel Pas. W8 —1J 75
(off Peel St.)
Peel Pl. Ilf —2C 34
Peel Precinct. NW6 —2J 59
Peel Rd. E18 —1H 33
Peel Rd. NW6 —3J 59
Peel Rd. W'stone —3K 23
(in two parts)
Peel Rd. Wemb —3D 40
Peel St. W8 —1J 75
Peerglow Est. Enf —5D 8
Peerless St. EC1
—3D 62 (2E 144)
Pegamoid Rd. N18 —3D 18
Pegasus Ct. King T —3D 118
Pegasus Pl. SE11
—6A 78 (7J 155)
Pegasus Tower. SE14 —7A 80
(off Woodpecker Rd.)
Pegg Rd. Houn —7B 70
Pegley Gdns. SE12 —2J 113
Pegwell St. SE18 —7J 83
Pekin Clo. E14 —6C 64
Pekin St. E14 —6C 64
Peldon Ct. Rich —5F 89
Peldon Pas. Rich —4F 89
Peldon Wlk. N1 —1B 62
(off Popham St.)
Pelham Av. Bark —1K 67
Pelham Clo. SE5 —3E 94
Pelham Cotts. Bex —1H 117
Pelham Ct. Sidc —3A 116
Pelham Cres. SW7
—4C 76 (4C 152)
Pelham Ho. W14 —4H 75
(off Mornington Av.)
Pelham Pl. SW7 —4C 76 (3C 152)
Pelham Rd. E18 —3K 33
Pelham Rd. N15 —4F 31
Pelham Rd. N22 —2A 30
Pelham Rd. SW19 —7J 107

Pelham Rd. Beck —2J 125
Pelham Rd. Bexh —3G 101
Pelham Rd. Ilf —2H 51
Pelham St. SW7
—4B 76 (3B 152)
Pelican Est. SE15 —1F 95
Pelican Ho. SE8 —4B 80
Pelican Pas. E1 —4J 63
Pelican Stairs. E1 —1J 79
Pelican Wlk. SW9 —4B 94
Pelier St. SE17 —6C 78 (7D 156)
Pelinore Rd. SE6 —2G 113
Pella Ho. SE11 —5K 77 (5H 155)
Pellant Rd. SW6 —7G 75
Pellatt Gro. N22 —1A 30
Pellatt Rd. SE22 —5F 95
Pellatt Rd. Wemb —2D 40
Pellerin Rd. N16 —5E 46
Pelling St. E14 —6C 64
Pellipar Clo. N13 —3F 17
Pellipar Gdns. SE18 —5D 82
Pelly Rd. E13 —1J 65
(in two parts)
Pelter St. E2 —3F 63 (1J 145)
Pelton Rd. SE10 —5G 81
Pembar Av. E17 —3A 32
Pember Rd. NW10 —3F 59
Pemberton Gdns. N19 —3G 45
Pemberton Gdns. Romf —5E 36
Pemberton Ho. SE26 —4G 111
(off High Level Dri.)
Pemberton Pl. E8 —7J 47
Pemberton Rd. N4 —5A 30
Pemberton Row. EC4
—6A 62 (7K 143)
Pemberton Ter. N19 —3G 45
Pembridge Av. Twic —1D 102
Pembridge Cres. W11 —7J 59
Pembridge Gdns. W2 —7J 59
Pembridge M. W11 —7J 59
Pembridge Pl. SW18 —5J 91
Pembridge Pl. W2 —7J 59
Pembridge Rd. W11 —7J 59
Pembridge Sq. W2 —7J 59
Pembridge Vs. W11 & W2
—7J 59
Pembroke Av. Enf —1C 8
Pembroke Av. Harr —3A 24
Pembroke Av. Surb —5H 119
Pembroke Bldgs. NW10 —3C 58
Pembroke Clo. SW1
—2E 76 (7H 147)
Pembroke Cotts. W8 —3J 75
(off Pembroke Sq.)
Pembroke Ct. W7 —6K 55
(off Copley Clo.)
Pembroke Gdns. W8 —4H 75
Pembroke Gdns. Dag —3H 53
Pembroke Gdns. Clo. W8 —3J 75
Pembroke Hall. NW4 —3E 26
(off Mulberry Clo.)
Pembroke Lodge. Stan —6H 11
Pembroke M. E3 —3A 64
Pembroke M. N10 —1F 29
Pembroke M. W8 —3J 75
Pembroke Pl. W8 —3J 75
Pembroke Pl. Edgw —7B 12
Pembroke Pl. Iswth —2J 87
Pembroke Rd. E6 —5D 66
Pembroke Rd. E17 —5D 32
Pembroke Rd. N8 —4J 29

Pembroke Rd. *N10* —1E **28**
Pembroke Rd. *N13* —3H **17**
Pembroke Rd. *N15* —5F **31**
Pembroke Rd. *SE25* —4E **124**
Pembroke Rd. *W8* —4H **75**
Pembroke Rd. *Brom* —2A **128**
Pembroke Rd. *Eri* —5J **85**
Pembroke Rd. *Gnfd* —4F **55**
Pembroke Rd. *Ilf* —1K **51**
Pembroke Rd. *Mitc* —2E **122**
Pembroke Rd. *Wemb* —3D **40**
Pembroke Sq. *W8* —3J **75**
Pembroke St. *N1* —1K **61**
Pembroke Vs. *Rich* —4D **88**
Pembroke Wlk. *W8* —4J **75**
Pembury Av. *Wor Pk* —1C **130**
Pembury Clo. *E5* —5H **47**
Pembury Clo. *Brom* —7H **127**
Pembury Cres. *Sidc* —2E **116**
Pembury Pl. *E5* —5H **47**
Pembury Rd. *E5* —5H **47**
Pembury Rd. *N17* —1F **31**
Pembury Rd. *SE25* —4G **125**
Pembury Rd. *Bexh* —7E **84**
Pemdevon Rd. *Croy* —7A **124**
Pemell Clo. *E1* —4J **63**
Pempath Pl. *Wemb* —2D **40**
Penally Pl. *N1* —1D **62**
Penang St. *E1* —1H **79**
Penarth Cen., The. *SE15* —6J **79**
Penarth St. *SE15* —6J **79**
Penberth Rd. *SE6* —2E **112**
Penbury Rd. *S'hall* —4D **70**
Pencombe M. *W11* —7H **59**
Pencraig Way. *SE15* —6H **79**
Pendall Clo. *Barn* —4H **5**
Penda Rd. *Eri* —7H **85**
Pendarves Rd. *SW20* —1E **120**
Penda's Mead. *E9* —4A **48**
Pendennis Ho. *SE8* —4A **80**
Pendennis Rd. *N17* —3D **30**
Pendennis Rd. *SW16* —4J **109**
Penderel Rd. *Houn* —5E **86**
Penderry Rise. *SE6* —2F **113**
Penderyn Way. *N7* —4H **45**
Pendle Ho. *SE26* —3G **111**
Pendle Rd. *SW16* —6F **109**
Pendlestone Rd. *E17* —5D **32**
Pendragon Rd. *Brom* —3H **113**
Pendragon Wlk. *NW9* —6A **26**
Pendrell Rd. *SE4* —2A **96**
Pendrell St. *SE18* —6H **83**
Pendula Dri. *Hayes* —4B **54**
Pendulum M. *E8* —5F **47**
Penerley Rd. *SE6* —1D **112**
Penfields Ho. *N7* —6J **45**
Penfold Clo. *Croy* —3A **134**
Penfold La. *Bex* —2D **116**
(in two parts)
Penfold Pl. *NW1*
—5C **60** (5C **140**)
Penfold Rd. *N9* —1E **18**
Penfold St. *NW8*
—4B **60** (4B **140**)
Penford Gdns. *SE9* —3B **98**
Penford St. *SE5* —2B **94**
Pengarth Rd. *Bex* —5D **100**
Penge La. *SE20* —7J **111**
Penge Rd. *E13* —1A **66**
Penge Rd. *SE25 & SE20*
—3G **125**
Penhall Rd. *SE7* —4B **82**
Penhill Rd. *Bex* —6C **100**
Penhurst Pl. *Ilf* —1F **35**

Penifather La. *Gnfd* —3H **55**
Penistone Rd. *SW16* —7J **109**
Penketh Dri. *Harr* —3H **39**
Penley Ct. *WC2* —7K **61** (2H **149**)
Penmon Rd. *SE2* —3A **84**
Pennack Rd. *SE15*
—6F **79** (7K **157**)
Pennant M. *W8* —4K **75**
Pennant Ter. *E17* —2B **32**
Pennard Rd. *W12* —2E **74**
Penn Clo. *Gnfd* —2F **55**
Penn Clo. *Harr* —4C **24**
Penn Ct. *NW9* —3K **25**
Penner Clo. *SW19* —2G **107**
Pennethorne Clo. *E9* —1J **63**
Pennethorne Rd. *SE15* —7H **79**
Penn Gdns. *Chst* —2F **129**
Penn Gdns. *Romf* —1G **37**
Pennine Dri. *NW2* —2F **43**
Pennine La. *NW2* —2G **43**
Pennine Pde. *NW2* —2G **43**
Pennine Way. *Bexh* —1K **101**
Pennington Clo. *SE27* —4D **110**
Pennington St. *SE16* —1A **80**
Pennington Dri. *N21* —5E **6**
Pennington St. *E1* —7H **63**
Pennington Way. *SE12* —2K **113**
Penninsular Pk. Rd. *SE7* —4J **81**
Penniston Clo. *N17* —2C **30**
Penn La. *Bex* —5D **100**
Penn Rd. *N7* —5J **45**
Penn St. *N1* —1D **62**
Pennycroft. *Croy* —7A **136**
Pennyfields. *E14* —7C **64**
Penny M. *SW12* —7F **93**
Pennymoor Wlk. *W9* —3H **59**
Penny Rd. *NW10* —3H **57**
Penny Royal. *Wall* —6H **133**
Pennyroyal Av. *E6* —6E **66**
Penpoll Rd. *E8* —6H **47**
Penpool La. *Well* —3B **100**
Penrhyn Av. *E17* —1B **32**
Penrhyn Cres. *E17* —1C **32**
Penrhyn Cres. *SW14* —4J **89**
Penrhyn Gdns. *King T* —4D **118**
Penrhyn Gro. *E17* —1C **32**
Penrhyn Rd. *King T* —4E **118**
Penrith Clo. *SW15* —5G **91**
Penrith Clo. *Beck* —1D **126**
Penrith Pl. *SE27* —2B **110**
Penrith Rd. *N15* —5D **30**
Penrith Rd. *N Mald* —4K **119**
Penrith Rd. *T Hth* —2C **124**
Penrith St. *SW16* —6G **109**
Penrose Gro. *SE17*
—5C **78** (6C **156**)
Penrose Ho. *SE17*
Penrose St. *SE17*
—5C **78** (6C **156**)
Penryn Ho. *SE11*
—5B **78** (5A **156**)
Penryn St. *NW1* —2H **61**
Penry Pl. *SE1* —5G **79**
Penry St. *SE1* —4E **78** (4H **157**)
Pensbury Pl. *SW8* —1G **93**
Pensbury St. *SW8* —2G **93**
Pensford Av. *Rich* —2G **89**
Penshurst. *NW5* —6E **44**
Penshurst Av. *Sidc* —6A **100**
Penshurst Gdns. *Edgw* —5C **12**
Penshurst Grn. *Brom* —5H **127**
Penshurst Ho. *SE15* —6J **79**
(off Lovelinch Clo.)
Penshurst Pl. *SE1*
—3K **77** (1H **155**)
Penshurst Rd. *E9* —7K **47**

Penshurst Rd. *N17* —7A **18**
Penshurst Rd. *Bexh* —1F **101**
Penshurst Rd. *T Hth* —5B **124**
Penshurst Wlk. *Brom* —5H **127**
Penshurst Way. *Sutt* —7J **131**
Pensilver Clo. *Barn* —4H **5**
Penstemon Clo. *N3* —6D **14**
Pentagon, The. *W13* —7A **56**
Pentavia Retail Pk. *NW7* —7G **13**
Pentire Rd. *E17* —1F **33**
Pentland Av. *Edgw* —2C **12**
Pentland Clo. *NW11* —2G **43**
Pentland Gdns. *SW18* —6A **92**
Pentland Pl. *N'holt* —1C **54**
Pentland St. *SW18* —6A **92**
Pentlow St. *SW15* —3E **90**
Pentlow Way. *Buck H* —1H **21**
Pentney Rd. *E4* —1A **20**
Pentney Rd. *SW12* —1G **109**
Pentney Rd. *SW19* —1G **121**
Penton Gro. *N1* —2A **62**
Penton Ho. *SE2* —1D **84**
Penton Pl. *SE17* —5B **78** (5B **156**)
Penton Rise. *WC1*
—3K **61** (1H **143**)
Penton St. *N1* —2A **62**
Pentonville Rd. *N1*
—2K **61** (1F **143**)
Pentrich Av. *Enf* —1B **8**
Pentridge St. *SE15* —7F **79**
Pentyre Av. *N18* —5J **17**
Penwerris Av. *Iswth* —7G **71**
Penwerris Ct. *Houn* —7G **71**
Penwith Rd. *SW18* —2J **107**
Penwood Ho. *SW15* —6B **90**
Penwortham Ct. *N22* —2A **30**
Penwortham Rd. *SW16* —6F **109**
Penylan Pl. *Edgw* —7B **12**
Penywern Rd. *SW5* —5J **75**
Penzance Pl. *W11* —1G **75**
Penzance St. *W11* —1G **75**
Peony Ct. *E4* —7B **20**
Peony Gdns. *W12* —7C **58**
Pepler Ho. *W10* —4G **59**
(off Wornington Rd.)
Peploe Rd. *NW6* —2F **59**
Pepper Clo. *E6* —5D **66**
Peppermead Sq. *SE13* —5C **96**
Peppermint Clo. *Croy* —7J **123**
Peppermint Pl. *E11* —3G **49**
Pepper St. *E14* —3D **80**
Pepper St. *SE1* —2C **78** (6C **150**)
Peppie Clo. *N16* —2E **46**
Pepys Ct. *SW4* —3F **93**
Pepys Cres. *E16* —1J **81**
Pepys Cres. *Barn* —5A **4**
Pepys St. *SE14* —1K **95**
Pepys Rd. *SW20* —1E **120**
Pepys St. *EC3* —7E **62** (2H **151**)
Perceval Av. *NW3* —5C **44**
Perceval Ct. *N'holt* —5E **38**
Perceval Ho. *W5* —7C **56**
Percheron Clo. *Iswth* —3K **87**
Perch St. *E8* —4F **47**
Percival Av. *N18* —7A **18**
Percival Gdns. *Romf* —6C **36**
Percival Rd. *SW14* —4J **89**
Percival Rd. *Enf* —4A **8**
Percival St. *EC1* —4B **62** (3A **144**)
Percy Cir. *WC1* —3K **61** (1H **143**)
Percy Gdns. *Enf* —5E **8**
Percy Gdns. *Iswth* —3A **88**
Percy Gdns. *Wor Pk* —1A **130**

Percy M. *W1* —5H **61** (6C **142**)
Percy Pas. *W1* —5H **61** (6C **142**)
Percy Pl. *W12* —2C **74**
Percy Rd. *E11* —7G **33**
Percy Rd. *E16* —5G **65**
Percy Rd. *N12* —5F **15**
Percy Rd. *N21* —7H **7**
Percy Rd. *NW6* —3J **59**
Percy Rd. *SE20* —1K **125**
Percy Rd. *SE25* —5G **125**
Percy Rd. *W12* —2C **74**
Percy Rd. *Bexh* —2E **100**
Percy Rd. *Hamp* —7E **102**
Percy Rd. *Ilf* —7A **36**
Percy Rd. *Iswth* —4A **88**
Percy Rd. *Mitc* —7E **122**
Percy Rd. *Romf* —3H **37**
Percy Rd. *Twic* —1F **103**
Percy St. *W1* —5H **61** (6C **142**)
Percy Way. *Twic* —1G **103**
Percy Yd. *WC1* —3K **61** (1H **143**)
Peregrine Clo. *NW10* —5K **41**
Peregrine Ct. *SE8* —6C **80**
(off Edward St.)
Peregrine Ct. *Well* —1K **99**
Peregrine Gdns. *Croy* —2A **136**
Peregrine Way. *SW19* —7E **106**
Perham Rd. *W14* —5G **75**
Peridot St. *E6* —5C **66**
Perifield. *SE21* —1C **110**
Perimeade Rd. *Gnfd* —2C **56**
Periton Rd. *SE9* —4B **98**
Perivale Gdns. *W13* —4B **56**
Perivale Grange. *Gnfd* —3A **56**
Perivale Ind. Pk. *Gnfd* —2B **56**
Perivale La. *Gnfd* —3A **56**
Perivale Lodge. *Gnfd* —3A **56**
(off Perivale La.)
Perivale New Bus. Cen. *Gnfd*
—2C **56**
Perkin Clo. *Wemb* —5B **40**
Perkin's Rents. *SW1*
—3H **77** (2C **154**)
Perkins Rd. *Ilf* —5H **35**
Perkins Sq. *SE1*
—1C **78** (4D **150**)
Perks Clo. *SE3* —3G **97**
Perpins Rd. *SE9* —6J **99**
Perran Rd. *SW2* —1B **110**
Perran Wlk. *Bren* —5E **72**
Perren St. *NW5* —6F **45**
Perrers Rd. *W6* —4D **74**
Perrin Rd. *Wemb* —4B **40**
Perrin's Ct. *NW3* —4A **44**
Perrin's La. *NW3* —4A **44**
Perrin's Wlk. *NW3* —4A **44**
Perronet Ho. *SE1*
—3B **78** (2B **156**)
Perrott St. *SE18* —4G **83**
Perry Av. *W3* —6K **57**
Perry Clo. *Rain* —2K **69**
Perry Ct. *N15* —6E **30**
Perryfield Way. *NW9* —6B **26**
Perryfield Way. *Rich* —3B **104**
Perry Gdns. *N9* —3K **17**
Perry Garth. *N'holt* —1A **54**
Perry Hall Rd. *Orp* —6K **129**
Perry Hill. *SE6* —3B **112**
Perry How. *Wor Pk* —1B **130**
Perrymans Farm Rd. *Ilf* —6H **35**
Perry Mead. *Enf* —2G **7**
Perrymead Gdns. *Gnfd* —2F **55**
Perrymead St. *SW6* —1J **91**
Perryn Ct. *Twic* —7A **88**

Perryn Ho. *W3* —7A **58**
Perryn Rd. *SE16* —3H **79**
Perryn Rd. *W3* —1K **73**
Perry Rise. *SE23* —3A **112**
Perry Rd. *Dag* —5F **69**
Perry's Pl. *W1* —6H **61** (7C **142**)
Perry St. *Chst* —7H **115**
Perry St. *Dart* —4K **101**
Perrystreete. *SE23* —2J **111**
Perry St. Gdns. *Chst* —6J **115**
Perry St. Shaw. *Chst* —7J **115**
Perry Vale. *SE23* —2J **111**
Persant Rd. *SE6* —2G **113**
Perseverance Pl. *SW9* —7A **78**
Perseverance Pl. *Rich* —4E **88**
Perseverance Works *E2*
—3E **62** (2H **145**)
(off Kingsland Rd.)
Perseverance Pl. *Rich* —4E **88**
Pershore Clo. *Ilf* —5F **35**
Pershore Gro. *Cars* —6B **122**
Pert Clo. *N10* —6A **16**
Perth Av. *NW9* —7K **25**
Perth Av. *Hayes* —4A **54**
Perth Clo. *SW20* —2C **120**
Perth Rd. *E10* —1A **48**
Perth Rd. *E13* —2K **65**
Perth Rd. *N4* —1A **46**
Perth Rd. *N22* —1B **30**
Perth Rd. *Bark* —2H **67**
Perth Rd. *Beck* —2E **126**
Perth Rd. *Ilf* —6E **34**
Perth Ter. *Ilf* —7G **35**
Perwell Av. *Harr* —1D **38**
Petauel Rd. *Tedd* —5J **103**
Peter Av. *NW10* —7D **42**
Peterboat Clo. *SE10* —4G **81**
Peterborough Ct. *EC4*
—6A **62** (1K **149**)
Peterborough Gdns. *Ilf* —7C **34**
Peterborough M. *SW6* —2J **91**
Peterborough Rd. *E10* —5E **32**
Peterborough Rd. *SW6* —2J **91**
Peterborough Rd. *Cars* —6C **122**
Peterborough Rd. *Harr* —1J **39**
Peterborough Vs. *SW6* —1K **91**
Peter Butler Ho. *SE1*
—2G **79** (6K **151**)
(off Wolseley St.)
Petergate. *SW11* —4A **92**
Peterhead Ct. *S'hall* —6G **55**
(off Osborne Rd.)
Peter James Enterprise Cen.
NW10 —3J **57**
Peterley Cen. *E2* —2H **63**
Peters Clo. *Dag* —1D **52**
Peters Clo. *Stan* —6J **11**
Peters Clo. *Well* —2J **99**
Peters Ct. *W2* —6K **59**
(off Porchester Rd.)
Petersfield Clo. *N18* —5H **17**
Petersfield Rise. *SW15* —1D **106**
Petersfield Rd. *W3* —2J **73**
Petersham Clo. *Rich* —2D **104**
Petersham Clo. *Sutt* —5J **131**
Petersham Dri. *Orp* —2K **129**
Petersham Gdns. *Orp* —2K **129**
Petersham La. *SW7* —3A **76**
Petersham M. *SW7* —3A **76**
Petersham Pl. *SW7* —3A **76**
Petersham Rd. *Rich* —6D **88**
Petersham Ter. *Mitc* —3J **133**
(off Richmond Grn.)
Peters Hill. *EC4* —7C **62** (2C **150**)
Peter's La. *EC1* —5B **62** (5B **144**)

Peter's Path. SE26 —4H 111
Peterstone Rd. SE2 —3B 84
Peterstow Clo. SW19 —2G 107
Peter St. W1 —7H 61 (2C 148)
Peterwood Pk. Croy —2K 133
Peterwood Way. Croy —2K 133
Petherton Ct. Harr —6K 23
(off Gayton Rd.)
Petherton Ho. N4 —1C 46
(off Woodberry Down Est.)
Petherton Rd. N5 —5C 46
Petiver Clo. E9 —7J 47
Petley Rd. W6 —6F 75
Peto Pl. NW1 —4F 61 (3K 141)
Peto St. N. E16 —6H 65
Peto St. S. E16 —7H 65
Petrie Clo. NW2 —6G 43
Petros Gdns. NW3 —6A 44
Petticoat La. E1 —5E 62 (7J 145)
Petticoat Sq. E1 —6F 63 (7J 145)
Petticoat Tower. E1
—6F 63 (7J 145)
Pettits Boulevd. Romf —1K 37
Pettits La. Romf —2K 37
Pettits La. N. Romf —1K 37
Pettits Pl. Dag —5G 53
Pettits Rd. Dag —5G 53
Pettiward Clo. SW15 —4E 90
Pettley Gdns. Romf —5K 37
Pettman Cres. SE28 —3H 83
Pettsgrove Av. Wemb —5D 40
Pett's Hill. N'holt —5F 39
Pett St. SE18 —4C 82
Petts Wood Rd. Orp —5G 129
Petty France. SW1
—3G 77 (1B 154)
Petworth Clo. N'holt —7D 38
Petworth Gdns. SW20 —3D 120
Petworth Rd. N12 —5H 15
Petworth Rd. Bexh —5G 101
Petworth St. SW11 —1C 92
Petyward. SW3 —4C 76 (4D 152)
Pevensey Av. N11 —5C 16
Pevensey Av. Enf —2K 7
Pevensey Clo. Iswth —7G 71
Pevensey Ct. W3 —2H 73
Pevensey Rd. E7 —4H 49
Pevensey Rd. SW17 —4B 108
Pevensey Rd. Felt —1C 102
Peverel. E6 —6E 66
Peverel Ho. Dag —2G 53
Peveret Clo. N11 —5A 16
Peveril Dri. Tedd —5H 103
Peveril Ho. SE1 —3E 78 (2F 157)
Pewsey Clo. E4 —5H 19
Peyton Pl. SE10 —7E 80
Pharaoh Clo. Mitc —7D 122
Pheasant Clo. E16 —6K 65
Phelp St. SE17 —6D 78 (7E 156)
Phene St. SW3 —6C 76 (7D 152)
Philbeach Gdns. SW5 —5J 75
Phil Brown Pl. SW8 —3F 93
(off Wandsworth Rd.)
Philchurch Pl. E1 —6G 63
Philimore Clo. SE18 —5J 83
Philip Av. Romf —1K 53
Philip Clo. Romf —1K 53
Philip Gdns. Croy —2B 136
Philip La. N15 —4D 30
Philipot Path. SE9 —6D 98
Philippa Gdns. SE9 —5B 98
Philips Clo. Cars —1E 132
Philip St. E13 —4J 65
Philip Wlk. SE15 —3G 95
(in three parts)

Phillimore Gdns. NW10 —1E 58
Phillimore Gdns. W8 —2J 75
Phillimore Gdns. Clo. W8 —3J 75
Phillimore Pl. W8 —2J 75
Phillimore Ter. W8 —3J 75
(off Allen St.)
Phillimore Wlk. W8 —3J 75
Phillipp St. N1 —1E 62
Phillips Ct. Edgw —6B 12
Philpot La. EC3 —7E 62 (2G 151)
Philpot Path. Ilf —3G 51
Philpot Sq. SW6 —3K 91
Philpot St. E1 —5H 63
(in two parts)
Phineas Pett Rd. SE9 —3C 98
Phipp's Bri. Rd. SW19 & Mitc
—2A 122
Phipps Hatch La. Enf —1H 7
Phipps Ho. W12 —7D 58
(off White City Est.)
Phipp's M. SW1 —4F 77 (2J 153)
Phipp St. EC2 —4E 62 (3G 145)
Phoebeth Rd. SE4 —5C 96
Phoenix Cen. Brom —4K 127
Phoenix Clo. E8 —1F 63
Phoenix Clo. W Wick —2F 137
Phoenix Ct. E4 —3J 19
Phoenix Ct. E14 —4C 80
Phoenix Ct. Houn —5B 86
Phoenix Ct. S Croy —9F 135
Phoenix Ct. Wemb —3H 41
Phoenix Dri. Kes —4B 138
Phoenix Ho. Sutt —4K 131
Phoenix Ind. Est. Harr —5K 23
Phoenix Pl. WC1
—4K 61 (3H 143)
Phoenix Rd. NW1
—3H 61 (1C 142)
Phoenix Rd. SE20 —6J 111
Phoenix St. WC2
—6H 61 (1D 148)
Phoenix Trad. Est. Gnfd —1C 56
Phoenix Trad. Pk. Bren —5D 72
Phoenix Way. Houn —6B 70
Phoenix Wharf Rd. SE1
—2F 79 (7K 151)
Phyllis Av. N Mald —5D 120
Physic Pl. SW3 —6D 76 (7E 152)
Picardy Manorway. Belv —3H 85
Picardy Rd. Belv —5G 85
Picardy St. Belv —3G 85
Piccadilly. W1 —1F 77 (5K 147)
Piccadilly Arc. SW1
—1G 77 (4A 148)
Piccadilly Cir. W1
—7H 61 (3C 148)
Piccadilly Pl. W1
—7G 61 (3B 148)
Pickard St. EC1 —3B 62 (1B 144)
Pickering Av. E6 —3E 66
Pickering Gdns. Croy —6F 125
Pickering Ho. W7 —4C 72
(off Windmill Rd.)
Pickering M. W2 —6K 59
Pickering Pl. SW1
—1G 77 (5B 148)
Pickering St. N1 —1B 62
Pickets Clo. Bush —1C 10
Pickets St. SW12 —7F 93
Pickett Croft. Stan —1D 24
Picketts Lock La. N9 —2D 18
Picketts Lock La. Ind. Est. N9
—2F 19
Pickford Clo. Bexh —2E 100
Pickford La. Bexh —2E 100

Pickford Rd. Bexh —3E 100
Pickfords Wharf. N1 —2C 62
Pickfords Wharf. SE1
—1D 78 (4E 150)
Pickfords Yd. N17 —6A 18
Pickhurst Grn. Brom —7H 127
Pickhurst La. W Wick & Brom
—5G 127
Pickhurst Mead. Brom —7H 127
Pickhurst Pk. Brom —5G 127
Pickhurst Rise. W Wick —1F 137
Pickwick Clo. Houn —5C 86
Pickwick Ho. SE16 —2G 79
(off George Row)
Pickwick M. N18 —5K 17
Pickwick Pl. Harr —7J 23
Pickwick Rd. SE21 —7D 94
Pickwick St. SE1
—2C 78 (7C 150)
Pickwick Way. Chst —6G 115
Pickworth Clo. SW8 —7J 77
Picton Pl. W1 —6E 60 (1H 147)
Picton St. SE5 —7D 78
Pied Bull Yd. WC1
—5J 61 (6E 142)
Piedmont Rd. SE18 —5H 83
Pier Head. E1 —1H 79
(off Wapping High St.)
Pier Ho. SW3 —6C 76 (7D 152)
Piermont Pl. Brom —2C 128
Piermont Rd. SE22 —5H 95
Pierpoint Rd. W3 —7H 57
Pierrepont Arc. N1 —2B 62
(off Pierrepont Row)
Pierrepont Row. N1 —2B 62
(off Camden Pas.)
Pier Rd. E16 —2D 82
Pier St. E14 —4E 80
Pier Ter. SW18 —4K 91
Pier Way. SE28 —3H 83
Pigeon La. Hamp —4E 102
Piggott St. E14 —6C 64
Pike Clo. Brom —5K 113
Pikemans Ct. SW5 —4J 75
(off W. Cromwell Rd.)
Pike Rd. NW7 —4E 12
Pikestone Clo. Hayes —4C 54
Pikethorne. SE23 —2K 111
Pilgrimage St. SE1
—2D 78 (7E 150)
Pilgrim Clo. Mord —7K 121
Pilgrim Hill. SE27 —4C 110
Pilgrims Clo. N13 —4E 16
Pilgrims Clo. N'holt —5G 39
Pilgrim's La. NW3 —4B 44
Pilgrim's Pl. NW3 —4B 44
Pilgrims Rise. Barn —5H 5
Pilgrim St. EC4 —6B 62 (1A 150)
Pilgrims Way. E6 —1C 66
(off High St. N.)
Pilgrims Way. N19 —1H 45
Pilgrims Way. S Croy —5F 135
Pilgrim's Way. Wemb —1H 41
Pilkington Rd. SE15 —2H 95
Pilot Clo. SE8 —6B 80
Pilot Ind. Cen. NW10 —4K 57
Pilsden Clo. SW19 —1F 107
Pilton Est., The. Croy —2B 134
Pilton Pl. SE17 —5C 78 (5D 156)
Pimento Ct. W5 —3D 72
Pimlico Rd. SW1
—5E 76 (5G 153)
Pimlico Wlk. N1 —3E 62 (1G 145)

Pinchin St. E1 —7G 63
Pincott Pl. SE4 —4K 95
Pincott Rd. SW19 —7A 108
Pincott Rd. Bexh —5G 101
Pindar St. EC2 —5E 62 (5G 145)
Pindock M. W9 —4K 59
Pine Apple Ct. SW1
—3G 77 (1B 154)
Pine Av. E15 —5F 49
Pine Av. W Wick —1D 136
Pine Clo. E10 —2D 48
Pine Clo. N14 —7B 6
Pine Clo. N19 —2G 45
Pine Clo. SE20 —1J 125
Pine Clo. Stan —4G 11
Pine Coombe. Croy —4K 135
Pine Ct. N21 —6E 6
Pine Ct. N'holt —4C 54
Pinecroft Ct. Well —7A 84
Pinecroft Cres. Barn —4B 4
Pine Dene. SE15 —1H 95
Pinefield Clo. E14 —7C 64
Pine Gdns. Ruis —1A 38
Pine Gdns. Surb —6G 119
Pine Glade. Orp —4D 138
Pine Gro. N4 —2J 45
Pine Gro. N20 —1C 14
Pine Gro. SW19 —5H 107
Pinehurst Ct. W11 —6H 59
(off Colville Gdns.)
Pinehurst Wlk. Orp —7H 129
Pinemartin Clo. NW2 —3E 42
Pine Ridge. Cars —7E 132
Pineridge Ct. Barn —4A 4
Pine Rd. N11 —2K 15
Pine Rd. NW2 —4E 42
Pines Rd. Brom —2C 128
Pines, The. N14 —5B 6
Pines, The. SE19 —7B 110
Pines, The. Wfd G —3D 20
Pine St. EC1 —4A 62 (3K 143)
Pine Tree Lodge. Short —4H 127
Pine Wlk. Surb —6G 119
Pinewood Av. Pinn —1A 22
Pinewood Av. Sidc —1J 115
Pinewood Clo. Croy —3A 136
Pinewood Clo. Pinn —6A 10
Pinewood Clo. SW4 —6H 93
Pinewood Ct. Enf —4G 7
Pinewood Gro. W5 —6C 56
Pinewood Lodge. Bush —1C 10
Pinewood Pl. Eps —4A 130
Pinewood Rd. SE2 —6D 84
Pinewood Rd. Brom —4J 127
Pinewood Rd. Felt —3A 102
Pinfold Rd. SW16 —4J 109
Pingle St. SE17 —5C 78 (5D 156)
Pinkerton Pl. SW16 —4H 109
Pinkham Mans. W4 —5G 73
Pinkham Way. N11 —7K 15
Pinley Gdns. Dag —1B 68
Pinnacle Hill. Bexh —4H 101
Pinnacle Hill N. Bexh —4H 101
Pinnacle Pl. Stan —4G 11
Pinnell Rd. SE9 —4B 98
Pinner Ct. Pinn —4C 22
Pinner Grn. Pinn —2A 22
Pinner Gro. Pinn —4C 22
Pinner Hill Farm. Pinn —1A 22
Pinner Hill Rd. Pinn —1A 22
Pinner Pk. Pinn —2E 22
Pinner Pk. Av. Harr —3F 23
Pinner Pk. Gdns. Harr —2G 23
Pinner Rd. Harr —4E 22
Pinner Rd. Pinn —4D 22

Pinner View. Harr —4G 23
Pintail Clo. E6 —5C 66
Pintail Ct. SE8 —6B 80
(off Pilot Clo.)
Pintail Rd. Wfd G —7E 20
Pintail Way. Hayes —5B 54
Pinter Ho. SW9 —2J 93
(off Grantham Rd.)
Pinto Way. SE3 —4K 97
Pioneer Clo. W12 —6D 58
Pioneer Mkt. Ilf —3F 51
(off Winston Way)
Pioneer Pl. Croy —7C 136
Pioneers Ind. Pk. Croy —1J 133
Pioneer St. SE15 —1G 95
Piper Clo. N7 —5K 45
Piper Rd. King T —3G 119
Piper's Gdns. Croy —7A 126
Pipers Grn. NW9 —5J 25
Pipers Grn. La. Edgw —3K 11
(in two parts)
Pipewell Rd. Cars —6C 122
Pippin Clo. NW2 —3D 42
Pippin Clo. Croy —1B 136
Piquet Rd. SE20 —2J 125
Pirbright Cres. New Ad —6E 136
Pirbright Rd. SW18 —1H 107
Pirie Clo. SE5 —3D 94
Pirie St. E16 —1K 81
Pitcairn Clo. Romf —4G 37
Pitcairn Ho. E9 —7J 47
Pitcairn Rd. Mitc —7D 108
Pitchford St. E15 —7F 49
Pitfield Cres. SE28 —1A 84
Pitfield Est. N1 —3E 62 (1G 145)
Pitfield St. N1 —3E 62 (1G 145)
Pitfield Way. NW10 —6J 41
Pitfield Way. Enf —1D 8
Pitfold Clo. SE12 —6K 97
Pitfold Rd. SE12 —6J 97
Pitlake. Croy —2B 134
Pitman Ho. SE8 —1C 96
Pitman St. SE5 —7C 78
(in two parts)
Pitsea Pl. E1 —6K 63
Pitsea St. E1 —6K 63
Pitshanger La. W5 —4B 56
Pitt Cres. SW19 —4K 107
Pittman Gdns. Ilf —5G 51
Pitt Rd. T Hth & Croy —5C 124
Pitt's Head M. W1
—1E 76 (5H 147)
Pittsmead Av. Brom —7J 127
Pitt St. SE15 —1F 95
Pitt St. W8 —2J 75
Pittville Gdns. SE25 —3G 125
Pixley St. E14 —6B 64
Pixton Way. Croy —7A 136
Place Farm Av. Orp —7H 129
Plaistow Gro. E15 —1H 65
Plaistow Gro. Brom —7K 113
Plaistow La. Brom —7J 113
(in two parts)
Plaistow Pk. Rd. E13 —2K 65
Plaistow Wharf. E16 —1J 81
Plane Ho. Short —2G 127
Plane St. SE26 —3H 111
Planetree Ct. W6 —4F 75
(off Brook Grn.)
Plane Tree Wlk. SE19 —6E 110
Plantagenet Clo. Wor Pk —4A 130
Plantagenet Gdns. Romf —7D 36
Plantagenet Pl. Romf —7D 36
Plantagenet Rd. Barn —4F 5

Plantain Gdns. E11 —3F 49
Plantain Pl. SE1 —2D 78 (6E 150)
Plantation Ho. EC3
　—7E 62 (2G 151)
Plantation, The. SE3 —2J 97
Plantation Wharf. SW11 —3A 92
Plasel Ct. E13 —1K 65
　(off Pawsey Clo.)
Plashet Gro. E6 —1A 66
Plashet Rd. E13 —1J 65
Plassy Rd. SE6 —7D 96
Platina St. EC2 —4D 62 (3F 145)
Plato Rd. SW2 —4J 93
Platt Halls. NW9 —2B 26
Platt's La. NW3 —4J 43
Platts Rd. Enf —1D 8
Platt St. NW1 —2H 61
Platt, The. SW15 —3F 91
Plawsfield Rd. Beck —1K 125
Plaxtol Clo. Brom —1A 128
Plaxtol Rd. Eri —7G 85
Plaxton Ct. E11 —3H 49
Playfair Mans. W14 —6G 75
　(off Qdeen's Club Gdns.)
Playfair St. W6 —5E 74
Playfield Av. Romf —1J 37
Playfield Cres. SE22 —5F 95
Playfield Rd. Edgw —2J 25
Playford Rd. N4 —2K 45
　(in two parts)
Playgreen Way. SE6 —3C 112
Playground Clo. Beck —2K 125
Playhouse Yd. EC4
　—6B 62 (1A 150)
Plaza Bus. Cen. Enf —2G 9
Plaza Pde. NW6 —2K 59
Plaza, The. W1 —6G 61 (7B 142)
Pleasance Rd. SW15 —5D 90
Pleasance, The. SW15 —4D 90
Pleasant Gro. Croy —3B 136
Pleasant Pl. N1 —7B 46
Pleasant Pl. S Harr —1H 39
Pleasant Row. NW1 —1F 61
Pleasant View. Eri —5K 85
Pleasant Way. Wemb —2C 56
Plender Pl. NW1 —1G 61
　(off Plender St.)
Plender St. NW1 —1G 61
Pleshey Rd. N7 —4H 45
Plesman Way. Wall —7J 133
Plevna Cres. N15 —6E 30
Plevna Rd. N9 —3B 18
Plevna St. E14 —3E 80
Pleydell Av. SE19 —7F 111
Pleydell Av. W6 —4B 74
Pleydell Est. EC1
　—3C 62 (2D 144)
Pleydell St. EC4 —6A 62 (1K 149)
Plimsoll Clo. E14 —6D 64
Plimsoll Rd. N4 —3A 46
Plough Clo. EC3 —7D 62 (2F 151)
Plough La. SE22 —6F 95
Plough La. SW19 & SW17
　—5K 107
Plough La. Purl —7K 133
Plough La. Wall —4J 133
Plough La. Clo. Wall —5J 133
Ploughmans Clo. NW1 —1H 61
Ploughmans End. Iswth —5H 87
Plough Pl. EC4 —6A 62 (7K 143)
Plough Rd. SW11 —3B 92
Plough Rd. Eps —7A 130
Plough St. E1 —6G 63 (7K 145)
Plough Ter. SW11 —4B 92
Plough Way. SE16 —4K 79

Plough Yd. EC2 —4E 62 (4H 145)
Plover Way. SE16 —3A 80
Plover Way. Hayes —6B 54
Plowden Bldgs. EC4
　—7A 62 (2J 149)
Plowman Clo. N18 —5J 17
Plowman Way. Dag —1C 52
Plumber's Row. E1 —5G 63
Plumbridge St. SE10 —1E 96
Plum Garth. Bren —4D 72
Plum La. SE18 —7F 83
Plummer La. Mitc —2D 122
Plummer Rd. SW4 —7H 93
Plumpton Clo. N'holt —6E 38
Plumpton Way. Cars —3C 132
Plums Clo. E16 —6D 64
Plumstead Comn. Rd. SE18
　—6F 83
Plumstead High St. SE18 —4H 83
Plumstead Rd. SE18 —4F 83
Plumtree Clo. Dag —6H 53
Plumtree Clo. Wall —7H 133
Plumtree Ct. EC4
　—6B 62 (7A 144)
Plymouth Ho. Bark —7A 52
　(off Keir Hardie Way)
Plymouth Rd. E16 —5J 65
Plymouth Rd. Brom —1K 127
Plymouth Wharf. E14 —4F 81
Plympton Av. NW6 —7H 43
Plympton Clo. Belv —3E 84
Plympton Rd. NW8
　—4C 60 (4C 140)
Plympton Rd. NW6 —7H 43
Plympton St. NW8
　—4C 60 (4C 140)
Plymstock Rd. Well —7C 84
Pocklington Clo. NW9 —2A 26
Pocklington Clo. W12 —3C 74
　(off Goldhawk Rd.)
Pocock St. SE1 —2B 78 (6A 150)
Podmore Rd. SW18 —4A 92
Poet's Rd. N5 —5D 46
Poets Way. Harr —4J 23
Pointalls Clo. N3 —2A 28
Point Clo. SE10 —1E 96
Pointer Clo. SE28 —6D 68
Pointers Clo. E14 —5D 80
Pointers Cotts. Rich —2C 104
Point Hill. SE10 —1E 96
Point Pl. Wemb —7H 41
Point Pleasant. SW18 —4J 91
Point Ter. E7 —5K 49
　(off Claremont Rd.)
Poland St. W1 —6G 61 (1B 148)
Polebrook Rd. SE3 —3A 98
Pole Cat All. Brom —2H 137
Polecroft La. SE6 —2B 112
Pole Hill Rd. E4 —7K 9
Polesden Gdns. SW20 —2D 120
Polesworth Ho. W2 —5J 59
　(off Alfred Rd.)
Polesworth Rd. Dag —7D 52
Police Sta. La. Bush —1A 10
Pollard Clo. E16 —7J 65
Pollard Clo. N7 —4K 45
Pollard Rd. N20 —2H 15
Pollard Rd. Mord —5B 122
Pollard Row. E2 —3G 63
Pollards Clo. Hill E. SW6 —3K 123
Pollards Hill N. SW16 —3J 123
Pollards Hill S. SW16 —3J 123
Pollards Hill W. SW16 —3K 123
Pollard St. E2 —3G 63

Pollards Wood Rd. SW16
　—3J 123
Pollard Wlk. Sidc —6C 116
Pollen St. W1 —6F 61 (1A 148)
Pollitt Dri. NW8 —4B 60 (3B 140)
Polperro Clo. Orp —6K 129
Polsted Rd. SE6 —7B 96
Polthorne Gro. SE18 —4H 83
Polworth Rd. SW16 —5J 109
Polygon Rd. NW1
　—2H 61 (1C 142)
Polygon, The. SW4 —4G 93
Polytechnic St. SE18 —4E 82
Pomell Way. E1 —6F 63 (7K 145)
Pomeroy St. SE14 —7J 79
Pomfret Rd. SE5 —3C 94
Pomoja La. N19 —2J 45
Pond Clo. N12 —6H 15
Pond Clo. SE3 —2J 97
Pond Cottage La. W Wick
　—1C 136
Pond Cotts. SE21 —1E 110
Ponders End Ind. Est. Enf —5F 9
Ponder St. N7 —7K 45
Pond Farm Est. E5 —3J 47
Pondfield Ho. SE27 —5C 110
Pondfield Rd. Brom —1G 137
Pondfield Rd. Dag —5H 53
Pond Hill Gdns. Sutt —6G 131
Pond Mead. SE21 —6D 94
Pond Path. Chst —6F 115
Pond Pl. SW3 —4C 76 (4C 152)
Pond Rd. E15 —2G 65
Pond Rd. SE3 —2H 97
Pond Sq. N6 —1E 44
Pond St. NW3 —5C 44
Pond Way. Tedd —6C 104
Pondwood Rise. Orp —7J 129
Ponler St. E1 —6H 63
Ponsard Rd. NW10 —3D 58
Ponsford St. E9 —6J 47
Ponsonby Pl. SW1
　—5H 77 (5D 154)
Ponsonby Rd. SW15 —7D 90
Ponsonby Ter. SW1
　—5H 77 (5D 154)
Pontefract Ct. N'holt —5F 39
　(off Newmarket Av.)
Pontefract Rd. Brom —5H 113
Ponton Rd. SW8
　—7H 77 (7D 154)
Pont St. SW1 —3D 76 (2E 152)
Pont St. M. SW1
　—3D 76 (2E 152)
Pontypool Pl. SE1
　—2B 78 (6A 150)
Pool Clo. Beck —5C 112
Pool Ct. SE6 —2C 112
Poole Ct. Rd. Houn —2C 86
Poole Ho. SE11 —3A 78 (3H 155)
Poole Rd. E9 —6K 47
Poole Rd. Eps —7A 130
Pooles Bldgs. WC1
　—4A 62 (4J 143)
Pooles Cotts. Rich —2D 104
Pooles La. SW10 —7A 76
Pooles La. Dag —2E 68
Pooles Pk. N4 —2A 46
Poole St. N1 —1D 62
Poolmans St. SE16 —2K 79
Pool Rd. Harr —7H 23
Poolsford Rd. NW9 —4A 26
Poonah St. E1 —6J 63
Pope Clo. SW19 —6B 108

Pope Rd. Brom —5B 128
Popes Av. Twic —2J 103
Popes Ct. Twic —2J 103
Popes Dri. N3 —1J 27
Popes Gro. Croy —3B 136
Popes Gro. Twic —2K 103
Pope's Head All. EC3
　—6D 62 (1F 151)
Popes La. W5 —3D 72
Pope's Rd. SW9 —3A 94
Pope St. SE1 —2E 78 (7H 151)
Popham Clo. Felt —3D 102
Popham Gdns. Rich —3G 89
Popham Rd. N1 —1C 62
Popham St. N1 —1B 62
　(in two parts)
Pop-In Commercial Cen. Wemb
　—5H 41
Popinjays Row. Cheam —5F 131
　(off Netley Clo.)
Poplar Av. Mitc —1D 122
Poplar Av. S'hall —3F 71
Poplar Bath St. E14 —6D 64
Poplar Bus. Pk. E14 —7E 64
Poplar Clo. E9 —5B 48
Poplar Clo. Pinn —1B 22
Poplar Ct. SW19 —5J 107
Poplar Ct. N'holt —2A 54
Poplar Gdns. SE28 —7C 68
Poplar Gdns. N Mald —2K 119
Poplar Gro. N11 —6K 15
Poplar Gro. W6 —2E 74
Poplar Gro. N Mald —2K 119
Poplar Gro. Wemb —3J 41
Poplar High St. E14 —7D 64
Poplar Ho. SE4 —4B 96
　(off Wickham Rd.)
Poplar M. W12 —1E 74
　(off Uxbridge Rd.)
Poplar Mt. Belv —4H 85
Poplar Pl. SE28 —7C 68
Poplar Pl. W2 —7K 59
Poplar Rd. SE24 —4C 94
Poplar Rd. SW19 —2J 121
Poplar Rd. Sutt —1H 131
Poplar Rd. S. SW19 —3J 121
Poplars Av. NW2 —6E 42
Poplars Rd. E17 —6D 32
Poplars, The. N14 —5A 6
Poplar St. Romf —4J 37
Poplar View. Wemb —2D 40
Poplar Wlk. SE24 —4C 94
Poplar Wlk. Croy —1C 134
Poplar Way. Ilf —4G 35
Poppins Ct. EC4 —6B 62 (1A 150)
Poppleton Rd. E11 —6G 33
Poppy Clo. Wall —1E 132
Poppy La. Croy —7J 125
Porchester Clo. SE5 —4D 94
Porchester Gdns. W2 —7K 59
Porchester Mead. Beck —6C 112
Porchester Pl. W2
　—6C 60 (1D 146)
Porchester Rd. W2 —6K 59
Porchester Rd. King T —2H 119
Porchester Sq. W2 —6K 59
Porchester Ter. W2 —7A 60
Porchester Ter. N. W2 —6K 59
Porch Way. N20 —3J 15
Porcupine Clo. SE9 —2C 114
Porden Rd. SW2 —4K 93
Porlock Av. Harr —1G 39
Porlock Ho. SE26 —3G 111

Porlock Rd. W10 —4F 59
Porlock Rd. Enf —7A 8
Porlock St. SE1 —2D 78 (6F 151)
Porrington Clo. Chst —1E 128
Porson Ct. SE13 —3D 96
Portal Clo. SE27 —3A 110
Portbury Clo. SE15 —1G 95
Port Cres. E13 —4K 65
Portcullis Lodge Rd. Enf —3J 7
Portelet Rd. E1 —3K 63
Porten Rd. W14 —3G 75
Porter Rd. E6 —6D 66
Porters Av. Dag —6B 52
Porter Sq. N19 —1J 45
Porter St. SE1 —1C 78 (4D 150)
Porter St. W1 —5D 60 (5F 141)
Porters Wlk. E1 —7H 63
　(off Pennington St.)
Porters & Walters Almshouses.
　N22 —7E 16
　(off Nightingale Rd.)
Porteus Rd. W2 —5A 60 (5A 140)
Portgate Clo. W9 —4H 59
Porthcawe Rd. SE26 —4A 112
Porthkerry Av. Well —4A 100
Portia Ct. Bark —7A 52
Portia Way. E3 —4B 64
Porticos, The. SW3
　—6B 76 (7A 152)
Portinscale Rd. SW15 —5G 91
Portland Av. N16 —1F 47
Portland Av. N Mald —7B 120
Portland Av. Sidc —6A 100
Portland Clo. Romf —5E 36
Portland Cres. SE9 —2C 114
Portland Cres. Gnfd —4F 55
Portland Cres. Stan —2D 24
Portland Dri. Enf —1G 7
Portland Gdns. N4 —6B 30
Portland Gdns. Romf —5D 36
Portland Gro. SW8 —1K 93
Portland M. W1
　—6G 61 (1B 148)
Portland Pl. SE25 —4G 125
　(off Portland Rd.)
Portland Pl. W1 —4F 61 (4J 141)
Portland Rise. N4 —1B 46
Portland Rise Est. N4 —1C 46
Portland Rd. N15 —4F 31
Portland Rd. SE9 —2C 114
Portland Rd. SE25 —4G 125
Portland Rd. W11 —7G 59
Portland Rd. Brom —4A 114
Portland Rd. King T —3E 118
Portland Rd. Mitc —2C 122
Portland Rd. S'hall —3D 70
Portland Sq. E1 —1H 79
Portland St. SE17
　—5D 78 (5E 156)
Portland Ter. Rich —4D 88
Portland Wlk. SE17
　—6D 78 (7F 157)
Portman Av. SW14 —3K 89
Portman Bldgs. NW1
　—4C 60 (4D 140)
Portman Clo. W1
　—6E 60 (7F 141)
Portman Clo. Bex —1K 117
Portman Clo. Bexh —3E 100
Portman Gdns. NW9 —2K 25
Portman M. S. W1
　—6E 60 (1G 147)
Portman Pl. E2 —3J 63
Portman Rd. King T —2F 119

Portman Sq. *W1*
　　　—6E **60** (7G **141**)
Portman St. *W1*—6E **60** (1G **147**)
Portman Towers. *W1*
　　　—6D **60** (7F **141**)
Portmeadow Wlk. *SE2* —2D **84**
Portmeers Clo. *E17*—6B **32**
Portnall Rd. *W9* —2H **59**
Portnoi Clo. *Romf* —2K **37**
Portobello Ct. Est. *W11*—6H **59**
Portobello M. *W11*—7J **59**
Portobello Rd. *W10*—5G **59**
Portobello Rd. *W11*—6H **59**
Portpool La. *EC1*
　　　—5A **62** (5J **143**)
Portree Clo. *N22* —7E **16**
Portree St. *E14*—6F **65**
Portrush Ct. S'hall —6G **55**
　(off Whitecote Rd.)
Portsdown. *Edgw* —5B **12**
Portsdown Av. *NW11*—6H **27**
Portsdown M. *NW11*—6H **27**
Portsea M. *W2*—6C **60** (1D **146**)
Portsea Pl. *W2*—6C **60** (1D **146**)
Portslade Rd. *SW8* —2G **93**
Portsmouth Av. *Th Dit*—7A **118**
Portsmouth Rd. *SW15*—7D **90**
Portsmouth Rd. *King T*—4D **118**
Portsmouth St. *WC2*
　　　—6K **61** (1G **149**)
Portsoken St. *E1*
　　　—7F **63** (2J **151**)
Portswood Pl. *SW15*—6B **90**
Portugal Gdns. *Twic* —2G **103**
Portugal St. *WC2*
　　　—6K **61** (1G **149**)
Portway. *E15*—1H **65**
Portway Gdns. *SE18*—7B **82**
Postern Grn. *Enf*—2F **7**
Postern, The. *EC2*
　　　—5C **62** (6D **144**)
Post La. *Twic*—1H **103**
Postmill Clo. *Croy*—3J **135**
Post Office App. *E7*—5K **49**
Post Office Way. *SW8*—6H **77**
Postway M. *Ilf*—3F **51**
　(in two parts)
Potier St. *SE1*—3D **78** (2F **157**)
Potter Clo. *Mitc*—2F **123**
Potteries, The. *Barn*—5D **4**
Potterne Clo. *SW19*—7F **91**
Potters Clo. *Croy*—1A **136**
Potters Field. Enf—4K **7**
　(off Lincoln Rd.)
Potter's Fields. SE1
　　　—1E **78** (5H **151**)
Potters Gro. *N Mald*—4J **119**
Potter's La. *SW16*—6H **109**
Potter's La. *Barn*—4D **4**
Potters Lodge. E14—5E **80**
　(off Manchester Rd.)
Potters Rd. *SW6*—2A **92**
Potter's Rd. *Barn*—4E **4**
Potter St. *Pinn*—1A **22**
Pottery La. *W11*—7G **59**
Pottery Rd. *Bex*—2J **117**
Pottery Rd. *Bren*—6E **72**
Pottery St. *SE16*—2H **79**
Pott St. *E2*—3H **63**
Poulett Gdns. *Twic*—1A **104**
Poulett Rd. *E6*—2D **66**
Poulner Way. *SE15*—7F **79**
　(in two parts)
Poulters Wood. *Kes*—5B **138**
Poulton Av. *Sutt*—3B **132**

Poulton Clo. *E8*—6H **47**
Poultry. *EC2*—6D **62** (1E **150**)
Pound Clo. *Surb*—7C **118**
Pound Grn. *Bex*—7G **101**
Pound La. *NW10*—6C **42**
Pound Pk. Rd. *SE7*—4B **82**
Pound Pl. *SE9*—6E **98**
Pound St. *Cars*—5D **132**
Pound Way. *Chst*—7G **115**
Pountney Rd. *SW11*—3E **92**
Poverest Rd. *Orp*—5K **129**
Powder Mill La. *Twic*—1D **102**
Powell Clo. *Edgw*—6A **12**
Powell Clo. *Wall*—7J **133**
Powell Ct. *E17*—3D **32**
Powell Gdns. *Dag*—4G **53**
Powell Rd. *E5*—3H **47**
Powell Rd. *Buck H*—1F **21**
Powell's Wlk. *W4*—6A **74**
Power Rd. *W4*—4G **73**
Powers Ct. *Twic*—7D **88**
Powerscroft Rd. *E5*—4J **47**
Powerscroft Rd. *Sidc*—6C **116**
Powis Gdns. *NW11*—7H **27**
Powis Gdns. *W11*—6H **59**
Powis M. *W11*—6H **59**
Powis Pl. *WC1*—4J **61** (4F **143**)
Powis Rd. *E3*—3D **64**
Powis Sq. *W11*—6H **59**
Powis Ter. *W11*—6H **59**
Powlett Pl. *NW1*—7E **44**
Pownall Gdns. *Houn*—4F **87**
Pownall Rd. *E8*—1G **63**
Pownall Rd. *Houn*—4F **87**
Pownsett Ter. *Ilf*—5G **51**
Powster Rd. *Brom*—5J **113**
Powys Clo. *Bexh*—6D **84**
Powys Ct. *N11*—5D **16**
Powys La. *N14 & N13*—4D **16**
Poynders Ct. *SW4*—6G **93**
Poynders Gdns. *SW4*—7G **93**
Poynders Rd. *SW4*—6G **93**
Poynings Rd. *N19*—3G **45**
Poynings Way. *N12*—5D **14**
Poyntell Cres. *Chst*—1H **129**
Poynter Ct. N'holt—2B **54**
　(off Gallery Gdns.)
Poynter Ho. W11—1F **75**
　(off Queensdale Cres.)
Poynter Rd. *Enf*—5B **8**
Poynton Rd. *N17*—2G **31**
Poyntz Rd. *SW11*—2D **92**
Poyser St. *E2*—2H **63**
Praed M. *W2*—6B **60** (7B **140**)
Praed St. *W2*—6B **60** (1A **146**)
Pragel St. *E13*—2A **66**
Pragnell Rd. *SE12*—2K **113**
Prague Pl. *SW2*—5J **93**
Prah Rd. *N4*—2A **46**
Prairie St. *SW8*—2E **92**
Pratt M. *NW1*—1G **61**
Pratts Pas. *King T*—2E **118**
Pratt St. *NW1*—1G **61**
Pratt Wlk. *SE11*—4K **77** (3H **155**)
Prayle Gro. *NW2*—1F **43**
Prebend Gdns. *W6 & W4*—3B **74**
　(in two parts)
Prebend Mans. W4—4B **74**
　(off Chiswick High Rd.)
Prebend St. *N1*—1C **62**
Precincts, The. *Mord*—6J **121**
Precinct, The. *N1*—1C **62**
Premier Corner. *W9*—2H **59**
Premier Ct. *Enf*—1D **8**

Premiere Pl. *E14*—7C **64**
Premier Pl. *SW15*—4G **91**
Prendergast Rd. *SE3*—3G **97**
Prentice Ct. *SW19*—5H **107**
Prentis Rd. *SW16*—4H **109**
Prentiss Ct. *SE7*—4B **82**
Presburg Rd. *N Mald*—5A **120**
Presburg St. *E5*—3K **47**
Prescelly Pl. *Edgw*—1F **25**
Prescot St. *E1*—7F **63** (2K **151**)
Prescott Av. *Orp*—6F **129**
Prescott Clo. *SW16*—7J **109**
Prescott Pl. *SW4*—3H **93**
Presentation M. *SW2*—1K **109**
Preshaw Cres. *Mitc*—3C **122**
President Dri. *E1*—1H **79**
President Ho. *EC1*
　　　—3B **62** (2B **144**)
President St. *EC1*
　　　—3C **62** (1C **144**)
Press Ho. *NW10*—3K **41**
Press Rd. *NW10*—3K **41**
Prestage Way. *E14*—7E **64**
Prestbury Rd. *E7*—7A **50**
Prestbury Sq. *SE9*—4D **114**
Prestbury St. *SE12*—4D **114**
Prested Rd. *SW11*—4C **92**
Prestige Way. *NW4*—5E **26**
Preston Av. *E4*—6A **20**
Preston Clo. *SE1*
　　　—4E **78** (3G **157**)
Preston Clo. *Twic*—3J **103**
Preston Ct. New Bar—4F **5**
Preston Ct. Sidc—4K **115**
　(off Crescent, The)
Preston Dri. *E11*—5A **34**
Preston Dri. *Bexh*—1D **100**
Preston Dri. *Eps*—6A **130**
Preston Gdns. *NW10*—6B **42**
Preston Gdns. *Ilf*—6C **34**
Preston Hill. *Harr*—7E **24**
Preston Ho. Dag—3G **53**
　(off Uvedale Rd.)
Preston Pl. *NW2*—6C **42**
Preston Pl. *Rich*—5E **88**
Preston Rd. *E11*—6G **33**
Preston Rd. *SE19*—6B **110**
Preston Rd. *SW20*—7B **106**
Preston Rd. Wemb & Harr
　　　—1E **40**
Preston's Rd. *E14*—7E **64**
Prestons Rd. *Brom*—3J **137**
Preston Waye. *Harr*—1E **40**
Prestwick Clo. *S'hall*—5C **70**
Prestwick Ct. S'hall—7G **55**
　(off Baird Av.)
Prestwood Av. *Harr*—4B **24**
Prestwood Clo. *SE18*—7A **84**
Prestwood Clo. *Harr*—4B **24**
Prestwood Gdns. *Croy*—7C **124**
Prestwood Ho. SE16—2H **79**
　(off Drummond Rd.)
Prestwood St. *N1*
　　　—2C **62** (1D **144**)
Pretoria Av. *E17*—4A **32**
Pretoria Clo. *N17*—7A **18**
Pretoria Cres. *E4*—1K **19**
Pretoria Rd. *E4*—1K **19**
Pretoria Rd. *E11*—1F **49**
Pretoria Rd. *E16*—4H **65**
Pretoria Rd. *N17*—7A **18**
Pretoria Rd. *SW16*—6F **109**
Pretoria Rd. *Ilf*—5F **51**
Pretoria Rd. *Romf*—4J **37**
Pretoria Rd. N. *N18*—6A **18**

Prevost Rd. *N11*—2K **15**
Price Clo. *NW7*—6B **14**
Price Clo. *SW17*—3D **108**
Price Rd. *Croy*—5B **134**
Price's St. *SE1*—1B **78** (5B **150**)
Price's Yd. *N1*—1K **61**
Price Way. *Hamp*—6C **102**
Prichard Ct. *N7*—5K **45**
Pricklers Hill. *Barn*—6E **4**
Prickley Wood. *Brom*—1H **137**
Priddy's Yd. *Croy*—2C **134**
Prideaux Pl. *W3*—7K **57**
Prideaux Pl. *WC1*
　　　—3K **61** (1H **143**)
Prideaux Rd. *SW9*—3J **93**
Pridham Rd. *T Hth*—4D **124**
Priestfield Rd. *SE23*—3A **112**
Priestlands Pk. Rd. *Sidc*—3K **115**
Priestley Clo. *N16*—7F **31**
Priestley Gdns. *Romf*—6B **36**
Priestley Ho. Wemb—3J **41**
　(off Barnhill Rd.)
Priestley Rd. *Mitc*—2E **122**
Priestley Way. *E17*—3K **31**
Priestley Way. *NW2*—1C **42**
Priest Pk. Av. *Harr*—2E **38**
Priests Av. *Romf*—2K **37**
Priest's Bri. *SW14 & SW13*
　　　—3A **90**
Priest's Ct. *EC2*
　　　—6C **62** (7C **144**)
Prima Rd. *SW9*—7A **78**
Primrose Av. *Enf*—1J **7**
Primrose Av. *Romf*—7B **36**
Primrose Clo. *SE6*—5E **112**
Primrose Clo. *Harr*—3D **38**
Primrose Clo. *Mitc*—7F **123**
Primrose Ct. *SW12*—7H **93**
Primrose Gdns. *NW3*—6C **44**
Primrose Gdns. *Bush*—1A **10**
Primrose Gdns. *Ruis*—5A **38**
Primrose Hill. *EC4*
　　　—6A **62** (1K **149**)
Primrose Hill Ct. *NW3*—7D **44**
Primrose Hill Rd. *NW3*—7C **44**
Primrose La. *Croy*—1J **135**
Primrose Mans. *SW11*—1E **92**
Primrose M. NW1—7D **44**
　(off Sharpleshall St.)
Primrose M. *SE3*—7J **81**
Primrose Rd. *E10*—1D **48**
Primrose Rd. *E18*—2K **33**
Primrose St. *EC2*
　　　—5E **62** (5G **145**)
Primrose Wlk. *Eps*—7B **130**
Primrose Way. *Wemb*—2D **56**
Primula St. *W12*—6C **58**
Prince Albert Rd. *NW8 & NW1*
　　　—3C **60** (1C **140**)
Prince Arthur M. *NW3*—4A **44**
Prince Arthur Rd. *NW3*—5A **44**
Prince Charles Dri. *NW4*—7E **26**
Prince Charles Rd. *SE3*—2H **97**
Prince Charles Way. *Wall*
　　　—3F **133**
Prince Consort Dri. *Chst*
　　　—1H **129**
Prince Consort Rd. *SW7*
　　　—3A **76** (1A **152**)
Princedale Rd. *W11*—1G **75**
Prince Edward Rd. *E9*—6B **48**
Prince George Av. *N14*—5C **6**
Prince George Rd. *N16*—4E **46**
Prince George's Av. *SW20*
　　　—2E **120**

Prince Georges Rd. *SW19*
　　　—1B **122**
Prince Henry Rd. *SE7*—7B **82**
Prince Imperial Rd. *SE18*—1D **98**
Prince Imperial Rd. *Chst*—1F **129**
Prince John Rd. *SE9*—5C **98**
Princelet St. *E1*—5F **63** (5K **145**)
Prince of Orange La. *SE10*
　　　—7E **80**
Prince of Wales Clo. *NW4*
　　　—4E **26**
Prince of Wales Dri. *SW11 & SW8*
　　　—1C **92**
Prince of Wales Mans. *SW11*
　　　—1E **92**
Prince of Wales Pas. *NW1*
　　　—3G **61** (2A **142**)
Prince of Wales Rd. *E16*—6A **66**
Prince of Wales Rd. *NW5*—6E **44**
Prince of Wales Rd. *SE3*—1H **97**
Prince of Wales Rd. Sutt
　　　—2B **132**
Prince of Wales Ter. *W4*—5A **74**
Prince of Wales Ter. *W8*—2K **75**
Prince Regent Ct. *NW8*—2C **60**
　(off Avenue Rd.)
Prince Regent La. *E13 & E16*
　　　—3K **65**
Prince Regent M. *NW1*
　　　—3G **61** (2A **142**)
Prince Regent Rd. *Houn*—3G **87**
Prince Rd. *SE25*—5E **124**
Prince Rupert Rd. *SE9*—4D **98**
Princes Arc. *SW1*
　　　—1G **77** (4B **148**)
Princes Av. *N3*—1J **27**
Princes Av. *N10*—3F **29**
Princes Av. *N13*—5F **17**
Princes Av. *N22*—1H **29**
Princes Av. *NW9*—4G **25**
Princes Av. *W3*—3G **73**
Princes Av. *Cars*—7D **132**
Prince's Av. Gnfd—6F **55**
Princes Av. *Orp*—5J **129**
Princes Av. Wfd G—4E **20**
Princes Cir. *WC2*
　　　—6J **61** (7E **142**)
Princes Clo. *N4*—1B **46**
Princes Clo. *NW9*—4G **25**
Princes Clo. *SW4*—3G **93**
Princes Clo. *Edgw*—5B **12**
Princes Clo. *Sidc*—3D **116**
Prince's Clo. Tedd—4H **103**
Princes Ct. *SE16*—3B **80**
Princes Ct. *Wemb*—5E **40**
Princes Dri. *Harr*—3J **23**
Prince's Gdns. SW7
　　　—3B **76** (1B **152**)
Princes Gdns. *W3*—5G **57**
Princes Gdns. *W5*—4C **56**
Prince's Ga. SW7
　　　—2B **76** (7B **146**)
Prince's Ga. Ct. SW7
　　　—2B **76** (7B **146**)
Prince's Ga. M. SW7
　　　—3B **76** (1B **152**)
Princes La. *N10*—3F **29**
Prince's M. *W2*—7K **59**
Princes Pde. NW11—6G **27**
　(off Golders Grn. Rd.)
Princes Pk. Av. *NW11*—6G **27**
Princes Pl. *SW1*
　　　—1G **77** (4B **148**)
Princes Pl. *W11*—1G **75**

Prince's Plain. *Brom* —7C **128**
Prince's Rise. *SE13* —2E **96**
Princes Riverside Rd. *SE16*
—1K **79**
Princes Rd. *N18* —4D **18**
Princes Rd. *SE20* —6K **111**
Princes Rd. *SW14* —3K **89**
Prince's Rd. *SW19* —6J **107**
Princes Rd. *W13* —1B **72**
Princes Rd. *Buck H* —2F **21**
Princes Rd. *Ilf* —4H **35**
Princes Rd. *Kew* —1F **89**
Princes Rd. *King T* —7G **105**
Princes Rd. *Rich* —5F **89**
Prince's Rd. *Tedd* —4H **103**
Princessa Ct. *Enf* —5J **7**
Princess Alice Ho. *W10* —4E **58**
Princess Ct. *N6* —7G **29**
Princess Ct. W2 —2J **59**
  (off Queensway)
Princess Cres. *N4* —2B **46**
Princess May Rd. *N16* —4E **46**
Princess M. *NW3* —5B **44**
Princess Pde. *Dag* —2G **69**
Princess Pde. *Orp* —3E **138**
Prince's Sq. *W2* —7K **59**
Princess Rd. *NW1* —1E **60**
Princess Rd. *NW6* —2J **59**
Princess Rd. *Croy* —6C **124**
Princess St. *SE1*
—3B **78** (2B **156**)
Prince's St. *EC2* —6D **62** (1E **150**)
Princes St. *N17* —6K **17**
Princes St. *W1* —6F **61** (1K **147**)
Princes St. *Bexh* —3F **101**
Princes St. *Rich* —4E **88**
Princes St. *Sutt* —4B **132**
Princes Ter. *E13* —1K **65**
Prince St. *SE8* —6B **80**
Princes Way. *SW19* —7F **91**
Princes Way. *Buck H* —2F **21**
Princes Way. *Croy* —5K **133**
Princes Way. *Ruis* —4C **38**
Princes Way. *W Wick* —4H **137**
Prince's Yd. W11 —1G **75**
  (off Princedale Rd.)
Princethorpe Ho. W2 —5K **59**
  (off Woodchester Sq.)
Princethorpe Rd. *SE26* —4K **111**
Princeton Ct. *SW15* —3F **91**
Princeton M. *King T* —1G **119**
Princeton St. *WC1*
—5K **61** (6G **143**)
Pringle Gdns. *SW16* —4G **109**
Pring St. *W10* —7F **59**
Printer St. *EC4* —6A **62** (7K **143**)
Printing Ho. Yd. E2
—3F **63** (1H **145**)
Priolo Rd. *SE7* —5A **82**
Prior Av. *Sutt* —7C **132**
Prior Bolton St. *N1* —6B **46**
Prioress Rd. *SE27* —3B **110**
Prioress St. *SE1* —3E **78** (2F **157**)
Prior Rd. *Ilf* —3E **50**
Priors Croft. *E17* —2A **32**
Priors Field. *N'holt* —6C **38**
Priors Gdns. *Ruis* —5A **38**
Priors Mead. *Enf* —1K **7**
Prior St. *SE10* —7E **80**
Priory Av. *E4* —3G **19**
Priory Av. *E17* —5C **32**
Priory Av. *N8* —4H **29**
Priory Av. *W4* —4A **74**
Priory Av. *Orp* —6H **129**
Priory Av. *Sutt* —4F **131**

Priory Av. *Wemb* —4K **39**
Priory Clo. *E4* —3G **19**
Priory Clo. *E18* —1J **33**
Priory Clo. *N3* —1H **27**
Priory Clo. *N14* —5A **6**
Priory Clo. *N20* —7C **4**
Priory Clo. *SW19* —1K **121**
Priory Clo. *Beck* —3A **126**
Priory Clo. *Chst* —1D **128**
Priory Clo. *Hamp* —7D **102**
Priory Clo. *Hayes* —7A **54**
Priory Clo. *Stan* —3E **10**
Priory Clo. *Wemb* —4K **39**
Priory Ct. *E6* —1B **66**
Priory Ct. *E9* —5K **47**
Priory Ct. *E17* —2B **32**
Priory Ct. *SW8* —1H **93**
Priory Ct. *Bush* —1B **10**
Priory Ct. *Eps* —7B **130**
Priory Ct. *Houn* —3F **87**
Priory Ct. *Sutt* —4G **131**
Priory Ct. *Wemb* —2E **56**
Priory Ct. Est. *E17* —2B **32**
Priory Cres. *SE19* —7C **110**
Priory Cres. *Sutt* —4F **131**
Priory Cres. *Wemb* —3A **40**
Priory Dri. *SE2* —5D **84**
Priory Dri. *Stan* —3E **10**
Prioryfield Dri. Edgw —4C **12**
Priory Gdns. *N6* —6F **29**
Priory Gdns. *SE25* —4F **125**
Priory Gdns. *SW13* —3B **90**
Priory Gdns. *W4* —4A **74**
Priory Gdns. *W5* —2E **56**
Priory Gdns. *Hamp* —7D **102**
Priory Gdns. *Wemb* —3A **40**
Priory Grange. N2 —3D **28**
  (off Fortis Grn.)
Priory Grn. Est. *N1* —2K **61**
Priory Gro. *SW8* —1J **93**
Priory Gro. *Barn* —5D **4**
Priory Hill. *Wemb* —4A **40**
Priory La. *SW15* —6A **90**
Priory La. *Rich* —7G **73**
Priory Leas. *SE9* —1C **114**
Priory M. *SW8* —1H **93**
Priory Pk. *SE3* —3H **97**
Priory Pk. Rd. *NW6* —1H **59**
  (in two parts)
Priory Pk. Rd. *Wemb* —4A **40**
Priory Rd. *E6* —1B **66**
Priory Rd. *N8* —4G **29**
Priory Rd. *NW6* —1K **59**
Priory Rd. *SW19* —7B **108**
Priory Rd. *W4* —3K **73**
Priory Rd. *Bark* —7H **51**
Priory Rd. *Croy* —7A **124**
Priory Rd. *Hamp* —7D **102**
Priory Rd. *Houn* —5G **87**
Priory Rd. *Rich* —6G **73**
Priory Rd. *Sutt* —4F **131**
Priory St. *E3* —3D **64**
Priory Ter. *NW6* —1K **59**
Priory, The. SE3 —4H **97**
Priory, The. *Croy* —4A **134**
Priory Vw. *Bush* —1D **10**
Priory Vs. N11 —6J **15**
  (off Colney Hatch La.)
Priory Wlk. *SW10* —5A **76**
Priory Way. *Harr* —4F **23**
Priory Way. *S'hall* —3B **70**
Pritchard's Rd. *E2* —1G **63**
Priter Rd. *SE16* —3G **79**
Priter Way. *SE16* —3G **79**
Private Rd. Enf —5J **7**

Probert Rd. *SW2* —5A **94**
Probyn Rd. *SW2* —2B **110**
Procter Ho. SE5 —7D **78**
  (off Picton St.)
Procter St. *WC1* —5K **61** (6G **143**)
Proctor Ho. *Mitc* —1E **122**
Progress Bus. Pk., The. *Croy*
—2K **133**
Progress Cen., The. *N9* —3K **17**
Progress Way. *N22* —1A **30**
Progress Way. *Croy* —2K **133**
Progress Way. *Enf* —5B **8**
Project Pk. E16 —4F **65**
Promenade App. Rd. *W4* —7A **74**
Promenade Mans. *Edgw* —5B **12**
Promenade, The. *W4* —1A **90**
Prospect Clo. *SE26* —4H **111**
Prospect Clo. *Belv* —4G **85**
Prospect Clo. *Houn* —2D **86**
Prospect Clo. *Ruis* —7B **22**
Prospect Cotts. *SW18* —4J **91**
Prospect Cres. *Twic* —6G **87**
Prospect Hill. *E17* —4D **32**
Prospect Ho. E17 —3E **32**
  (off Prospect Hill)
Prospect Ho. N1 —2A **62**
  (off Donegal St.)
Prospect Pl. *E1* —1J **79**
Prospect Pl. *N2* —4B **28**
Prospect Pl. *N7* —4J **45**
Prospect Pl. *N17* —7K **17**
Prospect Pl. *NW2* —3H **43**
Prospect Pl. *NW3* —4A **44**
Prospect Pl. *W4* —5K **73**
Prospect Pl. *Brom* —3K **127**
Prospect Pl. *Romf* —2J **37**
Prospect Quay. SW18 —4J **91**
  (off Point Pleasant)
Prospect Ring. *N2* —3B **28**
Prospect Rd. *NW2* —3H **43**
Prospect Rd. *Barn* —4D **4**
Prospect Rd. *Surb* —6C **118**
Prospect Rd. *Wfd G* —6F **21**
Prospect St. *SE16* —3H **79**
Prospect Vale. *SE18* —4C **82**
Prospero Rd. *N19* —1H **45**
Protheroe Ho. *N17* —3F **31**
Prothero Gdns. *NW4* —5D **26**
Prothero Rd. *SW6* —7G **75**
Prout Gro. *NW10* —4A **42**
Prout Rd. *E5* —3H **47**
Providence Ct. W1
—7E **60** (2H **147**)
Providence Pl. *N1* —1B **62**
Providence Pl. *Romf* —2F **37**
Providence Row. N1
—2K **61** (1G **143**)
Providence Sq. *SE1* —2G **79**
Province St. *N1* —2C **62**
Provost Est. *N1* —2D **62** (1E **144**)
Provost Rd. *NW3* —7D **44**
Provost St. *N1* —2D **62** (1E **144**)
Prowse Av. *Bush* —1B **10**
Prowse Pl. *NW1* —7G **45**
Proyers Path. *Harr* —7B **24**
Pruden Clo. *N14* —2B **16**
Prudent Pas. *EC2*
—6C **62** (7D **144**)
Prusom St. *E1* —1H **79**
Pryors, The. *NW3* —3B **44**
Pudding La. *EC3*
—7D **62** (3F **151**)
Pudding Mill La. *E15* —1D **64**
Puddle Dock. *EC4*
—7B **62** (2B **150**)

Puffin Clo. *Beck* —5K **125**
Pulborough Rd. *SW18* —7H **91**
Pulborough Way. *Houn* —4A **86**
Pulford Rd. *N15* —6D **30**
Pulham Av. *N2* —4A **28**
Pulham Ho. *SW8* —7K **77**
  (off Dorset Rd.)
Puller Rd. *Barn* —2B **4**
Pulleyns Av. *E6* —3C **66**
Pulleyns Ct. *SW2* —5J **93**
Pullman Gdns. *SW15* —6E **90**
Pullman Pl. *SE9* —5C **98**
Pulross Rd. *SW9* —3K **93**
Pulteney Clo. *E3* —1B **64**
Pulteney Rd. *E18* —3K **33**
Pulteney Ter. *N1* —1K **61**
Pulton Ho. *SE4* —4A **96**
  (off Turnham Rd.)
Pulton Pl. *SW6* —7J **75**
Puma Ct. *E1* —5F **63** (5J **145**)
Pump All. *Bren* —7D **72**
Pump Clo. *N'holt* —2E **54**
Pump Ct. *EC4* —6A **62** (1J **149**)
Pumping Sta. Rd. *W4* —7A **74**
Pump La. *SE14* —7J **79**
Pump Pail N. *Croy* —3C **134**
Pump Pail S. *Croy* —3C **134**
Punderson's Gdns. *E2* —3H **63**
Punjab La. *S'hall* —1D **70**
Purbeck Av. *N Mald* —6B **120**
Purbeck Dri. *NW2* —2F **43**
Purbeck Ho. SW8 —7K **77**
  (off Bolney St.)
Purbrook Est. *SE1*
—2E **78** (7H **151**)
Purbrook St. *SE1*
—3E **78** (1H **157**)
Purcell Cres. *SW6* —7G **75**
Purcell M. *NW10* —7A **42**
Purcell Rd. *Gnfd* —5F **55**
Purcells Av. *Edgw* —5B **12**
Purcell St. *N1* —2E **62**
Purchese St. *NW1* —2H **61**
Purdey Ct. *Wor Pk* —1C **130**
Purdon Ho. SE15 —1G **95**
  (off Oliver Goldsmith Est.)
Purdy St. *E3* —4D **64**
Purelake M. SE13 —3F **97**
  (off Marischal Rd.)
Purland Clo. *Dag* —1F **53**
Purland Rd. *SE28* —2K **83**
Purleigh Av. *Wfd G* —6H **21**
Purley Av. *NW2* —2G **43**
Purley Clo. *Ilf* —2E **34**
Purley Pl. *N1* —7B **46**
Purley Rd. *N9* —3K **17**
Purley Rd. *S Croy* —7D **134**
Purley View Ter. S Croy —7D **134**
  (off Sanderstead Rd.)
Purley Way. *Croy & Purl*
—7K **123**
Purley Way Cen., The. *Croy*
—2A **134**
Purley Way Corner. *Croy*
—7K **123**
Purley Way Cres. *Croy* —7K **123**
Purneys Rd. *SE9* —4B **98**
Purrett Rd. *SE18* —5K **83**
Purser Ho. *SW2* —6A **94**
  (off Tulse Hill)
Pursers Cross Rd. *SW6* —1H **91**
Purse Wardens Clo. *W13*
—1C **72**
Pursley Rd. *NW7* —7J **13**
Purves Rd. *NW10* —2D **58**

Putney Bri. *SW15 & SW6*
—3G **91**
Putney Bri. App. *SW6* —3G **91**
Putney Bri. Rd. *SW15 & SW18*
—4G **91**
Putney Comn. *SW15* —3E **90**
Putney Exchange Shop. Cen.
SW15 —4F **91**
Putney Gdns. *Chad H* —5B **36**
Putney Heath. *SW15* —7D **90**
Putney Heath La. *SW15* —6F **91**
Putney High St. *SW15* —4F **91**
Putney Hill. *SW15* —7F **91**
  (in two parts)
Putney Pk. Av. *SW15* —4C **90**
Putney Pk. La. *SW15* —4D **90**
Pycroft Way. *N9* —4A **18**
Pyecombe Corner. *N12* —4C **14**
Pylbrook Rd. *Sutt* —3J **131**
Pylon Trad. Est. *E16* —4G **65**
Pylon Way. *Croy* —1J **133**
Pym Clo. *E Barn* —5G **5**
Pymers Mead. *SE21* —1C **110**
Pym Ho. *SW9* —2A **94**
Pymmes Brook Ho. *N10* —7K **15**
Pymmes Clo. *N13* —5E **16**
Pymmes Clo. *N17* —1H **31**
Pymmes Gdns. N. *N9* —3A **18**
Pymmes Gdns. S. *N9* —3A **18**
Pymmes Grn. Rd. *N11* —4A **16**
Pymmes Rd. *N13* —6D **16**
Pymms Brook Dri. *Barn* —4H **5**
Pynfolds. *SE16* —2H **79**
Pynham Clo. *SE2* —3B **84**
Pynnacles Clo. *Stan* —5G **11**
Pynnersmead. *SE24* —5C **94**
Pyramid Ho. *Houn* —3C **86**
Pyrford Ho. *SW9* —4B **94**
Pyrland Rd. *N5* —5D **46**
Pyrland Rd. *Rich* —6F **89**
Pyrmont Gro. *SE27* —3B **110**
Pyrmont Rd. *W4* —6G **73**
Pytchley Cres. *SE19* —6C **110**
Pytchley Rd. *SE22* —3E **94**

Q

Quadrangle Clo. *SE1*
—4E **78** (3G **157**)
Quadrangle M. *Stan* —7H **11**
Quadrangle, The. *SE24* —5C **94**
Quadrangle, The. *SW10* —1A **92**
Quadrangle, The. W2
—6C **60** (7C **140**)
Quadrant Arc. *W1*
—7G **61** (3B **148**)
Quadrant Arc. *Romf* —5K **37**
Quadrant Gro. *NW5* —5D **44**
Quadrant Ho. SE1
—1B **78** (4A **150**)
Quadrant Rd. *Rich* —4D **88**
Quadrant Rd. *T Hth* —4B **124**
Quadrant, The. *NW4* —4E **26**
Quadrant, The. *SW20* —1G **121**
Quadrant, The. *W10* —3F **59**
Quadrant, The. *Bexh* —7D **84**
Quadrant, The. *Harr* —3H **23**
Quadrant, The. *Rich* —4E **88**
Quadrant, The. *Sutt* —6A **132**
Quad Rd. *Wemb* —3D **40**
Quaggy Wlk. *SE3* —4J **97**
Quainton St. *NW10* —3K **41**
Quaker La. *S'hall* —3E **70**
Quakers Course. *NW9* —1B **26**
Quakers La. *Iswth* —7K **71**
Quaker St. *E1* —4F **63** (4J **145**)

Quakers Wlk. N21 —6J 7
Quality Ct. WC2 —6A 62 (7J 143)
Quandrant Gro. NW5 —5D 44
Quantock Dri. Wor Pk —2E 130
Quantock Gdns. NW2 —2F 43
Quantock Ho. N16 —1F 47
Quarley Way. SE15 —7F 79
Quarrendon St. SW6 —2J 91
Quarr Rd. Cars —6C 122
Quarry Pk. Rd. Sutt —6H 131
Quarry Rise. Sutt —6H 131
Quarry Rd. SW18 —6A 92
Quarterdeck, The. E14 —2C 80
Quarter Mile La. E10 —4D 48
Quatre Ports. E4 —5A 20
Quayside Ho. E14 —1C 80
Quebec M. W1 —6D 60 (1F 147)
Quebec Rd. Hayes —6A 54
Quebec Rd. Ilf —7F 35
Quebec Way. SE16 —2K 79
Quedgeley Ct. SE15 —6F 79
  (off Ebley Clo.)
Queen Adelaide Ct. SE20 —6J 111
Queen Adelaide Rd. SE20
   —6J 111
Queen Alexandra's Ct. SW19
   —5H 107
Queen Anne Av. Brom —3H 127
Queen Anne M. W1
   —5F 61 (6K 141)
Queen Anne Rd. E9 —6K 47
Queen Anne's Clo. Twic —3H 103
Queen Anne's Gdns. W4 —3A 74
Queen Anne's Gdns. W5 —2E 72
Queen Anne's Gdns. Enf —6K 7
Queen Anne's Gdns. Mitc
   —3D 122
Queen Anne's Ga. SW1
   —2H 77 (7C 148)
Queen Anne's Ga. Bexh —3D 100
Queen Anne's Gro. W4 —3A 74
Queen Anne's Gro. W5 —2E 72
Queen Anne's Gro. Enf —7J 7
Queen Anne's Pl. Enf —6K 7
Queen Anne St. W1
   —5F 61 (6J 141)
Queen Anne's Wlk. WC1
   —4J 61 (4F 143)
Queenborough Gdns. Chst
   —6H 115
Queenborough Gdns. Ilf —4E 34
Queen Caroline St. W6 —4E 74
Queen Elizabeth Bldgs. EC4
   —7A 62 (2J 149)
Queen Elizabeth Gdns. Mord
   —4J 121
Queen Elizabeth Ho. SW12
   —7E 92
Queen Elizabeth Rd. E17 —3A 32
Queen Elizabeth Rd. King T
   —2F 119
Queen Elizabeth's Clo. N16
   —2D 46
Queen Elizabeth's Dri. N14
   —1D 16
Queen Elizabeth's Dri. New Ad
   —7F 137
Queen Elizabeth St. SE1
   —2E 78 (6H 151)
Queen Elizabeth's Wlk. N16
   —1D 46
Queen Elizabeth's Wlk. Wall
   —4H 133
Queen Elizabeth Wlk. SW13
   —1C 90

Queengate Ct. N12 —5E 14
Queenhithe. EC4
   —7C 62 (2D 150)
Queen Margaret's Gro. N1
   —5E 46
Queen Mary Av. Mord —5F 121
Queen Mary Rd. SE19 —6B 110
Queen Mary's Av. Cars —7D 132
Queen Marys Bldgs. SW1
   —4G 77 (3B 154)
  (off Stillington St.)
Queen of Denmark Ct. SE16
   —3B 80
Queens Acre. Sutt —7G 131
Queens Av. N3 —7F 15
Queens Av. N10 —3E 28
Queens Av. N20 —2G 15
Queens Av. N21 —1G 17
Queen's Av. Felt —4A 102
Queen's Av. Gnfd —6F 55
Queen's Av. Stan —3C 24
Queen's Av. Wfd G —5E 20
Queensberry M. W. SW7
   —4B 76 (3A 152)
Queensberry Pl. SW7
   —4B 76 (3A 152)
Queensberry Way. SW7
   —4B 76 (3A 152)
Queensborough Ct. N3 —4H 27
  (off N. Circular Rd.)
Queensborough M. W2 —7A 60
Queensborough Pas. W2 —7A 60
  (off Queensborough M.)
Queensborough Studios. W2
   —7A 60
  (off Queensborough M.)
Queensborough Ter. W2 —7K 59
Queensbridge Ct. E2 —1F 63
  (off Queensbridge Ct.)
Queensbridge Pk. Iswth —5J 87
Queensbridge Rd. E8 & E2
   —6F 47
Queensbury Circ. Pde. Harr &
   Stan —3E 24
Queensbury Ho. Rich —5D 88
Queensbury Rd. NW9 —7K 25
Queensbury Rd. Wemb —2F 57
Queensbury Sta. Pde. Edgw
   —3F 25
Queensbury St. N1 —7C 46
Queen's Cir. SW8 & SW11
   —7F 77
Queens Clo. Edgw —5B 12
Queens Clo. Wall —5F 133
Queen's Club Gdns. W14 —6G 75
Queens Clo. NW6 —5K 43
Queen's Ct. NW11 —5H 27
Queens Ct. SE23 —2J 111
Queen's Ct. W2 —7K 59
  (off Queensway)
Queens Ct. Rich —6F 89
Queen's Ct. W'stone —2C 24
Queenscourt. Wemb —4E 40
Queen's Cres. NW5 —6E 44
Queen's Cres. Rich —5F 89
Queenscroft Rd. SE9 —5B 98
Queensdale Cres. W11 —1F 75
Queensdale Pl. W11 —1G 75
Queensdale Rd. W11 —1F 75
Queensdale Wlk. W11 —1G 75
Queensdown Rd. E5 —4H 47
Queens Dri. E10 —7C 32
Queen's Dri. N4 —2B 46
Queen's Dri. W5 & W3 —6F 57
Queen's Dri. Surb —7G 119

Queen's Dri. Th Dit —6A 118
Queen's Elm Sq. SW3
   —5B 76 (6B 152)
Queens Ferry Wlk. N17 —4H 31
Queensfield Ct. Sutt —4E 130
Queen's Gdns. NW4 —5E 26
Queen's Gdns. W2 —7A 60
Queen's Gdns. W5 —4C 56
Queen's Gdns. Houn —1C 86
Queen's Gdns. Rain —2K 69
Queen's Ga. SW7 —2K 75
Queen's Ga. Gdns. SW7 —3A 76
Queens Ga. Gdns. SW15 —4D 90
Queensgate Gdns. Chst —1H 129
Queen's Ga. M. SW7 —3A 76
Queensgate Pl. NW6 —7J 43
Queen's Ga. Pl. SW7 —3A 76
Queen's Ga. Pl. M. SW7 —3A 76
Queen's Ga. Ter. SW7 —3A 76
Queen's Gro. NW8 —1B 60
Queens Gro. Rd. E4 —1A 20
Queen's Gro. Studios. NW8
   —1B 60
Queen's Head St. N1 —1B 62
Queen's Head Yd. SE1
   —1D 78 (5E 150)
Queens Ho. Tedd —6A 103
Queensland Av. N18 —6H 17
Queensland Av. SW19 —1K 121
Queensland Ho. E16 —1E 82
  (off Rymill St.)
Queensland Pl. N7 —4A 46
Queensland Rd. N7 —4A 46
Queens La. N10 —3F 29
Queens Mkt. E13 —1A 66
Queensmead. NW8 —1B 60
Queens Mead. Brom —2H 127
Queensmere Clo. SW19 —2F 107
Queensmere Rd. SW13 —6B 74
Queensmere Rd. SW19 —2F 107
Queen's M. W2 —7K 59
Queensmill Rd. SW6 —7F 75
Queens Pde. N8 —4B 30
Queen's Pde. N11 —5J 15
  (off Friern Barnet Rd.)
Queens Pde. W5 —6F 57
Queens Pde. Clo. N11 —5J 15
Queens Pas. Chst —6F 115
Queens Pl. Mord —4J 121
Queen's Promenade. King T
   —4D 118
Queen Sq. WC1 —4J 61 (4F 143)
Queen Sq. Pl. WC1
   —4J 61 (4F 143)
Queens Reach. King T —2D 118
Queens Ride. SW13 & SW15
   —3C 90
Queens Rise. Rich —6F 89
Queens Rd. E11 —7F 33
Queens Rd. E13 —1K 65
Queen's Rd. E17 —6B 32
Queens Rd. N3 —1A 28
Queens Rd. N9 —2C 18
Queen's Rd. N11 —7D 16
Queens Rd. NW4 —5E 26
Queen's Rd. SE15 & SE14
   —1H 95
Queens Rd. SW14 —3K 89
Queens Rd. SW19 —6H 107
Queen's Rd. W5 —6E 56
Queens Rd. Bark —6G 51
Queens Rd. Barn —3A 4
Queens Rd. Beck —2A 126

Queens Rd. Brom —2J 127
Queen's Rd. Buck H —2E 20
Queens Rd. Chst —6F 115
Queens Rd. Croy —6B 124
Queen's Rd. Enf —4K 7
Queen's Rd. Felt —1A 102
Queens Rd. Hamp —4F 103
Queen's Rd. Houn —3F 87
Queen's Rd. King T —7G 105
Queen's Rd. Mitc —3B 122
Queens Rd. Mord —4J 121
Queen's Rd. N Mald —4B 120
Queen's Rd. Rich —7F 89
Queen's Rd. S'hall —2B 70
Queen's Rd. Tedd —6K 103
Queen's Rd. Th Dit —5A 118
Queen's Rd. Twic —1A 104
Queen's Rd. Wall —5F 133
Queen's Rd. Well —2B 100
Queen's Rd. W. E13 —2J 65
Queen's Row. SE17
   —6D 78 (7E 156)
Queens Ter. E1 —4J 63
Queen's Ter. E13 —1K 65
Queen's Ter. NW8 —2B 60
Queen's Ter. Iswth —4A 88
Queen's Ter. Cotts. W7 —2J 71
Queensthorpe Rd. SE26 —4K 111
Queenstown M. SW8 —2F 93
Queenstown Rd. SW8 —6F 77
Queen St. EC4 —7C 62 (2D 150)
Queen St. N17 —6K 17
Queen St. W1 —1F 77 (4J 147)
Queen St. Bexh —3F 101
Queen St. Croy —4C 134
Queen St. Romf —6K 37
Queen St. Pl. EC4
   —7C 62 (3D 150)
Queensville Rd. SW12 —7H 93
Queens Wlk. E4 —1A 20
Queens Wlk. NW9 —2J 41
Queens Wlk. SW1
   —1G 77 (5A 148)
Queens Wlk. W5 —4C 56
Queens Wlk. Harr —4J 23
Queens Wlk. Ruis —2A 38
Queens Wlk. Ter. Ruis —3A 38
Queen's Wlk., The. SE1
   —1D 78 (4F 151)
  (off Borough High St.)
Queen's Wlk., The. SE1
   —1K 77 (3K 149)
  (off Waterloo Rd.)
Queen's Way. NW4 —5E 26
Queensway. W2 —6K 59
Queensway. Croy —5K 133
Queensway. Enf —4C 8
Queens Way. Felt —4A 102
Queensway. Orp —5G 129
Queensway. W Wick —3G 137
Queensway Ind. Est. Enf —4D 8
Queenswell Av. N20 —3H 15
Queens Wharf. W6 —5E 74
Queenswood Av. E17 —1E 32
Queenswood Av. Hamp —6F 103
Queenswood Av. Houn —2D 86
Queenswood Av. T Hth —5A 124
Queenswood Av. Wall —4H 133
Queenswood Ct. SE27 —4D 110
Queenswood Ct. SW4 —5J 93
Queenswood Gdns. E11 —1A 49
Queenswood Pk. N3 —2G 27
Queens Wood Rd. N10 —6F 29
Queenswood Rd. SE23 —3K 111
Queenswood Rd. Sidc —5K 99

Queen's Yd. WC1
   —4G 61 (4B 142)
Queen Victoria. (Junct.) —3E 130
Queen Victoria Av. Wemb —7D 40
Queen Victoria St. EC4
   —7B 62 (2A 150)
Quemerford Rd. N7 —5K 45
Quenington Ct. SE15 —6F 79
  (off Ebley Clo.)
Quentin Pl. SE13 —3G 97
Quentin Rd. SE13 —3G 97
Quernmore Clo. Brom —6J 113
Quernmore Rd. N4 —6A 30
Quernmore Rd. Brom —6J 113
Querrin St. SW6 —2A 92
Quested Ct. E8 —5H 47
  (off Brett Rd.)
Quex M. NW6 —1J 59
Quex Rd. NW6 —1J 59
Quick Pl. N1 —1B 62
Quick Rd. W4 —5A 74
Quicksilver Pl. N22 —2K 29
Quicks Rd. SW19 —7K 107
Quick St. N1 —2B 62
Quick St. M. N1 —2B 62
Quickswood. NW3 —7C 44
Quiet Nook. Brom —3B 138
Quill La. SW15 —4F 91
Quill St. N4 —3A 46
Quilp St. SE1 —2C 78 (6C 150)
Quilter St. E2 —3G 63 (1K 145)
Quilter St. SE18 —5K 83
Quinta Dri. Barn —5A 4
Quintin Av. SW20 —1H 121
Quinton Clo. Beck —3E 126
Quinton Clo. Houn —7A 84
Quinton Clo. Wall —4F 133
Quinton Ho. SW8 —7J 77
  (off Wyvil Rd.)
Quinton Rd. Th Dit —7A 118
Quinton St. SW18 —2A 108
Quixley St. E14 —7F 65
Quorn Rd. SE22 —4E 94

R

Rabbit Row. W8 —1J 75
Rabbits Rd. E12 —4C 50
Rabournmead Dri. N'holt —5C 38
Raby Rd. N Mald —4K 119
Raby St. E14 —6A 64
Raccoon Way. Houn —2A 86
Rachel Point. E5 —4G 47
Rackham M. SW16 —6G 109
Racton Rd. SW6 —6J 75
Radbourne Av. W5 —4C 72
Radbourne Clo. E5 —4K 47
Radbourne Ct. Harr —6B 24
Radbourne Cres. E17 —2F 33
Radbourne Rd. SW12 —7G 93
Radcliffe Av. NW10 —2C 58
Radcliffe Av. Enf —1H 7
Radcliffe Gdns. Cars —7C 132
Radcliffe Ho. SE16 —4G 79
  (off Anchor St.)
Radcliffe M. Hamp —5G 103
Radcliffe Rd. N21 —1G 17
Radcliffe Rd. SE1
   —3E 78 (1H 157)
Radcliffe Rd. Croy —2F 135
Radcliffe Rd. Harr —2A 24
Radcliffe Way. N'holt —3B 54
Radcot Point. SE23 —3K 111
Radcot St. SE11
   —5A 78 (6K 155)

Raddington Rd. *W10* —5G **59**
Radfield Way. *Sidc* —7H **99**
Radford Ho. *N7* —5K **45**
Radford Rd. *SE13* —6E **96**
Radford Way. *Bark* —3K **67**
Radipole Rd. *SW6* —1H **91**
Radland Rd. *E16* —6H **65**
Radlet Av. *SE26* —2H **111**
Radlett Clo. *E7* —6H **49**
Radlett Pl. *NW8* —1C **60**
Radley Av. *Ilf* —4A **52**
Radley Clo. *SE16* —2K **79**
Radley Gdns. *Harr* —4E **24**
Radley Ho. SE2 —2D **84**
   (off Wolvercote Rd.)
Radley M. *W8* —3J **75**
Radley Rd. *N17* —2E **30**
Radley's La. *E18* —2J **33**
Radleys Mead. *Dag* —6H **53**
Radley Sq. *E5* —2J **47**
Radley Ter. E16 —5H **65**
   (off Hermit Rd.)
Radlix Rd. *E10* —1C **48**
Radnor Av. *Harr* —5J **23**
Radnor Av. *Well* —5B **100**
Radnor Clo. *Chst* —6J **115**
Radnor Clo. *Mitc* —4J **123**
Radnor Ct. W7 —6K **55**
   (off Copley Clo.)
Radnor Ct. *Har W* —1K **23**
Radnor Cres. *SE18* —7A **84**
Radnor Cres. *Ilf* —5D **34**
Radnor Gdns. *Enf* —1K **7**
Radnor Gdns. *Twic* —2K **103**
Radnor M. *W2* —6B **60** (1B **146**)
Radnor Pl. *W2* —6C **60** (1C **146**)
Radnor Rd. *NW6* —1G **59**
Radnor Rd. *SE15* —7G **79**
Radnor Rd. *Harr* —5H **23**
Radnor Rd. *Twic* —1K **103**
Radnor St. *EC1* —3C **62** (2D **144**)
Radnor Ter. *W14* —4H **75**
Radnor Ter. *Sutt* —7J **131**
Radnor Wlk. E14 —4C **80**
   (off Copeland Dri.)
Radnor Wlk. *SW3*
   —5C **76** (6D **152**)
Radnor Wlk. *Croy* —6A **126**
Radnor Way. *NW10* —4H **57**
Radstock Av. *Harr* —3A **24**
Radstock St. *SW11* —7C **76**
Raeburn Av. *Surb* —7H **119**
Raeburn Clo. *NW11* —6A **28**
Raeburn Clo. *King T* —7D **104**
Raeburn Ho. N'holt —2B **54**
   (off Academy Gdns.)
Raeburn Rd. *Edgw* —1G **25**
Raeburn Rd. *Sidc* —6J **100**
Raeburn St. *SW2* —4J **93**
Raffles Ct. *NW4* —4D **26**
Rafford Way. *Brom* —2K **127**
Ragglesswood. *Chst* —1E **128**
Raglan Clo. *Houn* —5D **86**
Raglan Ct. *SE12* —5J **97**
Raglan Ct. *S Croy* —5B **134**
Raglan Ct. *Wemb* —4F **41**
Raglan Rd. *E17* —5E **32**
Raglan Rd. *SE18* —5G **83**
Raglan Rd. *Belv* —4F **85**
Raglan Rd. *Brom* —4A **128**
Raglan Rd. *Enf* —7A **8**
Raglan St. *NW5* —6F **45**
Raglan Ter. *Harr* —4F **39**
Raglan Way. *N'holt* —6G **39**
Ragley Clo. *W3* —2J **73**

Raider Clo. *Romf* —1G **37**
Railey M. *NW5* —5G **45**
Railshead Rd. *Iswth* —4B **88**
Railton Rd. *SE24* —4A **94**
Railway App. *N4* —6A **30**
Railway App. *SE1*
   —1D **78** (5F **151**)
Railway App. *Harr* —4K **23**
Railway App. *Twic* —7A **88**
Railway App. *Wall* —5F **133**
Railway Av. *SE16* —2J **79**
Railway Cotts. *SW19* —4K **107**
Railway Cotts. *Twic* —6E **86**
Railway Gro. *SE14* —7B **80**
Railway M. *E3* —3C **64**
   (off Wellington Way)
Railway M. *W10* —6G **59**
Railway Pas. *Tedd* —6A **104**
Railway Pl. *SW19* —6H **107**
Railway Pl. *Belv* —3G **85**
Railway Rise. *SE22* —4E **94**
Railway Rd. *Tedd* —4J **103**
Railway Side. *SW13* —3B **90**
Railway St. *N1* —2J **61**
Railway St. *Romf* —7C **36**
Railway Ter. *E17* —1E **32**
Railway Ter. *SE13* —5D **96**
Rainborough Clo. *NW10* —6J **41**
Rainbow Av. *E14* —5D **80**
Rainbow Quay. *SE16* —3A **80**
Rainbow St. *SE5* —7E **78**
Raine St. *E1* —1H **79**
Rainham Clo. *SE9* —6J **99**
Rainham Clo. *SW11* —6C **92**
Rainham Rd. *NW10* —3E **58**
Rainham Rd. N. *Dag* —2G **53**
Rainham Rd. S. *Dag* —4H **53**
Rainhill Way. *E3* —3C **64**
Rainsborough Av. *SE8* —4A **80**
Rainsford Clo. *Stan* —4H **11**
Rainsford Rd. *NW10* —2H **57**
Rainsford St. *W2*
   —6C **60** (7C **140**)
Rainton Rd. *SE7* —5J **81**
Rainville Rd. *W6* —6E **74**
Raisins Hill. *Pinn* —3A **22**
Raith Av. *N14* —3C **16**
Raleana Rd. *E14* —1E **80**
Raleigh Av. *Hayes* —5A **54**
Raleigh Av. *Wall* —4H **133**
Raleigh Clo. *NW4* —5E **26**
Raleigh Clo. *Pinn* —7B **22**
Raleigh Ct. *W13* —5B **56**
Raleigh Ct. *Beck* —1D **126**
Raleigh Ct. *Wall* —6F **133**
Raleigh Dri. *N20* —3H **15**
Raleigh Dri. *Surb* —7J **119**
Raleigh Gdns. *SW2* —6K **93**
Raleigh Gdns. *Mitc* —3D **122**
   (in two parts)
Raleigh Ho. E14 —2D **80**
   (off Admirals Way)
Raleigh M. N1 —1B **62**
   (off Queen's Head St.)
Raleigh Rd. *N2* —2C **28**
Raleigh Rd. *N8* —4A **30**
Raleigh Rd. *SE20* —7K **111**
Raleigh Rd. *Enf* —4J **7**
Raleigh Rd. *Rich* —3F **89**
Raleigh Rd. *S'hall* —5C **70**
Raleigh St. *N1* —1B **62**
Raleigh Way. *N14* —1C **16**
Raleigh Way. *Felt* —5A **102**
Ralph Ct. W2 —6K **59**
   (off Queensway)

Ralph Perring Ct. *Beck* —4C **126**
Ralston St. *SW3*
   —5D **76** (6E **152**)
Rama Clo. *SW16* —7J **109**
Rama Ct. *Harr* —2J **39**
Ramac Way. *SE7* —5K **81**
Rambler Clo. *SW16* —4G **109**
Rame Clo. *SW17* —5E **108**
Ramilles Clo. *SW2* —6J **93**
Ramillies Pl. *W1*
   —6G **61** (1A **148**)
Ramillies Rd. *NW7* —2F **13**
Ramillies Rd. *W4* —4K **73**
Ramillies Rd. *Sidc* —6B **100**
Ramillies St. *W1*
   —6G **61** (1A **148**)
Rampart St. *E1* —6H **63**
Ram Pas. *King T* —2D **118**
Rampayne St. *SW1*
   —5H **77** (5C **154**)
Ram Pl. *E9* —6J **47**
Rampton Clo. *E4* —3H **19**
Ramsay M. *SW3* —6C **76**
Ramsay Rd. *E7* —4G **49**
Ramsay Rd. *W3* —3J **73**
Ramscroft Clo. *N9* —7K **7**
Ramsdale Rd. *SW17* —5E **108**
Ramsden Dri. *Romf* —1G **37**
Ramsden Rd. *N11* —5J **15**
Ramsden Rd. *SW12* —6E **92**
Ramsden Rd. *Eri* —7K **85**
Ramsey Clo. *NW9* —6B **26**
Ramsey Clo. *Gnfd* —5H **39**
Ramsey Rd. *T Hth* —6K **123**
Ramsey St. *E2* —4G **63**
Ramsey Wlk. *N1* —6D **46**
Ramsey Way. *N14* —7B **6**
Ramsgate Clo. *E16* —1K **81**
Ramsgate St. *E8* —6F **47**
Ramsgill App. *Ilf* —4K **35**
Ramsgill Dri. *Ilf* —5K **35**
Rams Gro. *Romf* —4E **36**
Ram St. *SW18* —5K **91**
Ramulis Dri. *Hayes* —4C **54**
Rancliffe Gdns. *SE9* —4C **98**
Rancliffe Rd. *E6* —2C **66**
Randall Av. *NW2* —2A **42**
Randall Clo. *SW11* —1C **92**
Randall Clo. *Eri* —6J **85**
Randall Ct. *NW7* —7H **13**
Randall Pl. *SE10* —7E **80**
Randall Rd. *SE11*
   —5K **77** (4G **155**)
Randall Row. SE11
   —4K **77** (4G **155**)
Randell's Rd. *N1* —1J **61**
Randisbourne Gdns. *SE6*
   —3D **112**
Randle Rd. *Rich* —4C **104**
Randlesdown Rd. *SE6* —4C **112**
   (in two parts)
Randolph App. *E16* —6A **66**
Randolph Av. *W9* —2K **59**
Randolph Clo. *Bexh* —3J **101**
Randolph Clo. *King T* —5J **105**
Randolph Cres. *W9* —4A **60**
Randolph Gdns. *NW6* —2K **59**
Randolph Gro. *Romf* —5C **36**
Randolph M. *W9* —4A **60**
Randolph Rd. *E17* —5D **32**
Randolph Rd. *W9* —4A **60**
Randolph Rd. *Brom* —1D **138**
Randolph Rd. *S'hall* —2D **70**
Randolph St. *NW1* —7G **45**
Randon Clo. *Harr* —2F **23**

Ranelagh Av. *SW6* —3H **91**
Ranelagh Av. *SW13* —2C **90**
Ranelagh Bri. *W2* —5K **59**
Ranelagh Clo. *Edgw* —4B **12**
Ranelagh Dri. *Edgw* —4B **12**
Ranelagh Dri. *Twic* —5B **88**
Ranelagh Gdns. *E11* —5A **34**
Ranelagh Gdns. *SW6* —3G **91**
Ranelagh Gdns. *W4* —7J **73**
Ranelagh Gdns. *W6* —3B **74**
Ranelagh Gdns. *Ilf* —1D **50**
Ranelagh Gdns. Mans. SW6
   (off Ranelagh Gdns.) —3G **91**
Ranelagh Gro. *SW1*
   —5E **76** (5H **153**)
Ranelagh M. *W5* —2D **72**
Ranelagh Pl. *N Mald* —5A **120**
Ranelagh Rd. *E6* —1E **66**
Ranelagh Rd. *E11* —4G **49**
Ranelagh Rd. *E15* —2G **65**
Ranelagh Rd. *N17* —3E **30**
Ranelagh Rd. *N22* —1K **29**
Ranelagh Rd. *NW10* —2B **58**
Ranelagh Rd. *SW1*
   —5G **77** (6B **154**)
Ranelagh Rd. *W5* —2D **72**
Ranelagh Rd. *S'hall* —1B **70**
Ranelagh Rd. *Wemb* —6D **40**
Ranfurly Rd. *Sutt* —2J **131**
Rangbourne Ho. *N7* —5J **45**
Rangefield Rd. *Brom* —5G **113**
Rangemoor Rd. *N15* —5F **31**
Ranger's Rd. *E4* —1B **20**
Rangers Sq. *SE10* —1F **97**
Rangeworth Pl. *Sidc* —3K **115**
Rankin Clo. *NW9* —3A **26**
Ranleigh Gdns. *Bexh* —7F **85**
Ranmere St. *SW12* —1F **109**
Ranmoor Clo. *Harr* —4H **23**
Ranmoor Gdns. *Harr* —4H **23**
Ranmore Av. *Croy* —3F **135**
Ranmore Path. *Orp* —4K **129**
Ranmore Rd. *Sutt* —7F **131**
Rannoch Clo. *Edgw* —2C **12**
Rannoch Rd. *W6* —6E **74**
Rannock Av. *NW9* —7K **25**
Ransom Dri. *Enf* —4D **6**
Ransome's Dock Bus. Cen. *SW11*
   —7C **76**
Ransom Rd. *SE7* —5A **82**
Ransom Wlk. *SE7* —4A **82**
Ranston St. *NW1*
   —5C **60** (5C **140**)
Ranulf Rd. *NW2* —4H **43**
Ranwell Clo. *E3* —1B **64**
Ranworth Rd. *N9* —2D **18**
Rapesco Ho. SE14 —7A **80**
   (off Greenwood Rd.)
Raphael St. *SW7*
   —2D **76** (7E **146**)
Rashleigh Ct. *SW8* —2F **93**
Rasper Rd. *N20* —2F **15**
Rastell Av. *SW2* —2H **109**
Ratcliffe Clo. *SE12* —7J **97**
Ratcliffe Cross St. *E1* —6K **63**
Ratcliffe La. *E14* —6A **64**
Ratcliffe Orchard. *E1* —7K **63**
Ratcliff Gro. EC1
   —3C **62** (2D **144**)
Ratcliff Rd. *E7* —5A **50**
Rathbone Pl. *W1*
   —5H **61** (6C **142**)
Rathbone Point. *E5* —4G **47**
Rathbone Sq. *Croy* —4C **134**
Rathbone St. *E16* —6H **65**

Rathbone St. *W1*
   —5G **61** (6B **142**)
Rathcoole Av. *N8* —5K **29**
Rathcoole Gdns. *N8* —5K **29**
Rathfern Rd. *SE6* —1B **112**
Rathgar Av. *W13* —1B **72**
Rathgar Clo. *N3* —2H **27**
Rathgar Rd. *SW9* —3B **94**
Rathlin Wlk. *N1* —6C **46**
Rathmell Dri. *SW4* —6H **93**
Rathmore Rd. *SE7* —5K **81**
Rattray Rd. *SW2* —4A **94**
Raul Rd. *SE15* —2G **95**
Raveley St. *NW5* —4G **45**
Ravenet St. *SW11* —1F **93**
Ravenfield Rd. *SW17* —3D **108**
Ravenhill Rd. *E13* —2A **66**
Ravenings Pde. *Ilf* —1A **52**
Ravenna Rd. *SW15* —5F **91**
Ravenor Ct. *Gnfd* —4F **55**
Ravenor Pk. Rd. *Gnfd* —3F **55**
Raven Rd. *E18* —2A **34**
Raven Row. *E1* —5H **63**
Ravensbourne Av. *Beck & Brom*
   —7F **113**
Ravensbourne Ct. *SE6* —7C **96**
Ravensbourne Gdns. *W13*
   —5B **56**
Ravensbourne Gdns. *Ilf* —1E **34**
Ravensbourne Ho. *Brom*
   —5F **113**
Ravensbourne Pk. *SE6* —7C **96**
Ravensbourne Pk. Cres. *SE6*
   —7B **96**
Ravensbourne Pl. *SE13* —2D **96**
Ravensbourne Rd. *SE6* —7B **96**
Ravensbourne Rd. *Brom*
   —3J **127**
Ravensbourne Rd. *Twic* —6C **88**
Ravensbury Av. *Mord* —5A **122**
Ravensbury Ct. Mitc —4B **122**
   (off Ravensbury Gro.)
Ravensbury Gro. *Mitc* —4B **122**
Ravensbury La. *Mitc* —4B **122**
Ravensbury Path. *Mitc* —4B **122**
Ravensbury Rd. *SW18* —2K **107**
Ravensbury Rd. *Orp* —4K **129**
Ravensbury Ter. *SW18* —2K **107**
Ravenscar Rd. *Brom* —4G **113**
Ravens Clo. *NW9* —2A **26**
Ravens Clo. *Brom* —2H **127**
Ravens Clo. *Enf* —2K **7**
Ravenscourt Av. *W6* —4C **74**
Ravenscourt Gdns. *W6* —4C **74**
Ravenscourt Pk. *W6* —3C **74**
Ravenscourt Pk. Barn —4A **4**
Ravenscourt Pk. Mans. W6
   (off Paddenswick Rd.) —3D **74**
Ravenscourt Pl. *W6* —4D **74**
Ravenscourt Rd. *W6* —4D **74**
Ravenscourt Sq. *W6* —3C **74**
Ravenscraig Rd. *N11* —4B **16**
Ravenscroft Av. *NW11* —7H **27**
Ravenscroft Av. *Wemb* —1E **40**
Ravenscroft Clo. *E16* —5J **65**
Ravenscroft Cotts. Barn —4D **4**
Ravenscroft Cres. *SE9* —3D **114**
Ravenscroft Pk. Barn —3A **4**
Ravenscroft Rd. *E16* —5J **65**
Ravenscroft Rd. *W4* —4J **73**
Ravenscroft Rd. *Beck* —2J **125**
Ravenscroft St. *E2*
   —2F **63** (1K **145**)
Ravensdale Av. *N12* —4F **15**
Ravensdale Gdns. *SE19* —7D **110**

Ravensdale Rd. *N16* —7F **31**
Ravensdale Rd. *Houn* —3C **86**
Ravensdon St. *SE11*
    —5A **78** (6K **155**)
Ravensfield Clo. *Dag* —4D **52**
Ravensfield Gdns. *Eps* —5A **130**
Ravenshaw St. *NW6* —5H **43**
Ravenshill. *Chst* —1F **129**
Ravenshurst Av. *NW4* —4E **26**
Ravenside Clo. *N18* —5E **18**
Ravenside Retail Pk. *N18* —5E **18**
Ravenslea Rd. *SW12* —7D **92**
Ravensleigh Gdns. *Brom*
    —5K **113**
Ravensmead Rd. *Brom* —7F **113**
Ravensmede Way. *W4* —4B **74**
Ravens M. *SE12* —5J **97**
Ravenstone. *SE17*
    —5E **78** (6H **157**)
Ravenstone Rd. *N8* —3A **30**
Ravenstone Rd. *NW9* —6B **26**
Ravenstone St. *SW12* —1E **108**
Ravens Way. *SE12* —5J **97**
Ravenswood. *Bex* —1E **116**
Ravenswood Av. *W Wick*
    —1E **136**
Ravenswood Ct. *King T* —6H **105**
Ravenswood Cres. *Harr* —2D **38**
Ravenswood Cres. *W Wick*
    —1E **136**
Ravenswood Gdns. *Iswth* —1J **87**
Ravenswood Ind. Est. *E17*
    —4E **32**
Ravenswood Rd. *E17* —4E **32**
Ravenswood Rd. *SW12* —7F **93**
Ravenswood Rd. *Croy* —3B **134**
Ravensworth Rd. *NW10* —3D **58**
Ravensworth Rd. *SE9* —4D **114**
Ravent Rd. *SE11*
    —4K **77** (3H **155**)
Ravey St. *EC2* —4E **62** (3G **145**)
Ravine Gro. *SE18* —6J **83**
Rawalpindi Ho. *E16* —4H **65**
Rawchester Clo. *SW18* —1H **107**
Rawlings St. *SW3*
    —4D **76** (3E **152**)
Rawlins Clo. *N3* —3G **27**
Rawlins Clo. *S Croy* —7B **136**
Rawlinson Ct. *NW2* —7E **26**
Rawlinson Ho. *SE13* —4F **97**
    (off Mercator Rd.)
Rawlinson Point. *E16* —5H **65**
    (off Fox Rd.)
Rawlinson Ter. *N17* —3F **31**
Rawnsley Av. *Mitc* —5B **122**
Rawreth Wlk. *N1* —1C **62**
    (off Basire St.)
Rawson St. *SW11* —1E **92**
    (in two parts)
Rawsthorne Clo. *E16* —1D **82**
Rawsthorne Ct. *Houn* —4D **86**
Rawstone Wlk. *E13* —2J **65**
Rawstorne Pl. *EC1*
    —3B **62** (1A **144**)
Rawstorne St. *EC1*
    —3B **62** (1A **144**)
Raybell Ct. *Iswth* —2A **88**
Rayburne Ct. *W14* —3G **75**
Rayburne Ct. *Buck H* —1F **21**
Raydean Rd. *New Bar* —5E **4**
Raydons Gdns. *Dag* —5E **52**
Raydons Rd. *Dag* —5E **52**
Raydon St. *N19* —2F **45**
Rayfield Clo. *Brom* —6C **128**
Rayford Av. *SE12* —7H **97**

Ray Gdns. *Bark* —2A **68**
Ray Gdns. *Stan* —5G **11**
Ray Ho. *N1* —1E **62**
    (off Colville Est.)
Rayleas Clo. *SE18* —1F **99**
Rayleigh Av. *Tedd* —6J **103**
Rayleigh Clo. *N13* —3J **17**
Rayleigh Ct. *N22* —1C **30**
Rayleigh Ct. *King T* —2G **119**
Rayleigh Rise. *S Croy* —6E **134**
Rayleigh Rd. *N13* —3H **17**
Rayleigh Rd. *SW19* —1H **121**
Rayleigh Rd. *Wfd G* —6F **21**
Ray Lodge Rd. *Wfd G* —6F **21**
Ray Massey Way. *E6* —1C **66**
    (off High St. N.)
Raymead Av. *T Hth* —5A **124**
Raymede Towers. *W10* —5F **59**
    (off Treverton St.)
Raymere Gdns. *SE18* —7H **83**
Raymond Av. *E18* —3H **33**
Raymond Av. *W13* —3A **72**
Raymond Bldgs. *WC1*
    —5K **61** (5H **143**)
Raymond Clo. *SE26* —5J **111**
Raymond Ct. *N10* —7A **16**
Raymond Ct. *Sutt* —6K **131**
Raymond Postage Ct. *SE28*
    —7B **68**
Raymond Rd. *E13* —1A **66**
Raymond Rd. *SW19* —6G **107**
Raymond Rd. *Beck* —4A **126**
Raymond Rd. *Ilf* —7H **35**
Raymouth Ho. *SE16* —4J **79**
    (off Rotherhithe New Rd.)
Raymouth Rd. *SE16* —4H **79**
Raynald Ho. *SW16* —3J **109**
Rayne Ct. *E18* —4H **33**
Rayners Clo. *Wemb* —5D **40**
Rayners La. *Pinn & Harr* —5D **22**
Rayners Rd. *SW15* —5G **91**
Rayner Towers. *E10* —7C **32**
Raynes Av. *E11* —7A **34**
Raynes Pk. Bri. *SW20* —2E **120**
Raynham Av. *N18* —6B **18**
Raynham Rd. *W6* —4D **74**
Raynham Ter. *N18* —5B **18**
Raynor Clo. *S'hall* —1D **70**
Raynor Pl. *N1* —1C **62**
Raynton Clo. *Harr* —1C **38**
Rays Av. *N18* —4D **18**
Rays Rd. *N18* —4D **18**
Rays Rd. *W Wick* —7E **126**
Ray St. *EC1* —4A **62** (4K **143**)
Ray St. Bri. *EC1* —4A **62** (4K **143**)
Ray Wlk. *N7* —2K **45**
Reachview Clo. *NW1* —7G **45**
Read Ct. *E17* —6C **32**
Reade Ct. *W3* —3J **73**
    (off Stanley Rd.)
Reade Wlk. *NW10* —7A **42**
Read Ho. *SE11* —6A **78** (7J **155**)
Reading La. *E8* —6H **47**
Reading Rd. *N'holt* —5F **39**
Reading Rd. *Sutt* —5A **132**
Reading Way. *NW7* —5A **14**
Reads Clo. *Ilf* —3F **51**
Reapers Clo. *NW1* —1H **61**
Reapers Way. *Iswth* —5H **87**
Reardon Ct. *N21* —2H **17**
Reardon Path. *E1* —1H **79**
Reardon St. *E1* —1H **79**
Reaston St. *SE14* —7K **79**
Rebecca Ter. *SE16* —3J **79**

Reckitt Rd. *W4* —5A **74**
Record St. *SE15* —6J **79**
Recovery St. *SW17* —5C **108**
Recreation Av. *Romf* —5J **37**
Recreation Rd. *SE26* —4K **111**
Recreation Rd. *Brom* —2H **127**
Recreation Rd. *Sidc* —3J **115**
Recreation Rd. *S'hall* —4C **70**
Recreation Way. *Mitc* —3J **123**
Rector St. *N1* —1C **62**
Rectory Bus. Cen. *Sidc* —4B **116**
Rectory Clo. *E4* —3H **19**
Rectory Clo. *N3* —1H **27**
Rectory Clo. *SW20* —3E **120**
Rectory Clo. *Sidc* —4B **116**
Rectory Clo. *Stan* —5G **11**
Rectory Ct. *E18* —1H **33**
Rectory Ct. *Felt* —4A **102**
Rectory Ct. *Wall* —4G **133**
Rectory Cres. *E11* —6A **34**
Rectory Farm Rd. *Enf* —1E **6**
Rectory Field Cres. *SE7* —7A **82**
Rectory Gdns. *N8* —4J **29**
Rectory Gdns. *SW4* —3G **93**
Rectory Gdns. *Beck* —1C **126**
Rectory Gdns. *N'holt* —1D **54**
Rectory Grn. *Beck* —1B **126**
Rectory Gro. *SW4* —3G **93**
Rectory Gro. *Croy* —2B **134**
Rectory Gro. *Hamp* —4D **102**
Rectory La. *SW17* —6E **108**
Rectory La. *Edgw* —6B **12**
Rectory La. *Sidc* —4B **116**
Rectory La. *Stan* —5G **11**
Rectory La. *Surb* —7B **118**
Rectory La. *Wall* —4G **133**
Rectory Orchard. *SW19* —4G **107**
Rectory Pk. Av. *N'holt* —3C **54**
Rectory Pl. *SE18* —4E **82**
Rectory Rd. *E12* —5D **50**
Rectory Rd. *E17* —4D **32**
Rectory Rd. *N16* —2F **47**
Rectory Rd. *SW13* —2C **90**
Rectory Rd. *W3* —1H **73**
Rectory Rd. *Beck* —1C **126**
Rectory Rd. *Dag* —6H **53**
Rectory Rd. *Houn* —2A **86**
Rectory Rd. *Kes* —7B **138**
Rectory Rd. *S'hall* —3D **70**
Rectory Rd. *Sutt* —3J **131**
Rectory Sq. *E1* —5K **63**
Reculver Ho. *SE15* —6J **79**
    (off Lovelinch Clo.)
Reculver M. *N18* —4B **18**
Reculver Rd. *SE16* —5K **79**
Red Anchor Clo. *SW3*
    —6B **76** (7B **152**)
Redan Pl. *W2* —6K **59**
Redan St. *W14* —3F **75**
Redan Ter. *SE5* —2B **94**
Red Barracks Rd. *SE18* —4D **82**
Redberry Gro. *SE26* —3J **111**
Redbourne Av. *N3* —1J **27**
Redbridge Enterprise Cen. *Ilf*
    —2G **51**
Redbridge Gdns. *SE5* —7E **78**
Redbridge La. E. *Ilf* —6B **34**
Redbridge La. W. *E11* —6K **33**
Redbridge Roundabout. (Junct.)
    —6B **34**
Redburn St. *SW3*
    —6D **76** (7E **152**)
Redburn Trad. Est. *Enf* —6E **8**
Redcar Clo. *N'holt* —5F **39**
Redcar St. *SE5* —7C **78**

Redcastle Clo. *E1* —7J **63**
Red Cedars Rd. *Orp* —7J **129**
Redchurch St. *E2*
    —4F **63** (3J **145**)
Redcliffe Clo. *SW5* —5K **75**
Redcliffe Gdns. *SW5 & SW10*
    —5K **75**
Redcliffe Gdns. *Ilf* —1E **50**
Redcliffe M. *SW10* —5K **75**
Redcliffe Pl. *SW10* —6A **76**
Redcliffe Rd. *SW10* —5A **76**
Redcliffe Sq. *SW10* —5K **75**
Redcliffe St. *SW10* —6K **75**
Redcliffe Wlk. *Wemb* —3H **41**
Redclose Av. *Mord* —5J **121**
Redclyffe Rd. *E6* —1A **66**
Redcourt. *Croy* —3E **134**
Redcroft Rd. *S'hall* —7G **55**
Redcross Way. *SE1*
    —2C **78** (6D **150**)
Redding. *Sidc* —6B **116**
Reddings Clo. *NW7* —4G **13**
Reddings, The. *NW7* —3G **13**
Reddins Rd. *SE15* —7G **79**
Reddons Rd. *Beck* —7A **112**
Redenham Ho. *SW15* —7C **90**
    (off Tangley Gro.)
Rede Pl. *W2* —6J **59**
Redesdale Gdns. *Iswth* —7A **72**
Redesdale St. *SW3*
    —6C **76** (7D **152**)
Redfern Av. *Houn* —7E **86**
Redfern Ho. *E13* —1H **65**
    (off Redriffe Rd.)
Redfern Rd. *NW10* —7A **42**
Redfern Rd. *SE6* —7E **96**
Redfield La. *SW5* —4J **75**
Redfield M. *SW5* —4J **75**
Redford Av. *T Hth* —4K **123**
Redford Av. *Wall* —6J **133**
Redford Wlk. *N1* —1C **62**
    (off Popham St.)
Redgate Dri. *Brom* —2K **137**
Redgate Ter. *SW15* —6F **91**
Redgrave Clo. *Croy* —6F **125**
Redgrave Rd. *SW15* —3F **91**
Red Hill. *Chst* —5F **115**
Redhill Ct. *SW2* —2A **110**
Redhill Dri. *Edgw* —2H **25**
Redhill St. *NW1* —2F **61** (1K **141**)
Red Ho. La. *Bexh* —4D **100**
Red Ho. Sq. *N1* —7C **46**
    (off Ashby Gro.)
Redington Gdns. *NW3* —4K **43**
Redington Rd. *NW3* —3K **43**
Redlands. *N15* —4D **30**
Redlands. *Tedd* —6A **104**
Redlands Ct. *Brom* —7H **113**
Redlands Rd. *Enf* —1F **9**
Redlands, The. *Beck* —2D **126**
Redlands Way. *SW2* —7K **93**
Redleaf Clo. *Belv* —6G **85**
Redlees Clo. *Iswth* —4A **88**
Red Lion Clo. *SE17*
    —6D **78** (7E **156**)
Red Lion Clo. *EC4*
    —6A **62** (1K **149**)
Red Lion Ct. *SE1*
    —1C **78** (4D **150**)
Red Lion Hill. *N2* —2B **28**
Red Lion La. *SE18* —7E **82**
Red Lion Pde. *Pinn* —3C **22**
Red Lion Pl. *SE18* —1E **98**
Red Lion Rd. *Surb* —7G **119**

Red Lion Row. *SE17*
    —6C **78** (7D **156**)
Red Lion Sq. *SW18* —5J **91**
Red Lion Sq. *WC1*
    —5K **61** (6G **143**)
Red Lion St. *WC1*
    —5K **61** (5G **143**)
Red Lion St. *Rich* —5D **88**
Red Lion Yd. *W1*
    —1F **77** (4H **147**)
Red Lodge. *W Wick* —1E **136**
Red Lodge Cres. *Bex* —3K **117**
Red Lodge Rd. *Bex* —3K **117**
Red Lodge Rd. *W Wick* —1E **136**
Redman Clo. *N'holt* —2A **54**
Redman's Rd. *E1* —5J **63**
Redmead La. *E1* —1G **79**
Redmond Ho. *N1* —1K **61**
    (off Barnsbury Est.)
Redmore Rd. *W6* —4D **74**
Red Path. *E9* —6A **48**
Red Pl. *W1* —7E **60** (2G **147**)
Redpoll Way. *Eri* —3D **84**
Red Post Hill. *SE24 & SE21*
    —4D **94**
Red Post Ho. *E6* —7B **50**
Redriffe Rd. *E13* —1H **65**
Redriff Est. *SE16* —3B **80**
Redriff Rd. *SE16* —4K **79**
Redriff Rd. *Romf* —2H **37**
Redroofs Clo. *Beck* —1D **126**
Redrose Trad. Cen. *Barn* —5G **5**
Red Rover. (Junct.) —4C **90**
Redruth Clo. *N22* —7E **16**
Redruth Clo. *Sutt* —7K **131**
Redruth Rd. *E9* —1J **63**
Redstart Clo. *E6* —5C **66**
Redstart Clo. *SE14* —7A **80**
Redston Rd. *N8* —4H **29**
Redvers Rd. *N22* —2A **30**
Redvers St. *N1* —3E **62** (1H **145**)
Redwald Rd. *E5* —4K **47**
Redway Dri. *Twic* —7G **87**
Redwing Path. *SE28* —3H **83**
Redwood Clo. *N14* —7C **6**
Redwood Clo. *SE16* —1A **80**
Redwood Clo. *Buck H* —2E **20**
Redwood Clo. *Sidc* —3A **100**
Redwood Ct. *N19* —7H **29**
Redwood Ct. *NW6* —7G **43**
Redwood Ct. *N'holt* —3C **54**
Redwood Ct. *Surb* —7D **118**
Redwood Est. *Houn* —6A **70**
Redwood Mans. *W8* —3K **75**
    (off Chantry Sq.)
Redwoods. *SW15* —1C **106**
Redwood Way. *Barn* —5A **4**
Reece M. *SW7* —4B **76** (3A **152**)
Reed Clo. *E16* —5J **65**
Reed Clo. *SE12* —5J **97**
Reede Gdns. *Dag* —5H **53**
Reede Rd. *Dag* —6G **53**
Reede Way. *Dag* —6H **53**
Reedham Clo. *N17* —4H **31**
Reedham St. *SE15* —2G **95**
Reedholm Vs. *N16* —4D **46**
Reed Rd. *N17* —2F **31**
Reed's Pl. *NW1* —7G **45**
Reedworth St. *SE11*
    —4A **78** (4K **155**)
Reenglass Rd. *Stan* —4J **11**
Rees Dri. *Stan* —4K **11**
Rees Gdns. *Croy* —6F **125**
Reesland Clo. *E12* —5E **50**
Rees St. *N1* —1C **62**

Reets Farm Clo. *NW9* —6A **26**
Reeves Av. *NW9* —7K **25**
Reeves Corner. *Croy* —2B **134**
Reeves M. *W1* —7E **60** (3G **147**)
Reeves Rd. *E3* —4D **64**
Reeves Rd. *SE18* —6F **83**
Reform Row. *N17* —2F **31**
Reform St. *SW11* —2D **92**
Regal Clo. *E1* —5G **63**
Regal Clo. *W5* —5D **56**
Regal Ct. *N18* —5A **18**
Regal Cres. *Wall* —3F **133**
Regal Dri. *N11* —5K **15**
Regal La. *NW1* —1E **60**
Regal Pl. *E3* —3B **64**
Regal Pl. *SW6* —7K **75**
(off Maxwell Rd.)
Regal Row. *SE15* —1J **95**
Regal Way. *Harr* —6D **24**
Regan Ho. *N18* —4A **18**
Regan Way. *N1* —2E **62**
Regatta Ho. *Tedd* —4A **104**
Regency Clo. *W5* —6E **56**
Regency Clo. *Hamp* —5D **102**
Regency Ct. *Enf* —5J **7**
Regency Ct. *Sutt* —4K **131**
Regency Ct. *Tedd* —6B **104**
Regency Cres. *NW4* —2F **27**
Regency Lodge. *NW3* —7B **44**
(off Adelaide Rd.)
Regency Lodge. *Buck H* —2G **21**
Regency M. *NW10* —6C **42**
Regency M. *Back* —1E **126**
Regency M. *Iswth* —5J **87**
Regency Pl. *SW1*
—4H **77** (3C **154**)
Regency St. *SW1*
—4H **77** (3D **154**)
Regency Wlk. *Croy* —6A **126**
Regency Wlk. *Rich* —5E **88**
(off Grosvenor Av.)
Regency Way. *Bexh* —3D **100**
Regent Clo. *N12* —5F **15**
Regent Clo. *Harr* —6E **24**
Regent Clo. *Houn* —1A **86**
Regent Ct. *N3* —7E **14**
Regent Ct. *N20* —2F **15**
Regent Gdns. *Ilf* —7A **36**
Regent Pl. *SW19* —6A **108**
Regent Pl. *W1* —7G **61** (2B **148**)
Regent Pl. *Croy* —1F **135**
Regent Rd. *SE24* —6B **94**
Regent Rd. *Surb* —5F **119**
Regents Av. *N13* —5F **17**
Regent's Bri. Gdns. *SW8* —7J **77**
Regents Clo. *S Croy* —6E **134**
Regents Clo. *Stan* —4K **11**
Regents Ct. *Brom* —7H **113**
Regents M. *NW8* —2A **60**
Regents Pk. Est. *NW1*
—3G **61** (1A **142**)
Regent's Pk. Gdns. M. *NW1*
—1D **60**
Regents Pk. Rd. *N3* —3H **27**
Regent's Pk. Rd. *NW1* —1D **60**
(in two parts)
Regent's Pk. Ter. *NW1* —1F **61**
Regent's Pl. *SE3* —2J **97**
Regents Plaza. *NW6* —2J **59**
(off Kilburn High Rd.)
Regent Sq. *E3* —3D **64**
Regent Sq. *WC1* —3J **61** (2F **143**)
Regent Sq. *Belv* —4H **85**
Regent's Row. *E8* —1G **63**

Regent St. *NW10* —3F **59**
Regent St. *W1 & SW1*
—6F **61** (7K **141**)
Regent St. *W4* —5G **73**
Regents Wharf. E2 —1G **63**
(off Wharf Pl.)
Regents Wharf. *N1* —2K **61**
Regina Clo. *Barn* —3A **4**
Regina Ho. *SE18* —1K **125**
Reginald Rd. *E7* —6J **49**
Reginald Rd. *SE8* —7C **80**
Reginald Sq. *SE8* —7C **80**
Regina Rd. *N4* —1K **45**
Regina Rd. *SE25* —3G **125**
Regina Rd. *W13* —1A **72**
Regina Rd. *S'hall* —4C **70**
Regina Ter. *W13* —1A **72**
Regis Ct. *N8* —4K **29**
Regis Rd. *NW5* —5F **45**
Regnart Bldgs. *NW1*
—4G **61** (3B **142**)
Reidhaven Rd. *SE18* —4J **83**
Reigate Av. *Sutt* —1J **131**
Reigate Rd. *Brom* —3H **113**
Reigate Rd. *Ilf* —2K **51**
Reigate Way. *Wall* —5J **133**
Reighton Rd. *E5* —3G **47**
Reinickendorf Av. *SE9* —5G **99**
Relay Rd. *W12* —1E **74**
Relf Rd. *SE15* —3G **95**
Reliance Arc. *SW9* —4A **94**
Reliance Sq. *EC2*
—4E **62** (3H **145**)
Relko Gdns. *Sutt* —5B **132**
Relton M. *SW7* —3C **76** (1D **152**)
Rembrandt Clo. *E14* —3F **81**
Rembrandt Clo. *SW1*
—5E **76** (4G **153**)
Rembrandt Rd. *SE13* —4G **97**
Rembrandt Rd. *Edgw* —2G **25**
Rememberance Rd. *E7* —4B **50**
Remington Rd. *E6* —6C **66**
Remington Rd. *N15* —6D **30**
Remington St. *N1*
—2B **62** (1B **144**)
Remnant St. *WC2*
—6K **61** (7G **143**)
Rempstone M. *N1* —2D **62**
Remus Rd. *E3* —7C **48**
Rendle Clo. *Croy* —5F **125**
Rendlesham Rd. *E5* —4G **47**
Rendlesham Rd. *Enf* —1G **7**
Renforth St. *SE16* —2J **79**
Renfrew Clo. *E6* —7E **66**
Renfrew Ct. *Houn* —2C **86**
Renfrew Rd. *SE11*
—4B **78** (3A **156**)
Renfrew Rd. *Houn* —2C **86**
Renfrew Rd. *King T* —7H **105**
Renmuir St. *SW17* —6D **108**
Rennell St. *SE13* —3E **96**
Rennels Way. *Iswth* —2J **87**
Renness Rd. *E17* —3A **32**
Rennets Clo. *SE9* —5J **99**
Rennets Wood Rd. *SE9* —5H **99**
Rennie Ct. *SE1* —1E **78** (4A **149**)
Rennie Est. *SE16* —4H **79**
Rennie St. *SE1* —1B **78** (4A **150**)
Renown Clo. *Croy* —1B **134**
Renown Clo. *Romf* —1G **37**
Rensburg Rd. *E17* —5K **31**
Renshaw Clo. *Belv* —6F **85**
Renters Av. *NW4* —6E **26**
Renton Clo. *SW2* —6K **93**
Renwick Rd. *Bark* —4B **68**

Repens Way. *Hayes* —4B **54**
Rephidim St. *SE1*
—3E **78** (2G **157**)
Replingham Rd. *SW18* —1H **107**
Reporton Rd. *SW6* —7G **75**
Repository Rd. *SE18* —6D **82**
Repton Av. *Wemb* —4C **40**
Repton Clo. *Cars* —5C **132**
Repton Ct. *E5* —3A **48**
Repton Ct. *Beck* —1D **126**
Repton Ct. *Ilf* —1D **34**
Repton Gro. *Ilf* —1D **34**
Repton Rd. *Harr* —4F **25**
Repton St. *E14* —6A **64**
Repulse Clo. *Romf* —1H **37**
Reservoir Rd. *N14* —5B **6**
Reservoir Rd. *SE4* —2A **96**
Resolution Wlk. *SE18* —3D **82**
Resource Cen. *E6* —5E **66**
Restell Clo. *SE3* —6G **81**
Restmor Way. *Wall* —2E **132**
Reston Pl. *SW7* —2A **76**
Restons Cres. *SE9* —6H **99**
Restormel Clo. *Houn* —5E **86**
Restormel Ho. *SE11*
—4A **78** (4K **155**)
Retcar Clo. *NW5* —2F **45**
Retcar Pl. *N19* —2F **45**
(off Retcar Clo.)
Retford St. *N1* —2E **62** (1H **145**)
Retingham Way. *E4* —2J **19**
Retles Ct. *Harr* —7H **23**
Retreat Ho. *E9* —6J **47**
Retreat Pl. *E9* —6J **47**
Retreat Rd. *Rich* —5D **88**
Retreat, The. *NW9* —5K **25**
Retreat, The. *SW14* —3A **90**
Retreat, The. *Harr* —7E **22**
Retreat, The. *Surb* —6F **119**
Retreat, The. *T Hth* —4D **124**
Retreat, The. *Wor Pk* —3D **130**
Reubens Ct. *W4* —5H **73**
(off Chaseley Dri.)
Reunion Row. *E1* —7H **63**
Reveley Sq. *SE16* —2A **80**
Revell Rise. *SE18* —6K **83**
Revell Rd. *King T* —2H **119**
Revell Rd. *Sutt* —6H **131**
Revelon Rd. *SE4* —4A **96**
Revelstoke Rd. *SW18* —2H **107**
Reventlow Rd. *SE9* —1G **115**
Reverdy Rd. *SE1*
—4G **79** (4K **157**)
Reverend Clo. *Harr* —3F **39**
Revesby Rd. *Cars* —6C **122**
Review Rd. *NW2* —2B **42**
Review Rd. *Dag* —2H **69**
Rewell St. *SW6* —7A **76**
Rewley Rd. *Cars* —6B **122**
Rex Clo. *Romf* —1H **37**
Rex Pl. *W1* —7E **60** (3H **147**)
Reydon Av. *E11* —6A **34**
Reynard Clo. *SE4* —3A **96**
Reynard Clo. *Brom* —3E **128**
Reynard Dri. *SE19* —7F **111**
Reynard Mills Trad. Est. *Bren*
—5C **72**
Reynardson Rd. *N17* —7H **17**
Reynolds Av. *E12* —5E **50**
Reynolds Av. *Chad H* —7C **36**
Reynolds Clo. *NW11* —7K **27**
Reynolds Clo. *SW19* —1B **122**
Reynolds Clo. *Cars* —1D **132**
Reynolds Ct. *Romf* —3D **36**

Reynolds Dri. *Edgw* —3F **25**
Reynolds Pl. *SE3* —7K **81**
Reynolds Pl. *Rich* —6F **89**
Reynolds Rd. *SE15* —4J **95**
Reynolds Rd. *W4* —3J **73**
Reynolds Rd. *Hayes* —4A **54**
Reynolds Rd. *N Mald* —7K **119**
Reynolds Way. *Croy* —4E **134**
Rheidol M. *N1* —2C **62**
Rheidol Ter. *N1* —1C **62**
Rheingold Way. *Wall* —7J **133**
Rhein Ho. *N8* —3J **29**
(off Campsfield Rd.)
Rheola Clo. *N17* —1F **31**
Rhoda St. *E2* —4F **63** (3K **145**)
Rhodes Av. *N22* —1G **29**
Rhodes Ho. *W12* —1D **74**
(off White City Est.)
Rhodesia Rd. *E11* —2F **49**
Rhodesia Rd. *SW9* —2J **93**
Rhodesmoor Ho. Ct. *Mord*
—6J **121**
Rhodes St. *N7* —5K **45**
Rhodeswell Rd. *E14* —5A **64**
Rhondda Gro. *E3* —3A **64**
Rhyl Rd. *Gnfd* —2K **55**
Rhyl St. *NW5* —6E **44**
Rhys Av. *N11* —7C **16**
Rialto Rd. *Mitc* —2E **122**
Ribble Clo. *Wfd G* —6F **21**
Ribblesdale Av. *N'holt* —6F **39**
Ribblesdale Rd. *N8* —4K **29**
Ribblesdale Rd. *SW16* —6F **109**
Ribbon Dance M. *SE5* —1D **94**
Ribchester Av. *Gnfd* —3K **55**
Ribston Clo. *Brom* —1D **138**
Ricardo Path. *SE28* —1C **84**
Ricardo St. *E14* —6D **64**
Ricards Rd. *SW19* —5H **107**
Riccall Ct. *NW9* —1A **26**
(off Pageant Av.)
Rice Pde. *Orp* —5H **129**
Richard Clo. *SE18* —4C **82**
Richard Fell Ho. *E12* —4E **50**
(off Walton Rd.)
Richard Foster Clo. *E17* —7B **32**
Richard Ho. Dri. *E16* —7B **66**
Richards Av. *Romf* —6J **37**
Richards Clo. *Bush* —1C **10**
Richards Clo. *Harr* —5A **24**
Richard Sharples Ct. *Sutt*
—7A **132**
Richardson Clo. *E8* —1F **63**
Richardson Ct. *SW4* —2J **93**
(off Studley Rd.)
Richardson Rd. *E15* —2G **65**
Richardson's M. *W1*
—4G **61** (4A **142**)
Richards Pl. *E17* —3C **32**
Richard's Pl. *SW3*
—4C **76** (3D **152**)
Richard St. *E1* —6H **63**
Richbell Pl. *WC1*
—5K **61** (5G **143**)
Richborne Ter. *SW8* —7K **77**
Richborough Ho. *SE15* —6J **79**
(off Sharratt St.)
Richborough Rd. *NW2* —4G **43**
Riches Rd. *Ilf* —2G **51**
Richfield Rd. *Bush* —1B **10**
Richford Ga. *W6* —3E **74**
Richford Rd. *E15* —1H **65**
Richford St. *W6* —2E **74**
Richlands Av. *Eps* —4C **130**
Rich La. *SW5* —5K **75**

Richmond Av. *E4* —5A **20**
Richmond Av. *N1* —1K **61**
Richmond Av. *NW10* —6E **42**
Richmond Av. *SW20* —1G **121**
Richmond Bri. *Twic & Rich*
—6D **88**
Richmond Bldgs. *W1*
—6H **61** (1C **148**)
Richmond Circus. (Junct.)
—4E **88**
Richmond Clo. *E17* —6B **32**
Richmond Cotts. *W14* —4G **75**
(off Hammersmith Rd.)
Richmond Ct. *SW1*
—2D **76** (7F **147**)
(off Sloane St.)
Richmond Ct. *Wemb* —3F **41**
Richmond Cres. *E4* —5A **20**
Richmond Cres. *N1* —1K **61**
Richmond Cres. *N9* —1B **18**
Richmond Gdns. *NW4* —5C **26**
Richmond Gdns. *Harr* —6E **10**
Richmond Grn. *Croy* —3J **133**
Richmond Gro. *N1* —7B **46**
Richmond Gro. *Surb* —6F **119**
Richmond Hill. *Rich* —6E **88**
Richmond Hill Ct. *Rich* —6E **88**
Richmond Mans. *Twic* —6D **88**
Richmond M. *W1*
—6H **61** (1C **148**)
Richmond M. *Tedd* —5K **103**
Richmond Pde. Twic —6C **88**
(off Richmond Rd.)
Richmond Pk. Rd. *SW14* —5J **89**
Richmond Pk. Rd. *King T*
—7E **104**
Richmond Pl. *SE18* —4G **83**
Richmond Rd. *E4* —1A **20**
Richmond Rd. *E7* —5K **49**
Richmond Rd. *E8* —7F **47**
Richmond Rd. *E11* —2F **49**
Richmond Rd. *N2* —2A **28**
Richmond Rd. *N11* —6D **16**
Richmond Rd. *N15* —6E **30**
Richmond Rd. *SW20* —1D **120**
Richmond Rd. *W5* —2E **72**
Richmond Rd. *Croy* —3J **133**
Richmond Rd. *Ilf* —3G **51**
Richmond Rd. *Iswth* —3A **88**
Richmond Rd. *King T* —5D **104**
Richmond Rd. *New Bar* —5E **4**
Richmond Rd. *T Hth* —3B **124**
Richmond Rd. *Twic* —7B **88**
Richmond Ter. *SW1*
—2J **77** (6E **148**)
Richmond Ter. M. *SW1*
—2J **77** (6E **148**)
Richmond Way. *E11* —2J **49**
Richmond Way. *W12 & W14*
—2F **75**
Richmount Gdns. *SE3* —3J **97**
Rich St. *E14* —7B **64**
Rickard Clo. *NW4* —4D **26**
Rickard Clo. *SW2* —1A **110**
Rickett St. *SW6* —6J **75**
Rickman St. *E1* —4J **63**
Rickmansworth Rd. *Pinn* —2A **22**
Rick Roberts Way. *E15* —2E **64**
Rickthorne Rd. *N19* —2J **45**
Rickyard Path. *SE9* —4C **98**
Ridding La. *Gnfd* —5K **39**
Riddons Rd. *SE12* —3A **114**
Rideout St. *SE18* —4D **82**
Rider Clo. *Sidc* —6J **99**

Ride, The. *Bren* —4C **72**
Ride, The. *Enf* —4E **8**
Ridgdale St. *E3* —2D **64**
Ridge Av. *N21* —7H **7**
Ridgebrook Rd. *SE3* —3B **98**
Ridge Clo. *NW4* —2F **27**
Ridge Clo. *NW9* —4K **25**
Ridge Ct. *SE22* —7G **95**
Ridge Crest. *Enf* —1E **6**
Ridgecroft Clo. *Bex* —1J **117**
Ridge Hill. *NW11* —1G **43**
Ridgemont Gdns. *Edgw* —4D **12**
Ridgemount Av. *Croy* —1K **135**
Ridgemount Clo. *SE20* —7H **111**
Ridgemount Gdns. *Enf* —3G **7**
Ridge Rd. *N8* —6K **29**
Ridge Rd. *N21* —1H **17**
Ridge Rd. *NW2* —3H **43**
Ridge Rd. *Mitc* —7F **109**
Ridge Rd. *Sutt* —1G **131**
Ridge, The. *Barn* —5C **4**
Ridge, The. *Bex* —7F **101**
Ridge, The. *Surb* —5G **119**
Ridge, The. *Twic* —7H **87**
Ridgeview Clo. *Barn* —6A **4**
Ridgeview Rd. *N20* —3E **14**
Ridge Way. *SE19* —6E **110**
Ridgeway. *Brom* —2J **137**
Ridge Way. *Felt* —3C **102**
Ridgeway. *Rich* —6E **88**
Ridge Way. *Wfd G* —4F **21**
Ridgeway Av. *Barn* —6J **5**
Ridgeway Dri. *Brom* —4K **113**
Ridgeway E. *Sidc* —5K **99**
Ridgeway Gdns. *N6* —7H **29**
Ridgeway Gdns. *Ilf* —5C **34**
Ridgeway Rd. *Iswth* —7J **71**
Ridgeway Rd. N. *Iswth* —7J **71**
Ridgeways Pl. *EC2*
　—3E **62** (2G **145**)
Ridgeway, The. *E4* —1K **19**
Ridgeway, The. *N3* —7E **14**
Ridgeway, The. *N11* —4J **15**
Ridgeway, The. *N14* —2D **16**
Ridgeway, The. *NW7* —4J **13**
Ridgeway, The. *NW9* —4K **25**
Ridgeway, The. *NW11* —1H **43**
Ridgeway, The. *W3* —3G **73**
Ridgeway, The. *Croy* —3K **133**
Ridgeway, The. *Kent* —6C **24**
Ridgeway, The. *N Har* —5D **22**
(in two parts)
Ridgeway, The. *Pot B & Enf*
　—1E **6**
Ridgeway, The. *Stan* —6H **11**
Ridgeway Wlk. *N'holt* —6C **38**
(off Arnold Rd.)
Ridgeway W. *Sidc* —5J **99**
Ridgewell Clo. *N1* —1C **62**
Ridgewell Clo. *SE26* —4B **112**
Ridgewell Clo. *Dag* —1H **69**
Ridgmount Gdns. *WC1*
　—5H **61** (5C **142**)
Ridgmount Pl. *WC1*
　—5H **61** (5C **142**)
Ridgmount Rd. *SW18* —5K **91**
Ridgmount St. *WC1*
　—5H **61** (5C **142**)
Ridgway. *SW19* —7E **106**
Ridgway Ct. *SW19* —6F **107**
Ridgway Gdns. *SW19* —7F **107**
Ridgway Pl. *SW19* —6G **107**
Ridgway Rd. *SW9* —3B **94**
Ridgway, The. *Sutt* —6B **132**
Ridgwell Rd. *E16* —5A **66**

Riding Ho. St. *W1*
　—5F **61** (6K **141**)
Ridings Av. *N21* —5H **7**
Ridings Clo. *N6* —7G **29**
Ridings, The. *E11* —5J **33**
Ridings, The. *W5* —5F **57**
Ridings, The. *Barn* —7G **5**
Ridings, The. *Ewe* —7B **130**
Ridings, The. *Surb* —5G **119**
Riding, The. *NW11* —7H **27**
Ridler Rd. *Enf* —1K **7**
Ridley Av. *W13* —3B **72**
Ridley Clo. *SW16* —6J **109**
Ridley Rd. *E7* —4A **50**
Ridley Rd. *E8* —5F **47**
Ridley Rd. *NW10* —2C **58**
Ridley Rd. *SW19* —7K **107**
Ridley Rd. *Brom* —3H **127**
Ridley Rd. *Well* —1B **100**
Ridley Several. *SE3* —2J **97**
Ridsdale Rd. *SE20* —1H **125**
Riefield Rd. *SE9* —4G **99**
Riesco Dri. *Croy* —6J **135**
Riffel Rd. *NW2* —5E **42**
Rifle Ct. *SE11* —6A **78** (7K **155**)
Rifle Pl. *W11* —1F **75**
Rifle St. *E14* —5D **64**
Rigault Rd. *SW6* —2G **91**
Rigby Clo. *Croy* —3A **134**
Rigby M. *Ilf* —2E **50**
Rigden St. *E14* —6D **64**
Rigeley Rd. *NW10* —3C **58**
Rigg App. *E10* —1K **47**
Rigge Pl. *SW4* —4H **93**
Riggindale Rd. *SW16* —5H **109**
Riley Rd. *SE1* —3F **79** (1J **157**)
Riley Rd. *Enf* —1D **8**
Riley St. *SW10* —7B **76**
Rinaldo Rd. *SW12* —7F **93**
Ring Clo. *Brom* —7K **113**
Ringcroft St. *N7* —5A **46**
Ringers Rd. *Brom* —3J **127**
Ringford Rd. *SW18* —5H **91**
Ringles Ct. *E6* —1D **66**
Ringlet Clo. *E16* —5K **65**
Ringlewell Clo. *Enf* —2C **8**
Ringmer Av. *SW6* —1G **91**
Ringmer Gdns. *N19* —2J **45**
Ringmer Pl. *N21* —5J **7**
Ringmer Way. *Brom* —5C **128**
Ringmore Rise. *SE23* —7H **95**
Ring Rd. *W12* —1E **74**
Ringslade Rd. *N22* —2K **29**
Ringstead Rd. *SE6* —7D **96**
Ringstead Rd. *Sutt* —4B **132**
Ring, The. *W2* —1C **76** (2E **146**)
Ring Way. *N11* —6B **16**
Ringway. *S'hall* —5B **70**
Ringwold Clo. *Beck* —7A **112**
Ringwood Av. *N2* —2D **28**
Ringwood Av. *Croy* —7J **123**
Ringwood Clo. *Pinn* —3A **22**
Ringwood Gdns. *E14* —4C **80**
Ringwood Gdns. *SW15* —1C **106**
Ringwood Rd. *E17* —6B **32**
Ringwood Way. *N21* —1G **17**
Ringwood Way. *Hamp* —4E **102**
Ripley Clo. *Brom* —5D **128**
Ripley Clo. *New Ad* —6E **136**
Ripley Ct. *Mitc* —2B **122**
Ripley Gdns. *SW14* —3K **89**
Ripley Gdns. *Sutt* —4A **132**
Ripley M. *E11* —6G **33**
Ripley Rd. *E16* —6A **66**
Ripley Rd. *Belv* —4G **85**

Ripley Rd. *Enf* —1H **7**
Ripley Rd. *Hamp* —7E **102**
Ripley Rd. *Ilf* —2K **51**
Ripley Vs. *W5* —6C **56**
Ripon Clo. *N'holt* —5E **38**
Ripon Gdns. *Ilf* —7C **34**
Ripon Rd. *N9* —7C **8**
Ripon Rd. *N17* —3D **30**
Ripon Rd. *SE18* —6F **83**
Rippersley Rd. *Well* —1A **100**
Ripple Rd. *Bark & Dag* —7G **51**
Ripple Road Junction. (Junct.)
　—1A **68**
Rippleside Commercial Cen. *Bark*
　—2C **68**
Ripplevale Gro. *N1* —7K **45**
Rippolson Rd. *SE18* —5K **83**
Risboro' Clo. *N10* —3F **29**
Risborough Dri. *Wor Pk* —7C **120**
Risborough St. *SE1*
　—1B **78** (6B **150**)
Risdon St. *SE16* —2J **79**
Risedale Rd. *Bexh* —3J **101**
Riseholme Ct. *E9* —6B **48**
Riseldine Rd. *SE23* —6A **96**
Rise Pk. Pde. *Romf* —2K **37**
Rise, The. *E11* —5J **33**
Rise, The. *N13* —4F **17**
Rise, The. *NW7* —6G **13**
Rise, The. *NW10* —4K **41**
Rise, The. *Bex* —7C **100**
Rise, The. *Buck H* —1G **21**
Rise, The. *Edgw* —5C **12**
Rise, The. *Gnfd* —5A **40**
Risinghill St. *N1* —2K **61**
Risingholme Clo. *Bush* —1A **10**
Risingholme Clo. *Harr* —1J **23**
Risingholme Rd. *Harr* —2J **23**
Risings, The. *E17* —4F **33**
Rising Sun Ct. *EC1*
　—5B **62** (5B **144**)
Risley Av. *N17* —1C **30**
Rita Rd. *SW8* —6J **77**
Ritches Rd. *N15* —5C **30**
Ritchie Ho. *N19* —1H **45**
Ritchie Rd. *Croy* —6H **125**
Ritchie St. *N1* —2A **62**
Ritchings Av. *E17* —4A **32**
Ritherdon Rd. *SW17* —2E **108**
Ritson Ho. *N1* —1K **61**
(off Barnsbury Est.)
Ritson Rd. *E8* —6G **47**
Ritter St. *SE18* —6E **82**
Ritz Pde. *W5* —4F **57**
Rivaz Pl. *E9* —6J **47**
Rivenhall Gdns. *E18* —4H **33**
River Av. *N13* —3G **17**
River Av. *Th Dit* —7A **118**
River Bank. *N21* —7H **7**
River Bank. *Th Dit* —5A **118**
Riverbank Way. *Bren* —6C **72**
River Barge Clo. *E14* —2E **80**
River Brent Bus. Pk. *W7* —3J **71**
River Clo. *E11* —6A **34**
River Clo. *S'hall* —2G **71**
River Clo. *Surb* —5C **118**
Rivercourt Rd. *W6* —4D **74**
River Crane Way. *Felt* —2D **102**
Riverdale. *SE13* —3E **96**
Riverdale Ct. *N21* —5J **7**
Riverdale Dri. *SW18* —1K **107**
Riverdale Gdns. *Twic* —6C **88**
Riverdale Rd. *SE18* —5K **83**
Riverdale Rd. *Bex* —7F **101**
Riverdale Rd. *Eri* —5H **85**

Riverdale Rd. *Felt* —4C **102**
Riverdale Rd. *Twic* —6C **88**
Riverdene. *Edgw* —3D **12**
Riverdene Rd. *Ilf* —3E **50**
River Front. *Enf* —3K **7**
River Gdns. *Cars* —2C **132**
River Gdns. *Felt* —5A **86**
River Gdns. Bus. Cen. *Felt*
　—5A **86**
River Gro. Pk. *Beck* —1B **126**
Riverhead Clo. *E17* —2K **31**
Riverhill. *Wor Pk* —2A **130**
Riverholme Dri. *Eps* —7A **130**
River Ho. *SE26* —3H **111**
River La. *Rich* —1D **104**
Riverleigh Ct. *E4* —5G **19**
Rivermead. *King T* —5D **118**
Rivermead Clo. *Tedd* —5B **104**
Rivermead Ct. *SW6* —3H **91**
Rivermead Ho. *E9* —5A **48**
River Meads Av. *Twic* —3E **102**
River Pk. Gdns. *Brom* —7F **113**
River Pk. Rd. *N22* —2K **29**
River Pk. Trad. Est. *E14* —3C **80**
River Pl. *N1* —7C **46**
River Reach. *Tedd* —5C **104**
River Rd. *Bark* —2J **67**
River Rd. *Buck H* —1H **21**
River Rd. Bus. Pk. *Bark* —3K **67**
Riversdale Rd. *N5* —3B **46**
Riversdale Rd. *Romf* —1H **37**
Riversdale Rd. *Th Dit* —5A **118**
Riversfield Rd. *Enf* —3K **7**
Riverside. *NW4* —7D **26**
Riverside. *SE7* —3K **81**
Riverside. *Rich* —5D **88**
Riverside. *Twic* —1B **104**
Riverside Apartments. *N11*
　—5E **16**
Riverside Av. *Rich* —1E **88**
Riverside Bus. Cen. *SW18*
　—1K **107**
Riverside Bus. Cen. *Iswth*
　—4B **88**
Riverside Clo. *E5* —2J **47**
Riverside Clo. *W7* —4J **55**
Riverside Clo. *King T* —4D **118**
Riverside Clo. *Wall* —3F **133**
Riverside Cotts. *Bark* —2H **67**
Riverside Ct. *E4* —6H **9**
Riverside Ct. *SE3* —4H **97**
Riverside Ct. *E8* —6G **47**
Riverside Ct. *SW8*
　—6H **77** (7D **154**)
Riverside Ct. *Iswth* —2K **87**
(off Woodlands Rd.)
Riverside Dri. *NW11* —6G **27**
Riverside Dri. *W4* —7K **73**
Riverside Dri. *Mitc* —5C **122**
Riverside Dri. *Rich* —2B **104**
Riverside Gdns. *N3* —3G **27**
Riverside Gdns. *W6* —5D **74**
Riverside Gdns. *Enf* —2H **7**
Riverside Gdns. *Wemb* —2E **56**
Riverside Ind. Est. *SE10* —3H **81**
Riverside Ind. Est. *Bark* —3A **68**
Riverside Ind. Est. *Enf* —6F **9**
Riverside M. *Croy* —3J **133**
Riverside Rd. *E15* —2E **64**
Riverside Rd. *N15* —6G **31**
Riverside Rd. *SW17* —4K **107**
Riverside Rd. *Sidc* —3E **116**
Riverside Wlk. *N12 & N20*
　—3E **14**
Riverside Wlk. *SE10* —3G **81**

Riverside Wlk. *SW6* —3G **91**
Riverside Wlk. *W4* —6B **74**
Riverside Wlk. *Barn* —6A **4**
Riverside Wlk. *Iswth* —3J **87**
Riverside Wlk. *King T* —3D **118**
Riverside Wlk. *W Wick* —1D **136**
Riverside Works *Bark* —7F **51**
River St. *EC1* —3A **62** (1J **143**)
River Ter. *W6* —5E **74**
Riverton Clo. *W9* —3H **59**
River View. *Enf* —3H **7**
Riverview Gdns. *SW13* —6D **74**
Riverview Gdns. *Twic* —2K **103**
Riverview Gro. *W4* —6H **73**
Riverview Pk. *SE6* —2C **112**
Riverview Rd. *W4* —7H **73**
River Wlk. *W6* —7E **74**
Riverway. *N13* —4F **17**
River Way. *SE10* —3H **81**
River Way. *Eps* —5A **130**
River Way. *Twic* —2F **103**
River Wharf Bus. Pk. *Belv*
　—1K **85**
Riverwood La. *Chst* —1H **129**
Rivington Av. *Wfd G* —2B **34**
Rivington Bldgs. *EC2*
　—3E **62** (2G **145**)
Rivington Ct. *NW10* —1C **58**
Rivington Cres. *NW7* —7G **13**
Rivington Pl. *EC2*
　—3E **62** (2H **145**)
Rivington St. *EC2*
　—3E **62** (2G **145**)
Rivington Wlk. *E8* —1G **63**
Rivulet Rd. *N17* —7H **17**
Rixon St. *N7* —3A **46**
Rixsen Rd. *E12* —5C **50**
Roach Rd. *E3* —7C **64**
Roads Pl. *N19* —2J **45**
Roan St. *SE10* —6E **80**
Roants Clo. *Pinn* —6A **22**
Robb Rd. *Stan* —6F **11**
Robert Adam St. *W1*
　—6E **60** (7G **141**)
Roberta St. *E2* —3G **63**
Robert Clo. *W9* —4A **60**
Robert Dashwood Way. *SE17*
　—4C **78** (4C **156**)
Robert Keen Clo. *SE15* —1G **95**
Robert Lowe Clo. *SE14* —7K **79**
Robert Owen Ho. *SW6* —1F **91**
Robert Runcie Ct. *SW9* —4K **93**
Roberts All. *W5* —2D **72**
Robertsbridge Rd. *Cars* —1A **132**
Roberts Clo. *SE9* —1H **115**
Roberts Clo. *Sutt* —7F **131**
Roberts Ct. *SE20* —1J **125**
(off Maple Rd.)
Roberts M. *SW1*
　—3E **76** (1G **153**)
Roberts M. *Orp* —7K **129**
Robertson Rd. *E15* —1E **64**
Robertson St. *SW8* —3F **93**
Robert's Pl. *EC1*
　—4A **62** (3K **143**)
Roberts Rd. *E17* —1D **32**
Roberts Rd. *NW7* —6B **14**
Roberts Rd. *Belv* —5G **85**
Robert St. *E16* —1F **83**
Robert St. *NW1* —3F **61** (2K **141**)
Robert St. *SE18* —5H **83**
(in two parts)
Robert St. *WC2* —7J **61** (3F **149**)
Robert St. *Croy* —3C **134**

Robeson St. E3 —4B 64
Robina Clo. Bexh —4D 100
Robin Clo. NW7 —3F 13
Robin Clo. Hamp —5C 102
Robin Clo. Romf —1K 37
Robin Ct. E14 —3E 80
Robin Ct. SE16 —4F 79 (3K 157)
Robin Cres. E6 —5B 66
Robin Gro. N6 —2E 44
Robin Gro. Bren —6C 72
Robin Gro. Harr —6F 25
Robin Hill Dri. Chst —6C 114
Robin Hood. (Junct.) —3A 106
Robinhood Clo. Mitc —4G 123
Robin Hood Dri. Harr —7E 10
Robin Hood Gdns. E14 —7E 64
(off Robin Hood La.)
Robin Hood Grn. Orp —5K 129
Robin Hood La. E14 —7E 64
Robin Hood La. SW15 —4A 106
Robin Hood La. Bexh —5E 100
Robinhood La. Mitc —3G 123
Robin Hood La. Sutt —5J 131
Robin Hood Rd. SW19 & SW15 —5C 106
Robin Hood Way. SW15 & SW20 —3A 106
Robin Hood Way. Gnfd —6K 39
Robinia Cres. E10 —2C 48
Robins Ct. SE12 —3A 114
Robin's Ct. Beck —2F 127
Robinscroft M. SE10 —1D 96
Robins Gro. W Wick —3J 137
Robinson Cres. Bush —1B 10
Robinson Rd. E2 —2J 63
Robinson Rd. SW17 & SW19 —6C 108
Robinson Rd. Dag —4G 53
Robinson's Clo. W13 —5A 56
Robinson St. SW3 —6D 76 (7E 152)
Robinwood Pl. SW15 —4K 105
Robsart St. SW9 —2K 93
Robson Av. NW10 —1C 58
Robson Clo. E6 —6C 66
Robson Clo. Enf —2G 7
Robson Rd. SE27 —3B 110
Roch Av. Edgw —2F 25
Rochdale Rd. E17 —7C 32
Rochdale Rd. SE2 —5B 84
Rochdale Way. SE8 —7C 80
Rochelle Clo. SW11 —4B 92
Rochelle St. E2 —3F 63 (2J 145)
Roche Rd. SW16 —1K 123
Rochester Av. E13 —1A 66
Rochester Av. Brom —2K 127
Rochester Clo. SE3 —3A 98
Rochester Clo. SW16 —7J 109
Rochester Clo. Enf —1K 7
Rochester Clo. Sidc —6B 100
Rochester Dri. Bex —6F 101
Rochester Dri. Pinn —5B 22
Rochester Gdns. Croy —3E 134
Rochester Gdns. Ilf —7D 34
Rochester Ho. SE15 —6J 79
(off Sharratt St.)
Rochester M. NW1 —7G 45
Rochester M. W5 —4C 72
Rochester Pl. NW1 —6G 45
(in two parts)
Rochester Rd. NW1 —6G 45
Rochester Rd. Cars —4D 132
Rochester Row. SW1 —4G 77 (3B 154)
Rochester Sq. NW1 —7G 45

Rochester St. SW1 —3H 77 (2C 154)
Rochester Ter. NW1 —6G 45
Rochester Wlk. SE1 —1D 78 (4E 150)
Rochester Way. SE3 & SE9 —1K 97
Rochester Way. Dart —7K 101
Rochester Way Relief Rd. SE3 & SE9 —1K 97
Roche Wlk. Cars —6B 122
Rochford. N17 —2E 30
(off Griffin Rd.)
Rochford Av. Romf —5C 36
Rochford Clo. E6 —2B 66
Rochford Wlk. E8 —7G 47
Rochford Way. Croy —6J 123
Rochfort Ho. SE8 —5B 80
Rock Av. SW14 —3K 89
Rockbourne M. SE23 —1K 111
Rockbourne Rd. SE23 —1K 111
Rockell's Pl. SE22 —6H 95
Rockett Clo. SE8 —4A 80
Rockfield Ho. NW4 —4F 27
(off Belle Vue Est.)
Rockford Av. Gnfd —2A 56
Rock Gdns. Dag —5H 53
Rock Gro. Way. SE16 —4H 79
Rockhall Rd. NW2 —4F 43
Rockhampton Clo. SE27 —4A 110
Rockhampton Rd. SE27 —4A 110
Rockhampton Rd. S Croy —6E 134
Rock Hill. SE26 —4F 111
Rockingham Clo. SW15 —4B 90
Rockingham St. SE1 —3C 78 (2C 156)
Rockland Rd. SW15 —4G 91
Rocklands Dri. Stan —2B 24
Rockley Ct. W14 —2F 75
(off Rockley Rd.)
Rockley Rd. W14 —2F 75
Rockmount Rd. SE18 —5K 83
Rockmount Rd. SE19 —6D 110
Rocks La. SW13 —1C 90
Rock St. N4 —2A 46
Rockware Av. Gnfd —1H 55
Rockware Av. Bus. Cen. Gnfd —1H 55
Rockwell Gdns. SE19 —5E 110
Rockwell Rd. Dag —5H 53
Rockwood Pl. W12 —2E 74
Rocliffe St. N1 —2B 62
Rocombe Cres. SE23 —7J 95
Rocque Ho. SW6 —7H 75
(off Estcourt Rd.)
Rocque La. SE3 —3H 97
Rodborough Rd. NW11 —1J 43
Roden Gdns. Croy —6E 124
Rodenhurst Rd. SW4 —6G 93
Roden St. N7 —3K 45
Roden St. Ilf —3E 50
Roden Way. Ilf —3E 50
(off Roden St.)
Roderick Rd. NW3 —4D 44
Rodgers Ho. SW4 —7H 93
(off Clapham Pk. Est.)
Roding Av. Wfd G —6H 21
Roding Ho. N1 —1A 62
(off Barnsbury Est.)
Roding La. Buck H & Chig —1G 21
Roding La. N. Wfd G —6H 21
Roding La. S. Ilf —4B 34
Roding M. E1 —1G 79

Roding Rd. E5 —4K 47
Roding Rd. E6 —5F 67
Rodings, The. Wfd G —6F 21
Roding Trad. Est. Bark —7F 51
Roding View. Buck H —1G 21
Rodmarton St. W1 —5D 60 (6F 141)
Rodmell Clo. Hayes —4C 54
Rodmell Slope. N12 —5C 14
Rodmere St. SE10 —5G 81
Rodmill La. SW2 —7J 93
Rodney Clo. Croy —1B 134
Rodney Clo. N Mald —5A 120
Rodney Clo. Pinn —7C 22
Rodney Ct. W9 —4A 60
Rodney Ct. Barn —3C 4
Rodney Gdns. Pinn —5A 22
Rodney Gdns. W Wick —4J 137
Rodney Pl. E17 —2A 32
Rodney Pl. SE17 —4C 78 (3D 156)
Rodney Pl. SW19 —1A 122
Rodney Rd. E11 —4K 33
Rodney Rd. SE17 —4C 78 (3D 156)
Rodney Rd. Mitc —3C 122
Rodney Rd. N Mald —5A 120
Rodney Rd. Twic —6E 86
Rodney St. N1 —2K 61 (1H 143)
Rodney Way. Romf —1G 37
Rodsley St. SE1 —6G 79
Rodway Rd. SW15 —7C 90
Rodway Rd. Brom —1G 127
Rodwell Clo. Ruis —1A 38
Rodwell Pl. Edgw —6B 12
Rodwell Rd. SE22 —6F 95
Rodwell Rd. N'holt —1E 54
Roe. NW9 —1B 26
Roebourne Way. E16 —1E 82
Roebuck La. N17 —6A 18
Roebuck Rd. Buck H —1F 21
Roedean Av. Enf —1D 8
Roedean Clo. Enf —1D 8
Roedean Cres. SW15 —6A 90
Roe End. NW9 —4J 25
Roe Grn. NW9 —5J 25
Roehampton Clo. SW15 —4C 90
Roehampton Dri. Chst —6G 115
Roehampton Ga. SW15 —6A 90
Roehampton High St. SW15 —7C 90
Roehampton La. SW15 —4C 90
Roehampton Lane. (Junct.) —1D 106
Roehampton Vale. SW15 —3B 106
Roe Way. Wall —6J 133
Roffey St. E14 —2E 80
Rogate Ho. E5 —3G 47
Roger Dowley Ct. E2 —2J 63
Roger Harris Almshouses. E15 —1H 65
(off Gift La.)
Roger Reede's Almshouses. Romf —4K 37
Rogers Est. E2 —3J 63
Rogers Gdns. Dag —5G 53
Roger's Ho. Dag —3G 53
Rogers Rd. E16 —6H 65
Rogers Rd. SW17 —4B 108
Rogers Rd. Dag —5G 53
Rogers Wlk. N12 —3E 14
Rohere Ho. EC1 —3C 62 (1C 144)
Rojack Rd. SE23 —1K 111

Rokeby Gdns. Wfd G —1J 33
Rokeby Pl. SW20 —7D 106
Rokeby Rd. SE4 —2B 96
Rokeby Rd. Harr —3H 23
Rokeby St. E15 —1G 65
Rokell Ho. Beck —5D 112
(off Beckenham Hill Rd.)
Rokesby Clo. Well —2H 99
Rokesby Pl. Wemb —5D 40
Rokesly Av. N8 —5J 29
Roland Gdns. SW7 —5A 76
Roland M. E1 —5K 63
Roland Rd. E17 —4F 33
Roland Way. SE17 —5D 78 (6F 157)
Roland Way. SW7 —5A 76
Roland Way. Wor Pk —2B 130
Roles Gro. Romf —4D 36
Rolfe Clo. Barn —4H 5
Rolinsden Way. Kes —5B 138
Rolland Ho. W7 —5J 55
Rollesby Way. SE28 —6C 68
Rolleston Av. Orp —6F 129
Rolleston Clo. Orp —7F 129
Rolleston Rd. S Croy —7D 134
Roll Gdns. Ilf —5E 34
Rollins St. SE15 —6J 79
Rollit Cres. Houn —5E 86
Rollit St. N7 —5A 46
Rolls Bldgs. EC4 —6A 62 (7J 143)
Rollscourt Av. SE24 —5C 94
Rolls Pk. Av. E4 —5H 19
Rolls Pk. Rd. E4 —5J 19
Rolls Pas. EC4 —6A 62 (7J 143)
Rolls Rd. SE1 —5F 79 (5K 157)
Rolt St. SE8 —6A 80
Rolvenden Gdns. Brom —7B 114
Rolvenden Pl. N17 —1G 31
Roman Clo. W3 —2H 73
Roman Clo. Felt —5A 86
Roman Clo. Rain —2K 69
Romanfield Rd. SW2 —7K 93
Roman Ho. EC2 —5C 62 (6D 144)
Romanhurst Av. Brom —4G 127
Romanhurst Gdns. Brom —4G 127
Roman Ind. Est. Croy —7E 124
Roman Rise. SE19 —6D 110
Roman Rd. E2 & E3 —3J 63
Roman Rd. E6 —4C 66
Roman Rd. N10 —7A 16
Roman Rd. NW2 —3E 42
Roman Rd. W4 —4B 74
Roman Rd. Ilf —6F 51
Roman Sq. SE28 —1A 84
Roman Way. N7 —6K 45
Roman Way. SW15 —7J 79
Roman Way. Croy —2B 134
Roman Way. Enf —5A 8
Romany Gdns. E17 —1A 32
Romany Gdns. Sutt —7J 121
Roma Read Clo. SW15 —7D 90
Roma Rd. E17 —3A 32
Romayne Ho. SW4 —3H 93
Romberg Rd. SW17 —3E 108
Romborough Gdns. SE13 —5E 96
Romborough Way. SE13 —5E 96
Romero Clo. SW9 —3K 93
Romero Sq. SE3 —4A 98
Romeyn Rd. SW16 —3K 109
Romford Rd. E15, E7 & E12 —7G 49
Romford Rd. Romf —1E 36
Romford St. E1 —5H 63

Romilly Rd. N4 —2B 46
Romilly St. W1 —7H 61 (2D 148)
Romily Ct. SW6 —2G 91
Rommany Rd. SE27 —4D 110
(in two parts)
Romney Clo. N17 —2H 31
Romney Clo. NW11 —1A 44
Romney Clo. SE14 —7J 79
Romney Clo. Harr —7E 22
Romney Ct. W12 —2E 74
(off Shepherd's Bush Grn.)
Romney Dri. Brom —7B 114
Romney Dri. Harr —7E 22
Romney Gdns. Bexh —1F 101
Romney M. W1 —5E 60 (5G 141)
Romney Rd. SE10 —6F 81
Romney Rd. N Mald —6K 119
Romney St. SW1 —3J 77 (2E 154)
Romola Rd. SE24 —1B 110
Romsey Gdns. Dag —1D 68
Romsey Rd. W13 —7A 56
Romsey Rd. Dag —1D 68
Romulus Ct. Bren —7D 72
Ronald Av. E15 —3G 65
Ronald Clo. Beck —5B 126
Ronald Ct. New Bar —3E 4
Ronaldshay. N4 —1A 46
Ronalds Rd. N5 —5A 46
Ronalds Rd. Brom —1J 127
Ronaldstone Rd. Sidc —6J 99
Rona Rd. NW3 —4E 44
Ronart St. W'stone —3K 23
Rona Wlk. N1 —6D 46
(off Ramsey Wlk.)
Rondu Rd. NW2 —5G 43
Ron Leighton Way. E6 —1C 66
Ronver Rd. SE12 —1H 113
Rood La. EC3 —7E 62 (2G 151)
Rookby Ct. N21 —2G 17
Rookeries Clo. Felt —3A 102
Rookery Clo. NW9 —5B 26
Rookery Cres. Dag —7H 53
Rookery Dri. Chst —1E 128
Rookery La. Brom —6B 128
Rookery Rd. SW4 —4G 93
Rookery Way. NW9 —5B 26
Rooke Way. SE10 —5H 81
Rookfield Av. N10 —4G 29
Rookfield Clo. N10 —4G 29
Rookstone Rd. SW17 —5D 108
Rook Wlk. E6 —6B 66
Rookwood Av. N Mald —4C 120
Rookwood Av. Wall —4H 133
Rookwood Gdns. E4 —2C 20
Rookwood Ho. Bark —4C 67
Rookwood Ho. N16 —7F 31
Rookwood Rd. N16 —7F 31
Roosevelt Way. Dag —6K 53
Rootes Dri. W10 —5F 59
Ropemaker Rd. SE16 —2A 80
Ropemaker's Field. E14 —7B 64
Ropemaker St. EC2 —5D 62 (5E 144)
Roper La. SE1 —2E 78 (7H 151)
Ropers Av. E4 —5J 19
Roper St. SE9 —5D 98
Ropers Wlk. SW2 —7A 94
Roper Way. Mitc —2E 122
Ropery Bus. Pk. SE7 —4A 82
Ropery St. E3 —4B 64
Rope St. SE16 —4A 80
Rope Wlk. Gdns. E1 —6G 63
Rope Yd. Rails. SE18 —3F 83
Ropley St. E2 —2G 63

Rosa Alba M. *N5* —4C **46**
Rosalind Ct. Bark —7A **52**
(off Meadow Rd.)
Rosalind Ho. *N1* —2E **62**
(off Arden Ho.)
Rosaline Rd. *SW6* —7G **75**
Rosamond St. *SE26* —3H **111**
Rosamund Clo. *S Croy* —4D **134**
Rosamun St. *S'hall* —4C **70**
Rosary Clo. *Houn* —2C **86**
Rosary Gdns. *SW7* —4A **76**
Rosaville Rd. *SW6* —7H **75**
Roscoe St. *EC1* —4C **62** (4D **144**)
Roscoe St. Est. *EC1*
—4C **62** (4D **144**)
Roscoff Clo. *Edgw* —1J **25**
Roseacre Clo. *SW13* —5B **56**
Roseacre Rd. *Well* —3B **100**
Rose All. *EC2* —5E **62** (6H **145**)
(off Bishopsgate)
Rose All. *SE1* —1C **78** (4D **150**)
Rose Av. *E18* —2K **33**
Rose Av. *Mitc* —1D **122**
Rose Av. *Mord* —5A **122**
Rosebank. *SE20* —7H **111**
Rosebank. *W3* —6K **57**
Rosebank Av. *Wemb* —4K **39**
Rose Bank Clo. *N12* —5H **15**
Rosebank Clo. *Tedd* —6A **104**
Rosebank Gdns. *E3* —2B **64**
Rosebank Gdns. *W3* —6K **57**
Rosebank Gro. *E17* —3B **32**
Rosebank Rd. *E17* —6D **32**
Rosebank Rd. *W7* —2J **71**
Rosebank Vs. *E17* —4C **32**
Rosebank Wlk. *NW1* —7H **45**
Rosebank Wlk. *SE18* —4C **82**
Rosebank Way. *W3* —6K **57**
Rose Bates Dri. *NW9* —4G **25**
Roseberry Av. *N Mald* —2B **120**
Roseberry Av. *T Hth* —2C **124**
Roseberry Gdns. *N4* —6B **30**
Roseberry Pl. *E8* —6F **47**
Roseberry St. *SE16* —4H **79**
Roseberry Av. *E12* —6C **50**
Roseberry Av. *EC1*
—4A **62** (4J **143**)
Roseberry Av. *N17* —2G **31**
Roseberry Av. *Harr* —4C **38**
Roseberry Av. *Sidc* —7J **99**
Roseberry Clo. *Mord* —6F **121**
Roseberry Gdns. *N8* —5J **29**
Roseberry Gdns. *W13* —6A **56**
Roseberry Gdns. *Sutt* —4K **131**
Roseberry Ind. Est. *N17* —2H **31**
Roseberry Ind. Pk. *N17* —2H **31**
Roseberry M. *N10* —2G **29**
Roseberry Rd. *N9* —3B **18**
Roseberry Rd. *N10* —2G **29**
Roseberry Rd. *SW2* —6J **93**
Roseberry Rd. *Bush* —1A **10**
Roseberry Rd. *Houn* —5G **87**
Roseberry Rd. *King T* —2H **119**
Roseberry Rd. *Sutt* —6H **131**
Roseberry Sq. *EC1*
—4A **62** (4J **143**)
Roseberry Sq. *King T* —2H **119**
Rosebine Av. *Twic* —7H **87**
Rosebury Rd. *SW6* —2K **91**
Rose Bush Cl. *NW3* —5D **44**
Rose Ct. *E1* —5F **63** (6J **145**)
Rose Ct. *S Harr* —2G **39**
Rose Ct. Wemb —2E **56**
(off Vicars Bri. Clo.)
Rosecourt Rd. *Croy* —6K **123**

Rosecroft. *N14* —2C **16**
Rosecroft Av. *NW3* —3J **43**
Rosecroft Gdns. *NW2* —3C **42**
Rosecroft Gdns. *Twic* —1H **103**
Rosecroft Rd. *S'hall* —4E **54**
Rosecroft Wlk. *Pinn* —5B **22**
Rosecroft Wlk. *Wemb* —5D **40**
Rose & Crown Ct. *EC2*
—6C **62** (7D **144**)
Rose & Crown Pas. *Iswth*
—1A **88**
Rose & Crown Yd. *SW1*
—1G **77** (4B **148**)
Rosedale Clo. *SE2* —3B **84**
Rosedale Clo. *W7* —2K **71**
Rosedale Clo. *Stan* —6G **11**
Rosedale Ct. *N5* —4B **46**
Rosedale Ct. *Harr* —4K **39**
Rosedale Gdns. *Dag* —7B **52**
Rosedale Ho. *N16* —1D **46**
Rosedale Rd. *E7* —5A **50**
Rosedale Rd. *Dag* —7B **52**
Rosedale Rd. *Eps* —5C **130**
Rosedale Rd. *Rich* —4E **88**
Rosedale Rd. *Romf* —2J **37**
Rosedale Ter. *W6* —3D **74**
(off Dalling Rd.)
Rosedene. *NW6* —1F **59**
Rosedene Av. *SW16* —3K **109**
Rosedene Av. *Croy* —7J **123**
Rosedene Av. *Gnfd* —3E **54**
Rosedene Av. *Mord* —5J **121**
Rosedene Gdns. *Ilf* —4E **34**
Rosedene Ter. *E10* —2D **48**
Rosedew Rd. *W6* —6F **75**
Rose End. *Wor Pk* —1F **131**
Rosefield Clo. *Cars* —5C **132**
Rosefield Gdns. *E14* —7C **64**
Roseford Ct. *W12* —2F **75**
(off Shepherd's Bush Grn.)
Rose Garden Clo. *Edgw* —6K **11**
Rose Gdns. *W5* —3D **72**
Rose Gdns. *S'hall* —4E **54**
Rose Glen. *NW9* —4K **25**
Rose Glen. *Romf* —1K **53**
Rosehart M. *W11* —6J **59**
Rosehatch Av. *Romf* —3D **36**
Roseheath Rd. *Houn* —5D **86**
Rosehill. *Sutt* —2K **131**
Rosehill Av. *Sutt* —1A **132**
Rosehill Ct. *Mord* —7A **122**
(off St Helier Av.)
Rosehill Ct. Pde. *Mord* —7A **122**
(off St Helier Av.)
Rosehill Gdns. *Gnfd* —5K **39**
Rosehill Gdns. *Sutt* —2K **131**
Rose Hill Pk. W. *Sutt* —1A **132**
Rosehill Rd. *SW18* —6A **92**
Rose Hill Roundabout. (Junct.)
—7A **122**
Roseland Clo. *N17* —7J **17**
Rose La. *Romf* —3D **36**
Rose Lawn. *Bush* —1B **10**
Roseleigh Av. *N5* —4B **46**
Roseleigh Clo. *Twic* —6D **88**
Rosemary Av. *N3* —2K **27**
Rosemary Av. *N9* —1C **18**
Rosemary Av. *Enf* —1K **7**
Rosemary Av. *Houn* —2B **86**
Rosemary Clo. *Croy* —6J **123**
Rosemary Dri. *E14* —6F **65**
Rosemary Dri. *Ilf* —5B **34**
Rosemary Gdns. *SW14* —3J **89**
Rosemary Gdns. *Dag* —1F **53**

Rosemary Ho. *N1* —1D **62**
(off Colville Est.)
Rosemary La. *SW14* —3J **89**
Rosemary Rd. *SW17* —3A **108**
Rosemary Rd. *Well* —1K **99**
Rosemead. *NW9* —7B **26**
Rosemead Av. *Mitc* —3G **123**
Rosemead Av. *Wemb* —5E **40**
Rosemont Av. *N12* —6F **15**
Rosemont Rd. *NW3* —6A **44**
Rosemont Rd. *W3* —7H **57**
Rosemont Rd. *N Mald* —3J **119**
Rosemont Rd. *Rich* —6E **88**
Rosemont Rd. *Wemb* —1E **56**
Rosemoor St. *SW3*
—4D **76** (4E **152**)
Rosemount Clo. *Wfd G* —6J **21**
Rosemount Dri. *Brom* —4D **128**
Rosemount Point. *SE23* —3K **111**
Rosemount Rd. *W13* —6A **56**
Rosenau Cres. *SW11* —1D **92**
Rosenau Rd. *SW11* —1C **92**
Rosendale Rd. *SE21* —3D **110**
Rosendale Rd. *SE24 & SE21*
—7C **94**
Roseneath Av. *N21* —1G **17**
Roseneath Rd. *SW11* —6E **92**
Roseneath Wlk. *Enf* —4K **7**
Rosen's Wlk. *Edgw* —3C **12**
Rosenthal Rd. *SE6* —6D **96**
Rosenthorpe Rd. *SE15* —5K **95**
Rosepark Ct. *Ilf* —2D **34**
Roserton St. *E14* —2E **80**
Rosery, The. *Croy* —6K **125**
Roses, The. *Wfd G* —7C **20**
Rose St. *WC2* —7J **61** (2E **148**)
Rosethorn Clo. *SW12* —7H **93**
Rosetta Clo. *SW8* —7J **77**
Rosetti Ter. *Dag* —4B **52**
(off Marlborough Rd.)
Roseveare Rd. *SE12* —4A **114**
Roseville Av. *Houn* —5E **86**
Rosevine Rd. *SW20* —1E **120**
Rose Wlk. *Surb* —5H **119**
Rose Wlk. *W Wick* —2E **136**
Rose Way. *SE12* —5J **97**
Roseway. *SE21* —6D **94**
Rose Way. *Edgw* —4D **12**
Rosewell Clo. *SE20* —7H **111**
Rosewood Av. *Gnfd* —5A **40**
Rosewood Clo. *Sidc* —3C **116**
Rosewood Ct. *E8* —7F **47**
Rosewood Ct. *E11* —4F **49**
Rosewood Ct. *Brom* —1A **128**
Rosewood Gdns. *SE13* —2E **96**
Rosewood Gro. *Sutt* —2A **132**
Rosewood Ho. *SW8*
—6K **77** (7G **155**)
(off Vauxhall Gro.)
Rosewood Sq. *W12* —6C **58**
Rosher Clo. *E15* —7F **49**
Roshni Ho. *SW17* —6C **108**
Rosina St. *E9* —6K **47**
Roskell Rd. *SW15* —3F **91**
Roslin Rd. *W3* —3H **73**
Roslin Way. *Brom* —5J **113**
Roslyn Clo. *Mitc* —2B **122**
Roslyn M. *N15* —5E **30**
Roslyn Rd. *N15* —5D **30**
Rosmead Rd. *W11* —7G **59**
Rosoman Pl. *EC1*
—4A **62** (3K **143**)
Rosoman St. *EC1*
—3A **62** (2K **143**)

Rossall Cres. *NW10* —3F **57**
Ross Av. *NW7* —5B **14**
Ross Av. *Dag* —1F **53**
Ross Clo. *Harr* —7B **10**
Ross Ct. *NW9* —3A **26**
Ross Ct. *SW15* —7F **91**
Ross Ct. *W13* —5B **56**
(off Cleveland Rd.)
Rossdale. *Sutt* —5C **132**
Rossdale Dri. *N9* —6D **8**
Rossdale Dri. *NW9* —1J **41**
Rossdale Rd. *SW15* —4E **90**
Rosse M. *SE3* —1K **97**
Rossendale St. *E5* —2H **47**
Rossendale Way. *NW1* —7G **45**
Rossetti Rd. *SE16* —5H **79**
Rossignol Gdns. *Cars* —2E **86**
Rossindel Rd. *Houn* —5E **86**
Rossington St. *E5* —2G **47**
Rossiter Fields. *Barn* —6C **4**
Rossiter Rd. *SW12* —1F **109**
Rossland Clo. *Bexh* —5H **101**
Rosslyn Av. *E4* —2C **20**
Rosslyn Av. *SW13* —3A **90**
Rosslyn Av. *Dag* —7F **37**
Rosslyn Av. *E Barn* —6H **5**
Rosslyn Clo. *W Wick* —3H **137**
Rosslyn Cres. *Harr* —4K **23**
Rosslyn Cres. *Wemb* —4E **40**
Rosslyn Gdns. *Wemb* —3E **40**
(off Rosslyn Cres.)
Rosslyn Hill. *NW3* —4B **44**
Rosslyn M. *NW3* —4B **44**
Rosslyn Pk. M. *NW3* —5B **44**
Rosslyn Rd. *E17* —4E **32**
Rosslyn Rd. *Bark* —7H **51**
Rosslyn Rd. *Twic* —6C **88**
Rossmore Ct. *NW1*
—4D **60** (3E **140**)
Rossmore Rd. *NW1*
—4C **60** (4D **140**)
Ross Pde. *Wall* —6F **133**
Ross Rd. *SE25* —3D **124**
Ross Rd. *Twic* —1F **103**
Ross Rd. *Wall* —5G **133**
Ross Way. *SE9* —3C **98**
Rosswood Gdns. *Wall* —6G **133**
Ross Wyld Lodge. *E17* —3C **32**
(off Forest Rd.)
Rostella Rd. *SW17* —4B **108**
Rostrevor Av. *N15* —6F **31**
Rostrevor Gdns. *S'hall* —5C **70**
Rostrevor M. *SW6* —1H **91**
Rostrevor Rd. *SW6* —1H **91**
Rostrevor Rd. *SW19* —5J **107**
Rotary St. *SE1* —3B **78** (1A **156**)
Rothbury Gdns. *Iswth* —7A **72**
Rothbury Rd. *E9* —7B **48**
Rothbury Wlk. *N17* —7B **18**
Rotherfield Rd. *Cars* —4E **132**
Rotherfield St. *N1* —7C **46**
Rotherham Wlk. *SE1*
—1B **78** (5A **150**)
Rotherhill Av. *SW16* —6H **109**
Rotherhithe New Rd. *SE16*
—5G **79**
Rotherhithe Old Rd. *SE16* —3J **79**
Rotherhithe St. *SE16* —2J **79**
Rother Ho. *SE15* —4H **95**
Rothermere Rd. *Croy* —5K **133**
Rotherwick Hill. *W5* —4F **57**
Rotherwick Rd. *NW11* —7J **27**
Rotherwood Clo. *SW20* —1G **121**
Rotherwood Rd. *SW15* —3F **91**
Rothery St. *N1* —1B **62**
(off St Marys Path)

Rothesay Av. *SW20* —2G **121**
Rothesay Av. *Gnfd* —6G **39**
(in two parts)
Rothesay Av. *Rich* —4H **89**
Rothesay Ct. *SE11*
—6A **78** (7J **155**)
Rothesay Ct. *SE12* —3K **113**
Rothesay Rd. *SE25* —4D **124**
Rothsay Rd. *E7* —7A **50**
Rothsay St. *SE1*
—3E **78** (1G **157**)
Rothsay Wlk. *E14* —4C **80**
(off Charnwood Gdns.)
Rothschild Rd. *W4* —4J **73**
Rothschild St. *SE27* —4B **110**
Roth Wlk. *N7* —2K **45**
Rothwell Ct. *Harr* —5K **23**
Rothwell Gdns. *Dag* —7C **52**
Rothwell Ho. *Houn* —6E **70**
Rothwell Rd. *Dag* —1C **68**
Rothwell St. *NW1* —1D **60**
Rotten Row. *NW3* —1A **44**
Rotten Row. *SW7 & SW1*
—2B **76** (6B **146**)
Rotterdam Dri. *E14* —3E **80**
Rotunda, The. *Romf* —5K **37**
(off Yew Tree Gdns.)
Rouel Rd. *SE16* —3G **79** (1K **157**)
Rougemont Av. *Mord* —6J **121**
Roundacre. *SW19* —2F **107**
Roundaway Rd. *Ilf* —2D **34**
Roundel Clo. *SE4* —4B **96**
Round Gro. *Croy* —7K **125**
Roundhay Clo. *SE23* —2K **111**
Roundhedge Way. *Enf* —1E **6**
Round Hill. *SE26* —3J **111**
Roundhill Dri. *Enf* —4E **6**
Roundhouse, The. *NW1* —7E **44**
(off Chalk Farm Rd.)
Roundshaw Cen. *Wall* —7J **133**
(off Mollison Dri.)
Roundtable Rd. *Brom* —3H **113**
Roundtree Rd. *Wemb* —5B **40**
Roundway, The. *N17* —1D **30**
Roundwood. *Chst* —2F **129**
Roundwood Rd. *NW10* —6B **42**
Rounton Rd. *E3* —4C **64**
Roupel Ho. *SE15* —7G **79**
(off Sumner Est.)
Roupell Rd. *SW2* —1K **109**
Roupell St. *SE1* —1A **78** (5K **149**)
Rousden St. *NW1* —7G **45**
Rouse Gdns. *SE21* —4E **110**
Rous Rd. *Buck H* —1H **21**
Routemaster Clo. *E13* —3K **65**
Routh Rd. *SW18* —7C **92**
Routh St. *E6* —5D **66**
Rover Ho. *N1* —1E **62**
(off Whitmore Rd.)
Rowallan Rd. *SW6* —7G **75**
Rowallen Pde. *Dag* —1C **52**
Rowan. *N10* —2F **29**
Rowan Av. *E4* —6G **19**
Rowan Clo. *SW16* —1G **123**
Rowan Clo. *W5* —2E **72**
Rowan Clo. *N Mald* —2A **120**
Rowan Clo. *Stan* —6E **10**
Rowan Clo. *Wemb* —3A **40**
Rowan Ct. *E8* —7F **47**
Rowan Ct. *E13* —2K **65**
(off High St. Plaistow,)
Rowan Ct. *SE15* —7F **79**
(off Garnies Clo.)
Rowan Ct. *SW11* —6D **92**
Rowan Cres. *SW16* —1G **123**

Rowan Dri. NW9 —3C **26**
Rowan Gdns. Croy —3F **135**
Rowan Ho. Hay —2G **127**
Rowan Ho. Sidc —3K **115**
Rowan Rd. SW16 —2G **123**
Rowan Rd. W6 —4F **75**
Rowan Rd. Bexh —3E **100**
Rowan Rd. Bren —7B **72**
Rowans, The. N13 —3G **17**
Rowan Ter. W4 —4F **75**
  (off Rowan Rd.)
Rowantree Clo. N21 —1J **17**
Rowantree Rd. N21 —1J **17**
Rowantree Rd. Enf —2G **7**
Rowan Wlk. N2 —6A **28**
Rowan Wlk. N19 —2G **45**
Rowan Wlk. W10 —4G **59**
Rowan Wlk. Barn —5E **4**
Rowan Wlk. Brom —3D **138**
Rowan Way. Romf —3C **36**
Rowanwood Av. Sidc —1A **116**
Rowben Clo. N20 —1E **14**
Rowberry Clo. SW6 —7E **74**
Rowcross Pl. SE1
  —5F **79** (5J **157**)
Rowcross St. SE1
  —5F **79** (5J **157**)
Rowdell Rd. N'holt —1E **54**
Rowden Pk. Gdns. E4 —6H **19**
Rowden Rd. E4 —6J **19**
Rowden Rd. Beck —1A **126**
Rowditch La. SW11 —2E **92**
Rowdon Av. NW10 —7D **42**
Rowdown Cres. New Ad —7F **137**
Rowdowns Rd. Dag —1F **69**
Rowe Gdns. Bark —2K **67**
Rowe La. E9 —5J **47**
Rowena Cres. SW11 —2C **92**
Rowe Wlk. Harr —3E **38**
Rowfant Rd. SW17 —1E **108**
Rowhill Rd. E5 —4H **47**
Rowington Clo. W2 —5K **59**
Rowland Av. Harr —3C **24**
Rowland Ct. E16 —4H **65**
Rowland Gro. SE26 —3H **111**
Rowland Hill Av. N17 —7H **17**
Rowland Hill Ho. SE1
  —2B **78** (6A **150**)
Rowland Hill St. NW3 —5C **44**
Rowlands Av. Pinn —5A **10**
Rowlands Clo. N6 —6E **28**
Rowlands Clo. NW7 —7H **13**
Rowlands Rd. Dag —2F **53**
Rowland Way. SW19 —1K **121**
Rowley Av. Sidc —7B **100**
Rowley Clo. Wemb —7F **41**
Rowley Ct. Enf —5K **7**
  (off Wellington Rd.)
Rowley Gdns. N4 —7C **30**
Rowley Ind. Pk. W3 —3H **73**
Rowley Rd. N15 —5C **30**
Rowley Way. NW8 —1K **59**
Rowlls Rd. King T —3F **119**
Rowney Gdns. Dag —6C **52**
Rowney Rd. Dag —6B **52**
Rowntree Clifford Clo. E13
  —4K **65**
Rowntree Clo. NW6 —6J **43**
Rowntree Path. SE28 —1B **84**
Rowntree Rd. Twic —1J **103**
Rowse Clo. E15 —1E **64**
Rowsley Av. NW4 —3E **26**
Rowstock Gdns. N7 —5H **45**
Rowton Rd. SE18 —7G **83**
Roxborough Av. Harr —7H **23**

Roxborough Av. Iswth —7K **71**
Roxborough Pk. Harr —7J **23**
Roxborough Rd. Harr —5H **23**
Roxbourne Clo. N'holt —6C **38**
Roxburgh Rd. SE27 —5B **110**
Roxby Pl. SW6 —6J **75**
Roxeth Grn. Av. Harr —3F **39**
Roxeth Gro. Harr —4F **39**
Roxeth Hill. Harr —2H **39**
Roxley Rd. SE13 —6D **96**
Roxton Gdns. Croy —5C **136**
Roxwell Rd. W12 —2C **74**
Roxwell Rd. Bark —2A **68**
Roxwell Trad. Pk. E10 —7A **32**
Roxwell Way. Wfd G —7F **21**
Roxy Av. Romf —7C **36**
Royal Albert Way. E16 —7B **66**
Royal Arc. W1 —7G **61** (3A **148**)
Royal Av. SW3 —5D **76** (5E **152**)
Royal Av. Wor Pk —2A **130**
Royal Cir. SE27 —3A **110**
Royal Clo. N16 —1E **46**
Royal Clo. Iff —7A **36**
Royal Clo. Wor Pk —2A **130**
Royal College St. NW1 —7G **45**
Royal Ct. EC3 —6D **62** (1F **151**)
  (off Finch La.)
Royal Ct. SE16 —3B **80**
Royal Ct. Enf —6K **7**
Royal Cres. W11 —1F **75**
Royal Cres. Ruis —4C **38**
Royal Cres. M. W11 —1F **75**
Royal Docks Rd. E6 & Bark
  —5F **67**
Royal Exchange Av. EC3
  —6D **62** (1F **151**)
Royal Exchange Bldgs. EC3
  —6D **62** (1F **151**)
Royal Gdns. W7 —3A **72**
Royal Herbert Pavilions. SE18
  —1D **98**
Royal Hill. SE10 —7E **80**
Royal Hospital Rd. SW3
  —6D **76** (7E **152**)
Royal London Ind. Est. NW10
  —2K **57**
Royal Mint Ct. EC3
  —7F **63** (3K **151**)
Royal Mint Pl. E1
  —7G **63** (3K **151**)
Royal Mint St. E1
  —7F **63** (2K **151**)
Royal Naval Pl. SE14 —7B **80**
Royal Oak M. SE1
  —2E **78** (7G **151**)
Royal Oak Pl. SE22 —6H **95**
Royal Oak Rd. E8 —6H **47**
Royal Oak Rd. Bexh —5F **101**
Royal Opera Arc. SW1
  —1H **77** (4C **148**)
Royal Orchard Clo. SW18
  —7G **91**
Royal Pde. SE3 —2H **97**
Royal Pde. SW6 —7G **75**
Royal Pde. W5 —3E **56**
Royal Pde. Chst —7G **115**
Royal Pde. Dag —6H **53**
  (off Church St.)
Royal Pde. Rich —1G **89**
Royal Pde. M. Chst —7G **115**
  (off Royal Pde.)
Royal Pl. SE10 —7E **80**
Royal Rd. E16 —6A **66**
Royal Rd. SE17 —6B **78** (7A **156**)
Royal Rd. Sidc —3D **116**

Royal Rd. Tedd —5H **103**
Royal Route. Wemb —5F **41**
Royal St. SE1 —3K **77** (1H **155**)
Royalty M. W1 —6H **61** (1C **148**)
Royal Victoria Patriotic Building.
  SW18 —6B **92**
Royal Victor Pl. E3 —2K **63**
Royal Wlk. Wall —2F **133**
Roycraft Av. Bark —2K **67**
Roycroft Clo. E18 —1K **33**
Roycroft Clo. SW2 —1A **110**
Roydene Rd. SE18 —6J **83**
Roydon Clo. Lou —1H **21**
Roy Gdns. Iff —4J **35**
Roy Gro. Hamp —6F **103**
Royle Cres. W13 —4A **56**
Roymount Ct. Twic —3J **103**
Roy Sq. E14 —7A **64**
Royston Av. E4 —5H **19**
Royston Av. Sutt —3B **132**
Royston Av. Wall —4H **133**
Royston Ct. E13 —1J **65**
  (off Stopford Rd.)
Royston Ct. SE24 —6C **94**
Royston Ct. Rich —1F **89**
Royston Gdns. Iff —6B **34**
Royston Ho. N11 —4J **15**
Royston Pde. Iff —6B **34**
Royston Pk. Rd. Pinn —5A **10**
Royston Rd. SE20 —1K **125**
Royston Rd. Rich —5E **88**
Roystons, The. Surb —5H **119**
Royston St. E2 —2J **63**
Rozel Ct. N1 —1E **62**
Rozel Rd. SW4 —3G **93**
Rubastic Rd. S'hall —3A **70**
Rubens Rd. N'holt —2A **54**
Rubens St. SE6 —2B **112**
Ruberoid Rd. Enf —3G **9**
Ruby M. E17 —3C **32**
Ruby Rd. E17 —3C **32**
Ruby St. SE15 —6H **79**
Ruby Triangle. SE15 —6H **79**
Ruckholt Clo. E10 —3D **48**
Ruckholt Rd. E10 —4D **48**
Rucklidge Av. NW10 —2B **58**
Rucklidge Pas. NW10 —2B **58**
  (off Rucklidge Av.)
Rudall Cres. NW3 —4B **44**
Ruddington Clo. E5 —4A **48**
Ruddstreet Clo. SE18 —4F **83**
Ruddy Way. NW7 —6G **13**
Rudge Ho. SE16 —3G **79**
  (off Llewellyn St.)
Rudgwick Ct. SE18 —4C **82**
  (off Woodville St.)
Rudland Rd. Bexh —3H **101**
Rudloe Rd. SW12 —7G **93**
Rudolf Pl. SW8 —6J **77** (7F **155**)
Rudolph Rd. E13 —2H **65**
Rudolph Rd. NW6 —2J **59**
Rudyard Gro. NW7 —6D **12**
Ruffetts Clo. S Croy —7H **135**
Ruffetts, The. S Croy —7H **135**
Rufford Clo. Harr —6A **24**
Rufford St. N1 —1J **61**
Rufford Tower. W3 —1H **73**
Rufforth Ct. NW9 —1A **26**
  (off Pageant Av.)
Rufus Clo. Ruis —3C **38**
Rufus St. N1 —3E **62** (2G **145**)
Rugby Av. N9 —1A **18**
Rugby Av. Gnfd —6H **39**
Rugby Av. Wemb —5B **40**
Rugby Clo. Harr —4J **23**

Rugby Gdns. Dag —6C **52**
Rugby Rd. NW9 —4H **25**
Rugby Rd. W4 —2A **74**
Rugby Rd. Dag —7B **52**
Rugby Rd. Twic —5J **87**
Rugby St. WC1 —4K **61** (4G **143**)
Rugg St. E14 —7C **64**
Ruislip Clo. Gnfd —4F **55**
Ruislip Rd. Gnfd —3E **54**
Ruislip Rd. N'holt & S'hall
  —1A **54**
Ruislip Rd. E. Gnfd & W13 & W7
  —4H **55**
Ruislip St. SW17 —4D **108**
Rumbold Rd. SW6 —7K **75**
Rum Clo. E1 —7J **63**
Rumney Ct. N'holt —2B **54**
  (off Parkfield Dri.)
Rumsey Clo. Hamp —6D **102**
Rumsey M. N4 —3B **46**
Rumsey Rd. SW9 —3K **93**
Runbury Circ. NW9 —2K **41**
Runcorn Clo. N17 —4H **31**
Runcorn Pl. W11 —7G **59**
Rundell Cres. NW4 —5D **26**
Rundell Tower. SW8 —1K **93**
Runes Clo. Mitc —4B **122**
Runnel Field. Harr —3J **39**
Running Horse Yd. Bren —6E **72**
Runnymede. SW19 —1B **122**
Runnymede Clo. Twic —6F **87**
Runnymede Ct. SW15 —1C **106**
Runnymede Cres. SW16
  —1H **123**
Runnymede Gdns. Gnfd —2J **55**
Runnymede Gdns. Twic —6F **87**
Runnymede Ho. E9 —4A **48**
Runnymede Rd. Twic —6F **87**
Runway, The. Ruis —5A **38**
Rupack St. SE16 —2J **79**
Rupert Av. Wemb —5E **40**
Rupert Ct. W1 —7H **61** (2C **148**)
Rupert Gdns. SW9 —2B **94**
Rupert Ho. SE11
  —4A **78** (4K **155**)
Rupert Rd. N19 —3H **45**
Rupert Rd. NW6 —2H **59**
Rupert Rd. W4 —3A **74**
Rupert St. W1 —7H **61** (2C **148**)
Rural Way. SW16 —7F **109**
Ruscoe Rd. E16 —6H **65**
Rusham Rd. SW12 —6D **92**
Rushbrook Cres. E17 —1B **32**
Rushbrook Rd. SE9 —2G **115**
Rushbury Ct. Hamp —7E **102**
Rushcroft Rd. E4 —7J **19**
Rushcroft Rd. SW2 —4A **94**
Rushden Clo. SE19 —7D **110**
Rushdene. SE2 —3D **84**
  (in two parts)
Rushdene Av. Barn —7H **5**
Rushdene Clo. N'holt —2A **54**
Rushdene Cres. N'holt —2A **54**
Rushdene Rd. Pinn —6B **22**
Rushden Gdns. NW7 —6K **13**
Rushden Gdns. Iff —2E **34**
Rushen Wlk. Cars —1B **132**
Rushett Clo. Th Dit —7B **118**
Rushett Rd. Th Dit —7B **118**
Rushey Clo. N Mald —4K **119**
Rushey Grn. SE6 —7D **96**
Rushey Hill. Enf —4E **6**
Rushey Mead. SE4 —5C **96**
Rushford Rd. SE4 —6B **96**

Rush Grn. Gdns. Romf —1J **53**
Rush Grn. Rd. Romf —1H **53**
Rushgrove Av. NW9 —5A **26**
Rushgrove Pde. NW9 —5A **26**
Rushgrove St. SE18 —4D **82**
Rush Hill Rd. SW11 —3E **92**
Rushley Clo. Kes —4B **138**
Rushmead. E2 —3H **63**
Rushmead. Rich —3B **104**
Rushmead Clo. Croy —4F **135**
Rushmead Clo. Edgw —2C **12**
Rushmere Ct. Wor Pk —2C **130**
Rushmere Ho. SW19 —5F **107**
Rushmon Pl. Cheam —6G **131**
Rushmoor Clo. Pinn —4A **22**
Rushmore Clo. Brom —3C **128**
Rushmore Cres. E5 —4K **47**
Rushmore Rd. E5 —4J **47**
  (in three parts)
Rusholme Av. Dag —3G **53**
Rusholme Gro. SE19 —5E **110**
Rusholme Rd. SW15 —6F **91**
Rushout Av. Harr —6B **24**
Rush, The. SW19 —2H **121**
  (off Kingston Rd.)
Rushton Ho. SW8 —2H **93**
Rushton St. N1 —2D **62**
Rushworth Av. NW4 —3C **26**
Rushworth Gdns. NW4 —4C **26**
Rushworth St. SE1
  —2B **78** (6B **150**)
Rushy Meadow La. Cars
  —3C **132**
Ruskin Av. E12 —6C **50**
Ruskin Av. Rich —7G **73**
Ruskin Av. Well —3A **100**
Ruskin Clo. NW11 —6K **27**
Ruskin Ct. N21 —7E **6**
Ruskin Ct. SE5 —3D **94**
  (off Champion Hill)
Ruskin Dri. Well —3A **100**
Ruskin Dri. Wor Pk —2D **130**
Ruskin Gdns. W5 —4D **56**
Ruskin Gdns. Harr —5F **25**
Ruskin Gro. Well —1A **100**
Ruskin Mans. W14 —6G **75**
  (off Queen's Club Gdns.)
Ruskin Pk. Ho. SE5 —3D **94**
Ruskin Rd. N17 —1F **31**
Ruskin Rd. Belv —4G **85**
Ruskin Rd. Cars —5D **132**
Ruskin Rd. Croy —2B **134**
Ruskin Rd. Iswth —3K **87**
Ruskin Rd. S'hall —7C **54**
Ruskin Wlk. N9 —2B **18**
Ruskin Wlk. SE24 —5C **94**
Ruskin Wlk. Brom —6D **128**
Ruskin Way. SW19 —1B **122**
Rusland Heights. Harr —4J **23**
Rusland Pk. Rd. Harr —4J **23**
Rusper Clo. NW2 —3E **42**
Rusper Clo. Stan —4H **11**
Rusper Ct. SW9 —2J **93**
  (off Clapham Rd.)
Rusper Rd. N22 & N17 —2C **30**
Rusper Rd. Dag —6C **52**
Russell Av. N22 —2A **30**
Russell Clo. NW10 —7J **41**
Russell Clo. SE7 —7A **82**
Russell Clo. W4 —6B **74**
Russell Clo. Beck —3E **126**
Russell Clo. Bexh —4G **101**
Russell Clo. Ruis —2A **38**
Russell Ct. E10 —7D **32**

Russell Ct. *N14* —6C **6**
Russell Ct. *SE15* —2H **95**
(off Heaton Rd.)
Russell Ct. *SW1*
—1G **77** (5B **148**)
Russell Ct. *SW16* —5K **109**
Russell Ct. New Bar —4F **5**
Russell Ct. Wall —5G **133**
(off Ross Rd.)
Russell Courtyard. *Chst* —1E **128**
Russell Gdns. *N20* —2H **15**
Russell Gdns. *NW11* —6G **27**
Russell Gdns. *W14* —3G **75**
Russell Gdns. *Ilf* —7H **35**
Russell Gdns. *Rich* —2C **104**
Russell Gdns. M. *W14* —2G **75**
Russell Gro. *NW7* —5F **13**
Russell Gro. *SW9* —7A **78**
Russell Kerr Clo. *W4* —7J **73**
Russell La. *N20* —2H **15**
Russell Lodge. *E4* —2K **19**
Russell Mead. *Har W* —1K **23**
Russell Pde. *NW11* —6G **27**
(off Golders Grn. Rd.)
Russell Pl. *NW3* —5C **44**
Russell Pl. *SE16* —3A **80**
Russell Rd. *E4* —4G **19**
Russell Rd. *E10* —6D **32**
Russell Rd. *E16* —6J **65**
Russell Rd. *E17* —3B **32**
Russell Rd. *N8* —6H **29**
Russell Rd. *N13* —6E **16**
Russell Rd. *N15* —5E **30**
Russell Rd. *N20* —2H **15**
Russell Rd. *NW9* —6B **26**
Russell Rd. *SW19* —7J **107**
Russell Rd. *W14* —3G **75**
Russell Rd. Buck H —1E **20**
Russell Rd. Enf —1A **8**
Russell Rd. Mitc —3C **122**
Russell Rd. N'holt —5G **39**
Russell Rd. Twic —6K **87**
Russell's Footpath. *SW16*
—5J **109**
Russell Sq. *WC1*
—5J **61** (4E **142**)
Russell St. *WC2* —7J **61** (2F **149**)
Russell Wlk. Rich —6F **89**
Russell Way. Sutt —5K **131**
Russell Yd. *SW15* —4G **91**
Russet Cres. *N7* —5K **45**
Russet Dri. Croy —1A **136**
Russets Clo. *E4* —4A **20**
Russettings. Pinn —1D **22**
(off Westfield Pk.)
Russett Way. *SE13* —2D **96**
Russia Ct. *EC2* —6C **62** (7D **144**)
Russia Dock Rd. *SE16* —1A **80**
Russia La. *E2* —2J **63**
Russia Row. *EC2*
—6C **62** (1D **150**)
Russia Wlk. *SE16* —2A **80**
Rusthall Av. *W4* —4K **73**
Rusthall Clo. Croy —5J **125**
Rustic Av. *SW16* —7F **109**
Rustic Pl. Wemb —4D **40**
Rustic Wlk. *E16* —6K **65**
(off Lambert Rd.)
Rustington Wlk. Mord —7H **121**
Ruston Av. Surb —7H **119**
Ruston Gdns. *N14* —6A **6**
Ruston M. *W11* —6G **59**
Ruston Rd. *SE18* —3C **82**
Ruston St. *E3* —1B **64**
Rust Sq. *SE5* —7D **78**

Rutford Rd. *SW16* —5J **109**
Ruth Clo. Stan —4F **25**
Ruth Ct. *E3* —2A **64**
Rutherford Clo. Sutt —6B **132**
Rutherford Ho. Wemb —3J **41**
(off Barnhill Rd.)
Rutherford St. *SW1*
—4H **77** (3C **154**)
Rutherford Tower. S'hall —6F **55**
Rutherford Way. Bush —1C **10**
Rutherford Way. Wemb —4G **41**
Rutherglen Rd. *SE2* —6A **84**
Rutherwyke Clo. Eps —6C **130**
Ruthin Clo. *NW9* —6A **26**
Ruthin Rd. *SE3* —6J **81**
Ruthven St. *E9* —1K **63**
Rutland Av. Sidc —7A **100**
Rutland Clo. *SW14* —3H **89**
Rutland Clo. *SW19* —7C **108**
Rutland Clo. Bex —2D **116**
Rutland Ct. *EC1* —4G **62** (4C **144**)
Rutland Ct. *SE5* —4D **94**
Rutland Ct. *SE9* —2G **115**
Rutland Ct. *SW7*
—2C **76** (7D **146**)
Rutland Ct. *W3* —6G **57**
Rutland Ct. Chst —1E **128**
Rutland Ct. Enf —5C **8**
Rutland Dri. Mord —6H **121**
Rutland Dri. Rich —1E **104**
Rutland Gdns. *N4* —6B **30**
Rutland Gdns. *SW7*
—2C **76** (7D **146**)
Rutland Gdns. *W13* —5A **56**
Rutland Gdns. Croy —4E **134**
Rutland Gdns. Dag —5C **52**
Rutland Gdns. M. *SW7*
—2C **76** (7D **146**)
Rutland Ga. *SW7*
—2C **76** (7D **146**)
Rutland Ga. Belv —5H **85**
Rutland Ga. Brom —4H **127**
Rutland Ga. M. *SW7*
—2C **76** (7D **146**)
Rutland Gro. W6 —5D **74**
Rutland Ho. W8 —3K **75**
(off Marloes Rd.)
Rutland Ho. N'holt —6D **38**
(off Farmlands, The)
Rutland M. *NW8* —1K **59**
Rutland M. E. *SW7*
—3C **76** (1D **152**)
Rutland M. S. *SW7*
—3C **76** (1C **152**)
Rutland M. W. *SW7*
—3C **76** (1C **152**)
Rutland Pk. *NW2* —6E **42**
Rutland Pk. *SE6* —2B **112**
Rutland Pk. Mans. *NW2* —6E **42**
Rutland Pl. *EC1* —4B **62** (5B **144**)
Rutland Pl. Bush —1C **10**
Rutland Rd. *E7* —7B **50**
Rutland Rd. *E9* —1K **63**
Rutland Rd. *E11* —5K **33**
Rutland Rd. *E17* —6C **32**
Rutland Rd. *SW19* —7C **108**
Rutland Rd. Harr —6G **23**
Rutland Rd. *Ilf* —3F **51**
Rutland Rd. S'hall —5E **54**
Rutland Rd. Twic —2H **103**
Rutland St. *SW7*
—3C **76** (1D **152**)
Rutland Wlk. *SE6* —2B **112**
Rutley Clo. *SE17*
—6B **78** (7A **156**)

Rutlish Rd. *SW19* —1J **121**
Rutter Gdns. Mitc —4A **122**
Rutt's Ter. *SE14* —1K **95**
Rutts, The. Bush —1C **10**
Ruvigny Gdns. *SW15* —3F **91**
Ruxley Clo. Sidc —6D **116**
Ruxley Corner Ind. Est. Sidc
—6D **116**
Ruxley La. Eps —4A **130**
Ryalls Ct. *N20* —3J **15**
Ryan Clo. *SE3* —4A **98**
Ryan Ct. *SW16* —7J **109**
Ryan Dri. Bren —6A **72**
Rycott Path. *SE22* —7G **95**
Rycroft Way. *N17* —3F **31**
Ryculff Sq. *SE3* —2H **97**
Rydal Clo. *NW4* —2F **27**
Rydal Ct. Edgw —5A **12**
Rydal Ct. Wemb —7F **25**
Rydal Cres. Gnfd —3B **56**
Rydal Dri. Bexh —1G **101**
Rydal Dri. W Wick —2G **137**
Rydal Gdns. *NW9* —5A **26**
Rydal Gdns. Houn —6F **87**
Rydal Gdns. Wemb —1C **40**
Rydal Gdns. *SW15* —3A **106**
Rydal Rd. *SW16* —4H **109**
Rydal Water. *NW1*
—3G **61** (1A **142**)
Rydal Way. Enf —6D **8**
Rydal Way. Ruis —4A **38**
Rydens Ho. *SE9* —3A **114**
Ryde Pl. Twic —6D **88**
Ryder Clo. Brom —5K **113**
Ryder Ct. *E10* —2D **48**
Ryder Ct. *SW1* —1G **77** (4B **148**)
Ryder Dri. *SE16* —5H **79**
Ryder M. *E9* —5J **47**
Ryder's Ter. *NW8* —2A **60**
Ryder St. *SW1* —1G **77** (4B **148**)
Ryder Yd. *SW1* —1G **77** (4B **148**)
Ryde Vale Rd. *SW12* —2G **109**
Rydons Clo. *SE9* —3C **98**
Rydon St. *N1* —1C **62**
Rydston Clo. *N7* —7J **45**
Rye Clo. Bex —6H **101**
Ryecotes Mead. *SE21* —1E **110**
Ryecroft Av. *Ilf* —2F **35**
Ryecroft Av. Twic —7F **87**
Ryecroft Lodge. *SW16* —6B **110**
Ryecroft Rd. *SE13* —5E **96**
Ryecroft Rd. *SW16* —6A **110**
Ryecroft Rd. Orp —6H **129**
Ryecroft St. *SW6* —1K **91**
Ryedale. *SE22* —6H **95**
Ryefield Path. *SW15* —1C **106**
Ryefield Rd. *SE19* —6C **110**
Rye Hill Pk. *SE15* —4J **95**
Ryelands Cres. *SE12* —6A **98**
Rye La. *SE15* —1G **95**
Rye Pas. *SE15* —3G **95**
Rye Rd. *SE15* —4K **95**
Rye, The. *N14* —7C **6**
Rye Wlk. *SW15* —5F **91**
Rye Way. Edgw —6A **12**
Ryfold Rd. *SW19* —3J **107**
Ryhope Rd. *N11* —4A **16**
Rylandes Rd. *NW2* —3C **42**
Ryland Rd. *NW5* —6F **45**
Rylett Cres. *W12* —2B **74**
Rylett Rd. *W12* —2B **74**
Rylston Rd. *N13* —3J **17**
Rylston Rd. *SW6* —6H **75**
Rymer Rd. Croy —7E **124**
Rymer St. *SE24* —6B **94**

Rymill St. *E16* —1E **82**
Rysbrack St. *SW3*
—3D **76** (1E **152**)
Rythe Ct. Th Dit —7A **118**

S

Sabbarton St. *E16* —6H **65**
Sabella Ct. *E3* —2B **64**
Sabine Rd. *SW11* —3D **92**
Sable Clo. Houn —3A **86**
Sable St. *N1* —7B **46**
Sach Rd. *E5* —2H **47**
Sackville Av. Brom —1J **137**
Sackville Clo. Harr —3H **39**
Sackville Gdns. *Ilf* —1D **50**
Sackville Ho. *SW16* —3J **109**
Sackville Rd. Sutt —7J **131**
Sackville St. *W1*
—7G **61** (3B **148**)
Sackville Way. *SE22* —1G **111**
Saddlers Clo. Pinn —6A **10**
Saddlers M. *SW8* —1J **93**
Saddlers M. Hamp W —2C **118**
Saddlers M. Wemb —4K **39**
Saddlescombe Way. *N12* —5D **14**
Saddle Yd. *W1* —1F **77** (4J **147**)
Sadler Clo. Mitc —2D **122**
Saffron Av. *E14* —7F **65**
Saffron Clo. *NW11* —6H **27**
Saffron Clo. Croy —6J **123**
Saffron Ct. *E15* —5G **49**
(off Maryland Pk.)
Saffron Hill. *EC1*
—5A **62** (5K **143**)
Saffron Rd. Romf —2K **37**
Saffron St. *EC1* —5A **62** (5K **143**)
Sage Clo. *E6* —5D **66**
Sage St. *E1* —7J **63**
Sage Way. *WC1*
—3K **61** (2G **143**)
Sahara Clo. S'hall —7C **54**
Saigasso Clo. *E16* —6B **66**
Sail St. *SE11* —4K **77** (3H **155**)
Saimet. *NW9* —7G **13**
(off Satchell Mead)
Sainfoin Rd. *SW17* —2E **108**
Sainsbury Rd. *SE19* —5E **110**
St Agatha's Dri. King T —6F **105**
St Agatha's Gro. Cars —1D **132**
St Agnes Clo. *E9* —1J **63**
St Agnes Well. *EC1*
—4D **62** (3F **145**)
St Aidans Ct. Bark —2B **68**
St Aidan's Rd. *SE22* —6H **95**
St Aidan's Rd. *W13* —2B **72**
St Alban's Av. *E6* —3D **66**
St Alban's Av. *W4* —4K **73**
St Alban's Av. Felt —5B **102**
St Alban's Clo. *NW11* —1J **43**
St Albans Ct. *EC2*
—6C **62** (6D **144**)
St Alban's Cres. *N22* —1A **30**
St Alban's Cres. Wfd G —7D **20**
St Alban's Gdns. Tedd —5A **104**
St Alban's Gro. *W8* —3K **75**
St Alban's Gro. Cars —7C **122**
St Alban's La. *NW11* —1J **43**
St Albans Mans. *W8* —3K **75**
(off Kensington Ct. Pl.)
St Alban's M. *W2*
—5B **60** (5B **140**)
St Alban's Pl. *N1* —1B **62**
St Alban's Rd. *NW5* —3E **44**
St Alban's Rd. *NW10* —1A **58**
St Albans Rd. Barn —1A **4**

St Albans Rd. *Ilf* —1K **51**
St Alban's Rd. King T —6E **104**
St Alban's Rd. Sutt —4H **131**
St Alban's Rd. Wfd G —7D **20**
St Alban's *SW1*
—7H **61** (3C **148**)
St Alban's Ter. W6 —6G **75**
St Albans Vs. *NW5* —3E **44**
St Alfege Pas. *SE10* —6E **80**
St Alfege Rd. *SE7* —6B **82**
St Alphage Garden. *EC2*
—5C **62** (6D **144**)
St Alphage Highwalk. *EC2*
—5C **62** (6D **144**)
St Alphage Ho. *EC2*
—5D **62** (6E **144**)
St Alphage Wlk. Edgw —2J **25**
St Alphege Rd. *N9* —7D **8**
St Alphonsus Rd. *SW4* —4G **93**
St Amunds Clo. *SE6* —4C **112**
St Andrew's Av. Wemb —4A **40**
St Andrew's Clo. *N12* —4F **15**
St Andrew's Clo. *NW2* —3D **42**
St Andrew's Clo. *SE16* —5H **79**
(off Ryder Dri.)
St Andrew's Clo. Iswth —1J **87**
St Andrew's Clo. Ruis —2B **38**
St Andrew's Clo. Stan —2C **24**
St Andrew's Ct. *SW18* —2A **108**
St Andrews Dri. Stan —1C **24**
St Andrew's Gro. *N16* —1D **46**
St Andrew's Hill. *EC4*
—7B **62** (2B **150**)
St Andrews Mans. *W14* —5G **75**
(off St Andrews Rd.)
St Andrew's M. *N16* —1E **46**
St Andrew's M. *SE3* —7J **81**
St Andrew's Pl. *NW1*
—4F **61** (3K **141**)
St Andrew's Rd. *E11* —6G **33**
St Andrew's Rd. *E13* —3K **65**
St Andrew's Rd. *E17* —2K **31**
St Andrew's Rd. *N9* —7D **8**
St Andrew's Rd. *NW9* —1K **41**
St Andrew's Rd. *NW10* —6D **42**
St Andrew's Rd. *NW11* —6H **27**
St Andrews Rd. *W3* —7A **58**
St Andrews Rd. *W7* —2J **71**
St Andrews Rd. *W14* —6G **75**
St Andrews Rd. Cars —3C **132**
St Andrew's Rd. Croy —4C **134**
St Andrew's Rd. Enf —3J **7**
St Andrew's Rd. *Ilf* —7D **34**
St Andrew's Rd. Romf —6K **37**
St Andrew's Rd. Sidc —3D **116**
St Andrew's Rd. Surb —6D **118**
St Andrew's Sq. *W11* —6G **59**
St Andrew's Sq. Surb —6D **118**
St Andrew's Tower. S'hall
(off Baird Av.) —7G **55**
St Andrew St. *EC4*
—5A **62** (7K **143**)
St Andrews Way. *E3* —4D **64**
St Andrews Wharf. *SE1*
—2F **79** (6K **151**)
St Anna Rd. Barn —5A **4**
St Anne's Clo. *N6* —3E **44**
St Anne's Clo. *NW6* —1G **59**
St Anne's Ct. *W1*
—6H **61** (1C **148**)
St Anne's Ct. W Wick —4G **137**
St Anne's Gdns. *NW10* —3F **57**
St Anne's Pas. *SW13* —3A **90**
St Anne's Rd. *E11* —2F **49**

St Anne's Rd. *Wemb* —5D **40**
St Anne's Row. *E14* —6B **64**
St Anne's St. *E14* —6B **64**
St Ann's. *Bark* —1G **67**
St Ann's Ct. *NW4* —3D **26**
St Ann's Cres. *SW18* —6A **92**
St Ann's Gdns. *NW5* —6E **44**
St Ann's Hill. *SW18* —5K **91**
St Ann's La. *SW1*
　　　—3H **77** (7D **154**)
St Ann's Pk. Rd. *SW18* —6A **92**
St Ann's Pas. *E14* —6B **64**
St Ann's Rd. *N9* —2A **18**
St Ann's Rd. *N15* —5B **30**
St Ann's Rd. *SW13* —2B **90**
St Ann's Rd. *W11* —7F **59**
St Ann's Rd. *Bark* —1G **67**
St Ann's Rd. *Harr* —6J **23**
St Ann's Shop. Cen. *Harr* —6J **23**
St Ann's St. *SW1*
　　　—3H **77** (1D **154**)
St Ann's Ter. *NW8* —2B **60**
St Ann's Vs. *W11* —1F **75**
St Ann's Way. *S Croy* —6B **134**
St Anselm's Pl. *W1*
　　　—7F **61** (2J **147**)
St Anthony's Av. *Wfd G* —6F **21**
St Anthony's Clo. *E1* —1G **79**
St Anthony's Clo. *SW17* —2C **108**
St Antony's Rd. *E7* —7K **49**
St Arvan's Clo. *Croy* —3E **134**
St Asaph Rd. *SE4* —3K **95**
St Aubins Ct. *N1* —1E **62**
St Aubyn's Av. *SW19* —5H **107**
St Aubyn's Av. *Houn* —5E **86**
St Aubyn's Rd. *SE19* —6F **111**
St Audrey Av. *Bexh* —2G **101**
St Augustine's Av. *W5* —2E **56**
St Augustine's Av. *Brom* —5C **128**
St Augustine's Av. *S Croy*
　　　—6C **134**
St Augustines Av. *Wemb* —3E **40**
St Augustine's Path. *N5* —4C **46**
St Augustine's Rd. *NW1* —7H **45**
St Augustine's Rd. *Belv* —4F **85**
St Austell Clo. *Edgw* —2F **25**
St Austell Rd. *SE13* —2E **96**
St Awdry's Rd. *Bark* —7H **51**
St Awdry's Wlk. *Bark* —7G **51**
St Barnabas Clo. *Beck* —2E **126**
St Barnabas Ct. *Har W* —1G **23**
St Barnabas Rd. *E17* —6C **32**
St Barnabas Rd. *Mitc* —7E **108**
St Barnabas Rd. *Sutt* —5B **132**
St Barnabas Rd. *Wfd G* —1K **33**
St Barnabas St. *SW1*
　　　—5E **76** (5H **153**)
St Barnabas Ter. *E9* —5K **47**
St Barnabas Vs. *SW8* —1J **93**
St Bartholomew's Clo. *SE26*
　　　—4H **111**
St Bartholomew's Ct. E6 —2C **66**
　(off St Bartholomew's Rd.)
St Bartholomew's Rd. *E6* —2D **66**
St Benedict's Clo. *SW17* —5E **108**
St Benet's Clo. *SW17* —2C **108**
St Benet's Gro. *Cars* —7A **122**
St Benet's Pl. *EC3*
　　　—7D **62** (2F **151**)
St Bernards. *Croy* —3E **134**
St Bernard's Rd. *SE27* —4D **110**
St Bernard's Rd. *E6* —1B **66**
St Blaise Av. *Brom* —2K **127**
St Botolph Row. *EC3*
　　　—6F **63** (1J **151**)

St Botolph St. *EC3*
　　　—6F **63** (7J **145**)
St Brelades Ct. *N1* —1E **62**
St Briavel's Ct. SE15 —7E **78**
　(off Lynbrook Clo.)
St Bride's Av. *EC4*
　　　—6B **62** (1A **150**)
St Bride's Av. *Edgw* —1F **25**
St Brides Clo. *Eri* —2D **84**
St Bride's Pas. *EC4*
　　　—6B **62** (1A **150**)
St Bride St. *EC4* —6B **62** (7A **144**)
St Catherine's Clo. *SW17*
　　　—2C **108**
St Catherine's Ct. *W4* —3A **74**
St Catherine's Dri. *SE14* —2K **95**
St Catherine's M. *SW3*
　　　—4D **76** (3E **152**)
St Catherine's Rd. *E4* —2H **19**
St Catherines Tower. *E10* —7D **32**
St Chads Clo. *Surb* —7C **118**
St Chad's Gdns. *Romf* —7E **36**
St Chad's Pl. *WC1*
　　　—3K **61** (1F **143**)
St Chad's Rd. *Romf* —7E **36**
St Chad's St. *WC1*
　　　—3J **61** (1F **143**)
St Charles Pl. *W10* —5G **59**
St Charles Sq. *W10* —5F **59**
St Christopher's Clo. *Iswth*
　　　—1J **87**
St Christopher's Gdns. *T Hth*
　　　—3A **124**
St Christopher's M. *Wall* —5G **133**
St Christopher's Pl. *W1*
　　　—6E **60** (7H **141**)
St Clair Clo. *Ilf* —2D **34**
St Clair Dri. *Wor Pk* —3D **130**
St Clair Rd. *E13* —2K **65**
St Clair's Rd. *Croy* —2E **134**
St Clare Bus. Pk. *Hamp* —6G **103**
St Clare St. *EC3* —6F **63** (1J **151**)
St Clement's Clo. *EC4*
　　　—7D **62** (2F **151**)
St Clement's St. *N7* —6K **45**
St Clement's Heights. *SE26*
　　　—3G **111**
St Clement's La. *WC2*
　　　—6K **61** (1H **149**)
St Clements Mans. SW6 —6F **75**
　(off Lillie Rd.)
St Clement St. *N7* —7A **46**
St Cloud Rd. *SE27* —4C **110**
St Columbas Ho. *E17* —4D **32**
St Crispin's Clo. *NW3* —4C **44**
St Crispin's Clo. *S'hall* —6D **54**
St Cross St. *EC1* —5A **62** (5K **143**)
St Cuthbert's Rd. *NW2* —6H **43**
St Cyprian's St. *SW17* —4D **108**
St Davids Clo. SE16 —5H **79**
　(off Masters Dri.)
St David's Clo. *Wemb* —3J **41**
St David's Clo. *W Wick* —7D **126**
St David's Dri. *Edgw* —1F **25**
St David's Pl. *NW4* —7D **26**
St Denis Rd. *SE27* —4D **110**
St Dionis Rd. *SW6* —2H **91**
St Donatt's Rd. *SE14* —1B **96**
St Dunstan's. (Junct.) —6H **131**
St Dunstan's All. *EC3*
　　　—7E **62** (2G **151**)
St Dunstan's Av. *W3* —7K **57**
St Dunstan's Ct. *EC4*
　　　—6A **62** (1K **149**)
St Dunstan's Gdns. *W3* —7K **57**

St Dunstan's Hill. *EC3*
　　　—7E **62** (3G **151**)
St Dunstan's Hill. *Sutt* —5G **131**
St Dunstan's La. *EC3*
　　　—7E **62** (3G **151**)
St Dunstan's La. *Beck* —6E **126**
St Dunstan's Rd. *E7* —6A **50**
St Dunstan's Rd. *SE25* —4F **125**
St Dunstan's Rd. *W6* —5F **75**
St Dunstan's Rd. *W7* —2J **71**
St Dunstan's Rd. *Houn* —2A **86**
　(in two parts)
St Edmund's Clo. *NW8* —1D **60**
St Edmund's Clo. *SW17* —2C **108**
St Edmunds Clo. *Eri* —2D **84**
St Edmund's Dri. *Stan* —1A **24**
St Edmund's La. *Twic* —7F **87**
St Edmund's Rd. *N9* —7B **8**
St Edmund's Rd. *Ilf* —6D **34**
St Edmund's Ter. *NW8* —1C **60**
St Edward's Clo. *NW11* —6J **27**
St Edwards Ct. *E10* —7D **32**
St Edwards Ct. *NW8*
　　　—6H **77** (7D **154**)
St Egberts Way. *E4* —1K **19**
St Elizabeth Ct. *E10* —7D **32**
St Elmo Rd. *W12* —1B **74**
St Elmos Rd. *SE16* —2A **80**
St Erkenwald M. *Bark* —1H **67**
St Erkenwald Rd. *Bark* —1H **67**
St Ermin's Hill. *SW1*
　　　—3H **77** (1C **154**)
St Ervan's Rd. *W10* —5H **59**
St Faith's Clo. *Enf* —1H **7**
St Faith's Rd. *SE21* —1B **110**
St Fidelis Rd. *Eri* —5K **85**
St Fillans Rd. *SE6* —1E **112**
St Frances Way. *Ilf* —4H **51**
St Francis Clo. *Orp* —6J **129**
St Francis Rd. *SE22* —4E **94**
St Francis Rd. *Eri* —4K **85**
St Gabriel's Clo. *E11* —2K **49**
St Gabriel's Mnr. *SE5* —1B **94**
St Gabriels Rd. *NW2* —5F **43**
St George's Av. *E7* —7K **49**
St George's Av. *N7* —4H **45**
St George's Av. *NW9* —4K **25**
St George's Av. *W5* —2D **72**
St George's Av. *S'hall* —7D **54**
St George's Bldgs. SE1
　　　—2C **78** (6D **150**)
St George's Cir. *SE1*
　　　—3B **78** (1A **156**)
St George's Clo. *NW11* —6H **27**
St George's Clo. *SW8* —1G **93**
St George's Clo. *Wemb* —3A **40**
St George's Ct. *E6* —4D **66**
St George's Ct. *E17* —5F **33**
St Georges Ct. *EC4*
　　　—6B **62** (7A **144**)
St George's Ct. *SW15* —4H **91**
St Georges Ct. Harr —6A **24**
　(off Kenton Rd.)
St George's Ct. *Wemb* —3H **41**
St George's Dri. *SW1*
　　　—4F **77** (4K **153**)
St George's Fields. *W2*
　　　—6C **60** (1D **146**)
St George's Gro. *SW17* —3B **108**
St Georges Ind. Est. N17 —7G **17**
St George's Ind. Est. *King T*
　　　—5D **104**
St George's La. *EC3*
　　　—7D **62** (2F **151**)

St George's M. *NW1* —7D **44**
St George's M. *SE1*
　　　—3A **78** (1K **155**)
St George's Pl. *Twic* —1A **104**
St George's Rd. *E7* —7K **49**
St George's Rd. *E10* —3E **48**
St George's Rd. *N9* —3B **18**
St George's Rd. *N13* —2E **16**
St George's Rd. *NW11* —6H **27**
St George's Rd. *SE1*
　　　—3A **78** (1K **155**)
St George's Rd. *SW19* —6H **107**
　(in two parts)
St George's Rd. *W4* —2K **73**
St George's Rd. *W7* —1K **71**
St George's Rd. *Beck* —1D **126**
St George's Rd. *Brom* —2D **128**
　(in two parts)
St George's Rd. *Dag* —5E **52**
St George's Rd. *Enf* —1A **8**
St George's Rd. *Felt* —4B **102**
St George's Rd. *Ilf* —7D **34**
St George's Rd. *King T* —7G **105**
St George's Rd. *Mitc* —3F **123**
St George's Rd. *Orp* —6H **129**
St George's Rd. *Rich* —3F **89**
St George's Rd. *Sidc* —6D **116**
St George's Rd. *Twic* —5B **88**
St George's Rd. *Wall* —5F **133**
St George's Rd. W. *Brom*
　　　—2C **128**
St George's Shop. Cen. *Harr*
　　　—6J **23**
St George's Sq. *E7* —7K **49**
St George's Sq. *E14* —7A **64**
St George's Sq. *SE8* —4B **80**
St George's Sq. *SW1*
　　　—5H **77** (5C **154**)
St George's Sq. *N Mald* —3A **120**
St George's Sq. *SW1*
　　　—5H **77** (6C **154**)
St George's Ter. *NW1* —7D **44**
St George St. *W1*
　　　—7F **61** (1K **147**)
St George's Wlk. *Croy* —3C **134**
St George's Way. *SE15* —6E **78**
St Gerards Clo. *SW4* —5G **93**
St German's Pl. *SE3* —1J **97**
St German's Rd. *SE23* —1A **112**
St Giles Av. *Dag* —7H **53**
St Giles Cir. *W1* —6H **61** (7D **142**)
St Giles Clo. *Dag* —7H **53**
St Giles Ct. *WC2* —6J **61** (7E **142**)
St Giles High St. *WC2*
　　　—6H **61** (7D **142**)
St Giles Ho. *New Bar* —4F **5**
St Giles Pas. *WC2*
　　　—6H **61** (1D **148**)
St Giles Rd. *SE5* —7E **78**
St Gothard Rd. *SE27* —4D **110**
St Gregory Clo. *Ruis* —4A **38**
St Helena Rd. *SE16* —4K **79**
St Helena St. *WC1*
　　　—3A **62** (2J **143**)
St Helen's Cres. *SW16* —1K **123**
St Helen's Gdns. *W10* —5F **59**
St Helen's Pl. *EC3*
　　　—6E **62** (7G **145**)
St Helen's Rd. *SW16* —1K **123**
St Helen's Rd. *W13* —1B **72**
St Helen's Rd. *Eri* —2D **84**
St Helen's Rd. *Ilf* —7C **34**
St Helier Av. *Mord* —7A **122**
St Helier's Av. *Houn* —5E **86**
St Helier's Rd. *E10* —6E **32**

St Hilda's Clo. *NW6* —1F **59**
St Hilda's Clo. *SW17* —2C **108**
St Hilda's Rd. *SW13* —6D **74**
St Hughes Clo. *SW17* —2C **108**
St Hugh's Rd. *SE20* —1H **125**
St James Apartments. E17
　(off Pretoria Av.)　　—5A **32**
St James Av. *N20* —3H **15**
St James Av. *W13* —1A **72**
St James Av. *Beck* —3A **126**
St James Av. *Sutt* —5J **131**
St James Clo. *N20* —3H **15**
St James Clo. *SE18* —5G **83**
St James Clo. *Barn* —4G **5**
St James Clo. *N Mald* —5B **120**
St James Clo. *Ruis* —2A **38**
St James Ct. *SE3* —1K **97**
St James Ct. *SW1*
　　　—3G **77** (1B **154**)
St James' Gdns. Wemb —7E **40**
St James Ga. *NW1* —7H **45**
St James Ga. *Buck H* —1E **20**
St James Gro. *SW11* —2D **92**
St James M. *E14* —3E **80**
St James M. *E17* —5A **32**
St James Residences. W1
　　　—7H **61** (2C **148**)
　(off Brewer St.)
St James' Rd. *E15* —5H **49**
St James' Rd. *N9* —2C **18**
St James Rd. *Cars* —3C **132**
St James' Rd. *King T* —2D **118**
St James' Rd. *Mitc* —7E **108**
St James' Rd. *Sutt* —5J **131**
St James's. *SE14* —1A **96**
St James's. App. *EC2*
　　　—4E **62** (4G **145**)
St James's Av. *E2* —2J **63**
St James's Av. *Beck* —3A **126**
St James's Av. *Hamp* —5G **103**
St James's Clo. SW1 —1D **60**
　(off St James's Ter. M.)
St James's Clo. *SW17* —2D **108**
St James's Cotts. *Rich* —5D **88**
St James's Ct. St. N18 —5B **18**
　(off Fore St.)
St James's Ct. *Harr* —6A **24**
St James's Ct. *King T* —3E **118**
St James's Cres. *SW9* —3A **94**
St James's Dri. *SW17 & SW12*
　　　—1D **108**
St James's Gdns. *W11* —1G **75**
St James's La. *N10* —4F **29**
St James's Mkt. *SW1*
　　　—7H **61** (3C **148**)
St James's Pk. *Croy* —7C **124**
St James's Pas. *EC3*
　　　—6E **62** (1H **151**)
St James's Pl. *SW1*
　　　—1G **77** (5A **148**)
St James's Rd. *SE1* —6G **79**
St James's Rd. *SE16* —3G **79**
St James's Rd. *Croy* —7B **124**
St James's Rd. *Hamp* —5D **103**
St James's Rd. *Surb* —6D **118**
St James's Row. *EC1*
　　　—4B **62** (3A **144**)
St James's Sq. *SW1*
　　　—1G **77** (4B **148**)
St James's St. *SW1*
　　　—1G **77** (4A **148**)
St James's Ter. NW8 —2D **60**
　(off Prince Albert Rd.)
St James's Ter. M. *NW8* —1D **60**
St James St. *E17* —5A **32**

St James St. *W6* —5E **74**
St James's Wlk. *EC1*
—4B **62** (3A **144**)
St James Ter. *SW12* —1E **108**
St James Wlk. *SE15* —1F **95**
(off Pitt St.)
St James Way. *Sidc* —5E **116**
St Joan's Rd. *N9* —2A **18**
St John Fisher Rd. *Eri* —3D **84**
St John's Av. *N11* —5J **15**
St John's Av. *NW10* —1B **58**
St John's Av. *SW15* —5F **91**
St Johns Chu. Rd. *E9* —5J **47**
St Johns Clo. *N14* —6B **6**
St John's Clo. *N20* —3F **15**
(off Rasper Rd.)
St John's Clo. *SW6* —7J **75**
St John's Clo. *Wemb* —5E **40**
St John's Cotts. *SE20* —7J **111**
St John's Ct. *N4* —2B **46**
St John's Ct. *N5* —4B **46**
St John's Ct. *SE13* —2E **96**
St John's Ct. *W6* —4D **74**
(off Glenthorne Rd.)
St John's Ct. *Buck H* —1E **20**
St John's Ct. *Eri* —5K **85**
St John's Ct. *Harr* —6K **23**
St John's Ct. *Iswth* —2K **87**
St John's Cres. *SW9* —3A **94**
St Johns Dri. *SW18* —1K **107**
St John's Est. *SE1*
—2F **79** (6J **151**)
St John's Gdns. *W11* —7G **59**
St John's Gro. *N19* —2G **45**
St John's Gro. *SW13* —2B **90**
St John's Gro. *Rich* —4E **88**
St John's Hill. *SW11* —4B **92**
St John's Hill Gro. *SW11* —4B **92**
St John's La. *EC1*
—4B **62** (4A **144**)
St John's M. *W11* —6J **59**
St Johns Pde. *Sidc* —4B **116**
(off Sidcup High St.)
St John's Pk. *SE3* —7H **81**
St John's Pk. Mans. *N19* —3G **45**
St John's Pas. *SW19* —6G **107**
St John's Path. *EC1*
—4B **62** (4A **144**)
St Johns Pathway. *SE23* —1J **111**
St John's Pl. *EC1*
—4B **62** (4A **144**)
St John's Rd. *E4* —4J **19**
St John's Rd. *E6* —1C **66**
St John's Rd. *E16* —6J **65**
St John's Rd. *E17* —2D **32**
St John's Rd. *N15* —6E **30**
St John's Rd. *NW11* —6H **27**
St John's Rd. *SE20* —6J **111**
St John's Rd. *SW11* —4C **92**
St John's Rd. *SW19* —7G **107**
St John's Rd. *Bark* —1J **67**
St John's Rd. *Cars* —3E **150**
St John's Rd. *Croy* —3B **134**
St John's Rd. *Eri* —5K **85**
St John's Rd. *Felt* —4C **102**
St John's Rd. *Harr* —6K **23**
St John's Rd. *Ilf* —7J **35**
St John's Rd. *Iswth* —2J **87**
St John's Rd. *King T* —2C **118**
St John's Rd. *N Mald* —3J **119**
St John's Rd. *Orp* —6H **129**
St John's Rd. *Rich* —4E **88**
St John's Rd. *Sidc* —4B **116**
St John's Rd. *S'hall* —3C **70**
St John's Rd. *Sutt* —2K **131**

St John's Rd. *Well* —3B **100**
St John's Rd. *Wemb* —4D **40**
St John's Sq. *EC1*
(in two parts) —4B **62** (4A **144**)
St John's Ter. *E7* —6K **49**
St John's Ter. *SE18* —6G **83**
St John's Ter. *W10* —4F **59**
St John St. *EC1* —2A **62** (1K **143**)
St John's Vale. *SE8* —2C **96**
St John's Vs. *N11* —5J **15**
(off Friern Barnet Rd.)
St John's Vs. *N19* —2H **45**
St John's Vs. *W8* —3K **75**
St John's Way. *N19* —2G **45**
St John's Wood Ct. *NW8*
—3B **60** (2B **140**)
St John's Wood High St. *NW8*
—2B **60** (1C **140**)
St John's Wood Pk. *NW8* —1B **60**
St John's Wood Rd. *NW8*
—4B **60** (3A **140**)
St John's Wood Ter. *NW8*
—2B **60**
St John's Yd. *N17* —7A **18**
St Joseph's Clo. *W10* —5G **59**
St Josephs Ct. *SE7* —6K **81**
St Joseph's Dri. *S'hall* —1C **70**
St Joseph's Gro. *NW4* —4D **26**
St Joseph's Rd. *N9* —7C **8**
St Joseph's St. *SW8* —1F **93**
St Joseph's Vale. *SE3* —3F **97**
St Jude's Rd. *E2* —2H **63**
St Jude St. *N16* —5E **46**
St Julian's Clo. *SW16* —4A **110**
St Julian's Farm Rd. *SE27*
—4A **110**
St Julian's Rd. *NW6* —1H **59**
St Katharine's Precinct. *NW1*
—2F **61**
St Katharine's Way. *E1*
—1F **79** (4K **151**)
St Katherine's Rd. *Eri* —2D **84**
St Katherine's Row. *EC3*
—7E **62** (2H **151**)
St Katherines Wlk. *W11* —1F **75**
(off St Ann's Rd.)
St Keverne Rd. *SE9* —4C **114**
St Kilda Rd. *W13* —1A **72**
St Kilda Rd. *Orp* —7K **129**
St Kilda's Rd. *N16* —1D **46**
St Kilda's Rd. *Harr* —6J **23**
St Kitts Ter. *SE19* —5E **110**
St Laurence Clo. *NW6* —1F **59**
St Lawrence Clo. *Edgw* —7A **12**
St Lawrence Ct. *N1* —1E **62**
St Lawrence Dri. *Pinn* —5A **22**
St Lawrence Ter. *W10* —5G **59**
St Lawrence Way. *SW9* —2A **94**
St Leonard's Av. *E4* —6A **20**
St Leonard's Av. *Harr* —5C **24**
St Leonard's Clo. *Well* —3A **100**
St Leonard's Ct. *N1*
—3D **62** (1F **145**)
St Leonard's Gdns. *Houn* —1C **86**
St Leonard's Gdns. *Ilf* —5G **51**
St Leonard's Rd. *E14* —5E **64**
(in two parts)
St Leonard's Rd. *NW10* —4K **57**
St Leonard's Rd. *SW14* —3H **89**
St Leonard's Rd. *W13* —7C **56**
St Leonard's Rd. *Croy* —3B **134**
St Leonard's Rd. *Surb* —5D **118**
St Leonard's Ct. *N1*
St Leonard's Ter. *SW3*

St Leonards Sq. *Surb* —5D **118**
St Leonard's St. *E3* —3D **64**
St Leonard's Ter. *SW3*
—5D **76** (6E **152**)
St Leonard's Wlk. *SW16* —7K **109**
St Loo Av. *SW3* —6C **76** (7D **152**)
St Louis Rd. *SE27* —4D **110**
St Loy's Rd. *N17* —2E **30**
St Lucia Dri. *E15* —1H **65**
St Luke's Av. *SW4* —4H **93**
St Luke's Av. *Enf* —1J **7**
St Luke's Av. *Ilf* —5F **51**
St Luke's Clo. *EC1*
—4C **62** (3D **144**)
St Luke's Clo. *SE25* —6H **125**
St Lukes Ct. *E10* —7D **32**
(off Capworth St.)
St Luke's Est. *EC1*
—3D **62** (2E **144**)
St Luke's M. *W11* —6H **59**
St Luke's Pas. *King T* —1F **119**
St Luke's Path. *Ilf* —5F **51**
St Luke's Rd. *W11* —5H **59**
St Luke's Sq. *E16* —6H **65**
St Luke's St. *SW3*
—5C **76** (5D **152**)
St Luke's Yd. *W9* —2H **59**
St Malo Av. *N9* —3D **18**
St Margaret's. *Bark* —1H **67**
St Margaret's Av. *N15* —4B **30**
St Margaret's Av. *N20* —1F **15**
St Margaret's Av. *Harr* —3G **39**
St Margaret's Av. *Sidc* —3H **115**
St Margaret's Av. *Sutt* —3G **131**
St Margarets Bus. Cen. *Twic*
—6B **88**
St Margaret's Ct. *N11* —4K **15**
St Margaret's Ct. *SE1*
—1D **78** (5D **150**)
St Margarets Ct. *Edgw* —5C **12**
St Margaret's Cres. *SW15*
—5D **90**
St Margaret's Dri. *Twic* —5B **88**
St Margaret's Gro. *E11* —3H **49**
St Margaret's Gro. *SE18* —6G **83**
St Margaret's Gro. *Twic* —6A **88**
St Margaret's La. *W8* —3K **75**
St Margaret's Pas. *SE13* —3G **97**
St Margaret's Rd. *E12* —2A **50**
St Margaret's Rd. *N17* —3E **30**
St Margaret's Rd. *NW10* —3E **58**
St Margarets Rd. *SE4* —4B **96**
St Margaret's Rd. *W7* —2J **71**
St Margaret's Rd. *Edgw* —5C **12**
St Margarets Rd. *Iswth & Twic*
—4B **88**
St Margaret's Ter. *SE18* —5G **83**
St Margaret St. *SW1*
—2J **77** (7E **148**)
St Margarets Vicarage. *E11*
—3H **49**
St Mark's Clo. *SE10* —7E **80**
St Mark's Clo. *New Bar* —3E **4**
St Marks Ct. *E10* —7D **32**
(off Capworth St.)
St Marks Ct. *W7* —2J **71**
(off Lwr. Boston Rd.)
St Mark's Cres. *NW1* —1E **60**
St Mark's Ga. *E9* —7B **48**
St Mark's Gro. *SW10* —6K **75**
St Mark's Hill. *Surb* —6E **118**
St Marks Ind. Est. *E16* —1B **82**
St Mark's Pl. *SW19* —6H **107**
St Mark's Pl. *W11* —6G **59**
St Mark's Rise. *E8* —5F **47**

St Mark's Rd. *SE25* —4G **125**
St Mark's Rd. *W5* —1E **72**
St Mark's Rd. *W7* —2J **71**
St Mark's Rd. *W10 & W11*
—5F **59**
St Mark's Rd. *Brom* —3K **127**
St Marks Rd. *Enf* —6A **8**
St Marks Rd. *Mitc* —2D **122**
St Mark's Rd. *Tedd* —7B **104**
St Mark's Sq. *NW1* —1E **60**
St Mark St. *E1* —6F **63** (1K **151**)
St Martin's Av. *E6* —2B **66**
St Martin's Clo. *NW1* —1G **61**
St Martin's Clo. *Enf* —1C **8**
St Martin's Clo. *Eri* —2D **84**
St Martins Ct. *N1* —1E **62**
(off De Beauvoir Est.)
St Martin's Ct. *WC2*
—7J **61** (2E **148**)
St Martins Est. *SW2* —1A **110**
St Martin's La. *WC2*
—7J **61** (2E **148**)
St Martin's le Grand. *EC1*
—6C **62** (7C **144**)
St Martin's Pl. *WC2*
—7J **61** (3E **148**)
St Martin's Rd. *N9* —2C **18**
St Martin's Rd. *SW9* —2K **93**
St Martin's St. *WC2*
—7H **61** (3D **148**)
St Martins Way. *SW17* —3A **108**
St Mary Abbot's Ct. *W14* —3H **75**
(off Warwick Gdns.)
St Mary Abbot's Pl. *W8* —3H **75**
St Mary Abbot's Ter. *W14*
—3H **75**
St Mary at Hill. *EC3*
—7E **62** (3G **151**)
St Mary Av. *Wall* —3F **133**
St Mary Axe. *EC3*
—6E **62** (7H **145**)
St Marychurch St. *SE16* —2J **79**
St Mary Graces Ct. *E1*
—7F **63** (3K **151**)
St Mary Newington Clo. *SE17*
—5E **78** (5H **157**)
St Mary Rd. *E17* —4C **32**
St Mary's. *Bark* —1H **67**
St Mary's App. *E12* —5D **50**
St Mary's Av. *E11* —7K **33**
St Mary's Av. *N3* —2G **27**
St Mary's Av. *Brom* —3G **127**
St Mary's Av. *S'hall* —4F **71**
St Mary's Av. *Tedd* —6K **103**
St Mary's Clo. *N17* —1F **31**
St Mary's Clo. *Eps* —7B **130**
St Mary's Ct. *E6* —4D **66**
St Mary's Ct. *SE7* —7B **82**
St Mary's Ct. *W6* —2D **72**
St Mary's Ct. *W14* —3B **74**
St Mary's Ct. *Wall* —4G **133**
St Mary's Cres. *NW4* —3D **26**
St Mary's Cres. *Iswth* —7H **71**
St Mary's Gdns. *SE11*
—4A **78** (3K **155**)
St Mary's Ga. *W8* —3K **75**
St Mary's Grn. *N2* —2A **28**
St Mary's Gro. *N1* —6B **46**
St Mary's Gro. *SW13* —3D **90**
St Mary's Gro. *W4* —6H **73**
St Mary's Gro. *Rich* —4F **89**
St Mary's Mans. *W2*
—5B **60** (5A **140**)
St Mary's M. *NW6* —7K **43**
St Marys M. *Rich* —2C **104**

St Mary's Path. *N1* —1B **62**
St Mary's Pl. *SE9* —6E **98**
St Mary's Pl. *W5* —2D **72**
St Mary's Pl. *W8* —3K **75**
St Mary's Rd. *E10* —3E **48**
St Mary's Rd. *E13* —2K **65**
St Mary's Rd. *N8* —4J **29**
St Mary's Rd. *N9* —1C **18**
St Mary's Rd. *NW10* —1A **58**
St Mary's Rd. *NW11* —7G **27**
St Mary's Rd. *SE15* —1J **95**
St Mary's Rd. *SE25* —3E **124**
St Mary's Rd. *SW19* —5G **107**
St Marys Rd. *W5* —2D **72**
St Mary's Rd. *Barn* —7J **5**
St Mary's Rd. *Bex* —1J **117**
St Mary's Rd. *Dit H* —7C **118**
St Mary's Rd. *Ilf* —2G **51**
St Mary's Rd. *Surb* —6D **118**
St Mary's Rd. *Wor Pk* —2A **130**
St Mary's Sq. *W2*
—5B **60** (5A **140**)
St Mary's Sq. *W5* —2D **72**
St Mary's Ter. *W2*
—5B **60** (5A **140**)
St Mary's Tower. *EC1*
—4C **62** (4D **144**)
(off Fortune St.)
St Mary St. *SE18* —4D **82**
St Mary's View. *Harr* —5C **24**
St Mary's Wlk. *SE11*
—4A **78** (3K **155**)
St Mary's Way. *Chig* —5K **21**
St Matthew's Av. *Surb* —7E **118**
St Matthews Ct. *E10* —7D **32**
(off Capworth St.)
St Matthews Ct. *N10* —2E **28**
St Matthews Ct. *SE1*
—3C **78** (2C **156**)
St Matthew's Dri. *Brom* —3D **128**
St Matthew's Lodge. *NW1*
—2G **61**
(off Oakley Sq.)
St Matthew's Rd. *SW2* —4K **93**
St Matthew's Rd. *W5* —1E **72**
St Matthew's Row. *E2* —3G **63**
St Matthew St. *SW1*
—3H **77** (2C **154**)
St Matthias Clo. *NW9* —5B **26**
St Maur Rd. *SW6* —1H **91**
St Merryn Clo. *SE18* —7H **83**
St Merryn Ct. *Beck* —7C **112**
St Michael's All. *EC3*
—6D **62** (1F **151**)
St Michael's Av. *N9* —7D **8**
St Michael's Av. *Enf* —7D **8**
St Michael's Av. *Wemb* —6G **41**
St Michaels Clo. *E16* —5B **66**
St Michael's Clo. *N3* —2H **27**
St Michael's Clo. *N12* —5H **15**
St Michael's Clo. *Brom* —3C **128**
St Michael's Clo. *Eri* —2D **84**
St Michael's Clo. *Wor Pk*
—2B **130**
St Michaels Ct. *E14* —5E **64**
(off St Leonards Rd.)
St Michael's Cres. *Pinn* —6C **22**
St Michael's Gdns. *W10* —5G **59**
St Michael's Rise. *Well* —1B **100**
St Michael's Rd. *NW2* —4E **42**
St Michael's Rd. *SW9* —2K **93**
St Michael's Rd. *Croy* —1C **134**
St Michael's Rd. *Wall* —6G **133**
St Michael's Rd. *Well* —3B **100**
St Michael's St. *W2*
—6B **60** (7B **140**)

St Michael's Ter. N22 —1J 29
St Michael Tower. E17 —1B 32
St Mildred's Ct. EC2
—6D 62 (1E 150)
St Mildreds Rd. SE12 —7H 97
St Mirren Ct. New Bar —5F 5
St Nicholas Cen. Sutt —5K 131
St Nicholas Glebe. SW17
—6E 108
St Nicholas Rd. SE18 —5K 83
St Nicholas Rd. Sutt —5K 131
St Nicholas St. SE8 —1B 96
St Nicholas Way. Sutt —4K 131
St Nicolas La. Chst —1C 128
St Ninian's Ct. N2 —7H 15
St Norbert Grn. SE4 —4A 96
St Norbert Rd. SE4 —5K 95
St Olaf Ho. SE1 —1D 78 (4F 151)
St Olaf's Rd. SW6 —7G 75
St Olaf Stairs. SE1
—1D 78 (4F 151)
St Olave's Ct. EC2
—6D 62 (1E 150)
St Olave's Est. SE1
—2E 78 (6H 151)
St Olave's Gdns. SE11
—4A 78 (3J 155)
St Olave's Mans. SE11
—4A 78 (3J 155)
St Olave's Rd. E6 —1E 66
St Olave's Ter. SE1
—2E 78 (6H 151)
St Olaves Wlk. SW16 —2G 123
St Oswald's Pl. SE11
—5K 77 (6G 155)
St Oswald's Rd. SW16 —1B 124
St Oswulf St. SW1
—4H 77 (4D 154)
St Pancras Clo. N2 —2B 28
St Pancras Commercial Cen. NW1
(off Pratt St.) —1G 61
St Pancras Way. NW1 —7G 45
St Patrick's Ct. E4 —7B 20
St Patrick's Ct. SE4 —5C 96
St Paulinus Ct. Dart —4K 101
(off Manor Rd.)
St Paul's All. EC4
—6B 62 (1B 150)
St Paul's Av. NW2 —6E 42
St Paul's Av. SE16 —1K 79
St Paul's Av. Harr —4F 25
St Paul's Chyd. EC4
—6B 62 (1B 150)
St Pauls Clo. SE7 —5B 82
St Paul's Clo. W5 —2F 73
St Paul's Clo. Cars —1C 132
St Paul's Clo. Houn —2C 86
St Paul's Ct. SW4 —4H 93
St Paul's Ct. Houn —3C 86
St Pauls Courtyard. SE8 —7C 80
St Paul's Cray Rd. Chst —1H 129
St Paul's Cres. NW1 —7H 45
(in two parts)
St Paul's Dri. E15 —5F 49
St Paul's M. NW1 —7H 45
St Paul's Pl. N1 —6D 46
St Paul's Rise. N13 —6G 17
St Paul's Rd. N1 —6B 46
St Paul's Rd. N11 —5A 16
St Paul's Rd. N17 —7B 18
St Paul's Rd. Bark —1G 67
St Paul's Rd. Bren —6D 72
St Paul's Rd. Eri —7J 85
St Paul's Rd. Rich —3F 89
St Paul's Rd. T Hth —3C 124

St Paul's Shrubbery. N1 —6D 46
St Paul's Sq. Brom —2H 127
St Paul's Studios. W14 —5G 75
(off Talgarth Rd.)
St Paul's Ter. SE17
—6B 78 (7B 156)
St Pauls Tower. E10 —7D 32
St Paul St. N1 —1C 62
(in two parts)
St Paul's Wlk. King T —7G 105
St Pauls Way. E3 —5B 64
St Paul's Way. N3 —7E 14
St Paul's Wood Hill. Orp —2J 129
St Peter's Av. E2 —2G 63
St Peters Av. N2 —7H 15
St Peter's Av. N18 —4B 18
St Petersburgh M. W2 —7K 59
St Petersburgh Pl. W2 —7K 59
St Peter's Cen. E1 —1H 79
St Peters Chu. Ct. N1 —2B 62
(off Devonia Rd.)
St Peter's Clo. E2 —2G 63
St Peter's Clo. SW17 —2C 108
St Peters Clo. Bush —1C 10
St Peter's Clo. Chst —7H 115
St Peter's Clo. Ilf —4K 35
St Peter's Clo. Ruis —2B 38
St Peter's Ct. NW4 —5E 26
St Peter's Gdns. SE27 —3A 110
St Peters Gro. W6 —4C 74
St Peter's Pl. W9 —4K 59
St Peter's Rd. N9 —1C 18
St Peter's Rd. W6 —5C 74
St Peter's Rd. Croy —4D 134
St Peter's Rd. King T —2G 119
St Peter's Rd. S'hall —5E 54
St Peter's Rd. Twic —5B 88
St Peter's Sq. E2 —2G 63
St Peter's Sq. W6 —4B 74
St Peter's St. N1 —1B 62
St Peter's St. S Croy —5D 134
St Peter's St. M. N1 —2B 62
(off St Peters St.)
St Peter's Ter. SW6 —7H 75
St Peter's Vs. W6 —4C 74
St Peter's Way. N1 —7E 46
St Peter's Way. W5 —5D 56
St Peter's Wharf. W4 —5C 74
St Philips Av. N2 —7H 15
St Philip's Av. Wor Pk —2D 130
St Philip Sq. SW8 —2F 93
St Philip's Rd. E8 —6G 47
St Philip St. SW8 —2F 93
St Philip's Way. N1 —1C 62
St Phillips Rd. Surb —6D 118
St Quentin Rd. Well —3K 99
St Quintin Av. W10 —5E 58
St Quintin Gdns. W10 —5E 58
St Raphael's Way. NW10 —5J 41
St Regis Clo. N10 —2F 29
St Regis Heights. NW3 —3K 43
St Ronan's Clo. Barn —1G 5
St Ronan's Cres. Wfd G —7D 20
St Rule St. SW8 —2G 93
St Saviour's College.
—4D 110
St Saviour's Ct. N10 —2F 29
(off Alexandra Pk. Rd.)
St Saviours Ct. Harr —5J 23
St Saviour's Est. SE1
—3F 79 (1J 157)
St Saviour's Rd. SW2 —5K 93
St Saviour's Rd. Croy —6C 124
Saints Clo. SE27 —4B 110

Saints Dri. E7 —5B 50
St Silas Pl. NW5 —6E 44
St Simon's Av. SW15 —5E 90
St Stephen's Av. E17 —5E 32
St Stephen's Av. W12 —2D 74
St Stephen's Av. W13 —6B 56
St Stephen's Clo. E17 —5D 32
St Stephen's Clo. NW8 —1C 60
St Stephen's Clo. S'hall —5E 54
St Stephens Ct. N8 —6K 29
St Stephens Ct. Enf —6K 7
(off Park Av.)
St Stephen's Cres. W2 —6J 59
St Stephen's Cres. T Hth —3A 124
St Stephen's Gdns. SW15
—5H 91
St Stephen's Gdns. W2 —6J 59
(in two parts)
St Stephen's Gdns. Twic —6C 88
St Stephens Gro. SE13 —3E 96
St Stephen's M. W2 —5J 59
St Stephens Pde. E7 —7A 50
St Stephens Pde. SW1
—2J 77 (7F 149)
St Stephen's Pas. Twic —6C 88
St Stephen's Rd. E3 —1A 64
St Stephen's Rd. E6 —7A 50
St Stephen's Rd. E17 —5D 32
St Stephen's Rd. W13 —6B 56
St Stephen's Rd. Barn —5A 4
St Stephen's Rd. Houn —6E 86
St Stephen's Row. EC4
—6D 62 (1E 150)
St Stephens Ter. SW8 —7K 77
St Stephen's Wlk. SW7 —4A 76
St Swithin's La. EC4
—7D 62 (2E 150)
St Swithun's Rd. SE13 —6F 97
St Thomas Clo. Surb —7F 119
St Thomas Ct. Bex —7G 101
St Thomas Ct. Pinn —1C 22
St Thomas Dri. Orp —7G 129
St Thomas Dri. Pinn —1C 22
St Thomas Gdns. Ilf —6G 51
St Thomas Pl. NW1 —7H 45
(off Maiden La.)
St Thomas Rd. E16 —6J 65
St Thomas Rd. N14 —7C 6
St Thomas Rd. W4 —6J 73
St Thomas Rd. Belv —2J 85
St Thomas's Gdns. NW5 —6E 44
St Thomas's Pl. E9 —7J 47
St Thomas's Rd. N4 —2A 46
St Thomas Rd. NW10 —1A 58
St Thomas's Sq. E9 —7J 47
St Thomas St. SE1
—1D 78 (5E 150)
St Thomas's Way. SW6 —7H 75
St Timothys M. Brom —1K 127
St Ursula Gro. Pinn —5B 22
St Ursula Rd. S'hall —6E 54
St Vincent Clo. SE27 —5B 110
St Vincent Rd. Twic —6G 87
St Vincent St. W1
—5E 60 (6H 141)
St Wilfrid's Clo. Barn —5H 5
St Wilfrid's Rd. Barn —5H 5
St Winefride's Av. E12 —5D 50
St Winifred's Rd. Tedd —6B 104
Salamanca Pl. SE1
—4K 77 (4G 155)
Salamanca St. SE1 & SE11
—4K 77 (4G 155)

Salamander Clo. King T —5C 104
Salamander Quay. King T
—1D 118
Salcombe Dri. Mord —1F 131
Salcombe Dri. Romf —6F 37
Salcombe Gdns. NW7 —6K 13
Salcombe Rd. E17 —7B 32
Salcombe Rd. N16 —5E 46
Salcott Rd. SW11 —5C 92
Salcott Rd. Croy —3J 133
Salehurst Clo. Harr —5E 24
Salehurst Rd. SE4 —6B 96
Salem Pl. Croy —3C 134
Salem Rd. W2 —7K 59
Sale Pl. W2 —6C 60 (6C 140)
Sale St. E2 —4G 63
Salford Rd. SW2 —1H 109
Salisbury Av. N3 —3H 27
Salisbury Av. Bark —7H 51
Salisbury Av. Sutt —6H 131
Salisbury Clo. SE17
—4D 78 (4E 156)
Salisbury Clo. Wor Pk —3B 130
Salisbury Ct. EC4
—6B 62 (1A 150)
Salisbury Ct. Cars —5D 132
Salisbury Ct. N'holt —5F 39
(off Newmarket Av.)
Salisbury Gdns. SW19 —7G 107
Salisbury Gdns. Buck H —2G 21
Salisbury Hall Gdns. E4 —6H 19
Salisbury Ho. SW9 —7A 78
(off Cranmer Rd.)
Salisbury Ho. Stan —6F 11
Salisbury Mans. N15 —5B 30
Salisbury M. SW6 —7H 75
Salisbury Pas. SW6 —7H 75
(off Dawes Rd.)
Salisbury Pl. SW9 —7B 78
Salisbury Pl. W1
—5D 60 (5E 140)
Salisbury Rd. E4 —3H 19
Salisbury Rd. E7 —6J 49
Salisbury Rd. E10 —2E 48
Salisbury Rd. E12 —5B 50
Salisbury Rd. E17 —5E 32
Salisbury Rd. N4 —5B 30
Salisbury Rd. N9 —3B 18
Salisbury Rd. N22 —1B 30
Salisbury Rd. SE25 —6G 125
Salisbury Rd. SW19 —7G 107
Salisbury Rd. W13 —2B 72
Salisbury Rd. Barn —3B 4
Salisbury Rd. Bex —1G 117
Salisbury Rd. Brom —5C 128
Salisbury Rd. Cars —6D 132
Salisbury Rd. Dag —6H 53
Salisbury Rd. Felt —1A 102
Salisbury Rd. Harr —5J 23
Salisbury Rd. Houn —3A 86
Salisbury Rd. Ilf —2J 51
Salisbury Rd. N Mald —3K 119
Salisbury Rd. Rich —4E 88
Salisbury Rd. S'hall —4C 70
Salisbury Rd. Wor Pk —4A 130
Salisbury Sq. EC4
—6A 62 (1K 149)
Salisbury St. NW8
—4C 60 (4C 140)
Salisbury St. W3 —2J 73
Salisbury Wlk. N19 —2G 45
Salix Ct. N3 —6D 14
Salliesfield. Twic —6H 87

Sally Motland Ho. Wemb —7F 25
Salmen Rd. E13 —2H 65
Salmond Clo. Stan —6F 11
Salmon La. E14 —6A 64
Salmon Rd. Belv —5G 85
Salmons Rd. N9 —1B 18
Salmon St. E14 —6B 64
Salmon St. NW9 —1H 41
Salomons Rd. E13 —5A 66
Salop Rd. E17 —6K 31
Saltash Clo. Sutt —4H 131
Saltash Rd. Well —1C 100
Saltcoats Rd. W4 —2A 74
Saltcroft Clo. Wemb —1H 41
Saltdene. N4 —1K 45
Salter Clo. Harr —4D 38
Salterford Rd. SW17 —6E 108
Salter Rd. SE16 —1K 79
Salters Ct. EC4 —6C 62 (1D 150)
Salter's Hall Ct. EC4
—7D 62 (2E 150)
Salter's Hill. SE19 —5D 110
Salters Rd. E17 —4F 33
Salters Rd. W10 —4F 59
Salter St. E14 —7C 64
Salter St. NW10 —3C 58
Salterton Rd. N7 —3K 45
Saltley Clo. E6 —6C 66
Saltoun Rd. SW2 —4A 94
Saltram Clo. N15 —4F 31
Saltram Cres. W9 —3H 59
Saltwell St. E14 —7C 64
Saltwood Gro. SE17
—5D 78 (6E 156)
Saltwood Ho. SE15 —6J 79
(off Lovelinch Clo.)
Salusbury Rd. NW6 —1G 59
Salutation Rd. SE10 —4G 81
Salvador. SW17 —5D 108
Salva Gdns. Gnfd —2A 56
Salvia Gdns. Gnfd —2A 56
Salvin Rd. SW15 —3F 91
Salway Clo. Wfd G —7D 20
Salway Pl. E15 —6F 49
Salway Rd. E15 —6F 49
Samantha Clo. E17 —7B 32
Sam Bartram Clo. SE7 —5A 82
Sambrook Ho. SE11
—4A 78 (4J 155)
Sambruck M. SE6 —1D 112
Samels Ct. W6 —5C 74
Samford Ho. N1 —1A 62
(off Barnsbury Est.)
Samford St. NW8
—4B 60 (4C 140)
Samos Rd. SE20 —2H 125
Sampson Av. Barn —5A 4
Sampson Clo. Belv —3D 84
Sampson St. E1 —1G 79
Samsbrooke Ct. Enf —5A 8
Samson St. E13 —2A 66
Samuda Est. E14 —3E 80
Samuel Clo. E8 —1F 63
Samuel Clo. SE14 —6A 79
Samuel Clo. SE18 —4C 82
Samuel Johnson Clo. SW16
—4K 109
Samuel Jones Ind. Est. SE15
(off Peckham Gro.) —7E 78
Samuel Lewis Bldgs. N1 —6A 46
Samuel Lewis Trust Dwellings. E8
(Amhurst Rd.) —5G 47
Samuel Lewis Trust Dwellings. E8
(Dalston La.) —5G 47

Samuel Lewis Trust Dwellings.
  N16 —6E **30**
Samuel Lewis Trust Dwellings.
  (off Warner Rd.) SE5 —1C 94
Samuel Lewis Trust Dwellings.
  SW3 —4C **76** (4C **152**)
Samuel Lewis Trust Dwellings.
  (off Vanston Pl.) SW6 —7J 75
Samuel Lewis Trust Dwellings.
  (off Lisgar Ter.) W14 —4H 75
Samuel's Clo. W6 —4E **74**
Samuel St. SE18 —4D **82**
Sancroft Ho. NW2 —3D **42**
Sancroft Ho. SE11
  —5K **77** (5H **155**)
Sancroft Rd. Harr —2K **23**
Sancroft St. SE11
  —5K **77** (5H **155**)
Sanctuary St. SE1
  —2C **78** (6D **150**)
Sanctuary, The. SW1
  —3H **77** (1D **154**)
Sanctuary, The. Bex —6D **100**
Sanctuary, The. Mord —6J **121**
Sandale Ho. N16 —3D **46**
Sandall Clo. W5 —4E **56**
Sandall Rd. NW5 —6G **45**
Sandall Rd. W5 —4E **56**
Sandal Rd. N18 —5B **18**
Sandal Rd. N Mald —5K **119**
Sandal St. E15 —1G **65**
Sandalwood Clo. E1 —4A **64**
Sandalwood Ho. Sidc —3K **115**
Sandalwood Rd. Felt —3A **102**
Sandbach Pl. SE18 —4G **83**
Sandbourne Av. SW19 —2K **121**
Sandbourne Rd. SE4 —2A **96**
Sandbrook Clo. NW7 —6E **12**
Sandbrook Rd. N16 —3E **46**
Sandby Grn. SE9 —3C **98**
Sandcliff Rd. Eri —4K **85**
Sandcroft Clo. N13 —6G **17**
Sandell St. SE1 —2A **78** (6J **149**)
Sanderling Ct. SE8 —6B 80
  (off Abinger Gro.)
Sanderling Ct. SE28 —7C **68**
Sanders Clo. Hamp —5G **103**
Sanders La. NW7 —7K **13**
  (in three parts)
Sanderson Clo. NW5 —4F **45**
Sanderson Gdns. Wfd G —1A 34
Sanderson Shaw. SE28 —7D **68**
Sanderstead Av. NW2 —2G **43**
Sanderstead Clo. SW12 —7G **93**
Sanderstead Rd. E10 —1A **48**
Sanderstead Rd. S Croy —7D 134
Sanders Way. N19 —1H **45**
Sandfield Gdns. T Hth —3B **124**
Sandfield Rd. T Hth —3B **124**
Sandford Av. N22 —1C **30**
Sandford Clo. E6 —4D **66**
Sandford Ct. N16 —1E **46**
Sandford Ct. New Bar —3E 4
Sandford Rd. E6 —3C **66**
Sandford Rd. Bexh —4E **100**
Sandford Rd. Brom —4J **127**
Sandford St. SW6 —7K **75**
Sandgate Ho. Romf —7K **37**
Sandgate Ho. E5 —4H **47**
Sandgate Ho. W5 —5C **56**
Sandgate La. SW18 —1C **108**
Sandgate Rd. Well —7C **84**
Sandgate St. SE15 —6H **79**
Sandham Ct. SW4 —1J **93**
Sandhills. Wall —4H **133**

Sandhurst Av. Harr —6F **23**
Sandhurst Av. Surb —7H **119**
Sandhurst Clo. NW9 —3G **25**
Sandhurst Clo. S Croy —7E **134**
Sandhurst Ct. SW2 —4J **93**
Sandhurst Dri. Ilf —4K **51**
Sandhurst Rd. N9 —6D **8**
Sandhurst Rd. NW9 —3G **25**
Sandhurst Rd. SE6 —1F **113**
Sandhurst Rd. Bex —5D **100**
Sandhurst Rd. Sidc —3K **115**
Sandhurst Way. S Croy —7E 134
Sandiford Rd. Sutt —2H **131**
Sandiland Cres. Brom —2H **137**
Sandilands. Croy —2G **135**
Sandilands Rd. SW6 —1K **91**
Sandison St. SE15 —3G **95**
Sandland St. WC1
  —5K **61** (6H **143**)
Sandling Rise. SE9 —3E **114**
Sandlings Clo. SE15 —2H **95**
Sandlings, The. N22 —3B **30**
Sandmere Rd. SW4 —4H **93**
Sandown Av. Dag —6J **53**
Sandown Ct. Stan —5H **11**
Sandown Ct. Sutt —7K **131**
Sandown Dri. Cars —7E 132
Sandown Rd. SE25 —5H **125**
Sandown Way. N'holt —6C 38
Sandpiper Clo. E17 —7D **18**
Sandpiper Clo. SE16 —2B **80**
Sandpit Pl. SE7 —5C **82**
Sandpit Rd. Brom —5G **113**
Sandpits Rd. Croy —4K **135**
Sandpits Rd. Rich —2D **104**
Sandra Clo. N22 —1C **30**
Sandra Clo. Houn —5F **87**
Sandridge Clo. Harr —4J **23**
Sandridge Ct. N4 —2C **46**
Sandridge St. N19 —2G **45**
Sandringham Av. SW20 —1G **121**
Sandringham Clo. SW19 —7F **91**
Sandringham Clo. Enf —2K **7**
Sandringham Clo. Ilf —3G **35**
Sandringham Ct. W9 —3A 60
  (off Maida Vale)
Sandringham Ct. Sidc —6K **99**
Sandringham Cres. Harr —2E **38**
Sandringham Dri. Well —2J **99**
Sandringham Flats. WC2
  —7H **61** (2D **148**)
  (off Charing Cross Rd.)
Sandringham Gdns. N8 —6J **29**
Sandringham Gdns. N12 —6G **15**
Sandringham Gdns. Ilf —3C **35**
Sandringham M. W5 —7D **56**
Sandringham Rd. E7 —5A **50**
Sandringham Rd. E8 —5F **47**
Sandringham Rd. E10 —6F **33**
Sandringham Rd. N22 —3C **30**
Sandringham Rd. NW2 —6D **42**
Sandringham Rd. NW11 —7G **27**
Sandringham Rd. Bark —6K **51**
Sandringham Rd. Brom —5J **113**
Sandringham Rd. N'holt —7E **38**
Sandringham Rd. T Hth —5C **124**
Sandringham Rd. Wor Pk
  —3C **130**
Sandrock Pl. Croy —4K **135**
Sandrock Rd. SE13 —3C **96**
Sand's End La. SW6 —1K **91**
Sandstone Pl. N19 —2F **45**
Sandstone Rd. SE12 —2K **113**
Sands Way. Wfd G —6J **21**
Sandtoft Rd. SE7 —6K **81**

Sandwell Cres. NW6 —6J **43**
Sandwich St. WC1
  —3J **61** (2E **142**)
Sandycombe Rd. Rich —3F **89**
Sandycoombe Rd. Twic —6C **88**
Sandycroft. SE2 —6A **84**
Sandy Hill Av. SE18 —5F **83**
Sandy Hill Rd. SE18 —4E **82**
Sandyhill Rd. Ilf —4F **51**
Sandyhill Rd. Wall —7G **133**
Sandy La. Harr —6F **25**
Sandy La. Mitc —1E **122**
Sandy La. Orp —7K **129**
Sandy La. Rich —2C **104**
Sandy La. St P & Sidc —7D **116**
Sandy La. Sutt —7G **131**
Sandy La. Tedd & King T
  —7A **104**
Sandy La. N. Wall —5H **133**
Sandy La. S. Wall —7H **133**
Sandymount Av. Stan —5H **11**
Sandy Ridge. Chst —6E **114**
Sandy Rd. NW3 —2K **43**
Sandys Row. E1
  —5E **62** (6H **145**)
Sandy Way. Croy —3B **136**
Sanford La. N16 —2F **47**
  (in two parts)
Sanford St. SE14 —6A **80**
Sanford Ter. N16 —3F **47**
Sanford Wlk. N16 —2F **47**
Sanford Wlk. SE14 —6A **80**
Sangley Rd. SE6 —7D **96**
Sangley Rd. SE25 —4E **124**
Sangora Rd. SW11 —4B **92**
Sansom Rd. E11 —2H **49**
Sansom St. SE5 —7D **78**
Sans Wlk. EC1 —4A **62** (3K **143**)
Santley Ho. SE1 —2A **78** (7K **149**)
Santley St. SW4 —4J **93**
Santos Rd. SW18 —5J **91**
Santway, The. Stan —5D 10
Sapcote Trad. Est. NW10 —6B **42**
Saperton Wlk. SE11
  —4K **77** (3H **155**)
Sapperton Ct. EC1
  —4C **62** (3C **144**)
Sapphire Clo. E6 —6E **66**
Sapphire Clo. Dag —1C **52**
Sapphire Rd. SE8 —4A **80**
Saracen Clo. Croy —6D **124**
Saracen's Head Yd. EC3
  —6F **63** (1J **151**)
Saracen St. E14 —6C **64**
Sarah Ct. N'holt —1D **54**
Sarah St. N1 —3E **62** (1H **145**)
Saratoga Rd. E5 —4J **47**
Sardinia St. WC2
  —6K **61** (1G **149**)
Sarita Clo. Harr —2H **23**
Sarjant Path. SW19 —2F 107
  (off Blincoe Clo.)
Sark Clo. Houn —7E **70**
Sark Wlk. E16 —6K **65**
Sarnes Ct. N11 —4A 16
  (off Oakleigh Rd. S.)
Sarnesfield Ho. SE15 —6H 79
  (off Pencraig Way)
Sarnesfield Rd. Enf —4J **7**
Sarre Rd. NW2 —5H **43**
Sarsen Av. Houn —2E **86**
Sarsfeld Rd. SW12 —1D **108**
Sarsfield Rd. Gnfd —2B **56**
Sartor Rd. SE15 —4K **95**

Sassoon. NW9 —1B **26**
Satanita Clo. E16 —6B **66**
Satchell Mead. NW9 —1B **26**
Satchwell Rd. E2
  —3G **63** (2K **145**)
Satchwell St. E2 —3G **63**
Sattar M. N16 —3D 46
  (off Clissold Rd.)
Saul Ct. SE15 —6F 79
  (off Daniel Gdns.)
Sauls Grn. E11 —3G **49**
Saunders Hill. Wemb —7F **25**
Saunders Ho. W11 —1F **75**
Saunders Ness Rd. E14 —5E **80**
Saunders Rd. SE18 —5K **83**
Saunders St. SE11
  —4A **78** (3H **155**)
Saunders Way. SE28 —7B 68
Saunderton Rd. Wemb —5B **40**
Saunton Ct. S'hall —7G 55
  (off Haldane Rd.)
Savage Gdns. E6 —6D **66**
Savage Gdns. EC3
  —7E **62** (2H **151**)
Savernake Ct. Stan —6H **11**
Savernake Ho. N4 —7C **30**
Savernake Rd. N9 —6B **8**
Savernake Rd. NW3 —4D **44**
Savile Clo. N Mald —5A **120**
Savile Gdns. Croy —2F **135**
Savile Row. W1 —7G **61** (2A **148**)
Saville Gdns. Croy —2F **135**
Saville Rd. E16 —1C **82**
Saville Rd. W4 —3K **73**
Saville Rd. Romf —6F **37**
Saville Rd. Twic —1K **103**
Saville Row. Brom —1H **137**
Saville Row. Enf —2E **8**
Savill Gdns. SW20 —3C **120**
Savill Ho. E16 —1F 83
  (off Robert St.)
Savill Ho. SW4 —6H **93**
Savill Row. Wfd G —6C 20
Savin Lodge. Sutt —7A **132**
  (off Walnut M.)
Savona Clo. SW19 —7F **107**
Savona Ho. SW8 —7G **77**
Savona St. SW8 —7G **77**
Savoy Bldgs. WC2
  —7K **61** (3G **149**)
Savoy Clo. E15 —1G **65**
Savoy Clo. Edgw —5B **12**
Savoy Ct. NW3 —4A **44**
Savoy Ct. WC2 —7K **61** (3F **149**)
Savoy Hill. WC2
  —7K **61** (3G **149**)
Savoy Pde. Enf —3K **7**
Savoy Pl. WC2 —7J **61** (3F **149**)
Savoy Row. WC2
  —7K **61** (2G **149**)
Savoy Steps. WC2
  —7K **61** (3G **149**)
Savoy St. WC2 —7K **61** (3G **149**)
Savoy Way. WC2
  —7K **61** (3G **149**)
Sawbill Clo. Hayes —5B **54**
Sawkins Clo. SW19 —2G **107**
Sawley Rd. W12 —1B **74**
Sawtry Clo. Cars —7C **122**
Sawyer Clo. N9 —2B **18**
Sawyer Rd. SW10 —7K **41**
Sawyers Clo. Dag —6J **53**
Sawyers Hill. Rich —7F **89**
Sawyers Lawn. W13 —6A **56**
Sawyer St. SE1 —2C **78** (6C **150**)

Saxby Rd. SW2 —7J **93**
Saxham Rd. Bark —1J **67**
Saxlingham Rd. E4 —3A **20**
Saxon Av. Felt —2C **102**
Saxonbury Clo. Mitc —3B **122**
Saxonbury Ct. N7 —5J **45**
Saxonbury Gdns. Surb —7C **118**
Saxon Bus. Cen. SW19 —2A **122**
Saxon Clo. E17 —7C **32**
Saxon Clo. Surb —6D **118**
Saxon Dri. W3 —6G **57**
Saxonfield Clo. SW2 —1K **109**
Saxon Gdns. S'hall —7C **54**
Saxon Ho. Felt —2D **102**
Saxon Rd. E3 —2B **64**
Saxon Rd. E6 —4D **66**
Saxon Rd. N22 —1B **30**
Saxon Rd. SE25 —5D **124**
Saxon Rd. Brom —7H **113**
Saxon Rd. Ilf —6F **51**
Saxon Rd. S'hall —7C **54**
Saxon Rd. Wemb —3J **41**
Saxon Wlk. Sidc —6C **116**
Saxon Way. N14 —6C **6**
Saxton Clo. SE13 —3F **97**
Sayers Ho. N2 —2B 28
  (off Grange, The)
Sayer St. SE17 —4C **78** (3C **156**)
Sayer's Wlk. Rich —7F **89**
Sayes Ct. SE8 —5B **80**
Sayes Ct. St. SE8 —6B **80**
Scads Hill Clo. Orp —6K **129**
Scala St. W1 —5G **61** (5B **142**)
Scales Rd. N17 —3F **31**
Scampston M. W10 —6F **59**
Scandrett St. E1 —1H **79**
Scarba Wlk. N1 —6D 46
  (off Marquess Rd.)
Scarborough Rd. E11 —1F **49**
Scarborough Rd. N4 —1A **46**
Scarborough Rd. N9 —7D **8**
Scarborough St. E1
  —6F **63** (1K **151**)
Scarle Rd. Wemb —6D **40**
Scarlet Rd. SE6 —3G **113**
Scarlette Mnr. Way. SW2 —7A 94
Scarsbrook Rd. SE3 —3B **98**
Scarsdale Pl. W8 —3K **75**
Scarsdale Rd. Harr —3G **39**
Scarsdale Vs. W8 —3J **75**
Scarth Rd. SW13 —3B **90**
Scawen Rd. SE8 —5A **80**
Scawfell St. E2 —2F **63**
Sceaux Gdns. SE5 —1E **94**
Sceptre Ct. SE3 —7F 63 (3K 151)
  (off Tower Hill)
Sceptre Rd. E2 —3J **63**
Sceynes Link. N12 —4D **14**
Schofield Wlk. SE3 —7K **81**
Scholars Rd. E4 —1A **20**
Scholars Rd. SW12 —1G **109**
Scholefield Rd. N19 —1H **45**
Schonfeld Sq. N16 —1D **46**
School All. Twic —1A **104**
School App. E2 —3E **62** (1H **145**)
Schoolbell M. E3 —2A **64**
School Ho. La. E1 —7K **63**
School Ho. La. Tedd —7B **104**
School La. Bush —1A **10**
School La. King T —1C **118**
School La. Pinn —4C **22**
School La. Well —3B **100**
School Pas. King T —2F **119**
School Pas. S'hall —7D **54**

School Rd. E12 —4D 50
School Rd. NW10 —4K 57
School Rd. Chst —1G 129
School Rd. Dag —1G 69
School Rd. Hamp —6G 103
School Rd. Houn —3G 87
School Rd. King T —1C 118
School Rd. Av. Hamp —6G 103
School Way. N12 —6G 15
School Way. Dag —3C 52
Schooner Clo. SE16 —2K 79
Schubert Rd. SW15 —5H 91
Sclater St. E1 —4F 63 (3J 145)
Scoble Pl. N16 —4F 47
Scoles Cres. SW2 —1A 110
Scoresby St. SE1
—1B 78 (5A 150)
Scorton Av. Gnfd —2A 56
Scotch Comn. W13 —5A 56
Scotch House. (Junct.) —2D 76
Scoter Clo. Wfd G —7E 20
Scoter Ct. SE8 —6B 80
(off Abinger Gro.)
Scot Gro. Pinn —1B 22
Scotia Building. E1 —7K 63
(off Jardine Rd.)
Scotia Rd. SW2 —1A 110
Scotland Grn. N17 —2F 31
Scotland Grn. Rd. Enf —5E 8
Scotland Grn. Rd. N. Enf —4E 8
Scotland Pl. SW1
—1J 77 (5E 148)
Scotland Rd. Buck H —1F 21
Scotney Clo. Farn —4E 138
Scotney Ho. E9 —6J 47
Scotsdale Clo. Orp —4J 129
Scotsdale Clo. Sutt —7G 131
Scotsdale Rd. SE12 —5K 97
Scotswood St. EC1
—4A 62 (3K 143)
Scotswood Wlk. N17 —7B 18
Scott Clo. SW16 —1K 123
Scott Ct. W3 —2K 73
Scott Cres. Harr —1F 39
Scott Ellis Gdns. NW8
—3B 60 (2A 140)
Scottes La. Dag —1D 52
Scott Farm Clo. Th Dit —7B 118
Scott Gdns. Houn —7B 86
Scott Ho. E13 —2J 65
(off Queens Rd. W.)
Scott Ho. E14 —2C 80
(off Admirals Way)
Scott Ho. NW10 —7K 41
(off Stonebridge Pk.)
Scott Ho. Belv —5F 85
(off Albert Rd.)
Scott Lidgett Cres. SE16 —2G 79
Scott Russell Pl. E14 —5D 80
Scotts Av. Brom —2F 127
Scotts Dri. Hamp —7F 103
Scott's La. Brom —3F 127
Scotts Pas. SE18 —4F 83
Scott's Rd. E10 —1E 48
Scott's Rd. W12 —2D 74
Scotts Rd. Brom —7J 113
Scott's Rd. S'hall —3A 70
Scott St. E1 —4H 63
Scott's Yd. EC4 —7D 62 (2E 150)
Scott Trimmer Way. Houn
—2C 86
Scottwell Dri. NW9 —5B 26
Scoulding Rd. E16 —6J 65
Scouler St. E14 —7F 65
Scout App. NW10 —4A 42

Scout La. SW4 —3G 93
Scout Way. NW7 —4E 12
Scovell Cres. SE1
—2C 78 (7C 150)
Scovell Rd. SE1 —2C 78 (7C 150)
Scrattons Ter. Bark —1D 68
Scriven Ct. E8 —1F 63
Scriven St. E8 —1F 63
Scrooby St. SE6 —6D 96
Scrubs La. NW10 —3C 58
Scrutton Clo. SW12 —7H 93
Scrutton St. EC2
—4E 62 (4G 145)
Scudamore La. NW9 —4J 25
Scutari Rd. SE22 —5J 95
Scylla Rd. SE15 —3G 95
(in two parts)
Seabright Pas. E2 —2G 63
Seabright St. E2 —3H 63
Seabrook Dri. W Wick —2G 137
Seabrook Gdns. Romf —7G 37
Seabrook Rd. Dag —3D 52
Seaburn Clo. Rain —3K 69
Seacole Clo. W3 —5K 57
Seacourt Rd. SE2 —2D 84
Seafield Rd. N11 —4C 16
Seaford Rd. E17 —3D 32
Seaford Rd. N15 —5D 30
Seaford Rd. W13 —1B 72
Seaford Rd. Enf —4K 7
Seaford St. WC1 —3J 61 (2F 143)
Seaforth Av. N Mald —5D 120
Seaforth Cres. N5 —5C 46
Seaforth Gdns. N21 —7E 6
Seaforth Gdns. Eps —4B 130
Seaforth Gdns. Wfd G —5F 21
Seaforth Pl. SW1
—3G 77 (1B 154)
Seagrave Clo. E1 —5K 63
Seagrave Lodge. SW6 —6J 75
(off Seagrave Rd.)
Seagrave Rd. SW6 —6J 75
Seagry Rd. E11 —6J 33
Sealand Wlk. N'holt —3B 54
Seal St. E8 —4F 47
Searle Pl. N4 —1K 45
Searles Clo. SW11 —7C 76
Searles Rd. SE1 —4D 78 (3F 157)
Sears St. SE5 —7D 78
Seasprite Clo. N'holt —3B 54
Seaton Av. Ilf —5J 51
Seaton Clo. E13 —4J 65
Seaton Clo. SE11
—5B 78 (5K 155)
Seaton Clo. SW15 —1D 106
Seaton Clo. Twic —6H 87
Seaton Pl. NW1 —4G 61 (3A 142)
Seaton Point. E5 —4G 47
Seaton Rd. Mitc —2C 122
Seaton Rd. Twic —6G 84
Seaton Rd. Well —7C 84
Seaton Rd. Wemb —2E 56
Seaton St. N18 —5B 18
Sebastian St. EC1
—3B 62 (2B 144)
Sebastopol Rd. N9 —4B 18
Sebbon St. N1 —7B 46
Sebert Rd. E7 —5K 49
Sebright Pas. E2 —2G 63
Sebright Rd. Barn —2A 4
Secker Cres. Harr —1G 23
Secker Ho. SW9 —2B 94
(off Loughborough Est.)
Secker St. SE1 —1A 78 (5J 149)
Second Av. E12 —4C 50

Second Av. E13 —3J 65
Second Av. E17 —5C 32
Second Av. N18 —4D 18
Second Av. NW4 —4F 27
Second Av. SW14 —3A 90
Second Av. W3 —1B 74
Second Av. W10 —4G 59
Second Av. Dag —2H 69
Second Av. Enf —5A 8
Second Av. Romf —5C 36
Second Av. Wemb —2D 40
Second Cross Rd. Twic —2J 103
Second Way. Wemb —4H 41
Sedan Way. SE17
—5E 78 (5G 157)
Sedcombe Clo. Sidc —4B 116
Sedcote Rd. Enf —5D 8
Sedding St. SW1
—4E 76 (3G 153)
Seddon Ho. EC2
—5C 62 (5C 144)
Seddon Rd. Mord —5B 122
Seddon St. WC1
—3K 61 (2H 143)
Sedgebrook Rd. SE3 —3B 98
Sedgecombe Av. Harr —5C 24
Sedgefield Ct. N'holt —5F 39
(off Newmarket Av.)
Sedgeford Rd. W12 —1B 74
Sedgehill Rd. SE6 —4C 112
Sedgemere Av. N2 —3A 28
Sedgemere Rd. SE2 —3C 84
Sedgemoor Dri. Dag —4G 53
Sedge Rd. N17 —7D 18
Sedgeway. SE6 —1H 113
Sedgewood Clo. Brom —7H 127
Sedgmoor Pl. SE5 —7E 78
Sedgwick Rd. E10 —2E 48
Sedgwick St. E9 —5K 47
Sedleigh Rd. SW18 —6H 91
Sedlescombe Rd. SW6 —6J 75
Sedley Ct. SE26 —2H 111
Sedley Ho. SE11
—5K 77 (5H 155)
Sedley Pl. W1 —6F 61 (1J 147)
Seeley Dri. SE21 —4E 110
Seelig Av. NW9 —7C 26
Seely Rd. SW17 —6E 108
Seething La. EC3
—7E 62 (2H 151)
Seething Wells La. Surb —6C 118
Sefton Av. NW7 —5C 12
Sefton Av. Harr —2H 23
Sefton Clo. Orp —4K 129
Sefton Ct. Houn —1F 87
Sefton Rd. Croy —1G 135
Sefton Rd. Orp —4K 129
Sefton St. SW15 —3E 90
Sega Ho. SW5 —4J 75
(off Cromwell Rd.)
Segal Clo. SE23 —7A 96
Sekforde St. EC1
—4B 62 (4A 144)
Sekhon Ter. Felt —3E 102
Selah Dri. Swan —7J 117
Selbie Av. NW10 —5B 42
Selborne Av. E12 —4E 50
Selborne Av. Bex —1E 116
Selborne Gdns. NW4 —4C 26
Selborne Gdns. Gnfd —2A 56
Selborne Rd. E17 —5B 32
Selborne Rd. N14 —3D 16
Selborne Rd. SE5 —2D 94
Selborne Rd. Croy —3E 134
Selborne Rd. Ilf —2E 50

Selborne Rd. N Mald —2A 120
Selborne Rd. Sidc —4B 116
Selborne Wlk. E17 —4B 32
Selborne Wlk. Shop. Cen. E17
—4C 32
Selbourne Ho. SE1
—2D 78 (7E 150)
Selbourne Rd. N22 —1K 29
Selby Clo. E6 —5C 66
Selby Clo. Chst —6E 114
Selby Gdns. S'hall —4E 54
Selby Grn. Cars —7C 122
Selby Rd. E11 —3G 49
Selby Rd. E13 —5K 65
Selby Rd. N17 —7K 17
Selby Rd. SE20 —2G 125
Selby Rd. W5 —4B 56
Selby Rd. Cars —7C 122
Selby St. E1 —4G 63
Selden Ho. SE15 —2J 95
(off Selden Rd.)
Selden Rd. SE15 —2J 95
Selden Wlk. N7 —2K 45
Seldon Ho. SW8 —7G 77
(off Stewart's Rd.)
Selhurst Clo. SW19 —1F 107
Selhurst New Rd. SE25 —6E 124
Selhurst Pl. SE25 —6E 124
Selhurst Rd. N9 —3J 17
Selhurst Rd. SE25 —6E 124
Selinas La. Dag —7E 36
Selkirk Rd. SW17 —4C 108
Selkirk Rd. Twic —2G 103
Sellers Hall Clo. N3 —7D 14
Sellincourt Rd. SW17 —5C 108
Sellindge Clo. Beck —7B 112
Sellon M. SE11 —4K 77 (4G 155)
Sellons Av. NW10 —1B 58
Selsdon Av. S Croy —6D 134
Selsdon Clo. Romf —1J 37
Selsdon Clo. Surb —5E 118
Selsdon Pk. Rd. S Croy —7K 135
Selsdon Rd. E11 —7J 33
Selsdon Rd. E13 —1A 66
Selsdon Rd. NW2 —2B 42
Selsdon Rd. SE27 —3B 110
Selsdon Rd. S Croy —5D 134
Selsdon Way. E14 —3D 80
Selsea Pl. N16 —5E 46
Selsey Cres. Well —1D 100
Selsey St. E14 —5C 64
Selvage La. NW7 —5E 12
Selway Clo. Pinn —3A 22
Selwood Dri. Barn —5A 4
Selwood Pl. SW7
—5B 76 (5A 152)
Selwood Rd. Croy —2H 135
Selwood Rd. Sutt —1H 131
Selwood Ter. SW7
—5B 76 (5A 152)
Selworthy Clo. E11 —5J 33
Selworthy Rd. SE6 —3B 112
Selwyn Av. E4 —6A 19
Selwyn Av. Ilf —6K 35
Selwyn Av. Rich —3E 88
Selwyn Clo. Houn —4C 86
Selwyn Ct. E17 —5C 32
(off Yunus Khan Clo.)
Selwyn Ct. SE3 —3H 97
Selwyn Ct. Edgw —7C 12
Selwyn Cres. Well —3B 100
Selwyn Rd. E3 —2B 64
Selwyn Rd. E13 —1K 65

Selwyn Rd. NW10 —7K 41
Selwyn Rd. N Mald —5K 119
Semley Ga. E9 —6B 48
Semley Pl. SW1 —4E 76 (4H 153)
Semley Rd. SW16 —2J 123
Senate St. SE15 —2J 95
Senator Wlk. SE28 —3H 83
Seneca Rd. T Hth —4C 124
Senga Rd. Wall —1E 132
Senhouse Rd. Sutt —3F 131
Senior St. W2 —5K 59
Senlac Rd. SE12 —1K 113
Sennen Rd. Enf —7A 8
Sennen Wlk. SE9 —3C 114
Senrab St. E1 —6K 63
Sentinel Clo. N'holt —4C 54
Sentinel Sq. NW4 —4E 26
September Ct. S'hall —1F 71
(off Dormers Wells La.)
September Way. Stan —6G 11
Septimus Pl. Enf —5B 8
Sequoia Clo. Bush —1C 10
Sequoia Gdns. Orp —7K 129
Sequoia Pk. Pinn —6A 10
Serbin Clo. E10 —7E 32
Sergeant Ind. Est. SW18 —6K 91
Serica Ct. SE10 —7E 80
Serjeant's Inn. EC4
—6A 62 (1K 149)
Serle St. WC2 —6K 61 (7H 143)
Sermon La. EC4 —6C 62 (1C 150)
Serpentine Rd. W2
—1C 76 (5C 146)
Serviden Dri. Brom —1B 128
Servite Ho. Wor Pk —2B 130
(off Avenue, The)
Servius Ct. Bren —7D 72
Setchell Rd. SE1 —4F 79 (3J 157)
Setchell Way. SE1
—4F 79 (3J 157)
Seth St. SE16 —2J 79
Seton Gdns. Dag —7C 52
Settle Rd. E13 —2J 65
Settles St. E1 —5G 63
Settrington Rd. SW6 —2K 91
Seven Acres. Cars —2C 132
Seven Dials. WC2
—6J 61 (1E 148)
Seven Kings Rd. Ilf —2K 51
Sevenoaks Clo. Bexh —4H 101
Sevenoaks Rd. SE4 —6A 96
Sevenoaks Way. Sidc & Orp
—7C 116
Seven Sisters. (Junct.) —5F 31
Seven Sisters Rd. N7, N4 & N15
—3K 45
Seven Stars Corner. W12 —3C 74
Seventh Av. E12 —4D 50
Severnake Clo. E14 —4C 80
Severn Way. NW10 —5B 42
Severus Rd. SW11 —4C 92
Seville St. SW1 —2D 76 (7F 147)
Sevill M. N1 —7E 46
Sevington Rd. NW4 —6D 26
Sevington St. W9 —4K 59
Seward Rd. W7 —2A 72
Seward Rd. Beck —2K 125
Sewardstone Gdns. E4 —5J 9
Sewardstone Rd. E2 —2J 63
Sewardstone Rd. E4 —7J 9
Seward St. EC1 —3B 62 (3B 144)
Sewdley St. E5 —4K 47
Sewell Rd. SE2 —3A 84
Sewell St. E13 —3J 65
Sextant Av. E14 —4F 81

Seymer Rd. Romf —3K 37
Seymour Av. N17 —2G 31
Seymour Av. Eps —7D 130
Seymour Av. Mord —7F 121
Seymour Clo. EC1
  —4B 62 (4A 144)
Seymour Clo. Pinn —1D 22
Seymour Ct. E4 —2C 20
Seymour Ct. N10 —2E 28
Seymour Ct. N21 —6E 6
Seymour Ct. NW2 —2D 42
Seymour Dri. Brom —1D 138
Seymour Gdns. SE4 —3A 96
Seymour Gdns. Felt —4A 102
Seymour Gdns. Ilf —1D 50
Seymour Gdns. Ruis —1B 38
Seymour Gdns. Surb —5F 119
Seymour Gdns. Twic —7B 88
Seymour M. W1
  —6E 60 (7G 141)
Seymour Pl. SE25 —4H 125
Seymour Pl. W1
  —5D 60 (6E 140)
Seymour Rd. E4 —1J 19
Seymour Rd. E6 —2B 66
Seymour Rd. E10 —1B 48
Seymour Rd. N3 —7E 14
Seymour Rd. N8 —5A 30
Seymour Rd. N9 —2C 18
Seymour Rd. SW18 —7H 91
Seymour Rd. SW19 —3F 107
Seymour Rd. W4 —4J 73
Seymour Rd. Cars —5E 132
Seymour Rd. Hamp —5G 103
Seymour Rd. King T —1D 118
Seymour Rd. Mitc —7E 122
Seymour Rd. Ind. Est. E10
  —1B 48
Seymour St. W2 & W1
  —6D 60 (1E 146)
Seymour Ter. SE20 —1H 125
Seymour Vs. SE20 —1H 125
Seymour Wlk. SW10 —6A 76
Seyssel St. E14 —4E 80
Shaa Rd. W3 —7K 57
Shacklegate La. Tedd —4J 103
Shackleton Clo. SE23 —2H 111
Shackleton Ho. NW10 —7K 41
Shackleton Rd. S'hall —7D 54
Shacklewell Grn. E8 —4F 47
Shacklewell Ho. E8 —4F 47
Shacklewell La. E8 —5F 47
Shacklewell Rd. N16 —4F 47
Shacklewell Row. E8 —4F 47
Shacklewell St. E2
  —3F 63 (2K 145)
Shadbolt Clo. Wor Pk —2B 130
Shad Thames. SE1
  —1F 79 (5J 151)
Shadwell Ct. N'holt —2D 54
Shadwell Dri. N'holt —3D 54
Shadwell Gdns. E1 —7H 63
  (off Sutton St.)
Shadwell Pier Head. E1 —7J 63
Shadwell Pl. E1 —7J 63
Shadybush Clo. Bush —1B 10
Shaef Way. Tedd —7A 104
Shafter Rd. Dag —6J 53
Shaftesbury Av. W1 & WC2
  —7H 61 (3C 148)
Shaftesbury Av. Enf —2E 8
Shaftesbury Av. Kent —5D 24
Shaftesbury Av. New Bar —4F 5
Shaftesbury Av. S'hall —4E 70
Shaftesbury Av. S Harr —1F 39

Shaftesbury Circ. S Harr —1G 39
Shaftesbury Ct. E6 —6E 66
  (off Sapphire Clo.)
Shaftesbury Ct. SE5 —4D 94
Shaftesbury Ct. SW6 —1K 91
  (off Maltings Pl.)
Shaftesbury Ct. SW16 —3H 109
Shaftesbury Lodge. E14 —6D 64
  (off Upper N. St.)
Shaftesbury M. SW4 —5G 93
Shaftesbury M. W8 —3J 75
  (off Stratford Rd.)
Shaftesbury Pde. S Harr —1G 39
Shaftesbury Point. E13 —2J 65
  (off High St. Plaistow,)
Shaftesbury Rd. E4 —1A 20
Shaftesbury Rd. E7 —7A 50
Shaftesbury Rd. E10 —1C 48
Shaftesbury Rd. E17 —6D 32
Shaftesbury Rd. N18 —6K 17
Shaftesbury Rd. N19 —1J 45
Shaftesbury Rd. Beck —2B 126
Shaftesbury Rd. Cars —7B 122
Shaftesbury Rd. Rich —3E 88
Shaftesburys, The. Bark —2G 67
Shaftesbury St. N1 —2C 62
  (in two parts)
Shaftesbury Way. Twic —3H 103
Shaftesbury Way. Hayes —5A 54
Shafto M. SW1 —3D 76 (2F 153)
Shafton M. E9 —1K 63
Shafton Rd. E9 —1K 63
Shaftesbury Gdns. NW10 —4A 58
Shafts Ct. EC3 —6E 62 (1G 151)
Shakespeare Av. N11 —5B 16
Shakespeare Av. NW10 —1K 57
Shakespeare Av. Hayes —5A 54
  (in two parts)
Shakespeare Ct. New Bar —3E 4
Shakespeare Cres. E12 —6E 50
Shakespeare Cres. NW10 —1K 57
Shakespeare Dri. Harr —6F 25
Shakespeare Gdns. N2 —4D 28
Shakespeare Ho. N14 —2C 16
Shakespeare M. N16 —4E 46
Shakespeare Rd. E17 —2K 31
Shakespeare Rd. N3 —1J 27
Shakespeare Rd. NW7 —4G 13
Shakespeare Rd. SE24 —5B 94
Shakespeare Rd. W3 —1J 73
Shakespeare Rd. W7 —7K 55
Shakespeare Rd. Bexh —1E 100
Shakespeare Tower. EC2
  —5C 62 (5D 144)
Shakespeare Wlk. N16 —4E 46
Shakespeare Way. Felt —4A 102
Shalcomb St. SW10 —6A 76
Shalden Ho. SW15 —6B 90
Shaldon Dri. Mord —5G 121
Shaldon Dri. Ruis —3A 38
Shaldon Rd. Edgw —2F 25
Shalfleet Dri. W10 —7F 59
Shalford Ct. N1 —2B 62
  (off Charlton Pl.)
Shalford Ho. SE1
  —3D 78 (1F 157)
Shalimar Gdns. W3 —7J 57
Shalimar Rd. W3 —7J 57
Shallons Rd. SE9 —4F 115
Shalstone Rd. SW14 —3H 89
Shalston Vs. Surb —6F 119
Shamrock Rd. Croy —6K 123
Shamrock St. SW4 —3H 93
Shamrock Way. N14 —1A 16
Shandon Rd. SW4 —6G 93

Shand St. SE1 —2E 78 (6H 151)
Shandy St. E1 —5K 63
Shanklin Rd. N8 —5H 29
Shanklin Way. SE15 —7F 79
Shannon Clo. NW2 —3F 43
Shannon Clo. S'hall —5B 70
Shannon Corner. (Junct.)
  —4C 120
Shannon Corner Retail Pk. N Mald
  —4C 120
Shannon Ct. N16 —3E 46
Shannon Gro. SW9 —4K 93
Shannon Pl. NW8 —2C 60
Shannon Way. Beck —6D 112
Shanti Ct. SW18 —1J 107
Shap Cres. Cars —1D 132
Shap St. E2 —2F 63
Shardcroft Av. SE24 —5B 94
Shardeloes Rd. SE14 —2B 96
Shard's Sq. SE15 —6G 79
Sharland Clo. T Hth —6A 124
Sharman Ct. Sidc —4A 116
Sharnbrooke Clo. Well —3C 100
Sharon Clo. Surb —7D 118
Sharon Gdns. E9 —1J 63
Sharon Rd. W4 —5K 73
Sharon Rd. Enf —2F 9
Sharpe Clo. W7 —5K 55
Sharp Ho. SW8 —3F 93
Sharpleshall St. NW1 —7D 44
Sharpness Clo. Hayes —5C 54
Sharpness Ct. SE15 —7F 79
  (off Daniel Gdns.)
Sharratt St. SE15 —6J 79
Sharsted St. SE17
  —5B 78 (6A 156)
Sharvel La. N'holt —1A 54
Shaver's Pl. SW1
  —7H 61 (3C 148)
Shaw Av. Bark —2E 68
Shawbrooke Rd. SE9 —5A 98
Shawbury Rd. SE22 —5F 95
Shaw Clo. SE28 —1B 84
Shaw Clo. Bush —2D 10
Shaw Ct. W3 —3J 73
  (off All Saints Rd.)
Shawfield Pk. Brom —2B 128
Shawfield St. SW3
  —5C 76 (6D 152)
Shawford Ct. SW15 —7C 90
Shaw Gdns. Bark —2C 68
Shaw Ho. E16 —1E 82
  (off Claremont St.)
Shaw Ho. Belv —5F 85
  (off Albert Rd.)
Shaw Path. Brom —3H 113
Shaw Rd. SE22 —4E 94
Shaw Rd. Brom —3H 113
Shaw Rd. Enf —1E 8
Shaws Path. King T —1C 118
  (off High St. Hampton Wick,)
Shaw Sq. E17 —1A 32
Shaw Way. Wall —7J 133
Shearing Dri. Cars —7A 122
Shearling Way. N7 —6J 45
Shearman Rd. SE3 —4H 97
Shearwater Ct. SE8 —6B 80
  (off Abinger Gro.)
Shearwater Way. Hayes —6B 54
Sheaveshill Av. NW9 —4A 26
Sheaveshill Ct. NW9 —4K 25
Sheaveshill Pde. NW9 —4A 26
  (off Sheaveshill Av.)
Sheba St. E1 —4F 63 (4K 145)

Sheen Comn. Dri. Rich —4G 89
Sheen Ct. Rich —4G 89
Sheendale Rd. Rich —4F 89
Sheenewood. SE26 —4H 111
Sheen Ga. Gdns. SW14 —4J 89
Sheen Gro. N1 —1A 62
Sheen La. SW14 —5J 89
Sheen Pk. Rich —4E 88
Sheen Rd. Orp —4K 129
Sheen Rd. Rich —5E 88
Sheen Way. Wall —5K 133
Sheen Wood. SW14 —6A 89
Sheepcote La. SW11 —2D 92
Sheepcote Rd. Harr —6K 23
Sheepcotes Rd. Romf —4E 36
Sheephouse Way. N Mald
  —7K 119
Sheep La. E8 —1H 63
Sheep Wlk. M. SW19 —6F 107
Sheerwater Rd. E16 —5B 66
Sheffield Sq. E3 —3B 64
Sheffield St. WC2
  —6K 61 (1G 149)
Sheffield Ter. W8 —1J 75
Shelbourne Clo. Pinn —3D 22
Shelbourne Pl. Beck —7C 112
Shelbourne Rd. N17 —2H 31
Shelburne Rd. N7 —4K 45
Shelbury Clo. Sidc —4A 116
Shelbury Rd. SE22 —5H 95
Sheldon Av. N6 —7C 28
Sheldon Av. Ilf —2F 35
Sheldon Clo. SE12 —5K 97
Sheldon Clo. SE20 —1H 125
Sheldon Ct. SW8 —7J 77
  (off Lansdowne Grn.)
Sheldon Ct. Barn —4E 4
Sheldon Ho. N18 —4K 17
Sheldon Rd. NW2 —4F 43
Sheldon Rd. Bexh —1F 101
Sheldon Rd. Dag —7E 52
Sheldon St. Croy —3C 134
Sheldrake Clo. E16 —1D 82
Sheldrake Ct. E6 —2C 66
  (off St Bartholomew's Rd.)
Sheldrake Pl. W8 —2J 75
Sheldrick Clo. SW19 —2B 122
Shelduck Clo. E7 —5H 49
Shelduck Ct. SE8 —6B 80
  (off Pilot Clo.)
Sheldwich Ter. Brom —6C 128
Shelford Pl. N16 —3D 46
Shelford Rise. SE19 —7F 111
Shelford Rd. Barn —6A 4
Shelgate Rd. SW11 —5C 92
Shell Clo. Brom —6C 128
Shell Clo. NW9 —2A 26
Shelley. N8 —3J 29
  (off Boyton Rd.)
Shelley Av. E12 —6C 50
Shelley Av. Gnfd —3H 55
Shelley Clo. SE15 —2H 95
Shelley Clo. Edgw —4B 12
Shelley Clo. Gnfd —3H 55
Shelley Ct. E10 —7D 32
Shelley Ct. E11 —4J 33
  (off Makepiece Rd.)
Shelley Ct. N4 —1K 45
Shelley Cres. Houn —1B 86
Shelley Cres. S'hall —6D 54
Shelley Dri. Well —1J 99
Shelley Gdns. Wemb —2C 40
Shelley Ho. SE17
  —5C 78 (5D 156)
Shelley Way. SW19 —6B 108

Shellness Rd. E5 —5H 47
Shell Rd. SE13 —3D 96
Shellwood Rd. SW11 —2D 92
Shelmerdine Clo. E3 —5C 64
Shelton Rd. SW19 —1J 121
Shelton St. WC2 —6J 61 (1E 148)
Shenfield Rd. Wfd G —7E 20
Shenfield St. N1
  —2E 62 (1H 145)
Shenley Rd. SE5 —1E 94
Shenley Rd. Houn —1C 86
Shenstone W13 —1C 72
Shenstone Clo. Dart —4K 101
Shepherd Clo. W1
  (off Lees Pl.) —7E 60 (2G 147)
Shepherdess Pl. N1
  —3C 62 (1E 144)
Shepherdess Wlk. N1
  —2C 62 (1D 144)
Shepherd Mkt. W1
  —1F 77 (4J 147)
Shepherd's Bush Grn. W12
  —2E 74
Shepherd's Bush Mkt. W12
  —2E 74
Shepherd's Bush Pl. W12 —2F 75
Shepherd's Bush Rd. W6 —4E 74
Shepherd's Clo. N6 —6F 29
Shepherds Clo. Romf —5D 36
Shepherds Clo. W12 —2F 75
  (off Shepherd's Bush Grn.)
Shepherds Grn. Chst —7H 115
Shepherd's Hill. N6 —6F 29
Shepherds La. E9 —6A 47
Shepherds Lea. SE9 —4G 99
Shepherd's Path. NW3 —5B 44
  (off Lyndhurst Rd.)
Shepherds Path. N'holt —6C 38
  (off Arnold Rd.)
Shepherds Pl. W1
  —7E 60 (2G 147)
Shepherd St. W1
  —1F 77 (5J 147)
Shepherds Wlk. NW2 —2C 42
Shepherds Wlk. NW3 —5B 44
Shepherds Wlk. Bush —2C 10
Shepherds Way. S Croy —7K 135
Shepley Clo. Cars —3E 132
Sheppard Clo. Enf —1C 8
Sheppard Clo. King T —4E 118
Sheppard Dri. SE16 —5H 79
Sheppard Ho. SW2 —1A 110
Sheppard St. E16 —4H 65
Shepperton Rd. N1 —1D 62
Shepperton Rd. Orp —6G 129
Sheppey Gdns. Dag —7C 52
Sheppey Rd. Dag —7B 52
Sheppey Wlk. N1 —6C 46
Shepton Houses. E2 —3J 63
  (off Welwyn St.)
Sherard Rd. SE9 —5C 98
Sheraton Bus. Cen. Gnfd —2C 56
Sheraton St. W1
  —6H 61 (1C 148)
Sherborne Av. Enf —2D 8
Sherborne Av. S'hall —4E 70
Sherborne Clo. Hayes —6A 54
Sherborne Cres. Cars —7C 122
Sherborne Gdns. NW9 —3G 25
Sherborne Gdns. W13 —5B 56
Sherborne Ho. SW8 —7K 77
  (off Bolney St.)
Sherborne La. EC4
  —7D 62 (2E 150)
Sherborne Rd. Orp —5K 129

Sherborne Rd. Sutt —2J 131
Sherborne St. N1 —1D 62
Sherboro Rd. N15 —6F 31
Sherbourne Ct. Sutt —6A 132
Sherbourne Pl. Stan —6F 11
Sherbrooke Clo. Bexh —4G 101
Sherbrooke Rd. SW6 —7G 75
Sherbrook Gdns. N21 —7G 7
Sheredan Rd. E4 —5A 20
Shere Ho. SE1 —2D 78 (1E 156)
Shere Rd. Ilf —5E 34
Sherfield Gdns. SW15 —6B 90
Sheridan Ct. W7 —7K 55
(off Milton Rd.)
Sheridan Ct. Harr —6H 23
Sheridan Ct. Houn —5C 86
Sheridan Ct. N'holt —5F 39
Sheridan Cres. Chst —2F 129
Sheridan Gdns. Harr —6D 24
Sheridan Lodge. Brom —4A 128
(off Homesdale Rd.)
Sheridan Pl. SW13 —3B 90
Sheridan Pl. Hamp —7F 103
Sheridan Rd. E7 —3H 49
Sheridan Rd. E12 —5C 50
Sheridan Rd. SW19 —1H 121
Sheridan Rd. Belv —4G 85
Sheridan Rd. Bexh —3E 100
Sheridan Rd. Rich —3C 104
Sheridan St. E1 —6H 63
Sheridan Ter. N'holt —5F 39
Sheridan Wlk. NW11 —6J 27
Sheridan Wlk. Cars —5D 132
Sheridan Way. Beck —1B 126
Sheriden Pl. Harr —7J 23
Sheringham. NW8 —7B 44
Sheringham Av. E12 —4D 50
Sheringham Av. N14 —5C 6
Sheringham Av. Romf —6J 37
Sheringham Av. Twic —1D 102
Sheringham Ct. Enf —3G 7
Sheringham Dri. Bark —5K 51
Sheringham Ho. NW1
—5C 60 (5C 140)
Sheringham Rd. N7 —6K 45
Sheringham Rd. SE20 —3J 125
Sheringham Tower. S'hall —7F 55
Sherington Av. Pinn —1A 10
Sherington Rd. SE7 —6K 81
Sherland Rd. Twic —1K 103
Sherlock M. W1 —5E 60 (5G 141)
Sherman Rd. Brom —1J 127
Shernhall St. E17 —3E 32
Sherrard Rd. E7 & E12 —6A 50
Sherrards Way. Barn —5D 4
Sherrick Grn. Rd. NW10 —5D 42
Sherriff Rd. NW6 —6J 43
Sherringham Av. N17 —2G 31
Sherrin Rd. E10 —4D 48
Sherrock Gdns. NW4 —4C 26
Sherry M. Bark —7H 51
Sherston Ct. SE1
—4B 78 (3B 156)
Sherston Ct. WC1
—3A 62 (2J 143)
Sherwin Ho. SE11
—6A 78 (7J 155)
Sherwin Rd. SE14 —1K 95
Sherwood. NW6 —7G 43
Sherwood Av. E18 —3K 33
Sherwood Av. SW16 —7H 109
Sherwood Av. Gnfd —6J 39
Sherwood Clo. SW13 —3D 90
Sherwood Clo. W13 —1B 72
Sherwood Clo. Bex —6C 100

Sherwood Ct. SW11 —3A 92
Sherwood Ct. S Harr —2G 39
Sherwood Gdns. E14 —4C 80
Sherwood Gdns. SE16 —5G 79
Sherwood Gdns. Bark —7H 51
Sherwood Pk. Av. Sidc —7A 100
Sherwood Pk. Rd. Mitc —4G 123
Sherwood Pk. Rd. Sutt —5J 131
Sherwood Rd. NW4 —3E 26
Sherwood Rd. SW19 —7H 107
Sherwood Rd. Croy —7H 125
Sherwood Rd. Hamp —5G 103
Sherwood Rd. Harr —2G 39
Sherwood Rd. Ilf —4H 35
Sherwood Rd. Well —2J 99
Sherwood St. N20 —3G 15
Sherwood St. W1
—7G 61 (2B 148)
Sherwood Ter. N20 —3G 15
Sherwood Way. W Wick —2E 136
Shetland Rd. E3 —2B 64
Shield Dri. Bren —6A 72
Shieldhall St. SE2 —4C 84
Shifford Path. SE23 —3K 111
Shillaker Ct. W3 —1B 74
Shillibeer Pl. W1
—5C 60 (6D 140)
Shillingford St. N1 —7B 46
Shinfield St. W12 —6E 58
Shingle End. Bren —7C 72
Shinglewell Rd. Eri —7G 85
Shinners Clo. SE25 —5G 125
Ship All. W4 —6G 73
Ship & Half Moon Pas. SE18
—1F 97
Ship & Mermaid Row. SE1
—2D 78 (6F 151)
Ship St. SE8 —1C 96
Ship Tavern Pas. EC3
—7E 62 (2G 151)
Shipton Clo. Dag —3D 52
Shipton Pl. NW5 —6E 44
Shipton St. E2 —3F 63 (1K 145)
Shipway Ter. N16 —3F 47
Shipwright Rd. SE16 —2A 80
Shipwright Yd. SE1
—1E 78 (5G 151)
Ship Yd. E14 —5D 80
Shirburn Clo. SE23 —7J 95
Shirbutt St. E14 —7D 64
Shirebrook Rd. SE3 —3B 98
Shire Ct. Eps —7B 130
Shire Ct. Eri —3D 84
Shirehall Clo. NW4 —6F 27
Shirehall Gdns. NW4 —6F 27
Shirehall La. NW4 —6F 27
Shirehall Pk. NW4 —6F 27
Shire Horse Way. Iswth —3K 87
Shire La. Kes & Orp —7D 138
(in two parts)
Shire M. Whit —6G 87
Shire Pl. SW18 —7K 91
Shire Pl. Bren —7C 72
Shires, The. Ham —4E 104
Shirland M. W9 —3H 59
Shirland Rd. W9 —3H 59
Shirley Av. Bex —7D 100
Shirley Av. Croy —1J 135
Shirley Av. Sutt —4B 132
Shirley Chu. Rd. Croy —3K 135
Shirley Clo. Houn —5G 87

Shirley Ct. SW16 —7J 109
Shirley Cres. Beck —4A 126
Shirley Dri. Houn —5G 87
Shirley Gdns. W7 —1K 71
Shirley Gdns. Bark —6J 51
Shirley Gro. N9 —7D 8
Shirley Gro. SW11 —3E 92
Shirley Heights. Wall —7G 133
Shirley Hills Rd. Croy —5J 135
Shirley Ho. Dri. SE7 —7A 82
Shirley Oaks Rd. Croy —1K 135
Shirley Pk. Rd. Croy —1H 135
Shirley Rd. E15 —7G 49
Shirley Rd. W4 —2K 73
Shirley Rd. Croy —7H 125
Shirley Rd. Enf —3H 7
Shirley Rd. Sidc —3J 115
Shirley Rd. Wall —7G 133
Shirleys Clo. E17 —5D 32
Shirley St. E16 —6H 65
Shirley Way. Croy —3A 136
Shirlock Rd. NW3 —4D 44
Shobden Rd. N17 —1D 30
Shobroke Clo. NW2 —3E 42
Shoebury Rd. E6 —7D 50
Shoelands Ct. NW9 —3K 25
Shoe La. EC4 —6A 62 (7K 143)
Shooters Av. Harr —4C 24
Shooter's Hill. SE18 & Well
Shooters Hill Rd. SE3 & SE18
Shooters Rd. Enf —1G 7
Shoot Up Hill. NW2 —5G 43
Shore Clo. Hamp —6C 102
Shoreditch St. E8 —1F 63
(off Queensbridge Rd.)
Shoreditch High St. E1
—4E 62 (4H 145)
Shore Gro. Felt —2E 102
Shoreham Clo. SW18 —5K 91
Shoreham Clo. Bex —1D 116
Shoreham Clo. Croy —5J 125
Shoreham Way. Brom —6J 127
Shore Ho. SW8 —3F 93
Shore Pl. E9 —7J 47
Shore Rd. E9 —7J 47
Shorncliffe Rd. SE1
—5F 79 (5J 157)
Shorndean St. SE6 —1E 112
Shorne Clo. Sidc —6B 100
Shornefield Clo. Brom —3E 128
Shornells Way. SE2 —5C 84
Shorrold's Rd. SW6 —7H 75
Shortcroft Rd. Eps —7B 130
Shortcrofts Rd. Dag —6F 53
Shorter St. E1 —7F 63 (2K 151)
Short Ga. N12 —4C 14
Short Hedges. Houn —1E 86
Short Hill. Harr —1J 39
Shortlands. W6 —4F 75
Shortlands Clo. N18 —3J 17
Shortlands Clo. Belv —3F 85
Shortlands Gdns. Brom —2G 127
Shortlands Gro. Brom —3F 127
Shortlands Ho. E17 —5B 32
Shortlands Rd. E10 —7D 32
Shortlands Rd. Brom —3F 127
Shortlands Rd. King T —7F 105
Short Path. SE18 —6F 83
Short Rd. E11 —2G 49
Short Rd. E15 —1F 65
Short Rd. W4 —6A 74

Shorts Croft. NW9 —4H 25
Shorts Gdns. WC2
—6J 61 (1E 148)
Shorts Rd. Cars —4G 132
Short St. NW4 —4E 26
Short St. SE1 —2A 78 (6K 149)
Short Wall. E15 —3E 64
Short Way. N12 —6H 15
Short Way. SE9 —3C 98
Short Way. Twic —7G 87
Shotfield. Wall —6F 133
Shotfield Av. SW14 —4A 90
Shott Clo. Sutt —5A 132
Shottendane Rd. SW6 —1J 91
Shottery Clo. SE9 —3C 114
Shoulder of Mutton All. E14
—7A 64
Shouldham St. W1
—5C 60 (6D 140)
Shrapnel Clo. SE18 —7C 82
Shrapnel Rd. SE9 —3D 98
Shrewsbury Av. SW14 —4K 89
Shrewsbury Av. Harr —4E 24
Shrewsbury Ct. EC1
—4C 62 (4D 144)
Shrewsbury Cres. NW10 —1K 57
Shrewsbury Ho. SW8
—6K 77 (7H 155)
Shrewsbury La. SE18 —1F 99
Shrewsbury M. W2 —5J 59
(off Chepstow Rd.)
Shrewsbury Rd. E7 —5B 50
Shrewsbury Rd. N11 —6C 16
Shrewsbury Rd. W2 —6J 59
Shrewsbury Rd. Beck —3A 126
Shrewsbury Rd. Cars —7C 122
Shrewsbury St. W10 —4E 58
Shrewsbury Wlk. Iswth —3A 88
Shrewton Rd. SW17 —7D 108
Shroffold Rd. Brom —4G 113
Shropshire Clo. Mitc —4J 123
Shropshire Ct. W7 —6K 55
(off Copley Clo.)
Shropshire Pl. WC1
—4G 61 (4C 142)
Shropshire Rd. N22 —7E 16
Shroton St. NW1
—5C 60 (5D 140)
Shrubbary Clo. N1 —1C 62
Shrubberies, The. E18 —2J 33
Shrubbery Gdns. N21 —7G 7
Shrubbery Rd. N9 —3B 18
Shrubbery Rd. SW16 —4J 109
Shrubbery Rd. S'hall —1E 70
Shrubbery, The. E11 —5K 33
Shrubland Gro. Wor Pk —3E 130
Shrubland Rd. E8 —1G 63
Shrubland Rd. E10 —7C 32
Shrubland Rd. E17 —5C 32
Shrublands Av. Croy —3C 136
Shrublands Clo. N20 —1G 15
Shrublands Clo. SE26 —3J 111
Shrubsall Clo. SE9 —1C 114
Shuna Wlk. N1 —6D 46
Shurland Av. Barn —6G 5
Shurland Gdns. SE15 —7F 79
Shuters Sq. W14 —5H 75
Shuttle Clo. Sidc —7K 99
Shuttlemead. Bex —7F 101
Shuttle St. E1 —4G 63 (4K 145)
Shuttleworth Rd. SW11 —2C 92
Sibella Rd. SW4 —2H 93
Sibley Clo. Bexh —5E 100
Sibley Gro. E12 —7C 50
Sibthorpe Rd. SE12 —6K 97

Sibthorp Rd. Mitc —2D 122
Sibton Rd. Cars —7C 122
Sicilian Av. WC1 —5J 61 (6F 143)
Sickle Corner. Dag —3H 69
Sidbury St. SW6 —1G 91
Sidcup By-Pass. Chst & Sidc
—3H 115
Sidcup High St. Sidc —4A 116
Sidcup Hill. Sidc —4B 116
Sidcup Hill Gdns. Sidc —5C 116
Sidcup Pl. Sidc —5A 116
Sidcup Rd. SE12 & SE9 —6A 98
Sidcup Technical Cen. Sidc
—6D 116
Siddons La. NW1
—4D 60 (4F 141)
Siddons Rd. N17 —1G 31
Siddons Rd. SE23 —2A 112
Siddons Rd. Croy —3A 134
Side Rd. E17 —5B 32
Sidewood Rd. SE9 —1H 115
Sidford Ho. SE1 —3K 77 (2J 155)
Sidford Pl. SE1 —3A 78 (2H 155)
Sidgwick Ho. SW9 —2K 93
(off Stockwell Rd.)
Sidings M. N7 —3A 46
Sidings, The. E11 —1F 49
Sidlaw Ho. N16 —1F 47
Sidmouth Av. Iswth —2J 87
Sidmouth Ho. SE15 —7G 79
(off Friary Rd.)
Sidmouth Pde. NW10 —7E 42
Sidmouth Rd. E10 —3E 48
Sidmouth Rd. NW2 —7E 42
Sidmouth Rd. SE15 —1F 95
Sidmouth Rd. Well —7C 84
Sidmouth St. WC1
—3K 61 (2F 143)
Sidney. Sidc —6B 116
Sidney Av. N13 —5E 16
Sidney Boyd Ct. NW6 —7J 43
Sidney Elson Way. E6 —2E 66
Sidney Est. E1 —5J 63
(in two parts)
Sidney Gdns. Bren —6D 72
Sidney Gro. EC1
—2B 62 (1A 144)
Sidney Miller Ct. W3 —1H 73
(off Crown St.)
Sidney Rd. E7 —3J 49
Sidney Rd. N22 —7E 16
Sidney Rd. SE25 —5G 125
Sidney Rd. SW9 —2K 93
Sidney Rd. Beck —2A 126
Sidney Rd. Harr —3G 23
Sidney Rd. Twic —6A 88
Sidney Sq. E1 —5J 63
Sidney St. E1 —5H 63
Sidworth St. E8 —7H 47
Siebert Rd. SE3 —6J 81
Siemens Rd. SE18 —3B 82
Sigdon Pas. E8 —5G 47
Sigdon Rd. E8 —5G 47
Sigers, The. Pinn —6A 22
Signmakers Yd. NW1 —1F 61
(off Delancey St.)
Sigrist Sq. King T —1E 118
Silbury Av. Mitc —1C 122
Silbury Ho. SE26 —3G 111
Silbury St. N1 —3D 62 (1E 144)
Silchester Rd. W10 —6F 59
Silecroft Rd. Bexh —1G 101
Silesia Bldgs. E8 —7H 47
Silex St. SE1 —2B 78 (7B 150)
Silicone Bus. Cen. Gnfd —2C 56

Silk Clo. *SE12* —5J **97**
Silkfield Rd. *NW9* —5A **26**
Silk Ho. *NW9* —3K **25**
Silk Mills Path. *SE13* —2E **96**
Silkmills Sq. *E9* —6B **48**
Silks Ct. *E11* —1H **49**
Silkstream Pde. *Edgw* —1J **25**
Silkstream Rd. *Edgw* —1J **25**
Silk St. *EC2* —5C **62** (5D **144**)
Sillitoe Ho. N1 —1D **62**
 (off Colville Est.)
Silsoe Rd. *N22* —2K **29**
Silver Birch Av. *E4* —6G **19**
Silverbirch Clo. *N11* —6K **15**
Silver Birch Clo. *SE28* —1A **84**
Silver Birch Clo. *Dart* —4K **117**
Silverbirch Ct. *E8* —7F **47**
Silver Birch Gdns. *E4* —0D **66**
Silverburn Ho. SW9 —1B **94**
 (off Lothian Rd.)
Silver Chase Ct. *Enf* —1G **7**
Silvercliffe Gdns. *Barn* —4H **5**
Silver Clo. *SE14* —7A **80**
Silver Clo. *Harr* —7C **10**
Silver Cres. *W4* —4H **73**
Silverdale. *SE26* —4J **111**
Silverdale. *Enf* —4D **6**
Silverdale Av. *Ilf* —5K **35**
Silverdale Clo. *W7* —1J **71**
Silverdale Clo. *N'holt* —5D **38**
Silverdale Clo. *Sutt* —4H **131**
Silverdale Dri. *SE9* —2C **114**
Silverdale Rd. *E4* —6A **20**
Silverdale Rd. *Bexh* —2H **101**
Silverdale Rd. *Pet W* —4G **129**
Silverhall St. *Iswth* —3A **88**
Silverholme Clo. *Harr* —7E **24**
Silverland St. *E16* —1D **82**
Silver La. *W Wick* —2F **137**
Silverleigh Rd. *T Hth* —4K **123**
Silvermead. *E18* —1J **33**
Silvermere Rd. *SE6* —7D **96**
Silver Pl. *W1* —6G **61** (2B **148**)
Silver Rd. *W12* —7F **59**
Silver Spring Clo. *Eri* —6H **85**
Silverston Way. *Stan* —6H **11**
Silver St. *N18* —4J **17**
Silver St. *Enf* —3J **7**
Silverthorne Rd. *SW8* —2F **93**
Silverthorn Gdns. *E4* —2H **19**
Silverton Rd. *W6* —6F **75**
Silvertown Way. *E16* —6H **65**
Silvertree La. *Gnfd* —3H **55**
Silver Wlk. *SE16* —1B **80**
Silver Way. *Romf* —3H **37**
Silver Wing Ind. Est. *Croy*
 —6K **133**
Silverwood Clo. *Beck* —7C **112**
Silverwood Clo. *Croy* —7B **136**
Silvester Ho. W11 —6H **59**
 (off Basing St.)
Silvester Rd. *SE22* —5F **95**
Silvester St. *SE1*
 —2D **78** (7E **150**)
Silwood Est. *SE16* —4J **79**
Silwood St. *SE16* —4J **79**
Simla Clo. *SE14* —6A **80**
Simmons Clo. *N20* —2H **15**
Simmons La. *E4* —2A **20**
Simmons Rd. *SE18* —5F **83**
Simmons Way. *N20* —2H **15**
Simmott Rd. *E17* —1K **31**
Simms Clo. *Cars* —2C **132**
Simms Rd. *SE1* —4G **79**
Simnel Rd. *SE12* —7K **97**

Simon Clo. *W11* —7H **59**
Simonds Rd. *E10* —2C **48**
Simone Clo. *Brom* —1C **128**
Simone Ct. *SE26* —3J **111**
Simon Peter Ct. *Enf* —2G **7**
Simons Ct. *N16* —2F **47**
Simons Wlk. *E15* —5F **49**
Simpson Clo. *N21* —5E **6**
Simpson Dri. *W3* —6K **57**
Simpson Ho. *NW8*
 —3C **60** (2C **140**)
Simpson Ho. SE11
 —5K **77** (6H **155**)
Simpson Rd. *Houn* —6D **86**
Simpson Rd. *Rich* —4C **104**
Simpson's Rd. *E14* —7D **64**
Simpsons Rd. *Brom* —3J **127**
Simpson St. *SW11* —2C **92**
Simrose Ct. *SW18* —5J **91**
Sims Wlk. *SE3* —4H **97**
Sinclair Ct. *Croy* —2E **134**
Sinclair Dri. *Sutt* —7K **131**
Sinclair Gdns. *W14* —2F **75**
Sinclair Gro. *NW11* —6F **27**
Sinclair Mans. W12 —2F **75**
 (off Richmond Way)
Sinclair Rd. *E4* —5G **19**
Sinclair Rd. *W14* —2F **75**
Sinclare Clo. *Enf* —1A **8**
Singapore Rd. *W13* —1A **72**
Singer St. *EC2* —3D **62** (2F **145**)
Singleton Clo. *SW17* —7D **108**
Singleton Clo. *Croy* —7C **124**
Singleton Rd. *Dag* —5F **53**
Singleton Scarp. *N12* —5D **14**
Sinnott Rd. *E17* —1K **31**
Sion Ct. *Twic* —1B **104**
Sion Rd. *Twic* —1B **104**
Sippets Ct. *Ilf* —1H **51**
Sir Alexander Clo. *W3* —1B **74**
Sir Alexander Rd. *W3* —1B **74**
Sir Cyril Black Way. *SW19*
 —7J **107**
Sirdar Rd. *N22* —3B **30**
Sirdar Rd. *W11* —7F **59**
Sirdar Rd. *Mitc* —6E **108**
Sir Henry Floyd Ct. *Stan* —2G **11**
Sirinham Point. *SW8* —6K **77**
Sirius Building. E1 —7K **63**
 (off Jardine Rd.)
Sir Oswald Stoll Foundation, The.
 (off Fulham Rd.) *SW6* —7K **75**
Sir William Powell's Almshouses.
 SW6 —2G **91**
Sise La. *EC4* —6D **62** (1E **150**)
Sisley Rd. *Bark* —1J **67**
Sispara Gdns. *SW18* —6H **91**
Sissinghurst Rd. Croy —7G **125**
Sister Mabel's Way. SE15
 —7G **79**
Sisters Av. *SW11* —3D **92**
Sistova Rd. *SW12* —1F **109**
Sisulu Pl. *SW9* —3A **94**
Sittingbourne Av. *Enf* —6J **7**
Sittwell Gro. *Stan* —5E **10**
Siverst Clo. *N'holt* —6F **39**
Siviter Way. *Dag* —7H **53**
Siward Rd. *N17* —1D **30**
Siward Rd. *SW17* —3A **108**
Siward Rd. *Brom* —3K **127**
Six Acres Est. *N4* —2A **46**
Six Bridges Ind. Est. SE1 —5G **79**
 (off Marlborough Gro.)
Sixth Av. *E12* —4D **50**
Sixth Av. *W10* —3G **59**

Sixth Cross Rd. *Twic* —3G **103**
Skardu Rd. *NW2* —5G **43**
Skeena Hill. *SW18* —7G **91**
Skeffington Rd. *E6* —1D **66**
Skelbrook St. *SW18* —2A **108**
Skelgill Rd. *SW15* —4H **91**
Skelley Rd. *E15* —7H **49**
Skelton Clo. *E8* —6F **47**
Skelton Rd. *E7* —6J **49**
Skelton's La. *E10* —7D **32**
Skelwith Rd. *W6* —6E **74**
Skerne Rd. *King T* —1D **118**
Sketchley Gdns. *SE16* —5K **79**
Sketty Rd. *Enf* —3A **8**
Skiers St. *E15* —1G **65**
Skiffington Clo. *SW2* —1A **110**
Skillen Lodge. *Pinn* —1A **22**
Skinner Clo. *E2* —2H **63**
Skinner Pl. *SW1*
 —4E **76** (4G **153**)
Skinners La. *EC4*
 —7C **62** (2D **150**)
Skinners La. *Houn* —1F **87**
Skinner's Row. *SE10* —1D **96**
Skinner St. *EC1* —4A **62** (2K **143**)
Skipsey Av. *E6* —3D **66**
Skipton Ho. *SE4* —4A **96**
Skipworth Rd. *E9* —1J **63**
Skomer Wlk. *N1* —6C **46**
Skylines. *E14* —2E **80**
Sky Peals Rd. *Wfd G* —7A **20**
Sladebrook Rd. *SE3* —3B **98**
Slade Ct. *New Bar* —3E **4**
Sladedale Rd. *SE18* —5J **83**
Slade Ho. *Houn* —6D **86**
Sladen Pl. *E5* —4H **47**
Slades Clo. *Enf* —3F **7**
Slades Dri. *Chst* —4G **115**
Slades Gdns. *Enf* —2F **7**
Slades Hill. *Enf* —3F **7**
Slades Rise. *Enf* —3F **7**
Slade, The. *SE18* —6J **83**
Slade Tower. *E10* —2C **48**
Slade Wlk. *SE17*
 —6C **78** (7B **156**)
Slagrove Pl. *SE13* —5C **96**
Slaidburn St. *SW10* —6A **76**
Slaithwaite Rd. *SE13* —4E **96**
Slaney Pl. *N7* —5A **46**
Slatter. *NW9* —7G **13**
Slattery Rd. *Felt* —1A **102**
Sleaford Ind. Est. *SW8* —7G **77**
Sleaford St. *SW8* —7G **77**
Slewyn Ct. *Wemb* —3J **41**
Slievemore Clo. *SW4* —3H **93**
Slindon Ct. *N16* —3F **47**
Slingsby Pl. *WC2*
 —7J **61** (2E **148**)
Slippers Pl. *SE16* —3H **79**
Sloane Av. *SW3* —4C **76** (4D **152**)
Sloane Ct. E. *SW3*
 —5E **76** (5G **153**)
Sloane Ct. W. *SW3*
 —5E **76** (5G **153**)
Sloane Gdns. *SW1*
 —4E **76** (4G **153**)
Sloane Sq. *SW1* —4D **76** (4F **153**)
Sloane St. *SW1* —2D **76** (7F **147**)
Sloane Ter. *SW1*
 —4E **76** (3G **153**)
Sloane Wlk. *Croy* —6B **126**
Slocum Clo. *SE28* —7C **68**
Slough La. *NW9* —5J **25**
Sly St. *E1* —6H **63**
Smallberry Av. *Iswth* —2K **87**

Smallbrook M. *W2*
 —6B **60** (1A **146**)
Smalley Clo. *N16* —3F **47**
Smalley Rd. Est. N16 —3F **47**
 (off Smalley Clo.)
Smallwood Rd. *SW17* —4B **108**
Smarden Clo. *Belv* —5G **85**
Smarden Gro. *SE9* —4D **114**
Smart's Pl. *N18* —5B **18**
Smart's Pl. *WC2* —6J **61** (7F **143**)
Smart St. *E2* —3K **63**
Smeaton Ct. *SE1*
 —3C **78** (2C **156**)
Smeaton Rd. *SW18* —7J **91**
Smeaton Rd. *Wfd G* —5J **21**
Smeaton St. *E1* —1H **79**
Smedley St. *SW8 & SW4* —2H **93**
Smeed Rd. *E3* —7C **48**
Smiles Pl. *SE13* —2E **96**
Smith Clo. *SE16* —1K **79**
Smithfield St. *EC1*
 —5B **62** (6A **144**)
Smith Hill. *Bren* —6E **72**
Smithies Ct. *E15* —5E **48**
Smithies Rd. *SE2* —4B **84**
Smith's Ct. *W1* —7H **61** (2B **148**)
Smithson Rd. *N17* —1D **30**
Smiths Point. E13 —1J **65**
 (off Brooks Rd.)
Smith Sq. *SW1* —3J **77** (2E **154**)
Smith St. *SW3* —5D **76** (5E **152**)
Smith St. *Surb* —6F **119**
Smith's Yd. *SW18* —2A **108**
Smith Ter. *SW3* —5D **76** (6E **152**)
Smithwood Clo. *SW19* —1G **107**
Smithy St. *E1* —5J **63**
Smock Wlk. *Croy* —6C **124**
Smoothfield. *Houn* —4E **86**
Smugglers Way. *SW18* —4K **91**
Smyrk's Rd. *SE17*
 —5E **78** (6H **157**)
Smyrna Rd. *NW6* —7J **43**
Smythe St. *E14* —7D **64**
Snakes La. *Barn* —3A **6**
Snakes La. E. *Wfd G* —6F **21**
Snakes La. W. *Wfd G* —5D **20**
Snaresbrook Dri. *Stan* —4J **11**
Snaresbrook Hall. *E18* —4J **33**
Snaresbrook Rd. *E11* —4G **33**
Snarsgate St. *W10* —5E **58**
Sneath Av. *NW11* —7H **27**
Snells Pk. *N18* —6A **18**
Sneyd Rd. *NW2* —4E **42**
Snowbury Rd. *SW6* —2K **91**
Snowden Dri. *NW9* —6A **26**
Snowden St. *EC2*
 —4E **62** (4G **145**)
Snowdown Clo. *SE20* —1K **125**
Snowdrop Clo. *Hamp* —6E **102**
Snow Hill. *EC1* —5B **62** (6A **144**)
Snow Hill Ct. *EC1*
 —6B **62** (7B **144**)
Snowsfields. *SE1*
 —2D **78** (6F **151**)
Snowshill Rd. *E12* —5C **50**
Snowy Fielder Waye. Iswth
 —2B **88**
Soames St. *SE15* —3F **95**
Soames Wlk. *N Mald* —1A **120**
Socket La. *Hay* —6K **127**
Soho Sq. *W1* —6H **61** (7C **142**)
Soho St. *W1* —6H **61** (7C **142**)
Sojourner Truth Clo. *E8* —6H **47**
Solander Gdns. *E1* —7J **63**
Solar Ct. *N3* —7E **14**

Solarium Ct. *SE1*
 —4F **79** (3K **157**)
Soldene Ct. N7 —6K **45**
 (off Georges Rd.)
Solebay St. *E1* —4A **64**
Solent Rise. *E16* —3J **65**
Solent Rd. *NW6* —5J **43**
Soley M. *WC1* —3A **62** (1J **143**)
Solna Av. *SW15* —5E **90**
Solna Rd. *N21* —1J **17**
Soloman Av. *N9* —4B **18**
Solomon's Pas. *SE15* —4H **95**
Solon New Rd. *SW4* —4H **93**
Solon New Rd. Est. *SW4* —4J **93**
Solon Rd. *SW2* —4J **93**
Solway Clo. *E8* —6F **47**
 (off Queensbridge Rd.)
Solway Clo. *Houn* —3C **86**
Solway Rd. *N22* —1B **30**
Solway Rd. *SE22* —4G **95**
Somaford Gro. *Barn* —6G **5**
Somali Rd. *NW2* —5H **43**
Somerby Rd. *Bark* —7H **51**
Somercoates Clo. *Barn* —3H **5**
Somer Ct. SW6 —6J **75**
 (off Anselm Rd.)
Somerfield Ho. *SE8* —5K **79**
Somerfield Rd. *N4* —2B **46**
Somerford Gro. *N16* —4F **47**
Somerford Gro. *N17* —7B **18**
 (in two parts)
Somerford Gro. Est. *N16* —4F **47**
Somerford St. *E1* —4H **63**
Somerford Way. *SE16* —2A **80**
Somerhill Av. *Sidc* —7B **100**
Somerhill Rd. *Well* —2B **100**
Somerleyton Pas. *SW9* —4B **94**
Somerleyton Rd. *SW9* —4A **94**
Somersby Gdns. *Ilf* —5D **34**
Somers Clo. *NW1* —2H **61**
Somers Cres. *W2*
 —6C **60** (1C **146**)
Somerset Av. *SW20* —2D **120**
Somerset Av. *Well* —4K **99**
Somerset Clo. *N17* —2D **30**
Somerset Clo. *N Mald* —6A **120**
Somerset Clo. *Wfd G* —1J **33**
Somerset Ct. W7 —6K **55**
 (off Copley Clo.)
Somerset Ct. Buck H —2F **21**
Somerset Est. *SW11* —1B **92**
Somerset Gdns. *N6* —7E **28**
Somerset Gdns. *N17* —7K **17**
Somerset Gdns. *SE13* —2D **96**
Somerset Gdns. *SW16* —3K **123**
Somerset Gdns. *Tedd* —5J **103**
Somerset Hall. *N17* —7K **17**
Somerset Lodge. *Bren* —6D **72**
Somerset Rd. *E17* —6C **32**
Somerset Rd. *N17* —3F **31**
Somerset Rd. *N18* —5A **18**
Somerset Rd. *NW4* —4E **26**
Somerset Rd. *SW19* —3F **107**
Somerset Rd. *W4* —3K **73**
Somerset Rd. *W13* —1B **72**
Somerset Rd. *Bren* —6C **72**
Somerset Rd. *Harr* —6G **23**
Somerset Rd. *King T* —2F **119**
Somerset Rd. *New Bar* —5E **4**
Somerset Rd. *S'hall* —5D **54**
Somerset Rd. *Tedd* —5J **103**
Somerset Sq. *W14* —2G **75**
Somerset Waye. *Houn* —6C **70**
Somersham Rd. *Bexh* —2E **100**
Somers Pl. *SW2* —7K **93**

Somers Rd. *E17* —4B **32**
Somers Rd. *SW2* —6K **93**
Somerton Av. *Rich* —3H **89**
Somerton Rd. *NW2* —3G **43**
Somerton Rd. *SE15* —4H **95**
Somertrees Av. *SE12* —2K **113**
Somervell Rd. *Harr* —5D **38**
Somerville Rd. *SE20* —7K **111**
Somerville Rd. *Romf* —6C **36**
Sonderburg Rd. *N7* —2K **45**
Sondes St. *SE17*
　　　—6D **78** (7E **156**)
Sonia Ct. *Edgw* —7A **12**
Sonia Ct. *Harr* —6K **23**
Sonia Gdns. *N12* —4F **15**
Sonia Gdns. *NW10* —4B **42**
Sonia Gdns. *Houn* —7E **70**
Sonning Gdns. *Hamp* —6C **102**
Sonning Rd. *SE25* —6G **125**
Sontan Ct. *Twic* —1H **103**
Soper Clo. *E4* —5G **19**
Sophia Clo. *N7* —6K **45**
Sophia Rd. *E10* —1D **48**
Sophia Rd. *E16* —6K **65**
Sophia Sq. *SE16* —7A **64**
　　(off Sovereign Cres.)
Sopwith. *NW9* —7G **13**
Sopwith Clo. *King T* —5F **105**
Sopwith Rd. *Houn* —7A **70**
Sopwith Way. *SW8* —7F **77**
Sopwith Way. *King T* —1E **118**
Sorensen Ct. *E10* —2D **48**
Sorrel Clo. *SE28* —1A **84**
Sorrel Gdns. *E6* —5C **66**
Sorrel La. *E14* —6F **65**
Sorrel Clo. *SE14* —7A **80**
Sorrell Clo. *SW9* —2A **94**
Sorrento Rd. *Sutt* —3K **131**
Sotheby Rd. *N5* —3C **46**
Sotheran Clo. *E8* —1G **63**
Sotheron Rd. *SW6* —7K **75**
Soudan Rd. *SW11* —1D **92**
Souldern Rd. *W14* —3F **75**
S. Access Rd. *E17* —7A **32**
South Acre. *NW9* —2B **26**
Southacre Way. *Pinn* —1A **22**
S. Africa Rd. *W12* —1D **74**
Southall Ct. *S'hall* —7D **54**
Southall Enterprise Cen. *S'hall*
　　　—2E **70**
Southall La. *Houn & S'hall*
　　　—6A **70**
Southall Pl. *SE1* —2D **78** (7E **150**)
Southampton Bldgs. *WC2*
　　　—5A **62** (6J **143**)
Southampton Gdns. *Mitc*
　　　—5J **123**
Southampton Pl. *WC1*
　　　—5J **61** (6F **143**)
Southampton Rd. *NW5* —5D **44**
Southampton Row. *WC1*
　　　—5J **61** (5F **143**)
Southampton St. *WC2*
　　　—7J **61** (2F **149**)
Southampton Way. *SE5* —7D **78**
Southam St. *W10* —4G **59**
S. Audley St. *W1*
　　　—7E **60** (3H **147**)
South Av. *E4* —7J **9**
South Av. *N2* —4K **27**
South Av. *NW10* —4E **58**
South Av. *Cars* —7E **132**
South Av. *Rich* —2G **89**
South Av. *S'hall* —7D **54**
South Av. Gdns. *S'hall* —7D **54**

South Bank. *Chst* —4G **115**
South Bank. *Surb* —6E **118**
Southbank. *Th Dit* —7B **118**
Southbank Bus. Cen. *SW8*
　　　—6H **77**
Southbank Bus. Cen. *SW11*
　　　—1D **92**
S. Bank Ter. *Surb* —6E **118**
S. Birkbeck Rd. *E11* —3F **49**
S. Black Lion La. *W6* —5C **74**
S. Bolton Gdns. *SW5* —5A **76**
Southborough Clo. *Surb*
　　　—7D **118**
Southborough La. *Brom* —5C **128**
Southborough Rd. *E9* —1K **63**
Southborough Rd. *Brom*
　　　—3C **128**
Southborough Rd. *Surb* —7E **118**
S. Boundary Rd. *E12* —3D **50**
Southbourne. *Brom* —7J **127**
Southbourne Av. *NW9* —2J **25**
Southbourne Clo. *Pinn* —7C **22**
Southbourne Ct. *NW9* —2J **25**
Southbourne Cres. *NW4* —4G **27**
Southbourne Gdns. *SE12* —5K **97**
Southbourne Gdns. *Ilf* —5G **51**
Southbourne Gdns. *Ruis* —1A **38**
S. Branch Av. *NW10* —4E **58**
Southbridge Pl. *Croy* —4C **134**
Southbridge Rd. *Croy* —4C **134**
Southbridge Way. *S'hall* —2C **70**
Southbrook M. *SE12* —6H **97**
Southbrook Rd. *SE12* —6H **97**
Southbrook Rd. *SW16* —1J **123**
Southbury Av. *Enf* —4B **8**
Southbury Rd. *Enf* —3K **7**
S. Carriage Dri. *SW7 & SW1*
　　　—2B **76** (7B **146**)
Southchurch Ct. E6 —2D 66
　(off High St. S.)
Southchurch Rd. *E6* —2D **66**
South Clo. *N6* —6F **29**
South Clo. *Barn* —3C **4**
South Clo. *Dag* —1G **69**
South Clo. *Mord* —6J **121**
South Clo. *Pinn* —7D **22**
South Clo. *Twic* —3E **102**
Southcombe St. *W14* —4G **75**
Southcote Av. *Surb* —7H **119**
Southcote Rd. *E17* —5K **31**
Southcote Rd. *N19* —4G **45**
Southcote Rd. *SE25* —5H **125**
S. Countess Rd. *E17* —3B **32**
South Cres. *E16* —4F **65**
　　(in two parts)
South Cres. *WC1*
　　　—5H **61** (6C **142**)
Southcroft Av. *Well* —3J **99**
Southcroft Av. *W Wick* —2E **136**
Southcroft Rd. *SW17 & SW16*
　　　—6E **108**
S. Cross Rd. *Ilf* —5G **35**
S. Croxted Rd. *SE21* —3D **110**
Southdean Gdns. *SW19* —2H **107**
South Dene. *NW7* —3E **12**
Southdene Ct. *N11* —3A **16**
Southdown. *N7* —6J **45**
Southdown Av. *W7* —3A **72**
Southdown Cres. *Harr* —1G **39**
Southdown Cres. *Ilf* —5J **35**
Southdown Dri. *SW20* —7F **107**
Southdown Rd. *SW20* —1F **121**
Southdown Rd. *Cars* —7E **132**

South Dri. *E12* —3C **50**
S. Ealing Rd. *W5* —2D **72**
S. Eastern Av. *N9* —3A **18**
S. Eaton Pl. *SW1*
　　　—4E **76** (3H **153**)
S. Eden Pk. Rd. *Beck* —6D **126**
S. Edwardes Sq. *W8* —3H **75**
South End. *W8* —3K **75**
South End. *Croy* —4C **134**
S. End Clo. *NW3* —4C **44**
S. End Grn. *NW3* —4C **44**
Southend Clo. *SE9* —6F **99**
Southend Cres. *SE9* —6F **99**
S. End Row. *NW3* —4C **44**
Southend La. *SE26 & SE6*
　　　—4B **112**
Southend Rd. *E6* —7D **50**
Southend Rd. *E17 & E18* —1F **33**
S. End Rd. *NW3* —4C **44**
Southend Rd. *Beck* —1C **126**
Southend Rd. *Wfd G* —2A **34**
S. End Row. *W8* —3K **75**
Southerby Av. *Enf* —4B **8**
Southern Av. *Mitc* —4J **123**
Southern Av. *SE25* —3F **125**
Southerngate Way. *SE14* —7A **80**
Southern Gro. *E3* —3B **64**
Southern Rd. *E13* —2K **65**
Southern Rd. *N2* —4D **28**
Southern Row. *W10* —4G **59**
Southern St. *N1* —2K **61**
Southern Way. *Romf* —6G **37**
Southernwood Retail Pk. *SE1*
　　　—5F **79** (5J **157**)
Southerton Rd. *W6* —4E **74**
S. Esk Rd. *E7* —6A **50**
Southey Ho. *SE17*
　　　—5C **78** (5D **156**)
Southey M. *E16* —1K **81**
Southey Rd. *N15* —5E **30**
Southey Rd. *SW9* —1A **94**
Southey Rd. *SW19* —7J **107**
Southey St. *SE20* —7K **111**
Southfield. *Barn* —6A **4**
Southfield Cotts. *W7* —2K **71**
Southfield Pk. *Harr* —4F **23**
Southfield Rd. *N17* —2E **30**
Southfield Rd. *W4* —2K **73**
Southfield Rd. *Chst* —3K **129**
Southfield Rd. *Enf* —6C **8**
Southfields. *NW4* —3D **26**
Southfields Ct. *Sutt* —2J **131**
Southfields M. *SW18* —6J **91**
Southfields Pas. *SW18* —6J **91**
Southfields Rd. *SW18* —6J **91**
South Gdns. *SW19* —7B **108**
South Gdns. *Wemb* —2G **41**
Southgate Cir. *N14* —1C **16**
Southgate Gro. *N1* —7D **46**
Southgate Ind. Est. *N14* —7B **6**
Southgate Rd. *N1* —1D **62**
S. Gipsy Rd. *Well* —3D **100**
S. Glade, The. *Bex* —1F **117**
South Grn. *NW9* —1A **26**
South Gro. *E17* —5A **32**
South Gro. *N6* —1E **44**
South Gro. *N15* —5D **30**
South Gro. Ho. *N6* —1E **44**
S. Harrow Ind. Est. *S Harr*
　　　—2G **39**
South Hill. *Chst* —6D **114**
S. Hill Av. *S Harr & Harr* —3G **39**
S. Hill Gro. *Harr* —4J **39**
S. Hill Pk. *NW3* —4C **44**
S. Hill Pk. Gdns. *NW3* —4C **44**
S. Hill Rd. *Brom* —3G **127**

Southholme Clo. *SE19* —1E **124**
Southill Rd. *Hay* —5H **127**
Southill Ct. *Chst* —7C **114**
Southill St. *E14* —6D **64**
S. Island Pl. *SW9* —7K **77**
S. Lambeth Pl. *SW8*
　　　—6J **77** (7F **155**)
S. Lambeth Rd. *SW8*
　　　—7J **77** (7F **155**)
Southland Rd. *SE18* —7K **83**
Southlands Av. *SW19* —2F **107**
Southlands Gro. *Brom* —3C **128**
Southlands Rd. *Brom* —4B **128**
Southland Way. *Houn* —5H **87**
South La. *King T* —3D **118**
South La. *N Mald* —4K **119**
South La. W. *N Mald* —4K **119**
South Lodge. *NW8*
　　　—3B **60** (1A **140**)
S. Lodge. *Twic* —7G **87**
S. Lodge Av. *Mitc* —4J **123**
S. Lodge Cres. *Enf* —4C **6**
　　(in two parts)
S. Lodge Dri. *N14* —4C **6**
Southly Clo. *Sutt* —3J **131**
South Mall. N9 —3B 18
　(off Plevna Rd.)
South Mead. *NW9* —1B **26**
South Mead. *Eps* —7B **130**
S. Meadows. *Wemb* —5F **41**
Southmead Rd. *SW19* —1G **107**
S. Molton La. *W1*
　　　—6F **61** (1J **147**)
S. Molton Rd. *E16* —6J **65**
S. Molton St. *W1*
　　　—6F **61** (1J **147**)
Southmoor Way. *E9* —6B **48**
S. Norwood Hill. *SE19 & SE25*
　　　—2E **124**
S. Oak Rd. *SW16* —4A **109**
Southold Rise. *SE9* —3D **114**
Southolm St. *SW11* —1F **93**
Southover. *N12* —3D **14**
Southover. *Brom* —5J **113**
South Pde. *SW3*
　　　—5B **76** (5B **152**)
South Pde. *W4* —4K **73**
South Pde. *Edgw* —2G **25**
South Pde. *Wall* —6G **133**
South Pk. Ct. *Beck* —7C **112**
S. Pk. Cres. *SE6* —1H **113**
S. Pk. Cres. *Ilf* —3H **51**
S. Pk. Dri. *Bark & Ilf* —5J **51**
S. Pk. Gro. *N Mald* —4J **119**
South Pk. Hill Rd. *S Croy*
　　　—5D **134**
South Pk. M. *SW6* —3K **91**
South Pk. Rd. *SW19* —6J **107**
South Pk. Rd. *Ilf* —3H **51**
S. Pk. Ter. *Ilf* —3H **51**
South Pl. *EC2* —5D **62** (6F **145**)
South Pl. *Enf* —5D **8**
South Pl. *Surb* —7F **119**
South Pl. M. *EC2*
　　　—5D **62** (6F **145**)
Southport Rd. *SE18* —4H **83**
S. Quay Plaza. *E14* —2D **80**
Southridge Pl. *SW20* —7D **106**
South Rise. *W2* —7C **60** (2D **146**)
S. Rise. *Cars* —7C **132**
S. Rise Way. *SE18* —4H **83**

South Rd. *N9* —1B **18**
South Rd. *SE23* —2K **111**
South Rd. *SW19* —6A **108**
South Rd. *W5* —4D **72**
South Rd. *Chad H* —6E **36**
South Rd. *Edgw* —1H **25**
South Rd. *Felt* —5B **102**
South Rd. *Hamp* —6C **102**
South Rd. *L Hth* —5C **36**
South Rd. *S'hall* —2D **70**
South Rd. *Twic* —3H **103**
South Row. *SE3* —2H **97**
Southsea Rd. *King T* —4E **118**
S. Sea St. *SE16* —3B **80**
South Side. *N15* —4F **31**
South Side. *W6* —3B **74**
Southside Comn. *SW19* —6E **106**
Southspring. *Sidc* —7H **99**
South Sq. *NW11* —6K **27**
South Sq. *WC1* —5A **62** (6J **143**)
South St. *W1* —1E **76** (4H **147**)
South St. *Brom* —2J **127**
South St. *Enf* —5D **8**
South St. *Iswth* —3A **88**
South St. *Rain* —2J **69**
S. Tenter St. *E1* —7F **63** (2K **151**)
South Ter. *SW7* —4C **76** (3C **152**)
South Ter. *Surb* —6E **118**
Southvale. *SE19* —6E **110**
South Vale. *Harr* —4J **39**
Southvale Rd. *SE3* —2G **97**
South View. *Brom* —2A **128**
Southview Av. *NW10* —5B **42**
Southview Clo. *SW17* —5E **108**
S. View Ct. *Bex* —6F **101**
S. View Ct. *SE19* —7C **110**
Southview Cres. *Ilf* —6F **35**
S. View Dri. *E18* —3K **33**
Southview Gdns. *Wall* —7G **133**
Southview Pde. *Rain* —3K **69**
S. View Rd. *N8* —3H **29**
Southview Rd. *Brom* —4F **113**
S. View Rd. *Pinn* —1A **22**
South Vs. *NW1* —6H **45**
Southville. *SW8* —1H **93**
Southville Clo. *Eps* —7A **130**
Southville Rd. *Th Dit* —7B **118**
South Wlk. *W Wick* —3G **137**
Southwark Bri. *SE1 & EC4*
　　　—7C **62** (3D **150**)
Southwark Bri. Office Village. *SE1*
　　　—1C **78** (4D **150**)
Southwark Bri. Rd. *SE1*
　　　—3B **78** (1B **156**)
Southwark Gro. *SE1*
　　　—1C **78** (5C **150**)
Southwark Pk. Rd. *SE16*
　　　—4F **79** (3K **157**)
Southwark Pk. Rd. Est. *SE1*
　　　—4F **79** (3K **157**)
Southwark Pl. *Brom* —3D **128**
Southwark St. *SE1*
　　　—1B **78** (4A **150**)
Southwater Clo. *E14* —6B **64**
Southwater Clo. *Beck* —7D **112**
South Way. *E14* —3C **80**
South Way. *N9* —2D **18**
South Way. *N11* —6B **16**
Southway. *N20* —2D **14**
Southway. *NW11* —6K **27**
Southway. *SW20* —4E **120**
South Way. *Croy* —3A **136**
South Way. *Harr* —4E **22**
South Way. *Hay* —7J **127**
Southway. *Wall* —4G **133**

South Way. Wemb —5G 41
Southwell Av. N'holt —6E 38
Southwell Gdns. SW7 —3A 76
Southwell Gro. Rd. E11 —2G 49
Southwell Ho. SE16 —4H 79
  (off Anchor St.)
Southwell Rd. SE5 —3C 94
Southwell Rd. Croy —6A 124
Southwell Rd. Kent —6D 24
S. Western Rd. Twic —6A 88
S. W. India Dock Entrance. E14
  —2E 80
Southwest Rd. E11 —1F 49
S. Wharf Rd. W2
  —6B 60 (7A 140)
Southwick M. W2
  —6B 60 (7B 140)
Southwick Pl. W2
  —6C 60 (1C 146)
Southwick St. W2
  —6C 60 (7C 140)
Southwick Yd. W2
  —6C 60 (1C 146)
Southwold Dri. Bark —5A 52
Southwold Mans. W9 —3J 59
  (off Widley Rd.)
Southwold Rd. E5 —2H 47
Southwold Rd. Bex —6H 101
Southwood Av. N6 —7F 29
Southwood Av. King T —1J 119
Southwood Clo. Brom —4D 128
Southwood Clo. Wor Pk —1F 131
Southwood Ct. EC1
  —3B 62 (2A 144)
  (off Wynyatt St.)
Southwood Ct. NW11 —5K 27
Southwood Dri. Surb —7J 119
S. Woodford to Barking Relief Rd.
  E11 & E12 —5B 34
Southwood Gdns. Ilf —4F 35
Southwood Hall. N6 —6F 29
Southwood Heights. N6 —7F 29
Southwood La. N6 —1E 44
Southwood Lawn Rd. N6 —7E 28
Southwood Mans. N6 —6E 28
  (off Southwood La.)
Southwood Pk. N6 —7E 28
Southwood Rd. SE9 —2F 115
Southwood Rd. SE28 —1B 84
Southwood Smith St. N1 —1B 62
  (off Old Royal Free Sq.)
S. Worple Av. SW14 —3A 90
S. Worple Way. SW14 —3K 89
Southwyck Ho. SW9 —4B 94
Sovereign Bus. Cen. Enf —3G 9
Sovereign Clo. E1 —7H 63
Sovereign Clo. W5 —5C 56
Sovereign Ct. Houn —3E 86
Sovereign Cres. SE16 —7A 64
Sovereign Gro. Wemb —3D 40
Sovereign M. E2 —2F 63
Sovereign Pk. NW10 —4H 57
Sovereign Pk. Trad. Est. NW10
  —4H 57
Sovereign Rd. Bark —3C 68
Sowerby Clo. SE9 —5D 98
Spa Clo. SE19 —1E 124
Spa Ct. SW16 —4K 109
Spafield St. EC1 —4A 62 (3J 143)
Spa Grn. Est. EC1
  —3B 62 (1K 143)
Spa Hill. SE19 —1D 124
Spalding Ho. SE4 —4A 96
Spalding Rd. NW4 —7E 26
Spalding Rd. SW17 —5F 109

Spanby Rd. E3 —4C 64
Spaniards Clo. NW11 —1B 44
Spaniards End. NW3 —1A 44
Spaniards Rd. NW3 —2A 44
Spanish Pl. W1 —6E 60 (7H 141)
Spanish Rd. SW18 —5B 92
Spanswick Lodge. N15 —4B 30
Sparkbridge Rd. Harr —4J 23
Sparkes Clo. Harr —4J 23
Sparkes. Sidc —5B 116
Sparke Ter. E16 —6H 65
  (off Clarkson Rd.)
Sparkes Clo. W3 —6K 57
Sparks Clo. Dag —2D 52
Sparks Clo. Hamp —6C 102
Spa Rd. SE16 —3F 79 (2J 157)
Sparrick's Row. SE1
  —2D 78 (6F 151)
Sparrow Clo. Hamp —6C 102
Sparrow Dri. Orp —7G 129
Sparrow Farm Dri. Felt —7A 86
Sparrow Farm Rd. Eps —4C 130
Sparrow Grn. Dag —3H 53
Sparrows La. SE9 —7G 99
Sparrows Way. Bush —1B 10
Sparsholt Clo. Bark —1J 67
  (off Sparsholt Rd.)
Sparsholt Rd. N19 —1J 45
Sparsholt Rd. Bark —1J 67
Sparta St. SE10 —1E 96
Speakers Ct. Croy —1D 134
Speakman Ho. SE4 —3A 96
  (off Arica Rd.)
Spearman St. SE18 —6E 82
Spear M. SW5 —4J 75
Spearpoint Gdns. Ilf —5K 35
Spears Rd. N19 —1J 45
Speart La. Houn —7C 70
Spedan Clo. NW3 —3A 44
Speed Ho. EC2 —5D 62 (5D 144)
Speedwell Ho. N12 —5E 4
Speedwell St. SE8 —7C 80
Speedy Pl. WC1 —3J 61 (2E 142)
Speirs Clo. N Mald —6B 120
Speke Hill. SE9 —3D 114
Speke Rd. T Hth —2D 124
Speldhurst Clo. Brom —5J 127
Speldhurst Rd. E9 —7K 47
Speldhurst Rd. W4 —3K 73
Spellbrook Wlk. N1 —1C 62
  (off Basire St.)
Spelman St. E1 —5G 63 (5K 145)
Spence Clo. SE16 —2B 80
Spencer Av. N13 —6E 16
Spencer Clo. N3 —2J 27
Spencer Clo. NW10 —3F 57
Spencer Clo. Wfd G —5F 21
Spencer Dri. N2 —6A 28
Spencer Gdns. SE9 —5D 98
Spencer Gdns. SW14 —5J 89
Spencer Hill. SW19 —6G 107
Spencer Ho. NW4 —5D 26
Spencer M. SW9 —1K 93
Spencer M. W6 —6G 75
Spencer Pk. SW18 —5B 92
Spencer Pas. E2 —2H 63
  (off Coate St.)
Spencer Pl. N1 —7B 46
  (off Tyndale Ter.)
Spencer Pl. Croy —7D 124
Spencer Rise. NW5 —4F 45
Spencer Rd. E6 —1B 66
Spencer Rd. E17 —2E 32
Spencer Rd. N8 —5K 29
  (in two parts)

Spencer Rd. N11 —4A 16
Spencer Rd. N17 —1G 31
Spencer Rd. SW18 —4B 92
Spencer Rd. SW20 —1D 120
Spencer Rd. W3 —1J 73
Spencer Rd. W4 —7J 73
Spencer Rd. Brom —7H 113
Spencer Rd. Harr —2J 23
Spencer Rd. Ilf —1K 51
Spencer Rd. Iswth —1G 87
Spencer Rd. Mitc —3E 122
Spencer Rd. Mit J —7E 122
Spencer Rd. Rain —3K 69
Spencer Rd. S Croy —5E 134
Spencer Rd. Twic —3J 103
Spencer Rd. Wemb —2C 40
Spencer St. EC1
  —3B 62 (2A 144)
Spencer St. S'hall —2B 70
Spencer Wlk. NW3 —4B 44
Spencer Wlk. SW15 —4F 91
Spenlow Ho. SE16 —3G 79
  (off Jamaica Rd.)
Spenser Gro. N16 —5E 46
Spenser M. SE21 —2D 110
Spenser St. SE24 —5B 94
Spenser St. SW1
  —3G 77 (1B 154)
Spensley Wlk. N16 —3D 46
Speranza St. SE18 —5K 83
Sperling Rd. N17 —2E 30
Spert St. E14 —7A 64
Speyside. N14 —6B 6
Spey St. E14 —5E 64
Spey Way. Romf —1K 37
Spezia Rd. NW10 —2C 58
Spice Ct. E1 —7G 63
Spicer Clo. SW9 —2B 94
Spicer Ct. Enf —3K 7
Spice's Yd. Croy —4C 134
Spigurnell Rd. N17 —1D 30
Spikes Bri. Rd. S'hall —6C 54
Spilsby Clo. NW9 —1A 26
Spindle Clo. SE18 —3C 82
Spindlewood Gdns. Croy
  —4E 134
Spindrift Av. E14 —4C 80
Spinel Clo. SE18 —5H 83
Spinnells Rd. Harr —1D 38
Spinney Clo. N Mald —5A 120
Spinney Clo. Wor Pk —2B 130
Spinney Gdns. SE19 —5F 111
Spinney Gdns. Dag —5E 52
Spinney Oak. Brom —2C 128
Spinneys, The. Brom —1D 128
Spinney, The. N21 —7F 7
Spinney, The. SW13 —6D 74
Spinney, The. SW16 —3G 109
Spinney, The. Barn —2E 4
Spinney, The. Sidc —5E 116
Spinney, The. Stan —4K 11
Spinney, The. Sutt —4E 130
Spinney, The. Wemb —3A 40
Spires Shop. Cen., The. Barn
  —3B 4
Spirit Quay. E1 —1G 79
Spital Sq. E1 —5E 62 (5H 145)
Spital St. E1 —5G 63 (5K 145)
Spital Yd. E1 —5E 62 (5H 145)
Spitfire Est., The. Houn —5A 70
Spitfire Way. Houn —5A 70
Splendour Wlk. SE16 —5J 79
  (off Verne Rd.)
Spode Ho. SE11 —3A 78 (2J 155)
Spode Wlk. NW6 —5K 43

Spondon Rd. N15 —4G 31
Spoonbill Way. Hayes —5B 54
Spooner Ho. Houn —6E 70
Spooners M. W3 —1K 73
Spooner Wlk. Wall —5J 133
Sportsbank St. SE6 —7E 96
Spottons Gro. N17 —1C 30
Spout Hill. Croy —5C 136
Spratt Hall Rd. E11 —6J 33
Spray La. Twic —6J 87
Spray St. SE18 —4F 83
Sprimont Pl. SW3
  —4D 76 (5E 152)
Springall St. SE15 —7H 79
Spring Bank. N21 —6E 6
Springbank Rd. SE13 —6F 97
Springbank Wlk. NW1 —7H 45
Springbourne Ct. Beck —1E 126
  (in two parts)
Spring Bri. M. W5 —7D 56
Springbridge Rd. W5 —7D 56
Spring Clo. Barn —5A 4
Spring Clo. Dag —1D 52
Spring Clo. La. Sutt —6G 131
Spring Cotts. Surb —5D 118
Spring Ct. NW6 —6H 43
Spring Ct. Eps —7B 130
Spring Ct. Rd. Enf —1F 7
Springcroft Av. N2 —4D 28
Springdale M. N16 —4D 46
Springdale Rd. N16 —4D 46
Springfield. E5 —1H 47
Springfield. Bush —1C 10
Springfield Av. N10 —3G 29
Springfield Av. SW20 —3H 121
Springfield Av. Hamp —6F 103
Springfield Clo. N12 —5E 14
Springfield Clo. Stan —3F 11
Springfield Ct. Ilf —5F 51
Springfield Ct. Wall —5F 133
Springfield Dri. Ilf —5G 35
Springfield Gdns. E5 —1H 47
Springfield Gdns. NW9 —5K 25
Springfield Gdns. Brom —4D 128
Springfield Gdns. Ruis —1A 38
Springfield Gdns. W Wick
  —2D 136
Springfield Gdns. Wfd G —7F 21
Springfield Gro. SE7 —6A 82
Springfield La. NW6 —1K 59
Springfield Mt. NW9 —5A 26
Springfield Pde. M. N13 —4F 17
Springfield Pl. N Mald —4J 119
Springfield Rise. SE26 —3H 111
  (in two parts)
Springfield Rd. E4 —1B 20
Springfield Rd. E6 —7D 50
Springfield Rd. E15 —3G 65
Springfield Rd. E17 —6B 32
Springfield Rd. N11 —5A 16
Springfield Rd. N15 —4G 31
Springfield Rd. NW8 —1A 60
Springfield Rd. SE26 —5H 111
Springfield Rd. SW19 —5H 107
Springfield Rd. W7 —1J 71
Springfield Rd. Bexh —4H 101
Springfield Rd. Brom —4D 128
Springfield Rd. Harr —6J 23
Springfield Rd. Hayes —1A 70
Springfield Rd. King T —1E 118
Springfield Rd. Tedd —5A 104
Springfield Rd. T Hth —1C 124
Springfield Rd. Twic —6B 102
Springfield Rd. Wall —5F 133
Springfield Rd. Well —3B 100

Springfields. New Bar —5E 4
  (off Somerset Rd.)
Springfield Wlk. NW6 —1K 59
Springfield Wlk. Orp —7J 129
  (off Andover Rd.)
Spring Gdns. N5 —5C 46
Spring Gdns. SW1
  —1H 77 (4D 148)
Spring Gdns. Romf —5J 37
Spring Gdns. Wall —5G 133
Spring Gdns. Wfd G —7F 21
Spring Gro. SE19 —7F 111
Spring Gro. W4 —5G 73
Spring Gro. Mitc —1E 122
Spring Gro. Cres. Houn —1G 87
Spring Gro. Rd. Houn & Iswth
  —1F 87
Spring Gro. Rd. Rich —5F 89
Spring Hill. E5 —7G 31
Spring Hill. SE26 —4J 111
Springhill Clo. SE5 —3D 94
Springhurst Clo. Croy —4B 136
Spring Lake. Stan —4G 11
Spring La. E5 —7H 31
Spring La. N10 —3E 28
Spring La. SE25 —6H 125
Spring M. W1 —5D 60 (5F 141)
Spring Pk. Av. Croy —2K 135
Spring Pk. Dri. N4 —1C 46
Springpark Dri. Beck —3E 126
Spring Pk. Rd. Croy —2K 135
Spring Path. NW3 —5B 44
Spring Pl. N3 —2J 27
Spring Pl. NW5 —5F 45
Springpond Rd. Dag —5E 52
Springrice Rd. SE13 —6F 97
Spring Shaw Rd. Orp —7A 116
Spring St. W2 —6B 60 (1A 146)
Spring Ter. Rich —5E 88
Spring Tide Clo. SE15 —1G 95
Spring Vale. Bexh —4H 101
Springvale Av. Bren —5E 72
Spring Vale Ter. W14 —3F 75
Spring Villa Rd. Edgw —7B 12
Springwater. Clo. SE18 —1E 98
Springway. Harr —7H 23
Springwell Av. NW10 —1B 58
Springwell Clo. SW16 —4K 109
Springwell Ct. Houn —2B 86
Springwell Rd. SW16 —4A 110
Springwell Rd. Houn —1B 86
Springwood Ct. S Croy —4E 134
Springwood Cres. Edgw —2C 12
Sprowston M. E7 —6J 49
Sprowston Rd. E7 —5J 49
Spruce Clo. E4 —6G 19
Spruce Ct. E8 —7F 47
Spruce Clo. W5 —3E 72
Sprucedale Gdns. Croy —4K 135
Spruce Hills Rd. E17 —2E 32
Spruce Pk. Short —4H 127
Sprules Rd. SE4 —2A 96
Spurgeon Av. SE19 —1D 124
Spurgeon Rd. SE19 —1D 124
Spurgeon St. SE1
  —3D 78 (1E 156)
Spurling Rd. SE22 —4F 95
Spurling Rd. Dag —6F 53
Spurrell Av. Bex —4K 117
Spur Rd. N15 —4D 30
Spur Rd. SE1 —2A 78 (6J 149)
Spur Rd. SW1 —2G 77 (7A 148)
Spur Rd. Edgw —4K 11

Spur Rd. Felt —4A 86
Spur Rd. Iswth —7A 72
Spurstowe Rd. E8 —6H 47
Spurstowe Ter. E8 —5H 47
Square Rigger Row. SW11 —3A 92
Square, The. W6 —5E 74
Square, The. Cars —5E 132
Square, The. Ilf —7E 34
Square, The. Rich —5D 88
Square, The. Wfd G —5D 20
Squarey St. SW17 —3A 108
Squires Ct. SW4 —1J 93
Squires Ct. SW19 —4J 107
Squires La. N3 —2K 27
Squires Mt. NW3 —3B 44
Squires, The. Romf —6J 37
Squires Way. Dart —4K 117
Squires Wood Dri. Chst —7C 114
Squirrel Clo. Houn —3A 86
Squirrel M. W13 —7K 55
Squirrels Clo. N12 —4F 15
Squirrels Ct. Wor Pk —2B 130
(off Avenue, The)
Squirrels Drey. Short —2G 127
(off Park Hill Rd.)
Squirrels Grn. Wor Pk —2B 130
Squirrel's La. Buck H —3G 21
Squirrels, The. SE13 —3F 97
Squirrels, The. Pinn —3D 22
Squirries St. E2 —3G 63
Stable Clo. N'holt —2E 54
Stable M. SE27 —5C 110
Stables, The. W10 —6F 59
(off Bassett Rd.)
Stables, The. Buck H —1F 21
Stables Way. SE11 —5A 78 (5J 155)
Stable Wlk. N2 —1B 28
Stable Way. W10 —6E 58
Stable Yd. SW1 —2G 77 (6A 148)
Stable Yd. SW9 —2K 93
Stable Yd. SW15 —3E 90
Stable Yd. Rd. SW1 —2G 77 (6B 148)
Stacey Av. N18 —4D 18
Stacey Clo. E10 —5F 33
Stacey St. N7 —3A 46
Stacey St. WC2 —6H 61 (1D 148)
Stackhouse St. SW3 —3D 76 (1E 152)
Stacy Path. SE5 —7E 78
Stadbrook Clo. S Harr —3D 38
Stadium Bus. Cen. Wemb —3H 41
Stadium Rd. NW4 —7E 26
Stadium Rd. SE18 —7D 82
Stadium St. SW10 —7A 76
Stadium Way. Wemb —4F 41
Staffa Rd. E10 —1A 48
Stafford Clo. E17 —6B 32
Stafford Clo. N14 —5B 6
Stafford Clo. NW6 —3J 59
Stafford Clo. Sutt —6G 131
Stafford Ct. SW8 —7J 77
Stafford Ct. W7 —6K 55
(off Copley Clo.)
Stafford Cripps Ho. SW6 —6H 75
(off Clem Attlee Ct.)
Stafford Cross Bus. Pk. Croy —5K 133
Stafford Gdns. Croy —5K 133
Stafford Pl. SW1 —3G 77 (1A 154)
Stafford Pl. Rich —7F 89
Stafford Rd. E3 —2B 64

Stafford Rd. E7 —7A 50
Stafford Rd. NW6 —3J 59
Stafford Rd. Harr —7B 10
Stafford Rd. High Bar —3B 4
Stafford Rd. N Mald —3J 119
Stafford Rd. Sidc —4J 115
Stafford Rd. Wall & Croy —6G 133
Staffordshire St. SE15 —1G 95
Stafford St. W1 —1G 77 (4A 148)
Stafford Ter. W8 —3J 75
Staff St. EC1 —3D 62 (2F 145)
Stag Clo. Edgw —2H 25
Stag La. SW15 —3B 106
Stag La. Buck H —2E 20
Stag La. Edgw & NW9 —2H 25
Stag Lane. (Junct.) —2B 106
Stag Pl. SW1 —3G 77 (1A 154)
Stags Way. Iswth —7K 71
Stainbank Rd. Mitc —3F 123
Stainby Rd. N15 —4F 31
Stainer St. SE1 —1D 78 (5F 151)
Staines Av. Sutt —2F 131
Staines Rd. Felt & Houn —6A 86
Staines Rd. Ilf —4G 51
Staines Rd. Twic —3E 102
Staines Rd. E. Sun —7A 102
Staines Wlk. Sidc —6C 116
Stainforth Rd. E17 —4C 32
Stainforth Rd. Ilf —7H 35
Staining La. EC2 —6C 62 (7D 144)
Stainmore Clo. Chst —1H 129
Stainsbury St. E2 —2J 63
Stainsby Pl. E14 —6C 64
Stainsby Rd. E14 —6C 64
Stainton Rd. SE6 —6F 97
Stainton Rd. Enf —1D 8
Stalbridge St. NW1 —5C 60 (5D 140)
Stalham St. SE16 —3H 79
Stambourne Way. SE19 —7E 110
Stambourne Way. W Wick —2E 136
Stamford Brook Av. W6 —3B 74
Stamford Brook Gdns. W6 —3B 74
Stamford Brook Mans. W6
(off Goldhawk Rd.) —4B 74
Stamford Brook Rd. W6 —3B 74
Stamford Clo. N15 —5G 31
Stamford Clo. NW3 —3A 44
(off Heath St.)
Stamford Clo. Harr —7D 10
Stamford Clo. S'hall —7E 54
Stamford Ct. W6 —4C 74
Stamford Dri. Brom —4H 127
Stamford Gdns. Dag —7C 52
Stamford Gro. E. N16 —1G 47
Stamford Gro. W. N16 —1G 47
Stamford Hill. N16 —2F 47
Stamford Lodge. N16 —7F 31
Stamford Rd. E6 —1C 66
Stamford Rd. N1 —7E 46
Stamford Rd. N15 —5G 31
Stamford Rd. Dag —1B 68
Stamford St. SE1 —1A 78 (5J 149)
Stamford Wharf. SE1 —7A 62 (3K 149)
Stamp Pl. E2 —2F 63 (1J 145)
Stanard Clo. N16 —7E 30
Stanborough Clo. Hamp —6D 102
Stanborough Pas. E8 —6F 47
Stanborough Rd. Houn —3H 87

Stanbridge Pl. N21 —3G 17
Stanbridge Rd. SW15 —3E 90
Stanbrook Rd. SE2 —2B 84
Stanbury Ct. NW3 —6D 44
Stanbury Rd. SE15 —2H 95
(in two parts)
Stancroft. NW9 —5A 26
Standard Ind. Est. E16 —2D 82
Standard Pl. EC2 —3E 62 (2H 145)
Standard Rd. NW10 —4J 57
Standard Rd. Belv —5G 85
Standard Rd. Bexh —4E 100
Standard Rd. Houn —3D 86
Standen Rd. SW18 —7H 91
Standfield Gdns. Dag —6G 53
Standfield Rd. Dag —5G 53
Standish Ho. W6 —4C 74
(off St Peter's Gro.)
Standish Rd. W6 —4C 74
Standlake Point. SE23 —3K 111
Stane Clo. SW19 —7K 107
Stane Pas. SW16 —5J 109
Stane Way. SE18 —7B 82
Stanfield Ho. N'holt —2B 54
(off Academy Gdns.)
Stanfield Rd. E3 —2A 64
Stanford Clo. Hamp —6D 102
Stanford Clo. Romf —6H 37
Stanford Clo. Wfd G —5H 21
Stanford Ct. SW6 —1K 91
Stanford Ho. Bark —2B 68
Stanford Pl. SE17 —4E 78 (4G 157)
Stanford Rd. N11 —5J 15
Stanford Rd. SW16 —2H 123
Stanford Rd. W8 —3K 75
Stanford St. SW1 —4H 77 (4C 154)
Stanford Way. SW16 —2H 123
Stangate. SE1 —3K 77 (1H 155)
Stangate Gdns. Stan —4G 11
Stangate Lodge. N21 —7E 6
Stanger Rd. SE25 —4G 125
Stanhill Cotts. Dart —7K 117
Stanhope Av. N3 —3H 27
Stanhope Av. Brom —1H 137
Stanhope Av. Harr —1H 23
Stanhope Clo. SE16 —2K 79
Stanhope Gdns. N4 —6B 30
Stanhope Gdns. N6 —6F 29
Stanhope Gdns. NW7 —5G 13
Stanhope Gdns. SW7 —4A 76 (3A 152)
Stanhope Gdns. Dag —3F 53
Stanhope Gdns. Ilf —1D 50
Stanhope Ga. W1 —1E 76 (5H 147)
Stanhope Ho. SE8 —7B 80
(off Adolphus St.)
Stanhope M. E. SW7 —4A 76 (3A 152)
Stanhope M. S. SW7 —4A 76
Stanhope M. W. SW7 —4A 76
Stanhope Pde. NW1 —3G 61 (1A 142)
Stanhope Pk. Rd. Gnfd —4G 55
Stanhope Pl. W2 —7D 60 (1E 146)
Stanhope Rd. E17 —5D 32
Stanhope Rd. N6 —6G 29
Stanhope Rd. N12 —5F 15

Stanhope Rd. Barn —6A 4
Stanhope Rd. Bexh —2E 100
Stanhope Rd. Cars —7E 132
Stanhope Rd. Croy —3E 134
Stanhope Rd. Dag —2F 53
Stanhope Rd. Gnfd —5G 55
Stanhope Rd. Sidc —4A 116
Stanhope Row. W1 —1F 77 (5J 147)
Stanhope St. NW1 —3G 61 (1A 142)
Stanhope Ter. W2 —7B 60 (2B 146)
Stanier Clo. W14 —5H 75
Stanlake M. W12 —1E 74
Stanlake Rd. W12 —1E 74
Stanlake Vs. W12 —1E 74
Stanley Av. Bark —2K 67
Stanley Av. Beck —3E 126
Stanley Av. Dag —1F 53
Stanley Av. Gnfd —1G 55
Stanley Av. N Mald —5C 120
Stanley Av. Wemb —7E 40
Stanley Clo. SW8 —6K 77 (7G 155)
Stanley Clo. Wemb —7E 40
Stanley Cohen Ho. EC1 —4C 62 (4C 144)
(off Golden La. Est.)
Stanley Ct. W5 —5C 56
Stanley Ct. Cars —7E 132
Stanley Ct. Sutt —7K 131
Stanley Cres. W11 —7H 59
Stanleycroft Clo. Iswth —1J 87
Stanley Gdns. NW2 —5E 42
Stanley Gdns. W3 —2A 74
Stanley Gdns. W11 —7H 59
Stanley Gdns. Mitc —6E 108
Stanley Gdns. Wall —6G 133
Stanley Gdns. M. W11 —7H 59
(off Kensington Pk. Rd.)
Stanley Gdns. Rd. Tedd —5J 103
Stanley Gro. N17 —7A 18
Stanley Gro. SW8 —2E 92
Stanley Gro. Croy —6A 124
Stanley Pk. Dri. Wemb —1F 57
Stanley Pk. Rd. Cars & Wall —7D 132
Stanley Pas. NW1 —2J 61
Stanley Rd. E4 —1A 20
Stanley Rd. E10 —6D 32
Stanley Rd. E12 —5C 50
Stanley Rd. E15 —1F 65
Stanley Rd. E18 —1H 33
Stanley Rd. N2 —3B 28
Stanley Rd. N9 —1A 18
Stanley Rd. N10 —7A 16
Stanley Rd. N11 —6C 16
Stanley Rd. N15 —4B 30
Stanley Rd. NW9 —7C 26
Stanley Rd. SW14 —4H 89
Stanley Rd. SW19 —6J 107
Stanley Rd. W3 —3J 73
Stanley Rd. Brom —4A 128
Stanley Rd. Croy —7A 124
Stanley Rd. Enf —3K 7
Stanley Rd. Harr —2G 39
Stanley Rd. Houn —4G 87
Stanley Rd. Ilf —2H 51
Stanley Rd. Mitc —7E 108
Stanley Rd. Mord —4J 121
Stanley Rd. Orp —7K 129
Stanley Rd. Sidc —3A 116
Stanley Rd. S'hall —7C 54

Stanley Rd. Sutt —6K 131
Stanley Rd. Twic & Tedd —4H 103
Stanley Rd. Wemb —6F 41
Stanley Sidings. Harr —7F 45
Stanley Sq. Cars —7D 132
Stanley St. SE8 —7B 80
Stanley Ter. N19 —2J 45
Stanmer St. SW11 —2C 92
Stanmore Gdns. Rich —3F 89
Stanmore Gdns. Sutt —3A 132
Stanmore Hill. Stan —3F 11
Stanmore Lodge. Stan —4G 11
Stanmore Pk. Stan —5G 11
Stanmore Pl. NW1 —1F 61
Stanmore Rd. E11 —1H 49
Stanmore Rd. N15 —4B 30
Stanmore Rd. Belv —4J 85
Stanmore Rd. Rich —3F 89
Stanmore St. N1 —1K 61
Stanmore Ter. Beck —2C 126
Stannard Rd. E8 —6G 47
Stannary Pl. SE11 —5A 78 (6K 155)
Stannary St. SE11 —6A 78 (7K 155)
Stannet Way. Wall —4G 133
Stansfeld Rd. E6 —5B 66
Stansfield Rd. SW9 —3K 93
Stansfield Rd. Houn —2A 86
Stansgate Rd. Dag —2G 53
Stanstead Clo. Brom —6H 127
Stanstead Gro. SE6 —1B 112
Stanstead Mnr. Sutt —6J 131
Stanstead Rd. E11 —5K 33
Stanstead Rd. SE23 & SE6 —1K 111
Stansted Cres. Bex —1D 116
Stanswood Gdns. SE5 —7E 78
Stanthorpe Clo. SW16 —5J 109
Stanthorpe Rd. SW16 —5J 109
Stanton Av. Tedd —6J 103
Stanton Clo. Wor Pk —1F 131
Stanton Rd. SE26 —4B 112
Stanton Rd. SW13 —2B 90
Stanton Rd. SW20 —1F 121
Stanton Rd. Croy —7C 124
Stanton Sq. SE26 —4B 112
Stanton Way. SE26 —4B 112
Stanway Ct. N1 —2E 62 (1H 145)
Stanway Gdns. W3 —1G 73
Stanway Gdns. Edgw —5D 12
Stanway St. N1 —2E 62
Stanwick Rd. W14 —4H 75
Stanworth Ct. Houn —7E 70
Stanworth St. SE1 —3F 79 (7J 151)
Stanyhurst. SE23 —1A 112
Stapenhill Rd. Wemb —3B 40
Staple Clo. Bex —3K 117
Staplefield Clo. SW2 —1J 109
Staplefield Clo. Pinn —1C 22
Stapleford. N17 —2E 30
(off Willan Rd.)
Stapleford Av. Ilf —5J 35
Stapleford Clo. E4 —3K 19
Stapleford Clo. SW19 —7G 91
Stapleford Clo. King —7D 118
Stapleford Rd. Wemb —7D 40
Stapleford Way. Bark —3B 68
Staplehurst Rd. SE13 —5G 97
Staplehurst Rd. Cars —7C 132
Staple Inn. WC1 —5A 62 (6J 143)
Staple Inn Bldgs. WC1 —5A 62 (6J 143)

Staples Clo. *SE16* —1A **80**
Staples Corner. (Junct.) —1D **42**
Staples Corner Bus. Cen. *NW2*
    —1D **42**
Staples Ho. *E6* —6E **66**
    (off Savage Gdns.)
Staple St. *SE1* —2D **78** (7F **151**)
Stapleton Gdns. *Croy* —5A **134**
Stapleton Hall Rd. *N4* —1K **45**
Stapleton Rd. *SW17* —3E **108**
Stapleton Rd. *Bexh* —7F **85**
Stapley Rd. *Belv* —5G **85**
Stapylton Rd. *Barn* —3B **4**
Star All. *EC3* —7E **62** (2H **151**)
Starboard Way. *E14* —3C **80**
Star Bus. Cen. *Rain* —5K **69**
Starch Ho. La. *Ilf* —2H **35**
Starcross St. *NW1*
    —3G **61** (2B **142**)
Starfield Rd. *W12* —2C **74**
Star & Garter Hill. *Rich* —1E **104**
Star Hill. *Dart* —5K **101**
Star La. *E16* —4G **65**
Starling Clo. *Buck H* —1D **20**
Starling Clo. *Pinn* —3A **22**
Starling M. *SE28* —2H **83**
Starling Wlk. *Hamp* —5C **102**
Starmans Clo. *Dag* —1E **68**
Star Path. *N'holt* —2E **54**
    (off Brabazon Rd.)
Star Pl. *E1* —7F **63** (3K **151**)
Star Rd. *W14* —6H **75**
Star Rd. *Iswth* —2H **87**
Star St. *W2* —6C **60** (7B **140**)
Starts Clo. *Orp* —3E **138**
Starts Hill Rd. *Orp* —3E **138**
Star Yd. *WC2* —6A **62** (7J **143**)
Staten Gdns. *Twic* —1K **103**
Statham Gro. *N16* —4D **46**
Statham Gro. *N18* —5K **17**
Station App. *E4* —6A **20**
Station App. *E7* —4K **49**
Station App. *E11* —5J **33**
Station App. *E17* —5C **32**
    (in two parts)
Station App. *E18* —2J **33**
Station App. *N11* —5A **16**
Station App. *N12* —4E **14**
Station App. *NW10* —3B **58**
Station App. *SE3* —3K **97**
Station App. *SE26* —5B **112**
    (Lower Sydenham)
Station App. *SE26* —4J **111**
    (Sydenham)
Station App. *SW6* —3G **91**
Station App. *SW16* —5H **109**
Station App. *W7* —1J **71**
Station App. *Beck* —1C **126**
Station App. *Bex* —7G **101**
Station App. *Bexh* —2E **100**
Station App. *Brom* —3J **127**
Station App. *Buck H* —4G **21**
Station App. *Cheam* —7G **131**
Station App. *Chst* —1E **128**
    (Chislehurst)
Station App. *Chst* —6C **114**
    (Elmstead Woods)
Station App. *Ewe* —7B **130**
    (Ewell West)
Station App. *Gnfd* —7G **39**
Station App. *Hamp* —7E **102**
Station App. *Harr* —7J **23**
Station App. *Hay* —1J **137**
Station App. *King T* —2G **119**

Station App. *New Bar* —4F **5**
Station App. *Pinn* —3C **22**
Station App. *Rich* —1G **89**
Station App. *S Croy* —7D **134**
Station App. *S Ruis* —5A **38**
Station App. *S'leigh* —5C **130**
Station App. *Well* —2A **100**
    (in two parts)
Station App. *Wemb* —6B **40**
Station App. *W Wick* —7E **126**
Station App. *Wor Pk* —1C **130**
Station App. N. *Sidc* —2A **116**
Station App. Rd. *SE1*
    —2K **77** (7J **149**)
Station App. Rd. *W4* —7J **73**
Station Av. *SW9* —3B **94**
Station Av. *Eps* —7A **130**
Station Av. *N Mald* —3A **120**
Station Av. *Rich* —1G **89**
Station Clo. *N3* —1J **27**
Station Clo. *N12* —4E **14**
Station Clo. *Hamp* —7F **103**
Station Ct. *E10* —7D **32**
    (off Kings Clo.)
Station Cres. *N15* —4D **30**
Station Cres. *SE3* —5J **81**
Station Cres. *Wemb* —6B **40**
Stationers' Hall Ct. *EC4*
    —6B **62** (1B **150**)
Station Est. *Beck* —3K **125**
Station Garage M. *SW16*
    —6H **109**
Station Gdns. *W4* —7J **73**
Station Gro. *Wemb* —6E **40**
Station Hill. *Brom* —2J **137**
Station Ho. M. *N9* —4B **18**
Station Pde. *E11* —5J **33**
Station Pde. *N14* —1C **16**
Station Pde. *NW2* —6E **42**
Station Pde. *W3* —6G **57**
Station Pde. *W5* —1F **73**
Station Pde. *Bark* —7G **51**
Station Pde. *Barn* —4K **5**
Station Pde. *Dag* —6G **53**
Station Pde. *Edgw* —7K **11**
Station Pde. *Harr* —2A **24**
    (Belmont)
Station Pde. *Harr* —4F **39**
    (South Harrow)
Station Pde. *N'holt* —4F **39**
Station Pde. *Rich* —1G **89**
Station Pde. *Sidc* —2A **116**
Station Pas. *E18* —2K **33**
Station Pas. *SE15* —1J **95**
Station Path. *E8* —6H **47**
    (off Graham Rd.)
Station Pl. *N4* —2A **46**
Station Rise. *SE27* —2B **110**
Station Rd. *E4* —1A **20**
Station Rd. *E7* —4J **49**
Station Rd. *E10* —3E **48**
Station Rd. *E12* —4C **50**
Station Rd. *E17* —6A **32**
Station Rd. *N3* —1J **27**
Station Rd. *N11* —5A **16**
Station Rd. *N17* —3G **31**
Station Rd. *N19* —3G **45**
Station Rd. *N21* —1G **17**
Station Rd. *N22* —2J **29**
Station Rd. *NW4* —6C **26**
Station Rd. *NW7* —6F **13**
Station Rd. *NW10* —2B **58**
Station Rd. *SE13* —3E **96**
Station Rd. *SE20* —6J **111**
Station Rd. *SE25* —4F **125**

Station Rd. *SW13* —2B **90**
Station Rd. *SW19* —1A **122**
Station Rd. *W5* —6F **57**
Station Rd. *W7* —1J **71**
Station Rd. *B'side* —3H **35**
Station Rd. *Belv* —3G **85**
Station Rd. *Bexh* —3E **100**
Station Rd. *Brom* —1J **127**
Station Rd. *Cars* —4D **132**
Station Rd. *Croy* —2D **134**
Station Rd. *Dag & Chad* —7D **36**
Station Rd. *Edgw* —6B **12**
Station Rd. *Eri* —5K **85**
Station Rd. *Hamp* —7E **102**
Station Rd. *Hamp W* —1D **118**
Station Rd. *Harr* —4K **23**
Station Rd. *Houn* —4F **87**
Station Rd. *Ilf* —3F **51**
Station Rd. *King T* —1G **119**
Station Rd. *New Bar* —5E **4**
Station Rd. *N Mald* —5D **120**
Station Rd. *N Har* —5F **23**
Station Rd. *Short* —2G **127**
Station Rd. *Sidc* —2A **116**
Station Rd. *Tedd* —5K **103**
Station Rd. *Th Dit* —7A **118**
Station Rd. *Twic* —1K **103**
Station Rd. *W Wick* —1E **136**
Station Rd. N. *Belv* —3H **85**
Station Sq. *Pet W* —5G **129**
Station St. *E15* —7F **49**
Station St. *E16* —1F **83**
Station Ter. *NW10* —2E **58**
Station Ter. *SE5* —1C **94**
Station Ter. M. *SE3* —5J **81**
Station View. *Gnfd* —1H **55**
Station Way. *SE15* —2G **95**
Station Way. *Buck H* —4F **21**
Station Way. *Sutt* —6G **131**
Station Yd. *Twic* —7A **88**
Staunton Rd. *King T* —6E **104**
Staunton St. *SE8* —6B **80**
Staveley Clo. *E9* —5J **47**
Staveley Clo. *N7* —4J **45**
Staveley Clo. *SE15* —1J **95**
Staveley Gdns. *W4* —1K **89**
Staveley Rd. *W4* —6J **73**
Staverton Rd. *NW2* —7E **42**
Staw Yd. Rd. *SE16* —1A **80**
Stavordale Rd. *N5* —4B **46**
Stavordale Rd. *Cars* —7A **122**
Stayner's Rd. *E1* —4K **63**
Stayton Rd. *Sutt* —3J **131**
Steadfast Rd. *King T* —1D **118**
Steadman Ho. *Dag* —3G **53**
    (off Uvedale Rd.)
Stead St. *SE17* —4D **78** (4E **156**)
Stean St. *E8* —1F **63**
Stebbing Ho. *W11* —1F **75**
    (off Queensdale Cres.)
Stebbing Way. *Bark* —2A **68**
Stebondale St. *E14* —4E **80**
Stedham Pl. *WC1*
    —6J **61** (7E **142**)
Stedman Clo. *Bex* —3K **117**
Steedman St. *SE17*
    —4C **78** (4C **156**)
Steeds Rd. *N10* —1D **28**
Steele Ho. *E15* —2G **65**
    (off Eve Rd.)
Steele Rd. *E11* —4G **49**
Steele Rd. *N17* —3E **30**
Steele Rd. *NW10* —2J **57**
Steele Rd. *W4* —3J **73**
Steele Rd. *Iswth* —4A **88**

Steele's M. N. *NW3* —6D **44**
Steele's M. S. *NW3* —6D **44**
Steele's Rd. *NW3* —6D **44**
Steele Wlk. *Eri* —7H **85**
Steel's La. *E1* —6J **63**
Steelyard Pas. *EC4*
    —7D **62** (3E **150**)
Steen Way. *SE22* —5E **94**
Steep Hill. *SW16* —3H **109**
Steep Hill. *Croy* —4E **134**
Steeple Clo. *SW6* —2G **91**
Steeple Clo. *SW19* —5G **107**
Steeple Ct. *E1* —4H **63**
Steeplestone Clo. *N18* —5H **17**
Steeple Wlk. *N1* —1C **62**
    (off Basire St.)
Steerforth St. *SW18* —2A **108**
Steers Mead. *Mitc* —1D **122**
Steers Way. *SE16* —2A **80**
Stella Rd. *SW17* —6D **108**
Stelling Rd. *Eri* —7K **85**
Stellman Clo. *E5* —3G **47**
Stembridge Rd. *SE20* —2H **125**
Stephan Clo. *E8* —1G **63**
Stephendale Rd. *SW6* —3K **91**
Stephen Fox Ho. *W4* —5A **74**
    (off Chiswick La.)
Stephen M. *W1* —5H **61** (6C **142**)
Stephen Pl. *SW4* —3G **93**
Stephen Rd. *Bexh* —3J **101**
Stephens Ct. *E16* —4H **65**
Stephens Ct. *SE4* —3A **96**
Stephenson Ct. *Cheam* —7G **131**
    (off Station App.)
Stephenson Ho. *SE1*
    —3C **78** (1C **156**)
Stephenson Rd. *E17* —5A **32**
Stephenson Rd. *W7* —6K **55**
Stephenson Rd. *Twic* —7E **86**
Stephenson St. *E16* —4G **65**
Stephenson St. *NW10* —3A **58**
Stephenson Way. *NW1*
    —4G **61** (3B **142**)
Stephen's Rd. *E3* —2B **64**
Stephen's Rd. *E15* —1G **65**
Stephen St. *W1* —5H **61** (6C **142**)
Stepney Causeway. *E1* —6K **63**
Stepney Grn. *E1* —5J **63**
Stepney High St. *E1* —5K **63**
Stepney Way. *E1* —5H **63**
Sterling Av. *Edgw* —4A **12**
Sterling Gdns. *SE14* —6A **80**
Sterling Pl. *W5* —4E **72**
Sterling Rd. *Enf* —1J **7**
Sterling St. *SW7*
    —3C **76** (1D **152**)
Sterling Way. *N18* —5J **17**
Sterndale Rd. *W14* —3F **75**
Sterne St. *W12* —2F **75**
Sternhall La. *SE15* —3G **95**
Sternhold Av. *SW2* —2H **109**
Sterry Cres. *Dag* —5G **53**
Sterry Dri. *Eps* —4A **130**
Sterry Gdns. *Dag* —6G **53**
Sterry Rd. *Bark* —1K **67**
Sterry Rd. *Dag* —4G **53**
Sterry St. *SE1* —2D **78** (7E **150**)
Steucers La. *SE23* —1A **112**
Stevannie Ct. *Belv* —5G **85**
Steve Biko Ho. *Wemb* —7F **25**
Steve Biko La. *SE6* —4C **112**
Steve Biko Rd. *N7* —3A **46**
Steve Biko Way. *Houn* —3E **86**
Stevedale Rd. *Well* —2C **100**
Stevedore St. *E1* —1H **79**

Stevenage Rd. *E6* —6E **50**
Stevenage Rd. *SW6* —7F **75**
Stevens Av. *E9* —6J **47**
Stevens Clo. *Beck* —6C **112**
Stevens Clo. *Bex* —4K **117**
Stevens Clo. *Hamp* —5C **102**
Stevens Clo. *Pinn* —5A **22**
Stevens Grn. *Bush* —1B **10**
Stevenson Clo. *Barn* —7G **5**
Stevenson Cres. *SE16* —5H **79**
Stevens Rd. *Dag* —3B **52**
Stevens St. *SE1* —3E **78** (1H **157**)
Steventon Rd. *W12* —7B **58**
Stewards Holte Wlk. *N11* —4A **16**
Steward St. *E1* —5E **62** (5H **145**)
Stewart Clo. *NW9* —6J **25**
Stewart Clo. *Chst* —5F **115**
Stewart Clo. *Hamp* —6C **102**
Stewart Rainbird Ho. *E12* —5E **50**
    (off Parkhurst Rd.)
Stewart Rd. *E15* —4F **49**
Stewartsby Clo. *N18* —5H **17**
Stewart's Gro. *SW3*
    —5B **76** (5B **152**)
Stewart's Rd. *SW8* —7G **77**
Stewart St. *E14* —2E **80**
Stew La. *EC4* —7C **62** (2C **150**)
Steyne Ho. *W3* —1J **73**
    (off Horn La.)
Steyne Rd. *W3* —1H **73**
Steyning Gro. *SE9* —4D **114**
Steynings Way. *N12* —5D **14**
Steyning Way. *Houn* —4A **86**
Steynton Av. *Bex* —2D **116**
Stickland Rd. *Belv* —4G **85**
Stickleton Clo. *Gnfd* —3F **55**
Stilecroft Gdns. *Wemb* —3B **40**
Stile Hall Gdns. *W4* —5G **73**
Stile Hall Pde. *W4* —5G **73**
Stiles Clo. *Brom* —6D **128**
Stiles Clo. *Eri* —5H **85**
Stillingfleet Rd. *SW13* —6C **74**
Stillington St. *SW1*
    —4G **77** (3B **154**)
Stillness Rd. *SE23* —6A **96**
Stilton Cres. *NW10* —7K **41**
Stipularis Dri. *Hayes* —4B **54**
Stirling Clo. *SW16* —1G **123**
Stirling Ct. *W13* —7B **56**
Stirling Gro. *Houn* —2G **87**
Stirling Rd. *E13* —2K **65**
Stirling Rd. *E17* —3A **32**
Stirling Rd. *N17* —1G **31**
Stirling Rd. *N22* —1B **30**
Stirling Rd. *SW9* —2J **93**
Stirling Rd. *W3* —3H **73**
Stirling Rd. *Harr* —3K **23**
Stirling Rd. *Twic* —1E **102**
Stirling Rd. Path. *E17* —3A **32**
Stirling Wlk. *Surb* —6H **119**
Stirling Way. *Croy* —7J **123**
Stiven Cres. *Harr* —3D **38**
Stockbury Rd. *Croy* —6J **125**
Stockdale Rd. *Dag* —2F **53**
Stockdove Way. *Gnfd* —3K **55**
Stockfield Rd. *SW16* —3K **109**
Stockholm Rd. *SE16* —5J **79**
Stockholm Way. *E1* —1G **79**
Stockhurst Clo. *SW15* —2F **91**
Stockingswater La. *Enf* —3G **9**
Stockland Rd. *Romf* —6K **37**
Stock Orchard Cres. *N7* —5K **45**
Stock Orchard St. *N7* —5K **45**
Stockport Rd. *SW16* —1H **123**
Stocksfield Rd. *E17* —3E **32**

Stocks Pl. E14 —7B **64**
Stock St. E13 —2J **65**
Stockton Gdns. N17 —7H **17**
Stockton Gdns. NW7 —3F **13**
Stockton Ho. S Harr —1E **38**
Stockton Rd. N17 —7H **17**
Stockton Rd. N18 —6B **18**
Stockton Sq. Brom —3J **127**
Stockwell Av. SW9 —3K **93**
Stockwell Clo. Brom —2K **127**
Stockwell Gdns. SW9 —1K **93**
Stockwell Gdns. Est. SW9
—2J **93**
Stockwell Grn. SW9 —2K **93**
Stockwell Grn. Ct. SW9 —2K **93**
Stockwell La. SW9 —2K **93**
Stockwell M. SW9 —2K **93**
Stockwell Pk. Cres. SW9 —2K **93**
Stockwell Pk. Est. SW9 —2K **93**
Stockwell Pk. Rd. SW9 —1K **93**
Stockwell Pk. Wlk. SW9 —3K **93**
Stockwell Rd. SW9 —2K **93**
Stockwell St. SE10 —6E **80**
Stockwell Ter. SW9 —1K **93**
Stoddart Rd. SE20 —1J **125**
Stoddart Ho. SW8
—6K **77** (7H **155**)
Stofield Gdns. SE9 —3B **114**
Stoford Clo. SW19 —7G **91**
Stokenchurch St. SW6 —1K **91**
Stoke Newington Chu. St. N16
—3D **46**
Stoke Newington Comn. N16
—2F **47**
Stoke Newington High St. N16
—3F **47**
Stoke Newington Rd. N16
—5F **47**
Stoke Pl. NW10 —3B **58**
Stoke Rd. King T —7J **105**
Stokes Cotts. Ilf —1G **35**
Stokes Ct. N2 —4C **28**
Stokesley St. W12 —6B **58**
Stokes Rd. E6 —4C **66**
Stokes Rd. Croy —6K **125**
Stokley Ct. N8 —4J **29**
Stoll Clo. NW2 —3E **42**
Stoms Path. SE6 —5C **112**
Stonard Rd. N13 —3F **17**
Stonard Rd. Dag —5B **52**
Stondon Ho. E15 —1H **65**
(off John St.)
Stondon Pk. SE23 —6A **96**
Stondon Wlk. E6 —2B **66**
Stonebridge Comn. E8 —7F **47**
Stonebridge Pk. NW10 —7K **41**
Stonebridge Rd. N15 —5F **31**
Stonebridge Shop. Cen. NW10
—1K **57**
Stonebridge Way. Wemb —6H **41**
Stone Bldgs. WC2
—5K **61** (6H **143**)
Stonechat Sq. E6 —5C **66**
Stone Clo. SW4 —2G **93**
Stone Clo. Dag —2F **53**
Stonecot Clo. Sutt —1G **131**
Stonecot Hill. Sutt —1G **131**
Stonecroft Rd. Eri —7J **85**
Stonecroft Way. Croy —7J **123**
Stonecutter St. EC4
—6B **62** (7A **144**)
Stonefield. N4 —2K **45**
Stonefield Clo. Bexh —3G **101**
Stonefield Clo. Ruis —5C **38**
Stonefield St. N1 —1A **62**

Stonefield Way. SE7 —7B **82**
Stonefield Way. Ruis —5C **38**
Stonegrove. Edgw —4K **11**
Stone Gro. Ct. Edgw —5A **12**
Stonegrove Gdns. Edgw —5A **12**
Stonehall Av. Ilf —6C **34**
Stone Hall Gdns. W8 —3K **75**
Stone Hall Pl. W8 —3K **75**
Stone Hall Rd. N21 —7E **6**
Stoneham Rd. N11 —5B **16**
Stonehill Clo. SW14 —5K **89**
Stonehill Ct. E4 —7J **9**
Stonehill Rd. SW14 —5K **89**
Stone Hill Rd. W4 —5G **73**
Stonehills Ct. SE21 —3E **110**
Stonehill Woods Pk. Sidc
—6H **117**
Stonehorse Rd. Enf —5D **8**
Stone Ho. Ct. EC3
—6E **62** (7H **145**)
Stoneleigh Av. Enf —1C **8**
Stoneleigh Av. Wor Pk —4C **130**
Stoneleigh B'way. Eps —5C **130**
Stoneleigh Cres. Eps —5B **130**
Stoneleigh Pk. Av. Croy —6K **125**
Stoneleigh Pk. Rd. Eps —6B **130**
Stoneleigh Pl. W11 —7F **59**
Stoneleigh Rd. N17 —3F **31**
Stoneleigh Rd. Cars —7C **122**
Stoneleigh Rd. Ilf —3C **34**
Stoneleigh St. W11 —7F **59**
Stoneleigh Ter. N19 —2F **45**
Stonell's Rd. SW11 —6D **92**
Stonenest St. N4 —1K **45**
Stone Pk. Av. Beck —4C **126**
Stone Pl. Wor Pk —2C **130**
Stone Rd. Brom —5H **127**
Stones End St. SE1
—2C **78** (7C **150**)
Stone St. Croy —5A **134**
Stonewall E6 —5E **66**
Stonewold Ct. W5 —6D **56**
Stonewood Rd. Eri —5K **85**
Stoney All. SE18 —2E **98**
Stoneyard La. E14 —7D **64**
Stoneycroft Clo. SE12 —7H **97**
Stoneycroft Rd. Wfd G —6H **21**
Stoneydeep. Tedd —4A **104**
Stoneydown. E17 —4A **32**
Stoneydown Av. E17 —4A **32**
Stoneydown Ho. E17 —4A **32**
(off Blackhorse Rd.)
Stoneyfields Gdns. Edgw —4D **12**
Stoneyfields La. Edgw —5D **12**
Stoney La. E1 —6E **62** (7H **145**)
Stoney La. SE19 —6F **111**
Stoney St. SE1 —1D **78** (4E **150**)
Stonhouse St. SW4 —4H **93**
Stonor Rd. W14 —4H **75**
Stonycroft Clo. Enf —2F **9**
Stopes St. SE15 —7F **79**
Stopford Rd. E13 —1J **65**
Stopford Rd. SE17
—5B **78** (6B **156**)
Store Rd. E16 —2E **82**
Storers Quay. E14 —4F **81**
Store St. E15 —5F **49**
Store St. WC1 —5H **61** (6C **142**)
Storey Rd. E17 —4B **32**
Storey Rd. N6 —6D **28**
Storey's Ga. SW1
—2H **77** (7D **148**)
Storey St. E16 —1E **82**
Stories M. SE5 —2E **94**
Stories Rd. SE5 —3E **94**

Stork Rd. E7 —6J **49**
Storksmead Rd. Edgw —7F **13**
Stork's Rd. SE16 —3G **79**
Stormont Rd. N6 —7D **28**
Stormont Rd. SW11 —3E **92**
Storrington Rd. Croy —1F **135**
Story St. N1 —7K **45**
Stothard Pl. EC2
—5E **62** (5H **145**)
Stothard St. E1 —4J **63**
Stott Clo. SW18 —6B **92**
Stoughton Av. Sutt —5F **131**
Stoughton Clo. SE11
—4K **77** (4H **155**)
Stoughton Clo. SW15 —1C **106**
Stour Av. S'hall —3E **70**
Stour Clo. Kes —4A **138**
Stourhead Clo. SW19 —7F **91**
Stourhead Gdns. SW20 —3C **120**
Stour Rd. E3 —7C **48**
Stour Rd. Dag —2G **53**
Stourton Av. Felt —4D **102**
Stowage. SE8 —6C **80**
Stow Cres. E17 —7F **19**
Stowe Gdns. N9 —1A **18**
Stowe Ho. NW11 —6A **28**
Stowe Pl. N15 —3E **30**
Stowe Rd. W12 —2D **74**
Stoxmead. Harr —1H **23**
Stracey Rd. E7 —4J **49**
Stracey Rd. NW10 —1K **57**
Strachan Pl. SW19 —6E **106**
Stradbroke Dri. Chig —6K **21**
Stradbroke Gro. Buck H —1G **21**
Stradbroke Gro. Ilf —3C **34**
Stradbroke Pk. Chig —6K **21**
Stradbroke Rd. N5 —4C **46**
Stradbrook Clo. Harr —3D **38**
Stradella Rd. SE24 —6C **94**
Strafford Av. Ilf —2E **34**
Strafford Rd. W3 —2J **73**
Strafford Rd. Barn —3B **4**
Strafford Rd. Houn —3D **86**
Strafford Rd. Twic —7A **88**
Strafford St. E14 —2C **80**
Strahan Rd. E3 —3A **64**
Straightsmouth. SE10 —7E **80**
Straight, The. S'hall —2C **70**
Strait Rd. E6 —7C **66**
Strakers Rd. SE15 —4H **95**
Strale Ho. N1 —1E **62**
(off Whitmore Est.)
Strand. WC2 —7J **61** (3F **149**)
Strand Ct. SE18 —5J **83**
Strandfield Clo. SE18 —5J **83**
Strand La. WC2 —7K **61** (2H **149**)
Strand on the Grn. W4 —6G **73**
Strand Pl. N18 —4K **17**
Strand School App. W4 —6G **73**
Strang Ho. N1 —1C **62**
Strangways Ter. W14 —3H **75**
Stranraer Way. N1 —7K **45**
Strasburg Rd. SW11 —1E **92**
Stratfield Pk. Clo. N21 —7G **7**
Stratford Av. W8 —3J **75**
Stratford Cen. E15 —7F **49**
Stratford Clo. Bark —7A **52**
Stratford Clo. Dag —7J **53**
Stratford Ct. N Mald —4K **119**
Stratford Gro. SW15 —4F **91**
Stratford Ho. Av. Brom —3C **128**

Stratford Mkt. E15 —1F **65**
Stratford Office Village, The. E15
(off Romford Rd.) —7G **49**
Stratford Pl. W1 —6E **60** (1J **147**)
Stratford Rd. E13 —1H **65**
Stratford Rd. NW4 —4F **27**
Stratford Rd. W3 —2J **73**
Stratford Rd. W8 —3J **75**
Stratford Rd. Hayes —4A **54**
Stratford Rd. S'hall —4C **70**
Stratford Rd. T Hth —4A **124**
Stratford Vs. NW1 —7H **45**
Strathan Clo. SW18 —6H **91**
Strathaven Rd. SE12 —6K **97**
Strathblaine Rd. SW11 —4B **92**
Strathbrook Rd. SW16 —7K **109**
Strathcona Rd. Wemb —2D **40**
Strathdale. SW16 —5K **109**
Strathdon Dri. SW17 —3B **108**
Strathearn Av. Twic —1F **103**
Strathearn Pl. W2
—6C **60** (1C **146**)
Strathearn Rd. SW19 —5J **107**
Strathearn Rd. Sutt —5J **131**
Stratheden Pde. SE3 —7J **81**
Stratheden Rd. SE3 —7J **81**
Strathfield Gdns. Bark —6H **51**
Strathleven Rd. SW2 —5J **93**
Strathmore Gdns. N3 —1K **27**
Strathmore Gdns. W8 —1J **75**
Strathmore Gdns. Edgw —2H **25**
Strathmore Rd. SW19 —3J **107**
Strathmore Rd. Croy —7D **124**
Strathmore Rd. Tedd —4J **103**
Strathnairn St. SE1 —4G **79**
Strathray Gdns. NW3 —6C **44**
Strath Ter. SW11 —4C **92**
Strathville Rd. SW18 —2J **107**
Strathyre Av. SW16 —3A **124**
Stratton Clo. SW19 —2J **121**
Stratton Clo. Bexh —3E **100**
Stratton Clo. Edgw —6A **12**
Stratton Clo. Houn —1E **86**
Stratton Ct. Pinn —1D **22**
(off Devonshire Rd.)
Strattondale St. E14 —3E **80**
Stratton Dri. Bark —5J **51**
Stratton Gdns. S'hall —6D **54**
Stratton Rd. SW19 —2J **121**
Stratton Rd. Bexh —3E **100**
Stratton St. W1 —1F **77** (4K **147**)
Strauss Rd. W4 —2K **73**
Strawberry Hill. Twic —3K **103**
Strawberry Hill Clo. Twic —3K **103**
Strawberry Hill Rd. Twic —3K **103**
Strawberry La. Cars —3E **132**
Strawberry Ter. N10 —1D **28**
Strawberry Vale. N2 —1B **28**
Strawberry Vale. Twic —3A **104**
Streakes Field Rd. NW2 —2C **42**
Streamdale. SE2 —6B **84**
Stream La. Edgw —5C **12**
Streamside Clo. N9 —1A **18**
Streamside Clo. Brom —4J **127**
Stream Way. Belv —6F **85**
Streatfield Av. E6 —1D **66**
Streatfield Rd. Harr —3C **24**
Streatham Comn. N. SW16
—5J **109**
Streatham Comn. S. SW16
—6J **109**
Streatham Ct. SW16 —3J **109**
Streatham High Rd. SW16
—4J **109**

Streatham Hill. SW2 —2J **109**
Streatham Pl. SW2 —7J **93**
Streatham Rd. Mitc & SW16
—1E **122**
Streatham St. WC1
—6J **61** (7E **142**)
Streatham Vale. SW16 —1G **123**
Streathbourne Rd. SW17
—2E **108**
Streatley Pl. NW3 —4A **44**
Streatley Rd. NW6 —7H **43**
Streeters La. Wall —3H **133**
Streetfield M. SE3 —3J **97**
Streimer Rd. E15 —2E **64**
Strelley Way. W3 —7A **58**
Stretton Rd. Croy —7E **124**
Stretton Rd. Rich —2C **104**
Strickland Ct. SE15 —3G **95**
Strickland Row. SW18 —7B **92**
Strickland St. SE8 —1C **96**
Stride Rd. E13 —2H **65**
Stringer Ho. N1 —1E **62**
(off Whitmore Est.)
Strode Clo. N10 —7K **15**
Strode Rd. E7 —4J **49**
Strode Rd. N17 —2E **30**
Strode Rd. NW10 —6C **42**
Strode Rd. SW6 —7G **75**
Strone Rd. E7 & E12 —6A **50**
Strone Way. Hayes —4C **54**
Strongbow Cres. SE9 —5D **98**
Strongbow Rd. SE9 —5D **98**
Strongbridge Clo. Harr —1E **38**
Stronsa Rd. W12 —2B **74**
Strood Av. Romf —1K **53**
Stroud Cres. SW15 —3C **106**
Stroudes Clo. Wor Pk —7A **120**
Stroud Field. N'holt —6C **38**
Stroud Ga. Harr —4F **39**
Stroud Grn. Gdns. Croy —7J **125**
Stroud Grn. Rd. N4 —1K **45**
Stroud Grn. Way. Croy —7H **125**
Stroudley Wlk. E3 —3D **64**
Stroud Rd. SE25 —6G **125**
Stroud Rd. SW19 —3J **107**
Strouts Pl. E2 —3F **63** (1J **145**)
Strudwick Ct. SW4 —1J **93**
(off Binfield Rd.)
Strutton Ground. SW1
—3H **77** (1C **154**)
Strype St. E1 —5F **63** (6J **145**)
Stuart Av. NW9 —7C **26**
Stuart Av. W5 —1F **73**
Stuart Av. Brom —1J **137**
Stuart Av. Harr —3D **38**
Stuart Cres. N22 —1K **29**
Stuart Cres. Croy —3B **136**
Stuart Evans Clo. Well —3C **100**
Stuart Gro. Tedd —5J **103**
Stuart Mantle Way. Eri —7K **85**
Stuart Pl. Mitc —1D **122**
Stuart Rd. NW6 —3J **59**
(in two parts)
Stuart Rd. SE15 —4J **95**
Stuart Rd. SW19 —3J **107**
Stuart Rd. W3 —1J **73**
Stuart Rd. Bark —7K **51**
Stuart Rd. E Barn —7H **5**
Stuart Rd. Harr —3K **23**
Stuart Rd. Rich —2B **104**
Stuart Rd. T Hth —4C **124**
Stuart Rd. Well —1B **100**
Stubbs Clo. NW9 —5A **26**
Stubbs Dri. SE16 —5H **79**

Stubbs M. Dag —4B 52
(off Marlborough Rd.)
Stubbs Point. E13 —4K 65
Stubbs Way. SW19 —1B 122
Stucley Pl. NW1 —7F 45
Stucley Rd. Houn —7G 71
Studdridge St. SW6 —2J 91
Studd St. N1 —1B 62
Studholme Ct. NW3 —4J 43
Studholme St. SE15 —7H 79
Studio Pl. SW1 —2D 76 (7F 147)
Studland Clo. Sidc —3K 115
Studland Rd. SE26 —5K 111
Studland Rd. W7 —6H 55
Studland Rd. King T —6E 104
Studland St. W6 —4D 74
Studley Av. E4 —7A 20
Studley Clo. E5 —5A 48
Studley Ct. Sidc —5B 116
Studley Dri. Ilf —6B 34
Studley Est. SW4 —1J 93
Studley Grange Rd. W7 —2J 71
Studley Rd. E7 —6K 49
Studley Rd. SW4 —1J 93
Studley Rd. Dag —7D 52
Stukeley Rd. E7 —7K 49
Stukeley St. WC2
  —6J 61 (7F 143)
Stumps Hill La. Beck —6C 112
Sturdy Rd. SE15 —2H 95
Sturge Av. E17 —2D 32
Sturgeon Rd. SE17
  —5C 78 (6C 156)
Sturges Field. Chst —6H 115
Sturgess Av. NW4 —7D 26
Sturge St. SE1 —2C 78 (6C 150)
Sturmer Way. N7 —5K 45
Sturminster Clo. Hayes —6A 54
Sturminster Ho. SW8 —7K 77
(off Dorset Rd.)
Sturrock Clo. N15 —4D 30
Sturry St. E14 —6D 64
Sturt St. N1 —2C 62 (1D 144)
Stutfield St. E1 —6G 63
Styles Gdns. SW9 —3B 94
Styles Ho. SE1 —1B 78 (6A 150)
Styles Way. Beck —4E 126
Sudbourne Rd. SW2 —5J 93
Sudbrooke Rd. SW12 —6D 92
Sudbrook Gdns. Rich —3E 104
Sudbrook La. Rich —1E 104
Sudbury. E6 —6E 66
Sudbury Av. Wemb —3D 40
Sudbury Ct. E5 —4A 48
Sudbury Ct. SW8 —1J 93
Sudbury Ct. Dri. Harr —3K 39
Sudbury Ct. Rd. Harr —3K 39
Sudbury Cres. Brom —6J 113
Sudbury Cres. Wemb —5B 40
Sudbury Croft. Wemb —4K 39
Sudbury Gdns. Croy —4E 134
Sudbury Heights Av. Gnfd
  —5K 39
Sudbury Hill. Harr —2J 39
Sudbury Hill Clo. Wemb —3K 39
Sudbury Rd. Bark —5K 51
Sudbury Towers. Gnfd —5J 39
Sudeley St. N1 —2B 62
Sudlow Rd. SW18 —5J 91
Sudrey St. SE1 —2C 78 (7C 150)
Suez Av. Gnfd —2K 55
Suez Rd. Enf —4F 9
Suffield Rd. E4 —4J 19
Suffield Rd. N15 —5F 31
Suffield Rd. SE20 —2J 125

Suffolk Ct. E10 —7C 32
Suffolk Ct. Ilf —6J 35
Suffolk Ho. SE20 —7K 111
(off Croydon Rd.)
Suffolk La. EC4 —7D 62 (2E 150)
Suffolk Pk. Rd. E17 —4A 32
Suffolk Pl. SW1 —1H 77 (4D 148)
Suffolk Rd. E13 —3J 65
Suffolk Rd. N15 —5D 30
Suffolk Rd. NW10 —7A 42
Suffolk Rd. SE25 —4F 125
Suffolk Rd. SW13 —7B 74
Suffolk Rd. Bark —7H 51
Suffolk Rd. Dag —5J 53
Suffolk Rd. Enf —5C 8
Suffolk Rd. Harr —6D 22
Suffolk Rd. Ilf —6J 35
Suffolk Rd. Sidc —6C 116
Suffolk Rd. Wor Pk —2B 130
Suffolk St. E7 —4J 49
Suffolk St. SW1
  —7H 61 (3D 148)
Sugar Baker's Ct. EC3
  —6E 62 (1H 151)
Sugar Ho. La. E15 —2E 64
Sugar Loaf Wlk. E2 —3J 63
Sugar Quay. EC3
  —7E 62 (3H 151)
Sugar Quay Wlk. EC3
  —1C 78 (4C 150)
Sugden Rd. SW11 —3E 92
Sugden Rd. Th Dit —7B 118
Sugden Way. Bark —2K 67
Sulby Ho. SE4 —4A 96
(off Turnham Rd.)
Sulgrave Gdns. W6 —2E 74
Sulgrave Rd. W6 —3E 74
Sulina Rd. SW2 —7J 93
Sulivan Ct. SW6 —2J 91
Sulivan Enterprise Cen. SW6
  —3J 91
Sulivan Rd. SW6 —3J 91
Sullivan Av. E16 —5B 66
Sullivan Clo. SW11 —3C 92
Sullivan Ct. N16 —7F 31
Sullivan Rd. SE11
  —4B 78 (3K 155)
Sultan Rd. E11 —4K 33
Sultan St. SE5 —7C 78
Sultan St. Beck —2K 125
Sumatra Rd. NW6 —5J 43
Sumburgh Rd. SW12 —6E 92
Summercourt Rd. E1 —6J 63
Summerene Clo. SW16 —7G 109
Summerfield Av. NW6 —2G 59
Summerfield St. W5 —4B 56
Summerfields Av. N12 —6H 15
Summerfield St. SE12 —7H 97
Summer Hill. Chst —2E 128
Summerhill Gro. Enf —6K 7
Summerhill Rd. N15 —4D 30
Summerhill Vs. Chst —1E 128
Summerhill Way. Mitc —1E 122
Summerhouse Av. Houn —1C 86
Summerhouse Dri. Bex & Dart
  —4K 117
Summerhouse Rd. N16 —2E 46
Summerland Gdns. N10 —3F 29
Summerland Grange. N10
  —3F 29
Summerlands Av. W3 —7J 57
Summerlands Lodge. Orp
  —4E 138
Summerlee Av. N2 —4D 28
Summerlee Gdns. N2 —4D 28

Summerley St. SW18 —2K 107
Summer Rd. E Mol & Th Dit
  —6A 118
Summersby Rd. N6 —6F 29
Summers Clo. Sutt —7J 131
Summers Clo. Wemb —1H 41
Summers La. N12 —7G 15
Summers Row. N12 —6H 15
Summers St. EC1
  —4A 62 (4J 143)
Summerstown. SW17 —3A 108
Summerton Way. SE28 —6D 68
Summer Trees. Sun —7A 102
Summerville Gdns. Sutt —6H 131
Summerwood Rd. Iswth —5K 87
Summit Av. NW9 —5K 25
Summit Clo. N14 —2B 16
Summit Clo. NW9 —5K 25
Summit Clo. Edgw —7B 12
Summit Ct. NW2 —6G 43
Summit Dri. Wfd G —2B 34
Summit Est. N16 —7G 31
Summit Rd. E17 —4D 32
Summit Rd. N'holt —7E 38
Summit Way. N14 —2A 16
Summit Way. SE19 —7E 110
Sumner Av. SE15 —1F 95
Sumner Bldgs. SE1
  —1C 78 (4C 150)
Sumner Ct. SW8 —1J 93
Sumner Est. SE15 —7F 79
Sumner Gdns. Croy —1B 134
Sumner Pl. SW7
  —4B 76 (4B 152)
Sumner Pl. M. SW7
  —4B 76 (4B 152)
Sumner Rd. SE15
  —6F 79 (7K 157)
Sumner Rd. Croy —1A 134
Sumner Rd. Harr —6G 23
Sumner Rd. S. Croy —1A 134
Sumner St. SE1 —1B 78 (4B 150)
Sumpter Clo. NW3 —6A 44
Sun All. Rich —4E 88
Sunbeam Cres. W10 —4E 58
Sunbeam Rd. NW10 —4J 57
Sunbury Av. NW7 —5E 12
Sunbury Av. SW14 —4K 89
Sunbury Ct. Barn —4B 4
Sunbury Gdns. NW7 —5E 12
Sunbury La. SW11 —1B 92
Sunbury Rd. Sutt —3G 131
Sunbury St. SE18 —3D 82
Sunbury Way. Felt —5A 102
Sun Ct. EC3 —6D 62 (1F 151)
Suncroft Pl. SE26 —3J 111
Sunderland Mt. SE23 —2K 111
Sunderland Rd. SE23 —1K 111
Sunderland Rd. W5 —3D 72
Sunderland Ter. W2 —6K 59
Sunderland Way. E12 —2B 50
Sundew Av. W12 —7C 58
Sundew Ct. Wemb —2E 56
(off Elmore Clo.)
Sundial Av. SE25 —3F 125
Sundorne Rd. SE7 —5A 82
Sundra Wlk. E1 —4K 63
Sundridge Av. Brom & Chst
  —1B 128
Sundridge Av. Well —2H 99
Sundridge Pde. Brom —7K 113
Sundridge Pl. Croy —1G 135
Sundridge Rd. Croy —7F 125
Sunfields Pl. SE3 —7K 81
Sungate Cotts. Romf —1F 37

Sun-in-the-Sands. (Junct.)
  —7K 81
Sunkist Way. Wall —7J 133
Sunland Av. Bexh —4E 100
Sun La. SE3 —7K 81
Sunleigh Rd. Wemb —1E 56
Sunley Gdns. Gnfd —1A 56
Sunlight Clo. SW19 —6A 108
Sunningdale. N14 —5C 16
Sunningdale Av. W3 —7A 58
Sunningdale Av. Bark —1H 67
Sunningdale Av. Felt —2C 102
Sunningdale Av. Ruis —1A 38
Sunningdale Clo. E6 —3D 66
Sunningdale Clo. SE16 —5H 79
(off Ryder Dri.)
Sunningdale Clo. Stan —6F 11
Sunningdale Ct. Houn —6H 87
(off Whitton Dene)
Sunningdale Ct. S'hall —6G 55
(off Fleming Rd.)
Sunningdale Gdns. NW9 —5J 25
Sunningdale Gdns. W8 —3J 75
(off Stratford Rd.)
Sunningdale Rd. Brom —4C 128
Sunningdale Rd. Sutt —4H 131
Sunningfields Cres. NW4 —2D 26
Sunningfields Rd. NW4 —2D 26
Sunninghill Ct. W3 —2J 73
Sunninghill Rd. SE13 —2D 96
Sunny Bank. SE25 —3G 125
Sunny Cres. NW10 —7J 41
Sunnycroft Rd. SE25 —4G 125
Sunnycroft Rd. Houn —2F 87
Sunnycroft Rd. S'hall —5E 38
Sunnydale. Orp —2E 138
Sunnydale Gdns. NW7 —6E 12
Sunnydale Rd. SE12 —5K 97
Sunnydene Av. E4 —5A 20
Sunnydene Gdns. Wemb —6C 40
Sunnydene St. SE26 —4A 112
Sunnyfield. NW7 —4G 13
Sunnyfield Rd. Chst —3K 129
Sunny Gdns. Pde. NW4 —2D 26
Sunny Gdns. Rd. NW4 —2D 26
Sunny Hill. NW4 —3D 26
Sunnyhill Clo. E5 —4A 48
Sunnyhill Rd. SW16 —4J 109
Sunnyhurst Clo. Sutt —3J 131
Sunnymead Av. Mitc —3H 123
Sunnymead Rd. NW9 —7K 25
Sunnymead Rd. SW15 —5D 90
Sunnymede Av. Eps —7A 130
Sunnymede Dri. Ilf —5E 35
Sunny Nook Gdns. S Croy
  —6D 134
Sunny Rd., The. Enf —1E 8
Sunnyside. NW2 —3H 43
Sunnyside. SW19 —6G 107
Sunnyside Dri. E4 —7K 9
Sunnyside Houses. NW2 —3H 43
(off Sunnyside)
Sunnyside Pas. SW19 —6G 107
Sunnyside Rd. E10 —1C 48
Sunnyside Rd. N19 —7H 29
Sunnyside Rd. W5 —1D 72
Sunnyside Rd. Ilf —3G 51
Sunnyside Rd. Tedd —4H 103
Sunnyside Rd. E. N9 —3B 18
Sunnyside Rd. N. N9 —3A 18
Sunnyside Rd. S. N9 —3A 18
Sunnyside Ter. NW9 —3K 25
Sunny View. NW9 —5K 25

Sunny Way. N12 —7H 15
Sun Pas. SE16 —3G 79
(off Old Jamaica Rd.)
Sunray Av. E4 —4D 94
Sunray Av. Brom —6C 128
Sunrise Clo. Felt —3D 102
Sunrise View. NW7 —6G 13
Sun Rd. W14 —5H 75
Sunset Av. E4 —1J 19
Sunset Av. Wfd G —4C 20
Sunset Ct. Wfd G —7F 21
Sunset Gdns. SE25 —2F 125
Sunset Rd. SE5 —4C 94
Sunset Rd. SE28 —1A 84
Sunset View. Barn —2B 4
Sunshine Way. Mitc —2D 122
Sun St. EC2 —5D 62 (5F 145)
Sun St. Pas. EC2
  —5E 62 (6G 145)
Sun Wlk. E1 —7F 63 (3K 151)
Sunwell Clo. SE15 —1H 95
Surbiton Ct. Surb —6C 118
Surbiton Cres. King T —4E 118
Surbiton Hall Clo. King T
  —4E 118
Surbiton Hill Pk. Surb —5F 119
Surbiton Hill Rd. Surb —5E 118
Surbiton Pde. Surb —6E 118
Surbiton Rd. King T —4D 118
Surlingham Clo. SE28 —7D 68
Surma Clo. E1 —4H 63
Surrendale Pl. W9 —4J 59
Surrey Canal Rd. SE15 & SE14
  —6J 79
Surrey Ct. N3 —3G 27
Surrey Cres. W4 —5G 73
Surrey Gdns. N4 —6C 30
Surrey Gro. SE17
  —5E 78 (5G 157)
Surrey Gro. Sutt —3A 132
Surrey La. SW11 —1C 92
Surrey La. Est. SW11 —1C 92
Surrey M. SE27 —4E 110
Surrey Mt. SE23 —1H 111
Surrey Quays Rd. SE16 —3J 79
Surrey Quays Shop. Cen. SE16
  —3K 79
Surrey Rd. SE15 —5K 95
Surrey Rd. Bark —7J 51
Surrey Rd. Dag —5H 53
Surrey Rd. Harr —5G 23
Surrey Rd. W Wick —1D 136
Surrey Row. SE1
  —2B 78 (6A 150)
Surrey Sq. SE17
  —5E 78 (5G 157)
Surrey St. E13 —3K 65
Surrey St. WC2 —7K 61 (2H 149)
Surrey St. Croy —3C 134
Surrey Ter. SE17
  —5E 78 (5H 157)
Surrey Water Rd. SE16 —1K 79
Surridge Ct. SW9 —2J 93
(off Clapham Rd.)
Surridge Gdns. SE19 —6D 110
Surr St. N7 —5J 45
Susan Clo. Romf —3J 37
Susan Lawrence Ho. E12 —4E 50
(off Walton Rd.)
Susannah St. E14 —6D 64
Susan Rd. SE3 —2K 97
Susan Wood. Chst —1E 128
Sussex Av. Iswth —3J 87
Sussex Clo. N19 —2J 45
Sussex Clo. Ilf —5D 34

Sussex Clo. *N Mald* —4A **120**
Sussex Clo. *Twic* —6B **88**
Sussex Cres. *N'holt* —6E **38**
Sussex Gdns. *N4* —5C **30**
Sussex Gdns. *N6* —5D **28**
Sussex Gdns. *W2*
 —7B **60** (2A **146**)
Sussex Ga. *N6* —5D **28**
Sussex M. E. *W2*
 —6B **60** (1B **146**)
Sussex M. W. *W2*
 —7B **60** (2B **146**)
Sussex Pl. *NW1* —4D **60** (3E **140**)
Sussex Pl. *W2* —6B **60** (1B **146**)
Sussex Pl. *W6* —5E **74**
Sussex Pl. *Eri* —7H **85**
Sussex Pl. *N Mald* —4A **120**
Sussex Ring. *N12* —5D **14**
Sussex Rd. *E6* —1E **66**
Sussex Rd. *Cars* —7D **132**
Sussex Rd. *Eri* —7H **85**
Sussex Rd. *Harr* —5G **23**
Sussex Rd. *Mitc* —5J **123**
Sussex Rd. *N Mald* —4A **120**
Sussex Rd. *Sidc* —5B **116**
Sussex Rd. *S'hall* —3B **70**
Sussex Rd. *S Croy* —6D **134**
Sussex Rd. *W Wick* —1D **136**
Sussex Sq. *W2* —7B **60** (2B **146**)
Sussex St. *E13* —3K **65**
Sussex St. *SW1* —5F **77** (6K **153**)
Sussex Wlk. *SW9* —4B **94**
Sussex Way. *N19 & N7* —1J **45**
Sussex Way. *Barn* —5A **6**
Sutcliffe Clo. *NW11* —5K **27**
Sutcliffe Rd. *SE18* —6J **83**
Sutcliffe Rd. *Well* —2C **100**
Sutherland Av. *W9* —4J **59**
Sutherland Av. *W13* —6B **56**
Sutherland Av. *Orp* —6K **129**
Sutherland Av. *Well* —4J **99**
Sutherland Clo. *Barn* —4B **4**
Sutherland Ct. *N16* —3D **46**
Sutherland Ct. *NW9* —5H **25**
Sutherland Dri. *SW19* —1B **122**
Sutherland Gdns. *SW14* —3A **90**
Sutherland Gdns. *Wor Pk*
 —1D **130**
Sutherland Gro. *SW18* —6G **91**
Sutherland Gro. *Tedd* —5J **103**
Sutherland Ho. *W8* —3K **75**
Sutherland Pl. *W2* —6J **59**
Sutherland Point. *E5* —4H **47**
 (off Tiger Way)
Sutherland Rd. *E17* —3K **31**
Sutherland Rd. *N9* —1C **18**
Sutherland Rd. *N17* —1G **31**
Sutherland Rd. *W4* —6A **74**
Sutherland Rd. *W13* —6A **56**
Sutherland Rd. *Belv* —3G **85**
Sutherland Rd. *Croy* —7A **124**
Sutherland Rd. *Enf* —6E **8**
Sutherland Rd. *S'hall* —6D **54**
Sutherland Rd. Path. *E17* —3K **31**
Sutherland Row. *SW1*
 —5F **77** (5K **153**)
Sutherland Sq. *SE17*
 —5C **78** (6C **156**)
Sutherland St. *SW1*
 —5F **77** (5J **153**)
Sutherland Wlk. *SE17*
 —5C **78** (6D **156**)
Sutlej Rd. *SE7* —7A **82**
Sutterton St. *N7* —6K **45**
Sutton Arc. *Sutt* —5K **131**

Sutton Clo. *Beck* —1D **126**
Sutton Clo. *Lou* —1H **21**
Sutton Comn. Rd. *Sutt* —7H **121**
Sutton Ct. *W4* —6J **73**
Sutton Ct. *Sutt* —6A **132**
Sutton Ct. Rd. *E13* —3A **66**
Sutton Ct. Rd. *W4* —7J **73**
Sutton Ct. Rd. *Sutt* —6A **132**
Sutton Cres. *Barn* —5A **4**
Sutton Dene. *Houn* —1F **87**
Sutton Est. *EC1* —3D **62** (2F **145**)
Sutton Est. *W10* —5E **58**
Sutton Est., The. *N1* —7B **46**
Sutton Est., The. *SW3*
 —5C **76** (5D **152**)
Sutton Gdns. *SE25* —5F **125**
Sutton Gdns. *Bark* —1J **67**
Sutton Gdns. *Croy* —5F **125**
Sutton Grn. *Bark* —1K **67**
Sutton Gro. *Sutt* —4B **132**
Sutton Hall Rd. *Houn* —7E **70**
Sutton La. *Houn* —3D **86**
Sutton La. N. *W4* —5J **73**
Sutton La. S. *W4* —6J **73**
Sutton Pde. *NW4* —4E **26**
 (off Church Rd.)
Sutton Pk. Rd. *Sutt* —6K **131**
Sutton Pl. *E9* —5J **47**
Sutton Rd. *E13* —4H **65**
Sutton Rd. *E17* —1K **31**
Sutton Rd. *N10* —1E **28**
Sutton Rd. *Bark* —1J **67**
Sutton Rd. *Houn* —1E **86**
Sutton Row. *W1*
 —6H **61** (7D **142**)
Suttons Bus. Pk. *Rain* —3K **69**
Sutton Sq. *E9* —5J **47**
Sutton Sq. *Houn* —1D **86**
Sutton St. *E1* —7J **63**
Sutton's Way. *EC1*
 —4C **62** (4D **144**)
Sutton Way. *W10* —4E **58**
Sutton Way. *Houn* —1D **86**
Swaby Rd. *SW18* —1A **108**
Swaffham Way. *N17* —7G **17**
Swaffield Rd. *SW18* —7K **91**
Swain Clo. *SW16* —6F **109**
Swain Rd. *T Hth* —5C **124**
Swains La. *N6* —1E **44**
Swainson Rd. *Act V* —2B **74**
Swains Rd. *SW17* —7D **108**
Swalecliffe Rd. *Belv* —5H **85**
Swaillands Rd. *SE6* —3C **112**
 (in two parts)
Swallow Clo. *SE14* —1K **95**
Swallow Clo. *Bush* —1A **10**
Swallow Clo. *Eri* —1K **101**
Swallow Ct. *SE12* —7J **97**
Swallow Ct. *Ilf* —5F **35**
Swallow Ct. *Ruis* —1A **38**
Swallow Dri. *NW10* —6K **41**
Swallow Dri. *N'holt* —2E **54**
Swallowfield Rd. *SE7* —5K **81**
Swallow Gdns. *SW16* —5H **109**
Swallow Pl. *W1* —6F **61** (1K **147**)
Swallow St. *E6* —5C **66**
Swallow St. *W1* —7G **61** (3B **148**)
Swanage Ho. *SW8* —7K **77**
 (off Dorset Rd.)
Swanage Rd. *E4* —7K **19**
Swanage Rd. *SW18* —6A **92**
Swanage Waye. *Hayes* —6A **54**
Swan App. *E6* —5C **66**
Swanbridge Rd. *Bexh* —1G **101**
Swan Cen., The. *SW17* —3A **108**

Swan Clo. *E17* —1A **32**
Swan Clo. *Croy* —7E **124**
Swan Clo. *Felt* —4C **102**
Swan Ct. *SW3* —5C **76** (6D **152**)
Swan Ct. *Iswth* —3B **88**
 (off Swan St.)
Swandon Way. *SW18* —5K **91**
Swan Dri. *NW9* —2A **26**
Swanfield St. *E2* —3F **63** (2J **145**)
Swan La. *EC4* —7D **62** (3F **151**)
Swan La. *N20* —3F **15**
Swanley Rd. *Well* —1C **100**
Swan Mead. *SE1*
 —3E **78** (2G **157**)
Swan M. *SW9* —1K **93**
Swann Ct. *Iswth* —3A **88**
 (off South St.)
Swan & Pike Rd. *Enf* —1H **9**
Swan Pl. *SW13* —2B **90**
Swan Rd. *SE16* —2J **79**
Swan Rd. *SE18* —3B **82**
Swan Rd. *Felt* —5C **102**
Swan Rd. *S'hall* —6F **55**
Swanscombe Ho. *W11* —1F **75**
 (off St Ann's Rd.)
Swanscombe Point. *E16* —5H **65**
 (off Clarkson Rd.)
Swanscombe Rd. *W4* —5A **74**
Swanscombe Rd. *W11* —1F **75**
Swansea Rd. *Enf* —4D **8**
Swansland Gdns. *E17* —1A **32**
Swans Pas. *E1* —7G **63** (3K **151**)
Swan St. *SE1* —3C **78** (1D **156**)
Swan St. *Iswth* —3B **88**
Swan, The. (Junct.) —2E **136**
Swanton Gdns. *SW19* —1F **107**
Swanton Rd. *Eri* —7H **85**
Swan Wlk. *SW3* —6D **76** (7E **152**)
Swan Way. *Enf* —2E **8**
Swanwick Clo. *SW15* —7B **90**
Swan Yd. *N1* —6B **46**
Sward Rd. *Orp* —6K **129**
Swaton Rd. *E3* —4C **64**
Swaylands Rd. *Belv* —6G **85**
Swaythling Clo. *N18* —4C **18**
Swaythling Ho. *SW15* —6B **90**
 (off Tunworth Cres.)
Swedeland Ct. *E1*
 —5E **62** (6H **145**)
Swedenborg Gdns. *E1* —7H **63**
Sweden Ga. *SE16* —3A **80**
Swedish Quays Development,
 SE16 —3A **80**
Sweeney Cres. *SE1*
 —2F **79** (7K **151**)
Sweet Briar Grn. *N9* —3A **18**
Sweet Briar Gro. *N9* —3A **18**
Sweet Briar Wlk. *N18* —4A **18**
Sweetland Ct. *Dag* —6B **52**
Sweetmans Av. *Pinn* —3B **22**
Sweets Way. *N20* —2G **15**
Swell Ct. *E17* —6D **32**
Swetenham Wlk. *SE18* —5G **83**
Swete St. *E13* —2J **65**
Sweyn Pl. *SE3* —2J **97**
Swift Clo. *E17* —7F **19**
Swift Clo. *Harr* —2F **39**
Swift Ct. *Sutt* —7K **131**
Swift Rd. *Felt* —4B **102**
Swift Rd. *S'hall* —3E **70**
Swift St. *SW6* —1H **91**
Swinbrook Rd. *W10* —5G **59**
Swinburne Ct. *SE5* —4D **94**
 (off Basingdon Way)

Swinburne Cres. *Croy* —6J **125**
Swinburne Rd. *SW15* —4C **90**
Swinderby Rd. *Wemb* —6E **40**
Swindon Clo. *Ilf* —2J **51**
Swindon St. *W12* —1D **74**
Swinfield Clo. *Felt* —3C **102**
Swinford Gdns. *SW9* —3B **94**
Swingate La. *SE18* —6J **83**
Swinnerton St. *E9* —5A **48**
Swinton Clo. *Wemb* —1H **41**
Swinton Pl. *WC1*
 —3K **61** (1G **143**)
Swinton St. *WC1*
 —3K **61** (1G **143**)
Swires Shaw. *Kes* —4B **138**
Swiss Cottage. (Junct.) —7B **44**
Swiss Ct. *WC2* —7H **61** (3D **148**)
Swiss Ter. *NW6* —7B **44**
Swithland Gdns. *SE9* —4E **114**
Swyncombe Av. *W5* —4B **72**
Swynford Gdns. *NW4* —4C **26**
Sybil M. *N4* —6B **30**
Sybil Phoenix Clo. *SE8* —5K **79**
Sybourn St. *E17* —7B **32**
Sycamore Av. *W5* —3D **72**
Sycamore Av. *Sidc* —6K **99**
Sycamore Clo. *E16* —4G **65**
Sycamore Clo. *N9* —4B **18**
Sycamore Clo. *SE9* —2C **114**
Sycamore Clo. *W3* —1A **74**
Sycamore Clo. *Barn* —6G **5**
Sycamore Clo. *Cars* —4D **132**
Sycamore Clo. *N'holt* —1C **54**
Sycamore Clo. *Houn* —4C **86**
Sycamore Ct. *NW6* —1J **59**
 (off Bransdale Clo.)
Sycamore Ct. *Eri* —5K **85**
 (off Sandcliff Rd.)
Sycamore Ct. *Houn* —4C **86**
Sycamore Ct. *N Mald* —3A **120**
Sycamore Gdns. *W6* —2D **74**
Sycamore Gdns. *W12* —2D **74**
Sycamore Gdns. *Mitc* —2B **122**
Sycamore Gro. *NW9* —7J **25**
Sycamore Gro. *SE6* —6E **96**
Sycamore Gro. *SE20* —1G **125**
Sycamore Gro. *N Mald* —3K **119**
Sycamore Hill. *N11* —6K **15**
Sycamore Ho. *W6* —2D **74**
Sycamore Ho. *Brom* —2G **127**
Sycamore Ho. *Buck H* —2G **21**
Sycamore M. *SW4* —3G **93**
Sycamore M. *Eri* —5K **85**
 (off St John's Rd.)
Sycamore Rd. *SW19* —6E **106**
Sycamore St. *EC1*
 —4C **62** (4C **144**)
Sycamore Wlk. *W10* —4G **59**
Sycamore Wlk. *Ilf* —4G **35**
Sycamore Way. *Tedd* —6C **104**
Sycamore Way. *T Hth* —5A **124**
Sydcote. *SE21* —1C **110**
Sydenham Av. *N21* —5E **6**
Sydenham Av. *SE26* —5H **111**
Sydenham Cotts. *SE12* —2A **114**
Sydenham Hill. *SE26 & SE23*
 —4F **111**
Sydenham Pk. *SE26* —3J **111**
Sydenham Pk. Rd. *SE26* —3J **111**
Sydenham Pl. *SE27* —3B **110**
Sydenham Rise. *SE23* —2H **111**
Sydenham Rd. *SE26* —4J **111**
Sydenham Rd. *Croy* —1C **134**
Sydmons Ct. *SE23* —7J **95**
Sydner M. *N16* —4F **47**
Sydner Rd. *N16* —4F **47**

Sydney Clo. *SW3*
 —4B **76** (4B **152**)
Sydney Ct. *Hayes* —4A **54**
Sydney Gro. *NW4* —5E **26**
Sydney M. *SW3* —4B **76** (4B **152**)
Sydney Pl. *SW7* —4B **76** (4B **152**)
Sydney Rd. *E11* —6K **33**
Sydney Rd. *N8* —4A **30**
Sydney Rd. *N10* —1F **29**
Sydney Rd. *SE2* —3C **84**
Sydney Rd. *SW20* —2F **121**
Sydney Rd. *W13* —1A **72**
Sydney Rd. *Bexh* —4D **100**
Sydney Rd. *Enf* —4J **7**
 (in two parts)
Sydney Rd. *Ilf* —2G **35**
Sydney Rd. *Rich* —4E **88**
Sydney Rd. *Sidc* —4J **115**
Sydney Rd. *Sutt* —4J **131**
Sydney Rd. *Tedd* —5K **103**
Sydney Rd. *Wfd G* —4D **20**
Sydney St. *SW3*
 —5C **76** (5C **152**)
Sylvan Av. *N3* —2J **27**
Sylvan Av. *N22* —7E **16**
Sylvan Av. *NW7* —6F **13**
Sylvan Av. *Romf* —6F **37**
Sylvan Ct. *N12* —3E **14**
Sylvan Est. *SE19* —1F **125**
Sylvan Gdns. *Surb* —7D **118**
Sylvan Gro. *SE15* —6H **79**
Sylvan Hill. *SE19* —1E **124**
Sylvan Rd. *E7* —6J **49**
Sylvan Rd. *E11* —5J **33**
Sylvan Rd. *E17* —5C **32**
Sylvan Rd. *SE19* —1F **125**
Sylvan Wlk. *Brom* —3C **128**
Sylvan Way. *Dag* —4B **52**
Sylvan Way. *W Wick* —4G **137**
Sylverdale Rd. *Croy* —3B **134**
Sylvester Av. *Chst* —6D **114**
Sylvester Path. *E8* —6H **47**
Sylvester Rd. *E8* —6H **47**
Sylvester Rd. *E17* —7B **32**
Sylvester Rd. *N2* —2B **28**
Sylvester Rd. *Wemb* —5C **40**
Sylvestrus Clo. *King T* —1G **119**
Sylvia Ct. *Wemb* —7H **41**
Sylvia Gdns. *Wemb* —7H **41**
Sylvia Pankhurst Ho. *Dag* —3G **53**
 (off Wythenshawe Rd.)
Symes M. *NW1* —2G **61**
Symister M. *N1* —3E **62** (2G **145**)
Symons St. *SW3*
 —4D **76** (4F **153**)
Syon Ga. Way. *Bren* —7A **72**
Syon La. *Iswth* —6J **71**
Syon Lodge. *SE12* —7J **97**
Syon Pk. Gdns. *Iswth* —7K **71**
Syringa Ho. *SE4* —3B **96**

*T*abard Ct. *E14* —6E **64**
 (off Lodore St.)
Tabard Garden Est. *SE1*
 —3D **78** (7E **150**)
Tabard St. *SE1* —2D **78** (6D **150**)
Tabernacle Av. *E13* —4J **65**
Tabernacle St. *EC2*
 —4D **62** (4F **145**)
Tableer Av. *SW4* —5H **93**
Tabley Rd. *N7* —4J **45**
Tabor Ct. *Sutt* —6G **131**
Tabor Gdns. *Sutt* —7H **131**

Tabor Gro. *SW19* —7G **107**
Tabor Rd. *W6* —3D **74**
Tachbrook Est. *SW1*
　　　　—5H **77** (6C **154**)
Tachbrook M. *SW1*
　　　　—4G **77** (3A **154**)
Tachbrook Rd. *S'hall* —4B **70**
Tachbrook St. *SW1*
　　　　—4G **77** (4B **154**)
Tack M. *SE4* —3C **96**
Tadema Ho. *NW8*
　　　　—4B **60** (4B **140**)
Tadema Rd. *SW10* —7A **76**
Tadmor St. *W12* —1F **75**
Tadworth Av. *N Mald* —5B **120**
Tadworth Ho. *SE1*
　　　　—2B **78** (6A **150**)
Tadworth Rd. *NW2* —2C **42**
Taeping St. *E14* —4D **80**
Taffy's Row. *Mitc* —3C **122**
Taft Way. *E3* —3E **64**
Tailworth St. *E1* —5G **63**
　(off Chicksand St.)
Tailworth St. *E1* —5G **63** (6K **145**)
　(off Chicksand St.)
Tait Ct. *SW8* —1J **93**
　(off Lansdowne Grn.)
Tait Rd. *Croy* —7E **124**
Takeley Clo. *Romf* —2K **37**
Talacre Rd. *NW5* —6E **44**
Talbot Av. *N2* —3B **28**
Talbot Clo. *N15* —4F **31**
Talbot Ct. *EC3* —7D **62** (2F **151**)
Talbot Ct. *NW9* —3K **41**
Talbot Cres. *NW4* —5C **26**
Talbot Gdns. *Ilf* —2A **52**
Talbot Pl. *SE3* —2G **97**
Talbot Rd. *E6* —2E **66**
Talbot Rd. *E7* —4J **49**
Talbot Rd. *N6* —6E **28**
Talbot Rd. *N15* —4F **31**
Talbot Rd. *N22* —2G **29**
Talbot Rd. *SE22* —4E **94**
Talbot Rd. *W11 & W2* —6H **59**
　(in two parts)
Talbot Rd. *W13* —1A **72**
Talbot Rd. *Cars* —5E **132**
Talbot Rd. *Dag* —6F **53**
Talbot Rd. *Harr* —2K **23**
Talbot Rd. *Iswth* —4A **88**
Talbot Rd. *S'hall* —4C **70**
Talbot Rd. *T Hth* —4D **124**
Talbot Rd. *Twic* —1J **103**
Talbot Rd. *Wemb* —6D **40**
Talbot Sq. *W2* —6B **60** (1B **146**)
Talbot Wlk. *W11* —6G **59**
Talbot Wlk. *NW10* —6A **42**
Talbot Way. *NW10* —6A **42**
Talbot Yd. *SE1* —1D **78** (5E **150**)
Talcott Path. *SW2* —1A **110**
Talfourd Pl. *SE15* —1F **95**
Talfourd Rd. *SE15* —1F **95**
Talgarth Mans. *W14* —5G **75**
　(off Talgarth Rd.)
Talgarth Rd. *W6 & W14* —5F **75**
Talgarth Wlk. *NW9* —5A **26**
Talisman Clo. *Ilf* —1B **52**
Talisman Sq. *SE26* —4G **111**
Talisman Way. *Wemb* —3F **41**
Tallack Clo. *Harr* —7D **10**
Tallack Rd. *E10* —1B **48**
Tall Elms Clo. *Brom* —5H **127**
Talleyrand Ho. *SE5* —2C **94**
Tallis Clo. *E16* —6K **65**
Tallis Gro. *SE7* —6K **81**

Tallis St. *EC4* —7A **62** (2K **149**)
Tallis View. *NW10* —6K **41**
Tall Trees. *SW16* —4K **123**
Talma Gdns. *Twic* —6J **87**
Talmage Clo. *SE23* —7J **95**
Talman Gro. *Stan* —6J **11**
Talwin St. *E3* —3D **64**
Tamarind Yd. *E1* —1G **79**
Tamarisk Sq. *W12* —7B **58**
Tamar Sq. *W6* —6E **20**
Tamar St. *SE7* —4C **82**
Tamar Way. *N17* —3G **31**
Tamesis Gdns. *Wor Pk* —2A **130**
Tamian Ind. Est. *Houn* —4A **86**
Tamian Way. *Houn* —4A **86**
Tamworth. *N7* —6J **45**
Tamworth Av. *Wfd G* —6B **20**
Tamworth La. *Mitc* —2F **123**
Tamworth Pk. *Mitc* —3F **123**
Tamworth Pl. *Croy* —2C **134**
Tamworth Rd. *Croy* —2B **134**
Tamworth St. *SW6* —6J **75**
Tamworth Vs. *Mitc* —4G **123**
Tancred Rd. *N4* —7B **30**
Tandridge Dri. *Orp* —7H **129**
Tandridge Pl. *Orp* —7H **129**
Tanfield Av. *NW2* —4B **42**
Tanfield Rd. *Croy* —4C **134**
Tangier Rd. *Rich* —4G **89**
Tangleberry Clo. *Brom* —4D **128**
Tangle Tree Clo. *N3* —2K **27**
Tanglewood Clo. *Croy* —3J **135**
Tanglewood Clo. *Stan* —2D **10**
Tangley Gro. *SW15* —6B **90**
Tangley Pk. Rd. *Hamp* —5D **102**
Tangmere. *N17* —2D **30**
　(off Willan Rd.)
Tangmere Gdns. *N'holt* —2A **54**
　(in two parts)
Tangmere Gro. *King T* —5D **104**
Tangmere Way. *NW9* —2A **26**
Tanhurst Ho. *SW2* —7J **93**
　(off Redlands Way)
Tanhurst Wlk. *SE2* —3D **84**
Tankerton St. *WC1*
　　　　—3J **61** (2F **143**)
Tankerton Ter. *Croy* —6K **123**
Tankerville Rd. *SW16* —7H **109**
Tankridge Rd. *NW2* —2D **42**
Tanner Point. *E13* —1J **65**
　(off Pelly Rd.)
Tanners End La. *N18* —4K **17**
Tanner's Hill. *SE8* —1B **96**
Tanners La. *Ilf* —3G **35**
Tanner St. *SE1* —2E **78** (7H **151**)
Tanner St. *Bark* —6G **51**
Tannery Clo. *Beck* —4K **125**
Tannery Clo. *Dag* —3H **53**
Tannington Ter. *N5* —3A **46**
Tannsfeld Rd. *SE26* —5K **111**
Tansley Clo. *N7* —5H **45**
Tanswell St. *SE1* —2A **78** (7J **149**)
Tansy Clo. *E6* —6E **66**
Tantallon Rd. *SW12* —1E **108**
Tant Av. *E16* —6H **65**
Tantony Gro. *Romf* —3D **36**
Tanworth Gdns. *Pinn* —2A **22**
Tanyard La. *Bex* —7G **101**
Tanza Rd. *NW3* —4D **44**
Tapestry Clo. *Sutt* —7K **131**
Taplow. *SE17* —5D **78** (5F **157**)
Taplow Rd. *N13* —4G **17**
Taplow St. *N1* —2C **62** (1D **144**)
Tappesfield Rd. *SE15* —3J **95**

Tapp St. *E1* —4H **63**
Tapster St. *Barn* —3C **4**
Tara Ct. *Beck* —2D **126**
Tarbert Rd. *SE22* —5E **94**
Tarbert Wlk. *E1* —7J **63**
Target Ho. *W13* —1B **72**
　(off Sherwood Clo.)
Target Roundabout. (Junct.)
　　　　—1D **54**
Tariff Cres. *SE8* —4B **80**
Tariff Rd. *N17* —6B **18**
Tarleton Ct. *N22* —2A **30**
Tarleton Gdns. *SE23* —2H **111**
Tarling Clo. *Sidc* —3B **116**
Tarling Rd. *E16* —6H **65**
Tarling Rd. *N2* —2A **28**
Tarling St. *E1* —6J **63**
Tarling St. Est. *E1* —6J **63**
Tarn Bank. *Enf* —5D **6**
Tarn St. *SE1* —3C **78** (2C **156**)
Tarnwood Pk. *SE9* —1D **114**
Tarquin Ho. *SE26* —4G **111**
　(off High Level Dri.)
Tarragon Clo. *SE14* —7A **80**
Tarragon Gro. *SE26* —6K **111**
Tarranbrae. *NW6* —7G **43**
Tarrant Pl. *W1* —5D **60** (6E **140**)
Tarrington Clo. *SW16* —3H **109**
Tarry La. *SE8* —4A **80**
Tarver Rd. *SE17*
　　　　—5B **78** (5B **156**)
Tarves Way. *SE10* —7D **80**
Tash Pl. *N11* —5A **16**
Tasker Ho. *Bark* —2H **67**
Tasker Rd. *NW3* —5D **44**
Tasmania Ter. *N18* —6H **17**
Tasman Rd. *SW9* —3J **93**
Tasman Wlk. *E16* —6B **66**
Tasso Rd. *W6* —6G **75**
Tasso Yd. *W6* —6G **75**
　(off Tasso Rd.)
Tatam Rd. *NW10* —7K **41**
Tatchbury Ho. *SW15* —6B **90**
　(off Tunworth Cres.)
Tate Rd. *E16* —1D **82**
　(in two parts)
Tate Rd. *Sutt* —5J **131**
Tatnell Rd. *SE23* —6A **96**
Tattersall Clo. *SE9* —5C **98**
Tatton Cres. *N16* —7F **31**
Tatum St. *SE17* —4D **78** (4F **157**)
Taunton Av. *SW20* —2D **120**
Taunton Av. *Houn* —2G **87**
Taunton Clo. *Bexh* —2K **101**
Taunton Clo. *Sutt* —1J **131**
Taunton Dri. *N2* —1A **28**
Taunton Dri. *Enf* —3F **7**
Taunton M. *NW1*
　　　　—4D **60** (4E **140**)
Taunton Pl. *NW1*
　　　　—4D **60** (3E **140**)
Taunton Rd. *SE12* —5G **97**
Taunton Rd. *Gnfd* —1F **55**
Taunton Way. *Stan* —2E **24**
Tavern Clo. *Cars* —7C **122**
Taverners Clo. *W11* —1G **75**
Taverners Sq. *N5* —4C **46**
Taverner Way. *E4* —1B **20**
Tavern La. *SW9* —2A **94**
Tavern Quay. *SE16* —4A **80**
Tavistock Av. *E17* —3K **31**
Tavistock Av. *Gnfd* —2A **56**
Tavistock Clo. *N16* —5E **46**
Tavistock Cres. *W11* —5H **59**
　(in three parts)

Tavistock Cres. *Mitc* —4J **123**
Tavistock Gdns. *Ilf* —4J **51**
Tavistock Ga. *Croy* —1D **134**
Tavistock Gro. *Croy* —7D **124**
Tavistock Ho. *WC1*
　　　　—4H **61** (3D **142**)
Tavistock Ho. *Croy* —1D **134**
Tavistock M. *E18* —3J **33**
Tavistock M. *W11* —6H **59**
Tavistock Pl. *E18* —4J **33**
Tavistock Pl. *N14* —6A **6**
Tavistock Pl. *WC1*
　　　　—4J **61** (3E **142**)
Tavistock Rd. *E7* —4H **49**
Tavistock Rd. *E15* —6H **49**
Tavistock Rd. *E18* —3J **33**
Tavistock Rd. *N4* —6D **30**
Tavistock Rd. *NW10* —2B **58**
Tavistock Rd. *W11* —6H **59**
　(in two parts)
Tavistock Rd. *Brom* —4H **127**
Tavistock Rd. *Cars* —1B **132**
Tavistock Rd. *Croy* —1D **134**
Tavistock Rd. *Edgw* —1G **25**
Tavistock Rd. *Well* —1C **100**
Tavistock Sq. *WC1*
　　　　—4H **61** (3D **142**)
Tavistock St. *WC2*
　　　　—7J **61** (2F **149**)
Tavistock Ter. *N19* —3H **45**
Tavistock Tower. *SE16* —3A **80**
Tavistock Wlk. *Cars* —1B **132**
Taviton St. *WC1*
　　　　—4H **61** (3C **142**)
Tavy Bri. *SE2* —2C **84**
Tavy Bri. Cen. *SE2* —2C **84**
Tavy Clo. *SE11* —5A **78** (5K **155**)
Tawney Rd. *SE28* —7B **68**
Tawny Clo. *W13* —1B **72**
Tawny Way. *SE16* —4K **79**
Tayben Av. *Twic* —6J **87**
Taybridge Rd. *SW11* —3E **92**
Tay Bldgs. *SE1* —3E **78** (1G **157**)
Tayburn Clo. *E14* —6E **64**
Tayler Ct. *NW8* —1B **60**
　(off Dorman Way)
Taylor Av. *Rich* —2H **89**
Taylor Clo. *N17* —7B **18**
Taylor Clo. *Hamp* —5G **103**
Taylor Clo. *Houn* —1G **87**
Taylor Ct. *E15* —5E **48**
Taylor Ct. *SE20* —2J **125**
　(off Elmers End Rd.)
Taylormead. *NW7* —5H **13**
Taylor Rd. *Mitc* —7C **108**
Taylor Rd. *Wall* —5F **133**
Taylors Bldgs. *SE18* —4F **83**
Taylors Clo. *Sidc* —3K **115**
Taylors Grn. *W3* —6A **58**
Taylors La. *NW10* —7A **42**
Taylor's La. *SE26* —4H **111**
Taylors La. *Barn* —1C **4**
Taymount Grange. *SE23* —2J **111**
Taymount Rise. *SE23* —2J **111**
Tayport Clo. *N1* —7J **45**
Tayside Ct. *SE5* —4D **94**
Tayside Dri. *Edgw* —3C **12**
Taywood Rd. *N'holt* —3D **54**
Teak Clo. *SE16* —1A **80**
Tealby Ct. *N7* —6K **45**
　(off Georges Rd.)
Teal Clo. *E16* —5B **66**
Teal Clo. *NW10* —6K **41**
Teal Ct. *SE8* —6B **80**
　(off Abinger Gro.)

Teale St. *E2* —2G **63**
Teasel Clo. *Croy* —1K **135**
Teasel Way. *E15* —3G **65**
Tebworth Rd. *N17* —7A **18**
Teck Clo. *Iswth* —2A **88**
Tedder Rd. *S Croy* —7J **135**
Teddington Bus. Pk. *Tedd*
　　　　—6K **103**
　(off Station Rd.)
Teddington Pk. *Tedd* —5K **103**
Teddington Pk. Rd. *Tedd*
　　　　—4K **103**
Tedworth Gdns. *SW3*
　　　　—5D **76** (6E **152**)
Tedworth Sq. *SW3*
　　　　—5D **76** (6E **152**)
Tees Av. *Gnfd* —2J **55**
Tees Ct. *W7* —6H **55**
　(off Hanway Rd.)
Teesdale Av. *Iswth* —1A **88**
Teesdale Clo. *E2* —2H **63**
Teesdale Gdns. *SE25* —2E **124**
Teesdale Gdns. *Iswth* —1A **88**
Teesdale Rd. *E11* —7H **33**
Teesdale St. *E2* —2H **63**
Teesdale Yd. *E2* —2H **63**
　(off Teesdale St.)
Teeswater Ct. *Eri* —3D **84**
Tee, The. *W3* —6A **58**
Teevan Clo. *Croy* —7G **125**
Teevan Rd. *Croy* —1G **135**
Teignmouth Clo. *SW4* —4H **93**
Teignmouth Clo. *Edgw* —2F **25**
Teignmouth Gdns. *Gnfd* —2A **56**
Teignmouth Pde. *Gnfd* —2B **56**
Teignmouth Rd. *NW2* —5F **43**
Teignmouth Rd. *Well* —2C **100**
Telcote Way. *Ruis* —7A **22**
Telegraph Hill. *NW3* —3K **43**
Telegraph M. *Ilf* —1A **52**
Telegraph Pas. *SW2* —7J **93**
Telegraph Pl. *E14* —4D **80**
Telegraph Rd. *SW15* —7D **90**
Telegraph St. *EC2*
　　　　—6D **62** (7E **144**)
Teleman Sq. *SE3* —4K **97**
Telephone Pl. *SW6* —6H **75**
Telfer Clo. *W3* —2J **73**
Telferscot Rd. *SW12* —1H **109**
Telford Av. *SW2* —1H **109**
Telford Clo. *E17* —7A **32**
Telford Clo. *SE19* —6F **111**
Telford Rd. *N11* —5B **16**
Telford Rd. *NW9* —6C **26**
Telford Rd. *SE9* —2H **115**
Telford Rd. *W10* —5G **59**
Telford Rd. *S'hall* —7F **55**
Telford Rd. *Twic* —7E **86**
Telfords Yd. *E1* —7G **63**
Telford Ter. *SW1*
　　　　—6G **77** (7A **154**)
Telford Way. *Hayes* —5C **58**
Telford Way. *W'way E* —5A **58**
Telham Rd. *E6* —2E **66**
Tell Gro. *SE22* —4F **95**
Tellson Av. *SE18* —1B **98**
Temeraire St. *SE16* —2J **79**
Temperley Rd. *SW12* —7E **92**
Tempest Ho. *King T* —1E **118**
　(off Sigrist Sq.)
Templar Dri. *SE28* —6D **68**
Templar Ho. *NW2* —6H **43**
Templar Pl. *Hamp* —7E **102**
Templars Av. *NW11* —6H **27**

Templars Cres. *N3* —2J **27**
Templars Dri. *Harr* —6C **10**
Templars Ho. *E15* —5D **48**
Templar St. *SE5* —2B **94**
Temple. *EC4* —7A **62** (2J **149**)
Temple Av. *EC4* —7A **62** (2K **149**)
Temple Av. *Croy* —2B **136**
Temple Av. *Dag* —1G **53**
Temple Chambers. *EC4*
    —7A **62** (2K **149**)
Temple Clo. *E11* —7G **33**
Temple Clo. *N3* —2H **27**
Temple Clo. *SE28* —3G **83**
Templecombe Rd. *E9* —1J **63**
Templecombe Way. *Mord*
    —5G **121**
Temple Ct. *SW8* —7J **77**
    (off Thorncroft St.)
Temple Dwellings. *E2* —2H **63**
    (off Temple St.)
Temple Fortune Hill. *NW11*
    —5J **27**
Temple Fortune La. *NW11*
    —6H **27**
Temple Fortune Pde. *NW11*
    —5H **27**
Temple Gdns. *N21* —2G **17**
Temple Gdns. *NW11* —6H **27**
Temple Gdns. *Dag* —3D **52**
Temple Gro. *NW11* —6J **27**
Temple Gro. *Enf* —3G **7**
Temple Hall Ct. *E4* —2A **20**
Templehof Av. *NW4* —7E **26**
Temple La. *EC4* —6A **62** (1K **149**)
Templeman Rd. *W7* —5K **55**
Templemead Clo. *W3* —6A **58**
Temple Mead Clo. *Beck* —6J **11**
Templemead Ho. *E9* —4A **48**
Temple Mill La. *E10 & E15*
    (in two parts) —4D **48**
Temple Pl. *WC2*
    —7K **61** (2H **149**)
Temple Rd. *E6* —1C **66**
Temple Rd. *N8* —4K **29**
Temple Rd. *NW2* —4E **42**
Temple Rd. *W4* —3J **73**
Temple Rd. *W5* —3D **72**
Temple Rd. *Croy* —4D **134**
Temple Rd. *Houn* —4G **87**
Temple Rd. *Rich* —2F **89**
Temple Sheen. *SW14* —5J **89**
Temple Sheen Rd. *SW14* —4H **89**
Temple St. *E2* —2H **63**
Templeton Av. *E4* —4H **19**
Templeton Clo. *N15* —6D **30**
Templeton Clo. *N16* —5E **46**
Templeton Clo. *SE19* —1D **124**
Templeton Pl. *SW5* —4J **75**
Templeton Rd. *N15* —6D **30**
Temple Way. *Sutt* —3B **132**
Temple W. M. *SE11*
    —3B **78** (2A **156**)
Templewood. *W13* —5B **56**
Templewood Av. *NW3* —3K **43**
Templewood Gdns. *NW3* —3K **43**
Templewood Point. *NW2* —2H **43**
    (off Granville Rd.)
Tempo Ho. *N'holt* —3B **54**
Tempsford Clo. *Enf* —3H **7**
Tempsford Ct. *Harr* —6K **23**
Temsford Clo. *Harr* —2G **23**
Tenbury Clo. *E7* —5B **50**
Tenbury Ct. *SW12* —1H **109**
Tenby Av. *Harr* —2B **24**

Tenby Clo. *N15* —4F **31**
Tenby Clo. *Romf* —6E **36**
Tenby Ct. *E17* —5K **31**
Tenby Gdns. *N'holt* —6E **38**
Tenby Rd. *E17* —5A **32**
Tenby Rd. *Edgw* —1F **25**
Tenby Rd. *Enf* —4D **8**
Tenby Rd. *Romf* —6E **36**
Tenby Rd. *Well* —1D **100**
Tench St. *E1* —1H **79**
Tenda Rd. *SE16* —4H **79**
Tendring Way. *Romf* —5C **36**
Tenham Av. *SW2* —2H **109**
Tenison Ct. *W1* —7G **61** (2A **148**)
Tenison Way. *SE1*
    —1A **78** (5H **149**)
Tenniel Clo. *W2* —7A **60**
Tennison Rd. *SE25* —4F **125**
Tennis St. *SE1* —2D **78** (6E **150**)
Tenniswood Rd. *Enf* —1K **7**
Tennyson Av. *E11* —7J **33**
Tennyson Av. *E12* —7C **50**
Tennyson Av. *NW9* —3J **25**
Tennyson Av. *N Mald* —5D **120**
Tennyson Av. *Twic* —1K **103**
Tennyson Clo. *Well* —1J **99**
Tennyson Clo. *Enf* —6E **8**
Tennyson Ct. *SW6* —1K **91**
    (off Maltings Pl.)
Tennyson Ho. *SE17*
    —5C **78** (5D **156**)
Tennyson Ho. *Belv* —5F **85**
    (off Albert Rd.)
Tennyson Mans. *W14* —6G **75**
    (off Queen's Club Gdns.)
Tennyson Rd. *E10* —1D **48**
Tennyson Rd. *E15* —7G **49**
Tennyson Rd. *E17* —6B **32**
Tennyson Rd. *NW6* —1H **59**
    (in two parts)
Tennyson Rd. *NW7* —5H **13**
Tennyson Rd. *SE20* —7K **111**
Tennyson Rd. *SW19* —6A **108**
Tennyson Rd. *W7* —7K **55**
Tennyson Rd. *Houn* —2G **87**
Tennyson Rd. *SW8* —2F **93**
Tensing Rd. *S'hall* —3E **70**
Tentelow La. *S'hall* —5E **70**
Tenterden Clo. *NW4* —3F **27**
Tenterden Clo. *SE9* —4D **114**
Tenterden Clo. *SE12* —4C **114**
Tenterden Dri. *NW4* —3F **27**
Tenterden Gdns. *NW4* —3F **27**
Tenterden Gdns. *Croy* —7G **125**
Tenterden Gro. *NW4* —3F **27**
Tenterden Rd. *N17* —7A **18**
Tenterden Rd. *Croy* —7G **125**
Tenterden Rd. *Dag* —2F **53**
Tenterden St. *W1*
    —6F **61** (1K **147**)
Tenter Ground. *E1*
    —5F **63** (6J **145**)
Tent Peg La. *Pet W* —5G **129**
Tent St. *E1* —4H **63**
Terborch Way. *SE22* —5E **94**
Teredo St. *SE16* —3K **79**
Teresa M. *E17* —4C **32**
Teresa Wlk. *N10* —5F **29**
Terling Clo. *E11* —3H **49**
Terling Rd. *Dag* —2G **53**
Terling Wlk. *N1* —1C **62**
    (off Popham St.)
Terminal Ho. *Stan* —5J **11**
Terminus Pl. *SW1*
    —3F **77** (2K **153**)
Terrace Av. *NW10* —4E **58**

Terrace Gdns. *SW13* —2B **90**
Terrace La. *Rich* —6E **88**
Terrace Rd. *E9* —7K **47**
Terrace Rd. *E13* —2J **65**
Terrace, The. *E4* —3B **20**
Terrace, The. *EC4*
    —6A **62** (1K **149**)
Terrace, The. *N3* —2F **27**
Terrace, The. *NW6* —1J **59**
Terrace, The. *SE8* —4B **80**
    (off Longshore)
Terrace, The. *SW13* —2A **90**
Terrace, The. *Harr* —7B **24**
Terrace, The. *Wfd G* —6D **20**
Terrace Wlk. *SW11* —7D **76**
    (off Albert Bri. Rd.)
Terrace Wlk. *Dag* —5E **52**
Terrapin Rd. *SW17* —3F **109**
Terrence Ct. *Belv* —6F **85**
    (off Charton Clo.)
Terretts Pl. *N1* —7B **46**
Terrick Rd. *N22* —1J **29**
Terrick St. *W12* —6D **58**
Terrilands. *Pinn* —3D **22**
Territorial Ho. *SE11*
    —4A **78** (4K **155**)
Terront Rd. *N15* —4C **30**
Tessa Sanderson Pl. *SW8* —3F **93**
    (off Daley Thompson Way)
Tessa Sanderson Way. *Gnfd*
    —5H **39**
Testerton Wlk. *W11* —7F **59**
Testwood Ct. *W7* —7J **55**
Tetbury Pl. *N1* —1B **62**
Tetcott Rd. *SW10* —7A **76**
    (in two parts)
Tetherdown. *N10* —3E **28**
Tetty Way. *Brom* —2J **127**
Teversham La. *SW8* —1J **93**
Teviot Clo. *Well* —1B **100**
Teviot St. *E14* —5E **64**
Tewkesbury Av. *SE23* —7H **95**
Tewkesbury Av. *Pinn* —5C **22**
Tewkesbury Clo. *N15* —6D **30**
Tewkesbury Gdns. *NW9* —3H **25**
Tewkesbury Rd. *N15* —6D **30**
Tewkesbury Rd. *W13* —1A **72**
Tewkesbury Rd. *Cars* —1B **132**
Tewkesbury Ter. *N11* —6B **16**
Tewson Rd. *SE18* —5J **83**
Teynham Av. *Enf* —6J **7**
Teynham Ct. *Beck* —3E **126**
Teynham Grn. *Brom* —5J **127**
Teynton Ter. *N17* —1C **30**
Thackeray Av. *N17* —2G **31**
Thackeray Clo. *SW19* —7F **107**
Thackeray Clo. *Harr* —1E **38**
Thackeray Ct. *W14* —3G **75**
    (off Blythe Rd.)
Thackeray Dri. *Romf* —7A **36**
Thackeray Ho. *WC1*
    —4J **61** (3E **142**)
Thackeray Rd. *E6* —2B **66**
Thackeray Rd. *SW8* —2F **93**
Thackeray St. *W8* —3K **75**
Thackeray M. *E8* —6G **47**
Thackery Clo. *Iswth* —2A **88**
Thackrah Clo. *N2* —2A **28**
Thakeham Clo. *SE26* —4H **111**
Thalia Clo. *SE10* —6F **81**
Thame Rd. *SE16* —2K **79**
Thames Av. *SW10* —1A **92**
Thames Av. *Dag* —4H **69**
Thames Av. *Gnfd* —2K **55**
Thames Bank. *SW14* —2J **89**

Thamesbank Pl. *SE28* —6C **68**
Thames Barrier Ind. Area. *SE1*
    (off Faraday Way) —3B **82**
Thames Circ. *E14* —4C **80**
Thames Ct. *W7* —6J **55**
    (off Hanway Rd.)
Thames Cres. *W4* —7A **74**
Thames Exchange Building. *EC4*
    —7C **62** (3D **150**)
Thamesgate Clo. *Rich* —4B **104**
Thameshill Av. *Romf* —2J **37**
Thames Ho. *EC4*
    —7C **62** (2D **150**)
Thameside. *Tedd* —7D **104**
Thameside Cen. *Bren* —6F **73**
Thameside Ind. Est. *E16* —2B **82**
Thameside Wlk. *SE28* —6A **68**
Thamesmere Dri. *SE28* —7A **68**
Thames Pl. *SW15* —3F **91**
    (in two parts)
Thamespoint. *Tedd* —7D **104**
Thames Quay. *E14* —3D **80**
Thames Quay. *SW10* —1A **92**
    (off Chelsea Harbour)
Thames Rd. *E16* —1B **82**
Thames Rd. *W4* —6G **73**
Thames Rd. *Bark* —3K **67**
Thames Rd. *Rich* —6G **73**
Thames Rd. Ind. Est. *E16* —2B **82**
Thames Side. *King T* —1D **118**
Thames St. *SE10* —6D **80**
Thames St. *King T* —2D **118**
Thames Vale Clo. *Houn* —2E **86**
Thames Village. *W4* —1J **89**
Thanescroft Gdns. *Croy* —3E **134**
Thanet Ct. *W3* —6G **57**
Thanet Dri. *Kes* —3B **138**
Thanet Pl. *Croy* —4C **134**
Thanet Rd. *Bex* —7G **101**
Thanet St. *WC1* —3J **61** (2E **142**)
Thane Vs. *N7* —3K **45**
Thane Works. *N7* —3K **45**
Thant Clo. *E10* —3D **48**
Tharp Rd. *Wall* —5H **133**
Thatcham Ct. *N20* —7F **5**
Thatcham Gdns. *N20* —7F **5**
Thatchers Way. *Iswth* —5H **87**
Thatches Gro. *Romf* —4E **36**
Thavie's Inn. *EC1*
    —6A **62** (7K **143**)
Thaxted Ho. *Dag* —7H **53**
Thaxted Pl. *SW20* —7F **107**
Thaxted Rd. *SE9* —2G **115**
Thaxted Rd. *Buck H* —1H **21**
Thaxton Rd. *W14* —6H **75**
Thayers Farm Rd. *Beck* —1A **126**
Thayer St. *W1* —6E **60** (6H **141**)
Theatre St. *SW11* —3D **92**
Theberton St. *N1* —1A **62**
Theed St. *SE1* —1A **78** (5K **149**)
Thelma Gdns. *SE3* —1B **98**
Thelma Gro. *Tedd* —6A **104**
Theobald Cres. *Harr* —1G **23**
Theobald Rd. *E17* —7C **32**
Theobald Rd. *Croy* —2B **134**
Theobalds Av. *N12* —4F **15**
Theobalds Ct. *N4* —3C **46**
Theobald's Rd. *WC1*
    —5K **61** (5G **143**)
Theobald St. *SE1*
    —3D **78** (2E **156**)
Theodore Ct. *SE13* —6F **97**
Theodore Rd. *SE13* —6F **97**
Therapia La. *Croy* —7H **123**
    (in two parts)

Therapia Rd. *SE22* —6J **95**
Theresa Rd. *W6* —4C **74**
Therfield Ct. *N4* —2C **46**
Thermopylae Ga. *E14* —4D **80**
Thesiger Rd. *SE20* —7K **111**
Thessaly Ho. *SW8* —7G **77**
    (off Thessaly Rd.)
Thessaly Rd. *SW8* —7G **77**
Thetford Clo. *N13* —6G **17**
Thetford Gdns. *Dag* —7E **52**
Thetford Rd. *Dag* —7D **52**
Thetford Rd. *N Mald* —6K **119**
Thetis Ter. *Rich* —6G **73**
Theydon Gro. *Wfd G* —6F **21**
Theydon Rd. *E5* —2J **47**
Theydon St. *E17* —7B **32**
Thicket Cres. *Sutt* —4A **132**
Thicket Gro. *SE20* —7G **111**
Thicket Gro. *Dag* —6C **52**
Thicket Rd. *SE20* —7G **111**
Thicket Rd. *Sutt* —4A **132**
Thickett Gro. *Dag* —6C **52**
Third Av. *E12* —4C **50**
Third Av. *E13* —3J **65**
Third Av. *E17* —5C **32**
Third Av. *W3* —1B **74**
Third Av. *W10* —3G **59**
Third Av. *Dag* —1H **69**
Third Av. *Enf* —5A **8**
Third Av. *Romf* —6C **36**
Third Av. *Wemb* —2D **40**
Third Cross Rd. *Twic* —2H **103**
Third Way. *Wemb* —4H **41**
Thirleby Rd. *SW1*
    —3D **77** (2B **154**)
Thirleby Rd. *Edgw* —1K **25**
Thirlestane Ct. *N10* —2E **28**
Thirlmere Av. *Gnfd* —3G **56**
Thirlmere Gdns. *Wemb* —1C **40**
Thirlmere Rise. *Brom* —6H **113**
Thirlmere Rd. *N10* —1F **29**
Thirlmere Rd. *SW16* —4H **109**
Thirlmere Rd. *Bexh* —1J **101**
Thirsk Clo. *N'holt* —6E **38**
Thirsk Rd. *SE25* —4D **124**
Thirsk Rd. *SW11* —3F **92**
Thirsk Rd. *Mitc* —7E **108**
Thistlebrook. *SE2* —2C **84**
Thistlecroft Gdns. *Stan* —1D **24**
Thistledene Av. *Harr* —3C **38**
Thistle Gro. *SW10* —5A **76**
Thistlemead. *Chst* —2F **129**
Thistlewaite Rd. *E5* —3H **47**
Thistlewood Clo. *N7* —2K **45**
Thistlewood Clo. *Iswth* —5H **71**
Thistleworth Marina. *Iswth*
    (off Railshead Rd.) —4B **88**
Thistley Clo. *N12* —6H **15**
Thomas A'Beckett Clo. *Wemb*
    —4K **39**
Thomas Baines Rd. *SW11*
    —3B **92**
Thomas Ct. *E17* —5D **32**
Thomas Cribb M. *E6* —6E **66**
Thomas Dinwiddy Rd. *SE12*
    —2K **113**
Thomas Doyle St. *SE1*
    —3B **78** (1A **156**)
Thomas England Ho. *Romf*
    (off Waterloo Gdns.) —6K **37**
Thomas Hewlett Ho. *Harr* —4J **39**
Thomas Ho. *Sutt* —7K **131**
Thomas La. *SE6* —7C **96**
Thomas More Ho. *EC2*
    —5C **62** (6C **144**)

Thomas More St. *E1* —7G **63**
Thomas More Way. *N2* —3A **28**
Thomas Neals Shop. Mall. *WC2*
    —6J **61** (2E **148**)
Thomas N. Ter. E16 —5H **65**
  (off Barking Rd.)
Thomas Pk. *King T* —6J **105**
Thomas Pl. *W8* —3K **75**
Thomas Rd. *E14* —6B **64**
Thomas Rd. Ind. Est. *E14* —5C **64**
Thomas St. *SE18* —4F **83**
Thomas Turner Path. T Hth
  (off George St.) —3C **124**
Thomas Wall Clo. *Sutt* —5K **131**
Thompson Av. *Rich* —3G **89**
Thompson Clo. *Ilf* —2G **51**
Thompson Rd. *SE22* —6F **95**
Thompson Rd. *Dag* —3F **53**
Thompson's Av. *SE5* —7C **78**
Thomson Cres. *Croy* —1A **134**
Thomson Ho. *SW1*
    —5H **77** (6C **154**)
Thomson Ho. S'hall —7C **54**
  (off Broadway, The)
Thomson Rd. *Harr* —3J **23**
Thorburn Sq. *SE1* —4G **79**
Thorburn Way. *SW19* —1B **122**
Thoresby St. *N1*
    —3C **62** (1D **144**)
Thorkhill Gdns. *Th Dit* —7A **118**
Thorkhill Rd. *Th Dit* —7A **118**
Thornaby Gdns. *N18* —6B **18**
Thorn Av. *Bush* —1B **10**
Thorn Bank. *Edgw* —6B **12**
Thornbury. *NW4* —4E **26**
  (off Prince of Wales Clo.)
Thornbury Av. *Iswth* —7H **71**
Thornbury Clo. *N16* —5E **46**
Thornbury Ct. W11 —7J **59**
  (off Chepstow Vs.)
Thornbury Ct. *Iswth* —7J **71**
Thornbury Rd. *SW2* —6J **93**
Thornbury Rd. *Iswth* —7H **71**
Thornbury Sq. *N6* —1G **45**
Thornby Rd. *E5* —3J **47**
Thorncliffe Rd. *SW2* —6J **93**
Thorncliffe Rd. *S'hall* —5D **70**
Thorn Clo. *Brom* —6E **128**
Thorn Clo. *N'holt* —3D **54**
Thorncombe Rd. *SE22* —5E **94**
Thorncroft Rd. *Sutt* —4K **131**
Thorncroft St. *SW8* —7J **77**
Thorndean St. *SW18* —2A **108**
Thorndene. *SE28* —7B **68**
Thorndene Av. *N11* —1K **15**
Thorndike Av. *N'holt* —1B **54**
Thorndike Clo. *SW10* —7A **76**
Thorndike St. *SW1*
    —4H **77** (4C **154**)
Thorndon Clo. *Orp* —2K **129**
Thorndon Gdns. *Eps* —5A **130**
Thorndon Rd. *Orp* —2K **129**
Thorne Clo. *E11* —4G **49**
Thorne Clo. *E16* —6J **65**
Thorne Clo. *Eri* —6H **85**
Thorneloe Gdns. *Croy* —5A **134**
Thorne Pas. *SW13* —2A **90**
Thorne Rd. *SW8* —7J **77**
Thornes Clo. *Beck* —3E **126**
Thorne St. *SW13* —3A **90**
Thornet Wood Rd. *Brom*
    —3E **128**
Thorney Ct. W8 —2A **76**
  (off Palace Ga.)
Thorney Cres. *SW11* —7B **76**

Thorney Hedge Rd. *W4* —4H **73**
Thorney St. *SW1*
    —4J **77** (3E **154**)
Thornfield Av. *NW7* —1G **27**
Thornfield Ct. *NW7* —1G **27**
Thornfield Rd. *W12* —2D **74**
Thornford Rd. *SE13* —5E **96**
Thorngate Rd. *W9* —4J **59**
Thorngrove Rd. *E13* —1K **65**
Thornham Gro. *E15* —5F **49**
Thornham St. *SE10* —6D **80**
Thornhaugh M. *WC1*
    —4H **61** (4D **142**)
Thornhaugh St. *WC1*
    —4H **61** (4D **142**)
Thornhill Av. *SE18* —7J **83**
Thornhill Cres. *N1* —7K **45**
Thornhill Gdns. *E10* —2D **48**
Thornhill Gdns. *Bark* —7J **51**
Thornhill Gro. *N1* —7K **45**
Thornhill Ho. *N1* —7A **46**
Thornhill Ho. W4 —5A **74**
  (off Wood St.)
Thornhill Point. *E9* —7J **47**
Thornhill Rd. *E10* —2D **48**
Thornhill Rd. *N1* —7A **46**
Thornhill Rd. *Croy* —7C **124**
Thornhill Sq. *N1* —7K **45**
Thornicroft Ho. SW9 —2K **93**
  (off Stockwell Rd.)
Thornlaw Rd. *SE27* —4A **110**
Thornley Clo. *N17* —7B **18**
Thornley Dri. *Harr* —2F **39**
Thornley Pl. *SE10* —5G **81**
Thornsbeach Rd. *SE6* —1E **112**
Thornsett Pl. *SE20* —2H **125**
Thornsett Rd. *SE20* —2H **125**
Thornsett Rd. *SW18* —1K **107**
Thornsett Ter. *SE20* —2H **125**
  (off Croydon Rd.)
Thorn Ter. *SE15* —3J **95**
Thornton Av. *SW2* —1H **109**
Thornton Av. *W4* —4A **74**
Thornton Av. *Croy* —6K **123**
Thornton Dene. *Beck* —2C **126**
Thornton Gdns. *SW12* —1H **109**
Thornton Heath Pond. (Junct.)
    —5A **124**
Thornton Hill. *SW19* —7G **107**
Thornton Pl. *W1*
    —5D **60** (5E **140**)
Thornton Rd. *E11* —2F **49**
Thornton Rd. *N18* —4D **18**
Thornton Rd. *SW12* —7H **93**
Thornton Rd. *SW14* —4K **89**
Thornton Rd. *SW19* —6F **107**
Thornton Rd. *Barn* —3B **4**
Thornton Rd. *Belv* —4H **85**
Thornton Rd. *Brom* —5J **113**
Thornton Rd. *Cars* —1B **132**
Thornton Rd. *Croy & T Hth*
    —7K **123**
Thornton Rd. *Ilf* —4F **51**
Thornton Rd. E. *SW19* —6F **107**
Thornton Row. *T Hth* —5A **124**
Thorntons Farm Av. *Romf*
    —1J **53**
Thornton St. *SW9* —2A **94**
Thornton Way. *NW11* —5K **27**
Thorntree Ct. *W5* —5E **56**
Thorntree Rd. *SE7* —5B **82**
Thornville Gro. *Mitc* —2B **122**
Thornville St. *SE8* —1C **96**
Thornwell Ct. W7 —2J **71**
  (off Du Burstow Ter.)

Thornwood Clo. *E18* —2K **33**
Thornwood Ho. *Buck H* —1H **21**
Thornwood Rd. *SE13* —5G **97**
Thornycroft Ho. *W4* —5A **74**
  (off Fraser St.)
Thorogood Gdns. *E15* —5G **49**
Thorogood Way. *Rain* —1K **69**
Thorold Rd. *N22* —7D **16**
Thorold Rd. *Ilf* —2F **51**
Thorparch Rd. *SW8* —1H **93**
Thorpebank Rd. *W12* —1C **74**
Thorpe Clo. *W10* —6G **59**
Thorpe Ct. *Enf* —3G **7**
Thorpe Cres. *E17* —2B **32**
Thorpedale Gdns. *Ilf* —4E **34**
Thorpedale Rd. *N4* —2J **45**
Thorpe Hall Rd. *E17* —1E **32**
Thorpe Ho. N1 —1K **61**
  (off Barnsbury Est.)
Thorpe Rd. *E6* —1D **66**
Thorpe Rd. *E7* —4H **49**
Thorpe Rd. *E17* —2E **32**
Thorpe Rd. *N15* —6E **30**
Thorpe Rd. *Bark* —7H **51**
Thorpe Rd. *King T* —7E **104**
Thorpewood Av. *SE26* —2H **111**
Thorsden Way. *SE19* —5E **110**
Thorverton Rd. *NW2* —3G **43**
Thoydon Rd. *E3* —2A **64**
Thrale Rd. *SW16* —5G **109**
Thrale St. *SE1* —1C **78** (5D **150**)
Thrasher Clo. *E8* —1F **63**
Thrawl St. *E1* —5F **63** (6K **145**)
Thrayle Ho. SW9 —3K **93**
  (off Benedict Rd.)
Threadgold Ho. N1 —6D **46**
  (off Dovercourt Est.)
Threadneedle St. *EC2*
    —6D **62** (1F **151**)
Three Bridges Bus. Cen. *S'hall*
    —2G **71**
Three Colt Corner. E2 & E1
  (off Cheshire St.) —4G **63**
Three Colts La. *E2* —4H **63**
Three Colt St. *E14* —6B **64**
Three Corners. *Bexh* —2H **101**
Three Cranes Wlk. *EC4*
    —7C **62** (3D **150**)
Three Cups Yd. *WC1*
    —5K **61** (6H **143**)
Three Kings Yd. *W1*
    —7F **61** (2J **147**)
Three Mill La. *E3* —3E **64**
Three Oak La. *SE1*
    —2F **79** (6J **151**)
Three Quays. *EC3*
    —7E **62** (3H **151**)
Threshers Pl. *W11* —7G **59**
Thriftwood. *SE26* —3J **111**
Thring Ho. SW9 —2K **93**
  (off Stockwell Rd.)
Throckmorten Rd. *E16* —6K **65**
Throgmorton Av. *EC2*
    —6D **62** (7F **145**)
Throgmorton St. *EC2*
    —6D **62** (7F **145**)
Throwley Clo. *SE2* —3C **84**
Throwley Rd. *Sutt* —5K **131**
Throwley Way. *Sutt* —4K **131**
Thrupp Clo. *Mitc* —2F **123**
Thrush Grn. *Harr* —4E **22**
Thrush St. *SE17*
    —5C **78** (5C **156**)
Thruxton Way. *SE15* —7F **79**
Thurbarn Rd. *SE6* —5D **112**

Thurland Rd. *SE16* —3G **79**
Thurlby Clo. *Harr* —6A **24**
Thurlby Clo. *Wfd G* —5J **21**
Thurlby Croft. *NW4* —3E **26**
  (off Mulberry Clo.)
Thurlby Rd. *SE27* —4A **110**
Thurlby Rd. *Wemb* —6D **40**
Thurleigh Av. *SW12* —6E **92**
Thurleigh Rd. *SW12* —7D **92**
Thurleston Av. *Mord* —5G **121**
Thurlestone Av. *N12* —6H **15**
Thurlestone Av. *Ilf* —4K **51**
Thurlestone Ct. S'hall —6F **55**
  (off Howard Rd.)
Thurlestone Rd. *SE27* —3A **110**
Thurloe Clo. *SW7*
    —4C **76** (3C **152**)
Thurloe Pl. *SW7*
    —4B **76** (3B **152**)
Thurloe Pl. M. *SW7*
    —4B **76** (3B **152**)
Thurloe Sq. *SW7*
    —4C **76** (3C **152**)
Thurloe St. *SW7*
    —4B **76** (3B **152**)
Thurlow Clo. *E4* —6K **19**
Thurlow Gdns. *Wemb* —5D **40**
Thurlow Hill. *SE21* —1C **110**
Thurlow Ho. *SW16* —3J **109**
Thurlow Pk. Rd. *SE21* —2B **110**
Thurlow Rd. *NW3* —5B **44**
Thurlow Rd. *W7* —2A **72**
Thurlow St. *SE17*
    —5D **78** (5F **157**)
Thurlow Ter. *NW5* —5E **44**
Thurlow Wlk. *SE17*
    —5E **78** (5G **157**)
Thurnby Ct. *Twic* —3J **103**
Thursland Rd. *Sidc* —5C **116**
Thursley Cres. *New Ad* —7F **137**
Thursley Gdns. *SW19* —2F **107**
Thursley Ho. *SW2* —7K **93**
  (off Holmewood Gdns.)
Thursley Rd. *SE9* —3D **114**
Thurso Ho. *NW6* —2K **59**
Thurso St. *SW17* —4B **108**
Thurstan Rd. *SW20* —7D **106**
Thurston Ind. Est. *SE13* —3D **96**
Thurston Rd. *SE13* —2D **96**
Thurston Rd. *S'hall* —6D **54**
Thurtle Rd. *E2* —2F **63**
Thwaite Clo. *Eri* —6J **85**
Thyra Gro. *N12* —6E **14**
Tibbatts Rd. *E3* —4D **64**
Tibbenham Wlk. *E13* —2H **65**
Tibberton Sq. *N1* —7C **46**
Tibbet's Clo. *SW19* —1F **107**
Tibbet's Corner. (Junct.) —7F **91**
Tibbet's Ride. *SW15* —7F **91**
Tiber Gdns. *N1* —1J **61**
Ticehurst Clo. *Orp* —7A **116**
Ticehurst Rd. *SE23* —2A **112**
Tickford Clo. *SE2* —2C **84**
Tickford Ho. *NW8*
    —3C **60** (2C **140**)
Tidal Basin Rd. *E16* —7H **65**
Tidemore Ho. SW8 —7G **77**
  (off Savona St.)
Tidenham Gdns. *Croy* —3E **134**
Tideswell Rd. *SW15* —4E **90**
Tideswell Rd. *Croy* —3D **136**
Tideway Clo. *Rich* —4B **104**
Tideway Ind. Est. SW8 —6G **77**
  (off Kirtling St.)
Tideway Wlk. *SW8* —6G **77**

Tidey St. *E3* —5C **64**
Tidford Rd. *Well* —2K **99**
Tidworth Rd. *E3* —4C **64**
Tiepigs La. *W Wick & Brom*
    —2G **137**
Tierney Ct. *Croy* —2F **135**
Tierney Rd. *SW2* —1J **109**
Tiger La. *Brom* —4K **127**
Tiger Way. *E5* —4H **47**
Tiger La. Studios. *W10*
Tilbrook Rd. *SE3* —3A **98**
Tilbury Clo. *SE15* —7F **79**
Tilbury Rd. *E6* —2D **66**
Tilbury Rd. *E10* —7E **32**
Tildesley Rd. *SW15* —6E **90**
Tilehurst Point. *SE2* —2D **84**
Tilehurst Rd. *SW18* —1B **108**
Tilehurst Rd. *Sutt* —5G **131**
Tile Kiln La. *N6* —1F **45**
Tile Kiln La. *N13* —5H **17**
Tile Kiln La. *Bex* —2J **117**
  (in two parts)
Tile Kiln Studios. *N6* —1G **45**
Tile Yd. *E14* —6B **64**
Tileyard Rd. *N7* —7J **45**
Tilford Av. *New Ad* —7E **136**
Tilford Gdns. *SW19* —1F **107**
Tilford Ho. SW2 —7K **93**
  (off Holmewood Gdns.)
Tilia Rd. *E5* —4H **47**
Tiller Rd. *E14* —3C **80**
Tillett Clo. *NW10* —6J **41**
Tillett Sq. *SE16* —2A **80**
Tillett Way. *E2* —3G **63**
Tillingbourne Gdns. *N3* —3H **27**
Tillingbourne Grn. *Orp* —4K **129**
Tillingbourne Way. *N3* —4H **27**
Tillingham Way. *N12* —4D **14**
Tilling Rd. *NW2* —1E **42**
Tilling Way. *Wemb* —3D **40**
Tilman St. *E1* —6H **63**
Tilson Clo. *N1* —7K **45**
Tilson Gdns. *SW2* —7J **93**
Tilson Ho. *SW2* —7J **93**
Tilson Rd. *N17* —1G **31**
Tilston Clo. *E11* —3H **49**
Tilton St. *SW6* —6G **75**
Tiltwood, The. *W3* —7J **57**
Tilt Yd. App. *SE9* —6D **98**
Timber Clo. *Chst* —2E **128**
Timbercroft. *Eps* —4A **130**
Timbercroft La. *SE18* —6J **83**
Timberdene. *NW4* —2F **27**
Timberdene Av. *Ilf* —1F **35**
Timberland Clo. *SE15* —7G **79**
Timberland Rd. *E1* —6H **63**
Timber Mill Way. *SW4* —3H **93**
Timberslip Dri. *Wall* —7H **133**
Timber Wharf Rd. *N16* —6G **31**
Timbrell Pl. *SE16* —1B **80**
Time Sq. *E8* —5F **47**
Times Sq. *Sutt* —5K **131**

Timothy Clo. SW4 —5G 93
Timothy Clo. Bexh —5E 100
Timothy Ho. Eri —2E 84
(off Kale Rd.)
Timothy Rd. E3 —5B 64
Timsbury Wlk. SW15 —1C 106
Tindal St. SW9 —1B 94
Tinderbox All. SW14 —3K 89
Tinniswood Clo. N5 —5A 46
Tinsley Rd. E1 —5J 63
Tintagel Cres. SE22 —4F 95
Tintagel Dri. Stan —4J 11
Tintagel Gdns. SE22 —4F 95
Tintern Av. NW9 —3H 25
Tintern Clo. SW15 —5G 91
Tintern Clo. SW19 —6A 108
Tintern Ct. W13 —7A 56
Tintern Gdns. N14 —7D 6
Tintern Path. NW9 —6A 26
(off Fryent Gro.)
Tintern Rd. N22 —1C 30
Tintern Rd. Cars —1B 132
Tintern St. SW4 —4J 93
Tintern Way. Harr —1F 39
Tinto Rd. E16 —4J 65
Tinworth St. SE11
 —5K 77 (5F 155)
Tippett Ct. E6 —2D 66
Tippetts Clo. Enf —1H 7
Tipthorpe Rd. SW11 —3E 92
Tipton Dri. Croy —4E 134
Tiptree Clo. E4 —3K 19
Tiptree Cres. Ilf —3E 34
Tiptree Dri. Enf —4J 7
Tiptree Rd. Ruis —4A 38
Tiree Clo. Rich —1D 104
Tirlemont Rd. S Croy —7C 134
Tirrell Rd. Croy —6C 124
Tisbury Ct. W1 —7H 61 (2C 148)
Tisbury Rd. SW16 —2J 123
Tisdall Pl. SE17 —4D 78 (4F 157)
Titchborne Row. W2
 —6C 60 (1D 146)
Titchfield Rd. NW8 —2D 60
Titchfield Rd. Cars —1B 132
Titchfield Wlk. Cars —7B 122
Titchwell Rd. SW18 —1B 108
Tite St. SW3 —5D 76 (6E 152)
Tithe Barn Clo. King T —1F 119
Tithe Barn Way. N'holt —2A 54
Tithe Clo. NW7 —1C 26
Tithe Farm Av. Harr —3E 38
Tithe Farm Clo. Harr —3E 38
Tithe Wlk. NW7 —1C 26
Titian Av. Bush —1D 10
Titley Clo. E4 —5H 19
Titmuss Av. SE28 —7B 68
Titmuss St. W12 —2D 74
Tivendale. N8 —3J 29
Tiverton Av. Ilf —3E 34
Tiverton Dri. SE9 —1G 115
Tiverton Rd. N15 —6D 30
Tiverton Rd. N18 —5K 17
Tiverton Rd. NW10 —1F 59
Tiverton Rd. Edgw —2F 25
Tiverton Rd. Houn —2G 87
Tiverton Rd. T Hth —5A 124
Tiverton Rd. Wemb —2E 56
Tiverton St. SE1
 —3C 78 (2C 156)
Tivoli Ct. SE16 —1B 80
Tivoli Gdns. SE18 —4C 82
Tivoli Rd. N8 —5H 29
Tivoli Rd. SE27 —5C 110
Tivoli Rd. Houn —4C 86

Toad La. Houn —4D 86
Tobacco Dock. E1 —7H 63
Tobacco Quay. E1 —7H 63
Tobago St. E14 —2C 80
Tobin Clo. NW3 —7C 44
Toby Ct. N9 —7D 8
(off Tramway Av.)
Toby La. E1 —4A 64
Todd Ho. N2 —2B 28
(off Grange, The)
Todds Wlk. N7 —2K 45
Todhunter Ter. Barn —4D 4
Tokenhouse Yd. EC2
 —6D 62 (7E 144)
Token Yd. SW15 —4G 91
Tokyngton Av. Wemb —6G 41
Toland Sq. SW15 —5C 90
Tolcairn Ct. Belv —5G 85
Tolcarne Dri. Pinn —3A 22
Toley Av. Wemb —7E 24
Toll Bar Ct. Sutt —7K 131
Tollbridge Clo. W10 —4G 59
Tollesbury Gdns. Ilf —3H 35
Tollet St. E1 —4K 63
Tollgate Dri. SE21 —2E 110
Tollgate Gdns. NW6 —2K 59
Tollgate Rd. E16 & E6 —5A 66
Tollgate Sq. E6 —5D 66
Tollhouse Way. N19 —2G 45
Tollington Pk. N4 —2K 45
Tollington Pl. N4 —2K 45
Tollington Rd. N7 —4K 45
Tollington Way. N7 —3J 45
Tolmers Sq. NW1
 —4G 61 (3B 142)
Tolpaide Ho. SE11
 —5A 78 (4J 155)
Tolpuddle Av. E13 —1A 66
(off Queens Rd.)
Tolpuddle St. N1 —2A 62
Tolsford Rd. E5 —5H 47
Tolson Rd. Iswth —3A 88
Tolverne Rd. SW20 —1E 120
Tolworth Gdns. Romf —5D 36
Tolworth Pde. Chad H —5E 36
Tolworth Rise N. Surb —7H 119
Tolworth Rise S. Surb —7H 119
Tomahawk Gdns. N'holt —3B 54
Tom Coombs Clo. SE9 —4C 98
Tom Cribb Rd. SE28 —3G 83
Tom Groves Clo. E15 —5F 49
Tom Hood Clo. E15 —5F 49
Tom Jenkinson Rd. E16 —1K 81
Tomkyns Ho. SE11
 —4A 78 (3J 155)
Tomlins All. Twic —1A 104
Tomlin's Gro. E3 —3C 64
Tomlinson Clo. E2
 —3F 63 (2K 145)
Tomlinson Clo. W4 —5H 73
Tomlins Orchard. Bark —1G 67
Tomlins Ter. E14 —6A 64
Tomlins Wlk. N7 —2K 45
Tom Mann Clo. Bark —1J 67
Tom Nolan Clo. E15 —2G 65
Tom Oakman Cen. E4 —3A 20
Tompion St. EC1
 —3B 62 (2B 144)
Tom Smith Clo. SE10 —6G 81
Tomswood Ct. Ilf —1G 35
Tomswood Hill. Ilf —6C 21
Tomswood Rd. Chig —6K 21
Tom Williams Ho. SW6 —6H 75
(off Clem Attlee Ct.)
Tonbridge Cres. Harr —4E 24

Tonbridge Ho. SE15 —7F 79
(off Nutt St.)
Tonbridge St. WC1
 —3J 61 (1E 142)
Tonbridge Wlk. WC1
 —3J 61 (1E 142)
Tonfield Rd. Sutt —1H 131
Tonge Clo. Beck —5C 126
Tonge Vs. Beck —5C 126
Tonsley Hill. SW18 —5K 91
Tonsley Pl. SW18 —5K 91
Tonsley Rd. SW18 —5K 91
Tonsley St. SW18 —5K 91
Tonstall Rd. Mitc —2E 122
Tons Way. SW11 —3A 92
Tony Cannell M. E3 —3B 64
Tony Law Ho. SE20 —1H 125
Tooke Clo. Pinn —1C 22
Took's Ct. EC4 —6A 62 (7J 143)
Tooley St. SE1 —1D 78 (4F 151)
Toorack Rd. Harr —2H 23
Tooting Bec Gdns. SW16
 —4H 109
Tooting Bec Rd. SW17 & SW16
 —3E 108
Tooting B'way. SW17 —5C 108
Tooting Gro. SW17 —5C 108
Tooting High St. SW17 —5C 108
Tooting Mkt. SW17 —4D 108
Tootswood Rd. Brom —5G 127
Topaz Wlk. NW2 —7E 26
Topham Sq. N17 —1C 30
Topham St. EC1 —4A 62 (3J 143)
Top Ho. Rise. E4 —7K 9
Topiary Sq. Rich —3F 89
Topley St. SE9 —4A 98
Topmast Point. E14 —2C 80
Topp Wlk. NW2 —2E 42
Topsfield Clo. N8 —5H 29
Topsfield Pde. N8 —5J 29
Topsfield Rd. N8 —5J 29
Topsham Rd. SW17 —3D 108
Torbay Ct. NW1 —7F 45
Torbay Man. NW6 —1H 59
(off Willesden La.)
Torbay Rd. NW6 —7H 43
Torbay Rd. Harr —2C 38
Torbay St. NW1 —7F 45
Torbitt Way. Ilf —5K 35
Torbridge Clo. Edgw —7K 11
Torbrook Clo. Bex —6E 100
Torcross Dri. SE23 —2J 111
Torcross Rd. Ruis —3A 38
Tor Gdns. W8 —2J 75
Tor Ho. N6 —6F 29
Tormead Clo. Sutt —6J 131
Tormount Rd. SE18 —6J 83
Torney Ho. E9 —7J 47
Toronto Av. E12 —4D 50
Toronto Rd. E11 —4F 49
Toronto Rd. Ilf —1F 51
Torquay Gdns. Ilf —4B 34
Torquay St. W2 —5K 59
Torrance Clo. SE7 —6B 82
Torrens Ct. SE5 —3D 94
Torrens Rd. E15 —6H 49
Torrens Rd. SW2 —5K 93
Torrens Sq. E15 —6H 49
Torre Wlk. Cars —1C 132
Torriano Av. NW5 —5H 45
Torriano Cotts. NW5 —5H 45
Torriano M. NW5 —5G 45
Torridge Gdns. SE15 —4J 95
Torridge Rd. T Hth —5B 124

Torridon Ho. SE6 & SE13 —7F 97
Torrington Av. N12 —5G 15
Torrington Clo. N12 —4G 15
Torrington Ct. SE26 —5G 111
(off Crystal Pal. Pk. Rd.)
Torrington Dri. Harr —3F 39
Torrington Gdns. N11 —6C 16
Torrington Gdns. Gnfd —1C 56
Torrington Gro. N12 —5H 15
Torrington Pk. N12 —5F 15
Torrington Pl. E1 —1G 79
Torrington Pl. WC1
 —5H 61 (5C 142)
Torrington Rd. E18 —3J 33
Torrington Rd. Dag —1F 53
Torrington Rd. Gnfd —1C 56
Torrington Sq. WC1
 —4H 61 (4D 142)
Torrington Sq. Croy —7D 124
Torrington Way. Mord —6J 121
Tor Rd. Well —1C 100
Torr Rd. SE20 —7K 111
Torver Rd. Harr —4J 23
Torwood Rd. SW15 —5C 90
Tothill St. SW1 —2H 77 (7C 148)
Totnes Rd. Well —7B 84
Totnes Wlk. N2 —4B 28
Tottenhall Rd. N13 —6F 17
Tottenham Ct. Rd. W1
 —4G 61 (4B 142)
Tottenham Grn. E. N15 —4F 31
Tottenham Hale Gyratory. (Junct.)
 —3F 31
Tottenham Hale Retail Pk. N15
 —4G 31
Tottenham La. N8 —6J 29
Tottenham M. W1
 —5G 61 (5B 142)
Tottenham Rd. N1 —6E 46
Tottenham St. W1
 —5G 61 (6B 142)
Totterdown St. SW17 —4D 108
Totteridge Comn. N20 —7H 5
Totteridge Grn. N20 —2D 14
Totteridge La. N20 —2D 14
Totteridge Village. N20 —1B 14
Totternhoe Clo. Harr —5C 24
Totton Rd. T Hth —3A 124
Toulmin St. SE1 —2C 78 (7C 150)
Toulon St. SE5 —7C 78
Tournay Rd. SW6 —7H 75
Tours Pas. SW11 —4A 92
Toussaint Wlk. SE16 —3G 79
Tovil Clo. SE20 —2H 125
Towcester Rd. E3 —4D 64
Tower Bri. SE1 & E1
 —1F 79 (5J 151)
Tower Bri. App. E1
 —7F 63 (4J 151)
Tower Bri. Bus. Complex. SE16
(off Clement's Rd.) —3G 79
Tower Bridge Plaza. SE1
 —1F 79 (5J 151)
Tower Bri. Rd. SE1
 —3E 78 (2G 157)
Tower Bri. Sq. SE1
 —2F 79 (6J 151)
Tower Bri. Wharf. E1
 —1G 79 (5K 151)
Tower Bldgs. E1 —1H 79
Tower Clo. NW3 —5B 44
Tower Clo. SE20 —7H 111
Tower Ct. E5 —7F 31
Tower Ct. WC2 —6J 61 (1E 148)
Tower Gdns. Rd. N17 —1C 30

Tower Hamlets Rd. E7 —4H 49
Tower Hamlets Rd. E17 —3C 32
Tower Hill. EC3 —7E 62 (3H 151)
Tower Hill. (Junct.) —7F 63
Tower Hill Ter. EC3
 —7E 62 (3H 151)
Tower Ho. E1 —5G 63
(off Fieldgate St.)
Tower La. Wemb —3D 40
Tower M. E17 —4C 32
Tower Pl. EC3 —7E 62 (3H 151)
Tower Rise. Rich —3E 88
Tower Rd. NW10 —7C 42
Tower Rd. Belv —4J 85
Tower Rd. Bexh —4G 101
Tower Rd. Twic —3K 103
Tower Royal. EC4
 —7D 62 (2E 150)
Towers Bus. Pk. Wemb —4H 41
(off Carey Way)
Towers Pl. Rich —5E 88
Towers Rd. Pinn —1C 22
Towers Rd. S'hall —4E 54
Tower St. WC2 —6J 61 (1E 148)
Tower Ter. N22 —2K 29
Tower View. Croy —7A 126
Towgar Ct. N20 —7F 5
Towncourt Cres. Orp —5G 129
Towncourt La. Orp —6H 129
Towncourt Path. N4 —1C 46
Towney Mead. N'holt —2D 54
Towney Mead Ct. N'holt —2D 54
Town Field Way. Iswth —2A 88
Town Hall App. N16 —4D 46
(off Albion Rd.)
Town Hall App. Rd. N15 —4F 31
Town Hall Av. W4 —5K 73
Town Hall Rd. SW11 —3D 92
Townholm Cres. W7 —3K 71
Townley Ct. E15 —6H 49
Townley Rd. SE22 —5E 94
Townley Rd. Bexh —5F 101
Townley St. SE17
 —5D 78 (5E 156)
Townmead Bus. Cen. SW6
 —3A 92
Town Meadow. Bren —6D 72
Town Meadow Rd. Bren —7D 72
Townmead Rd. SW6 —3K 91
Townmead Rd. Rich —2H 89
Town Quay. Bark —1F 67
Town Rd. N9 —2C 18
Townsend Av. N14 —4C 16
Townsend Ind. Est. NW10 —2J 57
Townsend La. NW9 —7K 25
Townsend Rd. N15 —5F 31
Townsend Rd. S'hall —1C 70
Townsend St. SE17
 —4E 78 (3G 157)
Townsend Yd. N6 —1F 45
Townshend Clo. Sidc —6B 116
Townshend Ct. NW8 —2D 60
(off Townshend Rd.)
Townshend Est. NW8 —2C 60
Townshend Rd. NW8 —1C 60
Townshend Rd. Chst —5F 115
Townshend Rd. Rich —4F 89
Townshend Ter. Rich —4F 89
Towns Ho. SW4 —3H 93
Town Sq. Iswth —3B 88
(off Swan St.)

Town, The. *Enf* —3J **7**
Town Wharf. *Iswth* —3B **88**
Towpath, The. *SW10* —1B **92**
Towpath Wlk. *E9* —5B **48**
Towpath Way. *Croy* —6F **125**
Towton Rd. *SE27* —2C **110**
Toynbec Clo. *Chst* —4F **115**
Toynbee Rd. *SW20* —1G **121**
Toynbee St. *E1* —5F **63** (6J **145**)
Toyne Way. *N6* —6D **28**
Tracey Av. *NW2* —5E **42**
Tracey St. *SE11*
　　　　—5A **78** (5J **155**)
Tracy Ct. *Stan* —7H **11**
Trade Clo. *N13* —4F **17**
Trader Rd. *E6* —6F **67**
Tradescant Rd. *SW8* —7J **77**
Tradewinds Ct. *E1* —7G **63**
Trading Est. Rd. *NW10* —4J **57**
Trafalgar Av. *N17* —6K **17**
Trafalgar Av. *SE15*
　　　　—5F **79** (6K **157**)
Trafalgar Av. *Wor Pk* —1F **131**
Trafalgar Bus. Cen. *Bark* —4K **67**
Trafalgar Clo. *SE16* —4A **80**
Trafalgar Gdns. *E1* —5K **63**
Trafalgar Gro. *SE10* —6F **81**
Trafalgar Pl. *E11* —4J **33**
Trafalgar Pl. *N18* —5B **18**
Trafalgar Rd. *SE10* —6F **81**
Trafalgar Rd. *SW19* —7K **107**
Trafalgar Rd. *Twic* —2H **103**
Trafalgar Sq. *WC2* & *SW1*
　　　　—1H **77** (4D **148**)
Trafalgar St. *SE17*
　　　　—5D **78** (5E **156**)
Trafalgar Ter. *Harr* —1J **39**
Trafalgar Trad. Est. *Enf* —4F **9**
Trafalgar Way. *E14* —1E **80**
Trafalgar Way. *Croy* —2A **134**
Trafford Clo. *E15* —5D **48**
Trafford Ho. *N1* —2D **62**
　(off Cranston Est.)
Trafford Rd. *T Hth* —5K **123**
Tralee Ct. *SE16* —5H **79**
　(off Masters Dri.)
Tramway Av. *E15* —7G **49**
Tramway Av. *N9* —7C **8**
Tramway Path. *Mitc* —4C **122**
　(in two parts)
Tranley M. *NW3* —4C **44**
Tranmere Ct. *Sutt* —7A **132**
Tranmere Rd. *N9* —7A **8**
Tranmere Rd. *SW18* —2A **108**
Tranmere Rd. *Twic* —7F **87**
Tranquil Pas. *SE3* —2H **97**
Tranquil Vale. *SE3* —2G **97**
Transay Wlk. *N1* —6D **46**
Transept St. *NW1*
　　　　—5C **60** (6D **140**)
Transmere Clo. *Orp* —6G **129**
Transmere Rd. *Orp* —6G **129**
Transom Clo. *SE16* —4B **80**
Transom Sq. *E14* —5D **80**
Transport Av. *Bren* —5A **72**
Tranton Rd. *SE16* —3G **79**
Traps La. *N Mald* —1A **120**
Trash Pl. *N11* —5A **16**
Travellers Way. *Houn* —2A **86**
Travers Clo. *E17* —1K **31**
Travers Rd. *N7* —3A **46**
Travis Ho. *SE10* —1E **96**
Treacy Clo. *Bush* —2B **10**
Treadgold St. *W11* —7F **59**
Treadway St. *E2* —2H **63**

Treasury Pas. *SW1*
　　　　—2J **77** (6E **148**)
Treaty Cen. *Houn* —3F **87**
Treaty St. *N1* —1K **61**
Trebeck St. *W1* —1F **77** (4J **147**)
Trebovir Rd. *SW5* —5J **75**
Treby St. *E3* —4B **64**
Trecastle Way. *N7* —4H **45**
Tredegar M. *E3* —3B **64**
Tredegar Rd. *E3* —2B **64**
Tredegar Rd. *N11* —7C **16**
Tredegar Sq. *E3* —3B **64**
Tredegar Ter. *E3* —3B **64**
Trederwen Rd. *E8* —1G **63**
Tredown Rd. *SE26* —5J **111**
Tredwell Clo. *Brom* —4C **128**
Tredwell Rd. *SE27* —4B **110**
Tree Clo. *Rich* —1D **104**
Treen Av. *SW13* —3B **90**
Tree Rd. *E16* —6A **66**
Tree Top M. *Dag* —6K **53**
Treetops Clo. *SE2* —5E **84**
Treeview Clo. *SE19* —1E **124**
Treewall Gdns. *Brom* —4K **113**
Trefgarne Rd. *Dag* —2G **53**
Trefil Wlk. *N7* —4J **45**
Trefoil Ho. *Eri* —2E **84**
　(off Kale Rd.)
Trefoil Rd. *SW18* —5A **92**
Tregaron Av. *N8* —6J **29**
Tregaron Gdns. *N Mald* —4A **120**
Tregarvon Rd. *SW11* —4E **92**
Tregenna Av. *Harr* —4E **38**
Tregenna Clo. *N14* —5B **6**
Tregenna Ct. *S Harr* —4E **38**
Trego Rd. *E9* —7C **48**
Tregothnan Rd. *SW9* —3J **93**
Tregunter Rd. *SW10* —6A **76**
Trehearn Rd. *Ilf* —1H **35**
Treherne Ct. *SW9* —1B **94**
Treherne Ct. *SW17* —4E **108**
Trehern Rd. *SW14* —3K **89**
Trehurst St. *E5* —5A **48**
Trelawney Est. *E9* —6J **47**
Trelawney Rd. *Ilf* —1H **35**
Trelawn Rd. *E10* —3E **48**
Trelawn Rd. *SW2* —5A **94**
Trelawny Clo. *E17* —4D **32**
Trellis Sq. *E3* —3B **64**
Treloar Gdns. *SE19* —6D **110**
Tremadoc Rd. *SW4* —4H **93**
Tremaine Clo. *SE4* —2C **96**
Tremaine Rd. *SE20* —2H **125**
Trematon Pl. *Tedd* —7C **104**
Tremlett Gro. *N19* —3G **45**
Tremlett M. *N19* —3G **45**
Trenance Gdns. *Ilf* —3A **52**
Trenchard Clo. *NW9* —1A **26**
Trenchard Clo. *Stan* —6F **11**
Trenchard Ct. *NW4* —5C **26**
Trenchard St. *SE10* —5F **81**
Trenchold St. *SW8* —6J **77**
Trenholme Clo. *SE20* —7H **111**
Trenholme Rd. *SE20* —7H **111**
Trenholme Ter. *SE20* —7H **111**
Trenmar Gdns. *NW10* —3D **58**
Trent Av. *W5* —3C **72**
Trent Gdns. *N14* —6A **6**
Trentham St. *SW18* —1J **107**
Trent Ho. *SE15* —4J **95**
Trent Rd. *SW2* —5K **93**
Trent Rd. *Buck H* —1E **20**
Trent Way. *Wor Pk* —3E **130**
Trentwood Side. *Enf* —3E **6**

Treport St. *SW18* —7K **91**
Tresco Clo. *Brom* —6G **113**
Trescoe Gdns. *Harr* —7C **22**
Tresco Gdns. *Ilf* —2A **52**
Tresco Ho. *SE11*
　　　　—5A **78** (5J **155**)
Tresco Rd. *SE15* —4H **95**
Tresham Cres. *NW8*
　　　　—4C **60** (3C **140**)
Tresham Rd. *Bark* —7K **51**
Tresham Wlk. *E9* —5J **47**
Tresilian Av. *N21* —5E **6**
Tressell Clo. *N1* —7B **46**
Tressider Ho. *SW4* —7H **93**
Tressillian Cres. *SE4* —3C **96**
Tressillian Rd. *SE4* —4B **96**
Tress Pl. *SE1* —1B **78** (4A **150**)
Trestis Clo. *Hayes* —4B **54**
Treswell Rd. *Dag* —1E **68**
Tretawn Gdns. *NW7* —4F **13**
Tretawn Pk. *NW7* —4F **13**
Trevanion Rd. *W14* —5G **75**
Treve Av. *Harr* —7G **23**
Trevelyan Av. *E12* —4D **50**
Trevelyan Cres. *Harr* —7D **24**
Trevelyan Gdns. *NW10* —1E **58**
Trevelyan Rd. *E15* —4H **49**
Trevelyan Rd. *SW17* —5C **108**
Trevenna Ho. *SE23* —3K **111**
　(off Dacres Rd.)
Trevera Ct. *Enf* —5F **9**
Treveris St. *SE1* —1B **78** (5B **150**)
Treverton St. *W10* —5F **59**
Treverton Towers. *W10* —5F **59**
　(off Treverton St.)
Treville St. *SW15* —7D **90**
Treviso Rd. *SE23* —2K **111**
Trevithick St. *SE8* —6C **80**
Trevone Ct. *SW2* —7J **93**
　(off Doverfield Rd.)
Trevone Gdns. *Pinn* —6C **22**
Trevor Clo. *Brom* —7H **127**
Trevor Clo. *E Barn* —6G **5**
Trevor Clo. *Harr* —7E **10**
Trevor Clo. *Iswth* —5K **87**
Trevor Clo. *N'holt* —2A **54**
Trevor Gdns. *Edgw* —1K **25**
Trevor Gdns. *N'holt* —2A **54**
Trevor Pl. *SW7* —2C **76** (7D **146**)
Trevor Rd. *SW19* —7G **107**
Trevor Rd. *Edgw* —1K **25**
Trevor Rd. *Wfd G* —7D **20**
Trevor Sq. *SW7* —2D **76** (7E **146**)
Trevor St. *SW7* —2C **76** (7D **146**)
Trevose Rd. *E17* —1F **33**
Trewince Rd. *SW20* —1E **120**
Trewint St. *SW18* —2A **108**
Trewsbury Ho. *SE2* —1D **84**
Trewsbury Rd. *SE26* —5K **111**
Triandra Way. *Hayes* —5B **54**
Triangle Cen. *S'hall* —1H **71**
Triangle Ct. *E16* —5B **66**
Triangle Pas. *Barn* —4E **5**
Triangle Pl. *SW4* —4H **93**
Triangle Rd. *E8* —1H **63**
Triangle, The. *E8* —1H **63**
Triangle, The. *EC1*
　　　　—4B **62** (3B **144**)
Triangle, The. *N13* —4F **17**
Triangle, The. *Bark* —6G **51**
Triangle, The. *King T* —2J **119**
Trickett Ho. *Sutt* —7K **131**
Trident Gdns. *N'holt* —3B **54**
Trident St. *SE16* —4K **79**
Trident Way. *S'hall* —3A **70**

Trig La. *EC4* —7C **62** (2C **150**)
Trigon Rd. *SW8* —7K **77**
Trilby Rd. *SE23* —2K **111**
Trillo Ct. *Ilf* —7J **35**
Trimmer Wlk. *Bren* —6E **72**
Trinder Gdns. *N19* —1J **45**
Trinder Rd. *N19* —1J **45**
Trinder Rd. *Barn* —5A **4**
Tring Av. *W5* —1F **73**
Tring Av. *S'hall* —6D **54**
Tring Av. *Wemb* —6G **41**
Tring Clo. *Ilf* —5H **35**
Tring Ct. *Twic* —4A **104**
Trinidad Gdns. *Dag* —7K **53**
Trinidad St. *E14* —7B **64**
Trinity Av. *N2* —3B **28**
Trinity Av. *Enf* —6A **8**
Trinity Bus. Cen. *SE16* —2B **80**
Trinity Bus. Pk. *E4* —6G **19**
Trinity Chu. Pas. *EC4*
　　　　—6A **62** (7K **143**)
Trinity Chu. Pas. *SW13* —6D **74**
Trinity Chu. Rd. *SW13* —6D **74**
Trinity Chu. Sq. *SE1*
　　　　—3C **78** (1D **156**)
Trinity Clo. *E8* —6F **47**
Trinity Clo. *E11* —2G **49**
Trinity Clo. *NW3* —4B **44**
Trinity Clo. *SE13* —4F **97**
Trinity Clo. *SW4* —4G **93**
Trinity Clo. *Brom* —1C **138**
Trinity Clo. *Houn* —4C **86**
Trinity Clo. *S Croy* —7E **134**
Trinity Cotts. *Rich* —3F **89**
Trinity Ct. *N1* —1E **62**
Trinity Ct. *SE7* —4B **82**
Trinity Ct. *SE25* —6E **124**
Trinity Ct. *SE26* —3J **111**
Trinity Ct. *Croy* —2C **134**
Trinity Ct. *Enf* —2H **7**
Trinity Cres. *SW17* —2D **108**
Trinity Gdns. *SW9* —4K **93**
Trinity Gro. *SE10* —1E **96**
Trinity M. *SE20* —1H **125**
Trinity M. *W10* —6F **59**
Trinity Path. *SE26* —3J **111**
Trinity Pier. *E14* —7G **65**
Trinity Pl. *EC3* —7F **63** (2J **151**)
Trinity Pl. *Bexh* —4F **101**
Trinity Rise. *SW2* —1A **110**
Trinity Rd. *N2* —3B **28**
Trinity Rd. *N22* —7D **16**
Trinity Rd. *SW18* & *SW17*
　　　　—4A **92**
Trinity Rd. *SW19* —6J **107**
Trinity Rd. *Ilf* —3G **35**
Trinity Rd. *Rich* —3F **89**
Trinity Rd. *S'hall* —1C **70**
Trinity Sq. *EC3* —7E **62** (2H **151**)
Trinity St. *E16* —5H **65**
Trinity St. *SE1* —2C **78** (7D **150**)
Trinity St. *Enf* —2H **7**
Trinity Wlk. *NW3* —6A **44**
Trinity Way. *E4* —6G **19**
Trinity Way. *W3* —7A **58**
Trio Pl. *SE1* —2C **78** (7D **150**)
Tristan Sq. *SE3* —3G **97**
Tristram Clo. *E17* —3F **33**
Tristram Rd. *Brom* —4H **113**
Triton Sq. *NW1* —4G **61** (3A **142**)
Tritton Av. *Croy* —4J **133**
Tritton Rd. *SE21* —3D **110**
Triumph Ho. *Bark* —3A **68**
Triumph Rd. *E6* —6D **66**
Triumph Trad. Est. *N17* —6C **18**

Trojan Ct. *NW6* —7G **43**
Trojan Ind. Est. *NW10* —6B **42**
Trojan Way. *Croy* —3K **133**
Troon Clo. *SE16* —5H **79**
Troon St. *E1* —6A **64**
Trosley Rd. *Belv* —6G **85**
Trossachs Rd. *SE22* —5E **94**
Trothy Rd. *SE1* —4G **79**
Trotman Ho. *SE14* —1J **95**
　(off Pomeroy St.)
Trott Rd. *N10* —7J **15**
Trott St. *SW11* —1C **92**
Troughton Rd. *SE7* —5K **81**
Troutbeck Ho. *NW1*
　　　　—3F **61** (2K **141**)
Troutbeck Rd. *SE14* —1A **96**
Trouville Rd. *SW4* —6G **93**
Trowbridge Rd. *E9* —6B **48**
Trowlock Av. *Tedd* —6C **104**
Trowlock Way. *Tedd* —6D **104**
Troy Ct. *SE18* —4F **83**
Troy Ct. *W8* —3J **75**
　(off Kensington High St.)
Troy Ind. Est. *Harr* —5K **23**
Troy Rd. *SE19* —6D **110**
Troy Town. *SE15* —3G **95**
Truesdale Rd. *E6* —6D **66**
Trulock Ct. *N17* —7B **18**
Trulock Rd. *N17* —7B **18**
Truman Clo. *Edgw* —7D **12**
Trumans Rd. *N16* —5F **47**
Trumble Gdns. *T Hth* —4B **124**
Trumpers Way. *W7* —3J **71**
Trumpington Rd. *E7* —4H **49**
Trump St. *EC2* —6C **62** (1D **150**)
Trundlers Way. *Bush* —1D **10**
Trundle St. *SE1* —2C **78** (6C **150**)
Trundley's Rd. *SE8* —5K **79**
Trundley's Ter. *SE8* —4K **79**
Truro Gdns. *Ilf* —7C **34**
Truro Ho. *Pinn* —1D **22**
Truro Rd. *E17* —4B **32**
Truro Rd. *N22* —7D **16**
Truro St. *NW5* —6E **44**
Truslove Rd. *SE27* —5A **110**
Trussley Rd. *W6* —3E **74**
Trust Wlk. *SE21* —1B **110**
Tryfan Clo. *Ilf* —5B **34**
Tryon St. *SW3* —5D **76** (5E **152**)
Tuam Rd. *SE18* —6H **83**
Tubbs Rd. *NW10* —2B **58**
Tucklow Wlk. *SW15* —7B **90**
Tudor Av. *Hamp* —7E **102**
Tudor Av. *Wor Pk* —3D **130**
Tudor Clo. *N6* —7G **29**
Tudor Clo. *NW3* —5C **44**
Tudor Clo. *NW7* —6H **13**
Tudor Clo. *NW9* —2J **41**
Tudor Clo. *SW2* —6K **93**
Tudor Clo. *Chig* —4K **21**
Tudor Clo. *Chst* —1D **128**
Tudor Clo. *Hamp* —5G **103**
Tudor Clo. *Sutt* —6G **131**
Tudor Clo. *Wall* —7G **133**
Tudor Clo. *Wfd G* —5E **20**
Tudor Ct. *E17* —7B **32**
Tudor Ct. *N1* —6E **46**
Tudor Ct. *N22* —7D **16**
Tudor Ct. *SE9* —4C **98**
Tudor Ct. *W3* —2G **73**
Tudor Ct. *Felt* —4A **102**
Tudor Ct. *Sidc* —3A **116**

Tudor Ct. *Tedd* —6K **103**
Tudor Ct. N. *Wemb* —5G **41**
Tudor Ct. S. *Wemb* —5G **41**
Tudor Cres. *Enf* —1H **7**
Tudor Dri. *King T* —5D **104**
Tudor Dri. *Mord* —6F **121**
Tudor Enterprise Pk. *Harr* —3H **23**
Tudor Est. *NW11* —2H **57**
Tudor Gdns. *NW9* —2J **41**
Tudor Gdns. *SW13* —3A **90**
Tudor Gdns. *W3* —5G **57**
Tudor Gdns. *Harr* —2H **23**
Tudor Gdns. *Twic* —1K **103**
Tudor Gdns. *W Wick* —3E **136**
Tudor Gro. *E9* —7J **47**
Tudor Ho. Pinn —2A 22
(off Pinner Hill Rd.)
Tudor Pde. *Romf* —7D **36**
Tudor Pl. *Mitc* —7C **120**
Tudor Rd. *E4* —6J **19**
Tudor Rd. *E6* —1A **66**
Tudor Rd. *E9* —1H **63**
Tudor Rd. *N9* —7C **8**
Tudor Rd. *SE19* —7F **111**
Tudor Rd. *SE25* —5H **125**
Tudor Rd. *Bark* —1K **67**
Tudor Rd. *Barn* —3D **4**
Tudor Rd. *Beck* —3E **126**
Tudor Rd. *Hamp* —7E **102**
Tudor Rd. *Harr* —2H **23**
Tudor Rd. *Houn* —4H **87**
Tudor Rd. *King T* —7G **105**
Tudor Rd. *Pinn* —2A **22**
Tudor Rd. S'hall —7C 54
Tudor Stacks. *SE24* —4C **94**
Tudor St. *EC4* —7A **62** (2K **149**)
Tudor Wlk. *Bex* —6E **100**
Tudor Way. *N14* —1C **16**
Tudor Way. *W3* —2G **73**
Tudor Way. *Orp* —6H **129**
Tudor Well Clo. *Stan* —5G **11**
Tudway Rd. *SE3* —3K **97**
Tufnell Pk. Rd. *N19 & N7* —4G **45**
Tufton Rd. *E4* —4H **19**
Tufton St. *SW1* —3J **77** (1E **154**)
Tugboat St. *SE28* —2J **83**
Tugela Rd. *Croy* —6D **124**
Tugela St. *SE6* —2B **112**
Tulip Clo. *E6* —5D **66**
Tulip Clo. *Croy* —1K **135**
Tulip Clo. *Hamp* —6D **102**
Tulip Clo. *S'hall* —2G **71**
Tulip Gdns. *E4* —3A **20**
Tulip Gdns. *Ilf* —6F **51**
Tull St. *Mitc* —7D **122**
Tulse Clo. *Beck* —3E **126**
Tulse Hill. *SW2* —6A **94**
Tulse Hill Est. *SW2* —6A **94**
Tulse Ho. *SW2* —6A **94**
Tulsemere Rd. *SE27* —2C **110**
Tummons Gdns. *SE25* —2E **124**
Tunbridge Ho. EC1
—3B **62** (1A **144**)
Tuncombe Rd. *N18* —4K **17**
Tunis Rd. *W12* —1E **74**
Tunley Grn. *E14* —5B **64**
Tunley Rd. *NW10* —1A **58**
Tunley Rd. *SW17* —1E **108**
Tunmarsh La. *E13* —3A **66**
Tunnanleys. *E6* —6E **66**
Tunnel App. *E14* —7C **64**
Tunnel App. *SE10* —3G **81**
Tunnel App. *SE16* —2J **79**
Tunnel Av. *SE10* —2F **81**
(in two parts)

Tunnel Av. Trad. Est. *SE10*
—2F **81**
Tunnel Gdns. *N11* —7B **16**
Tunnel Rd. *SE16* —2J **79**
Tunstall Rd. *SW9* —4K **93**
Tunstall Rd. *Croy* —1E **134**
Tunstall Wlk. *Bren* —6E **72**
Tunstock Way. *Belv* —3F **85**
Tunworth Clo. *NW9* —6J **25**
Tunworth Cres. *SW15* —6B **90**
Tun Yd. *SW8* —2F **93**
Tupelo Rd. *E10* —2D **48**
Tupman Ho. SE16 —2G 79
(off Llewellyn St.)
Turenne Clo. *SW18* —4A **92**
Turin Rd. *N9* —7D **8**
Turin St. *E2* —3G **63** (2K **145**)
Turkey Oak Clo. *SE19* —1E **124**
Turk's Head Yd. *EC1*
—5B **62** (5A **144**)
Turk's Row. *SW3*
—5D **76** (5F **153**)
Turle Rd. *N4* —2K **45**
Turle Rd. *SW16* —2J **123**
Turlewray Clo. *N4* —1K **45**
Turley Clo. *E15* —1G **65**
Turnagain La. *EC4*
—6B **62** (7A **144**)
Turnage Rd. *Dag* —1E **52**
Turnberry Clo. SE16 —5H 79
(off Ryder Dri.)
Turnberry Quay. *E14* —3D **80**
Turnberry Way. *Orp* —7H **129**
Turnbull Ho. *N1* —1J **61**
Turnchapel M. *SW4* —3F **93**
Turner Av. *N15* —4E **30**
Turner Av. *Mitc* —1D **122**
Turner Av. *Twic* —3G **103**
Turner Clo. *NW11* —6K **27**
Turner Clo. *SE5* —1B **94**
Turner Clo. *Wemb* —6D **40**
Turner Dri. *NW11* —6K **27**
Turner Rd. *E17* —3E **32**
Turner Rd. *Edgw* —2E **24**
Turner Rd. *N Mald* —7K **119**
Turner's All. EC3
—7E **62** (2G **151**)
Turners Meadow Way. *Beck*
—1B **126**
Turners Rd. *E14 & E3* —5B **64**
Turners Rd. *N1* —2E **62**
Turner St. *E1* —5H **63**
Turner St. *E16* —6H **65**
Turner's Way. Croy —2A **134**
Turners Wood. *NW11* —1A **44**
Turneville Rd. *W14* —6H **75**
Turney Rd. *SE21* —7C **94**
Turnham Grn. Ter. *W4* —4A **74**
Turnham Grn. Ter. M. *W4* —4A **74**
Turnham Rd. *SE4* —5A **96**
Turnmill St. *EC1* —4B **62** (4A **144**)
Turnpike Clo. *SE8* —7B **80**
Turnpike Ho. EC1
—3B **62** (2B **144**)
Turnpike Ct. *Bexh* —4D **100**
Turnpike La. *N8* —4K **29**
Turnpike La. *Sutt* —5A **132**
Turnpike Link. *Croy* —2E **134**
Turnpike Pde. *N15* —3B **30**
(off Green Lanes)
Turnpike Way. *Iswth* —1A **88**
Turnpin La. *SE10* —6E **80**
Turnstone Clo. *E13* —3J **65**
Turnstone Clo. *NW9* —2A **26**
Turnstone Ct. *SE8* —6B **80**

Turpentine La. *SW1*
—5F **77** (5K **153**)
Turpington Clo. *Brom* —6C **128**
Turpington La. *Brom* —7C **128**
Turpin Ho. *SW11* —1F **93**
Turpin's La. Wfd G —5J **21**
Turpin Way. *N19* —2H **45**
Turpin Way. *Wall* —7F **133**
Turquand St. *SE17*
—4C **78** (4D **156**)
Turret Gro. *SW4* —3G **93**
Turtle Rd. *SW16* —2J **123**
Turton Rd. *Wemb* —5E **40**
Turville St. *E2* —4F **63** (3J **145**)
Tuscan Rd. *SE18* —5H **83**
Tuskar St. *SE10* —6G **81**
Tustin Est. *SE15* —6J **79**
Tutshill Ct. SE15 —7E 78
(off Lynbrook Clo.)
Tuttlebee La. *Buck H* —2D **20**
Tweedale Ct. *E15* —5E **48**
Tweed Ct. *W7* —6J **55**
(off Hanway Rd.)
Tweeddale Rd. *Cars* —1B **132**
Tweed Glen. *Romf* —1K **37**
Tweed Grn. *Romf* —1K **37**
Tweedmouth Rd. *E13* —2K **65**
Tweed Way. *Romf* —1K **37**
Tweedy Clo. *Enf* —5A **8**
Tweedy Rd. *Brom* —1J **127**
Tweezers All. WC2
—7A **62** (2J **149**)
Twelvetrees Cres. *E3 & E16*
—4E **64**
Twentyman Clo. *Wfd G* —5D **20**
Twickenham Bri. *Twic & Rich*
—5C **88**
Twickenham Clo. *Croy* —3K **133**
Twickenham Gdns. *Gnfd* —5A **40**
Twickenham Gdns. *Harr* —7D **10**
Twickenham Rd. *E11* —2F **49**
Twickenham Rd. *Felt* —3D **102**
Twickenham Rd. *Iswth* —5A **88**
Twickenham Rd. *Rich* —4C **88**
Twickenham Rd. *Tedd* —4A **104**
Twickenham Trad. Est. *Twic*
—6K **87**
Twigg Clo. *Eri* —7K **85**
Twilley St. *SW18* —7K **91**
Twin Bridges Bus. Pk. *S Croy*
—6D **134**
Twine Ct. *E1* —7J **63**
Twineham Grn. *N12* —4D **14**
Twining Av. *Twic* —3G **103**
Twinn Rd. *NW7* —6B **14**
Twins Clo. *Bark* —3B **68**
Twisden Rd. *NW5* —4F **45**
Twybridge Way. *NW10* —7J **41**
Twycross M. *SE10* —5G **81**
Twyford Abbey Rd. *NW10* —3F **57**
Twyford Av. *N2* —3D **28**
Twyford Av. *W3* —7G **57**
Twyford Ct. *Wemb* —2E **56**
(off Vicars Bri. Clo.)
Twyford Cres. *W3* —1G **73**
Twyford Ho. *N5* —3B **46**
Twyford Ho. N15 —6E 30
(off Chisley Rd.)
Twyford Pl. *WC2*
—6K **61** (7G **143**)
Twyford Rd. *Cars* —1B **132**
Twyford Rd. *Harr* —1F **39**
Twyford Rd. *Ilf* —5G **51**
Twyford St. *N1* —1K **61**

Tyas Rd. *E16* —4H **65**
Tybenham Rd. *SW19* —3J **121**
Tyberry Rd. *Enf* —3C **8**
Tyburn La. *Harr* —7K **23**
Tyburn Way. *W1*
—7D **60** (2F **147**)
Tyers Est. *SE1* —2E **78** (6G **151**)
Tyers Ga. *SE1* —2E **78** (7G **151**)
Tyers St. *SE11* —5K **77** (6G **155**)
Tyers Ter. *SE11* —5K **77** (6G **155**)
Tyeshurst Clo. *SE2* —5E **84**
Tylecroft Rd. *SW16* —2J **123**
Tylehurst Gdns. *Ilf* —5G **51**
Tyler Clo. *E2* —2F **63**
Tylers Ct. *E17* —4C **32**
(off Westbury Rd.)
Tyler's Ct. *W1* —6H **61** (1C **148**)
Tylers Ct. *Wemb* —2E **56**
Tylers Ga. *Harr* —6E **24**
Tylers Path. *Cars* —4D **132**
Tyler St. *SE10* —5G **81**
(in two parts)
Tylney Av. *SE19* —5F **111**
Tylney Rd. *E7* —4A **50**
Tylney Rd. *Brom* —2B **128**
Tyndale La. *N1* —7B **46**
Tyndale Mans. N1 —7B 46
(off Upper St.)
Tyndale Ter. *N1* —7B **46**
Tyndall Gdns. *E10* —2E **48**
Tyndall Rd. *E10* —2E **48**
Tyndall Rd. *Well* —3K **99**
Tyne Clo. W7 —6J 55
(off Hanway Rd.)
Tyneham Clo. *SW11* —3E **92**
Tyneham Rd. *SW11* —2E **92**
Tynemouth Clo. *E6* —6F **67**
Tynemouth Dri. *Enf* —1B **8**
Tynemouth Rd. *N15* —4F **31**
Tynemouth Rd. *Mitc* —7E **108**
Tynemouth Rd. *SW6* —2A **92**
Tyne St. *E1* —6F **63** (7K **145**)
Tynley Av. *SE19* —5F **111**
Tynwald Ho. *SE26* —3G **111**
Type St. *E2* —2K **63**
Tyrawley Rd. *SW6* —1K **91**
Tyre La. *NW9* —4A **26**
Tyrell Clo. *Harr* —4J **39**
Tyrell Ct. *Cars* —4D **132**
Tyrell Ho. Beck —5D 112
(off Beckenham Hill Rd.)
Tyrols Rd. *SE23* —1K **111**
Tyrone Rd. *E6* —2D **66**
Tyron Way. *Sidc* —4J **115**
Tyrrell Av. *Well* —5A **100**
Tyrrell Rd. *SE22* —4G **95**
Tyrrell Sq. *Mitc* —1C **122**
Tyrrel Way. *NW9* —7B **26**
Tyrwhitt Rd. *SE4* —3C **96**
Tysoe St. *EC1* —3A **62** (2K **143**)
Tyson Gdns. *SE23* —7J **95**
Tyson Rd. *SE23* —7J **95**
Tyssen Pas. *E8* —6F **47**
Tyssen Rd. *N16* —3F **47**
Tyssen St. *E8* —6F **47**
Tytherton Rd. *N19* —3H **45**

Uamvar St. *E14* —5D **64**
Uckfield Gro. *Mitc* —1E **122**
Udall St. *SW1* —4G **77** (4B **154**)
Udney Pk. Rd. *Tedd* —6A **104**
Uffington Rd. *NW10* —1C **58**
Uffington Rd. *SE27* —4A **110**

Ufford Clo. *Harr* —7A **10**
Ufford Rd. *Harr* —7A **10**
Ufford St. *SE1* —2A **78** (6K **149**)
Ufton Ct. *N'holt* —3B **54**
Ufton Gro. *N1* —7D **46**
Ufton Rd. *N1* —7D **46**
(in two parts)
Uhura Sq. *N16* —3E **46**
Ujima Ct. *SW16* —4J **109**
Ullathorne Rd. *SW16* —4G **109**
Ulleswater Rd. *N14* —3D **16**
Ullin St. *E14* —5E **64**
Ullswater Clo. *SW15* —4K **105**
Ullswater Clo. *Brom* —7G **113**
Ullswater Ct. *Harr* —7E **22**
Ullswater Cres. *SW15* —4K **105**
Ullswater Rd. *SE27* —2B **110**
Ullswater Rd. *SW13* —7C **74**
Ulster Gdns. *N13* —4H **17**
Ulster Pl. NW1 —4F 61 (4J **141**)
Ulster Ter. *NW1* —4E **60** (3H **141**)
Ulundi Rd. *SE3* —6G **81**
Ulva Rd. *SW15* —5F **91**
Ulverscroft Rd. *SE22* —5F **95**
Ulverstone Rd. *SE27* —2B **110**
Ulverston Rd. *E17* —2F **33**
Ulysses Rd. *NW6* —5H **43**
Umberston St. *E1* —6G **63**
Umbria St. *SW15* —6C **90**
Umfreville Rd. *N4* —6B **30**
Undercliff Rd. *SE13* —3C **96**
Underhill. *Barn* —5D **4**
Underhill Ct. *Barn* —5D **4**
Underhill Pas. NW1 —1F 61
(off Camden High St.)
Underhill Rd. *SE22* —5G **95**
Underhill St. *NW1* —1F **61**
Underne Av. *N14* —2A **16**
Undershaft. *EC3* —6E **62** (1G **151**)
Undershaw Rd. *Brom* —3H **113**
Underwood. *New Ad* —5E **136**
Underwood Ct. *E10* —1D **48**
Underwood Rd. *E1* —4G **63**
Underwood Rd. *E4* —5J **19**
Underwood Rd. Wfd G —7F 21
Underwood Row. *N1*
—3C **62** (1D **144**)
Underwood St. *N1*
—3C **62** (1D **144**)
Underwood, The. SE9 —3D 114
Undine Rd. *E14* —4D **80**
Undine St. *SW17* —5D **108**
Uneeda Dri. Gnfd —1H 55
Unicorn Building. E1 —7K 63
(off Jardine Rd.)
Unicorn Pas. SE1
—1E **78** (5H **151**)
Union Clo. *E11* —4F **49**
Union Cotts. *E15* —7G **49**
Union Ct. *EC2* —6E **62** (7G **145**)
Union Ct. *Rich* —5E **88**
Union Dri. *E1* —4A **64**
Union Gro. *SW8* —2H **93**
Union Rd. *N11* —6C **16**
Union Rd. *SW8 & SW4* —2H **93**
Union Rd. *Brom* —5B **128**
Union Rd. *Croy* —7C **124**
Union Rd. *N'holt* —2E **54**
Union Rd. *Wemb* —6E **40**
Union Sq. *N1* —1C **62**
Union St. *E15* —2F **65**
Union St. *SE1* —1B **78** (5A **150**)
Union St. *Barn* —3B **4**
Union St. *King T* —2D **118**
Union Wlk. *E2* —3E **62** (1H **145**)

Union Yd.—Varley Pde.

Union Yd. *W1* —6F **61** (1K **147**)
Unity Clo. *NW10* —7C **42**
Unity Clo. *SE19* —5C **110**
Unity Clo. *New Ad* —7D **136**
Unity Way. *SE18* —3B **82**
University Clo. *NW7* —7G **13**
University Gdns. *Bex* —7F **101**
University Pl. *Eri* —1J **85**
University Rd. *SW19* —6B **108**
University St. *WC1*
　　　　　　—4G **61** (4B **142**)
Unwin Clo. *SE15* —6G **79**
Unwin Mans. W14 —6G **75**
　(off Queen's Club Gdns.)
Unwin Rd. *SW7* —3B **76** (1A **152**)
Unwin Rd. *Iswth* —3J **87**
Upbrook M. *W2* —6A **60**
Upcerne Rd. *SW10* —7A **76**
Upchurch Clo. *SE20* —7H **111**
Upcroft Av. *Edgw* —5D **12**
Updale Rd. *Sidc* —4K **115**
Upfield. *Croy* —3H **135**
Upfield Rd. *W7* —5K **55**
Upgrove Mnr. Way. *SW2* —7A **94**
Uphall Rd. *Ilf* —5F **51**
Upham Pk. Rd. *W4* —4A **74**
Uphill Dri. *NW7* —5F **13**
Uphill Dri. *NW9* —5J **25**
Uphill Gro. *NW7* —4F **13**
Uphill Rd. *NW7* —4F **13**
Upland M. *SE22* —5G **95**
Upland Rd. *E13* —4J **65**
Upland Rd. *SE22* —5G **95**
Upland Rd. *Bexh* —3F **101**
Upland Rd. *S Croy* —5D **134**
Upland Rd. *Sutt* —7B **132**
Uplands. *Beck* —2C **126**
Uplands Av. *E17* —2K **31**
Uplands Bus. Pk. *E17* —3K **31**
Uplands Clo. *SW14* —5H **89**
Uplands Ct. N21 —7F **7**
　(off Green, The)
Uplands End. *Wfd G* —7H **21**
Uplands Pk. Rd. *Enf* —2F **7**
Uplands Rd. *N8* —5K **29**
Uplands Rd. *E Barn* —1K **15**
Uplands Rd. *Romf* —3D **36**
Uplands Rd. *Wfd G* —7H **21**
Uplands Way. *N21* —5F **7**
Upnall Ho. *SE15* —6J **79**
Upney La. *Bark* —6J **51**
Upnor Way. *SE17*
　　　　　　—5E **78** (5H **157**)
Uppark Dri. *Ilf* —6G **35**
Up. Abbey Rd. *Belv* —4F **85**
Up. Addison Gdns. *W14* —2G **75**
Up. Bardsey Wlk. N1 —6C **46**
　(off Bardsey Wlk.)
Up. Belgrave St. *SW1*
　　　　　　—3E **76** (1H **153**)
Up. Berkeley St. *W1*
　　　　　　—6D **60** (1E **146**)
Up. Beulah Hill. *SE19* —1E **124**
Up. Brighton Rd. *Surb* —6D **118**
Up. Brockley Rd. *SE4* —3B **96**
Up. Brook St. *W1*
　　　　　　—7E **60** (2G **147**)
Up. Caldy Wlk. N1 —6C **46**
　(off Caldy Wlk.)
Up. Camelford Wlk. W11 —6G **59**
　(off St Mark's Rd.)
Up. Cavendish Av. *N3* —3J **27**
Up. Cheyne Row. *SW3*
　　　　　　—6C **76** (7C **152**)

Up. Clapton Rd. *E5* —2H **47**
Up. Clarendon Wlk. W11 —6G **59**
　(off Clarendon Rd.)
Up. Dengie Wlk. N1 —1C **62**
　(off Basire St.)
Up. Elmers End Rd. *Beck*
　　　　　　—4A **126**
Up. Fosters. *NW4* —5E **26**
　(off New Brent St.)
Up. Green E. *Mitc* —3D **122**
Up. Green W. *Mitc* —2D **122**
Up. Grosvenor St. *W1*
　　　　　　—7E **60** (3G **147**)
Up. Grotto Rd. *Twic* —2K **103**
Up. Ground. *SE1*
　　　　　　—1A **78** (4J **149**)
Upper Gro. *SE25* —4F **125**
Up. Grove Rd. *Belv* —6F **85**
Up. Gulland Wlk. N1 —6C **46**
　(off Oronsay Wlk.)
Up. Ham Rd. *Rich* —4D **104**
Up. Handa Wlk. N1 —6D **46**
　(off Handa Wlk.)
Up. Harley St. *NW1*
　　　　　　—4E **60** (4H **141**)
Up. Hawkwell Wlk. N1 —1C **62**
　(off Maldon Clo.)
Up. Hilldrop Est. *N7* —5H **45**
Up. Holly Hill Rd. *Belv* —5H **85**
Up. James St. *W1*
　　　　　　—7G **61** (2B **148**)
Up. John St. *W1*
　　　　　　—7G **61** (2B **148**)
Up. Lismore Wlk. N1 —6C **46**
　(off Clephane St.)
Up. Mall. *W6* —5C **74**
　(in two parts)
Up. Marsh. *SE1* —3K **77** (1H **155**)
Up. Montagu St. *W1*
　　　　　　—5D **60** (5E **140**)
Up. Mulgrave Rd. *Sutt* —7G **131**
Up. North St. *E14* —5C **64**
Up. Park Rd. *N11* —5A **16**
Up. Park Rd. *NW3* —5D **44**
Up. Park Rd. *Belv* —4H **85**
Up. Park Rd. *Brom* —1K **127**
Up. Park Rd. *King T* —6G **105**
Up. Phillimore Gdns. *W8* —2J **75**
Up. Ramsey Wlk. N1 —6D **46**
　(off Ramsey Wlk.)
Up. Rawreth Wlk. N1 —1C **62**
　(off Basire St.)
Up. Richmond Rd. *SW15* —4B **90**
Up. Richmond Rd. W. *Rich* &
　　　　　　—4G **89**
Upper Rd. *E13* —3J **65**
Upper Rd. *Wall* —5H **133**
Up. St Martin's La. *WC2*
　　　　　　—7J **61** (2E **148**)
Up. Selsdon Rd. *S Croy* —7E **134**
Up. Sheppey Wlk. N1 —6C **46**
　(off Skomer Wlk.)
Up. Sheridan Rd. *Belv* —4G **85**
Up. Shirley Rd. *Croy* —3J **135**
Upper Sq. *Iswth* —3A **88**
Up. Staithe. *W4* —1J **89**
Upper St. *N1* —2A **62**
Up. Sutton La. *Houn* —7E **70**
Up. Tachbrook St. *SW1*
　　　　　　—4G **77** (3B **154**)
Up. Teddington Rd. *King T*
　　　　　　—7C **104**
Upper Ter. *NW3* —3A **44**
Up. Thames St. *EC4*
　　　　　　—7B **62** (2B **150**)

Up. Tollington Pk. *N4* —1A **46**
　(in two parts)
Upperton Rd. *Sidc* —5K **115**
Upperton Rd. E. *E13* —3A **66**
Upperton Rd. W. *E13* —3A **66**
Up. Tooting Pk. *SW17* —2D **108**
Up. Tooting Rd. *SW17* —4D **108**
Up. Town Rd. *Gnfd* —4F **55**
Up. Tulse Hill. *SW2* —7K **93**
Up. Vernon Rd. *Sutt* —5B **132**
Up. Walthamstow Rd. *E17*
　　　　　　—4E **32**
Up. Wickham La. *Well* —3B **100**
Up. Wimpole St. *W1*
　　　　　　—5E **60** (5H **141**)
Up. Woburn Pl. *WC1*
　　　　　　—3H **61** (2D **142**)
Uppingham Av. *Stan* —1B **24**
Upsdell Av. *N13* —6F **17**
Upstall St. *SE5* —1B **94**
Upton Av. *E7* —7J **49**
Upton Clo. *Bex* —6F **101**
Upton Ct. *SE20* —7J **111**
Upton Dene. *Sutt* —7K **131**
Upton Gdns. *Harr* —5B **24**
Upton La. *E7* —7J **49**
Upton Lodge. *E7* —6J **49**
Upton Lodge Clo. *Bush* —1B **10**
Upton Pk. Rd. *E7* —7K **49**
Upton Rd. *N18* —5B **18**
Upton Rd. *SE18* —6G **83**
Upton Rd. *Bexh & Bex* —4E **100**
Upton Rd. *Houn* —3D **86**
Upton Rd. *T Hth* —2D **124**
Upton Rd. S. *Bex* —6F **101**
Upton Vs. *Bexh* —4E **100**
Upway. *N12* —6H **15**
Upwood Rd. *SE12* —6J **97**
Upwood Rd. *SW16* —1J **123**
Urlwin St. *SE5* —6C **78**
Urlwin Wlk. *SW9* —1A **94**
Urmston Dri. *SW19* —1G **107**
Urquhart Ct. *Beck* —7B **112**
Ursula Lodges. *Sidc* —5B **116**
Ursula M. *N4* —1C **46**
Ursula St. *SW11* —1C **92**
Urswick Gdns. *Dag* —7E **52**
Urswick Rd. *E9* —5J **47**
Urswick Rd. *Dag* —7D **52**
Usborne M. *SW8* —7K **77**
Usher Rd. *E3* —1B **64**
Usher-Walker Ho. E16 —4F **65**
　(off South Cres.)
Usk Rd. *SW11* —4A **92**
Usk St. *E2* —3K **63**
Uvedale Rd. *Dag* —3G **53**
Uvedale Rd. *Enf* —5J **7**
Uverdale Rd. *SW10* —7A **76**
Uxbridge Rd. *W12* —1B **74**
Uxbridge Rd. *W13, W5 & W3*
　　　　　　—1B **72**
Uxbridge Rd. *Felt* —2A **102**
Uxbridge Rd. *Hamp* —4E **102**
Uxbridge Rd. *Harr & Stan* —7B **10**
Uxbridge Rd. *King T* —4D **118**
Uxbridge Rd. *Pinn* —2A **22**
Uxbridge Rd. *S'hall & W7* —1E **70**
Uxbridge Rd. *Uxb & Hay* —6A **54**
Uxbridge St. *W8* —1J **75**
Uxendon Cres. *Wemb* —1E **40**
Uxendon Hill. *Wemb* —1F **41**

Valance Av. *E4* —1B **20**
Valan Leas. *Brom* —3G **127**

Vale Clo. *N2* —3D **28**
Vale Clo. *W9* —3A **60**
Vale Clo. *Orp* —4E **138**
Vale Ct. *W3* —1B **74**
Vale Ct. W9 —3A **60**
　(off Maida Vale)
Vale Ct. *New Bar* —4E **4**
Vale Cres. *SW15* —4A **106**
Vale Croft. *Pinn* —5C **22**
Vale Dri. *Barn* —4C **4**
Vale End. *SE22* —4F **95**
Vale Est., The. *W3* —1A **74**
Vale Gro. *N4* —7C **30**
Vale Gro. *W3* —2K **73**
Vale La. *W3* —5G **57**
Vale Lodge. *SE23* —2J **111**
Valence Av. *Dag* —1D **52**
Valence Cir. *Dag* —3D **52**
Valence Rd. *Eri* —7K **85**
Valence Wood Rd. *Dag* —3D **52**
Valencia Rd. *Stan* —4H **11**
Valentia Pl. *SW9* —4A **94**
Valentine Av. *Bex* —2E **116**
Valentine Ct. *SE23* —2K **111**
　(in two parts)
Valentine Pl. *SE1*
　　　　　　—2B **78** (6A **150**)
Valentine Rd. *E9* —6K **47**
Valentine Rd. *Harr* —3G **39**
Valentines Rd. *Ilf* —1F **51**
Valentine's Way. *Romf* —2K **53**
Vale of Health. *NW3* —3B **44**
Valerian Way. *E15* —3G **65**
Valerie Ct. *Sutt* —7K **131**
Vale Rise. *NW11* —1H **43**
Vale Rd. *E7* —6K **49**
Vale Rd. *N4* —7C **30**
Vale Rd. *Brom* —1B **128**
Vale Rd. *Eps* —4B **130**
Vale Rd. *Mitc* —4H **123**
Vale Rd. *Sutt* —4K **131**
Vale Rd. *Wor Pk* —3B **130**
Vale Row. *N5* —3B **46**
Vale Royal. *N7* —7J **45**
Vale St. *SE27* —3D **110**
Valeswood Rd. *Brom* —5H **113**
Vale Ter. *N4* —6C **30**
Vale, The. *N10* —1E **28**
Vale, The. *N14* —6E **6**
Vale, The. *NW11* —2G **43**
Vale, The. *SW3*
　　　　　　—6B **76** (7B **152**)
Vale, The. *W3* —1B **74**
Vale, The. *Croy* —2K **135**
Vale, The. *Felt* —6A **86**
Vale, The. *Houn* —6C **70**
Vale, The. *Ruis* —4A **38**
Vale, The. *Wfd G* —7D **20**
Valetta Gro. *E13* —2J **65**
Valetta Rd. *W3* —2A **74**
Valette Ct. N10 —4F **29**
　(off St James's La.)
Valette St. *E9* —6J **47**
Valiant Clo. *N'holt* —3B **54**
Valiant Clo. *Romf* —2H **37**
Valiant Way. *E6* —5D **66**
Vallance Rd. *E2 & E1* —3G **63**
Vallance Rd. *N22* —2G **29**
Valley Av. *N12* —4G **15**
Valley Dri. *NW9* —6G **25**
Valleyfield Rd. *SW16* —5K **109**
Valley Fields Cres. *Enf* —2F **7**
Valley Gdns. *SW19* —7B **108**
Valley Gdns. *Wemb* —7F **41**

Valley Gro. *SE7* —5A **82**
Valleylink Est. *Enf* —6F **9**
Valley M. *Twic* —2K **103**
Valley Rd. *SW16* —5K **109**
Valley Rd. *Belv* —4H **85**
Valley Rd. *Eri* —4K **85**
Valley Rd. *Orp* —7B **116**
Valley Rd. *Short* —2G **127**
Valley Side. *E4* —2H **19**
Valley Side Pde. *E4* —2H **19**
Valley View. *Barn* —6B **4**
Valley Wlk. *Croy* —2J **135**
Valliere Rd. *NW10* —3C **58**
Valliers Wood Rd. *Sidc* —1H **115**
Vallis Way. *W13* —5A **56**
Valmar Rd. *SE5* —1C **94**
Valmar Trad. Est. *SE5* —1C **94**
Valnay St. *SW17* —5D **108**
Valognes Av. *E17* —1A **32**
Valonia Gdns. *SW18* —6H **91**
Vambery Rd. *SE18* —6G **83**
Vanbrough Cres. *N'holt* —1A **54**
Vanbrugh Clo. *E16* —5B **66**
Vanbrugh Ct. *SE11*
　　　　　　—4A **78** (4K **155**)
Vanbrugh Fields. *SE3* —6H **81**
Vanbrugh Hill. *SE10 & SE3*
　　　　　　—5H **81**
Vanbrugh Pk. *SE3* —7H **81**
Vanbrugh Pk. Rd. *SE3* —7H **81**
Vanbrugh Pk. Rd. W. *SE3*
　　　　　　—7H **81**
Vanbrugh Rd. *W4* —3K **73**
Vanbrugh Ter. *SE3* —1H **97**
Vanburgh Clo. *Orp* —7J **129**
Vanburgh Ct. *High Bar* —3B **4**
Vancouver Mans. *Edgw* —1H **25**
Vancouver Rd. *SE23* —2A **112**
Vancouver Rd. *Edgw* —1H **25**
Vancouver Rd. *Rich* —4C **104**
Vanderbilt Rd. *SW18* —1K **107**
Vandome Clo. *E16* —6K **65**
Vandon Pas. *SW1*
　　　　　　—3G **77** (1B **154**)
Vandon St. *SW1*
　　　　　　—3G **77** (1B **154**)
Van Dyck Av. *N Mald* —7K **119**
Vandyke Clo. *SW15* —7F **91**
Vandyke Cross. *SE9* —5C **98**
Vandy St. *EC2* —4G **62** (4G **145**)
Vane Clo. *NW3* —5B **44**
Vane Clo. *Harr* —6F **25**
Vanessa Clo. *Belv* —5G **85**
Vanessa Way. *Bex* —3K **117**
Vane St. *SW1* —4G **77** (3B **154**)
Van Gogh Ct. *E14* —3F **81**
Vanguard Clo. *E16* —5J **65**
Vanguard Clo. *Croy* —1B **134**
Vanguard Clo. *Romf* —2G **37**
Vanguard St. *SE8* —1C **96**
Vanguard Way. *Wall* —7J **133**
Vanoc Gdns. *Brom* —4J **113**
Vansittart Rd. *E7* —4H **49**
Vansittart St. *SE14* —6A **80**
Vanston Pl. *SW6* —7J **75**
Vantage W. *Bren* —4F **73**
Vant Rd. *SW17* —5D **108**
Vanweck Sq. *SW15* —5C **90**
Varcoe Rd. *SE16* —5H **79**
Vardens Rd. *SW11* —4B **92**
Varden St. *E1* —6H **63**
Vardon Clo. *W3* —6K **57**
Vardon Ho. *SE10* —1E **96**
Varley Pde. *NW9* —4A **26**

Varley Rd. E16 —6K 65
Varley Way. Mitc —2B 122
Varna Rd. SW6 —7G 75
Varndell St. NW1
　　　　—3G 61 (1A 142)
Varsity Dri. Twic —5J 87
Varsity Row. SW14 —2J 89
Vartry Rd. N15 —6D 30
Vassall Rd. SW9 —7A 78
Vauban Est. SE16
　　　　—3F 79 (2K 157)
Vauban St. SE16
　　　　—3F 79 (2K 157)
Vaudeville Ct. N4 —2A 46
Vaughan Av. NW4 —5C 26
Vaughan Av. W6 —4B 74
Vaughan Clo. Hamp —6C 102
Vaughan Est. E2 —3F 63 (1J 145)
Vaughan Gdns. Ilf —7D 34
Vaughan Ho. SW4 —7G 93
Vaughan Rd. E15 —6H 49
Vaughan Rd. SE5 —2C 94
Vaughan Rd. Harr —7G 23
Vaughan Rd. Th Dit —7B 118
Vaughan Rd. Well —2K 99
Vaughan St. SE16 —2B 80
Vaughan Way. E1 —7G 63
Vaughan Williams Clo. SE8
　　　　—7C 80
Vauxhall Bri. SW1 & SE1
　　　　—5J 77 (6E 154)
Vauxhall Bri. Rd. SW1
　　　　—3G 77 (2A 154)
Vauxhall Cross. SE1
　　　　—5J 77 (6F 155)
Vauxhall Cross. (Junct.) —5J 77
Vauxhall Gdns. S Croy —6C 134
Vauxhall Gro. SW8
　　　　—6K 77 (7G 155)
Vauxhall St. SE11
　　　　—5K 77 (5H 155)
Vauxhall Wlk. SE11
　　　　—5K 77 (5G 155)
Vawdrey Clo. E1 —4J 63
Veals Mead. Mitc —1C 122
Vectis Gdns. SW17 —6F 109
Vectis Rd. SW17 —6F 109
Veda Rd. SE13 —4C 96
Vega Rd. Bush —1B 10
Veldene Way. Harr —3D 38
Velde Way. SE22 —5E 94
Vellum Dri. Cars —3E 132
Venables Clo. Dag —4H 53
Venables St. NW8
　　　　—5B 60 (5B 140)
Vencourt Pl. W6 —4C 74
Venetian Rd. SE5 —2C 94
Venetia Rd. N4 —6B 30
Venetia Rd. W5 —2D 72
Venner Rd. SE26 —6J 111
Venn Ho. N1 —1K 61
　　　(off Barnsbury Est.)
Venn St. SW4 —4G 93
Ventnor Av. Stan —1B 24
Ventnor Dri. N20 —3E 14
Ventnor Gdns. Bark —6J 51
Ventnor Rd. SE14 —7K 79
Ventnor Rd. Sutt —7K 131
Venture Clo. Bex —7E 100
Venture Ct. SE12 —7J 97
Venue St. E14 —5E 64
Venus Rd. SE18 —3D 82
Vera Av. N21 —5F 7
Vera Lynn Clo. E7 —4J 49
Vera Rd. SW6 —1G 91

Verbena Clo. E16 —4H 65
Verbena Gdns. W6 —5C 74
Verdant Ct. SE6 —7G 97
　　　(off Verdant La.)
Verdant La. SE6 —7G 97
Verdayne Av. Croy —2K 135
Verdun Rd. SE18 —6A 84
Verdun Rd. SW13 —6C 74
Vereker Rd. W14 —5G 75
Vere St. W1 —6E 61 (1J 147)
Veritas Ho. Sidc —2A 116
　　　(off Station Rd.)
Verity Clo. W11 —7G 59
Ver Meer Ct. E14 —3F 81
Vermont Clo. Enf —4G 7
Vermont Rd. SE19 —6E 110
Vermont Rd. SW18 —6K 91
Vermont Rd. Sutt —3K 131
Verne Ct. W3 —3J 73
　　　(off Vincent Rd.)
Verney Gdns. Dag —4E 52
Verney Rd. SE16 —6G 79
Verney Rd. Dag —4E 52
　　　(in two parts)
Verney St. NW10 —3K 41
Verney Way. SE16 —5H 79
Vernham Rd. SE18 —6G 83
Vernon Av. E12 —4D 50
Vernon Av. SW20 —2F 121
Vernon Av. Wfd G —7E 20
Vernon Ct. NW2 —3H 43
Vernon Ct. W5 —7C 56
Vernon Cres. Barn —6K 5
Vernon Dri. Stan —1A 24
Vernon M. E17 —5B 32
Vernon M. W14 —4G 75
　　　(off Vernon St.)
Vernon Pl. WC1 —5J 61 (6F 143)
Vernon Rise. WC1
　　　　—3K 61 (1H 143)
Vernon Rise. Gnfd —5H 39
Vernon Rd. E3 —2B 64
Vernon Rd. E11 —1G 49
Vernon Rd. E15 —7G 49
Vernon Rd. E17 —5B 32
Vernon Rd. N8 —3A 30
Vernon Rd. SW14 —3K 89
Vernon Rd. Ilf —1K 51
Vernon Rd. Sutt —5A 132
Vernon Sq. WC1
　　　　—3K 61 (1H 143)
Vernon St. W14 —4G 75
Vernon Yd. W11 —7H 59
Veroan Rd. Bexh —2E 100
Verona Rd. E7 —7J 49
Veronica Gdns. SW16 —1G 123
Veronica Ho. SE4 —3B 96
Veronica Rd. SW17 —2F 109
Veronique Gdns. Ilf —5G 35
Verran Rd. SW12 —7F 93
Versailles Rd. SE20 —7G 111
Verulam Av. E17 —6B 32
Verulam Bldgs. WC1
　　　　—5K 61 (5H 143)
Verulam Ct. NW9 —7C 26
Verulam Ct. S'hall —6G 55
　　　(off Haldane Rd.)
Verulam Rd. Gnfd —4E 54
Verulam St. WC1
　　　　—5A 62 (5J 143)
Verwood Dri. Barn —3J 5
Verwood Rd. Harr —2G 23
Veryan Ct. N8 —5H 29
Vesey Path. E14 —6D 64

Vespan Rd. W12 —2C 74
Vesta Rd. SE4 —2A 96
Vestris Rd. SE23 —2K 111
Vestry M. SE5 —1E 94
Vestry Rd. E17 —4D 32
Vestry Rd. SE5 —1E 94
Vestry St. N1 —3D 62 (1E 144)
Vevey St. SE6 —2B 112
Veysey Gdns. Dag —3G 53
Viaduct Bldgs. EC1
　　　　—5A 62 (6K 143)
Viaduct Pl. E2 —3H 63
Viaduct Rd. N2 —2B 28
Viaduct St. E2 —3H 63
Viaduct, The. E18 —2K 33
Viaduct, The. Wemb —1E 56
Vian St. SE13 —3D 96
Viant Ho. NW10 —7K 41
Vibart Gdns. SW2 —7K 93
Vibart Wlk. N1 —1J 61
　　　(off Outram Pl.)
Vicarage Av. SE3 —7J 81
Vicarage Clo. Eri —6J 85
Vicarage Clo. N'holt —7D 38
Vicarage Ct. W8 —2K 75
Vicarage Ct. Beck —3A 126
Vicarage Ct. Ilf —5F 51
Vicarage Cres. SW11 —1B 92
Vicarage Dri. SW14 —5K 89
Vicarage Dri. Bark —5G 51
Vicarage Dri. Beck —1C 126
Vicarage Farm Ct. Houn —7D 70
Vicarage Farm Rd. Houn —2C 86
Vicarage Field Shop. Cen. Bark
　　　　—7G 51
Vicarage Gdns. W8 —1J 75
Vicarage Gdns. Mitc —3C 122
Vicarage Ga. W8 —1K 75
Vicarage Gro. SE5 —1D 94
Vicarage La. E6 —3D 66
Vicarage La. E15 —7G 49
Vicarage La. Eps —7C 130
Vicarage La. Ilf —1H 51
Vicarage M. NW9 —2K 41
Vicarage Pde. N15 —4C 30
Vicarage Pk. SE18 —5G 83
Vicarage Path. N8 —7H 29
Vicarage Rd. E10 —7C 32
Vicarage Rd. E15 —7H 49
Vicarage Rd. N17 —1G 31
Vicarage Rd. NW4 —6C 26
Vicarage Rd. SE18 —5G 83
Vicarage Rd. SW14 —5K 89
Vicarage Rd. Bex —1H 117
Vicarage Rd. Croy —3A 134
Vicarage Rd. Dag —7H 53
Vicarage Rd. Hamp W —1C 118
Vicarage Rd. King T —2D 118
Vicarage Rd. Sutt —3K 131
Vicarage Rd. Tedd —5A 104
Vicarage Rd. Twic —2J 103
Vicarage Rd. Whit —6G 87
Vicarage Rd. Wfd G —7H 21
Vicarage Wlk. SW11 —1B 92
Vicarage Way. NW10 —3K 41
Vicarage Way. Harr —2G 22
Vicars Bri. Clo. Wemb —2E 56
Vicar's Clo. E9 —1J 63
Vicars Clo. E15 —1J 65
Vicars Clo. Enf —2K 7
Vicar's Hill. SE13 —4D 96
Vicars Moor La. N21 —7F 7
Vicars Oak Rd. SE19 —6E 110
Vicar's Rd. NW5 —5E 44
Vicars Wlk. Dag —3B 52

Viceroy Clo. N2 —4C 28
Viceroy Ct. NW8 —2C 60
　　　(off Prince Albert Rd.)
Viceroy Ct. Croy —2D 134
Viceroy Pde. N2 —4C 28
　　　(off High Rd.)
Viceroy Rd. SW8 —1J 93
Vickers Rd. Eri —5K 85
V.I. Components Ind. Est. Eri
　　　　—5K 85
Victor Gro. Wemb —7E 40
Victoria Av. E6 —1B 66
Victoria Av. EC2 —5E 62 (6H 145)
Victoria Av. N3 —1H 27
Victoria Av. Barn —4G 5
Victoria Av. Houn —5E 86
Victoria Av. Surb —6D 118
Victoria Av. Wall —3E 132
Victoria Av. Wemb —6H 41
Victoria Clo. Barn —4G 5
Victoria Cotts. N10 —2E 28
Victoria Cotts. Rich —1F 89
Victoria Ct. E18 —3K 33
Victoria Ct. SE26 —6J 111
Victoria Ct. W3 —2G 73
Victoria Ct. Wemb —6G 41
Victoria Cres. N15 —5E 30
Victoria Cres. SE19 —6E 110
Victoria Cres. SW19 —7H 107
Victoria Dock Rd. E16 —6G 65
Victoria Dri. SW19 —7F 91
Victoria Embkmt. SW1, WC2 &
　　EC4 —2J 77 (6F 149)
Victoria Gdns. W11 —1J 75
Victoria Gdns. Houn —1C 86
Victoria Gro. N12 —5G 15
Victoria Gro. W8 —3A 76
Victoria Gro. M. W2 —7J 59
Victoria Ho. N1 —1K 61
　　　(off High Rd.)
Victoria Ho. SW8 —7J 77
　　　(off S. Lambeth Rd.)
Victoria Ho. Edgw —6C 12
Victoria Ind. Est. W3 —5A 58
Victoria La. Barn —4C 4
Victoria Mans. NW10 —7D 42
Victoria Mans. SW8 —7J 77
　　　(off S. Lambeth Rd.)
Victoria M. NW6 —1J 59
Victoria M. SW4 —4F 93
Victoria M. SW18 —1A 108
Victorian Gro. N16 —4E 46
Victorian Rd. N16 —3F 47
Victoria Pde. Rich —1G 89
　　　(off Sandycombe Rd.)
Victoria Pk. Ind. Cen. E9 —7C 48
　　　(off Rothbury Rd.)
Victoria Pk. Rd. E2 & E9 —1J 63
Victoria Pk. Sq. E2 —3J 63
Victoria Pas. NW8
　　　　—4B 60 (3B 140)
Victoria Pl. Rich —5D 88
Victoria Pl. Shop. Cen. SW1
　　　　—4F 77 (3K 153)
Victoria Point. E13 —2J 65
　　　(off Victoria Rd.)
Victoria Rise. SW4 —3F 93
Victoria Rd. E4 —1B 20
Victoria Rd. E11 —4G 49
Victoria Rd. E13 —2J 65
Victoria Rd. E17 —2E 32
Victoria Rd. E18 —2K 33
Victoria Rd. N4 —7K 29
Victoria Rd. N15 —4G 31
Victoria Rd. N18 & N9 —4A 18

Victoria Rd. N22 —1G 29
Victoria Rd. NW4 —4E 26
Victoria Rd. NW6 —2H 59
Victoria Rd. NW7 —5G 13
Victoria Rd. NW10 —5K 57
Victoria Rd. SW14 —3K 89
Victoria Rd. W3 —5K 57
Victoria Rd. W5 —5B 56
Victoria Rd. W8 —3A 76
Victoria Rd. Bark —6F 51
Victoria Rd. Barn —4G 5
Victoria Rd. Bexh —4G 101
Victoria Rd. Brom —5B 128
Victoria Rd. Buck H —2G 21
Victoria Rd. Bush —1A 10
Victoria Rd. Chst —5E 114
Victoria Rd. Dag —5H 53
Victoria Rd. Eri —6K 85
　　　(in two parts)
Victoria Rd. Gnfd —5B 56
Victoria Rd. King T —2F 119
Victoria Rd. Mitc —7C 108
Victoria Rd. Ruis —4A 38
Victoria Rd. Sidc —3K 115
Victoria Rd. S'hall —3D 70
Victoria Rd. Surb —6D 118
Victoria Rd. Sutt —5B 132
Victoria Rd. Tedd —6A 104
Victoria Rd. Twic —7B 88
Victoria Sq. SW1
　　　　—3F 77 (1K 153)
Victoria St. E15 —7G 49
Victoria St. SW1
　　　　—3G 77 (2K 153)
Victoria St. Belv —5F 85
Victoria Ter. N4 —1A 46
Victoria Ter. NW10 —4B 58
Victoria Ter. W5 —1D 72
Victoria Ter. Harr —1H 39
Victoria Vs. Rich —4F 89
Victoria Way. SE7 —5K 81
Victoria Wharf. E14 —7A 64
　　　(off Narrow St.)
Victoria Works. NW2 —2E 42
Victor Rd. NW10 —3D 58
Victor Rd. SE20 —7K 111
Victor Rd. Harr —3G 23
Victor Rd. Tedd —4J 103
Victors Dri. Hamp —6C 102
Victors Way. Barn —3C 4
Victor Vs. N9 —3J 17
Victory Av. Mord —5A 122
Victory Bus. Cen. Iswth —4K 87
Victory Pl. E14 —7A 64
Victory Pl. SE17 —4D 78 (3E 156)
Victory Pl. SE19 —7F 111
Victory Rd. E11 —4J 33
Victory Rd. SW19 —7A 108
Victory Rd. M. SW19 —7A 108
Victory Sq. SE5 —7D 78
Victory Wlk. SE8 —1C 96
Victory Way. SE16 —2A 80
Victory Way. Houn —5A 70
Victory Way. Romf —2H 37
Vienna Clo. Ilf —2B 34
View Clo. N6 —7D 28
View Clo. Harr —4H 23
View Cres. N8 —5H 29
Viewfield Clo. Harr —7E 24
Viewfield Rd. SW18 —6H 91
Viewfield Rd. Bex —1C 116
Viewland Rd. SE18 —5K 83
View Rd. N6 —7D 28
View, The. SE2 —5E 84
Vigar Ct. Barn —3B 4

Viga Rd. N21 —6F 7
Vigilant Clo. SE26 —4G 111
Vignoles Rd. Romf —7G 37
Vigo St. W1 —7G 61 (3A 148)
Viking Clo. E3 —2A 64
Viking Ct. SW6 —6J 75
Viking Gdns. E6 —4C 66
Viking Ho. SE5 —2C 94
Viking Pl. E10 —1B 48
Viking Rd. S'hall —7C 54
Viking Way. Eri —3J 85
Villacourt Rd. SE18 —7A 84
Village Arc. E4 —1A 20
Village Clo. E4 —5K 19
Village Clo. NW3 —5B 44
 (off Belsize La.)
Village Ct. SE3 —3G 97
 (off Hurren Clo.)
Village Gdns. Eps —7B 130
Village Heights. Wfd G —5C 20
Village M. NW9 —2K 41
Village Pk. Clo. Enf —6K 7
Village Rd. N3 —2G 27
Village Rd. Enf —7J 7
Village Row. Sutt —7J 131
Village Way. NW10 —4K 41
Village Way. SE21 —6D 94
Village Way. Pinn —7C 22
Village Way E. Harr —7E 22
Villa Rd. SW9 —3A 94
Villas on the Heath. NW3
 —3A 44
Villas Rd. SE18 —5G 83
 (in three parts)
Villa St. SE17 —5D 78 (6F 157)
Villa Wlk. SE17 —5D 78 (6F 157)
Villiers Av. Surb —5F 119
Villiers Av. Twic —1D 102
Villiers Clo. E10 —2C 48
Villiers Clo. Surb —4F 119
Villiers Gro. Sutt —7F 131
Villiers Path. Surb —5E 118
Villiers Rd. NW2 —6C 42
Villiers Rd. Beck —2K 125
Villiers Rd. Iswth —2J 87
Villiers Rd. King T —4F 119
Villiers Rd. S'hall —1D 70
Villiers St. WC2 —1J 77 (3E 148)
Vincam Clo. Twic —7E 86
Vincent Clo. SE16 —2A 80
Vincent Clo. SW9 —1K 93
Vincent Clo. Barn —3A 4
Vincent Clo. Brom —4K 127
Vincent Clo. Sidc —1J 115
Vincent Ct. N4 —1J 45
Vincent Ct. NW4 —4F 27
Vincent Gdns. NW2 —3B 42
Vincent M. E3 —2C 64
Vincent Rd. E4 —6A 20
Vincent Rd. N15 —4C 30
Vincent Rd. N22 —2A 30
Vincent Rd. SE18 —4F 83
Vincent Rd. W3 —3J 73
Vincent Rd. Croy —7E 124
Vincent Rd. Dag —7E 52
Vincent Rd. Houn —3B 86
Vincent Rd. Iswth —1H 87
Vincent Rd. King T —3G 119
Vincent Rd. Wemb —7F 41
Vincent Row. Hamp —6G 103
Vincents Path. N'holt —6C 38
 (off Arnold Rd.)
Vincent Sq. N22 —2A 30

Vincent Sq. SW1
 —4H 77 (3B 154)
Vincent St. E16 —5H 65
Vincent St. SW1
 —4H 77 (3C 154)
Vincent Ter. N1 —2B 62
Vince St. EC1 —3D 62 (2F 145)
Vine Clo. Surb —6F 119
Vine Clo. Sutt —3A 132
Vine Ct. E1 —5G 63
Vine Ct. Harr —6E 24
Vinegar All. E17 —4D 32
Vine Gdns. Ilf —5G 51
Vinegar St. E1 —1H 79
Vinegar Yd. SE1
 —2E 78 (6G 151)
Vine Hill. EC1 —4A 62 (4J 143)
Vine La. SE1 —1E 78 (5H 151)
Vine Pl. W5 —1E 72
 (off Grange Pk.)
Vine Pl. Houn —4F 87
Vineries Bank. NW7 —5J 13
Vineries Clo. Dag —6F 53
Vineries, The. N14 —6B 6
Vineries, The. SE6 —1C 112
Vineries, The. Enf —3K 7
Vine Rd. E15 —7H 49
Vine Rd. SW13 —3B 90
Vinery Way. W6 —3D 74
Vines Av. N3 —1K 27
Vine Sq. W14 —5H 75
 (off Star Rd.)
Vine St. EC3 —6F 63 (1J 151)
Vine St. W1 —7G 61 (3B 148)
Vine St. Romf —4J 37
Vine St. Bri. EC1
 —4A 62 (4K 143)
Vine Yd. SE1 —2C 78 (6D 150)
Vineyard Av. NW7 —7B 14
Vineyard Clo. SE6 —1C 112
Vineyard Clo. King T —3F 119
Vineyard Gro. N3 —1K 27
Vineyard Hill Rd. SW19 —4J 107
Vineyard M. EC1
 —4A 62 (3K 143)
Vineyard Pas. Rich —5E 88
Vineyard Path. SW14 —3K 89
Vineyard Row. Hamp W —1C 118
Vineyard, The. Rich —5E 88
Vineyard Wlk. EC1
 —4A 62 (3J 143)
Viney Bank. Croy —7B 136
Viney Rd. SE13 —3D 96
Vining St. SW9 —4A 94
Vinson Clo. Orp —7K 129
Vintners Hall. EC4
 —7C 62 (2D 150)
Vintner's Pl. EC4
 —7C 62 (2D 150)
Vintry M. E17 —4C 32
Viola Av. SE2 —4B 84
Viola Av. Felt —6A 86
Viola Sq. W12 —7B 58
Violet Av. Enf —1J 7
Violet Clo. E16 —4G 65
Violet Clo. Wall —1E 132
Violet Gdns. Croy —5B 134
Violet Hill. NW8 —2A 60
Violet La. Croy —6B 134
Violet Rd. E3 —4D 64
Violet Rd. E17 —6C 32
Violet Rd. E18 —2K 33
Violet St. E2 —3H 63
Virgil Pl. W1 —5D 60 (6E 140)
Virgil St. SE1 —3K 77 (1H 155)

Virginia Clo. N Mald —4J 119
Virginia Clo. Romf —1J 37
Virginia Gdns. Ilf —2G 35
Virginia Rd. E2 —3F 63 (2J 145)
Virginia Rd. T Hth —1B 124
Virginia St. E1 —7G 63
Virginia Wlk. SW2 —6K 93
Viscount Clo. N11 —5A 16
Viscount Dri. E6 —5D 66
Viscount Gro. N'holt —3B 54
Viscount St. EC1
 —4C 62 (4C 144)
Vista Av. Enf —2E 8
Vista Dri. Ilf —5B 34
Vista, The. SE9 —7C 98
Vista, The. Sidc —5K 115
Vista Way. Harr —6E 24
Vivian Av. NW4 —5D 26
Vivian Av. Wemb —5G 41
Vivian Ct. N12 —5E 14
Vivian Gdns. Wemb —5G 41
Vivian Mans. NW4 —5D 26
 (off Vivian Av.)
Vivian Rd. E3 —2A 64
Vivian Sq. SE15 —3H 95
Vivian Way. N2 —5B 28
Vivienne Clo. Twic —6D 88
Voce Rd. SE18 —7H 83
Voewood Clo. N Mald —6B 120
Vogans Wharf. SE1
 —2F 79 (6K 151)
Voltaire Rd. SW4 —3H 93
Volta Way. Croy —1K 133
Voluntary Pl. E11 —6J 33
Vorley Rd. N19 —2G 45
Voss Ct. SW16 —6J 109
Voss St. E2 —3G 63
Voyager Clo. SE28 —6C 68
Vulcan Clo. Wall —7K 133
Vulcan Ga. Enf —2F 7
Vulcan Rd. SE4 —2B 96
Vulcan Sq. E14 —4C 80
Vulcan Ter. SE4 —2B 96
Vulcan Way. N7 —6K 45
Vyner Rd. W3 —7K 57
Vyner St. E2 —1H 63
Vyne, The. Bexh —3H 101

Wadding St. SE17
 —4D 78 (4E 156)
Waddington Clo. Enf —4K 7
Waddington Rd. E15 —5F 49
Waddington St. E15 —6F 49
Waddington Way. SE19 —7C 110
Waddon Clo. Croy —3A 134
Waddon Ct. Rd. Croy —4A 134
Waddon Marsh Way. Croy
 —1K 133
Waddon New Rd. Croy —3B 134
Waddon Pk. Av. Croy —4A 134
Waddon Rd. Croy —3A 134
Waddon Way. Croy —6A 134
Wade Ct. N10 —7A 16
Wade Ho. Enf —5J 7
Wade Rd. E16 —6A 66
Wades Gro. N21 —7F 7
Wades Hill. N21 —6F 7
Wades La. Tedd —5A 104
Wadeson St. E2 —2H 63
Wade's Pl. E14 —7D 64
Wadeville Av. Romf —6E 36
Wadeville Clo. Belv —6G 85
Wadham Av. E17 —7J 19
Wadham Gdns. NW3 —1C 60

Wadham Gdns. Gnfd —6H 39
Wadham Rd. E17 —1D 32
Wadham Rd. SW15 —4G 91
Wadhurst Clo. SE20 —2H 125
Wadhurst Rd. SW8 —7J 77
Wadhurst Rd. W4 —3K 73
Wadley Rd. E11 —7G 33
Wadsworth Bus. Cen. Gnfd
 —2C 56
Wadsworth Clo. Enf —5E 8
Wadsworth Clo. Gnfd —2C 56
Wadsworth Rd. Gnfd —2B 56
Wager St. E3 —4B 64
Waggoners Roundabout. (Junct.)
 —1A 86
Waggon La. N17 —6B 18
Waggon M. N14 —1B 16
Waghorn Rd. E13 —1A 66
Waghorn Rd. Harr —3D 24
Waghorn St. SE15 —3G 95
Wagner St. SE15 —7J 79
Wagtail Clo. NW9 —2A 26
Waight's Ct. King T —1E 118
Wainfleet Av. Romf —2J 37
Wainford Clo. SW19 —7F 91
Wainwright Gro. Iswth —4H 87
Waite Davies Rd. SE12 —7H 97
Waite St. SE15 —6F 79 (7J 157)
Wakefield Ct. SE26 —6J 111
Wakefield Gdns. SE19 —7E 110
Wakefield Gdns. Ilf —6C 34
Wakefield M. WC1
 —3J 61 (2F 143)
Wakefield Rd. N11 —5C 16
Wakefield Rd. N15 —5F 31
Wakefield Rd. Rich —5D 88
Wakefield St. E6 —1B 66
Wakefield St. N18 —5B 18
Wakefield St. WC1
 —4J 61 (2F 143)
Wakehams Hill. Pinn —3D 22
Wakeham St. N1 —6D 46
Wakehurst Rd. SW11 —5C 92
Wakeling Rd. W7 —5K 55
Wakeling St. E14 —6A 64
Wakelin Ho. SE23 —7A 96
Wakelin Rd. E15 —2G 65
Wakeman Rd. NW10 —3E 58
Wakemans Hill Av. NW9 —5K 25
Wakering Rd. Bark —6G 51
Wakerings, The. Bark —6G 51
Wakerley Clo. E6 —6D 66
Wakley St. EC1 —3B 62 (1A 144)
Walberswick St. SW8 —7J 77
Walbrook. EC4 —7D 62 (2E 150)
Walbrook Ho. N9 —2D 18
 (off Huntingdon Rd.)
Walbrook Wharf. EC4
 —7C 62 (3D 150)
 (off Bell Wharf La.)
Walburgh St. E1 —6H 63
Walcorde Av. SE17
 —4C 78 (4D 156)
Walcot Gdns. SE11
 —4A 78 (3J 155)
Walcot Rd. Enf —2G 9
Walcot Sq. SE11
 —4A 78 (3K 155)
Walcott St. SW1
 —4G 77 (3B 154)
Waldair Ct. E16 —2F 83
Waldeck Gro. SE27 —3B 110
Waldeck Rd. N15 —4B 30
Waldeck Rd. SW14 —3J 89
Waldeck Rd. W4 —6G 73

Waldeck Rd. W13 —6B 56
Waldegrave Av. Tedd —5K 103
Waldegrave Ct. Bark —1H 67
Waldegrave Gdns. Twic —2K 103
Waldegrave Pk. Twic —4K 103
Waldegrave Rd. N8 —3A 30
Waldegrave Rd. SE19 —7F 111
Waldegrave Rd. W5 —7F 57
Waldegrave Rd. Brom —4C 128
Waldegrave Rd. Dag —2C 52
Waldegrave Rd. Twic & Tedd
 —4K 103
Waldegrove. Croy —4F 135
Waldemar Av. SW6 —1G 91
Waldemar Av. W13 —1C 72
Waldemar Rd. SW19 —5J 107
Walden Av. N13 —4H 17
Walden Av. Chst —4D 114
Walden Av. Rain —2K 69
Walden Clo. Belv —5F 85
Walden Ct. SW8 —1H 93
Walden Gdns. T Hth —3K 123
Walden Pde. Chst —6D 114
 (in two parts)
Walden Rd. N17 —1D 30
Walden Rd. Chst —6D 114
Waldenshaw Rd. SE23 —1J 111
Walden St. E1 —6H 63
Walden Way. NW7 —6A 14
Waldo Clo. SW4 —5G 93
Waldo Ind. Est. Brom —3B 128
Waldo Pl. Mitc —7C 108
Waldorf Clo. S Croy —7B 134
Waldo Rd. NW10 —3C 58
Waldo Rd. Brom —3B 128
Waldram Cres. SE23 —1J 111
Waldram Pk. Rd. SE23 —1K 111
Waldram Pl. SE23 —1J 111
Waldrist Way. Eri —2F 85
Waldron Gdns. Brom —3F 127
Waldronhyrst. S Croy —4B 134
Waldron M. SW3
 —6B 76 (7B 152)
Waldron Rd. SW18 —3A 108
Waldron Rd. Harr —1J 39
Waldron's Path. S Croy —4C 134
Waldrons, The. Croy —4B 134
Waldrons Yd. S Harr —2H 39
Waleran Clo. Stan —5E 10
Walerand Rd. SE13 —2E 96
Waleran Flats. SE1
 —4E 78 (3G 157)
Wales Av. Cars —5C 132
Wales Farm Rd. W3 —5K 57
Waleton Acres. Wall —6H 133
Waley St. E1 —5A 64
Walfield Av. N20 —7E 4
Walford Rd. N16 —4E 46
Walfrey Gdns. Dag —7E 52
Walham Grn. Ct. SW6 —7K 75
 (off Waterford Rd.)
Walham Gro. SW6 —7J 75
Walham Rise. SW19 —6G 107
Walham Yd. SW6 —7J 75
Walkato Lodge. Buck H —1F 21
Walkden Rd. Chst —5E 114
Walker Clo. N11 —4B 16
Walker Clo. SE18 —4G 83
Walker Clo. W7 —1J 71
Walker Clo. Hamp —6D 102
Walker's Ct. W1
 —7H 61 (2C 148)
Walkerscroft Mead. SE21
 —1C 110
Walkers Pl. SW15 —4G 91

Walkford Way. SE15 —7F 79
Walks, The. N2 —3B 28
Walk, The. N13 —3F 17
(off Fox La.)
Wallace Clo. SE28 —7D 68
Wallace Cres. Cars —5D 132
Wallace Ho. N7 —6K 45
(off Caledonian Rd.)
Wallace Rd. N1 —6C 46
Wallace Way. N19 —2H 45
(off St John's Way)
Wallbrook Bus. Cen. Houn
—3A 86
Wallbutton Rd. SE4 —2A 96
Wallcote Av. NW2 —1F 43
Wall Ct. N4 —1K 45
(off Stroud Grn. Rd.)
Wall End Ct. E6 —1E 66
(off Wall End Rd.)
Wall End Rd. E6 —7D 50
Waller Rd. SE14 —1K 95
Wallers Clo. Dag —1E 68
Wallers Rd. Wfd G —6J 21
Wallflower St. W12 —7B 58
Wallgrave Rd. SW5 —4K 75
Wallgrave Ter. SW5 —4J 75
(off Redfield La.)
Wallingford Av. W10 —6F 59
Wallington Corner. Wall —4F 133
(off Manor Rd. N.)
Wallington Ct. Wall —6F 133
(off Stanley Pk. Rd.)
Wallington Green. (Junct.)
—4F 133
Wallington Rd. Ilf —7K 35
Wallington Sq. Wall —6F 133
Wallis All. SE1 —2C 78 (6D 150)
Wallis Clo. SW11 —3B 92
Wallis Rd. E9 —6B 48
Wallis Rd. S'hall —6F 55
Wallis's Cotts. SW2 —7J 93
Wallman Pl. N22 —1K 29
Wallorton Gdns. SW14 —4K 89
Wallside. EC2 —5C 62 (6D 144)
Wall St. N1 —6D 46
Wallwood Rd. E11 —7F 33
Wallwood St. E14 —5B 64
Walmar Clo. Barn —1G 5
Walmer Clo. E4 —2J 19
Walmer Clo. Romf —2H 37
Walmer Gdns. W13 —2A 72
Walmer Pl. W1 —5D 60 (5E 140)
Walmer Rd. W10 —6E 58
Walmer Rd. W11 —7G 59
Walmer St. W1 —5D 60 (5E 140)
Walmer Ter. SE18 —4G 83
Walmgate Rd. Gnfd —1B 56
Walmington Fold. N12 —6D 14
Walm La. NW2 —6E 42
Walney Wlk. N1 —6C 46
Walnut Clo. SE8 —6B 80
Walnut Clo. Cars —5D 132
Walnut Clo. Ilf —4G 35
Walnut Clo. E17 —4E 32
Walnut Ct. W5 —2E 72
Walnut Ct. W8 —3K 75
(off St Marys Ga.)
Walnut Fields. Eps —7B 130
Walnut Gdns. E15 —4G 49
Walnut Gro. Enf —5J 7
Walnut M. Sutt —7A 132
Walnut Rd. E10 —2C 48
Walnut Tree Av. Mitc —3C 122
Walnut Tree Clo. SW13 —1B 90
Walnut Tree Clo. Chst —1H 129

Walnut Tree Cotts. SW19
—5G 107
Walnut Tree Rd. SE10 —5G 81
(in two parts)
Walnut Tree Rd. Bren —6E 72
Walnut Tree Rd. Dag —2D 52
Walnut Tree Rd. Houn —6D 70
Walnut Tree Wlk. SE11
—4A 78 (3J 155)
Walnut Way. Buck H —3G 21
Walnut Way. Ruis —6A 38
Walpole Av. Rich —2F 89
Walpole Clo. W13 —2C 72
Walpole Ct. Twic —2J 103
Walpole Cres. Tedd —5K 103
Walpole Gdns. W4 —5J 73
Walpole Gdns. Twic —2J 103
Walpole Lodge. W13 —1C 72
Walpole M. NW8 —1B 60
Walpole Pl. SE18 —4F 83
Walpole Pl. Tedd —5K 103
Walpole Rd. E6 —7A 50
Walpole Rd. E17 —4A 32
Walpole Rd. E18 —1H 33
Walpole Rd. N17 —2C 30
(in two parts)
Walpole Rd. SE14 —7B 80
Walpole Rd. SW19 —6B 108
Walpole Rd. Brom —5B 128
Walpole Rd. Croy —2D 134
Walpole Rd. Surb —7E 118
Walpole Rd. Tedd —5K 103
Walpole Rd. Twic —2J 103
Walpole St. SW3
—5D 76 (5E 152)
Walrond Av. Wemb —5E 40
Walsham Clo. N16 —1G 47
Walsham Clo. SE28 —7D 68
Walsham Ho. SE14 —2K 95
Walsham Rd. SE14 —2K 95
Walsham Rd. Felt —7A 86
Walsingham. NW8 —1B 60
Walsingham Gdns. Eps —4A 130
Walsingham Pk. Chst —2H 129
Walsingham Pl. SW11 —6E 92
Walsingham Rd. E5 —3G 47
Walsingham Rd. W13 —1A 72
Walsingham Rd. Enf —4J 7
Walsingham Rd. Mitc —5D 122
Walsingham Wlk. Belv —6G 85
Walter Geo. Ho. SE15 —1J 95
(off Lausanne Rd.)
Walter Hurford Pde. E12 —4E 50
Walter Rodney Clo. E6 —6D 50
Walter Sisulu Ho. Wemb —7F 25
Walters Rd. SE25 —4E 124
Walters Rd. Enf —4D 8
Walter St. E2 —3K 63
Walter St. King T —1E 118
Walters Way. SE23 —6K 95
Walters Yd. Brom —2J 127
Walter Ter. E1 —6K 63
Walterton Rd. W9 —4H 59
Walter Wlk. Edgw —6D 12
Waltham Av. NW9 —6G 25
Waltham Dri. Edgw —2G 25
Waltham Ho. NW8 —1A 60
Waltham Pk. Way. E17 —1C 32
Waltham Rd. Cars —7B 122
Waltham Rd. S'hall —3C 70
Waltham Rd. Wfd G —6H 21
Walthamstow Av. E4 —6F 19
Walthamstow Bus. Cen. E17
—2E 32
Waltham Way. E4 —3G 19

Waltheof Av. N17 —1D 30
Waltheof Gdns. N17 —1D 30
Walton Av. Harr —5D 38
Walton Av. N Mald —4B 120
Walton Av. Sutt —3H 131
Walton Clo. E5 —3K 47
Walton Clo. NW2 —2D 42
Walton Clo. SW8 —7J 77
Walton Clo. Harr —4H 23
Walton Ct. New Bar —5F 5
Walton Croft. Harr —4J 39
Walton Dri. NW10 —6K 41
Walton Dri. Harr —4H 23
Walton Gdns. W3 —5H 57
Walton Gdns. Wemb —2E 40
Walton Grn. New Ad —7D 136
Walton Ho. E4 —5H 19
Walton Ho. E17 —3D 32
(off Drive, The)
Walton Pl. SW3 —3D 76 (1E 152)
Walton Rd. E12 —4E 50
(in two parts)
Walton Rd. E13 —2A 66
Walton Rd. N15 —4F 31
Walton Rd. Harr —4H 23
Walton Rd. Romf —1F 37
Walton Rd. Sidc —3B 116
Walton St. SW3 —4C 76 (3D 152)
Walton St. Enf —1J 7
Walton Way. W3 —5H 57
Walton Way. Mitc —4G 123
Walt Whitman Clo. SE24 —4B 94
Walworth Pl. SE17
—5C 78 (6D 156)
Walworth Rd. SE1 & SE17
—4B 78 (3C 156)
Walwyn Av. Brom —3B 128
Wanborough Dri. SW15 —1D 106
Wanderer Dri. Bark —3C 68
Wandle Bank. SW19 —6A 108
Wandle Bank. Croy —3J 133
Wandle Ct. Croy —3J 133
Wandle Ct. Gdns. Croy —3J 133
Wandle Ho. Brom —5F 113
Wandle Pk. Trad. Est., The. Croy
—1A 134
Wandle Rd. SW17 —2C 108
Wandle Rd. Bedd —3J 133
Wandle Rd. Croy —3G 134
Wandle Rd. Mord —4A 122
Wandle Side. Croy —3K 133
Wandle Side. Wall —3F 133
Wandle Way. SW18 —1K 107
Wandle Way. Mitc —5D 122
Wandon Rd. SW6 —7K 75
Wandsworth Bri. SW6 & SW18
—3K 91
Wandsworth Bri. Rd. SW6
—1K 91
Wandsworth Comn. N. Side.
SW18 —5B 92
Wandsworth Comn. W. Side.
SW18 —5A 92
Wandsworth Enterprise Cen.
SW18 —4K 91
Wandsworth Gyratory. (Junct.)
—5K 91
Wandsworth High St. SW18
—5J 91
Wandsworth Plain. SW18
—5K 91
Wandsworth Rd. SW8
—3F 93 (7E 154)
Wangey Rd. Romf —7D 36

Wangford Ho. SW9 —4B 94
(off Loughborough Pk.)
Wanless Rd. SE24 —3C 94
Wanley Rd. SE5 —4D 94
Wanlip Rd. E13 —4K 65
Wannock Gdns. Ilf —1F 35
Wansbeck Ct. Enf —3G 7
(off Waverley Rd.)
Wansbeck Rd. E9 & E3 —7B 48
Wansdown Pl. SW6 —7K 75
Wansey St. SE17
—4C 78 (4C 156)
Wansford Rd. Wfd G —1A 34
Wanstead Clo. Brom —2A 128
Wanstead Gdns. Ilf —6B 34
Wanstead La. Ilf —6B 34
Wanstead Pk. Av. E12 —1B 50
Wanstead Pk. Rd. Ilf —6B 34
Wanstead Pl. E11 —6J 33
Wanstead Rd. Brom —2A 128
Wansunt Rd. Bex —1J 117
Wantage Rd. SE12 —5H 97
Wantz Rd. Dag —4H 53
Wapping Dock St. E1 —1H 79
Wapping High St. E1 —1G 79
Wapping La. E1 —7H 63
Wapping Wall. E1 —1J 79
Warbank La. King T —7B 106
Warbeck Rd. W12 —2D 74
Warberry Rd. N22 —2K 29
Warboys App. King T —6H 105
Warboys Cres. E4 —5K 19
Warboys Rd. King T —6H 105
Warburton Clo. N1 —6E 46
(off Culford Rd.)
Warburton Clo. Harr —6C 10
Warburton Rd. E8 —1H 63
Warburton Rd. Twic —1F 103
Warburton St. E8 —1H 63
Warburton Ter. E17 —2D 32
Wardalls Clo. SE14 —7J 79
Wardalls Ho. SE8 —6B 80
(off Staunton St.)
Ward Clo. Eri —6K 85
Ward Clo. S Croy —6E 134
Wardell Clo. NW7 —7F 13
Wardell Field. NW9 —1A 26
Warden Av. Harr —1D 38
Warden Rd. NW5 —6F 45
Wardens Gro. SE1
—1C 78 (5C 150)
Wardle St. E9 —5K 47
Wardley St. SW18 —7K 91
Wardo Av. SW6 —1G 91
Wardour M. W1
—6G 61 (1B 148)
Wardour St. W1
—6G 61 (7B 142)
Ward Point. SE11
—4A 78 (4J 155)
Ward Rd. E15 —1F 65
Ward Rd. N19 —3G 45
Ward Rd. SW19 —1A 122
Wardrobe Pl. EC4
—6B 62 (1B 150)
Wardrobe Ter. EC4
—7B 62 (2B 150)
Wards Rd. Ilf —7H 35
Ware Ct. Sutt —4H 131
Wareham Clo. Houn —4F 87
Wareham Ho. SW8 —7K 77
Waremead Rd. Ilf —5F 35
Warepoint Dri. SE28 —2H 83
Warfield Rd. NW10 —3F 59
Warfield Rd. Hamp —7F 103

Warfield Yd. NW10 —3F 59
(off Warfield Rd.)
Wargrave Av. N15 —6F 31
Wargrave Rd. Harr —3G 39
Warham Rd. N4 —5A 30
Warham Rd. Harr —2K 23
Warham Rd. S Croy —5B 134
Warham St. SE5 —7B 78
Waring & Gillow Est. W3 —4G 57
Waring Rd. Sidc —6C 116
Waring St. SE27 —4C 110
Warkworth Gdns. Iswth —7A 72
Warkworth Rd. N17 —7J 17
Warland Rd. SE18 —7H 83
Warley Av. Dag —7F 37
Warley Clo. E10 —1B 48
Warley Rd. N9 —2D 18
Warley Rd. Ilf —1E 34
Warley Rd. Wfd G —7E 20
Warley St. E2 —3K 63
Warlingham Rd. T Hth —4B 124
Warlock Rd. W9 —4H 59
Warlters Clo. N7 —4J 45
Warlters Rd. N7 —4J 45
Warltersville Mans. N19 —7J 29
Warltersville Rd. N19 —7J 29
Warmington Clo. E5 —3K 47
Warmington Rd. SE24 —6C 94
Warmington St. E13 —4J 65
Warmington Tower. SE14
—1A 96
Warminster Gdns. SE25
—2G 125
Warminster Rd. SE25 —2F 125
Warminster Sq. SE25 —2G 125
Warminster Way. Mitc —1F 123
Warmley Ct. SE15 —6E 78
(off Newent Clo.)
Warndon St. SE16 —4K 79
Warneford Rd. Harr —3D 24
Warneford St. E9 —1H 63
Warne Pl. Sidc —6B 100
Warner Av. Sutt —2G 131
Warner Clo. E15 —5G 49
Warner Clo. NW9 —7B 26
Warner Clo. Hamp —5D 102
Warner Pl. E2 —2G 63
Warner Rd. E17 —4A 32
Warner Rd. N8 —4H 29
Warner Rd. SE5 —1C 94
Warner Rd. Brom —7H 113
Warners Clo. Wfd G —5D 20
Warners La. Rich —4D 104
Warners Path. Wfd G —5D 20
Warner Ter. E14 —6D 64
(off Broomfield St.)
Warner Yd. EC1 —4A 62 (4J 143)
Warnford Ho. SW15 —6A 90
(off Tunworth Cres.)
Warnham Ct. Rd. Cars —7D 132
Warnham Ho. SW2 —7K 93
(off Up. Tulse Hill)
Warnham Rd. N12 —5H 15
Warple Way. W3 —2A 74
Warren Av. E10 —3E 48
Warren Av. Brom —7G 113
Warren Av. Rich —4H 89
Warren Av. S Croy —7K 135
Warren Clo. N9 —7E 8
Warren Clo. SE21 —7C 94
Warren Clo. Bexh —5G 101
Warren Clo. Hayes —5A 54
Warren Clo. Wemb —2D 40
Warren Ct. N17 —3G 31
(off High Cross Rd.)
Warren Ct. W5 —5C 56

Warren Ct. *Beck* —7C **112**
Warren Ct. *Croy* —1E **134**
Warren Cres. *N9* —7A **8**
Warren Cutting. *King T* —7K **105**
Warrender Rd. *N19* —4G **45**
Warren Dri. *Gnfd* —4F **55**
Warren Dri. *Ruis* —7B **22**
Warren Dri. N. *Surb* —7H **119**
Warren Dri. S. *Surb* —7J **119**
Warren Dri., The. *E11* —7A **34**
Warren Farm Cotts. *Romf*
—4F **37**
Warren Fields. *Stan* —4J **11**
Warren Footpath. *Twic* —1C **104**
Warren Gdns. *E15* —5F **49**
Warren La. *SE18* —3F **83**
Warren La. *Stan* —2F **11**
Warren M. *W1* —4G **61** (4A **142**)
Warren Pk. *King T* —6J **105**
Warren Pk. Rd. *Sutt* —6C **132**
Warren Pl. *E1* —6K **63**
(off Caroline St.)
Warren Pond Rd. *E4* —1C **20**
Warren Rise. *N Mald* —1K **119**
Warren Rd. *E4* —2K **19**
Warren Rd. *E10* —3E **48**
Warren Rd. *E11* —6A **34**
Warren Rd. *NW2* —2B **42**
Warren Rd. *SW19* —6C **108**
Warren Rd. *Bexh* —5G **101**
Warren Rd. *Brom* —2J **137**
Warren Rd. *Bush* —1B **10**
Warren Rd. *Croy* —1F **135**
Warren Rd. *Ilf* —5H **35**
Warren Rd. *King T* —6J **105**
Warren Rd. *Sidc* —3C **116**
Warren Rd. *Twic* —6G **87**
Warrens Shawe La. *Edgw*
—2C **12**
Warren St. *W1* —4F **61** (4A **142**)
Warren Ter. *Romf* —4D **36**
(in two parts)
Warren, The. *E12* —4C **50**
Warren, The. *Houn* —7D **70**
Warren, The. *Wor Pk* —3A **130**
Warren Wlk. *SE7* —6A **82**
Warren Way. *NW7* —6B **14**
Warren Wood Clo. *Brom*
—2H **137**
Warriner Gdns. *SW11* —1D **92**
Warrington Cres. *W9* —4A **60**
Warrington Gdns. *W9* —4A **60**
Warrington Pl. *E14* —1E **80**
(off Yabsley St.)
Warrington Rd. *Croy* —3B **134**
Warrington Rd. *Dag* —2D **52**
Warrington Rd. *Harr* —5J **23**
Warrington Rd. *Rich* —5D **88**
Warrington Sq. *Dag* —2D **52**
Warrior Sq. *E12* —4E **50**
Warsaw Clo. *Ruis* —6A **38**
Warspite Rd. *SE18* —3C **82**
Warton Rd. *E15* —7E **48**
Warwall. *E6* —6F **67**
Warwick. *Sidc* —5B **116**
Warwick Av. *W9 & W2* —4K **59**
Warwick Av. *Harr* —4D **38**
Warwick Chambers. *W8* —3J **75**
(off Pater St.)
Warwick Clo. *SW15* —7B **90**
Warwick Clo. *Barn* —5G **5**
Warwick Clo. *Bex* —7F **101**
Warwick Clo. *Bush* —1D **10**
Warwick Clo. *Hamp* —7G **103**

Warwick Ct. *W7* —6K **55**
(off Copley Clo.)
Warwick Ct. *WC1*
—5K **61** (6H **143**)
Warwick Ct. *Brom* —2G **127**
Warwick Ct. *Harr* —3J **23**
Warwick Ct. *New Bar* —5E **4**
(off Station Rd.)
Warwick Ct. *N'holt* —5E **38**
(off Newmarket Av.)
Warwick Cres. *W2* —5A **60**
Warwick Dene. *W5* —1E **72**
Warwick Est. *W2* —5K **59**
Warwick Gdns. *N4* —5C **30**
Warwick Gdns. *W14* —3H **75**
Warwick Gdns. *Barn* —1C **4**
Warwick Gdns. *Ilf* —1F **51**
Warwick Gdns. *T Hth* —3A **124**
Warwick Gro. *E5* —2H **47**
Warwick Gro. *Surb* —7F **119**
Warwick Ho. St. *SW1*
—1H **77** (4D **148**)
Warwick La. *EC4*
—6B **62** (7B **144**)
Warwick Lodge. *Twic* —3F **103**
Warwick Pde. *Harr* —2B **24**
Warwick Pas. *EC4*
—6B **62** (7B **144**)
(off Old Bailey)
Warwick Pl. *W5* —2D **72**
Warwick Pl. *W9* —5A **60**
Warwick Pl. *Th Dit* —6A **118**
Warwick Pl. N. *SW1*
—4G **77** (4A **154**)
Warwick Rd. *E4* —5H **19**
Warwick Rd. *E11* —5K **33**
Warwick Rd. *E12* —5C **50**
Warwick Rd. *E15* —6H **49**
Warwick Rd. *E17* —1B **32**
Warwick Rd. *N11* —6C **16**
Warwick Rd. *N18* —4K **17**
Warwick Rd. *SE20* —3H **125**
Warwick Rd. *W5* —2D **72**
Warwick Rd. *W14 & SW5*
—4H **75**
Warwick Rd. *Barn* —4E **4**
Warwick Rd. *Houn* —3A **86**
Warwick Rd. *King T* —1C **118**
Warwick Rd. *N Mald* —3J **119**
Warwick Rd. *Sidc* —5B **116**
Warwick Rd. *S'hall* —3D **70**
Warwick Rd. *Sutt* —4A **132**
Warwick Rd. *T Hth* —3A **124**
Warwick Rd. *Twic* —1J **103**
Warwick Rd. *Well* —3C **100**
Warwick Row. *SW1*
—3G **77** (1K **153**)
Warwickshire Path. *SE8* —7B **80**
Warwickshire Rd. *N16* —4E **46**
Warwick Sq. *EC4*
—6B **62** (7B **144**)
Warwick Sq. *SW1*
—5G **77** (5A **154**)
Warwick Sq. M. *SW1*
—4G **77** (4A **154**)
Warwick St. *W1*
—7G **61** (2B **148**)
Warwick Ter. *E17* —5F **33**
Warwick Ter. *SE18* —6H **83**
Warwick Way. *SW1*
—5F **77** (5J **153**)
Warwick Yd. *EC1*
—4C **62** (4D **144**)
Washington Av. *E12* —4C **50**

Washington Rd. *E6* —7A **50**
Washington Rd. *E18* —2H **33**
Washington Rd. *SW13* —7C **74**
Washington Rd. *King T* —2G **119**
Washington Rd. *Wor Pk*
—2D **130**
Wastdale Rd. *SE23* —1K **111**
Watchfield Ct. *W4* —5J **73**
Watcombe Cotts. *Rich* —6G **73**
Watcombe Pl. *SE25* —5H **125**
Watcombe Rd. *SE25* —5H **125**
Waterbank Rd. *SE6* —3D **112**
Waterbeach Rd. *Dag* —6C **52**
Water Brook La. *NW4* —5E **26**
Watercress Pl. *N1* —7E **46**
(off Hertford Rd.)
Waterdale Rd. *SE2* —6A **84**
Waterden Cres. *E15* —5C **48**
Waterden Rd. *E15* —5C **48**
Waterer Ho. *SE6* —4E **112**
Waterer Rise. *Wall* —6H **133**
Waterfall Clo. *N14* —3B **16**
Waterfall Cotts. *SW19* —6B **108**
Waterfall Rd. *N11 & N14* —4A **16**
Waterfall Rd. *SW19* —6B **108**
Waterfall Ter. *SW17* —6C **108**
Waterfield Clo. *SE28* —1B **84**
Waterfield Clo. *Belv* —3G **85**
Waterfield Gdns. *SE25* —4E **124**
Waterfield Gdns. *SE28* —1B **84**
Waterford Rd. *SW6* —7K **75**
Water Gdns. *Stan* —6G **11**
Water Gdns., The. *W2*
—6C **60** (7D **140**)
Watergardens, The. *King T*
—6J **105**
Watergate. *EC4* —7B **62** (2A **150**)
Watergate St. *SE8* —6C **80**
Watergate Wlk. *WC2*
—1J **77** (4F **149**)
Water Glade Cen., The. *W5*
—7D **56**
Waterhall Av. *E4* —4B **20**
Waterhall Clo. *E17* —1K **31**
Waterhouse Clo. *E16* —5B **66**
Waterhouse Clo. *NW3* —5B **44**
Waterhouse Clo. *W6* —4F **75**
Waterhouse Sq. *EC1*
—6A **62** (6J **143**)
Wateridge Clo. *E14* —3C **80**
Water La. *E15* —6G **49**
Water La. *EC3* —7E **62** (3H **151**)
Water La. *N9* —1C **18**
Water La. *NW1* —7F **45**
Water La. *SE14* —7J **79**
Water La. *Ilf* —3J **51**
Water La. *King T* —1D **118**
Water La. *Rich* —5D **88**
Water La. *Sidc* —3F **117**
(in two parts)
Water La. *Twic* —1A **104**
Water Lily Clo. *S'hall* —2G **71**
Waterloo Bri. *WC2 & SE1*
—7K **61** (3G **149**)
Waterloo Clo. *E9* —5J **47**
Waterloo Gdns. *E2* —2J **63**
Waterloo Gdns. *Romf* —6K **37**
Waterloo Pas. *NW6* —7H **43**
Waterloo Pl. *SW1*
—1H **77** (4C **148**)
Waterloo Pl. *Rich* —6G **73**
(Kew)
Waterloo Pl. *Rich* —4E **88**
(Richmond)
Waterloo Rd. *E6* —7A **50**

Waterloo Rd. *E7* —5H **49**
Waterloo Rd. *E10* —7C **32**
Waterloo Rd. *NW2* —1C **42**
Waterloo Rd. *SE1*
—2A **78** (4H **149**)
Waterloo Rd. *Ilf* —2G **35**
Waterloo Rd. *Romf* —5K **37**
Waterloo Rd. *Sutt* —5B **132**
Waterloo Ter. *N1* —7B **46**
Waterlow Ct. *NW11* —7K **27**
Waterlow Rd. *N19* —1G **45**
Watermans Clo. *King T* —7E **104**
Watermans Ct. *Bren* —6E **72**
Watermans M. *W5* —7E **56**
Waterman's Sq. *SE20* —7J **111**
Waterman St. *SW15* —3F **91**
Waterman's Wlk. *EC4*
—7D **62** (3E **150**)
Watermans Wlk. *SE16* —2A **80**
Waterman Way. *E1* —1H **79**
Watermead Ho. *E9* —5A **48**
Watermead La. *Cars* —7D **122**
Watermeadow La. *SW6* —2A **92**
Watermead Rd. *SE6* —4E **112**
Watermead Way. *N17* —3G **31**
Waterman's Sq. *SE20* —7J **111**
Water M. *SE15* —3J **95**
Watermill Bus. Cen. *Enf* —2G **9**
Watermill Clo. *Rich* —3C **104**
Water Mill Ho. *Felt* —2E **102**
Watermill La. *N18* —5K **17**
Watermill Way. *SW19* —1B **122**
Watermill Way. *Felt* —2D **102**
Watermint Quay. *N16* —7G **31**
Water Rd. *Wemb* —1F **57**
Watersfield Way. *Edgw* —7J **11**
Waters Gdns. *Dag* —5G **53**
Waterside. *E17* —6J **31**
Waterside. *Beck* —1B **126**
Waterside Clo. *SE16* —2G **79**
Waterside Clo. *Bark* —4A **52**
Waterside Clo. *N'holt* —3D **54**
Waterside Pl. *NW1* —1E **60**
Waterside Point. *SW11* —7C **76**
Waterside Rd. *S'hall* —3E **70**
Waterside Trad. Cen. *W7* —3J **71**
Waterside Way. *SW17* —4A **108**
Watersmeet Way. *SE28* —6C **68**
Waterson St. *E2*
—3E **62** (1H **145**)
Waters Pl. *SW15* —2E **90**
Watersplash Clo. *King T*
—3E **118**
Waters Rd. *SE6* —3G **113**
Waters Rd. *King T* —2H **119**
Waters Sq. *King T* —3H **119**
Water St. *WC2* —7A **62** (2J **149**)
Water Tower Hill. *Croy* —4D **134**
Water Tower Pl. *N1* —1B **62**
Waterworks Corner. (Junct.)
—2G **33**
Waterworks La. *E5* —2K **47**
Waterworks Rd. *SW2* —6K **93**
Waterworks Yd. *Croy* —3C **134**
Watery La. *SW20* —2H **121**
Watery La. *N'holt* —2A **54**
Watery La. *Sidc* —6B **116**
Wates Way. *Mitc* —6D **122**
Wateville Rd. *N17* —1C **30**
Watford By-Pass. *Stan & Edgw*
—1G **11**
Watford Clo. *SW11* —1C **92**
Watford Rd. *E16* —5J **65**
Watford Rd. *Harr & Wemb*
—7A **24**

Watford Way. *NW7 & NW4*
—4F **13**
Watkin Rd. *Wemb* —3H **41**
Watkins. *Sidc* —5B **116**
Watkinson Rd. *N7* —6K **45**
Watling Av. *Edgw* —1J **25**
Watling Ct. *EC4* —6C **62** (1D **150**)
Watling Farm Clo. *Stan* —1H **11**
Watling Gdns. *NW2* —6G **43**
Watling Ga. *NW9* —4K **25**
Watlings Clo. *Croy* —6A **126**
Watlings St. *EC4* —6C **62** (1D **150**)
Watling St. *Bexh* —4H **101**
Watlington Gro. *SE26* —5A **112**
Watney Mkt. *E1* —6H **63**
Watney Rd. *SW14* —3J **89**
Watney's Rd. *Mitc* —5H **123**
Watney St. *E1* —6H **63**
Watson Av. *E6* —7E **50**
Watson Av. *Sutt* —2G **131**
Watson Clo. *N16* —5D **46**
Watson Clo. *SW19* —6C **108**
Watson's M. *W1*
—5C **60** (6D **140**)
Watsons Rd. *N22* —1K **29**
Watson's St. *SE8* —7C **80**
Watson St. *E13* —2K **65**
Watsons Yd. *NW2* —2C **41**
Wattisfield Rd. *E5* —3J **47**
Watts Clo. *N15* —5E **30**
Watts Gro. *E3* —5D **64**
Watts La. *Chst* —1F **129**
Watts La. *Tedd* —5A **104**
Watts Point. *E13* —1J **65**
(off Brooks Rd.)
Watts Rd. *Th Dit* —7A **118**
Watts St. *E1* —1H **79**
Wat Tyler Rd. N8 —3J **29**
(off Boynton Rd.)
Wat Tyler Rd. *SE3 & SE10*
—2E **96**
Wauthier Clo. *N13* —5G **17**
Wavell Dri. *Sidc* —6J **99**
Wavel M. *N8* —4H **29**
Wavel M. *NW6* —7K **43**
Wavel Pl. *SE26* —4F **111**
Wavendon Av. *W4* —5K **73**
Waveney Av. *SE15* —4H **95**
Waveney Clo. *E1* —1G **79**
Waveney Ho. *SE15* —4H **95**
Waverley Av. *E4* —4G **19**
Waverley Av. *E17* —3F **33**
Waverley Av. *Surb* —6H **119**
Waverley Av. *Sutt* —2K **131**
Waverley Av. *Twic* —1D **102**
Waverley Av. *Wemb* —5F **41**
Waverley Clo. *E18* —1A **34**
Waverley Clo. *Brom* —5B **128**
Waverley Clo. *SE26* —5J **111**
Waverley Ct. *Enf* —3H **7**
Waverley Cres. *SE18* —5H **83**
Waverley Gdns. *E6* —5C **66**
Waverley Gdns. *NW10* —2F **57**
Waverley Gdns. *Bark* —2J **67**
Waverley Gdns. *Ilf* —2G **35**
Waverley Gro. *N3* —3G **27**
Waverley Ind. Est. *Harr* —3H **23**
Waverley Pl. *N4* —2B **46**
Waverley Pl. *NW8* —2B **60**
Waverley Rd. *E17* —3E **32**
Waverley Rd. *E18* —1A **34**
Waverley Rd. *N8* —6J **29**
Waverley Rd. *N17* —7C **18**
Waverley Rd. *SE18* —5H **83**
Waverley Rd. *SE25* —4H **125**

Waverley Rd. Enf —3G 7
Waverley Rd. Eps —5D 130
Waverley Rd. Harr —2C 38
Waverley Rd. S'hall —7E 54
Waverley Vs. N17 —2F 31
Waverley Way. Cars —6C 132
Waverton Rd. SW18 —7A 92
Waverton St. W1
—1E 76 (4J 147)
Wavertree Ct. SW2 —1J 109
Wavertree Rd. E18 —2J 33
Wavertree Rd. SW2 —1K 109
Waxlow Cres. S'hall —6E 54
Waxlow Ho. Hayes —5B 54
Waxlow Rd. NW10 —2J 57
Waxwell Clo. Pinn —2B 22
Waxwell Farm Ho. Pinn —2B 22
Waxwell La. Pinn —2B 22
Waxwell Ter. SE1
—2K 77 (7H 149)
Wayfarer Rd. N'holt —3B 54
Wayfield Link. SE9 —6H 99
Wayford St. SW11 —2C 92
Wayland Av. E8 —5G 47
Wayland Clo. E8 —5G 47
Wayland Ho. SW9 —2A 94
(off Robsart St.)
Waylands Mead. Beck —1D 126
Waylett Ho. SE11
—5K 77 (6J 155)
Waylett Pl. SE27 —3B 110
Waylett Pl. Wemb —4D 40
Wayne Kirkum Way. NW6
—5H 43
Waynflete Av. Croy —3B 134
Waynflete Sq. W10 —7F 59
Waynflete St. SW18 —2A 108
Wayside. NW11 —1G 45
Wayside. SW14 —5J 89
Wayside Clo. N14 —6B 6
Wayside Clo. Twic —6C 88
Wayside Ct. Wemb —3G 41
Wayside Gdns. SE9 —4D 114
Wayside Gdns. Dag —5G 53
Wayside Gro. SE9 —4D 114
Wayside M. Ilf —5E 34
Weald Clo. SE16 —5H 79
Weald Clo. Brom —2C 138
Weald La. Harr —2H 23
Weald Rise. Harr —7E 10
Weald Sq. E5 —2G 47
Wealdstone Rd. Sutt —2H 131
Weald, The. Chst —6D 114
Weald Way. Romf —6H 37
Wealdwood Gdns. Pinn —6A 10
Weale Rd. E4 —3A 20
Weall Ct. Pinn —4C 22
Weardale Gdns. Enf —1J 7
Weardale Rd. SE13 —4F 97
Wear Pl. E2 —3H 63
Wearside Rd. SE13 —4D 96
Weatherbury Ho. N19 —3H 45
(off Wedmore St.)
Weatherley Clo. E3 —5B 64
Weaver Clo. E6 —7F 67
Weavers Clo. Iswth —4J 87
Weavers Ho. E11 —6J 33
(off New Wanstead)
Weaver's La. SE1
—1E 78 (5H 151)
Weavers Ter. SW6 —6J 75
(off Micklethwaite Rd.)
Weavers Way. NW1 —1H 61
Weaver Wlk. SE27 —4C 110

Webber Row. SE1
(in two parts) —3A 78 (1K 155)
Webber St. SE1 —2A 78 (6K 149)
Webb Est. E5 —76 31
Webb Gdns. E13 —4J 65
Webb Ho. SW8 —7H 77
Webb Ho. Dag —3G 53
(off Kershaw Rd.)
Webb Ho. Felt —3C 102
Webb Pl. NW10 —3B 58
Webb Rd. SE3 —6H 81
Webbscroft Rd. Dag —4H 53
Webb's Rd. SW11 —4D 92
Webb St. SE1 —3E 78 (2G 157)
Webster Rd. E11 —3E 48
Webster Rd. SE16 —3G 79
Wedderburn Rd. NW3 —5B 44
Wedderburn Rd. Bark —1J 67
Wedgwood Ho. SE11
—3A 78 (2J 155)
(off Lambeth Wlk.)
Wedgwood M. W1
—6H 61 (1D 148)
Wedgwood Wlk. NW6 —5K 43
(off Dresden Clo.)
Wedgwood Way. SE19 —7C 110
Wedlake St. W10 —4G 59
Wedmore Av. Ilf —1E 34
Wedmore Ct. N19 —3H 45
Wedmore Gdns. N19 —2H 45
Wedmore M. N19 —3H 45
Wedmore Rd. Gnfd —3H 55
Wedmore St. N19 —3H 45
Weech Rd. NW6 —4J 43
Weedington Rd. NW5 —5E 44
Weedon Ho. W12 —6C 58
Weekley Sq. SW11 —3B 92
Weigall Rd. SE12 —5J 97
Weighhouse St. W1
—6E 60 (1H 147)
Weighton M. SE20 —2H 125
Weighton Rd. SE20 —2H 125
Weighton Rd. Harr —1H 23
Weihurst Ct. Sutt —5C 132
Weihurst Gdns. Sutt —5B 132
Weimar St. SW15 —3G 91
Weirdale Av. N20 —2J 15
Weir Hall Av. N18 —6J 17
Weir Hall Gdns. N18 —5J 17
Weir Hall Rd. N18 & N17 —5J 17
Weir Rd. SW12 —1G 109
Weir Rd. SW19 —3K 107
Weir Rd. Bex —7H 101
Weir's Pas. NW1
—3H 61 (1D 142)
Weiss Rd. SW15 —3F 91
Welbeck Av. Brom —4J 113
Welbeck Av. Sidc —1A 116
Welbeck Clo. N12 —5G 15
Welbeck Clo. Eps —7C 130
Welbeck Clo. N Mald —5B 120
Welbeck Rd. E6 —3B 66
Welbeck Rd. Barn —6H 5
Welbeck Rd. Harr —1F 39
Welbeck Rd. Sutt & Cars
—2B 132
Welbeck St. W1 —5E 60 (6H 141)
Welbeck Wlk. Cars —1C 132
Welbeck Way. W1
—6F 61 (7J 141)
Welbourne Rd. N17 —3F 31
Welby Ho. N19 —7H 29
Welby St. SE5 —1B 94
Welch Pl. Pinn —1A 22

Welcome Ct. E17 —7C 32
(off Saxon Clo.)
Weldon Clo. Ruis —6A 38
Weldon Ct. N21 —5E 6
Weld Pl. N11 —5A 16
Welfare Rd. E15 —7G 49
Welford Clo. E5 —3K 47
Welford Ct. SW8 —2G 93
Welford Rd. SW19 —4G 107
Welham Rd. SW17 & SW16
—5E 108
Welhouse Rd. Cars —1C 132
Wellacre Rd. Harr —6B 24
Welland Clo. Sidc —5B 100
Welland Ct. SE6 —2B 112
(off Oakham Clo.)
Welland Gdns. Gnfd —2K 55
Welland Ho. SE15 —4J 95
Welland M. E1 —1G 79
Wellands Clo. Brom —2D 128
Well App. Barn —5A 4
Wellbrook Rd. Orp —4E 138
Wellby Ct. E13 —1A 66
Well Clo. SW16 —4K 109
Well Clo. Ruis —3C 38
Wellclose Sq. E1 —7G 63
Well Cottage Clo. E11 —6A 34
Well Ct. EC4 —6C 62 (1D 150)
Weldon Ct. Harr —5J 23
Welldon Cres. Harr —5J 23
Weller Ho. SE16 —2G 79
(off George Row)
Weller St. SE1 —2C 78 (6C 150)
Wellesley Av. W6 —3D 74
Wellesley Ct. NW2 —2C 42
Wellesley Ct. W9 —3A 60
(off Maida Vale)
Wellesley Ct. Sutt —1G 131
Wellesley Ct. Rd. Croy —2D 134
Wellesley Cres. Twic —2J 103
Wellesley Gro. Croy —2D 134
Wellesley Lodge. Sutt —7K 131
(off Worcester Rd.)
Wellesley Pde. Twic —3K 103
Wellesley Pk. M. Enf —2G 7
Wellesley Pl. NW1
—3H 61 (2C 142)
Wellesley Rd. NW5 —5E 44
Wellesley Rd. E11 —5J 33
Wellesley Rd. E17 —6C 32
Wellesley Rd. N22 —2A 30
Wellesley Rd. NW5 —5E 44
Wellesley Rd. W4 —5G 73
Wellesley Rd. Croy —1C 134
Wellesley Rd. Harr —5J 23
Wellesley Rd. Ilf —2F 51
Wellesley Rd. Sutt —6A 132
Wellesley Rd. Twic —3H 103
Wellesley St. E1 —5K 63
Wellesley Ter. N1
—3C 62 (1D 144)
Wellfield Av. N10 —3F 29
Wellfield Rd. SW16 —4J 109
Wellfield Wlk. SW16 —5K 109
Wellfit St. SE24 —3B 94
Wellgarth. Gnfd —6B 40
Wellgarth Rd. NW11 —1K 43
Well Gro. N20 —1F 15
Well Hall Pde. SE9 —4D 98
Well Hall Rd. SE9 —3C 98
Well Hall Roundabout. (Junct.)
—4C 98
Wellhouse La. Barn —4A 4
Wellhouse Rd. Beck —4C 126

Welling High St. Well —3B 100
Wellington. N8 —4J 29
Wellington Av. E4 —2H 19
Wellington Av. N9 —3C 18
Wellington Av. N15 —6F 31
Wellington Av. Houn —5E 86
Wellington Av. Pinn —1D 22
Wellington Av. Sidc —6A 100
Wellington Av. Wor Pk —3E 130
Wellington Bldgs. SW1
—5F 77 (6H 153)
Wellington Clo. SE14 —1K 95
Wellington Clo. W11 —6J 59
Wellington Clo. Dag —7J 53
Wellington Ct. NW8 —2B 60
(off Wellington Rd.)
Wellington Ct. SW6 —1K 91
(off Maltings Pl.)
Wellington Ct. Hamp —5H 103
Wellington Ct. Pinn —1D 22
(off Wellington Rd.)
Wellington Cres. N Mald —3J 119
Wellington Dri. Dag —7J 53
Wellington Est. E2 —2J 63
Wellington Gdns. SE7 —6A 82
Wellington Gdns. Twic —4H 103
Wellington Gro. SE10 —7F 81
Wellington Ho. W5 —3E 56
Wellington Ho. N'holt —7E 38
(off Farmlands, The)
Wellington Mans. E11 —1C 48
Wellington M. SE7 —6A 82
Wellington M. SE22 —4G 95
Wellington Pde. Sidc —5A 100
Wellington Pk. Est. NW2 —2C 42
Wellington Pas. E11 —5J 33
(off Wellington Rd.)
Wellington Pl. N2 —6C 28
Wellington Pl. NW8
—3B 60 (1B 140)
Wellington Rd. E6 —1D 66
Wellington Rd. E7 —4H 49
Wellington Rd. E10 —1A 48
Wellington Rd. E11 —5J 33
Wellington Rd. E17 —4A 32
Wellington Rd. NW8
—2B 60 (1B 140)
Wellington Rd. NW10 —3F 59
Wellington Rd. SW19 —2J 107
Wellington Rd. W5 —3C 72
Wellington Rd. Belv —5F 85
Wellington Rd. Bex —5D 100
Wellington Rd. Brom —4A 128
Wellington Rd. Croy —7B 124
Wellington Rd. Enf —5K 7
Wellington Rd. Hamp & Twic
—5H 103
Wellington Rd. Harr —3J 23
Wellington Rd. Pinn —1D 22
Wellington Rd. N. Houn —3D 86
Wellington Rd. S. Houn —4D 86
Wellington Row. E2
—3F 63 (1K 145)
Wellington Sq. SW3
—5D 76 (5E 152)
Wellington St. SE18 —4E 82
Wellington St. WC2
—7J 61 (2D 149)
Wellington St. Bark —1G 67
Wellington Ter. E1 —1H 79
Wellington Ter. N8 —3A 30
(off Turnpike La.)
Wellington Ter. W2 —7J 59
Wellington Ter. Harr —1H 39
Wellington Way. E3 —3C 64

Welling Way. SE9 & Well —3G 99
Well La. SW14 —5J 89
Wellmeadow Rd. SE13 & SE6
(in two parts) —6G 97
Wellmeadow Rd. W7 —4A 72
Wellow Wlk. Cars —1B 132
Well Pl. NW3 —3B 44
Wells All. NW3 —3B 44
Well Rd. Barn —5A 4
Wells Clo. N'holt —3A 54
Wells Dri. NW9 —1K 41
Wells Gdns. Dag —5H 53
Wells Gdns. Ilf —7C 34
Wells Ho. W5 —7D 56
(off Grove Rd.)
Wells Ho. Bark —7A 52
(off Margaret Bondfield Av.)
Wells Ho. Brom —5K 113
Wells Ho. Rd. NW10 —5A 58
Wellside Clo. Barn —4A 4
Wellside Gdns. SW14 —4J 89
Wells M. W1 —5G 61 (6B 142)
Wellsmoor Gdns. Brom —3E 128
Wells Pk. Rd. SE26 —3G 111
Wellsprings Cres. Wemb —3H 41
Wells Rise. NW8 —1D 60
Wells Rd. W12 —2E 74
Wells Rd. Brom —2D 128
Wells Sq. WC1 —3K 61 (2G 143)
Wells St. W1 —5G 61 (6A 142)
Wellstead Av. N9 —7E 8
Wellstead Rd. E6 —2E 66
Wells Ter. N4 —2A 46
Wells, The. N14 —7C 6
Well St. E9 —7J 47
Well St. E15 —6G 49
Wells Way. SE5 —6D 78 (7F 157)
Wells Way. SW7
—3B 76 (1A 152)
Wells Yd. N7 —5A 46
Well Wlk. NW3 —4B 44
Wellwood Rd. Ilf —1A 52
Welsby Ct. W5 —5C 56
Welsford St. SE1 —5G 79
Welsh Clo. E13 —3J 65
Welshpool St. E8 —1G 63
(in two parts)
Welshside Wlk. NW9 —5A 26
Welsingham Lodge. SW13
—1C 90
Welstead Way. W4 —4B 74
Weltje Rd. W6 —4C 74
Welton Ct. SE5 —1E 94
Welton Rd. SE18 —7J 83
Welwyn St. E2 —3J 63
Wembley Commercial Cen. Wemb
—2D 40
Wembley Hill Rd. Wemb —5F 41
Wembley Pk. Bus. Cen. Wemb
—3H 41
Wembley Pk. Dri. Wemb —4H 41
Wembley Retail Pk. Wemb
—4G 41
Wembley Rd. Hamp —7E 102
Wembley Stadium Ind. Est. Wemb
—4H 41
Wembley Way. Wemb —6H 41
Wemborough Rd. Stan —1B 24
Wembury M. N6 —7G 29
Wembury Rd. N6 —7F 29
Wemyss Rd. SE3 —2H 81
Wendela Ct. Harr —2J 39
Wendell Rd. W12 —3B 74
Wendling Rd. Sutt —1B 132
Wendon St. E3 —1B 64

Wendover. *SE17*
—5E **78** (5G **157**)
Wendover Clo. *Hayes* —4C **54**
Wendover Ct. *NW2* —3J **43**
Wendover Ct. *W3* —4H **57**
Wendover Dri. *N Mald* —6B **120**
Wendover Rd. *NW10* —2B **58**
Wendover Rd. *SE9* —3B **98**
Wendover Rd. *Brom* —3K **127**
Wendover Way. *Well* —5A **100**
Wendy Clo. *Enf* —6A **8**
Wendy Way. *Wemb* —1E **56**
Wenham Ho. *SW8* —7G **77**
(off Ascalon St.)
Wenlock Barn Est. *N1* —2D **62**
(off Wenlock St.)
Wenlock Gdns. *NW4* —4C **26**
Wenlock Rd. *N1*
—2C **62** (1D **144**)
Wenlock Rd. *Edgw* —7C **12**
Wennington Rd. *E3* —2K **63**
Wensdale Ho. *E5* —2G **47**
Wensley Av. *Wfd G* —7C **20**
Wensley Clo. *SE9* —6D **98**
Wensleydale Av. *Ilf* —2C **34**
Wensleydale Gdns. *Hamp*
—7F **103**
Wensleydale Pas. *Hamp* —7E **102**
Wensleydale Rd. *Hamp* —7E **102**
Wensley Rd. *N18* —6C **18**
Wentland Clo. *SE6* —2F **113**
Wentland Rd. *SE6* —2F **113**
Wentworth Av. *N3* —7D **14**
Wentworth Clo. *N3* —7E **14**
Wentworth Clo. *Hay* —2J **137**
Wentworth Clo. *Mord* —7J **121**
Wentworth Ct. *W6* —6G **75**
(off Laundry Rd.)
Wentworth Ct. *Twic* —3J **103**
Wentworth Cres. *SE15* —7G **79**
Wentworth Gdns. *N13* —3G **17**
Wentworth Hill. *Wemb* —1F **41**
Wentworth M. *E3* —4A **64**
Wentworth Pk. *N3* —7D **14**
Wentworth Pl. *Stan* —6G **11**
Wentworth Rd. *E12* —4B **50**
Wentworth Rd. *NW11* —6H **27**
Wentworth Rd. *Barn* —3A **4**
Wentworth Rd. *Croy* —7A **124**
Wentworth Rd. *S'hall* —4A **70**
Wentworth St. *E1*
—6F **63** (7J **145**)
Wentworth Way. *Pinn* —4C **22**
Wenvoe Av. *Bexh* —2H **101**
Wernbrook St. *SE18* —6G **83**
Werndee Rd. *SE25* —4G **125**
Werneth Hall Rd. *Ilf* —3D **34**
Werrington St. *NW1*
—2G **61** (1C **142**)
Werter Rd. *SW15* —4G **91**
Wesleyan Pl. *NW5* —4F **45**
Wesley Av. *E16* —1J **81**
Wesley Av. *NW10* —3K **57**
Wesley Av. *Houn* —2C **86**
Wesley Clo. *N7* —2K **45**
Wesley Clo. *SE17*
—4B **78** (4B **156**)
Wesley Clo. *Harr* —2G **39**
Wesley Rd. *E10* —7E **32**
Wesley Rd. *N2* —1C **28**
Wesley Rd. *NW10* —1K **57**
Wesley Sq. *W11* —6G **59**
Wesley St. *W1* —5E **60** (6H **141**)
Wessex Av. *SW19* —3J **121**
Wessex Clo. *Ilf* —6J **35**

Wessex Clo. *King T* —1H **119**
Wessex Ct. *Barn* —4A **4**
Wessex Ct. *Beck* —1A **126**
Wessex Dri. *Pinn* —1C **22**
Wessex Gdns. *NW11* —1G **43**
Wessex Ho. *SE1*
—5F **79** (5K **157**)
Wessex La. *Gnfd* —3H **55**
Wessex St. *E2* —3J **63**
Wessex Way. *NW11* —1G **43**
West App. *Orp* —5G **129**
W. Arbour St. *E1* —6K **63**
West Av. *E17* —4D **32**
West Av. *N2* —4K **27**
West Av. *N3* —6D **14**
West Av. *NW4* —5F **27**
West Av. *Pinn* —6D **22**
West Av. *S'hall* —7D **54**
West Av. *Wall* —5J **133**
West Av. *E17* —4C **32**
West Bank. *N16* —7E **30**
West Bank. *Bark* —1F **67**
West Bank. *Enf* —2H **7**
West Bank Rd. *Hamp* —6G **103**
W. Barnes La. *N Mald & SW20*
—5D **120**
Westbeech Rd. *N22* —3A **30**
Westbere Dri. *Stan* —5J **11**
Westbere Rd. *NW2* —4G **43**
Westbourne Av. *W3* —6K **57**
Westbourne Av. *Sutt* —2G **131**
Westbourne Bri. *W2* —5A **60**
Westbourne Clo. *Hayes* —4A **54**
Westbourne Cres. *W2*
—7B **60** (2A **146**)
Westbourne Cres. M. *W2*
—7B **60** (2A **146**)
Westbourne Dri. *SE23* —2K **111**
Westbourne Gdns. *W2* —6K **59**
Westbourne Gro. *W11 & W2*
—7H **59**
Westbourne Gro. M. *W11* —6J **59**
Westbourne Gro. Ter. *W2*
—6K **59**
Westbourne Ho. *Houn* —6E **70**
Westbourne Pk. M. *W2* —6K **59**
Westbourne Pk. Pas. *W2* —5J **59**
Westbourne Pk. Rd. *W11 & W2*
—6G **59**
Westbourne Pk. Vs. *W2* —5J **59**
Westbourne Pl. *N9* —3C **18**
Westbourne Rd. *N7* —6K **45**
Westbourne Rd. *SE26* —6K **111**
Westbourne Rd. *Bexh* —7E **84**
Westbourne Rd. *Croy* —6F **125**
Westbourne St. *W2*
—7B **60** (2A **146**)
Westbourne Ter. SE23 —2K **111**
(off Waldram Pk. Rd.)
Westbourne Ter. *W2* —6A **60**
Westbourne Ter. M. *W2* —6A **60**
Westbourne Ter. Rd. *W2* —5K **59**
Westbridge Rd. *SW11* —1B **92**
Westbrook Av. *Hamp* —7D **102**
Westbrook Clo. *Barn* —3G **5**
Westbrook Cres. *Cockf* —3G **5**
Westbrooke Cres. *Well* —3C **100**
Westbrooke Rd. *Sidc* —2H **115**
Westbrooke Rd. *Well* —3B **100**
Westbrook Rd. *SE3* —1K **97**
Westbrook Rd. *Houn* —7D **70**
Westbrook Rd. *T Hth* —1D **124**
Westbrook Sq. *Barn* —3G **5**
Westbury Av. *N22* —3B **30**

Westbury Av. *S'hall* —4E **54**
Westbury Av. *Wemb* —7E **40**
Westbury Ct. Bark —1H **67**
(off Westbury Rd.)
Westbury Gro. *N12* —6D **14**
Westbury Ho. *E17* —4B **32**
Westbury La. *Buck H* —2F **21**
Westbury Lodge Clo. *Pinn*
—3B **22**
Westbury Pl. *Bren* —6D **72**
Westbury Rd. *E7* —6K **49**
Westbury Rd. *E17* —4C **32**
Westbury Rd. *N11* —6D **16**
Westbury Rd. *N12* —6D **14**
Westbury Rd. *SE20* —1K **125**
Westbury Rd. *W5* —6E **56**
Westbury Rd. *Bark* —1H **67**
Westbury Rd. *Beck* —3A **126**
Westbury Rd. *Brom* —1B **128**
Westbury Rd. *Buck H* —1F **21**
Westbury Rd. *Croy* —6D **124**
Westbury Rd. *Felt* —1B **102**
Westbury Rd. *Ilf* —2E **50**
Westbury Rd. *N Mald* —4K **119**
Westbury Rd. *Wemb* —7E **40**
Westbury St. *SW8* —2G **93**
Westbury Ter. *E7* —6K **49**
W. Carriage Dri. *W2*
—7C **60** (3C **146**)
W. Central St. *WC1*
—6J **61** (7E **142**)
W. Centre Av. *NW10* —4D **58**
W. Chantry. *Harr* —1F **23**
Westchester Dri. *NW4* —3F **27**
West Clo. *N9* —3A **18**
West Clo. *Cockf* —4K **5**
West Clo. *Gnfd* —2G **55**
West Clo. *Hamp* —6C **102**
West Clo. *Wemb* —1F **41**
Westcombe Av. *Croy* —7J **123**
Westcombe Dri. *Barn* —5D **4**
Westcombe Hill. *SE3* —7J **81**
Westcombe Pk. Rd. *SE3* —6G **81**
West Comn. Rd. *Hay & Kes*
—2J **137**
Westcoombe Av. *SW20* —1B **120**
Westcote Rd. *SW16* —5G **109**
West Cotts. *NW6* —5J **43**
Westcott Clo. *N15* —6F **31**
Westcott Clo. *Brom* —5C **128**
Westcott Cres. *W7* —6J **55**
Westcott Ho. *E14* —7C **64**
Westcott Rd. *SE17*
—6B **78** (7A **156**)
West Ct. *E17* —4D **32**
West Ct. *Houn* —7G **71**
West Ct. *Wemb* —2C **40**
Westcroft Clo. *NW2* —4G **43**
Westcroft Clo. *Enf* —1D **8**
Westcroft Gdns. *Mord* —4H **121**
Westcroft Rd. *Cars & Wall*
—4E **132**
Westcroft Sq. *W6* —4C **74**
Westcroft Way. *NW2* —4G **43**
W. Cromwell Rd. *W14 & SW5*
—5H **75**
W. Cross Cen. *Bren* —6A **72**
W. Cross Route. *W10, W11 &*
W12 —7F **59**
W. Cross Way. *Bren* —6B **72**
Westdale Pas. *SE18* —6F **83**
Westdale Rd. *SE18* —6F **83**
Westdean Av. *SE12* —1K **113**
W. Dean Clo. *SW18* —6K **91**

West Dene. *Sutt* —6G **131**
Westdown Rd. *E15* —4E **48**
Westdown Rd. *SE6* —7C **96**
West Dri. *SW16* —4G **109**
West Dri. *Harr* —6C **10**
West Dri. *Sutt* —7F **131**
West Dri. Gdns. *Harr* —6C **10**
W. Ealing Bus. Cen. *W13* —7A **56**
W. Eaton Pl. *SW1*
—4E **76** (3G **153**)
W. Eaton Pl. M. *SW1*
—4E **76** (2G **153**)
W. Ella Rd. *NW10* —7A **42**
W. End Av. *E10* —5F **33**
W. End Av. *Pinn* —4B **22**
W. End Ct. *Pinn* —4B **22**
W. End Gdns. *N'holt* —2A **54**
W. End La. *NW6* —5J **43**
W. End La. *Barn* —4A **4**
W. End La. *Pinn* —3B **22**
W. End Rd. *Ruis & N'holt*
—6A **38**
W. End Rd. *S'hall* —1C **70**
Westerdale Rd. *SE10* —5J **81**
Westerfield Rd. *N15* —5F **31**
Westergate. *W5* —5E **56**
Westergate Rd. *SE2* —6E **84**
Westerham Av. *N9* —3J **17**
Westerham Dri. *Sidc* —6B **100**
Westerham Ho. *SE1*
—3D **78** (1F **157**)
Westerham Lodge. Beck
(off Park Rd.) —7C **112**
Westerham Rd. *E10* —7D **32**
Westerham Rd. *Kes* —7B **138**
Westerley Cres. *SE26* —5B **112**
Western Av. *Gnfd, W5 & W3*
—1F **55**
Western Av. *NW11* —6F **27**
Western Av. *W3* —5J **57**
Western Av. *Dag* —6J **53**
Western Circus. (Junct.) —7B **58**
Western Ct. *N3* —6D **14**
Western Ct. NW6 —2H **59**
(off Carlton Vale)
Western Ct. *W3* —6K **57**
Western Gdns. *W5* —7G **57**
Western International Mkt. *S'hall*
—1A **124**
Western La. *SW12* —7E **92**
Western M. *W9* —4H **59**
Western Pde. *New Bar* —5D **4**
Western Pl. *SE16* —2J **79**
Western Rd. *E13* —2A **66**
Western Rd. *E17* —5E **32**
Western Rd. *N2* —4D **28**
Western Rd. *N22* —2K **29**
Western Rd. *NW10* —3J **57**
Western Rd. *SW9* —3A **94**
Western Rd. *SW19 & Mitc*
—1B **122**
Western Rd. *W5* —7D **56**
Western Rd. *S'hall* —4A **70**
Western Rd. *Sutt* —5J **131**
Western Ter. W6 —5C **74**
(off Chiswick Mall)
Westernville Gdns. *Ilf* —7G **35**
Western Way. *SE28* —3J **83**
Western Way. *Barn* —6D **4**
Westferry Cir. *E14* —1B **80**
Westferry Rd. *E14* —7C **64**
Westfield Clo. *NW9* —3J **25**
Westfield Clo. *SW10* —7A **76**
Westfield Clo. *Enf* —3F **9**
Westfield Clo. *Sutt* —4H **131**

Westfield Dri. *Harr* —4D **24**
Westfield Gdns. *Harr* —4D **24**
Westfield Ho. *SW18* —1K **107**
Westfield La. *Harr* —4D **24**
(in two parts)
Westfield Pk. *Pinn* —1D **22**
Westfield Pk. Dri. *Wfd G* —6H **21**
Westfield Rd. *NW7* —3E **12**
Westfield Rd. *W13* —1A **72**
Westfield Rd. *Beck* —2B **126**
Westfield Rd. *Bexh* —3J **101**
Westfield Rd. *Croy* —2B **134**
Westfield Rd. *Dag* —4E **52**
Westfield Rd. *Mitc* —2D **122**
Westfield Rd. *Surb* —5D **118**
Westfield Rd. *Sutt* —4H **131**
Westfields. *SW13* —3B **90**
Westfields Av. *SW13* —3A **90**
Westfields Rd. *W3* —5H **57**
Westfield St. *SE18* —3B **82**
Westfield Way. *E1* —3A **64**
W. Garden Pl. *W2*
—6C **60** (1D **146**)
West Gdns. *E1* —7H **63**
West Gdns. *SW17* —6C **108**
Westgate. *W5* —3E **56**
Westgate Ct. SE12 —1J **113**
(off Burnt Ash Hill)
Westgate Ct. *SW9* —3A **94**
(off Canterbury Cres.)
Westgate Rd. *SE25* —4H **125**
Westgate Rd. *Beck* —1E **126**
Westgate St. *E8* —1H **63**
Westgate Ter. *SW10* —5K **75**
Westglade Ct. *Kent* —5D **24**
West Grn. Pl. *Gnfd* —1H **55**
West Grn. Rd. *N15* —4B **30**
West Gro. *SE10* —1E **96**
West Gro. *Wfd G* —6F **21**
Westgrove La. *SE10* —1E **96**
W. Halkin St. *SW1*
—3E **76** (1G **153**)
W. Hallowes. *SE9* —1B **114**
W. Hall Rd. *Rich* —1H **89**
W. Ham La. *E15* —7F **49**
W. Hampstead M. *NW6* —6K **43**
W. Harding St. *EC4*
—6A **62** (7K **143**)
Westhay Gdns. *SW14* —5H **89**
W. Heath Av. *NW11* —1J **43**
W. Heath Clo. *NW3* —3J **43**
W. Heath Ct. *NW11* —1J **43**
W. Heath Dri. *NW11* —1J **43**
W. Heath Gdns. *NW3* —3J **43**
W. Heath Rd. *NW3* —2J **43**
W. Heath Rd. *SE2* —6D **84**
West Hill. *SW15 & SW18* —7F **91**
West Hill. *Harr* —2J **39**
West Hill. *S Croy* —7E **134**
West Hill. *Wemb* —1F **41**
W. Hill Ct. *N6* —3E **44**
Westhill Pk. *N6* —2D **44**
(in two parts)
W. Hill Rd. *SW18* —6H **91**
W. Hill Way. *N20* —1E **14**
Westholm. *NW11* —4K **27**
W. Holme. *Eri* —1J **101**
Westholme. *Orp* —7J **129**
Westhorne Av. *SE12 & SE9*
—7J **97**
Westhorpe Gdns. *NW4* —3E **26**
Westhorpe Rd. *SW15* —3E **90**
West Ho. Clo. *SW19* —1G **107**
West Ho. Cotts. *Pinn* —4B **22**
Westhurst Dri. *Chst* —5F **115**

W. India Av. *E14* —1C **80**
W. India Dock Rd. *E14* —7B **64**
W. Kensington Ct. *W14* —5H **75**
(off Edith Vs.)
W. Kensington Mans. *W14*
(off Beaumont Cres.) —5H **75**
Westlake Clo. *N13* —3F **17**
Westlake Clo. Hayes —4C **54**
Westlake Rd. Wemb —2D **40**
Westland Ct. N'holt —3B **54**
(off Seasprite Clo.)
Westland Dri. Brom —2H **137**
Westland Ho. *E16* —1E **82**
(off Rymill St.)
Westland Pl. *N1* —3D **62** (1E **144**)
Westlands Ter. *SW12* —6G **93**
West La. *SE16* —2H **79**
Westlea Rd. *W7* —3A **72**
Westleigh Av. *SW15* —5D **90**
Westleigh Ct. *E11* —5J **33**
Westleigh Dri. Brom —1C **128**
Westleigh Gdns. Edgw —1G **25**
W. Lodge Av. *W3* —1G **73**
W. Lodge Ct. *W3* —1G **73**
West Mall. *W8* —1J **75**
(off Palace Gdns. Ter.)
Westmead. *SW15* —6D **90**
West Mead. Eps —6A **130**
West Mead. Ruis —4A **38**
Westmead Corner. Cars —4C **132**
Westmead Rd. Sutt —4B **132**
Westmere Dri. NW7 —3E **12**
W. Mersea Clo. *E16* —1K **81**
West M. *N17* —6C **18**
West M. *SW1* —4G **77** (4A **154**)
Westmill Ct. *N4* —2C **46**
(off Brownswood Rd.)
Westminster Av. T Hth —2B **124**
Westminster Bri. *SW1 & SE1*
—2J **77** (7F **149**)
Westminster Bri. Rd. *SE1*
—2K **77** (7G **149**)
Westminster Bus. Sq. *SE11*
—5K **77** (6G **155**)
Westminster Clo. Ilf —2H **35**
Westminster Clo. Tedd —5A **104**
Westminster Ct. *E11* —6J **33**
(off Cambridge Pk.)
Westminster Dri. *N13* —5D **16**
Westminster Gdns. *E4* —1B **20**
Westminster Gdns. Bark —2J **67**
Westminster Gdns. Ilf —2G **35**
Westminster Ho. Har W —7E **10**
Westminster Ind. Est. *SE18*
—3B **82**
Westminster Pal. Gdns. *SW1*
—3H **77** (2C **154**)
Westminster Rd. *N9* —1C **18**
Westminster Rd. *W7* —1J **71**
Westminster Rd. Sutt —2B **132**
Westmoat Clo. Beck —7E **112**
Westmoor Gdns. Enf —2E **8**
Westmoor Rd. Enf —2E **8**
Westmoor St. *SE7* —3A **82**
Westmoreland Av. Well —4J **99**
Westmoreland Dri. Sutt —7K **131**
Westmoreland Pl. *SW1*
—5F **77** (6K **153**)
Westmoreland Pl. *W5* —5D **56**
Westmoreland Pl. Brom —3J **127**
Westmoreland Rd. NW9 —3F **25**
Westmoreland Rd. *SE17*
—6D **78** (7D **156**)
Westmoreland Rd. *SW13*
—1B **90**

Westmoreland Rd. Brom
—5G **127**
Westmoreland St. *W1*
—5E **60** (6H **141**)
Westmoreland Ter. *SW1*
—5F **77** (5K **153**)
Westmoreland Ter. *SE20*
—6D **78** (7E **156**)
Westmorland Clo. *E12* —2B **50**
Westmorland Clo. Twic —6B **88**
Westmorland Ct. Surb —7D **118**
Westmorland Rd. *E17* —6C **32**
Westmorland Rd. Harr —5F **23**
Westmorland Sq. Mitc —5J **123**
(off Westmorland Way)
Westmorland Ter. *SE20* —7H **111**
Westmorland Way. Mitc
—5H **123**
Westmount Ct. *W5* —6F **57**
Westmount Rd. *SE9* —2D **98**
West Oak. Beck —1F **127**
Westoe Rd. *N9* —2C **18**
Westonbirt Ct. *SE15* —6F **79**
(off Ebley Clo.)
Weston Ct. *N4* —3C **46**
Weston Dri. Stan —1B **24**
Westone Mans. Bark —7K **51**
(off Upney La.)
Weston Gdns. Iswth —1J **87**
Weston Grn. Dag —4F **53**
Weston Gro. Brom —1H **127**
Weston Ho. *E9* —1J **63**
(off King Edwards Rd.)
Weston Ho. NW6 —7G **43**
Weston Pk. *N8* —6J **29**
Weston Pk. King T —2E **118**
Weston Rise. *WC1*
—3K **61** (1H **143**)
Weston Rd. *W4* —3J **73**
Weston Rd. Brom —7H **113**
Weston Rd. Dag —4E **52**
Weston Rd. Enf —1J **7**
Weston St. *SE11* —2B **78**
Weston Wlk. *E8* —7H **47**
Westover Hill. NW3 —2J **43**
Westover Rd. *SW18* —7A **92**
Westow Hill. *SE19* —6E **110**
Westow St. *SE19* —6E **110**
West Pk. *SE9* —2C **114**
West Pk. Av. Rich —1H **89**
West Pk. Clo. Houn —6D **70**
West Pk. Clo. Romf —5D **36**
West Pk. Rd. Rich —1G **89**
West Pk. Rd. S'hall —1G **71**
West Pier. *E1* —1H **79**
West Pl. *SW19* —5E **106**
West Point. *SE1* —5G **79**
Westpoint Trad. Est. *W3* —5H **57**
Westpole Av. Barn —4K **5**
Westport Ct. Hayes —4A **54**
Westport Rd. *E13* —4K **65**
Westport St. *E1* —6K **63**
W. Poultry Av. *EC1*
—5B **62** (6A **144**)
W. Quarters. W12 —6C **58**
West Quay. *SW10* —1A **92**
W. Quay Dri. Hayes —5C **54**
W. Ridge Gdns. Gnfd —2G **55**
West Rise. *W2* —7C **60** (2D **146**)
West Rd. *E15* —1H **65**
West Rd. *N2* —2B **28**
West Rd. *N17* —6C **18**
West Rd. *SE1* —2K **77** (6H **149**)
West Rd. *SW3* —5D **76** (6F **153**)
West Rd. *SW4* —5H **93**

West Rd. *W5* —5E **56**
West Rd. Barn —1K **15**
West Rd. Chad H —6D **36**
West Rd. King T —1J **119**
West Rd. Rush G —7K **37**
Westrow. *SW15* —6E **90**
West Row. *W10* —4G **59**
Westrow Dri. Bark —6K **51**
Westrow Gdns. Ilf —2K **51**
W. Sheen Vale. Rich —4F **89**
Westside. *N2* —3D **28**
West Side. NW4 —2D **26**
W. Side Comn. *SW19* —5E **106**
W. Smithfield. *EC1*
—5B **62** (6A **144**)
West Sq. *SE11* —3B **78** (2A **156**)
West St. *E2* —2H **63**
West St. *E11* —3G **49**
West St. *WC2* —6H **61** (1D **148**)
West St. Bexh —3F **101**
West St. Bren —6C **72**
West St. Brom —1J **127**
West St. Cars —3D **132**
West St. Croy —4C **134**
West St. Eri —4K **85**
West St. Harr —1H **39**
West St. Sutt —5K **131**
West St. La. Cars —4D **132**
W. Temple Sheen. *SW14* —5H **89**
W. Tenter St. *E1* —6F **63** (1K **151**)
West Ter. Sidc —1J **115**
W. Towers. Pinn —6B **22**
Westvale M. *W3* —1A **74**
West View. NW4 —4E **26**
Westview. *W7* —6J **55**
W. View Clo. NW10 —5B **42**
Westview Clo. *W10* —6E **58**
Westview Cres. *N9* —7K **7**
Westview Dri. Wfd G —2B **34**
Westville Rd. *W12* —2C **74**
Westville Rd. Th Dit —7A **118**
West Wlk. E Barn —7K **5**
Westward Rd. *E4* —5G **19**
Westward Way. Harr —6E **24**
W. Warwick Pl. *SW1*
—4G **77** (4A **154**)
Westway. *N18* —4J **17**
West Way. NW10 —3K **41**
Westway. *SW20* —4D **120**
Westway. *W2* —5K **59**
Westway. *W12, W10 & W2*
—7B **58**
West Way. Croy —2A **136**
West Way. Edgw —6C **12**
West Way. Houn —1D **86**
Westway. Orp —5H **129**
West Way. Pinn —4B **22**
West Way. W Wick —6C **127**
Westway Clo. *SW20* —3D **120**
Westway Ct. N'holt —1E **54**
W. Way Gdns. Croy —2K **135**
Westways. Eps —4B **130**
Westwell M. *SW16* —6J **109**
Westwell Rd. *SW16* —6J **109**
Westwell Rd. App. *SW16*
—6J **109**
Westwick Gdns. W14 —2F **75**
Westwick Gdns. Houn —2C **86**
Westwood Av. *SE19* —1D **124**
Westwood Av. Harr —4F **39**
Westwood Clo. Brom —3B **128**
Westwood Ct. Gnfd —5H **39**
Westwood Ct. Wemb —4B **40**
Westwood Gdns. *SW13* —3B **90**
Westwood Hill. *SE26* —5G **111**
Westwood La. Sidc —5A **100**

Westwood La. Well —3K **99**
Westwood Pk. *SE23* —7H **95**
Westwood Pk. Trad. Est. *W3*
—5H **57**
Westwood Rd. *E16* —1K **81**
Westwood Rd. *SW13* —3B **90**
Westwood Rd. Ilf —1K **51**
W. Woodside. Bex —1E **116**
Wetheral Dri. Stan —1B **24**
Wetherby Clo. N'holt —6F **39**
Wetherby Gdns. SW5 —4A **76**
Wetherby Mans. SW5 —5K **75**
(off Earl's Ct. Sq.)
Wetherby M. SW5 —5K **75**
Wetherby Pl. SW7 —4A **76**
Wetherby Rd. Enf —1H **7**
Wetherden St. *E17* —7B **32**
Wetherell Rd. *E9* —1K **63**
Wetherill Rd. *N10* —1E **28**
Wevell Ho. N6 —7E **28**
(off Hillcrest)
Wexford Rd. *SW12* —7D **92**
Weybourne St. *SW18* —2A **108**
Weybridge Rd. T Hth —4A **124**
Weydown Clo. *SW19* —1G **107**
Weyhill Rd. *E1* —6G **63**
Weylond Rd. Dag —3F **53**
Weyman Rd. *SE3* —1A **98**
Weymarks, The. *N17* —6J **17**
Weymouth Av. NW7 —5F **13**
Weymouth Av. *W5* —3C **72**
Weymouth Clo. *E6* —6F **67**
Weymouth Ct. Sutt —7J **131**
Weymouth Ho. *SW8* —7K **77**
(off Bolney Rd.)
Weymouth M. *W1*
—5F **61** (5J **141**)
Weymouth St. *W1*
—5E **60** (6H **141**)
Weymouth Ter. *E2* —2F **63**
Weymouth Wlk. Stan —6F **11**
Whadcoat St. *N4* —2A **46**
Whalebone Av. Romf —6F **37**
Whalebone Ct. *EC2*
—6D **62** (7E **144**)
Whalebone Gro. Romf —6F **37**
Whalebone La. *E15* —7G **49**
Whalebone La. N. Romf —1E **36**
Whalebone La. S. Romf & Dag
—7F **37**
Whales Yd. *E15* —7G **49**
(off West Ham La.)
Wharfdale Rd. *N1* —2J **61**
Wharfedale Ct. *E5* —4A **48**
Wharfedale Gdns. T Hth —4K **123**
Wharfedale St. *SW10* —5K **75**
Wharf La. Twic —1A **104**
Wharf Pl. *E2* —1H **63**
Wharf Rd. *E15* —1F **65**
Wharf Rd. *N1* —2C **62** (1C **144**)
Wharf Rd. NW1 —7H **45**
Wharf Rd. Enf —6F **9**
Wharf Rd. Ind. Est. Enf —6F **9**
Wharfside Rd. *E16* —5G **65**
Wharf St. *E16* —5G **65**
Wharncliffe Dri. S'hall —1H **71**
Wharncliffe Gdns. *SE25* —2E **124**
Wharncliffe Rd. *SE25* —2E **124**
Wharton Clo. NW10 —6A **42**
Wharton Cotts. *WC1*
—3A **62** (2J **143**)
Wharton Rd. Brom —1K **127**
Wharton St. *WC1*
—3K **61** (2H **143**)
Whateley Rd. *SE20* —7K **111**

Whateley Rd. *SE22* —5F **95**
Whatley Av. SW20 —3F **121**
Whatman Rd. *SE23* —7K **95**
Wheatfields. *E6* —6F **67**
Wheatfields. Enf —1F **9**
Wheatfield Way. King T —2E **118**
Wheathill Rd. *SE20* —2H **125**
Wheatlands. Houn —6E **70**
Wheatlands Rd. *SW17* —3E **108**
Wheatley Clo. NW4 —2C **26**
Wheatley Gdns. N9 —2K **17**
Wheatley Ho. *SW15* —7C **90**
(off Tangley Gro.)
Wheatley Mans. Bark —7A **52**
(off Bevan Av.)
Wheatley Rd. Iswth —3K **87**
Wheatley St. *W1*
—5E **60** (6H **141**)
Wheat Sheaf Clo. *E14* —4D **80**
Wheatsheaf Clo. N'holt —5C **38**
Wheatsheaf La. SW6 —7E **74**
Wheatsheaf La. *SW8* —7J **77**
Wheatsheaf Ter. SW6 —7H **75**
Wheatstone Clo. Mitc —1C **122**
Wheatstone Rd. *W10* —5G **59**
Wheeler Clo. Wfd G —6J **21**
Wheeler Gdns. *N1* —1J **61**
(off Outram Pl.)
Wheelers Cross. Bark —2H **67**
Wheel Farm Dri. Dag —3J **53**
Wheelwright St. *N7* —7K **45**
Whelan Way. Wall —3H **133**
Wheler St. *E1* —4F **63** (4J **145**)
Whellock Rd. *W4* —3A **74**
Whenman Av. Bex —2J **117**
Whernside Clo. *SE28* —7C **68**
Whetstone Clo. *N20* —2G **15**
Whetstone Pk. *WC2*
—6K **61** (7G **143**)
Whetstone Rd. *SE3* —2A **98**
Whewell Rd. N19 —2J **45**
Whidborne Clo. *SE8* —2C **96**
Whidborne St. *WC1*
—3J **61** (2F **143**)
Whimbrel Clo. *SE28* —7C **68**
Whimbrel Way. Hayes —6A **54**
Whinchat Rd. *SE28* —3H **83**
Whinfell Clo. *SW16* —5H **109**
Whinyates Rd. *SE9* —3C **98**
Whipps Cross. *E17* —5F **33**
Whipps Cross Ho. *E17* —4F **33**
(off Wood St.)
Whipps Cross Rd. *E11* —5F **33**
Whiskin St. *EC1* —3B **62** (2A **144**)
Whisperwood Clo. Harr —1J **23**
Whistler Gdns. Edgw —2F **25**
Whistler M. Dag —5B **52**
(off Fitzstephen Rd.)
Whistlers Av. *SW11* —7B **76**
Whistler St. N5 —5B **46**
Whistler Tower. *SW10* —7A **76**
(off Worlds End Est.)
Whistler Wlk. *SW10* —7B **76**
Whiston Ho. *N1* —6B **30**
(off Richmond Gro.)
Whiston Rd. *E2* —2F **63**
(in two parts)
Whitbread Clo. *N17* —1G **31**
Whitbread Rd. *SE4* —4A **96**
Whitburn Rd. *SE13* —4D **96**
Whitby Av. NW10 —3H **57**
Whitby Ct. *N7* —4J **45**
Whitby Gdns. NW9 —3G **25**
Whitby Gdns. Sutt —2B **132**
Whitby Rd. *SE18* —4D **82**

319

Whitby Rd. *Harr* —3G **39**
Whitby Rd. *Ruis* —3A **38**
Whitby Rd. *Sutt* —2B **132**
Whitby St. *E1* —4F **63** (3J **145**)
Whitcher Clo. *SE14* —6A **80**
Whitcher Pl. *NW1* —6G **45**
Whitchurch Av. *Edgw* —7A **12**
Whitchurch Clo. *Edgw* —6A **12**
Whitchurch Gdns. *Edgw* —6A **12**
Whitchurch Ho. *W10* —6F **59**
(off Kingsdown Clo.)
Whitchurch La. *Edgw* —7J **11**
Whitchurch Pde. *Edgw* —7B **12**
Whitchurch Rd. *W11* —7F **59**
Whitcomb Ct. *WC2*
—7H **61** (3D **148**)
Whitcomb St. *WC2*
—7H **61** (3D **148**)
White Acre. *NW9* —2A **26**
Whiteadder Way. *E14* —4D **80**
Whitear Wlk. *E15* —6F **49**
White Av. *N2* —6B **28**
Whitebarn La. *Dag* —1G **69**
Whitebeam Av. *Brom* —7E **128**
Whitebeam Clo. *SW9* —7K **77**
White Bear Pl. *NW3* —4B **44**
White Bear Yd. *EC1*
—4A **62** (4J **143**)
(off Clerkenwell Rd.)
White Bri. Av. *Mitc* —3B **122**
White Butts Rd. *Ruis* —3B **38**
Whitechapel High St. *E1*
—6F **63** (7K **145**)
Whitechapel Rd. *E1*
—5G **63** (7K **145**)
Whitechurch La. *E1*
—6G **63** (7K **145**)
White City. (Junct.) *W12* —6E **58**
White City Clo. *W12* —7E **58**
White City Est. *W12* —7D **58**
White City Rd. *W12* —7E **58**
White Conduit St. *N1* —2A **62**
Whitecote Rd. *S'hall* —6G **55**
Whitecroft Clo. *Beck* —4F **127**
Whitecroft Way. *Beck* —5E **126**
Whitecross Pl. *EC2*
—5D **62** (5F **145**)
Whitecross St. *EC1 & EC2*
—4C **62** (3D **144**)
Whitefield Av. *NW2* —1E **42**
Whitefield Clo. *SW15* —6G **91**
Whitefoot La. *Brom* —4E **112**
Whitefoot Ter. *Brom* —3H **113**
Whitefriars Av. *Harr* —2J **23**
Whitefriars Ct. *N12* —5G **15**
Whitefriars Dri. *Harr* —2H **23**
Whitefriars St. *EC4*
—6A **62** (1K **149**)
Whitefriars Trad. Est. *Harr*
—3H **23**
White Gdns. *Dag* —6G **53**
Whitegate Gdns. *Harr* —7E **10**
Whitehall. *SW1* —1J **77** (4E **148**)
Whitehall Ct. *SW1*
—1J **77** (5E **148**)
Whitehall Gdns. *E4* —1B **20**
Whitehall Gdns. *SW1*
—1J **77** (5E **148**)
Whitehall Gdns. *W3* —1G **73**
Whitehall Gdns. *W4* —6H **73**
Whitehall La. *Buck H* —2D **20**
Whitehall Lodge. *N10* —2E **28**
Whitehall Pk. *N19* —1G **45**
Whitehall Pk. Rd. *W4* —6H **73**
Whitehall Pl. *E7* —5J **49**

Whitehall Pl. *SW1*
—1J **77** (5E **148**)
Whitehall Pl. *Wall* —4F **133**
Whitehall Rd. *E4 & Wfd G*
—2B **20**
Whitehall Rd. *W7* —2A **72**
Whitehall Rd. *Brom* —5B **128**
Whitehall Rd. *Harr* —7J **23**
Whitehall Rd. *T Hth* —5A **124**
Whitehall St. *N17* —7A **18**
White Hart Ct. *EC2*
—5E **62** (6G **145**)
White Hart La. *N22 & N17*
—1K **29**
White Hart La. *NW10* —6B **42**
White Hart La. *SW13* —2A **90**
White Hart La. *Romf* —1G **37**
White Hart Rd. *SE18* —4J **83**
White Hart Roundabout. *N'holt*
—2B **54**
White Hart Slip. *Brom* —2J **127**
White Hart St. *SE11*
—5A **78** (5K **155**)
White Hart Yd. *SE1*
—1D **78** (5E **150**)
Whitehaven Clo. *Brom* —4J **127**
Whitehaven St. *NW8*
—4C **60** (4C **140**)
Whitehead Clo. *N18* —5J **17**
Whitehead Clo. *SW18* —7A **92**
Whitehead's Gro. *SW3*
—5C **76** (4D **152**)
White Heron M. *Tedd* —6K **103**
Whitehorn Gdns. *Croy* —2H **135**
White Horse All. *EC1*
—5B **62** (5A **144**)
White Horse Hill. *Chst* —4E **114**
White Horse La. *E1* —4K **63**
Whitehorse La. *SE25* —4D **124**
Whitehorse M. *SE1*
—3A **78** (1K **155**)
White Horse Rd. *E1* —6A **64**
White Horse Rd. *E6* —3D **66**
Whitehorse Rd. *Croy & T Hth*
—7C **124**
White Horse St. *W1*
—1F **77** (5K **147**)
White Horse Yd. *EC2*
—6D **62** (7E **144**)
White Ho. *SW4* —7H **93**
(off Clapham Pk. Est.)
White Ho. Dri. *Stan* —4H **11**
White Ho. Dri. *Wfd G* —6C **20**
Whitehouse Est. *E10* —6E **32**
Whitehouse La. *Enf* —1H **7**
Whitehouse Way. *N14* —2A **16**
White Kennett St. *E1*
—6E **62** (7H **145**)
Whiteledges. *W13* —6C **56**
Whitelegg Rd. *E13* —2H **65**
Whiteley Rd. *SE19* —5D **110**
Whiteley's Cotts. *W14* —4H **75**
Whiteleys Shop. Cen. *W2* —6K **59**
Whiteley's Way. *Felt* —3E **102**
White Lion Ct. *EC3*
—6E **62** (1G **151**)
White Lion Ct. *SE15* —6J **79**
White Lion Ct. *Iswth* —3B **88**
White Lion Hill. *EC4*
—7B **62** (2B **150**)
White Lion St. *N1* —2A **62**
White Lion Yd. *W1*
(off Brook St.) —7F **61** (2J **147**)
White Lodge. *SE19* —7B **110**
White Lodge. *W5* —5C **56**

White Lodge Clo. *N2* —6B **28**
White Lodge Clo. *Sutt* —7A **132**
White Lyon Ct. *EC2*
—5C **62** (5C **144**)
White M. *Enf* —3J **7**
Whiteoak Ct. *Chst* —6E **114**
White Oak Dri. *Beck* —2E **126**
White Oak Gdns. *Sidc* —7K **99**
Whiteoaks La. *Gnfd* —3H **55**
White Orchards. *N20* —7C **14**
White Orchards. *Stan* —5F **11**
White Post La. *E9* —6C **48**
White Post St. *SE15* —7J **79**
White Rd. *E15* —7G **49**
Whites Av. *Ilf* —6J **35**
Whites Dri. *Brom* —6H **127**
White's Grounds. *SE1*
—2E **78** (7H **151**)
White's Grounds Est. *SE1*
—2E **78** (6H **151**)
White's Meadow. *Brom* —4E **128**
White's Row. *E1* —5F **63** (6J **145**)
Whites Sq. *SW4* —4H **93**
Whitestile Rd. *Bren* —5C **72**
Whitestone La. *NW3* —3A **44**
Whitestone Wlk. *NW3* —3A **44**
White St. *S'hall* —2B **70**
Whiteswan M. *W4* —5A **74**
Whitethorn Gdns. *Croy* —2H **135**
Whitethorn Gdns. *Enf* —5J **7**
Whitethorn St. *E3* —5C **64**
Whitewebbs Way. *Orp* —1K **129**
Whitfield Pl. *W1*
—4G **61** (4A **142**)
Whitfield Rd. *E6* —7A **50**
Whitfield Rd. *SE3* —2F **97**
Whitfield Rd. *Bexh* —7F **85**
Whitfield St. *W1*
—4G **61** (4A **142**)
Whitford Gdns. *Mitc* —3D **122**
Whitgift Av. *S Croy* —5D **134**
Whitgift Cen. *Croy* —2C **134**
Whitgift Ho. *SE11*
—4K **77** (3G **155**)
Whitgift Sq. *Croy* —2C **134**
Whitgift St. *SE11*
—4K **77** (3G **155**)
Whitgift St. *Croy* —3C **134**
Whiting Av. *Bark* —7F **51**
Whitings. *Ilf* —5J **35**
Whitings Rd. *Barn* —5A **4**
Whitings Way. *E6* —5E **66**
Whitland Rd. *Cars* —1B **132**
Whitley Rd. *N17* —2E **30**
Whitlock Dri. *SW19* —1G **107**
Whitman Rd. *E3* —4A **64**
Whitmead Clo. *S Croy* —6E **134**
Whitminster St. *SE15* —6E **78**
(off Brockworth Clo.)
Whitmore Clo. *N11* —5A **16**
Whitmore Est. *N1* —1E **62**
Whitmore Gdns. *NW10* —2E **58**
Whitmore Ho. *N1* —2E **62**
(off Whitmore Est.)
Whitmore Rd. *N1* —1E **62**
Whitmore Rd. *Beck* —3B **126**
Whitmore Rd. *Harr* —7G **23**
Whitnell Way. *SW15* —5E **90**
Whitney Av. *Ilf* —4B **34**
Whitney Rd. *E10* —7D **32**
Whitney Wlk. *Sidc* —6E **116**
Whitstable Clo. *Beck* —1B **126**
Whitstable Ho. *W10* —6F **59**
(off Silchester Rd.)
Whittaker Av. *Rich* —5D **88**

Whittaker Pl. *Rich* —5D **88**
(off Whittaker Av.)
Whittaker Rd. *E6* —7A **50**
Whittaker Rd. *Sutt* —3H **131**
Whittaker St. *SW1*
—4E **76** (4G **153**)
Whittaker Way. *SE1* —4G **79**
Whitta Rd. *E12* —4B **50**
Whittell Gdns. *SE26* —3J **111**
Whittingham. *N17* —7C **18**
Whittingham Ct. *W4* —7A **74**
Whittingstall Rd. *SW6* —1H **91**
Whittington Av. *EC3*
—6E **62** (1G **151**)
Whittington Ct. *N2* —5D **28**
Whittington M. *N12* —4K **15**
(off Fredericks Pl.)
Whittington Rd. *N22* —7D **16**
Whittington Way. *Pinn* —5C **22**
Whittlebury Clo. *Cars* —7D **132**
Whittle Clo. *E17* —6A **32**
Whittle Clo. *S'hall* —6F **55**
Whittle Rd. *Houn* —7A **70**
Whittlesea Clo. *Harr* —7B **10**
Whittlesea Path. *Harr* —1G **23**
Whittlesea Rd. *Harr* —7B **10**
Whittlesey St. *SE1*
—1A **78** (5J **149**)
Whitton Av. E. *Gnfd* —5J **39**
Whitton Av. W. *N'holt & Gnfd*
—5F **39**
Whitton Clo. *Gnfd* —6B **40**
Whitton Dene. *Houn & Iswth*
—5G **87**
Whitton Dri. *Gnfd* —6A **40**
Whitton Mnr. Rd. *Iswth* —6G **87**
Whitton Rd. *Houn* —4F **87**
Whitton Rd. *Twic* —6J **87**
Whitton Wlk. *E3* —3C **64**
Whitton Waye. *Houn* —6E **86**
Whitwell Rd. *E13* —3J **65**
Whitworth Ho. *SE1*
—3C **78** (2D **156**)
Whitworth Rd. *SE18* —7E **82**
Whitworth Rd. *SE25* —3E **124**
Whitworth St. *SE10* —5G **81**
Whorlton Rd. *SE15* —3H **95**
Whymark Av. *N22* —3A **30**
Whytecroft. *Houn* —7B **70**
Whyteville Rd. *E7* —6K **49**
Wickersley Rd. *SW11* —2E **92**
Wickers Oake. *SE19* —4F **111**
Wicker St. *E1* —6H **63**
Wicket Rd. *Gnfd* —3A **56**
Wicket, The. *Croy* —5C **136**
Wickfield Ho. *SE16* —2G **79**
(off Wilson Gro.)
Wickford St. *E1* —4J **63**
Wickford Way. *E17* —4K **31**
Wickham Av. *Croy* —2A **136**
Wickham Av. *Sutt* —5E **130**
Wickham Chase. *W Wick*
—1F **137**
Wickham Clo. *Enf* —3C **8**
Wickham Clo. *N Mald* —6B **120**
Wickham Ct. Rd. *W Wick*
—2E **136**
Wickham Cres. *W Wick* —2E **136**
Wickham Gdns. *SE4* —3B **96**
Wickham La. *SE2 & Well* —5A **84**
Wickham M. *SE4* —2B **96**
Wickham Rd. *E4* —7K **19**
Wickham Rd. *SE4* —4B **96**
Wickham Rd. *Beck* —2D **126**
Wickham Rd. *Croy* —2K **135**

Wickham Rd. *Harr* —2H **23**
Wickham St. *SE11*
—5K **77** (5G **155**)
Wickham St. *Well* —2J **99**
Wickham Way. *Beck* —4E **126**
Wick La. *E3* —1C **64**
(in two parts)
Wickliffe Av. *N3* —2G **27**
Wickliffe Av. *N3* —2G **27**
Wickliffe Gdns. *Wemb* —2H **41**
Wicklow St. *WC1*
—3K **61** (1G **143**)
Wick M. *E9* —6A **48**
Wick Rd. *E9* —6K **47**
Wick Rd. *Tedd* —7B **104**
Wicks Clo. *SE9* —4B **114**
Wick Sq. *E9* —6B **48**
Wicksteed Clo. *Bex* —3K **117**
Wicksteed Ho. *E2*
—3C **78** (2D **156**)
Wicksteed Ho. *Bren* —5F **73**
Wickway Ct. *SE15* —6F **79**
(off Cator St.)
Wickwood St. *SE5* —2B **94**
Widdecombe Av. *S Harr* —2C **38**
Widdenham Rd. *N7* —4K **45**
Widdin St. *E15* —7F **49**
Widecombe Gdns. *Ilf* —4C **34**
Widecombe Rd. *SE9* —3C **114**
Widecombe Way. *N2* —5B **28**
Widegate St. *E1* —5E **62** (6H **145**)
Widenham Clo. *Pinn* —5A **22**
Wide Way. *Mitc* —3H **123**
Widgeon Clo. *E16* —6K **65**
Widley Rd. *W9* —3J **59**
Widmer Ct. *Houn* —2C **86**
Widmore Lodge Rd. *Brom*
—2B **128**
Widmore Rd. *Brom* —2J **127**
Wigan Ho. *E5* —1H **47**
Wigeon Path. *SE28* —3H **83**
Wigeon Way. *Hayes* —6C **54**
Wiggins Mead. *NW9* —7G **13**
Wigginton Av. *Wemb* —6H **41**
Wightman Rd. *N8 & N4* —4A **30**
Wigley Rd. *Felt* —2B **102**
Wigmore Ct. *W13* —1A **72**
(off Singapore Rd.)
Wigmore Pl. *W1* —6F **61** (7J **141**)
Wigmore Rd. *Cars* —2B **132**
Wigmore St. *W1*
—6E **60** (7H **141**)
Wigmore Wlk. *Cars* —2B **132**
Wigram Rd. *E11* —6A **34**
Wigram Sq. *E17* —3E **32**
Wigston Clo. *N18* —5K **17**
Wigston Rd. *E13* —4A **65**
Wigton Gdns. *Stan* —1E **24**
Wigton Pl. *SE11*
—5A **78** (6K **155**)
Wigton Rd. *E17* —1B **32**
Wilberforce Rd. *N4* —2B **46**
Wilberforce Rd. *NW9* —6C **26**
Wilberforce Way. *SW19* —6F **107**
Wilbraham Pl. *SW1*
—4D **76** (3F **153**)
Wilbury Way. *N18* —5J **17**
Wilby M. *W11* —1H **75**
Wilcox Clo. *SW8* —7J **77**
(in two parts)
Wilcox Pl. *SW1* —3G **77** (2B **154**)
Wilcox Rd. *SW8* —7J **77**
Wilcox Rd. *Sutt* —4K **131**
Wilcox Rd. *Tedd* —4H **103**
Wild Ct. *WC2* —6K **61** (1G **149**)

Wildcroft Gdns. *Edgw* —6J **11**
Wildcroft Mnr. *SW15* —7E **90**
Wildcroft Rd. *SW15* —7E **90**
Wilde Clo. *E8* —1G **63**
Wilde Pl. *N13* —6G **17**
Wilde Pl. *SW18* —7B **92**
Wilderness Rd. *Chst* —7F **115**
Wilderness, The. *Hamp* —4F **103**
Wilde Rd. *Eri* —7H **85**
Wilderton Rd. *N16* —7E **30**
Wildfell Rd. *SE6* —7D **96**
Wild Goose Dri. *SE14* —1J **95**
Wild Hatch. *NW11* —6J **27**
Wild's Rents. *SE1*
   —3E **78** (1G **157**)
Wild St. *WC2* —6J **61** (1F **149**)
Wildwood Clo. *SE12* —7H **97**
Wildwood Gro. *NW3* —1A **44**
Wildwood Rise. *NW11* —1A **44**
Wildwood Rd. *NW11* —6K **27**
Wildwood Ter. *NW3* —1A **44**
Wilford Clo. *Enf* —3J **7**
Wilfred Owen Clo. *SW19*
   —6A **108**
Wilfred St. *SW1* —3G **77** (1A **154**)
Wilfrid Gdns. *W3* —5J **57**
Wilkes St. *E1* —5F **63** (5K **145**)
   (in two parts)
Wilkie Way. *SE22* —1G **111**
Wilkins Clo. *Mitc* —1C **122**
Wilkinson Ct. *SW17* —4B **108**
Wilkinson Ho. *N1* —2D **62**
   (off Cranston Est.)
Wilkinson Rd. *E16* —6A **66**
Wilkinson St. *SW8* —7K **77**
Wilkinson Way. *W4* —2K **73**
Wilkin St. *NW5* —6E **44**
Wilkin St. M. *NW5* —6F **45**
Wilks Gdns. *Croy* —1A **136**
Wilks Pl. *N1* —2E **62**
Willan Rd. *N17* —2D **30**
Willan Wall. *E16* —7H **65**
Willard St. *SW8* —3F **93**
Willcott Rd. *W3* —1H **73**
Will Crooks Gdns. *SE9* —4B **98**
Willenfield Rd. *NW10* —2J **57**
Willenhall Av. *New Bar* —6F **5**
Willenhall Ct. *New Bar* —6F **5**
Willenhall Rd. *SE18* —5F **83**
Willersley Av. *Sidc* —1K **115**
Willersley Clo. *Sidc* —1K **115**
Willesden La. *NW2 & NW6*
   —6E **42**
Willes Rd. *NW5* —6F **45**
Willett Clo. *N'holt* —3A **54**
Willett Clo. *Orp* —6J **129**
Willett Ho. *E13* —2K **65**
   (off Queens Rd. W.)
Willett Pl. *T Hth* —5A **124**
Willett Rd. *T Hth* —5A **124**
Willett Way. *Orp* —5H **129**
William Allen Ho. *Edgw* —7A **12**
William Banfield Ho. *SW6*
   (off Munster Rd.)   —2H **91**
William Barefoot Dri. *SE9*
   —4E **114**
William Bonney Est. *SW4* —4H **93**
William Booth Rd. *SE20* —1G **125**
William Carey Way. *Harr* —6J **23**
William Clo. *SW6* —7G **75**
   (off Dawes Rd.)
William Clo. *Romf* —1J **37**
William Clo. *S'hall* —2G **71**
William Cobbett Ho. *W8* —3K **75**
   (off Scarsdale Pl.)

William Ct. *Gnfd* —5C **56**
William Covell Clo. *Enf* —1E **6**
William Dromey Ct. *NW6* —7H **43**
William Ellis Way. *SE16* —3G **79**
William Evans Ho. *SE8* —4K **79**
   (off Haddonfield)
William IV St. *WC2*
   —7J **61** (3E **148**)
William Gdns. *SW15* —5D **90**
William Gunn Ho. *NW3* —5C **44**
William Guy Gdns. *E3* —3D **64**
William Margrie Clo. *SE15*
   —2G **95**
William M. *SW1* —2D **76** (7F **147**)
William Morley Clo. *E6* —1B **66**
William Morris Clo. *E17* —3B **32**
William Morris Ho. *W6* —6F **75**
   (off Margravine Rd.)
William Morris Way. *SW6*
   —3A **92**
William Paton Ho. *E16* —6K **65**
William Pike Ho. *Romf* —6K **37**
   (off Waterloo Gdns.)
William Pl. *E3* —2B **64**
William Rd. *NW1*
   —3F **61** (2K **141**)
William Rd. *SW19* —7G **107**
William Rd. *Sutt* —5A **132**
Williams Av. *E17* —1B **32**
Williams Clo. *N8* —6H **29**
Williams Gro. *N22* —1A **30**
Williams Ho. *NW2* —3E **42**
   (off Stoll Clo.)
William's La. *SW14* —3J **89**
Williams La. *Mord* —5A **122**
William Smith Ho. *Belv* —3G **85**
   (off Ambrooke Rd.)
Williamson Clo. *SE10* —5H **81**
Williamson Rd. *N4* —6B **30**
Williamson St. *N7* —4G **45**
Williamson Way. *NW7* —6B **14**
William Sq. *SE16* —7A **64**
   (off Sovereign Cres.)
Williams Rd. *W13* —1A **72**
Williams Rd. *S'hall* —4C **70**
Williams Ter. *Croy* —6A **134**
William St. *E10* —6D **32**
William St. *N17* —7A **18**
William St. *SW1*
   —2D **76** (7F **147**)
William St. *Bark* —7G **51**
William St. *Cars* —3C **132**
William White Ct. *E13* —1A **66**
   (off Green St.)
William Wood Ho. *SE26* —3J **111**
   (off Shrublands Clo.)
Willifield Way. *NW11* —4H **27**
Willingale Clo. *Wfd G* —6F **21**
Willingdon Rd. *N22* —2B **30**
Willingham Clo. *NW5* —5G **45**
Willingham Ter. *NW5* —5G **45**
Willington Ct. *E5* —3A **48**
Willington Rd. *SW9* —3J **93**
Willis Av. *Sutt* —6G **132**
Willis Ct. *T Hth* —6A **124**
Willis Rd. *E15* —2H **65**
Willis Rd. *Croy* —7C **124**
Willis Rd. *Eri* —4K **85**
Willis St. *E14* —6D **64**
Will Miles Ct. *SW19* —7A **108**
Willmore End. *SW19* —1K **121**
Willoughby Av. *Croy* —4K **133**
Willoughby Dri. *Rain* —7K **53**
Willoughby Gro. *N17* —7C **18**

Willoughby Ho. *EC2*
   —5D **62** (5E **144**)
Willoughby La. *N17* —6C **18**
Willoughby Pk. Rd. *N17* —7C **18**
   (in two parts)
Willoughby Rd. *N8* —3A **30**
Willoughby Rd. *NW3* —4B **44**
Willoughby Rd. *King T* —1F **119**
Willoughby Rd. *Twic* —5C **88**
Willoughbys, The. *SW14* —3A **90**
Willoughby St. *WC1*
   —5J **61** (6E **142**)
Willoughby Way. *SE7* —4K **81**
Willow Av. *SW13* —2B **90**
Willow Av. *Sidc* —6A **100**
Willow Bank. *SW6* —3G **91**
Willow Bank. *Rich* —3B **104**
Willow Bri. Rd. *N1* —6C **46**
Willow Brook Rd. *SE15* —7F **79**
Willowbrook Rd. *S'hall* —3E **70**
Willow Bus. Cen., The. *Mitc*
   —6D **122**
Willow Bus. Pk. *SE26* —3J **111**
Willow Clo. *SE6* —1H **113**
Willow Clo. *Bex* —6F **101**
Willow Clo. *Bren* —6C **72**
Willow Clo. *Brom* —5D **128**
Willow Clo. *Buck H* —3G **21**
Willow Cotts. *Hanw* —3C **102**
Willow Cotts. *Rich* —6G **73**
Willow Ct. *E11* —2G **49**
   (off Trinity Clo.)
Willow Ct. *EC2* —4E **62** (3G **145**)
Willow Ct. *W4* —7A **74**
   (off Corney Reach Way)
Willow Ct. *Edgw* —4K **11**
Willow Ct. *Harr* —1K **23**
Willowcourt Av. *Harr* —5B **24**
Willowdene. *N6* —7D **28**
Willowdene. *SE15* —1H **95**
Willow Dene. *Bush* —1D **10**
Willow Dene. *Pinn* —2B **22**
Willowdene Clo. *Twic* —7G **87**
Willowdene Ct. *N20* —7F **5**
   (off High Rd.)
Willow Dri. *Barn* —4B **4**
Willow End. *N20* —2D **14**
Willow End. *Surb* —7E **118**
Willow Farm La. *SW15* —3D **90**
Willow Gdns. *Houn* —1E **86**
Willow Grange. *Sidc* —3B **116**
Willow Grn. *NW9* —1A **26**
Willow Gro. *E13* —2J **65**
Willow Gro. *Chst* —6E **114**
Willowhayne Gdns. *Wor Pk*
   —3E **130**
Willow Ho. *Brom* —2G **127**
Willow La. *Mitc* —5D **122**
Willow Lodge. *SW6* —1E **90**
Willowmead Clo. *W5* —5D **56**
Willow Mt. *Croy* —3E **134**
Willow Pl. *SW1* —4G **77** (3B **154**)
Willow Rd. *E12* —3D **50**
Willow Rd. *NW3* —4B **44**
Willow Rd. *W5* —2E **72**
Willow Rd. *Enf* —3K **7**
Willow Rd. *N Mald* —4J **119**
Willow Rd. *Romf* —6E **36**
Willow Rd. *Wall* —7F **133**
Willows Av. *Mord* —5K **121**
Willows Clo. *Pinn* —2A **22**
Willowside Ct. *Enf* —3G **7**
Willows, The. *E6* —7E **50**
Willows, The. *Beck* —1C **126**
Willow St. *E4* —1A **20**

Willow St. *EC2* —4E **62** (3G **145**)
Willow St. *Romf* —4J **37**
Willow Tree Clo. *E3* —1B **64**
Willow Tree Clo. *SW18* —1K **107**
Willow Tree Clo. *Hayes* —4A **54**
Willow Tree Clo. *Sidc* —5K **115**
Willow Tree La. *Hayes* —4A **54**
Willow Tree Wlk. *Brom* —1K **127**
Willowtree Way. *T Hth* —1A **124**
Willow Vale. *W12* —1C **74**
Willow Vale. *Chst* —6F **115**
Willow View. *SW19* —1B **122**
Willow Wlk. *N2* —2B **28**
Willow Wlk. *N15* —4B **30**
Willow Wlk. *N21* —6E **6**
Willow Wlk. *SE1*
   —4E **78** (3H **157**)
Willow Wlk. *Ilf* —2F **51**
Willow Wlk. *Sutt* —3H **131**
Willow Way. *N3* —7E **14**
Willow Way. *SE26* —3J **111**
Willow Way. *W11* —7F **59**
Willow Way. *Eps* —6A **130**
Willow Way. *Twic* —2F **103**
Willow Way. *Wemb* —3A **40**
Willow Wood Cres. *SE25*
   —6E **124**
Willrose Cres. *SE2* —5B **84**
Willsbridge Ct. *SE15* —6F **79**
   (off Bibury Clo.)
Wills Cres. *Houn* —6F **87**
Wills Gro. *NW7* —5H **13**
Wilman Gro. *E8* —7G **47**
Wilmar Gdns. *W Wick* —1D **136**
Wilmcote Ho. *W2* —5K **59**
   (off Woodchester Sq.)
Wilmer Clo. *King T* —5F **105**
Wilmer Cres. *King T* —5F **105**
Wilmer Gdns. *N1* —1E **62**
Wilmer Lea Clo. *E15* —7F **49**
Wilmer Pl. *N16* —2F **47**
Wilmer Way. *N14* —5C **16**
Wilmington Av. *W4* —7K **73**
Wilmington Ct. *SW16* —7J **109**
Wilmington Gdns. *Bark* —6H **51**
Wilmington Sq. *WC1*
   —3A **62** (2J **143**)
Wilmington St. *WC1*
   —3A **62** (2J **143**)
Wilmot Clo. *N2* —2A **28**
Wilmot Clo. *SE15* —7G **79**
Wilmot Pl. *NW1* —7G **45**
Wilmot Pl. *W7* —1J **71**
Wilmot Rd. *E10* —2D **48**
Wilmot Rd. *N17* —3D **30**
Wilmot Rd. *Cars* —5D **132**
Wilmot St. *E2* —4H **63**
Wilmount St. *SE18* —4F **83**
Wilna Rd. *SW18* —7A **92**
Wilsham St. *W11* —1F **75**
Wilshaw Ho. *SE8* —7C **80**
Wilshaw St. *SE14* —1C **96**
Wilsmere Dri. *Har W* —7D **10**
Wilsmere Dri. *N'holt* —6C **38**
Wilson Av. *Mitc* —7C **108**
Wilson Clo. *S Croy* —5D **134**
Wilson Clo. *Wemb* —7F **25**
Wilson Dri. *Wemb* —7F **25**
Wilson Gdns. *Harr* —7G **23**
Wilson Gro. *SE16* —2H **79**
Wilson M. *SW15* —5C **90**
Wilson Rd. *E6* —3B **66**
Wilson Rd. *SE5* —1E **94**
Wilson Rd. *Ilf* —7D **34**
Wilson's Av. *N17* —2F **31**

Wilson's Pl. *E14* —6B **64**
Wilson's Rd. *W6* —5F **75**
Wilson St. *E17* —5E **32**
Wilson St. *EC2* —5D **62** (5F **145**)
Wilson St. *N21* —7F **7**
Wilson Wlk. *W4* —4B **74**
   (off Prebend Gdns.)
Wilson Wlk. *Stan* —5H **11**
Wilstone Clo. *Hayes* —4C **54**
Wilthorne Gdns. *Dag* —7H **53**
Wilton Av. *W4* —5A **74**
Wilton Cres. *SW1*
   —2E **76** (7G **147**)
Wilton Cres. *SW19* —7H **107**
Wilton Dri. *Romf* —1J **37**
Wilton Est. *E8* —6G **47**
Wilton Gro. *SW19* —7H **107**
Wilton Gro. *N Mald* —6B **120**
Wilton M. *SW1* —3E **76** (1H **153**)
Wilton Pl. *SW1* —2E **76** (7G **147**)
Wilton Rd. *N10* —2E **28**
Wilton Rd. *SE2* —4C **84**
Wilton Rd. *SW1*
   —3G **77** (2A **154**)
Wilton Rd. *SW19* —7C **108**
Wilton Rd. *Cockf* —4J **5**
Wilton Rd. *Houn* —3B **86**
Wilton Row. *SW1*
   —2E **76** (7G **147**)
Wilton Row. *SW6* —7G **75**
Wilton Sq. *N1* —1D **62**
Wilton St. *SW1* —3F **77** (1J **153**)
Wilton Ter. *SW1*
   —3E **76** (1G **153**)
Wilton Vs. *N1* —1D **62**
   (off Wilton Sq.)
Wilton Way. *E8* —6G **47**
Wiltshire Clo. *NW7* —5G **13**
Wiltshire Clo. *SW3*
   —4D **76** (3E **152**)
Wiltshire Ct. *N4* —1K **45**
   (off Marquis Rd.)
Wiltshire Ct. *Ilf* —6G **51**
Wiltshire Gdns. *N4* —6C **30**
Wiltshire Gdns. *Twic* —1G **103**
Wiltshire Rd. *N1* —1D **62**
Wiltshire Rd. *SW9* —3A **94**
Wiltshire Rd. *Orp* —7K **129**
Wiltshire Rd. *T Hth* —3A **124**
Wiltshire Row. *N1* —1D **62**
   (off Bridport Pl.)
Wilverley Cres. *N Mald* —6A **120**
Wimbart Rd. *SW2* —7K **93**
Wimbledon Bri. *SW19* —6H **107**
Wimbledon Hill Rd. *SW19*
   —6G **107**
Wimbledon Pk. Rd. *SW19 &*
   SW18 —2G **107**
Wimbledon Pk. Side. *SW19*
   —3F **107**
Wimbledon Park. *W4* —4A **108**
Wimbledon Stadium Bus. Cen.
   SW17 —3K **107**
Wimbolt St. *E2* —3G **63**
Wimborne Av. *Hayes* —6A **54**
Wimborne Av. *Orp & Chst*
   —4K **129**
Wimborne Av. *S'hall* —4E **70**
Wimborne Clo. *SE12* —5H **97**
Wimborne Clo. *Buck H* —2E **20**
Wimborne Clo. *Wor Pk* —1E **130**
Wimborne Ct. *N'holt* —6E **38**
Wimborne Dri. *NW9* —3G **25**
Wimborne Dri. *Pinn* —7B **22**

Wimborne Gdns. W13 —5B 56
Wimborne Ho. SW8 —7K 77
  (off Dorset Rd.)
Wimborne Rd. N9 —2B 18
Wimborne Rd. N17 —2E 30
Wimborne Way. Beck —3K 125
Wimbourne Ct. SW12 —3G 109
Wimbourne St. N1 —2D 62
Wimpole Clo. Brom —4A 128
Wimpole Clo. King T —2F 119
Wimpole M. W1 —5F 61 (5J 141)
Wimpole St. W1 —5F 61 (6J 141)
Wimshurst Clo. Croy —1J 133
Winans Wlk. SW9 —2A 94
Wincanton Cres. N'holt —5E 38
Wincanton Gdns. Ilf —3F 35
Wincanton Rd. SW18 —7H 91
Winchcombe Bus. Cen. SE15
  (off Lydney Clo.) —7E 78
Winchcombe Ct. SE15 —6E 78
  (off Lydney Clo.)
Winchcomb Gdns. Cars —7B 122
Winchcomb Gdns. SE9 —3B 98
Winchelsea Av. Bexh —7F 85
Winchelsea Clo. SW15 —5F 91
Winchelsea Rd. E7 —3J 49
Winchelsea Rd. N17 —3E 30
Winchelsea Rd. NW10 —1K 57
Winchelsey Rise. S Croy —6F 135
Winchendon Rd. SW6 —1H 91
Winchendon Rd. Tedd —4H 103
Winchester Av. NW6 —1G 59
Winchester Av. NW9 —3G 25
Winchester Av. Houn —6D 70
Winchester Clo. E6 —6D 66
Winchester Clo. SE17
  —4B 78 (4B 156)
Winchester Clo. Brom —3H 127
Winchester Clo. Enf —5K 7
Winchester Clo. King T —1H 105
Winchester Dri. Pinn —5B 22
Winchester Ho. SW3 —6B 76
Winchester Ho. SW9 —7A 78
Winchester Ho. Bark —7A 52
  (off Keir Hardie Way)
Winchester Pk. Brom —3H 127
Winchester Pl. E8 —5F 47
Winchester Pl. N6 —1F 45
Winchester Rd. E4 —7K 19
Winchester Rd. N6 —7F 29
Winchester Rd. N9 —1A 18
Winchester Rd. NW3 —7B 44
Winchester Rd. Bexh —2D 100
Winchester Rd. Brom —3H 127
Winchester Rd. Felt —3D 102
Winchester Rd. Harr —4E 24
Winchester Rd. Ilf —3H 51
Winchester Rd. Twic —6B 88
Winchester Sq. SE1
  —1D 78 (4E 150)
Winchester St. SW1
  —5F 77 (5K 153)
Winchester St. W3 —1J 73
Winchester Wlk. SE1
  —1D 78 (4E 150)
Winchet Wlk. Croy —6J 125
Winchfield Clo. Harr —6C 24
Winchfield Ho. SW15 —6B 90
Winchfield Rd. SE26 —5A 112
Winchmore Hill Rd. N14 & N21
  —1C 16
Winckley Clo. Harr —5F 25
Wincott St. SE11
  —4A 78 (4K 155)
Wincrofts Dri. SE9 —4H 99

Windall Clo. SE19 —1G 125
Windborough Rd. Cars —7E 132
Windermere Av. N3 —3J 27
Windermere Av. NW6 —1G 59
Windermere Av. SW19 —3K 121
Windermere Av. Ruis —7A 22
Windermere Av. Wemb —7C 24
Windermere Ct. SW13 —6B 74
Windermere Ct. Wemb —7C 24
Windermere Gdns. Ilf —5C 34
Windermere Gro. Wemb —1C 40
Windermere Hall. Edgw —5A 12
Windermere Ho. New Bar —4E 4
Windermere Point. SE15 —7J 79
  (off Old Kent Rd.)
Windermere Rd. N10 —1F 29
Windermere Rd. N19 —2G 45
Windermere Rd. SW15 —4A 106
Windermere Rd. SW16 —1G 123
Windermere Rd. W5 —3C 72
Windermere Rd. Bexh —2J 101
Windermere Rd. Croy —1F 135
Windermere Rd. S'hall —5D 54
Windermere Rd. W Wick
  —2G 137
Winders Rd. SW11 —2C 92
Windfield Clo. SE26 —4K 111
Windham Rd. Rich —3F 89
Winding Way. Dag —3C 52
Winding Way. Harr —4J 39
Windlass Pl. SE8 —4A 80
Windlesham Gro. SW19 —1F 107
Windley Clo. SE23 —2J 111
Windmill Av. S'hall —2G 71
Windmill Bus. Cen. S'hall —1G 71
Windmill Clo. SE1 —4G 79
Windmill Clo. SE13 —2E 96
Windmill Clo. Surb —7C 118
Windmill Ct. NW2 —6G 43
Windmill Ct. W7 —4C 72
  (off Windmill Rd.)
Windmill Dri. SW4 —5F 93
Windmill Dri. Kes —4A 138
Windmill Gdns. Enf —3F 7
Windmill Gro. Croy —6C 124
Windmill Hill. NW3 —3A 44
Windmill Hill. Enf —3G 7
Windmill La. E15 —6F 49
Windmill La. Bush —1D 10
Windmill La. Gnfd —5G 55
Windmill La. S'hall & Iswth
  —1G 71
Windmill La. Surb —6B 118
Windmill M. W4 —4A 74
Windmill Pas. W4 —4A 74
Windmill Rise. King T —7H 105
Windmill Rd. N18 —4J 17
Windmill Rd. SW18 —6B 92
Windmill Rd. SW19 —4D 106
Windmill Rd. W4 —4A 74
Windmill Rd. W5 & Bren —4C 72
Windmill Rd. Croy —7C 124
Windmill Rd. Hamp —5F 103
Windmill Rd. Mitc —5G 123
Windmill Row. SE11
  —5A 78 (6J 155)
Windmill St. W1
  (in two parts) —5H 61 (6C 142)
Windmill St. Bush —1D 10
Windmill Wlk. SE1
  —1A 78 (5K 149)
Windover Av. NW9 —4K 25
Windrose Clo. SE16 —2K 79
Windrush. SE28 —1B 84
Windrush Clo. SW11 —4B 92

Windrush Clo. W4 —1J 89
Windrush La. SE23 —3K 111
Windsock Clo. SE16 —4B 80
Windsor Av. E17 —2A 32
Windsor Av. SW19 —1A 122
Windsor Av. Edgw —4C 12
Windsor Av. N Mald —5J 119
Windsor Av. Sutt —3G 131
Windsor Cen., The. N1 —1B 62
  (off Windsor St.)
Windsor Clo. N3 —2G 27
Windsor Clo. SE27 —4C 110
Windsor Clo. Bren —6B 72
Windsor Clo. Chst —5F 115
Windsor Clo. Harr —3E 38
Windsor Ct. N11 —5J 15
Windsor Ct. N14 —7B 6
Windsor Ct. NW3 —3J 43
Windsor Ct. NW11 —6G 27
  (off Golders Grn. Rd.)
Windsor Ct. SW11 —2B 92
Windsor Ct. W10 —6F 59
  (off Darfield Way)
Windsor Ct. Pinn —3B 22
Windsor Cres. Harr —3E 38
Windsor Cres. Wemb —3H 41
Windsor Dri. Barn —6J 5
Windsor Gdns. W9 —5J 59
Windsor Gdns. Croy —3J 133
Windsor Gdns. SE27 —4C 110
Windsor Ho. N1 —2C 62
Windsor Ho. N'holt —6E 38
  (off Farmlands, The)
Windsor M. SE6 —1E 112
Windsor M. SE23 —1A 112
Windsor M. SW18 —7A 92
  (off Wilna Rd.)
Windsor Pl. SW1
  —4G 77 (3B 154)
Windsor Rd. E4 —4J 19
Windsor Rd. E7 —5K 49
Windsor Rd. E10 —2D 48
Windsor Rd. E11 —1J 49
Windsor Rd. N3 —2G 27
Windsor Rd. N7 —3J 45
Windsor Rd. N13 —3F 17
Windsor Rd. N17 —2G 31
Windsor Rd. NW2 —6D 42
Windsor Rd. W5 —7E 56
Windsor Rd. Barn —6A 4
Windsor Rd. Bexh —4E 100
Windsor Rd. Dag —3E 52
Windsor Rd. Harr —1G 23
Windsor Rd. Houn —2A 86
Windsor Rd. Ilf —4F 51
Windsor Rd. King T —7E 104
Windsor Rd. Rich —2F 89
Windsor Rd. S'hall —3D 70
Windsor Rd. Tedd —5H 103
Windsor Rd. T Hth —2B 124
Windsor Rd. Wor Pk —2C 130
Windsors, The. Buck H —2H 21
Windsor St. N1 —1B 62
Windsor Ter. N1
  —3C 62 (1D 144)
Windsor Wlk. SE5 —2D 94
Windsor Way. W14 —4F 75
Windsor Wharf. E9 —5B 48
Windspoint Dri. SE15 —6H 79
Windus Rd. N16 —1F 47
Windus Wlk. N16 —1F 47
Windy Ridge. Brom —1C 128
Windy Ridge Clo. SW19
  —5F 107
Wine Clo. E1 —7J 63

Wine Office Ct. EC4
  —6A 62 (7K 143)
Winery La. King T —3F 119
Winford Pde. S'hall —6F 55
  (off Brunel Pl.)
Winforton St. SE10 —1E 96
Winfrith Rd. SW18 —7A 92
Wingate Cres. Croy —6J 123
Wingate Rd. W6 —3D 74
Wingate Rd. Ilf —5F 51
Wingate Rd. Sidc —6C 116
Wingate Trad. Est. N17 —7B 18
Wingfield Ct. Sidc —2K 115
Wingfield Rd. E15 —4G 49
Wingfield Rd. E17 —5D 32
Wingfield Rd. King T —6F 105
Wingfield St. SE15 —3G 95
Wingfield Way. Ruis —6A 38
Wingford Rd. SW2 —6J 93
Wingmore Rd. SE24 —3C 94
Wingrave Rd. W6 —6E 74
Wingrove. E4 —7J 9
Wingrove Ct. Romf —5J 37
Wingrove Rd. SE6 —2G 113
Wings Clo. Sutt —4J 131
Winifred Pl. N12 —5F 15
Winifred Rd. SW19 —1J 121
Winifred Rd. Dag —2E 52
Winifred Rd. Eri —5K 85
Winifred Rd. Hamp —4E 102
Winifred St. E16 —1D 82
Winifred Ter. E13 —2J 65
  (off Victoria Rd.)
Winifred Ter. Enf —7A 8
Winkfield Rd. E13 —2K 65
Winkfield Rd. N22 —1A 30
Winkley Ct. S Harr —3E 38
Winkley St. E2 —2H 63
Winlaton Rd. Brom —4F 113
Winmill Rd. Dag —3F 53
Winnett St. W1 —7H 61 (2C 148)
Winnifred Mandela Ho. Wemb
  —7F 25
Winningales Ct. Ilf —3C 34
Winnings Wlk. N'holt —6C 38
Winnington Clo. N2 —6B 28
Winnington Ho. SE5 —7C 78
  (off Wyndham Est.)
Winnington Rd. N2 —6B 28
Winn Rd. SE12 —1J 113
Winns Av. E17 —3B 32
Winns Comn. Rd. SE18 —6J 83
Winns M. N15 —4E 30
Winns Ter. E17 —3C 32
Winsbeach. E17 —2F 33
Winscombe Cres. W5 —4D 56
Winscombe St. N19 —2F 45
Winscombe Way. Stan —5F 11
Winsford Rd. SE6 —3B 112
Winsford Ter. N18 —5J 17
Winsham Gro. SW11 —5E 92
Winslade Rd. SW2 —5J 93
Winslade Way. SE6 —7D 96
Winsland M. W2
  —6B 60 (7A 140)
Winsland St. W2
  —6B 60 (7A 140)
Winsley St. W1 —6G 61 (7B 142)
Winslow. SE17 —5E 78 (6G 157)
Winslow Clo. NW10 —3A 42
Winslow Clo. Pinn —6A 22
Winslow Gro. E4 —2B 20
Winslow Rd. W6 —6E 74
Winslow Way. Felt —3C 102
Winsmoor Ct. Enf —3G 7

Winsor Ter. E6 —5E 66
Winstanley Est. SW11 —3B 92
Winstanley Rd. SW11 —3B 92
Winstead Gdns. Dag —5J 53
Winston Av. NW9 —7A 26
Winston Clo. Harr —6E 10
Winston Clo. Romf —4H 37
Winston Ct. Brom —1K 127
Winston Ct. Harr —7A 10
Winston Ho. N1 —2D 62
  (off Cherbury St.)
Winston Ho. W13 —2A 72
Winston Rd. N16 —4D 46
Winston Wlk. W4 —3K 73
Winston Way. Ilf —3F 51
Winter Av. E6 —1C 66
Winterbourne Ho. W11 —7G 59
  (off Portland Rd.)
Winterbourne Rd. SE6 —1B 112
Winterbourne Rd. Dag —2C 52
Winterbourne Rd. T Hth —4A 124
Winter Box Wlk. Rich —5F 89
Winterbrook Rd. SE24 —6C 94
Winterfold Clo. SW19 —2G 107
Wintergreen Clo. E6 —5C 66
Winter Lodge. SE16 —5G 79
  (off Fern Wlk.)
Winter's Ct. E4 —3J 19
Winterslow Ho. SE5 —2C 94
Winterstoke Gdns. NW7 —5H 13
Winterstoke Rd. SE6 —1B 112
Winterton Ct. SE20 —2G 125
Winterton Pl. SW10
  —6A 76 (7A 152)
Winterwell Rd. SW2 —5J 93
Winthorpe Rd. SW15 —4G 91
Winthrop Wlk. Wemb —3E 40
Winton Av. N11 —7B 16
Winton Clo. N9 —7E 8
Winton Gdns. Edgw —7A 12
Winton Way. SW16 —5A 110
Wirrall Ho. SE26 —3G 111
Wirral Wood Clo. Chst —6E 114
Wisbeach Rd. Croy —5D 124
Wisborough Rd. S Croy —7F 135
Wisden Ho. SW8
  —6K 77 (7H 155)
Wisdom Ct. Iswth —3A 88
  (off South St.)
Wisdons Clo. Dag —1H 53
Wise La. NW7 —5H 13
Wiseman Rd. E10 —2C 48
Wise Rd. E15 —1F 65
Wiseton Rd. SW17 —1C 108
Wishart Rd. SE3 —2B 98
Wisley Rd. SW11 —5E 92
Wisley Rd. Orp —7A 116
Wisteria Clo. NW7 —5G 13
Wisteria Clo. Ilf —5F 51
Wisteria Rd. SE13 —4F 97
Witanhurst La. N6 —1E 44
Witan St. E2 —3H 63
Witham Ct. E10 —3D 48
Witham Rd. SE20 —3J 125
Witham Rd. W13 —1A 72
Witham Rd. Dag —6G 53
Witham Rd. Iswth —1H 87
Witherby Clo. Croy —4E 134
Witherby Clo. S Croy —5B 134
Witherington Rd. N5 —5A 46
Withers Mead. NW9 —1B 26
Withy Pl. EC1 —4C 62 (3D 144)
Witherston Way. SE9 —2E 114

Withington Ct. *SE15* —6E **78**
(off Brockworth Clo.)
Withycombe Rd. *SW19* —7F **91**
Withy Mead. *E4* —3A **20**
Witley Cres. *New Ad* —6E **136**
Witley Gdns. *S'hall* —4D **70**
Witley Ho. *SW2* —7K **93**
Witley Ind. Est. *S'hall* —4C **70**
Witley Rd. *N19* —2G **45**
Witney Path. *SE23* —3K **111**
Wittenham Way. *E4* —3A **20**
Wittering Clo. *King T* —5D **104**
Wittersham Rd. *Brom* —5H **113**
Wivenhoe Clo. *SE15* —3H **95**
Wivenhoe Ct. *Houn* —4D **86**
Wivenhoe-Rd. *Bark* —2A **68**
Wiverton Rd. *SE26* —6J **111**
Wix Rd. *Dag* —1D **68**
Wix's La. *SW4* —3F **93**
Woburn. *W13* —5B **56**
(off Clivedon Ct.)
Woburn Clo. *SW19* —6A **108**
Woburn Ct. *E18* —2J **33**
Woburn Ct. *SE16* —5H **79**
(off Masters Dri.)
Woburn M. *WC1*
—4H **61** (3D **142**)
Woburn Pl. *WC1*
—4H **61** (4E **142**)
Woburn Rd. *Cars* —1C **132**
Woburn Rd. *Croy* —1C **134**
Woburn Sq. *WC1*
—4H **61** (4D **142**)
Woburn Tower. *N'holt* —3A **54**
(off Broomcroft Av.)
Woburn Wlk. *WC1*
—3H **61** (2D **142**)
Wodehouse Ct. *W3* —3J **73**
(off Vincent Rd.)
Woffington Clo. *King T* —1C **118**
Woking Clo. *SW15* —4B **90**
Woldham Pl. *Brom* —4A **128**
Woldham Rd. *Brom* —4A **128**
Wolds Dri. *Orp* —4E **138**
Wolfe Clo. *Brom* —6J **127**
Wolfe Cres. *SE7* —5B **82**
Wolfe Cres. *SE16* —2K **79**
Wolfe Gdns. *Ilf* —7C **34**
Wolfe Ho. *W12* —7D **58**
(off White City Est.)
Wolferton Rd. *E12* —4D **50**
Wolffe Gdns. *E15* —6H **49**
Wolfington Rd. *SE27* —4B **110**
Wolfram Clo. *SE13* —5G **97**
Wolfson Rehabilitation Cen., The.
SW20 —7C **106**
Wolftencroft Clo. *SW11* —3C **92**
Wollaston Clo. *SE1*
—4C **78** (3C **156**)
Wolmer Clo. *Edgw* —4B **12**
Wolmer Gdns. *Edgw* —3B **12**
Wolseley Av. *SW19* —2J **107**
Wolseley Gdns. *W4* —6H **73**
Wolseley Rd. *E7* —7K **49**
Wolseley Rd. *N8* —6H **29**
Wolseley Rd. *N22* —1K **29**
Wolseley Rd. *W4* —4J **73**
Wolseley Rd. *Mitc* —7E **122**
Wolseley Rd. *Romf* —7K **37**
Wolseley Rd. *W'stone* —3J **23**
Wolseley St. *SE1*
—2F **79** (7K **151**)
Wolsey Av. *E6* —3E **66**
Wolsey Av. *E17* —3B **32**
Wolsey Clo. *SW20* —7D **106**

Wolsey Clo. *Houn* —4G **87**
Wolsey Clo. *King T* —1H **119**
Wolsey Clo. *S'hall* —3G **71**
Wolsey Clo. *Wor Pk* —4C **130**
Wolsey Cres. *Mord* —7G **121**
Wolsey Cres. *New Ad* —7E **136**
Wolsey Dri. *King T* —5E **104**
Wolsey Gro. *Edgw* —7E **12**
Wolsey M. *NW5* —6G **45**
Wolsey Rd. *N1* —5E **46**
Wolsey Rd. *Enf* —2C **8**
Wolsey Rd. *Hamp* —6F **103**
Wolsey Spring. *King T* —7J **105**
Wolsey St. *E1* —5J **63**
Wolstonbury. *N12* —5D **14**
Wolvercote Rd. *SE2* —2D **84**
Wolverley St. *E2* —3H **63**
Wolverton. *SE17*
—5E **78** (5G **157**)
Wolverton Av. *King T* —1G **119**
Wolverton Gdns. *W5* —7F **57**
Wolverton Gdns. *W6* —4F **75**
Wolverton Rd. *Stan* —6G **11**
Wolverton Way. *N14* —5B **6**
Wolves La. *N22 & N13* —7F **17**
Womersley Rd. *N8* —6K **29**
Wonersh Way. *Sutt* —7F **131**
Wonford Clo. *King T* —1A **120**
Wontner Clo. *N1* —7C **46**
Wontner Rd. *SW17* —2D **108**
Woodall Clo. *E14* —7D **64**
Woodall Ho. *N22* —1A **30**
Woodall Rd. *Enf* —6E **8**
Woodbank Rd. *Brom* —3H **113**
Woodbastwick Rd. *SE26*
—5K **111**
Woodberry Av. *N21* —2F **17**
Woodberry Av. *Harr* —4F **23**
Woodberry Cres. *N10* —3F **29**
Woodberry Down. *N4* —7C **30**
Woodberry Down Est. *N4* —7C **30**
Woodberry Gdns. *N12* —6F **15**
Woodberry Gro. *N4* —7C **30**
Woodberry Gro. *N12* —6F **15**
Woodberry Gro. *Bex* —3K **117**
Woodberry Way. *E4* —7K **9**
Woodberry Way. *N12* —6F **15**
Woodbine Clo. *Twic* —2H **103**
Woodbine Gro. *SE20* —7H **111**
Woodbine Gro. *Enf* —1J **7**
Woodbine La. *Wor Pk* —3E **130**
Woodbine Pl. *E11* —6J **33**
Woodbine Rd. *Sidc* —1J **115**
Woodbines Av. *King T* —3D **118**
Woodbine Ter. *E9* —6J **47**
Woodborough Rd. *SW15*
—4D **90**
Woodbourne Av. *SW16* —3H **109**
Woodbourne Clo. *SW16* —3J **109**
Woodbourne Gdns. *Wall* —7G **133**
Woodbridge Clo. *N7* —2K **45**
Woodbridge Ho. *E11* —1H **49**
Woodbridge Rd. *Bark* —5K **51**
Woodbridge St. *EC1*
—4B **62** (3A **144**)
Woodbrook Rd. *SE2* —6A **84**
Woodburn Clo. *NW4* —5E **27**
Woodbury Clo. *E11* —4K **33**
Woodbury Clo. *Croy* —2F **135**
Woodbury Pk. Rd. *W13* —4B **56**
Woodbury Rd. *E17* —4D **32**
Woodbury St. *SW17* —5C **108**
Woodchester Sq. *W2* —5K **59**

Woodchurch Clo. *Sidc* —3H **115**
Woodchurch Dri. *Brom* —7B **114**
Woodchurch Rd. *NW6* —7J **43**
Wood Clo. *E2* —4G **63**
Wood Clo. *NW9* —7K **25**
Wood Clo. *Harr* —7H **23**
Woodclyffe Dri. *Chst* —2E **128**
Woodcock Ct. *Harr* —7E **24**
Woodcock Dell Av. *Harr* —7D **24**
Woodcock Hill. *Harr* —5C **24**
Woodcocks. *E16* —5A **66**
Woodcombe Cres. *SE23* —1J **111**
Woodcote Av. *NW7* —6K **13**
Woodcote Av. *T Hth* —4B **124**
Woodcote Av. *Wall* —7F **133**
Woodcote Clo. *Enf* —6D **8**
Woodcote Clo. *King T* —5F **105**
Woodcote Ct. *Sutt* —6J **131**
Woodcote Dri. *Orp* —7H **129**
Woodcote Grn. *Wall* —7G **133**
Woodcote Ho. *SE8* —6B **80**
(off Prince St.)
Woodcote M. *Wall* —6F **133**
Woodcote Pl. *SE27* —5B **110**
Woodcote Rd. *E11* —7J **33**
Woodcote Rd. *Wall & Purl*
—6F **133**
Wood Crest. *Sutt* —7A **132**
(off Christchurch Pk.)
Woodcroft. *N21* —1F **17**
Woodcroft. *SE9* —3D **114**
Woodcroft. *Gnfd* —6A **40**
Woodcroft Av. *NW7* —6F **13**
Woodcroft Av. *Stan* —1K **23**
Woodcroft Rd. *T Hth* —5B **124**
Wood Dene. *SE15* —1H **95**
(off Queens Rd.)
Wood Dri. *Chst* —6C **114**
Woodedge Clo. *E4* —1C **20**
Woodend. *SE19* —6C **110**
Woodend. *Sutt* —2A **132**
Wood End Av. *Harr* —4F **39**
Wood End Clo. *N'holt* —5H **39**
Woodend Gdns. *Enf* —4D **6**
Wood End Gdns. *N'holt* —5G **39**
Wood End La. *N'holt* —6F **39**
(in two parts)
Woodend Rd. *E17* —2E **32**
Wood End Rd. *Harr* —4H **39**
Woodend, The. *Wall* —7F **133**
Wood End Way. *N'holt* —5G **39**
Wooder Gdns. *E7* —4J **49**
Wooderson Clo. *SE25* —4E **124**
Woodfall Av. *Barn* —5C **4**
Woodfall Rd. *N4* —2A **46**
Woodfall St. *SW3*
—5D **76** (6E **152**)
Woodfarrs. *SE5* —4D **94**
Wood Field. *NW3* —5D **44**
Woodfield Av. *NW9* —4A **26**
Woodfield Av. *SW16* —3H **109**
Woodfield Av. *W5* —4C **56**
Woodfield Av. *Cars* —6E **132**
Woodfield Av. *Wemb* —3C **40**
Woodfield Clo. *SE19* —7C **110**
Woodfield Clo. *Enf* —3K **7**
Woodfield Cres. *W5* —4C **56**
Woodfield Dri. *E Barn* —1H **15**
Woodfield Gdns. *W9* —5J **59**
Woodfield Gdns. *N Mald*
—5B **120**
Woodfield Gro. *SW16* —3H **109**
Woodfield Ho. *SE23* —3K **111**
(off Dacres Rd.)
Woodfield La. *SW16* —3H **109**

Woodfield Pl. *W9* —4H **59**
Woodfield Rise. *Bush* —1C **10**
Woodfield Rd. *W5* —4C **56**
Woodfield Rd. *W9* —5H **59**
Woodfield Rd. *Houn* —2A **86**
Woodfield Way. *N11* —7C **16**
Woodford Av. *Ilf* —3B **34**
Woodford Bri. Rd. *Ilf* —3B **34**
Woodford Ct. *W12* —2F **75**
(off Shepherd's Bush Grn.)
Woodford Cres. *Pinn* —2A **22**
Woodford Hall Path. *E18* —1H **33**
Woodford Ho. *E18* —4J **33**
Woodford New Rd. *E18, E17 &
Wfd G* —4G **33**
Woodford Pl. *Wemb* —1E **40**
Woodford Rd. *E7* —3K **49**
Woodford Rd. *E18* —4J **33**
Woodford Trad. Est. *Wfd G*
—3B **34**
Woodgate Dri. *SW16* —7H **109**
Woodger Rd. *W12* —2E **74**
Woodget Clo. *E6* —6C **66**
Woodgrange Av. *N12* —6G **15**
Woodgrange Av. *W5* —1G **73**
Woodgrange Av. *Enf* —6B **8**
Woodgrange Av. *Harr* —5C **24**
Woodgrange Clo. *Harr* —5D **24**
Woodgrange Gdns. *Enf* —6B **8**
Woodgrange Rd. *E7* —4K **49**
Woodgrange Ter. *Enf* —6B **8**
Wood Green Shop. City. *N22*
—2A **30**
Woodhall Av. *SE21* —3F **111**
Woodhall Av. *Pinn* —1C **22**
Woodhall Dri. *SE21* —3F **111**
Woodhall Dri. *Pinn* —1B **22**
Woodhall Ga. *Pinn* —1B **22**
Woodham Ct. *E18* —4H **33**
Woodham Rd. *SE6* —3E **112**
Woodhams Rd. *Barn* —3F **5**
Woodhatch Clo. *E6* —5C **66**
Woodhaven Gdns. *Ilf* —4G **35**
Woodhayes Rd. *SW19* —7E **106**
Woodhayes Rd. *NW10* —5K **41**
Woodhill. *SE18* —4C **82**
Woodhill Cres. *Harr* —6D **24**
Woodhouse Av. *Gnfd* —2K **55**
Woodhouse Clo. *Gnfd* —1K **55**
Woodhouse Gro. *E12* —6C **50**
Woodhouse Rd. *E11* —3H **49**
Woodhouse Rd. *N12* —6G **15**
Woodhurst Av. *Orp* —6G **129**
Woodhurst Rd. *SE2* —5A **84**
Woodhurst Rd. *W3* —7J **57**
Woodington Clo. *SE9* —6E **98**
Woodin St. *E14* —5D **64**
Woodison St. *E3* —4A **64**
Woodknoll Dri. *Chst* —1D **128**
Woodland App. *Gnfd* —6A **40**
Woodland Clo. *NW9* —6J **25**
Woodland Clo. *SE19* —6E **110**
Woodland Clo. *Eps* —6A **130**
Woodland Clo. *Wfd G* —3E **20**
Woodland Cres. *SE10* —6G **81**
Woodland Gdns. *N10* —5F **29**
Woodland Gdns. *Iswth* —3J **87**
Woodland Gro. *SE10* —5G **81**
Woodland Hill. *SE19* —6E **110**
Woodland Rise. *N10* —4F **29**
Woodland Rise. *Gnfd* —6A **40**
Woodland Rd. *E4* —1K **19**
Woodland Rd. *N11* —5A **16**
Woodland Rd. *SE19* —5E **110**
Woodland Rd. *T Hth* —4A **124**

Woodlands. *NW11* —5G **27**
Woodlands. *SW20* —4E **120**
Woodlands. *Harr* —4E **22**
Woodlands. *Short* —4H **127**
Woodlands Av. *E11* —1K **49**
Woodlands Av. *N3* —7F **15**
Woodlands Av. *W3* —1H **73**
Woodlands Av. *N Mald* —1J **119**
Woodlands Av. *Romf* —7E **36**
Woodlands Av. *Ruis* —7A **22**
Woodlands Av. *Sidc* —1J **115**
Woodlands Av. *Wor Pk* —2B **130**
Woodlands Clo. *NW11* —5G **27**
Woodlands Clo. *Brom* —2D **128**
Woodlands Ct. *SE23* —7H **95**
Woodlands Ct. *Brom* —1H **127**
Woodlands Ct. *Harr* —5K **23**
Woodlands Dri. *Stan* —6E **10**
Woodlands Ga. *SW15* —5H **91**
Woodlands Gro. *Iswth* —2J **87**
Woodlands Ho. *NW6* —7G **43**
Woodlands Pk. *Bex* —4K **117**
Woodlands Pk. Rd. *N15* —5B **30**
Woodlands Pk. Rd. *SE10* —6G **81**
Woodlands Rd. *E11* —2G **49**
Woodlands Rd. *E17* —3E **32**
Woodlands Rd. *N9* —1D **18**
Woodlands Rd. *SW13* —3B **90**
Woodlands Rd. *Bexh* —3E **100**
Woodlands Rd. *Brom* —2C **128**
Woodlands Rd. *Enf* —1J **7**
Woodlands Rd. *Harr* —5K **23**
Woodlands Rd. *Ilf* —3G **51**
Woodlands Rd. *Iswth* —3H **87**
Woodlands Rd. *S'hall* —1B **70**
Woodlands Rd. *Surb* —7D **118**
Woodlands St. *SE13* —7F **97**
Woodlands, The. *N5* —4C **46**
Woodlands, The. *N12* —6F **15**
Woodlands, The. *N14* —1A **16**
Woodlands, The. *SE13* —7F **97**
Woodlands, The. *SE19* —7C **110**
Woodlands, The. *Harr* —2J **39**
Woodlands, The. *Iswth* —2K **87**
Woodlands, The. *Stan* —5G **11**
Woodlands, The. *Wall* —7F **133**
Woodland St. *E8* —6F **47**
Woodlands Way. *SW15* —5H **91**
Woodland Ter. *SE7* —4C **82**
Woodland Wlk. *NW3* —5C **44**
Woodland Wlk. *SE10* —5G **81**
Woodland Wlk. *Brom* —4G **113**
(in two parts)
Woodland Way. *N21* —2F **17**
Woodland Way. *NW7* —6F **13**
Woodland Way. *SE2* —4D **84**
Woodland Way. *Croy* —1A **136**
Woodland Way. *Mitc* —7E **108**
Woodland Way. *Mord* —4H **121**
Woodland Way. *Orp* —4G **129**
Woodland Way. *W Wick*
—4D **136**
Woodland Way. *Wfd G* —3E **20**
Wood La. *N6* —6F **29**
Wood La. *NW9* —7K **25**
Wood La. *W12* —6E **58**
Wood La. *Dag* —4D **52**
Wood La. *Iswth* —6J **71**
Wood La. *Stan* —3F **11**
Wood La. *Wfd G* —4C **20**
Woodlawn Clo. *SW15* —5H **91**
Woodlawn Cres. *Twic* —2F **103**
Woodlawn Dri. *Felt* —2B **102**
Woodlawn Rd. *SW6* —7F **75**
Woodlea Dri. *Brom* —5G **127**

Woodlea Rd. *N16* —3E **46**
Woodleigh. *E18* —1J **33**
Woodleigh Av. *N12* —6H **15**
Woodleigh Gdns. *SW16* —3J **109**
Woodley Clo. *SW7* —7D **108**
Woodley La. *Cars* —3C **132**
Wood Lodge Gdns. *Brom*
　—7C **114**
Wood Lodge La. *W Wick*
　—3E **136**
Woodman Pde. *E16* —1E **82**
　(off Woodman St.)
Woodmans Gro. *NW10* —5B **42**
Woodman's M. *W12* —5D **58**
Woodmansterne Rd. *SW16*
　—7G **109**
Woodmansterne Rd. *Cars*
　—7C **132**
Woodman St. *E16* —1E **82**
　(in two parts)
Wood Mead. *N17* —6B **18**
Woodmere. *SE9* —1D **114**
Woodmere Av. *Croy* —7J **125**
Woodmere Clo. *SW11* —3E **92**
Woodmere Clo. *Croy* —7K **125**
Woodmere Ct. *N14* —7A **6**
Woodmere Gdns. *Croy* —7K **125**
Woodmere Way. *Beck* —5F **127**
Woodnook Rd. *SW16* —5F **109**
Woodpecker Clo. *N9* —6C **8**
Woodpecker Clo. *Bush* —1B **10**
Woodpecker Clo. *Harr* —1K **23**
Woodpecker Ct. *W7a* —136
Woodpecker Mt. *Croy* —7C **136**
Woodpecker Rd. *SE14* —6A **80**
Woodpecker Rd. *SE28* —7C **68**
Woodquest Av. *SE24* —5C **94**
Wood Retreat. *SE18* —7H **83**
Wood Ride. *Barn* —1G **5**
Wood Ride. *Orp* —4H **129**
Woodridge Clo. *NW2* —3D **42**
Woodridge Clo. *Enf* —2F **7**
Woodridings Av. *Pinn* —1D **22**
Woodridings Clo. *Pinn* —1C **22**
Woodridings Ct. *N22* —1H **29**
Woodriffe Rd. *E11* —7F **33**
Woodrow. *SE18* —4D **82**
Woodrow Clo. *Gnfd* —7B **40**
Woodrow Ct. *N17* —7C **18**
Woodrush Clo. *SE14* —7A **80**
Woodrush Way. *Romf* —4D **36**
Woodseer St. *E1*
　—5F **63** (5K **145**)
Woodsford Sq. *W14* —2G **75**
Woodshire Rd. *Dag* —3H **53**
Woodside. *N10* —3E **28**
Woodside. *SW19* —6H **107**
Woodside. *Buck H* —2F **21**
Woodside Av. *N6 & N10* —5D **28**
Woodside Av. *N12* —4F **15**
Woodside Av. *SE25* —6H **125**
Woodside Av. *Chst* —5G **115**
Woodside Av. *Wemb* —1E **56**
Woodside Av. *Bexh* —4K **101**
Woodside Clo. *Stan* —5G **11**
Woodside Clo. *Surb* —7J **119**
Woodside Clo. *Wemb* —1E **56**
Woodside Ct. *E12* —1A **50**
Woodside Ct. *N12* —4E **14**
Woodside Ct. *W5* —1E **72**
Woodside Ct. Rd. *Croy* —7G **125**
Woodside Cres. *Sidc* —3J **115**
Woodside Dri. *Dart* —4K **117**
Woodside End. *Wemb* —1E **56**
Woodside Gdns. *E4* —5J **19**

Woodside Gdns. *N17* —2E **30**
Woodside Grange. *N12* —4E **14**
Woodside Grange Rd. *N12*
　—4E **14**
Woodside Grn. *SE25* —6G **125**
　(in two parts)
Woodside Gro. *N12* —3F **15**
Woodside La. *N12* —3F **15**
Woodside La. *Bex* —6D **100**
Woodside Pk. *SE25* —6H **125**
Woodside Pk. Av. *E17* —4F **33**
Woodside Pk. Rd. *N12* —4E **14**
Woodside Pl. *Wemb* —1E **56**
Woodside Rd. *E13* —4A **66**
Woodside Rd. *N22* —7E **16**
Woodside Rd. *SE25* —6H **125**
Woodside Rd. *Bexh* —4K **101**
Woodside Rd. *Brom* —5C **128**
Woodside Rd. *King T* —7E **104**
Woodside Rd. *N Mald* —2K **119**
Woodside Rd. *Sidc* —3J **115**
Woodside Rd. *Sutt* —3A **132**
Woodside Rd. *Wfd G* —4D **20**
Woodside Way. *Croy* —6J **125**
Woodside Way. *Mitc* —1F **123**
Woods M. *W1* —7E **60** (2G **147**)
Woodsome Rd. *NW5* —3E **44**
Wood's Pl. *SE1* —3E **78** (2H **157**)
Woodspring Rd. *SW19* —2G **107**
Woods St. *SE15* —1H **95**
Woodstead Gro. *Edgw* —6K **11**
Woodstock Av. *NW11* —7G **27**
Woodstock Av. *W13* —3A **72**
Woodstock Av. *Iswth* —5A **88**
Woodstock Av. *S'hall* —3D **54**
Woodstock Av. *Sutt* —7H **121**
Woodstock Clo. *Bex* —7F **101**
Woodstock Clo. *Stan* —2E **24**
Woodstock Ct. *SE11*
　—5K **77** (5H **155**)
Woodstock Ct. *SE12* —6J **97**
Woodstock Cres. *N9* —6C **8**
Woodstock Gdns. *Beck* —1D **126**
Woodstock Gdns. *Ilf* —2A **52**
Woodstock Gro. *W12* —2F **75**
Woodstock M. *W1*
　—5E **60** (6H **141**)
Woodstock Rise. *Sutt* —7H **121**
Woodstock Rd. *E7* —7A **50**
Woodstock Rd. *E17* —2F **33**
Woodstock Rd. *N4* —1A **46**
Woodstock Rd. *NW11* —7H **27**
Woodstock Rd. *W4* —4A **74**
Woodstock Rd. *Cars* —5E **132**
Woodstock Rd. *Croy* —3D **134**
Woodstock Rd. *Wemb* —1F **57**
Woodstock St. *E16* —6G **65**
Woodstock St. *W1*
　—6F **61** (1J **147**)
Woodstock Ter. *E14* —7D **64**
Woodstock, The. (Junct.)
　—7H **121**
Woodstock Way. *Mitc* —1F **123**
Woodstone Av. *Eps* —5C **130**
Wood St. *E16* —7K **65**
Wood St. *E17* —3E **32**
Wood St. *EC2* —6C **62** (7D **144**)
Wood St. *W4* —5A **74**
Wood St. *Barn* —4A **4**
Wood St. *King T* —2D **118**
Wood St. *Mitc* —1E **122**
Wood Street. (Junct.) —3E **32**
Woodsyre. *SE26* —4F **111**
Woodthorpe Rd. *SW15* —4D **90**
Woodtree Clo. *NW4* —2F **27**

Wood Vale. *N10* —5G **29**
Wood Vale. *SE23* —1H **111**
Woodvale Av. *SE25* —3F **125**
Wood Vale Est. *SE23* —7H **95**
Woodvale Wlk. *SE27* —5C **110**
Woodvale Way. *NW11* —3F **43**
Woodview Av. *E4* —4K **19**
Woodview Clo. *N4* —7B **30**
Woodview Clo. *SW15* —4K **105**
Woodville. *SE3* —1K **97**
Woodville. *SE12* —5J **97**
Woodville Clo. *Tedd* —4A **104**
Woodville Clo. *SE19* —1F **125**
Woodville Gdns. *NW11* —7F **27**
Woodville Gdns. *W5* —6E **56**
Woodville Gdns. *Ilf* —3F **35**
Woodville Gdns. *Surb* —7D **118**
Woodville Gro. *Well* —3A **100**
Woodville Rd. *E11* —1H **49**
Woodville Rd. *E17* —4B **32**
Woodville Rd. *E18* —2K **33**
Woodville Rd. *N16* —5E **46**
Woodville Rd. *NW6* —2H **59**
Woodville Rd. *NW11* —7F **27**
Woodville Rd. *W5* —6D **56**
Woodville Rd. *Barn* —3E **4**
Woodville Rd. *Mord* —4J **121**
Woodville Rd. *Rich* —3B **104**
Woodville Rd. *T Hth* —4C **124**
Woodville St. *SE18* —4C **82**
Woodville, The. *W5* —6D **56**
　(off Woodville Rd.)
Woodward Av. *NW4* —5C **26**
Woodwarde Rd. *SE22* —6E **94**
Woodward Gdns. *Dag* —7C **52**
Woodward Gdns. *Stan* —7E **10**
Woodward Rd. *Dag* —7B **52**
Woodward's Footpath. *Twic*
　—6H **87**
Wood Way. *Orp* —2E **138**
Woodway Cres. *Harr* —6A **24**
Woodwell St. *SW18* —5A **92**
Wood Wharf Bus. Pk. *E14*
　—1D **80**
Woodyard Clo. *NW5* —5E **44**
Woodyard La. *SE21* —7E **94**
Woodyates Rd. *SE12* —6J **97**
Woolacombe Rd. *SE3* —2A **98**
Wooler St. *SE17*
　—5D **78** (6E **156**)
Woolf Clo. *SE28* —1B **84**
Woolf Ct. *W3* —3J **73**
　(off Vincent Rd.)
Woolf M. *WC1* —4H **61** (3D **142**)
　(off Burton Pl.)
Woolgar M. *N16* —5E **46**
Wollaston Rd. *N4* —6B **30**
Woolley Ho. *SW9* —3B **94**
　(off Loughborough Rd.)
Woolmead Av. *NW9* —7C **26**
Woolmer Gdns. *N18* —5B **18**
Woolmer Rd. *N18* —5B **18**
Woolmore St. *E14* —7E **64**
Woolneigh St. *SW6* —3K **91**
Woolridge Way. *E9* —7J **47**
Wool Rd. *SW20* —6D **106**
Woolstaplers Way. *SE16* —3G **79**
Woolston Clo. *E17* —2K **31**
Woolstone Rd. *SE23* —2A **112**
Woolwich Chu. St. *SE18* —3C **82**
Woolwich Comn. *SE18* —6E **82**
Woolwich Dockyard Ind. Est.
　SE18 —3C **82**
Woolwich High St. *SE18* —3E **82**

Woolwich Ind. Est. *SE28* —3J **83**
　(in two parts)
Woolwich Mnr. Way. *E6 & E16*
　—7F **67**
Woolwich New Rd. *SE18* —5E **82**
Woolwich Rd. *SE2 & Belv*
　—6D **84**
Woolwich Rd. *SE10 & SE7*
　—5H **81**
Woolwich Rd. *Bexh* —3G **101**
Wooster Gdns. *E14* —6F **65**
Wooster M. *Harr* —3G **23**
Wootton Gro. *N3* —1J **27**
Wootton St. *SE1*
　—1A **78** (5K **149**)
Worbeck Rd. *SE20* —2H **125**
Worcester Av. *N17* —7B **18**
Worcester Clo. *Croy* —2C **136**
Worcester Clo. *Mitc* —3F **123**
Worcester Ct. *N12* —5E **14**
Worcester Ct. *W7* —6K **55**
　(off Copley Clo.)
Worcester Ct. *Harr* —3J **23**
Worcester Ct. *Wor Pk* —3A **130**
Worcester Cres. *NW7* —3F **13**
Worcester Cres. *Wfd G* —5E **20**
Worcester Dri. *W4* —2A **74**
Worcester Gdns. *Gnfd* —6H **39**
Worcester Gdns. *Ilf* —7C **34**
Worcester Gdns. *Wor Pk*
　—3A **130**
Worcester Ho. *SW9* —7A **78**
　(off Cranmer Rd.)
Worcester M. *NW6* —6K **43**
Worcester Pk. Rd. *Wor Pk*
　—3A **130**
Worcester Rd. *E12* —3D **50**
Worcester Rd. *E17* —2K **31**
Worcester Rd. *SW19* —5H **107**
Worcester Rd. *Sutt* —7J **131**
Worcesters Av. *Enf* —1B **8**
Wordsworth Av. *E12* —7C **50**
Wordsworth Av. *E18* —3H **33**
Wordsworth Av. *Gnfd* —3H **55**
Wordsworth Ct. *Harr* —7J **23**
Wordsworth Dri. *Sutt* —4E **130**
Wordsworth Pde. *N8* —4B **30**
Wordsworth Pl. *NW5* —5D **44**
Wordsworth Rd. *N16* —4E **46**
Wordsworth Rd. *SE1*
　—4F **79** (4K **157**)
Wordsworth Rd. *SE20* —7K **111**
Wordsworth Rd. *Hamp* —4D **102**
Wordsworth Rd. *Wall* —6G **133**
Wordsworth Rd. *Well* —1J **99**
Wordsworth Wlk. *NW11* —4J **27**
Worfield St. *SW11* —7C **76**
Worgan St. *SE11*
　—5K **77** (5G **155**)
Worgan St. *SE16* —4K **79**
Worland Rd. *E15* —7G **49**
Worlds End Est. *SW10* —7B **76**
World's End La. *N21 & Enf* —5E **6**
World's End Pas. *SW10* —7B **76**
World's End Pl. *SW10* —7B **76**
World Trade Centre. *E1*
　—7F **63** (3K **151**)
Worlidge St. *W6* —5E **74**
Worlingham Rd. *SE22* —4F **95**
Wormholt Rd. *W12* —7C **58**
Wormwood St. *EC2*
　—6E **62** (7G **145**)
Wornington Rd. *W10* —4G **59**
　(in two parts)
Woronzow Rd. *NW8* —1B **60**

Worple Av. *SW19* —7F **107**
Worple Av. *Iswth* —5A **88**
Worple Clo. *Harr* —1D **38**
Worple Rd. *SW20 & SW19*
　—2E **120**
Worple Rd. *Iswth* —4A **88**
Worple Rd. M. *SW19* —6H **107**
Worple St. *SW14* —3K **89**
Worple Way. *Harr* —1D **38**
Worple Way. *Rich* —5E **88**
Worship St. *EC2*
　—4D **62** (4F **145**)
Worslade Rd. *SW17* —4B **108**
Worsley Bri. Rd. *SE26 & Beck*
　—4B **112**
Worsley Ho. *SE23* —2H **111**
Worsley Rd. *E11* —4G **49**
Worsopp Dri. *SW4* —5G **93**
Worthfield Clo. *Eps* —7A **130**
Worth Gro. *SE17*
　—5D **78** (6E **156**)
Worthing Clo. *E15* —1G **65**
Worthing Rd. *Houn* —6D **70**
Worthington Clo. *Mitc* —3F **123**
Worthington Rd. *Surb* —7F **119**
Wortley Rd. *E6* —7B **50**
Wortley Rd. *Croy* —7A **124**
Worton Ct. *Iswth* —4J **87**
Worton Gdns. *Iswth* —2H **87**
Worton Hall Ind. Est. *Iswth*
　—4J **87**
Worton Rd. *Iswth* —4J **87**
Worton Way. *Houn & Iswth*
　—2H **87**
Wotton Rd. *NW2* —3E **42**
Wotton Rd. *SE8* —6B **80**
Wouldham Rd. *E16* —6H **65**
Wragby Rd. *E11* —3G **49**
Wrampling Pl. *N9* —1B **18**
Wrangthorn Wlk. *Croy* —4A **134**
Wray Av. *Ilf* —3E **34**
Wrayburn Ho. *SE16* —2G **79**
　(off Llewellyn St.)
Wray Cres. *N4* —2J **45**
Wrayfield Rd. *Sutt* —3F **131**
Wray Rd. *Sutt* —7H **131**
Wraysbury Clo. *Houn* —5C **86**
Wrekin Rd. *SE18* —7G **83**
Wren Av. *NW2* —4E **42**
Wren Av. *S'hall* —4D **70**
Wren Clo. *E16* —6H **65**
Wren Clo. *N9* —1E **18**
Wren Cres. *Bush* —1B **10**
Wren Gdns. *Dag* —5D **52**
Wren Landing. *E14* —1C **80**
Wren Path. *SE28* —3H **83**
Wren Rd. *SE5* —1D **94**
Wren Rd. *Dag* —5D **52**
Wren Rd. *Sidc* —4C **116**
Wren's Pk. Ho. *E5* —2H **47**
Wren St. *WC1* —4K **61** (3H **143**)
Wrentham Av. *NW10* —2F **59**
Wrenthorpe Rd. *Brom* —4G **113**
Wrenwood Way. *Pinn* —4A **22**
Wrestlers Ct. *EC3*
　—6E **62** (7G **145**)
Wrexham Rd. *E3* —2C **64**
Wricklemarsh Rd. *SE3* —1K **97**
　(in two parts)
Wrigglesworth St. *SE14* —7K **79**
Wright Clo. *SE13* —4F **97**
Wright Rd. *N1* —6E **46**
Wright Rd. *Houn* —7A **70**
Wrights All. *SW19* —6E **106**
Wrights Clo. *Dag* —4H **53**

Wrights Grn. SW4 —4H 93
Wright's La. W8 —3K 75
Wrights Pl. NW10 —6J 41
Wright's Rd. E3 —2B 64
Wrights Rd. SE25 —3E 124
Wrights Wlk. SW14 —3K 89
Wrigley Clo. E4 —5A 20
Writtle Ho. NW9 —2B 26
Wrotham Ho. Beck —7B 112
  (off Sellindge Clo.)
Wrotham Rd. NW1 —7G 45
Wrotham Rd. W13 —1C 72
Wrotham Rd. Barn —2B 4
Wrotham Rd. Well —1C 100
Wrottesley Rd. NW10 —2C 58
Wrottesley Rd. SE18 —6G 83
Wroughton Rd. SW11 —6D 92
Wroughton Ter. NW4 —4D 26
Wroxall Rd. Dag —6C 52
Wroxham Gdns. N11 —7C 16
Wroxham Rd. SE28 —7D 68
Wroxton Rd. SE15 —2J 95
Wrythe Grn. Cars —3D 132
Wrythe Grn. Rd. Cars —3D 132
Wrythe La. Cars —1A 132
Wulfstan St. W12 —5B 58
Wyatt Clo. SE16 —2B 80
Wyatt Clo. Bush —1D 10
Wyatt Clo. Felt —1A 102
Wyatt Dri. SW13 —6D 74
Wyatt Ho. SE3 —2H 97
Wyatt Pk. Rd. SW2 —2J 109
Wyatt Rd. E7 —6J 49
Wyatt Rd. N5 —3C 46
Wyatts La. E17 —3E 32
Wybert St. NW1
  —4G 61 (3A 142)
Wyborne Ho. NW10 —7J 41
Wyborne Way. NW10 —7J 41
Wyburn Av. Barn —3C 4
Wyche Gro. S Croy —7C 134
Wych Elm Lodge. Brom —7H 113
Wych Elm Pas. King T —7F 105
Wycherley Clo. SE3 —7H 81
Wycherley Cres. New Bar —6E 4
Wychombe Studios. NW3
  —6D 44
Wychwood Av. Edgw —6J 11
Wychwood Av. T Hth —3C 124
Wychwood Clo. Edgw —6J 11
Wychwood End. N6 —7G 29
Wychwood Gdns. Ilf —4D 34
Wychwood Way. SE19 —6D 110
Wyclif Ct. EC1 —3B 62 (2A 144)
  (off Wyclif St.)
Wycliffe Clo. Well —1K 99
Wycliffe Rd. SW11 —2E 92
Wycliffe Rd. SW19 —6K 107
Wyclif St. EC1 —3B 62 (2A 144)
Wycombe Gdns. NW11 —2J 43
Wycombe Pl. SW18 —6A 92
Wycombe Rd. N17 —1G 31
Wycombe Rd. Ilf —5D 34
Wycombe Rd. Wemb —1G 57
Wydehurst Rd. Croy —7G 125
Wydell Clo. Mord —6F 121
Wydenhurst Rd. Croy —7G 125
Wydeville Mnr. Rd. SE12
  —4K 113
Wye Clo. Orp —7K 129
Wye Ct. W13 —5B 56
  (off Malvern Way)

Wyemead Cres. E4 —2B 20
Wye St. SW11 —2B 92
Wyfields. Ilf —1F 35
Wyfold Ho. SE2 —2D 84
  (off Wolvercote Rd.)
Wyfold Rd. SW6 —7G 75
Wyhill Wlk. Dag —7J 53
Wyke Clo. Iswth —6K 71
Wyke Gdns. W7 —3A 72
Wykeham Av. Dag —6C 52
Wykeham Grn. Dag —6C 52
Wykeham Hill. Wemb —1F 41
Wykeham Rise. N20 —1B 14
Wykeham Rd. NW4 —4E 26
Wykeham Rd. Harr —4B 24
Wyke Rd. E3 —7C 48
Wyke Rd. SW20 —2E 120
Wyldes Clo. NW11 —1A 44
Wyldfield Gdns. N9 —2A 18
Wyld Way. Wemb —6H 41
Wyleu St. SE23 —7A 96
Wylie Rd. S'hall —3E 70
Wyllen Clo. E1 —4J 63
Wymans Way. E7 —4A 50
Wymering Mans. W9 —3J 59
  (off Wymering Rd.)
Wymering Rd. W9 —3J 59
Wymond St. SW15 —3E 90
Wynan Rd. E14 —5D 80
Wynash Gdns. Cars —5C 132
Wynaud Ct. N22 —6E 16
Wyncham Av. Sidc —1J 115
Wyncham Ho. Sidc —2A 116
  (off Longlands Rd.)
Wynchgate. N14 & N21 —1C 16
Wynchgate. Harr —7D 10
Wynchgate. N'holt —5D 38
Wyncombe Av. W5 —4B 72
Wyncroft Clo. Brom —3D 128
Wyndale Av. NW9 —6G 25
Wyndcliff Rd. SE7 —6K 81
Wyndcroft Clo. Enf —3G 7
Wyndham Clo. Sutt —7J 131
Wyndham Ct. W7 —4A 72
Wyndham Cres. N19 —3G 45
Wyndham Cres. Houn —6E 86
Wyndham Est. SE5 —7C 78
Wyndham M. W1
  —5D 60 (6E 140)
Wyndham Pl. W1
  —5D 60 (6E 140)
Wyndham Rd. E6 —7B 50
Wyndham Rd. SE5 —7C 78
Wyndham Rd. W13 —3B 72
Wyndham Rd. Barn —1J 15
Wyndham Rd. King T —7F 105
Wyndham St. W1
  —5D 60 (5E 140)
Wyndham Yd. W1
  —5D 60 (6E 140)
Wyneham Rd. SE24 —5D 94
Wynell Rd. SE23 —3K 111
Wynford Pl. Belv —6G 85
Wynford Rd. N1 —2K 61
Wynford Way. SE9 —3D 114
Wynlie Gdns. Pinn —2A 22
Wynndale Rd. E18 —1K 33
Wynne Ho. SE14 —1K 95
Wynne Rd. SW9 —2A 94
Wynnstay Gdns. W8 —3J 75
Wynter St. SW11 —4A 92
Wynton Gdns. SE25 —5F 125
Wynton Pl. W3 —6H 57

Wynyard Ho. SE11
  —5K 77 (5H 155)
Wynyard Ter. SE11
  —5K 77 (5H 155)
Wynyatt St. EC1
  —3B 62 (2A 144)
Wyre Gro. Edgw —3C 12
Wyresdale Cres. Gnfd —3K 55
Wythburn Pl. W1
  —6D 60 (1E 146)
Wythenshawe Rd. Dag —3G 53
Wythens Wlk. SE9 —6F 99
Wythes Clo. Brom —2D 128
Wythes Rd. E16 —1C 82
Wythfield Rd. SE9 —6D 98
Wyvenhoe Rd. Harr —3G 39
Wyvern Est. N Mald —4C 120
Wyvil Rd. SW8 —6J 77
Wyvis St. E14 —5D 64

Xylon Ho. Wor Pk —2D 130

Yabsley St. E14 —1E 80
Yalding Rd. SE16
  —3G 79 (2K 157)
Yale Clo. Houn —5D 86
Yale Ct. NW6 —5K 43
Yaohan Plaza. NW9 —3K 25
Yarborough Rd. SW19 —1B 122
Yardley Clo. E4 —5J 9
Yardley Ct. Sutt —4E 130
Yardley La. E4 —5J 9
Yardley St. WC1 —3A 62 (2J 143)
Yarmouth Cres. N17 —5H 31
Yarmouth Pl. W1
  —1F 77 (5J 147)
Yarnfield Sq. SE15 —1G 95
Yarnton Way. SE2 & Eri —2C 84
Yarrow Cres. E6 —5C 66
Yateley St. SE18 —3B 82
Yeading Av. Harr —2C 38
Yeading Fork. Hayes —5A 54
Yeading Ho. Hayes —5B 54
Yeading La. Hayes & N'holt
  —6A 54
Yeading Wlk. N Har —5D 22
Yeames Clo. W13 —6A 56
Yeate St. N1 —7D 46
Yeatman Rd. N6 —6D 28
Yeats Clo. NW10 —5A 42
Yeats Clo. SE13 —2F 97
Yeldham Rd. W6 —5F 75
Yelverton Lodge. Twic —7C 88
Yelverton Rd. SW11 —2B 92
Yenston Clo. Mord —6J 121
Yeoman Clo. E6 —7F 67
Yeoman Clo. SE27 —3B 110
Yeoman Ct. Houn —7D 70
Yeomans M. Iswth —6H 87
Yeoman's Row. SW3
  —3C 76 (2D 152)
Yeoman St. SE8 —4A 80
Yeomans Way. Enf —2D 8
Yeoman's Yd. E1
  —7F 63 (2K 151)
Yeo St. E3 —5D 64
Yeovilton Pl. King T —5D 104
Yerbury Rd. N19 —3H 45
Yester Dri. Chst —7C 114
Yester Pk. Chst —7D 114

Yester Rd. Chst —7C 114
Yew Clo. Buck H —2G 21
Yew Ct. E4 —6G 19
Yewdale Clo. Brom —6G 113
Yewfield Rd. NW10 —6B 42
Yew Gro. NW2 —4F 43
Yew Tree Clo. N21 —7F 7
Yew Tree Clo. N22 —1G 29
Yew Tree Clo. N Har —4F 23
Yew Tree Clo. Well —1A 100
Yew Tree Clo. Wor Pk —1A 130
Yew Tree Ct. NW11 —5H 27
  (off Bridge La.)
Yew Tree Ct. Sutt —7A 132
  (off Walnut M.)
Yew Tree Gdns. Chad H —5E 36
Yew Tree Gdns. Romf —5K 37
Yew Tree Lodge. SW16 —4G 109
Yew Tree Lodge. Romf —5K 37
  (off Yew Tree Gdns.)
Yew Tree Rd. W12 —7B 58
Yewtree Rd. Beck —3B 126
Yew Tree Wlk. Houn —5D 86
Yew Tree Way. Croy —7B 136
Yew Wlk. Harr —1J 39
Yoakley Rd. N16 —2E 46
Yoke Clo. N7 —6J 45
Yolande Gdns. SE9 —5C 98
Yonge Pk. N4 —3A 46
York Av. SE17 —5C 78 (5D 156)
York Av. SW14 —5J 89
York Av. W7 —1J 71
York Av. Sidc —2J 115
York Av. Stan —1B 24
York Bri. NW1 —4E 60 (3G 141)
York Bldgs. WC2
  —7J 61 (3F 149)
York Clo. E6 —6D 66
York Clo. SE5 —2C 94
York Clo. W7 —1J 71
York Clo. Mord —4K 121
York Ct. N13 —3D 16
York Ga. N14 —7D 6
York Ga. NW1 —4E 60 (4G 141)
York Gro. SE15 —1J 95
York Hill. SE27 —3B 110
York Ho. SE1 —3K 77 (2H 155)
York Ho. Enf —1J 7
York Ho. Wemb —5G 41
York Ho. Pl. W8 —2K 75
Yorkland Av. Well —3A 100
York Mans. SW5 —5K 75
  (off Earl's Ct. Rd.)
York Mans. SW11 —1E 92
  (off Prince of Wales Dri.)
York M. NW5 —5F 45
York M. Ilf —3E 50
York Pde. Bren —5D 72
York Pl. SW11 —3C 92
York Pl. WC2 —7J 61 (3F 149)
York Pl. Dag —6J 53
York Pl. Ilf —2F 51
York Rise. NW5 —3F 45
York Rd. E4 —4H 19
York Rd. E7 —6J 49
York Rd. E10 —3E 48
York Rd. E17 —5K 31
York Rd. N11 —6C 16
York Rd. N18 —6C 18
York Rd. N21 —7J 7
York Rd. SE1 —2K 77 (7H 149)
York Rd. SW18 & SW11 —4A 92
York Rd. SW19 —6A 108

York Rd. W3 —6J 57
York Rd. W5 —3C 72
York Rd. Bren —5D 72
York Rd. Croy —7A 124
York Rd. Houn —3F 87
York Rd. Ilf —3E 50
York Rd. King T —7F 105
York Rd. New Bar —5F 5
York Rd. Rain —7K 53
York Rd. Rich —5F 89
York Rd. Sutt —6J 131
York Rd. Tedd —4J 103
York Rd. Uxb —3E 46
Yorkshire Clo. N16 —3E 46
Yorkshire Gdns. N18 —5C 18
Yorkshire Grey. (Junct.) —5B 98
Yorkshire Grey Pl. NW3 —4A 44
Yorkshire Grey Yd. WC1
  —5K 61 (6G 143)
Yorkshire Pl. E14 —6A 64
Yorkshire Rd. E14 —6A 64
Yorkshire Rd. Mitc —5J 123
York Sq. E14 —6A 64
York St. W1 —5D 60 (6E 140)
York St. Bark —1G 67
York St. Mitc —7E 122
York St. Twic —1A 104
York St. Chambers. W1
  (off York St.) —5D 60 (6E 140)
York Ter. Enf —1H 7
York Ter. Eri —1J 101
York Ter. E. NW1
  —4E 60 (4H 141)
York Ter. W. NW1
  —4E 60 (4G 141)
Yorkton St. E2 —2G 63
York Way. N7 & N1
  —6H 45 (1F 143)
York Way. N20 —3J 15
York Way. Felt —3D 102
  (in two parts)
York Way Est. N7 —6J 45
Young Ct. NW6 —7G 43
Youngmans Clo. Enf —1H 7
Young Rd. E16 —6A 66
Youngs Bldgs. EC1
  —4C 62 (3D 144)
Youngs Rd. Ilf —5H 35
Young St. W8 —2K 75
Yoxley App. Ilf —6G 35
Yoxley Dri. Ilf —6G 35
Yukon Rd. SW12 —7F 93
Yuletide Clo. NW10 —6A 42
Yunus Khan Clo. E17 —5C 32

Zampa Rd. SE16 —5J 79
Zander Ct. E2 —3G 63
Zangwill Rd. SE3 —1B 98
Zealand Ho. SE5 —2C 94
Zealand Rd. E3 —2A 64
Zenith Lodge. N3 —7E 14
Zennor Rd. SW12 —1G 109
Zenoria St. SE22 —4F 95
Zermatt Rd. T Hth —4C 124
Zetland Ho. W8 —3K 75
  (off Marloes Rd.)
Zetland St. E14 —5D 64
Ziggurat. EC1 —5A 62 (5K 143)
  (off Saffron Hill)
Zion Pl. T Hth —4D 124
Zion Rd. T Hth —4D 124
Zoar St. SE1 —1C 78 (4C 150)
Zoffany St. N19 —2H 45

INDEX TO SELECTED PLACES OF INTEREST
covered by this atlas

with their map square reference

Admiralty Arch. —1H **77** (4D **148**)
Albert Memorial. —2B **76** (7A **146**)
Alexander Fleming Museum.
　　　—6B **60** (7B **140**)
Alexandra Palace & Park. —2H **29**
All England Lawn Tennis Club &
　　　Museum. —3G **107**
Apsley House. —2E **76** (6H **147**)
Arsenal F.C. —3B **46**
Asgill House. —5C **88**

Bank of England. —6D **62** (1E **150**)
Bank of England Museum.
　　　—6D **62** (1E **150**)
Banqueting House. —1J **77** (5E **148**)
Barbican. —5C **62** (5D **144**)
Barbican Arts Centre. —5C **62** (5D **144**)
Barnet Museum. —4C **4**
Battersea Park. —7E **76**
BBC Broadcasting House & Experience.
　　　—5F **61** (6K **141**)
Bethnal Green Museum of Childhood.
　　　—3J **63**
Big Ben. —2J **77** (7F **149**)
Billingsgate Fish Market. —1D **80**
Billingsgate Market (Old).
　　　—7D **62** (3F **151**)
Bishopsgate Institute & Libraries.
　　　—5E **62** (6H **145**)
Black Heath. —1G **97**
Boston Manor. —5B **72**
Bourne Hall Museum. —7B **130**
Bramah Tea & Coffee Museum.
　　　—2F **79** (6K **151**)
Bramley Bank Nature Reserve. —6J **135**
Brent Cross Shopping Centre. —7E **26**
Brentford F.C. —6D **72**
British Library. —3H **61** (1D **142**)
British Museum. —5J **61** (6E **142**)
Broomfield House Museum. —4D **16**
Bruce Castle. —1E **30**
Buckingham Palace. —2G **77** (7A **148**)
Burgess Park. —7E **78** (7H **157**)
Bushy Park. —7K **103**
Business Design Centre. —1A **62**

Cabinet War Rooms. —2H **77** (6D **148**)
Camden Passage. —1B **62**
Canary Wharf Tower. —1D **80**
Carew Manor. —3H **133**
Catford Greyhound Stadium. —6C **96**
Central Criminal Court. —6B **62** (7B **144**)
Central Lending Library. —7J **61** (3E **148**)
Central Markets. —5B **62** (6A **144**)
Central Reference Library.
　　　—7H **61** (3D **148**)
Charlton Athletic F.C. —5A **82**
Charlton House (Library). —6B **82**
Chelsea Football Ground. —7K **75**
Chelsea Physic Garden.
　　　—6D **76** (7E **152**)
Chelsea Royal Hospital. —5E **76** (6G **153**)
Chislehurst Caves. —1E **128**
Chiswick House. —6A **74**

Church Farmhouse Museum. —3D **26**
Clarence House. —2G **77** (6B **148**)
College of Arms. —7B **62** (2B **150**)
Commonwealth Institute & Experience.
　　　(Closed) —3J **75**
County Hall (Former). —2K **77** (6G **149**)
Courtauld Institute & Galleries.
　　　—7K **61** (2G **149**)
Covent Garden. —7J **61** (2F **149**)
Covent Garden Market (New). —7H **77**
Crafts Council & Gallery. —2A **62**
Crane Park Island Nature Reserve.
　　　—2D **102**
Croydon Sports Arena. —5J **125**
Croydon Tourist Information Centre.
　　　—3C **134**
Croydon Water Palace. —6A **134**
Crystal Palace F.C. —4E **124**
Crystal Palace Museum. —6F **111**
Custom House. —7E **62** (3G **151**)
Cutty Sark. —6E **80**

Design Museum. —2F **79** (6K **151**)
Dickens House & Museum.
　　　—4K **61** (4H **143**)
Docklands Visitor Centre. —2E **80**
Dulwich College Art Gallery. —7E **94**

Earls Court Exhibition Centre. —5J **75**
Eastbury Manor House & Museum (NT).
　　　—1K **67**
Eastway Cycle Circuit. —5D **48**
Eltham Palace. —7C **98**

Fairfield Halls. (Croydon) —3D **134**
Faraday Museum. —7G **61** (3A **148**)
Flamsteed House. —7F **81**
Florence Nightingale Museum.
　　　—2K **77** (7G **149**)
Fulham F.C. —1F **91**
Fulham Palace & Museum. —2G **91**

Geffrye Museum. —2F **63**
Geographers' A-Z Map Shop.
　　　—5A **62** (5J **143**)
Globe Theatre, Shakespeare Centre.
　　　—7C **62** (3C **150**)
Globe Theatre, The. —7C **62** (3C **150**)
Gray's Inn. —5K **61** (6H **143**)
Green Park. —2F **77** (6K **147**)
Greenwich Park. —7F **81**
Guards Museum. —2G **77** (7B **148**)
Guildhall Library. —6C **62** (7D **144**)
Guildhall, The. —6C **62** (7D **144**)
Gunnersbury Park Museum. —3G **73**
Gunnersbury Triangle Nature Reserve.
　　　—4J **73**

Hackney Wick Stadium. —6C **48**
Hall Place & Gardens. —6J **101**
Ham House. —1C **104**

Ham Lands Nature Reserve. —2A **104**
Hampstead Heath. —2C **44**
Hampton Court Palace. —4A **118**
Harrow Museum & Heritage Centre.
　　　—3G **23**
Hayward Gallery. —1K **77** (4H **149**)
Heinz Gallery. —6D **60** (7F **141**)
Herne Hill Stadium. —6D **94**
HMS Belfast. —1E **78** (4H **151**)
Hogarth's House. —6A **74**
　　　(off Hogarth La.)
Holland Park. —2H **75**
Honeywood Heritage Centre. —4D **132**
Horniman Museum. —1H **111**
Horse Guards Parade. —1J **77** (5E **148**)
Hounslow Tourist Information Centre.
　　　—3F **87**
Houses of Parliament. —3J **77** (1F **155**)
Hyde Park. —1C **76** (4D **146**)
Hyde Park Corner. —2E **76** (6H **147**)

Imperial War Museum. —3A **78** (2K **155**)
Inner Temple. —7A **62** (2K **149**)
Isabella Plantation. —4H **105**
Iveagh Bequest. —1C **44**

Kempton Park Race Course. —7A **102**
Kensington Gardens. —1A **76** (5A **146**)
Kensington Palace. —1K **75**
Kenwood House. —1C **44**
Keston Postmill. —5B **138**
Kew Bridge Steam Museum. —5F **73**
Kew Gardens. —1E **88**
Kew Palace. —7E **72**
Kingston upon Thames Museum.
　　　—2E **118**

Leadenhall Market. —6E **62** (1G **151**)
Leighton House & Museum. —3H **75**
Leyton Orient F.C. —3D **48**
Lifetimes. —3C **134**
　　　(off Katharine St.)
Lincoln's Inn. —6K **61** (7H **143**)
Linford Christie Stadium. —5D **58**
Little Holland House. —7C **132**
Little Venice. —5A **60**
Livesey Museum. —6H **79**
Lloyds' Building. —6E **62** (1G **151**)
London Aquarium. —2K **77** (6G **149**)
London Butterfly House. —1B **88**
London Canal Museum. —2J **61**
London City Airport. —1C **82**
London Dungeon. —1D **78** (5F **151**)
London Eye. —2K **77** (6G **149**)
London Gas Museum. —4F **65**
London Library. —1G **77** (4B **148**)
London Planetarium. —4E **60** (4G **141**)
London Transport Museum.
　　　—7J **61** (2F **149**)
London Zoo. —2E **60**
London Wetland Heliport. —2B **92**
Lonsdale Road Nature Reserve. —7B **74**
Lord's Cricket Ground. —3B **60** (2B **140**)

Madame Tussaud's. —4E **60** (4G **141**)
Mansion House. —6D **62** (1E **150**)
Marble Arch. —7D **60** (2F **147**)
Marble Hill House. —7C **88**
Marlborough House. —1G **77** (5B **148**)
MCC Cricket Museum. —3B **60** (2A **140**)
Middle Temple. —7A **62** (2J **149**)
Mile End Park Stadium. —5B **64**
Millennium Experience Exhibition Site.
　　　—1G **81**
Millennium Wheel. —2K **77** (6G **149**)
Millwall F.C. —5J **79**
Morden Hall Park. —3K **121**
Motspur Park. —6C **120**
Mountaintop Ski Centre (Beckton Alps).
　　　—4E **66**
Museum of Gardening History.
　　　—3K **77** (2G **155**)
Museum of London. —5C **62** (6C **144**)
Museum of Richmond. —5D **88**
　　　(off Hill St.)
Museum of the Moving Image.
　　　(Closed until 2003) —1K **77** (4H **149**)
Museum of the Order of St John.
　　　—4B **62** (4A **144**)
Musical Museum, The. —6E **72**

Narwhal Inuit Art Gallery. —5K **73**
National Army Museum. —6D **76** (7F **153**)
National Film Theatre. —1K **77** (4H **149**)
National Gallery. —7H **61** (3D **148**)
National Maritime Museum. —6F **81**
National Portrait Gallery.
　　　—7H **61** (3D **148**)
National Postal Museum.
　　　—6B **62** (7B **144**)
National Recreation Centre. —6G **111**
　　　(Crystal Palace)
National Theatre (Royal).
　　　—1K **77** (4H **149**)
National Westminster Tower.
　　　—6E **62** (7G **145**)
Natural History Museum.
　　　—3B **76** (2A **152**)
Nonsuch Park. —6E **130**
　　　(and Palace site of)
North Woolwich Railway Museum.
　　　—2E **82**

Old Bailey. —6B **62** (7B **144**)
Old Royal Observatory. —7F **81**
Olympia. —4G **75**
Oratory, The. —3C **76** (2C **152**)
Orleans House Gallery. —1B **104**
Osterley Park House. —5H **71**
Oval Cricket Ground. —6K **77** (7H **155**)
Oxo Tower Wharf. —7A **62** (3K **149**)

Parliament Hill. —3D **44**
Percival David Foundation of.
　　　—4H **61** (4D **142**)
Petticoat Lane Market. —5F **63** (6J **145**)
　　　(Middlesex St.)

Piccadilly Circus. —7H **61** (3C **148**)
Planetarium. —4E **60** (4G **141**)
Portobello Road Market. —6H **59**
Purcell Room. —1K **77** (4H **149**)
  (within Queen Elizabeth Hall)

Queen Charlotte's Cottage. —2D **88**
Queen Elizabeth Hall. —1K **77** (4H **149**)
Queen Elizabeth II Conference Centre.
  —2H **77** (7D **148**)
Queen Elizabeth's Hunting Lodge &
  Museum. —1C **20**
Queen's Club, The. —5G **75**
Queen's Gallery. —2G **77** (7A **148**)
Queen's Park Rangers F.C. —1D **74**

Rangers House. —1F **97**
Regent's Park. —3E **60** (1G **141**)
Richmond Ice Rink. —6D **88**
Richmond Park. —1H **105**
Richmond Tourist Information Centre.
  —5D **88**
Romford Stadium. —6J **37**
Round Pond. —1A **76**
Royal Academy of Arts.
  —7G **61** (3A **148**)
Royal Air Force Museum. —2C **26**
Royal Albert Hall. —2B **76** (7A **146**)
Royal Artillery Museum. —5D **82**
Royal Botanic Gardens, Kew. —1E **88**
Royal Courts of Justice.
  —6K **61** (1H **149**)
Royal Exchange. —6D **62** (1F **151**)
Royal Festival Hall. —1K **77** (5H **149**)
Royal Geographical Society.
  —2B **76** (7B **146**)

Royal Hospital, Chelsea. —5E **76** (6G **153**)
Royal Mews, The. —3F **77** (1K **153**)
Royal National Theatre. —1K **77** (4H **149**)
Royal Opera House. —6J **61** (1F **149**)

St Bartholomew's Hospital.
  —5B **62** (6B **144**)
St James's Palace. —1G **77** (5B **148**)
St James's Park. —2H **77** (6C **148**)
St John's Gate. —4B **62** (4A **144**)
St Katherine's Dock & Yacht Haven.
  —1F **79** (4K **151**)
St Paul's Cathedral. —6C **62** (1C **150**)
Science Museum. —3B **76** (2B **152**)
Serpentine Gallery. —2B **76** (6B **146**)
Serpentine, The. —1C **76** (5D **146**)
Shakespeare Centre & Exhibition.
  —7C **62** (3C **150**)
Sherlock Holmes Museum.
  —4D **60** (4F **141**)
Shirley Towermill. —3J **135**
Sir John Soane's Museum.
  —6K **61** (7G **143**)
Smithfield Market. —5B **62** (6A **144**)
Somerset House. —7K **61** (2G **149**)
South Bank Centre. —1K **77** (4H **149**)
South Norwood Country Park, Albert Rd.
  —4J **125**
Southside House. —6E **106**
Southwark Cathedral. —1D **78** (4E **150**)
Spencer House. —1G **77** (5A **148**)
Spitalfields Market (Former).
  —5F **63** (5J **145**)
Spitalfields Market (New). —3C **48**
Staple Inn. —5A **62** (6J **143**)
Stock Exchange. —6D **62** (1F **151**)
Strawberry Hill. —3K **103**

Surrey County Hall. —3D **118**
Syon House. —1C **88**
Syon Park Gardens. —1C **88**

Tate British. —4J **77** (4E **154**)
Tate Modern. —1B **78** (4B **150**)
Teddington Lock. —4B **104**
Telecom Tower. —5G **61** (5A **142**)
Temple Bar. —6A **62** (1J **149**)
Temple, The. —7A **62** (2J **149**)
Terence McMilan Stadium. —4A **66**
Thames Ditton Miniature Railway.
  —7A **118**
Thames Flood Barrier. —2A **82**
Theatre Museum. —7J **61** (2F **149**)
Tottenham Hotspur F.C. —7B **18**
Tower Bridge. —1F **79** (4J **151**)
Tower Bridge Experience.
  —1F **79** (4J **151**)
Tower Hill Pageant. —7E **62** (3H **151**)
Tower of London. —7F **63** (3J **151**)
Trafalgar Square. —1J **77** (4E **148**)
Trocadero Centre. —7H **61** (3C **148**)
Twickenham Rugby Football Ground.
  —6J **87**
Twickenham Rugby Union Football
  Ground. —6J **87**
Twickenham Tourist Information Centre.
  —1B **104**

University of London. —4H **61** (4D **142**)
University of London Athletic Ground.
  —6C **120**

Valence House Museum. —2E **52**

Vestry House Museum. —4D **32**
Victoria & Albert Museum.
  —3B **76** (2B **152**)
Victoria Park. —1A **64**

Wallace Collection. —6E **60** (7G **141**)
Walthamstow Greyhound Race Track.
  —7J **19**
Wasps R.U.F.C. —4C **40**
Waterman's Arts Centre. (Brentford)
  —7E **72**
Wellcome Institute Exhibition.
  —4H **61** (3C **142**)
Wellington Museum. —2E **76** (6H **147**)
Wembley Arena. —4G **41**
Wembley Stadium. —5G **41**
Wesley's House, Chapel & Museum.
  —4D **62** (3F **145**)
West Ham United F.C. —2B **66**
Westminster Abbey. —3J **77** (1E **154**)
Westminster Cathedral.
  —3G **77** (2B **154**)
Westminster Hall. —2J **77** (7E **148**)
Whitehall. —6G **131**
Whitehall, Cheam. —6G **131**
Wigmore Hall. —6F **61** (7J **141**)
William Morris Gallery. —3C **32**
Wimbledon Common. —4C **106**
Wimbledon F.C. —5K **107**
Wimbledon Postmill & Museum.
  —3E **106**
Wimbledon Society Museum. —6G **107**
Wimbledon Stadium. —4A **108**
Wimbledon Tennis Courts & Museum.
  —3G **107**
Woolwich Stadium. —7D **82**

RAIL, CROYDON TRAMLINK, DOCKLANDS LIGHT RAILWAY AND LONDON UNDERGROUND STATIONS

with their map square reference

ABBEY WOOD, Rail —4C **84**
ACTON CENTRAL, Rail —1K **73**
ACTON MAIN LINE, Rail —6J **57**
ACTON TOWN, District & Piccadilly —2G **73**
ADDINGTON VILLAGE, Croydon Tramlink —6C **136**
ALBANY PARK, Rail —2D **116**
ALDGATE, Circle & Metropolitan —6F **63** (1J **151**)
ALDGATE EAST, District & Hammersmith & City
—6F **63** (7K **145**)
ALEXANDRA PALACE, Rail —2J **29**
ALL SAINTS, Docklands Light Railway —7D **64**
ALPERTON, Piccadilly —1D **56**
ANERLEY, Rail —1H **125**
ANGEL, Northern —2A **62**
ANGEL ROAD, Rail —5D **18**
ARCHWAY, Northern —2G **45**
ARENA, Croydon Tramlink —5J **125**
ARNOS GROVE, Piccadilly —5B **16**
ARSENAL, Piccadilly —3A **46**
AVENUE ROAD, Croydon Tramlink —2K **125**

BAKER STREET, Bakerloo, Circle, Hammersmith & City,
Jubilee & Metropolitan —4D **60** (4F **141**)
BALHAM, Rail & Northern —1F **109**
BANK, Central, Docklands Light Railway, Northern &
Waterloo & City —6D **62** (1E **150**)
BARBICAN, Rail, Circle, Hammersmith & City & Metropolitan
—5C **62** (5C **144**)
BARKING, Rail, District & Hammersmith & City —7G **51**
BARKINGSIDE, Central —3H **35**
BARNES, Rail —3C **90**
BARNEHURST, Rail —2J **101**
BARNES BRIDGE, Rail —2B **90**
BARONS COURT, District & Piccadilly —5G **75**
BATTERSEA PARK, Rail —7F **77**
BAYSWATER, Circle & District —7K **59**
BECKENHAM HILL, Rail —5E **112**
BECKENHAM JUNCTION, Rail & Croydon Tramlink —1C **126**
BECKENHAM ROAD, Croydon Tramlink —1A **126**
BECKTON, Docklands Light Railway —5E **66**
BECKTON PARK, Docklands Light Railway —7D **66**
BECONTREE, District —6D **52**
BEDDINGTON LANE, Croydon Tramlink —6G **123**
BELGRAVE WALK, Croydon Tramlink —3B **122**
BELLINGHAM, Rail —3D **112**
BELSIZE PARK, Northern —5C **44**
BELVEDERE, Rail —3H **85**
BERMONDSEY, Jubilee —3G **79**
BERRYLANDS, Rail —4H **119**
BETHNAL GREEN, Central —3J **63**
BETHNAL GREEN, Rail —4H **63**
BEXLEY, Rail —1G **117**
BEXLEYHEATH, Rail —2E **100**
BICKLEY, Rail —3C **128**
BINGHAM ROAD, Croydon Tramlink —1G **135**
BIRKBECK, Croydon Tramlink —3J **125**
BLACKFRIARS, Rail, Circle & District —7B **62** (2A **150**)
BLACKHEATH, Rail —3H **97**
BLACKHORSE LANE, Croydon Tramlink —7G **125**
BLACKHORSE ROAD, Rail & Victoria —4K **31**
BLACKWALL, Docklands Light Railway —7E **64**
BOND STREET, Central & Jubilee —6F **61** (1J **147**)
BOROUGH, Northern —2C **78** (7D **150**)
BOSTON MANOR, Piccadilly —4A **72**
BOUNDS GREEN, Piccadilly —6C **16**
BOW CHURCH, Docklands Light Railway —3C **64**
BOWES PARK, Rail —7D **16**

BOW ROAD, District & Hammersmith & City —3C **64**
BRENT CROSS, Northern —7F **27**
BRENTFORD, Rail —6C **72**
BRIMSDOWN, Rail —2F **9**
BRIXTON, Rail & Victoria —4A **94**
BROCKLEY, Rail —3A **96**
BROMLEY-BY-BOW, District & Hammersmith & City
—3E **64**
BROMLEY NORTH, Rail —1J **127**
BROMLEY SOUTH, Rail —3J **127**
BRONDESBURY, Rail —7H **43**
BRONDESBURY PARK, Rail —1G **59**
BRUCE GROVE, Rail —2F **31**
BUCKHURST HILL, Central —2G **21**
BURNT OAK, Northern —1J **25**
BUSH HILL PARK, Rail —6A **8**

CALEDONIAN ROAD, Piccadilly —6K **45**
CALEDONIAN ROAD & BARNSBURY, Rail —7K **45**
CAMBRIDGE HEATH, Rail —2H **63**
CAMDEN ROAD, Rail —7G **45**
CAMDEN TOWN, Northern —1F **61**
CANADA WATER, East London & Jubilee —2J **79**
CANARY WHARF, Docklands Light Railway & Jubilee
—1C **80**
CANNING TOWN, Rail & Docklands Light Railway & Jubilee
—5G **65**
CANNON STREET, Rail, Circle & District —7D **62** (2E **150**)
CANONBURY, Rail —5C **46**
CANONS PARK, Jubilee —7K **11**
CARSHALTON, Rail —4D **132**
CARSHALTON BEECHES, Rail —6D **132**
CASTLE BAR PARK, Rail —5K **55**
CATFORD, Rail —7C **96**
CATFORD BRIDGE, Rail —7C **96**
CHADWELL HEATH, Rail —7D **36**
CHALK FARM, Northern —7E **44**
CHANCERY LANE, Central —5A **62** (6J **143**)
CHARING CROSS, Rail, Bakerloo & Northern
—1J **77** (4E **148**)
CHARLTON, Rail —5A **82**
CHEAM, Rail —7G **131**
CHINGFORD, Rail —1B **20**
CHISLEHURST, Rail —2E **128**
CHISWICK, Rail —7J **73**
CHISWICK PARK, District —4J **73**
CHURCH STREET, Croydon Tramlink —2C **134**
CITY THAMESLINK, Rail —6B **62** (7A **144**)
CLAPHAM COMMON, Northern —4G **93**
CLAPHAM HIGH STREET, Rail —3H **93**
CLAPHAM JUNCTION, Rail —3C **92**
CLAPHAM NORTH, Northern —3J **93**
CLAPHAM SOUTH, Northern —6F **93**
CLAPTON, Rail —2H **47**
CLOCK HOUSE, Rail —1A **126**
COCKFOSTERS, Piccadilly —4K **5**
COLINDALE, Northern —3A **26**
COLLIERS WOOD, Northern —7B **108**
COOMBE LANE, Croydon Tramlink —5J **135**
COVENT GARDEN, Piccadilly —7J **61** (2F **149**)
CRICKLEWOOD, Rail —4F **43**
CROFTON PARK, Rail —5B **96**
CROSSHARBOUR, Docklands Light Railway —3D **80**
CROUCH HILL, Rail —7K **29**
CROYDON CENTRAL, Croydon Tramlink —2C **134**
CRYSTAL PALACE, Rail —6G **111**
CUSTOM HOUSE, Rail & Docklands Light Railway —7K **65**

CUTTY SARK, Docklands Light Railway —6E **80**
CYPRUS, Docklands Light Railway —7E **66**

DAGENHAM DOCK, Rail —3F **69**
DAGENHAM EAST, District —5J **53**
DAGENHAM HEATHWAY, District —6F **53**
DALSTON KINGSLAND, Rail —5E **46**
DENMARK HILL, Rail —2D **94**
DEPTFORD, Rail —7C **80**
DEPTFORD BRIDGE, Docklands Light Railway —1C **96**
DEVONS ROAD, Docklands Light Railway —4D **64**
DOLLIS HILL, Jubilee —5C **42**
DRAYTON GREEN, Rail —6K **55**
DRAYTON PARK, Rail —4A **46**
DUNDONALD ROAD, Croydon Tramlink —7H **107**

EALING BROADWAY, Rail, Central & District —7D **56**
EALING COMMON, District & Piccadilly —1F **73**
EARL'S COURT, District & Piccadilly —4K **75**
EARLSFIELD, Rail —1A **108**
EAST ACTON, Central —6B **58**
EASTCOTE, Metropolitan & Piccadilly —7A **22**
EAST CROYDON, Rail & Croydon Tramlink —2D **134**
EAST DULWICH, Rail —4E **94**
EAST FINCHLEY, Northern —4C **28**
EAST HAM, District & Hammersmith & City —7C **50**
EAST INDIA, Docklands Light Railway —7F **65**
EAST PUTNEY, District —5G **91**
EDEN PARK, Rail —5C **126**
EDGWARE, Northern —6C **12**
EDGWARE ROAD, Bakerloo —5C **60** (5C **140**)
EDGWARE ROAD, Circle, District & Hammersmith & City
—5C **60** (6C **140**)
EDMONTON GREEN, Rail —2B **18**
ELEPHANT & CASTLE, Rail, Bakerloo & Northern
—4C **78** (3C **156**)
ELMERS END, Rail & Croydon Tramlink —4K **125**
ELMSTEAD WOODS, Rail —6C **114**
ELTHAM, Rail —5D **98**
ELVERSON ROAD, Docklands Light Railway —2D **96**
EMBANKMENT, Bakerloo, Circle, District & Northern
—1J **77** (4F **149**)
ENFIELD CHASE, Rail —3H **7**
ENFIELD TOWN, Rail —3K **7**
ERITH, Rail —5K **85**
ESSEX ROAD, Rail —7C **46**
EUSTON, Rail, Northern & Victoria —3H **61** (2C **142**)
EUSTON SQUARE, Circle, Hammersmith & City &
Metropolitan —4G **61** (3B **142**)
EWELL WEST, Rail —7A **130**

FAIRLOP, Central —1H **35**
FALCONWOOD, Rail —4H **99**
FARRINGDON, Rail, Circle, Hammersmith & City &
Metropolitan —5B **62** (5A **144**)
FENCHURCH STREET, Rail —7E **62** (2J **151**)
FIELDWAY, Croydon Tramlink —7D **136**
FINCHLEY CENTRAL, Northern —1J **27**
FINCHLEY ROAD & FROGNAL, Rail —5A **44**
FINCHLEY ROAD, Jubilee & Metropolitan —6A **44**
FINSBURY PARK, Rail, Piccadilly & Victoria —2A **46**
FOREST GATE, Rail —5J **49**
FOREST HILL, Rail —2J **111**
FULHAM BROADWAY, District —7J **75**
FULWELL, Rail —4H **103**

Rail, Croydon Tramlink, Docklands Light Railway & London Underground Stations

GALLIONS REACH, Docklands Light Railway —7F **67**
GANTS HILL, Central —6E **34**
GIPSY HILL, Rail —5E **110**
GLOUCESTER ROAD, Circle, District & Piccadilly —4A **76**
GOLDERS GREEN, Northern —1J **43**
GOLDHAWK ROAD, Hammersmith & City —2E **74**
GOODGE STREET, Northern —5H **61** (5C **142**)
GOODMAYES, Rail —1A **52**
GORDON HILL, Rail —1G **7**
GOSPEL OAK, Rail —4E **44**
GRANGE PARK, Rail —5G **7**
GRAVEL HILL, Croydon Tramlink —6A **136**
GREAT PORTLAND STREET, Circle, Hammersmith & City &
    Metropolitan —4F **61** (4K **141**)
GREENFORD, Rail & Central —1H **55**
GREEN PARK, Jubilee, Piccadilly & Victoria
    —1G **77** (4K **147**)
GREENWICH, Rail & Docklands Light Railway —7D **80**
GROVE PARK, Rail —3K **113**
GUNNERSBURY, Rail & District —5H **73**

HACKBRIDGE, Rail —2F **133**
HACKNEY CENTRAL, Rail —6H **47**
HACKNEY DOWNS, Rail —5H **47**
HACKNEY WICK, Rail —6C **48**
HADLEY WOOD, Rail —1F **5**
HAMMERSMITH, District, Hammersmith & City & Piccadilly
    —4E **74**
HAMPSTEAD, Northern —4A **44**
HAMPSTEAD HEATH, Rail —4C **44**
HAMPTON, Rail —7E **102**
HAMPTON WICK, Rail —1C **118**
HANGER LANE, Central —3E **56**
HANWELL, Rail —7J **55**
HARLESDEN, Rail & Bakerloo —2K **57**
HARRINGAY, Rail —6A **30**
HARRINGAY GREEN LANES, Rail —6B **30**
HARRINGTON ROAD, Croydon Tramlink —3H **125**
HARROW & WEALDSTONE, Rail & Bakerloo —4J **23**
HARROW-ON-THE-HILL, Rail & Metropolitan —6J **23**
HATCH END, Rail —1E **22**
HAYDONS ROAD, Rail —5A **108**
HAYES, Rail —1J **137**
HEADSTONE LANE, Rail —1F **23**
HENDON, Rail —6C **26**
HENDON CENTRAL, Northern —5D **26**
HERNE HILL, Rail —6B **94**
HERON QUAYS, Docklands Light Railway —1C **80**
HIGHAMS PARK, Rail —6A **20**
HIGH BARNET, Northern —4D **4**
HIGHBURY & ISLINGTON, Rail & Victoria —6B **46**
HIGHGATE, Northern —6F **29**
HIGH STREET, KENSINGTON, Circle & District —2K **75**
HITHER GREEN, Rail —6G **97**
HOLBORN, Central & Piccadilly —6K **61** (6G **143**)
HOLLAND PARK, Central —1H **75**
HOLLOWAY ROAD, Piccadilly —5K **45**
HOMERTON, Rail —6K **47**
HONOR OAK PARK, Rail —6K **95**
HORNSEY, Rail —4K **29**
HOUNSLOW, Rail —5F **87**
HOUNSLOW CENTRAL, Piccadilly —3F **87**
HOUNSLOW EAST, Piccadilly —2G **87**
HOUNSLOW WEST, Piccadilly —2C **86**
HYDE PARK CORNER, Piccadilly —2E **76** (6H **147**)

ILFORD, Rail —3F **51**
ISLAND GARDENS, Docklands Light Railway —5E **80**
ISLEWORTH, Rail —2K **87**

KENNINGTON, Northern —5B **78** (5A **156**)
KENSAL GREEN, Rail & Bakerloo —3E **58**
KENSAL RISE, Rail —2F **59**
KENSINGTON (OLYMPIA), Rail & District —3G **75**

KENT HOUSE, Rail —1A **126**
KENTISH TOWN, Rail & Northern —5G **45**
KENTISH TOWN WEST, Rail —6F **45**
KENTON, Rail & Bakerloo —6B **24**
KEW BRIDGE, Rail —5F **73**
KEW GARDENS, Rail & District —1G **89**
KIDBROOKE, Rail —3K **97**
KILBURN, Jubilee —6H **43**
KILBURN HIGH ROAD, Rail —1K **59**
KILBURN PARK, Bakerloo —2J **59**
KINGSBURY, Jubilee —5G **25**
KING'S CROSS, Rail —2J **61** (1F **143**)
KING'S CROSS SAINT PANCRAS, Circle, Hammersmith &
    City, Metropolitan, Northern, Piccadilly & Victoria
    —3J **61** (1E **142**)
KING'S CROSS THAMESLINK, Rail —3K **61** (1F **143**)
KINGSTON, Rail —1E **118**
KNIGHTSBRIDGE, Piccadilly —2D **76** (7F **147**)

LADBROKE GROVE, Hammersmith & City —6G **59**
LADYWELL, Rail —5D **96**
LAMBETH NORTH, Bakerloo —3A **78** (1J **155**)
LANCASTER GATE, Central —7B **60** (2A **146**)
LATIMER ROAD, Hammersmith & City —7F **59**
LEBANON ROAD, Croydon Tramlink —2E **134**
LEE, Rail —6J **97**
LEICESTER SQUARE, Northern & Piccadilly
    —7J **61** (2D **148**)
LEWISHAM, Rail & Docklands Light Railway —3E **96**
LEYTON, Central —3E **48**
LEYTON MIDLAND ROAD, Rail —1E **48**
LEYTONSTONE, Central —1G **49**
LEYTONSTONE HIGH ROAD, Rail —2G **49**
LIMEHOUSE, Rail & Docklands Light Railway —6A **64**
LIVERPOOL STREET, Rail, Central, Circle, Hammersmith &
    City & Metropolitan —5E **62** (6G **145**)
LLOYD PARK, Croydon Tramlink —4F **135**
LONDON BRIDGE, Rail, Northern & Jubilee
    —1D **78** (5F **151**)
LONDON FIELDS, Rail —7H **47**
LOUGHBOROUGH JUNCTION, Rail —3B **94**
LOWER SYDENHAM, Rail —5B **112**

MAIDA VALE, Bakerloo —3K **59**
MALDEN MANOR, Rail —7A **120**
MANOR HOUSE, Piccadilly —7C **30**
MANOR PARK, Rail —4B **50**
MANSION HOUSE, Circle & District —7C **62** (2D **150**)
MARBLE ARCH, Central —6D **60** (1F **147**)
MARYLAND, Rail —6G **49**
MARYLEBONE, Rail & Bakerloo —5D **60** (4E **140**)
MAZE HILL, Rail —6G **81**
MERTON PARK, Croydon Tramlink —1J **121**
MILE END, Central, District & Hammersmith & City
    —3B **64**
MILL HILL BROADWAY, Rail —6F **13**
MILL HILL EAST, Northern —7B **14**
MITCHAM, Croydon Tramlink —4C **122**
MITCHAM JUNCTION, Rail & Croydon Tramlink —5E **122**
MONUMENT, Circle & District —7D **62** (2F **151**)
MOORGATE, Rail, Circle, Hammersmith & City, Northern &
    Metropolitan —5D **62** (6E **144**)
MORDEN, Northern —3K **121**
MORDEN ROAD, Croydon Tramlink —2K **121**
MORDEN SOUTH, Rail —5J **121**
MORNINGTON CRESCENT, Northern —2G **61**
MORTLAKE, Rail —3J **89**
MOTSPUR PARK, Rail —5D **120**
MOTTINGHAM, Rail —1D **114**
MUDCHUTE, Docklands Light Railway —4D **80**

NEASDEN, Jubilee —5A **42**
NEW BARNET, Rail —5G **5**
NEW BECKENHAM, Rail —7B **112**

NEWBURY PARK, Central —6H **35**
NEW CROSS, Rail & East London —7B **80**
NEW CROSS GATE, Rail & East London —7A **80**
NEW ELTHAM, Rail —1G **115**
NEW MALDEN, Rail —3A **120**
NEW SOUTHGATE, Rail —5A **16**
NORBITON, Rail —1G **119**
NORBURY, Rail —1K **123**
NORTH ACTON, Central —5K **57**
NORTH DULWICH, Rail —5D **94**
NORTH EALING, Piccadilly —6F **57**
NORTHFIELDS, Piccadilly —3C **72**
NORTH GREENWICH, Jubilee —2G **81**
NORTH HARROW, Metropolitan —5F **23**
NORTHOLT, Central —6E **38**
NORTHOLT PARK, Rail —4F **39**
NORTH SHEEN, Rail —4G **89**
NORTHUMBERLAND PARK, Rail —7C **18**
NORTH WEMBLEY, Rail & Bakerloo —3D **40**
NORTHWICK PARK, Metropolitan —7B **24**
NORTH WOOLWICH, Rail —2E **82**
NORWOOD JUNCTION, Rail —4G **125**
NOTTING HILL GATE, Central, Circle & District —1J **75**
NUNHEAD, Rail —2J **95**

OAKLEIGH PARK, Rail —7G **5**
OAKWOOD, Piccadilly —5B **6**
OLD STREET, Rail & Northern —4D **62** (3F **145**)
OSTERLEY, Piccadilly —7H **71**
OVAL, Northern —6A **78**
OXFORD CIRCUS, Bakerloo, Central & Victoria
    —6G **61** (1A **148**)

PADDINGTON, Bakerloo, Rail, Circle, District &
    Hammersmith & City —6B **60** (1A **146**)
PALMERS GREEN, Rail —4E **16**
PARK ROYAL, Piccadilly —4G **57**
PARSONS GREEN, District —1J **91**
PECKHAM RYE, Rail —2G **95**
PENGE EAST, Rail —6J **111**
PENGE WEST, Rail —6H **111**
PERIVALE, Central —2A **56**
PETTS WOOD, Rail —5G **129**
PHIPPS BRIDGE, Croydon Tramlink —3B **122**
PICCADILLY CIRCUS, Bakerloo & Piccadilly
    —7H **61** (3C **148**)
PIMLICO, Victoria —5H **77** (5C **154**)
PINNER, Metropolitan —4C **22**
PLAISTOW, District & Hammersmith & City —2H **65**
PLUMSTEAD, Rail —4H **83**
PONDERS END, Rail —5F **9**
POPLAR, Docklands Light Railway —7D **64**
PRESTON ROAD, Metropolitan —1E **40**
PRINCE REGENT, Docklands Light Railway —7A **66**
PUDDING MILL LANE, Docklands Light Railway —1D **64**
PUTNEY, Rail —4G **91**
PUTNEY BRIDGE, District —3H **91**

QUEENSBURY, Jubilee —3F **25**
QUEENS PARK, Rail & Bakerloo —2H **59**
QUEEN'S ROAD (PECKHAM), Rail —1J **95**
QUEENSTOWN ROAD (BATTERSEA), Rail —1F **93**
QUEENSWAY, Central —7K **59**

RAVENSBOURNE, Rail —7F **113**
RAVENSCOURT PARK, District —4D **74**
RAYNERS LANE, Metropolitan & Piccadilly —7D **22**
RAYNES PARK, Rail —2E **120**
RECTORY ROAD, Rail —3F **47**
REDBRIDGE, Central —6B **34**
REGENT'S PARK, Bakerloo —4F **61** (4J **141**)
RICHMOND, Rail & District —4E **88**
RODING VALLEY, Central —4G **21**

329

Rail, Croydon Tramlink, Docklands Light Railway & London Underground Stations

ROTHERHITHE, East London —2J **79**
ROYAL ALBERT, Docklands Light Railway —7C **66**
ROYAL OAK, Hammersmith & City —5K **59**
ROYAL VICTORIA, Docklands Light Railway —7J **65**
RUSSELL SQUARE, Piccadilly —4J **61** (4E **142**)

SAINT HELIER, Rail —6J **121**
SAINT JAMES'S PARK, Circle & District —3H **77** (1C **154**)
SAINT JAMES STREET, WALTHAMSTOW, Rail —5A **32**
SAINT JOHNS, Rail —2C **96**
SAINT JOHN'S WOOD, Jubilee —2B **60**
SAINT MARGARETS, Rail —6B **88**
SAINT PANCRAS, Rail —3J **61** (1E **142**)
SAINT PAUL'S, Central —6C **62** (7C **144**)
SANDERSTEAD, Rail —7D **134**
SANDILANDS, Croydon Tramlink —2F **135**
SELHURST, Rail —5E **124**
SEVEN KINGS, Rail —1J **51**
SEVEN SISTERS, Rail & Victoria —5E **30**
SHADWELL, Docklands Light Railway & East London
—7H **63**
SHEPHERD'S BUSH, Central —2F **75**
SHEPHERD'S BUSH, Hammersmith & City —1E **74**
SHOREDITCH, East London —4F **63** (4K **145**)
SHORTLANDS, Rail —2G **127**
SIDCUP, Rail —2A **116**
SILVER STREET, Rail —4A **18**
SILVERTOWN & CITY AIRPORT, Rail —1B **82**
SLOANE SQUARE, Circle & District —4E **76** (4G **153**)
SNARESBROOK, Central —5J **33**
SOUTH ACTON, Rail —3J **73**
SOUTHALL, Rail —2D **70**
SOUTH BERMONDSEY, Rail —5J **79**
SOUTHBURY, Rail —4C **8**
SOUTH CROYDON, Rail —5D **134**
SOUTH EALING, Piccadilly —3D **72**
SOUTHFIELDS, District —1H **107**
SOUTHGATE, Piccadilly —1C **16**
SOUTH GREENFORD, Rail —3J **55**
SOUTH HAMPSTEAD, Rail —7A **44**
SOUTH HARROW, Piccadilly —3G **39**
SOUTH KENSINGTON, Circle, District & Piccadilly
—4B **76** (3B **152**)
SOUTH KENTON, Rail & Bakerloo —1C **40**
SOUTH MERTON, Rail —3H **121**
SOUTH QUAY, Docklands Light Railway —2D **80**
SOUTH RUISLIP, Rail & Central —5A **38**
SOUTH TOTTENHAM, Rail —5F **31**
SOUTHWARK, Rail & Jubilee —1B **78** (5A **150**)
SOUTH WIMBLEDON, Northern —7K **107**
SOUTH WOODFORD, Central —2K **33**
STAMFORD BROOK, District —4B **74**
STAMFORD HILL, Rail —7E **30**
STANMORE, Jubilee —4J **11**
STEPNEY GREEN, District & Hammersmith & City —4K **63**
STOCKWELL, Northern & Victoria —2J **93**
STOKE NEWINGTON, Rail —2F **47**
STONEBRIDGE PARK, Rail & Bakerloo —7H **41**

STONELEIGH, Rail —5C **130**
STRATFORD, Rail, Central & Docklands Light Railway &
Jubilee —7F **49**
STRATFORD (LOW LEVEL), Rail —7F **49**
STRAWBERRY HILL, Rail —3K **103**
STREATHAM, Rail —5H **109**
STREATHAM COMMON, Rail —7H **109**
STREATHAM HILL, Rail —2J **109**
SUDBURY & HARROW ROAD, Rail —5B **40**
SUDBURY HILL, Piccadilly —4J **39**
SUDBURY HILL, HARROW, Rail —4J **39**
SUDBURY TOWN, Piccadilly —6B **40**
SUNDRIDGE PARK, Rail —7K **113**
SURBITON, Rail —6E **118**
SURREY QUAYS, East London —4K **79**
SUTTON, Rail —6A **132**
SUTTON COMMON, Rail —2K **131**
SWISS COTTAGE, Jubilee —7B **44**
SYDENHAM, Rail —4J **111**
SYDENHAM HILL, Rail —3F **111**
SYON LANE, Rail —7A **72**

TEDDINGTON, Rail —6A **104**
TEMPLE, Circle & District —7K **61** (2H **149**)
THERAPIA LANE, Croydon Tramlink —7J **123**
THORNTON HEATH, Rail —4C **124**
TOOTING, Rail —6D **108**
TOOTING BEC, Northern —3E **108**
TOOTING BROADWAY, Northern —5C **108**
TOTTENHAM COURT ROAD, Central & Northern
—6H **61** (7D **142**)
TOTTENHAM HALE, Rail & Victoria —3H **31**
TOTTERIDGE & WHETSTONE, Northern —2F **15**
TOWER GATEWAY, Docklands Light Railway
—7F **63** (2J **151**)
TOWER HILL, Circle & District —7F **63** (2J **151**)
TUFNELL PARK, Northern —4G **45**
TULSE HILL, Rail —2B **110**
TURNHAM GREEN, District & Picaddilly —4A **74**
TURNPIKE LANE, Piccadilly —3B **30**
TWICKENHAM, Rail —7A **88**

UPNEY, District —7K **51**
UPPER HOLLOWAY, Rail —2H **45**
UPTON PARK, District & Hammersmith & City —1A **66**

VAUXHALL, Rail & Victoria —5J **77**
VICTORIA, Coach Station —4F **77** (4J **153**)
VICTORIA, Rail, Circle, District & Victoria —4F **77** (3K **153**)

WADDON, Rail —4A **134**
WADDON MARSH, Croydon Tramlink —1K **133**
WALLINGTON, Rail —6F **133**
WALTHAMSTOW CENTRAL, Rail & Victoria —5C **32**
WALTHAMSTOW QUEENS ROAD, Rail —5C **32**

WANDLE PARK, Croydon Tramlink —2A **134**
WANDSWORTH COMMON, Rail —1D **108**
WANDSWORTH ROAD, Rail —2G **93**
WANDSWORTH TOWN, Rail —4K **91**
WANSTEAD, Central —6K **33**
WANSTEAD PARK, Rail —4K **49**
WAPPING, East London —1J **79**
WARREN STREET, Northern & Victoria —4G **61** (3A **142**)
WARWICK AVENUE, Bakerloo —4A **60**
WATERLOO, Rail, Bakerloo, Northern, Waterloo & City &
Jubilee —2A **78** (6J **149**)
WATERLOO (EAST), Rail —1A **78** (5K **149**)
WATERLOO INTERNATIONAL, Rail —2K **77** (6H **149**)
WELLESLEY ROAD, Croydon Tramlink —2D **134**
WELLING, Rail —2A **100**
WEMBLEY CENTRAL, Rail & Bakerloo —5E **40**
WEMBLEY PARK, Jubilee & Metropolitan —3G **41**
WEMBLEY STADIUM, Rail —5F **41**
WEST ACTON, Central —6G **57**
WESTBOURNE PARK, Hammersmith & City —5H **59**
WEST BROMPTON, Rail & District —6J **75**
WESTCOMBE PARK, Rail —5J **81**
WEST CROYDON, Rail & Croydon Tramlink —1C **134**
WEST DULWICH, Rail —2D **110**
WEST EALING, Rail —7B **56**
WESTFERRY, Docklands Light Railway —7C **64**
WEST FINCHLEY, Northern —6E **14**
WEST HAM, District, Hammersmith & City & Jubilee —3G **65**
WEST HAM, Rail —3G **65**
WEST HAMPSTEAD, Jubilee —6K **43**
WEST HAMPSTEAD, Rail —6J **43**
WEST HAMPSTEAD THAMESLINK, Rail —6J **43**
WEST HARROW, Metropolitan —6G **23**
WEST INDIA QUAY, Docklands Light Railway —7C **64**
WEST KENSINGTON, District —5H **75**
WESTMINSTER, Circle, District & Jubilee —2J **77** (7F **149**)
WEST NORWOOD, Rail —4B **110**
WEST SUTTON, Rail —4J **131**
WEST WICKHAM, Rail —7E **126**
WHITECHAPEL, District, Hammersmith & City & East London
—5H **63**
WHITE CITY, Central —7E **58**
WHITE HART LANE, Rail —7A **18**
WHITTON, Rail —7G **87**
WILLESDEN GREEN, Jubilee —6E **42**
WILLESDEN JUNCTION, Rail & Bakerloo —3B **58**
WIMBLEDON, Rail, District & Croydon Tramlink —6H **107**
WIMBLEDON CHASE, Rail —2G **121**
WIMBLEDON PARK, District —3J **107**
WINCHMORE HILL, Rail —7G **7**
WOODFORD, Central —6E **20**
WOODGRANGE PARK, Rail —5B **50**
WOOD GREEN, Piccadilly —2A **30**
WOODSIDE, Croydon Tramlink —6H **125**
WOODSIDE PARK, Northern —4E **14**
WOOD STREET, WALTHAMSTOW, Rail —4F **33**
WOOLWICH ARSENAL, Rail —4F **83**
WOOLWICH DOCKYARD, Rail —4D **82**
WORCESTER PARK, Rail —1C **130**

HOSPITALS, HEALTH CENTRES and HOSPICES
covered by this atlas
with their map square reference

N.B. Where Hospitals and Health Centres are not named on the map, the reference given is for the road in which they are situated.

Acton Health Centre —2J **73**
Church Rd., Acton, London. W3 8QE
Tel: 020 8896 0473

ACTON HOSPITAL —2G **73**
Gunnersbury La., London. W3 8EG
Tel: 020 8383 1133

Albion Street Health Centre —2J **79**
87 Albion St., London. SE16 1JX
Tel: 020 7231 2296

Annie Prendergast Health Centre —6E **36**
Ashton Gdns., Chadwell Heath, Essex. RM6 6RT
Tel: 020 8590 1086

ATHLONE HOUSE —1D **44**
Hampstead La., Highgate, London. N6 4RX
Tel: 020 8348 5231

ATKINSON MORLEY'S HOSPITAL —7D **106**
31 Copse Hill, Wimbledon, London. SW20 0NE
Tel: 020 8946 7711

Avenue House Mental Health Centre —2J **73**
Avenue Rd., Acton, London. W3 8NJ
Tel: 020 8993 7781

Aylesbury Health Centre —5D **78** (5F **157**)
Taplow House, Thurlow St., London. SE17 2UN
Tel: 020 7701 4251

Balham Health Centre —2F **109**
120 Bedford Hill, Balham, London. SW12 9HP
Tel: 020 8700 0600

BARKING HOSPITAL —7K **51**
Upney La., Barking, Essex. IG11 9LX
Tel: 020 8594 3898

BARNES HOSPITAL —3A **90**
South Worple Way, London. SW14 8SU
Tel: 020 8878 4981

BARNET COMMUNITY HOSPITAL —4A **4**
Wellhouse La., Barnet, Herts. EN5 3DJ
Tel: 020 8440 5111

Barton House Health Centre —2D **46**
233 Albion Rd., Stoke Newington, London. N16 9JT
Tel: 020 7249 5511

Bath Street Health Centre —3D **62** (2E **144**)
60 Bath St., London. EC1V 9JX
Tel: 020 7253 2806

BECKENHAM HOSPITAL —2B **126**
379 Croydon Rd., Beckenham, Kent. BR3 3QL
Tel: 020 8289 6600

BECONTREE DAY HOSPITAL —3E **52**
Becontree Av., Dagenham, Essex. RM8 3HR
Tel: 020 8984 1234

BEECHLAWN DAY HOSPITAL —7G **93**
Belthorn Cres., Weir Rd., London. SW12 0NS
Tel: 020 8675 3415

Belmont Health Centre —2A **24**
516 Kenton La., Kenton, Middx. HA3 7LT
Tel: 020 8863 8647

Belsize Priory Health Centre —1K **59**
208 Belsize Rd., London. NW6 4DJ
Tel: 020 7530 2600

BELVEDERE DAY HOSPITAL —1C **58**
341 Harlesden Rd., London. NW10 3RX
Tel: 020 8459 3562

BELVEDERE PRIVATE CLINIC —5C **84**
Knee Hill, Abbey Wood, London. SE2 0AT
Tel: 020 8311 4464

Bermondsey Health Centre —4F **79** (3K **157**)
108 Grange Rd., London. SE1 2BW
Tel: 020 7231 9031

BETHLEM ROYAL HOSPITAL, THE —7C **126**
Monks Orchard Rd., Eden Park,
Beckenham, Kent. BR3 3BX
Tel: 020 8777 6611

Bethnal Green Health Centre —3G **63**
60 Florida St., Bethnal Green, London. E2 6LL
Tel: 020 7739 1440

BEXLEY HOSPITAL —2K **117**
Old Bexley La., Bexley, Kent. DA5 2BW
Tel: (01322) 526282

BLACKHEATH HOSPITAL —3H **97**
40-42 Lee Ter., Blackheath, London. SE3 9UD
Tel: 020 8318 7722

BOLINGBROKE HOSPITAL —5C **92**
Bolingbroke Gro., Wandsworth Common,
London. SW11 6HN
Tel: 020 7223 7411

Bounds Green Health Centre —7C **16**
Gordon Rd., London. N11 2PA
Tel: 020 8889 1961

Bourne Hall Health Centre —7B **130**
Chessington Rd., Ewell, Surrey. KT17 1TG
Tel: 020 8394 1301

B. P. A. S. ST ANN'S —6C **30**
Ward K2, St Ann's Hospital, St Ann's Rd.,
South Tottenham, London. N15 3TH
Tel: 020 8809 6600

Brentford Health Centre —6C **72**
Boston Manor Rd., Brentford, Middx. TW8 8DR
Tel: 020 8321 3800

Bridge Lane Health Centre —1C **92**
20 Bridge La., Battersea, London. SW11 3AD
Tel: 020 7441 0730

BRITISH HOME & HOSPITAL FOR INCURABLES —6B **110**
Crown La., Streatham, London. SW16 3JB
Tel: 020 8670 8261

Broadwater Farm Community Health Centre —2D **30**
Adams Rd., London. N17 6HE
Tel: 020 8801 4115

Brocklebank Health Centre —7K **91**
249 Garratt La., Wandsworth,
London. SW18 4DU
Tel: 020 8870 1341

BROMLEY HOSPITAL —4K **127**
Cromwell Av., Bromley, Kent. BR2 9AJ
Tel: 020 8289 7000

Brunswick Park Health Centre —2K **15**
Brunswick Park Rd., London. N11 1EY
Tel: 020 8368 2828

BUSHEY BUPA HOSPITAL —1E **10**
Heathbourne Rd., Bushey, Watford, Herts. WD2 1RD
Tel: 020 8950 9090

CAMDEN MEWS DAY HOSPITAL —6G **45**
5 Camden Mews, London. NW1 9DB
Tel: 020 7530 4780

CARSHALTON WAR MEMORIAL HOSPITAL —6D **132**
The Park, Carshalton, Surrey. SM5 3DB
Tel: 020 8647 5534

CASSEL HOSPITAL, THE —4D **104**
1 Ham Comn., Richmond, Surrey. TW10 7JF
Tel: 020 8940 8181

Castlewood Therapy Centre —1E **98**
25 Shooter's Hill, London. SE18 4LG
Tel: 020 8856 4970

Central Lewisham Health Centre —6D **96**
410 Lewisham High St., London. SE13 6LL
Tel: 020 8690 9723

CENTRAL MIDDLESEX HOSPITAL —3J **57**
Acton La., Park Royal, London. NW10 7NS
Tel: 020 8965 5733

CHADWELL HEATH HOSPITAL —6B **36**
Grove Rd., Chadwell Heath, Essex. RM6 4XH
Tel: 020 8983 8000

Chalkhill Health Centre —3G **41**
Chalkhill Rd., Wembley, Middx. HA9 9BQ
Tel: 020 8904 0911

CHARING CROSS HOSPITAL —6F **75**
Fulham Palace Rd., London. W6 8RF
Tel: 020 8383 0000

CHARTER NIGHTINGALE HOSPITAL —5C **60** (5D **140**)
11-19 Lisson Gro., London. NW1 6SH
Tel: 020 7258 3828

CHASE FARM HOSPITAL —1F **7**
127 The Ridgeway, Enfield, Middx. EN2 8JL
Tel: 020 8366 6600

CHELSEA & WESTMINSTER HOSPITAL —6A **76**
369 Fulham Rd., Chelsea, London. SW10 9NH
Tel: 020 8746 8000

Cherington House Mental Health Centre —1K **71**
Cherington Rd., Hanwell, London. W7 3HL
Tel: 020 8566 2777

Chingford Health Centre —4G **19**
109 York Rd., London. E4 8LF
Tel: 020 8529 1660

Chiswick Health Centre —4K **73**
Fishers La., Chiswick, London. W4 1RX
Tel: 020 8995 8051

Hospitals, Health Centres & Hospices

Chrisp Street Health Centre —6D **64**
100 Chrisp St., London. E14 6PG
Tel: 020 7515 4860

CHURCHILL CLINIC —3A **78** (2K **155**)
80 Lambeth Rd., London. SE1 7PW
Tel: 020 7928 5633

CLAYPONDS HOSPITAL —4E **72**
Sterling Pl., South Ealing, London. W5 4RN
Tel: 020 8560 4013

CLEMENTINE CHURCHILL HOSPITAL, THE —3K **39**
Sudbury Hill, Harrow, Middx. HA1 3RX
Tel: 020 8872 3872

Coleridge Road Special Health Centre —4B **32**
Coleridge Rd., London. E17 6QU
Tel: 020 8521 0337

COLINDALE HOSPITAL —3A **26**
Colindale Av., London. NW9 5HG
Tel: 020 8200 1555

Colville Health Centre —6H **59**
51 Kensington Pk. Rd., London. W11 1PA
Tel: 020 7221 2650

COPPETTS WOOD HOSPITAL —1D **28**
Coppetts Rd., Muswell Hill, London. N10 1JN
Tel: 020 8883 9792

COTTAGE DAY HOSPITAL —3C **108**
Springfield University Hospital,
61 Glenburnie Rd., London. SW17 7DJ
Tel: 020 8682 6514

Covent Garden Health Centre —6J **61** (1F **149**)
8-12 Neal St., London. WC2H 9LZ
Tel: 020 7240 8484

Craven Park Health Centre —1K **57**
Shakespeare Cres., London. NW10 8XW
Tel: 020 8965 0151

Crawford Avenue Health Centre —5D **40**
Crawford Av., Wembley, Middx. HA0 2HX
Tel: 020 8903 6411

CROMWELL HOSPITAL, THE —4K **75**
162-174 Cromwell Rd., London. SW5 0TU
Tel: 020 7460 2000

Crouch End Health Centre —5J **29**
45 Middle La., London. N8 8PH
Tel: 020 8341 2045

Crowndale Health Centre —2G **61**
59 Crowndale Rd., London. NW1 1TY
Tel: 020 7530 3800

David Cousins Mental Health Centre —5G **55**
Windmill La., Greenford,
Middx. UB6 9DZ
Tel: 020 8575 5550

DEVONSHIRE HOSPITAL —5E **60** (5H **141**)
29 Devonshire St., London. W1N 1RF
Tel: 020 7486 7131

Downham Health Centre —4H **113**
24 Churchdown, Downham, Bromley, Kent. BR1 5PT
Tel: 020 8695 6644

Ealing Day Treatment Centre —6E **54**
Britten Dri., Southall, Middx. UB1 2SH
Tel: 020 8571 1143

EALING HOSPITAL —2H **71**
Uxbridge Rd., Southall, Middx. UB1 3HW
Tel: 020 8574 2444

East Barnet Health Centre —5G **5**
149 East Barnet Rd., Barnet, London. EN4 8QZ
Tel: 020 8440 1251

Eastcote Health Centre —1A **22**
Devonshire Lodge, Abbotsbury Gdns.,
Eastcote, Middx. HA5 1TG
Tel: 020 8868 1166

EAST HAM MEMORIAL HOSPITAL —7B **50**
Shrewsbury Rd., Forest Gate, London. E7 8QR
Tel: 020 8586 5000

EASTMAN DENTAL HOSPITAL & EASTMAN DENTAL
INSTITUTE, THE —4K **61** (3G **143**)
256 Gray's Inn Rd., London. WC1X 8LD
Tel: 020 7915 1000

Edenhall Marie Curie Centre —5B **44**
11 Lyndhurst Gdns., Hampstead, London. NW3 5NS
Tel: 020 7794 0066

EDGWARE COMMUNITY HOSPITAL —7C **12**
Burnt Oak Broadway, Edgware, Middx. HA8 0AD
Tel: 020 8952 2381

Elsdale Street Health Centre —7J **47**
28 Elsdale St., Hackney, London. E9 6QY
Tel: 020 8533 0031

ENFIELD COMMUNITY CARE CENTRE —1J **7**
Chase Side Cres., Enfield, Middx. EN2 0JB
Tel: 020 8366 6600

ERITH & DISTRICT HOSPITAL —6K **85**
Park Cres., Erith, Kent. DA8 3EE
Tel: 020 8302 2678

FARNBOROUGH HOSPITAL —3E **138**
Farnborough Comn., Locksbottom,
Orpington, Kent. BR6 8ND
Tel: (01689) 814000

FINCHLEY MEMORIAL HOSPITAL —7F **15**
Granville Rd., North Finchley,
London. N12 0JE
Tel: 020 8349 3121

Finsbury Health Centre —4A **62** (3J **143**)
Pine St., London. EC1R 0JH
Tel: 020 7530 4200

Five Elms Health Centre —3F **53**
Five Elms Rd., Dagenham, Essex. RM9 5TT
Tel: 020 8593 7241

FLORENCE HOUSE DAY HOSPITAL —5C **60** (5D **140**)
1 Harewood Row, London. NW1 6SE
Tel: 020 7724 5430

Forest Road Health Centre —1C **18**
2a Forest Rd., London. N9 8RX
Tel: 020 8804 7757

Fountayne Road Health Centre —2G **47**
Fountayne Rd., London. N16 7EA
Tel: 020 8806 3311

Fulwell Cross Health Centre —2G **35**
1 Tomswood Hill, Ilford, Essex. IG6 2HL
Tel: 020 8491 1580

Gallions Reach Health Centre —7A **68**
Bentham Rd., Thamesmead,
London. SE28 8BE
Tel: 020 8311 1010

GARDEN HOSPITAL, THE —3E **26**
46-50 Sunny Gdns. Rd., Hendon,
London. NW4 1RX
Tel: 020 8203 0111

Gill Street Health Centre —7B **64**
11 Gill St., London. E14 8HQ
Tel: 020 7987 4433

GOLDIE LEIGH HOSPITAL —6C **84**
Bostall House, Lodge Hill, Abbey Wood, London. SE2 0AY
Tel: 020 8319 7111

Goodinge Health Centre —6J **45**
Goodinge Clo., North Rd., London. N7 9EW
Tel: 020 7530 4900

GOODMAYES HOSPITAL —5A **36**
Barley La., Goodmayes, Ilford, Essex. IG3 8XJ
Tel: 020 8983 8000

GORDON HOSPITAL —4H **77** (4C **154**)
Bloomburg St., London. SW1V 2RH
Tel: 020 8746 8710

Grahame Park Health Centre —1B **26**
The Concourse, Grahame Park Est., London. NW9 5XT
Tel: 020 8205 6204

GREAT ORMOND STREET HOSPITAL FOR CHILDREN
—4J **61** (4F **143**)
Gt. Ormond St., London. WC1N 3JH
Tel: 020 7405 9200

Greenwich & Bexley Cottage Hospice —5C **84**
185 Bostall Hill, Abbey Wood, London. SE2 0QX
Tel: 020 8312 2244

GREENWICH DISTRICT HOSPITAL —5H **81**
Vanbrugh Hill, Greenwich, London. SE10 9HE
Tel: 020 8858 8141

GROVELANDS PRIORY HOSPITAL —1D **16**
The Bourne, Southgate, London. N14 6RA
Tel: 020 8882 8191

GUY'S HOSPITAL —1D **78** (5E **150**)
St Thomas St., London. SE1 9RT
Tel: 020 7955 5000

GUY'S NUFFIELD HOUSE —2D **78** (6E **150**)
Newcomen St., London. SE1 1YR
Tel: 020 7955 5000

HAMMERSMITH HOSPITAL —6C **58**
Du Cane Rd., London. W12 0HS
Tel: 020 8383 1000

Hampton Community Health Centre —6D **102**
Tangley Park Rd., Hampton Nurserylands,
Hampton, Middx. TW12 3YH
Tel: 020 8979 1726

Handsworth Avenue Health Centre —6A **20**
Handsworth Av., London. E4 9PD
Tel: 020 8527 0913

HARLEY STREET CLINIC, THE —5F **61** (5J **141**)
35 Weymouth St., London. W1N 4BJ
Tel: 020 7935 7700

HARROW HOSPITAL —2H **39**
Roxeth Hill, Harrow, Middx. HA2 0JX
Tel: 020 8864 5432

HAYES GROVE PRIORY HOSPITAL —2J **137**
Prestons Rd., Hayes, Bromley, Kent. BR2 7AS
Tel: 020 8462 7722

HEART HOSPITAL, THE —5E **60** (6H **141**)
Westmoreland St., London. W1M 7HN
Tel: 020 7573 8888

Heathside Health Centre —1E **96**
Landale Ct., Sparta St., London. SE10 8DY
Tel: 020 8692 1757

HENDERSON HOSPITAL —7K **131**
Homeland Dri., Sutton, Surrey. SM2 5LY
Tel: 020 8661 1611

Heston Health Centre —7C **70**
Cranford La., Heston, Middx. TW5 9ER
Tel: 020 8570 5891

Highbury Grange Health Centre —4C **46**
Highbury Grange, London. N5 2QB
Tel: 020 7530 2888

HIGHGATE PRIVATE HOSPITAL —6D **28**
17-19 View Rd., Highgate, London. N6 4DJ
Tel: 020 8341 4182

HOLLY HOUSE HOSPITAL —2E **20**
High Rd., Buckhurst Hill, Essex. IG9 5HX
Tel: 020 8505 3311

HOMERTON HOSPITAL —5K **47**
Homerton Row, Homerton, London. E9 6SR
Tel: 020 8919 5555

Honor Oak Health Centre —4A **96**
20 Turnham Rd., London. SE4 2LA
Tel: 020 7639 8811

HORNSEY CENTRAL HOSPITAL —5H **29**
Park Rd., Crouch End, London. N8 8JL
Tel: 020 8219 1702

Hornsey Rise Health Centre —7J **29**
Hornsey Rise, London. N19 3YU
Tel: 020 8530 2400

HOSPITAL FOR TROPICAL DISEASES —1H **61**
4 St Pancras Way, London. NW1 0PE
Tel: 020 7530 3500

HOSPITAL OF ST JOHN & ST ELIZABETH —2B **60**
60 Grove End Rd., St John's Wood, London. NW8 9NH
Tel: 020 7286 5126

Hunter Street Health Centre —4J **61** (3F **143**)
8 Hunter St., London. WC1N 1BN
Tel: 020 7530 4300

Hurst Road Health Centre —3D **32**
36a Hurst Rd., London. E17 3BL
Tel: 020 8520 8513

Island Health Centre —3D **80**
145 East Ferry Rd., Isle of Dogs,
London. E14 3BQ
Tel: 020 7363 1111

Jenner Health Centre —1A **112**
201 Stanstead Rd., London. SE23 1HU
Tel: 020 7771 4110

John Scott Health Centre —1C **46**
Green Lanes, London. N4 2NU
Tel: 020 8800 0111

Julia Engwell Health Centre —7C **52**
Woodward Rd., Dagenham, Essex. RM9 4SR
Tel: 020 8592 2588

Kennard Street Health Centre —1D **82**
1 Kennard St., North Woolwich, London. E16 2HR
Tel: 020 7445 7150

Kentish Town Health Centre —6G **45**
2 Bartholomew Rd., London. NW5 2AJ
Tel: 020 7530 4700

KING EDWARD VII'S HOSPITAL —5E **60** (5H **141**)
Beaumont House, 10 Beaumont St.,
London. W1N 2AA
Tel: 020 7486 4411

KING GEORGE HOSPITAL —5A **36**
Barley La., Goodmayes, Ilford, Essex. IG3 8YB
Tel: 020 8983 8000

KINGSBURY COMMUNITY HOSPITAL —4G **25**
Honeypot La., Kingsbury, London. NW9 9QY
Tel: 020 8903 1323

KING'S COLLEGE HOSPITAL —2D **94**
Denmark Hill, London. SE5 9RS
Tel: 020 7737 4000

KING'S COLLEGE HOSPITAL, DULWICH —4E **94**
East Dulwich Gro., London. SE22 8PT
Tel: 020 7737 4000

KING'S OAK HOSPITAL —1F **7**
The Ridgeway, Enfield, Middx. EN2 8SD
Tel: 020 8364 5520

KINGSTON HOSPITAL —1H **119**
Galsworthy Rd., Kingston-upon-Thames,
Surrey. KT2 7QB
Tel: 020 8546 7711

Lakeside Health Centre —2D **84**
Tavy Bri., Thamesmead, London. SE2 9UQ
Tel: 020 8310 3281

LANGTHORNE HOSPITAL —4F **49**
1 Langthorne Rd., London. E11 4HJ
Tel: 020 8539 5511

LATIMER DAY HOSPITAL —5G **61** (5A **142**)
40 Hanson St., London. W1P 7DE
Tel: 020 7380 9187

Lee Health Centre —5H **97**
2 Handen Rd., London. SE12 8NE
Tel: 020 8318 4431

Lewin Road Community Mental Health Centre —6H **109**
55-57 Lewin Rd., London. SW16 6JZ
Tel: 020 8664 6406

LEWISHAM HOSPITAL —5D **96**
Lewisham High St., Lewisham,
London. SE13 6LH
Tel: 020 8333 3000

Lisson Grove Health Centre —4C **60** (4C **140**)
Gateforth St., London. NW8 8EG
Tel: 020 7724 2391

Lister Health Centre —1F **95**
1 Camden Sq., London. SE15 5LW
Tel: 020 7701 6291

LISTER HOSPITAL, THE —6F **77** (7J **153**)
Chelsea Bridge Rd., London. SW1W 8RH
Tel: 020 7730 3417

LONDON BRIDGE HOSPITAL —1D **78** (4F **151**)
27 Tooley St., London. SE1 2PR
Tel: 020 7407 3100

LONDON CHEST HOSPITAL —2J **63**
Bonner Rd., London. E2 9JX
Tel: 020 8980 4433

LONDON CLINIC, THE —4E **60** (4H **141**)
20 Devonshire Pl., London. W1N 2DH
Tel: 020 7935 4444

LONDON FOOT HOSPITAL —5G **61** (5A **142**)
33 Fitzroy Sq., London. W1P 6AY
Tel: 020 7530 4500

LONDON INDEPENDENT HOSPITAL —5K **63**
1 Beaumont Sq., Stepney Green, London. E1 4NL
Tel: 020 7790 0990

London Lighthouse —6G **59**
111-117 Lancaster Rd., Ladbroke Gro.,
London. W11 1QT
Tel: 020 7792 1200

LONDON WELBECK HOSPITAL —5E **60** (6H **141**)
27 Welbeck St., London. W1M 7PG
Tel: 020 7224 224

Lord Lister Health Centre —4J **49**
121 Woodgrange Rd., Forest Gate,
London. E7 0EP
Tel: 020 8250 7200

Lower Clapton Health Centre —5J **47**
36 Lower Clapton Rd., Clapton,
London. E5 0PQ
Tel: 020 8986 7111

MAITLAND DAY HOSPITAL —4J **47**
143-153 Lower Clapton Rd.,
Clapton, London. E5 8EQ
Tel: 020 8919 5600

Manor Drive Health Centre —1C **130**
3 The Manor Dri., Worcester Park,
Surrey. KT4 7LG
Tel: 020 8337 0246

Manor Gardens Health Centre —3J **45**
6-9 Manor Gdns., London. N7 6LA
Tel: 020 7275 4231

Manor Gate Mental Health Centre —7C **38**
1a Manor Ga., Northolt, Middx. UB5 5TG
Tel: 020 8841 5271

Manor Health Centre —3H **93**
Clapham Manor St., London. SW4 6EB
Tel: 020 7622 2293

MANOR HOUSE HOSPITAL —1K **43**
North End Rd., Golders Green,
London. NW11 7HX
Tel: 020 8455 6601

Marks Gate Health Centre —3E **36**
Lawn Farm Gro., Chadwell Heath,
Essex. RM6 5LL
Tel: 020 8590 9181

Marvels Lane Health Centre —2K **113**
37 Marvels La., Grove Park,
London. SE12 9PN
Tel: 020 8857 0042

Maswell Park Health Centre —5G **87**
Hounslow Av., Hounslow,
Middx. TW3 2DY
Tel: 020 8898 2321

Mattock Lane Health Centre —1C **72**
78 Mattock La., Ealing, London. W13 9NZ
Tel: 020 8574 2444

MAUDSLEY HOSPITAL, THE —2D **94**
Denmark Hill, London. SE5 8AZ
Tel: 020 7703 6333

Mawbey Brough Health Centre —7J **77**
39 Wilcox Clo., London. SW8 2UD
Tel: 020 7627 4444

MAYDAY UNIVERSITY HOSPITAL —6B **124**
Mayday Rd., Thornton Heath,
Surrey. CR7 7YE
Tel: 020 8401 3000

Meadow House Hospice —2H **71**
Uxbridge Rd., Southall, Middx. UB1 3EU
Tel: 020 8967 5179

Hospitals, Health Centres & Hospices

MEMORIAL HOSPITAL —2E **98**
Shooters Hill, Woolwich, London. SE18 3RZ
Tel: 020 8856 5511

MIDDLESEX HOSPITAL, THE —5G **61** (6A **142**)
Mortimer St., London. W1N 8AA
Tel: 020 7636 8333

Mildmay Mission Hospital —3F **63** (2J **145**)
Hackney Rd., Bethnal Green, London. E2 7NA
Tel: 020 7739 2331

Milson Road Health Centre —3F **75**
1-13 Milson Rd., London. W14 0LJ
Tel: 020 8846 6262

Mollison Drive Health Centre —7J **133**
Mollison Dri., Wallington,
Surrey. SM6 9HF
Tel: 020 8773 2820

MONTPELIER HOSPITAL, THE —5E **56**
19 Montpelier Rd., Ealing, London. W5 2QT
Tel: 020 8998 2848

Moorfield Road Health Centre —1D **8**
Moorfield Rd., Enfield, Middx. EN3 5TU
Tel: 020 8805 5500

MOORFIELDS EYE HOSPITAL —3D **62** (2E **144**)
162 City Rd., London. EC1V 2PD
Tel: 020 7253 3411

MORLAND ROAD DAY HOSPITAL —1G **69**
Morland Rd., Dagenham, Essex. RM10 9HU
Tel: 020 8593 2343

Mortimer Market Centre —4G **61** (4B **142**)
Mortimer Mkt., London. WC1E 6AU
Tel: 020 7530 5000

Myatts Field Health Centre —1B **94**
Patmos Rd., London. SW9 6SE
Tel: 020 7735 9171

NATIONAL HOSPITAL FOR NEUROLOGY &
                        NEUROSURGERY (FINCHLEY) , THE —4C **28**
Gt. North Rd., East Finchley, London. N2 0NW
Tel: 020 7837 3611

NATIONAL HOSPITAL FOR NEUROLOGY &
                        NEUROSURGERY, THE —5J **61** (5F **143**)
Queen Sq., London. WC1N 3BG
Tel: 020 7837 3611

NATIONAL TEMPERANCE HOSPITAL —3J **61** (2A **142**)
108-110 Hampstead Rd., London. NW1 2LT
Tel: 020 7530 3000

NELSON HOSPITAL —2H **121**
Kingston Rd., Merton,
London. SW20 8DB
Tel: 020 8296 2000

Newbury Park Health Centre —6H **35**
40 Perrymans Farm Rd., Newbury Park,
Ilford, Essex. IG2 7LB
Tel: 020 8491 1550

Newby Place Health Centre —7E **64**
21 Newby Pl., Poplar, London. E14 0EY
Tel: 020 7515 8893

NEWHAM GENERAL HOSPITAL —4A **66**
Glen Rd., Plaistow, London. E13 8SL
Tel: 020 7476 4000

NEW VICTORIA HOSPITAL —1A **120**
184 Coombe La. W., Kingston-upon-Thames,
Surrey. KT2 7EG
Tel: 020 8949 9000

Norbury Health Centre —2K **123**
2b Pollards Hill N., Norbury, London. SW16 4NL
Tel: 020 8679 1700

NORMANSFIELD HOSPITAL —7C **104**
Kingston Rd., Teddington, Middx. TW11 9JH
Tel: 020 8977 7583

North London Hospice —4F **15**
47 Woodside Av., North Finchley,
London. N12 8TF
Tel: 020 8343 8841

NORTH LONDON NUFFIELD HOSPITAL, THE —2F **7**
Cavell Dri., Uplands Pk. Rd.,
Enfield, Middx. EN2 7PR
Tel: 020 8366 2122

NORTH MIDDLESEX HOSPITAL, THE —5K **17**
Sterling Way, London. N18 1QX
Tel: 020 8887 2000

NORTHWICK PARK HOSPITAL —7A **24**
Watford Rd., Harrow, Middx. HA1 3UJ
Tel: 020 8864 3232

Oakhill Health Centre —6E **118**
Oakhill Rd., Surbiton, Surrey. KT6 6EN
Tel: 020 8390 6755

Oakleigh Road Health Centre —3J **15**
Oakleigh Rd. N., Whetstone,
London. N20 0DH
Tel: 020 8368 8350

OBSTETRIC HOSPITAL, THE —4G **61** (4B **142**)
Huntley St., London. WC1E 6DH
Tel: 020 7387 9300

OLDCHURCH HOSPITAL —6K **37**
Oldchurch Rd., Romford, Essex. RM7 0BE
Tel: (01708) 746090

Orchards Health Centre —1G **67**
Gascoigne Rd., Barking, Essex. IG11 7RS
Tel: 020 8594 1311

PADDINGTON COMMUNITY HOSPITAL —5J **59**
7a Woodfield Rd., London. W9 2BB
Tel: 020 7286 6669

PARKSIDE HOSPITAL —3F **107**
53 Parkside, Wimbledon,
London. SW19 5NX
Tel: 020 8971 8000

Parson's Green Health Centre —1J **91**
5-7 Parson's Grn., London. SW6 4UL
Tel: 020 8846 6767

Paxton Green Health Centre —4E **110**
1 Alleyn Pk., London. SE21 8AU
Tel: 020 8761 1923

PENNY SANGHAM DAY HOSPITAL —3D **70**
Osterley Park Rd., Southall, Middx. UB2 4EU
Tel: 020 8571 9676

PLAISTOW HOSPITAL —2A **66**
Samson St., Plaistow, London. E13 9EH
Tel: 020 8586 6200

Plumstead Health Centre —5J **83**
Tewson Rd., Plumstead,
London. SE18 1BH
Tel: 020 8855 9341

PORTLAND HOSPITAL FOR WOMEN & CHILDREN, THE
                                —5F **61** (5K **141**)
209 Gt. Portland St., London. W1N 6AH
Tel: 020 7580 4400

PRINCESS GRACE HOSPITAL —4E **60** (4G **141**)
42-52 Nottingham Pl., London. W1M 3FD
Tel: 020 7486 1234

PRINCESS LOUISE HOSPITAL —5F **59**
St Quintin Av., London. W10 6DL
Tel: 020 8969 0133

PRIORY HOSPITAL —4B **90**
Priory La., Roehampton,
London. SW15 5JJ
Tel: 020 8876 8261

PUTNEY HOSPITAL —3E **90**
Commondale, Lower Richmond Rd.,
Putney, London. SW15 1HW
Tel: 020 8789 6633

QUEEN CHARLOTTE'S & CHELSEA HOSPITAL —4C **74**
Goldhawk Rd., London. W6 0XG
Tel: 020 8383 1111

QUEEN ELIZABETH HOSPITAL —7C **82**
Stadium Rd., Woolwich, London. SE18 4QH
Tel: 020 8856 5533

QUEEN ELIZABETH HOSPITAL FOR CHILDREN —2G **63**
Hackney Rd., London. E2 8PS
Tel: 020 7377 7000

QUEEN MARY'S HOSPITAL —3A **44**
124 Heath St., Hampstead, London. NW3 1DU
Tel: 020 7431 4111

QUEEN MARY'S HOSPITAL —6A **116**
Frognal Av., Sidcup, Kent. DA14 6LT
Tel: 020 8302 2678

QUEEN MARY'S HOSPITAL FOR CHILDREN —1A **132**
Wrythe La., Carshalton, Surrey. SM5 1AA
Tel: 020 8296 2000

QUEEN MARY'S UNIVERSITY HOSPITAL —6C **90**
Roehampton La., Roehampton, London. SW15 5PN
Tel: 020 8789 6611

QUEENS HOSPITAL —6C **124**
66a Queens Rd., Croydon, Surrey. CR9 2PQ
Tel: 020 8401 3000

Queen's Park Health Centre —3G **59**
Dart St., London. W10 4LD
Tel: 020 8968 8899

Railton Road Health Centre —5B **94**
143-149 Railton Rd., London. SE24 0LT
Tel: 020 7274 1083

Rathmell Drive Health Centre —6H **93**
9A Rathmell Dri., London. SW4 8JG
Tel: 020 8674 7400

REDFORD LODGE HOSPITAL —2B **18**
15 Church St., Edmonton, London. N9 9DY
Tel: 020 8956 1234

RICHMOND HEALTHCARE HAMLET —3E **88**
Kew Foot Rd., Richmond, Surrey. TW9 2TE
Tel: 020 8940 3331

River Place Health Centre —7C **46**
River Pl., Essex Rd., London. N1 2DE
Tel: 020 7530 2900

Robin Hood Lane Health Centre —5K **131**
Camden Rd., Sutton, Surrey. SM1 2RJ
Tel: 020 8643 8611

RODING HOSPITAL (BUPA) —3B **34**
Roding La. S., Redbridge, Essex. IG4 5PZ
Tel: 020 8551 1100

Rosslyn Clinic —6C **88**
15 Rosslyn Rd., East Twickenham,
Middx. TW1 2AR
Tel: 020 8891 3173

Roxbourne Complex —2F **39**
Rayners La., South Harrow,
Middx. HA2 0UE
Tel: 020 8422 5602

ROYAL BROMPTON HOSPITAL —5C **76** (5C **152**)
Sydney St., London. SW3 6NP
Tel: 020 7352 8121

ROYAL BROMPTON HOSPITAL (ANNEXE) —5B **76** (5B **152**)
Fulham Rd., London. SW3 6HP
Tel: 020 7352 8121

ROYAL FREE HOSPITAL, THE —5C **44**
Pond St., London. NW3 2QG
Tel: 020 7794 0500

ROYAL HOSPITAL FOR NEURO-DISABILITY —7G **91**
West Hill, Putney,
London. SW15 3SW
Tel: 020 8780 4500

ROYAL LONDON HOMOEOPATHIC HOSPITAL, THE
—5J **61** (5F **143**)
Gt. Ormond St., London. WC1N 3HR
Tel: 020 7833 7220

ROYAL LONDON HOSPITAL MILE END —5K **63**
Bancroft Rd., London. E1 4DG
Tel: 020 7377 7000

ROYAL LONDON HOSPITAL ST CLEMENT'S —4B **64**
3a Bow Rd., London. E3 4LL
Tel: 020 7377 7000

ROYAL LONDON HOSPITAL WHITECHAPEL —5H **63**
Whitechapel Rd., London. E1 1BB
Tel: 020 7377 7000

ROYAL MARSDEN HOSPITAL (FULHAM) , THE
—5B **76** (5B **152**)
Fulham Rd., London. SW3 6JJ
Tel: 020 7352 8171

ROYAL NATIONAL ORTHOPAEDIC HOSPITAL —2G **11**
Brockley Hill, Stanmore, Middx. HA7 4LP
Tel: 020 8954 2300

ROYAL NATIONAL ORTHOPAEDIC HOSPITAL
(OUTPATIENTS) —4F **61** (4K **141**)
45-51 Bolsover St.,
London. W1P 8AQ
Tel: 020 7387 5070

ROYAL NATIONAL THROAT, NOSE & EAR HOSPITAL
—3K **61** (1G **143**)
330 Gray's Inn Rd., London. WC1X 8DA
Tel: 020 7915 1300

ROYAL NATIONAL THROAT, NOSE & EAR HOSPITAL-
SPEECH & LANGUAGE UNIT —5C **56**
6 Castlebar Hill, Ealing, London. W5 1TD
Tel: 020 8997 8480

ST ANDREW'S AT HARROW —2J **39**
Bowden House Clinic, London Rd.,
Harrow, Middx. HA1 3JL
Tel: 020 8966 7000

ST ANDREW'S HOSPITAL —4D **64**
Devons Rd., Bow, London. E3 3NT
Tel: 020 7476 4000

ST ANN'S HOSPITAL —6C **30**
St Ann's Rd., Sth. Tottenham,
London. N15 3TH
Tel: 020 8442 6000

ST ANTHONY'S HOSPITAL —2F **131**
London Rd., North Cheam, Surrey. SM3 9DW
Tel: 020 8337 6691

ST BARTHOLOMEW'S AT SMITHFIELD —6B **62** (7B **144**)
West Smithfield, London. EC1A 7BE
Tel: 020 7601 8888

ST BERNARD'S HOSPITAL —2H **71**
Uxbridge Rd., Southall, Middx. UB1 3EU
Tel: 020 8574 2444

ST CHARLES HOSPITAL —5F **59**
Exmoor St., London. W10 6DZ
Tel: 020 8969 2488

St Christopher's Hospice —5J **111**
51 Lawrie Pk. Rd., Sydenham, London. SE26 6DZ
Tel: 020 8778 9252

ST GEORGE'S HOSPITAL —5B **108**
Blackshaw Rd., Tooting, London. SW17 0QT
Tel: 020 8672 1255

ST HELIER HOSPITAL —1A **132**
Wrythe La., Carshalton, Surrey. SM5 1AA
Tel: 020 8296 2000

St James Health Centre —5A **32**
47 St James's St., London. E17 7NH
Tel: 020 8520 9286

St John's Health Centre —7A **88**
Oak La., Twickenham, Middx. TW1 3PH
Tel: 020 8891 3101

St John's Hospice —2B **60**
Hospital of St John & St Elizabeth, 60 Grove End Rd.,
St John's Wood, London. NW8 9NH
Tel: 020 7286 5126 ext 321

ST JOHN'S HOUSE HOSPITAL —7A **88**
Strafford Rd., London. SW1 3HQ
Tel: 020 8744 9943

St Joseph's Hospice —1H **63**
Mare St., Hackney, London. E8 4SA
Tel: 020 8985 0861

St Leonards Primary Care Centre —2E **62**
Nuttall St., London. N1 5LZ
Tel: 020 7790 4711

St Luke's Hospice —5H **23**
59 Harrow View, Harrow, Middx. HA1 1RF
Tel: 020 8427 1713 / 6755

ST LUKE'S HOSPITAL FOR THE CLERGY —4G **61** (4A **142**)
14 Fitzroy Sq., London. W1P 6AH
Tel: 020 7388 4954

ST LUKE'S WOODSIDE HOSPITAL —4E **28**
Woodside Av., London. N10 3HU
Tel: 020 8219 1800

St Mark's Health Centre —6F **83**
24 Wrottesley Rd., Plumstead,
London. SE18 3EP
Tel: 020 8317 3540

ST MARY'S HOSPITAL —6B **60** (7B **140**)
Praed St., London. W2 1NY
Tel: 020 7725 6666

ST PANCRAS HOSPITAL —1H **61**
4 St Pancras Way, London. NW1 0PE
Tel: 020 7530 3500

St Quintin Avenue Health Centre —5F **59**
St Quintin Av., London. W10 6PU
Tel: 020 8960 5677

St Raphael's Hospice —1F **131**
London Rd., North Cheam, Surrey. SM3 9DX
Tel: 020 8337 7475

ST THOMAS' HOSPITAL —3K **77** (1G **155**)
Lambeth Palace Rd., London. SE1 7EH
Tel: 020 7928 9292

Seven Kings Health Centre —2J **51**
1 Salisbury Rd., Seven Kings, Ilford, Essex. IG3 8BE
Tel: 020 8924 6290

Sheen Lane Health Centre —3J **89**
Sheen La., London. SW14 8LP
Tel: 020 8878 7561

SHIRLEY OAKS HOSPITAL —1J **135**
Poppy La., Shirley Oaks, Croydon,
Surrey. CR9 8AB
Tel: 020 8655 2255

Shotfield Health Centre —5F **133**
Shotfield, Wallington, Surrey. SM6 0HY
Tel: 020 8647 0031

Shrewsbury Road Health Centre —7B **50**
East Ham Memorial Hospital, Shrewsbury Rd.,
Forest Gate, London. E7 8QP
Tel: 020 8586 5142

Sidcup Health Centre —4A **116**
43 Granville Rd., Sidcup, Kent. DA14 4TA
Tel: 020 8302 7811

Silverthorne Health Centre —3K **19**
2 Friars Clo., Larkshall Rd., Chingford,
Essex. E4 6UN
Tel: 020 8529 3706

SLOANE HOSPITAL, THE —1F **127**
125-133 Albemarle Rd.,
Beckenham, Kent. BR3 5HS
Tel: 020 8466 6911

Solent Road Health Centre —6J **43**
9 Solent Rd., London. NW6 1TP
Tel: 020 7530 2550

Somerford Grove Health Centre —4F **47**
Somerford Gro., London. N16 7UA
Tel: 020 7249 2071

Sorsby Health Centre —4A **48**
Mandeville St., London. E5 0DH
Tel: 020 8985 7671

Southall Norwood Mental Health Centre —3D **70**
The Green, Southall, Middx. UB2 4BH
Tel: 020 8571 6110

South Kensington & Chelsea Mental Health Centre —6A **76**
1 Nightingale Pl., London. SW10 8RP
Tel: 020 8846 6025

South Lewisham Health Centre —4E **112**
50 Conisborough Cres., London. SE6 2SP
Tel: 020 8698 8921

SOUTH WESTERN HOSPITAL —3J **93**
108 Landor Rd., London. SW9 9NT
Tel: 020 7346 5400

South Westminster Health Centre —4H **77** (3C **154**)
St George's House, 82 Vincent Sq.,
London. SW1P 2PF
Tel: 020 8746 5757

South Woodford Health Centre —1J **33**
114 High Rd., South Woodford,
Essex. E18 2QS
Tel: 020 8491 3333

SOUTHWOOD HOSPITAL —7E **28**
70 Southwood La., Highgate,
London. N6 5SP
Tel: 020 8340 8778

Speedwell Mental Health Centre —7C **80**
Speedwell St., Deptford,
London. SE8 4AT
Tel: 020 8691 4535

Spindrift Medical Centre —4C **80**
100 Spindrift Av., Isle of Dogs,
London. E14 9WU
Tel: 020 7537 0071

Spitalfields Health Centre —5F **63** (6K **145**)
9-11 Brick La., London. E1 6PU
Tel: 020 7247 8251

SPRINGFIELD UNIVERSITY HOSPITAL —3C **108**
61 Glenburnie Rd.,
London. SW17 7DJ
Tel: 020 8672 9911

Steel's Lane Health Centre —6J **63**
384-388 Commercial Rd.,
London. E1 0LR
Tel: 020 7790 7171

STEPNEY DAY HOSPITAL —6J **63**
Ronald St., London. E1 0DT
Tel: 020 7702 8199

Stuart Crescent Health Centre —1A **30**
Stuart Cres., London. N22 5NJ
Tel: 020 8889 4311

SURBITON HOSPITAL —6E **118**
Ewell Rd., Surbiton, Surrey. KT6 6EZ
Tel: 020 8399 7111

Surrey Docks Health Centre —2A **80**
Downtown Rd., London. SE16 1NP
Tel: 020 7231 3085

Sydenham Green Health Centre —4A **112**
26 Holmshaw Clo., London. SE26 4TH
Tel: 020 8778 1333

Tavistock Clinic —6B **44**
120 Belsize La., London. NW3 5BA
Tel: 020 7435 7111

TEDDINGTON MEMORIAL HOSPITAL —6J **103**
Hampton Rd., Teddington, Middx. TW11 0JL
Tel: 020 8977 2212

Temple Fortune Health Centre —6J **27**
23 Temple Fortune La.,
London. NW11 7TE
Tel: 020 8458 4431

Thames View Health Centre —2K **67**
Bastable Av., Barking,
Essex. IG11 0LG
Tel: 020 8594 4233

Thornton Heath Health Centre —4D **124**
61a Gillett Rd., Thornton Heath,
Surrey. CR7 8RL
Tel: 020 8684 2424

THORPE COOMBE HOSPITAL —3E **32**
714 Forest Rd., Walthamstow,
London. E17 3HP
Tel: 020 8520 8971

Tollgate Health Centre —5D **66**
220 Tollgate Rd., Beckton,
London. E6 4JS
Tel: 020 7474 5656

Torrington Park Health Centre —5F **15**
16 Torrington Pk.,
London. N12 9SS
Tel: 020 8446 4201

Trinity Hospice —4F **93**
30 Clapham Comn. N. Side,
Clapham, London. SW4 0RN
Tel: 020 7622 9481

Tudor Lodge Health Centre —1F **107**
8c Victoria Dr., Wimbledon Park,
London. SW19 6AE
Tel: 020 8788 1525

Tynemouth Road Health Centre —4F **31**
24 Tynemouth Rd.,
London. N15 4RH
Tel: 020 8275 4000

UNITED ELIZABETH GARRETT ANDERSON & SOHO
HOSPITALS FOR WOMEN —3Hb **61** (2D **142**)
144 Euston Rd., London. NW1 2AP
Tel: 020 7387 2501

UNIVERSITY COLLEGE HOSPITAL —4G **61** (4B **142**)
Gower St., London. WC1E 6AU
Tel: 020 7387 9300

UPTON ROAD DAY HOSPITAL —4E **100**
14 Upton Rd., Bexleyheath,
Kent. DA6 8LQ
Tel: 020 8301 7900

Vanbrugh Hill Health Centre —5H **81**
Vanbrugh Hill, Greenwich,
London. SE10 9HE
Tel: 020 8853 3434

Vicarage Fields Health Centre —7G **51**
Vicarage Dri., Barking,
Essex. IG11 7NR
Tel: 020 8591 5466

Waldron Health Centre —7B **80**
Stanley St., London. SE8 4BS
Tel: 020 8691 4621

Walpole House Mental Health Centre —7C **56**
13 Mattock La., Ealing, London. W5 5BG
Tel: 020 8840 6900

Wapping Health Centre —1H **79**
22 Wapping La., London. E1 9RL
Tel: 020 7488 0404

WELLINGTON HOSPITAL, THE —2B **60**
Wellington Pl., London. NW8 9LE
Tel: 020 7586 5959

Wellington Way Health Centre —3C **64**
1a Wellington Way, London. E3 4NE
Tel: 020 8980 3510

WEMBLEY COMMUNITY HOSPITAL —6D **40**
Fairview Av., Wembley, Middx. HA0 4UH
Tel: 020 8903 1323

West Beckton Health Centre —5B **66**
90 Lawson Clo., West Beckton,
London. E16 3LU
Tel: 020 7445 7080

WESTERN OPHTHALMIC HOSPITAL —5D **60** (5E **140**)
Marylebone Rd., London. NW1 5QH
Tel: 020 7402 4211

West Ham Health Centre —1G **65**
84 West Ham La., Stratford,
London. E15 4PT
Tel: 020 8250 7300

WEST MIDDLESEX UNIVERSITY HOSPITAL —2A **88**
Twickenham Rd., Isleworth,
Middx. TW7 6AF
Tel: 020 8560 2121

WHIPPS CROSS HOSPITAL —6F **33**
Whipps Cross Rd., Leytonstone,
London. E11 1NR
Tel: 020 8539 5522

White City Health Centre —7D **58**
Australia Rd., London. W12 7PH
Tel: 020 8846 6464

WHITTINGTON HOSPITAL —2G **45**
Highgate Hill, London. N19 5NF
Tel: 020 7272 3070

Wick Health Centre —6A **48**
200 Wick Rd., Hackney,
London. E9 5AN
Tel: 020 8986 6341

WILLESDEN COMMUNITY HOSPITAL —1C **58**
Harlesden Rd., Willesden,
London. NW10 3RY
Tel: 020 8459 1292

Woodside Health Centre —5G **125**
3 Enmore Rd., South Norwood,
London. SE25 5NT
Tel: 020 8656 0213

World's End Health Centre —7A **76**
529 King's Rd., London. SW10 0UD
Tel: 020 8846 6333